THE PRINCIPLES OF THE LAW OF
RESTITUTION

D1382089

THE PRINCIPLES OF
THE LAW OF
RESTITUTION

GRAHAM VIRGO

CLARENDON PRESS · OXFORD
1999

OXFORD

UNIVERSITY PRESS

Great Clarendon Street, Oxford OX2 6DP

Oxford University Press is a department of the University of Oxford
It furthers the University's objective of excellence in research, scholarship,
and education by publishing worldwide in

Oxford New York

Athens Auckland Bangkok Bogotá Buenos Aires Calcutta
Cape Town Chennai Dar es Salaam Delhi Florence Hong Kong Istanbul
Karachi Kuala Lumpur Madrid Melbourne Mexico City Mumbai
Nairobi Paris São Paulo Singapore Taipei Tokyo Toronto Warsaw

and associated companies in Berlin Ibadan

Oxford is a registered trade mark of Oxford University Press
in the UK and in certain other countries

Published in the United States
by Oxford University Press Inc., New York

© Graham Virgo 1999

British Library Cataloguing in Publication Data
Data available

Library of Congress Cataloging in Publication Data
Data available

ISBN 0-19-876377-8

1 3 5 7 9 10 8 6 4 2

Typeset by Hope Services (Abingdon) Ltd.
Printed in Great Britain
on acid-free paper by

Biddles Ltd, Guildford and King's Lynn

For my mother
and in memory of my father

Preface

The Law of Restitution is like a mountain. From a distance it may appear somewhat insignificant, indeed some have dismissed it simply as a hill, a minor bump on the legal landscape. But on closer inspection, it is definitely a mountain. It is big and complex and it is very easy to get lost on its slopes. It has been explored many times recently. Some explorers have recorded the mountain's features in great detail. Others have sought to understand how the mountain was formed and why its various features have developed. Others have simply tried to find the safest and quickest routes to the summit. But although many explorers have visited the mountain recently, it has been inhabited for a much longer time. These inhabitants know the mountain well, even though they may not understand all its features, because they work on it every day. They know the quick routes to the summit. The explorers have created new routes, which may be better. But for explorers and inhabitants alike, there is only one true objective: to reach the summit safely. This textbook seeks to provide a map for those who are trying to climb to the top of the mountain. In doing so it attempts to identify the best routes to the summit, where restitutionary remedies can be awarded to the conqueror. But it also seeks to explain the features which are passed on the way and identify the holes and swamps which will catch the unwary.

This book owes a great deal to those who have explored the subject before, particularly the works of Lord Goff, Professor Gareth Jones, Professor Peter Birks and Professor Andrew Burrows; but it does seek to do something different. It does not seek to describe the law in an encyclopaedic way as Goff and Jones have done in each of the five editions of their seminal work 'The Law of Restitution'. Neither does it solely seek to identify a theoretical structure to assist in the organisation of the subject, particularly if such a structure has not been expressly recognised in the cases. This is what Birks sought to do in his book 'An Introduction to the Law of Restitution'. But neither of these works can be characterised as textbooks. The very nature of the law of restitution requires the textbook writer both to describe the law and to identify a coherent and consistent structure which assists in the description and understanding of the subject. This is what Burrows sought to do so successfully in his work on the subject, which was explicitly founded on the theoretical structure identified by Birks.

A particular problem for any textbook writer is whether he or she should simply seek to follow the law, by stating it as it is, or seek to lead it on by suggesting the direction in which the law should go. It is both an advantage and a disadvantage of the approach adopted by Birks and Burrows that they are prepared to lead the judges on. If they are dissatisfied with the analysis adopted in the cases, they are prepared to develop their own analysis and make the cases fit. But sometimes they take this too far and create categories of restitution which are inconsistent with the cases. The textbook writer is a map-reader whose function is to direct the explorer to the desired destination by the best route. Usually, that route will be well established and well sign-posted. Sometimes, however, the most convenient route is one that goes along the by-ways, along roads which have been forgotten or are rarely used. Occasionally, the map-reader must cut across new country, forging a new route. Maybe others will follow and the authorities may eventually recognise that route as legitimate, as giving those who follow a right of way, but they are unlikely to do so if there is another perfectly serviceable route nearby.

A further advantage of the approach adopted by Birks and Burrows is that their analysis of the subject is elegant and symmetrical. But the law of restitution is not a work of art; something to be looked at and admired. It is a body of law which must operate in the real world. Elegance and function do not always go together. Far better that the body of law works, even if it has some rough edges. Consequently, some of the conclusions reached in this book lack the elegance of those of Burrows and Birks, but if they work and, equally importantly, are likely to be recognised and adopted by the judges, then the loss of elegance is a small price to pay.

What marks this book as different from those which have come before is that those books assume that the law of restitution is about the reversal of unjust enrichment. In other words, it is the unjust enrichment principle which defines the ambit of the law of restitution. I do not think that that is correct. For when the law of restitution is examined from a principled perspective there are in fact three principles which trigger the award of restitutionary remedies, namely the reversal of unjust enrichment, ensuring that a wrongdoer does not profit from the commission of a wrong and the vindication of proprietary rights. The rules themselves are complex and for detailed description of them the reader is referred to Goff and Jones's work on the subject. However, this book does not seek to concentrate wholly on the theory and policy behind the law, but seeks to adopt a balance between identification and analysis of the rules themselves and how they operate in practice.

This book could not have been written without the help and support of many friends and colleagues. My interest in the subject was first triggered at Oxford by Andrew Burrows, Jack Beatson and John Cartwright. At Cambridge my interest has been nurtured by Gareth Jones. I have had the privilege of teaching Restitution at Cambridge with the best of colleagues and I particularly wish to thank Janet O'Sullivan and Richard

Nolan for their good humour and support. I also want to thank all those students who have helped me formulate my ideas about the subject, often without knowing it. I am also grateful for the support and encouragement of the Fellows and students at Downing College, particularly that of John Hopkins and Charles Harpum. In addition to all these people who have helped me in writing this book in numerous ways, I wish to express my thanks to the following who have always been willing to answer my questions and read draft chapters: Neil Andrews, Mark Armitage, David Capper, Ian Carnochan, Mindy Chen-Wishart, Steve Hedley, Richard Hooley, Cherry Hopkins, Roger Kaye QC, Omar Rashid, Clare Stanley and Janet Ulph. The team at Oxford University Press have been very supportive and helpful and I particularly wish to express my gratitude to Michaela Coulthard, Myf Milton and Kate Elliott. Finally, the support of my family throughout the period I have been writing this book is something for which I am most grateful. My children, Elizabeth and Jonathan, have brought me down to earth whenever I became obsessed by the subject. My wife, Cally, has been doctored and reverenced whilst this book was written, but has remained a constant source of encouragement and strength. To you all, thank you.

I have attempted to state the law as of 31 January 1999, but it has been possible to incorporate references to some more recent developments. After the text of the book had been completed the new civil procedure rules were brought into force. One consequence of this has been the introduction of new terminology in respect of civil litigation. In particular the 'plaintiff' is now to be described as 'claimant'. It has not been possible to incorporate this new language into the text, but, for the avoidance of doubt, it should be stressed that whenever the word 'plaintiff' is used this means the 'claimant'.

Graham Virgo
Downing College, Cambridge
1st June 1999

Outline Contents

Contents

Contents

Table of Cases

UK

US

Table of Statutes

UK

PART I

THE FUNDAMENTAL PRINCIPLES

1

The Essence of Restitution

1. WHAT IS THE LAW OF RESTITUTION ABOUT?

Before the principles and rules which form the law of restitution are examined it is vital to ask what this body of law is actually about. The answer is simple, but it is an answer which has rarely been articulated by judges or commentators. The law of restitution is about the award of a generic group of remedies which have one common function, namely to deprive the defendant of a gain rather than to compensate the plaintiff for loss suffered.[1] These are called the restitutionary remedies.[2] Whilst there is a great deal more to the subject than this remedial aspect, since it is also vital to determine what circumstances will trigger the award of restitutionary remedies, it is only because there are a group of remedies which have a common function of depriving defendants of gains that we are able to assert that there is an independent body of law which can be called the law of restitution. To understand what these remedies are, how they operate and when they are available requires examination of a complex body of law. To assist in the understanding of this law it is necessary to identify and analyse the principles which underlie the rules. That is the aim of this book.

2. WHAT IS THE NATURE OF RESTITUTIONARY REMEDIES?

(a) The categories of restitutionary remedy

The restitutionary remedies themselves fall into two distinct categories.

(i) Personal restitutionary remedies

These are those remedies which restore to the plaintiff the value of a benefit which the defendant has received. These remedies are said to operate *in personam*. This means that the defendant is liable to pay the value of the benefit to the plaintiff rather than transfer the benefit itself to the plaintiff. So, for example, if the plaintiff pays £100 to the defendant by

---

[1] See Lord Wright of Durley, 'Legal Essays and Addresses' (Cambridge: Cambridge University Press, 1939) p. 6. See also Barker, 'Rescuing Remedialism in Unjust Enrichment Law: Why Remedies are Right' (1998) 57 *CLJ* 301.

[2] The range of restitutionary remedies is considered at pp. 20–8 below.

mistake the defendant will be liable to pay £100 to the plaintiff, even if the defendant no longer has the money which he or she received from the plaintiff.[3] It follows that the award of a personal restitutionary remedy creates a relationship of creditor and debtor between the parties, since the defendant owes money to the plaintiff. Crucially, this category of remedy does not depend on the defendant retaining the benefit which he or she had received from the plaintiff.

(ii) Proprietary restitutionary remedies

The function of these remedies[4] is to enable the plaintiff to assert his or her property rights in or over an asset which is held by the defendant. These remedies are said to operate *in rem*. There are two types of proprietary restitutionary remedy: first, remedies by virtue of which the plaintiff can recover the property which is held by the defendant; secondly, remedies which recognise that the plaintiff has a security interest in property which is held by the defendant. The key advantage of both types of remedy is that, since the plaintiff has a proprietary interest in an asset which is held by the defendant, the plaintiff's claim to the asset ranks above other creditors of the defendant, with the result that the plaintiff is more likely to recover the property or its value if the defendant becomes insolvent. Crucially, this category of remedy does depend on the defendant retaining the property in which the plaintiff has a proprietary interest.[5]

(b) The characteristics of restitutionary remedies

(i) Restoring what the plaintiff lost

Since restitutionary remedies are assessed by reference to the defendant's gain, they operate in a very different way from compensatory remedies where the measure of relief is assessed by reference to the plaintiff's loss. Despite this, in many cases the effect of a restitutionary remedy will be to restore to the plaintiff what he or she has lost, because the extent of the defendant's gain will reflect exactly what the plaintiff lost. 'Restitutionary' is clearly the most appropriate word to describe these remedies, since their function is to restore to the plaintiff the value of the thing, the thing itself or its substitute which the plaintiff had lost.

The award of such restitutionary remedies to the plaintiff can be justified on the ground that, where the defendant has obtained a benefit at the plaintiff's expense, justice demands that this should be restored to

---

[3] Subject to the application of defences, such as change of position. See Chapter 24.
[4] See Chapter 21.   [5] See Chapter 20.

the plaintiff.[6] The importance of restitutionary remedies as a mechanism for securing justice between the parties was recognised by Fuller and Perdue:

If, following Aristotle, we regard the purpose of justice as the maintenance of an equilibrium of goods among members of society, the restitution interest presents twice as strong a claim to judicial intervention as the reliance interest, since if A not only causes B to lose one unit but appropriates that unit to himself, the resulting discrepancy between A and B is not one unit but two.[7]

The award of restitutionary remedies consequently operates as a mechanism to secure corrective justice by rectifying an imbalance between the plaintiff and the defendant.[8]

(ii) Disgorgement

But in some cases the remedy which is awarded, although it is still assessed by reference to the defendant's gain, results in the plaintiff obtaining property which he or she never had before. For example, the defendant may have obtained some money from a third party in breach of duty to the plaintiff. In such circumstances the plaintiff may be able to bring a restitutionary claim in respect of the money[9] but, since it has not been taken from the plaintiff, it is inappropriate to describe the remedy which enables the plaintiff to obtain this money as restitutionary because it is not possible to restore to the plaintiff what he or she never had in the first place. It is often more appropriate, therefore, to describe the function of such remedies as being to require the defendant to disgorge benefits to the plaintiff rather than to restore to the plaintiff what he or she has lost.[10] Even though the description of these remedies as 'restitutionary' is not always felicitous, it is still appropriate to treat them as falling within the law of restitution, simply because the remedy is assessed by reference to a benefit obtained by the defendant.[11]

Can the award of this type of restitutionary remedy also be justified on the basis that they operate as a mechanism to secure corrective justice between the parties? The answer is 'yes' and this is simply because the

---

[6] See *Moses* v. *Macferlan* (1760) 2 Burr. 1005, 1012; 97 ER 676, 681 (Lord Mansfield) and *Fibrosa Spolka Akcyjna* v. *Fairbairn Lawson Combe Barbour Ltd.* [1943] AC 32, 61 (Lord Wright).

[7] 'The Reliance Interest in Contract Damages' (1936–37) 46 *Yale LJ* 52, 56. See Aristotle, 'Nichomachean Ethics', Book V, ch. 2, 4.

[8] See Barker, 'Unjust Enrichment: Containing the Beast' (1995) 15 *OJLS* 457, 468. See also *Peel* v. *Canada* (1992) 98 DLR (4th) 140, 165 (McLachlin J).

[9] See Part IV.

[10] Smith, 'The Province of the Law of Restitution' (1992) 71 *CBR* 672, 696.

[11] Birks has suggested that the description of these remedies as restitutionary is justified because the 'underlying Latin "*restituere/restitutio*" indicates that the word can include both "give up" and "give back"': 'Equity in the Modern Law: An Exercise in Taxonomy' (1996) 26 *Univ. WALR* 1, 28.

only cases where the defendant will be liable to make restitution to the plaintiff of benefits which have not been subtracted from the plaintiff is where the defendant owes duties to the plaintiff and obtains the benefits in breach of these duties. In other words, the defendant will only be liable to make restitution of such benefits where he or she has committed a wrong against the plaintiff.[12] Justice demands that the defendant should disgorge these benefits because of a fundamental principle of the law of restitution that no defendant should profit from his or her wrongdoing. Justice also demands that the defendant should disgorge these benefits to the plaintiff because the plaintiff is the victim of the wrong and the award of restitutionary relief is a mechanism for protecting the plaintiff's rights.[13]

3. WHEN WILL RESTITUTIONARY REMEDIES BE AWARDED?

Although the rationale of corrective justice can be relied on to justify the award of restitutionary remedies it is too uncertain to operate as an underlying principle on which the law of restitution can be built. For if the question whether restitutionary remedies can be awarded depended simply on whether it is just to require the defendant to restore what he or she has gained to the plaintiff, then the law of restitution would be unpredictable and unworkable, to such an extent that it would effectively be void for uncertainty. Consequently, it is necessary to identify more specific principles which provide the basis for determining whether he or she may obtain restitutionary relief.

Orthodox learning about the law of restitution suggests that there is only one principle on which the law of restitution is dependent, namely the principle of unjust enrichment. The main academic works on the subject consider that restitutionary remedies will be awarded only where the defendant has been unjustly enriched.[14] This is particularly well expressed by Goff and Jones who say that:

The law of restitution is the law relating to all claims . . . which are founded upon the principle of unjust enrichment.[15]

This equation of the law of restitution with the principle of reversing the defendant's unjust enrichment has been recognised by the judiciary

12 See Chapter 15.
13 Barker, 'Unjust Enrichment: Containing the Beast' (1995) 15 *OJLS* 457, 473.
14 See, for example, Birks, *An Introduction to the Law of Restitution* (revised edn., Oxford: Clarendon Press, 1989) p. 17 and Burrows, *The Law of Restitution* (London: Butterworths, 1993) p. 1.
15 Goff and Jones, *The Law of Restitution* (5th edn., London: Sweet and Maxwell, 1998) p. 3.

as well. For example, in the case which can be regarded as the source of the modern law of restitution, *Moses* v. *Macferlan*,[16] Lord Mansfield recognised that 'the gist of this kind of action is, that the defendant, upon the circumstances of the case, is obliged by the ties of natural justice and equity to refund the money'. Lord Wright, one of the leading proponents of an independent law of restitution, recognised that:[17]

It is clear that any civilised system of law is bound to provide remedies for cases of what has been called unjust enrichment or unjust benefit, that is to prevent a man from retaining the money of or some benefit derived from another which it is against conscience that he should keep. Such remedies in English law are generically different from remedies in contract or tort, and are now recognised to fall within a third category of the common law which has been called quasi-contract or restitution.

But it was not until the decisions of the House of Lords, first in *Lipkin Gorman (a firm)* v. *Karpnale Ltd.*[18] and then in *Woolwich Equitable Building Society* v. *Inland Revenue Commissioners*[19] that we could be certain that there is a body of law which can be called the law of restitution and which exists to secure the reversal of unjust enrichment.[20] Probably the most important *dictum* of the modern law of restitution is that of Lord Goff in *Lipkin Gorman*, who recognised that:

The recovery of money in restitution is not, as a general rule, a matter of discretion for the court. A claim to recover money at common law is made as a matter of right; and even though the underlying principle of recovery is the principle of unjust enrichment, nevertheless, where recovery is denied, it is denied on the basis of legal principle.[21]

Despite the recognition by the House of Lords that the law of restitution equates with the reversal of the defendant's unjust enrichment, such an interpretation of the law is in fact too simplistic and does not accurately reflect the true operation of the law of restitution.[22] For careful analysis of the case law suggests that the law of restitution is not

---

[16] (1776) 2 Burr. 1005, 1012; 97 ER 976, 981.

[17] *Fibrosa Spolka Akcyjna* v. *Fairbairn Lawson Combe Barbour Ltd.* [1943] AC 32, 61.

[18] [1991] 2 AC 548. See in particular Lord Bridge at p. 558, Lord Templeman at p. 559 and Lord Goff at p. 578.

[19] [1993] AC 70, 197 (Lord Browne-Wilkinson).

[20] See also *Westdeutsche Landesbank Girozentrale* v. *Islington LBC* [1996] AC 669, 710 (Lord Browne-Wilkinson); *Kleinwort Benson Ltd.* v. *Glasgow CC* [1997] 3 WLR 923, 931 (Lord Goff) and 947 (Lord Clyde); *Banque Financière de la Cité* v. *Parc (Battersea) Ltd.* [1998] 2 WLR 475; and *Kleinwort Benson Ltd.* v. *Lincoln CC* [1998] 3 WLR 1095, 1113 (Lord Goff), 1144 (Lord Hope).

[21] [1991] 2 AC 548, 578.

[22] That the law of restitution should not be equated with the unjust enrichment principle has also been recognised by Birks, 'Misnomer' in 'Restitution: Past, Present and Future' (ed. Cornish, Nolan, O'Sullivan and Virgo, Oxford: Hart Publishing, 1998) p. 7. See also Birks, 'The Law of Restitution at the End of an Epoch' (1999) 28 *Univ. WALR* 13, 19.

founded upon one principle but rather is founded on three different principles, namely:

(1) the reversal of unjust enrichment;
(2) the prevention of a wrongdoer from profiting from his or her wrong; and
(3) the vindication of property rights with which the defendant has interfered.

Restitutionary remedies are available in respect of each of these three principles, but it is vital that they are kept separate and are not brought together within one general principle of unjust enrichment, for the award of restitutionary remedies depends on very different considerations depending on which principle the plaintiff relies. Each of these three principles requires careful description at the outset.

(a) The reversal of unjust enrichment

The reversal of the defendant's unjust enrichment is without doubt the most important principle in the law of restitution, since it is the principle which underlies the award of restitutionary relief in the majority of cases. It is therefore crucial to determine exactly what unjust enrichment means. Two different senses of the phrase can be identified, and it is the failure to distinguish between these different senses which has resulted in the assumption by many that the reversal of unjust enrichment is the only principle on which the award of restitutionary remedies is dependent.

(i) The descriptive sense of unjust enrichment

Unjust enrichment may be used simply to describe a state of affairs where the defendant can be said to have been enriched in circumstances of injustice. Since restitutionary remedies will only be awarded where the defendant has received some sort of benefit in circumstances where he or she is required to transfer that benefit or its value to the plaintiff, this descriptive notion of unjust enrichment can be treated as underlying the whole of the law of restitution. Indeed, it is this idea of unjust enrichment which was recognised by Lord Wright in the *Fibrosa* case[23] and which had earlier been adopted by Lord Mansfield in *Moses* v. *Macferlan*[24] where the judges referred to good conscience. This descriptive sense of unjust enrichment was recently recognised by Lord Clyde who said that the unjust enrichment principle 'is equitable in the sense

---

[23] [1943] AC 32, 61.   [24] (1760) 2 Burr. 1005, 1012; 97 ER 676, 681.

that it seeks to secure a fair and just determination of the rights of the parties concerned in the case'.[25]

Whilst the award of restitutionary remedies can be justified *ex post facto* on the ground that it is just to require the defendant to make restitution, unjust enrichment in this descriptive sense can hardly be considered to be a legal principle which is sufficiently certain to determine when restitutionary remedies should be awarded. Indeed, the assumption in a number of cases that the award of restitutionary remedies depended simply on whether or not the defendant had been enriched in circumstances of injustice was one of the main obstacles to the recognition of the law of restitution as an independent body of law. This is illustrated by the *dictum* of Hamilton LJ in *Baylis* v. *Bishop of London*[26] that the judges 'are not now free in the twentieth century to administer that vague jurisprudence which is sometimes attractively styled "justice as between man and man"'.

(ii) The substantive sense of unjust enrichment

Alternatively, and much more acceptably, unjust enrichment has been relied on as a substantive principle which can be used to determine when restitutionary remedies should be available. To establish this substantive sense of unjust enrichment four questions must be examined:[27]

(a) the defendant must have received an enrichment;[28]
(b) the enrichment must have been received at the plaintiff's expense;[29]
(c) the enrichment must have been received in circumstances of injustice, meaning that the plaintiff's claim falls within one of the recognised grounds of restitution;[30] and
(d) the defendant is not able to rely on a defence which defeats the plaintiff's claim.[31]

If the first three requirements are satisfied, and the defendant does not have a defence, then a restitutionary remedy will be awarded to enable the plaintiff to recover the value of any enrichment which had been received by the defendant. The only remedies which are available for actions founded on the reversal of unjust enrichment are restitutionary

---

[25] *Banque Financière de la Cité* v. *Parc (Battersea) Ltd.* [1998] 2 WLR 475, 488.

[26] [1913] 1 Ch. 127, 140. See also *Holt* v. *Markham* [1913] 1 Ch. 127, 140 where Scrutton LJ described the history of restitution as a 'history of well-meaning sloppiness of thought'.

[27] *Banque Financière de la Cité* v. *Parc (Battersea) Ltd.* [1998] 2 WLR 475, 479 (Lord Steyn).

[28] See Chapter 4.   [29] See Chapter 5.

[30] See Part III. A number of commentators call these grounds of restitution 'unjust factors'. 'Grounds of restitution' is the expression which will be used in this book simply because it is more elegant.

[31] See Part VI.

remedies and, even then, only personal restitutionary remedies are available.

The justification for the award of restitutionary remedies where the defendant has been unjustly enriched at the plaintiff's expense is that, by virtue of the relevant ground of restitution, the defendant cannot be considered to have any right to retain the value of the benefit.[32]

(b) The deprivation of benefits from a wrongdoer [33]

(i) The nature of restitution for wrongs

In certain cases where a wrong has been committed the victim of the wrong may be able to bring a restitutionary claim to recover the value of the benefit obtained by the defendant as a result of the wrongdoing. For example, sometimes where the defendant commits a tort against the plaintiff the remedial response is not necessarily assessed by reference to the plaintiff's loss, but may alternatively be assessed by reference to the defendant's gain.[34] A similar response may also arise in respect of benefits accruing to the defendant as a result of a breach of contract,[35] the commission of equitable wrongs such as breach of fiduciary duty[36] and the commission of criminal offences.[37]

Although a number of commentators have argued that the restitutionary response in such circumstances arises because the defendant has been unjustly enriched at the plaintiff's expense,[38] this is correct only to the extent that unjust enrichment is used in its descriptive and not its substantive sense. But where the defendant has received a benefit as a result of the commission of a wrong it is not possible to say that the defendant has been unjustly enriched in any substantive sense for two reasons:[39] first, because the plaintiff's restitutionary claim will succeed even though the defendant's benefit was not obtained directly from the plaintiff, so it is not possible to show that the defendant has been enriched at the plaintiff's expense, save in the most artificial sense that the defendant's benefit was obtained from the commission of a wrong and the plaintiff was the victim; secondly, because it is not necessary to show that the plaintiff's restitutionary claim falls within one of the recognised grounds of restitution. It is sufficient that the defendant has com-

---

[32] *Moses* v. *Macferlan* (1760) 2 Burr. 1005, 1007; 97 ER 676, 650 (Lord Mansfield).
[33] See Part IV.   [34] See Chapter 16.   [35] See Chapter 17.
[36] See Chapter 18.   [37] See Chapter 19.
[38] See, in particular, Burrows, *The Law of Restitution* at p. 376 and the report of the Law Commission, *Aggravated, Exemplary and Restitutionary Damages* (Law Com. No. 247, 1997) p. 51. Birks at one time shared this view (Birks, *An Introduction to the Law of Restitution*, p. 26) but he has since changed his mind: *Restitution: Past, Present and Future* (ed. Cornish, Nolan, O'Sullivan and Virgo) p. 14.
[39] See Smith, 'The Province of the Law of Restitution' (1992) 71 *CBR* 672, 683.

mitted a wrong against the plaintiff and that this wrong is of a type which has been recognised as triggering a restitutionary response. It is this wrongdoing, and not unjust enrichment, which constitutes the cause of action for which the relevant remedy may be restitutionary, although compensatory remedies may also be available.

(ii) The nature of the restitutionary remedy

Where the plaintiff seeks a restitutionary remedy in respect of a wrong committed by the defendant the remedy will usually be personal. There are, however, cases where the defendant has been awarded a proprietary restitutionary remedy and where the event which triggered this was a wrong.[40] In such cases there is clearly an overlap between the principle of restitution for wrongs and the principle of vindicating property rights. It is preferable, however, to treat such claims as ultimately founded on the wrong, since it is the wrong which triggers the recognition of the plaintiff's proprietary right.[41]

The justification for the award of restitutionary remedies where the defendant has committed a wrong is the fundamental principle that wrongdoers should not be allowed to profit from their wrongdoing.[42]

(c) The vindication of property rights with which the defendant has interfered

(i) The nature of restitutionary claims founded on the vindication of property rights

Where the plaintiff has a proprietary interest in property which has been received by the defendant, whether that proprietary interest previously existed or has been created by operation of law, then the plaintiff will be able to make a claim to obtain a restitutionary remedy to vindicate this proprietary right.[43] Such proprietary restitutionary claims may take two forms.

(1) Where the defendant received property in which the plaintiff has a proprietary interest and the defendant has retained that property, or has substituted other property for it, then the plaintiff can obtain a proprietary restitutionary remedy in respect of that property itself, the cause of action being the vindication of the plaintiff's continuing property rights.

(2) Where the defendant received property in which the plaintiff had a proprietary interest at the time of receipt, but that interest has since been lost, then the only restitutionary remedy available to the plaintiff is a

---

[40] See, for example, *Attorney-General for Hong Kong* v. *Reid* [1994] 1 AC 324 where the Privy Council awarded the plaintiff a restitutionary proprietary remedy for the defendant's breach of fiduciary duty.

[41] See *ibid.*   [42] See Chapter 15.   [43] See Part V.

personal one, representing the value of the property which the defendant had received. But the plaintiff's cause of action can still be the vindication of property rights, since the plaintiff can show that the property which the defendant received belonged to the plaintiff at the time of receipt.

(ii) Is a proprietary restitutionary claim founded on the unjust enrichment principle?

It is often assumed that where the plaintiff seeks to recover property in which he or she has a proprietary interest then the recovery of the property or its proceeds can be justified only by reference to the principle that the defendant has been unjustly enriched at the expense of the plaintiff. But, again, this is true only to the extent that 'unjust enrichment' is used in a descriptive sense to indicate that the defendant has property which it is just for him or her to return to the plaintiff. 'Unjust enrichment' in its substantive sense is completely irrelevant in this context because the action to vindicate property rights forms part of the law of property and has nothing to do with the principle of reversing the defendant's unjust enrichment.[44] Once it has been shown that the defendant has received or has retained property in which the plaintiff has a proprietary interest then nothing else needs to be proved to establish the plaintiff's cause of action. If the defendant has the plaintiff's property he or she should return it, or its value, to the plaintiff, without the plaintiff first having to establish that the defendant has been unjustly enriched at his or her expense.

It should be acknowledged immediately, however, that the argument that proprietary restitutionary claims are not founded on the principle of unjust enrichment has little support amongst commentators[45] and appears to have little support from the judiciary, because of the prevalent notion that all restitutionary claims are founded on the reversal of unjust enrichment.[46] They argue that, since property is an enrichment which generally cannot be subjectively devalued,[47] it is possible to establish that the defendant has been enriched. Also, if the plaintiff had a proprietary interest in the property or its substitute then this shows that the property was received at the plaintiff's expense. The stumbling block with this analysis relates to the identification of the ground of restitution. Some authors suggest that the applicable grounds of restitution are the

---

[44] See Chapter 20.

[45] For arguments against, see in particular Birks, 'Property and Unjust Enrichment: Categorical Truths' [1997] *NZ Law Rev.* 623. For arguments in favour, see Grantham and Rickett, 'Property and Unjust Enrichment: Categorical Truths or Unnecessary Complexity?' [1997] *NZ Law Rev.* 668.

[46] See in particular Millett LJ in *Boscawen* v. *Bajwa* [1996] 1 WLR 328, 334.

[47] See Chapter 4.

same as those which apply to unjust enrichment.[48] Other authors create new grounds of restitution to enable them to explain the decided cases. For example, Burrows is forced to rely on the ground of ignorance and to create a ground of restitution which he calls 'retention of property belonging to the plaintiff without his consent'.[49] But such artifice is completely unnecessary. The reported cases do not use such reasoning and they have no need to do so, simply because it is sufficient to establish that the defendant has received property in which the plaintiff has a proprietary interest.

There is, in fact, growing evidence to suggest that the unjust enrichment principle cannot explain why restitutionary relief is awarded where the plaintiff brings a proprietary claim. Crucially, in *Macmillan Inc.* v. *Bishopsgate Investment Trust plc. (No. 3)*,[50] the Court of Appeal appeared to assume that proprietary restitutionary claims are not necessarily founded on the unjust enrichment principle. Although this was a case which was concerned with conflict of law issues, and so should be treated with some caution because of the tendency to manipulate legal concepts in order to identify the appropriate choice of law, it is still a very useful decision on the proper characterisation of proprietary restitutionary claims in a domestic context. In *Macmillan* the plaintiff wished to recover shares from the defendants which had been transferred to them by a third party in breach of trust. The defendants pleaded the defence that they were *bona fide* purchasers for value.[51] The issue before the court concerned the choice of law rule for this type of restitutionary action. It was agreed that the plaintiff's claim should be characterised as restitutionary and the argument then related to whether this claim was based on an obligation or property. The Court of Appeal unanimously held that it was a matter of property and so proprietary choice of law rules were applicable. The importance of this case is that the court implicitly recognised that a cause of action could be restitutionary even though the action was not founded upon the reversal of an unjust enrichment. For example, Auld LJ emphasised that the issue in the case was essentially a proprietary one and stated that 'it is difficult to see what unjust enrichment the [defendants] have had'[52] and Aldous LJ accepted that, although the claim arose in equity for restitution, the issue was one of priority of title to shares, without making any reference to the unjust enrichment principle.[53] At the very least the decision of the Court of

---

[48] This is the approach of both Birks (*An Introduction to the Law of Restitution*) and Goff and Jones (*The Law of Restitution*).

[49] Burrows, *The Law of Restitution*, Chapter 13.

[50] [1996] 1 WLR 387. See Virgo, 'Reconstructing the Law of Restitution' (1996) 10 *TLI* 20 and Swadling, 'A Claim in Restitution?' [1996] LMCLQ 63 for further discussion of this case.

[51] See Chapter 22.   [52] [1996] 1 WLR 387, 409.

[53] *Ibid*, p. 418.

Appeal in *Macmillan* is consistent with the assertion that the unjust enrichment principle is not the only principle which justifies the award of restitutionary remedies.

If proprietary restitutionary claims do form a different part of the law of restitution from those claims founded on unjust enrichment, this has profound consequences for the proper analysis of *Lipkin Gorman (a firm)* v. *Karpnale*,[54] where the House of Lords, following the lead of Lord Goff, agreed that all restitutionary claims are founded on the unjust enrichment principle. But *Lipkin Gorman* is not in fact a case which is founded upon the reversal of unjust enrichment, save in the broadest and least useful descriptive sense of the defendant having received a benefit which should be returned to the plaintiff as a matter of justice. Rather, *Lipkin Gorman* was a case which was primarily concerned with the vindication of the plaintiff's proprietary rights.[55] This explains why none of the judges expressly identified all of the elements which are required to establish that the defendant had been unjustly enriched, most notably the ground of restitution, an omission which has been a serious cause of concern for some commentators.[56] This is not a problem if the basis for awarding restitutionary remedies was the vindication of property rights rather than the reversal of unjust enrichment, because where the plaintiff wishes to vindicate property rights it is only necessary to identify the property right and not a ground of restitution.

The facts of *Lipkin Gorman* were straightforward. A partner of the plaintiff firm of solicitors stole money from the firm over a period of time and then used this money to gamble at the defendant's casino. The plaintiff brought a restitutionary claim against the defendant to recover the value of the money which it had received. The plaintiff's action succeeded. Lord Templeman and Lord Goff emphasised the plaintiff's continuing proprietary interest in the money from the moment it was stolen by the partner until it, or its substitute, was received by the defendant.[57] Consequently, a continuing proprietary interest was clearly recognised and appears to have proved vital to the success of the plaintiff's claim.

If this analysis is correct we are left with a nice irony. Whilst the decision of the House of Lords in *Lipkin Gorman* v. *Karpnale* is of prime importance as the case in which the unjust enrichment principle was

---

[54] [1991] AC 548.

[55] This view appears to have been adopted by Ferris J in *Box* v. *Barclays Bank plc.*, *The Times*, 30 April 1998.

[56] See Birks. 'The English Recognition of Unjust Enrichment' [1991] LMCLQ 473, McKendrick, 'Restitution, Misdirected Funds and Change of Position' (1992) 55 MLR 377 and Burrows, *The Law of Restitution*, pp. 148–50. These commentators all consider that the ground of restitution was that of ignorance, even though none of the judges referred to any such ground. See Chapter 7 for further discussion of ignorance as a ground of restitution.

[57] See Lord Templeman at p. 560 and Lord Goff at p. 572.

accepted as forming part of English law, that case is not itself authority for the application of the unjust enrichment principle on the facts of the case.

(iii) Criticisms of the vindication of proprietary rights principle

The recognition of a vindication of proprietary rights principle as distinct from an unjust enrichment principle can be criticised on three grounds.

(1) One criticism of the vindication of property rights principle is that, whereas unjust enrichment is an event for which restitutionary remedies are available, it is not possible to treat proprietary rights as an event and so it is not possible to contrast unjust enrichment and property rights as triggers of restitutionary remedies.[58] But this is not the relevant contrast which should be made. The use of the phrase 'property rights' is neutral and does not suggest that any event has occurred. But the crucial feature of the property rights principle is that the defendant has interfered with the plaintiff's property rights by not allowing the plaintiff the exclusive benefit of his or her rights. It is this interference which justifies the award of restitutionary remedies.[59]

(2) A second criticism is that unjust enrichment and the vindication of property rights cannot be considered to be distinct principles since the plaintiff's property right may arise by operation of law as a response to the defendant's unjust enrichment at the plaintiff's expense. This is particularly the view of Birks,[60] who has argued that personal and proprietary rights exist by virtue of one of four events, namely consent, wrongs, unjust enrichment and other events. Whilst this classification may be of some merit, it is not obviously reflected in the case law. Although in particular it is clear that property rights may exist by virtue of consent, such as the express trust, or wrongs,[61] it is not clear that property rights can derive from the defendant's unjust enrichment. No case has expressly recognised that property rights can arise simply because the defendant has been unjustly enriched at the plaintiff's expense.[62] Also, there is no need to rely on the substantive unjust enrichment principle to explain why the plaintiff has a proprietary interest in property. It is sufficient that the plaintiff's case falls within one of the recognised categories of case by

---

[58] Birks, 'Property and Unjust Enrichment: Categorical Truths' [1997] *NZ Law Rev.* 623, 627–8.

[59] See Grantham and Rickett, 'Property and Unjust Enrichment: Categorical Truths or Unnecessary Complexity?' [1997] *NZ Law Rev.* 668, 680.

[60] Birks, 'Property and Unjust Enrichment: Categorical Truths' [1997] *NZ Law Rev.* 623 and 'Misnomer' in *Restitution: Past, Present and Future* (ed. Cornish, Nolan, O'Sullivan and Virgo).

[61] See, for example, *Reid* v. *Attorney-General for Hong Kong* [1994] 1 AC 324.

[62] Birks only cites *Chase-Manhattan Bank NA* v. *Israel-British Bank (London) Ltd.* [1981] Ch. 105 as an example, but unjust enrichment reasoning was not specifically mentioned in that case.

virtue of which property rights arise and none of these cases requires the plaintiff to establish specifically that the defendant has been unjustly enriched at the expense of the plaintiff.[63] It follows that the substantive unjust enrichment principle should be considered as triggering only personal and not proprietary restitutionary claims.

(3) A final criticism of the vindication of property rights principle is the use of the word 'vindication'. Certainly, the use of the word can be criticised on the technical ground that vindication refers to a specific remedy by virtue of which property, which is in the possession of the defendant but belongs to the plaintiff, is restored to the plaintiff. This *vindicatio* is not recognised at common law and even in equity it is not the only remedy where the defendant has interfered with the plaintiff's property rights,[64] so it could be concluded that it is not appropriate to refer to the vindication of property rights, since property rights are not necessarily vindicated. But despite this, the use of the word 'vindication' does serve a useful function. This is because it describes, albeit in general terms, the nature of the remedy where property rights have been interfered with by the defendant. The word 'vindication' relates to the phrase 'property rights' in the same way that the word 'reversal' relates to 'unjust enrichment'.[65] Because of the technical meaning of vindication an alternative word could be suggested, such as 'protection', but this too lacks precision since it suggests that the restitutionary remedy will be awarded before the proprietary right has been interfered with, to ensure that such interference does not occur, whereas typically the property right has already been interfered with, hence the need for a restitutionary remedy. Consequently, the word 'vindication' will be used in this book, as the most useful word, albeit not the most accurate, to describe the award of restitutionary remedies where the defendant has interfered with the plaintiff's property rights.[66]

(iv) Justifying the award of restitutionary remedies to vindicate property rights

The justification for the award of restitutionary remedies to vindicate the plaintiff's property rights stems from the fundamental principle of English law the property rights are of such importance that they are deserving of particular protection.[67]

---

[63] See Chapter 20.   [64] See Chapter 21.
[65] The equivalent word for wrongdoing is the not very useful 'remedy'.
[66] The use of the word 'vindication' does have some judicial support: see, for example, *Tinsley* v. *Milligan* [1994] 1 AC 340, 368 (Lord Lowry).
[67] See Chapter 20.

(d) Summary of the key principles

Although the matter cannot be considered to be free from doubt, the law of restitution should properly be analysed in the following way. The law of restitution is concerned with all claims where the remedy which the plaintiff seeks is a restitutionary remedy which is assessed by reference to the defendant's gain. Restitutionary remedies are available in three situations: first, where it can be shown that the defendant has been unjustly enriched—here the only remedies which are available are personal restitutionary remedies; secondly, where the defendant has committed a wrong for which restitutionary relief may be available—here the remedy may be restitutionary but it can also be compensatory; finally, where the plaintiff wishes to vindicate his or her property rights—here the remedy is typically restitutionary and, depending on whether or not the defendant retains property in which the plaintiff has a proprietary interest, the restitutionary remedy will either be proprietary or personal.

4. WHAT IS THE JUSTIFICATION FOR RECOGNISING AN INDEPENDENT LAW OF RESTITUTION?

Where the law of restitution is equated with the law of unjust enrichment the justification for recognising an independent body of law called the law of restitution is clear, since it is a distinct subject different from contract, tort and the law of property. But once it is accepted that the law of restitution is not the law of unjust enrichment, but is simply a body of law concerning the types of remedies which may be awarded in particular circumstances, the justification for recognising an independent law of restitution is more difficult to find. It might be thought better to stop talking about and studying the law of restitution and instead concentrate our efforts on the law of unjust enrichment[68] and, where relevant, wrongdoing and vindication of proprietary rights. This would be a mistake.

The main reason for identifying any legal category, such as contract, equity or company law, is that, by grouping cases together which are concerned with the same legal issues, common principles can be identified which assist in the better understanding and prediction of the law. This is true of the law of restitution as well. There are a number of common principles and questions of policy which underlie all restitutionary claims regardless of the cause of action.[69] So, for example, there are important questions of relevance to all restitutionary claims concerning

---

[68] See Birks in *Restitution: Past, Present and Future* (ed. Cornish, Nolan, O'Sullivan and Virgo) Chapter 1.
[69] These are identified and examined in Chapter 2.

how restitutionary remedies should be assessed. Similarly, there are defences and bars which are generally applicable to all restitutionary claims regardless of the principle on which that claim is founded. Also, as a mechanism for analysis of the law, the law of restitution remains a useful hook on which to hang disparate areas of law. It forces us to make connections which might otherwise be ignored, and so the subject remains of great use for the purposes of exposition. For all of these reasons much is to be gained by recognising the law of restitution as an independent body of law in its own right, where the only common characteristic is that it is concerned with the award of remedies which are assessed by reference to the benefit obtained by the defendant.

5. THE OBSTACLES OF HISTORY

Although this book is not the place for a detailed examination of the history of the law of restitution,[70] the essential features of that history remain of vital importance to a proper understanding of the modern subject, particularly because this explains why an independent law of restitution has only recently been fully recognised by the House of Lords in *Lipkin Gorman (a firm)* v. *Karpnale Ltd.*[71]

(a) The implied contract theory

The law of restitution had its origins in the old forms of action, particularly the action of *indebitatus assumpsit* which was developed in the seventeenth century. The function of this action was to enable the plaintiff to recover a sum of money from the defendant after he or she had established that the defendant owed a debt to the plaintiff which the defendant had promised to repay to the plaintiff. Although the essential feature of the action was that a debt was owed by the defendant, the promise was required to enable the action to be accommodated within the system of formal pleading which existed at the time. Although initially the defendant's promise to repay the plaintiff had to be proved expressly, increasingly it was implied from the circumstances of the case, so that the promise became a fiction.[72] This was recognised by Barry J in *William Lacey (Hounslow) Ltd.* v. *Davis*[73] who said that:

---

[70] For detailed analysis of the history of restitution see Jackson's *The History of Quasi-Contract in English Law* (Cambridge: Cambridge University Press,1936). See also Baker, 'The History of Quasi-Contract in English Law' in *Restitution: Past, Present and Future* (ed. Cornish, Nolan, O'Sullivan and Virgo) Chapter 3.

[71] [1991] 2 AC 548.

[72] See *Fibrosa Spolka Akcyjna* v. *Fairbairn Lawson Combe Barbour Ltd.* [1943] AC 32, 63 (Lord Wright).

[73] [1957] 1 WLR 932, 936.

In these quasi-contractual cases the court will look at the true facts and ascertain from them whether or not a promise to pay should be implied, irrespective of the actual views or intentions of the parties at the time when the work was done or the services rendered.

In fact the award of restitution in these cases can, in retrospect, be justified by reference to the principle of unjust enrichment. But, until the middle of the twentieth century, the plaintiff's claim depended on whether it was possible to imply a promise by the defendant to repay the plaintiff. If the facts of the case were inconsistent with the implication of a promise to repay it followed that the plaintiff's restitutionary claim had to fail. So, for example, restitutionary remedies could not be awarded where there was an express contract in existence which prevented a contract from being implied or where one of the parties was incapacitated from making a contract.

(b) Rejection of the implied contract theory

It was this emphasis on promise and the notion of an implied contract theory that proved to be the main obstacle to the recognition of an independent law of restitution. For analysis in terms of implied promises meant that the question whether restitutionary remedies were available was treated simply as an appendix to the law of contract, as was reflected by the fact that such restitutionary liability was characterised as quasi-contractual.[74] The law of restitution has, however, been emancipated from its reliance on contract. This occurred in the crucial case of *United Australia Ltd.* v. *Barclays Bank Ltd.*[75] where Lord Atkin memorably said:

These fantastic resemblances of contracts invented in order to meet requirements of the law as to forms of action which have now disappeared should not in these days be allowed to affect actual rights. When these ghosts of the past stand in the path of justice clanking their medieval chains the proper course for the judge is to pass through them undeterred.[76]

It follows that restitutionary claims will succeed even though it is not possible to imply a contract between the parties. But this rejection of the implied contract theory as the principle which underlies the award of restitutionary remedies does not prevent a plaintiff from suing the defendant on an implied contract. The effect of the *United Australia* case is to remove the fiction of an implied contract from English law, it does not prevent the implication of a contract from the facts where the evidence is consistent with the implication of a contract.

[74] An expression which had been recognised by Lord Mansfield in *Moses* v. *Macferlan* (1760) 2 Burr. 1005, 1008; 97 ER 976, 978.
[75] [1941] AC 1.   [76] *Ibid*, p. 28.

(c) The legacy of the implied contract theory

The legacy of the fictional implied contract does unfortunately live on since judges still sometimes consider whether a contract can be implied when determining whether restitutionary relief should be available to the plaintiff. One of the most blatant examples of such reliance on the implied contract theory is contained in the judgment of Millett LJ in *Taylor* v. *Bhail*.[77] One of the questions for the court in that case was whether a builder could recover the reasonable value of his building work from a customer after the builder had inflated the estimated price of the work to enable the customer to defraud his insurance company. This inflation of the price made the transaction illegal and, since the courts will not enforce illegal transactions,[78] the plaintiff's action on the contract failed. But Millett LJ also concluded that the plaintiff's restitutionary claim should fail because:

The illegality renders any implied promise to pay a reasonable sum unenforceable—just as it renders the express promise to pay the contract price unenforceable.

Such reliance on quasi-contract reasoning should have no part to play in the modern law of restitution. The obligation to make restitution is imposed as a matter of law and does not involve enforcement of any fictional promise of the defendant.[79]

6. THE PRINCIPAL TYPES OF RESTITUTIONARY REMEDY

There are a number of different restitutionary remedies which will be examined throughout this book. At this stage it is sufficient to identify the most important ones. Whilst the remedy which is available for a particular restitutionary claim will vary according to the circumstances of the case, the function of all restitutionary remedies is 'to effect a fair and just balance between the rights and interests of the parties concerned'.[80]

---

[77] [1996] CLC 377. See also *Guinness plc.* v. *Saunders* [1990] 2 AC 663, 689 (Lord Templeman).

[78] *Holman* v. *Johnson* (1775) 1 Cowp. 341; 98 ER 1120. See Chapter 26.

[79] This view has been endorsed in the House of Lords in *Westdeutsche Landesbank Girozentrale* v. *Islington LBC* [1996] 2 AC 669, 710 (Lord Browne-Wilkinson).

[80] *Banque Financière de la Cité* v. *Parc (Battersea) Ltd.* [1998] 2 WLR 475, 489 (Lord Clyde).

(a) Money had and received

Although money had and received was one of the common counts which is still referred to today when pleading a restitutionary claim, it is more appropriate to treat money had and received as a restitutionary remedy rather than as a cause of action. This is a restitutionary remedy which is available where the plaintiff simply wishes to recover money which had been paid to the defendant. It is a personal remedy which exists only at common law and enables the plaintiff to recover the value of money received by the defendant rather than the actual notes and coins.

(b) Reasonable value of property and services

Where the plaintiff has transferred property to the defendant or has provided a service for the benefit of the defendant, and the plaintiff successfully brings a restitutionary claim in respect of these benefits, then the typical remedy which he or she will be awarded is a financial one, assessed by reference to the value of the benefit received by the defendant. Where the plaintiff's claim is for the reasonable value of the property transferred this is called a *quantum valebat*, and where the claim is for the reasonable value of services this is called a *quantum meruit*. The question of valuation of goods and particularly services is one which is fraught with difficulty.[81]

(c) Account of profits[82]

Where the defendant has committed a wrong against the plaintiff, such as a breach of fiduciary duty, and the defendant makes a profit as a result, then one of the restitutionary remedies which may be awarded is that of an account of profits. This involves an account being taken to ascertain the profit made by the defendant as a result of the wrongdoing, which the defendant is then liable to pay to the plaintiff. This is a personal remedy, since the defendant is required to transfer only the value of the profit made.[83]

---

[81] See Chapter 4.
[82] See Chapter 15.
[83] The profit may, however, be held on constructive trust so that the plaintiff has an equitable proprietary interest in it. See Chapter 18.

(d) Restitutionary damages[84]

An alternative remedy which may be available where the defendant has committed a wrong is that of restitutionary damages. Whereas compensatory damages are assessed by reference to the loss suffered by the plaintiff as a result of the wrongdoing, restitutionary damages are assessed by reference to the value of the defendant's benefit obtained from the commission of the wrong. Sometimes the term 'restitutionary damages' is interpreted as covering all pecuniary restitutionary remedies which are awarded following the commission of a wrong.[85] Alternatively, the term is confined to the award of a pecuniary remedy where the defendant has saved money as a result of the wrongdoing, to distinguish it from the award of an account of profits where the defendant has obtained a profit as a result of the wrongdoing.

(e) Recognition of a beneficial interest

Where the defendant has received and retains property in which the plaintiff has a continuing equitable proprietary interest, the defendant may be required to hold that property on resulting or constructive trust for the plaintiff.[86] This means that the plaintiff can call for the return of the property whenever he or she wishes.[87] This type of proprietary restitutionary remedy involving the transfer of property is not available at common law. Consequently, if the defendant has property in which the plaintiff has retained a legal proprietary interest the plaintiff is able to obtain only the value of the property and is not able to recover the property itself.

(f) Equitable charge[88]

Where the defendant has property in which the plaintiff has an equitable proprietary interest an alternative restitutionary remedy to that of recognising that the plaintiff has a beneficial interest in the property is for the courts to impose an equitable charge over it. This is a proprietary restitutionary remedy since it recognises that the plaintiff has a proprietary interest in the property to secure repayment of what the defendant owes to the plaintiff. Consequently, the plaintiff cannot compel the defendant

---

[84] See Chapter 15 and Law Commission Paper No. 247 (1997) entitled 'Aggravated, Exemplary and Restitutionary Damages' p. 51. The term 'restitutionary damages' has been recognised by the Court of Appeal in *Attorney-General* v. *Blake* [1998] 2 WLR 805, 817.

[85] Birks, 'Equity in the Modern Law: An Exercise in Taxonomy' (1996) 26 *Univ. WALR* 1, 29.

[86] See Chapter 21.   [87] See *Saunders* v. *Vautier* (1841) 4 Beav 115; 49 ER 282.

[88] See Chapter 21.

to transfer the property to him or her, but the plaintiff's claim for repayment is given priority over unsecured creditors of the defendant.

(g) Subrogation[89]

(i) The relevance of subrogation within the law of restitution

Subrogation is a restitutionary remedy which is designed to ensure 'a transfer of rights from one person to another . . . by operation of law'.[90] Essentially the function of subrogation is to enable the plaintiff to rely on the rights of a third party against a defendant, or the rights of a defendant against a third party. This will be a particularly useful remedy where, for example, the plaintiff lends money to the defendant in circumstances where the plaintiff thinks that the loan is secured by a charge so that he or she has priority over the defendant's other creditors. If the charge is invalid the plaintiff will simply be an unsecured creditor and so will not have priority over other creditors. In such a case the plaintiff could be subrogated to the rights of another secured creditor of the defendant, even though that security has been discharged. The security in such circumstances is treated as though it has been assigned to the plaintiff,[91] so that he or she is able to rely on it as against the defendant and so gain priority over the defendant's unsecured creditors. Since subrogation is a restitutionary remedy, this notional assignment of the charge is only effective as against a defendant who is liable to make restitution to the plaintiff.

In the leading case of *Banque Financière de la Cité* v. *Parc (Battersea) Ltd.*[92] the House of Lords recognised that there are essentially two forms of subrogation which are recognised in English law.

(1) Contractual

The first type is that which arises by virtue of the express or implied intentions of the parties, as occurs in contracts of insurance where a term is implied that insurers are subrogated to the rights of the assured against the party who caused loss.[93] Since this right to subrogation arises by virtue of contract, it has nothing to do with the law of restitution.[94]

---

[89] See Mitchell, *The Law of Subrogation* (Oxford: Clarendon Press, 1995).

[90] *Orakpo* v. *Manson Investments Ltd.* [1978] AC 95, 104 (Lord Diplock).

[91] *Banque Financière de la Cité* v. *Parc (Battersea) Ltd.* [1998] 2 WLR 475, 488 (Lord Hoffmann).

[92] [1998] 2 WLR 475.

[93] See, for example, *Lord Napier and Ettrick* v. *Hunter* [1993] AC 713.

[94] *Hobbs* v. *Marlowe* [1978] AC 16, 39 (Lord Diplock).

(2) Restitutionary

The other type of subrogation is the equitable remedy which is available by operation of law as a restitutionary remedy specifically to reverse the defendant's unjust enrichment.[95] It may also be used to prevent the defendant's unjust enrichment.[96] Although the matter was not discussed by the House of Lords, subrogation will also be available where the plaintiff's restitutionary claim is founded on the vindication of proprietary rights, and is in fact most likely to arise in such circumstances.[97] Whilst the remedy is in principle available where the plaintiff's claim is founded on the commission of a wrong, there are no cases where such a remedy has been awarded and it is difficult to conceive of a case where such a remedy would be appropriate.

The function of the remedy of subrogation is illustrated by the facts of the *Banque Financière* case itself. In that case the plaintiff had lent a sum of money to the debtor company, which used the money to pay off part of a debt owed by it to a third party, this debt having been secured by a charge over property. The defendant company, which was in the same group as the debtor, had a second charge over the same property. When the plaintiff lent the money to the debtor company the plaintiff received a letter of postponement which stated that the plaintiff's debt would be paid off in priority to that of any other company in the group. Clearly the intention behind this letter was to give the plaintiff priority over the defendant, but the letter was ineffective to give the plaintiff priority as a matter of law. The debtor company became insolvent, and the question for the House of Lords to resolve was whether the debt which that company owed to the plaintiff should be discharged before that which was owed to the defendant. The court concluded that the defendant had been unjustly enriched at the expense of the plaintiff. The defendant was enriched at the plaintiff's expense because the plaintiff's money was used partially to discharge the liability of the third party, and this improved the chances of the defendant being repaid. This enrichment was unjust because the plaintiff had mistakenly believed that the effect of the letter of postponement was that it had priority over the defendant and, had it not made this mistake, it would not have lent the money in the first place.[98] The court concluded that the most appropriate remedy to reverse the defendant's unjust enrichment was to subrogate the plaintiff to the rights of the third party against the debtor company. This meant that, as between the plaintiff and the defendant, the plaintiff had the benefit of the third party's charge so that the plain-

---

[95] *Banque Financière de la Cité* v. *Parc (Battersea) Ltd.* [1998] 2 WLR 475, 483 (Lord Hoffmann).
[96] *Ibid.*   [97] See Chapter 21.
[98] See Chapter 8 for examination of mistake as a ground of restitution.

tiff obtained priority over the defendant. The particularly important feature of the remedy of subrogation in this case was that it operated as a personal remedy, since the plaintiff obtained priority only over the defendant and not as regards any of the other creditors of the debtor company.[99] In other circumstances it might be appropriate to treat the remedy of subrogation as having proprietary consequences, by giving the plaintiff priority over other creditors of the debtor.[100]

(ii) The principles underlying the award of the remedy of subrogation

(1) The restitutionary remedy of subrogation arises by operation of law and does not depend on the parties' intention that the remedy should be available.[101]

(2) The remedy of subrogation may however be defeated by the intention of the parties. In particular, the plaintiff cannot obtain a remedy which is better than that for which he or she had bargained. So, for example, in *Paul* v. *Speirway Ltd.*,[102] where the plaintiff had lent money to the defendant, he could not be subrogated to the security of a third party, in respect of a debt owed by the defendant to the third party, because the plaintiff had intended his loan to the defendant to be unsecured. Although it has sometimes been suggested that where the plaintiff's money has been used to discharge a secured liability then the plaintiff should be presumed to have intended that the security should be kept alive for the plaintiff's benefit,[103] the preferable view is that there is no role for such a presumption in this context. Consequently, the burden of proving that the parties intended the plaintiff's loan to be secured should be on the plaintiff, since this is consistent with basic principles concerning the establishment of causes of action for the purposes of the law of restitution.[104]

(3) Subrogation will also be denied to the plaintiff for reasons of policy, as is illustrated by *Orakpo* v. *Manson Investments Ltd.*[105] where the plaintiff was not subrogated to the rights of a third party because this would have been contrary to the policy of the Moneylenders Acts.

(h) The award of interest

Since it is a function of restitutionary remedies that the defendant should be deprived of those gains obtained as a result of being unjustly

---

[99] [1998] 2 WLR 475, 480 (Lord Steyn) and 489 (Lord Clyde).
[100] See Chapter 21. [101] [1998] 2 WLR 475, 483 (Lord Hoffmann).
[102] [1976] Ch. 220.
[103] *Ghana Commercial Bank* v. *Chandiram* [1960] AC 732, 745 (Lord Jenkins) and *Boodle Hatfield and Co.* v. *British Films Ltd.* [1986] PCC 176.
[104] *Banque Financière de la Cité* v. *Parc (Battersea) Ltd.* [1998] 2 WLR 475, 486 (Lord Hoffmann).
[105] [1978] AC 95.

enriched, having committed a wrong or receiving property in which the plaintiff has a proprietary interest, it should follow automatically that whenever pecuniary restitutionary remedies are awarded the plaintiff should also receive interest. This is because, immediately the defendant has received a benefit which he or she is liable to restore to the plaintiff, the defendant is not entitled to the benefit and so he or she should pay the plaintiff for its use. The law of restitution accepts this argument, and so the defendant is liable to pay the plaintiff for the use of the benefit by means of the award of interest.

But when it comes to assessing the interest which the defendant is liable to pay to the plaintiff the law becomes much more controversial. Should simple or compound interest be awarded?

Simple interest may be awarded by virtue of section 35A of the Supreme Court Act 1981. It is awarded on the amount of money which is owed by the defendant to the plaintiff.

Compound interest has traditionally been awarded in equity where money has been obtained or retained by fraud or where money has been withheld or misapplied by a fiduciary.[106] Compound interest is awarded both on the amount of money which is owed by the defendant to the plaintiff and on the amount of interest which is already due to the plaintiff. Consequently, the award of compound interest is more favourable to the plaintiff.

In *Westdeutsche Landesbank Girozentrale* v. *Islington LBC*[107] the issue for the House of Lords was whether compound interest was available in respect of all restitutionary claims. By a majority it was decided that, since the jurisdiction to award compound interest was an equitable jurisdiction, it followed that compound interest could only be awarded in respect of equitable restitutionary claims. Consequently, where the plaintiff's claim was for money had and received then, because this was a common law claim, the plaintiff could only obtain simple interest.

The majority supported their conclusion by reference to a number of different arguments. In particular, they asserted that, since Parliament had decided in 1981 that simple interest should be awarded on claims at common law, it was not for the House of Lords to award compound interest in respect of such claims.[108] But the Supreme Court Act 1981 does not specifically exclude the award of compound interest in respect of common law claims. Rather, it recognises that the court can award simple interest to such claims. The equitable jurisdiction to award compound interest is still available in appropriate cases.

---

[106] *President of India* v. *La Pintada Compania Navigacion SA* [1985] AC 104, 116 (Lord Brandon).
[107] [1996] AC 669.   [108] *Ibid*, p. 717 (Lord Browne-Wilkinson), p. 718 (Lord Slynn).

In two very strong dissenting judgments Lords Goff and Woolf rejected the argument of the majority. They asserted that, since the policy of the law of restitution was to remove benefits from the defendant, it follows that compound interest should be available in respect of all restitutionary claims, regardless of whether they arise at law or in equity.[109] This argument can be illustrated by the following example. In the straightforward case where the plaintiff pays money to the defendant by mistake and the defendant is liable to repay that money to the plaintiff, the defendant's liability arises from the moment the money is received from the plaintiff. The defendant has the use of that money and consequently should pay the plaintiff for that benefit. This was accepted by all the judges in the case. The difficulty relates to the valuation of this benefit. If the defendant were to borrow an equivalent amount of money from a financial institution then the defendant would be liable to pay compound interest to that institution. It followed that the defendant has saved that amount of money, and so this is the value of the benefit which the defendant should restore to the plaintiff, in addition to the value of the money which the defendant received in the first place.[110] If it could be shown that, had the defendant borrowed the equivalent amount of money, it would only have paid simple interest then it would be appropriate for the interest awarded to the plaintiff to be simple rather than compound interest.[111] Usually, however, the interest awarded in commercial transactions will be compound interest.

The approach of the minority is much more attractive than that of the majority since the award of compound interest is consistent with the fundamental principles underlying all restitutionary claims, especially that, where the defendant has obtained a benefit from the plaintiff in circumstances in which the plaintiff can bring a restitutionary claim, the defendant should be required to make full restitution of all benefits obtained, regardless of the nature of the cause of action. The essential question relating to the award of interest turns on the valuation of the benefit which the defendant has obtained. Where the defendant has been saved paying compound interest to a financial institution as a result of receiving a benefit from the plaintiff, it is entirely appropriate that this benefit should be valued by reference to what the defendant has saved, namely the compound interest.

But despite the attraction of the views of the minority, the decision of the majority represents the law. It follows that compound interest is only available where the plaintiff brings a restitutionary equitable claim. This is indefensible. It is clear that a majority of the House of Lords did not feel that it is for the judiciary to change the law on the award of interest, so we

---

[109] *Ibid*, p. 696 (Lord Goff), p. 736 (Lord Woolf).
[110] *Ibid*, p. 719 (Lord Woolf).   [111] *Ibid*, p. 728 (Lord Woolf).

must look to Parliament for statutory reform. What is needed is a statute which extends the equitable jurisdiction to award compound interest to include claims brought at common law.

7. THE ROLE OF RESCISSION WITHIN THE LAW OF RESTITUTION

One of the most difficult questions facing the modern law of restitution concerns how the doctrine of rescission should be fitted within the structure of the subject.

(a) Rescission as a restitutionary remedy

Where a transaction, usually a contract,[112] is voidable for some reason, such as mistake,[113] misrepresentation[114] or undue influence,[115] then the plaintiff can set the transaction aside and recover any benefits which have been transferred to the defendant under it. The mechanism for setting a transaction aside is rescission. Once the plaintiff has rescinded the transaction it is treated as vitiated, and it follows that the parties should be returned to the position which they occupied before the transaction was entered into. This involves restitution of benefits transferred pursuant to the transaction.

Rescission has been described as a remedy[116] and it may certainly be treated as a restitutionary remedy since a function of rescission is that the plaintiff can recover 'the property with which he has parted under the contract and [must return] the benefit which he received' to the defendant.[117] This remedy will be available once the plaintiff has satisfied the conditions for setting the transaction aside and the plaintiff will not need to establish that the defendant was unjustly enriched, had committed a wrong or that the plaintiff had a proprietary interest which he or she wished to vindicate. It is sufficient that the plaintiff can establish that the transaction was voidable, and then the restitutionary consequence will follow automatically. This analysis of rescission has recently been recognised by Millett LJ in *Portman BS* v. *Hamlyn Taylor and Neck*:[118]

The obligation to make restitution must flow from the ineffectiveness of the transaction under which the money was paid and not from a mistake or misrepresentation which induced it . . . If the payer exercises his right of rescission in

---

[112] But the transaction may also be a gift or a voluntary settlement.
[113] See Chapter 8.   [114] *Ibid.*   [115] See Chapter 10.
[116] *Dunbar Bank plc.* v. *Nadeem* [1998] 3 All ER 876, 884 (Millett LJ).
[117] *Smith New Court Securities Ltd.* v. *Scrimgeour Vickers (Asset Management) Ltd.* [1994] 2 BCLC 212, 221 (Nourse LJ).
[118] [1998] 4 All ER 202, 208.

time and before the recipient deals with the money in accordance with his instructions, the obligation to make restitution may follow.

Even if rescission can be considered to operate as a restitutionary remedy, it is clear that it does not always have restitutionary consequences. For example, sometimes the court may order rescission on terms, such as requiring the parties to enter into a new, more appropriate contract.[119] Where an executory contract is rescinded it appears that rescission is not operating as a restitutionary remedy since the defendant has not received any tangible benefit under the contract which he or she is required to restore to the plaintiff. But even rescission of an executory contract can be analysed as a restitutionary remedy, since the consequence of rescission in such circumstances is that the defendant is required to restore the personal right against the plaintiff which derived from the contract.[120] This personal right is a benefit which was obtained under the contract and, if the contract is to be rescinded, this right ought to be restored to the plaintiff.

(b) What principles trigger the award of the remedy of rescission?

If the remedy of rescission is available whenever a contract is voidable, as determined by the law of contract, it appears that there is a fourth principle by reference to which restitutionary remedies are available, in addition to the principles of unjust enrichment, wrongdoing and the vindication of proprietary rights. In fact, this is not the case. The restitutionary consequences which are implicit within the remedy of rescission can be analysed with reference to both the principle of vindicating property rights and the unjust enrichment principle depending on whether the consequence of rescission is proprietary or personal.

The proprietary consequences of rescission will be that, if the transaction is rescinded at law, then legal title to property will be vested in the plaintiff.[121] Where the plaintiff rescinds the transaction in equity, the consequence will be that the property which the plaintiff transferred to the defendant will be held on trust for the plaintiff so that the plaintiff has an equitable proprietary interest in it. It follows that the plaintiff will be able to bring a proprietary restitutionary claim to vindicate his or her property right.

Where the plaintiff has transferred property to the defendant under a voidable transaction and that transaction is rescinded, the defendant

[119] See, for example, *Solle* v. *Butcher* [1950] 1 KB 671 and *Grist* v. *Bailey* [1967] Ch. 532, discussed in Chapter 8.

[120] Nahan, 'Rescission: A Case For Rejecting the Classical Model?' (1997) 27 *Univ. WALR* 66, 72.

[121] *Car and Universal Finance Co. Ltd.* v. *Caldwell* [1965] 1 QB 525. See Chapter 20.

may not have retained the property, so that a proprietary restitutionary claim will not be available to the plaintiff. The plaintiff will, however, be able to recover the value of the benefits transferred. This restitutionary response can be justified on the basis that, if the defendant was not required to make restitution to the plaintiff, the consequence of the plaintiff setting the transaction aside would be that the defendant would become unjustly enriched at the plaintiff's expense. This is because the defendant would have obtained a benefit from the plaintiff in circumstances where the defendant's retention of that benefit was unjust because the plaintiff had not intended the defendant to receive the benefit in those circumstances. Consequently, the real relevance of the unjust enrichment principle for the purposes of rescission is that it has a negative function. In other words, restitution forms an integral part of the remedy of rescission to prevent the defendant from becoming unjustly enriched as a result of the setting aside of a transaction.[122]

(c) The process of rescission

The method by which the plaintiff rescinds a transaction depends on whether he or she is rescinding the transaction at law or in equity.

Where the plaintiff wishes to rescind a transaction at law he or she can do so without obtaining a court order.[123] Consequently, rescission at law can be characterised as a self-help mechanism. Where the plaintiff wishes to rescind a transaction it is usually necessary that he or she communicates his or her wish to rescind to the defendant. But in certain exceptional circumstances such direct communication is not required. For example, in *Car and Universal Finance Co. Ltd.* v. *Caldwell*[124] the plaintiff wanted to rescind a contract to sell a car, but he could not trace the purchaser of the vehicle. It was held to be sufficient to rescind the contract that the plaintiff had notified both the AA and the police that he wished them to assist him in finding the car. Alternatively, if there is a dispute about the right to rescind and the plaintiff commences judicial proceedings to resolve the matter, the statement in the pleadings that the transaction has been or should be set aside will in itself be sufficient to rescind the transaction.[125] It is a matter of some uncertainty when a transaction can be rescinded at law. The preferable view is that rescis-

---

[122] That the unjust enrichment principle can function in this negative way was recognised by the House of Lords in *Banque Financière de la Cité* v. *Parc (Battersea) Ltd.* [1998] 2 WLR 475 where the remedy of subrogation was awarded to prevent the defendant from becoming unjustly enriched.

[123] *Car and Universal Finance Co. Ltd.* v. *Caldwell* [1965] 1 QB 525, 532 (Lord Denning MR).

[124] [1965] 1 QB 525.   [125] *TSB Bank plc.* v. *Camfield* [1995] 1 WLR 430, 438 (Roch LJ).

sion is available at law only where the plaintiff was induced to enter into a transaction as a result of a fraudulent misrepresentation.[126]

Rescission in equity is more common than rescission at law. It seems that rescission in equity only occurs by order of the court. Or, perhaps more accurately, the plaintiff rescinds the transaction and the function of the court is to determine whether he or she has rescinded the transaction or is entitled to do so.[127] Once such an order has been obtained, rescission will operate retrospectively to the date when the plaintiff commenced legal proceedings.[128]

Regardless of whether the transaction is rescinded at law or in equity, once it has been rescinded restitution follows automatically. The policy of the law is to return the parties to the position which they occupied before entering into the transaction. Consequently, the defendant will be obliged to return to the plaintiff all benefits which he or she received under the transaction and the plaintiff must make counter-restitution to the defendant. The justification for restitution following rescission will either be that the defendant has property in which the plaintiff has a proprietary interest or that the defendant would become unjustly enriched at the plaintiff's expense.

The award of restitutionary remedies following the rescission of a contract is illustrated by *Newbigging* v. *Adam*,[129] where a contract had been rescinded for misrepresentation. The Court of Appeal held that the defendant was required to make restitution in respect of all benefits which he had received under the transaction. Consequently, the defendant was required to repay to the plaintiff the money which the plaintiff had put into a partnership business, as well as the money he had paid to discharge the debts of the business, minus those sums which the plaintiff had received from the partnership. The plaintiff had also assumed liability in respect of partnership debts, consequently the defendant was required to indemnify the plaintiff against all liabilities which he was, or would be, liable to pay under the contract.[130] The defendant was not required to compensate the plaintiff for losses which he had suffered as a result of entering into the contract.[131] We can justify this conclusion on the basis that the loss suffered by the plaintiff was not mirrored by any benefit gained by the defendant.

---

[126] Cp. *ibid*, where Roch LJ suggested that rescission as a self-help mechanism was available in all cases of misrepresentation.

[127] *TSB Bank plc.* v *Camfield* [1995] 1 WLR 430, 438 (Roch LJ).

[128] *Reese Silver Mining Co.* v. *Smith* (1869) LR 4 HL 64.

[129] (1886) 34 Ch.D 582.   [130] (1886) 34 Ch.D 582, 594.

[131] *Ibid*, 592–3 (Bowen LJ). See also *Whittington* v. *Seale-Hayne* (1900) 82 LT 49.

(d) Bars to rescission

Although the plaintiff has a right to rescind the transaction whenever that transaction is voidable, this right will be barred in four specific situations. Where the relevant transaction is a contract the question whether rescission is barred is essentially contractual, since if rescission is barred the contract will continue to exist. But clearly this has consequences for restitutionary claims, particularly because of a fundamental principle of the law of restitution that restitutionary relief cannot be awarded where a contract subsists.[132] It follows that, if rescission is barred, then it is not possible for the plaintiff to obtain restitution from the defendant.

(i) Counter-restitution is impossible[133]

The plaintiff will be barred from rescinding a transaction where he or she is not able to restore benefits to the defendant which the plaintiff has received under the transaction.[134]

Traditionally this bar has been interpreted as barring the right to rescind whenever the plaintiff is unable to make exact counter-restitution to the defendant. So, for example, it has been held that, where the plaintiff has consumed or disposed of property which was received from the defendant under a voidable contract, the plaintiff will be barred from rescinding the contract.[135] In *Smith New Court Securities Ltd.* v. *Scrimgeour Vickers (Asset Management) Ltd.*[136] the plaintiff had been induced to buy shares as a result of the defendant's fraudulent misrepresentation. The Court of Appeal held that the plaintiff was unable to rescind the contract and recover the full purchase price of the shares from the defendant, because it had sold the shares to a third party and so was unable to make 'substantial restitution in specie of the property' which it had received.[137]

Despite this, the requirement that the plaintiff must make counter-restitution has been interpreted much more liberally where the plaintiff wishes to rescind a transaction in equity, so that the plaintiff is not barred from rescinding the transaction if he or she cannot make exact counter-restitution so long as it is possible to make substantial counter-

---

[132] See Chapter 2.

[133] This principle is also known as the bar of *restitutio in integrum* being impossible. It is criticised by Nahan, '*Rescission: A Case for Rejecting the Classical Model?*' (1997) 27 *Univ. WALR* 66, 76–9.

[134] *Spence* v. *Crawford* [1939] 3 All ER 271, 288–9 (Lord Wright); *Smith New Court Securities Ltd.* v. *Scrimgeour Vickers (Asset Management) Ltd.* [1994] 2 BCLC 212, 221 (Nourse LJ) and *Dunbar Bank plc.* v. *Nadeem* [1998] 3 All ER 876, 884 (Millett LJ).

[135] *Clarke* v. *Dickson* (1858) EB and E 148; 120 ER 463.

[136] [1994] 2 BCLC 212.

[137] *Ibid*, at p. 221 (Nourse LJ). This issue was not raised on appeal before the House of Lords [1997] AC 254.

restitution. Essentially what this means is that it does not matter that the plaintiff cannot return the particular benefit which he or she has received so long as he or she is prepared to pay the reasonable value of this benefit to the defendant. So, for example, if the defendant sold a car to the plaintiff pursuant to a contract which was voidable for some reason and the plaintiff damaged the car in an accident, the plaintiff should still be able to rescind the contract so long as he or she returns the car to the defendant with a sum of money to reflect its decreased value after the damage. Rescission should only be denied where it is not possible to value the benefit which has been provided.

Support for this more flexible approach to counter-restitution can be found in a number of cases.[138] It is illustrated by *Erlanger* v. *New Sombrero Phosphate Co.*[139] where the plaintiff wished to rescind a contract for the purchase of a phosphate mine on the ground of non-disclosure of a material fact by the defendant. The problem was that the plaintiff had worked the mine and obtained some benefit from it. The House of Lords held that the plaintiff was able to rescind the contract, so long as it returned the mine to the defendant and accounted for the profits it had made from working the mine. As Lord Blackburn said, a court of equity will grant relief 'whenever, by the use of its powers, it can do what is practically just, though it cannot restore the parties precisely to the state they were in before the contract'.[140]

The consequence of such decisions is that rescission will hardly ever be defeated in equity by the bar of counter-restitution not being possible, since the plaintiff will be able to make counter-restitution in respect of benefits received from the defendant in virtually every case, as long as it is possible to value the benefit which was received, even if it is not possible to return the specific benefit to the defendant.[141] It is consequently most unfortunate that a similar approach was not recognised for rescission at common law by the Court of Appeal in *Smith New Court Securities Ltd.* v. *Scrimgeour Vickers (Asset Management) Ltd.*[142] Surely it would have been sufficient for the plaintiff to pay the value of these shares to the defendant or buy substitute shares which could be returned to the defendant. This was, in fact, recognised by Lord Browne-Wilkinson when the case was heard on appeal, although the question of rescission

---

[138] See, in particular, *O'Sullivan* v. *Management Agency and Music Ltd.* [1985] AC 686; *Cheese* v. *Thomas* [1994] 1 WLR 129 and *Mahoney* v. *Purnell* [1996] 3 All ER 61.

[139] (1878) 3 App. Cas. 1218.

[140] *Ibid*, p. 1278. In the exercise of this power the court will also be prepared to grant the defendant an allowance in respect of the deterioration in value of any property which is returned to him or her.

[141] See *Dunbar Bank plc.* v. *Nadeem* [1998] 3 All ER 876, 888 where Morritt LJ contemplated that, on the exceptional facts of that case, counter-restitution would not be possible.

[142] [1994] 2 BCLC 212.

was not specifically considered by that court. Lord Browne-Wilkinson said that:

if the current law in fact provides (as the Court of Appeal thought) that there is no right to rescind the contract for the sale of quoted shares once the specific shares purchased have been sold, the law will need to be closely looked at hereafter. Since in such a case other, identical, shares can be purchased on the market, the defrauded purchaser can offer substantial restitutio in integrum which is normally sufficient.[143]

This is surely the more just approach. It should follow that the bar of not being able to make counter-restitution should only be relevant where the plaintiff cannot restore the value of any benefit received to the defendant. Consequently, rescission should only be barred where the benefit obtained from the defendant cannot be valued.[144]

(ii) Bona fide *purchase for value*

Rescission will be barred where a third party acquires an interest in assets other than money which were transferred under the voidable transaction, so long as the interest is acquired for some consideration and without notice of the defect which provides the reason for the plaintiff wishing to rescind it. This bar to rescission[145] is, however, difficult to defend. Whilst it is clear that, if a third party has acquired proprietary rights in good faith and for value, then the plaintiff should not be able to bring a proprietary claim against that property, it should not follow that the acquisition of third party proprietary rights should prevent the plaintiff from rescinding the transaction with the defendant and from recovering the value of the benefit which had been transferred to the defendant.[146]

(iii) Affirmation

Where the plaintiff has affirmed the transaction then he or she cannot rescind it. Two conditions must be satisfied before the transaction can be considered to have been affirmed.

(1) The plaintiff must know of the circumstances which enable him or her to rescind the transaction, as will be the case where the plaintiff discovers that he or she was induced to enter into the contract by virtue of the defendant's misrepresentation.[147] But rescission will not be barred simply because the plaintiff had the means of discovering that there was

---

[143] [1997] AC 254, 262.

[144] See Halson, 'Rescission for Misrepresentation' (1997) 5 RLR 89, 91.

[145] Cp. the *defence* of *bona fide* purchase for value which operates to defeat restitutionary claims which are founded on the vindication of property rights. See Chapter 22.

[146] Nahan, '*Rescission: A Case for Rejecting the Classical Model?*' (1997) 27 *Univ. WALR* 66, 74.

[147] *Car and Universal Finance Co. Ltd.* v. *Caldwell* [1965] 1 QB 525.

a ground for rescinding the transaction, even if this could have been discovered with due diligence.[148]

(2) The plaintiff must show by words or conduct that he or she has decided not to rescind the contract.[149] It is not necessary for the plaintiff to communicate this affirmation to the defendant.[150] So, for example, in *Sharpley* v. *Louth and East Coast Ry. Co.*[151] the plaintiff was induced by a misrepresentation of the defendant company to purchase shares in that company. The plaintiff sought to rescind the contract but was unable to do so because, having discovered that the defendant's representations had been untrue, he continued to act as a shareholder, for example by attending general meetings of the company. This was conduct which was considered to show that he intended to affirm the contract.

(iv) Lapse of time

The plaintiff will also be barred from rescinding a transaction if a reasonable period of time has elapsed before he or she has attempted to rescind it.[152] What constitutes a reasonable period of time is a question of fact which depends on the particular circumstances of the case. This bar is often difficult to distinguish from the bar of affirmation since, if the plaintiff delays unnecessarily before he or she seeks to rescind the transaction, this may be treated as affirmation of it.[153]

(e) Rescission on terms

Where the plaintiff wishes to rescind a transaction in equity it is accepted that he or she can rescind on terms that he or she makes restitution of any benefit received from the defendant.[154] But can rescission be subject to other terms imposed by the court, such as terms that the plaintiff can rescind only part of a transaction or is required to enter into a new transaction? In *TSB Bank plc.* v. *Camfield*[155] it was held, in the context of a case in which the plaintiff wished to rescind a transaction for undue influence, that such rescission on terms was not possible in English law. But rescission on terms has been recognised in other contexts, such as where a plaintiff wishes to rescind a transaction for mistake.[156] It has even been recognised where the plaintiff has sought to rescind a transaction by virtue of undue influence.[157]

---

[148] *Redgrave* v. *Hurd* (1881) 20 Ch.D 1.
[149] *Clough* v. *London and North Western Rly. Co.* (1871) LR 7 Exch. 26.
[150] *Car and Universal Finance Co. Ltd.* v. *Caldwell* [1965] 1 QB 525.
[151] (1876) 2 Ch.D 663.   [152] *Leaf* v. *International Galleries* [1950] 2 KB 86.
[153] *Clough* v. *London and North Western Rly. Co.* (1871) LR 7 Exch. 26.
[154] See p. 32 above.   [155] [1995] 1 WLR 430.
[156] See *Solle* v. *Butcher* [1950] 1 KB 671 and *Grist* v. *Bailey* [1967] Ch. 532.
[157] *Cheese* v. *Thomas* [1994] 1 WLR 129.

There is no obvious reason why the court cannot impose terms as a condition of the plaintiff rescinding a transaction. This would be particularly important where it could be shown, for example, that the defendant had induced the plaintiff to enter into a transaction as a result of a misrepresentation but the plaintiff would have entered into an aspect of the transaction anyway even had the defendant not made a misrepresentation. Surely, in such circumstances, the plaintiff should be bound by the transaction to the extent that he or she had not been influenced by the misrepresentation?

2

Themes and Controversies

The previous chapter was concerned with identifying the bare bones of the law of restitution, by identifying the essential structure of the subject. This chapter is concerned with putting some flesh on those bones, by identifying the key principles and policies which affect the operation and structure of the law of restitution. These principles and policies affect the whole of the law of restitution, but their application will vary depending on the principle on which the plaintiff's restitutionary claim is founded. The chapter will also identify some of the issues about which there is particular controversy, the resolution of which will be decisive for the future development of the subject.

1. THE RELEVANCE OF FAULT

(a) Fault is generally irrelevant

One of the most important issues concerning the structure of the law of restitution relates to the role of the fault of both the plaintiff and the defendant in determining whether restitutionary remedies should be awarded. The orthodox approach is that the restitutionary action is generally one of strict liability. In other words, the defendant will be liable to make restitution to the plaintiff without any need to show fault on the part of the defendant. This is generally true of claims founded on the reversal of the defendant's unjust enrichment, where the plaintiff's claim can succeed once it has been established that the defendant has been enriched at the plaintiff's expense in circumstances which fall within one of the recognised grounds of restitution, and it is not necessary to show that the defendant was at fault in anyway. So, for example, if the plaintiff pays money to the defendant mistakenly believing that he or she is liable to the defendant, where the defendant has done nothing to encourage this belief and actually shares it, the defendant is liable to repay the plaintiff.[1] Similarly, where the plaintiff's restitutionary claim is founded on the vindication of property rights, the defendant will be liable to make restitution to the plaintiff regardless of the fault of the defendant.

[1] See Chapter 8.

But the apparent simplicity of this orthodox analysis of restitutionary claims, where the difficulties involving the definition and proof of fault do not appear to intrude, is misleading. In fact, issues of fault are important to many different aspects of the law of restitution.

(b) Circumstances when the fault of either party is relevant

(1) Where the plaintiff wishes to found a restitutionary claim on the commission of a wrong then the fault of the defendant may be important when considering whether the defendant has committed a wrong. But whether fault needs to be proved to establish that the defendant has committed a wrong and, if it does need to be proved, the degree of fault which needs to be shown will depend on the nature of the wrong which has been committed. Some wrongs can be committed without proof of fault, such as breach of contract or breach of fiduciary duty. Other wrongs, especially some torts and serious criminal offences, will only be committed if the defendant was at fault in some way.

(2) Some of the defences which apply to restitutionary claims will only succeed if the plaintiff was acting in good faith. So, for example, if the defendant acted in bad faith he or she will not be able to rely on the defences of change of position[2] or *bona fide* purchase.[3] What is meant by bad faith for these purposes is a matter of controversy, but certainly neither defence will be available to the defendant if he or she knew of the plaintiff's restitutionary claim.

(3) In the context of certain restitutionary claims founded on the reversal of the defendant's unjust enrichment the fault of both the plaintiff and the defendant may be relevant when considering whether a ground of restitution can be established. For example, some grounds of restitution will only be established if the defendant is considered to be more at fault than the plaintiff.[4] For other grounds of restitution it is not necessary to prove that the defendant was necessarily at fault, but such fault is implicit in the nature of the ground of restitution, such as where the defendant has compelled the plaintiff to transfer a benefit[5] or the defendant has exploited the plaintiff's weaker position.[6] The fault of the defendant may also be a relevant consideration when identifying and valuing an enrichment.[7]

(4) It is in the context of equitable restitutionary claims that the question of fault is often explicit. For example, where the defendant has received property in breach of trust or fiduciary duty the defendant may

---

[2] See Chapter 24.   [3] See Chapter 22.
[4] Such as the ground of the defendant being more responsible for participation in an illegal transaction than the plaintiff. See Chapter 10.
[5] See Chapter 9.   [6] See Chapter 10.   [7] See Chapter 4.

be liable to the beneficiary of the trust or the principal to whom the fiduciary duties were owed in an action for knowing receipt. But the defendant's liability will depend on the plaintiff proving that the defendant was at fault in some way.[8] Again, the degree of fault which must be proved is a matter of controversy, as is the need to prove fault at all, but this is clearly a situation where, as the law stands, the defendant will be liable to make restitution to the plaintiff only if the defendant was at fault in some way.

2. OFFICIOUSNESS AND VOLUNTARINESS

It is a fundamental principle of the law of restitution that where the plaintiff has acted officiously in transferring a benefit to the defendant then any restitutionary claim of the plaintiff must fail.[9] This is sometimes expressed in the aphorism that restitution will not assist a volunteer. Whilst this principle has clearly been recognised in English law,[10] its ambit remains a matter of great uncertainty. The application of the principle is illustrated by *Re Rhodes*[11] where a nephew paid for his aunt, who was of unsound mind, to be kept in a lunatic asylum. Since there was no evidence that the nephew intended to be repaid, there was no restitutionary liability as against the aunt's estate after she had died. Restitutionary relief was unavailable because the nephew had acted voluntarily in paying the aunt.

The plaintiff will generally be considered to have acted officiously where he or she transferred a benefit to the defendant in circumstances in which the defendant had not requested the benefit to be transferred.[12]

A number of reasons can be identified to explain the need for a principle to deny restitution to the plaintiff where he or she had acted voluntarily.

(1) If the plaintiff voluntarily makes a gift to the defendant there is no reason why the plaintiff should be allowed to change his or her mind and recover the gift. The donee should be secure in the validity of his or her receipt of the gift and the law of restitution should not be used to unsettle this security. The only exception to this is where there are particular circumstances which undermine the validity of the gift, such as where

---

[8] See Chapter 21.

[9] See Hope, 'Officiousness' (1929) *Cornell LQ* 25 and Wade, 'Restitution for Benefits Conferred Without Request' (1966) *Vanderbilt LR* 1183. See also Evans, 'An Essay on the Action for Money Had and Received' (1998) 6 RLR 1, 8.

[10] See, for example, *Falcke* v. *Scottish Imperial Insurance* (1886) 34 Ch.D 234, 248 (Bowen LJ).

[11] (1890) 44 Ch.D 94.   [12] See *Owen* v. *Tate* [1976] QB 402.

the plaintiff was mistaken[13] or had been compelled to make the gift to the defendant.[14] But where the gift can be undermined in this way it is not possible to conclude that the plaintiff had acted voluntarily in making the gift.

(2) Where the plaintiff can be considered to have taken the risk either that the transfer of the benefit to the defendant was valid or that the defendant may pay for the benefit without being obliged to do so, it is not for the law of restitution to reallocate the risks so that the defendant is required to make restitution to the plaintiff. Where the plaintiff has taken the risk he or she should be considered to have acted officiously.

(3) Where the plaintiff has voluntarily paid the defendant to settle a demand for payment made by the defendant, the payment cannot be recovered because the defendant who has received the payment to settle the claim should be secure in the validity of the payment.[15]

3. THE PRINCIPLE OF SANCTITY OF CONTRACT

One of the most important principles in the law of restitution is that restitutionary remedies cannot be awarded where their effect would be to subvert a contract; the sanctity of the agreement between the parties is of paramount importance. If the parties have entered into a valid agreement which is to regulate their relationship it is vital that the law of restitution does not undermine what they have decided. It is only where the agreement does not operate or has ceased to operate that the law of restitution should have a role to play in any dispute between the parties.

(a) The application of the principle

This principle has a number of implications throughout the law of restitution.

(i) Restitutionary remedies are unavailable if a contract subsists

Where the plaintiff has transferred a benefit to the defendant under a contract and the plaintiff expected to receive something from the defendant in return which was not forthcoming, the plaintiff cannot bring a restitutionary claim against the defendant to recover the benefit which had been transferred unless the contract has first been discharged.[16]

---

[13] See Chapter 8.   [14] See Chapter 9.   [15] See Chapter 23.
[16] See Chapter 12. See *Foran* v. *Wright* (1989) 64 ALJR 1, 13 (Mason CJ) and *Guinness plc.* v. *Saunders* [1990] 2 AC 663, 697–8 (Lord Goff).

(ii) Exclusion of restitution by contract

If a contract excludes the possibility of the plaintiff recovering a benefit from the defendant then it is not for the law of restitution to subvert the contract and enable the plaintiff to obtain restitution of the benefit.[17] The contract may exclude restitution expressly or impliedly. So where, for example, the plaintiff transfers a benefit to the defendant pursuant to an agreement which is subject to contract, this operates to exclude the right to restitution as a general rule, because the inclusion of the phrase 'subject to contract' allocates the risk of a contract not being made to the person who transfers a benefit before a contract is made.[18] It is even possible for the plaintiff's right to restitution to be excluded in a contract between the plaintiff and a third party to which the defendant is not a party.[19]

(iii) Provision for restitution by contract

It is also possible for the contract to provide, either expressly or impliedly, for restitution of benefits transferred under the contract.[20] Consequently, it may be possible for the plaintiff to obtain what looks like restitution from the defendant by relying on the terms of the contract. But such an apparently restitutionary claim should not be considered to fall within the law of restitution, since the obligation to make restitution does not arise by operation of law but arises simply by operation of the agreement between the parties. It is consequently the contractual regime which governs the plaintiff's restitutionary claim. This is important because it means, for example, that the plaintiff does not need to establish that any of the three principles which underlie restitutionary claims are applicable. Also it will follow that the general defences which apply to all restitutionary claims are not applicable to the contractual claim to restitution.

(b) Limits to the sanctity of contract principle

But the principle of sanctity of contracts does have limits. In the same way that the law of restitution should not be used to undermine contracts, the law of contract should not be used to undermine the legitimate award of restitutionary relief. This is most likely to happen by means of an implied contract. Whilst an implied contract is a useful device to respect the intentions of the parties even where these have not

[17] *Pan Ocean Shipping Co. Ltd.* v. *Creditcorp Ltd. (The Trident Beauty)* [1994] 1 WLR 161, 164 (Lord Goff).

[18] See, for example, *Regalian Properties plc.* v. *London Docklands Development Corporation* [1995] 1 WLR 212. See Chapter 12.

[19] *Pan Ocean Shipping Co. Ltd.* v. *Creditcorp Ltd. (The Trident Beauty)* [1994] 1 WLR 161.

[20] See *Sebel Products Ltd.* v. *Customs and Excise Commissioners* [1949] Ch. 409.

been clearly expressed, a contract should only be implied where it is tolerably clear that the parties did intend the contract to be made or would have intended it to be made had they thought about the matter. If contracts are implied in circumstances beyond this then contract will become a fiction, with consequent uncertainty. It does not follow that implied contracts have no role to play in the law of obligations; clearly they do, but the crucial point is that their role must not be abused by artificial extension.

4. THE NATURE OF THE RELATIONSHIP BETWEEN THE PARTIES

In certain circumstances the nature of the relationship between the parties may influence the court's decision to award restitutionary relief. The most important circumstance is whether the relationship between the parties can be characterised as a commercial relationship. This will be significant in two particular circumstances, where the fact that the relationship is commercial means that restitutionary claims are less likely to succeed.

(a) Relevance to unjust enrichment claims

The nature of the relationship between the plaintiff and the defendant may determine whether one of the recognised grounds of restitution is applicable. So for example in the context of the grounds of duress and undue influence, restitution is much more likely to be awarded where the plaintiff is a consumer and the defendant a commercial trader, than if both parties are trading companies which have entered into arm's length commercial transactions.[21] The law of restitution is much more reluctant to intervene where the parties have entered into commercial transactions, because of the fear that this will introduce undesirable uncertainty into the commercial bargaining process and could 'enable bona fide settled accounts to be reopened when parties to commercial dealings fall out'.[22] This was recognised by the Privy Council in *Pao On* v. *Lau Yiu Long*[23] where Lord Scarman held that 'justice requires that men, who have negotiated at arm's length, be held to their bargains unless it can be shown that their consent was vitiated by fraud, mistake or duress'. Even so, exceptionally restitution is prepared to intervene in such commercial transactions, primarily because the nature of the defendant's conduct is so unconscionable that restitution is appropriate to protect the plaintiff from unscrupulous exploitation.[24]

[21] See in particular *CTN Cash and Carry Ltd.* v. *Gallaher Ltd.* [1994] 4 All ER 714.
[22] *Ibid*, p. 719 (Steyn LJ).   [23] [1980] AC 614, 634.   [24] See Chapters 9 and 10.

(b) Relevance to the identification of a fiduciary relationship

Where a defendant owes fiduciary duties to the plaintiff and breaches those duties the defendant will typically be liable to make restitution to the plaintiff of any benefits obtained as a result of his or her wrongdoing. It is consequently important to determine whether the defendant owes fiduciary duties to the plaintiff. But the courts are generally reluctant to recognise that parties to a purely commercial transaction are subject to such duties.[25] It does not necessarily follow, however, that just because the relationship between the parties is purely commercial one of the parties will not owe fiduciary duties to the other, but this will only be recognised in exceptional circumstances.

5. THE PRINCIPLE AGAINST FICTIONS

For a long time the law of restitution was founded on the fiction of the implied contract, whereby the right to obtain a restitutionary remedy depended on whether or not it was possible to imply a contract between the plaintiff and the defendant.[26] Such a fiction has now been abandoned,[27] but it is essential that such fictions do not reappear. There is, however, evidence that the judges do still rely on fictions to achieve what they perceive to be the just result. The best example of this is the way the courts have been prepared to identify fiduciary relationships between the parties as a means of securing restitutionary remedies.[28]

The reason reliance on fictions is dangerous is because it results in muddled thinking and uncertainty. It is also an easy step to treating a fiction as a requirement which must be satisfied before restitutionary remedies can be awarded, rather than simply as a means to an end, once the original reason for the fiction has been forgotten. It is far better that the award of restitutionary remedies is transparent, founded on clear principles, and does not happen behind the smoke-screen of a fiction. If the law of restitution is founded on a clear theoretical basis there should be no need to rely on fictions to secure the desired result.[29]

---

[25] See Chapter 18.   [26] See Chapter 1.
[27] *United Australia* v. *Barclays Bank Ltd.* [1941] AC 1.   [28] See Chapters 18 and 20.
[29] See Baker, 'The History of Quasi-Contract in English Law' and Langbein, 'The Later History of Restitution' in *Restitution: Past, Present and Future* (ed. Cornish, Nolan, O'Sullivan and Virgo, Oxford: Hart Publishing, 1998) pp. 41 and 57–8 respectively.

6. THE ROLE OF PUBLIC POLICY

It is the basic thesis of this book that there are a number of principles which underlie the law of restitution and, once they have been identified, it is possible to predict whether or not restitutionary remedies will be available. But it would be foolish to assert that the law of restitution is so principled, both because many of these principles are poorly developed and lack explicit judicial recognition and also because the decision to award restitutionary remedies is often affected by policy decisions. Numerous examples of this policy orientated approach can be identified throughout the law of restitution. So, for example, the law is reluctant to assist a plaintiff who is party to an illegal transaction.[30] The law also seeks to encourage the highest standard of behaviour on the part of those people who are in a relationship of trust and confidence with the plaintiff.[31] There is also a general policy in favour of depriving wrongdoers of the benefits obtained from the commission of their wrongdoing.

7. THE RELATIONSHIP BETWEEN LAW AND EQUITY

Law and equity were supposed to have been fused into a single system as a result of the Judicature Acts 1873–5. But many aspects of the law of restitution show that this 'fusion' was merely a matter of form rather than substance. It is often still necessary to consider whether the plaintiff's claim is brought in equity or in the common law, since the applicable rules are subtly, sometimes even fundamentally, different. This difference between legal and equitable claims is probably most important in the context of restitutionary proprietary claims. For the purposes of such claims it is vital to determine whether the plaintiff is seeking to vindicate a legal or equitable proprietary interest, since this will affect the plaintiff's ability to trace his or her proprietary right into substitute assets[32] and will also affect the nature of the plaintiff's claim and the remedy which is available.[33] Another consequence of the plaintiff's claim being brought at law or in equity is that this will determine the type of interest which the court can award, since compound interest is only available in respect of equitable claims.[34]

One of the most important challenges facing the modern law of restitution is to determine to what extent the disparate approaches of

[30] See Chapter 26.   [31] See Chapter 18.   [32] See Chapter 20.
[33] See also *MCC Proceeds Inc.* v. *Lehman Bros. International (Europe)* [1998] 4 All ER 675 where it was held that the plaintiff could not sue the defendant for the tort of conversion where the defendant had interfered with the plaintiff's equitable proprietary right.
[34] *Westdeutsche Landesbank Girozentrale* v. *Islington LBC* [1996] AC 669. See Chapter 1.

common law and equity to the award of restitutionary remedies can be assimilated. Such assimilation is particularly difficult because of the different policies, principles and terminology in these two areas, but there is a growing recognition that assimilation is vital. This was recognised by Deane and Dawson JJ in *Baltic Shipping Co.* v. *Dillon*:[35]

> In a modern context where common law and equity are fused with equity prevailing, the artificial constraints imposed by the old forms of action can, unless they reflect coherent principle, be disregarded where they impede the principled enunciation and development of the law. In particular, the notions of good conscience, which both the common law and equity recognized as the underlying rationale of the law of unjust enrichment, now dictate that, in applying the relevant doctrines of law and equity, regard be had to matters of substance rather than technical form.

Such assimilation of legal and equitable regimes is increasingly being advocated in this country, most notably in the context of the tracing rules for the identification of the plaintiff's proprietary interest in substitute assets.[36]

8. RULES VERSUS DISCRETION

One of the most controversial questions facing the modern law of restitution concerns exactly how the laws which form that body of law called restitution should be formulated. In particular, should they be formulated as rules, with consequent certainty and predictability but also inflexibility, or should the laws be formulated in such a way as to give the judge a discretion as to the appropriate result, with consequent flexibility but also uncertainty?

This question has been particularly important in the context of determining how restitutionary remedies should be formulated,[37] and especially whether a remedial constructive trust should be recognised in English law. Currently, English law recognises the institutional constructive trust where the defendant's conduct falls within one of the recognised categories of unconscionable behaviour and consequently the defendant holds property on trust for the plaintiff by operation of law.[38] Although the circumstances in which such a trust is recognised may be

[35] (1992) 176 CLR 344, 376.
[36] See, for example, *Trustees for the Estate of Jones* v. *Jones* [1997] Ch. 159, 170 (Millett LJ). See Chapter 20. For a note of caution see Barker, 'Equitable Title and Common Law Conversion: The Limits of the Fusionist Ideal' (1998) 6 RLR 150, 156.
[37] See especially Finn, 'Equitable Doctrine and Discretion in Remedies' in *Restitution: Past, Present and Future* (ed. Cornish, Nolan, O'Sullivan and Virgo) Chapter 17.
[38] See Chapter 20.

poorly defined it is at least clear that the judge's decision that the defendant holds property on constructive trust derives from the application of rules rather than the judge's discretion. But increasingly judges and commentators have been suggesting that a remedial constructive trust should be recognised, the consequence of which would be that the recognition that the defendant holds property on constructive trust for the plaintiff would arise from the exercise of the judge's discretion rather than operation of law.[39]

The approach which is adopted in this book is that the law of restitution should be as principled as possible. Certainty and predictability of the law is a virtue. For this reason it will be argued that the remedial constructive trust should not be recognised in English law.[40] There are a number of advantages in having a rule-based, principled law of restitution, notably it makes exposition of the law clearer and encourages settlement out of court rather than litigation. But it must not be forgotten that a degree of judicial discretion does have advantages, particularly if principles and rules can be identified to constrain the exercise of this discretion.[41] Ultimately, the proper formulation of the law of restitution involves a balancing exercise between certain rules and flexible discretions. Throughout this book it will be seen that the law is constantly trying to balance these two objectives.

[39] See Chapter 20.   [40] See pp. 635–7 below.
[41] Barker, 'Rescuing Remedialism in Unjust Enrichment Law: Why Remedies are Right' (1998) 57 CLJ 301, 317.

PART II

UNJUST ENRICHMENT

3

The Principle of Unjust Enrichment

1. THE RECOGNITION OF THE UNJUST ENRICHMENT PRINCIPLE

The unjust enrichment principle was first recognised by the House of Lords in *Lipkin Gorman (a firm)* v. *Karpnale Ltd.*[1] Subsequently that court has recognised that there are three questions which must be examined before it can be concluded that the principle is applicable,[2] namely that the defendant received an enrichment[3] at the expense of the plaintiff[4] and in circumstances of injustice.[5] Once the plaintiff has established that the defendant was unjustly enriched the emphasis shifts to determine whether the plaintiff's claim will be defeated or qualified by one of the general defences to restitutionary claims.[6] Although usually the unjust enrichment principle operates positively, in the sense that the plaintiff must establish that the defendant has been unjustly enriched before restitutionary relief is available, sometimes the principle may operate negatively, since restitutionary relief may be awarded to prevent the defendant from becoming unjustly enriched.[7]

Even though the unjust enrichment principle has been clearly recognised at the highest level, the place of that principle within the law of restitution and the function of the principle still requires careful consideration.

(a) The place of unjust enrichment within the law of obligations

The unjust enrichment principle has a vital and distinct role within the law of obligations.[8] Whenever it can be shown that the defendant has been unjustly enriched at the expense of the plaintiff then, by operation of law, the defendant will be obliged to restore to the plaintiff the value of the benefit which he or she has received. Consequently, liability for unjust enrichment is properly regarded as falling within the law of obligations and it should be treated as being on a par with the law of tort and

---

[1] [1991] AC 548.

[2] *Banque Financière de la Cité* v. *Parc (Battersea) Ltd.* [1998] 2 WLR 475, 479 (Lord Steyn).

[3] See Chapter 4.   [4] See Chapter 5.   [5] See Part III.   [6] See Part VI.

[7] See *Banque Financière de la Cité* v. *Parc (Battersea) Ltd.* [1998] 2 WLR 475. This may also help to explain how the remedy of rescission fits within the law of restitution. See p. 30 above.

[8] Burrows, 'Contract, Tort and Restitution—A Satisfactory Division or Not?' (1983) 99 LQR 217.

law of contract.[9] But, crucially, liability for unjust enrichment is very different from these other aspects of the law of obligations, hence the justification for treating it separately. The law of tort is concerned with the identification of wrongdoing, whereas liability for unjust enrichment does not depend on proof of any wrongdoing. Equally, whereas liability for breach of contract arises from the agreement itself, liability for unjust enrichment is imposed by operation of law and does not depend on any agreement having been made between the parties. Indeed, liability for unjust enrichment will be excluded if a contract between the parties is subsisting.[10]

(b) Alternative theories

Even though the unjust enrichment principle has been recognised by the House of Lords, the validity and usefulness of the principle continues to be a source of controversy. A number of commentators have rejected it and have suggested that restitutionary liability should be based on some other theoretical foundation.

(i) Proprietary theory

One of the most important critiques of the unjust enrichment principle was made by Stoljar, who advocated a proprietary theory of the law of restitution.[11] The essence of this theory is that restitution is justified where the defendant has received property which belonged to the plaintiff. Stoljar's recognition of a proprietary theory of restitution is consistent with the principle of vindicating proprietary rights, where the plaintiff is able to obtain restitution if he or she can establish a continuing proprietary interest in property which was received by the defendant.[12] But Stoljar took his proprietary theory much further since he considered that it even encompassed unjust enrichment claims. But this is unacceptable for the following reasons.

(1) In most cases where the plaintiff transfers property to the defendant the plaintiff cannot be said to have a proprietary interest in the property when it was received by the defendant since the plaintiff's title to the property will usually have passed to the defendant at the time of receipt.[13] It follows that the plaintiff's claim cannot be based on the fact that the defendant has received property which belongs to the plaintiff,

---

[9] This was recognised by Lord Wright in *Fibrosa Spolka Akcyjna* v. *Fairbairn Lawson Combe Barbour Ltd.* [1943] AC 32, 61. See also *Banque Financière de la Cité* v. *Parc (Battersea) Ltd.* [1998] 2 WLR 475, 479 (Lord Steyn).

[10] See p. 41 above.

[11] *The Law of Quasi-Contract* (2nd edn., Sydney: The Law Book Co. Ltd., 1989) pp. 9–10 and 250.

[12] See Part V.   [13] See Chapter 20.

because the property no longer belonged to the plaintiff when it was received. It is for this reason that there is a role for the unjust enrichment principle, since this does not depend on proof that the plaintiff has retained a proprietary interest in the property which was received by the defendant.

(2) The fact that the defendant received property which belonged to the plaintiff before it was transferred is hardly a convincing justification for the award of restitutionary remedies where the consequence of the receipt is that the property then belongs to the defendant. Something else needs to be shown to justify the award of such remedies such as the application of one of the recognised grounds of restitution for the purposes of a claim founded on the defendant's unjust enrichment.

(3) Stoljar's proprietary theory also does not explain how restitutionary remedies can be awarded where the defendant is enriched by the receipt of services, since the plaintiff has no proprietary interest in the provision of a service. Although Stoljar accepted that his theory did not cover such claims, he adopted an alternative explanation, namely that a remedy is awarded to the plaintiff in respect of the services which he or she had provided to the defendant on the basis of the plaintiff's loss rather than the defendant's gain, this being called the principle of 'unjust sacrifice'.[14] But this is highly artificial, particularly when the principle of reversing the defendant's unjust enrichment explains why restitutionary remedies can be available where the defendant has benefited from the plaintiff's services.

(ii) No unifying principle of unjust enrichment

An alternative critique of the unjust enrichment principle is that it is of little or no utility to our understanding of when restitutionary remedies will be awarded.[15] This is both because unjust enrichment is not sufficiently recognised by the courts and also because the principle is artificial in bringing together disparate areas of the law which are not sufficiently similar, so that it is not possible to identify a coherent independent body of law founded on the reversal of the defendant's unjust enrichment. This rejection of the unjust enrichment principle can itself be rejected on two grounds. First, because the principle has now been recognised in a number of decisions of the House of Lords. Secondly, because the unjust enrichment principle does indeed have an important,

---

[14] 'Unjust Enrichment and Unjust Sacrifice' (1987) 50 MLR 603. See Chapter 4 for further discussion of this principle.

[15] See especially Atiyah, *The Rise and Fall of Freedom of Contract* (Oxford: Clarendon Press, 1979) p. 768 and Hedley 'Unjust Enrichment as the Basis of Restitution—an Overworked Concept' (1985) 5 LS 56, 'Unjust Enrichment' (1995) 54 CLJ 578 and 'Ten Questions for "Unjust Enrichment" Theorists' [1997] 3 *Web JCL* 1.

but not a universal, function in explaining when restitutionary remedies can be awarded.[16] It is a principle which explains earlier cases and can be used to predict results in future cases. It also enables disparate areas of the law to be brought together. The proof of the usefulness of the unjust enrichment principle will be found in the remaining chapters of this Part and in Part III of this book.

2. THE FUNCTION OF THE UNJUST ENRICHMENT PRINCIPLE

(a) Possible functions of the unjust enrichment principle

Once it has been recognised that there is a principle of unjust enrichment in English law, it is then necessary to determine the function of that principle. It can be interpreted as having two alternative functions, which can usefully be called the formulaic and the normative function.

(i) The formulaic function

According to the formulaic function of the unjust enrichment principle the defendant will only be considered to have been unjustly enriched where the circumstances of the case satisfy the formula for unjust enrichment, namely that the defendant has received an enrichment at the expense of the plaintiff and in circumstances which fall within one of the recognised grounds of restitution. Crucially, restitutionary relief will only be available to the plaintiff according to this interpretation of the principle if restitutionary liability has previously been recognised in similar circumstances.

(ii) The normative function

According to the normative function of the principle the defendant can be considered to have been unjustly enriched whenever the court decides that the circumstances of the enrichment were unjust. The normative function is much more discretionary, involving the judge considering the facts of the case without regard to whether restitutionary relief has previously been awarded in similar circumstances.

(b) The approach adopted by English law

English law considers the unjust enrichment principle to have a formulaic rather than a normative function. Consequently, the defendant will be considered to have been unjustly enriched only where the circum-

---

[16] See Birks, 'Restitution and the Freedom of Contract' (1983) 38 *CLP* 141.

stances of the enrichment fall within one of the recognised grounds of restitution. This approach was accepted by Lord Diplock in *Orakpo* v. *Manson Investments Ltd.*[17] when he said that:

There is no general doctrine of unjust enrichment recognised in English law. What it does is to provide specific remedies in particular cases of what might be classified as unjust enrichment in a legal system that is based on the civil law.

It follows from this that the decision that the defendant has been unjustly enriched is made by reference to principle rather than to vague notions that, as a matter of justice, the defendant ought to return a benefit which he or she has received to the plaintiff. This emphasis on principle rather than discretion was particularly well expressed by Deane J in a decision of the High Court of Australia in *Pavey and Matthews Pty. Ltd.* v. *Paul*:[18]

To identify the basis of such actions as restitution and not genuine agreement is not to assert a judicial discretion to do whatever idiosyncratic notions of what is fair and just might dictate . . . That is not to deny the importance of the concept of unjust enrichment in the law of this country. It constitutes a unifying legal concept which explains why the law recognizes, in a variety of distinct categories of case, an obligation on the part of a defendant to make fair and just restitution for a benefit derived at the expense of a plaintiff and which assist in the determination, by the ordinary processes of legal reasoning, of the question whether the law should, in justice, recognise such an obligation in a new or developing category of case.

(c) Should the unjust enrichment principle have a normative function?

Although the unjust enrichment principle has traditionally been treated as having a formulaic function there is some evidence that the principle may be shifting towards having a more normative function. The trigger for this shift may be an important dictum of Lord Goff in *Westdeutsche Landesbank Girozentrale* v. *Islington LBC*[19] where he recognised that:

An action of restitution appears to me to provide an almost classic case in which the jurisdiction should be available to enable the courts to do full justice . . . The seed is there, but the growth has hitherto been confined within a small area. That growth should now be permitted to spread naturally elsewhere within this newly recognised branch of the law. No genetic engineering is required, only that the warm sun of judicial creativity should exercise its benign influence rather than remain hidden behind the dark clouds of legal history.

[17] [1978] AC 95, 104. See also Lord Goff in *Lipkin Gorman (a firm)* v. *Karpnale Ltd.* [1991] 2 AC 548, 578.
[18] (1987) 162 CLR 221, 256–7. See also *David Securities Pty. Ltd.* v. *Commonwealth Bank of Australia* (1992) 175 CLR 353, 379.
[19] [1996] AC 669, 697.

Whilst it cannot follow from this that we must throw away the recognised principles which underlie the award of restitutionary relief, this dictum does suggest that there is a shift of emphasis away from a backward-looking principled approach towards a forward-looking approach which is much more prepared to enter new territory and award restitutionary relief in circumstances where such relief has not been awarded before. Is this desirable?

Such an approach has been adopted in Canada, where the courts have been much more prepared to award restitutionary remedies by reference to a general principle of unjust enrichment rather than the pre-existing grounds of restitution.[20] But such an approach is surely unsatisfactory. The virtually unconstrained discretion of the judge to decide whether or not the receipt of an enrichment was in circumstances of injustice will result in great uncertainty. Such discretion is alien to the common law tradition where judges reach their decision by reference to what has gone before. Rather, judges would be more concerned with the circumstances of the case and balancing the conduct of the parties to see where the balance of justice lies. This danger is particularly well illustrated by the decision of Knox J in *Hillsdown plc.* v. *Pensions Ombudsman*[21] who said that:

As to its being unjust . . . one only has to compare the position of Hillsdown who successfully wielded a big but misguided stick with that of the members of the . . . scheme who were never told anything of what was being done as regards the payment of surplus to Hillsdown to see which way the scales of justice fall.

Although judges must be allowed a degree of discretion when determining whether the defendant should be liable to make restitution and what the nature of the restitutionary remedy should be, this discretion must never be at the expense of principle.

(d) The middle way

It does not, however, follow from this emphasis on principle rather than discretion that the grounds of restitution are closed. The recognised grounds of restitution must be adapted and, if necessary, new grounds of restitution must be recognised to ensure that the law of restitution remains relevant to the demands of the late twentieth century.[22] There is,

---

[20] See, in particular, *Deglman* v. *Guaranty Trust of Canada* [1954] SCR 725 and *Pettkus* v. *Becker* [1980] 2 SCR 834, both decisions of the Supreme Court of Canada. See also Klippert, 'The Juridical Nature of Unjust Enrichment' (1980) 30 *University of Toronto LJ* 356. Cp. *Peel* v. *Canada* (1993) 98 DLR (4th) 180, examined at p. 55 below.

[21] [1997] 1 All ER 862, 903.

[22] *CTN Cash and Carry Ltd.* v. *Gallaher Ltd.* [1994] 4 All ER 714, 720 (Sir Donald Nicholls V-C).

in fact, evidence that the law of restitution is able to adapt by developing the notion of what constitutes injustice for the purposes of the unjust enrichment principle. This is exemplified by the decision of the House of Lords in *Woolwich Equitable Building Society* v. *Inland Revenue Commissioners*[23] where the plaintiff was able to recover overpaid tax from the Inland Revenue on the newly recognised ground that a public authority was not authorised to receive such an *ultra vires* payment. Another example of a newly recognised ground of restitution is that of absence of consideration which has been applied where the plaintiff pays money to the defendant pursuant to a transaction which is null and void.[24]

There is, therefore, a middle way between the formulaic and normative functions of the unjust enrichment principle. That principle cannot be allowed to be a strait-jacket to restitutionary claims, since it needs to adapt to changing circumstances. But this adaptation must be by reference to the established principles, rather than simply by referring to the justice of the case. This 'middle way' has been expressly recognised by the Supreme Court of Canada in *Peel* v. *Canada*[25] where McLachlin J said:

we must choose a middle path; one which acknowledges the importance of proceeding on general principles but seeks to reconcile the principles with the established categories of recovery . . . [26]

This notion of a 'middle path' is reflected in English law as well. It is vital that new grounds of restitution are recognised or that the existing grounds are reinterpreted where it is appropriate to do so, but this recognition and development should always occur in a piece-meal fashion and be continuously informed by the existing and well-established grounds of restitution.

3. THE ROLE OF THE UNJUST ENRICHMENT PRINCIPLE IN PRACTICE

It is one thing to recognise the unjust enrichment principle as a means of analysing certain types of restitutionary claim, but how does this principle operate in practice? Most importantly, how does the plaintiff plead a restitutionary claim founded on unjust enrichment? This raises a further question, namely what is the cause of action when the plaintiff's claim is founded on unjust enrichment?

---

23 [1993] AC 70. See Chapter 14.   24 See Chapter 12.
25 (1993) 98 DLR (4th) 140.   26 *Ibid*, p. 153.

(a) Current practice

In practice where the plaintiff wishes to being a restitutionary claim at common law founded on the defendant's unjust enrichment that claim will still be pleaded with reference to the old forms of action, known as the common counts, even though they were abolished in the nineteenth century.[27] There are four types of action:

(1) the action for money had and received by the defendant to the use of the plaintiff;
(2) the action for money paid to the defendant;
(3) *quantum valebat*, to recover the reasonable value of goods which had been transferred to the defendant; and
(4) *quantum meruit* to recover the reasonable value of services which the defendant had received from the plaintiff.

Which action is pleaded depends on the type of enrichment which the plaintiff alleges the defendant has received and the circumstances in which it has been received. Even though the plaintiff's claim is formulated in terms of the old forms of action, it does not follow that the claim is unrelated to the unjust enrichment principle. In fact, the forms of action are explicable only by reference to that principle. This was recognised by Clarke J in *South Tyneside MBC* v. *Svenska International plc.*[28] who accepted that the recognition of unjust enrichment does not constitute the recognition of a new cause of action different from that of money had and received and the other forms of action. Rather, unjust enrichment 'is simply another way of describing the same thing'.

(b) A preferable approach

Rather than formulating the plaintiff's claim with reference to the old forms of action it would be preferable to formulate the claim with explicit reference to the unjust enrichment principle. As yet, unjust enrichment cannot be pleaded as a 'cause of action' in its own right, and as a term on its own it is probably too vague to be acceptable.[29] But since the unjust enrichment principle will be applicable only where the plaintiff's claim falls within one of the recognised grounds of restitution, such as mistake, duress or total failure of consideration, the better view is that it should be sufficient for the plaintiff to plead that the defendant had been unjustly enriched at the plaintiff's expense on the ground of mistake or duress, for example, without needing to assert that the plaintiff's action falls within

---

[27] By s. 3 of the Common Law Procedure Act 1852.   [28] [1995] 1 All ER 545, 557.
[29] As was recognised by Dawson J in *David Securities Pty. Ltd.* v. *Commonwealth Bank of Australia* (1992) 175 CLR 353, 406.

one of the forms of action such as money had and received or *quantum meruit*. It follows that the plaintiff's cause of action is not unjust enrichment as such, that is merely a principle on which the claim is based; rather the cause of action is that the defendant has been enriched at the plaintiff's expense in circumstances which fall within one of the recognised grounds of restitution.[30] This is consistent with the other two principles which trigger restitutionary remedies. So, where the plaintiff's claim is founded on the defendant's wrongdoing, it is not sufficient merely to say that the plaintiff's claim is founded on a wrong, it is necessary to identify the particular type of wrongdoing which is alleged. Similarly, where the claim is founded on the vindication of property rights, it is necessary to identify the right which the plaintiff seeks to vindicate, and sometimes to formulate the claim with some precision, as is the case where, for example, the claim is founded on the action for knowing receipt.[31]

***

[30] *Ibid.* [31] See Chapter 21.

4

Enrichment

1. THE RELEVANCE OF ENRICHMENT

The identification of an enrichment goes to the very heart of a restitutionary action which is founded on reversal of the defendant's unjust enrichment, for until an enrichment has been identified and valued it is not possible to ascertain exactly what should be returned to the plaintiff. Usually the need to identify an enrichment causes no difficulty for the plaintiff. So, in a typical claim where the defendant has received money from the plaintiff, the defendant is always regarded as enriched by the money since it is the measure of value.[1] But in those restitutionary actions where the plaintiff seeks to recover the value of non-money benefits, such as goods or services, the identification of an enrichment and its valuation is a matter of some complexity. It must not be forgotten that, even though it can be shown that the defendant has been enriched, it does not follow that the plaintiff's restitutionary claim will necessarily succeed, since it must also be established that the enrichment was received at the plaintiff's expense[2] and that one of the recognised grounds of restitution is applicable.[3]

The law concerning the identification and valuation of an enrichment is particularly difficult and uncertain, primarily because of the paucity of the case law in this area. It follows that much of the discussion of the law in this chapter has to be speculative, with particular emphasis placed on academic commentaries rather than cases. This does not mean that the issue of how an enrichment is defined is not important; rather that, in an underdeveloped law of restitution, many of the controversial questions concerning enrichment have either been ignored or have not yet arisen. Now that we have a clearly defined structure founded, at least in part, on the reversal of unjust enrichment, the discussion is increasingly being focused on the enrichment issue, as exemplified by the growing number of recent cases where judges have explicitly analysed the definition of enrichment.[4]

---

[1] See p. 67 below.   [2] See Chapter 5.   [3] See Part III.
[4] See, for example, *BP Exploration Co. (Libya) Ltd.* v. *Hunt (No. 2)* [1979] 1 WLR 783; *Marston Construction Co. Ltd.* v. *Kigass* (1989) 15 Con. LR 116; *Ministry of Defence* v. *Ashman* [1993] 40 EG 144.

(a) Unjust enrichment or unjust benefit?

Whilst the principle of reversing unjust enrichment clearly assumes that it is a precondition of liability that the defendant has been enriched, sometimes the restitutionary action is analysed in terms of whether or not the defendant has been unjustly benefited rather than enriched. For example, in the *Fibrosa* case[5] Lord Wright referred to the principles of both unjust enrichment and unjust benefit. The Law Reform (Frustrated Contracts) Act 1943[6] uses the word 'benefit' in the context of a statutory scheme which comes into operation once a contract has been frustrated and which exists to reverse the defendant's unjust enrichment.[7] Does it make any difference whether 'enrichment' or 'benefit' is used or can these words be used indiscriminately?

Linguistically there is an important difference between 'enrichment' and 'benefit', and consequently the word which is used may have an important effect upon the ambit of the restitutionary action. This is because 'enrichment' can be interpreted as being limited to those benefits which can be assessed only in terms of monetary value. In other words, a defendant will only be enriched when he or she has received money or money's worth. Consequently, Beatson[8] has assumed that enrichment equates with wealth and concludes that a defendant will only be enriched where he or she has received something which has an exchange value, so that on receipt of the enrichment the defendant is better off than he or she would have been had he or she not received the enrichment. This may be acceptable as an economic definition of what constitutes an enrichment, but is it really acceptable as a legal definition? Colloquially, a defendant may say that he or she was enriched even though he or she had not received something which itself had an exchange value. This is particularly relevant where the defendant has received a 'pure service', namely a service which leaves no marketable residuum,[9] such as attendance at a concert or receiving a massage. Beatson, by virtue of his rigorously economic approach to the definition of enrichment, concludes that pure services cannot be treated as enrichments, save where the service anticipates expenditure which the defendant would necessarily have incurred.[10]

[5] *Fibrosa Spolka Akcyjna* v. *Fairbairn Lawson Combe Barbour Ltd* [1943] AC 32, 61. See also *Brook's Wharf and Bull Wharf Ltd.* v. *Goodman Brothers* [1937] 1 KB 534, 545 (Lord Wright MR).

[6] See Chapter 12.

[7] *BP Exploration Co. (Libya) Ltd.* v. *Hunt (No. 2)* [1979] 1 WLR 783, 799 (Robert Goff J).

[8] *The Use and Abuse of Unjust Enrichment* (Oxford: Clarendon Press, 1991) pp. 29 ff.

[9] A marketable residuum will be left where the effect of the service is to leave a valuable end-product, for example a service which improves the defendant's property and so increases its value.

[10] *The Use and Abuse of Unjust Enrichment*, p. 32.

Since, however, there will often be a demand for pure services in the market where reasonable people are prepared to pay for the service, this suggests that the service is a valuable benefit.[11] It is for this reason that 'benefit' is a better expression than 'enrichment', since it emphasises that the unjust enrichment principle should not be limited by the artificial restrictions of economic analysis.

The fact that 'benefit' is a more flexible and wider expression than 'enrichment' has been recognised before. For example, Fuller and Perdue in their essay on 'The Reliance Interest in Contract Damages'[12] recognised that 'enrichment' is a narrower term than benefit, which, if it is used, will have the effect of narrowing the potential ambit of the restitutionary response. Also Goff and Jones stress[13] that 'the concept of *benefit* is in English law not synonymous with that of objective enrichment (in the sense that the wealth of the defendant has increased) . . . '.

Despite this preference for the use of 'benefit', the terms 'enrichment' and 'benefit' will be used interchangeably throughout this book for two reasons:

(1) This reflects the practice in the cases where the words are used indiscriminately without any obvious intention that they have different senses.
(2) The word 'enrichment' is explicitly incorporated in the principle of reversing unjust enrichment. It is probably too late now to rename this the unjust benefit principle, even though this is the more accurate expression. But where 'enrichment' is referred to, it must always be remembered that it should be given a wide interpretation, one which is not constrained by economic definitions of wealth, so that it should include pure services.

(b) The essence of enrichment

The essential feature of an enrichment is that it must be capable of being measured in monetary terms. The need to value the enrichment is vital since, as the only remedy for unjust enrichment is personal, it follows that the plaintiff will be able to recover only the value of the enrichment itself from the defendant and this remedy can only be expressed in mon-

---

[11] Edward Nugee QC, sitting as a Deputy High Court Judge in *Re Berkeley Applegate (Investment Consultants) Ltd.* [1989] Ch. 32, appears to have rejected Beatson's contention when, at p. 50, he said that the suggestion that services would constitute an enrichment only where the work added to the assets of the defendant was 'too narrow a view of the principles'. See also Birks, 'In Defence of Free Acceptance' in *Essays on the Law of Restitution* (ed. Burrows, Oxford: Clarendon Press, 1991) p. 134.

[12] (1936) 46 *Yale LJ* 52, 72.

[13] Goff and Jones, *The Law of Restitution*, p. 16 (emphasis in original).

etary terms. Resorting to value as the indicator of enrichment does not mean that Beatson's notion of exchange value is being recognised. This is because something may be regarded as valuable without necessarily having an exchange value. For example, a pure service may be valuable, in that reasonable people would pay for it, even though the defendant is left with nothing of any value.

Much of the uncertainty concerning the definition of enrichment stems from the lack of consensus about where the analysis should start. Essentially there are two options available. Either we start with an objective test, ascertained by asking whether reasonable people would consider the defendant to have received something of value, or we start with a subjective test, by considering whether the defendant considers that he or she has received something of value. Most commentators have assumed that the subjective test prevails. Birks, for example, assumes that the question whether the defendant has been enriched should be determined by reference to the defendant's own perception of whether or not he or she has received something of value.[14] But, whilst both objective and subjective tests are relevant to the identification of an enrichment, the better view is that it is the objective test which should always be considered first, for four reasons.

(1) The most important reason for the initial emphasis on the objective test is that it makes more sense for the plaintiff to establish that the defendant has received an objective benefit and then for the burden to shift to the defendant to disprove this by arguing that he or she did not subjectively value what had been received. To require the plaintiff at the outset to show that the defendant actually valued what was received is difficult and illogical.

(2) Also, the emphasis on the objective test is justified by the fact that the subjective test of enrichment has usually been formulated in terms of the principle of subjective devaluation,[15] whereby the defendant is allowed to show that he or she did not value the benefit which had been received. But, for the principle of subjective devaluation to work, the defendant must first be shown to have received an objective benefit; otherwise there is nothing to devalue.

[14] Birks, *An Introduction to the Law of Restitution*, pp. 112 and 114. See also p. 125 where he says of the objective approach that it is 'exactly the opposite technique from that with which the common law has grown up'. More recently Birks appears to have accepted that the objective test provides the underlying test of enrichment, although he stresses that this may be displaced in appropriate cases by the subjective test. See Birks, 'In Defence of Free Acceptance' in *Essays on the Law of Restitution* (ed. Burrows) p. 134.

[15] Birks, *An Introduction to the Law of Restitution*, p. 109. This principle was recognised by the Court of Appeal in *Ministry of Defence* v. *Ashman* [1993] EG 144, 147 (Hoffmann LJ).

(3) The objective test is the test which is generally relied on when valuing the enrichment and so, for consistency, that test should also be adopted, at least initially, when identifying the enrichment.[16]

(4) Finally, there is some evidence that the objective test is adopted in practice. So, for example, it is the objective test which is adopted for the purposes of determining whether the defendant has received a valuable benefit under a frustrated contract.[17] Also, the objective test was initially applied in *Leigh* v. *Dickeson*[18] where the Court of Appeal accepted that the defendant had been benefited by repairs to the house of which he was a tenant, but denied that he was liable to pay for the repairs, apparently by virtue of the subjective devaluation principle. In other words, the court initially assumed that the defendant had received an objective benefit and then considered the question whether the defendant valued what had been received.

The question whether the objective or subjective test of enrichment determines the essential nature of an enrichment is not simply a matter of semantics; it can have profound consequences on the determination of whether the defendant was enriched and in explaining the true function of the different principles which assist in the identification of an enrichment.

(i) The objective test of enrichment

The objective test of enrichment assesses whether the defendant has received anything of value by asking whether reasonable people would have been prepared to pay money for the benefit which the defendant received. This objective enrichment may take many forms. Often the enrichment will be positive, such as where the defendant receives a chattel or benefits from a services which increases the value of a defendant's property. Alternatively, a defendant may be negatively enriched, for example where the defendant has been saved an expense which he or she would otherwise have incurred. This is illustrated by the facts of *Craven-Ellis* v. *Canons Ltd.*,[19] where the plaintiff director of the defendant company provided services to that company. These services were described as necessary to the running of the company, and so it is possible to conclude that the company had been enriched by them, because it had been saved money which it would otherwise necessarily have incurred had the plaintiff not provided the services.

---

[16] See *Rover International Ltd.* v. *Cannon Film Sales Ltd. (No. 3)* [1989] 1 WLR 912, discussed at p. 101 below.

[17] By virtue of the Law Reform (Frustrated Contracts) Act 1943. See *BP Exploration Co. (Libya) Ltd.* v. *Hunt (No. 2)* [1979] 1 WLR 783, 802 (Robert Goff J).

[18] (1884) 15 QBD 60.   [19] [1936] 2 KB 403. See p. 75 below.

The defendant cannot be considered to have been enriched objectively unless he or she has actually received a putative benefit. It is not sufficient for the plaintiff to have supplied a benefit to the defendant. This follows logically from the essential nature of restitutionary actions, where the restitutionary remedy is assessed by reference to the value of the benefit obtained by the defendant. This will be particularly important where the plaintiff argues that the defendant has been enriched by a service. Even where the alleged benefit takes the form of pure services, the defendant can be considered to be benefited only if he or she received the service. So, for example, if the defendant goes to a concert he or she can be regarded as benefited by the musicians' services only if the defendant actually hears the music.

It follows from the requirement that the defendant must have received a benefit that the defendant cannot be considered to have been enriched simply because the plaintiff commenced work in providing a service. But not every case is consistent with this principle. This is illustrated by the difficult case of *Planché* v. *Colburn*,[20] where the plaintiff had entered into a contract with the defendant to write a book on costume and ancient armour to be published by the defendant in a series called *The Juvenile Library*. After the plaintiff had commenced research for the book, by visiting museums and consulting reference books, but before he had delivered any part of the manuscript to the defendant, the defendant abandoned the series and refused to pay the plaintiff for the work which he had done. The plaintiff successfully sued the defendant and recovered a sum representing the reasonable value of his work. The court particularly stressed that the remedy was a *quantum meruit* and was not awarded for breach of contract.[21] It appears therefore that the plaintiff was awarded a restitutionary remedy by virtue of which the defendant was required to pay for the reasonable value of the services provided by the plaintiff. But this cannot have been a case where the remedy was awarded to reverse the defendant's unjust enrichment, since the defendant had received no benefit.[22] The remedy which was awarded is much easier to justify if it is characterised as the award of reliance damages for breach of contract.[23] Alternatively, the award of a restitutionary remedy

---

[20] (1831) 5 Car. and P 58; 172 ER 876. See also *Prickett* v. *Badger* (1856) 1 CB (NS) 296; 140 ER 123.

[21] See Tindal CJ in (1831) 5 Car. and P 58, 61; 172 ER 876, 877.

[22] Birks in *Essays on the Law of Restitution* (ed. Burrows), p. 141 suggests that the contract might be construed as one which commissioned both the research and the work of writing the book, rather than just delivery of the complete manuscript. This is highly unlikely on the facts, and even if this construction of the contract is correct, how can the defendant be regarded as having received the benefit of the plaintiff's work?

[23] A count for breach of contract was included as part of the plaintiff's claim.

could, perhaps, be justified if it was possible to estop the defendant from denying that he or she had received a benefit.[24]

(ii) The subjective test of enrichment

Once the plaintiff has established that the defendant had received an objective benefit the burden shifts to the defendant to show that he or she did not value what was received.[25] This is the subjective test of enrichment which is called the principle, or sometimes the defence,[26] of 'subjective devaluation'.[27] Usually, if the reasonable person would regard the benefit as valuable, the defendant will agree; but this is not always the case because 'different people value different things according to their own tastes and priorities'.[28]

The defendant may subjectively devalue an objective benefit for a number of different reasons. The defendant might simply wish to be perverse. For example, if the plaintiff had washed the defendant's dirty windows without being requested to do so, the reasonable person would consider this to be an objective benefit but the defendant, for some perverse reason, might have preferred the windows to remain dirty.[29] Consequently, the objective enrichment is defeated by subjective devaluation.[30] Another motive for subjective devaluation is that the defendant might have a different priority for expenditure. For example, if the plaintiff installed a fitted kitchen in the defendant's house which should have been fitted in the house next door, the defendant would presumably acknowledge that the fitted kitchen was an objective benefit but might not wish to pay for it because he or she was saving to buy a new car, something which he or she considered to be a much more urgent expenditure.

One of the best examples of subjective devaluation in operation arises from the facts of *Boulton* v. *Jones*.[31] In this case the defendant ordered and received a quantity of pipe. This pipe was supplied by the plaintiff, although the defendant had not made a contract with him but with his predecessor in title. Consequently, when the plaintiff sued the defendant under the contract for the price of the pipe, his action was defeated because there was no contract between the plaintiff and the defendant. No restitutionary liability would have arisen on these facts either.

---

[24] See pp. 88–91 below.

[25] Garner, 'The Role of Subjective Benefit in the Law of Unjust Enrichment' (1990) 10 *OJLS* 42, 63.

[26] See *ibid*, 51; Carter, 'Ineffective Transactions' in *Essays on Restitution* (ed. Finn, Sydney: The Law Book Co. Ltd., 1990) p. 216.

[27] See Birks, *An Introduction to the Law of Restitution*, pp. 109 ff.

[28] Birks in *Essays on the Law of Restitution* (ed. Burrows) p. 127.

[29] Garner (1990) 10 *OJLS* 42, 44.

[30] Subject to the limitations on the operation of subjective devaluation. See pp. 70–86 below.   [31] (1857) 2 H and N 564; 157 ER 232.

Although the defendant was objectively enriched by the receipt of the pipe, he did not actually value it. This was because the predecessor in title of the plaintiff owed money to the defendant. The defendant had ordered the pipe from the plaintiff's predecessor in title in the expectation that he would be able to set off what was due to him against the price of the pipe. Since the money was still due from the predecessor in title, the defendant could legitimately say that he had not actually been enriched by the receipt of the pipe from the plaintiff.[32]

(1) The rationale of subjective devaluation

The principle of subjective devaluation originates from the forms of action which required the defendant to have requested a particular benefit before a restitutionary remedy could be awarded. Although this request eventually became a fiction, the policy behind it, namely that the defendant would be liable only for benefits which he or she wanted, remains valid. This principle was identified in a number of cases. For example, in *Falcke* v. *Scottish Imperial Insurance Co.*[33] Bowen LJ said:

Liabilities are not to be forced upon people behind their backs any more than you can confer a benefit upon a man against his will.

In other words, the defendant should be given the opportunity to decide whether or not he or she wants the putative benefit. Similarly, in *Ministry of Defence* v. *Ashman*[34] Hoffmann LJ specifically recognised that the underlying rationale of the subjective devaluation principle was that the defendant could not be considered to have been enriched if he or she had not been given the opportunity to reject the benefit.

But why should the defendant be given the opportunity to decide whether he or she valued the objective benefit which he or she had received? The justification derives from the principle of individual autonomy or freedom of choice, a principle which is of fundamental importance to much of English law. Where the defendant is not given a free choice about the receipt of a particular benefit, it is perfectly legitimate for the defendant to say that he or she did not value the benefit. It is for this reason that, when the defendant relies on the subjective devaluation principle, it is not necessary to show why he or she did not value what was received; it is sufficient that the defendant can show that he or she had not chosen to receive the benefit. The defendant may recognise that what he or she has received is potentially valuable to reasonable

---

[32] Although the defendant might have freely accepted the benefit. See pp. 79–86 below. See Birks, *An Introduction to the Law of Restitution*, p. 116.

[33] (1886) 34 Ch.D 234, 248. See also *Taylor* v. *Laird* (1856) 25 LJ Exch. 320, 332 (Pollock CB) and *Stocker* v. *The Planet Building Society* (1879) 27 WR 793, 794 (Jessel MR).

[34] [1993] 40 EG 144, 147.

people, but this recognition does not mean that the defendant valued it. Even if the defendant used what had been received it does not necessarily follow that he or she valued it because '[if the plaintiff] cleans another's shoes, what can the other do but put them on?'[35]

(2) Implications of recognising subjective devaluation

The recognition of the subjective devaluation principle has a number of implications.

(1) It has been assumed so far that the subjective test of enrichment will apply only to enable the defendant to devalue an objective benefit which has been received. But logically and for reasons of consistency it should be possible to use the defendant's own valuation of what has been received to identify an enrichment, even though the reasonable person would not regard the defendant as having received anything of value. This principle of subjective revaluation raises additional problems which will be discussed later.[36]

(2) The analysis of the subjective devaluation principle which has been adopted so far assumes that the principle can be used to defeat completely the argument that the defendant has been enriched. This will be its usual function. But subjective devaluation could also be relevant in those cases where the defendant has clearly been enriched, to determine the extent of that enrichment. For the reasonable person might value the enrichment at a certain price, but the defendant might value it at a lesser price. The role of subjective devaluation in valuing the enrichment will also be discussed later.[37]

(3) If we are prepared to adopt a subjective test to ascertain whether the defendant has been enriched, why should this test be confined to the defendant's own perception of the value of what he or she has received? Surely, the plaintiff's perception of the value of what he or she has provided should also be taken into account? For example, imagine a case where the defendant has taken the plaintiff's ring without the plaintiff's consent. This ring is actually cheap cosmetic jewellery, but it was given to the plaintiff by his mother who has recently died and so it is of great sentimental value. The defendant has lost the ring and so the plaintiff seeks to recover its value. Should the plaintiff's perception of the value of the ring be taken into account in assessing whether, and the extent to which, the defendant has been enriched? The answer must be 'no' for the simple reason that it is not the function of the law of restitution to assess relief by reference to the plaintiff's loss. The law of restitution assesses restitutionary remedies only by reference to the defendant's gain. Therefore, in assessing that particular gain the defendant's own valua-

---

[35] *Taylor* v. *Laird* (1856) 25 LJ Ex. 320, 332 (Pollock CB).
[36] See p. 86 below.   [37] See p. 95 ff below.

tion is relevant. It is the function of compensatory remedies to take into account the plaintiff's particular circumstances and compensation is not a function of the law of restitution.

2. PARTICULAR TYPES OF ENRICHMENT

Enrichments may take many different forms, but generally they fall into one of four categories, which reflect the historic division between the four common counts, namely the actions for money had and received, *quantum valebat* (the reasonable value of goods), *quantum meruit* (the reasonable value of services) and money paid.

(a) Money

Most restitutionary claims involve the plaintiff seeking to recover money from the defendant to whom the plaintiff has paid it. In these circumstances the enrichment question is not of critical importance, because money is always regarded as an enrichment. This was recognised by Robert Goff J in *BP Exploration Co. (Libya) Ltd.* v. *Hunt (No. 2)*[38] who stressed that, because money is the universal medium of exchange, it always constitutes an enrichment.[39] Consequently, it is never possible for the defendant to rely on the subjective devaluation principle and argue that he or she did not value the money which has been received. In the vast majority of cases 'money' refers to coins and notes which are legal tender. But 'money' may also include a sum credited to the account of the defendant. This is deemed to be equivalent to a payment[40] and will similarly always be regarded as an enrichment.

(b) Property

Generally where the defendant receives property, such as land or chattels, he or she will acknowledge that the property is a valuable benefit and so constitutes an enrichment. But it is possible subjectively to devalue property. This will especially be the case where the defendant argues that he or she would not wish to have spent money on such property, preferring instead to spend the money on something which was of more use to him or her. For example, if the defendant already has a car and is given another car by the plaintiff by mistake, the defendant could rely on subjective devaluation and assert that he or she did not value the

[38] [1979] 1 WLR 783, 789.
[39] In other words it is an incontrovertible benefit. See pp. 72–9 below.
[40] *Ward and Co.* v. *Wallis* [1900] 1 QB 675, 679 (Kennedy J).

car. Such subjective devaluation would, however, be subject to those principles which operate to limits its application.[41]

(c) Services

The issue of whether the receipt of services constitutes an enrichment for the purposes of the law of restitution is highly controversial. The reason for this was identified by Robert Goff J in *BP Exploration Co. (Libya) Ltd. v. Hunt (No. 2)*[42] when he stressed that services, unlike money, cannot be restored and 'the identity and value of the resulting benefit to the recipient may be debatable'.[43] A particular problem relating to the determination of whether the receipt of services constitutes an enrichment arises where the services were provided without being requested by the defendant. In such circumstances the defendant will be able subjectively to devalue the service because the defendant had no choice but to accept them.[44]

Whether a particular service constitutes an enrichment will depend upon the type of service which is being provided. Essentially, the provision of services fall into two groups.

(i) Services resulting in an end-product

The first category is those services which increase the value of the defendant's property and so result in some end-product, as occurs where the plaintiff improves the defendant's property. This end-product can be regarded as an objective benefit, though it may still be subject to subjective devaluation. Where the service has resulted in an end-product the nature of the enrichment which has been received is a matter of controversy. It has sometimes been argued that the true enrichment is the service itself, rather than the end-product.[45] But such a conclusion is highly artificial. Where, for example, the defendant employs the plaintiff to explore for oil and the plaintiff eventually finds oil, it is surely more accurate to conclude that the benefit which was eventually received by the defendant is the end-product, namely the oil found, rather than the provision of the service itself, namely the cost of the exploration. Since we are concerned with identifying the benefit which the defendant had received, rather than the loss suffered by the plaintiff,[46] that benefit should be considered to be what the defendant actually received after

---

[41] See pp. 70–86 below.   [42] [1979] 1 WLR 783, 799.
[43] Robert Goff J recognised that a similar problem arises with the provision of goods where the goods are consumed or transferred to somebody else.
[44] *Taylor* v. *Laird* (1856) 25 LJ Ex. 329, 332 (Pollock CB).
[45] See *BP Exploration Co. (Libya) Ltd.* v. *Hunt (No. 2)* [1979] 1 WLR 783, 801 (Robert Goff J).
[46] See *Kleinwort Benson Ltd.* v. *Birmingham CC* [1996] 4 All ER 733. See Chapter 5.

the plaintiff had finished his or her work, even if the end-product was worth less than the services which the plaintiff had provided. Whilst it is true that the service was a means to the end of finding oil, since oil was found this was the direct benefit to the defendant. The provision of the services by the plaintiff was too remote.

(ii) Pure services

The second category of services is those services which leave no end-product, known as 'pure services', such as the provision of lessons and entertainments. Beatson has argued that, because of the absence of an end-product, such services cannot constitute an enrichment, except where the defendant has been saved a necessary expense.[47] But this is to adopt a highly artificial definition of enrichment, grounded upon economic principles, which is contrary to common sense.[48] The provision of pure services can be objectively beneficial since reasonable people are prepared to pay for such services, and so they should be regarded as an objective enrichment,[49] although this is also subject to subjective devaluation.

(d) Payment made to a third party on behalf of the defendant

If the plaintiff pays money to a third party this may constitute a benefit to the defendant. For example, if the defendant owes money to the third party and the plaintiff pays off this debt, then, to the extent that this payment discharges the debt,[50] this will constitute an objective benefit to the defendant, since reasonable people would regard this as valuable.[51] Such a benefit is a non-money benefit, because it is the effect on the defendant and not the third party which characterises its nature. This benefit could be regarded as a service,[52] but since it concerns the payment of money, albeit to a third party, it is useful to examine it separately from the provision of services. Also this type of benefit has traditionally been kept separate from the provision of services, as reflected by the structure of the common counts. The count for the provision of services was a *quantum meruit*, whereas that for payments made to third parties was brought specifically under the action for money paid. Since this enrichment is characterised as a non-money benefit it may be subjectively devalued by the defendant if, for example, the defendant could have

---

[47] Beatson, *The Use and Abuse of Unjust Enrichment*, p. 23.   [48] See p. 60 above.

[49] See *BP Exploration Co. (Libya) Ltd.* v. *Hunt (No. 2)* [1979] 1 WLR 783, 801–2 (Robert Goff J). See also Birks, *An Introduction to the Law of Restitution*, p. 450.

[50] The question of when a debt is discharged is discussed in Chapter 9.

[51] See, for example, *Exall* v. *Partridge* (1799) 8 TR 303; 101 ER 1405.

[52] This was how the benefit was characterised in *Procter and Gamble Phillipine Manufacturing Corp.* v. *Peter Cremer GmbH and Co. (The Manila)* [1988] 3 All ER 843.

relied on a set-off or a counterclaim to negate his or her liability to the third party.

3. METHODS OF OVERRIDING SUBJECTIVE DEVALUATION

Once the plaintiff has established that the defendant has received an objective benefit, the burden then shifts to the defendant to show that he or she did not value the benefit. The only hope for the plaintiff then is to find some way to trump the defendant's reliance on the subjective deval-uation principle. There are four methods by which the plaintiff can over-ride the defendant's reliance on the principle.

(a) Contract

(i) Express contracts

Where the court can conclude that the plaintiff has transferred a benefit to the defendant under a contract the contractual regime will be applic-able and, if the defendant is liable to pay the plaintiff for the value of the benefit under the contract, he or she must do so even though the defen-dant may not value the benefit which was received. This is because of the fundamental principle that the law of restitution is subordinate to the law of contract.[53] Such contractual liability may take the form of an express ancillary contract[54] or the defendant may be held liable to pay for the benefit under the contract by which the benefit was provided, even though that contract had been discharged for the defendant's breach.[55]

(ii) Implied contracts

More controversially, the court may be able to imply a genuine contract to pay for the benefit from the facts of the case. A rare example of a case in which it was possible to imply a genuine contract is *Empirnall Holdings Pty. Ltd.* v. *Machon Paull Partners Pty. Ltd.*,[56] where the plain-tiff architects were engaged in an extensive property development for which the defendant property developer had refused to execute a printed contract. The New South Wales Court of Appeal was able to infer that the

[53] See Chapter 2.

[54] *Turniff Construction Ltd.* v. *Regalia Knitting Mills* [1972] EG (Dig.) 257, where a letter of intent was regarded as an ancillary contract for the preparatory work which had been done by the plaintiff. The effect of this was that the defendant was required to pay for the preparatory work once the negotiations for a main contract had collapsed.

[55] See, for example, *Inchbold* v. *The Western Neilgherry Coffee, Tea and Chinchora Plantation Co. Ltd.* (1864) 17 CB (NS) 753; 144 ER 293.

[56] (1988) 14 NSWLR 523. See also *Batis Maritime Corp.* v. *Petroleos del Mediterranea* [1990] 1 Lloyd's Rep. 345.

defendant had accepted the terms of this contract by virtue of its conduct, even though it had not signed the contract. Consequently, the
plaintiffs were able to sue on the contract for the value of the benefits
which had been provided. The ratio of the case can be found in a dictum
of McHugh JA who said that:[57]

Where an offeree with a reasonable opportunity to reject the offer of goods or services takes the benefit of them under circumstances which indicate that they
were to be paid for in accordance with the terms of the offer, it is open to the tribunal of fact to hold that the offer was according to its terms.

This case seems to fall just above the threshold of what constitutes an
acceptable implication of a contract. But this dictum shows the danger of
implied contracts. Since the decision essentially turns upon an analysis
of the facts of the case to identify the real intentions of the parties, there
is clearly scope for the courts to manipulate the facts to secure what they
believe to be the just result. This could easily escalate into the fiction of
implying a contract as a matter of law where the justice of the case
demands it. This is unacceptably uncertain and should be rejected. The
implication of a contract to pay for benefits which have been received
should be confined to those exceptional cases where it is possible to conclude that the relationship between the parties really was governed by a
contract. Consequently, a contract cannot be implied where the facts as
found negate the existence of such a contract. For example, if two parties
are negotiating a contract and the plaintiff, encouraged by the defendant, incurs expenditure in preparing to perform the contract, it will not
be possible to imply a contractual obligation that the defendant should
reimburse the plaintiff for this expenditure if the parties intended that
the reimbursement for this expenditure would be paid for out of the proceeds of the contract. Nevertheless, there may still be scope for the imposition of restitutionary liability.[58]

(iii) The relationship between implied contracts and free acceptance

When the implied contract theory within the law of restitution was at its
height, the fiction of the implied contract was the method by which restitution for goods or services was achieved.[59] Many of these cases can
today be justified using other principles. Whilst some of them would still
be treated as involving a genuine implied contract, many others would
today be decided by reference to the principle of free acceptance.[60]
Indeed, the language used by McHugh JA in *Empirnall Holdings* reflects

---

[57] *Ibid*, at p. 535.
[58] See *William Lacey (Hounslow) Ltd.* v. *Davis* [1957] 1 WLR 932, discussed at p. 362
below.
[59] See, for example, *Re Rhodes* (1890) 44 Ch.D 94, 107 (Lopes LJ).
[60] See pp. 79–86 below.

the principle of free acceptance. This suggests that there is a very fine line between the contractual and restitutionary response where the defendant receives goods or services in circumstances where there is an opportunity to reject them.

(b) Incontrovertible benefit

It is unclear to what extent a principle of incontrovertible benefit exists in English law, although this type of principle has been recognised in a few cases.[61] Recognition has been advocated by Goff and Jones and Birks.[62] The essence of the principle of incontrovertible benefit was identified by McLachlin J in *Regional Municipality of Peel* v. *Her Majesty the Queen in Right of Canada*,[63] where she described it as:

> an unquestionable benefit, a benefit which is demonstrably apparent and not subject to debate and conjecture. Where the benefit is not clear and manifest it would be wrong to make the defendant pay, since he or she might well have preferred to decline the benefit if given the choice.

Consequently, the incontrovertible benefit principle defeats the subjective devaluation principle because it identifies those circumstances in which it can be presumed that the defendant would not have declined the benefit even if he or she had been given the choice to do so. In other words, the defendant will be incontrovertibly benefited where the only possible conclusion is that he or she has received a valuable benefit. Obviously proof of incontrovertible benefit is not sufficient in its own right to establish unjust enrichment, since the other elements of the claim must also be identified.[64] The incontrovertible benefit principle is simply relevant to the identification of an enrichment.

Whether the benefit which has been received by the defendant can be regarded as incontrovertibly beneficial is ultimately a question of fact, but three, and possibly four, tests can be identified which will assist in determining what can constitute an incontrovertible benefit.

---

[61] *The Manila* [1988] 3 All ER 843, 855 (Hirst J); *Marston Construction Ltd.* v. *Kiglass Ltd.* (1989) 15 Con. LR 116, 129 (Judge Bowsher QC). The notion of incontrovertible benefit was recognised in *Re Berkeley Applegate (Investment Consultants) Ltd.* [1989] Ch. 32, although the expression was not specifically used. See also the Australian case of *Monks* v. *Poynice Pty. Ltd.* (1987) 11 ACLR 637, 639 (Young J) and the decision of the Supreme Court of Canada in *Regional Municipality of Peel* v. *Her Majesty the Queen in Right of Canada* (1993) 98 DLR (4th) 140, 159 (McLachlin J).

[62] Goff and Jones, *The Law of Restitution*, p. 23 and Birks, *An Introduction to the Law of Restitution*, p. 116.

[63] (1993) 98 DLR (4th) 140, 159.

[64] See McKendrick, 'Incontrovertible Benefit—A Postscript' [1989] *LMCLQ* 401. It seems that this was ignored in *Marston Construction Ltd.* v. *Kiglass Ltd.* (1989) 15 Con. LR 116.

(i) Money

The simplest and most common example of an incontrovertible benefit is the receipt of money, because no reasonable person would ever regard the receipt of money as anything other than beneficial.[65] It is with the non-money benefits that the greatest difficulties arise. What needs to be identified are those non-money benefits which are so unequivocally enriching that their receipt can be treated as equivalent in effect to the receipt of money.[66]

(ii) Anticipation of necessary expenditure

Where the defendant receives a benefit which saves him or her from incurring expenditure which he or she would otherwise necessarily have incurred then the defendant should be treated as incontrovertibly benefited. Such a defendant cannot convincingly argue that he or she did not value what had been received, because he or she would have paid for the particular benefit anyway had the plaintiff not provided it. Because of the circumstances of necessity the defendant has no choice whether or not to accept the benefit. Consequently, treating the defendant as enriched does not infringe the autonomy principle.

The circumstances of necessity may arise in two different ways.

(1) Operation of law

The expenditure which the defendant needed to make may arise by operation of law. For example, in *Exall* v. *Partridge*[67] the plaintiff's carriage, which was on the defendant's premises, was distrained by the defendant's landlord because the defendant's rent was in arrears. To recover his carriage the plaintiff was compelled to pay the outstanding rent to the landlord. He then successfully recovered this money from the defendant. Clearly the defendant was enriched, since the money paid to the landlord discharged the debt which the defendant owed. The defendant could never argue that he did not value this benefit because, if the plaintiff had not paid the money, the defendant would have been legally obliged to pay the landlord, and so the expenditure was necessary.[68] Similarly, in *County of Carleton* v. *City of Ottawa*,[69] a decision of the Supreme Court of Canada, the plaintiff, thinking that an indigent was resident within its boundaries, paid for board, lodging and medical assistance to be provided to her. In fact, the indigent was resident within the defendant's boundaries, so that the defendant was liable to make

---

[65] *BP Exploration Co. (Libya) Ltd.* v. *Hunt* [1979] 1 WLR 783, 799 (Robert Goff J).
[66] Birks, *An Introduction to the Law of Restitution*, p. 117.
[67] (1799) 8 TR 308; 101 ER 1405. See Chapter 9.
[68] On the question of the ground for restitution, see Chapter 9.
[69] (1965) 52 DLR (2d.) 220.

provision for her. It was held that the defendant was liable to repay the plaintiff. The defendant was incontrovertibly benefited since the plaintiff had discharged the defendant's legal liability. It seems that if the defendant is to be characterised as incontrovertibly benefited by the discharge of a liability, this must have been a legal rather than a moral liability.[70]

(2) Factually necessary expenditure

Alternatively, the expenditure may be factually necessary. This will arise where, although the defendant is not compelled by law to incur the expenditure, he or she would have incurred it had the plaintiff not provided the benefit. So, for example, if whilst the defendant is on holiday, burglars break into his house and break a window, the plaintiff, who is a neighbour, may arrange for the window to be replaced to ensure that the property is protected. When the defendant returns from holiday he or she is obliged to reimburse the plaintiff. The defendant cannot argue that he or she was not benefited by what the plaintiff did, because if the plaintiff had not replaced the window the defendant would inevitably have done so.[71] This is illustrated by *Re Berkeley Applegate (Investment Consultants) Ltd.*[72] where services provided by a liquidator in administering trust property were held to have been of substantial benefit to the investors because 'if the liquidator had not done this work, it is inevitable that the work, or at all events a great deal of it, would have had to be done by someone else, and on application to the court a receiver would have been appointed whose expenses and fees would necessarily have had to be borne by the trust assets'.

Other examples of factually necessary expenditure being anticipated by the plaintiff arise in the context of the supply of necessaries to the incapacitated, such as infants and the mentally disturbed.[73] By the very definition of 'necessaries', their supply constitutes an incontrovertible benefit. In *Falcke* v. *Scottish Imperial Insurance Co.*[74] it was recognised that, in the context of maritime salvage, services which have been provided to preserve or benefit property belonging to somebody else will result in a restitutionary obligation being imposed on that person to

[70] *Regional Municipality of Peel* v. *Her Majesty the Queen in Right of Canada* (1993) 98 DLR (4th) 140, 156 (McLachlin J).
[71] See Chapter 11 for consideration of the relevant ground of restitution in such circumstances.
[72] [1989] Ch. 32, 50 (Edward Nugee QC). See also *Re Allison, Johnson and Foster Ltd., ex p. Birkinshaw* [1904] 2 KB 327, 331 (Kennedy J), *Craven-Ellis* v. *Canons Ltd.* [1936] 2 KB 403, 412 (Greer LJ), *Re Duke of Norfolk's Settlement Trusts* [1982] Ch. 61 and *Monks* v. *Poynice Pty. Ltd.* (1987) 11 ACLR 637.
[73] See for example *Re Rhodes* (1890) 44 Ch.D 94, discussed in Chapter 13. See also *Clarke* v. *The Guardians of the Cuckfield Union* (1852) 21 LJ (QB) 349, concerning the supply of toilets to a work-house; the toilets were held to be necessary.
[74] (1886) 34 Ch.D 234, 248 (Bowen LJ).

reimburse the plaintiff. To the extent that recovery within maritime salvage can be regarded as restitutionary the defendant is enriched because he or she was incontrovertibly benefited.[75]

One specific problem which arises in respect of factually necessary expenditure relates to the determination of what is meant by necessity in this context. This is not a problem for legally necessary expenditure, since the law either requires the expenditure to be incurred or it does not. But in the context of factual necessity it may be possible for the defendant to carry on without incurring the expenditure. If so, the benefit received should not be regarded as incontrovertibly beneficial. But, when considering whether the expenditure was necessary, unrealistic or fanciful possibilities of the defendant doing without the enrichment should be ignored.[76] So, for example, in *Craven-Ellis* v. *Canons Ltd.*,[77] where it was recognised that the services of the managing director of a company were necessary to the company,[78] it might be argued that the company could have continued to function without the managing director's services, but this is surely unrealistic. So long as it can be shown that in the ordinary course of events the defendant would have incurred the expenditure it should be possible to conclude that the defendant had been incontrovertibly benefited.[79]

(iii) Benefit realised in money

If the defendant has received a benefit in kind which is then realised in money, it should be possible to conclude that the defendant has been incontrovertibly benefited. In such circumstances the defendant should not be allowed subjectively to devalue the benefit because the value of the benefit has been converted into money and the receipt of money is always an enrichment. So, for example, if the plaintiff repairs the defendant's damaged car, which is then sold by the defendant, he or she will be regarded as enriched to the extent that the car has increased in value as a result of the plaintiff's services.

Some support for the notion that the defendant can be incontrovertibly benefited by realising a benefit in money can be identified in the decision of the Court of Appeal in *Greenwood* v. *Bennett*.[80] This is a difficult case to analyse since, although the award of restitutionary remedies appears to have been considered, the court assumed without comment

---

[75] See Chapter 11.

[76] Birks, *An Introduction to the Law of Restitution*, p. 120. See *Monks* v. *Poynice Pty. Ltd.* (1987) 11 ACLR 637, 640 (Supreme Court of New South Wales).

[77] [1936] 2 KB 403.   [78] *Ibid*, 412 (Greer LJ).

[79] Birks in *Essays on the Law of Restitution* (ed. Burrows) suggests, at p. 127, that the test should be whether 'it would be wholly unrealistic to deny that, had the plaintiff not furnished [the benefit], the recipient would have laid out money to secure it . . . '.

[80] [1973] QB 195. See also *Munro* v. *Willmott* [1949] 1 KB 295.

that the recipient of a benefit in kind was objectively enriched and there was no apparent reliance on subjective devaluation. Despite this, the facts of the case provide a useful scenario for analysis of the incontrovertible benefit principle. The facts of *Greenwood* v. *Bennett* were complex. Bennett, who managed a car dealership, sent one of the cars to be repaired. The repairer drove the car and crashed it. He then sold it to Harper, who bought the car thinking that he had good title to it. Harper repaired and improved the car and sold it on to a finance company who let it on hire-purchase. The police recovered the car and then brought interpleader proceedings to ascertain who had the better claim to the vehicle. Essentially, the dispute boiled down to one between Bennett, who sought to recover the car, and Harper, who wished to be paid for his work in repairing and improving it. The trial judge held that Bennett had a better claim to the car and so ordered it to be restored to him, without making any order for Harper to be reimbursed for his services. Harper appealed to the Court of Appeal. Before that appeal was heard Bennett sold the car. The Court of Appeal affirmed that Bennett had the better title to the car, but held that, as a condition of recovery, Harper should be reimbursed for the cost of the repairs and improvements.

The imposition of the condition that Harper should be reimbursed for his services can be interpreted as compensating Harper for his loss or ensuring that Bennett made restitution of a gain. But if this restitutionary analysis is to succeed, it needs to be established that Bennett had been unjustly enriched. This raises three separate questions.

(1) Identifying an enrichment

Bennett had clearly been objectively enriched by Harper's work in repairing and improving Bennett's car, and he could be prevented from subjectively devaluing this benefit by virtue of establishing an incontrovertible benefit. But in considering the application of this principle it is necessary to draw a subtle but important distinction between the different types of work which Harper had undertaken.

In respect of the repairs needed to restore the car to its condition before the crash, Bennett can be regarded as incontrovertibly benefited since Harper had presumably anticipated expenditure which Bennett would necessarily have incurred once he had regained possession of the vehicle. For Bennett was a commercial dealer in cars and presumably would have repaired the car so that he could have sold it, which he in fact did once the car had been recovered.

Harper also improved the car. This cannot be regarded as necessary expenditure because there was nothing to suggest that Bennett would have improved the car once he had recovered it. But the improvement could still be considered to have incontrovertibly benefited Bennett because he had realised the value of the improvement by selling the car. The difficulty with this analysis is that when the case came before the trial judge it was not open to him to say that the value of the improvement had been realised, since at that point the car had not been sold. Perhaps, therefore, it is sufficient that the value of the services would be realised in the ordinary course of events.[81] This is a fair conclusion on the facts, since Bennett was in the motor trade and so he would be expected to sell the car at some stage.

(2) Identifying the ground of restitution

Once it could be shown that Bennett had been enriched at Harper's expense, Harper would need to identify a ground of restitution before Bennett could be considered to have been unjustly enriched. This could easily be established, since Harper had mistakenly believed that the car belonged to him, and, had he not made this mistake, he would not have undertaken the work on it.[82]

(3) Passive or active claim?

Even though Harper could have established that Bennett was unjustly enriched, he was not bringing a claim to recover the value of the services which he had provided. Rather, Harper's restitutionary claim was passive, since it took the form of a condition that he be reimbursed before Bennett could recover the car. This passive claim was recognised by all three members of the Court of Appeal. But the more controversial question is whether Harper could have brought an active restitutionary claim on these facts. For example, if Bennett had recovered possession of the car without recourse to the courts, could Harper have instigated an action against him to recover the value of the services? Although Cairns LJ expressly rejected such a claim,[83] Lord Denning MR was adamant that such a claim could be brought.[84] Surely Lord Denning was correct. Harper could have established that Bennett had been unjustly enriched and so should have been able to recover the reasonable value of the services which he had provided.

Since the decision of the Court of Appeal in *Greenwood* v. *Bennett* the law has been clarified to some extent by the enactment of the Torts (Interference with Goods) Act 1977. The gist of this statute is to create a new tort of wrongful interference with goods, which covers the torts of conversion, trespass and negligence as they apply to goods. Section 6(1) of this statute makes specific provision for a passive restitutionary claim. By virtue of this provision, when the court is assessing the damages

---

[81] See p. 78 below. [82] See Chapter 8. [83] [1973] QB 195, 203.
[84] *Ibid*, 202. Phillimore LJ agreed with Denning LJ but did not expressly consider whether an active restitutionary claim could be brought.

which are due for the tort of wrongful interference with goods, it must award the defendant an allowance in respect of his or her work in improving the goods, as long as the defendant did so in the honest belief that he or she had title to the goods. This allowance is assessed by reference to the increase in the value of the goods which is attributable to their improvement by the defendant.

This statute would not, however, have resolved the dispute in *Greenwood* v. *Bennett* since Bennett did not recover damages but recovered his car, and section 6(1) of the 1977 Act only applies where the plaintiff is awarded damages. Also the statute only provides for a passive restitutionary claim, presumably because its purpose is to ensure that the plaintiff is not overcompensated.[85] What is needed now is either statutory reform or express judicial recognition that a person who repairs or improves property belonging to somebody else, mistakenly thinking that the property belongs to him or her, can recover the value of the services from the owner where it can be shown that the owner was unjustly enriched at the repairer's expense. There is some evidence for the existence of such an active claim in the decision of the Court of Appeal in *Rover International Ltd.* v. *Cannon Film Sales Ltd. (No. 3)*,[86] where the plaintiff successfully recovered the value of its services which had mistakenly been provided for the benefit of the defendant. Counsel for the defendant had conceded that the defendant had received a benefit and this concession was correct because, as Kerr LJ recognised, the services provided by the plaintiff had generated money for the defendant. In other words, the defendant had been incontrovertibly benefited since the services provided by the plaintiff had been realised in money.[87]

(iv) Benefit realisable in money

Whether a final category of incontrovertible benefit should be recognised is a highly controversial question. Goff and Jones in particular have suggested that the defendant should be considered to be incontrovertibly benefited where the plaintiff has improved the defendant's property and even though the defendant has not yet converted this enrichment into money.[88] This is because the fact that the benefit is potentially realisable in money should be sufficient to conclude that the defendant must have been enriched.

This interpretation of incontrovertible benefit was in fact accepted by Judge Bowsher QC in *Marston Construction Co. Ltd.* v. *Kigass Ltd.*[89] and it may also be used to explain the success of the passive restitutionary claim in *Greenwood* v. *Bennett*.[90] Despite this, the conclusion that the

---

[85] Burrows, *The Law of Restitution*, p. 122.   [86] [1989] 1 WLR 912.
[87] *Ibid*, p. 922.   [88] Goff and Jones, *The Law of Restitution*, p. 23.
[89] (1989) 15 Con. LR 116, 129.   [90] [1973] QB 195. See p. 77 above.

defendant has been incontrovertibly benefited simply because he or she has received something which could be sold is generally unacceptable, because it unnecessarily subverts the principle of individual autonomy.[91] Analysis of the different categories of incontrovertible benefit shows that, with the exception of the test of whether the benefit is realisable in money, the principle does not subvert the autonomy of the individual which underlies the principle of subjective devaluation. This is because, where it is proved that the defendant had received an incontrovertible benefit within one of these other categories, it is clear that either the defendant had no free choice to exercise whether to accept the benefit, as in the category of anticipation of necessary expenditure, or had exercised that choice, where the benefit has been realised in money. The difficulty with the test of whether the benefit is realisable in money arises precisely because in that situation the defendant does have a free choice whether or not to accept the benefit, and there is no acceptable basis on which we can exercise that choice for him or her. Therefore, the better view is that this test of incontrovertible benefit should be rejected save, perhaps, where it is inevitable that the defendant will realise the benefit, for in such a situation there will be no free choice to exercise. Such inevitability will, however, be virtually impossible to prove.

(c) Free acceptance

The term 'free acceptance' was first coined by Goff and Jones[92] who, with Birks, are the doctrine's strongest advocates. Goff and Jones define free acceptance as arising where the defendant

as a reasonable man, should have known that the plaintiff who rendered the services expected to be paid for them, and yet he did not take a reasonable opportunity open to him to reject the proffered services.[93]

Such a principle defeats the defendant's reliance on the subjective devaluation principle since, where the defendant had the opportunity to reject the proffered benefit but failed to do so, he or she was exercising a voluntary choice.[94] Consequently, the fact that the defendant freely accepted the benefit is in itself an expression of freedom of choice and so is consistent with the principle of the autonomy of the individual to decide whether he or she values the benefit which has been received.

[91] Cp. Verse, 'Improvements and Enrichments: A Comparative Analysis' (1998) 6 *RLR* 85, 96, who suggests that the defendant should be considered to have been incontrovertibly benefited if the asset is realisable, but only if it is not unique and is easily replaced.

[92] *The Law of Restitution* (1966) p. 30.

[93] Goff and Jones, *The Law of Restitution*, p. 18. See also Birks, *An Introduction to the Law of Restitution*, p. 265.

[94] Birks in *Essays on the Law of Restitution* (ed. Burrows) p. 129.

The principle of free acceptance has developed from the requirement that the defendant would only be liable to pay for a benefit which he or she had requested. Today, the defendant can be considered to have freely accepted a benefit even though he or she had not requested it, since it is sufficient that the defendant knowingly acquiesced in the provision of the benefit.[95] Where, however the benefit was requested this indicates that the defendant had freely accepted the benefit because the request shows that the defendant valued the benefit which had been received. But the existence of a request by the defendant must be treated with caution, since it may provide the basis for implying a contract to pay for the benefit. Where such a contract can be implied the defendant will be liable on the contract rather than in the law of restitution.[96]

At the outset it is important to recognise that, in the literature at least, the doctrine of free acceptance is sometimes regarded as having a dual function in the law of restitution. This is particularly the view of Birks[97] and Goff and Jones agree.[98] This dual function involves free acceptance operating both to establish an enrichment and a ground of restitution in its own right. This dual function is highly controversial, and Birks has now accepted that free acceptance has a much reduced role as a ground for restitution than he had originally suggested.[99] There is in fact no role for free acceptance as a ground of restitution in its own right, by virtue of the wide interpretation which is given to the doctrine of failure of consideration.[100] But this does not affect the validity of free acceptance as an important principle to assist in the identification of whether or not the defendant has been enriched.

Whilst the phrase 'free acceptance' is rarely mentioned by judges,[101] the elements of free acceptance, and even some of the language of free acceptance, can be identified. For example, some judges refer to the fact that the defendant stood by whilst the plaintiff was providing the benefit,[102] whilst others are clearly influenced by the fact that the defendant had requested a benefit knowing that it was to be paid for and then

---

[95] See *Leigh* v. *Dickeson* (1884) 15 QBD 60; *Falcke* v. *Scottish Imperial Insurance* (1886) 34 Ch.D 234.

[96] See pp. 70–1 above.

[97] See, for example, *Restitution—The Future* (Sydney: The Foundation Press, 1992) pp. 98–9.

[98] Goff and Jones, *The Law of Restitution*, p. 18, who assert that where a defendant has freely accepted an enrichment 'he cannot deny that he has been *unjustly* enriched' (emphasis in the original).

[99] Birks in *Essays on the Law of Restitution* (ed. Burrows) pp. 109–20. But he still asserts that free acceptance does have a continuing role as a ground for restitution.

[100] See Chapter 6.

[101] It has, however, been recognised in New Zealand: *Van den Berg* v. *Giles* [1979] 2 NZLR 111, 120 (Jeffries J).

[102] See, for example, *Weatherby* v. *Banham* (1832) 5 Car. and P 228; 172 ER 950.

refused to pay for it.[103] Four cases in particular can be used to show that the principle of free acceptance exists in English law even though it has never been expressly recognised. Also, certain statutory provisions can be explained as incorporating a principle of free acceptance.

(1) In *Lamb* v. *Bunce*[104] the plaintiff was a surgeon who had been called in to administer to an injured patient, who was a pauper. The practice at the time was that a surgeon in such circumstances could recover the cost of the services he had provided from the parish where the pauper lived, but this depended upon the surgeon being invited to attend by the parish officer who was responsible. In *Lamb* v. *Bunce* the plaintiff was not called by the relevant parish officer who consequently argued that his parish was not liable to pay the plaintiff for his services. Since the parish had a legal duty to look after paupers within it, it followed that the provision of the plaintiff's services constituted an objective benefit to the parish.[105] The defendant effectively denied that an enrichment had been received, but this argument failed specifically because the parish officer was aware that the plaintiff was attending the patient and he had failed to say that the plaintiff's services were not required. In other words, the parish officer had freely accepted the plaintiff's services.

(2) In *Leigh* v. *Dickeson*[106] the plaintiff sought to recover rent from the defendant who was initially the plaintiff's tenant but who then became a co-owner with the plaintiff of a house. The defendant counter-claimed for money spent to the use of the plaintiff in respect of repairs to the house. The counter-claim failed, essentially because, despite the fact that the plaintiff had received an objective benefit by virtue of the repairs which were considered to be reasonable and proper, the defendant's expenditure had been incurred voluntarily and it could not be shown that the plaintiff valued it. In other words, the plaintiff resorted to subjective devaluation, which the defendant was unable to defeat. In reaching this conclusion, Brett MR in particular identified the essence of free acceptance. He emphasised[107] that if a person receives a benefit in circumstances where there is an option to adopt or decline it, and the recipient adopts the benefit, then the expenditure incurred by the other party must be repaid. If the recipient declines the benefit he or she will not be liable to make restitution to the other party. But if the recipient has no choice but to accept the benefit then, because there is no opportunity to exercise an option as to whether to adopt or decline the benefit, the

---

[103] See, for example, *Lawford* v. *The Billericay RDC* [1903] 1 KB 772.

[104] (1815) 4 M and S 275; 105 ER 836. See also *Paynter* v. *Williams* (1833) 1 C and M 810; 149 ER 626.

[105] Since the plaintiff had discharged the parish's legal liability the parish could also be regarded as incontrovertibly benefited since it had been saved a necessary expense. See p. 73 above.

[106] (1884) 15 QBD 60.   [107] *Ibid*, p. 64.

recipient will not be liable to the other party. Since on the facts the plaintiff had no choice but to accept the benefit, because she continued to live in the house, she was not liable to the defendant who had incurred the expenditure.[108] This is a perfect example of a case where it was not possible to defeat reliance on subjective devaluation, simply because there was no evidence that the recipient of the benefit had chosen it and so it could not be concluded that the recipient valued the benefit.

(3) In *Falcke* v. *Scottish Imperial Insurance Co.*[109] the plaintiff, having paid premiums on a life assurance policy mistakenly believing that he had acquired an interest in the policy, sought to recover the expenditure from the defendant who did have an interest in the policy. Clearly the defendant had received an objective benefit, since the plaintiff's payments preserved the policy,[110] but there was insufficient evidence to defeat the defendant's reliance on arguments of subjective devaluation. In particular, the defendant was unaware of the plaintiff's payments, so she could not be regarded as having chosen to accept the benefit. But it was expressly recognised that if the defendant had been aware of the payment and had failed to intervene then she would have been liable to reimburse the plaintiff.[111]

(4) In *Re Cleadon Trust Ltd.*[112] the secretary of the defendant company had requested the plaintiff, a director of the company, to pay a sum of money to meet the financial obligations of two of the defendant's subsidiaries. The plaintiff paid the money which was due on the footing that his payment was a loan to the defendant.[113] A meeting of the defendant's board of directors purported to confirm that the money had been paid at the defendant's request. The defendant was wound up and the plaintiff sought to recover the loan. His claim was unsuccessful because the directors' meeting which purported to confirm that the money had been paid at the company's request was inquorate. This meant that there was no organ of the company which was capable of freely accepting the benefit. It was, however, accepted that if the directors' meeting had been quorate then the plaintiff's claim would have succeeded by reason of the defendant's acceptance of the benefit.[114]

---

[108] But since the repairs had been considered to be necessary and proper it could be concluded that the plaintiff had been incontrovertibly benefited since she had been saved a necessary expenditure.

[109] (1886) 34 Ch.D 234.

[110] Again, it could have been concluded that the defendant had been incontrovertibly benefited by the plaintiff's expenditure, which constituted a necessary expense to preserve the insurance policy.

[111] (1886) 34 Ch.D 234, 249 (Bowen LJ).   [112] [1939] Ch. 286.

[113] This was not money paid to the defendant, which would have been an incontrovertible benefit, but money paid on behalf of and for the benefit of the defendant, so it was possible for the defendant subjectively to devalue it.

[114] [1939] Ch. 286, 298 (Sir Wilfrid Greene MR).

(5) The free acceptance principle is also implicitly recognised by certain statutory provisions. For example, section 30(3) of the Sale of Goods Act 1979 states that where a vendor delivers more goods to the purchaser than he or she has contracted to sell and the purchaser accepts all of the goods delivered then the purchaser will be liable to pay for all of the goods.

(i) The elements of free acceptance

Analysis of these four cases shows that an embryonic principle of free acceptance is recognised in English law. Three conditions need to be satisfied before it can be concluded that the defendant has freely accepted the benefit.[115]

(1) Since free acceptance depends on the defendant having chosen to accept the benefit it is vital that the defendant had the opportunity to reject it before it was provided. It follows that the defendant cannot be considered to have freely accepted the benefit if he or she lacked the capacity to accept it.[116]

(2) The defendant will only be considered to have freely accepted the benefit if he or she knew that the plaintiff either expected to receive something in return for it, typically that the plaintiff expected to be paid for it, or that the plaintiff thought he or she was doing something of benefit to him or herself rather than the defendant, such as where the plaintiff improved the defendant's property in the mistaken belief that the plaintiff owned it.[117] This is a subjective test since it depends on the defendant knowing that the benefit was not provided gratuitously. Goff and Jones, however, have suggested that an objective test should be adopted, so that it should be sufficient that the reasonable person would have realised that the plaintiff expected to be paid for the benefit even if the defendant did not know this.[118] The cases, however, suggest that a subjective test is applicable,[119] and such a test is consistent with the true function of free acceptance, namely to prevent the defendant from relying on the principle of subjective devaluation by deeming that the defendant did value the benefit which was received.

(3) The final condition is that, even though the defendant had the opportunity to reject the benefit and knew that it was not provided gratuitously, he or she failed to reject it.

How the principle of free acceptance will operate in practice is illustrated by the following example suggested by Birks.[120] If the plaintiff

---

[115] Birks, *An Introduction to the Law of Restitution*, pp. 280–6.
[116] See *Re Cleadon Trust Ltd.* [1939] Ch. 286. [117] See p. 86 below.
[118] Goff and Jones, *The Law of Restitution*, p. 19.
[119] See especially *Falcke* v. *Scottish Imperial Insurance Co.* (1886) 34 Ch.D 234, 249 (Bowen LJ) and *Re Cleadon Trust Ltd.* [1939] Ch. 286.
[120] Birks, *An Introduction to the Law of Restitution*, p. 265.

cleaned the defendant's windows without being requested to do so, presumably the reasonable person would regard the defendant as having received an objective benefit. For this is the type of service which is commonly paid for and so it has a market value. The defendant, however, might subjectively devalue this benefit, perhaps because he or she usually cleans the windows him or herself and does not see the need to pay somebody else to do it. The plaintiff would then need to find some way of defeating the defendant's reliance on the subjective devaluation principle. The defendant does not appear to have been incontrovertibly benefited, save if it could be shown that he or she was about to pay somebody to clean the windows and so the plaintiff had saved the defendant a factually necessary expense.[121] If this cannot be established, the plaintiff's only hope is to prove that the defendant had freely accepted the benefit. This would be established if the plaintiff could show that, when he or she was cleaning the windows, the defendant was in the house, was aware of what was going on, knew that the plaintiff expected to be paid for the service and had failed to make it clear to the plaintiff that he or she did not want the windows cleaned by the plaintiff.

Although this example illustrates how the free acceptance principle might operate in practice, it should be emphasised that, even if the defendant had freely accepted the benefit, it does not follow that restitution would be awarded. Indeed, it is most unlikely that the plaintiff's restitutionary claim would succeed, because there is no apparent ground for restitution and, most importantly, the plaintiff was acting officiously, by taking the risk that the defendant might not pay for the window cleaning. It is a fundamental principle of the law of restitution that officious plaintiffs should not be able to obtain restitutionary remedies.

(ii) The function of free acceptance

Even though there is some evidence that a principle of free acceptance is recognised in English law, the very existence and function of the principle remain a matter of controversy. Some commentators deny the existence of such a principle, asserting that there is a much narrower principle instead, the function of which is to ascertain that the defendant did positively value the benefit which was received.[122] But other commentators, notably Birks and Goff and Jones, recognise the existence of the free acceptance principle and assert that it has a negative function,

---

[121] Interpreting what constitutes 'necessary' expenditure broadly, as was examined at p. 75 above.

[122] For example, Burrows, 'Free Acceptance and the Law of Restitution' (1988) 104 *LQR* 576. See also Garner, 'The Role of Subjective Benefit in the Law of Unjust Enrichment' (1990) 10 *OJLS* 42.

namely to defeat the defendant's reliance on the principle of subjective devaluation.

To assess which of these views is preferable, it is necessary to examine what the function of free acceptance actually is. The question whether the defendant had freely accepted the benefit is significant only where the defendant seeks to argue that he or she did not value the benefit. It follows, therefore, that the function of the principle is not necessarily to show that the defendant did positively value the benefit but, rather, because of the defendant's conduct in failing to reject the benefit knowing that it was not provided gratuitously, its function is to prevent the defendant from subjectively devaluing the benefit. Consequently, it has a negative function of preventing the defendant from relying on the subjective devaluation principle because the defendant has acted unconscientiously in saying that he or she did not value the benefit after he or she had freely accepted it.[123] Where the defendant freely accepted the benefit and then seeks to turn round and say that he or she did not value it, the defendant's conduct prevents him or her from relying on subjective devaluation; it deprives him or her of the opportunity to assert individual autonomy. It follows that the free acceptance principle is triggered by the defendant's fault.

The flaw in the arguments of commentators such as Burrows, who asserts that what is needed is a doctrine to show that the defendant positively valued the benefit which had been received, is that it ignores the question whether the defendant is in receipt of a benefit objectively determined. If the defendant has received an objective benefit, then we are only concerned with the question whether he or she can resort to subjective devaluation, and that principle is inapplicable where the defendant freely accepted the benefit. If, however, the defendant has not received an objective benefit then the free acceptance principle can be of no use in identifying an enrichment because, as Burrows correctly asserts, the free acceptance principle is ambiguous as to whether or not the defendant actually valued what was received. This ambiguity arises because there are many reasons why the defendant might acquiesce in the provision of goods or services by the plaintiff, including pure indifference. Just because the defendant cannot be bothered to prevent the plaintiff from acting does not mean that the defendant values what is being provided. Clearly, therefore, there is a role for some other principle to show that the defendant did subjectively value a benefit even though it was not objectively valuable,[124] but free acceptance cannot do this since it only has a negative function.

---

[123] See Birks, *Restitution—the Future*, p. 97.   [124] See pp. 86–8 below.

This analysis of free acceptance as a principle which is triggered by the defendant's unconscionable conduct and prevents him or her from relying on the subjective devaluation principle, indicates what free acceptance is, namely a form of estoppel.[125] By freely accepting the benefit the defendant is estopped from asserting that he or she did not value it. This also justifies the assertion that free acceptance is triggered by the defendant's unconscionable conduct, since unconscionable conduct is vital to the recognition of estoppel.[126] But free acceptance is a peculiar form of estoppel because, although the defendant will either have requested the benefit or, more usually, acquiesced in its provision, it is not necessary to show that the plaintiff had detrimentally relied on the defendant's representation. For example, in the illustration of the plaintiff cleaning the defendant's windows, the defendant can be considered to have freely accepted the benefit even though the plaintiff did not know that the defendant was in the house at the time, so the plaintiff could not have relied on the defendant's acquiescence. But this is simply because free acceptance is concerned only with the question whether the defendant was enriched, so only the conduct of the defendant is relevant. Whether or not the plaintiff relied on the defendant's acquiescence is of no relevance to the question whether the defendant's conduct is such that he or she is estopped from relying on the subjective devaluation principle.

4. SUBJECTIVE REVALUATION

(a) Recognising the principle of subjective revaluation

In most cases a defendant will only be considered to have been enriched where he or she has received an objective benefit. But, exceptionally, the defendant may still be considered to be enriched even though he or she had not received anything which was objectively valuable, if it can be shown that the defendant positively valued what had been received. This is the principle of subjective revaluation.[127] Such a principle has been recognised by Burrows in the form of proof that the defendant has bar-

---

[125] See Birks, *An Introduction to the Law of Restitution*, p. 276.

[126] See Chapter 18. See *Appleby* v. *Myers* (1867) LR 2 CP 651, 659–60 (Blackburn J); *Willmott* v. *Barber* (1880) 15 Ch.D 96; and *Salvation Army Trustee Co. Ltd.* v. *West Yorkshire Metropolitan County Council* (1980) 41 P and CR 179, 198.

[127] Garner, 'The Role of Subjective Benefit in the Law of Unjust Enrichment' (1990) 10 *OJLS* 42, 43: '[t]hus a defendant may "subjectively revalue" something done for him by the plaintiff even though the plaintiff's work may be objectively valueless.' Mead, 'Restitution within Contract?' (1991) *LS* 172, 186 calls this concept 'subjective valuation'.

gained for the benefit,[128] since if the defendant has actually bargained for the benefit this suggests that he or she really valued it. This principle of subjective revaluation will be of very limited importance in identifying an enrichment, since in the vast majority of cases the benefit which the defendant received will be characterised as objectively valuable. But the subjective revaluation principle may be of some exceptional relevance is identifying an enrichment and it will be of particular significance when considering the value of an enrichment.[129]

There is no reason why a subjective test should not be used to identify an enrichment even though a reasonable person would not have considered the benefit to be valuable. For example, to use a scenario suggested by Robert Goff J,[130] if the defendant requested the plaintiff to decorate the rooms of his house, which were already in good decorative order, to suit the defendant's execrable taste, presumably the reasonable person would not regard the plaintiff's work as valuable, but, as evidenced by the fact that the defendant had specifically requested the work, he clearly valued it and so should be regarded as enriched. The essence of this subjective revaluation principle is that, by virtue of the defendant's conduct, it is possible for the plaintiff to presume that the defendant valued the benefit.

(b) Establishing subjective revaluation

The subjective revaluation principle will be established whenever it can be shown positively that the defendant valued the benefit which had been received. This may be a difficult matter for the plaintiff to prove, so there is scope for adopting a presumption. It might be argued that the defendant should be presumed to value the benefit which he or she had received if the defendant had requested it. But mere request does not necessarily suggest that the defendant was willing to pay for the benefit and such willingness to pay is of vital importance since, without it, there is nothing to suggest that the defendant actually valued the goods or services which had been provided. It follows, therefore, that if the defendant is to be presumed to have valued the benefit then two conditions need to be satisfied:

(1) The defendant requested the benefit.

---

[128] Burrows, 'Free Acceptance and the Law of Restitution' (1988) 104 *LQR* 576. Burrows argues that this 'bargained-for benefit principle' should replace the principle of free acceptance. This argument was rejected at p. 85 above but it does not follow that there is no role for a principle of subjective valuation at all. There is such a role, but it is much more limited than Burrows suggests.

[129] See pp. 95–104 below.

[130] *BP Exploration Co. (Libya) Ltd.* v. *Hunt (No. 2)* [1979] 1 WLR 783, 803.

(2) It can be shown that the defendant valued the benefit when it was provided, because, for example, the defendant was willing to pay for it.[131]

5. RESTITUTION WITHOUT ENRICHMENT

Although it seems obvious that if the plaintiff is to obtain restitutionary
relief by virtue of the defendant's unjust enrichment it must be established that the defendant has indeed been enriched, there are two situations where it might be argued that the plaintiff's claim for restitution
should succeed even though the defendant has not been enriched.

(a) The defendant is estopped from denying the enrichment

(i) The function of estoppel

Although the defendant may not have received an objective benefit and
the principle of subjective revaluation is inapplicable, it may still be possible to show that the defendant has been enriched by establishing that
he or she is estopped from asserting that he or she has not received a
benefit at the plaintiff's expense. There is growing evidence that estoppel
constitutes a form of wrongdoing, since it is founded on the defendant's
unconscionable conduct.[132] But, even though restitutionary remedies
are available for the commission of such a wrong, they are rare and lie in
the discretion of the court. If estoppel is being used to establish enrichment, it does not automatically establish the plaintiff's cause of action,
since it will still be necessary for the plaintiff to establish that one of the
recognised grounds of restitution is applicable. Rather, the function of
the estoppel is simply to enable the plaintiff to pursue a restitutionary
cause of action by negating some of the required elements of that
action.[133] This notion of estoppel is different from the principle of free
acceptance, since it must be shown that the defendant made a representation of fact on which the plaintiff relied to his or her detriment.

(ii) The conditions for establishing an estoppel

Three conditions will need to be satisfied before the defendant can be
estopped from denying that he or she has been enriched.

(1) The defendant must have represented to the plaintiff that he or she
wanted to receive the benefit and would pay the plaintiff for it. Evidence
of a request will typically satisfy this condition, but passive acquiescence
in the provision of the service will also be sufficient.

---

[131] Garner (1990) 10 *OJLS* 42, 50.   [132] See Chapter 18.
[133] See Brandon LJ in *Amalgamated Investment and Property Co. Ltd.* v. *Texas Commerce International Bank Ltd.* [1982] QB 84, 131–2.

(2) The plaintiff must have acted to his or her detriment in reliance upon the defendant's representation that he or she would pay for the benefit.

(3) The defendant must have falsified the representation in some way. It is this condition which is the most important since it establishes that the defendant was at fault, and this provides the justification for preventing the defendant from denying that he or she was enriched.[134] If the defendant's representation is falsified without the fault of the defendant, he or she should not be estopped from denying the enrichment since he or she will not have acted unconscionably. So where, for example, the defendant encourages the plaintiff to incur expenditure in anticipation of a contract and no contract is made simply because the parties are unable to agree, the defendant is not at fault, and so should not be estopped from denying that he or she had been enriched.[135]

(iii) The application of the estoppel principle

Although the estoppel principle has never been expressly recognised as a way of satisfying the plaintiff's need to establish that the defendant was enriched, the operation of this principle can be discerned in a few cases. Its most important role will be in those cases where the plaintiff has spent time and money doing work for the defendant which has not yet been received by the defendant, or where the plaintiff has done work on behalf of the defendant which has been received by a third party. In both situations the defendant has not received any benefit, so a restitutionary claim founded on the reversal of the defendant's unjust enrichment can only succeed if he or she is estopped from denying that he or she has been enriched.

The most important context in which this estoppel principle can be used to justify the award of restitutionary remedies is where the plaintiff has acted in anticipation of a contract which is not forthcoming.[136] In some of these cases the defendant received an objective benefit which he or she would have been unable subjectively to devalue because it was incontrovertibly beneficial or had been freely accepted.[137] In other cases, however, the plaintiff was awarded a restitutionary remedy even though there was no evidence that the defendant had received an objective benefit. This is particularly well illustrated by *Brewer Street Investments Ltd.* v. *Barclays Woollen Co. Ltd.*,[138] where the defendant had been

---

[134] The requirement of fault has been stressed in a number of cases. See in particular *Brewer Street Investments Ltd.* v. *Barclays Woollen Co. Ltd.* [1954] 1 QB 428 and *Sabemo Pty. Ltd.* v. *North Sydney Municipal Council* [1977] 2 NSWLR 880.

[135] *Ibid*, p. 901(Sheppard J). See also p. 903.   [136] See Chapter 12.

[137] See, for example, *William Lacey (Hounslow) Ltd.* v. *Davis* [1957] 1 WLR 932.

[138] [1954] 1 QB 428.

negotiating with the plaintiff for a lease of the plaintiff's property. Before a contract had been signed, the defendant requested the plaintiff to do some work on the property, which the plaintiff did. No contract was ever signed and so the plaintiff brought a restitutionary claim against the defendant to recover the value of the work which it had done. The plaintiff's claim succeeded. The problem with this case is that the defendant had not received any benefit from the plaintiff's work, because the work had occurred on the plaintiff's own property and the defendant had never entered into possession of it, but the defendant was still held liable to pay the plaintiff for the reasonable value of its services. A majority of the Court of Appeal explained this restitutionary liability by virtue of the fact that no contract had been made because of the defendant's conduct,[139] namely the defendant's insistence on the granting of an option when it knew at the outset that the plaintiff would never grant an option. Although none of the judges stated that the defendant was estopped from denying enrichment, the language they did use is consistent with that principle. The defendant had requested the plaintiff to do the work, the plaintiff had done so in reliance on this request and the failure to make the contract was due to the fault of the defendant. It followed that the defendant could not have asserted that he had not been enriched.

Similarly, in the Australian case of *Sabemo Pty. Ltd.* v. *North Sydney Municipal Council*[140] the defendant had requested the plaintiff to do some work for it in anticipation of a contract being made. This contract was not forthcoming due to the fault of the defendant, in that it unilaterally decided to drop the proposal.[141] So, even though the trial judge held that the defendant had not been unjustly enriched since it had not received a benefit,[142] the restitutionary remedy which was awarded could still be justified by reference to the principle of unjust enrichment, with the enrichment element being assumed, since the defendant's conduct, on which the plaintiff had relied, estopped it from denying that it had been enriched.

In *Jennings and Chapman Ltd.* v. *Woodman Matthews and Co.*,[143] on the other hand, although the facts were similar to those of *Brewer Street*, restitution was denied. The preferable explanation for this is simply that in *Jennings* the reason no contract was forthcoming was because of a mutual breakdown in negotiations; there was no evidence that the

---

[139] This was the conclusion of both Somervell and Romer LJJ. Denning LJ did not find that the defendant was at fault, though he did find that the defendant had agreed to take responsibility for the plaintiff's work: *ibid*, p. 437.

[140] [1977] 2 NSWLR 880.

[141] *Ibid*, p. 901 where Sheppard J said that 'the defendant's decision to drop the proposal is the determining factor'.

[142] *Ibid*, p. 897.   [143] [1952] 2 TLR 409.

defendant was at fault in any way and so there was no basis for preventing the defendant from denying that it had been enriched.[144]

This estoppel principle may also be relevant to explain the difficult case of *Planché* v. *Colburn*.[145] In that case the plaintiff had contracted with the defendant to research and write a book, but the defendant terminated the contract after the plaintiff had done a lot of the research and writing but before anything had been received by the defendant. The plaintiff successfully brought an action to recover the reasonable value of his services. Although the plaintiff's action should properly have been founded on breach of contract, it is still possible to justify the award of a restitutionary remedy by reference to the estoppel principle. This was because the defendant had requested the plaintiff's performance on the understanding that the plaintiff would be paid for it, the plaintiff had acted in reliance on this request and then the defendant by his own act falsified the representation that the performance would be paid for under the contract by terminating the contract.[146] Consequently, even though the defendant had not received an enrichment, it might still have been possible to assume that the defendant had been enriched because he would have been estopped by his conduct from denying that this was the case.

(b) Unjust sacrifice

(i) *The significance of recognising the unjust sacrifice principle*

It has sometimes been argued that remedies may be available even though a defendant has not received any benefit and cannot be estopped from denying that he or she has been enriched, without founding an action in contract or tort. Rather, it has been argued that liability should be founded on the principle of unjust sacrifice, whereby the plaintiff has suffered a loss without the defendant necessarily obtaining a benefit.[147] If such liability exists, clearly it cannot be founded on the principle of reversing unjust enrichment, because of the lack of an enrichment. But also the remedies consequent upon such liability cannot be termed restitutionary, since if the defendant has not been enriched and cannot be assumed to have been enriched there is no actual or deemed benefit which the defendant can restore to the plaintiff. It might therefore be

---

[144] See also *Regalian Properties plc.* v. *London Docklands Development Corporation* [1995] 1 WLR 212 where Rattee J specifically distinguished *Sabemo* on the basis that in that case the anticipated contract failed to materialise because of the defendant's conduct, whereas in *Regalian* no contract was forthcoming due to a mutual inability to agree a price.

[145] (1831) 8 Bing. 14; 131 ER 305. See p. 63 above. See also *Prickett* v. *Badger* (1856) 1 CB (NS) 296; 140 ER 123.

[146] See in particular the report of the case at (1831) 1 LJCP 7.

[147] See especially Stoljar, 'Unjust Enrichment and Unjust Sacrifice' (1987) 50 *MLR* 603.

thought that analysis of unjust sacrifice has no place in a textbook on the law of restitution. Its analysis can be justified, however, because if such a principle is recognised it will have an important influence on the question of how enrichment is defined. For if unjust sacrifice liability does exist, it will not be so important to adopt a wide definition of enrichment to ensure that the plaintiff obtains a remedy. Equally, if the notion of enrichment is defined widely, as has been argued in this chapter, there is little, if any role, for unjust sacrifice liability to play.[148]

(ii) Is the principle recognised in English law?

The unjust sacrifice principle has not been expressly recognised in any English decision. Many of the situations which might be covered by a principle of unjust sacrifice are better regarded as falling within the principle of unjust enrichment, essentially because of the wide interpretation of incontrovertible benefit. For many of the cases of supplying necessaries or discharging liabilities of the defendant can be regarded as cases where the defendant has been incontrovertibly benefited.[149]

(iii) Should the principle be recognised in English law?

Despite the absence of case law support for the unjust sacrifice principle, can a case be made for its recognition? Stoljar provides an example of a situation in which this principle would have a useful role to play, namely where the plaintiff attends to the defendant's child injured in an accident, but the child dies.[150] Clearly the defendant cannot be regarded as benefited by the plaintiff's services in these circumstances, so a restitutionary remedy cannot lie. But should the defendant be held liable to recompense or reimburse the plaintiff for the reasonable value of his or her services? Stoljar suggests the answer is 'yes', so long as those services were provided in the expectation that they would be paid for, otherwise the plaintiff would be a mere volunteer, and so long as the services are 'manifestly necessary or urgent or useful' for the defendant, so that the provision of those services cannot be regarded as officious.[151] Stoljar's justification for the defendant's liability in these circumstances is that the plaintiff's non-gratuitous provision of services requires protection as though it were his or her property. But this justification is not convincing. Where the defendant has not been benefited why should he or she be required to recompense the plaintiff? Where the plaintiff attempted to save the life of the defendant's child but failed, perhaps this was due to the fault of the plaintiff. Also where the defendant has not received any

---

[148] Birks, *Restitution—The Future*, p. 103.   [149] See p. 73 above.

[150] (1987) 50 *MLR* 603, 612. See for example *Cotnam* v. *Wisdom* (1907) 104 SW 164 and *Matheson* v. *Smiley* [1932] 2 DLR 787.

[151] *Ibid* at p. 613.

benefit at all, it is difficult to conclude that the plaintiff's officiousness has been displaced. Although we want people to try to save the lives of children, we must not be misled by the emotive nature of this example. Where the defendant has not been benefited in any way, then no obligation to pay the plaintiff should be imposed, despite the policy that society wishes to encourage intervention in an emergency. It is for this reason that the unjust sacrifice principle should be rejected.

6. PART-PERFORMANCE OF A CONTRACT

There is an additional problem which relates to the identification of an enrichment. This involves the situation where the plaintiff has done some of the work which is required to be done under a contract, but he or she did not complete it. Can the defendant in such circumstances be regarded as enriched so that the plaintiff can recover the reasonable value of the work which he or she has done in a restitutionary action? It should be emphasised that the restitutionary claim will only be relevant once the contract has been discharged for whatever reason, because of the principle that restitutionary claims are always subordinate to contractual claims.[152]

Where the defendant has received the benefit of the plaintiff's partial performance of the contract the defendant will typically have received an objective benefit. So, for example, if the plaintiff agreed to build a house for the defendant and, after having done half of the work, the plaintiff fails, for whatever reason, to complete the house, the defendant is in receipt of a benefit, namely half a house, which is of some objective value. But, of course, because the defendant wanted a whole house it would be perfectly proper for him or her subjectively to devalue the benefit which had been received. Will it be possible for the plaintiff to defeat the defendant's reliance on this principle? This will depend on the circumstances of the case and five different circumstances need to be considered.

(a) The defendant completed the work

Where the defendant has completed the work which had been started by the plaintiff, this adoption of the benefit should defeat the defendant's reliance on subjective devaluation. For the defendant's voluntary acceptance of the benefit shows that he or she values what the plaintiff has provided, and so it is inconsistent for the defendant to turn round and say

---

[152] See Chapter 2. See also Chapter 12 for examination of the ground of restitution where a contract has been discharged after the plaintiff has partly performed it.

that he or she did not value what the plaintiff had done.[153] This is consistent with the principle of subjective revaluation.[154]

(b) The defendant prevented the plaintiff from performing

Where the defendant has prevented the plaintiff from completing the performance then this should be sufficient to prevent the defendant from subjectively devaluing the benefit.[155] But it is difficult to show that the defendant has freely accepted the benefit, since it does not necessarily follow from the fact that the defendant has prevented the plaintiff from continuing to perform that the defendant values what the plaintiff has done already. It might be argued that the defendant should be considered to be enriched because he or she had requested the plaintiff to do the work in the first place,[156] but the defendant's request only shows that he or she valued the whole and not necessarily the part performance. But, despite this, it should still be possible to establish that the defendant was enriched in these circumstances by virtue of the estoppel principle.[157] This principle will be applicable because the defendant had represented that he or she would pay for the benefit, the plaintiff detrimentally relied on this representation and the defendant's representation was falsified because it was the defendant who prevented the plaintiff from performing the contract.

(c) The plaintiff breached the contract

Where the reason the plaintiff failed to perform the contract was that he or she had breached it, it will be very difficult to prevent the defendant from relying on the subjective devaluation principle, save where it can be shown that the defendant voluntarily accepted the benefit or the benefit was incontrovertibly beneficial.

(d) The contract was frustrated

Where the plaintiff was unable to perform his side of the bargain because the contract was frustrated, it will still be possible to establish that the defendant has been enriched by virtue of the statutory regime under the Law Reform (Frustrated Contracts) 1943, section 1(3).[158]

---

[153] See *Lodder* v. *Slowey* [1904] AC 442.
[154] See p. 86 above.
[155] Birks in *Essays on the Law of Restitution* (ed. Burrows), p. 140.
[156] Burrows, 'Free Acceptance and the Law of Restitution' (1988) 104 *LQR* 576, 586.
[157] See p. 88 above.
[158] See Chapter 12.

(e) Entire contract

Where the contract is an entire contract, meaning that the terms are such that the defendant is not liable to pay the plaintiff until the plaintiff has performed his or her side of the bargain, then, even though the defendant could be considered to have been enriched by the part performance of the contract, the plaintiff's restitutionary claim will fail.[159] This is because the effect of making the contract entire is that the plaintiff takes the risk of not fully performing the contract, so the right to obtain restitution is effectively excluded by the contract.[160]

7. THE VALUATION OF THE ENRICHMENT

Once it has been shown that the defendant received an enrichment it is then necessary to value this enrichment, because this value forms the basis for assessing the restitutionary remedy which is awarded to reverse the defendant's unjust enrichment. A number of questions need to be examined when valuing the enrichment.

(a) Timing of the valuation

In order to value the defendant's enrichment it is first necessary to consider at what point it should be valued. In particular, should it be valued at the time of receipt or the time of the trial? This is an important question, since the test of timing which is adopted could have a profound effect upon the value which is actually restored to the plaintiff. The importance of the timing question is illustrated by *Appleby* v. *Myers*,[161] where the plaintiff partly performed a contract to build machinery for the defendant, but before he was able to complete the work the machinery was destroyed by fire, so frustrating the contract. If the enrichment was valued at the time it was received it would have been a substantial amount, but if the enrichment was valued at the time of the trial it would have been worth nothing since the enrichment no longer existed.

English law recognises that the enrichment should be valued at the time it was received by the defendant.[162] Events which take place after receipt can have no effect on the determination of the enrichment question as such, but such events may enable the defendant to establish a

---

[159] *Sumpter* v. *Hedges* [1898] 1 QB 673.   [160] See p. 357 below.

[161] (1867) LR 2 CP 651. The case would today be governed by the Law Reform (Frustrated Contracts) Act 1943. See Chapter 12.

[162] *BP Exploration Co. (Libya) Ltd.* v. *Hunt* [1979] 1 WLR 783, 802 (Robert Goff J). See also *Flett* v. *Deniliquin Publishing Co. Ltd.* [1964–5] NSWLR 383, 386 (Heron CJ).

defence, such as estoppel or change of position,[163] and so negate or reduce the value of the enrichment which must be restored to the plaintiff. It might be concluded, therefore, that there is no point in distinguishing between the value of the benefit at the time it was received and valuation at the time of the trial if events after the benefit was received are taken into account in determining its value. But this distinction is of vital importance since it affects the burden of proof. The plaintiff must prove that the defendant was in receipt of an enrichment and must establish the value of the enrichment at the time it was received. The burden then shifts to the defendant to establish whether any defences are applicable to negate or reduce the value of the enrichment by virtue of events which happened after receipt. This distinction was ignored by Rattee J in *Regalian Properties plc.* v. *London Docklands Development Corp.*,[164] who assumed that the defendant had not been enriched by the plaintiff's work relating to the redevelopment of the defendant's land which the plaintiff had done in anticipation of a contract being made, but no contract was forthcoming. The judge justified his conclusion by asserting that, once negotiations between the plaintiff and the defendant had collapsed, property values had fallen so that no-one would wish to develop the defendant's land. Consequently, the plaintiff's preparatory work which related to the redevelopment of the land was ultimately worthless.[165] But the judge assumed that, in determining whether or not the defendant was enriched, events which reduce or negate its value after receipt should be taken into account. Such considerations are irrelevant to the determination of the question whether the defendant has been enriched, but will be highly relevant with regard to the defence of change of position. But it is for the defendant to show that the conditions for establishing that defence have been established and there was nothing to indicate that that defence was applicable to the facts of the case.

(b) The test of valuation

The question of valuing the enrichment is something which has generally been ignored in the leading texts on restitution,[166] presumably because the valuation question usually causes no difficulty. So, for example, where the benefit conferred on the defendant consists of the payment of money the defendant is benefited by the amount received or applied for his or her benefit, and it is this amount which must be repaid to the plaintiff.[167] This does not mean that there can never be valuation

---

[163] See Chapter 24.   [164] [1995] 1 WLR 212.   [165] *Ibid.*, at p. 225.
[166] Though it is discussed by Goff and Jones, *The Law of Restitution*; see especially pp. 27–33.
[167] Subject to the operation of the general defences.

problems when the enrichment is money received or applied for the defendant's benefit, since there may be particular problems relating to inflation, the payment of interest for the use of the money[168] and the valuation of foreign currency.[169]

These problems are nothing, however, when compared with those which can arise in connection with the valuation of goods supplied or services rendered.[170] The general test of valuation which should be adopted is an objective test, namely the reasonable value of the benefit in kind, since this is the basic test which is relied on when identifying whether or not the defendant has actually been enriched.[171] This reasonable value is usually ascertained by reference to the market value, which is the sum 'a willing supplier and buyer would have agreed upon' for the provision of the benefit in kind.[172] Where, however, the principle of subjective revaluation[173] is relied on to establish that the defendant has been enriched even though he or she has not received an objectively valuable benefit, there is no scope for valuing the benefit by an objective test, so a subjective test of valuation will have to be adopted.

Although where the defendant is in receipt of an objective benefit the initial test of valuation will be the objective value of the benefit, this test may be qualified by the subjective devaluation principle.[174] Consequently, if the defendant does not value the enrichment as much as the reasonable person would, this should be taken into account when valuing the benefit. But, in the same way as the principle of subjective devaluation may be defeated by the principles of incontrovertible benefit and free acceptance for the purpose of identifying an enrichment, the defendant's reliance on that principle should similarly be circumscribed for the purposes of valuing the enrichment. This means that, if it can be shown that the defendant had been incontrovertibly benefited or had freely accepted the benefit then the objective value of the benefit should be adopted and the defendant's own valuation of the benefit should be considered to be irrelevant. In the context of identifying the appropriate test for valuing benefits there are three issues which require particular consideration.

---

[168] See Chapter 1.
[169] *BP Exploration Co. (Libya) Ltd.* v. *Hunt* [1979] 1 WLR 783, 839–41 (Robert Goff J).
[170] *Ibid.*   [171] See p. 61 above.
[172] Goff and Jones, *The Law of Restitution*, p. 28. See *Flett* v. *Deniliquin Publishing Co. Ltd.* [1964–5] NSWLR 383.
[173] See p. 86 above.
[174] In *Scarisbrick* v. *Parkinson* (1869) 20 LT 175 Kelly CB, at p. 177, emphasised that the court was concerned with how the defendant valued the services which he had received. See also *Ministry of Defence* v. *Thompson* [1993] 40 EG 148, 149 (Hoffmann LJ). See also Arrowsmith. 'Ineffective Transactions and Unjust Enrichment' (1989) 9 *LS* 121, 126.

(i) Valuing services

Where the plaintiff has provided a service which the defendant is unable subjectively to devalue the objective value of the benefit will be adopted. Where the benefit takes the form of services it should follow that the defendant's enrichment should be assessed as the reasonable value of the services.[175] But what of the case where the plaintiff has improved the defendant's property with the effect that he or she has increased its value? If the increase in value of the property is greater than the value of the services, should the defendant's enrichment be treated as the value of the services or the increased value in the property? Ultimately, this is not a question of valuation but one concerning the identification of the enrichment. Where the effect of the plaintiff's services is to increase the value of the defendant's property it is the benefit to that property which is the end-product of the services, and so this should constitute the enrichment.[176] The value of the enrichment is therefore the amount by which the defendant's property increased in value. Logically, where the increase in the value of the defendant's property is less than the value of the services, the enrichment should still be treated as the improvement to the defendant's property rather than the services, because the improvement is the end-product. The value of the services should be taken into account only where they constitute pure services which do not have any end-product.

This analysis of the valuation of services is illustrated, but not supported, by the decision of the Court of Appeal in *Greenwood* v. *Bennett*[177] where it has been argued that the owner of the car had been incontrovertibly benefited by the repairer's work. What was the value of this incontrovertible benefit? The owner of the car, Bennett, had originally entrusted the car to a repairer, and at this point the car was worth between £400 and £500. The repairer then crashed the car and sold it to Harper for £75. Harper spent £226 on labour and materials. The car was eventually sold by Bennett for £400. Harper was awarded an allowance of £226 in respect of the services which he had provided. Is this correct? Since we are concerned only with the value of Bennett's incontrovertible benefit, it might be argued that, looking at the complete course of events, he had not been enriched at all, since at the beginning of the story the car was worth at least £400 and, at the end, he sold it for that figure. But it is also necessary to consider the intermediate events. Since Bennett had entrusted the car to the repairer he should bear the risk of the repairer damaging the car. So the test of initial value of the car should be regarded as its value at the time Harper gained possession, namely £75. Since the

---

[175] See also Chapter 11.   [176] See p. 68 above.
[177] [1973] 1 QB 195. See p. 76 above.

car was eventually sold for £400, it had increased in value by £325. So this should be regarded as the value of Bennett's benefit, since this was the value of the end-product which Bennett had eventually received rather than the value of the services which Harper had provided. The only way that the award of £226 can be defended is that, since Harper had committed the tort of conversion by interfering with the car which belonged to Bennett, it follows that Harper was a wrongdoer and it is a fundamental principle of the law that wrongdoers should not be allowed to profit from their wrong.[178] If this principle is applied strictly it follows that the award of an allowance of £226 was correct.[179] This means that Bennett was still enriched to the sum of £174, being the difference between the value of the services provided by Harper and the amount for which the car was sold, but this can be justified on the basis that, since Harper was a wrongdoer, Bennett had a better claim to that sum.

(ii) Free acceptance

Where the defendant has freely accepted the benefit from the plaintiff, this should mean that the objective valuation of the enrichment is adopted because the defendant is unable to rely on the subjective devaluation principle.[180] Birks has, however, suggested that where the free acceptance principle applies then '[a]utomatic valuation of the freely accepted benefit is qualified to the extent that the free acceptance was itself qualified'.[181] What this means is that if, for example, the defendant had freely accepted a benefit believing that it was being offered at £10, when in fact it had a market value of £20, the valuation of the enrichment should not exceed £10. Although Birks is correct in his assumption that the free acceptance principle is relevant both to the identification of the enrichment and its valuation, there is no basis for asserting that, at the valuation stage, the extent of the free acceptance can be qualified by the defendant's own belief as to the value of the enrichment. Surely the purpose of free acceptance is simply to prevent the defendant from resorting to the subjective devaluation argument, because his or her conduct was unconscionable. Where free acceptance applies it should defeat the subjective devaluation argument completely, meaning that valuation of the enrichment should occur solely by reference to the objective test.[182] This is consistent with the view that free acceptance is closely related to estoppel and, as Birks has acknowledged, a 'freely accepting recipient must acknowledge the objective valuation of the benefit'.[183]

---

[178] See Chapter 15.   [179] See Goff and Jones, *The Law of Restitution*, p. 248.
[180] *Ibid*, p. 28.   [181] Birks in *Essays on the Law of Restitution* (ed. Burrows) p. 129.
[182] Goff and Jones, *The Law of Restitution*, p. 29.
[183] Birks in *Essays on the Law of Restitution* (ed. Burrows) p. 129.

(iii) Estoppel

Where the defendant is estopped from denying that he or she has been enriched, it follows that he or she is deemed to have received a benefit. Since no benefit will actually have been received the measure of the enrichment should be assessed by reference to the market value of the plaintiff's work.[184] So, in a case such as *Planché* v. *Colburn*,[185] if the estoppel principle is adopted to identify an enrichment then the value of the defendant's deemed benefit should be assessed by reference to the objective value of the plaintiff's work in researching and preparing the manuscript.

(c) The role of the contract in the valuation of the enrichment

One of the most controversial matters relating to the valuation of bene-fits, and one which is closely related to the question whether a subjective or an objective test of valuation should be adopted, concerns the effect of a contract upon the valuation of a benefit. If the defendant receives a benefit under a contract and that contract is subsequently set aside so that the plaintiff is forced to sue the defendant in restitution rather than on the contract, should the value of the benefit be assessed by reference to its market value or to the price which the parties had agreed in the con-tract? This will be a particularly important question where the objective value of the benefit is greater than the value of the benefit as determined by the contract. In such circumstances should the contract price operate as a ceiling on the value of the benefit? There are mixed views in the cases and amongst the commentators on the role of the contract price in valu-ing benefits.

(i) The contract price should operate as a ceiling to the valuation of the benefit

One view[186] is that the price determined by the contract should, at least as a general rule, operate as a ceiling upon the price of the services or goods provided. Goff and Jones accept that the price agreed by the par-ties should at least be treated as evidence of the reasonable value of the benefit which was provided.[187] There are a number of situations where

---

[184] This was the test of valuation which was adopted in *Sabemo Pty. Ltd.* v. *North Sydney Municipal Council* [1977] 2 NSWLR 880, 903.

[185] (1831) 8 Bing. 14; 131 ER 305. See p. 91 above.

[186] As exemplified by the decision of Deane J of the High Court of Australia in *Pavey and Matthews Pty. Ltd.* v. *Paul* (1987) 162 CLR 221, 257. Birks, *An Introduction to the Law of Restitution*, p. 288, agreed with this but he has since changed his mind: *Essays on the Law of Restitution* (ed. Burrows) p. 136.

[187] Goff and Jones, *The Law of Restitution*, p. 30. This was also the view of Robert Goff J in *BP Exploration Co. (Libya) Ltd.* v. *Hunt (No. 2)* [1979] 1 WLR 783 in respect of the

the contract price has been taken into account in valuing the benefit which the defendant had received. So, for example, the contract price has been taken into account to value the defendant's benefit even where the contract itself was unenforceable.[188] Where the plaintiff delivers more goods to the defendant than he or she contracted to sell and the defendant accepts these goods, the excess will be valued at the contract price rather than their reasonable value.[189] Even if the parties have not agreed on a specific price for the work or the property, the course of the parties' negotiations has been of considerable assistance in determining the value of the benefit. As Lord Atkin said in *Way* v. *Latilla*:[190]

[the] court may take into account the bargainings between the parties, not with a view to completing the bargain for them, but as evidence of the value which each of them puts upon the services. If the discussion had ranged between three per cent. on the one side and five per cent. on the other, all else being agreed, the court would not be likely to depart from somewhere about those figures, and would be wrong in ignoring them altogether and fixing remuneration on an entirely different basis, upon which, possibly, the services would never have been rendered at all.

This emphasis on the contract price as being a ceiling on the value of the defendant's benefit is consistent with the subjective approach to the valuation of benefits.[191] If the essential test for determining whether or not the defendant has been enriched is whether he or she values the benefit, then logic demands that the defendant's perception should be referred to when valuing the enrichment, and this perception can be discovered from the price which has been agreed by the parties and is contained in the contract.

(ii) The contract price should not operate as a ceiling to the valuation of the benefit

The most recent judicial discussion of the function of the actual or possible contract price suggests that it should not be used to restrict the valuation of the enrichment received by the defendant.[192] In *Rover*

valuation of the just sum to be awarded in respect of benefits in kind which have been provided under a contract subsequently frustrated. See p. 386 below. See also *Flett* v. *Denilquin Publishing Co. Ltd.* [1964–5] NSWLR 383, 386 (Herron CJ).

[187] *Scarisbrick* v. *Parkinson* (1869) 20 LT 175 and *Pavey and Matthews Pty.* v. *Paul* (1987) 162 CLR 221.

[188] Sale of Goods Act 1979, s. 30(3).

[189] [1937] 3 All ER 759, 764. In *Renard Constructions (ME) Pty. Ltd.* v. *Minister for Public Works* (1992) 26 NSWLR 234 Meagher JA regarded the contract price as strong evidence but not conclusive evidence of the value of the benefit.

[190] Birks, *An Introduction to the Law of Restitution*, p. 467.

[191] This approach is endorsed by Birks in *Essays on the Law of Restitution* (ed. Burrows) p. 136. See also *Renard Constructions (ME) Pty. Ltd.* v. *Minister for Public Works* (1992) 26 NSWLR 234.

International Ltd. v. *Cannon Film Sales (No. 3) Ltd.*[193] the valuation of the services provided by the plaintiff for the benefit of the defendant was not restricted to the price which had been agreed by the parties in the contract. *Rover International* concerned, amongst other claims, a *quantum meruit* claim to recover the value of services provided in respect of a contract for the dubbing and distribution of films in Italy. Unfortunately the contract was void *ab initio* since it was made before the plaintiff company had been incorporated. Counsel for the defendant conceded that the plaintiff's claim could be established, so the only remaining issue related to the valuation of the benefit. Kerr LJ, with whom Nicholls LJ concurred,[194] held that the valuation of the benefit received by the defendant was not constrained by the amount which the plaintiff would have received under the contract for the provision of the service. Kerr LJ provided three reasons for this conclusion.[195]

(1) It would not be just for the defendant to rely on the contract to restrict the valuation of the benefit when it was the defendant who had initially relied on the invalidity of the contract to discontinue its performance of the contract. In other words, the defendant's conduct had been such that it could not ignore the contract at one stage of the proceedings and rely on its terms when it was in its own interest to do so.[196]

(2) If the contract terms did constitute a ceiling on the restitutionary claim this would result in undesirable inconsistency in the law of restitution, particularly because when relief is awarded following the frustration of a contract then the contract terms do not restrict the plaintiff's restitutionary claim.[197]

(3) It would be unprincipled to rely on the contract to restrict the plaintiff's restitutionary claim when that contract was null and void. Since such claims arise from the fact that the contract was non-existent, it would be illogical then to rely on that contract when valuing the benefit.

The first two of the judge's reasons are unconvincing. The first reason, concerning the relative merits of the parties' conduct, should not be relevant when considering the role of the contract in valuing the benefits provided, for that is the route to palm-tree justice and consequent uncertainty. As regards the second reason, any inconsistency with the law concerning frustrated contracts may be undesirable but might be inevitable, since the implications of a contract being frustrated are now governed by statute. But the third reason is surely relevant in concluding that the plaintiff's claim should not have been circumscribed by the contract

---

[193] [1989] 1 WLR 912.   [194] The other judge, Dillon LJ, did not consider the matter.
[195] [1989] 1 WLR 912, 927–8.
[196] See also *Renard Constructions (ME) Pty. Ltd.* v. *Minister for Public Works* (1992) 26 NSWLR 234, 278 (Meagher JA).
[197] Law Reform (Frustrated Contracts) Act 1943, s. 1(3). See Chapter 12.

price. If the contract is null and void then how can its terms be relevant to the restitutionary claim? This explains why in *Pavey and Matthews Pty. Ltd.* v. *Paul*[198] the High Court of Australia held that the contract price operated as a ceiling on the restitutionary claim, because in that case the contract was merely unenforceable and not void, so the contract price continued to be relevant.

(iii) When the contract price should be relevant to the valuation of the benefit

The preferable view is that the contract price should simply be treated as evidence of valuation.[199] Since the starting point for valuation of the benefit is the objective value test, the contract price may provide some evidence of what the market price for the benefit was, but it cannot be conclusive evidence, because the market value may have changed by the time the benefit was provided. Equally, if the defendant wishes subjectively to devalue the benefit, the contract price may be quite strong evidence of how the defendant values the benefit and so, usually, the contract price will determine the value of the benefit. But it may not be possible to rely on the contract price in two particular circumstances.

(1) Where the contract is null and void it may be considered to be unreliable evidence of how the defendant valued the benefit. But this may itself depend on why the contract was null and void. If, for example, the contract was void because of the incapacity of the defendant, then the contract price must be treated as unreliable evidence of how the defendant valued the benefit, since the defendant lacked capacity to enter into the contract and so cannot be considered to have consented to any of its terms. Where, however, the contract was void because of the plaintiff's incapacity, as was the case in *Rover International*, it is much more difficult to justify the failure to treat the contract price as evidence of the defendant's valuation of the benefit, since the defendant had the capacity to enter into the contract and did so voluntarily. Ultimately, whether the contract price is taken into account should depend on how reliable it is as evidence of either the objective value of the benefit or the defendant's valuation of the benefit.

(2) Where the objective value of the benefit is greater than the price agreed in the contract for the provision of the benefit, the defendant should be unable to rely on the contract price subjectively to devalue the benefit if the defendant is prevented from relying on the subjective devaluation principle at all. So where it can be shown that the defendant

---

[198] (1987) 162 CLR 221.
[199] See *Mohamed* v. *Alaga and Co. (a firm)* [1998] 2 All ER 720, 726 (Lightman J).

has been incontrovertibly benefited or has freely accepted the benefit, then the defendant's own valuation of the benefit is irrelevant.[200]

(d) Inadequate performance

Where the plaintiff provides a service to the defendant but the service is performed inadequately or late,[201] should this be a matter which is taken into account when valuing the benefit received by the defendant? As a matter of principle the answer should be 'yes' since the defendant should be able subjectively to devalue the benefit which was received. Consequently, if the defendant considers the service to be less valuable because it was poorly performed or was performed late so that the defendant incurred additional expense or liabilities to third parties, this should be taken into account when valuing the service. Of course, if the defendant had freely accepted the service or the enrichment was treated as incontrovertibly beneficial, then the objective value of the benefit should be adopted. Some judicial support for this approach can be found in the decision of the Court of Appeal in *Crown House Engineering Ltd.* v. *Amec Projects Ltd.*[202] Although Bingham LJ said[203] that he was agnostic on the point, he suggested that the courts should have regard to the plaintiff's acts or omissions in the provision of the service if they depreciated or even eliminated the value of the services to the defendant. This is an entirely appropriate response to the problem since it is consistent with the fundamental principles concerning the identification and valuation of an enrichment.

---

[200] Burrows, 'Free Acceptance and the Law of Restitution' (1988) 104 *LQR* 576, 588; Garner, 'The Role of Subjective Benefit in the Law of Unjust Enrichment' (1990) 10 *OJLS* 42, 55.

[201] As occurred in *British Steel Corporation* v. *Cleveland Bridge and Engineering Co. Ltd.* [1984] 1 All ER 504. The question whether a deduction should be made for inadequate performance was not considered because the parties had agreed the reasonable value of the services.

[202] (1989) 48 BLR 37.

[203] *Ibid*, at p. 58. Slade LJ, at p. 54, described this as 'a difficult question' but did not provide any assistance on how to resolve it.

5

At the Expense of the Plaintiff

1. GENERAL PRINCIPLES

Where the plaintiff wishes to obtain restitution from the defendant on the ground of unjust enrichment it is not enough to show that the defendant has been enriched in circumstances which fall within one of the grounds of restitution; the plaintiff must also establish that this enrichment was obtained at the plaintiff's expense. This requires the plaintiff to establish a connection between the receipt of an enrichment by the defendant and the plaintiff's loss so as to justify the plaintiff's claim against the defendant.[1] This is usually easily established. For example, if the plaintiff pays £1,000 to the defendant by mistake it is obvious that the defendant was enriched at the plaintiff's expense, because the money was obtained directly from the plaintiff and the defendant's gain mirrors the plaintiff's loss exactly. There are, however, certain types of case in which the question whether the benefit was obtained at the plaintiff's expense is much more difficult to answer and raises some fundamentally important questions about the ambit of the law of restitution. The most important question is whether the benefit obtained by the defendant must have been obtained directly from the plaintiff or can be obtained indirectly via a third party.

Although the requirement that the defendant's enrichment was received at the plaintiff's expense serves to show that the defendant's gain is reflected by a loss suffered by the plaintiff,[2] it does not follow that the defendant is liable to make restitution only to the extent that the plaintiff has suffered a loss. This is because the function of the requirement that the benefit was obtained at the plaintiff's expense is simply to show that there is a causal link between the plaintiff's loss of an enrichment and the defendant's gain. Once this causal link has been established it is no longer necessary to consider the 'at the plaintiff's expense' requirement since the law of restitution is concerned only with the identification and valuation of the benefit which was received by the defendant. It is for this reason that if, following the receipt of a benefit by the defendant, the plaintiff passes on the loss which he or she has suffered to

---

[1] See *Chase Manhattan NA* v. *Israel British Bank (London) Ltd.* [1981] Ch. 105, 125 (Goulding J) and *Banque Financière de la Cité* v. *Parc (Battersea) Ltd.* [1998] 2 WLR 475, 488 (Lord Clyde).

[2] *Ibid.*

a third party then this will not operate as a defence to the plaintiff's restitutionary claim.[3]

2. THE PRIVITY PRINCIPLE

(a) The nature of the privity principle

If the requirement that an enrichment was obtained at the expense of the plaintiff is interpreted strictly it means that the plaintiff can only establish that the defendant has been unjustly enriched where the defendant has obtained a benefit directly from the plaintiff.[4] It follows that where the defendant obtains a benefit indirectly via a third party then the defendant will not have been enriched at the plaintiff's expense. So, for example, if the plaintiff pays £1,000 to a third party to pay that money to X but the money is mistakenly paid by the third party to the defendant, the defendant is enriched at the expense of the third party rather than the plaintiff, even though the defendant's gain is mirrored by an equivalent loss suffered by the plaintiff. This strict interpretation of the 'at the plaintiff's expense' requirement appears to be generally recognised as a fundamental principle of unjust enrichment claims.[5] This principle can be called the 'privity' principle and its general effect is that the plaintiff can bring a restitutionary claim only against the direct recipient of a benefit.[6] Indirect recipients will not generally be liable to make restitution, at least on the ground of reversing the defendant's unjust enrichment.

(b) The rationale of the privity principle

The reason for the imposition of this privity requirement is fundamental to our understanding of the action to reverse the defendant's unjust enrichment. Crucially, where the plaintiff seeks to obtain restitution on the ground of unjust enrichment, the action depends on the plaintiff showing that he or she has a stronger claim to the value received by the defendant than the defendant has to retain that value. But where, for example, the plaintiff's money is paid to a third party and then it is received by the defendant the plaintiff's claim for restitution is much

---

[3] *Kleinwort Benson Ltd.* v. *Birmingham CC* [1996] 4 All ER 733. See Chapter 25. See also Verse, 'Improvements and Enrichments: A Comparative Analysis' (1998) 6 *RLR* 85, 102. Cp. McInnes 'At the Plaintiff's Expense—Quantifying Restitutionary Relief' (1998) 57 *CLJ* 472.

[4] *Re Byfield* [1982] 1 All ER 249, 256 (Goulding J) and *Kleinwort Benson Ltd.* v. *Birmingham CC* [1996] 4 All ER 733, 749 (Morritt LJ).

[5] See, in particular, *The Colonial Bank* v. *The Exchange Bank of Yarmouth, Nova Scotia* (1885) 11 App.Cas. 84, 85 (Lord Hobhouse).

[6] See Millett, 'Tracing the Proceeds of Fraud' (1991) 107 *LQR* 71, 79.

weaker. The enrichment obtained by the defendant was obtained directly from the third party, and so the defendant appears to have been enriched at that party's expense rather than at the plaintiff's expense. Consequently, as a general rule, the plaintiff would not be able to establish standing to sue the defendant.

In an important contribution to the understanding of this privity principle, Tettenborn has provided a further explanation of why a defendant who has received a benefit from a third party should not generally be required to make restitution to the plaintiff.[7] Tettenborn suggests that the reason for this principle is that the defendant has lawfully received the benefit from the third party when the benefit was the unencumbered property of the third party.[8] It follows that, where the defendant has lawfully received a benefit, he or she cannot be considered to be unjustly enriched. The recognition of this principle of lawful receipt is to be welcomed, both because it explains why the privity principle should be generally recognised and also because it is consistent with a policy of general application in English law, namely that it is important to encourage transactional security by protecting those who are involved in permissible activities.[9] Ultimately, where the defendant has lawfully obtained a benefit from a third party, albeit that it was derived from the plaintiff, it is not for the law of restitution to unsettle the defendant's security in the lawful receipt of the benefit.

Although the days of the privity doctrine in the context of contract appear to be numbered,[10] the privity principle within the context of unjust enrichment is a very different creature. It is implicit within the principle of unjust enrichment itself. Consequently, any future reform of the contractual doctrine of privity is of no consequence to the continued existence of the different notion of privity in restitution.

(c) Exceptions to the privity principle

This doctrine of privity within the law of restitution is apparently subject to a number of exceptions, whereby the plaintiff can obtain a restitutionary remedy against the indirect recipient of a benefit. In fact, careful analysis of these so-called exceptions show that there are few true limits on the operation of the principle.

---

[7] 'Lawful Receipt—A Justifying Factor?' (1997) 5 *RLR* 1.   [8] *Ibid*, p. 12.
[9] *Ibid*, p. 7.

[10] The Law Commission has recommended the abolition of that doctrine within the contractual context: 'Privity of Contract: Contracts for the Benefit of Third Parties' (Law Com. No. 242, 1996). The Law Commission makes no reference to the privity doctrine within the law of restitution. Now see the Contracts (Rights of Third Parties) Bill 1999.

(i) Restitutionary claims to vindicate the plaintiff's proprietary rights

Where the defendant has received property in which the plaintiff retains a proprietary interest the plaintiff will be able to bring a restitutionary claim against the defendant even though the defendant received the benefit indirectly. In fact, most claims involving the vindication of proprietary rights are brought against the indirect recipients of property. This is illustrated by the decision of the House of Lords in *Lipkin Gorman (a firm)* v. *Karpnale Ltd.*[11] where a partner in the plaintiff firm of solicitors stole money from it which he then used to gamble at the defendant's casino. The plaintiff's restitutionary claim against the defendant succeeded, even though the defendant had not received the benefit directly from the plaintiff. But this is not an exception to the privity requirement simply because the restitutionary claim to vindicate property rights is not founded on the unjust enrichment principle.[12]

(ii) Restitutionary claims founded on wrongdoing

Where the plaintiff's restitutionary claim is founded on a wrong it is irrelevant that the defendant obtained a benefit indirectly, it being sufficient that the enrichment arose from the commission of a wrong by the defendant against the plaintiff, without there being any need to show that the benefit necessarily represents a loss suffered by the plaintiff. So, for example, where the defendant owes fiduciary duties to the plaintiff and receives a bribe from a third party to induce him or her to breach this fiduciary duty, the plaintiff has a restitutionary claim to this money even though he or she has not suffered any loss.[13] But again this is not an exception to the privity principle simply because restitution in such circumstances is not founded on the reversal of unjust enrichment, but on the wrongdoing itself.[14]

(iii) Agency

Where a benefit is transferred from the plaintiff to the defendant by the plaintiff's agent the plaintiff will be able to bring a restitutionary claim against the defendant even though he or she is an indirect recipient of the enrichment.[15] This is simply a function of the law of agency whereby the agent acts on behalf of his or her principal and so the transfer is deemed to have been directly at the plaintiff's expense. Similarly, where the benefit was received by the defendant's agent directly from the plaintiff and then transmitted to the defendant, the plaintiff can bring a

---

[11] [1991] 2 AC 546. [12] See Chapter 20.
[13] See *Attorney-General for Hong Kong* v. *Reid* [1994] 1 AC 324. [14] See Chapter 15.
[15] *Colonial Bank* v. *Exchange Bank of Yarmouth, Nova Scotia* (1885) 11 App. Cas. 84, 90 (Lord Hobhouse).

restitutionary claim against the defendant simply because the benefit received by the defendant's agent is deemed to have been received by the defendant directly from the plaintiff. This is a true exception to the privity requirement, since the defendant is considered to have been enriched at the plaintiff's expense even though the enrichment was received directly from a third party.

(iv) Interceptive subtraction[16]

In some cases the defendant may be enriched by the receipt of money which can be considered to be at the plaintiff's expense even though it was not received directly from the plaintiff. This will occur, for example, where a third party transmits money to the plaintiff and this money is intercepted by the defendant before the plaintiff receives it. This could be treated as a case where the defendant has obtained a benefit at the plaintiff's expense since, if the defendant had not intervened, the benefit would have been received by the plaintiff. Consequently, the plaintiff should be able to bring a restitutionary claim against the defendant in respect of the benefit which he or she had intercepted if it is possible for the plaintiff to establish that one of the recognised grounds of restitution is applicable.[17]

In the typical case where the defendant has intervened and subtracted a benefit which the third party was intending to transfer to the plaintiff, the third party will be seeking to discharge a liability which was owed to the plaintiff. In such circumstances it cannot be assumed that the defendant has necessarily been enriched at the plaintiff's expense because he or she has received the benefit. This will, in fact, turn on whether or not the liability has been discharged. If the liability has not been discharged, the third party will continue to be liable to the plaintiff and so the defendant cannot be considered to have been enriched at the plaintiff's expense, simply because the plaintiff will not have suffered any loss. In this situation the defendant will be enriched at the third party's expense who consequently will be able to bring a restitutionary claim against the defendant.

Where, however, the third party's payment to the defendant has discharged the liability which the third party owed to the plaintiff, the defendant will have been enriched at the plaintiff's expense and so the plaintiff will able to seek restitution from the defendant. It is in this case that the principle of interceptive subtraction will be important. Ultimately, therefore, it is necessary to determine whether the third

---

[16] See Birks, *An Introduction to the Law of Restitution*, pp. 133–9. This principle is examined rigorously and critically by Smith, 'Three-Party Restitution: A Critique of Birks's Theory of Interceptive Subtraction' (1991) 11 *OJLS* 481.

[17] Ignorance or failure of consideration would be most appropriate.

party's payment has discharged the liability. Although the law on discharge of liabilities is uncertain it seems that the debt is discharged if the
creditor accepts that the debt has been discharged.[18]

The advantage of recognising the principle of interceptive subtraction
is that it avoids multiplying proceedings. If the third party's payment to
the defendant does discharge the third party's liability to the plaintiff it
follows that the only claim in this type of case is one brought by the plaintiff against the defendant for restitution. If the payment does not discharge the liability, however, the third party will continue to be liable to
the plaintiff and the third party will need to seek restitution from the
defendant. This pragmatic advantage of enabling the plaintiff to obtain
restitution from the defendant was recognised by Nourse J in *Official
Custodian for Charities* v. *Mackey (No. 2)*[19] who said that the rationale for
restitution in these cases is to avoid circuity of actions, to ensure that the
person who is ultimately entitled to receive the money can recover it
directly.

(1) Establishing interceptive subtraction

Two conditions must be satisfied before the plaintiff can establish that
the defendant has been enriched at the plaintiff's expense by means of
the principle of interceptive subtraction.

(a) Inevitability of receipt

It must first be shown that the benefit received by the defendant would
inevitably have come to the plaintiff had the defendant not intervened,
for otherwise it is not possible to conclude that the defendant's enrichment had effectively been subtracted from the plaintiff. This notion of
inevitability of receipt may be interpreted in two separate ways.

(1) Where the third party was legally obliged to transfer the benefit to
the plaintiff and this benefit was intercepted by the defendant it is possible to conclude that the defendant has indeed been enriched at the
plaintiff's expense simply because, had the defendant not intervened, it
would have been inevitable that the plaintiff would have received the
benefit. The third party's obligation to transfer the benefit to the plaintiff
may have arisen by operation of law or by agreement between the
parties.

(2) Where the third party was not obliged to transfer the benefit to the
plaintiff but it can be established that, had the defendant not intervened,
the benefit would definitely have been received by the plaintiff, it might
also be possible to conclude that the defendant has been enriched at the
plaintiff's expense. Although Birks has argued that this test of factual
inevitability is supported by case law, this is not so. In particular, he relies

---

[18] See pp. 225–30 below.   [19] [1985] 1 WLR 1308, 1315.

on the decision of the Privy Council in *Cook* v. *Deeks*[20] where the directors of a company were negotiating on its behalf for a lucrative contract. Just before the contract was signed some of the directors intervened and took the contract for themselves. The directors were then sued for the profit they had made and their claim succeeded. Birks says that this is an example of interceptive subtraction because it was accepted that, had the directors not intervened, the company would have received the contract and so the directors' profits can be considered to have been obtained at the company's expense. But in fact this case has nothing to do with the reversal of the defendant's unjust enrichment, since liability was founded on the defendants' breach of fiduciary duty. Consequently, it is an example of restitution for wrongdoing.[21]

In fact, the proper interpretation of the notion of inevitable receipt is that of legal inevitability, as was recognised by Nourse J in *Official Custodian for Charities* v. *Mackey (No. 2)*:[22]

[A] defendant, intervening without right between the plaintiff and a third party, renders himself accountable to the plaintiff for the sum which he receives from the third party. It seems to me that it is of the essence of all [such] cases . . . that there is a contract or some other current obligation between the third party and the plaintiff on which the defendant intervenes . . .

The application of this test of legal inevitability is particularly well illustrated by the *Mackey* case. In this case the plaintiff landlord had forfeited a lease and then sought to recover rent which had mistakenly been paid by sub-tenants to receivers on behalf of the tenant's mortgagee. Since the sub-tenants were liable to pay the plaintiff mesne profits whilst they occupied the premises after the lease had been forfeited, the plaintiff sued the receivers in an action for money had and received to recover the money which had been paid to them by the sub-tenants. The plaintiff's action failed on the ground that it could not be assumed that the mesne profits which the sub-tenants were liable to pay to the plaintiff were necessarily precisely equivalent to the rent which the sub-tenants had paid to the receivers. Although Nourse J did not refer specifically to the principle of interceptive subtraction, his analysis is consistent with that principle. For the plaintiff's restitutionary claim to succeed it had to be shown that the money paid by the sub-tenants to the receivers would inevitably have been paid to the plaintiff had the receivers not intervened. It was not possible to show this, simply because the sub-tenants were not liable to pay rent to the plaintiff but were only liable to pay mesne profits and, crucially, the sub-tenants were not liable to pay this sum until the plaintiff had sued for it and judgment had been entered.

---

[20] [1916] 1 AC 554. See Birks, *An Introduction to the Law of Restitution*, p. 137.
[21] See p. 540 below.   [22] [1985] 1 WLR 1308, 1314.

(b) The defendant must not have earned the benefit

The plaintiff will not be able to rely on the interceptive subtraction principle if the defendant who received a benefit from a third party had earned it, since in such a case the defendant cannot be considered to have intercepted the benefit from the plaintiff but will instead have received it in his or her own right. This is illustrated by *Boyter* v. *Dodsworth*[23] where the plaintiff had been appointed to the office of Sexton of Salisbury Cathedral for life. He did not receive any regular fees for this office, but it was usual for him to be paid by those visitors for whom he gave a tour of the cathedral. The defendant usurped the plaintiff's office and was paid by visitors for guided tours. The plaintiff then brought an action for money had and received to recover these fees. The plaintiff's claim failed on the ground that the money paid to the defendant had taken the form of gratuities for the services he had provided and which the visitors were not obliged to pay him. The money paid to the defendant had therefore been paid as a result of the work which he had done and it could not be shown that the plaintiff would necessarily have received this money if he had shown visitors round the Cathedral.

(2) Application of the principle

The principle of interceptive subtraction has been applied in a number of disparate areas. In each of these areas the ground of restitution may be a matter of some controversy, although the better view is that restitution can be justified on the ground of ignorance[24] or, sometimes, on the ground of mistake.

Where the plaintiff is entitled to receive fees from a third party by virtue of the plaintiff's office and the defendant has collected this money by usurping that office, the plaintiff has an action for money and received to recover what had been paid to the defendant, even though this money was received directly from the third party rather than the plaintiff. Such an action will succeed so long as it can be shown that the fees were certain and were annexed to the discharge of duties relating to the office.[25] Clearly, where it is certain that the money received by the defendant would have been received by the plaintiff had the defendant not intervened, these cases illustrate the principle of interceptive subtraction. That these cases relate to the award of restitutionary remedies is supported by *King* v. *Alston*[26] where it was recognised that the plaintiff could recover the money which had actually been paid to the defendant usurper but had no

---

[23] (1796) 6 TR 682; 101 ER 770.   [24] See Chapter 7.

[25] *Boyter* v. *Dodsworth* (1796) 6 TR 682, 683; 101 ER 770, 771 (Lord Kenyon CJ). See also *Arris* v. *Stukley* (1677) 2 Mod. 260; 86 ER 1060, *Howard* v. *Wood* (1679) 2 Lev. 245; 83 ER 540 and *Jacob* v. *Allen* (1703) 1 Salkeld 27; 91 ER 26.

[26] (1848) 12 QB 971; 116 ER 1134.

claim against the defendant in respect of any greater sum which the plaintiff might have earned had the defendant not intervened. In other words, the plaintiff's claim is confined to the amount which the defendant had gained rather than what the plaintiff might have lost.

In these cases where the defendant has usurped the plaintiff's office it is possible to conclude that the defendant has been enriched because of the long recognised rule that the acts of the usurper of the office are binding on the true holder of that office.[27] It follows that where the third party pays the defendant rather than the plaintiff the defendant's receipt of the payment discharges the third party's liability to the plaintiff. Consequently, it is clear that the defendant has been enriched and that this enrichment was at the expense of the plaintiff.

Although these cases recognise that the plaintiff has a restitutionary claim founded on the reversal of the defendant's unjust enrichment, in the form of an action for money had and received, the award of the restitutionary remedy is also consistent with restitution founded on wrongdoing since usurpation of an office constitutes a proprietary tort.[28]

The principle of interceptive subtraction can be identified in other contexts as well. So, for example, in *Jacob* v. *Allen*[29] the defendant had acted as administrator of the deceased's estate until the deceased's will was found. Whilst he had been acting as administrator the defendant had received money from the estate. The plaintiff executor then sued the defendant in an action for money had and received and successfully recovered this money. Similarly where a defendant acts as an executor *de son tort* he or she is liable to the rightful representatives of the deceased for what the defendant had received from the estate.[30] Indeed, Goff and Jones argue that the categories of cases where the creditor is able to recover what has erroneously been paid by his or her debtor are not closed.[31]

[27] See Smith, 'Three-Party Restitution: A Critique of Birks's Theory of Interceptive Subtraction' (1991) 11 *OJLS* 481, 494.

[28] See Chapter 16. [29] (1703) 1 Salkeld 27; 91 ER 26.

[30] *Yardley* v. *Arnold* (1842) Car. and M 434; 174 ER 577.

[31] Goff and Jones, *The Law of Restitution*, p. 698. Birks has suggested that the principle of interceptive subtraction operates in two other cases as well, namely attornment and secret trusts: Birks, *An Introduction to the Law of Restitution*, pp. 134–6. This is not correct. Attornment arises where the defendant acknowledges that goods or money, which were transferred by a third party to the defendant to be transferred to the plaintiff, are held for the plaintiff's use. Where attornment has occurred legal title in the goods is transferred to the plaintiff (*Henderson and Co.* v. *Williams* [1895] 1 QB 521, 528 *per* Lord Halsbury) or the plaintiff has an equitable interest in the money (Goff and Jones, p. 39). Consequently, the plaintiff's claim for restitution is founded on the vindication of property rights rather than the reversal of unjust enrichment. Similarly, where a secret trust is created, being a trust where a settlor transfers property to the defendant apparently as an absolute gift but accompanied by instructions to transfer the property to particular people, the property will be held on trust for those people. Consequently, the plaintiff beneficiary has an equitable interest and will obtain restitution by vindicating that proprietary right rather than by arguing that the defendant trustee has been unjustly enriched.

3. NON-MONEY BENEFITS

Where the enrichment received by the defendant is money it will usually be obvious whether or not the money was received directly from the plaintiff. Where, however, the defendant has received a non-money benefit it may be more difficult to show that this benefit was received at the plaintiff's expense. This is illustrated by the facts of *Rowland* v. *Divall*[32] where the vendor purported to sell a car to the purchaser, when the car actually belonged to a third party. After the purchaser had used the car for a few months he discovered that the vendor had not been able to transfer title to him and he successfully recovered the purchase price from the vendor. At first sight it seems that the vendor might have had a restitutionary claim against the purchaser, who had clearly benefited from the use of the car, and this benefit had been obtained at the vendor's expense simply because the car had been obtained directly from the vendor. But this is not strictly correct. The benefit had in fact been obtained at the expense of the true owner, since it was the true owner of the car who suffered the real loss through the purchaser's use of the car.

Sometimes the defendant may be considered to have received a non-money benefit directly from the plaintiff even though the plaintiff only dealt with a third party. The best example of this is where the plaintiff has discharged the defendant's liability to a third party by paying off a debt which the defendant owed to the third party. As long as this payment was effective to discharge the debt,[33] the defendant can be considered to have been enriched at the plaintiff's expense even though the defendant did not receive any money from the plaintiff, because the negative enrichment of the defendant mirrors the loss suffered by the plaintiff.

This realistic approach to the determination of whether or not the defendant has been enriched at the plaintiff's expense when a debt is discharged is particularly well illustrated by the decision of the House of Lords in *Banque Financière de la Cité* v. *Parc (Battersea) Ltd.*[34] In this case the plaintiff had entered into a refinancing transaction where it paid a sum of money to the chief financial officer of a holding company to be transmitted to a subsidiary of that company to discharge a debt which the subsidiary owed. It was conceded that the discharge of this debt enriched the defendant, another subsidiary of the holding company, which was also owed money by the first subsidiary, because the discharge of the first debt meant that the defendant's debt was more likely

---

[32] [1923] 2 KB 500.   [33] This is discussed at pp. 225–30 below.
[34] [1998] 2 WLR 475.

to be repaid.[35] One of the questions for the House of Lords was whether this enrichment could be considered to have been at the plaintiff's expense, when the money paid by the plaintiff had been paid to the chief financial officer rather than to the first subsidiary directly. The reason the transaction had been structured in this way was to avoid the need to report the transaction to the Swiss financial authorities. Consequently, the court was prepared to consider the realities of the case and the role of the financial officer was ignored, so that the benefit obtained by the defendant, namely the reduction of the other subsidiary's liabilities, was considered to have been obtained directly at the plaintiff's expense, so the privity principle was not infringed.

[35] The first debt was secured by a first legal charge over the subsidiary's property and the defendant's debt was secured by a second legal charge over the same property. Consequently, the discharge of the first debt meant that the defendant's charge became the first legal charge so that the defendant's position was much more secure.

PART III

THE GROUNDS OF RESTITUTION FOR THE PURPOSE OF ESTABLISHING UNJUST ENRICHMENT

6

Principles Underlying the Recognition of Grounds of Restitution

Since a restitutionary claim founded on the reversal of the defendant's unjust enrichment will only succeed if the plaintiff's claim falls within one of the recognised grounds of restitution, or within a ground of restitution which can be deduced from one of the recognised grounds of restitution, it is vital to be aware of what the grounds of restitution are and also why they have been recognised.

The main grounds of restitution were recognised by Lord Mansfield in *Moses* v. *Macferlan*:[1]

[This action of money had and received] lies for money paid by mistake; or upon a consideration which happens to fail; or for money got through imposition, (express, or implied); or extortion; or oppression; or an undue advantage taken of the plaintiff's situation, contrary to laws made for the protection of persons under those circumstances.

These are still the main grounds of restitution for purposes of establishing unjust enrichment. But why have these grounds been recognised? The answer is that the receipt of a benefit by the defendant in the circumstances recognised by Lord Mansfield can be considered to be unjust. This notion of injustice derives from three different principles, which can usefully be summarised as plaintiff oriented, defendant oriented and policy oriented.[2] Every ground of restitution can be explained by reference to at least one of these principles, but quite often more than one of them may be operating.

1. PLAINTIFF-ORIENTED GROUNDS OF RESTITUTION

Most of the grounds of restitution are plaintiff-oriented in the sense that, to determine whether the receipt of a benefit by the defendant can be considered to be unjust, it is necessary to consider the circumstances from the perspective of the plaintiff. Usually what this means is that a ground of restitution will only be applicable where the circumstances of

---

[1] (1760) 2 Burr. 1005, 1012; 97 ER 676, 681.

[2] See Birks, ' No Consideration: Restitution after Void Contracts' (1993) 23 *Univ. WALR* 195, 206.

the transfer are such that the plaintiff's intention to transfer the benefit to the defendant can be considered to be absent, vitiated or qualified. Where the plaintiff's intention has been affected in some way he or she cannot be considered to have voluntarily transferred a benefit to the defendant and so the defendant can be considered to have been unjustly enriched.

(a) Absence of intention

The simplest grounds of restitution to explain are those where the defendant received a benefit in circumstances in which the plaintiff had no intention that the defendant should receive the benefit. This absence of intention may arise as a matter of fact, as where the benefit was stolen from the plaintiff without his or her knowledge,[3] or it may arise as a matter of law, as where the plaintiff is incapable of forming the necessary intention because of incapacity.[4]

(b) Vitiated intention

The best example of a ground of restitution which operates where the plaintiff's intention can be considered to be vitiated is the ground of mistake. Where the plaintiff transfers a benefit to the defendant as a result of an operative mistake then the plaintiff's intention to transfer the benefit is considered to have been vitiated by virtue of the mistake.[5] Similarly, where the plaintiff is compelled to transfer a benefit to the defendant, the plaintiff is not able to exercise a free choice by virtue of the compulsion, and so again his or her intention to transfer the benefit will be considered to have been vitiated.[6]

(c) Qualified intention

Where the plaintiff transfers a benefit to the defendant in the expectation that he or she will receive a benefit in return, then the plaintiff's intention that the defendant should receive the benefit has been qualified. Consequently, if the expected benefit is not forthcoming the plaintiff's intention can be considered to have been negated by the failure of the condition, and this will constitute the ground of restitution, which is called total failure of consideration.[7]

The crucial distinction between vitiated intention and qualified intention is that the plaintiff's intention can only be vitiated by the circumstances which exist when the defendant received the benefit, whereas

---

[3] See Chapter 7.   [4] See Chapter 13.   [5] See Chapter 8.
[6] See Chapter 9.   [7] See Chapter 12.

where the plaintiff's intention is qualified the question whether a ground of restitution can be established arises after the receipt of the benefit by the defendant.

2. DEFENDANT-ORIENTED GROUNDS OF RESTITUTION

Grounds of restitution can be considered to be defendant-oriented if it is necessary to consider the conduct of the defendant or his or her intention when considering whether he or she received a benefit in circumstances of injustice.

(a) Exploitation

The best examples of defendant-oriented grounds of restitution are those which are founded on the principle of exploitation, such as undue influence and unconscionable conduct.[8] Whether these grounds of restitution are defendant-oriented has proved to be a particularly controversial matter since it has been argued that, where the defendant has exploited the plaintiff, it follows that the plaintiff's intention to benefit the defendant can be considered to be vitiated.[9] The better view is that these grounds of restitution are both plaintiff- and defendant-oriented, because the effect of the exploitation is to vitiate the plaintiff's intention, but this requires proof that the defendant had actually exploited the plaintiff's weaker position or can be presumed to have done so.[10] The same is also true of the grounds of restitution which are founded on compulsion which also require proof that the defendant compelled the plaintiff to transfer a benefit.

(b) Free acceptance

A number of commentators have argued that there is another ground of restitution which can only be characterised as defendant-oriented, namely free acceptance or, a more accurate description, unconscientious receipt of a non-money benefit.[11] Such a ground of restitution would be established where the defendant accepts a benefit, knowing that the plaintiff expects to be paid for it in circumstances where the

---

[8] See Chapter 10.   [9] See p. 252 below.

[10] It will be sufficient that the plaintiff has been exploited by a third party, so in such a case the ground of restitution cannot be considered to be defendant-oriented at all. See pp. 265–78 below.

[11] See, for example, Birks, *An Introduction to the Law of Restitution*, Chapter 8 and Tettenborn, *The Law of Restitution in England and Ireland* (2nd edn., London: Cavendish Publishing Ltd., 1996), Chapter 5.

defendant has an opportunity to reject it.[12] Whether such a ground of
restitution is recognised is a highly contentious matter, particularly
because, if it exists, its characteristics are very different from the majority of the other grounds of restitution since it is defendant-oriented and
depends upon proof of fault, namely that the defendant had acted
unconscientiously.

The strongest proponent of free acceptance as a ground of restitution
has been Birks, but he has since tempered his views and has recognised
that many of the cases which he once argued were explicable by reference to free acceptance are better explained as cases where there was a
total failure of consideration.[13] So, for example, where the defendant has
requested the plaintiff to transfer a benefit to him or her, and the plaintiff does so on the condition that the defendant will pay for it but the
defendant fails to do so, then the ground of restitution will be total failure of consideration because the basis for the plaintiff's transfer of the
benefit to the defendant has failed.[14]

Where, however, the plaintiff transfers a benefit to the defendant in the
hope or expectation that the defendant will pay for it, but without any
request from the defendant or previous communication between the
parties, it will not be possible for the plaintiff to ground a claim on total
failure of consideration.[15] Consequently, Birks has argued that it is in this
limited context that there is a role for the ground of free acceptance. He
calls this the 'secret acceptance' case and it is characterised by the facts
that the defendant had the opportunity to reject the benefit and knew
that the plaintiff expected to be paid for it but the plaintiff did not know
that the defendant knew this.[16] The operation of this principle may be
illustrated by reference to Birks's notorious example of the window
cleaner who cleaned the defendant's windows without being requested
to do so.[17] If the defendant was in the house at the time, knew that the
plaintiff expected to be paid for cleaning the windows and failed to stop
him from continuing with the work even though the defendant had the

[12] See Birks, n. 11 above, p. 104.

[13] Birks, 'In Defence of Free Acceptance' in *Essays on the Law of Restitution* (ed. Burrows)
p. 111. See also Simester, 'Unjust Free Acceptance' [1997] *LMCLQ* 103, 104.

[14] See Chapter 12. Birks, *Essays on the Law of Restitution* (ed. Burrows) p. 111. Similarly,
where the benefit was transferred to the defendant without the defendant's request but the
plaintiff had told the defendant that he or she expected to be paid for it and the defendant
had the opportunity to reject the benefit before it was received. Here too the plaintiff's
claim for restitution can be grounded on total failure of consideration. *Ibid*, p. 115.

[15] The conditions for establishing total failure of consideration are examined at
pp. 329–36 below.

[16] Birks, *Essays on the Law of Restitution* (ed. Burrows) p. 118. If the plaintiff thought that
the defendant *probably* knew that the benefit was to be paid for and the defendant did in
fact know this, it may be possible to conclude that the plaintiff's expectation of payment
did indeed constitute consideration which could fail.

[17] Birks, *An Introduction to the Law of Restitution*, p. 265.

opportunity to do so, then Birks concludes that the defendant had received the benefit unconscientiously and restitution should follow. Unconscientious receipt would only be established in such a case if the defendant thought that the plaintiff would have stopped cleaning had the defendant said that he or she would not pay for the work[18] and so long as the defendant had decided at the time of the cleaning that he or she would not pay the plaintiff.

Two arguments can be identified for rejecting this notion of free acceptance as a ground of restitution.

(1) Burrows in particular is opposed to restitution being awarded on the ground of free acceptance, essentially because the plaintiff took the risk that the defendant would not pay for the work.[19] It is a fundamental principle of the law of restitution that the plaintiff who acts officiously or voluntarily should not be able to obtain restitutionary relief.[20] Burrows argues that the plaintiff's risk-taking cancels out the shabbiness of the defendant's behaviour in unconscientiously accepting the benefit. Consequently, there is no injustice in the law of restitution failing to require the defendant to pay for the benefit. It is unclear why, according to Birks, the defendant's unconscientious behaviour in receiving the benefit should necessarily outweigh the plaintiff's behaviour in providing the benefit, for it is easy enough for the plaintiff to check whether or not the defendant wanted the benefit and was prepared to pay for it.[21]

Burrows's argument is consistent with a number of cases which recognise that a plaintiff who provides a benefit which has not been requested by the defendant should not be able to obtain restitution from the defendant, if none of the other recognised grounds of restitution is applicable.[22] Although Birks relies on a number of cases which appear to support his argument that free acceptance should be recognised,[23] none of these cases explicitly recognise such a ground of restitution and those cases where restitutionary remedies were awarded can all be explained by reference to other grounds, particularly mistake,[24] total failure of consideration[25] and necessity.[26] In fact, mistake may explain why the

---

[18] Birks, *Essays on the Law of Restitution* (ed. Burrows) p. 121. It is for this reason that the defendant who refuses to put money in a busker's hat after listening to the busker's music cannot be regarded as unconscientiously receiving a benefit, since the busker would have carried on playing music even if he or she knew that the defendant would not pay.

[19] Burrows, 'Free Acceptance and the Law of Restitution' (1988) 104 *LQR* 576, 578.

[20] See pp. 39–40 above.

[21] Simester, 'Unjust Free Acceptance' [1997] *LMCLQ* 103, 116.

[22] See, for example, *Taylor* v. *Laird* (1856) 25 LJ Ex. 329, 332 (Pollock CB).

[23] See, for example, *Leigh* v. *Dickeson* (1884) 15 QBD 60, 64–5 (Brett MR); *Falcke* v. *Scottish Imperial Insurance Co.* (1886) 34 Ch.D 234, 249 (Bowen LJ); and *Re Cleadon Trust Ltd.* [1939] 1 Ch. 287. But the plaintiff's restitutionary claim failed in each of these cases.

[24] *Weatherby* v. *Banham* (1832) 5 C and P 228; 172 ER 950.

[25] *Alexander* v. *Vane* (1836) 1 M and W 511; 150 ER 537 and *Paynter* v. *Williams* (1833) 1 C and M 810; 149 ER 626.　　　　[26] *Lamb* v. *Bunce* (1815) 4 M and S 275; 105 ER 836.

window cleaner who cleans the defendant's windows might be able to obtain restitution, if the plaintiff honestly but mistakenly believed that the defendant might be prepared to pay for the plaintiff's services when the defendant had already decided that he or she would not pay the plaintiff. Although mispredictions of the future do not constitute mistakes, the plaintiff has surely made a mistake of existing fact as to the present state of the defendant's mind and consequently in principle restitution should lie.[27]

(2) A further criticism of free acceptance as a ground of restitution is that, if it was recognised, liability would be placed on the defendant for his or her failure to act, and this is contrary to the general approach of English law which is opposed to imposing liability for omissions, save in the most exceptional and well-defined circumstances where it is possible to conclude that the defendant was under a duty to act.[28]

It follows that the preferable view is that there is no need to recognise free acceptance as a ground of restitution. Failure of consideration and other grounds of restitution should be available in many of the cases where the plaintiff has provided a non-money benefit to the defendant and, to the extent that the plaintiff is a risk-taker, the award of restitutionary remedies cannot be justified anyway.

3. POLICY-ORIENTED GROUNDS OF RESTITUTION

Some of the recognised grounds of restitution may be justified by reference to the principle that public policy considers the benefit to have been received in circumstances of injustice. Examples of this type of ground of restitution include the grounds of necessity[29] and recovery of *ultra vires* payments from public authorities.[30]

This justification for the recognition of grounds of restitution is clearly open to criticism since it is too vague. There is a particular danger that all grounds of restitution may ultimately be justified by reference to public policy, and this would lead to the unjust enrichment principle being interpreted as a normative principle, since restitution would be justified whenever the circumstances of receipt were considered to be unjust. To guard against this argument, it is vital to identify with some precision the policy which is being fulfilled in respect of each ground of restitution which is considered to be policy-oriented. So, for example, necessity constitutes a ground of restitution because of the policy of encouraging

---

[27] See p. 140 below. Cp. Simester, 'Unjust Free Acceptance' [1997] *LMCLQ* 103, 114.
[28] See Mead, 'Free Acceptance: Some Further Considerations' (1989) 105 *LQR* 460 and Simester, 'Unjust Free Acceptance' [1997] *LMCLQ* 103, 116–20.
[29] See Chapter 11.   [30] See Chapter 14.

people to help those who are in urgent need of assistance. Similarly, recovery of *ultra vires* payments from public authorities is justified because of the constitutional principle that a public authority cannot legitimately receive a benefit unless it is authorised to do so.

4. FOUR ADDITIONAL CONSIDERATIONS

(a) The dangers of over-simplification

Although it is useful to identify the three different principles which justify the recognition of grounds of restitution, there is a great danger of over-simplification of analysis.[31] For in reality some of the existing grounds can be explained by reference to more than one of these principles. So, for example, the ground of undue influence, which applies where the defendant has exploited a relationship of influence between him or her and the plaintiff, should be treated as both a plaintiff- and a defendant-oriented ground of restitution.[32] This is because, to establish undue influence, it is necessary to show both that the plaintiff's intention to transfer a benefit to the defendant can be treated as vitiated and that the defendant's conduct can be considered to be unconscientious in some way. Similarly, the necessity principle can be analysed as both plaintiff- and policy-oriented.[33] It is important that this overlap between the principles is acknowledged, otherwise the principles become artificial straitjackets to the proper analysis of each ground of restitution.

(b) The grounds of restitution are not closed

In *CTN Cash and Carry Ltd.* v. *Gallaher Ltd.*[34] Sir Donald Nicholls V-C recognised that the grounds of restitution are not closed. This is evident from the fact that recently two new grounds of restitution have been recognised, namely the recovery of *ultra vires* payments from public authorities[35] and absence of consideration.[36] Consequently, there is nothing to stop new grounds of restitution being recognised in the future, but it is vital that their existence and definition can be justified by reference to at least one of the three underlying principles which justify the recognition of grounds of restitution.

---

[31] See Simester, 'Unjust Free Acceptance' [1997] *LMCLQ* 103, 120.
[32] See Chapter 10.   [33] See Chapter 11.   [34] [1994] 4 All ER 714, 720.
[35] See Chapter 14.
[36] See Chapter 12, although the validity of this ground of restitution has been challenged.

(c) The relevance of the type of enrichment

One of the most controversial issues concerning the structure and development of the unjust enrichment principle concerns its application to different types of enrichment. The issue is essentially whether each ground of restitution should be applicable regardless of the type of enrichment which is involved, or whether certain grounds of restitution are only applicable to particular types of enrichment. This issue has proven to be particularly significant in the context of restitutionary claims which are founded on total failure of consideration, where traditionally the ground has only been applicable in respect of claims to recover money. The issue is also significant in respect of claims grounded on mistake.

Whilst every ground of restitution clearly applies to money claims, it is not possible to be certain whether every ground of restitution can apply where the plaintiff seeks restitution of a non-money benefit. This is largely because judicial analysis of restitutionary claims in respect of non-money benefits is limited due to excessive reliance on the old forms of action. Typically the decision to award restitutionary remedies is expressed simply in terms of granting a *quantum valebat* for goods or a *quantum meruit* for services. The incantation of these Latin phrases appears to avoid the need for real legal analysis. But it is not acceptable for a principled law of restitution to rely on such an approach. It is vital to identify the ground of restitution involved, since the simple fact that the defendant has received a non-money benefit from the plaintiff does not in itself provide any reason why the plaintiff's restitutionary claim should succeed.

There is no reason why the application of any of the grounds of restitution should depend on the nature of the enrichment which the defendant has received.[37] In fact, careful analysis of those cases where a *quantum valebat* or *quantum meruit* have been awarded suggests that the court could have awarded the plaintiff a restitutionary remedy by reference to one of the recognised grounds of restitution such as mistake[38] or total failure of consideration.[39]

(d) Restitution and third parties

Although the usual case of unjust enrichment will involve the defendant having received a benefit from the plaintiff in circumstances where the

---

[37] Birks, *Restitution—The Future*, p. 87.
[38] See, for example, *Boulton* v. *Jones* (1857) 2 H and N 564; 157 ER 232; *Greenwood* v. *Bennett* [1973] QB 195; and *Rover International Ltd.* v. *Cannon Film Sales Ltd. (No. 3)* [1989] 1 WLR 912.
[39] See, for example, *Pulbrook* v. *Lawes* (1876) 1 QBD 284.

ground of restitution operates between the plaintiff and the defendant, this is not necessarily the case. Although the defendant must usually have received the benefit directly from the plaintiff,[40] the ground of restitution may relate to a third party. It should be irrelevant that the defendant is not tainted by the ground of restitution, so long as the defendant has been enriched at the plaintiff's expense and the plaintiff can establish that one of the grounds of restitution is applicable. So, for example, in *Barclays Bank Ltd.* v. *W.J. Simms, Son and Cooke (Southern) Ltd.*[41] the plaintiff paid money to the defendant in the mistaken belief that it had been authorised to pay this money to the defendant by a third party. The plaintiff was able to recover the money from the defendant on the ground of mistake, even though the mistake related to the authorisation by the third party. Similarly, if the plaintiff provides a benefit to the defendant in the expectation that he or she will be paid by a third party and such payment is not forthcoming, the plaintiff should be able to bring a restitutionary claim against the defendant on the ground of total failure of consideration, even though the payment was expected to come from another party.[42] This principle is also applicable where the grounds of restitution are duress or undue influence, so where the plaintiff was compelled or unduly influenced by a third party to transfer a benefit to the defendant, restitution founded on reversing the defendant's unjust enrichment should be available.[43]

[40] See Chapter 5. [41] [1980] QB 677, see p. 152 below.

[42] But see the decision of the House of Lords in *Pan Ocean Shipping Co. Ltd.* v. *Creditcorp Ltd. (The Trident Beauty)* [1994] 1 WLR 161, discussed at pp. 344–6 below, which suggests that a restitutionary claim would not lie against the defendant in such circumstances.

[43] But, as regards undue influence by a third party, the defendant's liability to make restitution will depend on him or her having notice of the undue influence. See pp. 265–78. The same is true where the plaintiff has transferred a benefit to the defendant as the result of misrepresentation by the third party. See pp. 184–6 below.

7

Ignorance

1. IS IGNORANCE A GROUND OF RESTITUTION?

Although ignorance has never been recognised by the courts as a ground of restitution in its own right, a number of commentators have resorted to the principle to explain why restitution has been ordered in a number of cases.[1] This lack of judicial recognition is initially surprising since it has been acknowledged for many years that, if a plaintiff has paid money to a defendant under the influence of a mistaken belief that he or she is liable to pay the defendant, then the plaintiff will be able to obtain restitution of the money.[2] This is because the plaintiff's intention that the defendant should receive the money can be regarded as vitiated by the operation of the mistake. If a mistake is regarded as sufficient to vitiate the plaintiff's intent that the defendant should receive the money, then it should be even easier to justify restitution where the defendant received the plaintiff's money in circumstances in which the plaintiff was ignorant of the transfer. This is because where the plaintiff mistakenly pays money to the defendant there is at least an intention that the defendant receive the money, albeit one which may be vitiated, whereas, where the plaintiff is ignorant that his or her money has been transferred, there is not even an intention that needs to be vitiated. This will occur, for example, where the plaintiff's money has been stolen and received by the defendant. In such circumstances the plaintiff cannot argue that he or she made any mistake in respect of the transfer to the defendant, since the plaintiff was unaware of the transfer. But, at least as a matter of general principle, the plaintiff should be able to recover the value of the money from the defendant because there was no intention that the defendant should receive it. In the light of this it is surprising that ignorance has not been explicitly endorsed by the judges as a ground for restitution, and that some commentators reject it or ignore it completely.[3]

Although this argument for the recognition of ignorance as a ground of restitution is superficially convincing, it is subject to a fatal flaw which

---

[1] See in particular Burrows, *The Law of Restitution*, chapter 4 and Birks, *An Introduction to the Law of Restitution*, pp. 140–6.

[2] See Chapter 8.

[3] Goff and Jones state, in *The Law of Restitution* at p. 176, that they 'doubt whether ignorance can properly be of itself the ground of a restitutionary claim'. See also Swadling, 'A Claim in Restitution?' [1996] *LMCLQ* 63.

largely explains why ignorance has not been judicially recognised and is unlikely ever to be recognised as an independent ground of restitution save in the most exceptional circumstances. The flaw arises from the fact that, where the plaintiff is ignorant that his or her property has been taken by the defendant, title in that property will remain with the plaintiff, there being no intent whatsoever that the property be transferred to the defendant.[4] Hence, when the plaintiff wishes to recover the property, he or she has no need to resort to the principle of reversing unjust enrichment, rather the restitutionary action will be founded upon the vindication of the plaintiff's continuing proprietary interest.[5]

In many cases it will in fact make no difference whether the plaintiff's restitutionary claim is founded on unjust enrichment, with ignorance constituting the ground for restitution, or on the vindication of property rights, with the plaintiff's ignorance being used to explain why title did not pass to the defendant. For example, it will make no difference which principle is relied on where the plaintiff only seeks a personal remedy and where it is clear that the defendant has been enriched at the expense of the plaintiff, as will be the case where the plaintiff's money is transferred directly to the defendant. Where, however, the plaintiff's property is transferred indirectly to the defendant without the plaintiff's knowledge, the unjust enrichment action cannot assist the plaintiff, primarily because of the insurmountable obstacle of showing that the enrichment received by the defendant was received at the expense of the plaintiff.[6] In this situation the plaintiff's only hope is to found his or her action upon the vindication of property rights.[7] This action will also be the only relevant one where the plaintiff seeks a proprietary restitutionary remedy, a remedy which will be particularly important to the plaintiff where the defendant is insolvent and so the plaintiff wishes to secure priority over the other creditors of the defendant, or where the benefit has increased in value.

2. RELYING ON IGNORANCE AS A GROUND OF RESTITUTION

In certain very exceptional circumstances it might, however, be possible for the plaintiff to bring a restitutionary claim founded on unjust enrichment, where the ground of restitution is ignorance, in circumstances

---

[4] *Ibid*, 65.   [5] See Chapter 20.   [6] See Chapter 5.
[7] See, for example, *Clarke* v. *Shee and Johnson* (1774) 1 Cowp. 197; 98 ER 1041; *Marsh* v. *Keating* (1834) 1 Bing. NC 198; 131 E.R. 1094; *Calland* v. *Loyd* (1840) 6 M and W 26; 151 ER 307; *Banque Belge pour l'Etranger* v. *Hambrouck* [1912] 1 KB 321; *Nelson* v. *Larholt* [1948] 1 KB 339; *Lipkin Gorman* v. *Karpnale* [1991] 2 AC 548.

where the plaintiff will not be able to bring a claim founded on the vindication of proprietary rights.

(a) Services provided in circumstances of ignorance

In principle, if the plaintiff has provided a service to the defendant which constitutes an enrichment and it can be shown that the plaintiff was ignorant that the service was provided, then he or she can bring a restitutionary claim founded on the reversal of the defendant's unjust enrichment. In such a case a claim founded on the vindication of property rights is out of the question, simply because there is no proprietary interest in the provision of a service. It would, however, be possible to establish that the defendant had been unjustly enriched at the expense of the plaintiff. The problem, of course, is that it is highly unlikely that the plaintiff would ever provide a service in circumstances where he or she was unaware that a service had been provided. But it is possible to conceive of some exceptional circumstances where the ignorant provision of a service could be established. For example, the defendant may have entered a theatre without paying and seen a play. Or the plaintiff may have been giving a presentation at a conference in the course of which he disclosed the results of some recent research and the defendant may have overheard this information and relied on it in the course of his business. So long as it can be shown in each of these cases that the defendant had received an enrichment[8] it would be possible to show that he or she had been unjustly enriched at the expense of the plaintiff who was ignorant of the fact that the defendant had received the benefit.

(b) Interceptive subtraction

Where the defendant has intervened and taken a benefit from a third party in circumstances where that benefit was intended to be transferred to the plaintiff, it may exceptionally be possible for the plaintiff to found a restitutionary claim on unjust enrichment, with the ground of restitution being ignorance. Alternatively, it might be possible, in such a case, to show that the defendant had committed a wrong in taking the benefit for him or herself, as would occur if the defendant owed fiduciary duties to the plaintiff so that the plaintiff's claim would be founded on the wrong rather than unjust enrichment.[9] It might even be possible for the plaintiff to bring a proprietary claim to vindicate his or her proprietary rights in the property which was transferred to the defendant, although there might be some difficulty in the plaintiff establishing that he or she

---

[8] See Chapter 4.   [9] See Chapter 18.

did indeed have a proprietary interest in the property before it was received. It certainly does not necessarily follow from the fact that the third party had intended the property to be received by the plaintiff that the plaintiff has a property interest in it when it was transferred to the defendant.[10] Consequently, if a claim founded on wrongdoing and a claim founded on vindication of property rights are unavailable, the only hope for the plaintiff is to base a claim on the defendant's unjust enrichment, with the ground of restitution being that the plaintiff was ignorant that the benefit had been transferred by the third party to the defendant. The requirement that the benefit was obtained at the plaintiff's expense would be satisfied by the fact that the defendant had intercepted the transfer of the benefit.[11]

However, in many cases of interceptive subtraction it will be possible for the plaintiff to establish a proprietary interest in the property which was received by the defendant, typically an equitable proprietary interest. This will particularly be the case where the defendant has obtained the money in a fiduciary capacity. This is well illustrated by *Lyell* v. *Kennedy*[12] where land which had been let to tenants was managed by the defendant for the landowner. The defendant received rents from the tenants which were paid into a separate ear-marked account at his own bank. After the death of the landowner the defendant continued to receive the rents. The plaintiff, who was the landowner's heir, then sought to recover the rent which had been received by the defendant. The plaintiff's claim succeeded because it was held that, since the defendant had received the money in a fiduciary capacity, he held it on trust for the plaintiff. A personal restitutionary remedy was ordered in the form of an account of the rent and profits. The Earl of Selborne, with whom the other members of the House of Lords concurred, emphasised that the money in the account had never been the property of the defendant, so presumably on the death of the landowner it belonged to the heir, even though he was ignorant of the fact that the defendant had been receiving the money from the tenants. This proprietary analysis is also the preferable explanation of the decision of the House of Lords in *Ministry of Health* v. *Simpson*,[13] where personal representatives had mistakenly paid money to the defendants rather than the beneficiaries and the beneficiaries were able to recover the value of the money which the defendants had received. Although the personal representatives had made a mistake of law, this did not form the basis of the beneficiaries' claim. Rather, the beneficiaries were ignorant of the receipt by the

[10] See *Asher* v. *Wallis* (1707) 11 Mod. 146; 88 ER 956. See also *Arris and Arris* v. *Stukely* (1677) 2 Mod. 260; 86 ER 1060 and *Howard* v. *Wood* (1679) 2 Shaw. KB 21; 89 ER 767.
[11] See pp. 109–13 above. [12] (1889) 14 App. Cas. 437.
[13] [1951] AC 251 (*sub nom. Re Diplock*).

defendants. However, since the beneficiaries had an equitable proprietary interest in the money which the defendants received, vindication of
this interest was the true basis of their claim.[14]

3. ELECTION BETWEEN PRINCIPLES

Where the plaintiff is ignorant that his or her property has been taken by
the defendant so that he or she retains legal title in the property, it is clear
that the plaintiff can bring a claim for restitution grounded on the vindication of this legal title. But can the plaintiff alternatively bring a claim
grounded on the defendant's unjust enrichment, even though the plaintiff has legal title in the property? It is difficult to conceive of reasons why
the plaintiff would wish to bring such a claim when a proprietary claim is
available, but the plaintiff might think that it is easier to establish that the
defendant has been unjustly enriched at his or her expense or the plaintiff might simply be poorly advised and think that the only claim available is one grounded on unjust enrichment. The issue is essentially
whether the plaintiff's claim in unjust enrichment will be barred by the
fact that he or she has retained legal title.

A number of commentators have concluded that where the plaintiff
does indeed retain legal title to the property then a claim grounded on
unjust enrichment is barred.[15] One suggested reason for this is that,
where the plaintiff has retained title in the property he or she will not be
able to establish that the defendant has been enriched.[16] This argument
assumes that the notion that whether or not the defendant has been
enriched is a legal test rather than a factual test.[17] The consequence of
this is that, if the plaintiff continues to own the property which the defendant has received, it is not possible to conclude that the defendant has
been enriched because the property does not belong to the defendant. In
other words, the plaintiff has not lost anything. Birks, on the other hand,
considers that the notion of enrichment is a factual test.[18] Consequently,
it is sufficient for the plaintiff to establish that the defendant has received
a benefit, which is assessed by showing that value has passed from the

[14] See Chapter 20.
[15] Swadling, 'A Claim in Restitution?' [1996] *LMCLQ* 63, 65; Grantham and Rickett,
'Property and Unjust Enrichment: Categorical Truth or Unnecessary Complexity?' [1997]
NZ Law Rev. 668, 682–3.
[16] Grantham and Rickett, 'Restitution, Property and Mistaken Payments' (1997) 5 *RLR*
83, 87.
[17] See Grantham and Rickett, 'Trust Money as an Unjust Enrichment: A Misconception'
[1998] *LMCLQ* 514, 517–18. See also *Ilich* v. *R.* (1987) 162 CLR 110, 140–1 (Brennan J).
[18] Birks, 'Property and Unjust Enrichment: Categorical Truths' [1997] *NZ Law Rev.* 623,
654 and, 'On Taking Seriously the Difference Between Tracing and Claiming' (1997) 11 *TLI*
2, 7–8.

defendant to the plaintiff. If the defendant steals the plaintiff's car it is clear that the defendant is now in possession of a car, a valuable benefit, which he or she did not have before. It follows that the defendant should be considered to be enriched and this enrichment should be considered to derive from the plaintiff. The question whether the defendant is legally enriched should be of no significance to the question whether the defendant has been unjustly enriched at the expense of the plaintiff; it is only of significance when determining whether the plaintiff has title to property as a matter of law for purposes of bringing a claim to vindicate his or her property rights.

If it is possible to show that the defendant has received an enrichment, even though the plaintiff has retained title in the property received by the defendant, and it can be shown that the defendant has obtained this benefit directly from the plaintiff, it should be possible to bring a restitutionary claim founded on the reversal of the defendant's unjust enrichment so long as it can be shown that the plaintiff was ignorant of the transfer. It is no bar to a restitutionary claim founded on unjust enrichment that the plaintiff could have brought a claim founded on the commission of a wrong,[19] and neither should it matter that the plaintiff's claim could alternatively have been founded on the vindication of proprietary rights.

4. THE ROLE OF IGNORANCE AS A GROUND OF RESTITUTION

It follows from this analysis that there is no reason of principle or law which should prevent the plaintiff from bringing a restitutionary claim where the ground of restitution is ignorance. But, as has been seen in this chapter, such a claim will be highly exceptional. It is no wonder that ignorance has not yet been recognised as a ground of restitution in its own right, simply because where the plaintiff was ignorant that property had been transferred to the defendant, the plaintiff will have retained a proprietary interest in the property and a proprietary restitutionary claim has many advantages over a claim founded on the reversal of the defendant's unjust enrichment.[20]

---

[19] See Chapter 15.   [20] See p. 4 above.

8

Mistake

1. GENERAL PRINCIPLES

(a) The significance of mistake as a ground of restitution

A claim to recover money mistakenly paid by the plaintiff to the defendant is often regarded as the paradigm example of a restitutionary claim founded on the principle of unjust enrichment. In such a case there is clearly an enrichment at the plaintiff's expense and, at least where the reason for the plaintiff making the payment arose from a mistaken belief that he or she was liable to pay the money to the defendant, there is a clear justification for restoring the value of the money to the plaintiff, since the plaintiff's intention to make the payment can readily be treated as vitiated by the mistake. It is, however, unfortunate that mistake is regarded as the paradigm ground of restitution, because there is a consequent tendency to underestimate the complex policy issues which arise in determining whether the defendant's enrichment really can be considered to be unjust.

The complexity of mistake as a ground of restitution arises for two reasons. First, the law is still uncertain about what is the appropriate test for determining when a mistake can operate to vitiate the plaintiff's intention to benefit the defendant. Secondly, even where it is possible to show that the plaintiff's intention was vitiated by the mistake, it does not necessarily follow that restitutionary relief should be available. This is because the circumstances of the defendant's receipt of a benefit and his or her subsequent conduct may be such that it would not be just to require the defendant to make restitution. As Birks has said, 'in seeking to do justice to mistaken payers the action [for money had and received] often seems to tremble on the brink of doing injustice to the recipient of the payment'.[1] Consequently, the respective interests of the parties need to be balanced when determining whether restitutionary relief is appropriate, and this requires careful consideration of issues of policy.

---

[1] 'The Recovery of Carelessly Mistaken Payments' (1972) 25 CLP 179.

(b) The key policies which determine when a mistake should ground a restitutionary claim

There are four policies which are relevant when identifying the appropriate test for determining when mistake should operate as a ground of restitution.

(i)   *Security of transactions:* restitution for mistake should not be used to undermine transactions unnecessarily. Defendants need to have a degree of security that, when they receive benefits, they will not be required to make restitution unless there is a good reason to do so. This policy favours a restrictive interpretation of mistake as a ground of restitution.

(ii) *Risk allocation:* where the parties to a contract have expressly or implicitly allocated the risk that one or both of them may be mistaken as to particular facts it is not for the law of restitution to intrude and subvert the allocation of risk. This policy also favours a restrictive interpretation of mistake.

(iii) *Concoction of claims:* there is a danger that plaintiffs will concoct claims that they were mistaken when they transferred a benefit. It is easy for the plaintiff to assert that he or she was mistaken, since this simply depends on the state of his or her mind at the time the benefit was transferred, and it is difficult for the defendant to deny this. Again, this policy favours a restrictive interpretation of mistake.

(iv) *Relative conduct of the parties:* when determining whether it is just for the defendant to make restitution to the plaintiff the relative conduct of the parties should be taken into account. Since, until recently, it was not possible to take into account the conduct of the defendant after he or she had received the benefit, save in exceptional circumstances,[2] this policy also favoured a restrictive interpretation of mistake as a ground of restitution. However, with the recognition of the defence of change of position,[3] it is possible to balance the interests of the parties more fairly. In *Lipkin Gorman (a firm)* v. *Karpnale Ltd.*[4] Lord Goff accepted that 'the recognition of change of position will enable a more generous approach to be taken to the recognition of the right to restitution'. In fact, the history of mistake as a ground of restitution is a history of development of the law from a starting point at which mistake was interpreted

---

[2] Such as where the defendant had relied on the plaintiff's representation that the benefit was properly received, and so the plaintiff was estopped from asserting that he or she had been mistaken. See Chapter 24.

[3] *Lipkin Gorman (a firm)* v. *Karpnale Ltd.* [1991] AC 548. See Chapter 24.

[4] *Ibid*, p. 581.

very restrictively to the position today where it appears that the notion of an operative mistake is interpreted much more widely. But it remains vital to ensure that this generous approach to the interpretation of mistake does not infringe the other three policies.

(c) Different types of enrichment

Where the plaintiff has mistakenly paid money to the defendant the only difficult question concerns whether the mistake was of a type to ground restitution. There are no difficulties regarding the identification of an enrichment, since money is incontrovertibly beneficial, and if the money has been paid directly to the defendant by the plaintiff it was obviously received at the plaintiff's expense. Other types of claim will, however, raise more complex issues. So, for example, where the alleged enrichment is the receipt of goods[5] or a service provided by the plaintiff,[6] it will also be necessary to consider carefully whether the defendant has actually been enriched. But the fact that the identification of the enrichment is more complicated in such cases has no effect upon the test for identifying those mistakes which are sufficient to ground restitution, since the same type of mistake will ground restitution regardless of whether the enrichment is money or benefits in kind.

(d) Mistakes of law and fact

(i) The mistake of law bar[7]

It has been a fundamental rule of English law for nearly 200 years that where the plaintiff has made a mistake of law then usually he or she could not base a restitutionary claim on the mistake.[8] It followed that only mistakes of fact would be sufficient to ground a restitutionary claim. This mistake of law bar was interpreted widely. The phrase covered both cases where the plaintiff was ignorant of what the state of the law was and cases where the plaintiff had a positive but incorrect belief as to the state of the law.[9] Mistakes of law related to all aspects of the law, including judicial

---

[5] See, for example, *Boulton* v. *Jones* (1857) 2 H and N 564; 157 ER 232.

[6] See, for example, *Greenwood* v. *Bennett* [1973] QB 195 and *Rover International Ltd.* v. *Cannon Film Sales Ltd. (No. 3)* [1989] 1 WLR 912.

[7] See *Kleinwort Benson Ltd.* v. *Lincoln CC* [1998] 3 WLR 1095, 1108–15 (Lord Goff).

[8] See, in particular, *Bilbie* v. *Lumley* (1802) 2 East 469; 102 ER 448; *Brisbane* v. *Dacres* (1813) 5 Taunt. 143; 128 ER 641; *Henderson* v. *Folkestone Waterworks Co.* (1885) 1 TLR 329; *R.* v. *Tower Hamlets London Borough Council, ex p. Chetnik Developments Ltd.* [1988] AC 858, 876–7 (Lord Bridge); and *Friends' Provident Life Office* v. *Hillier Parker May and Rowden (a firm)* [1995] 4 All ER 260, 267 (Auld LJ).

[9] Winfield, 'Mistake of Law' (1943) 59 *LQR* 327. See also *David Securities* v. *Commonwealth Bank of Australia* (1992) 175 CLR 353, 372.

decisions, the existence of statutory powers, the interpretation of statutes and the construction of covenants.[10]

The distinction between mistakes of law and fact was notoriously difficult to draw, and this created much scope for manipulation of the plaintiff's claim to ensure that it was founded on a mistake of fact.[11] The mistake of law bar was also subject to a number of exceptions. Of particular importance was the rule that the plaintiff was not barred from obtaining restitution simply because he or she had made a mistake of law if it was possible to rely on another ground of restitution, such as duress.[12] Even if that was not possible, the plaintiff's mistake of law might still operate as a ground of restitution in its own right in certain exceptional circumstances. So, for example, restitutionary claims grounded on mistake of law would succeed where money had been paid to an officer of the court, such as a trustee in bankruptcy.[13] The plaintiff could claim restitution by virtue of a mistake of law where the defendant had acted in bad faith, as would be the case where the defendant knew of the plaintiff's mistake[14] or had fraudulently induced the mistake.[15] Restitution would also be available where the defendant could be considered to be more responsible for the mistake of law than the plaintiff.[16] Even certain statutes have made specific provision for restitution of money which had been paid as a result of a mistake of law.[17]

(ii) Justifications for the mistake of law bar

A number of justifications can be identified for the mistake of law bar. Ultimately, none of them is convincing.

(1) In *Bilbie* v. *Lumley*[18] Lord Ellenborough CJ justified the recognition of the mistake of law bar by reference to the principle that:

[e]very man must be taken to be cognisant of the law; otherwise there is no saying to what extent the excuse of ignorance might not be carried. It would be urged in almost every case.[19]

---

[10] *Re Hatch* [1919] 1 Ch. 351.

[11] See, for example, *George (Porky) Jacobs Enterprises Ltd.* v. *City of Regina* (1964) 44 DLR (2d.) 179 (Supreme Court of Canada) and *Avon County Council* v. *Howlett* [1983] 1 WLR 65. Note also the rule that mistakes as to private rights could be characterised as mistakes of fact: *Cooper* v. *Phibbs* (1867) LR 2 HL 149.

[12] *Westdeutsche Landesbank Girozentrale* v. *Islington LBC* [1994] 4 All ER 890, 933 (Hobhouse J). See also *Woolwich Building Society* v. *IRC* [1993] AC 70, 177 (Lord Goff) and 205 (Lord Slynn).

[13] *Ex parte James* (1874) LR 9 Ch. App. 609; *Ex parte Simmonds* (1885) 16 QBD 308.

[14] *Ward and Co.* v. *Wallis* [1900] 1 QB 675, 678. See also *Friends' Provident Life Office* v. *Hillier Parker May and Rowden (a firm)* [1995] 4 All ER 260, 268 (Auld LJ).

[15] *Henderson* v. *Folkestone Waterworks Co.* (1885) TLR 329.

[16] *Kiriri Cotton Co. Ltd.* v. *Dewani* [1960] AC 192, 204 (Lord Denning).

[17] See, for example, s. 33(1) of the Taxes Management Act 1970 which provides for the recovery of income tax *inter alia* which has been paid as the result of a mistake of law.

[18] (1802) 2 East 469; 102 ER 448.   [19] *Ibid*, p. 472; p. 449.

This principle that ignorance of the law is no excuse[20] is particularly important in the law of tort and in the criminal law where a defendant is not allowed to argue that he or she should be excused from liability because he or she was ignorant of the law.[21] But it does not follow that this general principle of ignorance of law should be interpreted to mean that a plaintiff's mistake of law should bar a claim for restitution, for the policy of the criminal law and the law of tort is not necessarily applicable to the law of restitution. Within the context of the criminal law, for example, it is vitally important that defendants should not be allowed to rely on their ignorance of the criminal law to excuse their liability, for otherwise many criminals could not be convicted, the complexity of the criminal law being such that many defendants are unaware that their conduct may be criminal. But there is no equivalent problem within the law of restitution. This is because, where the plaintiff wishes to rely on mistake of law within the law of restitution, he or she is not doing so to excuse liability but rather to establish the defendant's liability. Reference to the ignorance of law principle is consequently an unsatisfactory explanation of the mistake of law bar.

(2) Lord Ellenborough also justified the mistake of law rule in *Bilbie* v. *Lumley* by asserting that restitution had never previously been granted where there was a mistake of law; but this was not the case.[22]

(3) A particular concern about allowing restitution for mistake of law is that it would open the floodgates and this would result in restitution being awarded in undeserving cases. There is a particular fear that it would be too easy for a plaintiff to assert that he or she had made a mistake of law by exploiting any uncertainty as to the interpretation of the law. But this is a very weak argument, because the mistake of law rule itself was uncertain and was riddled with exceptions of uncertain ambit. It is more accurate to say that the mistake of law rule created rather than removed uncertainty in the law.

(4) Another argument which has been used to justify the mistake of law rule is that it is necessary to preserve the security of transactions.[23] There has been a real concern that a consequence of allowing restitution for

---

[20] A more accurate statement of this principle than stating that everyone is presumed to know the law, something which is patently untrue, is that nobody 'can excuse himself from doing his duty by saying that he did not know the law on the matter': *Kiriri Cotton Co.* v. *Dewani* [1960] AC 192, 204 (Lord Denning). This was recognised in an important dissenting judgment by Chambre J in *Brisbane* v. *Dacres* (1813) 5 Taunt. 143, 159; 128 ER 641, 647. See also *David Securities* v. *Commonwealth Bank of Australia* (1992) 175 CLR 353, 402 (Dawson J).

[21] Ashworth, *Principles of Criminal Law* (2nd edn., Oxford: Clarendon Press, 1995) p. 233. But even in this context the mistake of law rule is subject to a number of exceptions.

[22] See, for example, *Farmer* v. *Arundel* (1772) 2 W Black. 824, 825; 96 ER 485, 486 and *Bize* v. *Dickason* (1786) 1 TR 285; 99 ER 1097.

[23] See *Rogers* v. *Ingham* (1876) 3 Ch.D 351, 357 (James LJ).

mistake of law would be the overturning of commercial transactions with major fiscal consequences,[24] especially where the defendant is a public authority.[25] But this concern for the interests of the recipient of the benefit can surely be catered for by developing general and specific defences to restitutionary claims. Indeed, with the development of defences such as change of position, this concern for the security of the defendant's receipt has become a much less serious cause for concern.

(5) Goff and Jones have justified many of the decisions in which restitution was denied on the ground of mistake of law on the basis that the plaintiff had voluntarily submitted to the defendant's honest claim.[26] Whilst the notions of voluntary payment and settlement of the defendant's honest claim clearly do underlie a number of the mistake of law cases,[27] and sometimes such notions are even expressly relied on to justify the denial of restitutionary relief,[28] it must not be forgotten that most of these mistake cases were decided expressly by reference to the mistake of law rule.[29]

(iii) The abolition of the mistake of law bar

In *Kleinwort Benson Ltd.* v. *Lincoln City Council*[30] the House of Lords abolished the mistake of law bar. It follows that the plaintiff will be able to obtain restitution of benefits transferred to the defendant on the ground of mistake regardless of whether the mistake was one of fact or one of law. This brings English law into line with virtually all other common law countries, which have similarly abolished the bar.[31] Abolition had also been recommended by the Law Commission.[32]

---

[24] *Hydro-Electric Commission for the Township of Nepean* v. *Ontario-Hydro* (1982) 132 DLR (3d.) 193, 243 (Estey J). See also *David Securities* v. *Commonwealth Bank of Australia* (1992) 175 CLR 353, 394 (Brennan J).

[25] See *Air Canada* v. *British Columbia* (1989) 59 DLR (4d.) 161. See Chapter 14.

[26] Goff and Jones, *The Law of Restitution*, p. 214. See also *Woolwich Equitable Building Society* v. *IRC* [1993] AC 70, 166 (Lord Goff).

[27] Though by no means all of these cases. See *David Securities* v. *Commonwealth Bank of Australia* (1992) 175 CLR 353, 404 (Dawson J).

[28] See, for example, *Brisbane* v. *Dacres* (1813) Taunton 143, 152–3; 128 ER 641, 645 (Gibbs J).

[29] See, for example, *Holt* v. *Markham* [1923] 1 KB 504.   [30] [1998] 3 WLR 1095.

[31] The rule was abolished by the Supreme Court of Canada in *Air Canada* v. *British Columbia* (1989) 59 DLR (4d.) 161, by the High Court of Australia in *David Securities Pty. Ltd.* v. *Commonwealth Bank of Australia* (1992) 175 CLR 353, by the Appellate Division of the Supreme Court of South Africa in *Willis Faber Enthoven (Pty.) Ltd.* v. *Receiver of Revenue* 1992 (4) SA 202(A) and by the Inner House of the Court Session in Scotland in *Morgan Guaranty Trust Co. of New York* v. *Lothian Regional Council*, 1995 SLT 299. The rule was also abolished in New Zealand by the Judicature Act 1908, s. 94A, as inserted by the Judicature Amendment Act 1958, s. 2.

[32] 'Restitution: Mistakes of Law and *Ultra Vires* Public Authority Receipts and Payments' (Law Commission No. 227, 1994). See Virgo, 'Striking the Balance in the Law of Restitution' [1995] *LMCLQ* 362 and Beatson, 'Mistakes of Law and *Ultra Vires* Public Authority Receipts: The Law Commission Report' (1995) 3 *RLR* 280.

(iv) Justifications for the abolition of the mistake of law bar

The abolition of the mistake of law bar was correct for the following reasons.

(1) Where the plaintiff's claim is founded on the reversal of unjust enrichment it is impossible to justify a distinction which allows restitution in cases of mistake of fact but denies it where restitution is founded on mistake of law. The receipt of an enrichment can be unjust regardless of whether the mistake is characterised as one of law or fact.[33] This is simply because the crucial question with which we are concerned, when determining whether the plaintiff's mistake should ground a restitutionary claim, is whether the plaintiff's intention to transfer a benefit to the defendant can be considered to have been vitiated by the mistake. The plaintiff's intention is just as likely to be vitiated where he or she made a mistake of law as where he or she made a mistake of fact.

(2) Before the mistake of law rule was abolished the state of the law created great uncertainty on two counts. First, it was notoriously difficult to distinguish between mistakes of law and fact, and the consequent uncertainty created much scope for manipulation of the characterisation of the mistake to secure what was considered to be a just result. Secondly, the mistake of law bar was riddled with exceptions, often of uncertain ambit. There was also no identifiable principle which could be considered to underlie all of the exceptions to the mistake of law rule. This meant that the law was unnecessarily complex and that there were numerous ways of avoiding the rule, making those cases where it could not be avoided even more unjust.

(e) Some fundamental distinctions

(i) Mistakes and mispredictions

Mistakes are concerned with present facts or laws, whereas mispredictions are concerned with future events. If the plaintiff has made a mistake as to a present fact or law this will constitute a ground of restitution. Where, however, the plaintiff has made a misprediction as to the defendant's future actions this will not justify restitution in its own right.[34] This is because, where the plaintiff has transferred a benefit to the defendant having made a misprediction as to a future event occurring, the plaintiff will be considered to be an officious intervener and to have taken the risk

---

[33] See *Baylis* v. *Bishop of London* [1913] 1 Ch. 127, 133 (Cozens-Hardy MR); *Hydro-Electric Commission of Nepean* v. *Ontario Hydro* (1982) 132 DLR (3d.) 193, 209, *per* Dickson J; *David Securities* v. *Commonwealth Bank of Australia* (1992) 175 CLR 353, 375; *Kleinwort Benson Ltd.* v. *Lincoln CC* [1998] 3 WLR 1095, 1145 (Lord Hope).

[34] See *Kleinwort Benson Ltd.* v. *Lincoln CC* [1998] 3 WLR 1095, 1137 (Lord Hoffmann), 1147 (Lord Hope).

that the future event may not occur.[35] It is a fundamental principle of the law of restitution that restitutionary relief will not be available to a plaintiff who has acted officiously or as a volunteer.[36] So, for example, if the plaintiff cleans the defendant's windows without being asked to do so, in the hope that when the defendant sees the clean windows she will pay him for the work, he will not be able to claim that he was mistaken, since he only mispredicted the defendant's future reaction.[37] Similarly, if the plaintiff is negotiating a contract with the defendant and, anticipating that the contract will be made, the plaintiff spends money in preparation for performance of the contract, then if no contract is signed the plaintiff cannot found a restitutionary claim on mistake.[38] This is because the plaintiff was not mistaken as to present facts but had simply made a misprediction as to what might happen in the future.

The only qualification to this distinction between mistakes and mispredictions arises from the recognition that a mistake of law can constitute a ground of restitution. If the plaintiff transferred a benefit to the defendant on the correct assumption that he or she was liable to do so by operation of law, and the law was subsequently changed by judicial decision, the effect of the declaratory theory of law-making is that the plaintiff had indeed made a mistake when he or she transferred the benefit to the defendant. This is because the subsequent judicial decision is deemed to be operating at the time the benefit was transferred, so the plaintiff was in fact mistaken in his or her belief that he or she was liable to transfer the benefit to the defendant. This could be characterised as a misprediction, because the plaintiff's error related to the law in the future rather than in the present when the benefit was transferred. But this argument is incorrect because of the declaratory theory of law-making. The effect of that theory is that the plaintiff was not liable to transfer the benefit when he or she did so, and so this is deemed to be a present mistake as to the law at the time of the transfer.[39]

(ii) Different types of claim

Where a plaintiff has mistakenly transferred a benefit to the defendant, the test of mistake varies depending on the nature of the plaintiff's claim. There are two routes to the recovery of such benefits. First, the plaintiff

---

[35] Though restitution may lie even though the plaintiff mispredicted what the defendant would do, if the plaintiff can found his or her claim on another ground of restitution, such as that of total failure of consideration. See Chapter 12.

[36] See pp. 39–40 above.

[37] There would also be difficulties in showing that the defendant had been enriched. See p. 84 above.

[38] A restitutionary claim may, however, be founded on total failure of consideration. See p. 362 below.

[39] *Kleinwort Benson Ltd.* v. *Lincoln CC* [1998] 3 WLR 1095, 1139 (Lord Hoffmann).

may have transferred a benefit to the defendant by mistake and the plaintiff simply wishes to recover the value of this benefit from the defendant. Alternatively, the plaintiff may have entered into a transaction, usually a contract, by mistake, and the plaintiff wishes to recover a benefit which he or she has transferred to the defendant pursuant to the transaction. In this situation the plaintiff must set the transaction aside before he or she can recover the benefit which was transferred to the defendant. It is vital to distinguish between these two routes to the recovery of benefits which have been mistakenly transferred because the definition of mistake varies depending on the route which is adopted.

(iii) Ignorance and mistake

There is no satisfactory legal definition of what constitutes an operative mistake for the purposes of the law of restitution. Mistake could be given a very wide definition so that it even encompasses those cases which have already been treated as involving ignorance.[40] But it is important to distinguish between those cases where the plaintiff is unaware of the transfer of a benefit to the defendant and those where the plaintiff is aware of the transfer but makes an error in respect of what is being transferred or why the benefit is being transferred to the defendant. This distinction should be made because, where the plaintiff is unaware of the transfer, there is no intention to transfer a benefit which needs to be vitiated before the plaintiff can obtain restitution. But where the plaintiff is aware of the transfer there is an apparent intention to transfer the benefit and so, if the plaintiff is to obtain restitution on the ground of mistake, it must be shown that the mistake vitiated the plaintiff's intention. The key question is which types of mistake can be considered to vitiate this intention. Since we are only concerned with the effect of the mistake on the plaintiff, it is irrelevant that the defendant did not share the mistake.[41]

(iv) Passive and active mistakes

In those cases where the plaintiff is aware that he or she has transferred a benefit to the defendant but the plaintiff has made a mistake, this mistake may take two forms. First, the plaintiff may either have forgotten certain facts, including the state of the law, which, if they had been remembered, would have meant that the benefit would not have been transferred, or the plaintiff may be ignorant of a relevant circumstance relating to the transaction, and this ignorance may relate either to a mat-

---

[40] See Chapter 7. This is the view of Goff and Jones, *The Law of Restitution*, p. 176.
[41] Although the defendant's belief may be relevant when considering the applicability of defences, such as change of position. See Chapter 24.

ter of fact or law. This has been called 'passive mistake'.[42] Secondly, the plaintiff may have been consciously relying on certain facts at the time of transfer, when those facts were untrue, or the plaintiff may have been consciously relying on a belief that he or she was required by law to transfer a benefit to the defendant, when this belief was untrue. Such mistakes could be called 'active mistakes'. Although some judges have suggested that only an active mistake can ground a restitutionary claim,[43] most judges accept that no distinction should be drawn between passive and active mistakes.[44] This is surely right, because, apart from the fact that the distinction between the two types of mistake is difficult to draw, regardless of whether the plaintiff had made an active or a passive mistake he or she was still intending to transfer a benefit to the defendant in circumstances which were different from those which the plaintiff believed to be in existence. Consequently, the plaintiff's intention to transfer the benefit could be considered to have been vitiated regardless of whether he or she had made an active or passive mistake.

(v) Spontaneous and induced mistakes

Usually the plaintiff's mistake will arise spontaneously, but sometimes it may have been induced by the defendant.[45] It is important to distinguish between spontaneous and induced mistakes because the nature of the mistakes may be such that different tests should be adopted to determine whether the mistake was sufficient to vitiate the plaintiff's intention to transfer a benefit to the defendant.

2. RESTITUTION OF BENEFITS TRANSFERRED BY MISTAKE

(a) Spontaneous mistakes

Where the plaintiff wishes to recover a benefit which has been transferred to the defendant as a result of a spontaneous mistake, the appropriate test for determining when such a mistake will ground a restitutionary claim remains a matter of controversy. It is, however, possible to identify three principal tests which have been recognised as

---

[42] *Barrow* v. *Isaacs and Son* [1891] 1 QB 417, 420 (Lord Esher MR).   [43] *Ibid.*

[44] *Lady Hood of Avalon* v. *Mackinnon* [1909] 1 Ch. 476, 482 (Eve J). See also Kay and Lopes LJJ in *Barrow* v. *Issacs and Son* [1891] 1 QB 417, 428; *Home and Colonial Insurance Co. Ltd.* v. *London Guarantee and Accident Co. Ltd.* (1928) 45 TLR 134, 135 (Wright J). A number of important cases involving restitution of money paid under a mistake concerned passive mistakes. See, for example, *Kelly* v. *Solari* (1841) 9 M and W 54; 152 ER 24.

[45] Birks, *An Introduction to the Law of Restitution*, p. 146. For analysis of the effect of induced mistakes see pp. 166–7 below.

grounding such claims, namely liability mistakes, fundamental mistakes and causative mistakes.

(i) Liability mistakes

In the first cases to recognise that the plaintiff's spontaneous mistake could ground a restitutionary claim, relief was confined to those cases where the plaintiff mistakenly believed that he or she was liable to pay the defendant. In such circumstances it is tolerably clear that the plaintiff's intention to benefit the defendant can be considered to have been vitiated. This is because, had the plaintiff not mistakenly believed that he or she was liable to pay the defendant, the money would not have been paid because there would usually be no other explanation of why the money was paid.

It is possible to identify four different types of liability mistake which have been recognised as sufficient to operate as grounds of restitution.

(1) Existing legal liabilities

If the plaintiff can show that he or she transferred a benefit to the defendant because of a mistaken belief that he or she was subject to an existing legal liability to do so then this will ground a restitutionary claim. This was recognised in *Aiken* v. *Short*[46] where Bramwell B said:[47]

> In order to entitle a person to recover back money paid under a mistake of fact, the mistake must be as to a fact which, if true, would make the person paying liable to pay the money; not where, if true, it would merely make it desirable that he should pay the money.

The application of this principle is illustrated by *Kelly* v. *Solari*[48] where the plaintiff insurance company had paid money to the executrix of the assured believing that it was liable to pay her the money under a life insurance policy. In fact, there was no liability to pay this money because the policy had lapsed as a result of the assured failing to pay the premiums on the policy. Such a mistake as to the existence of the liability meant that in principle the plaintiff could recover the money,[49] since, as Parke B recognised, where money was paid on the assumption of certain mistaken facts which, if true, would mean that the recipient was entitled to the money, it followed that restitution should be awarded where those

---

[46] (1856) 1 H and N 210; 156 ER 1180. Affirmed in *Re the Bodega Company Ltd.* [1904] 1 Ch. 276.

[47] *Aiken* v. *Short*, n. 46 above, p. 215; *ibid*, p. 1182. On the facts the plaintiff's claim failed both because there was no mistaken belief as to a liability to pay and because the defendant had provided good consideration for the payment. See p. 172 below.

[48] (1841) 9 M and W 54; 152 ER 24. See also *Home and Colonial Insurance Co. Ltd.* v. *London Guarantee and Accident Co. Ltd.* (1928) 45 TLR 134, 135 (Wright J).

[49] A retrial was ordered to determine whether the plaintiff really had made a mistake of fact.

facts were not true.[50] It was also held to be irrelevant that the means of discovering that the policy had lapsed were available to the plaintiff. Consequently, the plaintiff's carelessness did not prevent it from obtaining restitution.

Usually, as in *Kelly* v. *Solari*, the mistaken belief in liability relates to a contractual liability to pay the defendant, but this is not always the case. So, in *Baylis* v. *Bishop of London*,[51] although the plaintiff's mistaken belief concerned a non-contractual liability to pay ecclesiastical tithes to the Bishop of London, restitution of the money was still ordered.

Even where the plaintiff has made a mistake as to the existence of a legal liability, restitution only lies if the plaintiff can show that, if the mistake had not been made, he or she would not have transferred the benefit to the defendant. In other words, the liability mistake must be shown to have been the cause of the transfer being made, in the sense that, but for the mistake, the benefit would not have been transferred to the defendant. For example, in *Home and Colonial Insurance Co. Ltd.* v. *London Guarantee and Accident Co. Ltd.*[52] the payment made by the plaintiff had been influenced by a mistake of law as well as one of fact. It followed that restitution was denied because the plaintiff could not show that his decision to make the payment had only been influenced by the mistake of fact. Of course, with the abolition of the mistake of law bar, where the plaintiff's mistake is both a mistake of law and one of fact then restitutionary relief will be awarded because both types of mistake can now operate as grounds of restitution. But it must still be shown that, had the plaintiff not been mistaken as to liability, he or she would not have paid the money to the defendant.

(2) Liabilities owed to third parties

Whether restitution can be awarded where the plaintiff transfers a benefit to the defendant in the mistaken belief that he or she is under an existing legal liability to a third party to do so has been a matter of some controversy. Restitution in such circumstances has sometimes been rejected specifically because the plaintiff mistakenly believed that he or she was liable to a third party rather than the defendant,[53] whereas in other cases restitution has been awarded even though the plaintiff had

---

[50] (1841) 9 M and W 54, 58; 152 ER 24, 26. But Parke B did not suggest that a mistaken belief as to liability to pay the money was the only type of mistake which would ground restitution. See *Barclays Bank Ltd.* v. *W.J. Simms Son and Cooke (Southern) Ltd.* [1980] 1 QB 677, 687 (Robert Goff J).

[51] [1913] 1 Ch. 127.   [52] (1928) 45 TLR 134.

[53] *Deutsche Bank (London Agency)* v. *Beriro and Co.* (1895) 73 LTR 669. See also *Barclay and Co. Ltd.* v. *Malcolm and Co.* (1925) 133 LT 512 and *Weld-Blundell* v. *Synott* [1940] 2 KB 107.

such a mistaken belief.[54] The better view is that the fact that the plaintiff believed the liability was owed to a third party rather than to the defendant should not bar the plaintiff's restitutionary claim, since the transfer is still caused by the plaintiff's mistaken belief that he or she was liable to make the transfer, albeit that this liability was not owed to the recipient of the benefit.[55] To insist that the mistaken liability can only be owed by the plaintiff to the defendant is to impose a requirement of privity between the parties. Whilst such privity is generally crucial when considering whether the defendant has been enriched at the plaintiff's expense,[56] it is a very different matter to impose a privity requirement for the purposes of establishing a ground of restitution. Such a requirement could only be justified if the right to restitution was dependent upon an implied contract.[57] Since the implied contract theory has been rejected,[58] it is not possible to defend any limitation on recovery which is founded on privity. Consequently, restitution should lie whenever the plaintiff mistakenly believed that he or she was under a legal liability to transfer a benefit to the defendant, regardless of whether that liability was believed to be owed to the defendant or a third party.

(3) Future liabilities

Restitution has also been granted where the plaintiff's mistake related to a future liability to transfer a benefit to the defendant. This was the result in *Kerrison* v. *Glyn, Mills, Currie and Co.*[59] where the plaintiff agreed with a bank that he would reimburse it in respect of any payments which were made by it on his behalf. In anticipation of such liability to reimburse the bank arising in the future, the plaintiff transferred money to the defendant to be paid to the bank when the liability arose. The plaintiff was not, however, aware that at the time of his payment to the defendant the bank was insolvent. Consequently the plaintiff sought to recover the money which he had paid to the defendant on the ground that he had made a mistake of fact, namely that no liability to reimburse the bank would have arisen. Although there was no existing liability to pay the money to the bank, it was held that the plaintiff could recover the amount paid to the defendant because of a mistaken belief that liability to pay the money would arise in the future.

This case does cause some serious difficulties though, since a mistaken belief that a liability to pay money will arise in the future is not a mistake

---

[54] See, for example, *Colonial Bank* v. *Exchange Bank of Yarmouth, Nova Scotia* (1885) 11 App. Cas. 84 ; *Kleinwort, Sons and Co.* v. *Dunlop Rubber Co.* (1907) 97 LT 263 ; *R.E. Jones Ltd.* v. *Waring and Gillow Ltd.* [1926] AC 670; *Barclays Bank* v. *Simms* [1980] 1 QB 677.
[55] This was the view of Robert Goff J in *ibid*.
[56] See Chapter 5.   [57] Goff and Jones, *The Law of Restitution*, p. 184.
[58] *United Australia Ltd.* v. *Barclays Bank Ltd.* [1941] AC 1.   [59] (1911) 81 LJKB 465.

at all but is a misprediction, and so it appears that the plaintiff in the *Kerrison* case had acted voluntarily in paying the defendant, so the plaintiff took the risk of the bank's insolvency. Consequently, the ratio of the case, that restitutionary relief should be available if the plaintiff's 'mistake' relates to a liability arising in the future, should be rejected. It does not follow, however, that the result of the case is necessarily wrong. The success of the plaintiff's claim can be justified on two alternative grounds. First, the plaintiff can be considered to have made a mistake as to an existing fact, namely that the bank was solvent, and this mistake caused the plaintiff to pay the defendant. In other words, the plaintiff's mistake was not a liability mistake but was simply a causative mistake, in the sense that, but for the plaintiff's mistake as to the solvency of the bank, the plaintiff would not have paid the money.[60] It therefore follows that the success of the plaintiff's restitutionary claim can be justified, but not on the ground that the plaintiff had made a liability mistake, but only because the mistake had caused the plaintiff to make the payment. Alternatively, the success of the plaintiff's claim can be justified on the ground that the basis for the plaintiff paying the defendant, namely that the defendant would pay the bank, could never be satisfied because the bank was insolvent. In other words, the plaintiff could have relied on an alternative ground of restitution, namely total failure of consideration.[61]

(4) Moral duties

It has sometimes been suggested that if the plaintiff transferred a benefit to the defendant in the mistaken belief that there was a moral duty to do so, then such a mistake would enable the plaintiff to recover the benefit from the defendant. So, for example, in *Larner* v. *London County Council*[62] the London County Council had decided to pay its employees who had entered the armed services during the Second World War the difference between their war service pay and their civil pay. The Council made such a payment to Larner, but overpaid him because he had failed to disclose changes in his war service pay. It was held by the Court of Appeal that the Council could recover the overpayment, even though it never believed that it was legally liable to make the payment in the first place. Denning LJ emphasised that it was sufficient, on the facts as the Council believed them to be, that there was a moral duty to pay Larner.

It remains unclear how the court in *Larner* was able to conclude that there was a moral duty to pay the defendant. There are two possible explanations of the case. The first is that the duty to pay arose from national policy at the time which sought to encourage men to engage in war service by removing some of the financial risks of doing so. But this

---

[60] See p. 151 below.   [61] See Chapter 12.   [62] [1949] 2 KB 683.

is a vague basis for identifying a moral duty to pay.[63] The alternative, and preferable, interpretation of the case is that the duty arose from the fact that the Council had already promised Larner that it would pay him the money.[64] So a moral duty to pay would appear to be triggered by an antecedent promise to pay, regardless of the absence of any contractual liability. But if an antecedent promise creates a moral liability to pay then it follows that it will sometimes be possible to recover gifts by reason of mistake, so long as the plaintiff has promised to make the gift in the first place. If this were possible then it would make a mockery of any notion of restitution being confined to liability mistakes. Consequently, *Larner* is better treated as a case where the mistake did not depend on any belief on the part of the plaintiff that it was liable to pay the defendant. The acceptance that the Council could recover the overpayment is much easier to justify by reference to a test that the Council's mistake was fundamental or simply that it had caused the Council to make the payment to Larner.

(5) Is restitution confined to liability mistakes?

Even though it is clear that, where the plaintiff has made a mistake as to an existing liability to pay either the defendant or a third party, this is sufficient to establish a ground of restitution, it does not follow that restitution on the ground of mistake is confined to such circumstances. It is clear from those cases which have recognised that mistakes as to future liability and as to non-contractual liabilities can ground restitutionary claims, that there must be some other test of mistake, simply because the mistakes in those cases cannot properly be characterised as liability mistakes.

(ii) Fundamental mistakes

The test of fundamental mistake was recognised by the Court of Appeal in *Morgan* v. *Ashcroft*,[65] where the plaintiff was a bookmaker whose clerk had mistakenly overpaid the defendant his winnings after he had laid bets on a horse race. The plaintiff sought to recover the overpayment on the ground that his clerk had made a mistake of fact. The plaintiff's claim failed because betting was illegal and the court would not assist a plaintiff to recover a benefit where he or she had participated in an illegal transaction.[66] Despite this, the judges did analyse the proper test for

---

[63] Goff and Jones, *The Law of Restitution*, p. 187.

[64] Needham, 'Mistaken Payments: A New Look at an Old Theme' (1979) 12 *Univ. of Brit. Col. LR* 159, 168.

[65] [1938] 1 KB 49. Cp. *Gilks* [1972] 3 All ER 280.

[66] By virtue of the Gaming Act 1845, s. 18. For analysis of the defence of illegality see Chapter 26.

determining when a mistake would ground a restitutionary claim. Whilst they accepted that a mistaken belief in a liability to pay the money would be sufficient to establish a restitutionary claim, they emphasised that the ground for recovery was not restricted to liability mistakes. Rather, the cases where restitution was awarded on the basis of a liability mistake formed part of a wider principle, namely that it was sufficient that the mistake could be characterised as a fundamental mistake.[67] On the facts of the case it was considered that the plaintiff's mistake was not fundamental.

In *Morgan* v. *Ashcroft* Sir Wilfred Greene MR specifically relied on the decision of the Privy Council in *Norwich Union Fire Insurance Society Ltd.* v. *Price*[68] as authority for this test of fundamental mistake. In the *Norwich Union* case the defendant had claimed money from the plaintiff insurance company in respect of a cargo of lemons which the defendant asserted had been damaged by a peril which had been insured against, and which was subsequently sold at a loss. The plaintiff paid the defendant the insured value of the cargo, but it later discovered that the lemons were not sold because they had been damaged but because they were ripening, and this was a risk which was not covered by the insurance policy. The plaintiff recovered the money it had paid on the basis that it had made a mistake of fact. Although the success of the claim could have been justified by virtue of the mistaken liability principle, since the plaintiff mistakenly believed that it was liable to pay on the insurance policy, Lord Wright justified the result on the ground that the plaintiff's mistake was fundamental and such a mistake prevented there being the necessary intention to pay the money.[69]

In the *Norwich Union* case Lord Wright described a fundamental mistake as one 'in respect of the underlying assumption of the contract or transaction or as being fundamental or basic'.[70] He went on to add that '[w]hether the mistake does satisfy this description may often be a matter of great difficulty'. Despite the inherent uncertainty of the fundamental mistake test, it is possible to clarify what is meant by a mistake as to the 'underlying assumption' for the transfer of the benefit to the defendant. In *Morgan* v. *Ashcroft* two types of fundamental mistake were identified: first, those mistakes which are concerned with the nature of the transfer—the best example of this are those cases where the plaintiff mistakenly believed that he or she was liable to pay the defendant; secondly, where the mistake is one of identity—this is illustrated by a case where the plaintiff paid money to the defendant mistakenly thinking that he or she was somebody else. In both cases the plaintiff's intention that

---

[67] [1938] 1 KB 49, 66 (Sir Wilfred Greene MR) and 74 (Scott LJ).
[68] [1934] AC 455.   [69] *Ibid*, p. 462.   [70] *Ibid*, p. 463.

the defendant should receive the money is vitiated by this fundamental mistake and so restitution will lie.[71]

The effect of the recognition of fundamental mistake as the test to determine when a mistake can operate as a ground of restitution is that even gifts are recoverable in those cases where the reason for the gift can be regarded as undermined by the mistake.

Although the test of fundamental mistake has been recognised as a means of establishing a ground of restitution, whether such a test should be adopted is a particularly difficult matter. The key question of principle which needs to be considered when determining the most appropriate test of mistake is what degree of vitiation of intention is considered appropriate before the mistake can operate as a ground of restitution. This in turn depends on a question of policy, namely how easy should it be for a plaintiff to claim that he or she has made a mistake and so is entitled to restitutionary relief? This is something which has often been ignored by the courts in those cases which advocate the test of fundamental mistake. That restrictive test is entirely appropriate where it is necessary to vitiate a contract for mistake,[72] since a bargain should be treated as vitiated only where it can be concluded that the effect of the mistake was such that the parties cannot be considered to have truly made a bargain at all. But a test which is appropriate in the context of vitiation of contracts is not necessarily appropriate where the plaintiff wishes to recover benefits without setting a transaction aside.[73] Where a contract is set aside for mistake what needs to be shown is that the intention to contract was vitiated by the mistake. Where the plaintiff simply wishes to recover benefits from the defendant all we are concerned with is whether the plaintiff's intention to transfer the benefit was vitiated by the mistake. The policy of the law is very different in the two contexts as well. For there is a clear reluctance to set contracts aside for mistake because of the principle of law that parties should be held to their bargains wherever possible. There is no similar policy in operation where the plaintiff wishes to recover the value of a benefit from the defendant.

One possible argument which can be used to explain why the test of fundamental mistake has been adopted to determine whether a ground of

---

[71] [1938] 1 KB 49, 66 (Sir Wilfred Greene MR). Fundamental mistake as to identity may have been the ground of restitution in *Greenwood* v. *Bennett* [1973] QB 195 where the repairer of a car, who repaired it because he mistakenly believed that he owned it, recovered from the car's owner the value of the services he had provided in repairing and improving it.

[72] See pp. 175–87 below.

[73] See *Citibank NA* v. *Brown Shipley and Co. Ltd.* [1991] 2 All ER 690, 700 (Waller J). Cp. Birks, *An Introduction to the Law of Restitution*, who tentatively supports the fundamental mistake test because of concerns about opening the floodgates of litigation and consequent insecurity of receipts: Birks, p. 159.

restitution is available, even though the plaintiff did not need to set a transaction aside, is founded on the implied contract theory. At a time when it was believed that restitutionary relief would only be available if it were possible to imply a contract between the parties to make restitution, the contractual test of mistake would appear to have been an entirely appropriate test of mistake, even though the plaintiff did not seek to set a contract aside. But with the rejection of the implied contract theory,[74] any analogy drawn from the law of contract is clearly inappropriate.

The fundamental mistake test is also adopted in respect of claims to vindicate proprietary rights where such a mistake operates to prevent title to property from passing to the defendant.[75] Such a restrictive test is appropriate because it is only where the effect of the mistake was to negate the plaintiff's intention completely that it is proper to conclude that title did not pass to the defendant, so that the plaintiff can rely on his or her continuing title to recover property from the direct or indirect recipient. Where, however, the plaintiff simply wishes to recover the value of a benefit mistakenly transferred to the defendant in a personal restitutionary claim founded on the reversal of unjust enrichment it is not necessary to show that the mistake is so serious that it prevents title from passing. If the same test of fundamental mistake were adopted for both types of restitutionary claim then, since fundamental mistakes prevent title from passing to the defendant, there would be no need for the plaintiff to base his or her restitutionary claim on the principle of unjust enrichment. For the plaintiff will necessarily have retained a proprietary interest whenever he or she has made a fundamental mistake and the vindication of this interest can form the basis of a restitutionary action, for which the plaintiff may obtain either a personal or a proprietary restitutionary remedy. If there is to be an independent restitutionary action founded on reversing unjust enrichment where the ground for restitution is mistake, the test of mistake needs to be wider than the equivalent test for proprietary restitutionary claims.

The obvious conclusion from these arguments is that the test of mistake for the purposes of restitutionary claims founded on the unjust enrichment principle should be wider than the test of fundamental mistake,[76] and so some other test of mistake needs to be identified. That other test is the test of operating cause.

(iii) Causative mistakes

The operating cause test of mistake will be satisfied whenever the plaintiff's mistake caused him or her to transfer a benefit to the defendant.

---

[74] See *United Australia Ltd.* v. *Barclays Bank Ltd.* [1941] AC 1.

[75] See pp. 607–10 below.

[76] Robert Goff J in *Barclays Bank* v. *Simms* [1980] 1 QB 677, 689.

Although there are few cases where this test has been expressly adopted, it is increasingly being recognised by the courts.

In *Kelly* v. *Solari*[77] whilst Parke B recognised that a mistaken belief as to liability to pay the defendant would constitute a ground for restitution,[78] he did not suggest that this was the only type of mistake which would ground such claims.[79] The judgment of Rolfe B in the same case supports a very wide test for recovery, one which is not restricted to mistaken beliefs as to liability to transfer a benefit to the defendant. He said:

wherever [money] is paid under a mistake of fact, and the party would not otherwise have paid it if the fact had been known to him, it cannot be otherwise than unconscientious to retain it.[80]

The statement in this dictum that the plaintiff would not have paid the defendant had he or she not been mistaken constitutes an implicit recognition that it is sufficient to show that the mistake had caused the plaintiff to pay the money.

The leading case which recognised and applied the operating cause test of mistake is *Barclays Bank* v. *W.J. Simms (Southern) Ltd.*,[81] a decision of Robert Goff J. In this case a customer of the plaintiff bank drew a cheque on its account with the plaintiff in favour of the defendant. The customer discovered subsequently that the defendant had just entered into receivership and telephoned the plaintiff requesting that it stop the cheque. The receiver presented the cheque to the plaintiff for payment. The paying official, forgetting about the existence of the stop order, paid the money to the receiver. The plaintiff then sought to recover the money from the defendant and succeeded because the paying official's mistake had been an operating cause of the payment. This was because, but for the fact that the official had forgotten about the stop order, the money would not have been paid to the defendant. Although restitution could have been awarded by reference to the liability principle, since the plaintiff had mistakenly believed that it was liable to pay the defendant, Robert Goff J used the case to stress that the liability principle was only an example of a wider principle by virtue of which it was sufficient that the mistake had caused the plaintiff to transfer a benefit to the defendant.

---

[77] (1841) 9 M and W 54; 152 ER 24.   [78] *Ibid*, p. 58–9; 26.

[79] As was recognised by Robert Goff J in *Barclays Bank* v. *Simms* [1980] 1 QB 677, 687.

[80] (1841) 9 M and W 54, 58–9; 152 ER 24, 26. See also *Kleinwort, Sons and Co.* v. *Dunlop Rubber Co.* (1907) 97 LT 263, 264 (Lord Loreburn LC); *Kerrison* v. *Glyn, Mills, Currie and Co.* (1911) 81 LJ KB 465, 470 (Lord Atkinson), 471 (Lord Shaw of Dunfermline); *R.E. Jones Ltd.* v. *Waring and Gillow Ltd.* [1926] AC 670, 679–80 (Viscount Cave LC). None of these judges specified that the plaintiff must have mistakenly believed that he or she was under a liability to pay the defendant.

[81] [1980] QB 677. See also *Saronic Shipping Co. Ltd.* v. *Huron Liberian Co.* [1979] 1 Lloyd's Rep. 341, 362–6 (Mocatta J), affirmed by the Court of Appeal without reference to mistake: [1980] 2 Lloyd's Rep. 26.

The test of operative causation was further considered by the Court of Appeal in *Rover International Ltd.* v. *Cannon Film Sales Ltd. (No. 3)*.[82] In this case the plaintiff had agreed to dub the defendant's films and then distribute them in Italy. The agreement with the defendant also required the plaintiff to make advance payment of a number of instalments to the defendant. After the plaintiff had paid some of the instalments and done a lot of work in dubbing and distributing the films, the relationship between the parties broke down. The plaintiff sought to recover the money paid to the defendant, and its restitutionary claim succeeded on the ground of mistake of fact.[83] The mistake arose from the fact that the plaintiff believed that the money was due to the defendant under the agreement, when in fact the agreement was void *ab initio*, since it was made before the plaintiff had been incorporated.[84] Although the plaintiff's mistake related to a belief that it was liable to pay the defendant,[85] and none of the judges explicitly adopted the test of operating cause, at no point did any of the judges specifically restrict the ground of recovery to liability mistakes or fundamental mistakes. Indeed, Dillon LJ[86] specifically approved the analysis of Robert Goff J in *Barclays Bank* v. *Simms*.[87] Dillon LJ accepted that where 'money is repayable because it was paid under a mistake of fact, that is because the mistake falsified the assumption on which the payment was made',[88] the false assumption on the facts of the *Rover International* case being that the money was paid 'under and to comply with a valid contract'.[89] Similarly, Kerr LJ emphasised that '[i]t is obvious that the payments would not have been made unless [the plaintiff] had believed that there was a binding contract' between the parties.[90] In other words, the mistaken belief that the contract was valid caused the payments to be made. As Dillon LJ said, '[i]t is impossible to suggest any other reason for the payments'.[91]

Although the decision of the Court of Appeal in *Rover International* is important, since nothing said by any of the judges contradicts the test of operating cause and much that is said can be regarded as supporting that

[82] [1989] 1 WLR 912.

[83] The claim also succeeded on the alternative ground of total failure of consideration. See Chapter 12. The plaintiff also successfully recovered reasonable remuneration in respect of its work in dubbing and distributing the films.

[84] See the Companies Act 1985, s. 36C, as inserted by the Companies Act 1989, s. 130(4).

[85] As was recognised by Dillon LJ at [1989] 1 WLR 912, 933.   [86] *Ibid.*

[87] [1980] 1 QB 677. Dillon LJ also approved the dictum of Parke B in *Kelly* v. *Solari* (1841) 9 M and W 54, 58–9; 152 ER 24, 26 which does not confine recovery for mistake to cases where the mistake relates to liability to transfer a benefit. No reference is made by any of the judges in the *Rover International* case to the dictum of Bramwell B in *Aiken* v. *Short* (1856) 1 H and N 210, 215; 156 ER 1180, 1182 which provides the strongest support for restitution for mistake being confined to liability mistakes.

[88] [1989] 1 WLR 912, 934.   [89] *Ibid.*

[90] *Ibid*, p. 925. Nicholls LJ agreed with the judgments of both Kerr and Dillon LJJ.

[91] *Ibid*, p. 933.

test, the success of the plaintiff's restitutionary claim in the case on the ground of mistake of fact is difficult to justify.[92] This is because a mistaken belief that money is due under a contract which is void *ab initio* as a matter of law should surely be characterised as a mistake of law.[93] Although with the abolition of the mistake of law bar this would no longer constitute an obstacle to the plaintiff's claim for restitution, at the time the case was decided the mistake of law bar still existed and so the result of the case is difficult to justify.

The test of operative causation also appears to have been accepted by the House of Lords in *Banque Financière de la Cité* v. *Parc (Battersea) Ltd*.[94] In this case the plaintiff had lent money to the debtor company to be used to discharge a liability of the debtor to a third party. The plaintiff's loan to the debtor was unsecured because the plaintiff had received a letter of postponement which stated that the debt owed to the plaintiff would be paid off in priority to any debts which were owed by the debtor company to any other company in the group. The defendant was another company in the same group which was also owed money by the debtor company, but the defendant's debt was secured. This meant that the defendant's debt had priority over that of the plaintiff, and this was important since the debtor had gone into liquidation. The question for the House of Lords concerned the effect of the letter of postponement on the priorities of the claims of the plaintiff and the defendant. It was held that, although the letter of postponement did not bind the defendant, the plaintiff could successfully bring a restitutionary claim for which the remedy was that the plaintiff could be subrogated to the rights of the third party against the debtor and so obtain priority over the defendant.[95] The court concluded that the defendant had been enriched at the plaintiff's expense, because the plaintiff's money had been used to discharge part of the debt owed to the third party, so improving the chances of the defendant being repaid. It was then necessary to consider the ground of restitution. Whilst not all the members of the House of Lords considered this matter, those that did clearly considered the ground to be the plaintiff's mistake in lending the money to the debtor in the belief that the letter of postponement was effective to give the plaintiff priority over the defendant. Clearly the plaintiff's mistake was not a mistake as to a liability, nor could it be considered to be a fundamental mistake. Rather the mistake was simply an operating cause of the plaintiff lending the money to the debtor company. This was specifically acknowledged by

---

[92] Although the result of the case is defensible by reference to the alternative ground of total failure of consideration.

[93] Although Kerr LJ did commend the decision of counsel not to argue that the mistake of law bar applied: [1989] 1 WLR 912, 925.   [94] [1998] 2 WLR 475.

[95] See pp. 23–5 above for analysis of the remedy of subrogation.

Lord Hoffmann who stated that:

The [plaintiff] advanced [the money] upon the mistaken assumption that it was obtaining a postponement letter which would be effective to give it priority over any intra-group indebtedness. It would not otherwise have done so.[96]

Although the court did not specifically examine the different theories of the appropriate test for identifying which mistakes can ground restitutionary claims, this is the clearest indication so far that the appropriate test is that of causation: but for the mistake the plaintiff would not have transferred the benefit to the defendant.

Further support for the operating cause test can be found in some of the judgments in the House of Lords in *Kleinwort Benson Ltd.* v. *Lincoln City Council.*[97] The most important judgment in this respect is that of Lord Hope who stated that:

Subject to any defences that may arise from the circumstances, a claim for restitution of money paid under a mistake raises three questions. (1) Was there a mistake? (2) Did the mistake cause the payment? And (3) did the payee have a right to receive the sum which was paid to him?[98]

This is the clearest recognition in this country at the highest level that it is sufficient that the plaintiff's mistake has simply caused him or her to transfer a benefit to the defendant, even though the mistake did not relate to a belief that the plaintiff was liable to pay the defendant. The significance of this dictum is weakened somewhat because the plaintiff's mistake in that case was a liability mistake, namely that the plaintiff believed that it was liable to pay money to the defendant under an interest rate swap contract which was null and void. Nevertheless, Lord Hope's dictum makes no reference to the mistake concerning a liability to pay the defendant; it is sufficient that the mistake caused the payment to be made.

Recent developments in some Commonwealth countries show that there is a growing recognition that the test of causation is the most appropriate one for identifying those mistakes which will ground restitutionary claims. Most importantly, in the decision of the High Court of Australia in *David Securities Pty. Ltd.* v. *Commonwealth Bank of Australia*[99] the test of fundamental mistake, which had previously been accepted as the appropriate one for determining which mistakes would ground restitutionary claims, was rejected in favour of a causation test. The court stressed that where the mistake has caused the plaintiff to pay the defendant then the plaintiff's intention has been vitiated for

---

[96] [1998] 2 WLR 475, 486. See also Lord Steyn at p. 479.

[97] [1998] 3 WLR 1095, 1100 (Lord Browne-Wilkinson), 1112 (Lord Goff), 1137 (Lord Hoffmann).

[98] *Ibid*, p. 1145.   [99] (1992) 175 CLR 353, 378.

purposes of the law of restitution and this was all that needed to be shown.[100] In the decision of the New Zealand High Court in *University of Canterbury* v. *Attorney-General*[101] the plaintiff recovered a gift of shares which he had transferred to an educational trust in the mistaken belief that such a gift was necessary because the trust fund had been seriously depleted, when this was not in fact the case. It was held that the plaintiff could recover the shares because he would not have made the gift but for the mistake.[102]

The question whether the test of causation is the appropriate one for determining whether the plaintiff's mistake constitutes a ground of restitution, is still a matter of controversy. The leading case on the appropriate test for mistake is still the decision of the House of Lords in *Kerrison* v. *Glyn, Mills, Currie and Co.*[103] where the test of liability mistake was endorsed. That case has not yet been formally overruled. But despite this, the recent decisions of the House of Lords in the *Banque Financière* and *Kleinwort Benson* cases strongly suggest that the proper test is that of operating cause, and it is not necessary to confine restitution on the ground of mistake to where the plaintiff's mistake concerned his or her liability to pay the defendant. *Kerrison* v. *Glyn, Mills, Currie and Co.* is a highly dubious authority anyway, since the plaintiff's mistake related to liability to pay in the future, so the case involved a misprediction rather than a mistake. The result of the case can, however, be justified on the basis that, but for the mistake, the plaintiff would not have paid the money to the bank.[104] Consequently, although the matter is not yet completely free from doubt, the preferable view is that English law now recognises the test of operating cause to determine whether the plaintiff's mistake can ground a restitutionary claim.

If the test of operating cause is adopted, those cases in which restitution was granted by reference to the alternative tests of liability mistake or fundamental mistake will still have been decided the same way. This is because it is inconceivable that cases where a benefit was transferred because the plaintiff believed that he or she was liable to transfer it, or because the plaintiff had made a fundamental mistake, could be treated as cases where the mistaken belief was not an operating cause of the transfer. Some other cases can only be explained by reference to a test of operating cause, even though the court did not articulate why the mistake constituted a ground of restitution. For example, in *Greenwood* v. *Bennett*[105] the person who had repaired and improved a car, mistakenly

---

[100] (1992) 175 CLR 353, 378.   [101] [1995] 1 NZLR 78.

[102] *Ibid*, p. 81 (Williamson J). Williamson J also endorsed the test of fundamental mistake, but it is is difficult to see how the plaintiff's mistake on the facts was fundamental when it related simply to his motive for making the gift.

[103] (1911) 81 LJKB 465.   [104] See p. 147 above.   [105] [1973] QB 195.

believing that he owned it, succeeded in recovering the value of his services in an action where the true owner sought to recover the car, even though the repairer did not think that he was liable to make the repairs. The mistaken belief that the repairer owned the car might be characterised as a fundamental mistake as to the identity of the person who benefited from the work, the repairer thinking that it was himself when in fact it was the owner, but it is definitely a causative mistake, since, but for that mistake, the repairer would not have undertaken the repairs.[106] Similarly, some of the earlier cases in which the plaintiff succeeded in recovering money paid, by virtue of a somewhat artificial extension of the notion of mistaken belief as to a legal liability to pay the defendant, are more easily explained by reference to a test of operating cause.[107]

Some of the previous cases in which restitution was denied because no liability mistake had been made would often have been decided differently if a test of operating cause had been recognised. For example, in *Aiken* v. *Short*[108] restitutionary relief was denied because the plaintiff had not made any mistake as to its liability to pay money to the defendant. Rather, the plaintiff had made the payment because it thought that it was discharging the defendant's supposed interest in the plaintiff's property, when in fact the defendant did not have such an interest. This mistake was an operating cause of the payment, since if the plaintiff had been aware at the time of the payment that the defendant did not have an interest in the property it would not have made the payment. This was effectively recognised by Bramwell B who, whilst concluding that the plaintiff had acted voluntarily because it had not satisfied the mistaken liability test, recognised that the purchase of the defendant's supposed interest in the property 'turned out to be different to, and of less value than, what [the plaintiff] expected'.[109] Consequently, if *Aiken* v. *Short* were decided today restitution could be granted, subject to argument about any defences which might be relied on by the defendant.[110]

(1) Justifications for the operating cause test

The ground of restitution for mistake has developed gradually from the core case of liability mistakes, where it is easy to conclude that the defendant was unjustly enriched, to the extraction of a general principle that it suffices that the mistake was an operating cause of the benefit being

[106] Another case which cannot be explained by reference to a mistaken belief as to liability to pay the defendant is *Colonial Bank* v. *Exchange Bank of Yarmouth, Nova Scotia* (1885) 11 App. Cas. 84.

[107] See, for example, *Kleinwort, Sons and Co.* v. *Dunlop Rubber Co.* (1907) 97 LT 263 where the plaintiff did not believe that it was under any liability to the defendant, but that it was liable to a third party to pay the defendant.

[108] (1856) 1 H and N 210; 156 ER 1180.   [109] *Ibid*, 215; 1182.

[110] Such as the defence of good consideration. See pp. 169–73 below.

transferred. This development of the ground of mistake mirrors the development of the tort of negligence. In the same way that, before the leading case of *Donoghue* v. *Stevenson*,[111] the tort of negligence arose in specific and limited categories, so too the ground of mistake was confined to specific categories of case where the nature of the mistake justified the award of restitutionary relief. The importance of the decision of the House of Lords in *Donoghue* v. *Stevenson* was to extract a general principle from the disparate categories of negligence, and this general principle has been the touchstone against which all claims in negligence are determined. If the analogy with the tort of negligence is a true one it means that the decision of Robert Goff J in *Barclays Bank* v. *Simms* should be considered to be the *Donoghue* v. *Stevenson* of restitution for mistake, for it was in that case that Robert Goff J extracted a general principle from the previous cases which would serve to determine when a mistake could constitute a ground of restitution. The only serious drawback with this analogy is that *Donoghue* v. *Stevenson* was a decision of the House of Lords, whereas *Barclays Bank* v. *Simms* was merely the decision of a trial judge, albeit one whose decisions are highly influential. Despite dicta in recent decisions of the House of Lords which support the operating cause test of mistake, we still need a decision from that court to dispel any lingering doubts about what the proper test of mistake should be.

The recognition of the operating cause test of mistake can, however, be justified by reference to the principles underlying the recognition of grounds of restitution. A ground of restitution serves to show that the benefit received by the defendant was unjustly received. This will be the case in the context of mistake where it is possible to conclude that the effect of the plaintiff's mistake was to vitiate his or her intention to transfer the benefit to the defendant.[112] But this notion of vitiation of intention must be treated with caution, because vitiation of intention is a matter of degree and the effect of the different tests of mistake is that the plaintiff's intention is vitiated to differing extents. So, for example, where the plaintiff makes a fundamental mistake as to the identity of the defendant it can be concluded that the mistake is so extreme that the plaintiff's intention to transfer the benefit can be considered to have been utterly negated.[113] Where the plaintiff makes a mistake which is not even an

---

[111] [1932] AC 562.

[112] This was recognised by Waller J in *Midland Bank plc.* v. *Brown Shipley and Co. Ltd.* [1991] 2 All ER 690, 700–1.

[113] But see Williams, 'Mistake in the Law of Theft' (1977) 36 *CLJ* 62, 64, where he asserts that the notion that a fundamental mistake negatives the plaintiff's consent 'is in varying degrees a legal fiction: there is always an element of consent in the transfer'. But he goes on to recognise, at p. 65, that where there is a fundamental mistake 'the element of non-consent bulks so large that it seems more reasonable to deny consent rather than to affirm it'.

operating cause of the benefit being transferred, so that even if the plaintiff had not made the mistake the benefit would still have been transferred, the intention to make the transfer clearly outweighs any element of lack of intention. In the middle are those mistakes which are causative of the transfer, where the mistake is not so severe that it can be regarded as effectively negating any intention that the defendant receive the benefit, but is sufficiently important to be able to conclude that the plaintiff's intention to transfer the benefit was so affected by the mistake that it should be treated as vitiated, without necessarily being utterly negated. This distinction between complete negation and partial vitiation of intent is illustrated by *Barclays Bank* v. *Simms* where the mistake relating to the existence of the stop order did not negate the plaintiff's intention completely, so title to the money did pass to the defendant, but the mistake was sufficiently serious so that, had the plaintiff not been mistaken, it would not have paid the money. Consequently, it was possible to conclude that the plaintiff's intention had been vitiated to some extent so that its claim founded on unjust enrichment was successful.

(2) Defining the operating cause test

If the test of causation is adopted to determine when a mistake will ground a restitutionary claim it is then necessary to define causation for these purposes. There are two alternative tests which may be adopted.

(1) The first test is the 'but for' test, by virtue of which the plaintiff's mistake will only be considered to have caused the plaintiff to transfer a benefit to the defendant if the plaintiff can show that the benefit would not have been transferred but for the mistake.[114] If the plaintiff would still have transferred the benefit even if he or she had not been mistaken the mistake cannot be considered to have caused the benefit to be transferred.

(2) The second test is the 'contributory cause' test by virtue of which it is sufficient for the plaintiff to establish that the mistake contributed to his or her decision to transfer the benefit to the defendant, but it is not necessary to show that, had the plaintiff not been mistaken, he or she would not have transferred the benefit to the defendant. This test of causation has been adopted where the transfer of the benefit was induced by a misrepresentation of the defendant[115] or was compelled by the defendant.[116]

---

[114] See Burrows, *The Law of Restitution*, pp. 25–7. This 'but for' test has alternatively been called the 'necessary' cause: Arrowsmith, 'Mistake and the Role of the "Submission to an Honest Claim" ' in *Essays on the Law of Restitution* (ed. Burrows) p. 21.

[115] *Edgington* v. *Fitzmaurice* (1880) 25 Ch.D 459. See p. 166 below.

[116] *Barton* v. *Armstrong* [1976] AC 104. See Chapter 8.

Where the plaintiff's claim is based on a mistake the appropriate test of causation is that of 'but for' cause. Any analogy with the test which is adopted where the defendant has induced the plaintiff's mistake or has compelled the benefit to be transferred is a false one. For in those cases a more flexible test of causation is justified by virtue of the defendant's conduct, which makes it easier to conclude that any enrichment received by the defendant was received in circumstances of injustice. But where the plaintiff's mistake occurred spontaneously it is more difficult to establish that the defendant has been unjustly enriched. Consequently, restitution should only be awarded where the plaintiff would not have transferred the benefit had he or she not been mistaken, because this is sufficient to vitiate the plaintiff's intention to benefit the defendant. This analysis is supported by a number of cases. For example, in *Kelly* v. *Solari*[117] Parke B stressed that restitution should be awarded because 'the money would not have been paid if it had been known to the payer that the fact was untrue'. Whereas in *Holt* v. *Markham*[118] one reason for the denial of restitution where the plaintiff had paid the defendant too much money was because the plaintiff would have paid the money anyway even if it had known the true facts.

If the test whether the plaintiff had been caused to transfer a benefit by mistake depends on whether the plaintiff would have transferred the benefit had he or she not been mistaken, should this be formulated as a subjective or an objective test? In other words, should the test of causation be assessed by reference to what the plaintiff would have done had he or she known the truth or what the reasonable person would have done? Tettenborn prefers the objective test,[119] but this is surely inconsistent with the rationale of mistake as a ground of restitution. What we are trying to show is that the plaintiff's intention to transfer a benefit to the defendant was vitiated by the mistake. Whilst considerations of what the reasonable person might have done in the circumstances may be useful evidence of what the plaintiff would have done, we are ultimately only concerned with how the plaintiff would have acted had he or she not been mistaken. So a subjective test of causation is more appropriate. Of course, the more unreasonable the plaintiff's mistake appears to be then the more likely it is that the court will conclude that the alleged mistake was not a 'but for' cause of the benefit being transferred.[120] For example, if the plaintiff pays £100 to the defendant because she thinks that he has blue eyes, when in fact he has brown eyes, the plaintiff will be able to recover the money if it can be shown that but for the mistake about the

---

[117] (1814) 9 M and W 54, 58; 152 ER 24, 26.   [118] [1923] 1 KB 504.

[119] Tettenborn, *The Law of Restitution in England and Ireland*, p. 65.

[120] See Needham, 'Mistaken Payments: A New Look at an Old Theme' (1979) 12 *Univ. of Brit. Col. LR* 159, 221–2.

colour of the defendant's eyes the money would not have been paid. But it will be very hard for the plaintiff to convince the court that but for such a mistake the payment would not have been made.

If the plaintiff voluntarily transferred a benefit to the defendant he or she cannot be considered to have been mistaken.[121] Whether the plaintiff acted voluntarily depends on what the plaintiff was thinking at the time the benefit was transferred. This requires some subtle distinctions to be drawn.

(1) *Knowledge.* The easiest case is where the plaintiff knows all of the facts. This automatically negates the mistake.[122]

(2) *Recklessness.* Where the plaintiff transfers a benefit to the defendant being suspicious of the circumstances but he or she decides to take the risk that he or she is mistaken, the plaintiff will be considered to have acted voluntarily and so will not be mistaken. The test of recklessness for these purposes is a matter of some controversy. Arrowsmith has suggested that the plaintiff should be treated as acting recklessly where he or she failed to make a full inquiry to allay his or her suspicions or where, even though the plaintiff had made such an inquiry, it did not produce any clear conclusions but the plaintiff transferred the benefit anyway.[123] Alternatively, McKendrick[124] has suggested that a plaintiff should only be considered to have acted recklessly if he or she thought that it was more probable than not that he or she was mistaken. Whether the approach of Arrowsmith or McKendrick is preferred is ultimately a question of policy as to how much of an onus we wish to place on the plaintiff to allay any suspicions that he or she may be mistaken. Arrowsmith's view does, however, seem more workable and so preferable. Consequently, the plaintiff should be considered to have acted voluntarily whenever he or she was aware that there was a possibility that he or she had been mistaken.

(3) *Negligence.* Where the plaintiff has made a mistake which would not have been made by a reasonable person, such negligence will not prevent the plaintiff from arguing that the mistake has caused him or her to transfer the benefit to the defendant.[125]

If the 'but for' test of causation is adopted to identify when a mistake will ground a restitutionary claim then it will be possible for the plaintiff

---

[121] *Kleinwort Benson Ltd.* v. *Lincoln CC* [1998] 3 WLR 1095, 1140 (Lord Hoffmann).

[122] *Brisbane* v. *Dacres* (1813) 5 Taunt. 143, 159–60; 128 ER 641, 647–8 (Gibbs J).

[123] In *Essays on the Law of Restitution* (ed. Burrows) p. 26.

[124] 'Mistake of Law—Time for a Change' in *The Limits of Restitutionary Claims: A Comparative Analysis* (ed. Swadling) p. 224.

[125] *Banque Financière de la Cité* v. *Parc (Battersea) Ltd.* [1998] 2 WLR 475, 487 (Lord Hoffmann). See also *Kelly* v. *Solari* (1841) 9 M and W 54; 152 ER 24.

to recover a benefit mistakenly transferred to the defendant even though the plaintiff intended the benefit to be a gift. This is because if, but for the mistake, the plaintiff would not have made the gift to the defendant, the plaintiff's intention to make the gift can be treated as vitiated. Restitutionary relief will also be available according to the 'but for' test where the mistake relates to a third party rather than the defendant, as will occur where the plaintiff believes that he or she is liable to a third party to pay the defendant. This is exactly what happened in *Barclays Bank* v. *Simms*[126] where the plaintiff's claim succeeded.

(3) Mistakes of law

Even though the effect of the decision of the House of Lords in *Kleinwort Benson Ltd.* v. *Lincoln City Council*[127] should be that there is no longer any need to distinguish between mistakes of law and mistakes of fact for the purposes of identifying a ground of restitution, it is still necessary to draw such a distinction, since peculiar considerations need to be borne in mind when determining whether the plaintiff transferred a benefit as the result of a mistake of law.

For reasons of consistency with the ground of mistake of fact, restitution for mistake of law should only lie if the mistake was a 'but for' cause of the benefit being transferred.[128] But the particular difficulty relating to the identification of a mistake of law which caused the plaintiff to transfer a benefit to the defendant arises where the plaintiff correctly believed that he or she was obliged by operation of law to transfer the benefit, but the law was subsequently changed. Can the change in the law operate retrospectively to create a mistake of law? This depends on the circumstances in which the law was changed.

As the result of a long-standing principle, when a judge's decision effects a change in the law this is deemed to operate retrospectively because of the fiction that judges do not purport to change the law but simply declare the law to be what it has always been.[129]

Whether the effect of this fiction is sufficient to create an artificial mistake of law was the central issue in the decision of the House of Lords in

---

[126] [1980] QB 677. Cp. *National Westminster Bank Ltd.* v. *Barclays Bank International Ltd.* [1974] 3 All ER 834, 831 (Kerr LJ).

[127] [1998] 3 WLR 1095.

[128] In Australia, where the mistake of law bar has been abolished, the 'but for' test of causation applies to all restitutionary claims founded on mistake, regardless of whether the mistake is one of fact or law: *David Securities Pty. Ltd.* v. *Commonwealth Bank of Australia* (1992) 175 CLR 353. This has now been recognised in this country by Neuberger J in *Nurdin and Peacock plc.* v. *D.B. Ramsden and Co. Ltd.* [1999] 1 All ER 941.

[129] That this principle is a fiction is emphasised by the fact that recently the House of Lords has accepted that in the context of particular cases it is purporting to change the law rather than simply declaring what the law always was. See in particular *R.* v. *R.* [1992] 1 AC 599 and *Woolwich Equitable Building Society* v. *IRC* [1993] AC 70.

Kleinwort Benson Ltd. v. *Lincoln City Council.*[130] The plaintiff bank in that case had paid money to the defendant local authority pursuant to an interest rate swap transaction which had been made in the 1980s. In 1990 the House of Lords held that such transactions were *ultra vires* the local authorities, and so they were null and void. The plaintiff sought restitution of the money which it had paid to the defendant and, because of the law relating to limitation periods,[131] the plaintiff was forced to found its claim on mistake. Although the plaintiff's mistake was one of law this did not automatically defeat its claim because the judges in the House of Lords unanimously abolished the mistake of law bar. But it was still necessary for the plaintiff to establish that it had paid the defendant as a result of a mistake. The crucial questions for the House of Lords to decide were whether the plaintiff could be considered to have been mistaken and what was the effect of the declaratory theory of law-making on the identification of a mistake to ground a restitutionary claim. The court identified two different scenarios which required consideration.

(1) *The court overrules an earlier decision.* Where the plaintiff relies on a judicial decision to transfer a benefit and that decision is subsequently overruled, the House of Lords held that this is sufficient to establish a mistake of law. This is because of the effect of the declaratory theory of judicial law-making. Since the consequence of that theory is that the change in the law operates retrospectively, it can be assumed that the plaintiff has been caused to transfer a benefit to the defendant as a result of a mistake which is deemed to have been operating at the time the payment was made.

(2) *The court clarifies existing practice.* On the facts of *Kleinwort Benson* itself the courts had not overruled an earlier decision. There was no decision which stated that interest rate swap transactions made with local authorities were valid. Rather, practitioners had assumed that such transactions were probably valid. Consequently, when the House of Lords decided in 1990 that such transactions were null and void, the court was not changing the law; it was simply declaring the law. The House of Lords in *Kleinwort Benson* held, however, that this was a distinction without a difference. Since the plaintiff had assumed that the transaction was valid, the effect of the decision of the House in 1990 was to falsify this assumption and this was sufficient to create a mistake for the purposes of the restitutionary claim.

Where a statute changes the law this usually operates only prospectively, so it cannot be used to create a mistake. Exceptionally a statute may change the law retrospectively but the statute may make provision for whether restitutionary claims are available as a result of the change of

---

[130] [1998] 3 WLR 1095.   [131] See Chapter 28.

the law. If no such provision is made, is it possible to create a mistake? Lord Goff held in *Kleinwort Benson*[132] that it was not possible to identify a mistake in such circumstances, but this is very difficult to justify because it is surely inconsistent with the court's approach to judicial changes in the law.

Lords Browne-Wilkinson and Lloyd in *Kleinwort Benson* rejected the decision of the majority that the plaintiff had paid the money to the defendant as a result of a mistake of law. The conclusion of the minority seems preferable for two main reasons:

(1) A serious consequence of the decision of the House of Lords is that defendants may be liable to make restitution to the plaintiff by reason of mistake of law many years after the plaintiff had paid money to the defendant. This is because the limitation period for mistakes will begin to run only from the period when the plaintiff discovered the mistake.[133] So, for example, if the plaintiff paid £10,000 to the defendant in 1930 because, as the law stood at the time, he was liable to do so, if the law was subsequently changed by a decision of the Court of Appeal in 1995 it follows that the plaintiff had made a mistake of law in 1930. Consequently, the plaintiff can sue the defendant for repayment of the money, plus interest, since the limitation period did not start to run until 1995 when the plaintiff discovered the mistake. Such a result is patently unacceptable because it undermines the security of transactions. The only restriction on restitution in such circumstances derives from the potential application of the defence of change of position, but since that defence is defined restrictively because the change of position must be extraordinary,[134] its influence in curtailing restitutionary claims many years after a benefit has been transferred is likely to be minimal. It follows that there is an urgent need for statutory intervention to ensure that the security of transactions is not undermined unnecessarily. This statutory intervention should take the form of an appropriately drawn limitation statute.[135]

(2) The decision of the majority confuses the distinction between mistakes and mispredictions and undermines the fundamental principle concerning mistake as a ground of restitution, namely that the mistake is to be determined at the time the benefit was received by the defendant.[136] By applying the declaratory theory of judicial law-making the House of Lords has condoned the artificial manufac-

---

[132] [1998] 3 WLR 1095, 1121 (Lord Goff). Cp. Lord Hoffmann at p. 1139.
[133] Limitation Act 1980, s. 32(1)(c).   [134] See Chapter 24.
[135] See the Law Commission Consultation Paper, 'Limitation of Actions' (No. 151, 1998) examined in Chapter 28.
[136] *Baker* v. *Courage and Co.* [1910] 1 KB 56.

ture of a mistake at the time when the benefit was transferred.[137] The flaw in the opinion of the majority is that they underestimate the crucial feature of mistake as a ground of restitution, namely that it is simply concerned with the plaintiff's state of mind at the time the benefit was transferred to the defendant.[138] Since later changes in the substantive law by judges, although they operate retrospectively, cannot change the plaintiff's state of mind at the time of the transfer it follows that the plaintiff cannot be considered to have been mistaken. In reality, if at the time the plaintiff paid money to the defendant he or she was liable to do so and it was only subsequently that the law changed, the plaintiff cannot be considered to have made a mistake as to the existing law. Rather, he or she had made a misprediction as to what would happen in the future.[139] The plaintiff should be considered to bear the risk that the law might change in the future and so should not be allowed to obtain restitution on the ground of mistake. Such a conclusion would result in a consistent approach for mistakes of law and fact.[140] It follows that restitution on the ground of mistake should only be available where at the time the benefit was transferred it can be shown that the plaintiff was mistaken as to the state of the law at that time.

The strength of these criticisms and the failure of the majority to engage with them leads to a startling conclusion. Despite the very strong case for the abolition of the mistake of law bar in the first place, the House of Lords was not the proper forum to abolish it.[141] Because of the numerous implications of abolition, raising some difficulty policy questions, reform should have been left to Parliament.[142] Since the House of Lords has abolished the mistake of law bar and left a great deal of uncertainty there is still an urgent need for Parliamentary intervention to provide stability and clarity.

[137] This declaratory theory of law-making has been described as a 'fairy tale in which no one any longer believes': [1998] 3 WLR 1095, 1100 (Lord Browne-Wilkinson) citing Lord Reid's article, 'The Judge as Law Maker' (1972–1973) 12 *JSPTL* (*NS*) 22. See also Lord Lloyd: [1998] 3 WLR 1095, 1133.

[138] See in particular Lord Hoffmann: [1998] 3 WLR 1095, 1137.

[139] [1998] 3 WLR 1095, 1101 (Lord Browne-Wilkinson), 1133 (Lord Lloyd). This had previously been recognised in *Henderson* v. *The Folkestone Waterworks Co.* (1885) 1 TLR 329 and *Derrick* v. *Williams* [1939] 2 All ER 559. See also *Commissioner of State Revenue* v. *Royal Insurance Australia Ltd.* (1995) 182 CLR 51 which adopted a similar approach in respect of a retrospective change of the law by statute.

[140] See pp. 140–1 above.

[141] This was the view of the minority: [1998] 3 WLR 1095, 1106 (Lord Browne-Wilkinson) and 1136 (Lord Lloyd).

[142] In the criminal case of *C. (a minor)* v. *DPP* [1996] 1 AC 1 Lord Lowry identified a number of guidelines to determine when the judiciary should engage in law-making. According to these guidelines the House of Lords should not have abolished the mistake of law bar, but should have left reform to Parliament.

(4) Illegality

Where the plaintiff transfers a benefit to the defendant in circumstances in which the transfer is illegal, the illegality generally operates as a defence to the plaintiff's restitutionary claim.[143] But where the plaintiff is unaware of the illegality it is possible to bring a restitutionary claim on the ground of mistake.[144] But the plaintiff's claim will succeed only if the mistake relates to the existence of the illegality. If it does not then the illegality will still operate as a defence to the restitutionary claim.[145] The reason for this is that it is only where the plaintiff's mistake relates to the fact of the illegality that he or she will be considered not to have been tainted by that illegality so that his or her restitutionary claim should succeed. So, for example, in *Oom* v. *Bruce*,[146] goods which were to be transferred from Russia to England had been insured at a time when hostilities between England and Russia had just commenced. This made the contract of insurance illegal. But because both parties were unaware of the outbreak of hostilities it was held that the premiums paid under the insurance contract could be recovered by the plaintiff. The ground of restitution was mistake, because the mistake related to the fact that war had been declared.

(b) Induced mistakes

If the plaintiff transfers a benefit to the defendant as a result of a mistake which was induced by a misrepresentation by the defendant, it is not necessary to show that the mistake was a 'but for' cause of the benefit being transferred. Rather, it is enough that the mistake was simply a contributory cause of the transfer.[147] This means that the mistake need only have been a contributory factor to the plaintiff's decision to transfer the benefit to the defendant without necessarily being a reason but for which the benefit would not have been transferred. The reason for the adoption of this different test of causation where the plaintiff's mistake was induced by the defendant is that the defendant is to blame for creating the plaintiff's mistake, regardless of whether the misrepresentation was made fraudulently, negligently or innocently. It follows from the defendant's conduct in inducing the mistake that it is easier to conclude that the benefit received by him or her was unjustly received as a result of the mistake.

---

[143] See *Holman* v. *Johnson* (1775) 1 Cowp. 341, 343; 98 ER 1120, 1121 (Lord Mansfield). See Chapter 26.

[144] After the abolition of the mistake of law bar by the House of Lords in *Kleinwort Benson Ltd.* v. *Lincoln CC* [1998] 3 WLR 1095 this principle should apply regardless of whether the plaintiff's mistake was one of fact or law.

[145] See *Morgan* v. *Ashcroft* [1938] 1 KB 49.   [146] (1810) 12 East 225; 104 ER 87.

[147] *Edgington* v. *Fitzmaurice* (1885) 29 Ch.D 459.

Where the plaintiff has mistakenly transferred a benefit to the defendant in circumstances in which the transfer was illegal and the mistake was induced by the defendant's fraudulent conduct, the plaintiff will be able to obtain restitution despite the usual rule that participation in an illegal transaction bars a restitutionary claim.[148] This is because in such a case the defendant can be considered to be more blameworthy than the plaintiff for entering into the transaction.[149] Consequently, the plaintiff's claim will succeed only where he or she is considered to be less blameworthy than the defendant. This is illustrated by *Parkinson* v. *College of Ambulance*[150] where restitution of a charitable donation was denied because, although the plaintiff had been induced to give the money by means of a fraudulent representation that by making the gift the defendant charity could arrange for him to receive a knighthood, the plaintiff knew throughout that such an arrangement was illegal. The plaintiff was therefore an equal participant in the illegality and so was *in pari delicto* with the defendant.

(c) Should mistake be recognised as a ground of restitution?

Some commentators have argued that there is no need to recognise mistake as a ground of restitution, since the ground of total failure of consideration is applicable in all cases of mistake.[151] Failure of consideration in this context is not concerned with the consideration which is required when making a contract, but rather with the question whether the basis for the plaintiff's transfer of a benefit to the defendant has been satisfied in any way.[152] So, for example, if the plaintiff sells a car to the defendant in the expectation that £3,000 will be received for it, and the plaintiff does not receive any money at all, then the consideration for the transfer of the car will have failed totally. Those commentators who argue that the mistake cases are better interpreted as cases where there was a total failure of consideration base their argument on the fact that, where the plaintiff transfers a benefit to the defendant mistakenly believing that certain facts exist then, because those facts do not exist, the expected consequence of the transfer will not be achieved and so the consideration for the transfer will often have failed totally. So, for example, where

---

[148] See *Holman* v. *Johnson* (1775) 1 Cowp. 341, 343; 98 ER 1120, 1121 (Lord Mansfield). See Chapter 26.

[149] *Hughes* v. *Liverpool Victoria Legal Friendly Society* [1916] 2 KB 482.

[150] [1923] 2 KB 1.

[151] See, for example, Matthews, 'Money Paid Under Mistake of Fact' (1980) 130 *NLJ* 587 and 'Stopped Cheques and Restitution' [1982] *JBL* 281. See also Butler, 'Mistaken Payments, Change of Position and Restitution' in *Essays on Restitution* (ed. Finn, Sydney: The Law Book Co. Ltd., 1990) Chapter 4.

[152] See Chapter 12.

the plaintiff pays a sum of money to the defendant in the mistaken belief that it will discharge an existing liability then, if there was no such liability, the consideration for the payment will have failed totally, since it is not possible to discharge a liability which does not exist.

Whilst the award of restitutionary remedies in some cases can be justified by reference to both total failure of consideration and mistake,[153] the two grounds cannot be equated for three reasons.

(1) The state of the case law does not support the argument that the ground of mistake should not be recognised. Mistake is clearly accepted as a ground of restitution in its own right, independently of the ground of total failure of consideration.[154] This has been recognised decisively by the House of Lords in *Kleinwort Benson Ltd.* v. *Lincoln CC*[155] where the success of the plaintiff's claim depended on the ground of mistake because the plaintiff needed to rely on the rule extending the limitation period for cases of mistake where the plaintiff has not been able to discover the mistake. The plaintiff could not have relied on the ground of total failure of consideration, because the plaintiff had received some of the expected consideration from the defendant.[156]

(2) The plaintiff cannot rely on the ground of total failure of consideration where he or she has received some consideration for the benefit which he or she has transferred to the defendant. In such circumstances the plaintiff's only chance of bringing a restitutionary claim within the principle of unjust enrichment will be on the ground of mistake. Although even this cause of action is affected by consideration being provided by the defendant,[157] this will only bar restitution to the extent that consideration has been provided, whereas the ground of total failure of consideration will be completely barred if any consideration for the transfer has been provided.[158]

(3) The grounds of restitution for mistake and failure of consideration are recognised for very different reasons. Mistake is a ground of restitution because the mistake operates to vitiate the plaintiff's intention to

---

[153] See, for example, *Re the Bodega Company Ltd.* [1904] 1 Ch. 276 and *Rover International Ltd.* v. *Cannon Film Sales Ltd. (No. 3)* [1989] 1 WLR 912.

[154] As was recognised by Lord Wright in *Fibrosa Spolka Akcyjna* v. *Fairbairn Lawson Combe Barbour Ltd.* [1943] AC 32, 61.

[155] [1998] 3 WLR 1095.

[156] The plaintiff could have relied in principle on the alternative ground of absence of consideration (see Chapter 12) but did not wish to do so because a restitutionary claim founded on that ground of restitution would have been statute barred.

[157] See pp. 169–73 below.

[158] See Chapter 12. If partial failure of consideration is ever recognised as a ground of restitution in its own right the distinction between the grounds of mistake and failure of consideration will be less apparent, since in respect of both grounds of restitution the plaintiff's claim will only fail to the extent that consideration has been provided. See pp. 342–3 below.

transfer a benefit to the defendant. Where, however, there has been a total failure of consideration the plaintiff's intention is always valid but this intention is qualified by the plaintiff's expectation that some benefit will be provided by the defendant in return. Once it is clear that no benefit will be provided the ground of restitution is established. There is consequently a fundamental difference in approach between mistake and total failure of consideration as grounds of restitution. For whether the plaintiff has made a mistake can be determined only at the time the benefit is transferred to the defendant, whereas the question whether there has been a failure of consideration can be determined only after the benefit has been transferred.[159] Mistake and failure of consideration are consequently determined at different times. They both have a useful, albeit different, role to play within the law of restitution.

(d) Specific defences to restitutionary claims founded on mistake

Restitutionary claims founded on mistake are subject to the general defences which apply to all restitutionary claims, such as change of position,[160] estoppel[161] and transfer by an agent.[162] There is, however, one defence which is peculiarly applicable to restitutionary claims founded on mistake, and it is therefore appropriate to examine it in this chapter. It is also necessary to consider whether any specific defences should be available where the plaintiff's claim is grounded on a mistake of law.

(i) Good consideration provided by the defendant

In *Barclays Bank* v. *Simms*[163] Robert Goff J recognised that the plaintiff would not be able to recover money on the ground of mistake if the defendant had provided consideration for the payment. Presumably consideration in this context has the same meaning as it does in the context of total failure of consideration,[164] namely the benefit which the plaintiff expects to receive in return for transferring a benefit to the

---

[159] This distinction was recognised by Lord Shaw in *Jones Ltd.* v. *Waring and Gillow Ltd.* [1926] AC 670, 690: 'when . . . a payment [is] made under a mistake of fact, that mistake has reference to occurrences which have taken place or things which have been done prior to or at the time of the transaction . . . on the other hand the imposition of a condition upon the making of a payment . . . that affects the future'. See also Brennan J in *David Securities* v. *Commonwealth Bank of Australia* (1992) 175 CLR 353, 390.

[160] This defence was specifically recognised by Robert Goff J in *Barclays Bank* v. *Simms* [1980] QB 677, 695. See Chapter 24 for discussion of the defence.

[161] See Chapter 24. One of the leading cases on estoppel in the context of restitution, is *Avon County Council* v. *Howlett* [1983] 1 WLR 605, a case which concerned restitution of money paid by mistake.   [162] See Chapter 24.

[163] [1980] QB 677, 695. See also *Bank of New South Wales* v. *Murphett* [1983] VR 489 and *Lloyds Bank Plc* v. *Independent Insurance Co. Ltd.* [1999] 2 WLR 986.

[164] See Chapter 12.

defendant. The consideration which is provided must be 'good' consideration, so, for example, if the consideration is illegal or contrary to public policy, as will be the case where the defendant pays money to the plaintiff under a gaming contract, the defence of good consideration will not be applicable.[165]

Although the defence of good consideration has been judicially recognised, its role within the modern law of restitution is a matter of particular controversy. This is because, since the decision of Robert Goff J in the *Simms* case, the House of Lords has recognised the defence of change of position.[166] Both defences have a similar function, namely to limit the defendant's liability to make restitution to the plaintiff by reference to events following the receipt of a benefit from the plaintiff. Consequently, it might be concluded that the narrower defence of good consideration should be subsumed within the wider defence of change of position. At the very least this would remove the aberration of a defence existing within the law of restitution which is confined to a specific restitutionary claim, namely claims founded on mistake. Despite the attraction of this assimilation of the defences the apparent differences between them means that they must continue to be analysed separately. Indeed, in *Barclays Bank* v. *Simms* itself Robert Goff J considered the two defences to be different.

Two features distinguish the defences of the provision of good consideration and change of position:

(1) Whereas the defence of change of position will only arise where the defendant has changed his or her position in an unusual way, for example by incurring extraordinary expenditure in reliance on the validity of the benefit received from the plaintiff,[167] the defence of good consideration is not constrained by any such requirement. It is sufficient that the defendant has simply provided some consideration, however mundane, in return for the benefit received from the plaintiff.

(2) The defence of good consideration is applicable only where the defendant has provided consideration for the benefit which he or she received from the plaintiff. It follows from the definition of 'consideration' that the consideration provided by the defendant must have been expected by the plaintiff. For the defence of change of position on the other hand, it is necessary to show only that the defendant's position has changed in some extraordinary way; it is not necessary to show that the plaintiff expected the defendant's circumstances to change.

---

[165] *Lipkin Gorman (a firm)* v. *Karpnale Ltd.* [1991] 2 AC 548, 575 (Lord Goff).
[166] *Ibid*, pp. 579–80.   [167] See Chapter 24.

Despite these differences between the two defences they do share three common characteristics.

(1) In *Barclays Bank* v. *Simms*[168] Robert Goff J recognised that the defence of good consideration would not be applicable if the plaintiff's mistake had been induced by the defendant or if the defendant had not received the benefit from the plaintiff in good faith, as would be the case where the defendant was aware of the plaintiff's mistake. Similarly, the change of position defence is inapplicable if the defendant had not been acting in good faith.[169]

(2) The provision of good consideration should be treated as a defence to a restitutionary claim rather than a bar to that claim, since this is how change of position is treated. It follows that the defence of good consideration must be pleaded by the defendant.

(3) The defence of good consideration and that of change of position have a similar rationale, namely that where the defendant has provided consideration or his or her position has changed it is not just and equitable that the defendant should be required to make full restitution to the plaintiff. This common rationale assists in the resolution of a particular uncertainty about the ambit of the defence of good consideration, namely whether the defence defeats the plaintiff's restitutionary claim completely or only to the extent of the consideration provided. The better view is that, by analogy with the defence of change of position, the plaintiff's claim should be barred only to the extent that consideration has been provided.[170] So, for example, if the plaintiff mistakenly pays £1,000 to the defendant who provides goods worth £150 in return, the plaintiff's restitutionary claim will only be barred to the extent of £150.

It has recently been suggested by Peter Cribson LJ that the defence of good consideration can properly be characterised as a form of the defence of *bona fide* purchase for value.[171] This is, however, incorrect since the defence of *bona fide* purchase has a very specific function, namely make good defects in the defendant's title to property.[172] Where the plaintiff's restitutionary claim is founded on the unjust enrichment

---

[168] [1980] QB 677, 695.

[169] *Lipkin Gorman (a firm)* v. *Karpnale Ltd.* [1991] 2 AC 548, 580 (Lord Goff).

[170] *David Securities* v. *Commonwealth Bank of Australia* (1992) 175 CLR 353, 392 (Brennan J). Cp *Barclays Bank Ltd.* v. *W.J. Simms and Cooke (Southern) Ltd.* [1980] QB 677, 695 (Robert Goff J).

[171] *Lloyds Bank plc.* v. *Independent Insurance Co. Ltd.*, [1999] 2 WLR 986, 1005. Cp. Waller LJ who assumed that the defence of good consideration is a form of change of position: [1999] 2 WLR 986, 999. See Chapter 22 for discussion of the defence of *bona fide* purchase for value.

[172] See *Boscawen* v. *Bajwa* [1996] 1 WLR 328, 334 (Millett LJ).

principle the question whether or not the defendant has title to the property which he or she received is irrelevant. It follows that the defences of good consideration and *bona fide* purchase are different.

The most common situation in which the defence of good consideration may be applicable is where the plaintiff mistakenly pays a sum of money which has the effect of discharging a debt owed to the defendant. It is the discharge of the debt which constitutes the provision of good consideration by the defendant.[173] Whether the plaintiff's payment will have discharged a debt depends on whether the payment is authorised by the debtor.[174] This is particularly important in the context of banking transactions. In *Barclays Bank* v. *Simms*,[175] for example, the plaintiff bank had mistakenly paid money to the defendant in respect of a cheque drawn on a customer's account. If, which did not occur on the facts of the case, the mistake which the plaintiff had made was that the customer had sufficient funds in the account then, since the customer had authorised the payment, the debt which the customer owed to the defendant would have been discharged and the plaintiff would be forced to recover the money from the customer.[176] The plaintiff would not have been able to sue the defendant for the money because good consideration would have been provided for the payment, namely the discharge of the debt which was owed to the defendant. But, as occurred on the facts of the case, since the customer had countermanded the payment, the payment ceased to be authorised and so did not discharge the debt.[177] Consequently, the plaintiff was able to recover the money from the defendant by reason of the mistake. This seems perfectly fair since, as the debt was not discharged, the defendant could still sue the customer on that debt.[178]

A case in which the defence of good consideration defeated the plaintiff's restitutionary claim was *Aiken* v. *Short*[179] where the plaintiff bank paid money to the defendant to discharge a debt which was owed to the defendant by a third party, the bank mistakenly thinking that it was discharging an incumbrance on property which it owned. The plaintiff was unable to recover the money from the defendant since the third party debtor had authorised the payment and so the debt was discharged. The discharge of the debt was held to constitute the provision of considera-

---

[173] *David Securities* v. *Commonwealth Bank of Australia* (1992) 175 CLR 353, 406 (Dawson J). See *Lloyds Bank plc.* v. *Independent Insurance Co. Ltd.* [1999] 2 WLR 986

[174] This is examined in Chapter 9.   [175] [1980] QB 677.

[176] See *Lloyds Bank plc.* v. *Independent Insurance Co. Ltd.* [1999] 2 WLR 986 for an example of an authorised payment which discharged a debt.

[177] Cp. Goode, 'The Bank's Right to Recover Money Paid on a Stopped Cheque' (1981) 97 *LQR* 254 who suggests that the bank had apparent authority to pay the money to the defendant.

[178] [1980] QB 677, 703 (Robert Goff J).

[179] (1856) 1 H and N 210; 156 ER 1180. See also *Porter* v. *Latec Finance (Qld) Pty. Ltd.* (1964) 111 CLR 177.

tion by the defendant.[180] One point of particular importance about this case was that the consideration provided by the defendant, the discharge of the debt, could not be regarded as benefiting the plaintiff, since having made the payment it discovered that it did not own the property which was the subject of the incumbrance. The true beneficiary of the payment was the third party debtor. This does not matter, for the defence of good consideration is only concerned with the provision of some consideration by the defendant; it is not necessary to show that this was received by, or benefited, the plaintiff.[181] This is logically correct, since the defence of good consideration, like that of change of position, is concerned with changes in the defendant's circumstances following the receipt of a benefit. If the debt which was owed to the defendant has been discharged it is not just that the defendant must return the payment to the plaintiff, since the defendant will have lost the money and will no longer be able to sue the debtor on the debt. If the defence of good consideration succeeds in such a case, the plaintiff will be forced to bring a restitutionary claim against the third party debtor who was the actual beneficiary of the debt being discharged, the ground of restitution being the plaintiff's mistake.

(ii) Defences to claims founded on mistake of law

Now that it has been recognised that mistake of law can constitute a ground of restitution in its own right, it is necessary to consider whether any particular defences should be recognised where the plaintiff's claim is founded on a mistake of law. In *Kleinwort Benson* v. *Lincoln CC*[182] Lord Goff recognised that 'the law must evolve appropriate defences which can, together with the defence of change of position, provide protection where appropriate for recipients of money paid under a mistake of law in those cases in which justice or policy does not require them to refund the money'. Despite this, the House of Lords was generally reluctant to recognise any specific defence to claims founded on mistake of law. A number of potential defences to such claims have been suggested.

---

[180] See especially Pollock CB at *ibid*, p. 214; p. 1181 (ER). Cp. *Jones Ltd.* v. *Waring and Gillow Ltd.* [1926] AC 670 where the money received by the defendant from the plaintiff was not received in discharge of the debt which the fraudulent third party owed to it, so no consideration was provided for the payment.

[181] This point was ignored by the High Court of Australia in *David Securities* v. *Commonwealth Bank of Australia* (1992) 175 CLR 353 where the majority of the court consistently refer to the defence as involving the receipt of consideration. See especially *ibid*, p. 383.

[182] [1998] 3 WLR 1095, 1114.

(1) Settled view of law

The Law Commission has recommended that a restitutionary claim founded on mistake of law should be barred where the plaintiff acted in accordance with a settled view of the law which was subsequently departed from by a decision of a court of tribunal.[183] The House of Lords refused to recognise such a defence, simply because a change in a settled view of the law was considered to constitute a mistake of law in its own right.[184] Whilst the rejection of this defence is correct, since there are serious difficulties in defining the defence, the reason for its rejection is incorrect. For the preferable view is that where the plaintiff transfers a benefit to the defendant on the basis of a settled view of law, and the law is later changed or clarified, it is simply not possible to conclude that the plaintiff made a mistake at the time he or she transferred the benefit.[185]

(2) Defendant's honest receipt

In *David Securities Pty. Ltd.* v. *Commonwealth Bank of Australia*[186] Brennan CJ suggested that the defendant should have a defence to a restitutionary claim founded on mistake of law if he or she honestly believed that he or she was entitled to receive or retain the benefit from the plaintiff. The reason for advocating this defence was to maintain the security of receipts. The House of Lords in *Kleinwort Benson*[187] rejected such a defence simply because it would be so wide that it would under-mine the abolition of the mistake of law bar. This is because in most cases the defendant would honestly believe that he or she was entitled to the benefit since the defendant will typically share the plaintiff's mistake of law.

(3) Completed transactions

The House of Lords also held that there was no defence that the money has been paid pursuant to a transaction which has been fully per-formed.[188] Professor Birks had suggested that if the transaction has been completed then the force of the mistake was spent.[189] This argument was rejected, primarily because the right to restitution of benefits transferred by mistake arises at the time the benefit is transferred to the defendant. The fact that the transaction is subsequently completed should not deprive the plaintiff of his or her accrued cause of action.

---

[183] 'Restitution: Mistakes of Law and Ultra Vires Public Authority Receipts and Payments' (Law Com. No. 227, 1994) para. 5.13. This was also advocated by Lord Browne-Wilkinson: [1998] 3 WLR 1095, 1105.

[184] [1998] 3 WLR 1095, 1122 (Lord Goff).   [185] See p. 163 above.

[186] (1992) 175 CLR 353, 399.   [187] [1998] 3 WLR 1095, 1124 (Lord Goff).

[188] *Ibid*, p. 1126 (Lord Goff).

[189] 'No Consideration: Restitution after Void Contracts' (1993) 23 *Univ. WALR* 195, 230.

(4) Defendant entitled to the benefit

Lord Hope recognised that the plaintiff could not recover a benefit transferred to the defendant by reason of a mistake if the defendant was entitled to receive the benefit.[190] So, for example, if the defendant was entitled to receive money pursuant to a court order the plaintiff cannot recover it, even though the plaintiff had been mistaken as to the grounds on which the sum was due to the defendant.

3. RELIEF FROM TRANSACTIONS ENTERED INTO UNDER MISTAKE

Where the plaintiff enters into a transaction, usually a contract, because of a mistaken belief and then transfers a benefit to the defendant pursuant to this transaction, if the plaintiff wishes to recover this benefit he or she must first show that the transaction has been vitiated by the mistake. This is because the plaintiff must establish that he or she was not subject to a valid contractual obligation to transfer the benefit to the defendant before he or she can obtain restitution from the defendant.[191] In this type of case the mistake relates to the contract rather than the transfer of the benefit to the defendant. Although the question of the effect of mistake on the validity of the contract is a matter for the law of contract, it is still important to be aware of the doctrine of contractual mistake in a book on the law of restitution for two reasons: first, because where a benefit has been transferred to the defendant pursuant to a contract which was made by mistake, the question whether the plaintiff can obtain restitution of the benefit cannot be considered until it can be shown that the contract is no longer operating;[192] secondly, the definition of mistake for the purposes of the law of contract may have some implications for how mistake should be defined as a ground of restitution. Since, however, the doctrine of contractual mistake is adequately dealt with in textbooks on contract,[193] this book will only identify the key principles in outline.

When analysing the circumstances in which a contract may be vitiated for mistake it is necessary to distinguish between those cases where the contract is made void *ab initio* by the mistake and those where the mistake merely makes the contract voidable. Essentially this distinction derives from the different approaches at common law and equity. Where

---

[190] [1998] 3 WLR 1095, 1146.

[191] *Barclays Bank* v. *Simms* [1980] 1 QB 677, 695 (Robert Goff J).

[192] See p. 40 above.

[193] See especially Anson's *Law of Contract* by J. Beatson (27th edn., Oxford: Oxford University Press, 1998) Chapter 8.

a mistake has been made which the common law regards as sufficient to vitiate the contract that contract is automatically treated as null and void. Consequently the plaintiff can normally recover any benefits which have been transferred under it, with the ground of restitution being either mistake or total failure of consideration. Where equity regards the mistake as sufficient to vitiate the contract this will make it only voidable. For the plaintiff to avoid the contract it must be rescinded and then he or she will be able to recover the benefits which had been transferred to the defendant.[194]

(a) Transactions which are void for mistake

Although the common law recognises that a contract may be void by virtue of mistake[195] this will occur only in the most exceptional circumstances. This is because the policy of the law seeks to ensure that contracts, once made, are binding on the parties[196] for reasons of certainty and commercial convenience.[197] In certain situations, however, the plaintiff's mistake is so extreme that his or her intention to enter into a contract can be considered to be vitiated, so it is not possible to conclude that there was a true agreement between the parties.[198] There are two types of mistake which the law recognises as vitiating the intention to enter into the contract, namely mutual mistakes and unilateral mistakes. There is a related doctrine of *non est factum* which also renders a contract void. The plaintiff will not, however, be able to rely on the doctrine of mistake at common law in two circumstances: first, where there are no reasonable grounds for the plaintiff's mistaken belief;[199] secondly, the contract itself may expressly or impliedly state which party bears the risk of the mistake and this will exclude the operation of the common law doctrine.[200]

(i) Mutual mistakes

Mutual mistakes are mistakes which are shared by the parties to the contract. The test which is adopted to identify when a mutual mistake will

---

[194] See pp. 28–36 above.

[195] See *Associated Japanese Bank (International) Ltd.* v. *Crédit du Nord SA* [1989] 1 WLR 255. Cp. Lord Denning MR in *Magee* v. *Pennine Insurance Co. Ltd.* [1969] 2 QB 507, 514; *Chitty on Contracts* (27th edn., London: Sweet & Maxwell, 1994).

[196] This is traditionally expressed by reference to the Latin maxim *pacta sunt servanda*. See *Bell* v. *Lever Bros. Ltd.* [1932] AC 161, 224 (Lord Atkin); *Associated Japanese Bank (International) Ltd.* v. *Crédit du Nord SA* [1989] 1 WLR 255, 268 (Steyn J).

[197] Needham, 'Mistaken Payments: A New Look at an Old Theme' (1979) 10 *Univ. Brit. Col. LR* 159, 164.

[198] This is sometimes described as the parties not being *ad idem*—not of one mind.

[199] *Associated Japanese Bank (International) Ltd.* v. *Crédit du Nord SA* [1989] 1 WLR 255, 268–9 (Steyn J).

[200] *Ibid*, at p. 268.

render a contract void is that of fundamental mistake.[201] In *Kennedy* v. *Panama, New Zealand and Australian Royal Mail Co.*[202] Blackburn J recognised that such a mistake must relate to 'the substance of the whole consideration, going, as it were, to the root of the matter'. Examples of such mistakes include mistakes as to the existence, identity or quantity of the subject-matter of the contract, mistakes as to the title to the subject-matter of the contract and mistakes relating to the possibility of performing the contract.

In every case it is a matter of degree whether the mutual mistake of the parties is so important that it relates to the very foundation of the contract. If the mistake is not as serious as this it will not operate to vitiate the parties' intention to enter into the contract. This is illustrated by the decision of the House of Lords in *Bell* v. *Lever Brothers Ltd.*[203] In this case an employer wished to terminate the service contracts of two employees, and it agreed to make them compensation payments. In fact the employer could have sacked the employees summarily without compensation because they had breached their contract of employment by working on their own account when they should have been working for it. The House of Lords held that the employer's mistaken assumption that it could terminate the employees' contracts only if compensation was paid, a mistake which was shared by the employees, was not a fundamental mistake. This was presumably because the mistake did not relate to the validity or operation of the contract, but merely related to the employer's motivation for entering into it. In other words, there was no mistake as to what was paid but only as to the reason for making the payment. Consequently, the employer was not able to recover the compensation payments which it had paid to the employees.

(ii) Unilateral mistakes

A unilateral mistake arises where there is a mistake in the communications between the parties to the contract so that no genuine contract is formed between them. This will be the case where there is no correspondence between the offer of one party and the acceptance of the other. So, for example, where one party offers to sell his bicycle for £5,000 and the other party agrees to purchase it for £2,000 there is no genuine agreement between them and the contract is void. The main examples of such unilateral mistakes include mistakes as to the terms of the contract[204] or the identity of the other party to the agreement.[205]

---

[201] *Bell* v. *Lever Bros. Ltd.* [1932] AC 161, 224 (Lord Atkin). See also *Norwich Union Fire Insurance Society Ltd.* v. *Price* [1934] AC 455 and *Midland Bank plc.* v. *Brown Shipley and Co. Ltd.* [1991] 2 All ER 690.

[202] (1876) LR 2 QB 580, 588.   [203] [1932] AC 161.

[204] See *Smith* v. *Hughes* (1871) LR 6 QB 597.

[205] *Boulton* v. *Jones* (1857) 2 H and N 564; 157 ER 232 and *Cundy* v. *Lindsay* (1878) 3 App.

(iii) The doctrine of non est factum

The essence of the common law doctrine of *non est factum* is that a writ-ten contract will be considered to be void where one of the signatories to it was misled into signing a document which was radically different from that which he or she intended to sign. This doctrine is restrictively inter-preted, since it will apply only where the plaintiff who wishes to rely on it can be considered to have acted reasonably in signing the document.[206] The leading case on the operation of the doctrine is the decision of the House of Lords in *Saunders* v. *Anglia Building Society*[207] where the plain-tiff, an old woman, was induced to sign a deed which she thought assigned the lease of her house to her nephew, when in fact the deed assigned the lease to her nephew's business associate. Since the plain-tiff's spectacles were broken she was unable to read the document but relied on the assignee's representation that the deed involved a gift to her nephew. The plaintiff claimed that the deed was void, but the claim failed for two reasons: first, because there was no radical difference between what the plaintiff thought she was signing and what she actually signed[208]—this was because the plaintiff was not mistaken in thinking that the deed assigned the lease of her house, the mistake only related to the identity of the assignee; secondly, since the plaintiff could have taken the trouble to find out what the effect of the document was, her failure to do so meant that she had acted unreasonably in signing it and so her sig-nature was valid. It would have been different if she were blind or illiter-ate since then she would have been compelled to rely on someone else to explain to her the effect of the deed. The consequence of this decision is that it is very difficult for the plaintiff to establish that a transaction is void by virtue of the *non est factum* doctrine.

(iv) The consequences of a contract being void for mistake

Once the contract has been held to be void for mistake or by virtue of the *non est factum* doctrine, the plaintiff can secure restitution of any bene-fits transferred under it. The plaintiff's claim may be founded either on the vindication of property rights, if the mistake was so fundamental that title to property did not pass to the defendant,[209] or on the reversal of the defendant's unjust enrichment. As regards the latter principle, it follows

---

Cas. 459. The so-called *inter praesentes* exception applies here, so that if the plaintiff and the defendant make a contract in each other's presence a mistake as to identity will not viti-ate it, since the parties can see with whom they are contracting: see *Phillips* v. *Brooks Ltd.* [1919] 2 KB 243.

[206] *Avon Finance Co. Ltd.* v. *Bridger* [1985] 2 All ER 281.   [207] [1971] AC 1004.
[208] *Ibid*, p. 1017 (Lord Reid). See also Lord Hodson at p. 1019 who said that the difference must go to the substance of the whole consideration or to the root of the matter.
[209] See pp. 607–10 below.

from the fact that the contract has been vitiated for mistake that any benefit which has been received by the defendant from the plaintiff pursuant to the transaction will have been received in circumstances of injustice. Where, for example, the plaintiff has paid the defendant under a contract believing that he or she was obliged to do so, and this contract is avoided by reason of a mutual or unilateral mistake, it is possible to show that the defendant was enriched at the plaintiff's expense and the ground for restitution is usually the mistake. For if the plaintiff's mistake was sufficient to vitiate the contract it must follow that the plaintiff's mistaken belief in the validity of the contract was the operating cause of his or her payment to the defendant.[210]

(b) Transactions which are voidable for mistake

Whereas the doctrine of mistake at common law operates to make the contract void, a mistake in equity will make the contract only voidable, so the plaintiff must then seek to rescind it if he or she wishes it to be set aside. Consequently, if the parties have made a fundamental mistake, as defined by the common law, the contract will be void and there is no function for the equitable doctrine of mistake, simply because there is no contract to rescind. In equity a mistake will be relevant only if it is a common mistake shared by both parties.[211]

Confusingly, the test which is used by equity to identify those mistakes which are capable of avoiding a contract is characterised as a test of fundamental mistake, but analysis of the case law shows that this test is interpreted much more liberally than the equivalent test of the common law. The leading case on the equitable doctrine of mistake is *Solle* v. *Butcher*,[212] where the defendant let a flat to the plaintiff. Both parties mistakenly believed that the Rent Acts did not apply to the lease. Since the Acts were in fact applicable the defendant had charged the plaintiff too much rent for the flat. The Court of Appeal set the lease aside because the parties had made a fundamental mistake. The essence of this equitable jurisdiction to set aside a contract for mistake can be found in the judgment of Denning LJ, who said that:

[a] contract is . . . liable in equity to be set aside if the parties were under a common misapprehension either as to facts or as to their relative and respective

---

[210] Alternatively the plaintiff may rely on the ground of total failure of consideration: see *Strickland* v. *Turner* (1852) 7 Ex. 208; 155 ER 919; or absence of consideration. See Chapter 12.

[211] *Cooper* v. *Phibbs* (1867) LR 2 HL 147, 170 (Lord Westbury). For detailed analysis of the equitable doctrine of mistake, see *Chitty's Law of Contract* (27th edn.) pp. 328–31.

[212] [1950] 1 KB 671.

rights, provided that the misapprehension was fundamental and that the party seeking to set it aside was not himself at fault.[213]

He went on to add that a court would set aside a contract for mistake when it was of opinion that it was 'unconscientious for the other party to avail himself of the legal advantage' which he or she had obtained.[214] Goff and Jones conclude from this and subsequent decisions that 'the courts have an equitable jurisdiction to set aside contracts where the parties' mistake is substantial but not so fundamental as to render the contract void at law. But it is not clear how substantial the mistake must be before relief is granted in equity'.[215]

Three cases decided after *Solle* v. *Butcher* provide little assistance in determining what constitutes a sufficient mistake to trigger the equitable jurisdiction to set a contract aside. In *Grist* v. *Bailey*[216] the parties had entered into a contract to sell a house, where the contract was expressly subject to an existing tenancy. Both parties mistakenly thought this was a protected tenancy. Goff J held that this mistake was not sufficient to make the contract void at law, but it did trigger the equitable jurisdiction to rescind the contract.[217] In *Magee* v. *Pennine Insurance Co. Ltd.*[218] a compromise of an insurance claim made by an insurance company was set aside because both the insurer and the assured mistakenly believed that the insurance policy was binding, when in fact it was voidable for innocent misrepresentation. This common mistaken belief that the policy was valid was regarded by a majority of the Court of Appeal as a fundamental mistake, even though the mistake did not relate to the nature of the compromise, since no mistake was made as to the terms of the settlement, but only as to whether there was a dispute which could be compromised. In other words, the mistake related to the need to make a settlement rather than the substance of the settlement itself. Finally, in *Laurence* v. *Lexcourt Holdings Ltd.*[219] a mistake that planning permission was available to enable particular premises to be used as offices was characterised as a fundamental mistake in equity, even though the mistake related to the legal suitability of the land for a particular use rather than its physical description.

---

[213] [1950] 1 KB 671, pp. 692–3. Presumably, with the abolition of the mistake of law bar, mistakes as to law can also constitute a fundamental mistake.

[214] *Ibid*, p. 693.   [215] Goff and Jones, *The Law of Restitution*, p. 293.

[216] [1967] Ch. 532.

[217] This result was doubted by Hoffmann LJ in *William Sindall plc.* v. *Cambridgeshire CC* [1994] 1 WLR 1016, 1035 on the ground that Goff J had not considered whether the contract had allocated the risk of mistake to the plaintiff.

[218] [1969] 2 QB 507.

[219] [1978] 1 WLR 1128. This case was also doubted by Hoffmann LJ in *William Sindall plc.* v. *Cambridgeshire CC* [1994] 1 WLR 1016, 1035 because the trial judge failed to consider whether the contract had allocated the risk of mistake to the plaintiff.

Analysis of these cases brings us no nearer to identifying which types of mistake will be sufficient to set aside a contract in equity. In *Gibbon* v. *Mitchell*,[220] however, Millett J emphasised that the mistake must relate to the effect of the transaction rather than to the consequences of it or the advantages to be gained from entering into it. In other words, the mistake must relate to the substance of the transaction itself rather than the plaintiff's motive for entering into it. If this is correct it means that the decision in *Magee* v. *Pennine Insurance Co. Ltd.* is particularly difficult to justify.

One further matter of uncertainty arises from Denning LJ's suggestion in *Solle* v. *Butcher*[221] that the plaintiff would not be able to rescind the contract for mistake if he or she were at fault, but it remains unclear what constitutes fault in this context.[222] Clearly if the plaintiff knew of the mistake then he or she could not rescind the contract, simply because there was no common mistake shared by the plaintiff and the defendant.[223] Presumably if the plaintiff suspected a mistake had been made, he or she would also be prevented from rescinding the contract. A further limitation on the right to rescind the contract for mistake arises where the contract provides which party bears the risk of mistake, regardless of whether this is provided for expressly, impliedly or by operation of law. If the contract allocates the risk of mistake to the plaintiff he or she will not be able to rescind the contract by virtue of the mistake.[224]

Transactions which involve the plaintiff making a gift by deed may also be avoided in equity by virtue of mistake. This was recognised in *Ogilvie* v. *Littleboy*,[225] although the mistake in that case was insufficiently serious to allow the court to set aside two deeds which had created a charitable trust. In *Lady Hood of Avalon* v. *Mackinnon*,[226] however, a deed was set aside where the plaintiff had appointed property for the benefit of one of her daughters, forgetting that she had made provision for the daughter previously. This was regarded as a sufficiently serious mistake to enable the court to rescind the deed, since the plaintiff had never intended to make double provision for the daughter.

Where a contract may be rescinded in equity for mistake, it continues to be valid until it is rescinded.[227] Once rescinded, the policy of the law is

---

[220] [1990] 1 WLR 1304, 1309.   [221] [1950] 1 KB 671, 693.

[222] *Grist* v. *Bailey* [1967] Ch. 532, 542 (Goff J).

[223] *Magee* v. *Pennine Insurance Co. Ltd.* [1969] 2 QB 507, 516 (Lord Denning MR).

[224] *William Sindall plc.* v. *Cambridgeshire CC* [1994] 1 WLR 1016, 1035 (Hoffmann LJ).

[225] (1897) 12 TLR 399, CA; affirmed by the House of Lords (1899) 15 TLR 294.

[226] [1909] 1 Ch. 476.

[227] An alternative remedy to rescission is rectification of the contract. See *Gibbon* v. *Mitchell* [1990] 1 WLR 1304 and *Commissioner for the New Towns* v. *Cooper (Great Britain) Ltd.* [1995] 2 Ch. 259. Rectification is not a restitutionary remedy since it involves the court imposing a new bargain on the parties rather than restoring them to the position they occupied before entering into the agreement.

to ensure that the parties are returned to the position they occupied before entering into the contract, so there may be restitutionary conse- quences.[228] But the nature of rescission is such that the consequences of rescission are not necessarily restitutionary. For example, in *Solle* v. *Butcher*[229] the contract was rescinded on condition that the defendant allowed the plaintiff to remain in the flat as a licensee pending the grant of a new lease.

(c) Misrepresentation[230]

(i) The test of misrepresentation

Where the plaintiff enters into a contract in reliance on a misrepresenta- tion the contract will be either void or voidable depending on the nature of the plaintiff's induced mistake.[231] Where the plaintiff's mistake which has been induced by the misrepresentor can be characterised as fraudu- lent, the contract will be voidable at common law.[232] Where the misrep- resentation did not induce a fraudulent mistake the contract may still be rescinded in equity if the misrepresentation materially contributed to the plaintiff's decision to contract with the defendant, even though the plaintiff may have been influenced by other considerations.[233] Consequently, it is not necessary to show that the misrepresentation was the 'but for' cause of the plaintiff entering into the contract; it suffices that it was a contributory cause. The reason for this generous test of cau- sation is simply that the misrepresentor has interfered with the risks involved in the bargaining process between the parties, and this makes it easier to justify setting the contract aside. Equally there are no dangers of the plaintiff fabricating the mistake where the mistake was induced by a clear misrepresentation of another party.

The law on what constitutes a misrepresentation for these purposes is complex. Essentially, the defendant must have made a representation which is false. The representation must usually relate to existing facts, rather than opinion or law, though a contract may be rescinded for mis- representation of law where the defendant has acted fraudulently.[234] A

---

[228] Whether rescission is a restitutionary remedy in its own right is considered at p. 28 above.

[229] [1950] 1 KB 671. See also *Grist* v. *Bailey* [1967] Ch. 532 where the contract of sale of a house was set aside on terms that a new contract was entered into for the sale of the house at an appropriate price.

[230] For detailed analysis of the law see Chitty, *The Law of Contract*, Chapter 6.

[231] If the misrepresentation is included as a term of the contract the plaintiff may be able to terminate it for breach and recover damages for loss, but only if the breach is sufficiently serious.

[232] See p. 31 above.   [233] *Edgington* v. *Fitzmaurice* (1885) 29 Ch.D 459.

[234] *West London Commercial Bank* v. *Kitson* (1884) 13 QBD 360. Although the matter was not discussed by the House of Lords in *Kleinwort Benson Ltd.* v. *Lincoln City Council* [1998]

promise made by the defendant may constitute a misrepresentation where the promise involves a statement of the defendant's existing state of mind which is untrue. So, in *Edgington* v. *Fitzmaurice*[235] a statement in a company's prospectus, which invited subscriptions for debentures, stated that the purpose of the debentures was to enable the company to complete building operations and to develop its trade. In fact, the real purpose of the debentures was to enable the directors to discharge pressing liabilities. The Court of Appeal held that the statement in the prospectus was a representation of fact rather than intention and, since the directors never intended to use the money raised in the way they had suggested in the prospectus, the statement constituted a misrepresentation. Usually a misrepresentation involves a false statement being made by the defendant, but misrepresentations may also arise from the defendant's conduct or where the defendant fails to correct a representation which was initially true but was falsified by subsequent events.[236]

(ii) The consequences of misrepresentation

Once it has been established that there is an operative misrepresentation which has induced the plaintiff to enter into a contract, the remedies which are available are complex and are not necessarily restitutionary. If the misrepresentation was made fraudulently or negligently, the plaintiff may recover damages to compensate him or her for loss suffered.[237] There is also a statutory right to damages if the misrepresentation was made other then fraudulently, save where the misrepresentor can prove that he or she had reasonable grounds for believing and did believe up to the time when the contract was made that the representation was true.[238] The plaintiff alternatively has a right to rescind the contract, regardless of whether the representation was made fraudulently, negligently or innocently.

The right to rescind a contract for misrepresentation is subject to the usual bars.[239] In addition, it may be excluded by the contract, so long as the provision is clear and reasonable[240] and reasonable steps have been taken to draw it to the notice of the plaintiff. There is also one specific bar to rescission which arises where the plaintiff was induced to enter into a contract by the defendant's innocent or negligent misrepresentation. In

---

3 WLR 1095, presumably the abolition of the mistake of law bar in that case will mean that all types of misrepresentation can encompass representations as to the law, regardless of whether the misrepresentation was fraudulent, negligent or innocent.

[235] (1885) 29 Ch.D 459.   [236] *Briess* v. *Woolley* [1954] AC 333.
[237] For the torts of deceit and negligent misrepresentation see *Doyle* v. *Olby (Ironmongers) Ltd.* [1969] 2 QB 158 and *Hedley Byrne and Co. Ltd.* v. *Heller and Partners Ltd.* [1964] AC 465 respectively.
[238] Misrepresentation Act 1967, s. 2(1).   [239] See pp. 32–6 above.
[240] *Walker* v. *Boyle* [1982] 1 WLR 495.

such circumstances section 2(2) of the Misrepresentation Act 1967 provides that the court may order that damages be awarded in lieu of rescission. Section 2(2) identifies certain factors which should particularly be considered by the court when deciding whether to exercise this discretion, namely the nature of the misrepresentation, the loss to the misrepresentee if the contract is not rescinded and the loss to the misrepresentor which would arise from rescission. Consequently, the court would probably award damages in lieu of rescission where the misrepresentation can be characterised as trivial or where the harm to the misrepresentor if rescission were ordered clearly outweighs any advantages of rescission to the plaintiff.[241] Where the court orders that damages should be awarded in lieu of rescission, the plaintiff's remedy will be compensatory rather than restitutionary. This power to award damages will be available even though the plaintiff is no longer able to rescind the contract as long as he or she had been able to rescind the contract at some point in the past.[242]

(iii) Misrepresentation and third parties

Where the plaintiff is induced to enter into a contract by virtue of a misrepresentation but he or she enters into a contract with a third party and not with the misrepresentor, the question whether the plaintiff can rescind the contract is particularly complex. This scenario has arisen most frequently recently where a husband makes a misrepresentation to his wife to induce her to enter into a transaction with a bank whereby the wife agrees to act as surety for her husband's debts. Usually this security takes the form of a charge over the matrimonial home in which the wife has a proprietary interest. Where the husband fails to pay his debts the bank will wish to enforce its security by requiring the matrimonial home to be sold. The resolution of this dispute is particularly difficult because it is between two innocent parties, the wife and the bank, with the husband not being a party to the proceedings. The policy question is therefore which of two innocent parties should bear the loss. The House of Lords decided in *Barclays Bank plc.* v. *O'Brien*[243] that the wife would be able to rescind the transaction if she could show the bank had actual or constructive notice of the misrepresentation. This is because where the bank has notice of the wife's equity to set the transaction aside the bank can be considered to be more responsible for entering into the transac-

---

[241] See *William Sindall plc.* v. *Cambridgeshire CC* [1994] 1 WLR 1016, 1036–8 (Hoffmann LJ).

[242] *Thomas Witter Ltd.* v. *TBP Industries Ltd.* [1996] 2 All ER 573, 590 (Jacob J). Cp. *Atlantic Lines and Navigation* v. *Hallam* [1983] 1 Lloyd's Rep. 188. See Beale, 'Points on Misrepresentation' (1995) 111 *LQR* 385.

[243] [1994] 1 AC 180. See pp. 265–77 below.

tion and so should bear the loss. A bank will have such constructive notice where the transaction is not on its face to the wife's advantage and there is a substantial risk that the husband has made a misrepresentation to induce the wife to enter into the transaction. Where, however, the bank can show that it has taken reasonable steps to ensure that the wife has not been induced to act by a misrepresentation then it will not be bound by the wife's equity to set the transaction aside. This is because the nature of the bank's conduct is such that it should not be considered to bear the responsibility for the misrepresentation. The bank will be considered to have taken reasonable steps where, for example, it receives confirmation from a solicitor that the wife has received legal advice before she entered into the transaction.[244]

Although the decision of the House of Lords in *O'Brien* concerned a wife who entered into a transaction with the bank as a result of her husband's misrepresentation, that decision also applies where the wife entered into the transaction as a result of her husband's undue influence. The role of the constructive notice doctrine where the wife has been unduly influenced to enter into the transaction is generally defensible, but the application of that doctrine to cases where the wife entered into the transaction as a result of a misrepresentation has been criticised,[245] most notably by Lord Jauncey, dissenting, in *Smith* v. *Bank of Scotland*,[246] a decision of the House of Lords in an appeal from the Scottish Court of Session. Lord Jauncey said:

I have the greatest difficulty in seeing why such constructive knowledge should extend to misrepresentation. There has so far as I am aware never been any suggestion in the law of Scotland that any particular class of persons is more likely to misrepresent in relation to a contract than any other class.[247]

The real concern about the application of the *O'Brien* principle to cases involving misrepresentation is that a bank will be found to have constructive notice of the husband's conduct only where there was an emotional relationship of trust and confidence between the wife and her husband, and such a relationship hints at a risk of undue influence and not misrepresentation.[248] But this argument is not convincing. Whilst it

---

[244] *Royal Bank of Scotland* v. *Etridge (No. 2)* [1998] 4 All ER 705. For more detailed discussion of when a bank will be deemed to have constructive notice of the wife's equity to set the transaction aside and what constitutes the taking of reasonable steps, see pp. 268–74 below.

[245] See in particular O'Sullivan, 'Undue Influence and Misrepresentation after *O'Brien*: Making Security Secure' in *Restitution and Banking Law* (ed. Rose, Oxford: Mansfield Press, 1998) pp. 46–8.

[246] 1997 SCLR 765.

[247] *Ibid*, p. 769. Despite this criticism, the House of Lords decided that the *O'Brien* principle should apply in Scotland, even as regards cases involving misrepresentation.

[248] O'Sullivan in *Restitution and Banking Law* (ed. Rose), pp. 46–7. O'Sullivan also criticises the application of the *O'Brien* principle to cases involving misrepresentation because

may indeed be true that a relationship of trust and confidence is more likely to suggest that the husband has unduly influenced his wife than that he has made a misrepresentation to her, this simply means that it will be more difficult to establish that the bank had constructive notice of the husband's conduct in making a misrepresentation. But this is a question of evidence and not substance. There is no reason in principle why a bank should not be considered to have constructive notice of the husband's misrepresentation.

It is right that the *O'Brien* principle should apply to cases of misrepresentation as well as to undue influence. Indeed, it would be much more difficult to justify confining the principle to cases of undue influence where the issue in both contexts is the same, namely which of two innocent parties should suffer loss arising from the husband's misconduct. The doctrines of actual and constructive notice are entirely appropriate in identifying who should suffer this loss, regardless of whether the factor which vitiates the transaction is undue influence or misrepresentation.

Although the *O'Brien* principle has so far only been applied to cases in which the relationship between the misrepresentor and the misrepresentee has been a relationship of trust and confidence, there is no obvious reason why the principle should be confined to such cases. The principle should be applicable in any case where the misrepresentee enters into a transaction as a result of a misrepresentation from a person who is not a party to the transaction, regardless of the nature of the relationship between the misrepresentor and misrepresentee. In all such cases it should be necessary to consider whether the other party to the transaction had actual or constructive notice of the misrepresentation. It will, of course, be much more difficult to show that that party did have notice where the relationship between the misrepresentor and misrepresentee was not based on trust and confidence and was, for example, a purely commercial relationship. But it does not follow from the fact that this will be difficult to establish that the *O'Brien* principle should be artificially restricted to cases involving relationships of trust and confidence.

(d) Non-disclosure

Usually a failure by the defendant to disclose material facts to the plaintiff will not enable the plaintiff to rescind the contract.[249] However, in certain limited circumstances the defendant's failure to disclose material facts

---

this is inconsistent with the restrictive rules on pre-contract disclosure. But this argument is not convincing. See Virgo, 'A Commentary' in *Restitution and Banking Law* (ed. Rose), pp. 74–5.

[249] See *Smith* v. *Hughes* (1871) LR 6 QB 597.

will make the contract voidable where the plaintiff was induced to enter into the contract by reason of the non-disclosure. The duty to disclose material facts will arise only in special circumstances, most notably in the context of contracts of insurance[250] or surety transactions where the creditor is under a duty to disclose any unusual feature of the contract between the debtor and the creditor which makes the contract materially different in a potentially disadvantageous respect from that which the surety would naturally expect.[251]

The role of rescission for non-disclosure of material facts is illustrated by *Sybron* v. *Rochem*[252] where the plaintiff employer had made a contract with the defendant whereby the defendant agreed to take early retirement in return for a payment of £13,000. The defendant had, however, failed to disclose the fraudulent misconduct of his subordinate employees as he was required to do, so making the contractual settlement voidable. The plaintiff was held to be able to rescind the contract and recover the money which had been paid to the defendant because the defendant had failed to disclose material facts.

4. REFORM OF THE LAW

Even though the mistake of law rule has been abolished, we are still left with a body of law which is confused and uncertain, since, as the Law Commission has acknowledged, 'many questions . . . have still to be conclusively resolved by the common law in relation to mistake of fact'.[253] It is still not possible to say with complete confidence exactly what the test is for identifying those mistakes which will operate as grounds for restitution. The notion that restitutionary claims founded on mistake are barred where the plaintiff acted voluntarily is also too uncertain. Probably the most important question which needs to be clarified relates to the relevance of the plaintiff's fault when considering whether restitution should be ordered. These uncertainties are such that there is still a need for a comprehensive statutory scheme concerning restitution for all types of mistake.

---

[250] See, for example, *Cornhill Insurance Co. Ltd.* v. *L and B. Assenheim* (1937) 58 Ll. L Rep. 27 and *Pan Atlantic Insurance Co. Ltd.* v. *Pine Top Insurance Co. Ltd.* [1995] 1 AC 501.

[251] *Levett* v. *Barclays Bank plc.* [1995] 1 WLR 1260. [252] [1984] Ch. 112.

[253] 'Restitution: Mistakes of Law and *Ultra Vires* Public Authority Receipts and Payments' (Law Com. No. 227, 1994) para. 4.2.

9

Compulsion

1. GENERAL PRINCIPLES

(a) The principle of compulsion

Although compulsion is not a ground of restitution in its own right, it is a general principle which underlies a number of specific grounds of restitution, most notably duress. The essence of the principle of compulsion is that it arises where pressure has been placed on the plaintiff to transfer a benefit to the defendant. Compulsion operates in a similar way to mistake as an explanation of why the receipt of an enrichment by the defendant can be regarded as unjust, namely that the effect of the pressure is treated as vitiating the plaintiff's intention that the defendant should receive the enrichment. This is because, where the plaintiff is pressurised into transferring a benefit to the defendant, his or her freedom of choice has been interfered with to such an extent that he or she cannot be considered to have wanted the defendant to receive the benefit.

(b) Different types of enrichment

Although the reported cases have all concerned claims for the restitution of money paid as a result of compulsion, there is no reason why restitutionary claims cannot be founded on this principle where the plaintiff has been compelled to transfer non-money benefits to the defendant. Where the plaintiff has been compelled to transfer goods or to provide services it is still possible to conclude that the plaintiff's intention to transfer the benefit has been vitiated as a result of the compulsion. Although it is usually more difficult to establish that the defendant has been enriched by the receipt of goods or services,[1] this is less so where the defendant compelled the plaintiff to transfer the benefit to him or her, simply because the fact of compulsion suggests that the defendant valued the benefit, and so he or she will not be able to rely on the principle of subjective devaluation.[2]

---

[1] See Chapter 4.   [2] See p. 64 above.

(c) Vitiation of contracts for compulsion

Whereas the definition of mistake as a ground of restitution differs depending on whether it is necessary to set aside a contract before the plaintiff can obtain restitution,[3] this is not the case with those grounds of restitution which are founded on compulsion. These grounds are defined in exactly the same way regardless of whether the plaintiff simply wishes to bring a pure restitutionary claim or first needs to set a contract aside for compulsion before restitution is available.[4] This is presumably because, unlike cases where the plaintiff entered into a contract as a result of a spontaneous mistake but like cases where the plaintiff entered into a contract as a result of an induced mistake, the defendant's conduct in compelling the plaintiff to enter into a contract is such that it is easier to set the contract aside. Consequently, the grounds of restitution which are used to show that the plaintiff's intention to transfer a benefit to the defendant was vitiated by the compulsion can also be used to show that the plaintiff did not intend to contract with the defendant, without any difference of definition.

Even though the grounds of restitution are the same, it is still necessary to distinguish between those cases where the plaintiff transferred a benefit to the defendant pursuant to a contract and those where there was no contract in existence for two reasons.

(i) The time factor

The time at which the compulsion must have been operating depends on the nature of the claim. For the purposes of setting aside a contract the compulsion must have been operating when the contract was made. Where, however, the plaintiff wishes to recover a non-contractual payment it is simply sufficient to show that the compulsion was operative at the time of the payment.

(ii) The contract must cease to operate before restitutionary remedies can be awarded

If the plaintiff has transferred a benefit to the defendant pursuant to a contract which he or she was compelled to enter into the plaintiff cannot obtain restitution until the contract has been set aside. This is because of the fundamental principle of the law of restitution that restitutionary relief cannot be used to subvert contracts.[5] Where the defendant

---

[3] See Chapter 8.

[4] In *CTN Cash and Carry Ltd.* v. *Gallaher Ltd.* [1994] 4 All ER 714, 717 Steyn LJ said that it did not matter, for the purposes of defining economic duress, whether the plaintiff had agreed to pay money to the defendant or had simply paid the money unilaterally, since the same definition of duress applied.

[5] See p. 40 above.

compelled the plaintiff to make a contract, this renders the contract voidable and not void.[6] Consequently, if the plaintiff wishes to recover benefits transferred under such a contract by reason of compulsion it is first necessary to rescind the contract.[7] Rescission will be barred, however, if the plaintiff affirmed it after the compulsion had ceased to operate,[8] if rescission has been unreasonably delayed, if third party rights have intervened or if the plaintiff is unable to make counter-restitution to the defendant of benefits which the plaintiff had received from the defendant.[9]

(d) The grounds of restitution

A number of different grounds of restitution can be considered to be founded on the principle of compulsion. Chief amongst these are the grounds of duress of the person, duress of goods and economic duress. But the principle of compulsion also underlies other restitutionary grounds such as undue pressure and legal compulsion.

The principle can also be interpreted to underlie other grounds of restitution, where the plaintiff has been pressurised to transfer a benefit to the defendant, but for reasons of convenience these grounds of restitution are considered in separate chapters because they are also affected by other principles. This is true of three grounds of restitution in particular.

(i) Necessity

There are cases in which the plaintiff is compelled to provide a benefit to the defendant, not because of threats made by the defendant, but by virtue of the pressure of surrounding circumstances. This necessitous intervention is clearly related to the principle of compulsion but it deserves to be treated separately because of the complex policy issues which are raised in determining in what circumstances necessity should operate as a ground of restitution.[10]

---

[6] *The Universe Sentinel* [1983] 1 AC 366, 383 (Lord Diplock) and 400 (Lord Scarman). See also *The Evia Luck* [1992] 2 AC 152, 168 (Lord Goff). In *Barton* v. *Armstrong* [1976] AC 104, 120, the Privy Council found that threats to kill the plaintiff avoided a deed which was entered into as a result of the threats. This decision is explicable either because of the extreme nature of the threats or, more likely, because the plaintiff had sought a declaration that the deed was void and the form of the declaration which was granted had not been challenged by the defendant.

[7] See p. 28 above.

[8] *Mutual Finance Ltd.* v. *John Wetton and Sons Ltd.* [1937] 2 KB 389, 397 (Porter J.). In *The Atlantic Baron* [1979] QB 705 affirmation of a contract prevented the plaintiff from rescinding it for economic duress.

[9] See pp. 32–5 above.   [10] See Chapter 11.

(ii) Undue influence

Where the plaintiff has transferred a benefit to the defendant as a result of undue influence, this influence may sometimes involve the exercise of pressure on the plaintiff to transfer the benefit. But this is not necessarily the case, and consequently undue influence is more accurately analysed in terms of exploitation rather than compulsion.[11]

(iii) Colore officii

The ground of *colore officii* arises where a plaintiff is compelled to pay the defendant to secure the performance of a public duty which the defendant should perform for nothing or for less than the sum demanded.[12] Whilst this ground of restitution is clearly founded on notions of compulsion, because it is a necessary condition that the public officer exerted illegitimate pressure to obtain the payment, it is more convenient to consider it in the context of restitutionary claims from public authorities.[13] This is primarily because recent developments in this area of the law of restitution may mean that the ground of *colore officii* has been subsumed within a general ground of restitution involving the recovery of unauthorised payments made to public authorities.[14]

(e) Illegality

Despite the general principle that the plaintiff's restitutionary claim will be defeated by the defence of illegality if the transfer of a benefit to the defendant is illegal,[15] the plaintiff will be able to bring a restitutionary claim by virtue of compulsion despite the illegality. So, for example, in *Astley* v. *Reynolds*[16] the plaintiff was able to recover interest payments which he had paid to the defendant to recover his goods which the defendant had threatened to hold onto until the interest was paid. The ground of restitution in this case was duress of goods, and it made no difference to the plaintiff's claim that the interest payments were illegal. Similarly, in *Davies* v. *London and Provincial Marine Insurance Co.*[17] it was held that the plaintiff was able to recover money which he had been compelled to pay to the defendant as a result of the defendant's threat to prosecute the plaintiff, even though the transaction was illegal for stifling a prosecution.

---

[11] See Chapter 10.
[12] See, for example, *Steele* v. *Williams* (1853) 8 Ex. 625; 155 ER 1502.
[13] See Chapter 14.
[14] *Woolwich Equitable Building Society* v. *IRC* [1993] AC 70, 198 (Lord Browne-Wilkinson).
[15] See Chapter 26. [16] (1731) 2 Stra. 915; 93 ER 939.
[17] (1878) 8 Ch.D 469.

2. DURESS

(a) Its rationale as a ground of restitution

Essentially duress operates as a ground of restitution where the plaintiff has transferred a benefit to the defendant as a result either of the exercise of actual pressure or the making of an illegitimate threat. This illegitimate threat may be made either expressly or implied from surrounding circumstances,[18] but it must take the form of 'do this or else . . . '.

The reason a plaintiff who succumbs to the illegitimate threat or pressure by transferring a benefit to the defendant should be able to obtain restitution is usually considered to be that the effect of the threat or pressure is to vitiate the plaintiff's intention that the defendant should receive the benefit.[19] But this notion that the duress vitiates intent is not strictly accurate, since the plaintiff has a choice whether or not to transfer the benefit to the defendant; the plaintiff does not need to submit to the threat or the pressure, but chooses to do so.[20] The real reason, therefore, that duress should be recognised as a ground of restitution is simply that the effect of the duress is that the plaintiff cannot be regarded as having exercised a free choice when he or she transferred a benefit to the defendant. In other words, the duress interferes with the plaintiff's autonomy to benefit whom he or she wishes without constraint. This was recognised by Lord Scarman in *The Universe Sentinel*:

> The classic case of duress is . . . not the lack of will to submit but the victim's intentional submission arising from the realisation that there is no other practical choice open to him.[21]

(b) The elements of duress

When determining whether the plaintiff can rely on duress as a ground of restitution, two separate questions always need to be examined.[22]

---

[18] *Woolwich Equitable Building Society* v. *IRC* [1993] AC 70, 165 (Lord Goff).

[19] See, for example, *Barton* v. *Armstrong* [1976] AC 104, 121 (Lords Wilberforce and Simon).

[20] This was recognised by the House of Lords in *DPP for Northern Ireland* v. *Lynch* [1975] AC 653. Lord Simon, at p. 695, said that 'duress is not inconsistent with act and will, the will being deflected and not destroyed'.

[21] [1983] 1 AC 366, 400.

[22] As was recognised by the Privy Council in *Barton* v. *Armstrong* [1976] AC 104, 121 (Lords Wilberforce and Simon). See also *The Universe Sentinel* [1983] 1 AC 366, 400 (Lord Scarman) and *The Evia Luck* [1992] 2 AC 152, 165 (Lord Goff).

(i) Illegitimate threats and pressure

Duress involves either the defendant threatening to do something unless the plaintiff transfers a benefit to him or her or the actual exertion of pressure until the benefit is transferred.

A useful definition of 'threats' has been suggested by Smith who says that

[a] threat is a proposal to bring about an unwelcome event unless the recipient of the proposal does something (e.g. enter a contract), where the proposal is made because the event is unwelcome and in order to induce the recipient to do the thing requested.[23]

It is possible in principle to distinguish a threat from a warning, on the basis that the person making the warning does not have control over whether the unwelcome consequence will occur.[24] Similarly, a threat is different from a request, which involves the defendant asking for something. Although a theoretical distinction can readily be drawn between threats, warnings and requests, in practice it is much more difficult to make such distinctions. Threats are normally made expressly, but they can also be implicit.[25] For example, if the defendant goes to the plaintiff's house and asks for money and the defendant has three thugs with him, the implicit threat is that, unless the plaintiff pays the defendant, the thugs will beat him up.

Where the defendant has threatened to do something to the plaintiff unless the plaintiff transfers a benefit to him or her it is clear that the plaintiff will be able to establish duress only if the threat was illegitimate,[26] but this provides little assistance since it is still necessary to determine what makes a threat illegitimate. In assessing this, both the nature of the threat and the nature of what the defendant demands need to be considered.

Duress can be established only where the defendant's threat is unlawful.[27] The threat can be unlawful for two reasons: first, and most usually, because what the defendant threatens to do is unlawful—so, threats to commit crimes or torts, such as threats to injure the person or to interfere with property, are unlawful, as are threats to breach a contract; secondly, the defendant may actually be threatening to do something which is lawful, but in circumstances where the making of the threat is unlawful. The best example of this is where the threat constitutes the crime of

---

[23] 'Contracting under Pressure: A Theory of Duress' (1997) 56 *CLJ* 343, 346.
[24] *Ibid.*   [25] *The Alev* [1989] 1 Lloyd's Rep. 138, 142 (Hobhouse J).
[26] *Barton* v. *Armstrong* [1976] AC 104. See also *The Universe Sentinel* [1983] 1 AC 366, 384 (Lord Diplock).
[27] *Mutual Finance Ltd.* v. *John Wetton and Sons Ltd.* [1937] 2 KB 389, 395 (Porter J).

blackmail,[28] which is defined as the making of an unwarranted demand with menaces. This offence can be committed even where what the defendant is threatening to do is lawful, such as threatening to report someone to the police, but he or she uses menaces to strengthen the threat.

It is not sufficient for the plaintiff to establish that the threat is unlawful, since it must also be shown that what the defendant demands from the plaintiff is not lawfully due to the defendant.[29] For example, if the plaintiff owes the defendant £1,000, and the defendant threatens to seize the plaintiff's property unless he or she pays up, although the threat is unlawful, the demand is not, because the debt is owed to the defendant. Duress can be established only where what the defendant seeks from the plaintiff is something to which the defendant is not entitled. Where some money is lawfully due to the defendant and he or she receives more because of duress, then the plaintiff will be able to recover only the excess amount.[30] Where, however, the plaintiff owes money to the defendant, but that money is not lawfully due to the defendant, because it was a gambling debt for example, then the defendant's demand for payment of the money can be considered to be unlawful.

Where the defendant actually exerts pressure to obtain a benefit from the defendant, rather than simply threatening to exert pressure, the pressure exerted must be illegitimate. Whether it is illegitimate is determined in a similar way to illegitimate threats. First, the pressure must involve the commission of an unlawful act, such as a crime or tort or breach of contract. Secondly, it must be shown that what the defendant seeks from the exertion of the pressure is not lawfully due to him or her. So, for example, if the defendant falsely imprisons the plaintiff until he pays £1,000 which is not otherwise due to the defendant, the plaintiff will be able to establish that the defendant exerted illegitimate pressure.

(ii) Causation

Once it has been established that the defendant has made an illegitimate threat or exerted illegitimate pressure, the plaintiff must then show that he or she was induced to transfer a benefit to the defendant as a result or, where relevant, that he or she was induced to enter into a contract. This is a question of causation. It is obvious that, where the plaintiff has not perceived any threats made or pressure exerted by the defendant or

[28] Contrary to s. 21 of the Theft Act 1968.

[29] Cp. Goff and Jones, *The Law of Restitution*, p. 309 who suggest that duress may be established even though the defendant's demand is lawful. But, as they recognise, this is an academic question since, even if the plaintiff could secure restitution for duress founded on a lawful demand, as the money was actually due to the defendant he or she would still have a counter-claim for the debt.

[30] See *Astley* v. *Reynolds* (1731) 2 Strange 915; 93 ER 939.

where the plaintiff discounted the threats, then the defendant's conduct cannot be regarded as the operative cause of any transaction entered into with the defendant.[31] But where the plaintiff did perceive the threats or the pressure, the difficult question concerns what test of causation should be adopted to determine whether the duress was a sufficient cause for the plaintiff to transfer the benefit. In the context of spontaneous mistakes it was concluded that the mistake would be considered as constituting a ground of restitution only if the plaintiff could show that, but for the mistake, he or she would not have transferred a benefit to the defendant.[32] But where the mistake had been induced by the defendant, a more lenient test of causation is adopted, namely that it is sufficient that the mistake was a contributory cause of the payment without needing to show that it was the 'but for' cause.[33] This is because where the defendant has induced the mistake his or her conduct makes it easier to conclude that the plaintiff's claim to restitution is stronger than the defendant's claim to retain the enrichment. In principle, a similar argument should apply where the defendant has compelled the plaintiff to transfer a benefit. The key case on causation in the context of duress, *Barton* v. *Armstrong*,[34] has adopted such an approach, with explicit reliance on the misrepresentation cases.

In *Barton* v. *Armstrong* the defendant wanted the plaintiff to buy his shares in a company of which the plaintiff was managing director. The defendant had made numerous threats to kill the plaintiff if he did not purchase the shares, but it appeared that the main reason for the plaintiff agreeing to the purchase was commercial necessity. Despite this, the Privy Council held that the threats to kill the plaintiff were sufficient to vitiate the deed for the transfer of the shares. Lord Cross for the majority said that the test of causation for the purposes of duress was the same as that where a contract was induced by fraudulent misrepresentation, namely that it was sufficient that the threat or misrepresentation was a reason the plaintiff executed the deed, but it did not have to be the predominant reason. Consequently, the plaintiff was 'entitled to relief even though he might well have entered into the contract if [the defendant] had uttered no threats to induce him to do so'.[35] In other words, it was not necessary to show that but for the threats the plaintiff would not have agreed to buy the shares. It did not matter that the plaintiff would have agreed to buy the shares even if the threat had not been made, as long as it could be shown that, since the threat was made, this was a factor which influenced the plaintiff's decision to buy the shares. As Lord Cross said,

[31] See *Twyford* v. *Manchester Corporation* [1946] Ch. 236 and *Crescendo Management Pty. Ltd.* v. *Westpac Banking Corporation* (1988) 19 NSWLR 40.
[32] See p. 160 above.   [33] See p. 166 above.   [34] [1976] AC 104, PC.
[35] *Ibid*, p. 119.

'in this field the court does not allow an examination into the relative importance of contributory causes'.[36] The minority, Lords Wilberforce and Simon, accepted this formulation of the test of causation for the purposes of duress, though they did not agree that the test was satisfied on the facts of the case, because the trial judge's finding of fact that the threats had not even been a reason for the plaintiff's decision to execute the deed meant that the plaintiff had been motivated only by the commercial advantages of purchasing the defendant's shareholding and was not influenced by the threat at all.

Although the test of causation for the purposes of duress appears to be the same as that for induced mistakes, namely a test of operative rather than 'but for' cause, this test may be applied differently in two respects in the context of duress.

(1) Lord Cross in *Barton* v. *Armstrong*[37] suggested that the burden of proof is on the defendant to show that the threats did not contribute to the plaintiff's decision to transact with the defendant. If this is correct it means that, once the plaintiff has established that the defendant has exercised duress, there is a presumption that the duress caused the plaintiff to transact with the defendant. The defendant must then seek to rebut the presumption by showing that the duress did not contribute to the plaintiff's decision to transact with him or her.[38] This would be a particularly difficult presumption to rebut, since the defendant would be required to show why the plaintiff entered into the transaction. Even so, this presumption of causation is justifiable, at least where the duress is particularly serious, for example where it involves the actual or threatened commission of a crime against the person. Where the defendant commits or threatens to commit such a serious unlawful act, the defendant's conduct can be characterised as so unconscionable that the test of causation for purposes of restitution should be weighted in the plaintiff's favour.

(2) *Barton* v. *Armstrong* itself involved duress against the person, the most serious type of duress, so it is relatively easy to conclude that the defendant's conduct was sufficiently reprehensible to justify the recognition of a lenient test of causation. But it does not necessarily follow that the same test of causation should be adopted in respect of all types of duress. Consequently, for each type of duress it will be necessary to consider whether the test of operative causation should be adopted or whether an alternative test, such as that of 'but for' cause, is more appropriate.

---

[36] [1976] AC 104, PC, p. 118.   [37] [1976] AC 104, 120.
[38] See *Crescendo Management Pty. Ltd.* v. *Westpac Banking Corporation* (1988) 19 NSWLR 40, 46 (McHugh JA).

(c) Duress and third parties

In most cases duress will involve threats made or actual pressure exerted by the defendant who obtains a benefit as a result. But it is possible that the duress emanated from a third party and this resulted in a benefit being received by the defendant. Should this make any difference to whether the defendant is liable to make restitution to the plaintiff? Although this question has never been raised in any reported case, it can be answered by reference to the principles which underlie the grounds of restitution. The better view is that it should be irrelevant that the duress came from a third party. All we are concerned with is the particular effect of the threats upon the plaintiff's freedom of choice to transfer a benefit to the defendant, and whether the duress was exerted by the defendant or a third party has no effect on this question. Where, however, the plaintiff transferred a benefit to the defendant as a result of duress exerted by a third party, the liability of the defendant to make restitution may depend on whether he or she had actual or constructive notice of the duress. This would be consistent with the cases where the plaintiff seeks restitution of benefits transferred as a result of a third party's misrepresentation or undue influence.[39]

(d) The heads of duress

There are three types of duress which will operate as grounds of restitution.[40] Of these, the definition of the first two, duress against the person and against property, is not controversial since they have long been recognised and clearly involve the use of illegitimate pressure. The definition of the third head, economic duress, is controversial, however, primarily because this head has only recently been recognised and because the line between what is and what is not regarded as legitimate economic pressure is particularly difficult to draw.

(e) Duress of the person

Duress of the person involves actual or threatened unauthorised interference with the person, whether by endangering life, personal safety or liberty. The test of causation which is applicable to this type of duress is clearly the test of contributory cause, as was recognised in *Barton* v. *Armstrong*,[41] a case which involved threats to kill. Consequently, it is

---

[39] *Barclays Bank plc.* v. *O'Brien* [1994] 1 AC 180. See pp. 184–7 above and pp. 265–77 below.

[40] In *Crescendo Management Pty. Ltd.* v. *Westpac Banking Corporation* (1988) 19 NSWLR 40, 46 McHugh JA suggested that the categories of duress are not closed.

[41] [1976] AC 104.

sufficient that the duress of the person contributed to the plaintiff's decision to transfer a benefit to the defendant without necessarily being a
cause but for which the benefit would not have been transferred.

Usually duress of the person will take the form of the defendant threatening to interfere with the person of the plaintiff or somebody else unless
the plaintiff transfers a benefit to the defendant. These threats can take
one of three different forms. In each case the threat is unlawful, either
because it involves a threat to commit a crime or a tort or, usually, both.

(1) *Threats to kill.* It remains unclear whether a threat to kill made by
the defendant will be relevant only where the defendant threatens to kill
the plaintiff or whether it is sufficient that the defendant simply threatens to kill somebody. The better view is that the threat to kill need not be
directed at the plaintiff, as long as it can be shown to have influenced the
plaintiff's decision to transfer a benefit to the defendant. So, for example,
if the defendant threatens to kill the plaintiff's spouse and children if he
or she does not pay some money to the defendant, it is clear that such an
extreme threat must have removed the plaintiff's freedom of choice as to
what he or she would do with the money.

(2) *Threats to injure.* If the defendant threatens to injure the plaintiff or
presumably anyone else then, so long as the threat was a contributory
cause of the plaintiff's decision to transfer a benefit to the defendant, this
will operate as a ground of restitution.

(3) *Threats to interfere with liberty.* Where the defendant unlawfully
threatens to interfere with the liberty of the plaintiff or presumably anyone else, and this influenced the plaintiff's decision to transfer a benefit
to the defendant, this too is a form of duress of the person. This is illustrated by *Duke de Cadaval* v. *Collins*[42] where the plaintiff had been
unlawfully arrested by the defendant on the ground that he owed the
defendant £10,000. This was a fraudulent claim made by the defendant,
but, to secure his release, the plaintiff paid £500 to him. The plaintiff then
sought to recover the money in an action for money had and received
and succeeded, because the arrest had been wrongful and the defendant
knew that he had no legitimate claim against the plaintiff. This is a good
example of a case where the defendant actually exerted pressure against
the plaintiff, rather than merely threatening it, because the plaintiff's liberty had already been infringed and would continue to be infringed until
he paid the defendant. The plaintiff had paid the money to remove this
pressure and this was a sufficient reason for restitution to be awarded.[43]

---

[42] (1836) 4 Ad. and E 858; 111 ER 1006. See also *Pitt* v. *Coomes* (1835) 2 Ad. and E 459; 111
ER 478.

[43] *Ibid*, at p. 864; p. 1009 (ER) (Lord Denman CJ). In fact, Lord Denman held that title to
the money never passed to the defendant, so he regarded this as a proprietary restitutionary claim. See p. 611 below. See also *Clark* v. *Woods, Smith and Cooper* (1848) 2 Ex. 395; 154
ER 545.

(f) Duress of property

Where the defendant threatens to seize[44] or to retain[45] property, which belongs to the plaintiff or in which he or she has a proprietary interest,[46] unless the plaintiff fails to transfer a benefit to the defendant, then the plaintiff is able to recover the benefit by virtue of duress of property. This is because threats to seize or retain property are unlawful, being threats to commit torts, such as the tort of conversion.

But duress of property will operate as a ground of restitution only if the duress caused the plaintiff to transfer a benefit to the defendant. Although no case has specifically considered what the test of causation should be for this particular ground of restitution, there is no reason to suppose that the test of operative causation in *Barton* v. *Armstrong*[47] does not apply where the ground of restitution is duress of property. This is because the reasons which justify the use of that test where the duress relates to the person are also applicable where the duress relates to property, namely that the exercise of duress by the defendant can be regarded as constituting unconscionable behaviour, even though duress of property is less serious than duress of the person. Consequently, the test of operative causation, with such causation being presumed, should be applicable even where the duress relates to property.[48]

An old rule that only duress of the person could be relied on to set aside any contract which was entered into as a result of the threats[49] no longer represents the law.[50] Consequently, the defendant's threats to seize or retain property are a sufficient ground for setting aside contracts entered into as a result of such threats, with the consequence that it is then possible to recover any benefits which were transferred under the contract.

The best example of duress of property operating as a ground of restitution is *Astley* v. *Reynolds*[51] where the plaintiff pawned silver plate to the defendant for £20 and then wished to recover his property. The plaintiff tendered the money to redeem the loan but the defendant refused to

[44] *Maskell* v. *Horner* [1915] 3 KB 106.

[45] *Spanish Government* v. *North of England Steamship Co. Ltd.* (1938) 54 TLR 852, 856 (Lewis J).

[46] In *Fell* v. *Whittaker* (1871) LR 7 QB 120 it was sufficient that the plaintiff had possession of the property which had been seized.

[47] [1976] AC 104.

[48] Such a presumption appeared to be in operation in *Maskell* v. *Horner* [1915] 3 KB 106, 122 (Lord Reading CJ). See Goff and Jones, *The Law of Restitution*, p. 353.

[49] *Skeate* v. *Beale* (1841) 11 Ad. and E 983; 113 ER 688.

[50] *The Siboen and The Sibotre* [1976] 1 Lloyd's Rep. 293, 335 (Kerr J); *The Atlantic Baron* [1979] QB 705, 719 (Mocatta J); *Pao On* v. *Lau Yiu Long* [1980] AC 614, 636 (Lord Scarman); *The Evia Luck* [1992] 2 AC 152, 165 (Lord Goff).

[51] (1731) 2 Strange 915; 93 ER 939. See also *Somes* v. *British Empire Shipping Co.* (1860) 8 HLC 838; 11 ER 459.

return the plate to him unless he paid £10 interest, which was more than the interest which was legally due. The plaintiff tendered £4, but the defendant refused to take it. Consequently, the plaintiff was forced to pay the additional £10 demanded by the defendant as well as the money to redeem the loan. He then successfully brought an action for money had and received to recover this amount, the ground of restitution being that the plaintiff had paid the money to the defendant because of the defendant's refusal to return the plaintiff's property. The plaintiff only recovered the amount which was not lawfully due to the defendant, since the defendant's demand for the rest of the money was lawfully made.

(g) Economic duress[52]

(i) The essential features of economic duress

Economic duress has been recognised as a ground of restitution in its own right only relatively recently,[53] and the requirements for establishing it remain a matter of some uncertainty. Essentially economic duress arises where the defendant resorts to illegitimate commercial threats, whether express or implied from circumstances, in support of his or her demands, whether these demands are for payment from the plaintiff or that the plaintiff is to enter into a contract or to vary an existing one.

The key issue relates to the determination of what constitutes illegitimate commercial pressure for these purposes, since it is clear that commercial pressure alone cannot constitute economic duress.[54] What is needed are threats which are unlawful, typically threats to break a contract[55] or to commit a tort.[56] So, for example, if the defendant threatens to breach a contract with the plaintiff unless the plaintiff pays double the agreed contract price and the plaintiff succumbs to this threat because he or she requires immediate performance of this contract to be able to perform a sub-contract, this could constitute economic duress and the plaintiff would be able to recover the extra amount which had been paid to the defendant by virtue of the threatened breach of contract. It must also be shown that the threat caused the plaintiff to enter into the contract, to vary an existing contract or to pay money to the defendant, and it is the identification of the appropriate test of causation for these purposes which has proved to be particularly controversial.

---

[52] Dawson, 'Economic Duress: An Essay in Perspective' (1947) 48 *Mich. LR* 253.
[53] *The Siboen and The Sibotre* [1976] 1 Lloyd's Rep. 293. For analysis of the previous history see *The Atlantic Baron* [1979] QB 705, 715–16 (Moccata J).
[54] *Pao On* v. *Lau Yiu Long* [1980] AC 614, 635 (Lord Scarman).
[55] *The Atlantic Baron* [1979] QB 705.
[56] *The Universe Sentinel* [1983] AC 366; *The Evia Luck* [1992] 2 AC 152.

Before the definition of economic duress is examined, it is useful to consider two preliminary matters which have an important effect on the practical role of the economic duress doctrine in practice.

(1) Avoiding contracts for economic duress

Although some of the cases which are concerned with economic duress involve non-contractual restitutionary claims, the majority of them involve a plaintiff entering into a contract with the defendant or renegotiating an existing contract as a result of the duress. In such circumstances, if the plaintiff wishes to obtain restitution from the defendant it will first be necessary to set the contract aside. This can occur in two ways.

First, the plaintiff can specifically rely on the doctrine of economic duress to show that the contract is voidable and then rescind it. This will depend on whether it is possible to establish economic duress.

The plaintiff might alternatively be able to show that in the circumstances of the case there was no consideration provided by the defendant for the contract which was made as a result of the threats. This is important because, if no consideration can be identified, then the contract will be void[57] and the plaintiff will be able to recover any money paid to the defendant pursuant to the contract by virtue of the restitutionary grounds of total failure of consideration or absence of consideration.[58] This is a potentially important principle in the context of contracts which are renegotiated as a result of duress, where the effect of the pressure placed on the plaintiff is that he or she agrees to pay more money to the defendant but the defendant does not agree to provide any additional benefits to the plaintiff under the contract. If no consideration has been provided for this renegotiated contract it will cease to operate, and so the plaintiff can bring a restitutionary claim without having to establish economic duress and, bearing in mind the uncertainties as to the ambit of economic duress, this is a major advantage to the plaintiff.

Whether the plaintiff is able to establish that the contract is void because no consideration has been provided by the defendant will depend on what is meant by consideration for these purposes. Traditionally past consideration, such as a promise to perform an existing duty, has not been considered to be good consideration for a contract.[59] The significance of this is illustrated by the following example. The plaintiff and the defendant entered into a contract in which the defendant agreed to supply the plaintiff with building materials for a big

---

[57] *D and C Builders* v. *Rees* [1966] 2 QB 617.

[58] Chapter 12. Whether either of these grounds of restitution can be established will depend on a careful analysis of the facts of the case.

[59] *Stilk* v. *Meyrick* (1809) 2 Camp. 317; 170 ER 1168.

project which the plaintiff was developing. After the plaintiff had begun building, the defendant said that she would refuse to supply any more materials unless the plaintiff paid twice the price agreed and, because the plaintiff could not find the materials anywhere else, he agreed to the defendant's demands. Since the defendant had not promised to supply anything other than what she had originally agreed to supply, no new consideration had been provided for the renegotiated contract, and so the renegotiated contract would be void. However, the courts are increasingly able to find ways of identifying consideration for the new contract,[60] with the consequence that the plaintiff can only set it aside by relying on the doctrine of economic duress. This judicial manipulation of the doctrine of consideration reached its high point in the decision of the Court of Appeal in *Williams* v. *Roffey Bros. and Nicholls (Contractors) Ltd.*[61] where, although the Court of Appeal affirmed the basic requirement that a promise will only be enforceable if consideration is provided by the promisee, it went on to limit dramatically the function of consideration by recognising that the receipt of practical benefits by the promisor from the promisee could constitute good consideration.

In *Williams* v. *Roffey* the plaintiff, who was working for the defendant under a sub-contract to refurbish a block of flats, had set his contract price too low, making it impossible for him to make a profit and meaning that he had no incentive to complete the contract on time. If there was a delay in completing the contract, the defendant would have been liable to pay a penalty under the main contract. Consequently, to ensure that the plaintiff completed his work on time, the defendant promised to pay him a substantial extra amount when the work on each flat was completed. The issue before the court was whether the defendant was liable to make these additional payments. Since it was the defendant who took the initiative, it was clear that there was no ground for saying that the agreement was voidable for economic duress, since the plaintiff had not threatened to refuse to perform the contract unless the extra money was paid. But the Court of Appeal held that the defendant's promise to pay these extra amounts was enforceable because it had received consideration from the plaintiff in the form of practical benefits. It did not matter that the defendant had not received any benefits in law because the plaintiff was not promising to do any more than he had originally agreed to do. These practical benefits included that the plaintiff continued to work and did not stop in breach of the sub-contract, that there was a much reduced risk that the penalty clause would be triggered by delay and that the defendant had avoided the trouble and expense of engaging other people to complete the plaintiff's work.

---

[60] *The Atlantic Baron* [1979] QB 705 and *Pao On* v. *Lau Yiu Long* [1980] AC 614, 629.
[61] [1991] 1 QB 1. See Birks, 'The Travails of Duress' [1990] *LMCLQ* 342, 344–7.

Despite the Court of Appeal's affirmation of the requirement that the promisor must receive some benefit from the promisee for the promise to be valid, the effect of its decision is to make the requirement of consideration a very easy hurdle to overcome, at least where the parties renegotiate the price for the performance of an existing obligation, because the consideration in *Williams* v. *Roffey* were 'the routine benefits which flow from agreeing to make an extra payment'.[62] As a result, where there is an agreement to make an additional payment for the performance of an existing obligation, this will be enforceable unless it can be avoided on the ground of fraud or economic duress. Indeed, the recent recognition of economic duress proved to be the main justification for the Court of Appeal's decision in *Williams* v. *Roffey*.[63] This is because consideration is a blunt tool for setting aside renegotiated contracts. The doctrines of fraud and, particularly, economic duress are much better tools, being more sophisticated in balancing the interests of the parties.

(2) Threats not to contract with the plaintiff

The requirement that the defendant must threaten to do something which is unlawful before economic duress can be established means that a threat by the defendant not to contract with the plaintiff will not be sufficient to establish economic duress, simply because such a threat is perfectly lawful.[64] This was the effect of the decision of the High Court of Australia in *Smith* v. *Charlick (William) Ltd.*,[65] where it was held that the defendant, the Wheat Harvest Board which occupied a monopolistic position as regards the supply of wheat in South Australia, was acting legitimately in threatening that it would refuse to supply the plaintiff miller any more wheat if he refused to pay a surcharge on wheat which had already been supplied to him. This money was not lawfully due to the defendant, but the High Court held that the plaintiff could not recover the money he had paid as a result of the defendant's threats.[66] This must be correct, since a defendant who threatens not to contract with the plaintiff is not threatening to do anything unlawful. Admittedly, the facts of *Smith* v. *Charlick* were rather extreme since the defendant had a monopoly, so the plaintiff had no choice but to contract with the defendant on the terms which it demanded if he wished to carry on business as a miller. The defendant's monopolistic position may mean that a ground of restitution could be identified after all, not economic

---

[62] *Ibid*, p. 345. [63] [1991] QB 1, 13 (Glidewell LJ), 21 (Purchas LJ).
[64] *CTN Cash and Carry Ltd.* v. *Gallaher Ltd.* [1994] 4 All ER 714.
[65] (1924) 34 CLR 38.
[66] Today restitution might be awarded on the ground of unauthorised receipt by a public authority. See Chapter 14.

duress due to the absence of an unlawful threat, but rather undue pressure.[67]

Dicta in a recent decision of the Court of Appeal appear to qualify the contention made here that economic duress is confined to where the threat or pressure emanating from the defendant is unlawful. In *CTN Cash and Carry Ltd.* v. *Gallaher Ltd.*[68] the defendant supplied cigarettes to the plaintiff for sale to the public. The defendant was the sole supplier in the United Kingdom of particular brands of cigarettes, including Benson and Hedges and Silk Cut. The commercial arrangement between the parties was that each sale of cigarettes to the plaintiff was under a separate contract. The defendant had also arranged credit facilities for the plaintiff. The dispute between the parties arose from the supply of one particular consignment of cigarettes to the plaintiff which the defendant mistakenly delivered to the wrong warehouse. When the plaintiff informed the defendant of this, the defendant agreed to pick up the cigarettes and take them to the correct warehouse. But before it was able to do this the cigarettes were stolen. The defendant mistakenly, but honestly and reasonably, believed that title to the cigarettes had passed to the plaintiff so that they were at the plaintiff's risk at the time of the theft, and so it invoiced the plaintiff for the price of the stolen cigarettes. The plaintiff refused to pay, but the defendant threatened that it would withdraw the credit facilities in respect of future transactions if the plaintiff failed to pay for the cigarettes. Consequently, the plaintiff paid the money. It then sought to recover this money on the ground of economic duress. The Court of Appeal held that this action failed because economic duress had not been established on the facts, primarily because it was lawful for the defendant to withdraw credit facilities in respect of future dealings.[69] The court also recognised that a threat not to enter into future contracts with the plaintiff would have been lawful as well.[70]

The result of the *CTN Cash and Carry* case is therefore consistent with the principle that economic duress will only be established where the defendant's threats are unlawful. Unfortunately, Steyn LJ stated that 'the fact that the defendants have used lawful means does not by itself remove the case from the scope of the doctrine of economic duress'.[71] This suggests that the ground of economic duress can encompass lawful threats. Whilst Steyn LJ was reluctant to extend the notion of 'lawful act duress', as he called it, to commercial transactions which involved *bona fide* claims, for fear of unsettling bargains, he was prepared to admit that even in the commercial context 'lawful act duress' might have a role to play, although it would be more important in the field of protected

---

[67] See pp. 218–23 below.   [68] [1994] 4 All ER 714.   [69] *Ibid*, p. 717–18 (Steyn LJ).
[70] *Ibid*, p. 718 (Steyn LJ).
[71] *Ibid*. See also *The Universe Sentinel* [1983] AC 366, 401 (Lord Scarman).

relationships, such as where the dispute arose in the context of dealings between a supplier and consumer. Does this mean that we must now recognise the notion of 'lawful act duress'? The answer should be a resounding 'no'. Duress should be restricted to where the defendant's threats are unlawful. But this does not mean that, where the defendant's threats are lawful, there is no possibility of relief for the plaintiff. There is, but only by reference to the more restricted equitable doctrine of undue pressure which is established where the defendant's conduct can be characterised as unconscionable.[72] That this is the doctrine which Steyn LJ was actually referring to is supported by his statement that 'the critical inquiry is not whether the conduct is lawful but whether it is morally or socially acceptable'.[73] This ground of restitution would also have been unavailable on the facts of the case because there was nothing to suggest that the defendant had acted unconscionably, since it believed that its demand was lawfully made.

(ii) Establishing Economic Duress

Whenever a plaintiff wishes to rely on economic duress as a ground of restitution, there are always two questions which must be examined: first, whether the defendant's conduct, which invariably involves a threat, can be regarded as illegitimate;[74] and secondly whether this was a sufficient cause of the plaintiff doing what the defendant demanded.[75] Whilst it is clear that both these questions will always need to be examined, their relative importance remains a matter of great uncertainty. Two distinct theoretical bases for establishing economic duress can be identified; the first emphasises the illegitimacy of the threat and the second concentrates on the issue of causation.[76]

---

[72] See pp. 218–23 below.

[73] [1994] 4 All ER 714, 719. He also relied on cases which are properly analysed as involving undue pressure rather than duress, most notably *Mutual Finance Ltd.* v. *John Wetton and Sons Ltd.* [1937] 2 All ER 657.

[74] *Universe Tankships Inc. of Monrovia* v. *International Transport Workers Federation (The Universe Sentinal)* [1983] AC 366, 400 (Lord Scarman).

[75] See in particular Lord Goff in *The Evia Luck* [1992] 2 AC 152, 165.

[76] A third theoretical basis, advocated by Smith in 'Contracting under Pressure: A Theory of Duress' (1997) 56 *CLJ* 343, is that there are two forms of economic duress, one emphasising the defendant's wrongdoing and the other emphasising impairment of the plaintiff's consent. Whilst this clear distinction is theoretically attractive, it does not represent the law. However, the distinction recognised by Smith can be used to explain the difference of approach to duress of the person and goods and economic duress. This is because it appears easier to obtain restitution for duress of the person and goods, presumably because the defendant's wrongdoing is paramount in such cases. In the context of economic duress, the defendant's wrongdoing is less obvious, and so greater emphasis is placed on the validity of the plaintiff's consent. This distinction can also be used to explain why different tests of causation should be adopted for duress of the person and goods on the one hand and economic duress on the other.

(1) Illegitimacy of the threat

According to this theory of economic duress, it is not sufficient that the defendant's threat is either intrinsically unlawful or a threat to do an unlawful act; it is also necessary to consider whether the particular threat involves illegitimate pressure. The essential feature of this theory is that something extra must be shown before the threat can be classified as illegitimate, but the identification of that additional element is uncertain. Although this theory has never been specifically recognised, a few of the key decisions on economic duress appear to support it,[77] although the judges provide little assistance in identifying what additional factors would make the threat illegitimate, since typically they recognise that it depends on the particular circumstances of the case.[78] Once the court is satisfied that the threat was illegitimate it is presumably sufficient that the duress was a contributory cause of the plaintiff transferring a benefit to the defendant, rather than the 'but for' cause.[79]

If it is accepted that more needs to be shown than simply a threat to commit an unlawful act before economic duress is established, it is vital that a test is recognised which enables the courts to identify the additional factors which make a threat illegitimate. Two alternative tests have been suggested as being appropriate.

According to the first test an unlawful threat is characterised as illegitimate only when it was made in bad faith.[80] This is a notoriously vague concept, but Birks suggests that a defendant would be acting in bad faith if he or she 'intended to exploit the plaintiff's weakness rather than to solve financial or other problems of the defendant'.[81] This is not a satisfactory test for three reasons.

(1) It would be very difficult for the plaintiff to show what the motive of the defendant was in making the threat.

---

[77] See, for example, *Universe Tankships Inc. of Monrovia* v. *International Transport Workers Federation (The Universe Sentinel)* [1983] 1 AC 366 and *Dimskal Shipping Co. SA* v. *International Transport Workers Federation (The Evia Luck)* [1992] 2 AC 152.

[78] *The Universe Sentinel* [1983] 1 AC 366, 385 (Lord Diplock), 391 (Lord Cross), 400 (Lord Scarman) and *The Evia Luck* [1992] 2 AC 152, 166 (Lord Goff).

[79] *Ibid*, where Lord Goff approved the *Barton* v. *Armstrong* [1976] AC 104 test of causation.

[80] Burrows regards this as the preferable test: *The Law of Restitution*, at p. 181.

[81] Birks, *An Introduction to the Law of Restitution*, p. 183. An alternative test suggested by Birks at p. 183 is to distinguish between a threat and a warning and to deny restitution where the defendant was simply communicating to the plaintiff that he or she was subject to a pressure which was not of the defendant's own making, whereas restitution would lie where the defendant had 'threatened the plaintiff with a pressure of his own making'. This distinction between threats and warning is just a more specific attempt to identify when a defendant was acting in bad faith. Birks has since said that the distinction between threats and warnings is too fine and too easily abused: 'The Travails of Duress' [1990] *LMCLQ* 342, 346.

(2) As Burrows correctly asserts, this test 'reverses traditional contract values in that bad faith in breaking a contract has traditionally been afforded no importance (e.g. it does not affect the measure of damages) precisely because the self-interested pursuit of profit is regarded as acceptable'.[82] In other words, since the defendant's motive in breaking a contract to obtain profit has no effect on the assessment of damages, there is no reason why a different approach should be adopted where the defendant threatens to break a contract to obtain profit.

(3) By emphasising the defendant's motives for making the threat rather than considering the effect of the threat on the plaintiff, the test of bad faith is inconsistent with the majority of the other grounds of restitution which are plaintiff-oriented, in the sense that they are concerned with the effect of the particular ground on the plaintiff. This is true of mistake, where we are concerned only with the question whether the plaintiff was mistaken, without any need to consider whether the defendant was at fault. Similarly with duress of the person and property, where we are concerned only with whether the effect of the duress was to rob the plaintiff of his or her freedom of choice. There is no reason why this approach should not be adopted in the context of economic duress as well.

There is virtually no case law to support this test of bad faith, save perhaps for the decision of the Court of Appeal in *CTN Cash and Carry Ltd.* v. *Gallaher Ltd.*[83] where one reason for the failure of the plaintiff to establish economic duress was that the defendant had acted in good faith in claiming that the plaintiff was required to pay for goods which had been stolen. But the real reason the plaintiff's claim failed in that case was because the defendant's threat to withdraw credit facilities was not a threat to do an unlawful act. Without this vital element it is simply not possible to establish duress.

Although some of the cases in which economic duress has been established are consistent with the test of bad faith, this is a test which cannot be used to explain all the cases where economic duress has been recognised, since in a number of them restitution on the basis of economic duress was awarded even though there was nothing to suggest bad faith

---

[82] Burrows, *The Law of Restitution*, p. 179.

[83] [1994] 4 All ER 714. See p. 204 above. The decision of the Court of Appeal in *D and C Builders* v. *Rees* [1966] 2 QB 617 also appears to support a good faith test, since the plaintiff was not estopped from denying that it had agreed to accept a lesser sum of money for building work, because the defendant had acted in bad faith since he knew that the plaintiff was facing bankruptcy and so took advantage of his stronger bargaining position by threatening to pay nothing unless the plaintiff agreed to accept a lesser amount of money for the work. But this case can just as easily be analysed as involving exploitation rather than compulsion, and this is more consistent with the approach adopted by the judges.

on the part of the defendant.[84] Consequently, bad faith should be rejected as a test to determine whether the defendant's threat was illegitimate.

The alternative test of illegitimacy of threats is that a threat made by the defendant will be regarded as illegitimate where the terms proposed by him or her are substantively unfair.[85] As with the test of bad faith, this is inherently uncertain. To determine whether there was substantive unfairness it would be necessary to engage in a detailed analysis of all of the surrounding circumstances and the nature of the relationship between the parties. Surely there is a danger that such an approach would result in unpredictability and give the judiciary an unrestrained discretion to reach the 'just' solution. Such uncertainty is totally unacceptable in the context of commercial disputes. In addition, this test lacks any clear judicial support.

Failure to identify a satisfactory test of illegitimacy of threats means that this theory must be rejected. Particularly in the sphere of commercial transactions, any test which is inherently uncertain and provides an unrestricted discretion for the judges must be rejected as unworkable, and this is true of both the test of bad faith and that of substantive unfairness.

(2) Coercion of the will[86]

The alternative and preferable theory of economic duress is to treat all unlawful threats as illegitimate and then determine whether the threat was sufficiently serious to deprive the plaintiff of a free choice when deciding whether or not to enter into a contract with the defendant, or to renegotiate an existing contract or simply to transfer a benefit to the defendant. In other words, as was recognised by Lords Wilberforce and Simon in *Barton* v. *Armstrong*,[87] whether a threat is illegitimate simply depends on whether it is 'one of a kind which the law does not regard as legitimate'. So all threats to breach a contract or to commit torts or crimes are illegitimate. Whether such threats operate as a ground of restitution depends on whether they were a sufficient cause of the plaintiff's actions. The test which has been adopted for determining whether the threats were a sufficient cause is expressed by asking whether the threats coerced the plaintiff's will so as to vitiate his or her consent.[88] The

---

[84] See, for example, *The Atlantic Baron* [1979] QB 705 and *Atlas Express Ltd.* v. *Kafco (Importers and Distributors) Ltd.* [1989] QB 833.

[85] Burrows, *The Law of Restitution*, pp. 180–1.

[86] This is sometimes called the overborne will theory.   [87] [1976] AC 104, 121.

[88] *The Siboen and The Sibotre* [1976] 1 Lloyd's Rep. 293, 336 (Kerr J). See also *Pao On* v. *Lau Yiu Long* [1980] AC 614, 635 (Lord Scarman); *Hennessy* v. *Craigmoyle and Co. Ltd.* [1986] ICR 461, 468 (Sir John Donaldson MR); *The Alev* [1989] 1 Lloyd's Rep. 138, 145 (Hobhouse J).

most important statement of this coerced will principle can be found in the judgment of Lord Scarman in *Pao On* v. *Lau Yiu Long*:[89]

In determining whether there was a coercion of will such that there was no true consent, it is material to inquire whether the person alleged to have been coerced did or did not protest; whether, at the time he was allegedly coerced into making the contract, he did or did not have an alternative course open to him such as an adequate legal remedy; whether he was independently advised; and whether after entering the contract he took steps to avoid it. All these matters are . . . relevant in determining whether he acted voluntarily or not.

It is the final sentence which identifies the essential concern of the coerced will principle. If the plaintiff's will was coerced he or she did not act voluntarily and this will be the case only where the threats were a contributory cause of the plaintiff's actions. What Lord Scarman is doing in this dictum is to identify the types of factors which should be taken into account when determining whether the defendant's threats really can be regarded as a sufficient cause of the plaintiff's conduct, so that it is possible to conclude that he or she did not freely intend to transact with the defendant.

So if the emphasis is on causation, what test of causation should be adopted? This raises a crucial question of policy as to whether restitution for economic duress should be defined restrictively or widely. In the most common situation of economic duress, where the defendant threatens to breach a contract, the apparent policy of the courts is to adopt a restrictive interpretation of economic duress due to a fear of unsettling commercial transactions. So, for example, in *The Universe Sentinel*,[90] Lord Brandon said that only '*severe* economic pressure could amount to duress in law'.[91] This restrictive approach should be reflected in the test for causation. There are three possible tests of causation which may be applicable.

(1) The defendant's threats were the sole cause of the plaintiff's actions. This test would be unworkable, since it would be virtually impossible to prove that the plaintiff was influenced only by the threats and nothing else. In addition, there is no obvious reason why restitutionary relief should be denied to the plaintiff simply because he or she was influenced in doing what the defendant demanded by factors other than the defendant's threats, even though these factors might have had only a minor influence on the plaintiff's decision to transact with the defendant.

(2) The threats were a contributory cause of the plaintiff's actions. According to this test of causation it would be sufficient that the threats were a cause of the plaintiff's actions, without necessarily being the 'but for' cause. This test has received some support in the academic

---

[89] [1980] AC 614, 635.   [90] [1983] AC 366.   [91] *Ibid*, p. 405 (emphasis added).

literature[92] and has been implicitly recognised in certain key cases where the test in *Barton* v. *Armstrong*[93] was assumed to be applicable to economic duress.[94] But this test of causation is surely inappropriate in the context of economic duress since it does not follow from the fact that the defendant's threats contributed to the plaintiff's actions that the threats necessarily had a sufficiently serious effect on the plaintiff, as should be required if economic duress is to be restrictively interpreted as policy suggests it should be. Also the *Barton* v. *Armstrong* test probably incorporates a presumption that the threats were a cause of the plaintiff's acts, with the burden of rebutting this being placed on the defendant. This too is inappropriate in respect of economic duress, where such a presumption would result in economic duress being too easily established. The *Barton* v. *Armstrong* presumption is justifiable where the defendant's threats are themselves particularly serious, as where the threats relate to the person or even property, making it acceptable to presume that the threats influenced the plaintiff's conduct, since this is highly likely to have been the case. But commercial or economic threats are of a very different kind, especially because the plaintiff is more likely to have been influenced by other factors when deciding what the appropriate course of action should be.

(3) *The 'but for' test of causation.* The preferable test of causation is therefore the 'but for' test, where it must be shown that the plaintiff would not have acted in the way which he or she did had the defendant not made the threats. The recognition of this test of causation would mean that a different test of causation is adopted for economic duress than for duress of the person or goods, but this is justified because economic threats tend to be much less blameworthy than threats to interfere with the person or property. For example, economic duress usually takes the form of a threat to break a contract. Although such a threat is unlawful, it lacks the serious wrongfulness of threats to interfere with the person or property. Consequently, something else needs to be established beyond the wrongfulness of the threat before restitution may be awarded, and that extra element is proof that, had the threat not been made, the plaintiff would not have acted in the way which he or she did. This stricter test of causation also fulfils the policy of the law which seeks to restrict liability for duress in commercial transactions.

Birks has rejected the 'but for' test of causation because it involves 'an impossible and inscrutable inquiry into the metaphysics of the will'.[95]

---

[92] MacDonald, 'Duress by Threatened Breach of Contract' [1989] *JBL* 460, 472 and Birks, 'The Travails of Duress' [1990] *LMCLQ* 342.

[93] [1976] AC 104.

[94] See, for example, Lord Goff in *The Evia Luck* [1992] 2 AC 152, 165 and McHugh JA in *Crescendo Management Pty. Ltd.* v. *Westpac Banking Corporation* (1988) 19 NSWLR 40, 46.

[95] Birks, *An Introduction to the Law of Restitution*, p. 183.

But, so long as the test of causation is not confined to showing that the threat was the sole reason for the plaintiff's actions, it is a test which is perfectly workable, particularly because the courts have identified a number of factors to assist in determining whether the defendant's threats were indeed a 'but for' cause of the plaintiff's actions. Also this test of causation is not unique to economic duress, since it has also been recognised as applying in the context of spontaneous mistakes,[96] where it appears to operate perfectly satisfactorily. But the most important argument in favour of the 'but for' test of causation is that it accords with the notion of coercion of the will. For it will be possible to conclude that a plaintiff's will has been coerced by the defendant's threats only where, but for the threats, the plaintiff would not have acted as he or she did. It is only in this situation that it can be concluded that the plaintiff had no free choice whether or not to submit to the defendant's demands.

The application of the 'but for' test of causation is illustrated by the decision of the Privy Council in *Pao On* v. *Lau Yiu Long*.[97] In this case the plaintiff had agreed to sell its shares in a private company to a public company in exchange for shares in the public company. To ensure that it did not suffer from a fall in the value of the shares in this public company the plaintiff entered into a subsidiary agreement with the defendant, who was a majority shareholder in the public company, whereby the defendant agreed to buy a majority of the allotted shares at $2.50 a share. The purpose of this subsidiary agreement was to ensure that the plaintiff would not suffer any loss if the value of the shares fell below $2.50. Surprisingly the plaintiff had failed to realise that the effect of the agreement was such that, if the shares increased in value, the defendant would benefit since it would still be able to purchase the shares at $2.50 each. Consequently, the plaintiff refused to perform the main agreement unless the defendant agreed to cancel the subsidiary agreement and replace it with a guarantee to indemnify the plaintiff against loss. The defendant submitted to this threat because it feared that the public would lose confidence in the public company if it did not complete the agreement quickly. After the shares had been allotted their value dropped rapidly and the plaintiff sought to enforce the defendant's promise to indemnify it against this loss. The defendant argued that the guarantee was voidable for economic duress, but this claim failed because it could not be shown that the commercial pressure to which the defendant had been subjected by the plaintiff caused it to sign the guarantee. This conclusion was reached by reference to a number of different factors, the most important of which was that the defendant had taken a calculated risk that the value of the shares would not fall.[98] Since this was

---

[96] *Barclays Bank Ltd.* v. *W.J. Simms and Son and Cooke (Southern) Ltd.* [1980] QB 677.
[97] [1980] AC 614.   [98] *Ibid*, p. 627.

a purely commercial decision it was concluded that the plaintiff's threats had not caused the defendant to do as the plaintiff demanded. Presumably the plaintiff's threats were taken into account by the defendant when deciding whether to agree to the guarantee, but it could not be shown that it was the 'but for' cause of the defendant's action.

In *Pao On* and the later case of *The Universe Sentinel*[99] Lord Scarman identified a number of factors which might be used to determine, as he put it, whether the plaintiff had no choice but to submit to the defendant's demands. These factors include protesting about the validity of the demand, either at the time of entering the contract or making the payment or shortly afterwards,[100] the failure to obtain independent advice and a declaration by the plaintiff that he or she would go to law to recover money paid or property transferred as a result of the duress. But Lord Scarman emphasised that these are merely evidential factors, so if any are absent it does not mean that the plaintiff necessarily did exercise a free choice. So, for example, if the plaintiff failed to protest about the validity of the defendant's demand it does not follow that he or she must have acted voluntarily,[101] since the plaintiff may fail to protest for a number of reasons, for example, because the defendant is not available when the plaintiff wishes to protest or because the defendant's threats are such that the plaintiff is constrained from making a protest.[102] As Lord Scarman memorably said in *The Universe Sentinel*:[103] '[t]he victim's silence will not assist the bully, if the lack of any practicable choice but to submit is proved'.

There is one other factor which Lord Scarman emphasised in *Pao On* v. *Lau Yiu Long*[104] as being relevant to the assessment of whether the defendant's threats were a sufficient cause of the plaintiff's actions, namely whether the plaintiff had a reasonable alternative course open to him or her rather than submit to the defendant's threat. For if the plaintiff did have an alternative course available then he or she should have taken that course rather than submit to the threat. This factor is of such importance to the question whether the plaintiff can rely on economic duress that it should not be treated simply as an evidential factor to assist the court in determining whether the test of causation is satisfied, but it should rather be characterised as a rule of substance.[105] Consequently, if

---

[99] [1983] AC 366, 400.

[100] See also *The Siboen and The Sibotre* [1976] 1 Lloyd's Rep. 293, 336 (Kerr J).

[101] *Maskell* v. *Horner* [1915] 3 KB 106, 124 (Buckley LJ). In *Atlas Express Ltd.* v. *Kafco Ltd.* [1989] QB 833 economic duress was established despite the absence of any protest.

[102] See Halson, 'Opportunism, Economic Duress and Contractual Modifications' (1991) 107 *LQR* 649, 667–8.

[103] [1983] AC 366, 400.   [104] [1980] AC 614, 627.

[105] Phang, 'Economic Duress: Recent Difficulties and Possible Alternatives' (1997) 5 RLR 53, 59.

the plaintiff did have a reasonable alternative to submitting to the defendant's threats, this in itself should prevent the plaintiff from relying on economic duress because, as a matter of law, the defendant's threats will not have been a sufficient cause of the plaintiff's actions. It does not automatically follow, however, that just because there was no reasonable alternative open to the plaintiff but to submit to the defendant's demands, that economic duress will have been established, since it will still be necessary to show that the threats were the 'but for' cause of the plaintiff's actions, although it will be possible to prove this in most cases.

Despite the suggestion in some of the cases that the question whether there was a reasonable alternative open to the plaintiff is a subjective test,[106] so that it is sufficient that the plaintiff thought that he or she had no choice but to submit to the threat, the better view is that this is a matter which is to be assessed objectively, by reference to what the reasonable person would have done if he or she had been in the plaintiff's position. This objective approach was adopted in *B and S Contracts and Design Ltd.* v. *Victor Green Publications Ltd.*[107] where Kerr LJ recognised that a threat to break a contract 'will only constitute duress if the consequences of a refusal would be serious and immediate so that there is no reasonable alternative open, such as by legal redress, obtaining an injunction, etc.'.[108] The application of this 'no reasonable alternative' principle is illustrated by *Hennessy* v. *Craigmyle and Co. Ltd.*[109] In this case the plaintiff was unable to set aside an agreement, in which he had promised not to bring proceedings before an industrial tribunal in respect of his summary dismissal, because he had a real, albeit unattractive, alternative to signing the agreement, which was to make an immediate complaint to an industrial tribunal and draw social security benefit until his complaint was heard. A case in which there was held to be no reasonable alternative open to the plaintiff but to submit to the defendant's demands is *The Alev*,[110] where the owners of cargo which was being retained by shipowners had no reasonable alternative but to pay money as demanded by the shipowners. This was primarily because the only possible alternative course of action open to the plaintiffs was to seek an injunction to restrain the threatened breach of contract, but this would have been of no practical use because the cargo and the shipowners were outside the jurisdiction at the time, so this alternative course of action was objectively unreasonable.

Although the most usual alternative course of action open to the plaintiff is to resort to legal redress, other considerations can be taken into

---

[106] See in particular Lord Scarman in *The Universe Sentinel* [1983] 1 AC 366, 400.
[107] [1984] ICR 419.
[108] *Ibid* at p. 428. See also *The Alev* [1989] 1 Lloyd's Rep. 138, 147 (Hobhouse J).
[109] [1986] ICR 461.   [110] [1989] 1 Lloyd's Rep. 138.

account in determining whether the plaintiff's submission to the defendant's threats really was reasonable. For example, if the defendant, having entered into a contract to build an extension onto the plaintiff's house next month for £4,000, refuses to do so one week before performance is required unless the plaintiff pays an extra £1,000, it is not reasonable for the plaintiff to pay the money if it is possible to arrange for another builder to do the work at relatively short notice at no substantially greater cost than the original contract price. Similarly, if the benefit which is to be rendered to the plaintiff by the defendant is wholly disproportionate to the seriousness of the threat, restitution should also be denied because it is not reasonable for the plaintiff to have submitted to the demand. For example, if the defendant had demanded that the plaintiff pay him £1,000 otherwise he would refuse to deliver goods worth £100, it is surely unreasonable for the plaintiff to have succumbed to such a demand, which is wholly disproportionate to the value of the goods, and so restitution should be denied. A different result would probably be reached if the goods were required by the plaintiff to satisfy a lucrative contract with a third party. In such circumstances it might be considered that the plaintiff did indeed have no reasonable alternative but to submit to the threats.

It is this requirement of no reasonable alternative being open to the plaintiff which is of such crucial importance in determining whether the defendant's threats constitute economic duress. For where there is no reasonable alternative but to submit to the defendant's demands the economic pressure placed on the plaintiff is so extreme that he or she can be regarded as having no free choice in deciding whether to do what the defendant wanted. This is the reason this test is not required for the other heads of duress, where restitution is available even though the plaintiff may have had a reasonable alternative to submitting to the defendant's threats.[111] In the different context of economic duress, restitutionary relief should be denied to the plaintiff if a reasonable person would not have succumbed to the defendant's threats. This is because typically the dispute is between two commercial organisations, where the defendant's demands, usually for more money, occur in the context of a continuing contractual relationship. Where the plaintiff succumbs to the defendant's demands in circumstances in which there is a reasonable alternative open to it, that submission should be regarded as a legitimate part of the bargaining process and the law should not interfere with such commercial arrangements. It is only where the defendant can be

---

[111] For example, in *Astley* v. *Reynolds* (1731) 2 Strange 915; 93 ER 939 the defendant obtained restitution on the ground of duress of property even though he could have brought an action in trover rather than pay the extra money which the defendant demanded.

regarded as taking unfair advantage of the plaintiff that the law should intervene. The key characteristic of unfair advantage is that the defendant's threats caused the plaintiff to pay the defendant in circumstances where he or she had no reasonable alternative. If the plaintiff is not a commercial organisation, without the resources to challenge the defendant's threats, it would presumably be less reasonable for such a person to resort to litigation rather than submit to the defendant's demands. Consequently, the notion of what is reasonable will vary depending on who the plaintiff is. So the question which must be asked is what it would be reasonable for the particular plaintiff to have done in the circumstances.

Whilst the theory, which is founded on showing that the plaintiff's will has been coerced or overborne, identifies accurately those cases in which restitution should be awarded for economic duress, it does suffer from one major drawback arising from the very use of the terms 'coerced' or 'overborne' will. The requirement that the plaintiff's will be coerced or overborne has a tendency to mislead, since, if interpreted literally, it suggests that the plaintiff's intention must have been completely vitiated by the defendant's threats so that he or she was acting involuntarily in doing what the defendant demanded.[112] If such an interpretation is adopted, economic duress would be impossible to establish, since in these cases the plaintiff does have a choice whether or not to comply with the defendant's demands. This was recognised by the House of Lords in the criminal case of *Lynch* v. *DPP of Northern Ireland*[113] which unanimously rejected the overborne will theory in respect of the operation of the defence of duress. This interpretation of a coerced or overborne will should consequently be rejected for the law of restitution as well, but this does not mean that the test of coerced will should be rejected completely, because it does have a legitimate and workable function once it is recognised that the crucial issue before the court is not whether the plaintiff had no choice at all but to submit to the defendant's threats, but rather whether the plaintiff's choice was freely exercised. This will be established if the defendant's threats were unlawful and were a 'but for' cause of the plaintiff's actions because there was no reasonable alternative for the plaintiff but to submit to the defendant's demands. Whilst the use of language such as an 'overborne' or 'coerced' will can be described

[112] The test was interpreted in this way by McHugh JA in *Crescendo Management Pty Ltd.* v. *Westpac Banking Corpn.* (1988) 19 NSWLR 40, 45, who consequently rejected it. See also Lord Goff in *The Evia Luck* [1992] 2 AC 152, 166 and Lord Diplock in *The Universe Sentinel* [1983] 1 AC 366, 384.

[113] [1975] AC 653. See especially Lord Simon at p. 461. See also Atiyah, 'Economic Duress and the "Overborne Will" ' (1982) 98 *LQR* 197 and Dawson, 'Economic Duress—An Essay in Perspective' (1947) 45 *Michigan LR* 253.

as overdramatic it is perfectly intelligible,[114] although 'coercion' of the will is more accurate than the will being 'overborne'.

But to what extent is this theory of the plaintiff's will being coerced reflected in the cases? Although the theory has been expressly rejected in certain cases,[115] all of the reported cases on economic duress either support the theory, or at least are not inconsistent with it. For example, in *B and S Contracts and Design Ltd.* v. *Victor Green Publications Ltd.*[116] the plaintiff agreed to erect an exhibition stand for the defendant at Olympia. The plaintiff's employees, who had already received redundancy notices, demanded severance pay of £9,000 to which they were not entitled. Since the plaintiff was only able to offer the employees severance pay of £4,500, it threatened the defendant that if it did not pay the remaining £4,500 itself the plaintiff would not be able to complete the contract. Since the defendant required the stands to be erected urgently it paid the money as requested. When the defendant came to pay the plaintiff for its work in erecting and dismantling the stands it treated the £4,500 which it had already paid to the plaintiff as an advance payment, and it deducted this sum from the contract price. The plaintiff sued to recover the £4,500 from the defendant and failed, because the Court of Appeal found that the defendant had no choice but to pay the money, since cancellation of the contract to erect the stands would have caused it severe financial damage. Therefore, it was proper to treat the money paid as an advance payment and deduct it from the contract price. The finding of economic duress on these facts was surely correct. The plaintiff had made a veiled threat to commit an unlawful act, namely that it would breach the contract if the defendant failed to pay the sum demanded. This threat was the 'but for' cause of the defendant making the payment, since, as Eveleigh LJ put it, the defendant had 'been influenced against [its] will to pay the money'.[117] It was also expressly found that the defendant had no reasonable alternative but to pay the money.[118] This was because there was no chance that the defendant could have found another source of labour to erect the stands and, if the stands were not erected, it would be liable to a number of exhibitors who had leased exhibition space.

Similarly, in *The Atlantic Baron*[119] a shipbuilder agreed to build a ship for a fixed price in United States dollars. After the purchaser had paid the first instalment, the US dollar was devalued by 10 per cent and the

---

[114] Smith, 'Contracting under Pressure: A Theory of Economic Duress' (1997) 56 *CLJ* 343, 365.

[115] See, for example, *Crescendo Management Pty. Ltd.* v. *Westpac Banking Corporation* (1988) 19 NSWLR 40, 45 (McHugh JA) and *The Evia Luck* [1992] 2 AC 152, 166 (Lord Goff).

[116] [1984] ICR 419.   [117] *Ibid*, p. 423.   [118] *Ibid*, p. 426 (Griffiths LJ).

[119] *North Ocean Shipping Co. Ltd.* v. *Hyundai Construction Co. Ltd. (The Atlantic Baron)* [1979] QB 705.

builder demanded an increase of 10 per cent on the remaining instalments which were due to it, threatening to breach the contract if it did not receive the extra payments. The purchaser needed the ship urgently since it was negotiating a lucrative contract for its charter, and so it paid the additional amounts when it paid the remaining instalments to the builder. For all but one of these payments the purchaser said that the payments were made without prejudice to its right to recover the additional amount paid, although it did pay the final instalment without protest. The purchaser did not commence proceedings for restitution of the excess amounts until over two years later. It was held that the builder's threat to break the contract constituted economic duress. Clearly the builder had made an unlawful threat, and this was presumably the 'but for' cause of the purchaser paying the extra amount demanded. The purchaser had no reasonable alternative but to pay this amount because it needed the ship urgently for the purpose of the charterparty, and in the circumstances it would have been unreasonable to take the matter to arbitration because of the 'inherent unavoidable uncertainties of litigation'.[120] Despite this, the purchaser was not able to rescind the contract because its conduct in making the final payment without protest and its delay in seeking rescission were considered to constitute affirmation of the variation of the contract.

One of the best examples of the coerced will theory in operation is *The Olib*,[121] where the defendant had chartered its ship for the transport of the plaintiff's cargo but, once it had been transported to the nominated destination, nobody accepted delivery. The defendant told the plaintiff that it would sell the cargo if the plaintiff did not collect it and pay the sums which were outstanding. Eventually the plaintiff paid the sums demanded and then sought to recover them on the ground of duress. The question before the trial judge was whether the plaintiff had a good arguable case of economic duress, for the purposes of serving a writ on the defendant out of the jurisdiction.[122] The judge held that the plaintiff had not established a good arguable case for two main reasons. First, it had not shown that the defendant's threat to sell the goods was unlawful as a breach of the charterparty, because the condition of the cargo was such that immediate sale was essential, and, secondly, it had not established that the defendant's threats had induced it to make the payments. The judge's reasoning identifies the two essential features of the coerced will theory, namely an unlawful threat which was the 'but for' cause of the plaintiff's actions.

---

[120] *Ibid*, p. 719 (Mocatta J).
[121] *Enimont Overseas AG* v. *Rojugotanker Zadar (The Olib)* [1991] 2 Lloyd's LR 108.
[122] Under RSC Order 11.

(iii) Summary of the law on economic duress

Clearly the law relating to economic duress remains in a state of some confusion, but the preferable view is that this form of duress will be established where the defendant threatened to commit an unlawful act, whether this was a tort or breach of contract or even a crime, in circumstances in which the threat coerced the will of the plaintiff. To show coercion of the will it must be established that but for the threat the plaintiff would not have acted in the way the defendant demanded, and this but for test requires proof, at the very least, that the plaintiff had no reasonable alternative open to him or her but to submit to the defendant's demands.

3. UNDUE PRESSURE

(a) The essence of undue pressure

In some circumstances the defendant might threaten the plaintiff that, unless the plaintiff contracts with the defendant on particular terms or renegotiates an existing contract or pays the defendant a sum of money which is not due to the defendant, the defendant will do something which is perfectly lawful. If the plaintiff wishes to set the transaction aside or recover the money, he or she will generally not be able to rely on duress because the defendant is not threatening to do anything unlawful. The only exception to this will arise where, although the defendant threatens to do something which is lawful, the making of the threat is itself unlawful because it constitutes the crime of blackmail. Such a threat would be sufficient to found a restitutionary claim on the ground of duress. But the defendant will only commit blackmail where the threat involves the making of an unwarranted demand with menaces.[123] If the defendant thinks that he or she has reasonable grounds for making the demand or that the use of menaces is a proper way of reinforcing the demand, then the defendant will not be guilty of blackmail and so the threat will not be unlawful. In such circumstances the plaintiff will not be able to obtain restitution on the ground of duress but may rely on another ground of restitution instead, namely undue pressure.

Undue pressure was a term which was first recognised by Lord Denning MR in *Lloyds Bank Ltd.* v. *Bundy*,[124] although it is an expression which has rarely been used by judges.[125] Undue pressure is a ground of

---

[123] Theft Act 1968, s. 21.   [124] [1975] QB 326, 338.
[125] It was, however, a term used by Lord Chelmsford in *Williams* v. *Bayley* (1866) LR 1 HL 200, 214. See also Lord Westbury at p. 216.

restitution which is founded on the principle of compulsion, since it arises where the defendant has obtained a benefit from the plaintiff as a result of threats, albeit that the threats are lawful. Undue pressure should be distinguished from the ground of undue influence, which is founded on the principle of exploitation rather than compulsion since undue influence does not involve the defendant obtaining a benefit as a result of making threats.[126] Despite this, the grounds of undue pressure and undue influence are closely related, because they are both equitable doctrines which are triggered because the defendant's conduct can be characterised as unconscionable.

(b) The recognised heads of undue pressure

There are three particular circumstances in which restitution is available on the ground of undue pressure. Although the threats which are involved in these cases relate to lawful activity, the development of the law of tort may mean that some cases which were once characterised as involving undue pressure would today be treated as economic duress, because the defendant's threats relate to what is now an unlawful act.[127]

The plaintiff will not be able to establish undue pressure in any of these cases if the benefit which the defendant demanded from the plaintiff was lawfully due to the defendant.[128] A similar restriction applies to the ground of duress.

(i) Threats to invoke the criminal process

Where the defendant has threatened to prosecute the plaintiff or a relative of the plaintiff and, as a result of this, the plaintiff has paid money to the defendant or entered into a contract with him or her, the money can be recovered or the contract set aside on the ground of undue pressure. Although the cases which can be used to illustrate this ground of restitution tend to refer to the ground being either duress or undue influence,[129] the better view is that the ground of restitution is that of undue pressure because the threat will tend to be lawful since it is generally clear that the person who might be prosecuted has committed a crime.

The application of undue pressure in this context is illustrated by *Williams* v. *Bayley*[130] where the defendant bankers procured the plaintiff

---

[126] See Chapter 10.

[127] Particularly following the recognition and development of the tort of intimidation.

[128] *Flower* v. *Sadler* (1882) 10 QBD 572; *Mutual Finance Ltd.* v. *John Wetton and Sons Ltd.* [1937] 2 KB 389.

[129] Alternatively the ground of restitution may be that the parties are not *in pari delicto*, if the agreement to compromise criminal proceedings is held to be illegal. See pp. 297–9 below and Goff and Jones, *The Law of Restitution*, p. 315.

[130] (1866) LR 1 HL 200. See also *Kaufman* v. *Gerson* [1904] 1 KB 591 and *Société des Hôtels Réunis* v. *Hawker* (1913) 29 TLR 578.

to execute an equitable mortgage of his property by threatening that, if he failed to do so, they would prosecute his son for forgery with the morally certain consequence of the son being transported for life. As a result of the pressure applied by the defendant the mortgage was set aside. As Lord Chelmsford said, equity would set aside an agreement 'where there is inequality between the parties, and one of them takes unfair advantage of the situation of the other, and uses undue influence to force an agreement from him'.[131] Despite the express reference to undue influence this case is still better treated as one involving undue pressure because the defendant had induced the plaintiff to enter into the mortgage as a result of a threat, albeit a lawful one.[132] Similarly, in *Mutual Finance Ltd.* v. *John Wetton and Sons Ltd.*[133] a guarantee had been entered into by the defendant company for the benefit of the plaintiff as a result of the threats made by the plaintiff that it would prosecute the brother of one of the directors of the defendant company for forgery. This director signed the guarantee on behalf of the defendant because he feared that if his sick father found out about the forgery the shock might kill him. The judge set aside the guarantee specifically because the plaintiff's conduct amounted to undue influence in equity, but again a lawful threat had been made. In this case it was recognised that the facts were not sufficient to establish duress at common law, because the threats in each case were lawful,[134] but this did not prevent the intervention of equity.

It does not matter what the relationship is between the person who entered into the contract or paid the money and the person who is liable to be prosecuted. Essentially the only question before the court is whether the threats or pressure caused a contract to be made or money to be paid. In *Mutual Finance Ltd.* v. *John Wetton and Sons Ltd.*[135] Porter J held that the doctrine 'extended to any case where the persons entering into the undertaking were in substance influenced by the desire to prevent the prosecution or possibility of prosecution of the person implicated, and were known and intended to have been so influenced by the person in whose favour the undertaking was given'. This notion of substantial influence by the pressure suggests that it is sufficient that the pressure was a contributory cause of the plaintiff's actions, without needing to be a 'but for' cause of those actions.

---

[131] (1866) LR 1 HL 200, 216.

[132] Although the actual receipt of money in return for the agreement not to disclose material information relating to a serious offence is a crime (see the Criminal Law Act 1967, s. 5(1)) the threat to disclose the information is not unlawful.

[133] [1937] 2 KB 389.   [134] *Ibid*, p. 395 (Porter J).   [135] *Ibid*, p. 396.

(ii) Threats to sue

Usually, where the defendant threatens to sue the plaintiff if he or she refuses to pay money or enter into a contract, this will not in itself constitute compulsion,[136] because the plaintiff is expected to resist the threat and to defend the proceedings in court.[137] However, in certain exceptional cases a threat by the defendant that he or she will sue the plaintiff if money is not paid has been treated as grounding a restitutionary claim, and the ground of restitution is most appropriately characterised as undue pressure. This ground of restitution will be triggered in this type of case only where the defendant can be regarded as abusing the legal process. So, for example, in *Unwin* v. *Leaper*[138] it was held that the defendant had abused the legal process by threatening to bring proceedings to secure payment in respect of a matter which was unrelated to the threatened proceedings.

(iii) Threats to publish information

Where the defendant threatens to publish information which would detrimentally affect the plaintiff or someone known to the plaintiff, any contract which is entered into as a result of the threat may be set aside or any money paid as a result of the threat may be recovered. *Norreys* v. *Zeffert*[139] illustrates the potential application of this head of compulsion. Zeffert was not able to pay money on his gambling debts and he was interviewed by the National Turf Protection Society with a view to their securing a promise from him that he would pay his creditor. In order to induce Zeffert to make this promise his creditor threatened to have him reported to Tattersalls, which was a normal and legitimate threat to make in such circumstances. However, the creditor went on to threaten to report him to trade protection societies and to notify his social club of his refusal to pay. As a result of these threats Zeffert promised to pay his creditor. Although the trial judge held that this promise was not enforceable for lack of consideration, he went on to state, *obiter*, that if Zeffert had made a legally enforceable promise to pay his creditor, this would not have been enforced by the courts because it was obtained by threats and it was irrelevant that it was lawful to divulge the information as the creditor threatened to do. As Atkinson J said, just because 'a person may have a legal right to do something which will injure another is not sufficient justification for the demand of money as the price of not doing it'.[140]

---

[136] *Williams* v. *Bayley* (1866) LR 1 HL 200.
[137] See *Mason* v. *New South Wales* (1959) 102 CLR 108, 144 (Windeyer J). See also *Woolwich Equitable Building Society* v. *IRC* [1993] AC 70, 165 (Lord Goff).
[138] (1840) 1 Man. and G 747; 133 ER 533.　　　　　　[139] [1939] 2 All ER 187.
[140] *Ibid*, p. 189.

Although the money which the creditor was seeking to recover from Zeffert was actually due to it, this did not make the threats legitimate. This was presumably because the money was due pursuant to a gambling transaction and, since such transactions are themselves unlawful, the creditor could not sue Zeffert for breach of the gambling contract, hence the need to get Zeffert to promise to pay the gambling debts so that the creditor could enforce that promise. So, *Norreys* v. *Zeffert* should be treated as a case in which the money which the creditor sought to recover was not *legally* due to him. The result of the case would presumably have been different if Zeffert's debt had arisen from a lawful commercial transaction. In such circumstances, the threat to divulge to relevant organisations the information that Zeffert had failed to pay would probably have been regarded as an acceptable way of securing the payment of a debt which was legally due to the threatener.

Although the point has never been expressly determined, as a matter of principle this type of undue pressure should be applicable regardless of the type of information and the person to whom the information is threatened to be divulged. These issues will, however, be relevant in assessing whether the threat to divulge the information to a particular person or organisation actually caused the plaintiff to act as the defendant had demanded.

(c) Is there a general ground of undue pressure?

Although the notion of undue pressure has been implicitly recognised in these three particular circumstances, is it possible to extract a general ground of restitution which can be called undue pressure and which is applicable beyond these discrete areas? The preferable view is that there is such a general ground of restitution, as was recognised by Lord Denning in *Lloyds Bank Ltd.* v. *Bundy*.[141] Since undue pressure is an equitable doctrine it is clear that the main trigger for its application relates to the unconscientious behaviour of the defendant in threatening the defendant, without any need to show that the defendant's threats were unlawful.[142] To determine whether the defendant acted unconscientiously it will be necessary to examine all the circumstances of the case, especially the nature of the relationship between the parties and whether the defendant had acted in good faith. These were factors which were expressly recognised in *CTN Cash and Carry Ltd.* v. *Gallaher Ltd.*,[143]

---

[141] [1975] QB 326, 338.

[142] This was implicitly recognised by McHugh JA in *Crescendo Management Pty. Ltd.* v. *Westpac Banking Corporation* (1988) 19 NSWLR 40, 46, although the judge described the notion of unconscionable, but lawful, conduct as duress rather than undue pressure. But duress should be confined to where unlawful threats are made.

[143] [1994] 4 All ER 714, 717–18 (Steyn LJ).

although the Court of Appeal in that case assumed that they assisted in the identification of economic duress. They should instead be used to determine whether the defendant was unduly pressurising the plaintiff.

The difficulty with recognising a ground of restitution which is founded on the defendant's unconscionable conduct is that it is an inherently uncertain concept. This is unavoidable, but to mitigate the uncertainty it is vital that the application of this ground of restitution is confined to the most exceptional cases of extreme unconscionable conduct. This is particularly true where the parties are commercial entities which are trading at arm's length. Despite the general principle that there is no doctrine of unfair use of a dominant bargaining position,[144] even in the commercial context undue pressure may be applicable, at least where the defendant is aware that there are no grounds for his or her claiming a benefit from the plaintiff and where the nature of the relationship is such that the defendant can be regarded as taking unfair advantage of the plaintiff.[145] This might be the case, for example, where the defendant was occupying a monopolistic position and the plaintiff had no choice but to succumb to the defendant's threats.[146] The dual test involving consideration of the nature of the relationship between the parties and the *bona fides* of the defendant's belief as to the legitimacy of his or her claim can also be used to explain the result in the earlier decisions where the defendant's threats involved prosecution, suing or disclosure of information.

4. LEGAL COMPULSION

(a) The essential characteristics of legal compulsion

Whereas duress depends on the defendant making unlawful threats or threats to do unlawful acts and undue pressure depends on the defendant's conduct being characterised as unconscionable, there is a third and independent ground of restitution, called legal compulsion, which is also clearly founded on the general principle of compulsion. Unlike duress and undue pressure, legal compulsion is applicable where a benefit is demanded by somebody to whom it is lawfully due.

[144] *Pao On* v. *Lau Yiu Long* [1980] AC 614, 634.

[145] In *Lloyds Bank Ltd.* v. *Bundy* [1975] 1 QB 326, 339, Lord Denning MR recognised that abuse of a longstanding commercial relationship might constitute an illegitimate act for the purposes of undue influence.

[146] This argument could have been used to enable a restitutionary remedy to be awarded in *Smith* v. *William Charlick Ltd.* (1924) 34 CLR 38: see p. 203 above. But, although the defendant realised that it had no legal right to demand payment of a surcharge on wheat which it had supplied, it thought that it had a moral right to do so and so it would presumably have been found to have acted in good faith.

Legal compulsion will arise where the plaintiff is compelled to transfer a benefit to someone in circumstances in which, if the plaintiff does not transfer the benefit, it will be taken from him or her by recourse to the legal process. This pressure may derive, for example, from an express or implicit threat to resort to litigation or to exercise a court order or to execute a judgment. Where legal compulsion operates as a ground of restitution it does so because, as with all grounds of restitution which are founded on compulsion, the effect of the pressure is that the plaintiff has no choice but to transfer the benefit. But even though the plaintiff's intention to transfer the benefit may be treated as vitiated by the pressure, it does not automatically follow that the plaintiff can obtain restitution from the recipient of the benefit. This is because the pressure to transfer a benefit to prevent the other party from having recourse to legal process is 'a normal and necessary incident of social life'.[147] Consequently, the person who receives money or property as a result of the exercise of such threats will not be considered to have been *unjustly* enriched. This suggests that there is no role for legal compulsion as a ground of restitution. But legal compulsion may constitute a ground of restitution where three parties are involved. For example, where a creditor is owed money by the defendant and the plaintiff is lawfully compelled to discharge this liability, it is the defendant, rather than the third party, who can be considered to have been unjustly enriched at the expense of the plaintiff. This is because, where the plaintiff's payment discharges the defendant's liability to the third party,[148] the defendant will have received a negative incontrovertible benefit, since the payment has saved the defendant money which he or she would otherwise inevitably have had to pay to the third party, and this benefit was received at the plaintiff's expense since he or she paid the money to discharge the liability. Whether the plaintiff can successfully bring a restitutionary claim against the defendant in these circumstances will depend on whether the plaintiff can establish a ground of restitution, the most important of which is that of legal compulsion. The plaintiff's restitutionary claim against the defendant may take two forms. First, where the plaintiff is not ultimately liable to pay the creditor any money at all, the plaintiff will wish to recover from the defendant all of the money which he or she has paid to the creditor. This is called reimbursement or recoupment. Secondly, where the plaintiff and the defendant share a common liability, but the plaintiff has paid what he or she owed and some, or all, of what the defendant owed, then the plaintiff will wish to recover the amount he or she paid on behalf of the defendant. This is called contribution. In both cases the remedy which is awarded is resti-

---

[147] Birks, *An Introduction to the Law of Restitution*, p. 185.
[148] For discussion of when the debt will be discharged see pp. 225–30 below.

tutionary, since the plaintiff recovers what has been paid for the benefit of the defendant.[149]

Where the plaintiff seeks reimbursement or contribution from the defendant, the plaintiff will usually sue the defendant directly. But the plaintiff may be able to seek restitution using another route, namely the remedy of subrogation.[150] Subrogation enables the plaintiff to rely on the rights of the third party against the defendant even though the defendant's liability to the creditor has been discharged by the plaintiff's payment.[151] The main advantage of this is that it enables the plaintiff to take advantage of any security which the creditor had in respect of his or her claim against the defendant, or it may be relied on where a direct restitutionary claim against the defendant is not possible. Although subrogation raises more complex questions, it will only be available once the plaintiff has established that the defendant has been unjustly enriched at his or her expense.[152]

(b) Determining whether a debt has been discharged[153]

If the plaintiff is to establish a restitutionary claim against the defendant where the plaintiff has paid money to the creditor purportedly to discharge a debt owed by the defendant, it must be shown that the defendant has been enriched. Although the discharge of an existing liability will usually constitute an enrichment, since it generally amounts to an incontrovertible benefit, the difficult question to determine is actually when the debt will be discharged. This is a particularly controversial question, but a number of principles can be identified which will assist in its determination.

(i) Request by the defendant

Where the defendant requested the plaintiff to discharge the debt by paying the creditor, this will be effective to discharge the debt if the creditor accepted payment.[154]

---

[149] As regards recoupment see *Owen* v. *Tate* [1976] QB 402, 409 (Scarman LJ). As regards contribution see *Deering* v. *The Earl of Winchelsea* (1787) 2 Bos. and Pul. 270, 272; 126 ER 1276, 1277 (Eyre CB).

[150] See pp. 23–5 above.

[151] *Esso Petroleum Ltd.* v. *Hall Russell and Co. Ltd.* [1989] AC 643.

[152] *Banque Financière de la Cité* v. *Parc (Battersea) Ltd.* [1998] 2 WLR 475.

[153] Although this is essentially a question of enrichment which should properly have been considered in Chapter 4, it is more appropriate to consider it in this chapter, since the question whether a debt has been discharged will typically be relevant in the context of a restitutionary claim founded on the ground of legal compulsion.

[154] *Simpson* v. *Eggington* (1855) 10 Ex. 845; 156 ER 683.

(ii) Acceptance by the defendant

Where the plaintiff pays the creditor, purporting to discharge the debt, but without any request by the defendant to make the payment, this will discharge the debt if the creditor accepts payment and if the defendant accepted that the payment has discharged the debt.[155] Such acceptance of the payment is effective to perfect the discharge of the debt only where the plaintiff intends this to be the effect of the payment.[156] Also, when the defendant accepts the payment he or she must know that the plaintiff does not intend the payment to be a gift, since this is a condition of establishing free acceptance of a benefit.

(iii) Performance of an act which the defendant was liable to perform

Where the plaintiff performs an act which the defendant was liable to perform, this must discharge the defendant's liability, at least where the act is irrevocable.[157] So, for example, if the defendant was under a legal liability to keep a road in a good state of repair and the plaintiff mended the road, the plaintiff clearly discharged the defendant's liability. The defendant's liability must have been discharged in these circumstances because the person to whom the liability was owed cannot restore the benefit which has been received.[158]

(iv) Automatic discharge by an unrequested payment

The controversial question is whether the plaintiff's payment to the creditor, which was unrequested by the defendant and which has not subsequently been ratified by him or her, ever operates to discharge the debt automatically. The case law on this question is confused and contradictory. One line of cases suggests, either expressly or implicitly, that the plaintiff's payment discharges the defendant's liability only where the defendant has accepted the discharge, suggesting that there is no doctrine of automatic discharge by mere payment to the creditor.[159] This view was recently endorsed, obiter, by Hirst J in *Guardian Ocean Cargoes Ltd.* v. *Banco de Brasil SA.*[160] However, there are a number of other cases where it has been accepted, again either explicitly or implicitly, that the plaintiff's payment will automatically discharge the debt and it is irrele-

---

[155] *Simpson* v. *Eggington* (1855) 10 Ex. 845; 156 ER 683.
[156] *Re Rowe* [1904] 2 KB 483.   [157] See *Gebhardt* v. *Saunders* [1892] 2 QB 452.
[158] Friedmann, 'Payment of Another's Debt' (1983) 99 *LQR* 534, 541.
[159] See, for example, *Belshaw* v. *Bush* (1851) 11 CB 190; 138 ER 444; *Simpson* v. *Eggington* (1855) 10 Ex. 845; 156 ER 683; *City Bank of Sydney* v. *McLaughlin* (1909) 9 CLR 615; *Barclays Bank Ltd.* v. *W.J. Simms, Son and Cooke (Southern) Ltd.* [1980] QB 677.
[160] [1991] 2 Lloyd's Rep. 68, 87. See also *Esso Petroleum Co. Ltd.* v. *Hall Russell and Co. Ltd.* [1989] AC 643, 663 (Lord Goff).

vant that the defendant had not accepted the payment.[161] All that is needed is for the creditor to accept the payment. The debt will be discharged even where the creditor accepts a lesser amount.[162] A number of these cases arise in the specific context of legal compulsion, where the plaintiff was compelled by the creditor to pay money which was assumed to discharge the debt.[163] Sutton has identified another group of cases which recognise the principle of automatic discharge of liability where a part-owner of property has discharged a debt which was charged on the property.[164]

The views of academics are also contradictory. For example, Goff and Jones,[165] in an attempt to reconcile as many of these cases as possible, argue that the debt will be discharged automatically by an unrequested payment only when it was paid under legal compulsion. Birks and Beatson[166] have tentatively suggested that a payment does not automatically discharge the debt, save where the plaintiff is not a volunteer and has no immediate right of recovery against the creditor. Friedmann,[167] Stoljar[168] and Burrows[169] on the other hand argue that, so long as the plaintiff's payment was accepted by the creditor, it should automatically discharge the debt, regardless of the particular ground of restitution on which the plaintiff relies, and Birks now regards this approach as providing 'a much more stable basis from which to begin the enquiry'.[170]

Since the cases provide little assistance in determining when the plaintiff's payment will discharge the defendant's debt, and the views of academics are so contradictory, it is necessary to consider the fundamental principles which underlie the law of restitution to see if they provide any answers. Essentially the question when a debt is discharged concerns the identification of an enrichment, since once the debt has been discharged the defendant will have received an incontrovertible benefit. Since the basic test for identifying an enrichment depends on whether the defendant has received an objective benefit, we are not at this stage concerned with the defendant's reaction to the payment by the plaintiff. Rather

---

[161] *Welby* v. *Drake* (1821) 1 C and P 557; 171 ER 1315; *Re Barnes* (1861) 4 LTNS 60; *Cook* v. *Lister* (1863) 13 CB (NS) 543, 594–5; 143 ER 215, 235 (Willes J); *Hirachand Punamchand* v. *Temple* [1911] 2 KB 330; *Liggett (Liverpool) Ltd.* v. *Barclays Bank Ltd.* [1928] 1 KB 48.

[162] *Hirachand Punamchand* v. *Temple* [1911] 2 KB 330.

[163] See, for example, *Exall* v. *Partridge* (1799) 8 Term Rep. 308; 101 ER 1405; *Edmunds* v. *Wallingford* (1885) 14 QBD 811; *Moule* v. *Garrett* (1872) LR 7 Exch. 101; *Brook's Wharf and Bull Wharf* v. *Goodman* [1937] 1 KB 534; *Owen* v. *Tate* [1976] QB 402.

[164] 'Payments of Debts Charged Upon Property' in *Essays on the Law of Restitution* (ed. Burrows, 1991) p. 71.

[165] Goff and Jones, *The Law of Restitution*, pp. 16–18.

[166] 'Unrequested Payment of Another's Debt' (1976) 92 *LQR* 188, 211.

[167] 'Payment of Another's Debt' (1983) 99 *LQR* 534, 556.

[168] Stoljar, *The Law of Quasi-Contract*, p. 166.

[169] Burrows, *The Law of Restitution*, p. 223.

[170] Birks, *An Introduction to the Law of Restitution*, p. 191.

than concentrating on the relationship between the plaintiff and the debtor, the focus should be on the relationship between the plaintiff and the creditor. If the plaintiff pays the creditor who accepts the payment, then, as a general rule and as between the plaintiff and the creditor, the debt should be considered to have been discharged.[171] Does this constitute an objective benefit to the defendant? The answer must be 'yes', since the discharge of a debt clearly has an objective value. The next question is whether the defendant can argue that he or she did not value the benefit, the so-called principle of 'subjective devaluation'. But surely, subject to one qualification, no reasonable person would accept the defendant's argument that he or she did not value the discharge of a debt, simply because any reasonable person would regard the discharge as valuable. Therefore, the defendant should be considered to be enriched by the discharge of the debt, by virtue of the principle of incontrovertible benefit, in the sense that the defendant has been saved necessary expenditure.[172] There is no need to resort to request or free acceptance to defeat the defendant's reliance on subjective devaluation, since it is sufficient that the discharge was incontrovertibly beneficial.

The only qualification to the application of the principle of incontrovertible benefit in this context would occur where the defendant had a defence to the creditor's claim or had a counterclaim.[173] In either case the objective value of the benefit would be reduced or eliminated depending on the nature of the defence or counterclaim. If the defendant had a complete defence to the creditor's claim the plaintiff's payment to the creditor would not have discharged a debt, since there would have been no debt to discharge. Consequently, the plaintiff would have to bring a restitutionary claim against the creditor, on the ground of total failure of consideration,[174] since the plaintiff expected the payment to discharge the debt and this did not occur. If the defendant's defence only reduced his or her liability to the creditor, or where the defendant has a counterclaim against the creditor, the plaintiff's payment to the creditor has still discharged the defendant's liability. If the plaintiff then seeks restitution from the defendant, who argues that the effect of the defence or counterclaim was that the payment was of less or no value to him or her, in principle this should reduce or eliminate the amount which the defendant should pay to the plaintiff. What should the plaintiff do then? By the plaintiff overpaying the creditor, it is the creditor who has been

---

[171] Or, as Birks and Beatson analyse it, the acceptance of the payment by the creditor means that a benefit has already been executed: 'Unrequested Payments of Another's Debt' (1976) 92 *LQR* 188, 197. See also Friedmann, 'Payment of Another's Debt' (1983) 99 *LQR* 534, 537.

[172] Birks, *An Introduction to the Law of Restitution*, p. 186.

[173] See Beatson, *The Use and Abuse of Unjust Enrichment*, p. 203.

[174] See Chapter 12.

enriched. Can the plaintiff secure restitution from him or her? Since the debt has been discharged there has been no total failure of consideration. But since the overpayment was not lawfully due to the creditor, it would be appropriate for the plaintiff to rely on the ground of legal compulsion to recover this amount.

This analysis depends on the debt being treated as discharged between the plaintiff and the creditor, for then this will be treated as a benefit as regards the defendant. But this is only the case if the creditor is entitled to keep the payment.[175] The creditor will not be entitled to keep the payment if it can be shown that the plaintiff's intention that the creditor should received the payment has been vitiated in some way, as occurs where the payment was made as the result of an operative mistake or the creditor has used unlawful threats to secure payment of money which was not due. Where, however, the plaintiff has been legally compelled to pay the creditor then, as between the plaintiff and the creditor, the debt will be treated as discharged because legal compulsion cannot operate as a ground of restitution as against the person to whom the money is lawfully due. In other words, the plaintiff's intention to pay the creditor cannot be treated as vitiated by reason of legal compulsion where the creditor is entitled to payment. Where, however, the plaintiff purports to discharge the defendant's debt for reasons of necessity, this should not be regarded as sufficient automatically to discharge the debt, since the effect of the necessity is to vitiate the plaintiff's intention that the creditor should receive the payment.[176] It follows that the circumstances of the payment need to be analysed carefully to determine whether the plaintiff has a claim against the creditor to recover the money.

If it is accepted that the debt is automatically discharged by the plaintiff's payment once it has been accepted by the creditor and there are no grounds for the plaintiff to secure restitution from him or her, it is still possible for the plaintiff and the creditor together to agree that the contract of discharge should be set aside. This would have the effect of reviving the debt so that the defendant would no longer be considered to have been enriched by the plaintiff's payment. This was recognised in *Walter v. James*.[177] However, once the defendant has accepted the payment as discharging the debt, this should prevent the plaintiff and the creditor from agreeing to revive it.[178] Beatson regards the notion that the debt may be revived by the plaintiff and the creditor as 'enabling parties to

---

[175] Friedmann, 'Payment of Another's Debt' (1983) 99 *LQR* 534, 537. See also Birks and Beatson, 'Unrequested Payments of Another's Debt' (1976) 92 *LQR* 188, 201.

[176] See pp. 303–4 below. But it will be virtually impossible for the plaintiff to establish that money was paid for reasons of necessity. See pp. 311–12 below.

[177] (1871) LR 6 Exch. 124.

[178] Friedmann, 'Payment of Another's Debt' (1983) 99 *LQR* 534, 542.

impose a burden on a non-consenting third party'.[179] But what burden has been imposed? All that the parties have done is to restore their position to what it was before the plaintiff paid the creditor. No burden is being placed on the defendant beyond that which already existed. The only qualification to this should arise where the defendant has relied on the discharge of the debt in some way, so that the plaintiff and creditor should be estopped from arguing that the debt has been revived.

There is one potential difficulty with the argument that the payment of the defendant's debt by the plaintiff will automatically discharge the debt because the discharge is incontrovertibly beneficial to the debtor, namely that the plaintiff might be a volunteer whose motive in discharging the debt was to harass the defendant.[180] But this does not make the discharge of the debt itself of less value; it just means that the plaintiff is placed in a position in which he or she may exploit the defendant. It is for this reason that the fact that the plaintiff was a volunteer should be an irrelevant consideration when determining whether the plaintiff's payment discharged the defendant's debt. Rather, this is a separate consideration, of relevance generally to the plaintiff's restitutionary claim, which needs to be examined in the context of identifying a relevant ground of restitution.

The preferable interpretation of the law on the automatic discharge of debts can be summarised as follows. Where the plaintiff pays money to the creditor purporting to discharge a debt which is owed by the defendant this will automatically discharge the debt once the payment has been accepted by the creditor, regardless of the fact that the plaintiff was a volunteer, except where the plaintiff's intention that the creditor should receive the payment can be treated as vitiated by virtue of a recognised ground of restitution such as mistake or duress.

(c) Restitution from the debtor

Where the plaintiff has discharged the defendant's liability to the creditor the plaintiff will wish to obtain restitution from the defendant, and this will require the plaintiff to establish that the claim falls within one of the recognised grounds of restitution. In many cases this will be legal compulsion, though another potential ground of restitution may be necessity.[181] To establish legal compulsion it is necessary to show that the plaintiff was 'compellable by law' to make the payment.[182] Usually this takes the form of the creditor expressly threatening the plaintiff with the legal process if he or she does not pay the money as demanded. But legal compulsion may also be established where the threats derive

---

[179] Beatson, *Use and Abuse of Unjust Enrichment*, p. 202.
[180] See the American case of *Norton* v. *Haggett* (1952) 85 A 2d. 571.
[181] See Chapter 11.   [182] *Moule* v. *Garrett* (1872) LR 7 Ex. 101, 104.

implicitly from the circumstances in which the plaintiff finds him- or herself. Whether the plaintiff can be considered to have been legally compelled to pay the creditor ultimately depends on whether the plaintiff exercised a free choice in discharging the liability.

Where the plaintiff can be regarded as having been legally compelled to pay the money, he or she may either seek to be reimbursed by the defendant, where the defendant was wholly or ultimately liable for the debt, or may seek to recover a contribution, where the parties were jointly liable.

(i) Reimbursement

Where the plaintiff has been compelled by law to discharge the defendant's liability the general principle is that the defendant will be required to reimburse the plaintiff for his or her expenditure if the defendant bears the ultimate, or primary, liability for it.[183] The defendant will bear the ultimate liability as between the plaintiff and the defendant, either where the defendant bears the whole of the liability and the plaintiff bears none of it or where the plaintiff's liability is subordinate to that of the defendant. Generally, the defendant's liability will be characterised as ultimate where any benefit which was derived from it has been enjoyed by the defendant.[184] For example, since a borrower has the use of the borrowed money rather than the guarantor, it is the borrower who will bear the ultimate liability for the debt.

(1) The defendant bears the whole of the liability

Where the defendant bears the whole liability and this liability has been discharged by the plaintiff it is clearly appropriate that the defendant should make restitution to the plaintiff. This is illustrated by *Exall* v. *Partridge*[185] where the plaintiff left his carriage on land which was leased by the defendant for the defendant to repair. The defendant had not paid his rent to his landlord who entered the defendant's premises and lawfully seized the plaintiff's carriage in distress of rent. Since the plaintiff wanted to recover his carriage he was compelled to pay the rent to the landlord. The plaintiff then sought to recover the money he had paid to the landlord from the defendant. It was assumed that the plaintiff's payment had discharged the defendant's liability to the landlord, so clearly the defendant had been benefited. But it was still necessary to identify a ground of restitution. Duress of goods could not be established both

[183] *Re Downer Enterprises Ltd.* [1974] 1 WLR 1460, 1468 (Pennycuick V-C).
[184] Birks, *An Introduction to the Law of Restitution*, p. 192.
[185] (1799) 8 Term Rep. 308; 101 ER 1405. See also *Johnson* v. *Royal Mail Steam Packet Co.* [1867] LR 3 CP 38; *Edmunds* v. *Wallingford* (1885) 14 QBD 811 and *Whitham* v. *Bullock* [1939] 2 KB 81.

because the landlord had not acted unlawfully in seizing the carriage and because the money demanded was lawfully due to the landlord. But it was held that the plaintiff could recover from the defendant what he had paid to the landlord on the ground that he had not paid the money voluntarily but had been compelled to do so by the landlord seizing his property.[186] Le Blanc J even described this as 'compulsion of law'.[187] This compulsion derived from the fact that the landlord had seized the plaintiff's goods by legitimate application of the legal process and, if the plaintiff wished to recover his carriage, he had no choice but to pay the money which the landlord sought. Although the landlord never exactly said to the plaintiff that he must pay the debt, this was implicit since the landlord's actions clearly suggested that if the debt was not paid by someone he would retain the plaintiff's carriage. Since the defendant was not going to pay the rent, the plaintiff had no choice but to do so. Presumably, for reasons of consistency at least with economic duress and much of the rest of the law of restitution, the 'but for' test of causation is applicable in this type of case. If this is so it follows that, where the plaintiff would have paid off the defendant's debts even if his or her goods had not been seized by the third party, then restitution will be denied, simply because there is insufficient evidence that the compulsion of law had deprived the plaintiff of a free choice as to how to spend his or her money.

In *Exall* v. *Partridge* the plaintiff's property had actually been seized by the third party. Exactly the same analysis should be possible where the third party has simply threatened to seize the plaintiff's goods if the money is not paid. In the context of duress of property no distinction is drawn between threats to seize goods and the actual seizure, so there is no reason why such a distinction should be drawn in respect of legal compulsion.[188] Also, it makes no difference whether the plaintiff has paid money to the third party to recover his or her goods or the plaintiff's goods have been sold by the third party to pay off the debt, for in each case the defendant's liability will have been discharged and the plaintiff will have been deprived of a free choice whether he or she should discharge the liability.[189]

In *Exall* v. *Partridge* it was relatively straightforward to establish that the plaintiff was compelled to discharge the defendant's liability, since the fact that the plaintiff's property was taken by the third party was clearly outside his or her control since the carriage was under the control of the defendant. Crucially, there was no question of the plaintiff acting voluntarily in leaving the carriage on the defendant's premises because the defendant had requested the plaintiff to do this so that he could

---

[186] See in particular Grose J, n. 185 above, p. 311; 1406 (ER).
[187] *Ibid*, p. 311; 1407 (ER).   [188] See *Maskell* v. *Horner* [1915] 3 KB 106.
[189] *Edmunds* v. *Wallingford* (1885) 14 QBD 811.

repair it. But what about a case where the plaintiff has left his property on the defendant's premises without being requested to do so? In *England* v. *Marsden*[190] this was held to be sufficient to distinguish *Exall* v. *Partridge*. In that case the plaintiff had legitimately seized the defendant's goods but left them on the defendant's premises without being requested to do so and without any benefit to the defendant. The defendant's landlord then seized the goods as distress for rent which was owed by the defendant. The plaintiff paid the rent to recover the goods and then sought to recover the rent from the defendant, but his claim failed because he had acted voluntarily in leaving the goods on the defendant's premises. But this distinction, which depends on whether the defendant has requested the goods to be left on the premises or has benefited from the goods being left, was later doubted in *Edmunds* v. *Wallingford*.[191] Any such distinction should be completely rejected because it does not follow from the fact that the plaintiff has left his or her property on the defendant's premises without being requested to do so that the plaintiff is necessarily acting voluntarily when he or she discharges the defendant's liability. Rather, given that the plaintiff's property has been seized, regardless of the reason for which it was on the defendant's property, the question is whether the plaintiff had any real choice but to discharge the liability to recover his or her property, and since usually the plaintiff had no reasonable alternative but to discharge the liability, the defendant should reimburse the plaintiff. The only possible qualification to this might arise where the plaintiff left his property on the defendant's premises knowing that there was a possibility that it might be seized by a landlord. Only in such a case could it be concluded that the plaintiff had taken the risk of seizure and so was acting voluntarily.[192]

(2) The plaintiff's liability is ancillary to that of the defendant

The alternative situation in which the plaintiff will seek to be reimbursed by the defendant is where, although he or she is liable to the third party, that liability is ancillary to that of the defendant. Typically this will arise where the plaintiff is acting as surety for the defendant's debts and the creditor threatens to sue the plaintiff unless the debt is discharged. The plaintiff will be liable to the third party to discharge the defendant's debt by virtue of the guarantee but, because the defendant bears the ultimate liability in respect of the debt, the defendant will be required to reimburse the plaintiff.[193]

---

[190] (1866) LR 1 CP 529.

[191] (1885) 14 QBD 811. Although it was suggested that restitution would be denied if the plaintiff left the goods on the defendant's premises without the defendant's express consent.

[192] By analogy with *Esso Petroleum Ltd.* v. *Hall Russell and Co. Ltd.* [1989] AC 643.

[193] *Anson* v. *Anson* [1953] 1 QB 636. See also *Re a Debtor* [1937] Ch. 156, 163 (Greene LJ).

This form of liability also arises in respect of the assignment of leases. This is illustrated by *Moule* v. *Garrett*[194] where the plaintiff was a tenant who had covenanted with his landlord that he would keep the leased property in repair. The plaintiff assigned the lease to an assignee who subsequently assigned it to the defendant. The defendant failed to keep the property in repair. The landlord sued the plaintiff for breach of covenant, since this liability to keep the property in repair continued despite the assignment. The plaintiff then brought an action against the defendant to recover what he had paid to the landlord. Since the plaintiff had not assigned the lease directly to the defendant he could not sue on an implied covenant to indemnify him, simply because there was no privity of contract between the plaintiff and the defendant. Despite this, the defendant was required to reimburse the plaintiff because his payment had discharged the defendant's liability to the landlord. The defendant bore the ultimate liability since he had the immediate obligation to keep the property in repair and it was his default which resulted in the landlord suing the plaintiff for breach of the covenant. Cockburn CJ specifically justified the reimbursement by reference to the fact that the plaintiff had been compelled to pay the landlord.[195]

The principle in *Moule* v. *Garrett* is applicable only where the plaintiff's payment to the landlord has discharged a liability owed by the defendant, for otherwise the defendant will not have been enriched. It is for this reason that *Moule* v. *Garrett* was distinguished in *Bonner* v. *Tottenham and Edmonton Permanent Investment Building Society*,[196] where the plaintiff tenant had assigned his lease to Price who had then mortgaged it to the defendant. When Price went bankrupt the defendant took possession, but failed to pay rent to the landlord. The landlord then sued the plaintiff for breach of his covenant to pay rent. The plaintiff was compelled to pay the landlord and then sought to recover this sum from the defendant. The plaintiff's claim failed because it was held that he had not discharged any liability of the defendant. This was because, unlike the defendant in *Moule* v. *Garrett* who was an assignee, the defendant in *Bonner* was a sub-lessee and consequently was not liable to the landlord to pay the rent. Since the plaintiff had not discharged any liability of the defendant it could not be shown that the defendant had received any benefit from the plaintiff.[197]

---

[194] (1872) LR 7 Exch. 101. See also *Selous Street Properties Ltd.* v. *Oronel Fabrics Ltd.* [1984] 270 EG 643, 749 and *Beckton Dickinson UK Ltd.* v. *Zwebner* [1989] QB 208.

[195] (1872) LR 7 Exch. 101, 104.

[196] [1899] 1 QB 161. See also *Re Nott and Cardiff Corp.* [1918] 2 KB 146; *Receiver for the Metropolitan Police District* v. *Croydon Corp.* [1957] 2 QB 154; and *Esso Petroleum Co. Ltd.* v. *Hall Russell and Co. Ltd.* [1989] AC 643.

[197] See particularly Vaughan-Williams LJ [1899] 1 QB 161, 177.

Although the principle involving the discharge of the defendant's ulti-mate liability is particularly important in respect of sureties and assign-ments of leases, it is applicable in a wide variety of situations. For example, in *Brook's Wharf and Bull Wharf Ltd.* v. *Goodman Bros.*,[198] the defendant stored a number of packages of squirrel skins, which had been imported from Russia, in the plaintiff's bonded warehouse, from where they were stolen without negligence on the part of the plaintiff. The defendant remained liable to pay customs duties on the skins, but refused to pay. As a result the plaintiff was compelled under statute to pay the duties and then sought to recover the amount he had paid from the defendant. The plaintiff's action succeeded because, although it was legally obliged to pay the custom duties, this liability was ancillary to that of the defendant who remained primarily liable for the duties. Lord Wright MR recognised that, if the plaintiff was not reimbursed by the defendant, the result would be that the defendant would be 'unjustly benefited at the cost of the plaintiffs'.[199]

Whilst the vast majority of the cases which are concerned with the dis-charge of the defendant's ultimate liability involve discharge simply by payment of money to the creditor, there are some examples of cases where the discharge of liability occurs by the plaintiff expending money on work. So, for example, in *Gebhardt* v. *Saunders*[200] the plaintiff, who was the tenant of the defendant's house, had received a notice from the sanitary authority which required either the owner or the occupier to abate a nuisance arising from water and sewage collecting in the cellar of the house, with a financial penalty if the nuisance was not abated. The notice was directed at both the owner and the occupier because it was unclear what the cause of the problem was. If it was due to blocked drains, the plaintiff as occupier would have been liable to abate the nui-sance, but if it arose from structural problems, the defendant as owner would have been liable. Since the problem needed to be resolved urgently, the plaintiff did the necessary work in the course of which it was discovered that the problem arose from a structural defect in the drains, so the defendant was liable. The plaintiff then sought to recover the costs and expenses in abating the nuisance from the defendant, and suc-ceeded. The exact ground for restitution in this case is somewhat uncer-tain. It could have been mistake as to an existing liability to do the work,[201] or even necessity,[202] but the judges assumed that the ground was legal compulsion.[203] This was particularly because, since the notice

---

[198] [1937] 1 KB 534.   [199] *Ibid*, p. 545.   [200] [1892] 2 QB 452.
[201] This is Birks's preferred explanation of the case. See Birks, *An Introduction to the Law of Restitution*, p. 191.
[202] See Chapter 11.
[203] See also *Andrew* v. *St Olave's Board of Works* [1898] 1 QB 775.

from the sanitary authority was directed to the plaintiff as well as the defendant, if the plaintiff had failed to do anything he would have been liable to pay a penalty. To avoid paying the penalty, the plaintiff incurred expenditure on the work.[204] Since it eventually turned out that the plaintiff was not liable at all, this case could be treated as falling within the first category of cases, where the defendant bears the whole liability. Whichever category the case falls within is of no legal importance, because it is clear that it was the defendant who bore the ultimate liability, and this is sufficient justification for the award of restitution on the ground of legal compulsion.

(3) Voluntary payments

One problem which has arisen particularly in respect of the plaintiff discharging the defendant's liability to a creditor concerns the role of voluntariness or officiousness.[205] It is obvious that a plaintiff, who voluntarily discharges the defendant's liability in circumstances in which the plaintiff would not suffer in any way if he or she did not discharge the liability, is unable to establish a restitutionary claim based on legal compulsion, simply because of the absence of any compulsion. But a difficult question arises where, for example, the plaintiff has voluntarily become surety for the defendant's liability without being requested to do so by the defendant, and is then compelled by the creditor to discharge the liability. Can the plaintiff rely on legal compulsion to obtain restitution from the defendant in these circumstances? It is obvious that the plaintiff was compellable by law to pay the creditor, but does it, and should it, make any difference that the plaintiff voluntarily became the surety?

This question arose in *Owen* v. *Tate*[206] where the plaintiff, without consulting the defendant, deposited a sum of money with the defendant's creditor as security for a loan. The reason for this was that the defendant's previous surety wished to recover the title deeds of her property which had been surrendered to the creditor and, as a favour to her, the plaintiff agreed to become surety. When the defendant discovered that the plaintiff had become the surety it protested, but when it was pressed for payment by the creditor, it asked the creditor to have recourse to the money which the plaintiff had deposited. The plaintiff then sought to be reimbursed by the defendant. The Court of Appeal assumed that the

---

[204] It might be doubted whether the threat of the penalty was a sufficient cause of the plaintiff incurring the expenditure. It is just as likely that he incurred the expenditure out of necessity, to stop sewage leaking into the cellar. But where two grounds of restitution are operating the plaintiff should be able to rely on both of them to show that they jointly caused him or her to benefit the defendant.

[205] See pp. 39–40 above.

[206] [1976] QB 402. See also *Esso Petroleum Co. Ltd.* v. *Hall Russell and Co. Ltd.* [1989] AC 643.

plaintiff's payment had discharged the defendant's debt and, whether or not the principle of automatic discharge is accepted, this must have been correct, if only because the defendant had requested the creditor to resort to the plaintiff's payment to discharge the debt. The only question remaining for the court concerned the relevance of the fact that the plaintiff had voluntarily become the surety in the first place. Scarman LJ identified two relevant principles. First, where the plaintiff is compelled to pay money which the defendant is liable to pay, the plaintiff has a right to be reimbursed by the defendant. Secondly, this is subject to the principle that the plaintiff will not be reimbursed where he or she voluntarily paid the money or voluntarily assumed the obligation to pay.[207] The plaintiff acted voluntarily where he or she paid money or incurred liability in circumstances where there was 'no antecedent request, no consideration or consensual basis' to do so.[208] Since this second principle qualifies the first, and because the plaintiff had voluntarily guaranteed the defendants' liability, it followed that he had no right to be reimbursed by the defendant.[209] The only exception to this would arise where the plaintiff voluntarily incurred the liability in circumstances where it was reasonably necessary in the interests of the plaintiff or the defendant or both of them to do so.[210] The effect of this decision is that, where a plaintiff has incurred liability as a surety, he or she will be able to seek reimbursement from the defendant only where the defendant had expressly or impliedly requested the plaintiff to act as surety or where it was necessary for the plaintiff to become surety.

A similar approach was adopted in *Esso Petroleum Ltd.* v. *Hall Russell and Co. Ltd.*[211] where restitution was denied because the plaintiff was compelled to discharge the defendant's liability pursuant to an agreement with the creditor which the plaintiff had made voluntarily. Since the plaintiff had voluntarily incurred the liability in the first place it was not possible for it then to claim that it had been legally compelled to pay the third party.[212]

Owen v. *Tate* has generally been considered to be wrongly decided.[213] The result appears to be unjust since the plaintiff had conferred a benefit on the defendant by discharging the debt, but the defendant was still not required to reimburse the plaintiff. If the case was analysed simply in

---

[207] *Re National Motor Mail-Coach Co. Ltd.* [1908] 2 Ch. 515, 520 (Swinfen Eady J).

[208] *Owen* v. *Tate* [1976] QB 402, 408 (Scarman LJ).

[209] See also *Re National Motor Mail-Coach Co. Ltd.* [1908] 2 Ch. 515.

[210] *Owen* v. *Tate* [1976] QB 402, 409–10 (Scarman LJ).

[211] [1989] AC 643.

[212] The plaintiff's claim also failed because it could not be established that it had discharged any liability of the defendant.

[213] See Birks, *An Introduction to the Law of Restitution*, p. 311 and Goff and Jones, *The Law of Restitution*, at p. 446.

terms of causation then it is difficult to defend, since, at the time the plaintiff's money was taken to discharge the debt, legal compulsion was operating. Ultimately, the validity of the decision is a matter of policy. Should we regard somebody who has voluntarily assumed a liability as acting in such a way that restitution should be denied to them? The particular difficulty with *Owen* v. *Tate* is that there is nothing to suggest that the plaintiff had done anything which was detrimental to the interests of the defendant. Even though, as Scarman LJ found,[214] the plaintiff had acted behind the back of the defendant in the interests of another party, the plaintiff had not harmed the defendant in any way. Despite this, Ormrod LJ[215] did suggest that the defendant's position was worsened by the intrusion of the plaintiff. If this really was shown to be the case, it would have been possible to conclude that the defendant had not in fact benefited from the discharge of the liability, so the necessary element of enrichment would have been missing from the unjust enrichment claim.

Voluntariness, as defined in *Owen* v. *Tate*, does not defeat restitutionary claims in other areas where the ground of restitution is legal compulsion. So, for example, in *Edmunds* v. *Wallingford*[216] the fact that the plaintiff's goods which were seized had been voluntarily left on the defendant's premises was held to be irrelevant. It is also inconsistent with the law on contribution whereby a surety is entitled to contribution from his or her co-surety regardless of whether the plaintiff was requested by the defendant to become a surety. The emphasis in *Owen* v. *Tate* on the defendant requesting the plaintiff to act as surety, whether expressly or impliedly, appears to arise from an unfortunate misunderstanding of the earlier cases on discharge of liability. In these cases[217] the plaintiff's action was typically founded on the count for money paid, which required the plaintiff to plead that the defendant had requested the payment. In many of these cases this request was implied in highly artificial circumstances. Rather than rejecting the need for a request, *Owen* v. *Tate* has affirmed it as a requirement. This is unacceptable and should be rejected. It is yet another example of the forms of action continuing to rule us from their graves.

The validity of *Owen* v. *Tate* is therefore in doubt. The preferable view is that, where the plaintiff has been legally compelled to discharge the defendant's liability, the fact that he or she has not been requested to do so should be irrelevant. In those rare cases where the reason for the plaintiff voluntarily discharging the liability is so that the plaintiff can harass the defendant, it should be possible to deny restitution simply by virtue of the principle that the plaintiff had been acting officiously.

---

[214] [1976] QB 402, 412.   [215] *Ibid*, p. 413.   [216] (1885) 14 QBD 811.
[217] See in particular *Exall* v. *Partridge* (1799) 8 Term Rep. 308; 101 ER 1405.

(ii) Contribution[218]

Where both the plaintiff and the defendant are under a common and equal liability to the creditor, so that neither of them bears the ultimate liability, and the creditor compels the plaintiff to discharge the liability, the plaintiff will have a restitutionary claim against the defendant in the form of a claim for contribution. If there were no doctrine of contribution in English law it would follow that which of the debtors was ultimately liable to discharge the debt would simply be a matter of chance depending on which debtor the creditor decided to sue, a result which is inequitable in the light of the fact that the debtors were equally liable to the creditor. There are two main restitutionary routes for contribution, one at common law and in equity and the other by statute, both of which remain relevant. Contribution, rather than recoupment, is relevant where the parties are under a common liability simply because, where the plaintiff has discharged his or her liability as well as that of the defendant, it would be inappropriate for the defendant to reimburse the plaintiff the whole amount spent, since the plaintiff also benefited from the payment by the discharge of his or her own liability. The rationale of contribution is that it provides a mechanism whereby the burden of liability is shared equally between the parties.

Contribution can be analysed as embodying a restitutionary claim which is founded on the reversal of the defendant's unjust enrichment. This is because the consequence of the plaintiff discharging the defendant's liability is that the defendant has been enriched by the receipt of a negative benefit and, since the plaintiff was compellable by law to discharge the liability, it follows that the ground of restitution is legal compulsion. That contribution involves restitution grounded on legal compulsion is exemplified by *Spiers and Son Ltd.* v. *Troup*[219] where the plaintiff and the defendant both received a notice to pull down a party wall because it was in a dangerous condition. The plaintiff pulled down the wall and built a new wall which was taller and thicker than the old one, and then he sought a contribution from the defendant in respect of the cost of demolition and rebuilding. It was held that, since the plaintiff had not been legally compelled to *rebuild* the wall, he could not obtain contribution from the defendant in respect of that expenditure. However, since both parties were equally liable to *demolish* the wall it followed that the plaintiff could obtain contribution in respect of the cost of demolition, simply because the plaintiff had been legally compelled to incur this expenditure.

[218] For more detailed analysis of contribution see Goff and Jones, *The Law of Restitution*, chapter 14.

[219] (1915) 84 LJKB 1986. See also *Legal and General Assurance Society Ltd.* v. *Drake Insurance Co. Ltd.* [1992] QB 887.

(1) Contribution at common law and equity

The right to contribution at common law and equity arises where the plaintiff and defendant are under a common liability to the same creditor in respect of the same debt,[220] regardless of whether they are jointly liable in the same instrument or severally liable in different instruments,[221] and the plaintiff pays a sum of money to the creditor in respect of that debt. Where the plaintiff discharges the liability completely, the defendant is required to make contribution in respect of his or her own share of the liability. So, if the plaintiff and defendant were jointly liable to pay the creditor £1,000 and the plaintiff discharged this liability completely, the defendant's contribution would be £500. The right to contribution is not confined, however, to where the plaintiff has discharged the common liability completely, but applies in all cases in which the plaintiff has paid a sum which is more than his or her proportionate share of the common debt.

Although the right to contribution was first established in respect of co-sureties,[222] it now extends to all types of cases where there is a common liability for the same debt. So the right to contribution is also applicable in respect of co-insurers,[223] co-partners,[224] co-mortgagors,[225] co-trustees[226] and joint contractors.[227] But in addition to these recognised categories the right to contribution may arise from the particular facts of a case. This was recognised by Lord Kenyon CJ in *Child* v. *Morley*:[228]

> I remember a case in Rolle's Abridgement, where a party met to dine at a tavern, and after dinner all but one of them went away without paying their quota of the reckoning, and that one paid for all the rest; and it was holden that he might recover from the others their aliquot proportions.

A matter of some recent controversy has concerned at what point the liability to make contribution arises. This has been a particularly important issue in respect of double insurance where the assured has obtained insurance cover from different insurers in respect of the same risk, so that each insurer would be liable to the assured for the whole of any loss

---

[220] *Cooper* v. *Twynam* (1823) Turn. and R 424; 37 ER 1164.

[221] *Deering* v. *The Earl of Winchelsea* (1787) 2 Bos. and Pul. 270; 126 ER 1276. As regards apportionment of liability in respect of liability insurance, see *Commercial Union Assurance Co. Ltd.* v. *Hayden* [1977] QB 804.

[222] *Deering* v. *The Earl of Winchelsea* (1787) 2 Bos. and Pul. 270; 126 ER 1276.

[223] *North British and Mercantile Insurance Co.* v. *London, Liverpool and Globe Insurance Co.* (1876) 5 Ch.D 569.

[224] *Re The Royal Bank of Australia, Robinson's Executors* (1856) 6 De G M and G 572; 43 ER 1356.

[225] *Re Mainwaring* [1937] Ch. 96.   [226] *Chillingworth* v. *Chambers* [1898] 1 Ch. 685.

[227] *Boulter* v. *Peplow* (1850) 9 CB 493; 137 ER 984.

[228] (1800) 8 TR 610, 614; 101 ER 1574, 1576.

which had occurred. If one insurance company was compelled to pay on the policy it would then seek contribution from the other company, since the first company would have discharged the second company's liability. But what if the second insurance policy had a clause which stated that it would not be liable unless the assured had notified it of any event which might give rise to a claim, and the assured had not done this? In this situation the Court of Appeal decided in *Legal and General Assurance Society Ltd.* v. *Drake Insurance Co. Ltd.*[229] that the failure to notify the second company would not defeat the first insurance company's right to contribution, since that right had already accrued at the time the loss was suffered. So the second insurance company was liable to make contribution simply because it was potentially liable to the assured. But this view was rejected by the Privy Council in *Eagle Star Insurance Co. Ltd.* v. *Provincial Insurance plc.*[230] which held that the liability of the insurers was to be assessed by reference to the respective contracts of insurance. This meant that, if the assured had not notified the second insurance company of the claim, then that company was not liable to make contribution to the first company, simply because the first company had not discharged an existing liability of the second company. But if, as occurred in the *Eagle Star* case itself, both companies were entitled to repudiate their contractual liability to the assured but remained statutorily liable for the loss, then the normal equitable rule of equal sharing of the liability would be applicable. This emphasis on the parties' actual rather than their potential liability is a much more realistic approach to the determination of when a liability to make contribution arises and therefore it is the preferable approach.

The general principle that where the parties are equally liable they must make an equal contribution can be modified by contract, so the parties may agree that they are liable to contribute different sums.[231] It is even possible to exclude the right to contribution by contract.[232]

The right to contribution is also qualified where any of the people who are potentially liable to the creditor are insolvent[232] or cease to be liable for the debt. Such people are not liable to make contribution and so, where their liability has been discharged by the plaintiff, the remaining solvent parties must contribute equally to the common debt.[234] So, for example, where A, B and C are sureties for a debt of £1,000 and the debtor and C become insolvent then, if A pays the whole debt, he can recover £500 from B, though this is subject to any contractual modification of the general principle of equal contribution. If the plaintiff pays only his or

[229] [1992] QB 887.   [230] [1994] 1 AC 130.   [231] *Ibid.*
[232] *Pendlebury* v. *Walker* (1841) 4 Y and C Ex. 424; 160 ER 1072.
[233] *Deering* v. *The Earl of Winchelsea* (1787) 2 Bos. and Pul. 270; 126 ER 1276.
[234] Goff and Jones, *The Law of Restitution*, p. 404.

her share of the common debt which the creditor accepts in full settlement of the debt, the plaintiff can only claim a rateable contribution from the other people who are liable.[235]

(2) Civil Liability (Contribution) Act 1978[236]

The effect of the Civil Liability (Contribution) Act 1978 is to extend the ambit of contribution beyond those cases where the plaintiff and the defendant are jointly liable in respect of the same debt, where contribution is still governed by the common law, to where they are jointly or otherwise liable in respect of the same damage which has been suffered by another person.[237] This means that where the plaintiff and the defendant are liable to pay compensation in respect of the same damage to a third party, whether it arises from tort, breach of contract, breach of trust, unjust enrichment[238] or any other form of liability,[239] and the plaintiff discharges the defendant's liability, then the plaintiff is able to recover such contribution from the defendant as the court considers to be 'just and equitable having regard to the extent of [the defendant's] responsibility for the damage in question'.[240] When determining the defendant's responsibility for the damage, the court should consider the relative culpability of the plaintiff and the defendant and the causative potency of their conduct.[241] The court may determine that equal division of the liability is equitable or that the defendant is not liable to make any contribution or even that the defendant should be required to indemnify the plaintiff completely.[242]

The 1978 Act has a potentially wide ambit, since it relates to any person who has caused damage to another person. So, apart from the obvious cases of tortfeasors, joint contractors who are in breach of contract and breach of trust by trustees, the Act is also applicable, for example, to directors who have caused damage to their company. Where a contribution is claimed the fact that the claimant participated in an illegal activity does not, at least as a matter of principle, defeat the defendant's right to contribution.[243] But the relative blameworthiness of the parties will be a relevant consideration when the court is assessing what a just and equitable award should be. Consequently, if the effect of the

---

[235] *Ex p. Snowden* (1881) 17 Ch.D 44, 47 (James LJ).

[236] Mitchell, 'The Civil Liability (Contribution) Act 1978' (1997) 5 *RLR* 2.

[237] Civil Liability (Contribution) Act 1978, s. 1(1). The parties must be liable to the same person: *Birse Construction Ltd.* v. *Haiste Ltd.* [1996] 1 WLR 675.

[238] *Friends' Provident Life Office* v. *Hillier Parker May and Rowden (a firm)* [1995] 4 All ER 260.

[239] Civil Liability (Contribution) Act 1978, s. 6(1). This is to be interpreted widely, but it does not include exemplary damages. See *K* v. *P* [1993] Ch. 140, 148 (Ferris J).

[240] Civil Liability (Contribution) Act 1978, s. 2(1).

[241] *Madden* v. *Quirk* [1989] 1 WLR 702.

[242] Civil Liability (Contribution) Act 1978, s. 2(2).   [243] *K* v. *P* [1993] Ch. 140.

contribution would be to enable the plaintiff to retain the proceeds of fraud, then, at least where the defendant was not party to the fraud, it is unlikely that it would be just and equitable to require the defendant to make any contribution to the plaintiff.[244]

Although the 1978 Act will generally be applicable only where the plaintiff was legally compellable to pay the third party, there is an important exception to this where the plaintiff has *bona fide* settled or compromised the claim against him or her, since such a person can claim contribution from the defendant even though it was not clear on the facts, rather than as a matter of law, whether he or she was personally liable to the third party.[245]

The relationship between unjust enrichment claims and contribution under the 1978 Act was examined by the Court of Appeal in *Friends' Provident Life Office* v. *Hillier Parker May and Rowden (a firm)*.[246] In this case the plaintiff had appointed the defendant chartered surveyors to check and authorise payment in respect of the developer's claims for the plaintiff's share of the costs arising from the development of a shopping centre. The defendant had recommended that the plaintiff pay the developer's claims which included sums for 'notional interest'. In fact, it was not necessary for the plaintiff to pay anything for notional interest under the development agreement and so it sought to recover this sum from the developer. This litigation settled and the plaintiff then sued the defendant for damages for negligence and breach of contract arising from the defendant's failure to advise the plaintiff that the notional interest was not payable. The defendant claimed a contribution from the developer under the 1978 Act on the basis that the developer was liable to repay the money it had received to the plaintiff on the ground of mistake or absence of consideration. The question for the Court of Appeal was whether a restitutionary claim by the plaintiff against the developer could be treated as a claim in respect of the same damage as that alleged by the plaintiff against the defendant. This turned on whether the restitutionary remedy could be characterised as compensatory within section 6(1) of the 1978 Act. The Court of Appeal held that both a claim for restitution and one for damages could be a claim for compensation for damage, so that contribution could be awarded under the 1978 Act. This

---

[244] *Ibid*, p. 149 (Ferris J).

[245] Civil Liability (Contribution) Act 1978, s. 1(4). In addition, s. 1(2) enables the plaintiff to seek contribution even though he or she has ceased to be liable in respect of the damage in question since it occurred, but only if he or she was so liable immediately before making or agreeing to make the payment in respect of which the contribution is sought. By s. 1(3) the defendant remains liable to make contribution to the plaintiff even though he or she has ceased to be liable in respect of the damage in question, save where this extinction of liability occurred by virtue of the expiry of a limitation period.

[246] [1997] QB 85.

would also be the case if the plaintiff's restitutionary claim against the developer was founded on the vindication of proprietary rights. As Auld LJ said:[247]

[The Act] clearly spans a variety of causes of action, forms of damage in the sense of loss of some sort, and remedies, the last of which are gathered together under the umbrella of 'compensation'.

It did not matter that the liability of the defendant and the developer derived from different causes of action, namely tort and breach of contract on the one hand and unjust enrichment on the other, since it was sufficient that the liabilities arose from the same event, namely the plaintiff's payment for notional interest.

This is yet another example of a problem concerning the application of a statute to restitutionary claims where the terms of the statute do not clearly cover such claims.[248] The dispute would not have arisen in this case if the 1978 Act made specific reference to restitutionary liability. But despite this, the court's interpretation of the 1978 Act is acceptable, albeit rather artificial. The issue before the court was whether a restitutionary remedy could be characterised as compensatory. Even though a restitutionary remedy is assessed by reference to the defendant's gain rather than the plaintiff's loss, it is still possible to treat that remedy as compensating the plaintiff, at least where the plaintiff's claim is founded on the reversal of the defendant's unjust enrichment, since such a restitutionary claim depends on a benefit being subtracted from the plaintiff. The effect of the restitutionary remedy is to restore the benefit to the plaintiff, and so this could be considered to have a compensatory function. Crucially, the court's interpretation of the 1978 Act is defensible on policy grounds, since there is no reason why contribution should be denied to a plaintiff where the liability which is discharged derives from unjust enrichment, tort or breach of contract.

Even though the result of the *Friends' Provident* case is correct, there is one remaining difficulty. In *Friends' Provident* the restitutionary remedy which the plaintiff sought against the developer would have been equivalent to what it had lost, since the plaintiff's loss was equal to the defendant's gain. This would also be the case where the plaintiff sought to vindicate property rights. But it is possible for a plaintiff to bring a restitutionary claim even though it has not suffered a loss, as will be the case where a fiduciary has made a profit from his or her position as fiduciary.

---

[247] [1997] QB 85, p. 103.
[248] See also the interpretation of the Limitation Act 1980, discussed in Chapter 28, and the application of the Civil Jurisdiction and Judgments Act 1982 to restitutionary claims as examined by the House of Lords in *Kleinwort Benson Ltd.* v. *Glagow City Council* [1999] 1 AC 153.

The fiduciary is liable to account for this profit to the person to whom the fiduciary duties are owed.[249] It is not possible to conclude that the restitutionary remedy in such circumstances is compensatory because the plaintiff is not seeking to recover the value of something which he or she has lost. Consequently, if a third party was liable for assisting the fiduciary to breach his or her duty to the plaintiff, and was sued by the plaintiff, he or she would not be able to seek a contribution from the fiduciary because the plaintiff is not entitled to recover compensation. There is no convincing policy reason for this and so it is an unacceptable lacuna in the law of contribution.

(d) Restitution from the creditor

The plaintiff's payment to a creditor will automatically discharge a debt owed by the defendant to the creditor once the creditor has accepted payment, save where the plaintiff's intention to pay the creditor can be treated as vitiated.[250] This will be the case, for example, where the plaintiff paid the creditor as a result of a mistake or duress. Since the debt owed by the defendant will not be discharged in such circumstances the plaintiff is unable to obtain restitution from the defendant simply because he or she will not have been enriched. Rather, the creditor will have been enriched, since he or she received the plaintiff's money and can still sue the defendant for payment. The plaintiff must then establish a ground of restitution to secure recovery of this money. Usually, the reason the plaintiff's payment did not discharge the debt will also constitute the ground of restitution. So, for example, if the plaintiff paid the money to the creditor due to the effect of an operative mistake, the mistake will prevent the debt from being discharged and will also ground the plaintiff's restitutionary claim against the creditor. This was what happened in *Barclays Bank* v. *Simms*[251] where the plaintiff bank had mistakenly paid the creditor of its customer once the customer had revoked the authority to do so. Robert Goff J assumed that the payment had not discharged the customer's liability to the creditor and so the customer was not considered to have received any benefit from the payment. But the plaintiff successfully secured restitution from the creditor who had received the payment. This case must have been correctly decided. The customer's debt could not be regarded as discharged by the plaintiff since its intention that the customer receive the payment was vitiated by the mistake, and this mistake also provided the ground for restitution from the creditor.

Alternatively, where the plaintiff pays money to the creditor purporting to discharge the defendant's debt and the debt is not discharged then

---

[249] See Chapter 18.　　　　　　　　　　　　　　　[250] See p. 229 above.
[251] [1980] QB 677. Cp. *B. Liggett (Liverpool) Ltd.* v. *Barclays Bank Ltd.* [1928] 1 KB 48.

the plaintiff may found restitution on the ground of total failure of consideration,[252] since the expected effect of the payment, namely the discharge of the liability, has not occurred.[253] Whether the consideration
did fail totally depends on whether the payment was effective in any way
and this turns on what the plaintiff expected the payment to achieve. If,
as will usually be the case, the plaintiff simply intended the payment to
discharge the debt, and the debt has not been discharged, then there will
have been a total failure of consideration, and it should be irrelevant that
the creditor treated the debt as being discharged and has refrained from
suing the defendant.[254]

5. THREATS TO SECURE THE PERFORMANCE OF A STATUTORY DUTY

A final ground of restitution which is founded on the principle of compulsion is of limited importance, but it does have an independent existence, namely where the defendant demands payment to secure the
performance of a statutory duty.[255] In the usual case in which a defendant receives payment from the plaintiff where that payment has not
been authorised by statute, restitution of the unauthorised payment will
cause little difficulty, because the vast majority of such cases involve
payments made to public authorities. The decision of the House of Lords
in *Woolwich Equitable Building Society* v. *Inland Revenue Commissioners*[256] recognises a right to restitution in such circumstances.[257] But
this ground of restitution is confined to restitution from public authorities. In certain exceptional cases the defendant may be a private body
which has received payments in excess of that which has been authorised by statute. This situation is most likely to arise where the defendant
is in a monopolistic position,[258] such as a recently privatised company
which imposes charges for the provision of essential services in excess of
that which is authorised by statute or a regulator. In such circumstances
it appears that the ground of restitution cannot be the fact that the company has received money which is not due to it, which would be sufficient to ground the claim if the defendant were a public authority.
Rather, restitution is triggered by the implied threats which may accom-

---

[252] See Chapter 12.   [253] *Walter* v. *James* (1871) LR 6 Ex. 124, 127 (Kelly CB).
[254] Beatson, *Use and Abuse of Unjust Enrichment*, p. 202. Cp. Friedmann, 'Payment of
Another's Debt' (1983) 99 *LQR* 534, 539.
[255] See Burrows, *The Law of Restitution*, pp. 172–3. This was recognised as a distinct
ground of restitution founded on the principle of compulsion by Lord Goff in *Woolwich
Equitable Building Society* v. *IRC* [1993] AC 170, 165.
[256] [1993] AC 70.   [257] See Chapter 14.
[258] Goff and Jones, *The Law of Restitution*, p. 325.

pany the defendant's demand for payment. Since these threats accompany demands for a payment which is not due to the defendant, the threats should be considered to be illegitimate and restitution should follow if the threats caused the plaintiff to pay the defendant.

The leading case on this ground of restitution is *Great Western Railway* v. *Sutton*[259] where the defendant was a railway company which had charged the plaintiff more for carrying goods than it was charging other customers. This was in contravention of a statute which required all similar customers to be charged on the same basis. The plaintiff was able to recover the excess payment in an action for money had and received on the ground that he had been compelled to make the payment, for if the plaintiff had not paid the excess amount he would not have been able to procure the defendant to perform its duty of carrying the plaintiff's goods.

This is in fact a highly artificial ground of restitution, primarily because, whilst the emphasis is placed upon the assumed compulsion derived from the defendant refusing to perform a statutory duty unless it is paid more than it can legitimately receive, the real reason for restitution is that the excess money received by the defendant was not due to it. The better approach is that adopted by the House of Lords in *Woolwich*, namely to justify restitution by virtue of the *ultra vires* receipt of the defendant. This principle should be developed to cover even private bodies where they receive more than is authorised by statute. Restitution would still lie in cases such as *Great Western Railway* v. *Sutton*, but not because of artificially constructed compulsion, deduced from implied threats, but rather because of the defendant's unauthorised receipt. Alternatively, this type of case may be analysed with reference to the ground of absence of consideration, at least where the plaintiff was not required to pay anything to the defendant,[260] or by the ground of mistake, it now being irrelevant that the mistake was one of law.[261]

---

[259] (1869) LR 4 HL 226. See also *South of Scotland Electricity Board* v. *British Oxygen Co. Ltd. (No. 2)* [1959] 1 WLR 587.

[260] Chapter 12.   [261] See Chapter 8.

10

Exploitation

1. GENERAL PRINCIPLES

(a) The essence of exploitation

It was seen in the last chapter that compulsion is not a ground of restitution in its own right but is a general principle on which a number of specific grounds of restitution are founded. Exactly the same is true of exploitation. Exploitation is a useful general principle to recognise, since it enables a number of disparate grounds of restitution to be treated together. These grounds have the common characteristic that the defendant has actually taken advantage of the plaintiff's weaker position in some way, or can at least be presumed to have taken advantage of the plaintiff. The essence of exploitation consequently involves the actual or potential abuse of power by the defendant. The grounds of restitution which are founded on the principle of exploitation can be considered to be both plaintiff- and defendant-oriented. They are primarily plaintiff-oriented in the sense that the effect of the actual or presumed exploitation means that the plaintiff's intent to transfer a benefit to the defendant can be treated as vitiated. But the grounds of restitution are also defendant-oriented in the sense that it is the actual or presumed conduct of the defendant which constitutes the exploitation of the plaintiff's weaker position.[1]

(b) The relationship between exploitation and other principles

The boundary between exploitation and compulsion is particularly difficult to draw, primarily because the grounds of restitution which are founded on these two principles operate in a similar way, to vitiate the plaintiff's intention to benefit the defendant by virtue of the defendant's conduct. This is because the defendant's conduct in compelling the plaintiff to act or in exploiting his or her weakness deprives the plaintiff of the opportunity to exercise a sufficiently free choice whether to provide a benefit to the defendant.[2] Despite this apparent similarity

---

[1] Sometimes, however, the exploitation comes from a third party. See p. 265 below.
[2] See Birks and Chin, 'On the Nature of Undue Influence' in *Good Faith and Fault in Contract Law* (ed. Beatson and Friedmann, Oxford: Clarendon Press, 1995) p. 58.

between the two principles, they are crucially different. The essential feature of compulsion is that the plaintiff is not able to exercise a free choice to transfer a benefit because of threats made by the defendant, whether express or implied from the circumstances. The essential feature of exploitation, on the other hand, is that the plaintiff's lack of a free choice arises from the fact that the defendant occupied a superior position to that of the plaintiff which the defendant either actually exploited or was able to exploit. To establish exploitation it is not necessary to show that the defendant has threatened the plaintiff in any way.

There will, however, be cases where the defendant in threatening the plaintiff will also have exploited him or her so grounds of restitution founded on both compulsion and exploitation will be applicable. Usually, in such circumstances, it will be more appropriate for the plaintiff to emphasise the threats and so rely on grounds of restitution which are founded on the principle of compulsion. There will also be some cases where the defendant has exploited the plaintiff's weaker position by making a misrepresentation and so induced the plaintiff to make a mistake.[3] In such cases the plaintiff could rely on the mistake as an alternative ground of restitution. In most cases of exploitation, however, the plaintiff will be sufficiently aware of the circumstances so that it is not possible to conclude that he or she was mistaken, leaving only the grounds of restitution founded on exploitation as relevant for the establishment of the plaintiff's restitutionary claim.

(c) Identifying the enrichment

Where the plaintiff wishes to seek restitution of a benefit which has been transferred to the defendant as a result of the defendant's exploitation of the plaintiff's weaker position, the enrichment will usually be in the form of money. But it is possible that, as a consequence of the defendant's exploitation, he or she will have received non-monetary benefits from the plaintiff, such as goods or even services.[4] Restitution will be available by reason of the exploitation, regardless of the type of enrichment received by the defendant, although with goods and services the question of whether or not the defendant has actually been enriched may be more difficult to establish.[5]

---

[3] See Chapter 8. Similarly the *non est factum* doctrine, also examined in Chapter 8, could be justified by reference to the principle of exploitation.

[4] See *O'Sullivan* v. *Management Agency and Music Ltd.* [1985] QB 428 where the plaintiff successfully brought an action for restitution in respect of services received by the defendant as a result of undue influence.

[5] See Chapter 4.

(d) Vitiation of transactions for exploitation

Usually the effect of the defendant's exploitation is that the plaintiff enters into a transaction with the defendant and transfers a benefit to him or her pursuant to it. If the plaintiff is to recover such benefits it is first necessary for him or her to establish that the transaction has been vitiated by reason of the exploitation. This is because of the principle that restitutionary remedies will not be awarded to subvert transactions.[6] These transactions will usually involve contracts but they may also involve voluntary dispositions such as gifts.[7] The courts are more prepared to set aside gifts for exploitation than they are to set aside contracts.[8] This accords with the general policy of the law, which is to uphold agreements wherever possible and only to set them aside in extreme cases. Gifts are more readily set aside for another reason, namely that where the plaintiff has made a gift to the defendant without receiving anything in return this suggests that the plaintiff may have been exploited by the defendant.

Most of the cases which arise in the context of exploitation are concerned with the vitiation of contracts. The effect of exploitation on the part of the defendant is generally to render the contract voidable,[9] so if the plaintiff wishes to set it aside he or she must rescind it.[10] As a consequence of rescission the defendant must make restitution to the plaintiff of any benefits which he or she has received pursuant to the transaction and the plaintiff will be required to make counter-restitution to the defendant of the value of any benefit which the plaintiff has received pursuant to it.[11] These restitutionary consequences of rescission can be explained by reference to the unjust enrichment principle, for without restitution the defendant would be unjustly enriched as a result of the contract being rescinded.

(e) The relationship between exploitation and wrongdoing

In some situations where the defendant has obtained a benefit as a result of the exploitation of the plaintiff, the plaintiff's restitutionary claim may

---

[6] See p. 40 above.

[7] See, for example, *Allcard* v. *Skinner* (1887) 36 Ch.D 145 and *Louth* v. *Diprose* [1992] 75 CLR 621.

[8] *Wright* v. *Carter* [1903] 1 Ch. 27, 50 (Vaughan Williams LJ).

[9] Save where the contract is already void by virtue of illegality. See p. 297 below.

[10] On rescission generally see pp. 28–36 above. Rescission is subject to the usual bars of affirmation, lapse of time, intervention of third parties and counter-restitution being impossible.

[11] *O'Sullivan* v. *Management Agency and Music Ltd.* [1985] AC 686. See also *Cheese* v. *Thomas* [1994] 1 WLR 129 and *Mahoney* v. *Purnell* [1996] 3 All ER 61.

be founded on two alternative restitutionary principles. First, he or she may be able to establish that one of the recognised grounds of restitution is applicable, so that restitution will be founded on the principle of reversing the defendant's unjust enrichment. Alternatively, the plaintiff's claim may be founded explicitly on the defendant's wrongdoing. This is particularly true where the defendant is a fiduciary and exploits his or her position at the expense of the plaintiff. This will constitute a breach of fiduciary duty for which a number of remedies are available, including restitution.[12] In such circumstances the plaintiff may bring alternative claims founded on unjust enrichment and wrongdoing, although he or she will need to elect between them once judgment has been given.[13]

2. UNDUE INFLUENCE

(a) The essence of undue influence as a ground of restitution

(i) The types of undue influence

Undue influence is an equitable ground of restitution which applies where the defendant is in a relationship of influence with the plaintiff[14] and the defendant either abuses that relationship to induce the plaintiff to transfer a benefit to him or her, or he or she is presumed to have abused that relationship to induce the transfer of a benefit. There are consequently two forms of undue influence, actual and presumed.[15] Both kinds of undue influence may be applicable in one case with the consequence that they should both be pleaded.[16]

(ii) The rationale of undue influence as a ground of restitution

Undue influence constitutes a ground of restitution because the effect of the actual or presumed abuse of the defendant's relationship of influence with the plaintiff is that the plaintiff's decision to transact with the defendant cannot be regarded as freely exercised.[17] This was well expressed by Eldon LC in *Huguenin* v. *Baseley*,[18] who said that the

---

[12] See pp. 283–6 below and Chapter 18.   [13] See p. 476 below.

[14] Where there is no relationship of influence between the parties, a transaction may still be set aside on the alternative ground of the defendant's unconscionable conduct. See pp. 286–97 below.

[15] *Allcard* v. *Skinner* (1887) 36 Ch.D 145, 171 (Cotton LJ).

[16] See, for example, *Re Craig* [1971] Ch. 95 and *BCCI* v. *Aboody* [1990] 1 QB 923, 953 (Slade LJ).

[17] *National Westminster Bank plc.* v. *Morgan* [1985] AC 686, 705 (Lord Scarman), relying on a dictum of Lindley LJ in *Allcard* v. *Skinner* (1887) 36 Ch.D 145, 182. See also *The Commercial Bank of Australia Ltd.* v. *Amadio* (1983) 151 CLR 447, 461 (Mason J).

[18] (1807) 14 Ves. Jun. 273, 300; 33 ER 526, 536.

'question is not whether [the plaintiff] knew what she was doing, had done, or proposed to do, but how the intention was produced'. Consequently, where the plaintiff has been induced to transact with the defendant by actual or presumed undue influence his or her intention to enter into the transaction can be regarded as vitiated. The policy behind undue influence as a ground of restitution is to protect the vulnerable from exploitation by those who are in a stronger position than them-selves,[19] rather than a policy to set aside transactions on the ground of the plaintiff's folly, imprudence or lack of foresight.[20]

(iii) Is undue influence plaintiff- or defendant-oriented?

There has been much discussion recently whether undue influence is a ground of restitution which is plaintiff- or defendant-oriented. If it is plaintiff-oriented the justification for its existence as a ground of restitu-tion is that the effect of the undue influence is to impair the plaintiff's capacity to make decisions, so that his or her intention to transfer a ben-efit to the defendant can be regarded as vitiated.[21] If undue influence is defendant-oriented then it is justified as a ground of restitution by virtue of the defendant's conduct which can variously be described as 'wicked' or simply 'unconscionable'.[22] This was recognised by Millett LJ in *Dunbar Bank plc. v. Nadeem*:[23]

The court of equity is a court of conscience. It sets aside transactions obtained by the exercise of undue influence because such conduct is unconscionable.

But whether undue influence is a plaintiff- or defendant-oriented ground of restitution is ultimately a sterile debate because undue influ-ence can be characterised as both plaintiff- and defendant-oriented. Undue influence should principally be treated as impairing the plain-tiff's ability to exercise a free choice to enter into the transaction, since this is consistent with other grounds of restitution, such as mistake and duress, which similarly result in a vitiated intent to participate in the transaction. But it is dangerous to conclude from this that undue influ-ence is entirely plaintiff-oriented, since this implies that the nature of the defendant's conduct is not relevant to the identification of undue influ-ence. This is incorrect. To establish actual undue influence it is essential to establish some degree of responsibility for the undue influence on the part of the defendant, and for the purposes of presumed undue influence

---

[19] *Royal Bank of Scotland* v. *Etridge (No. 2)* [1998] 4 All ER 705, 712 (Stuart-Smith LJ).

[20] *Allcard* v. *Skinner* (1887) 36 Ch.D 145, 183 (Lindley LJ).

[21] Birks and Chin, in *Good Faith and Fault in Contract Law* (ed. Beatson and Friedmann) p. 57.

[22] See Bigwood, 'Undue Influence: "Impaired Consent" or "Wicked Exploitation"?' (1996) 16 *OJLS* 503.

[23] [1998] 3 All ER 876, 884.

such responsibility is presumed, with the burden being placed on the defendant to rebut the presumption by showing that the plaintiff was not induced to act by means of undue influence. Consequently, both forms of undue influence can be considered to be defendant-oriented as well as plaintiff-oriented and nothing can usefully be gained from treating them as being either one or the other.

(iv) Is undue influence a form of wrongdoing?

It has sometimes been suggested that where the plaintiff transferred a benefit to the defendant as a result of undue influence the defendant can be considered to have committed a wrong. If this is correct it follows that the plaintiff's restitutionary claim can be founded on the wrong rather than on the defendant's unjust enrichment. There is not, however, any justification for treating undue influence as a wrong. As Birks has said:

there is no case which suggests that undue influence may be characterised as a breach of duty or gives rise to actions for damages or indeed to any liability beyond the primary duty to surrender whatever is so acquired.[24]

But, despite this, there are cases which have characterised the person who unduly influenced the plaintiff, either actually or presumptively, as a wrongdoer.[25] Such a characterisation is unfortunate and misleading, because it does not follow that a plaintiff who has been unduly influenced by the defendant can bring a restitutionary claim founded on wrongdoing; he or she is confined to a restitutionary claim founded on unjust enrichment.

(b) Actual undue influence

A crucial distinction needs to be drawn between two grounds of restitution, although they are often both called undue influence. The first ground arises where the defendant compels the plaintiff to pay a sum of money or to enter into a contract as a result of lawful threats. This ground is founded upon the principle of compulsion, rather than exploitation, and for this reason it is analysed in Chapter 9. Since the essential feature of this ground is that the defendant has pressurised the plaintiff, it should properly be called undue pressure[26] to distinguish it from undue influence. The other ground of restitution, which is called actual undue influence, is concerned with those cases where the defendant is shown to have unfairly exploited his or her position of influence over the

---

[24] 'Equity in the Modern Law: An Exercise in Taxonomy' (1996) 26 *Univ. WALR* 1, 42.
[25] *Barcalys Bank plc.* v. *O'Brien* [1994] AC 180, 196 (Lord Browne-Wilkinson) and *Royal Bank of Scotland* v. *Etridge (No. 2)* [1998] 4 All ER 705, 711 (Stuart-Smith LJ).
[26] *Lloyds Bank Ltd.* v. *Bundy* [1975] QB 326, 338 (Lord Denning MR).

plaintiff. This ground of restitution is properly treated as founded on the exploitation principle. Restitution on the ground of actual undue influence has been justified on the basis that the defendant should not 'be allowed to retain any benefit arising from his own fraud or wrongful act'.[27] But this ground of restitution is better justified on the basis that the plaintiff's intention to benefit the defendant can be treated as vitiated by the exploitation. That actual undue influence is not founded on the principle of compulsion was recognised by Millett LJ in *Dunbar Bank plc.* v. *Nadeem*[28] who stated that 'neither coercion, nor pressure, nor deliberate concealment is a necessary element in a case of actual undue influence'.

(i) Establishing actual undue influence

To establish actual undue influence the plaintiff must show that a number of conditions have been satisfied. These conditions were identified by the Court of Appeal in *Bank of Credit and Commerce International SA* v. *Aboody.*[29]

(1) The defendant[30] must have had the ability to influence the plaintiff. This will require evidence that the relationship between the parties was such that the plaintiff trusted and had confidence in the defendant. This is illustrated by *Morley* v. *Laughnan*,[31] where it was held that the deceased had become completely dependent on the defendant, who had converted the deceased to become a member of an exclusive and secluded religious sect, known as 'The Exclusive Brethren'. The deceased was found to have been particularly susceptible to influence, being impressionable, physically weak, highly strung and morbidly religious. The ability of the defendant to influence the deceased was so extreme that he became the deceased's temporal and spiritual adviser and even regulated his diet and medicine.

(2) The defendant must have exercised this influence over the plaintiff. This will require evidence that the defendant had actually dominated the plaintiff. This was described by Sir Eric Sachs in *Lloyds Bank Ltd.* v. *Bundy*[32] as arising 'when the will of one person has become so dominated by that of another that . . . "the person was the mere puppet of the dominator"'. It was, however, emphasised in *Aboody* that actual undue

---

[27] *Allcard* v. *Skinner* (1887) 36 Ch.D 145, 171 (Cotton LJ).

[28] [1998] 3 All ER 876, 883.

[29] [1990] 1 QB 923, 967. The Court of Appeal characterised actual undue influence as 'Class 1', to distinguish it from presumed undue influence, which they characterised as 'Class 2'. Such numerical characterisation can be confusing, so it is safer to characterise the grounds of restitution simply by reference to the terms 'actual' and 'presumed'.

[30] Or, where relevant, a third party who induced the plaintiff to transact with the defendant. See p. 265 below.

[31] [1893] 1 Ch. 736.   [32] [1975] QB 326, 342.

influence did not necessarily depend on proof of some positive act of coercion being exercised over the plaintiff; undue influence can be more subtle.

(3) The influence must have been exercised unduly,[33] as is the case where the defendant has victimised the plaintiff in some way, for example by forcing, tricking or misleading the plaintiff into parting with his or her property, or agreeing to part with the property.[34] It is not necessary to prove that the defendant intended to injure the plaintiff.

(4) The exercise of the influence must have been a sufficient cause of the transaction which the plaintiff seeks to set aside or the transfer of the benefit to the defendant. The test of causation for these purposes is that of 'but for' cause, as was recognised by Slade LJ in *Aboody*,[35] who said that a transaction would not be set aside for undue influence 'where the evidence establishes that on the balance of probabilities the complainant would have entered into the transaction in any event'. In other words, it must be shown that but for the undue influence the plaintiff would not have entered into a transaction with the defendant or transferred the benefit. But is this test of causation justified, bearing in mind that the test of causation where the ground of restitution is induced mistake[36] or duress of the person or property[37] is a test of operative causation where it is sufficient that the mistake or duress simply contributed to the plaintiff's actions? Whether a test of 'but for' causation is appropriate for the ground of actual undue influence depends on how blameworthy we consider the defendant's conduct to be. The test of 'but for' causation was justified in its application to economic duress[38] because the defendant's conduct may be considered to be less blameworthy than where the duress relates to the person or property, so requiring a more stringent test of causation to be satisfied before restitutionary relief could be awarded. In other words where the defendant's conduct can be considered to be more blameworthy, the attitude of the law is to allow restitutionary relief to be granted more easily through the operation of a test of causation which is easier to satisfy, namely that of operative causation. When the test of causation is analysed in these terms, it suggests that a test of operative rather than 'but for' causation should be available where the ground of restitution is actual undue influence, simply because the requirement of influence being exercised unduly implies a sufficient degree of blameworthiness to justify the award of restitutionary relief without needing to satisfy a stringent test of causation as well.

[33] *Dunbar Bank plc.* v. *Nadeem* [1998] 3 All ER 876, 883 (Millett LJ).
[34] See *Allcard* v. *Skinner* (1887) 36 Ch.D 145, 181 (Lindley LJ).
[35] [1990] 1 QB 923, 971.   [36] See p. 166 below.
[37] See pp. 197–200 below.   [38] See p. 210 below.

(ii) The identification of actual undue influence

The facts of *Aboody* itself illustrate how the requirements for establishing actual undue influence are applied. In that case the defendant's husband had induced her to execute three charges on the matrimonial home as security for loans to a company in which they both owned shares. The house was registered in the wife's name only. The husband had induced his wife's consent to the execution of the charges by deliberately concealing crucial matters from her. The wife wanted the charges to be set aside on the ground of actual undue influence. The Court of Appeal accepted that the husband had the capacity to influence his wife since, because she trusted her husband, she habitually signed documents relating to the company without considering their contents. The husband had exercised this influence by inviting his wife to enter into the relevant transactions. This influence was found to have been unduly exercised because the husband had deliberately concealed from his wife the risks involved in the transactions. Finally, the exercise of this undue influence was a sufficient cause of the wife signing the relevant documents since it was accepted that, if the husband had not unduly influenced his wife, she would not have signed them. Therefore, the four requirements for establishing actual undue influence were satisfied. But the Court of Appeal went on to hold that there was a fifth requirement which needed to be satisfied before a transaction could be set aside for undue influence, namely that the particular transaction was manifestly and unfairly disadvantageous to the plaintiff, and since this had not been established on the facts the charges were not set aside.

(iii) The requirement of manifest and unfair disadvantage

A requirement that the transaction was manifestly and unfairly disadvantageous to the plaintiff, as recognised in *Aboody*, involves consideration of whether the transaction itself was unfair, so-called substantive unfairness or contractual imbalance, rather than that the means by which the transaction was procured were unfair, so-called procedural unfairness.[39] This requirement of manifest disadvantage was, however, later rejected by the House of Lords in *CIBC Mortgages plc. v. Pitt.*[40] Burrows has argued that a requirement of manifest disadvantage is necessary before actual undue influence can be established since, without it, there is insufficient evidence of unacceptable exploitation of the plaintiff by the defendant.[41] It is true that the fact that the transaction itself was manifestly disadvantageous may be of some evidential significance in establishing undue influence, since the terms of the transac-

---

[39] See *Hart* v. *O'Connor* [1985] AC 1000, 1018, PC.   [40] [1994] 1 AC 200.
[41] Burrows, *The Law of Restitution*, p. 195.

tion might assist the court in determining whether there was procedural unfairness. For example, the more unreasonable the terms of the agreement the less likely it is that the plaintiff will have freely agreed to them. But there are likely to be a number of cases where the terms of the particular transaction are perfectly reasonable but the defendant will still have unacceptably taken advantage of the plaintiff's weaker position. This is illustrated by the facts of *CICB Mortgages plc.* v. *Pitt* itself, where a husband obtained his wife's consent to using their home, which was registered in their joint names, as security for a loan from a mortgage company. The House of Lords accepted that the husband had actually used undue influence to procure his wife's consent and so, as against him, the transaction was invalid.[42] It made no difference that the terms of the transaction itself were perfectly fair. The transaction was in principle invalid simply because of the methods to which the husband had resorted to procure the consent of his wife. The House of Lords was therefore correct to reject a requirement that the plaintiff must show that the transaction itself was manifestly disadvantageous before it is possible to conclude that there had been actual undue influence.

This rejection of manifest disadvantage as an element of actual undue influence means that the true nature of this ground of restitution becomes apparent. This ground is invoked, not because the terms of the transaction are unfair, but rather because the means by which the defendant procured the plaintiff's consent to the transaction are regarded as unfair. Consequently, actual undue influence is concerned with the procedure by which the plaintiff consented to the transaction and not with the substance of the transaction itself. The essence of actual undue influence was encapsulated in an important dictum of Lord Browne-Wilkinson in the *Pitt* case:

Actual undue influence is a species of fraud. Like any other victim of fraud, a person who has been induced by undue influence to carry out a transaction which he did not freely and knowingly enter into is entitled to have that transaction set aside as of right . . . The effect of the wrongdoer's conduct is to prevent the wronged party from bringing a free will and properly informed mind to bear on the proposed transaction which accordingly must be set aside in equity as a matter of justice.[43]

---

[42] Whether the husband's undue influence affected the mortgage company was a separate question. See p. 270 below.

[43] [1994] 1 AC 200, 209.

(c) Presumed undue influence[44]

(i) The essential features of presumed undue influence

Sometimes it will not be possible for the plaintiff to show that he or she was actually unduly influenced to enter into a transaction with the defendant or to transfer a benefit to the defendant. Instead, the circumstances of the case may be such that undue influence can be presumed to have caused the plaintiff to enter into such a transaction or to transfer a benefit. Once undue influence is presumed, the defendant then bears the burden of proving that it was not the cause of the plaintiff's actions.[45] Restitution is justified in these circumstances, not because the defendant has actually exploited the plaintiff, but because he or she is presumed to have done so.[46]

It is possible to presume undue influence only when two conditions are satisfied. First, the relationship between the parties must be such that the plaintiff can be treated as being under the defendant's influence, so that the plaintiff was not a free agent. Secondly, the transaction with the defendant must be manifestly disadvantageous to the plaintiff. Since the satisfaction of these tests means that the plaintiff is presumed to have been induced by undue influence to have entered into a transaction, there is no separate question of causation to be examined. Indeed, it is because it is difficult or impossible for the plaintiff to prove that he or she was induced to enter into the transaction as a result of undue influence that there is a role for a presumption of undue influence.

(ii) Relationships of influence

A relationship of influence is one in which the plaintiff has placed his or her trust and confidence in the defendant so that the defendant is in a position which enables him or her to influence the plaintiff to enter into the particular transaction without necessarily dominating the plaintiff.[47] There are two methods for ascertaining which relationships will trigger the presumption. The first requires the relationship to fall within a recognised group of relationships which are always treated as those in which the plaintiff is under the defendant's influence, whereas the second method requires a relationship of trust and confidence to be established by reference to the particular facts of the case.

---

[44] This is called relational undue influence by Birks, *An Introduction to the Law of Restitution*, p. 184.

[45] *Allcard* v. *Skinner* (1887) 36 Ch.D 145, 170 (Cotton LJ).

[46] *National Westminster Bank* v. *Morgan* [1985] AC 686, 704 (Lord Scarman).

[47] *Goldsworthy* v. *Brickell* [1987] Ch. 338, 401 (Nourse LJ).

(1) Recognised relationships of influence[48]

Where the relationship between the parties is recognised by law as being a relationship of influence, it is sufficient that the plaintiff establishes that his or her relationship with the defendant falls within one of these established categories without any need to prove that he or she placed trust and confidence in the defendant. So, for example, it will always be presumed that a parent has influence over his or her minor child,[49] that a guardian has influence over his or her ward[50] and that a doctor has influence over his or her patient.[51] Other relationships have been treated as presumed relationships of influence, notably that a solicitor has influence over his or her client,[52] and that a trustee has influence over his or her beneficiary,[53] but such cases are better treated as involving an abuse of a fiduciary relationship of confidence, with restitution founded on wrongdoing rather than unjust enrichment.[54] Crucially, the relationship between a husband and wife is not one which falls within these established categories of influence,[55] although a relationship of influence might be identified from the particular facts of the case.

(2) Factual relationship of influence[56]

If the relationship between the plaintiff and the defendant does not fall within one of the recognised relationships of influence, the plaintiff must prove that the actual relationship between the parties was such that he or she placed such a degree of trust and confidence in the defendant that he or she was under the defendant's influence so that the defendant could take advantage of the plaintiff.[57] Such factual relationships of influence have been identified in a wide variety of different contexts. For example, such a relationship has been found to exist between a housekeeper and her elderly employer,[58] between a junior employee and her employer's agent,[59] between a farm manager and the elderly owner of

---

[48] In *BCCI* v. *Aboody* [1990] 1 QB 923, 953 this was characterised as Class 2(A).
[49] *Lancashire Loans Ltd.* v. *Black* [1934] 1 KB 380. Where the child has passed the age of majority it seems that there will be an automatic presumption of influence for a short time afterwards and thereafter a relationship of influence will need to be established on the particular facts of the case: at p. 419 (Greer LJ). See also *Bainbrigge* v. *Browne* (1880) 18 Ch.D 188.
[50] *Hatch* v. *Hatch* (1804) 9 Ves. 292; 32 ER 615.
[51] *Mitchell* v. *Homfray* (1881) 8 QBD 587; *Radcliffe* v. *Price* (1902) 18 TLR 466.
[52] *Wright* v. *Carter* [1903] 1 Ch. 27.
[53] *Ellis* v. *Barker* (1870) LR 7 Ch.App. 104.
[54] See pp. 283–6 below and Chapter 18.
[55] *National Westminster Bank plc.* v. *Morgan* [1985] AC 686, 703 (Lord Scarman). See also *Barclays Bank plc.* v. *O'Brien* [1994] 1 AC 180, 190 (Lord Browne-Wilkinson).
[56] In *BCCI* v. *Aboody* [1990] 1 QB 923, 953 this was characterised as Class 2(B).
[57] *Re Brocklehurst* [1978] Ch. 14.   [58] *Re Craig* [1971] Ch. 95.
[59] *Crédit Lyonnais Bank Nederland NV* v. *Burch* [1997] 1 All ER 144.

the farm[60] and between a mother superior and a nun in her convent.[61] Such a relationship has even been recognised between a bank and a potential guarantor of debts owed to the bank, where the assistant bank manager had gone beyond the normal commercial role of the bank and had advised on general matters relating to the wisdom of the particular transaction.[62] But it does not follow from the fact that relationships of influence have previously been recognised in these situations that all similar relationships can be treated as relationships of influence; everything turns on the facts of the particular case. For example, in *National Westminster Bank plc.* v. *Morgan*[63] the House of Lords held that undue influence could not be presumed between a bank manager and the wife of one of his customers. The court stressed that the relationship between a banker and his or her customer will trigger the presumption of undue influence only in the exceptional case where there is evidence that the relationship between the parties went beyond the normal business relationship of banker and customer.[64]

The most important relationship in practice which may be shown to involve trust and confidence is that between a wife and her husband, and similar relationships which are founded on sexual and emotional ties, regardless of whether they are heterosexual[65] or homosexual. As regards such relationships it can never be assumed that, for example, a wife does repose trust and confidence in her husband as regards the management of their mutual financial affairs; this is something which needs to be established on the facts of each individual case. However, in *Barclays Bank plc.* v. *O'Brien*[66] Lord Browne-Wilkinson did suggest that 'the risk of undue influence affecting a voluntary disposition by a wife in favour of a husband is greater than in the ordinary run of cases where no sexual or emotional ties affect the free exercise of the individual's will'.[67] Although it is usually the husband who is presumed to have unduly influenced the wife, it is sometimes possible to presume that the wife unduly influenced the husband. This is illustrated by *Simpson* v. *Simpson*[68] where the trans-

---

[60] *Goldsworthy* v. *Brickell* [1987] Ch. 378. See also *O'Sullivan* v. *Management Agency and Music Ltd.* [1985] QB 428 where a relationship of influence was identified between a manager and a young singer-songwriter. Since the relationship was also characterised as a fiduciary relationship the case is better regarded as one involving abuse of a fiduciary relationship of confidence rather than undue influence. See Chapter 18.

[61] *Allcard* v. *Skinner* (1887) 36 Ch.D 145.

[62] *Lloyds Bank Ltd.* v. *Bundy* [1975] 1 QB 326. See also *Harry* v. *Tate and Lyle Refineries Ltd.* [1982] 2 Lloyd's Rep. 416, where a so-called 'fiduciary relationship' was identified between an employee and his employer's insurers.

[63] [1985] AC 686.   [64] As occurred in *Lloyds Bank Ltd.* v. *Bundy* [1975] 1 QB 326.

[65] See, for example, *Zamet* v. *Hyman* [1961] 1 WLR 1442 where the relationship between an engaged couple was treated as a relationship of influence.

[66] [1994] 1 AC 180, 191.

[67] Cp. *Crédit Lyonnais Bank Nederland NV* v. *Burch* [1997] 1 All ER 144, 155 (Millet LJ).

[68] [1992] 1 FLR 601.

fer of property by a husband to his wife was set aside because the husband was increasingly dependent on his wife by virtue of a terminal illness, suggesting that there was a particular relationship of trust and confidence between them.

In determining whether there is a relationship of trust and confidence between the plaintiff and the defendant, the burden is placed on the plaintiff, but he or she can have regard to all of the circumstances of the case to identify such a relationship. Whilst the terms of the transaction itself will never be sufficient evidence to establish the necessary relationship, where the relationship between the parties is of a type which may involve trust and confidence the terms of the transaction will be of particular significance in confirming the conclusion that such a relationship did indeed exist.[69]

(iii) Manifest and unfair disadvantage

It is not sufficient that the relationship between the parties is such that the plaintiff can be presumed to have been under the influence of the defendant. The plaintiff must also show that the transaction between the parties was manifestly and unfairly disadvantageous to him or her.[70] A transaction will be considered to be manifestly disadvantageous to the plaintiff if it was so improvident that it cannot reasonably be accounted for by ordinary motives on which reasonable people act, motives such as charity, friendship or family relationships.[71] This is an objective test, to be judged by asking whether a reasonable and independent person, who knew all of the relevant facts at the time of the transaction, would have considered the transaction to be obviously disadvantageous to the plaintiff.[72] It is not sufficient that the disadvantage was unfair, it must also be manifest as was recognised by Slade LJ in *BCCI* v. *Aboody*:[73]

the overall disadvantageous nature of a transaction cannot be said to be manifest, if it only emerges after a fine and close evaluation of its various beneficial and detrimental features. It must be obvious.

Evidence that the transaction was manifestly disadvantageous can take many forms. For example, the plaintiff may have entered into an agreement with the defendant which was inequitable, irrational or unconscionable, for example because it was a sale at an undervalue.[74] A gift is more likely to be regarded as manifestly disadvantageous to the plaintiff than a contract, simply because the plaintiff will not have

---

[69] *Crédit Lyonnais Bank Nederland NV* v. *Burch* [1997] 1 All ER 144, 154–5 (Millett LJ).
[70] *National Westminster Bank plc.* v. *Morgan* [1985] AC 686.
[71] See *Goldsworthy* v. *Brickell* [1987] Ch. 378, 407 (Nourse LJ). See also *Allcard* v. *Skinner* (1887) 36 Ch.D 145, 185 (Lindley LJ).
[72] *BCCI* v. *Aboody* [1990] QB 923, 965 (Slade LJ).   [73] *Ibid*, p. 964.
[74] *National Westminster Bank plc.* v. *Morgan* [1985] AC 486, 704 (Lord Scarman).

received any consideration in return. As Lord Scarman recognised in *National Westminster Bank plc.* v. *Morgan*,[75] 'gifts are transactions in which the donor by parting with his property accepts a disadvantage or a sacrifice'. This will usually be a matter of degree, since the greater the size of the gift the easier it will be to conclude that there was no good motive for the gift being made.[76] Where the transaction involved the creation of a security interest then, to determine whether it was manifestly disadvantageous to the plaintiff, it is necessary to balance the likelihood at the time the security was executed that it would be enforced against the benefits gained by the plaintiff in executing the security.[77] Whether the transaction was manifestly disadvantageous is to be judged by reference to the circumstances which existed at the time the transaction was entered into, without reference to subsequent events.[78] A transaction will not be considered to be manifestly disadvantageous if it was beneficial to the plaintiff, even though part of the transaction was not for the plaintiff's benefit.[79]

The decision of the Court of Appeal in *Cheese* v. *Thomas*[80] illustrates how manifest disadvantage is determined. In this case the plaintiff's contribution of £43,000 to the purchase of a house, which was registered in the name of someone else, was characterised as manifestly disadvantageous, even though the plaintiff had the right to live rent-free in the house for the rest of his life. The manifest disadvantage arose because there were a number of drawbacks to the transaction, including that the plaintiff had put all his capital into the house, he could not compel the owner to sell the house if he wished to recover his contribution and move elsewhere and he was at risk of losing possession if the owner of the house failed to keep up with mortgage payments to the building society. This case illustrates that all the facts of the case need to be examined and the advantages of the transaction need to be carefully balanced against the disadvantages.

A particularly extreme example of manifest disadvantage occurred in *Crédit Lyonnais Bank Nederland NV* v. *Burch*[81] where an employee agreed to give a charge over her flat and an unlimited guarantee for all of her employer's debts. This meant that she had committed herself to a liability which was well beyond her means, and she risked the loss of her home and personal bankruptcy for the company which employed her, even though she had no interest in the company either as shareholder or

---

[75] [1985] AC 486, 704.
[76] *BCCI* v. *Aboody* [1990] 1 QB 923, 961 (Slade LJ). See also *Allcard* v. *Skinner* (1887) 36 Ch.D 145, 185 (Lindley LJ).
[77] *BCCI* v. *Aboody* [1990] 1 QB 923, 965 (Slade LJ). [78] *Ibid*, p. 964 (Slade LJ).
[79] *Dunbar Bank plc.* v. *Nadeem* [1998] 3 All ER 876.
[80] [1994] 1 WLR 129. See also *Bank of Scotland* v. *Bennett* [1997] 1 FLR 801.
[81] [1997] 1 All ER 144. See also *Steeples* v. *Lea* [1998] 1 FLR 138.

director. Such a transaction was so disadvantageous to the employee that it was characterised as an unconscionable bargain.[82]

With the rejection of manifest disadvantage as a requirement for establishing actual undue influence[83] it might be considered that there is no longer a role for this requirement in respect of presumed undue influence, but this is not correct. The requirement of manifest disadvantage is justifiable in this context simply because the features of presumed undue influence are fundamentally different from those of actual undue influence. Where the defendant has been shown to have actually unduly influenced the plaintiff, this in itself is sufficient evidence that the plaintiff was not able to exercise a free choice to enter into a transaction with the defendant or to transfer a benefit. But, for presumed undue influence to constitute a ground of restitution, the mere fact that the nature of the relationship between the parties was such that the defendant had influence over the plaintiff is not in itself sufficient evidence to justify the conclusion that the plaintiff was unable to exercise a free choice. Something else needs to be shown before such a conclusion can be reached, and that extra element is proof that the transaction was manifestly disadvantageous to the plaintiff. It is this requirement of manifest and undue disadvantage which makes it possible to presume that the influence was unduly asserted.[84] For if the plaintiff has entered into a transaction which was manifestly disadvantageous this surely suggests, at the very least, that he or she might not have had a free choice to enter into the transaction.[85]

(iv) Rebutting the presumption of undue influence

Once the plaintiff has established that he or she was under the influence of the defendant and that the transaction was manifestly and unfairly disadvantageous, undue influence will be presumed and the burden will then shift to the defendant to rebut this presumption. To do this the defendant must show that the transaction 'was the spontaneous act of the [plaintiff] acting under circumstances which enabled him to exercise an independent will and which justified the court in holding that [the

---

[82] *Burch*, n. 81 above, 151 (Nourse LJ). Cp. Millett LJ at p. 152. On the equitable jurisdiction to relieve against unconscionable bargains see pp. 286–97 below. This jurisdiction could have been relied on in the *Burch* case without any need to rely on undue influence, but since this had not been pleaded the Court of Appeal was not prepared to base its decision on this basis. On this aspect of the case see Chen-Wishart, 'The *O'Brien* Principle and Substantive Unfairness' (1997) 56 *CLJ* 60.

[83] *CIBC Motgages plc.* v. *Pitt* [1994] AC 200.

[84] *BCCI* v. *Aboody* [1990] 1 QB 923, 957 (Slade LJ).

[85] Birks and Chin prefer a test of whether the transaction was ill-advised, in the sense that an adult *sui iuris* would not have entered into the transaction in the circumstances: in *Good Faith and Fault in Contract Law* (ed. Beatson and Friedmann) p. 84.

transaction] was the result of a free exercise of the [plaintiff's] will'.[86] This raises an issue of causation, since the defendant must show that the plaintiff entered into the transaction voluntarily and was not induced to do so by the defendant's influence.

Whether the defendant can rebut the presumption of undue influence depends upon all the facts of the case. By far the most common method of rebutting the presumption is by showing that the plaintiff has received independent advice about the transaction, since if the plaintiff entered into the transaction even after having received such advice this suggests that the plaintiff has freely exercised his or her will. The adviser need not be a lawyer[87] but he or she must be independent of any influence from the defendant.[88] The advice must be fully informed and competent.[89] This means that the adviser should be qualified to give advice and he or she must be fully aware of the facts of the case. The function of the adviser is not simply to ensure that the plaintiff understands the trans-action, since the adviser must also be satisfied that the transaction is one which the plaintiff could sensibly enter into if he or she was not being improperly influenced. If the adviser is not satisfied of this then he or she must advise the plaintiff not to enter into the transaction.[90] The pre-sumption will not be rebutted if the plaintiff had the opportunity to obtain legal advice but failed to avail him- or herself of the opportunity. The defendant must show that the plaintiff did obtain the advice and acted on it for, as Millett LJ has recognised, if it was simply sufficient that the plaintiff obtained the advice, the influence which produced the plaintiff's desire to enter into the transaction in the first place would cause the plaintiff to disregard any advice that he or she should not enter into the transaction.[91] It follows that, if the presumption of undue influ-ence is to be rebutted, it must be shown that the plaintiff was free from such influence, and simply taking independent advice does not show this; the advice must actually be that the transaction is a sensible one for the plaintiff to enter into.

But showing that the plaintiff has received and acted on independent advice is not the only method of rebutting the presumption of undue influence.[92] The defendant can rely on any available evidence to show

---

[86] *Allcard* v. *Skinner* (1887) 36 Ch.D 145, 171 (Cotton LJ). In *Zamet* v. *Hyman* [1961] 1 WLR 1442, 1446, Lord Evershed MR said the presumption will only be rebutted if the defen-dant establishes that the plaintiff entered into the transaction 'after full, free and informed thought about it'.

[87] *Inche Noriah* v. *Shaik Allie Bin Omar* [1929] AC 127, 135 (Lord Hailsham LC).

[88] *Ibid.*   [89] *Wright* v. *Carter* [1903] 1 Ch. 27.

[90] *Crédit Lyonnais Bank Nederland NV* v. *Burch* [1997] 1 All ER 144, 156 (Millett LJ). Cp. where an adviser is being used to insulate a third party from the effects of another's undue influence, where it is not necessary to show that the advice was acted on. See pp. 272–4 below.

[91] *Ibid.* Cp. *Inche Noriah* v. *Shaik Allie Bin Omar* [1929] AC 127, 135 (Lord Hailsham LC).

[92] *Inche Noriah* v. *Shaik Allie Bin Omar* [1929] AC 127.

that the plaintiff has acted voluntarily and as a free agent. For example, in *Re Brocklehurst*[93] a majority of the Court Appeal held that the defendant could rebut the presumption of undue influence by showing that the deceased's gift to him of valuable shooting rights arose from the free and independent exercise of the deceased's will, motivated by the close friendship between the parties.

(d) Undue influence and third parties[94]

It has been assumed so far that the plaintiff has entered into a transaction or transferred a benefit as a result of the defendant's undue influence, but this is not always the case. By far the most controversial and practically important question relating to the role of undue influence as a ground of restitution arises where the plaintiff has entered into a transaction with the defendant as a result of the undue influence of a third party. In such circumstances the plaintiff's weakness is exploited by the third party and it is necessary to determine which of the two innocent parties, the plaintiff or the defendant, should suffer from this exploitation.[95] Typically this problem arises where a husband has induced his wife to act as surety for his debts, or those of his business, by unduly influencing her to execute a charge over the matrimonial home in which she has a proprietary interest and, when the creditor wishes to enforce the charge, the wife argues that it was not valid because of undue influence. Although the problem will arise in all cases where actual and presumed undue influence has been established, regardless of the nature of the relationship between the parties, the case of the husband unduly influencing the wife to enter into a transaction with a bank will be used as the basis for examining the law. These were essentially the facts of the leading case in this area, the decision of the House of Lords in *Barclays Bank plc.* v. *O'Brien*,[96] save that the wife had been induced to consent to a second mortgage on the family home not because of undue influence, but by reason of the husband's misrepresentation as to the extent and duration of the charge.[97] The fact that the case was concerned with an induced mistake does not make any difference to its application to cases of undue influence. This is because misrepresentations like undue influence, constitute unconscionable behaviour, and consequently the

[93] [1978] Ch. 14.
[94] See O'Sullivan, 'Undue Influence and Misrepresentation after *O'Brien*: Making Security Secure' in *Restitution and Banking Law* (ed. Rose, Oxford: Mansfield Press, 1998), Chapter 3.
[95] *Barclays Bank plc.* v. *O'Brien* [1994] 1 AC 180, 195 (Lord Browne-Wilkinson).
[96] [1994] 1 AC 180.
[97] See pp. 184–6 above.

effect of both grounds of restitution is the same, regardless of whether the misrepresentation is fraudulent, negligent or innocent.[98]

(i) What does the O'Brien principle have to do with the reversal of unjust enrichment?

Where the wife is able to set aside a transaction with a bank because of the undue influence of her husband the relevance to the law of restitution, and particularly the unjust enrichment principle, may not be obvious. The real difficulty concerns the identification of an enrichment. Two different types can be identified depending on the nature of the transaction between the wife and the bank. Where the bank acquires a security interest in the matrimonial home the bank can be considered to be presently enriched to the extent of this interest. Alternatively, where the wife simply enters into a personal guarantee with the bank it should be considered to be enriched because it has a valuable right to sue the wife on the guarantee. This analysis of the enrichment question also explains why the wife's claim that she can rescind the transaction as against the bank involves restitutionary relief. This is because a consequence of the rescission will be that the bank has to give up its right either to the matrimonial home or to sue the wife on the guarantee, rights which had been obtained from the wife as a result of her husband's undue influence.[99]

Once it has been established that the bank has indeed been enriched at the wife's expense it is then necessary to show that a ground of restitution applies. The ground of restitution will be undue influence, but the difficulty relates to showing that the bank was tainted by the undue influence so that its enrichment can be treated as unjust. This is what the *O'Brien* principle seeks to establish.

The conclusion that the wife's claim to rescind the transaction as against the bank can be analysed in terms of reversing the bank's unjust enrichment does have one important consequence, which has not yet been considered in any of the myriad cases which have examined the *O'Brien* principle. If the wife's claim for rescission of the transaction can be analysed in terms of unjust enrichment, it follows that the bank should be able to plead the defence of change of position, and typically the bank could argue that it has changed its position because, as a result of the wife's transaction with the bank, the bank lent money to the husband. The application of such a defence would dramatically restrict the ambit of the *O'Brien* principle. So why has the defence of change of posi-

---

[98] In *TSB Bank plc.* v. *Camfield* [1995] 1 WLR 430 the security was set aside where the wife's consent had been induced by her husband's innocent misrepresentation.

[99] See Nahan, 'Rescission: A Case for Rejecting the Classical Model?' (1997) *Univ. WALR* 66, 72–3.

tion not been relied on in any of these cases? A number of reasons can be identified.

(1) It is a requirement of the defence of change of position that the change in the defendant's position was extraordinary.[100] Consequently, it could be concluded that the lending of money by the bank to the husband in the ordinary course of commercial business was not an extraordinary change of position and so the defence will not be available to the bank.

(2) The defence of change of position will succeed only where the defendant acted in good faith. Where the *O'Brien* principle applies, it does so because the bank had actual or constructive notice of the wife's equity to set the transaction aside because of the undue influence and so it might be concluded that the bank was not acting in good faith. It is, however, unclear whether the defence will be unavailable to the defendant if he or she had constructive notice of the plaintiff's restitutionary claim.[101]

(3) In some cases the bank may have lent money to the husband and entered into the security transaction with the wife only subsequently. In this type of case it is clear that the defence of change of position is unavailable to the bank because it has been held that the defence cannot be relied on where the defendant changes its position before it has received an enrichment.[102]

(ii) Determining the validity of the transaction

When determining whether the particular transaction which the wife entered into with the bank is binding on the wife, two distinct questions will need to be considered.

First, the wife must have been induced to enter into the particular transaction by virtue of the husband's undue influence. Consequently, the normal rules for establishing undue influence, whether actual or presumed, must be satisfied. It follows from this that the wife will in principle have an equity to set this transaction aside as against the bank, because the effect of the undue influence is that the wife did not freely choose to enter into the transaction with the bank.

Since it was not the bank which unduly influenced the wife to enter into the transaction with it, it is necessary to consider a second condition before the wife is able to enforce her equity to set the transaction with the

---

[100] See pp. 714–15 below.

[101] See p. 721 below. Stuart-Smith LJ in *Royal Bank of Scotland* v. *Etridge (No. 2)* [1998] 4 All ER 705, 718 stated that there were difficulties with this argument because there was no trace of it in *O'Brien*.

[102] *South Tyneside MBC* v. *Svenska International plc.* [1995] 1 All ER 545. See pp. 717–20 below.

bank aside. This condition effectively requires consideration of whether the bank has been tainted by the husband's undue influence. There are two ways of establishing such a taint: first, by showing that the husband was acting as the agent of the bank and secondly by showing that the bank had notice of the wife's equity to set the transaction aside.

(1) Agency

If the husband was acting as the bank's agent the wife's equity to set the transaction aside will be enforceable against it. But it is only in the most exceptional circumstances that it will be possible to establish such an agency relationship.[103] To show that the husband was the agent of the bank it must be established that the bank had entrusted the husband with the task of obtaining the wife's consent to participate in the transaction. Where the wife is induced to act as surety for her husband this agency relationship will be particularly difficult to identify since normally, as the House of Lords recognised in *O'Brien*, the bank informs the husband that there must be a surety before it will lend him any money, and the husband arranges for somebody to act as a surety on his own account.[104] This does not create an agency relationship between the husband and the bank.

(2) Notice

Alternatively, and much more importantly, the wife's equity to set the transaction aside will be enforceable against the bank if it had notice of the facts which gave rise to the wife's equity. This notice may take two different forms. The first is actual notice, where the bank knew of the facts which gave rise to the equity, as will be the case where the bank was aware that the husband had obtained his wife's consent to participate in the transaction through undue influence. The second type is constructive notice, which will be established where the bank:

> knows of certain facts which put it on inquiry as to the possible existence of the rights of [the wife] and it fails to make such inquiry or take such steps as are reasonable to verify whether [the wife's] earlier right does or does not exist.[105]

In *Barclays Bank plc.* v. *Boulter*[106] the Court of Appeal held that the burden of proof is on the bank to plead and show that it did not have notice of the wife's equity to set the transaction aside, rather than being

---

[103] *Barclays Bank plc.* v. *O'Brien* [1994] 1 AC 180, 195 (Lord Browne-Wilkinson). See *Kings North Trust Ltd.* v. *Bell* [1986] 1 WLR 119.

[104] *Barclays Bank plc.* v. *O'Brien*, n. 103 above, p. 194 (Lord Browne-Wilkinson).

[105] *Ibid*, pp. 195–6 (Lord Browne-Wilkinson). On the doctrine of notice in this context see Mee, 'Undue Influence, Misrepresentation and the Doctrine of Notice' (1995) 54 *CLJ* 536. See also O'Dell, 'Restitution, Coercion by a Third Party and the Proper Role of Notice' (1997) 56 *CLJ* 71.   [106] [1998] 1 WLR 1.

on the wife to show that the bank had notice of her equity. It follows that, once the wife has established that she entered into the transaction as a result of undue influence, the transaction will be set aside unless the bank can establish that it did not have constructive notice of her equity. The bank will be able to establish this either by showing that there was nothing to put it on inquiry as to the possible existence of the wife's claim or, if there was, by showing that it had taken reasonable steps to avoid being fixed with constructive notice.

The decision in *Boulter* is, however, highly dubious.[107] The Court of Appeal drew an analogy with the doctrine of notice as it operates in the context of the defence of *bona fide* purchase for value without notice.[108] Since the burden of proof is on the defendant to establish the defence of *bona fide* purchase it was assumed that the same must be true for the doctrine of constructive notice.[109] But such reasoning is fundamentally flawed. This is because the doctrine of *bona fide* purchase has a very specific function, namely to ensure that where a *bona fide* purchaser for value receives a defective title that defect can be made good.[110] The doctrine of notice in the undue influence context has a very different function, namely to determine which of two innocent parties should bear the loss arising from the husband's undue influence.[111] Since the dispute is between the wife and the bank, it is surely appropriate that the wife bears the burden of proving that the bank had constructive notice of her equity to set the transaction aside before she can rescind the transaction with the bank. Only once this has been established should the burden shift to the bank to establish that it has taken reasonable steps to avoid being fixed with constructive notice. This would mean that the question of reasonable steps becomes a defence, but the element of notice forms part of the wife's cause of action.[112]

The introduction of the doctrine of notice to determine whether the bank should be considered to be tainted by the husband's undue influence has been criticised, primarily because it is assumed that a doctrine which was developed in the context of land law is inappropriate in the

---

[107] See Birks, 'Notice and Onus in *O'Brien*' (1998) 12 TLI 2 and Barker, '*O'Brien*, Notice and the Onus of Proof' in *Restitution and Banking Law* (ed. Rose), Chapter 5.

[108] See Chapter 22.

[109] See O'Dell, 'Restitution, Coercion by a Third Party and the Proper Role of Notice' (1997) 56 *CLJ* 71.

[110] This was recognised by Stuart-Smith LJ in *Royal Bank of Scotland* v. *Etridge (No. 2)* [1998] 4 All ER 705, 717–18, but the judge still affirmed the allocation of the burden of proof on the bank as held in *Barclays Bank plc.* v. *Boulter*.

[111] Cp. Birks, 'Notice and Onus in *O'Brien*' (1998) 12 TLI 2, 13 who suggests that the function of the notice requirement is 'to protect and give expression to the general interest in facilitating and upholding bargains'.

[112] This was the view of Nourse LJ when deciding whether to grant leave to appeal in *Steeples* v. *Lea* [1998] 1 FLR 138, 141, a view with which Millett LJ did not disagree.

context of an *O'Brien* dispute.[113] But such criticism is unfounded. It is, perhaps, unfortunate that Lord Browne-Wilkinson used the word 'notice' to describe the relevant test, because of the connotations of the word, but so long as it is realised that the doctrine of notice has a unique interpretation in this context, because it can be rebutted by proof that the bank had taken reasonable steps, it can do no harm.[114]

Although a wide variety of factors might put the bank on notice of the existence of the wife's equity to set the transaction aside, two matters are particularly important. The first is whether there was a substantial risk that the husband had procured the wife to enter into the particular transaction by undue influence.[115] The second is that the transaction was not to the financial advantage of the wife, as will be the case where, for example, a wife agrees to act as surety in respect of a loan from which she will not receive any benefit.[116] In *O'Brien* itself the bank was fixed with constructive notice of the husband's misrepresentation, particularly because the wife would not benefit financially by agreeing to act as surety in respect of the debts of a company in which her husband, but not herself, had an interest. In *CICB Mortgages* v. *Pitt*,[117] another decision of the House of Lords which was handed down on the same day as *O'Brien*, the financial institution was not fixed with constructive notice of the wife's equity. This was primarily because the transaction involved a second mortgage of the family home, which was registered in the name of both the husband and the wife, and the transaction was purportedly entered into to enable the couple to purchase a holiday home and so appeared to be in the wife's financial interests. If *O'Brien* and *Pitt* are analysed together, it seems that a transaction is more likely to be unenforceable by the bank where it involves the wife agreeing to act as surety for debts owed by her husband or his business, than where it involves the creation of a charge to secure joint borrowing made by the husband and wife, simply because in the former case the suretyship does not appear to be for the wife's benefit.

One further point needs to be emphasised in connection with *Pitt*. Although it was established in that case that the husband had actually unduly influenced his wife, and so there was no additional requirement that the transaction had been manifestly disadvantageous to her, it seems that where the issue before the court is whether the bank has constructive notice of the wife's equity, the fact that the transaction was manifestly disadvantageous to the wife will be particularly relevant. For,

[113] See, for example, Rickett, 'The Financier's Duty of Care to a Surety' (1998) 114 *LQR* 17, 19. Cp. Gardner, 'Wives' Guarantees of their Husbands' Debts' (1999) 115 *LQR* 1, 5.

[114] See O'Sullivan, in *Restitution and Banking Law* (ed. Rose) pp. 43–6.

[115] [1994] 1 AC 180, 196 (Lord Browne-Wilkinson).

[116] See *Crédit Lyonnais Nederland NV* v. *Burch* [1997] 1 All ER 144, 150 (Nourse LJ).

[117] [1994] 1 AC 200. See also *BCCI* v. *Aboody* [1990] QB 923, 974.

if the transaction appears to be manifestly disadvantageous this suggests that the bank should have inquired as to the possible existence of the wife's equity to set the transaction aside.

Even where the wife has a direct financial interest in the transaction, it may be possible to show that the bank has constructive notice of her equity to set the transaction aside. For example, in *Goode Durant Administration* v. *Biddulph*[118] the wife agreed to act as surety for a loan to a company in which she owned 2.5 per cent of the shares. It was held that the bank had constructive notice of the wife's equity to set the transaction aside on the basis that it should have noticed the discrepancy between the extensive personal liability which she had taken for the whole of the company's indebtedness when compared with the small stake which she had in the company. The degree of participation of the wife in the company's affairs should be a matter of particular interest to the bank to determine to what extent the wife might benefit from the transaction. Quite often the wife will have an indirect financial interest in the transaction where the effect of the transaction is to enable the husband to pursue a business career which finances the family's lifestyle, but such indirect advantages are not usually considered to be relevant to the question of notice.[119]

Where a bank has been put on inquiry to investigate whether the wife's equity exists it will be fixed with constructive notice of this equity, save where it has taken reasonable steps to satisfy itself that the wife's consent to enter into the particular transaction was obtained freely and with knowledge of the true facts. There has been a great deal of discussion in the cases about what constitute reasonable steps for these purposes. There are two distinct routes by which the bank can show that it has taken reasonable steps to ensure that the wife fully appreciated the consequences of the particular transaction.[120]

(1) Actions of the bank. In *O'Brien* itself Lord Browne-Wilkinson accepted that a bank has taken reasonable steps where one of its representatives has met the wife at a private meeting[121] which the husband does not attend, and informs her of her potential liability by entering into the transaction and the risk she is taking by entering it.[122] In addition, the representative must *advise* the wife that she should seek independent advice.[123] If the institution thinks that the husband has probably unduly influenced the wife then it must *insist* that she obtains independent

---

[118] [1994] 2 FLR 551. See also *Bank of Scotland* v. *Bennett* [1997] 1 FLR 801.

[119] *Barclays Bank plc.* v. *Caplan* [1998] 1 FLR 532, 542 (Jonathan Sumption QC).

[120] *Royal Bank of Scotland* v. *Etridge (No. 2)* [1998] 4 All ER 705, 721 (Stuart-Smith LJ).

[121] Written warnings are not sufficient, because the wife might not read them or they might be intercepted by her husband: *Barclays Bank plc.* v. *O'Brien* [1994] 1 AC 180, 198 (Lord Browne-Wilkinson).

[122] *Ibid*, p. 196 (Lord Browne-Wilkinson).   [123] *Ibid.*

advice.[124] Similarly, where the transaction is so manifestly disadvanta-geous to the wife that it can be characterised as an unconscionable bar-gain, the bank must insist that the wife obtains independent legal advice.[125] The difference between advising and insisting that the wife obtains independent advice is that to advise the wife it is not necessary for the bank to check that the wife did obtain advice, whereas to insist that the wife obtains independent advice requires the bank to be satisfied that such advice was taken, as evidenced, for example, by the receipt of a cer-tificate from the independent adviser. In such a case the bank should not proceed with the transaction until it knows that the wife has received independent advice. Presumably where the bank has advised the wife to obtain advice and then discovers that she has not done so, it will not have taken all reasonable steps to ensure that the wife was fully aware of the consequences of the transaction. The bank in *O'Brien* was unable to establish that it had taken such reasonable steps since nobody had sug-gested to the wife that she should seek independent legal advice and she was not warned about the risks involved in becoming a surety.

(2) *Confirmation that independent legal advice has been obtained.* Decisions of the Court of Appeal after *O'Brien* have emphasised that Lord Browne-Wilkinson's statement, that the bank must have had a private meeting with the wife in the absence of the husband, is not a require-ment but merely a suggestion of what might constitute reasonable steps.[126] Alternatively, the bank can be considered to have taken reason-able steps if it receives confirmation from a firm of solicitors that the wife has received legal advice from the firm.[127] If the bank knows that the wife has seen a reputable firm of solicitors, and has received confirmation from the firm that the transaction was explained[128] to her, it has no duty to inquire into what actually happened at the interview and can properly assume that the solicitors have acted honestly, without there being a conflict of interest, and that proper advice has been given.[129] So, in *Massey* v. *Midland Bank plc.*[130] the fact that the solicitor had been cho-sen by the debtor, who had given instructions and attended the interview with the surety, did not mean that the bank had not taken all reasonable steps, since there was nothing to put the bank on notice that the surety

---

[124] *Barclays Bank plc.* v. *O'Brien* [1994] 1 AC 180, 198 (Lord Browne-Wilkinson), p. 197.
[125] *Crédit Lyonnais Bank Nederland NV* v. *Burch* [1997] 1 All ER 144, p. 151–2 (Nourse LJ) and p. 158 (Swinton Thomas LJ).
[126] *Massey* v. *Midland Bank plc.* [1995] 1 All ER 929; *Banco Exterior Internacional* v. *Mann* [1995] 1 All ER 936.
[127] *Royal Bank of Scotland* v. *Etridge (No. 2)* [1998] 4 All ER 705.
[128] There being no clear dividing line between explanation and advice: *Banco Exterior Internacional* v. *Mann* [1995] 1 All ER 936, p. 950 (Sir Thomas Bingham MR).
[129] *Royal Bank of Scotland* v. *Etridge (No. 2)* [1998] 4 All ER 705, 721 (Stuart-Smith LJ).
[130] [1995] 1 All ER 929.

had not been properly advised. It is not necessary for the bank or the independent adviser to investigate the motives of the wife for entering into the transaction.[131] Where, however, the bank has some reason to suppose that the particular solicitor could not be trusted to achieve the standards of his or her profession in advising the wife, the bank cannot assume that proper advice has been given.[132] Equally, the bank will still be fixed with constructive notice of the wife's equity if it has not disclosed all material circumstances to the solicitor[133] or if it knew that no competent solicitor could advise the wife to enter into the transaction on the terms on which she did.[134]

Where a solicitor is giving legal advice to the wife he or she acts exclusively for the wife, even if the solicitor has been instructed by the bank and even if the solicitor also acts for the husband.[135] It follows that if the solicitor obtains information from the wife which suggests that she has been unduly influenced by her husband, such information cannot be imputed to the bank, because the solicitor is not acting as agent for the bank.[136]

Although this second route for identifying whether the bank has taken reasonable steps appears to dilute Lord Browne-Wilkinson's test in *O'Brien*, because the bank is simply allowed to rely on the solicitor's certificate without being required to check on the nature of the advice which is given, such a conclusion is incorrect. It must never be forgotten why a bank must take reasonable steps to ensure that the wife exercised a free and informed choice in entering into the transaction. This is required simply to prevent the bank from being fixed with constructive notice of the husband's undue influence.[137] The role of independent advice is consequently different in this context from that in which it is used to rebut the presumption of undue influence.[138] For in that context independent advice has a much more important role, to show that the

---

[131] *Banco Exterior SA* v. *Thomas* [1997] 1 WLR 221.
[132] *Barclays Bank plc.* v. *Caplan* [1998] 1 FLR 332, 344 (Jonathan Sumption QC).
[133] *Royal Bank of Scotland* v. *Etridge (No. 2)* [1998] 4 All ER 705, 722 (Stuart-Smith LJ). It was held in *Crédit Lyonnais Bank Nederland NV* v. *Burch* [1997] 1 All ER 144 that the bank is required to inform the wife of the current state of the husband's borrowing. This requirement had previously been explicitly rejected in *Bank of Baroda* v. *Rayarel* [1995] 2 FLR 376 and *Midland Bank plc.* v. *Kidwai* [1995] 4 Bank. LR 227. See also *Bank of Scotland* v. *Bennett* [1997] 1 FLR 801. For criticism of the approach adopted in the *Crédit Lyonnais* case see Hooley and O'Sullivan, 'Undue Influence and Unconscionable Bargains' [1997] *LMCLQ* 17, 20. See also O'Sullivan in *Restitution and Banking Law* (ed. Rose) at p. 62, who recommends that banks should produce standard disclosure forms.
[134] *Royal Bank of Scotland* v. *Etridge (No. 2)* [1998] 4 All ER 705, 722 (Stuart-Smith LJ) and *Crédit Lyonnais Bank Nederland NA* v. *Burch* [1997] 1 All ER 144, 157 (Millett LJ).
[135] *Royal Bank of Scotland* v. *Etridge (No. 2)* [1998] 4 All ER 705, 721 (Stuart-Smith LJ).
[136] *Ibid.*
[137] *Banco Exterior Internacional* v. *Mann* [1995] 1 All ER 936, 944 (Morritt LJ).
[138] *Royal Bank of Scotland* v. *Etridge (No. 2)* [1998] 4 All ER 705, 715 (Stuart-Smith LJ).

wife was not being unduly influenced when she entered into the transaction, with the emphasis being placed on the nature of the advice which
the wife has received.[139] In the context of a bank being fixed with constructive notice, however, we are concerned only with the conduct of the
bank itself. If it has taken all reasonable steps to ensure that the wife was
fully informed when she entered into the transaction it will not be fixed
with notice of the wife's equity to set the transaction aside. As between
the two innocent parties the bank will have the stronger claim. This
difference is reflected by the fact that, for the purposes of rebutting the
presumption of undue influence, the legal adviser must be truly independent,[140] whereas for the purposes of taking reasonable steps it is sufficient that the adviser is a reputable firm of solicitors, even if the adviser
is acting for other parties to the transaction, including the bank.[141]

(iii) Enforceability of the transaction

Where the husband has induced his wife to enter into a transaction by
virtue of undue influence but he was not acting as agent for the bank and
the bank did not have actual or constructive notice of the wife's equity to
set the transaction aside, the wife will not be able to rescind the transaction. But where the husband was the bank's agent or the bank had notice
of the wife's equity then the transaction will be set aside completely and
cannot be set aside partially or on terms.[142] The only qualification to this
arises where the wife is required to make counter-restitution to the bank
in respect of benefits which she had received from the transaction.[143]
Since the dispute in all of these cases is which of two innocent parties
should suffer from the husband's undue influence, it is surely right that
if the transaction is set aside, so that the bank bears the loss, the wife
should still be required to pay for any benefit she has received. This is
consistent with fundamental principles of the law of restitution, particularly that rescission is barred unless the party wishing to rescind the
transaction makes restitution of benefits received under it.[144]

The qualification to the right to rescind that the wife must make
counter-restitution of benefits she has received will generally not be relevant since the wife is unlikely to have received any benefit from the
transaction. Whether the wife can be considered to have received a benefit from the transaction was considered by the Court of Appeal in
Dunbar Bank plc. v. *Nadeem*.[145] In this case the husband used money
which he had borrowed from the bank to buy a lease jointly with his wife.

---

[139] *Crédit Lyonnais Bank Nederland NV* v. *Burch* [1997] 1 All ER 144, 156 (Millett LJ).
[140] *Re Coomber* [1911] 1 Ch. 723.
[141] *Barclays Bank plc.* v. *Thompson* [1997] 4 All ER 816.
[142] *TSB Bank plc.* v. *Camfield* [1995] 1 WLR 430.
[143] *Dunbar Bank plc.* v. *Nadeem* [1998] 3 All ER 876.   [144] See pp. 32–4 above.
[145] [1998] 3 All ER 876.

The bank sought to enforce a charge over the property which the wife resisted on the ground of presumed undue influence of which the bank had constructive notice. It was held that the presumption had not been established because it could not be shown that the wife had suffered manifest disadvantage as a result of the transaction. Despite this, the court went on to consider whether, if the presumption of undue influence had been established, the wife had received a benefit under the transaction. It was accepted that the wife had to restore any benefits which she had received under the transaction, otherwise she would be unjustly enriched if the transaction was rescinded without counter-restitution being made, and if she could not make counter-restitution she would be barred from rescinding the transaction. It was held that the wife had obtained a benefit, namely the beneficial interest in the lease which the wife obtained, with her husband, by the use of money lent by the bank.[146]

(iv) Relationships other than that of husband and wife

Although many of the reported cases involve wives being unduly influenced by their husbands, exactly the same principles will be applicable even where the couple are unmarried and regardless of whether the relationship is heterosexual or homosexual, so long as one party reposes trust and confidence in the other and the bank is aware of this.[147] In *Massey* v. *Midland Bank plc.*,[148] for example, it was accepted that the bank was put on notice of the fact that there was a relationship of trust and confidence between the defendant and her lover, even though they had never cohabited, because there was a longstanding sexual and emotional relationship between them, and he was the father of her two children. The relationship was such that the defendant's judgmental capacity was just as likely to be impaired as if she had been married to or cohabited with her lover. It is even possible for a relationship of trust and confidence to be established although the relationship could not be characterised as sexual or emotional, as was recognised by the Court of Appeal in *Crédit Lyonnais Bank Nederland NV* v. *Burch*,[149] where a relationship of trust and confidence was identified between an employee and the agent of her employer.[150]

---

[146] There was a difference of view amongst the judges as to whether the wife could have made counter-restitution on the facts of the case. Millett LJ thought she could, whereas Morritt LJ thought she could not and Potter LJ did not express a view.

[147] *Barclays Bank plc.* v. *O'Brien* [1994] 1 AC 180, 198 (Lord Browne-Wilkinson).

[148] [1995] 1 All ER 929.   [149] [1997] 1 All ER 144.

[150] Although this relationship appears to have been inferred from the fact that the transaction was manifestly disadvantageous to the employee. See Chen-Wishart, 'The *O'Brien* Principle and Substantive Unfairness' (1997) 56 CLJ 60, 67. See also *Avon Finance Co. Ltd.* v. *Bridger* [1985] 2 All ER 281 where a son misled his elderly parents to stand as surety for his debts. Since the financial institution should have been aware that the parents trusted the son in their financial dealings, so that he could be expected to have influence over them, the guarantee was held to be unenforceable by the institution against the parents.

(v) Critique of the law after O'Brien

The law after the House of Lords decision in *O'Brien* is broadly acceptable. Certainly, as a matter of policy, it should be warmly welcomed. For
the effect of the decision is to balance two competing social needs. On
the one hand there is a need to protect the wife against unacceptable
exploitation by her husband, where the wife depends on her husband for
financial advice and guidance.[151] If the security which she was induced
to sign is declared valid, the consequence will often be that she loses the
matrimonial home since the security is usually a second mortgage on the
home. The wife, and others who are similarly dependent on their partner, needs protection against such extreme consequences of exploitation. But, on the other hand, it is necessary to ensure that the legal
requirements which are imposed to ensure that the wife does not suffer
from exploitation are not so rigorous as to deter banks from entering into
transactions with spouses from a fear that the transactions may easily be
set aside for reasons outside their control. This would result in institutions refusing to grant loans on the security of matrimonial homes,
which would reduce 'the flow of loan capital to business enterprises'.[152]
The requirement that the bank can treat the transaction as valid so long
as it has taken reasonable steps to ensure that the wife was fully informed
and freely consented to the transaction, appears to be a happy compromise between these two interests, since it gives the wife a degree of
protection against exploitation without making the acceptance of an
interest in the matrimonial home a security interest which is unacceptably insecure for the bank.

But is this compromise solution really workable in practice? Will a wife
who is subject to the undue influence of her husband really be protected
by obtaining legal advice? Probably the decision in *O'Brien* is the only
acceptable solution to what is ultimately an insoluble problem. It will
never be possible to ensure that all transactions which have been
obtained through undue influence or misrepresentation will be invalidated without unnecessarily deterring banks from lending money to co-
habitees. As Cretney has said, the House of Lords decisions in *O'Brien*
and *Pitt* provide an:

ingenious, and pragmatically effective, short term response to what was evi-
dently becoming a significant social problem. But much remains conceptually
uncertain, and the cases leave much room for the further analysis of the principles which should govern the giving of relief against the consequences of a transaction into which the parties apparently freely entered.[153]

---

[151] *Barclays Bank plc.* v. *O'Brien* [1994] 1 AC 180, 188 (Lord Browne-Wilkinson).
[152] *Ibid.*
[153] 'Mere Puppets, Folly and Imprudence: Undue Influence for the Twenty First
Century' (1994) 2 *RLR* 3, 13.

There is, however, much greater certainty in the application of the *O'Brien* principle as a result of the important decision of the Court of Appeal in *Royal Bank of Scotland* v. *Etridge (No. 2)*,[154] particularly as regards the determination of whether the bank has taken reasonable steps.

One consequence of the recent shift to advice being given by solicitors rather than the financial institution itself is that the wife is more likely to seek redress from her legal adviser than from the financial institution.[155] A further consequence will be that legal advisers will increasingly seek more information from the bank to ensure that they give full and accurate advice.[156] The consequent increase in costs in the preparation and supply of this information is presumably justified to ensure that the wife receives adequate, but not excessive, protection, without deterring banks from accepting the matrimonial home as security for loans.

(vi) The special equity theory

The *O'Brien* principle has been rejected in Australia. In *Garcia* v. *National Australia Bank Ltd.*[157] the High Court of Australia preferred to rely on a so-called 'special equity theory'. According to this theory, where, for example, a wife agrees to guarantee her husband's debts in circumstances in which the transaction is of no benefit to her and with an incomplete understanding of the nature of the transaction, then the guarantee is invalid unless the bank has taken sufficient steps to ensure that the wife's lack of understanding is rectified.[158] The chief differences between this theory and the *O'Brien* principle is that the theory does not require proof of any factor, such as undue influence or misrepresentation, which vitiated the transaction with the bank. Also the effect of the special equity theory is that the transaction is presumed to be invalid simply because of the wife's incomplete understanding of it and without proof that the husband was the bank's agent or that the bank had notice of her lack of understanding.

Should this theory be recognised in this country in place of the *O'Brien* principle? The answer is emphatically 'no' because the special equity theory is open to a number of objections. The crucial objection is that the effect of the theory would make it easier to undermine transactions with banks, with the consequence that banks would be less likely to lend

---

[154] [1998] 4 All ER 705.

[155] As was acknowledged by Stuart-Smith LJ in *Royal Bank of Scotland* v. *Etridge (No. 2)* [1998] 4 All ER 705, 722. He also suggested that the solicitor may owe a duty of care to the bank.

[156] See Hooley, 'Taking Security after *O'Brien*' [1995] *LMCLQ* 346.

[157] (1998) 72 ALJR 1242. See Gardner, 'Wives' Guarantees of their Husbands' Debts' (1999) 115 *LQR* 1.

[158] *Ibid*, pp. 1–2.

money on the security of the matrimonial home or the wife's guarantee. In addition, why should wives, and presumably others who are emotionally dependent on the debtor, receive special treatment simply because they have an incomplete understanding of the transaction, where that incomplete understanding is not induced by their husband in any way? It is surely unacceptable to assume that all wives are in need of special protection when they enter into commercial transactions. Finally, the essence of the special equity theory, as interpreted by the High Court of Australia, is that it is unconscionable for the bank to rely on the transaction where the wife had an incomplete understanding of it. But the notion of unconscionability is defined much more restrictively in English law.[159] If a wider principle of unconscionability was recognised in this country it would result in commercial uncertainty. It is, anyway, difficult to see how the bank's conduct can be considered to be unconscionable where the wife had an incomplete understanding of the transaction of which the bank did not even have constructive notice. The special equity theory fails to balance adequately the interests of two innocent parties, namely the interests of the wife and the bank, since the transaction is assumed to be invalid unless the bank took sufficient steps. The *O'Brien* principle is much more successful in balancing these interests, because, subject to the question about the burden of proof, the transaction can only be vitiated if the bank is tainted in some way by the husband's conduct.

(e) The nature of the relief

Where a transaction is rescinded for undue influence it can usually only be set aside in its entirety and not partially, so that part of the transaction remains valid. Also the transaction cannot be set aside on terms, for example by setting aside the whole transaction and substituting a new one for it. In *Zamet* v. *Hyman*[160] it was held that the relief for undue influence is confined to setting aside the particular transaction and that the court could not substitute some other, fairer, transaction. This approach was endorsed by the Court of Appeal in *TSB Bank plc*. v. *Camfield*[161] where it was held that a mortgage would be set aside completely as a result of a husband's misrepresentation and would not be treated as valid to the extent of the maximum liability which the wife had accepted. This general principle against rescission on terms is, however, subject to an apparent exception where rescission is conditional on the plaintiff

---

[159] See pp. 286–97 below.   [160] [1961] 1 WLR 1442.
[161] [1995] 1 WLR 430. See also *Allied Irish Banks plc*. v. *Byrne* [1995] 1 FCR 453. In Australia partial rescission is accepted: *Vadasz* v. *Pioneer Concrete (SA) Pty. Ltd.* (1995) 184 CLR 102. See Proksch, 'Rescission on Terms' (1996) 4 *RLR* 71.

making counter-restitution to the defendant of any benefits received under the transaction.[162] But this is consistent with rescission operating to set the transaction aside completely and so restore both parties to the position they occupied before entering into the transaction, by ensuring that they return any benefits received, or the value of any benefits received, to the other party.

The apparent reason for the courts' refusal to allow partial rescission or rescission on terms stems from the nature of rescission itself. Rescission is not a form of equitable relief to which terms can be attached, but is a form of self-help. The plaintiff rescinds the transaction and the only role for the courts is to determine whether he or she has rescinded the transaction or is entitled to do so.[163] There is consequently no scope for any half-way house; either the plaintiff is or is not entitled to rescind the transaction in question. But this is highly dubious reasoning for two reasons: first, because, even though a contract may be rescinded by the act of the aggrieved party,[164] it does not follow that the restitutionary consequences which follow from rescission are achieved without the intervention of the court;[165] secondly, even if rescission can occur without the intervention of the court, it does not follow that there cannot be rescission on terms for, as O'Sullivan has recognised, 'if the law allows rescission on terms, then they are the terms on which the plaintiff's own act of rescission will take effect and the plaintiff must submit to those terms, even if rescission is triggered by her own act'.[166]

In fact some cases show that rescission on terms is available.[167] The most important of these is *Cheese* v. *Thomas*,[168] where the Court of Appeal set aside a transaction on terms where the transaction had been entered into through the exercise of undue influence. In this case the defendant, who was the plaintiff's great-nephew, was presumed to have unduly influenced the plaintiff into entering into a transaction to buy a house, to which the plaintiff contributed all of his capital, amounting to £43,000. The parties had agreed that the plaintiff would occupy the house

[162] See *TSB Bank plc.* v. *Camfield* [1995] 1 WLR 430, 434–5 (Nourse LJ). For an example of such conditional rescission see *Midland Bank plc.* v. *Greene* [1994] 2 FLR 82. English law only requires the parties to the transaction in question to make restitution to each other. If a third party has received a benefit under the transaction, as will be the case where a bank has lent money to a third party as a result of the plaintiff agreeing to act as surety, the guarantee can be rescinded even though the bank cannot recover what it had lent to the third party.

[163] See Roch LJ, in *TSB Bank plc.* v. *Camfield*, n. 162 above, at p. 438.

[164] *Car and Universal Finance Co. Ltd.* v. *Caldwell* [1964] 1 QB 525.

[165] O'Sullivan in *Restitution and Banking Law* (ed. Rose) at p. 66.

[166] *Ibid*, pp. 66–7.

[167] In some of the cases on rescission for mistake the plaintiff was permitted to rescind the transaction but only on condition that a new contract was offered: *Solle* v. *Butcher* [1950] 1 KB 671 and *Grist* v. *Bailey* [1967] Ch. 532.

[168] [1994] 1 WLR 129.

for the rest of his life and then it would pass to the defendant, in whose name the house was registered. The balance of the purchase price and expenses, amounting to £40,000 in total, was funded by a building society loan made to the defendant and secured by a mortgage over the property. The defendant was to pay off this loan but he failed to keep up with the mortgage payments and the plaintiff then sought to set the transaction aside. It was conceded that there was a relationship of trust and confidence between the parties and the court held that the transaction was manifestly disadvantageous to the plaintiff, so it was possible to presume that the plaintiff had entered into the transaction as a result of the defendant's undue influence. The court then needed to consider what remedy was appropriate. Since the value of the house had fallen by over £27,500, the real issue for the court was which party should bear this loss. If the orthodox approach to rescission was adopted, the transaction would be set aside in its entirety, so the plaintiff would recover his contribution to the purchase price plus interest and the defendant would suffer the loss. But the court imposed a condition on rescission, namely that the loss should be apportioned between the parties in proportion to their respective contributions to the purchase price. In reaching this conclusion the court emphasised the importance of characterising the transaction involved.[169] In this case the transaction did not simply involve a payment by the plaintiff for the right to occupy the house. Rather, it was a joint venture between the plaintiff and the defendant, since the parties had agreed to contribute money to buy a house in which they would both have an interest. Since it is a feature of a joint venture that both parties participate equally in the transaction, it was held that the loss arising from the transaction would be apportioned between both of them.

But this identification of a joint venture is difficult to defend. The court emphasised that the parties should be treated as equal participants in the venture, particularly because the defendant was exonerated of any reprehensible behaviour in inducing the plaintiff to participate. But such a conclusion was not open to the court, simply because it had been presumed that the defendant had unduly influenced the plaintiff to enter into the transaction, and this presumption had not been rebutted. Consequently, the parties should have been treated as unequal participants in the transaction, with the result that the transaction should have been set aside in its entirety. The court did acknowledge that, had there not been a joint venture, the transaction would have been set aside completely, so that the plaintiff would have recovered what he had contributed and the defendant would have suffered the loss in value of the property.

[169] [1994] 1 WLR 129, p. 136 (Sir Donald Nichols V-C).

A further difficulty with the analysis of rescission in this case arises from the principle that rescission is traditionally barred where the plaintiff has received benefits under a transaction which he or she is unable to restore to the defendant.[170] This was in fact the situation in *Cheese* v. *Thomas* since the plaintiff had received benefits under the transaction, namely rent-free occupation of the house. This benefit was received at the defendant's expense, since the defendant was the registered owner of the house and the plaintiff was merely a contractual licensee. Nevertheless, the fact that the plaintiff received this benefit should not have barred rescission, since courts are increasingly prepared to award the defendant an allowance which is assessed by reference to the reasonable value of the benefit received by the plaintiff, especially where the equitable doctrine of rescission is concerned.[171] Since this benefit was the use of the house, it could have been valued and a sum of money equivalent to rent been paid to the defendant. In fact the Court of Appeal procured this counter-restitution by offsetting the rent which the plaintiff should have paid for occupation against the interest which the defendant should have paid to the plaintiff on the money which he had received once the house had been sold. This is a highly inaccurate method of securing counter-restitution. The court should simply have valued the rent which the plaintiff owed and deducted this from the £43,000 plus interest which the defendant owed to the plaintiff.[172]

In most cases of rescission for undue influence the only terms which are appropriate to impose as a condition for rescission are that the plaintiff must make counter-restitution to the defendant for any benefits obtained under the transaction. It is difficult to conceive of any other terms being appropriate. If the plaintiff entered into a transaction as a result of undue influence, but it can be shown that he or she would have entered into a version of the transaction but on different terms had there not been undue influence, it should be possible, in principle, to impose terms that the plaintiff can rescind the first transaction but only if he or she enters into the alternative transaction. But where the plaintiff has been induced to enter into a transaction by reason of undue influence it will be very difficult to establish that he or she would freely have entered into part of the transaction, simply because undue influence will

---

[170] See the decision of the Court of Appeal in *Smith New Court Securities Ltd.* v. *Scrimgeour Vickers (Asset Management) Ltd.* [1994] 1 WLR 1271 where the requirement that the plaintiff must make complete counter-restitution was interpreted strictly. Whilst this question did not arise in the House of Lords, Lord Browne-Wilkinson did suggest that it was open to review: [1997] AC 254, 262.

[171] See, for example, *O'Sullivan* v *Management Agency and Music Ltd.* [1985] QB 428.

[172] For an alternative analysis of the case as involving an implicit application of the defence of change of position, see Chen-Wishart, 'Loss Sharing, Undue Influence and Manifest Disadvantage' (1994) 110 *LQR* 173. See p. 714 below.

generally taint the whole transaction. Consequently, there is little scope for imposing terms as a condition for rescinding the transaction save where this is necessary to achieve counter-restitution.[173] One exceptional circumstance has, however, been recognised where rescission on terms is possible, namely where part of a complex transaction which was formed in stages has been obtained by undue influence and this part can be severed from the rest, which has not been obtained by undue influence, without adding to or modifying the rights and obligations in that part of the transaction which remains.[174]

The question of the appropriate relief for undue influence has been further examined in the difficult case of *Mahoney* v. *Purnell*.[175] In this case it was held that, where a transaction was liable to be set aside by reason of undue influence, but it was not possible to restore the parties to their original position because the relevant transaction had involved the sale of shares in a company which had subsequently been wound up, then rescission was barred but the court had a power to award the plaintiff equitable compensation. This is a highly dubious decision since it appears that the judge was treating undue influence as a form of wrong-doing, hence the award of a compensatory remedy, whereas undue influence can be established without any need to prove the commission of a wrong.[176] In fact, even though the case was treated as involving undue influence, the judge characterised the relationship of the parties, where a son-in-law purchased his father-in-law's shares in a company, as a fiduciary relationship. Since he concluded that this relationship had been abused it was entirely appropriate for equitable compensation to be awarded, although the finding of a fiduciary relationship on the facts of the case is very difficult to justify since the requisite element of dependence appears to have been lacking.[177] Despite this conclusion, closer analysis of the case suggests that what the judge was in fact authorising was restitutionary relief, since the so-called 'equitable compensation' took the form of the plaintiff recovering from the defendant the value of the shares he had surrendered minus what he had received from the defendant.[178] Such restitutionary relief is available without proof of

---

[173] Cp. where the plaintiff entered into a transaction as a result of misrepresentation, where the plaintiff thought, for example, that he or she had entered into a surety transaction for £5,000 but in fact the transaction was for £50,000. In such circumstances the actual surety transaction should be rescinded but terms could be imposed that a £5,000 surety transaction should be substituted since this is the amount which the plaintiff actually consented to guarantee. See further Virgo, 'A Commentary' in *Restitution and Banking Law* (ed. Rose) p. 77.

[174] *Barclays Bank plc.* v. *Caplan* [1998] 1 FLR 532.   [175] [1996] 3 All ER 61.

[176] See p. 253 above.   [177] See p. 531 below.

[178] The judge apparently assumed that compensation was the only remedy where the defendant no longer retained the shares which he had acquired from the plaintiff: [1996] 3 All ER 61, 90. But the remedy which was awarded was assessed by reference to the value

wrongdoing, so the identification of a fiduciary relationship was unnecessary.

3. ABUSE OF FIDUCIARY RELATIONSHIPS OF CONFIDENCE

Sometimes the relationship between the plaintiff and the defendant is such that it is possible to identify a duty of confidence owed by one of the parties to the other. The relationships which are relevant for these purposes are those which can be characterised as fiduciary, notably those between solicitor and client,[179] trustee and beneficiary, agent and principal, and any other similar relationship.[180] Where there is a transaction between the fiduciary and the principal to whom he or she owes fiduciary duties, it is presumed that the fiduciary exploited the other party, and so the burden is on him or her to establish that the transaction was fair[181] and that there has been full disclosure of everything which was or might be material to the other party's decision to enter into the transaction.[182] Whether the principal was advised to obtain independent and competent advice will be a particularly important consideration in determining whether the transaction was fair. In *Tate* v. *Williamson*[183] Lord Chelmsford LC identified the essential features of this principle:

> Wherever two persons stand in such a [fiduciary] relation that, while it continues, confidence is necessarily reposed by one, and the influence which necessarily grows out of that confidence is possessed by the other, and this confidence is abused, or the influence is exerted to obtain an advantage at the expense of the confiding party, the person so availing himself of his position will not be permitted to retain the advantage, although the transaction could not have been impeached if no such confidential relation had existed.[184]

(a) The identification of fiduciary relationships of confidence

The terms 'fiduciary relationship' and 'relationships of confidence' have been used indiscriminately in some cases which should properly have been treated as involving undue influence,[185] whereas in other cases the courts have relied on undue influence when the doctrine of abuse of

---

of the shares received by the defendant, and this can clearly be characterised as restitutionary.

[179] See *Wright* v. *Carter* [1903] 1 Ch. 27. [180] *BCCI* v. *Aboody* [1990] QB 923, 964.
[181] *Moody* v. *Cox and Hatt* [1917] 2 Ch. 71.
[182] *Demerara Bauxite Co. Ltd.* v. *Hubbard* [1923] AC 673.
[183] (1866) LR 2 Ch. App. 55. [184] At 61.
[185] *National Westminster Bank plc.* v. *Morgan* [1985] AC 686, 703 (Lord Scarman). For an example of indiscriminate use of these terms see *Lloyds Bank Ltd.* v. *Bundy* [1975] QB 326, 341 (Sir Eric Sachs) and *Roche* v. *Sherrington* [1982] 1 WLR 599.

fiduciary relationships of confidence was more appropriate. Although the line between undue influence and abuse of a fiduciary relationship of confidence is a fine one, essentially a distinction needs to be drawn between those relationships where the defendant influences the plaintiff and those where the plaintiff is totally dependent on the defendant. The doctrine of abuse of fiduciary relationships of confidence will only apply as regards the latter group of relationships.

(b) The relationship between undue influence and abuse of fiduciary relationships of confidence

The boundary between the doctrine of abuse of fiduciary relationships of confidence and undue influence is uncertain,[186] particularly because where there is a relationship of confidence there will also be the potential for undue influence. So, typically both may be pleaded on the same set of facts. But although the two principles overlap, they do not coincide.[187] The doctrine of abuse of fiduciary relationships of confidence has two important advantages over undue influence. First, it is not necessary to show that the plaintiff was, or might be, under the influence of the defendant. Thus, in *Moody* v. *Cox and Hatt*[188] a transaction between a solicitor and his client was set aside by reason of the solicitor's non-disclosure of material details about the transaction and it was irrelevant that the plaintiff was an independent man of business who would not have looked to the defendant for advice. All that needed to be established was that there was a fiduciary relationship between the parties. The second advantage which the doctrine of abuse of a fiduciary relationship of confidence has, at least over the doctrine of presumed undue influence, is that there is no need to show that the transaction was manifestly disadvantageous to the plaintiff. Once the relationship of confidence has been identified, manifest disadvantage is assumed and the burden is on the defendant to show that the transaction was not unfair to the plaintiff. The heavy burden of proving that the transaction is fair is shifted where there is a relationship of confidence simply because of the potential for abuse of such relationships by the fiduciary.[189]

The different roles of undue influence and breach of a fiduciary relationship of confidence are illustrated by an example which was

---

[186] *CICB Mortgages plc.* v. *Pitt* [1994] 1 AC 200, 209 (Lord Browne-Wilkinson).

[187] *BCCI* v. *Aboody* [1990] QB 923, 962. In *Moody* v. *Cox and Hatt* [1917] 2 Ch. 71, 79 Lord Cozens-Hardy MR specifically held that relief in equity was given by reason of a breach of a relationship of confidence and not for undue influence.

[188] *Ibid.*

[189] *Ibid*, p. 963. See also *CICB Mortgages plc.* v. *Pitt* [1994] 1 AC 200, 209 (Lord Browne-Wilkinson).

suggested by the Court of Appeal in *BCCI* v. *Aboody*[190] involving an 'old lady who was induced by her solicitor under strong pressure to sell him a large and inconvenient family home at full market value'. Although it might be possible to establish that the old lady had actually been unduly influenced by the solicitor to sell him her house, it would be much easier for her to base her claim on abuse of a fiduciary relationship of confidence, since then she would need to establish only that the solicitor owed her fiduciary duties, which is obvious. There would be no need to show that she was influenced by her solicitor. The burden is then on the solicitor to establish that the transaction was perfectly fair and that he or she had made full disclosure to her.

(c) The place of the doctrine of abuse of fiduciary relationships of confidence within the law of restitution

The place of the doctrine of abuse of fiduciary relationships of confidence within the law of restitution itself remains unclear. The better view is that, where the fiduciary has abused his or her relationship of confidence, this constitutes wrongdoing on the part of the defendant. So the plaintiff's restitutionary action will be founded on the wrongdoing, rather than the action of reversing unjust enrichment. Therefore, this principle is fully considered in the context of restitution for wrongs.[191] Whether a particular restitutionary claim is founded on unjust enrichment or wrongdoing will be important, since where the claim is based on wrongdoing the remedies are not necessarily restitutionary[192] and the defences may differ.

That the doctrine of abuse of fiduciary relationships of confidence is better treated as founded on wrongdoing rather than the reversal of the defendant's unjust enrichment is illustrated by *O'Sullivan* v. *Management Agency and Music Ltd.*[193] where the plaintiff had entered into an exclusive management agreement with the defendant. Although the defendant had conceded that the agreement was voidable because the relationship between the parties was such that undue influence was presumed, the approach adopted by the Court of Appeal suggests that the case is better regarded as one where the plaintiff's restitutionary action was founded on the defendant's wrongdoing, namely breach of fiduciary duty. The court recognised that the relationship between the parties was a fiduciary one and, if the defendant had not conceded that undue influence could be presumed, the existence of this fiduciary relationship would have meant that the transactions could have been presumed to be unfair without any need to show manifest disadvantage.

[190] [1990] QB 923, 962.

[191] See pp. 531–4 below.

[192] See *Mahoney* v. *Purnell* [1996] 3 All ER 61.

[193] [1985] QB 428.

The burden would then have been on the defendant to prove that the agreements were fair and reasonable.[194] The defendant would not have been able to show this because the terms of the agreement were such that the defendant was not in fact obliged to do any work for the plaintiff and because the defendant had not advised the plaintiff to obtain independent advice.

4. UNCONSCIONABLE CONDUCT[195]

The recognition of undue influence as a ground of restitution has sometimes been justified on the basis that it involves unconscionable conduct on the part of the defendant. Whilst unconscionable conduct may be presumed where a relationship of trust and confidence has been abused, it is incorrect to assume that restitution is justified for this reason where the plaintiff relies on undue influence. This is because undue influence is principally, but not completely, a plaintiff-oriented ground of restitution, in the sense that restitution is justified because the effect of the undue influence is that the plaintiff was unable to exercise a free choice whether or not to transact with the defendant. There is, however, evidence of another equitable ground of restitution which, whilst founded on the principle of exploitation, is primarily defendant-oriented, in the sense that it will be established only where the defendant is considered to have been at fault.[196] This is the ground of unconscionable conduct. There is a further difference between this ground of restitution and undue influence in that unconscionable conduct does not depend on the identification of an existing relationship of influence or dependency between the plaintiff and the defendant.[197]

The essential features of unconscionable conduct were identified by Lord Hardwicke in *Earl of Chesterfield* v. *Janssen*[198] as involving:

fraud presumed or inferred from the circumstances or conditions of the parties contracting: weakness on one side, usury on the other, or extortion or advantage taken of that weakness. There has always been the appearance of fraud from the nature of the bargain.

---

[194] This was in fact recognised by Dunn LJ at *ibid*, p. 463.

[195] See Bamforth, 'Unconscionability as a Vitiating Factor' [1995] *LMCLQ* 538 and Capper, 'Unconscionable Bargains' in *One Hundred and Fifty Years of Irish Law* (ed. Dawson, Greer and Ingrams (SLS/Round Hall Sweet and Maxwell, 1996) p. 45.

[196] See *Commercial Bank of Australia Ltd.* v. *Amadio* (1983) 151 CLR 447, 474 (Deane J). See also *Morrison* v. *Coast Finance Ltd.* (1965) 55 DLR (2d.) 710, 713 (Davey JA).

[197] Capper has argued that undue influence should be subsumed within the broader ground of unconscionability: 'Undue Influence and Unconscionability: A Rationalisation' (1998) 114 *LQR* 479 but this would only result in a loss of certainty in the definition and application of the law.

[198] (1751) 2 Ves. Sen. 125, 157; 28 ER 82, 101

So a transaction will be set aside for reasons of unconscionable conduct, or a benefit recovered, where the defendant has unconscientiously exploited his or her superior bargaining position to the detriment of the plaintiff who is in a much weaker position.

(a) The general principle of unconscionable conduct

In *Lloyds Bank Ltd.* v. *Bundy*[199] Lord Denning MR recognised a general principle of inequality of bargaining power, which he said arose where the plaintiff:

without independent advice, enters into a contract upon terms which are very unfair or transfers property for a consideration which is grossly inadequate, when his bargaining power is grievously impaired by reasons of his own needs or desires, or by his own ignorance or infirmity, coupled with undue influences or pressures brought to bear on him by or for the benefit of the other.[200]

This principle of inequality of bargaining power has subsequently been doubted[201] but, to the extent that this principle forms part of the general power of equity to relieve against transactions induced by uncon-scionable conduct, it has a useful function. In *National Westminster Bank plc.* v. *Morgan*[202] Lord Scarman considered that the principle of undue influence is now sufficiently well developed to remove the need for any doctrine of inequality of bargaining power, but this is not con-vincing since undue influence will only operate where there is an estab-lished relationship between the parties, and this is simply not the case in many situations where two parties have entered into a bargain. The prin-ciple which underlies undue influence, namely that of exploitation, should be applicable even where there is no existing relationship between the parties. Although Lord Denning in *Lloyds Bank Ltd.* v. *Bundy* said that this justified the recognition of a general principle of inequality of bargaining power, which encompassed all cases of duress, *colore officii*,[203] unconscionable transactions, undue pressure and undue influ-ence, this is apt to mislead, since these specific grounds of restitution are so different from each other that nothing can usefully be gained from treating them together. But Lord Denning did identify a gap in the recog-nised grounds of restitution where 'an unfair advantage has been gained by an unconscientious use of power by a stronger party against a weaker'.[204] Consequently, there is a need to recognise a new ground of restitution, which can usefully be called 'unconscionable conduct'. Although the name of this ground of restitution is new, the principles

---

[199] [1975] QB 326.   [200] *Ibid*, p. 339.
[201] See *National Westminster Bank plc.* v. *Morgan* [1985] AC 686, 708 (Lord Scarman).
[202] *Ibid*.   [203] See pp. 427–9 below.   [204] [1975] QB 326, 337.

underlying it are not, for they have been recognised by equity for a very long time and have recently been confirmed by the Court of Appeal.[205]

The biggest drawback to a principle of unconscionability is that its vagueness will make it unworkable. Bamforth in particular has warned against the danger of using pejorative terms such as 'unconscionability', and has called for precision and clarity when identifying criteria for assessing whether a transaction is unconscionable.[206] But it is possible to identify certain key principles which define the application of the principle of unconscionable conduct with some certainty. Crucially, it is clear that equity will not set aside a transaction simply because it is harsh. As Sir Raymond Evershed MR said in *Tufton* v. *Sperni*,[207] 'extravagant liberality and immoderate folly do not of themselves provide a passport to equitable relief'. To secure the intervention of equity[208] by reason of the defendant's unconscionable conduct the plaintiff needs to prove that two conditions have been satisfied, as was recognised by the High Court of Australia in the important decision of *Commercial Bank of Australia Ltd.* v. *Amadio*.[209]

(i) Special disability

The first requirement is that the plaintiff was suffering from a special disability or was placed in a special situation of disadvantage as against the defendant, so that there is a reasonable degree of inequality between the parties. It is not possible to draw up a complete list of all situations where there will be a sufficient degree of inequality, since ultimately this is a question of fact. However, in *Blomley* v. *Ryan*[210] Fullagar J did usefully describe the type of disability or disadvantage which is involved:

Among [these situations] are poverty or need of any kind, sickness, age, sex, infirmity of body or mind, drunkenness, illiteracy or lack of education, lack of assistance or explanation where assistance or explanation is necessary. The common characteristic seems to be that they have the effect of placing one party at a serious disadvantage vis-a-vis the other.

To this list may be added those cases where the plaintiff does not understand English very well,[211] where the plaintiff is in an emotional

---

[205] *Crédit Lyonnais Bank Nederland NV* v. *Burch* [1997] 1 All ER 144, 151 (Nourse LJ).

[206] 'Unconscionability as a Vitiating Factor' [1995] *LMCLQ* 538, 544.

[207] (1952) 2 TLR 516, 519.

[208] It is clear that there is no common law doctrine of inequality of bargaining power or anything equivalent to such a doctrine. See *CTN Cash and Carry Ltd.* v. *Gallaher Ltd.* [1994] 4 All ER 714, 717 (Steyn LJ).

[209] (1983) 151 CLR 447. See especially the judgment of Deane J at p. 474. See also *Earl of Aylseford* v. *Morris* (1873) LR 8 Ch. App. 484.

[210] (1956) 99 CLR 362, 405. For analysis of some of these situations see pp. 293–7 below.

[211] *The Commercial Bank of Australia Ltd.* v. *Amadio* (1983) 151 CLR 447. See also *Barclays Bank plc.* v. *Schwartz, The Times,* 2 August 1995.

state following the breakdown of his or her marriage[212] and even where the plaintiff is infatuated with the defendant.[213]

(ii) Unconscionable conduct

The second requirement is that the defendant's conduct must have been unconscionable.[214] The test for determining unconscionability has been a matter of some controversy. The orthodox approach assesses it by reference to the nature of the defendant's conduct and the fairness of the transaction. So, for example, a number of cases have relied on the fact that property was sold at a gross undervalue as evidence of unconscionable conduct.[215] More recently the emphasis has shifted to a test whereby unconscionability is identified by reference to whether the particular defendant was at fault in some way.

The leading case on this modern approach to unconscionability is the decision of the Privy Council in *Hart* v. *O'Connor*,[216] which concerned whether a transaction for the sale of land could be set aside where the vendor of the property was suffering from senile dementia but the purchaser was unaware of this disability. The decision of the Privy Council concerned two separate grounds for setting the transaction aside, namely the common law ground of contractual incapacity[217] and the alternative equitable ground that the defendant's conduct was unconscionable. It was held that, to establish either ground, it was not sufficient for the plaintiff to show that the terms of the transaction were unfair; rather it was necessary to establish that the defendant had committed equitable, or constructive, fraud. So this is now the test of unconscionable conduct. But the decision of the Privy Council does not provide much assistance on what this actually means. Lord Brightman, who delivered the Board's judgment, said that equitable fraud 'is victimisation, which can consist either of the active extortion of a benefit or the passive acceptance of a benefit in unconscionable circumstances'.[218] He went on to suggest that the defendant must have been in bad faith or had taken advantage of the plaintiff in some way.[219]

The preferable interpretation of *Hart* v. *O'Connor* is that what must be shown is that the defendant was at fault in some way, either because he

---

[212] *Backhouse* v. *Backhouse* [1978] 1 WLR 243.

[213] *Louth* v. *Diprose* (1992) 75 CLR 621.

[214] *Alec Lobb (Garages) Ltd.* v. *Total Oil (GB) Ltd.* [1985] 1 WLR 173, 182 (Dillon LJ).

[215] *Longmate* v. *Ledger* (1860) 2 Giff. 157; 66 ER 67; *Fry* v. *Lane* (1888) 40 Ch.D 312, 322 (Kay J); *Blomley* v. *Ryan* (1956) 99 CLR 362, 405 (Fullagar J). See especially the judgment of Peter Millett QC in *Alec Lobb (Garages) Ltd.* v. *Total Oil (GB) Ltd.* [1983] 1 WLR 87, 95.

[216] [1985] AC 1000.   [217] See Chapter 13.

[218] [1985] AC 1000, 1028.

[219] *Ibid.* See also *Boustany* v. *Piggott* (1993) 69 P and CR 298 (PC) noted by Cartwright, 'Unconscionable Bargains' (1993) 109 *LQR* 530.

or she actually knew of the plaintiff's special disability or disadvantage or because he or she should have known this since he or she was aware of particular facts which would have put the reasonable person on notice that the plaintiff had a special disability or disadvantage.[220] This does not mean that questions of substantive unfairness, such as the fact that the transaction is at a gross undervalue, are completely irrelevant, since such unfairness will provide strong evidence that the defendant was put on notice that the plaintiff was suffering from a special disability or disadvantage and so should have been advised to obtain independent legal advice.[221] But despite this, the real significance of *Hart* v. *O'Connor* is to emphasise that unconscionable conduct is primarily to be assessed by reference to the fault of the defendant, rather than simply by referring to the objective facts of the case. Consequently, the mere fact that there was a contractual imbalance between the parties or that the terms of the transaction were unfair is not sufficient evidence of unconscionability.[222] Equally, just because the transaction appears to be fair, in that the plaintiff did not suffer any loss or detriment as a result of it, does not mean that the defendant was acting without fault.[223]

(iii) Whether the transaction was fair, just and reasonable

Once the plaintiff has shown that he or she was suffering from a special disability or disadvantage and that the defendant's conduct was unconscionable, the transaction will be set aside, unless the defendant can show that the transaction was fair, just and reasonable.[224] The defendant will be able to establish this by showing, for example, that the plaintiff obtained independent legal advice, since this can place the parties on equal terms.[225] But the obtaining of such advice will only be relevant if its effect really is to place the parties on equal terms. So, for example, in *Boustany* v. *Piggott*[226] a renegotiated lease was set aside by reason of the defendant's unconscionable conduct even though the disadvantages of

---

[220] *Owen and Gutch* v. *Homan* (1853) 4 HLC 997, 1035; 10 ER 752, 767 (Lord Cranworth LC); *The Commercial Bank of Australia Ltd.* v. *Amadio* (1983) 151 CLR 447, 467 (Mason J); *Nichols* v. *Jessup* [1986] 1 NZLR 226, 236 (Somers J). Cp. *Louth* v. *Diprose* (1992) 175 CLR 621 where the High Court of Australia adopted a subjective test of fault. On the general question of whether a subjective or an objective test of fault should be adopted see Bamforth, 'Unconscionability as a Vitiating Factor' [1995] *LMCLQ* 538, 550. Bamforth cogently argues that a subjective test of fault should be adopted since this ground of restitution is defendant-oriented and so should depend on clear proof of fault: *ibid*, p. 557.

[221] See McMullin J in *Nichols* v. *Jessup* [1986] 1 NZLR 226, 234: 'I do not read *O'Connor* v. *Hart* as negating entirely the importance of objective considerations or insisting upon over-reaching as necessary to establish an unconscionable bargain'. See also *Alec Lobb (Garages) Ltd.* v. *Total Oil (GB) Ltd.* [1983] 1 WLR 87, 95 (Peter Millett QC).

[222] *Boustany* v. *Piggott* (1993) 69 P and CR 298, 303.

[223] *Blomley* v. *Ryan* (1956) 99 CLR 362, 405 (Fullagar J).

[224] *Earl of Aylesford* v. *Morris* (1873) LR 8 Ch. App. 484, 491 (Lord Selborne LC).

[225] *Fry* v. *Lane* (1888) 40 Ch.D 312. [226] (1993) 69 P and CR 298.

the transaction had been forcibly pointed out to the plaintiff by a barrister, because the defendant was present and was taking advantage of the plaintiff when the advice was given.[227]

(b) Identifying unconscionable conduct

The application of this ground of restitution is illustrated by *Hart* v. *O'Connor*[228] itself, where it was held that unconscionable conduct had not been established on the facts because the defendant, who had bought land from the plaintiff, was not aware of the plaintiff's dementia, and there was nothing to put him on notice of this since it appeared that the vendor was acting in accordance with the most full and careful legal advice. Neither was there any evidence of objective unfairness since the terms of the bargain had been proposed by the plaintiff's solicitor and the land had been independently valued. As Lord Brightman concluded:

There was no equitable fraud, no victimisation, no taking advantage, no over-reaching or other description of unconscionable doings which might have justified the intervention of equity.[229]

The decision in *Hart* v. *O'Connor* may usefully be contrasted with the later decision of the New Zealand Court of Appeal in *Nichols* v. *Jessup*,[230] where the plaintiff had agreed to grant the defendant a right of way over her land, the effect of which was to increase the value of the defendant's land by $45,000 and to decrease the value of the plaintiff's land by $3,000. The trial judge found that the consideration which the plaintiff had received for the transaction had been grossly inadequate, that she had not received legal advice and that she was unintelligent and muddle-headed. The Court of Appeal held that, where the defendant knew or should have known that the plaintiff was at a significant disadvantage in appreciating the relative consequences of the transaction, then the marked imbalance of benefit arising from it was evidence that the defendant had acted unconscionably. When the case was returned to the trial judge for reconsideration he concluded that the defendant had indeed acted unconscionably because 'although [the transaction was] not originally extorted by an unconscientious exercise of power [it] should be set aside in exercise of the Court's equitable jurisdiction on the ground that in all the circumstances it is not consistent with equity and good conscience that the [defendant] should enforce or retain the benefit of the transaction'.[231] The trial judge's decision is open to two main criticisms.

---

[227] For a similar approach to the role of independent advice for the purposes of establishing undue influence see p. pp. 263–5 above.

[228] [1985] AC 1000.   [229] *Ibid*, p. 1024.   [230] [1986] 1 NZLR 226.

First, his decision was based on the fact that the transaction was 'on any objective view ... so manifestly one-sided' even though he had actually found that there was no moral fraud on the part of the defendant.[232] This is surely contrary to the decision of the Privy Council in *Hart* v. *O'Connor*, where emphasis was specifically placed on the need to establish that the defendant had been at fault. Secondly, the question of unconscionable conduct should be judged at the time the defendant entered into the transaction with the plaintiff.[233] The judge's conclusion that the agreement had not been extorted by unconscientious use of power should have meant that the transaction would not be set aside.

(c) Unconscionable conduct and third parties

Where the plaintiff is induced to enter into a transaction with the defendant as a result of the unconscionable conduct of a third party, and the defendant's conduct cannot be characterised as unconscionable, then the defendant will be able to enforce the transaction unless he or she had notice, whether actual or constructive, of the plaintiff's equity to set the transaction aside.[234] This reflects exactly the situation in which a defendant wishes to enforce a transaction which a party had been induced to enter as a result of undue influence exerted by a third party.[235] So, for example, if an employer induces an employee to provide security for the employer's debts in favour of a bank and this can be characterised as unconscionable by virtue of the employer's conduct, the bank will still be able to enforce the security unless it has notice of the employer's impropriety.[236]

(d) Vitiation of gifts by unconscionable conduct

Although it has been held that the doctrine of unconscionable conduct will only be available where the plaintiff has entered into a contract as a result of the unconscionable conduct and not where the plaintiff has made a gift,[237] because otherwise the donee bears the burden of proving that the gift was fair, just and reasonable, this is a conclusion which is difficult to defend. For it is perfectly possible to conceive of cases where

---

[231] *Nichols* v. *Jessup (No. 2)* [1986] 1 NZLR 237, 240 (Prichard J).   [232] *Ibid*, p. 239.
[233] As is the case where the plaintiff relies on undue influence. See *Allcard* v. *Skinner* (1887) 36 Ch.D 145, 191 (Bowen LJ).
[234] This has been recognised in Australia: see, for example, *Atkins* v. *National Australia Bank Ltd.* (1994) 34 NSWLR 155 and *National Australia Bank Ltd.* v. *Garcia* (1995) 39 NSWLR 577.
[235] See p. 265 above.
[236] See *Crédit Lyonnais Nederland NV* v. *Burch* [1997] 1 All ER 144, 153 (Millett LJ).
[237] *Langton* v. *Langton*, *The Times*, 24 February 1995.

the plaintiff has been induced to make a gift to the defendant or another party as a result of unconscionable conduct where the benefit transferred should be restored to the plaintiff.[238] It seems that too much emphasis has been placed on the notion of unconscionable bargains, which would exclude gifts, where the real issue concerns the effect of the defendant's unconscionable conduct.

(e) Examples of special disability or disadvantage

There are a number of well recognised categories of special disability or disadvantage. The potential for abuse in the first two categories, involving transactions with the poor and ignorant and with expectant heirs, might be so great that unconscionability on the part of the defendant may even be presumed.[239] If so, once the plaintiff has established the special disability or disadvantage then the burden will be on the defendant to show that the transaction was fair, just and reasonable.

(i) Transactions with the poor and ignorant

Equity is prepared to set aside certain transactions if they are made with somebody who is both poor and ignorant, because such people are assumed to be particularly vulnerable to exploitation. So, for example, in *Fry* v. *Lane*[240] a contract for sale at an undervalue was set aside where the vendor was characterised as poor and ignorant, because the temptation of receiving a sum of money immediately might mean that such a person did not consider the consequences of transacting with the defendant. This category of special disability continues to be relevant, although the notions of poverty and ignorance were reinterpreted in *Cresswell* v. *Potter*,[241] so that poor meant 'a member of the lower income group' and ignorant was to be interpreted as meaning 'less highly educated'. In *Cresswell* the plaintiff, who was a telephonist, had released her interest in the matrimonial home to her husband on her divorce from him. This release was set aside because she was characterised as being poor and ignorant, it being sufficient that she was ignorant as to the operation of property transactions. It was also of crucial significance that the transaction had been at a significant undervalue and that she had not received any independent legal advice, something which was considered to be of

---

[238] *Louth* v. *Diprose* (1992) 175 CLR 621. See Capper, 'Undue Influence and Unconscionability: A Rationalisation' (1998) 114 *LQR* 479, 492.

[239] See *Alec Lobb (Garages) Ltd.* v. *Total Oil (GB) Ltd.* [1985] 1 WLR 173, 182 (Dillon LJ).

[240] (1888) 40 Ch.D 312. See also *Evans* v. *Llewellin* (1787) 1 Cox 333; 29 ER 1191.

[241] [1978] 1 WLR 255n. See also *Crédit Lyonnais Bank Nederland NV* v. *Burch* [1997] 1 All ER 144.

particular importance in a conveyancing transaction.

In neither of these cases was the defendant's conduct specifically characterised as unconscionable. Indeed, in *Fry* v. *Lane* it was held that there
was no evidence of moral fraud or misconduct on the part of the defendant. This suggests that, where the defendant has transacted with somebody who is poor and ignorant then, at least where the transaction is at a
considerable undervalue, it will be presumed that the defendant had
acted unconscionably and then he or she will bear the burden of proving
that the transaction was fair, just and reasonable. This is because the fact
that a transaction with somebody who was poor and ignorant was at a
gross undervalue is itself evidence of equitable fraud.[242]

(ii) Transactions with expectant heirs

Where someone is expecting to receive an inheritance at some point in
the future, his or her desire to receive money as soon as possible makes
him or her peculiarly susceptible to moneylenders, who will lend him or
her money at extortionate rates of interest or purchase his or her inheritance at a gross undervalue. Such expectant heirs are characterised as
being disadvantaged by a special disability; what Lord Selborne LC called
'the follies and vice of unprotected youth, inexperience and imbecil-
ity'.[243] If the defendant's conduct in transacting with such people can be
characterised as unconscionable then the transaction is liable to be set
aside. The operation of this principle is illustrated by *Earl of Aylesford* v.
Morris[244] where the plaintiff stood to inherit his father's estate and took
out a loan from the defendant to pay off his debts at an interest rate of 60
per cent. This was set aside because the nature of the relationship
between the parties and the terms of the transaction were such that the
defendant was presumed to have acted fraudulently. As a condition of
setting the transaction aside the plaintiff was required to repay the principal sum and a reasonable interest rate of 5 per cent. One of the crucial
factors which influenced the court in characterising this transaction as
unconscionable was the fact that the plaintiff was inexperienced and
immature. It was accepted that the presumption of unconscionability
could have been rebutted if the defendant could prove that the plaintiff
had obtained independent legal advice.

(iii) Salvage agreements

Where a ship is in danger of sinking and urgently needs help, the rescuer
is in a strong position to exploit the situation. If the salvage agreement
which is entered into is manifestly unfair and unjust then the court will

---

[242] *Fry* v. *Lane* (1888) 40 Ch.D 312, 321 (Kay J).
[243] *Earl of Aylesford* v. *Morris* (1873) LR 8 Ch. App. 484.
[244] *Ibid*. See also *O'Rorke* v. *Bolingbroke* (1877) 2 App. Cas. 814.

set it aside.[245] For example, in *The Port Caledonia and The Anna*[246] a rescuer refused to provide a rope to assist with the rescue unless he was paid
£1,000. The agreement to pay this sum was set aside on the ground that
it was manifestly unfair and unjust.

(iv) Gross inequality of bargaining power

In addition to these specific types of disability or disadvantage, it seems
that the courts are prepared to identify a special disadvantage where on
the particular facts of the case there is a gross inequality of bargaining
power between the parties. In an exceptional case where the difference
in the relative bargaining power of the parties is such that the defendant
is at a great advantage and the defendant's conduct is characterised as
unconscionable the transaction is liable to be set aside. For example,
where a husband and wife divorce and are suffering from emotional
strain, if the husband retains the matrimonial home he is in a position of
particular advantage, so if the wife agrees to transfer her interest in the
house to her husband for little or no consideration, the transaction is
liable to be set aside if she is not encouraged to obtain independent legal
advice.[247] This is further illustrated by *The Commercial Bank of Australia
v. Amadio*,[248] where the defendants were induced to provide a guarantee
so that the bank would be prepared to increase the approved overdraft
limit of their son's company. It has already been seen that this type of
transaction might be set aside on the basis of the son's undue influence
if the son acted as the bank's agent or the bank had notice of the son's
conduct.[249] However, in the *Amadio* case the guarantee was set aside
specifically because of the bank's unconscionable conduct. Although the
High Court of Australia recognised that the bank's duty to make disclosure to its intending surety was very limited, it found that, on the particular and exceptional facts of this case, there was a gross inequality of
bargaining power between the bank and the parents, so that the parents
stood in a position of special disadvantage *vis-à-vis* the bank. This gross
inequality of bargaining power arose from a number of different factors,
including the defendants' reliance on their son, their age, 71 and 76
respectively, their limited command of written English and relative inexperience of business in which the son was engaged. The bank's conduct
was regarded as unconscionable primarily because the bank manager,
who had visited the defendants to obtain their signatures for the guarantee, knew of the circumstances which amounted to a special disadvantage, particularly that the defendants clearly did not understand the
nature of the document which they were signing. Also, because the bank

---

[245] See Lord Denning MR in *Lloyds Bank Ltd.* v. *Bundy* [1975] QB 326, 339.
[246] [1903] P 184.   [247] *Backhouse* v. *Backhouse* [1978] 1 WLR 243.
[248] (1983) 151 CLR 447.   [249] See pp. 268–74 above.

manager knew that the transaction was improvident from the viewpoint
of the defendants it was 'inconceivable that the possibility did not occur
to [him] that the [parents'] entry into the transaction was due to their
inability to make a judgment as to what was in their best interests'.[250] But
another feature which enabled the court to conclude that the bank's conduct was unconscionable was the fact that the relationship between the
bank and the son was more than an ordinary business relationship. This
was because the son's company was a major client of the bank and, crucially, the bank's wholly-owned subsidiary. So it was in the bank's best
interests that the company was able to continue trading.

It is even possible that gross inequality of bargaining power may arise
in a purely commercial context, as was recognised in *Multiservice Bookbinding Ltd.* v. *Marden*,[251] where Browne-Wilkinson J accepted that
there might be gross inequality of bargaining power between a borrower
and a lender, so that, if the borrowing transaction was unfair and unconscionable, it could be set aside. It was subsequently recognised that if a
purely commercial transaction were to be set aside on this ground then
three conditions needed to be satisfied.[252] First, the plaintiff must be at a
serious disadvantage as against the defendant. Secondly, the plaintiff's
weakness must have been exploited by the defendant in a morally culpable manner and, finally, the resulting transaction must have been over-
reaching and oppressive. Consequently, unconscionability in a purely
commercial context is assessed by reference both to the defendant's
conduct and the particular terms of the transaction. It is for this reason
that the borrowing transaction in *Multiservice Bookbinding* was not set
aside. This was because the plaintiff borrower in that case had obtained
independent legal advice, there was no evidence of sharp practice and,
crucially, the plaintiff was only seeking the loan in order to expand, so
that if it did not like the lender's terms it could have refused to enter the
transaction without the risk of becoming insolvent. Where the solvency
of the borrower is dependent upon the obtaining of the loan, it may be
possible to identify gross inequality of bargaining power, but unconscionability will still need to be identified and this will be difficult to
establish.

(v) Statutory regimes[253]

A money-lending transaction may also be set aside by virtue of certain
statutory provisions. For example, section 1 of the Moneylenders Act
1900 authorises the court to grant relief to a borrower who is charged an

---

[250] (1983) 151 CLR 447, 466–7 (Mason J).   [251] [1979] Ch. 84.
[252] Peter Millett QC sitting as a Deputy High Court Judge in *Alec Lobb (Garages) Ltd.* v.
Total Oil (GB) Ltd. [1983] 1 WLR 87, 95, affirmed by the Court of Appeal [1985] 1 WLR 173.
[253] See Bamforth, 'Unconscionability as a Vitiating Factor' [1995] *LMCLQ* 538, 557–9.

excessive rate of interest, if he or she establishes that the transaction is harsh or unconscionable or that there are other reasons why equity should grant relief. The court's powers to grant relief include that it may require the creditor to repay the amount of interest which is unreasonable, or it may even create a new bargain between the parties. The most important statutory provision however is the Consumer Credit Act 1974, which gives the court extensive powers to reopen extortionate credit transactions to secure justice between the parties,[254] including the power to require the creditor to repay the whole or part of any sum paid under the agreement.[255]

5. THE PARTIES ARE NOT *IN PARI DELICTO*

It is a fundamental principle of the law of restitution that restitutionary claims will fail where the plaintiff has participated in an illegal transaction.[256] This was recognised by Lord Mansfield in *Holman* v. *Johnson*[257] in the form of the *in pari delicto* defence, whereby if the parties are equally at fault in participating in the illegal transaction then the loss will lie where it falls. But if a defence to restitutionary claims is founded on the principle of equal fault, it should follow that if the plaintiff is less at fault than the defendant then the restitutionary claim should not be defeated by the taint of illegality. That this is implicit within the *in pari delicto* defence was recognised by Lord Mansfield in *Smith* v *Bromley*.[258] Consequently, where it can be shown that the defendant is more blameworthy than the plaintiff for entering into the transaction then restitution will lie, and the ground of restitution in such cases is the fact that the parties are not *in pari delicto*, in other words that they are not equally to blame.

There are three categories of cases in which the plaintiff will be able to establish that the parties are not *in pari delicto* and so will be able to obtain restitution even though he or she has participated in an illegal transaction. Of these, the fact that the plaintiff was induced to transfer a benefit to the defendant as a result of the defendant's fraudulent conduct is properly treated as involving restitution for an induced mistake.[259] The other two categories, however, of oppression and statutory protection of the plaintiff, should be analysed as being founded on the principle of exploitation, whether actual or potential, by the defendant of the plaintiff. That this is the preferable explanation of this ground of restitution is supported by a dictum of Lord Mansfield in *Smith* v. *Bromley*,[260] the case

---

[254] Consumer Credit Act 1974, s. 137(1).   [255] *Ibid*, s. 139(2).
[256] See Chapter 26.   [257] (1775) 1 Cowp. 341, 343; 98 ER 1120, 1121.
[258] (1760) 2 Doug. 696n, 697; 99 ER 441, 442.   [259] See p. 167 above.

which first recognised this ground of restitution:

But there are other laws, which are calculated for the protection of the subject against oppression, extortion, deceit etc. If such laws are violated and the defendant takes advantage of the plaintiff's condition or situation, then the plaintiff shall recover . . .

Such laws may exist by virtue of common law or statute. The fact that where the plaintiff is not *in pari delicto* with the defendant then this is a ground of restitution in its own right was recognised by Lord Denning in *Kiriri Cotton Co. Ltd.* v. *Dewani*,[261] where he treated it on a par with restitution for mistake or total failure of consideration.

(a) Oppression

Where the defendant has exploited the plaintiff's weakness oppressively restitution will be awarded to the plaintiff by reason of the oppression even though the plaintiff participated in an illegal transaction. This is particularly well illustrated by a line of cases involving creditors who refused to enter into a composition agreement unless they received preferential treatment from the debtor, such preferential treatment being illegal. This is illustrated by *Smith* v. *Cuff*[262] where the plaintiff was allowed to recover money from the defendant creditor in an action for money had and received. As Lord Ellenborough CJ said, the parties are not '*par delictum* where one holds the rod and the other bows to it'.[263]

What the courts are looking for in such cases is sufficient evidence of inequality between the parties to enable them to ignore the plaintiff's turpitude in entering into the illegal transaction in the first place. If the plaintiff's conduct is regarded as voluntary because there was insufficient oppression the restitutionary claim will fail.[264] Oppression arising from the particular circumstances of the case rather than from the defendant's actions is not sufficient to show that the parties are not *in pari delicto*. So, for example, in *Bigos* v. *Bousted*[265] the plaintiff was forced to enter into a loan agreement which contravened the exchange control regulations because he was desperate for money to be able to send his daughter abroad to improve her health. Despite the difficult circumstances in which the plaintiff found himself, the court still held that the parties were *in pari delicto* and the plaintiff was not able to recover the security he had provided for the loan.

---

[260] (1760) 2 Doug. 696n., 697; 99 ER 441, 443.
[262] (1817) 6 M and S 160; 105 ER 1203.
[264] *Wilson* v. *Ray* (1839) 10 Ad. and E 82; 113 ER 32.

[261] [1960] AC 102, 205.
[263] *Ibid*, p. 165; 1205.
[265] [1951] 1 All ER 92.

(b) Statutory protection of the plaintiff

Sometimes a statutory provision which makes a transaction illegal is regarded as existing for the purposes of protecting a particular group of people to which the plaintiff belongs. In such a case the plaintiff is regarded as not being *in pari delicto* with the defendant and so restitution will be allowed. This is illustrated by *Kiriri Cotton Co. Ltd.* v. *Dewani,*[266] where the plaintiff tenant paid a premium to his landlord in circumstances in which both parties were unaware that such a payment was illegal by virtue of a statute. The plaintiff was allowed to recover the premium because it was held that the statute existed to protect tenants like him and so the parties were not *in pari delicto*. In other words, the responsibility for ensuring compliance with the law was placed on the landlord rather than the tenant. Although this was not a case where the landlord had set out to exploit the plaintiff in contravention of the statute, it is at least a case in which there was a potential for exploitation, as reflected by the fact that a statute was enacted to protect tenants.

For restitution to be awarded on this ground it is necessary to determine whether the policy of the statute is to protect people like the plaintiff. So, for example, in *Green* v. *Portsmouth Stadium Ltd.*[267] it was held that money paid by a bookmaker to the owner of a racecourse in excess of the amount authorised by statute was an illegal payment, but that it could not be recovered because the relevant statutory provision had not been enacted for the purpose of protecting bookmakers, but sought simply to regulate racecourses.

[266] [1960] AC 192.   [267] [1953] 2 QB 190.

11

Necessity

1. GENERAL PRINCIPLES

(a) The principle of necessity

In the same way that there are general principles of compulsion and exploitation on which a number of specific grounds of restitution are based, there is also a general principle of necessity by reference to which a number of specific grounds of restitution can be identified. Although the existence of a general principle of necessity is beyond doubt in English law,[1] the principle is not well developed in common law legal systems, unlike civil law systems which have a well developed doctrine of *negotiorum gestio* which is applicable where the plaintiff has provided a benefit to the defendant in circumstances of necessity.[2] Consequently, in English law the ambit and rationale of necessity within the law of restitution is a matter of great uncertainty. The predominant reason for the underdeveloped nature of the necessity principle is the importance of the principle of officiousness which operates to bar restitutionary claims.[3] The success of restitutionary claims grounded on necessity will depend on how the principle of officiousness is defined.

(b) The principle of officiousness

In *Falcke* v. *Scottish Imperial Insurance Co.*[4] Bowen LJ identified the essence of the officiousness principle when he stated that:

The general principle is, beyond all question, that work or labour done or money expended by one man to preserve or benefit the property of another do not according to English law create any lien upon the property saved or benefited, nor even, if standing alone, create any obligation to repay the expenditure. Liabilities are not to be forced on people behind their backs any more than you can confer a benefit upon a man against his will.[5]

---

[1] It was recognised by the House of Lords in *Re F (Mental Patient: Sterilisation)* [1990] 2 AC 1.

[2] See Dawson, '*Negotiorum Gestio*: The Altruistic Intermeddler' (1961) 74 *Harv. LR* 817.

[3] See pp. 39–40 above. For discussion of the notion of 'officiousness' see in particular Hope, 'Officiousness' (1929) 15 *Cornell LQ* 5 and Birks, '*Negotiorum Gestio* and the Common Law' (1971) 24 *CLP* 110.   [4] (1886) 34 Ch.D 234.

[5] *Ibid*, p. 248. Bowen LJ went on to recognise an exception to this principle in the context of maritime salvage. See p. 320 below.

According to this definition the plaintiff will have been acting officiously where he or she acted without the consent or knowledge of the defendant. Restitution will be denied because the plaintiff will be deemed to have taken the risk that he or she would not be reimbursed by the defendant for the work done or the money which had been expended. If this is the correct interpretation of the officiousness principle it follows that it will be virtually impossible to obtain restitution in the context of claims grounded on necessity because typically the defendant will be unaware that the plaintiff had intervened. It seems, however, that the definition of the officiousness principle can be defined further, although the cases are not consistent as to what this definition should be. The cases suggest that there are two distinct interpretations of the principle in the context of necessity.

(i) The plaintiff acted selfishly rather than benevolently

The first interpretation, as exemplified by *Falcke* itself, suggests that the plaintiff will be considered to have acted officiously if he or she acted selfishly rather than benevolently for the defendant. In *Falcke* the plaintiff was the mortgagor of a life insurance policy who had paid a large annual premium to ensure that the policy did not lapse. Although it might be argued that it was necessary for the plaintiff to act to preserve the insurance policy, it was held that he was not able to recover the amount he had paid from the defendant, who was the executrix of the mortgagee of the policy, because the plaintiff had been acting as an officious volunteer, motivated as he was by a desire to protect his own proprietary interest in the policy rather than that of the defendant.

(ii) The plaintiff intervened when he or she was not legally obliged to do so

The alternative interpretation of officiousness in the context of necessity limits the ambit of the plaintiff's claim much more dramatically. Under this interpretation the plaintiff will be able to rely on necessity only where he or she was legally obliged to intervene. The recognition and application of this interpretation of officiousness are illustrated by *Macclesfield Corporation* v. *Great Central Railway*[6] where the defendant railway company was obliged by statute to keep a bridge in good repair. The plaintiff highway authority requested the defendant to repair the bridge, but the defendant refused to do so. Since the bridge was in a dangerous state of disrepair the plaintiff undertook the necessary repairs and then sought restitution of its expenses from the defendant. The plaintiff's claim failed. The Court of Appeal did not examine whether the

---

[6] [1911] 2 KB 528. See also *Binstead* v. *Buck* (1777) 2 Black. W 1117; 96 ER 660.

plaintiff had acted in circumstances of necessity, but concluded that the plaintiff's claim should fail simply because it considered that the plaintiff had acted voluntarily since it was not under any legal liability to carry out the work.[7] This interpretation of the officiousness principle had previously been recognised by Eyre CJ in *Nicholson* v. *Chapman*[8] who suggested that 'perhaps it is better for the public that these voluntary acts of benevolence from one man to another, which are charities and moral duties, but not legal duties, should depend altogether for their reward upon the moral duty of gratitude'.[9]

(iii) The preferable interpretation of officiousness

Of these two interpretations of the principle of officiousness the former is the preferable since there is no obvious reason why a plaintiff who has acted in the interests of the defendant should be denied restitutionary relief simply because he or she was not legally obliged to act. Where, however, the plaintiff has acted for his or her own selfish reasons, then the plaintiff should be considered to have acted officiously and his or her claim for restitution grounded on necessity should be defeated.

(c) The rationale of the necessity principle

Even where a plaintiff who has transferred a benefit to the defendant can be considered not to have been acting officiously, it is still important to determine whether the plaintiff was indeed acting in circumstances of necessity. If grounds of restitution founded on necessity are to be recognised then we need to be able to identify the reason such grounds of restitution should be recognised. Two possible justifications can be identified.

(i) Public Policy

The first justification is that grounds of restitution founded on necessity should be recognised for reasons of public policy to encourage the plaintiff to intervene to assist others who are in need of help.[10] This seems to be the reason a doctrine of maritime salvage exists,[11] as Eyre CJ accepted in *Nicholson* v. *Chapman*[12] when he said that:

Principles of public policy dictate to civilised and commercial countries, not only the propriety, but even the absolute necessity, of establishing a liberal recompense for the encouragement of those who engage in so dangerous a service.

---

[7] [1911] 2 KB 528, p. 539 (Farwell LJ), p. 540 (Kennedy LJ).
[8] (1793) 2 Hy. Bl. 254, 259; 126 ER 536, 539.   [9] But see p. 314 below.
[10] See Burrows, *The Law of Restitution*, p. 249.   [11] See p. 320 below.
[12] (1793) 2 Hy. Bl. 254, 257; 126 ER 536, 538.

But the doctrine of maritime salvage has usually been treated as *sui generis* and may not even have anything to do with the law of restitution at all.[13] More generally, whilst public policy can be used to explain why grounds of restitution founded on necessity ought to be recognised, the notion of public policy is not sufficiently certain to predict when the plaintiff was acting in circumstances of necessity. Reliance on public policy by itself lays the law of restitution open to the charge of palm-tree justice.

(ii) Interference with the plaintiff's free choice

The preferable explanation of why necessity should constitute a principle by reference to which grounds of restitution can be recognised is that the effect of the necessity is to vitiate the plaintiff's intention to provide a gratuitous benefit to the defendant. The crucial question when determining whether the plaintiff indeed acted in circumstances of necessity is whether he or she had a free choice in providing a benefit for the defendant. Where, for example, there is an emergency which requires immediate action on the part of the plaintiff, whether it be to rescue the defendant or his or her property or to perform an act which the defendant has a duty to perform, then the circumstances which create the emergency may operate to constrain the plaintiff's freedom of choice to intervene, so that it is possible to conclude that the plaintiff did not intend to provide a gratuitous benefit to the defendant. This explanation was specifically recognised in *The Great Northern Railway Company* v. *Swaffield*[14] where it was held to be reasonable for a railway company to incur expenditure in stabling a horse which it had transported but which had not been collected by the defendant. Kelly CB justified the plaintiff's conduct in the following terms:[15]

I think we need do no more than ask ourselves, as a question of common sense and common understanding, had they any choice? They must either have allowed the horse to stand at the station—a place where it would have been extremely improper and dangerous to let it remain; or they must have put it in safe custody, which was in fact what they did ...

It has sometimes even been suggested that where the plaintiff acts in circumstances of necessity he or she has no choice but to act.[16] Although this may be true in certain cases, for example, where the plaintiff reacts instinctively to save the defendant, in most cases, particularly those in which the plaintiff brings a restitutionary claim, he or she will have had the opportunity to decide whether or not to intervene. So, rather than

---

[13] See p. 321 below.   [14] (1874) LR 9 Ex. 132.   [15] *Ibid*, p. 135.
[16] This was the view of Lord Simon of Glaisdale in *DPP for Northern Ireland* v. *Lynch* [1975] AC 653, 690.

confining necessity to those very rare cases in which the plaintiff has no choice but to intervene, it is more accurate to define necessity as arising where the plaintiff's freedom of choice was constrained by the circumstances facing the defendant, so that there was no real choice open to the plaintiff but to intervene. This was recognised by Sir Montague Smith in *Australasian Steam Navigation Co.* v. *Morse*,[17] who said that:

the word 'necessity' when applied to mercantile affairs . . . cannot of course mean an irresistible compelling power—what is meant by it in such cases is, the force of circumstances which determines the course a man ought to take.

This justification for the recognition of the necessity principle has the added advantage that it reconciles the principle of denying restitution where the plaintiff is an officious volunteer with allowing restitution in circumstances of necessity. This is because it will only be the most exceptional cases in which the circumstances are such that the plaintiff had no real choice but to intervene and, where this is the case, it will not be possible to show that the plaintiff was an officious volunteer, simply because he or she would be acting benevolently.

(iii) Distinguishing between necessity and compulsion

This justification for the existence of necessity as a ground of restitution is virtually identical to the justification for those grounds of restitution which are founded on compulsion, so much so that it is very difficult to make a clear distinction between compulsion and necessity. But there is a key difference between the two principles which justifies their separate treatment. Compulsion involves threats being made against the plaintiff, whether explicitly or implicitly, by the words or actions of the defendant, or sometimes a third party. Such threats can be classified as being of the 'do this, or else . . . ' variety. In other words, the threat takes the form that some detriment will be suffered by somebody if the plaintiff does not do what the defendant or a third party demands. Necessity, on the other hand, does not involve threats or pressure of the 'do this, or else . . . ' variety. Rather, the circumstances of the case require the plaintiff to act to prevent harm being suffered. Typically, the pressure will derive from some form of disaster, whether natural or man-made. So, to take a mundane example, if the defendant's house was burgled whilst she was on holiday, the defendant's neighbour may have incurred expenditure to ensure that a window which was broken in the course of the burglary was repaired, so that no-one else would break in. The pressure on the neighbour in these circumstances was not of the kind that if he did not repair the window some detrimental consequence would inevitably result at the hands of a person who had made threats. Consequently, this is a case

[17] (1872) LR 4 PC 222, 230.

of necessity rather than compulsion. This is a subtle, but legitimate, distinction which needs to be drawn because the policy issues concerning the existence and ambit of the principle of necessity are different from those which relate to compulsion.

(d) Determining whether the plaintiff acted in circumstances of necessity

Although necessity is defined subjectively, in the sense that we are concerned with whether the plaintiff had no real choice but to assist the defendant, this is a matter which is particularly difficult to prove. Consequently, the courts often refer to an objective test, namely whether, had he or she been in the same situation as the plaintiff, a reasonable person would have acted in the same way.[18] A number of principles can be identified which will assist in the determination of whether the plaintiff's intervention really was reasonable.[19] Whilst many of these principles have been recognised as relevant in those cases in which necessity has been examined in the context of restitutionary claims, it is not necessary to establish all of them before restitutionary relief will be awarded.[20] Rather, they should be treated as characteristics of what constitutes reasonable conduct on the part of the plaintiff so that he or she can be considered to have acted in circumstances of necessity. Consideration of these principles will also assist the court in determining whether the plaintiff had acted officiously.

(1) The plaintiff's intervention is invariably reasonable where the circumstances were such that intervention was urgently required to protect life, health or property. Generally this means that there must have been an emergency which required immediate action, otherwise the person or property would be lost or at least suffer serious injury or damage. Whether there was an emergency is to be determined at the time when the emergency becomes apparent.[21] But it is possible in exceptional cases for the plaintiff's intervention to be justified by reason of necessity even though an immediate response may not be required. This will be the case where there is no immediate danger, 'but there was a possible contingency that serious consequences might have ensued',[22] such as

[18] See *The Australasian Steam Navigation Co.* v. *Morse* (1872) LR 4 PC 222, 230 (Sir Montague Smith) and *Re F (Mental Patient: Sterilisation)* [1990] 2 AC 1, 75 (Lord Goff).
[19] See Rose, 'Restitution for the Rescuer' (1989) 9 *OJLS* 167, esp. 182–99 and Jones, *Restitution in Public and Private Law* (London: Sweet and Maxwell Ltd., 1991) p. 128.
[20] Rose, 'Restitution from the Rescuer' (1989) 9 *OJLS* 167, 182.
[21] *The Winson* [1982] AC 939, 965 (Lord Simon).
[22] *The Ella Constance* (1864) 33 LJ Adm. 189, 193 (Dr. Lushington). Jones, in *Restitution in Public and Private Law* at p. 145, suggests that, where the plaintiff intervenes to preserve the defendant's property 'the contingency of serious consequences should be *probable*

where the plaintiff is in a permanent or semi-permanent condition whereby he or she is unable to consent to necessary, but not urgent, medical treatment.[23] It is for this reason that the underlying principle for the purposes of restitution is necessity rather than emergency. As Lord Goff has said:

> the relevance of an emergency is that it may give rise to a necessity to act in the interests of the assisted person without first obtaining his consent. Emergency is, however, not the criterion or even a prerequisite; it is simply a frequent origin of the necessity which impels intervention.[24]

(2) A key factor in the identification of circumstances of necessity is that it was impractical, but not necessarily impossible, for the plaintiff to communicate with the defendant and obtain his or her consent or instructions before intervening.[25] Where it is possible for the plaintiff to communicate with the defendant, the plaintiff can still be considered to have acted in circumstances of necessity if he or she asked the defendant for instructions and none were forthcoming.[26] If the plaintiff could have communicated with the defendant before intervening but failed to do so, then he or she could be considered to have acted officiously.

(3) The plaintiff should have been an appropriate person to intervene, otherwise his or her action will appear to be officious.[27] Whether the plaintiff was an appropriate person to intervene will depend upon the particular facts of the case, but the plaintiff is more likely to have been such a person if there was a pre-existing relationship between the plaintiff and the defendant, such as where the plaintiff was a friend or relative of the defendant, or the plaintiff possessed particular skills which were relevant. If the plaintiff was aware that there was a more appropriate person who was ready and willing to intervene then this strongly suggests that the plaintiff's restitutionary claim should fail.[28]

(4) Even though it was reasonable for the plaintiff to have intervened, it should also be shown that the plaintiff's actions were reasonable since they were in the defendant's best interests.[29] Relevant factors which should be considered when determining whether the plaintiff's conduct was reasonable include the potential consequences if the plaintiff had

---

rather than *possible*', whereas if the plaintiff intervenes to preserve life or health, it should be sufficient that there was a possible risk of serious consequences: *ibid* at p. 159. Jones justifies this distinction on the ground that life is more precious than property.

[23] See *Re F (Mental Patient: Sterilisation)* [1990] 2 AC 1 where the court allowed a sexually active mental patient to be sterilised on the ground that this was necessary for her own well-being.

[24] *Ibid*, p. 75.   [25] *Ibid*.   [26] *The Winson* [1982] AC 939, 961 (Lord Diplock).

[27] *Re F (Mental Patient: Sterilisation)* [1990] 2 AC 1, 76 (Lord Goff).

[28] Goff and Jones, *The Law of Restitution*, p. 472.

[29] *Re F (Mental Patient: Sterilisation)* [1990] 2 AC 1, 75 (Lord Goff).

not intervened and the relative cost of the intervention relative to the benefit to the defendant.

(5) Restitution for reasons of necessity should be denied in all cases in which the plaintiff was aware that the defendant did not wish him or her to intervene.[30] In particular, where the defendant has asked the plaintiff not to provide the benefit then restitution should be denied, since this suggests that the plaintiff was acting officiously.[31]

(6) Restitution should be denied where the plaintiff intended to act gratuitously, because if the plaintiff never expected to be remunerated for the benefit which he or she provided he or she is considered to have acted as a volunteer. Consequently it should be highly relevant to the determination of whether a restitutionary remedy should be awarded that the plaintiff always intended to charge the defendant for the benefit which he or she had received.[32] Where the plaintiff has provided services in a professional capacity the intention to charge the defendant for the services should be presumed.

(7) Restitution should be denied if the predominant reason for the plaintiff's intervention is to protect his or her own personal interests, for this means that the plaintiff was an officious volunteer.[33] Similarly, restitution should be denied where the plaintiff's misconduct contributed to the emergency arising in the first place. So, for example, if the plaintiff intentionally created the risk of harm so that he or she could intervene and then claim remuneration from the defendant, the claim should fail on the ground that the plaintiff had been acting officiously.

(e) The defendant must have been enriched at the plaintiff's expense

(i) Identifying the enrichment

Restitution should be awarded by virtue of necessity regardless of the type of enrichment which has been received by the defendant. Even where the alleged enrichment takes the form of goods or services it will be relatively easy to establish that the defendant has been enriched because necessity will be established only where a reasonable person would have intervened, so it will usually be the case that the defendant will have been incontrovertibly benefited by the intervention since the defendant will have been saved an inevitable expense.[34]

---

[30] Goff and Jones, *The Law of Restitution*, p. 472.
[31] *Re F (Mental Patient: Sterilisation)* [1990] 2 AC 1, 76 (Lord Goff).
[32] See *Re Rhodes* (1890) 44 Ch.D 94.
[33] *Falcke* v. *Scottish Imperial Insurance Co.* (1886) 34 Ch.D 234.
[34] See pp. 74–5.

(ii) Valuing the enrichment[35]

When assessing what the extent of the defendant's enrichment actually is a distinction needs to be drawn between three different measures, namely reward, reimbursement and remuneration. Where the plaintiff has acted in circumstances of necessity it is not appropriate to reward the plaintiff for doing so within the law of restitution, simply because a reward does not assist in the reversal of an unjust enrichment.[36] But it will be appropriate to reimburse the plaintiff his or her expenditure incurred in intervening, and it may be appropriate to remunerate the plaintiff for the provision of his or her services, at least where the plaintiff is a professional, because these sums will reflect the extent of the defendant's enrichment.[37] So, for example, if the plaintiff is a vet who saves the life of the defendant's valuable racehorse in circumstances of necessity after the horse has been injured in an accident, the defendant's enrichment can legitimately be regarded as being the value of any drugs or materials used by the vet as well as the reasonable value of his or her services, since the defendant would have had to pay these sums if the plaintiff had not intervened. It would not be appropriate, however, to award an additional sum to reward the vet for his or her intervention, since such a sum will not reverse the defendant's enrichment.

(iii) Determining whether the enrichment was received at the expense of the plaintiff

Although it will often be easy to establish that the defendant was enriched by the plaintiff's intervention, it may be more difficult to establish that this enrichment was received at the expense of the plaintiff. This can be illustrated by reference to the example of the plaintiff who intervenes to save the life of the defendant's racehorse. Can the defendant be considered to be enriched at the plaintiff's expense if the plaintiff was not a professional vet? Clearly such a plaintiff should be entitled to recover the expenditure which he or she has reasonably incurred, since this is expenditure which the defendant has saved and this benefit was received at the plaintiff's expense, since the plaintiff suffered a loss in providing the benefit. But should such a plaintiff be entitled to receive any remuneration for his or her services? In principle, the answer should be 'yes' since the defendant will have been saved this amount by not needing to employ a professional vet. It follows that the defendant can be considered to have been enriched by the amount he or she has saved, but it does not follow that the plaintiff will necessarily be able to recover the

---

[35] See generally pp. 95–104 above.
[36] See the discussion of maritime salvage at p. 321 below.
[37] This was recognised by Ralph Gibson LJ in *The Goring* [1987] QB 687, 708.

value of this benefit from the defendant. This is because, where the plaintiff was not a professional vet, it may not be possible to establish that this enrichment had actually been obtained at the plaintiff's expense. To establish this, the plaintiff must show that the defendant's benefit is mirrored by some loss which had been suffered by the plaintiff.[38] Where the plaintiff is a professional vet it should be possible to establish that the benefit of the plaintiff's services reflected an identifiable loss to the plaintiff, simply because he or she would have wished to enter into a contract with the defendant to provide the service had the circumstances of necessity not existed. The failure of the plaintiff to enter into a contract for the provision of the service can be considered to be a financial loss which he or she has suffered. Where, however, the plaintiff was not a professional vet he or she would presumably not have entered into a contract to provide the service and so it will not be possible to conclude that he or she has suffered any financial loss in providing the service to the defendant.

(iv) Limiting the extent of the restitutionary remedy

Where the plaintiff has intervened to preserve the defendant's property, it would be unacceptable if the restitutionary award exceeded the value of the property, simply because the effect would be to cause the defendant to suffer a loss rather than simply to reverse the defendant's enrichment. Consequently, the 'value of the property preserved should be the ceiling of any restitutionary award'.[39]

2. NECESSITOUS INTERVENTION BY A STRANGER

There are two main grounds of restitution which can be considered to be founded on the principle of necessity, namely where there is a pre-existing legal relationship between the plaintiff and the defendant and where there is no such pre-existing relationship. This latter ground of restitution will be considered first. In certain established categories the plaintiff will be able to obtain restitution from the defendant by virtue of necessitous intervention, even though there is no pre-existing legal relationship between the parties. The plaintiff in these circumstances is conveniently characterised as a 'stranger' even though he or she may have been known to the defendant, simply because there is no legal relationship between the parties.

---

[38] See p. 105 above. [39] Jones, *Restitution in Public and Private Law*, p. 154.

(a) Discharge of the defendant's legal liability

Restitution has been awarded in a number of cases where the consequence of the plaintiff's necessitous intervention is the discharge of a legal liability which was owed by the defendant.

(i) Burial

If the person who is ultimately responsible for arranging the burial of the deceased[40] is not able to do so then it is necessary for somebody to intervene and make the arrangements. The reason the necessity principle applies in such circumstances was identified in *Rogers* v. *Price*[41] as arising from '[the] common principles of decency and humanity, the common impulses of our nature . . . and to do that which is immediately necessary upon the subject in order to avoid what, if not provided against, may become an inconvenience to the public'. In such circumstances the person who incurred expenditure or provided professional services is entitled to be reimbursed or remunerated by the defendant who was under a duty to arrange the burial. This is illustrated by *Jenkins* v. *Tucker*[42] where the deceased had died whilst her husband was in Jamaica. The deceased's father arranged for his daughter's funeral and was able to recover the expenditure incurred because he had 'acted in discharge of a duty which the defendant was under a strict legal necessity of himself performing, and which common decency required at his hands . . . '.[43] Although today there is a statutory right of restitution which is applicable where a local authority is obliged to bury or cremate a person, whereby the authority can recover the expenditure incurred from the deceased person's estate,[44] the old cases at common law continue to be a very good illustration of the recognition and application of the doctrine of necessity in a restitutionary context.

Where the plaintiff has arranged for the burial of the deceased restitution of expenditure will only be allowed if two conditions are satisfied.

(1) The plaintiff who made the arrangements for the burial must have been a proper person to respond to the necessity. This may be a parent,[45] a sibling[46] or even a professional undertaker, so long as he or she was engaged by an appropriate person.[47]

---

[40] Today this is the personal representative of the deceased, but the husband used to be responsible for the burial of his wife (*Jenkins* v. *Tucker* (1788) 1 H Bl. 91; 126 ER 55). Where a child dies a parent is probably responsible for arranging his or her burial.

[41] (1829) 3 Y and J 28, 34; 148 ER 1080, 1082 (Garrow B).

[42] (1788) 1 H Bl. 91; 126 ER 55.   [43] *Ibid*, p. 93; 57 (Lord Loughborough).

[44] Public Health (Control of Disease) Act 1984, ss. 46–48.

[45] *Jenkins* v. *Tucker* (1788) 1 H Bl. 91; 126 ER 55.

[46] *Bradshaw* v. *Beard* (1862) 12 CB (NS) 344; 142 ER 1175.

[47] *Rogers* v. *Price* (1829) 3 Y and J 28; 148 ER 1080 where the undertaker was engaged by the defendant's brother.

(2) The benefit which the plaintiff provided must have been reasonable. So, for example, the plaintiff would only be able to recover expenditure which he or she had incurred in arranging for the funeral if it was reasonably incurred. An important factor which indicates what may be reasonable expenditure is to consider what the defendant would have paid for the funeral, considering his or her rank and fortune.[48]

(ii) Provision of medical treatment

In the same way that the burial cases recognise that the plaintiff may be able to obtain restitutionary relief based on the fact that it was necessary to arrange for the funeral, there is another group of cases which recognise that if the plaintiff provides medical treatment to the victim of an accident who is in immediate need of such treatment, the plaintiff may obtain restitution from the defendant who was liable to arrange for the services to be provided. This group of cases concerned the provision of urgent medical treatment to paupers where the parish officer of the parish where the pauper was at the time of the illness or injury was under a legal obligation to care for the pauper. In these cases the plaintiff, in providing necessary medical treatment for the pauper, was discharging the parish officer's legal duty and this was regarded as a sufficient basis to enable the plaintiff to be reimbursed for the expenses incurred.[49] The fact that the plaintiff had discharged the defendant's legal liability meant that the defendant had been benefited by the plaintiff's intervention. The ground of restitution in these cases was clearly founded on necessity, because the paupers were in urgent need of medical attention.

(iii) Discharge of a debt

Where the plaintiff discharges the defendant's debt in circumstances of necessity the plaintiff can obtain restitution from the defendant, with the ground of restitution being founded on the principle of necessity. This was recognised in *Owen* v. *Tate*[50] in which Scarman LJ suggested that, where there was some necessity for the plaintiff to assume an obligation, such as a guarantee of the defendant's liability, and the plaintiff was required to pay money under the guarantee to discharge the defendant's liability, then the defendant would be required to make restitution to the plaintiff 'if it is just and reasonable to do so'.[51] This dictum was applied

[48] *Jenkins* v. *Tucker* (1788) 1 H Bl. 91; 126 ER 55.

[49] *Lamb* v. *Bunce* (1815) 4 M and S 273; 105 ER 836. See also *Simmons* v. *Wilmot* (1800) 3 Esp. 91; 170 ER 549 and *Tomlinson* v. *Bentall* (1826) 5 B and C 737; 108 ER 738.

[50] [1976] QB 402, 409.

[51] There is no reason why the court should have a discretion to award restitutionary relief where it is considered to be just and reasonable to do so. Such a discretion is not recognised in respect of any other claims founded on the reversal of the defendant's unjust enrichment.

in *The Zuhal K and Selin*[52] where the plaintiff had entered into a guarantee with a third party since this was the only practical way that it could secure the release of the defendant's ship which had been arrested by the owners of cargo. If the ship had not been released the consequent delay would have been very costly for the plaintiff. When the plaintiff was compelled to pay on the guarantee it was able to recover the amount paid from the defendant. Even though the restitutionary claim succeeded, no ground of restitution was identified. Although it could have been concluded that the ground of restitution was founded on necessity, the case is better analysed as an example of legal compulsion, since the plaintiff had been compelled to pay money to the defendant's creditor by virtue of the guarantee.[53] Even if legal compulsion had been relied on to secure restitution, there would still have been a role for the necessity principle in that the need for the plaintiff to release the ship would have defeated any argument that the plaintiff had entered into the guarantee officiously.

There are other cases in which the plaintiff's conduct in discharging the defendant's liability can be regarded as arising in circumstances of necessity, so that this could constitute a ground of restitution. For example, in *Gebhardt* v. *Saunders*[54] where the plaintiff had repaired a sewer even though the obligation to repair it was placed on the defendant, the plaintiff's restitutionary claim succeeded. Again the ground of restitution was not identified but the result is clearly consistent with the application of the principle of necessity.

(b) Preservation of life, health and property

There are a number of cases in which restitutionary relief has been awarded by reason of necessity where the effect of the plaintiff's intervention is to preserve the defendant's life, health or property, even though the plaintiff has not discharged any liability of the defendant.

(i) Preservation of life or health

Although there is little authority on the point, in principle a plaintiff who has intervened to save the defendant's life or the life of somebody for whom the defendant is legally responsible, such as the defendant's child, or to preserve the health of such a person, should be entitled to restitution. But restitution will only be awarded in such circumstances if the plaintiff has intervened in circumstances of necessity[55] and to the extent that the defendant has been enriched at the expense of the plaintiff. This will depend on whether the plaintiff has incurred reasonable expendi-

---

[52] [1987] 1 Lloyd's Rep. 151.   [53] See pp. 223–46 below   [54] [1892] 2 QB 452.
[55] *Shallcross* v. *Wright* (1850) 12 Beav. 558; 50 ER 1174.

ture or has rendered professional services for which he or she is entitled to reasonable remuneration.

(ii) Supply of necessaries

Where the plaintiff has supplied necessaries to somebody affected by some form of incapacity, such as mental disorder or infancy, then the supplier will be able to recover the value of the necessaries from the person who was incapacitated by means of a restitutionary action,[56] at least where he or she intended to charge for the necessaries.[57] What constitutes necessaries is a question of fact, with relevant considerations being the reasonable requirements of the incapacitated person, his or her station in life and his or her means.[58] The definition of necessaries is not confined to those which the defendant requires to keep alive. Necessaries include the provision of both goods and beneficial services. Today, where the necessaries take the form of goods, there is a statutory right for the supplier to recover the reasonable value of them.[59] In *Re Rhodes*[60] it was accepted that the provision of a room in a private lunatic asylum for a woman of unsound mind did constitute the provision of necessaries, whereas in *Nash* v. *Inman*[61] the supply of a large number of waistcoats of 'extravagant and ridiculous style' to an undergraduate were not necessaries.[62]

The difficulty with this ground of restitution relates to why there is a requirement that the plaintiff must have intended to charge for the supply of the necessaries, when the fact that the plaintiff did not intend to charge the defendant for the benefit is not relevant in other contexts, such as where the plaintiff arranges for the burial of the deceased. Perhaps the reason is simply that, in the context of the burial cases, there is less scope for officious intervention and taking advantage of the defendant,[63] whereas there is much more scope for this in respect of the provision of necessaries for those who are incapacitated. Consequently, to dispel any notion that the plaintiff was an officious volunteer it must be shown that the plaintiff intended to charge for the benefit provided. This will usually be the case where the plaintiff is a professional who is supplying the necessaries in the course of his or her profession. Such a person is less likely to be an officious volunteer than is a relative who is presumed, as was the case in *Re Rhodes*, to have supplied the benefit gratuitously. This presumption was particularly appropriate in that case simply because the annual cost of keeping the woman in the asylum was

---

[56] *Nash* v. *Inman* [1908] 2 KB 1.   [57] *Re Rhodes* (1890) 44 Ch.D 94.
[58] *Ibid*, p. 107 (Lopes LJ).   [59] Sales of Goods Act 1979, s. 3(2).
[60] (1890) 44 Ch.D 94.   [61] [1908] 2 KB 1.
[62] Even though the student was studying at Trinity College, Cambridge.
[63] See Stoljar, *The Law of Quasi-Contract*, p. 202.

£140, whereas her annual income was only £96. Since the benefit which was provided was beyond the woman's means it was assumed that it was provided gratuitously by her relatives and so the restitutionary claim failed.

(iii) Preservation of property

Even though restitution was denied in *Falcke* v. *Scottish Imperial Insurance Co.*,[64] where the plaintiff had paid premiums to preserve an insurance policy which would otherwise have lapsed, this was only because the plaintiff was acting to protect his own interest in the property rather than that of the defendant.[65] It could therefore be concluded that the plaintiff had been acting officiously. It does not follow that restitution will automatically be denied where the plaintiff has intervened to protect the defendant's property, so long as the plaintiff was not acting officiously, even though some cases assume that there is a blanket rule denying restitution in such circumstances. An example of a case in which restitution was denied is *Binstead* v. *Buck*[66] where the plaintiff looked after the defendant's stray dog for 20 weeks but was unable to recover any expenditure incurred in so doing.

There are, however, a number of other cases in which it was recognised that restitution should be, or could have been, awarded where the plaintiff has intervened in circumstances of necessity to protect the defendant's property. For example, in *Nicholson* v. *Chapman*[67] timber which had been left on the bank of the River Thames was carried away by the tide and was left on a towing path where it was found by the defendant, who carried it away to safety beyond the reach of the tide. The defendant's claim that he had a lien over the timber as security for the expenditure incurred in rescuing it was rejected. But Eyre CJ did suggest that the defendant should be entitled to recover his reasonable expenditure in rescuing the timber from the owner and that a court would 'go as far as it could go towards enforcing' such payment.[68] In *Jenkins* v. *Tucker*[69] Lord Loughborough suggested that where the defendant's goods had been seized for payment of tax and the plaintiff had redeemed the goods by paying the tax for the defendant then the plaintiff could recover the money paid from the owner. This action nicely mirrors an equivalent restitutionary action where the *plaintiff's* goods have been seized by a third party in respect of a liability owed by the defendant and the plaintiff discharged the defendant's debt to recover the goods. Here the

---

[64] (1886) 34 Ch.D 234. [65] *Ibid*, p. 251 (Bowen LJ). See p. 300 above.
[66] (1777) 2 Black. W 1117; 96 ER 660. See also *Sorrell* v. *Paget* [1950] 1 KB 252.
[67] (1793) 2 H. Bl. 254; 126 ER 536. [68] *Ibid*, p. 257; 538.
[69] (1788) 1 H Bl. 91; 126 ER 55.

ground of restitution would be legal compulsion.[70] Where the *defendant's* goods have been seized and the plaintiff intervenes to discharge the liability the ground of restitution would presumably be characterised as founded on the necessity principle.

These cases therefore suggest that, where the plaintiff intervenes to protect the defendant's property in circumstances of necessity, it may be possible to establish a restitutionary claim. It must follow that this claim will be a personal one and the plaintiff will not be awarded a proprietary remedy such as a lien over the property which has been protected,[71] since there is no reason why the plaintiff should be given priority over the defendant's other creditors. The personal remedy will lie only to the extent that the plaintiff has intervened to protect and preserve property and will not lie to the extent that the plaintiff has improved the property, because the improvement cannot be justified by the need to act urgently. As Stoljar has said, '[m]any, probably most, common law instances of officious conduct are in fact those of a volunteer merely improving property, his acts going well beyond what urgent preservation would demand'.[72] It is for this reason that restitution was denied in such cases as *Taylor* v. *Laird*,[73] where the plaintiff had improved property in which the defendant had an interest as a tenant in common and the plaintiff then sought restitution from the defendant.

(c) A general principle of necessitous intervention

There is no reason why restitutionary claims founded on the circumstances of necessity should be confined to these established categories. Whilst the facts of a number of these cases will not occur again, particularly with the introduction of the welfare state and a national health service, the principles which are embodied in them will continue to be of general relevance. So long as the plaintiff's conduct in assisting the defendant can be regarded as reasonable, as assessed by reference to the established principles, then restitution should lie even though the facts do not fall within one of the established categories of necessity.

3. AGENCY AND OTHER PRE-EXISTING LEGAL RELATIONSHIPS

The only difference between this ground of restitution and that of necessitous intervention by a stranger is that this ground depends on there

---

[70] *Exall* v. *Partridge* (1799) 8 Term Rep. 308; 101 ER 1405. See p. 231 above.

[71] *Nicholson* v. *Chapman* (1793) 2 H Bl. 254; 126 ER 536. See also *Falcke* v. *Scottish Imperial Insurance Co.* (1886) 34 Ch.D 234, 248 (Bowen LJ).

[72] Stoljar, *The Law of Quasi-Contract*, p. 208.   [73] (1856) 25 LJ Ex. 329.

being some form of pre-existing legal relationship between the parties.[74] The importance of this difference is simply that where there is such a pre-existing relationship then, when the plaintiff intervenes in circumstances of necessity, he or she will generally be considered to have been an appropriate person to intervene, with the effect that it will be much more difficult to characterise him or her as an officious volunteer.[75] Nevertheless, even though there is a pre-existing legal relationship between the parties, the plaintiff must show that his or her conduct was reasonable before restitution can be awarded and the general principles as to what constitutes reasonable conduct are relevant here as in the case where a stranger has intervened.[76]

The origins of the doctrine of necessitous intervention by someone who is in a legal relationship with the defendant lie in the principle of agency of necessity, where an agent went beyond his or her authority by intervening on behalf of the principal in an emergency. Because of the circumstances of necessity, particularly the impracticability of the agent communicating with the principal, the courts were prepared to treat the agent as though he or she had the necessary authority to do what was reasonably necessary to save the principal's property. If an agency of necessity was established, the agent would be reimbursed for the expense incurred in rescuing the principal's property.

The doctrine of agency of necessity was initially relevant only in respect of the carriage of goods by sea, where the master took action to save the ship or cargo in an emergency. It was then extended to those cases which concerned the carriage of goods by land. This is illustrated by *The Great Northern Railway Co.* v. *Swaffield*[77] where the plaintiff railway company had transported a horse to a station on behalf of the defendant. When the horse arrived there was nobody to collect it, so the plaintiff sent it to a stable. A number of months later the plaintiff paid the stabling charges and then sought to recover what it had paid from the defendant. The plaintiff's restitutionary claim succeeded even though this involved the extension of the doctrine of agency of necessity to include carriers of goods by land. There was an agency of necessity because the plaintiff was found to have had no choice but to arrange for the proper care of the horse.

The doctrine of agency of necessity was then extended beyond cases involving carriage of goods to other cases in which the plaintiff had been forced by an emergency to act beyond his or her existing authority. This extension of the principle was recognised in *Prager* v. *Blatspiel, Stamp*

---

[74] *Jebara* v. *Ottoman Bank* [1927] 2 KB 254, 271 (Scrutton LJ).
[75] *The Winson* [1982] AC 939, 961 (Lord Diplock).   [76] See pp. 305–7 above.
[77] (1874) LR 9 Ex. 132. See also *Sims and Co.* v. *Midland Railway Co.* [1913] 1 KB 103, 112 (Scrutton LJ).

and Heacock Ltd.,[78] although the element of emergency was not established on the facts. In *Prager* the defendant, who was a fur merchant, bought and dressed skins on behalf of the plaintiff to be delivered to Romania. The outbreak of the First World War made it impossible for the defendant either to send the skins to Romania or to communicate with the plaintiff. The defendant then sold the skins. When the plaintiff eventually asked the defendant to transport the skins to him, the defendant argued that it had been forced to sell the skins because they were deteriorating, making it necessary that the skins were sold forthwith. On the facts of the case it was held that the defendant was not an agent of necessity, simply because, since the skins were dressed, they were in no danger of deteriorating. But it was accepted that if the skins had been deteriorating rapidly the defendant would have been authorised to sell them by virtue of an agency of necessity.

The principle underlying the doctrine of agency of necessity has now been extended beyond those cases where there was a pre-existing relationship of principal and agent to where there was any form of pre-existing legal relationship, such as the relationship of bailor and bailee. This was recognised in *The Winson*,[79] where the plaintiff, who was a professional salvor, had entered into an agreement to salvage the defendant's cargo of wheat after its ship had been stranded on a reef. The cargo was salvaged and taken to Manila where it was stored under cover to ensure that it did not deteriorate. The plaintiff informed the defendant that it was going to put the wheat into storage and the defendant did not object. The plaintiff then sought to recover the storage expenses from the defendant. Since the storage was not covered by the salvage agreement, the plaintiff could not sue under the contract. However, once the wheat had arrived in the Philippines the relationship between the parties was one which was founded on a gratuitous bailment. Consequently, the plaintiff argued that, in storing the wheat, it was acting as an agent of necessity. The plaintiff's claim for restitution of the storage expenses which had been incurred succeeded before the House of Lords, because the plaintiff's conduct was considered to have been reasonable. But Lord Diplock, who gave the leading judgment, stressed that the plaintiff should not be characterised as an agent of necessity, since he considered that the notion of agency should be confined to where the agent was deemed to have authority to create contractual rights and obligations between the principal and a third party. He did not regard the term as being appropriate where the plaintiff's claim was for reimbursement, as it was here. Despite this change in terminology, it is still important to draw a distinction between those cases in which a stranger has intervened in

[78] [1924] 1 KB 566.
[79] *China Pacific SA* v. *Food Corporation of India (The Winson)* [1982] AC 939.

circumstances of necessity and those in which the plaintiff who intervened has a pre-existing relationship with the defendant. The change in
terminology in respect of the latter doctrine emphasises that the pre-
existing relationship between the parties need not have been an agency
relationship. Lord Diplock did suggest that the conditions which need to
be satisfied before an agency of necessity is established will not necessarily have to be satisfied before the plaintiff obtains reimbursement
from the defendant. Consequently, for example, restitution will not be
denied simply because the plaintiff was in fact able to communicate with
the defendant, it being sufficient, as occurred in *The Winson* itself, that,
despite the communication with the defendant by the plaintiff, the
defendant had failed to give any instructions to the plaintiff as to what to
do with the wheat.

Where there is a pre-existing legal relationship between the parties,
restitution may be awarded by reason of necessity if certain conditions
are satisfied, as was recognised in *The Choko Star*.[80] However, as Lord
Diplock recognised in *The Winson*,[81] the key issue for the courts to determine is whether the plaintiff's conduct was reasonable, so the fact that
one of these conditions is not satisfied does not mean that the plaintiff's
conduct must automatically be considered to have been unreasonable.

(1) There must be an actual and definite commercial necessity for the
plaintiff to intervene having regard to the particular circumstances of the
case.[82] It was for this reason that an agency of necessity was not established in *Sachs* v. *Miklos*[83] where the defendant had agreed to store the
plaintiff's furniture free of charge. After a considerable time the plaintiff
had not reclaimed the furniture and, since the defendant wished to rent
out the room where it was stored, the defendant attempted to contact the
plaintiff. Despite numerous attempts to make contact, the defendant
could not find the plaintiff and so he sold the furniture. The plaintiff then
returned to claim his furniture and, when he discovered that it had been
sold, he sued the defendant in conversion. The defendant argued that he
was an agent of necessity but the Court of Appeal held that this had not
been established, simply because there was no need for the furniture to
be sold. Similarly, in *Munro* v. *Willmott*[84] the defendant sold the plaintiff's car which had been left on his premises for a number of years. Again
the defendant was not characterised as an agent of necessity because the
sale of the car was not required as a matter of real urgency but was done
simply for the defendant's convenience. It would have been different in
both cases if the plaintiff's property had been perishable, such as fruit

---

[80] [1990] 1 Lloyd's Rep. 516.   [81] [1982] AC 939, 961.
[82] *Prager* v. *Blatspeil, Stamp and Heacock Ltd.* [1924] 1 KB 566, 572 (McCardie J).
[83] [1948] 2 KB 23.   [84] [1949] 1 KB 295.

and vegetables,[85] so that there was a commercial necessity for the property to be disposed of, otherwise it would have perished.

(2) It must have been practically impossible to obtain the defendant's instructions about what should be done in time.[86] Restitutionary relief may, however, still be awarded where the plaintiff asks the defendant for instructions and the defendant fails to respond.[87]

(3) The burden is on the plaintiff to show that he or she was acting in good faith in the best interests of the defendant.[88] It follows that the plaintiff's action must have been reasonable and prudent in the particular circumstances of the case and must have been taken to protect the interests of the defendant, otherwise it will smack of officiousness.[89]

The problem with the action for reimbursement in circumstances of necessity where there is a pre-existing legal relationship between the parties is whether it really forms part of the law of restitution. The difficulty arises from the requirement that there must be a pre-existing relationship, whether it be agency or bailment or whatever. The effect of the doctrine is that the plaintiff's authority under this relationship is extended to include the reaction to the emergency.[90] This suggests that the doctrine is part of the law governing the pre-existing relationship, such as contract, rather than the law of restitution, with the consequence that, if the plaintiff has a remedy, it will be contractual rather than restitutionary. Whilst this may be true in most cases, there is still a role for the doctrine to apply within the law of restitution. This will particularly be the case where, as in *The Winson*, the pre-existing relationship between the parties is not contractual but arises, for example, from a gratuitous bailment or where the previous contractual relationship may have ended. In these circumstances the law of restitution intervenes to impose an obligation on the defendant by operation of law to ensure that the defendant does not receive an enrichment without reimbursing or remunerating the plaintiff.

---

[85] Now see the Torts (Interference with Goods) Act 1977, ss. 12, 13 and Sched. 1 which enables a bailee to sell uncollected goods provided the bailor has been notified or the bailee has been unable to trace the bailor.

[86] *Sims and Co.* v. *Midland Railway Co.* [1913] 1 KB 103, 112 (Scrutton LJ). See *Springer* v. *Great Western Railway Company* [1921] 1 KB 257.

[87] *The Winson* [1982] AC 939, 961 (Lord Diplock).

[88] *Prager* v. *Blatspeil, Stamp and Heacock Ltd.* [1924] 1 KB 566, 572 (McCardie J).

[89] See *Springer* v. *Great Western Railway Company* [1921] 1 KB 257.

[90] *De Bussche* v. *Alt* (1878) 8 Ch.D 286, 310.

4. NECESSITY IN THE CONTEXT OF MARITIME ADVENTURES

(a) Salvage[91]

The law on salvage is highly complex but, to the extent that it involves restitution, it can be considered to be founded on the principle of necessity. Although the doctrine of maritime salvage can be analysed, at least to some extent, by reference to the unjust enrichment principle, it is not possible to justify the award of restitutionary remedies in terms of an absence of a freely exercised choice to intervene on the part of the salvors, unlike the other grounds of restitution which are founded on the principle of necessity. This is particularly because most salvors today are professionals who do not find themselves in circumstances of necessity but actually seek out such emergencies. Indeed, in *Falcke* v. *Scottish Imperial Insurance Co.*[92] Bowen LJ specifically excluded maritime salvage from the principle that liabilities are not to be forced upon people behind their backs. The salvage award which such salvors receive is primarily justified by public policy[93] to encourage salvage services to be provided.

(i) Establishing maritime salvage

The essential features of maritime salvage are that when a ship or cargo is in danger those people who reasonably incur expenditure in successfully rescuing it are entitled to remuneration from the owners.[94] It is crucial that the salvage is successful; there is no reward for failure.[95] So a salvage award will only be made if and to the extent that property has been saved by the salvor. The salvor must be acting voluntarily, which means that he or she must not be under a pre-existing duty to carry out the salvage. So, for example, the crew of a ship will generally not be able to claim salvage from its owners since their terms of employment will require them to salvage the vessel or its cargo.

(ii) Characterising the salvage award

Whilst maritime salvage is often dependent on contract,[96] this is not essential, and to the extent that salvage work is effected outside contract

---

[91] For detailed examination of salvage see Goff and Jones, *The Law of Restitution*, chapter 18.

[92] (1886) 34 Ch.D 234, 249.

[93] *Nicholson* v. *Chapman* (1793) 2 H Bl. 254; 126 ER 536.

[94] The doctrine of maritime salvage does not extend to non-tidal waters (*The Goring* [1988] AC 831) nor to the rescue of property on land: (*Sorrell* v. *Paget* [1950] 1 KB 252, 260 (Bucknill LJ)). Salvage has been extended to include the salvage of lives and aircraft.

[95] *Semco Salvage and Marine Pte. Ltd.* v. *Lancer Navigation Co. Ltd.* [1997] AC455, 459 (Lord Mustill).

[96] For an example see *ibid.*

aspects of the salvage award may be considered to be restitutionary to reverse the defendant's unjust enrichment. This is supported by the fact that the owner of cargo or a ship will only be liable to pay for salvage if he or she has actually received a benefit. Crucially, however, the remedy which the salvor is awarded is not necessarily restitutionary, since it can also include an element of reward. The rationale behind the salvage award is to compensate the salvor for the services provided but also 'in the interests of public policy, encourage other mariners in like circumstances to perform like services'.[97] It is because of the element of reward which is included in the salvage award that maritime salvage cannot be regarded as falling four square within the law of restitution, simply because the remedy which is awarded does not seek only to reverse the defendant's unjust enrichment. That the salvage award is not completely restitutionary is illustrated by the types of factors which the courts take into account when fixing it.[98] For example, the court is to consider such matters as the value of the property saved, the degree of danger involved and the particular skill of the salvor. In fact, professional salvors are entitled to a more generous award than those salvors who act on the spur of the moment, because the law seeks to encourage professional salvors as a matter of public policy. Similarly, the salvage award may include an additional sum for saving life. Even though the salvage award may be made up in part of a restitutionary remedy to enable the salvor to recover the reasonable value of the services provided, even this amount lies in the discretion of the court.

Maritime salvage is better treated as being *sui generis*. Whilst it involves elements which are clearly restitutionary, particularly because the doctrine will only be triggered where the defendant has received a benefit, it must not be artificially squeezed into the law of restitution. There are different considerations of policy at play in respect of salvage, which do not apply in other cases of necessitous intervention.

(b) General average[99]

The doctrine of general average also arises in the context of maritime emergencies. An act of general average is committed where an extraordinary sacrifice or expenditure is incurred in the course of a maritime adventure for the benefit of the adventure. The doctrine of general average can be analysed in restitutionary terms since it can be considered to be founded on the reversal of unjust enrichment. This is because

[97] *The Telemachus* [1957] P 47, 49 (Willmer J).
[98] See Steel and Rose, *Kennedy's Law of Salvage* (5th edn., London: Stevens, 1985) pp. 458–9.
[99] See Rose, 'General Average as Restitution' (1997) 113 *LQR* 569.

a defendant will be liable to those plaintiffs who suffered loss or incurred expenditure in the course of the maritime adventure, but only if the defendant was a party to the maritime adventure and benefited from the plaintiff's acts.[100] Crucially, the defendant is only liable if the consequence of the plaintiff's intervention is that the defendant's property has been preserved.[101] It follows that the ground of restitution will be founded on the principle of necessity. Consequently, the doctrine of general average can be considered to fall within the law of restitution, although in practice provision is typically made for it by contract.

[100] See *Birkley* v. *Presgrave* (1801) 1 East 220, 228; 102 ER 86, 89 (Lawrence J) and the Marine Insurance Act 1906, s. 66(1), (2).
[101] See *Chellew* v. *Royal Commission on the Sugar Supply* [1921] 2 KB 627.

12

Failure of Consideration

1. GENERAL PRINCIPLES

(a) The principle of failure of consideration

The essence of failure of consideration is that, where the plaintiff transfers a benefit to the defendant pursuant to a transaction which is subject to a condition, this condition has not been wholly or partly satisfied. This failure of condition may occur for a number of different reasons, including that the defendant fails to do what he or she had promised to do or is prevented by a change of circumstances from satisfying the condition. Failure of consideration is not a ground of restitution in its own right but is rather a general principle which underlies the existence of a number of particular grounds of restitution. These grounds of restitution are especially important in the modern law of restitution.

The particular grounds of restitution which are founded on the principle of failure of consideration operate in broadly the same way as the other recognised grounds of restitution, namely that restitution is awarded because the plaintiff's intention that the defendant should receive the benefit has been vitiated. This was recognised by Lord Wright in *Fibrosa Spolka Akcyjna* v. *Fairbairn Lawson Combe Barbour Ltd.*:[1]

There was no intent to enrich [the defendant] in the events which happened . . . The payment was originally conditional. The condition of retaining it is eventual performance. Accordingly, when that condition fails, the right to retain the money must simultaneously fail.

But, whereas for grounds of restitution such as mistake and duress the plaintiff's intention is vitiated when the defendant receives the benefit, this is not generally the case where the plaintiff relies on grounds of restitution which are founded on the principle of failure of consideration. This is because in such cases the plaintiff does intend the defendant to receive the benefit at the time of the transfer. The plaintiff's intention is vitiated only because of subsequent events. Consequently, the effect of the consideration failing is retrospectively to vitiate the plaintiff's intention that the defendant should receive the benefit.[2]

[1] [1943] AC 32, 64–5.
[2] The only exception to this analysis of failure of consideration is where there never was any possibility of the condition for the transfer of the benefit being satisfied.

The grounds of restitution which are founded on failure of consideration are most likely to operate in a contractual context, where the usual
basis for the transfer of a benefit to the defendant is that he or she
promises to do something in return, such as to pay for the benefit. As a
result, it is vitally important to ensure that the law of restitution is not
used to subvert the law of contract. In this area of the law of restitution
more than any other the fundamental principle that the law of contract
prevails must be respected.[3] It is for this reason that the question of the
award of restitutionary remedies will arise only once the contract has
been set aside. However, even though the contract itself may have been
set aside, its terms may still be considered to be relevant in assessing the
remedy which is appropriate. For example, when valuing the enrichment
which has been received by the defendant the terms of the contract
under which the benefit was transferred may have a useful role to play.[4]
The terms of the contract may also exclude or modify the plaintiff's right
to obtain restitution.[5]

(b) The grounds of restitution which are founded on the principle of failure of consideration

There are essentially three grounds of restitution which are founded on
the principle of failure of consideration, namely where the consideration
has totally failed, where the consideration has partially failed and where
the consideration failed as a matter of law, typically known as absence of
consideration. Whilst the ground of total failure of consideration has
long been recognised,[6] the role of partial failure of consideration as a
ground of restitution is much less certain. Although it is clear that partial
failure of consideration is the recognised ground of restitution where a
contract has been discharged by frustration,[7] there is increasing evidence that the ground of total failure of consideration is itself being
watered down, through a growing manipulation of the notion of when
consideration can be considered to have failed totally, with the consequence that we are moving ever closer to the recognition of partial failure of consideration as a general ground of restitution in its own right.
The existence of a third ground of restitution which arises where there is
an absence of consideration is highly controversial, although this ground
has received some judicial recognition.[8]

---

[3] See pp. 40–2 above.   [4] See pp. 100–4 above.
[5] *Pan Ocean Shipping Co. Ltd.* v. *Creditcorp Ltd. (The Trident Beauty)* [1994] 1 WLR 161.
[6] See *Moses* v. *Macferlan* (1760) 2 Burrows 1005, 1012; 97 ER 676, 681.
[7] See p. 373 below.   [8] See pp. 394–403 below.

(c) The definition of consideration

It is most unfortunate that this principle has been called failure of consideration, since the contractual connotations of the expression are misleading. When we talk about consideration failing we are not using 'consideration' as it is used in the law of contract to mean the *quid pro quo* for there to be a binding contract.[9] Rather, consideration for the purposes of the law of restitution refers to the condition which formed the basis for the plaintiff transferring a benefit to the defendant. It is when this condition fails that it is possible to conclude that the consideration has failed. It is not sufficient, however, that the plaintiff imposed the condition for the transfer of a benefit to the defendant without, at the very least, communicating this condition to the defendant.[10] So, for example, consideration will not have failed where the plaintiff cleaned the defendant's car without his or her knowledge but in the expectation that the defendant would pay for the work. The plaintiff cannot claim that the consideration has failed if the defendant refused to pay, since there was no understanding between the parties that it was a condition of the plaintiff doing the work that the defendant would pay. Denial of restitution in such circumstances is consistent with the general principle that no plaintiff can obtain restitution where he or she is a volunteer who has taken the risk of not being paid for doing the work.[11]

Whenever it is necessary to decide whether the consideration for the transfer of a benefit has failed, 'consideration' can be used in two different ways, depending on whether or not the condition involves performance by the defendant.

(i) Failure of the defendant to perform his or her part of the bargain

By far the most common meaning of consideration in the restitutionary context relates to where the condition on which the transfer of the benefit is contingent is performance by the defendant for which the plaintiff had bargained.[12] Usually, the defendant's promise will be contractual. So, for example, if the plaintiff and the defendant entered into a contract whereby the defendant agreed to sell a car to the plaintiff for £5,000 and the plaintiff paid the full price in advance but the defendant failed to supply the car, the consideration will have failed because the plaintiff did not receive

[9] *Rover International Ltd.* v. *Cannon Film Sales Ltd. (No. 3)* [1989] 1 WLR 912, 923 (Kerr LJ).

[10] See *Craven-Ellis* v. *Canons Ltd.* [1936] 2 KB 403, discussed at p. 393 below.

[11] See pp. 39–40 above.

[12] *Fibrosa Spolka Akcyjna* v. *Fairbairn Lawson Combe Barbour Ltd.* [1943] AC 32, 48 (Viscount Simon LC). See also Kerr LJ in *Rover International* v. *Cannon Film Sales Ltd. (No. 3)* [1989] 1 WLR 912, 923 and Lord Goff in *Stocznia Gdanska SA* v. *Latvian Shipping Co.* [1998] 1 WLR 574, 588.

from the defendant what he or she had promised to provide. In such a situation the plaintiff would usually sue for breach of contract, but a restitutionary remedy would be more attractive if the value of the car was less than £5,000, since damages for breach of contract would be assessed by reference to the value of the car which the plaintiff should have received.

The defendant's expected performance need not, however, arise in a contractual context for the plaintiff to establish that consideration has failed. So, for example, if the plaintiff provided a benefit for the defendant on the understanding that it would be paid for under a contract which the parties were negotiating, but the negotiations failed, then the plaintiff should be able to recover the value of the benefit on the ground of total failure of consideration,[13] even though the defendant was not obliged by contract to pay for the benefit.

(ii) Failure of a contingent condition

The alternative meaning of consideration relates to where the transfer of the benefit to the defendant is subject to a condition which does not involve performance by the defendant. Restitution is justified in such a case because the basis for the transfer of the benefit will have been removed if the condition is not satisfied. But it is not sufficient that the plaintiff simply imposed this condition in his or her own mind, since the condition for the transfer of the benefit must have been communicated to the defendant.

This type of contingent condition is illustrated by *Chillingworth* v. *Esche*,[14] where the plaintiff agreed to buy land from the defendant subject to contract and paid a deposit to the defendant. A contract was drawn up by the defendant, but the plaintiff refused to sign it and claimed repayment of the deposit. The plaintiff's claim succeeded because the money had been paid on the condition that a binding contract would be made and, since no contract had been signed, the contingency failed. Consequently the basis for the defendant receiving the money disappeared. Crucially the failure of the condition was due to the failure of the plaintiff, rather than the defendant, to sign the contract.

This secondary interpretation of consideration means that a plaintiff who, for example, gives money to the defendant on condition that he or she marries a particular person, will be able to recover the gift if the defendant does not marry that person.[15] This is also illustrated by *Re*

---

[13] See p. 361 below.

[14] [1924] 1 Ch. 97. See also *Guardian Ocean Cargoes Ltd.* v. *Banco de Brazil SA* [1991] 2 Lloyd's Rep. 68.

[15] See also the Law Reform (Miscellaneous Provisions) Act 1970, s. 3(2) by virtue of which the gift of an engagement ring is presumed to be an absolute gift, but this presumption may be rebutted by proving that the ring was given on condition, whether express or implied, that it would be returned if the marriage does not take place.

Ames' Settlement,[16] where a marriage settlement was established whereby the settlor covenanted to pay £10,000 within one year of the parties' marriage. Although the marriage did take place it was held to be void *ab initio* since the husband was incapable of consummating it. Consequently the consideration had failed since the marriage, on which the settlement was conditional, was deemed never to have been made.

(d) The nature of the enrichment

Traditionally, those grounds of restitution which are founded on the principle of failure of consideration have only been invoked to obtain restitution of money from the defendant. This is because total failure of consideration originated as a ground of restitution in the action for money had and received. But, with the abolition of the forms of action, there is no longer any reason why this ground of restitution should be inapplicable where the enrichment received by the defendant takes the form of goods or services. Recognition of the principle of symmetry[17] in particular suggests that restitutionary remedies should be available regardless of the type of benefit received by the defendant.[18] The state of the authorities is such that it is not yet possible to assert with confidence that restitution will lie where consideration has failed regardless of the type of enrichment involved. There are, however, a number of cases which implicitly support the proposition that restitutionary remedies are available where consideration has failed even where the enrichment is goods or services.[19] It will consequently be assumed in this chapter that the nature of the enrichment will not affect the success of the plaintiff's restitutionary claim, although this is subject to the caveat that there is still some doubt as to whether the grounds of restitution founded on failure of consideration are applicable to non-money claims.

(e) The relationship between damages for breach of contract and restitution to reverse unjust enrichment

Where the plaintiff has paid money in advance to the defendant in pursuance of a contract which the defendant breaches, the plaintiff has two remedial options open to him or her. First, the plaintiff may sue the defendant for breach of contract and recover damages. These damages

---

[16] [1946] Ch. 217. See also *P* v. *P* [1916] 2 IR 400. [17] See p. 126 above.

[18] See Birks, 'Failure of Consideration' in *Consensus Ad Idem* (ed. Rose, London: 1996) pp. 185–6.

[19] See in particular *Pulbrook* v. *Lawes* (1876) 1 QBD 284, discussed at p. 368 below. Where a contract is frustrated restitution will lie in respect of money and non-money benefits. See pp. 377–88 below.

will usually be compensatory, but it is now possible for restitutionary damages to be awarded to deprive the defendant of any gain made as a result of breaching the contract.[20] The award of such damages has nothing, however, to do with the reversal of the defendant's unjust enrichment, since the plaintiff's restitutionary claim is founded on the wrong of the breach of contract.[21] Alternatively the plaintiff may seek to recover the advance payment on the ground of failure of consideration. Such a claim would be founded on the reversal of the defendant's unjust enrichment.

In *Baltic Shipping* v. *Dillon*[22] the High Court of Australia held that the award of compensatory damages for breach of contract and restitutionary remedies to reverse the defendant's unjust enrichment are incompatible and so they can only be awarded as alternatives. In principle this must be correct. The usual function of compensatory damages for breach of contract was to fulfil the plaintiff's expectations by placing him or her in the position which he or she would have occupied had the contract not been breached. The function of restitutionary remedies on the other hand is to return the plaintiff to the position which he or she occupied before the contract was breached. If the plaintiff was awarded expectation damages it appears to follow that he or she could not be awarded a restitutionary remedy on the ground of failure of consideration as well. This is because if, by awarding compensatory damages, the plaintiff is deemed to be placed in the position which he or she would have occupied had the contract not been breached, it will not be possible to show that consideration has failed since the plaintiff will be considered to have received what he or she expected to receive under the contract. Similarly, if the plaintiff has been awarded a restitutionary remedy on the ground of failure of consideration it appears not to be possible to award him or her damages for loss arising from the defendant's failure to perform his or her side of the bargain. This is because, if the plaintiff has recovered the benefit which he or she had transferred to the defendant under the contract, then the basis for the plaintiff requiring the defendant to perform the contract will have been removed, since it was conditional on receipt of the benefit from the plaintiff.[23] If the defendant is not required to perform his or her side of the bargain there is no ground for holding him or her liable for breach of contract.

But this dichotomy between damages for breach and restitution for failure of consideration is not as clear-cut as the High Court of Australia implies. Rather than saying that compensatory damages and restitution-

---

[20] *Attorney-General* v. *Blake* [1998] 2 WLR 805.   [21] See Chapter 17.

[22] (1993) 176 CLR 344. See also *Walstab* v. *Spottiswode* (1846) 15 M and W 501, 514; 153 ER 952, 953 (Pollock CB).

[23] *Baltic Shipping Co.* v. *Dillon* (1993) 176 CLR 344, 359 (Mason CJ).

ary remedies are incompatible, it is preferable to assert that both types of remedy may be awarded in the same action so long as there is no double recovery.[24] If the plaintiff is awarded a restitutionary remedy it should still in principle be possible to award him or her a compensatory remedy as well, but in assessing the loss suffered by the plaintiff it is vital to take into account the effect of the restitutionary remedy which has been awarded. So, for example, if the plaintiff is able to recover the value of any benefit transferred under the contract to the defendant by virtue of failure of consideration it should still be possible for the plaintiff to claim damages to compensate for loss such as personal injury or disappointment.[25]

2. TOTAL FAILURE OF CONSIDERATION

By far the most important ground of restitution which is founded on the principle of failure of consideration arises where the consideration has totally failed. In other words, restitution will lie where no part of the condition on which the transfer of a benefit to the defendant is contingent has been fulfilled. So, for example, if the plaintiff contracts to buy a car from the defendant for which the plaintiff pays in advance, but the defendant does not deliver the car to the plaintiff then, because the plaintiff failed to receive any benefit, the defendant will be required to repay the advance payment.

(a) The requirements for establishing total failure of consideration

Where a plaintiff wishes to obtain restitution on the ground of total failure of consideration certain requirements will need to be satisfied. Whether a particular requirement applies depends on the nature of the plaintiff's claim.

(i) The contract must cease to be operative

Where the plaintiff has transferred a benefit to the defendant pursuant to a contract and wishes to recover the benefit on the ground of total failure of consideration it is first necessary to show that the contract has ceased to operate.[26] The contract may no longer be operative for a number of

---

[24] See Barker, 'Restitution of Passenger Fare' [1993] *LMCLQ* 291. Compensatory damages and restitutionary damages may both be awarded for breach of contract so long as there is no double recovery. See p. 461 below.

[25] This had been recognised by Lord Denning MR in *Heywood* v. *Wellers (a firm)* [1976] QB 446, 458. See also *Millar's Machinery Co. Ltd.* v. *David Way and Son* (1935) 40 Com. Cas. 204.

[26] This has been recognised by the Court of Session in *ERDC Construction Ltd.* v. *H.M. Lane* (1994) 70 BLR 67, 90 (the Lord Justice Clerk). See also *The Olanda* [1919] QB 728 and *Re Richmond Gate Property Ltd.* [1965] 1 WLR 335.

reasons, the most important being that it was discharged for breach or was frustrated. It will not be possible, however, to discharge a contract for breach once the plaintiff has affirmed it. It follows that affirmation will prevent the plaintiff from bringing a restitutionary claim.[27] This requirement that the contract must cease to be operative before a restitutionary remedy can be awarded is an important safeguard against the abuse of the law of restitution by undermining the law of contract. For, until the contract has been discharged, the contractual regime still operates to determine what remedies can be awarded.

But it does not necessarily follow from the fact that a contract has been discharged for breach that the contractual regime is inapplicable to the restitutionary claim. This is illustrated by the decision of the House of Lords in *The Trident Beauty*.[28] In this case the plaintiff had chartered a vessel from a shipowner, which then assigned to the defendant its right to receive payments for hiring the vessel from the plaintiff. The plaintiff was informed of this assignment and paid an instalment to the defendant. The shipowner breached the contract and the plaintiff accepted the repudiation. The plaintiff then sought to obtain restitution of the payment it had made to the defendant on the ground of total failure of consideration, since the ship had been out of action for the whole period in respect of which the instalment was paid. The plaintiff's claim failed because there was a clause in the contract which was made between the plaintiff and the shipowner to the effect that any overpaid hire had to be repaid at once. Since this contractual provision had come into operation before the contract was discharged it still applied despite the discharge. This meant that the shipowner was obliged to repay the hire to the plaintiff by virtue of the contract, even though the hire had been paid to the defendant. As Lord Goff emphasised:

as between shipowner and charterer, there is a contractual regime which legislates for the recovery of overpaid hire. It follows that, as a general rule, the law of restitution has no part to play in the matter; the existence of the agreed regime renders the imposition by the law of a remedy in restitution both unnecessary and inappropriate.[29]

The denial of restitution in these circumstances may seem unjust because the defendant was allowed to retain the instalment even though

---

[27] *Kwei Tek Chao* v. *British Traders and Shippers Ltd.* [1954] 2 QB 459. See also *Goodman* v. *Pocock* (1850) 15 QB 576; 117 ER 577.

[28] *Pan Ocean Shipping Co. Ltd.* v. *Creditcorp Ltd.* [1994] 1 WLR 161.

[29] *Ibid*, p. 164. Other reasons were given for the failure of the plaintiff's claim, including that a plaintiff should not be given a choice of which party to sue, whether the charterer in contract or the defendant in restitution. See Lord Woolf at p. 171. But if the plaintiff can establish a claim in restitution the fact that there is an alternative claim against another party, or even the same party, in contract is irrelevant, so long as the remedies which are awarded are compatible and do not result in double recovery.

the plaintiff had received no benefit in respect of that payment. Although the plaintiff did have a cause of action against the shipowner in contract, this was worthless because the shipowner was not considered to be worth suing. Nevertheless, the decision of the House of Lords is correct, since it implicitly accepts that the law of restitution is subservient to the law of contract. The plaintiff had agreed to the inclusion of the clause which required the shipowner to repay overpaid hire payments, and so the plaintiff bore the risk that the shipowner would not be able to repay the money. This risk had been allocated by the contract and it is not for the law of restitution to reallocate such risks.

(ii) The defendant is no longer ready, willing and able to perform his or her part of the bargain

It has sometimes been suggested that there is an additional requirement which must be satisfied before restitution can be awarded on the ground of total failure of consideration, namely that the defendant is no longer ready, able and willing to perform his or her part of the bargain. The leading case where this requirement was recognised is *Thomas* v. *Brown*[30] where the plaintiff contracted to buy a shop from the defendant and paid him a deposit. This contract was unenforceable since the vendor's name had not been disclosed as was required by the Statute of Frauds. Before the shop was conveyed to the plaintiff he sought to recover the deposit on the ground of total failure of consideration, but he was unable to do so. Two reasons were given for this: first, because the plaintiff had voluntarily paid the deposit with full knowledge that the vendor's name was not disclosed in the contract. It was not considered to be acceptable for the purchaser in such circumstances subsequently to object to the non-disclosure. Secondly, the defendant always remained ready and willing to execute the conveyance, so there was nothing unconscientious in the defendant retaining the deposit.

The difficulty with the requirement that the defendant must no longer be ready, willing and able to perform is whether it is additional to the requirement that the contract must be discharged or whether it is a separate requirement which only arises in certain circumstances. The latter is the better view. Where a contract has been discharged for breach, for example, it is clear that the defendant is no longer able to perform his or her contractual promise because there is no longer such an obligation to perform. It follows automatically from the fact that the contract has been discharged that the defendant is unable to perform his or her side of the bargain and so this is not an additional requirement which must be satisfied before the plaintiff can rely on total failure of consideration.

---

[30] (1876) 1 QBD 714. See also *Monnickendam* v. *Leanse* (1923) 39 TLR 445.

Where, however, the contract is unenforceable, as in *Thomas* v. *Brown*, the policy of the law which makes the contract unenforceable means that it is not necessary to show that the contract has been discharged,[31] but the plaintiff must instead show that the defendant is no longer ready, able and willing to perform the contract.

The requirement that the defendant is no longer ready, able and willing to perform is also applicable where the consideration for the transfer of the benefit to the defendant by the plaintiff is non-contractual performance. This is because in this type of case there is no contract which needs to be set aside, so some other test needs to be relied on to determine at what point the consideration should be regarded as having failed. It is sufficient instead simply to show that the defendant is not ready, able or willing to perform.

Where the consideration for the transfer of a benefit to the defendant involves the satisfaction of a condition which is not contractual and which does not involve performance by the defendant there is no contract which needs to be set aside. But in this type of case the requirement that the defendant is unable to perform is inapplicable because the condition does not depend on performance by the defendant. This is illustrated by *Chillingworth* v. *Esche*[32] where the plaintiff recovered a deposit which he had paid to the defendant pursuant to an agreement which was 'subject to contract'. Although it was the plaintiff who refused to sign the contract and the defendant remained ready, able and willing to sell his land, the plaintiff recovered the deposit simply because the condition on which the deposit was contingent, namely the signing of the contract, had not been satisfied. Since the defendant had never promised that he would sign the contract, his continued willingness to sign it did not prevent the consideration from failing totally.

It follows from this analysis that there are three different types of consideration which may fail and the requirements to establish total failure of consideration will vary depending on the consideration which is involved. The question which we are trying to determine in these cases is simply from what point the plaintiff can assert that the consideration has failed:

(1) Where the consideration involves the performance of a contractual obligation or the satisfaction of a contractual contingency restitutionary relief will only be available where the contract has been discharged.

(2) Where the consideration arises under a contract which is unenforceable or involves non-contractual performance by the defendant it is

---

[31] As was recognised by Deane J in *Pavey and Matthews Pty. Ltd.* v. *Paul* (1987) 162 CLR 221, 256.

[32] [1924] 1 Ch. 97.

not necessary to show that the contract ceases to operate but it is necessary to show that the defendant is no longer ready, able or willing to perform his or her side of the bargain.

(3) Where the consideration involves the satisfaction of a non-contractual condition which does not involve performance on the part of the defendant there are no requirements which need to be satisfied other than to show that the consideration has failed totally.

(iii) The consideration must have failed totally

Regardless of the type of consideration which forms the condition for the transfer of a benefit to the defendant, whether it is the performance of a contractual or non-contractual promise or the satisfaction of a non-promissory condition, restitution of the benefit will depend on whether the consideration has failed totally, save where one of the other recognised grounds of restitution is applicable.

(1) Determining whether the consideration has failed

The proper test for determining whether the consideration has failed has proved to be a controversial matter. However, this has now been resolved by the decision of the House of Lords in *Stocznia Gdanska SA* v. *Latvian Shipping Co.*[33] where Lord Goff recognised that:

> the test is not whether the promisee has received a specific benefit, but rather whether the promisor has performed any part of the contractual duties in respect of which the payment is due.[34]

Although this dictum related to a case involving performance of a contractual obligation, it is of relevance to all types of consideration. The key point is that consideration will not have failed totally if any part of the condition by reference to which the plaintiff has transferred a benefit to the defendant has been satisfied. Quite often this condition will be satisfied to some extent by the receipt of a benefit by the plaintiff, but, as Lord Goff acknowledged, this will not always be the case.[35] If consideration were provided only where the plaintiff received a benefit there would be many cases in which consideration could never be furnished. For example, if the plaintiff paid the defendant to paint the house of the plaintiff's daughter, the plaintiff would never receive a benefit. The importance of Lord Goff's dictum is that, in the contractual context at least, whether consideration has failed totally will depend on the terms of the contract. This is another example, therefore, of a situation in which the ambit of the restitutionary claim is circumscribed by the contract.

But Lord Goff's dictum cannot be regarded as an exclusive definition of the notion of consideration for the purposes of determining whether it

---

[33] [1998] 1 WLR 574.   [34] *Ibid*, p. 588.   [35] *Ibid*.

has totally failed. This is because it is clear that consideration need not involve the performance of a promise by the defendant, but may simply involve the occurrence of an event or some other condition precedent. Consequently, although Lord Goff's dictum expands our understanding of 'consideration' for the purposes of the law of restitution, it cannot be treated as a complete definition of that concept. The definition of consideration which is appropriate in each case will ultimately depend on what it is that the plaintiff has bargained for under the transaction[36] and, in a contractual context at least, whether the defendant has performed any part of his or her 'essential obligation' under the contract.[37] Consequently, the nature of the transaction is of decisive importance when determining whether or not the consideration has failed totally.

(2) Distinguishing between contracts to sell and contracts to build and sell

Since the effect of the *Stocznia* case means that whether consideration has failed totally will depend on the terms of the contract this can raise some difficult questions of contractual construction. This has been particularly difficult in the context of contracts in which the defendant agrees to sell goods to the plaintiff which the defendant is to make. It was recognised in the *Stocznia* case that, if the contract is construed simply as an agreement where the defendant promises to sell goods to the plaintiff, then the plaintiff will be able to rely on the ground of total failure of consideration only if he or she has not received any goods from the defendant, since the supply of goods is all that the defendant promises to do. Where, however, the contract is construed as one where the defendant agrees both to manufacture and supply the goods, the plaintiff will not be able to rely on the ground of total failure of consideration once the defendant has started to manufacture the goods, because this is what the defendant promised to do. It is irrelevant in this type of case that the plaintiff has not actually received a specific benefit from the defendant.[38] Lord Lloyd did recognise that the distinction between these two types of contracts is fine, but it is decisive to the success or failure of the plaintiff's restitutionary claim.[39] This distinction between contracts of sale and contracts of service and sale can be illustrated by analysing two decisions of the House of Lords.

In *Fibrosa Spolka Ackyjna* v. *Fairbairn Lawson Combe Barbour Ltd.*[40]

---

[36] *Rover International* v. *Cannon Film Sales Ltd. (No. 3)* [1989] 1 WLR 912, 923 (Kerr LJ).

[37] *Guinness Mahon Co. Ltd.* v. *Chelsea and Kensington LBC* [1998] 2 WLR 272, 294 (Robert Walker LJ).

[38] *Stocznia Gdanska SA* v. *Latvian Shipping Co.* [1998] 1 WLR 574, 589 (Lord Goff), p. 600 (Lord Lloyd).

[39] See Kerr LJ in *Rover International* v. *Cannon Film Sales Ltd. (No. 3)* [1989] 1 WLR 912, 931.

[40] [1943] AC 32. Today the defendant's loss could be apportioned under the Law Reform (Frustrated Contracts) Act 1943. See pp. 377–80 below.

the plaintiff had entered into a contract with the defendant to purchase machinery, which the defendant manufactured. The plaintiff made an advance payment to the defendant. The contract was frustrated by the outbreak of the Second World War before the defendant was able to deliver the machines to the plaintiff, but after the defendant had incurred expenditure in manufacturing them. The House of Lords held that the plaintiff could recover the advance payments on the ground of total failure of consideration, because it had not received any of the machinery which had been promised by the defendant. It was irrelevant that the defendant had incurred expenditure under the contract, simply because the contract was construed as an ordinary contract for the sale of goods. The manufacture of the machinery was not considered to form part of the consideration for the plaintiff's payment.[41]

This case can be compared with *Hyundai Heavy Industries Co. Ltd.* v. *Papadopoulos.*[42] In *Hyundai* the plaintiff contracted to build and sell a ship to the purchaser, who agreed to pay for the ship in instalments, with these payments being guaranteed by the defendant. The purchaser paid the first instalment as had been agreed, but defaulted on the second instalment, and consequently the plaintiff treated the contract as discharged. The plaintiff then sued the defendant on the guarantee for payment of the second instalment. The judges unanimously held that the defendant was liable under the terms of the guarantee, but three of the judges said that the defendant's liability could also be founded on the fact that, despite the discharge of the contract, the purchaser remained liable to pay the second instalment because the liability to pay this had already accrued before the contract was discharged. In reaching this decision the majority assumed that the purchaser could not have claimed repayment of the instalments on the ground of total failure of consideration. This was relevant because, if the purchaser had a right to obtain restitution of the payments had the instalments been paid, it would not have been liable to pay the instalments once the contract had been discharged. Whilst the court recognised that, had this simply been a contract of sale, the purchaser could have obtained restitution of the instalments which had already been paid on the ground of total failure of consideration, it was accepted that, because this was a contract to build and sell, the consideration would not have failed totally once the builder had incurred expenditure in building the ship before the contract was discharged, even though the purchaser had not received any benefit from this expenditure.

---

[41] *Ibid*, p. 56 (Lord Russell), p. 64 (Lord Wright) and p. 83 (Lord Porter).
[42] [1980] 1 WLR 1129. This case was affirmed in *Stocznia Gdanska SA* v. *Latvian Shipping Co.* [1998] 1 WLR 574 which also concerned a contract to build and sell ships.

The result of this case can be justified on the basis that, since the purchaser was required to pay instalments to the plaintiff before receiving
any specific benefit, this effectively meant that the purchaser was
expected to take the risk of default, so that if the contract was discharged
he or she should suffer the loss. If the contract allocates the risks in this
way then it is not for the law of restitution to re-allocate the risks.

(3) Contracts to provide services

Where the contract involves the provision of a service by the defendant
the plaintiff will not be able to rely on the ground of total failure of consideration if he or she has benefited from this service in any way. This is
illustrated by *Hunt* v. *Silk*[43] where the plaintiff leased a house from the
defendant for £10 on condition that the defendant executed the lease
and arranged for certain repairs to be done to the property within a certain period of time. The plaintiff paid the money and took immediate
possession of the property, but the defendant failed to execute the lease
or to repair the premises as he had promised. The plaintiff remained in
possession for two days after the time by which the defendant should
have executed the lease and completed the repairs. The plaintiff then
sought to recover the money, but was unable to do so because he had
remained in possession of the property after the time the defendant was
expected to do what he had promised to do. Consequently the plaintiff
had received a benefit and so the consideration for the payment had not
failed totally.

The application of this principle is also illustrated by the decision of
the High Court of Australia in *Baltic Shipping Co.* v. *Dillon*,[44] where the
plaintiff had paid in advance for a 14-day cruise. On the eighth day the
ship capsized and, although the defendant had repaid the fare in respect
of the remaining six-day period, the plaintiff sought restitution of the
whole fare which she had paid on the ground of total failure of consideration. Her claim failed because the consideration had not failed totally,
since she had received the benefit of the cruise for eight days.

(b) Manipulating the notion of total failure of consideration

Although this ground of restitution depends on the consideration failing
totally, the courts have manipulated the notion of *total* failure of consideration. There are, in particular, two judicial techniques by virtue of
which certain benefits received by the plaintiff can be discounted so that
they will not prevent the consideration from failing totally. The first tech-

---

[43] (1804) 5 East. 449; 102 ER 1142. See also *Brooks* v. *Beirnstein* [1909] 1 KB 98 and
Chatterton v. *Maclean* [1951] 1 All ER 761.
[44] (1993) 176 CLR 344.

nique involves ignoring the receipt of collateral benefits and the second involves the apportionment of the consideration.

(i) Receipt of collateral benefits

Where the plaintiff has received a benefit from the defendant this will only be considered to be a relevant benefit for the purposes of establishing whether or not the consideration has failed totally where it was a benefit for which the plaintiff had bargained. Any benefit which was received by the plaintiff and which can be characterised as collateral can be discounted, and so will not prevent the consideration from failing totally. The application of this principle is well illustrated by *Rowland* v. *Divall*[45] where the plaintiff had bought a car from the defendant and, having used it for over four months, discovered that it had been stolen, and so he was compelled to return it to its true owner. He then sought to recover the purchase price from the defendant on the ground of total failure of consideration and succeeded, even though he had used the car for a substantial period of time. This period of use was characterised as a collateral benefit since the real benefit for which the plaintiff had bargained was lawful possession of the car with good title and he had not obtained this at all. This is a somewhat strange conclusion, since anybody who purchases a car presumably expects to be able to use it, but the decision illustrates a desire to prevent the rigours of the total failure of consideration doctrine from preventing restitution where the award of a restitutionary remedy appears appropriate.[46]

Rowland v. *Divall* can be contrasted with *Yeoman Credit Ltd.* v. *Apps*,[47] where the defendant had entered into a hire purchase agreement with the plaintiff by virtue of which the defendant obtained possession of a car in an unroadworthy condition. Despite its condition he used the car for six months. The defendant failed to keep up with the hire payments and the plaintiff recovered the car. The plaintiff then sued the defendant for arrears and the defendant counterclaimed for recovery of the hire payments he had made on the ground of total failure of consideration. The defendant's counterclaim failed because he had obtained some benefit from the use of the car. *Rowland* v. *Divall* was distinguished because, in that case, the contract was one of purchase, and so the plaintiff had not obtained that for which he had bargained, namely good title, whereas in *Yeoman Credit Ltd.* v. *Apps*, the contract was one of hire

---

[45] [1923] 2 KB 500. See also *Warman* v. *Southern Counties Car Finance Co. Ltd.* [1949] 2 KB 576, and *Barber* v. *NWS Bank plc.* [1996] 1 WLR 641.

[46] *Rowland* v. *Divall* was followed in *Butterworth* v. *Kingsway Motors* [1954] 1 WLR 1286 where the plaintiff recovered the purchase price of the car on the ground of total failure of consideration even though he had used the car for 11 months.

[47] [1962] 2 QB 508.

purchase, so the plaintiff was assumed simply to have bargained for the use of the car, and this he had obtained, albeit that the quality of the use was not what he had expected.

Rowland v. Divall was followed by the Court of Appeal in *Rover International Ltd.* v. *Cannon Film Sales Ltd. (No. 3)*[48] where the plaintiff was able to recover money which it had paid to the defendant in respect of a contract for the distribution of films in Italy. One ground for restitution of this sum of money was that the consideration for the payment had totally failed, even though the plaintiff had received films from the defendant under the contract. This was because the receipt of these films was not considered to constitute the receipt of a benefit under the contract since 'delivery and possession [of the films] were not what [the plaintiff] had bargained for'.[49] Rather, the plaintiff was deemed to have bargained for the opportunity to earn a substantial share of the gross receipts from the distribution contract and it had not been able to earn anything because the contract, being a pre-incorporation contract, was void. Consequently, since the plaintiff got nothing of what it had bargained for, the court was able to order restitution of the money it had paid to the defendant.

The interpretation of total failure of consideration in both *Rowland* v. *Divall* and *Rover International* is open to criticism, since the benefit which was received in both cases surely formed a necessary part of the bargain. In *Rowland* v. *Divall*, for example, the use of the car was surely a crucial benefit which the plaintiff expected to obtain as an essential part of the contract to purchase the car. Similarly, in *Rover International* the plaintiff could not make any profit from the distribution of the films if it had not received them in the first place. The cynical interpretation of these cases is that the court considered that restitution should be awarded and did not wish to be defeated in this objective by the fact that the consideration must fail totally if it is to constitute a ground of restitution. This covert manipulation of the concept of consideration by characterising the receipt of certain benefits as collateral is unsatisfactory, leading as it does to great uncertainty. It would have been so much easier in these cases if it were acknowledged that partial failure of consideration is a satisfactory ground of restitution in its own right. For that is the effect of these decisions, namely that restitution is being awarded on the ground of failure of consideration even though the plaintiff had received some benefit by virtue of the defendant's performance of his or her side of the bargain.

(ii) Apportionment of the consideration

An alternative mechanism for avoiding the strict rigours of the requirement that the consideration must have totally failed before it can consti-

---

[48] [1989] 1 WLR 912.   [49] *Ibid*, p. 925 (Kerr LJ).

tute a ground of restitution is to apportion the consideration. What this means is that where, for example, the plaintiff has purchased a number of different items from the defendant and paid for them in advance, if the defendant fails to supply one of these items and the plaintiff accepts those which have been delivered, then the plaintiff can claim repayment of the price of the item which was not delivered on the ground that, as regards that item, the consideration has totally failed.[50]

This principle of apportionment has now been recognised by the Privy Council in the important case of *Goss* v. *Chilcott*[51] where a finance company had lent money to the defendants on the security of a mortgage over their property. In a separate transaction the defendants lent this money to a director of the finance company. The purpose of this transaction was effectively to enable the director to borrow money from the company of which he was director, which he was prohibited from doing. The director, in his capacity as agent of the finance company, altered the mortgage instrument without the consent of the defendants. This meant that the security was unenforceable as against the defendants, so their contractual liability to repay the money to the finance company was automatically discharged. The finance company having gone into liquidation, the plaintiff liquidator sought to recover the amount of the loan from the defendants in a restitutionary claim founded on the ground of total failure of consideration. The difficulty for the plaintiff was that the defendants had already made two payments to the finance company in respect of interest, so they argued that the consideration for the transaction had not totally failed. Lord Goff delivered the judgment of the Privy Council and held that the consideration for the transaction had failed totally. This was because the plaintiff's restitutionary claim related to repayment of capital and no part of the capital had been repaid; rather the defendants had simply been repaying interest. This is a perfectly acceptable conclusion since, although the defendant's obligation to pay interest and capital arose under the same transaction, the obligations arose for different reasons, interest payments being payments for the use of the capital rather than involving the return of the capital. To the extent that it is possible to say, as it was in this case, that the money paid by the defendants related either to interest or to capital and that only interest had been repaid then the decision is correct.

[50] As was recognised by Bovill CJ in *Whincup* v. *Hughes* (1871) LR 6 CP 78, 81. See also *Devaux* v. *Connolly* (1849) 8 CB 640; 137 ER 658.

[51] [1996] AC 788. The principle has also been recognised by the High Court of Australia in *David Securities* v. *Commonwealth Bank of Australia* (1992) 175 CLR 353, 383. See also *Fibrosa Spolka Ackyjna* v. *Fairbairn Lawson Combe Barbour Ltd.* [1943] AC 32, 77 (Lord Porter).

However, Lord Goff did say in addition that:

even if part of the capital sum had been repaid, the law would not hesitate to hold that the balance of the loan outstanding would be recoverable on the ground of failure of consideration; for at least in those cases in which apportionment can be carried out without difficulty, the law will allow partial recovery on this ground.[52]

But this is much more difficult to justify. Where, for example, the plaintiff lends £1,000 to the defendant who repays £400, can it really be said that, as regards the outstanding amount, the consideration has failed totally? What is being apportioned in this case? Surely it would only be possible to apportion consideration in this way if, for example, the contract of loan itself provided for repayment by instalments. As the High Court of Australia said in *David Securities Pty. Ltd.* v. *Commonwealth Bank of Australia*,[53] it is only where the parties have impliedly acknowledged that the consideration may be apportioned by the structure of the transaction that apportionment will be possible. In such circumstances if two of five instalments have been paid it could still be argued that the consideration has failed totally in respect of the final three instalments, which would then be recoverable. But in *Goss* v. *Chilcott* the whole loan was repayable three months after it was made; it was only the interest which was payable in instalments. There is therefore no justification for saying that, if the defendants had repaid part of the loan, then the consideration would have failed totally in respect of the outstanding sum, simply because there was nothing in the loan transaction to suggest that the consideration could be apportioned in this way.

If Lord Goff's dictum, which was *obiter* and in a decision of the Privy Council, is taken as representing English law then surely the doctrine of total failure of consideration is dead and buried. It is not possible, however, on the basis of that one dictum to reach such a conclusion. Nevertheless, at the very least the decision of the Privy Council constitutes another nail in the coffin of total failure of consideration. This had been recognised by the High Court of Australia in *David Securities* v. *Commonwealth Bank of Australia*,[54] where the majority acknowledged that once it is accepted that the consideration can be apportioned then 'any rationale for adhering to the traditional rule requiring *total* failure of consideration disappears'.[55] Although it is not yet possible to say that partial failure of consideration is generally a sufficient ground of restitution in its own right, particularly because the Privy Council in *Goss* v. *Chilcott* affirmed that the consideration must totally fail,[56] the recognition that consideration can be apportioned means that the requirement

---

[52] *Goss* v. *Chilcott* [1996] AC 788, 798.   [53] (1992) 175 CLR 353, 383.
[54] *Ibid.*   [55] *Ibid*, emphasis in the original.   [56] [1996] AC 788, 797.

that consideration must fail totally is less of an obstacle to the plaintiff's restitutionary claim.

The fact that recognition of a principle of apportionment will inexorably lead to recognition of partial failure of consideration as a ground of restitution is illustrated by the bizarre decision of the Court of Appeal in *D.O. Ferguson* v. *Sohl*.[57] In this case the plaintiff had paid £6,268.75 to the defendant, of which £4,673 constituted an overpayment. It was held that the plaintiff could recover the overpayment on the ground of total failure of consideration. Hirst LJ specifically stated[58] that the overpayment was recoverable even though it formed part of a larger payment. But it is an abuse of language to say that the money was recoverable on the ground of total failure of consideration since clearly the consideration had not failed totally. The result might be explained on the ground of apportionment of consideration, but there was nothing in the contract which enabled such an apportionment to be made. Consequently, the case is better analysed as one in which restitution was awarded on the ground of partial failure of consideration. The importance of the case is that the Court of Appeal clearly considered that restitution should follow as a matter of common sense because the plaintiff had paid money to the defendant for work which had never been done.

(c) Is the requirement that the consideration must totally fail defensible?

The reliance of the courts on mechanisms such as characterisation of benefits as collateral and apportionment of consideration stems from a desire to award restitutionary remedies, even where the consideration for a particular transaction has only partially failed. As the law stands, restitution on the ground of partial failure of consideration will only be awarded in one situation.[59] It would surely make the law of restitution more just if partial failure of consideration were recognised as a ground of restitution in its own right.[60]

(i) Arguments in favour of recognising partial failure of consideration

There are a number of reasons why the law of restitution should recognise partial failure of consideration as a ground of restitution which is generally available:

(1) Where the plaintiff has transferred a benefit to the defendant and has received part of the expected consideration in return, restitution can

---

[57] (1992) 62 BLR 95. Surprisingly, no reference was made to mistake as a possible ground of restitution.
[58] *Ibid*, p. 105.   [59] See p. 373 below.
[60] See Birks in *Consensus Ad Idem* (ed. Rose), p. 179.

still be justified since the plaintiff's intention that the defendant should retain the benefit, which is contingent on the fulfilment of a condition, has still been vitiated where that condition has not been completely fulfilled.

(2) Recognising partial failure of consideration would also mean that there would no longer be any need for the courts to manipulate the concept of consideration to enable it to conclude that the consideration had totally failed where it was felt that restitution was justified.

(3) Partial failure of consideration is already recognised as a ground of restitution where a contract has been frustrated.[61] There is no reason why the ground of restitution following the discharge of a contract should differ depending on whether the contract has been discharged for frustration or for breach. Indeed, the fact that Parliament in the Law Reform (Frustrated Contracts) Act 1943 has accepted the legitimacy of partial failure of consideration as a ground of restitution should mean that there is no reason why the common law should not extend this ground of restitution to other areas where the contract has ceased to operate.

(ii) Arguments against recognising partial failure of consideration

The main reason the courts have traditionally emphasised that the consideration must fail totally is the difficulty of apportioning benefits to reflect the fact that the plaintiff has received some benefit from the defendant. This stems primarily from a long-standing reluctance to value non-money benefits. But with a more sophisticated law of restitution which is prepared to value non-money benefits for the purposes of making counter-restitution, as is now recognised where the plaintiff wishes to rescind a contract,[62] there is no longer any reason why the fact that the plaintiff has received some benefit should operate as a bar to restitution. Consequently, restitution should be awarded on the ground of partial failure of consideration, so long as the value of any benefits received by the plaintiff is repaid to the defendant.

(iii) The consequences of recognising partial failure of consideration

If partial failure of consideration were recognised as a general ground of restitution in its own right the consequence would be that, to the extent that any part of the consideration had failed, restitution should be avail-

---

[61] Law Reform (Frustrated Contracts) Act 1943, s. 1(2), (3). See p. 373 below.

[62] See, for example, *O'Sullivan* v. *Management Agency and Music Ltd.* [1985] QB 428. See pp. 32–4 above. For analysis of the issues concerning the relationship between 'counter-restitution' and total failure of consideration see McKendrick, 'Total Failure of Consideration and Counter-restitution: Two Issues or One?' in *Laundering and Tracing* (ed. Birks, Oxford: Clarendon Press, 1995) pp. 217ff. and Birks in *Consensus Ad Idem* (ed. Rose) pp. 193–8.

able. Where the plaintiff had received some benefit from the defendant then this benefit would need to be valued and the plaintiff would be required to make counter-restitution to the defendant. There would still be an advantage for the plaintiff to show that the consideration had totally failed because then there would be no question that the plaintiff had received any benefit from the transaction, so the plaintiff could recover the value of all of the benefits which had been transferred to the defendant pursuant to the transaction without any obligation to make counter-restitution.

If partial failure of consideration were recognised as a general ground of restitution its operation could potentially cause difficulties in those cases in which the consideration had not failed totally but the plaintiff had received no specific benefit from the defendant, as illustrated by the case in which the defendant has agreed to build and deliver a ship which he or she had started to build when the contract was discharged.[63] Although the plaintiff should be able to obtain restitution of the benefit which he or she transferred to the defendant, on the ground of partial failure of consideration, how should the work done by the defendant be taken into account? Should this work be valued and this amount be deducted from what the defendant is required to restore to the plaintiff? This would mean that the plaintiff is required to make counter-restitution to the defendant in respect of a benefit which the plaintiff has not actually received. Consequently, since the plaintiff has not received any benefit, it could be argued that the plaintiff is not required to make counter-restitution to the defendant, because the plaintiff has not been unjustly enriched. Perhaps the solution should depend on the construction of the contract. If the defendant's promised performance includes work as well as sale, then the plaintiff should be considered to have freely accepted the work done by the defendant even though the plaintiff has not actually received a specific benefit from the defendant. Such a result would at least be consistent with the rationale of the build and sell cases, where the plaintiff is considered to take the risk that the ship will not be built.

(iv) Will the courts be prepared to recognise partial failure of consideration?

There is some suggestion in the decision of the House of Lords in *Westdeutsche Landesbank Girozentrale* v. *Islington London Borough Council*[64] of a greater willingness to accept partial failure of consideration as a ground of restitution. As Lord Goff said:[65]

---

[63] See *Stocznia Gdanska SA* v. *Latvian Shipping Co.* [1998] 1 WLR 574.
[64] [1996] AC 669. [65] *Ibid*, p. 682.

There has long been a desire among restitution lawyers to escape from the unfortunate effects of the so-called rule that money is only recoverable at common law on the ground of failure of consideration where the failure is total, by reformulating the rule upon a more principled basis; and signs that this will in due course be done are appearing in judgments throughout the common law world.

Although it is likely, particularly in the light of decisions such as *Goss* v. *Chilcott*,[66] that it will not be long before the House of Lords recognises that partial failure of consideration is a ground of restitution in its own right, we have not yet reached that position. Indeed, in the most recent decision of the House of Lords where the principle of failure of consideration was considered, Lord Goff appeared to sound a note of caution when he said of the ground of total failure of consideration:[67]

This rule has been subject to considerable criticism in the past; but it has to be said that in a comparatively recent Report (Law Com. No. 121(1983) concerned with Pecuniary Restitution on Breach of Contract) the Law Commission has declined to recommend a change in the rule, though it was there considering recovery by the innocent party rather than by the party in breach.

The House of Lords had the opportunity in that case to reject the requirement that consideration must fail totally, but it declined to do so. Consequently, although a very strong case can be made for the recognition of partial failure of consideration as a general ground of restitution, this recognition is still some way off.

(d) Two problems in the application of total failure of consideration

The application of the ground of total failure of consideration faces two particular difficulties which require careful analysis, namely whether restitution is available from third parties on this ground and whether a plaintiff who has participated in an illegal transaction can rely on this ground of restitution.

(i) Restitution from parties who were not expected to provide the consideration

In *The Trident Beauty*[68] it was seen that the plaintiff, who had paid money to the defendant, was unable to recover that money by claiming that there had been a total failure of consideration, because of a term in the contract between the plaintiff and the shipowner which excluded the right to restitution. But would the plaintiff's restitutionary claim have succeeded had there been no provision in the contract to exclude a resti-

---

[66] [1996] AC 788.
[67] *Stocznia Gdanska SA* v. *Latvian Shipping Co.* [1998] 1 WLR 574, 590.
[68] *Pan Ocean Shipping Co. Ltd.* v. *Creditcorp Ltd.* [1994] 1 WLR 161. See p. 330 above.

tutionary claim? The defendant was clearly enriched at the plaintiff's expense and there was total failure of consideration, since the plaintiff had not received the benefit for which it had bargained, namely the use of the ship. The problem was that the plaintiff was seeking to obtain restitution from a party who was never intended to provide the consideration for the payment, since the ship did not belong to the defendant. Lord Woolf considered this to be a reason to deny restitution,[69] whereas Lord Goff accepted that the matter was open for debate.[70] The matter should be beyond debate now and restitution should be awarded even though the defendant who was enriched was not a party to the contract between the plaintiff and the party who was expected to provide the consideration. Restitution on the ground of mistake is not barred where the benefit is mistakenly transferred to the defendant rather than a third party,[71] so why should restitution for total failure of consideration be treated any differently? Burrows has argued that restitution should be denied in such circumstances because the contract of assignment between the shipowner and the defendant did not contemplate an obligation on the part of the defendant to repay the instalment.[72] But why should this bar the plaintiff's restitutionary claim? The plaintiff was not a party to this contract so, as long as the contract which the plaintiff had made did not bar the restitutionary claim, the contract of assignment should have no effect on the plaintiff's restitutionary claim against the defendant. In principle restitution should lie on the ground of total failure of consideration even against a party who was not expected to provide the consideration for the benefit which the plaintiff had transferred, simply because the consequence of the failure of consideration is that the plaintiff's intention that the defendant should receive the benefit is vitiated. The fact that the consideration failed due to the failure of a third party rather than the defendant who actually received the benefit is of no significance to whether the plaintiff's intention can be treated as vitiated.

Even if it is accepted that restitution can lie on the ground of total failure of consideration against a defendant who has received a benefit even though he or she was not expected to provide the consideration, whether this is of any practical significance depends on the nature of the case in which the issue arises. This is illustrated by the following example. The defendant contracted with a third party to build a house and the third party entered into a sub-contract with the plaintiff to install the windows. If the plaintiff installed the windows but the third party failed to pay him or her under the sub-contract because the third party had

---

[69] *Ibid*, p. 171.   [70] *Ibid*, p. 166.
[71] *Barclays Bank Ltd.* v. *W.J. Simms Son and Cooke (Southern) Ltd.* [1980] QB 677. See p. 152 above.
[72] Burrows 'Restitution from Assignees' (1994) 2 *RLR* 52, 55.

become bankrupt, could the plaintiff bring a restitutionary claim against the defendant? The defendant would have been enriched by the installation of the windows, since the work was both incontrovertibly beneficial and had been freely accepted,[73] and this enrichment would have been at the plaintiff's expense. There has also been a total failure of consideration since the plaintiff received no payment from the third party, this being the consideration which the plaintiff expected to receive for the work he had done. But the obstacle to a restitutionary claim in such a case is that it would involve unacceptable interference by the law of restitution in the contractual relationships for two reasons. First, the defendant will continue to be liable to pay the third party under the head contract and, secondly, the third party remains liable to the plaintiff under the sub-contract.[74] Where there is existing contractual liability it is not possible for restitutionary liability to be imposed as well, something which was recognised in *The Trident Beauty* itself. The only way that a restitutionary claim could be available in this scenario is if it could be shown somehow that both the head contract and the sub-contract had ceased to operate. The relevant ground of restitution would therefore be total failure of consideration, since the condition on which the installation of the windows was contingent has not been satisfied. There is no reason why an artificial privity requirement should be imposed upon the concept of total failure of consideration, particularly because it is a restitutionary and not a contractual concept.[75] But it is only in the most exceptional circumstances that it will be possible to show that both the head contract and the sub-contract have ceased to be operative.

(ii) Denial of restitution where the plaintiff has participated in an illegal transaction

Where the plaintiff has participated in an illegal transaction it is usually possible for him or her to obtain a restitutionary remedy by relying on one of the established grounds of restitution, such as mistake or duress. This is not, however, possible where the plaintiff relies on the ground of total failure of consideration, despite dicta in certain cases to the contrary.[76] So, for example, in *Parkinson* v. *College of Ambulance*[77] the plaintiff had paid a sum of money to a charity on the understanding that the charity would be able to arrange for him to receive a knighthood. This was an illegal transaction. The knighthood was not forthcoming and the

---

[73] Cp. Burrows, *The Law of Restitution*, p. 271.

[74] See Watts, 'Does a Subcontractor have Restitutionary Rights against the Employer?' [1995] *LMCLQ* 398, 399.

[75] Burrows, 'Restitution from Assignees' (1994) 2 *RLR* 52, 53.

[76] See, for example, *Bloxsome* v. *Williams* (1824) 3 B and C 232, 235; 107 ER 720, 721 (Bayley J) and *Shaw* v. *Shaw* [1965] 1 WLR 537, 539 (Lord Denning MR).

[77] [1923] 2 KB 1. See also *Berg* v. *Sadler and Moore* [1937] 2 KB 158.

plaintiff sought to recover the money. Clearly the consideration for the payment had totally failed, but, because the plaintiff had participated in an illegal transaction, he was unable to recover his money.

That restitution will be denied in such cases was recently confirmed by the Court of Appeal in *Taylor* v. *Bhail*,[78] a case which is unsatisfactory for a number of reasons. In this case the plaintiff builder had entered into a building contract with the defendant. At the defendant's request the plaintiff's estimate for the work was inflated by £1,000 to enable the defendant to perpetrate a fraud on his insurance company. The plaintiff completed the work and, after the defendant had refused to pay for all the work he had done, the plaintiff sued for breach of contract. His action failed on the ground that he had been tainted by illegality since he was a party to a conspiracy to defraud. Millett LJ also considered whether he could have brought a restitutionary claim for the reasonable value of his services and concluded that he could not, again by virtue of the fact that he was tainted by illegality. Millett LJ identified two reasons for this conclusion.[79]

(1) The illegality rendered unenforceable any implied promise by the defendant to pay the reasonable value of the services, in the same way that the express promise to pay is unenforceable. But this is outdated reasoning founded on notions of quasi-contract which no longer have any part to play in the law of restitution.[80] The obligation to make restitution is imposed by operation of law and does not depend upon the implication of any promise to pay. It does not follow, therefore, that because the plaintiff could not sue on the illegal contract he was necessarily prevented from bringing a restitutionary claim.

(2) Where the transaction is illegal any enrichment received by the defendant is not unjust, since 'it is the price which the plaintiff must pay for having entered into an illegal transaction in the first place'.[81] This is the crux of the issue. Where the plaintiff has not received any of the expected consideration for the benefit which he or she has transferred to the defendant there is, at the very least, the appearance of an unjust enrichment. The real question is whether the plaintiff can be considered to have been so tainted by the illegality that he or she is prevented from asserting that the defendant has been unjustly enriched. Traditionally restitution has been denied to the plaintiff on the ground of total failure of consideration where he or she has participated in an illegal transaction simply because it does not follow from the fact that the consideration has failed that the plaintiff ceases to be tainted by the illegality, and the policy of the law is not to assist a plaintiff to obtain restitution where

---

[78] [1996] CLC 377.   [79] *Ibid*, 383.
[80] See *United Australia Ltd.* v. *Barclays Bank Ltd.* [1941] AC 1, discussed at p. 19 above.
[81] [1996] CLC 377, 383.

he or she has been so tainted. It is for this reason that restitution has been awarded where the plaintiff has withdrawn from the transaction before any part of it has been executed. But, as will be seen below,[82] the inter- pretation of this withdrawal principle today means that it is virtually indistinguishable from the ground of total failure of consideration. In fact, the denial of the plaintiff's restitutionary claim founded on total fail- ure of consideration where he or she has participated in an illegal trans- action is increasingly difficult to defend. It would be preferable to allow restitution on this ground even if the plaintiff has been tainted by illegal- ity, so long as it is not of a particularly serious kind.[83]

(e) The role of total failure of consideration

Total failure of consideration is the relevant ground of restitution in a number of different contexts, including where a contract has been breached, where a benefit has been provided in respect of an anticipated contract and where a contract is unenforceable for failure to comply with formalities. The application of total failure of consideration in each of these situations raises particular problems which will be examined in turn.

(f) Contracts which are discharged for breach[84]

Where a contract has been breached there are two remedial options available. First, the plaintiff may seek a remedy for the breach itself. Normally this will be compensatory damages, assessed by reference to the plaintiff's loss, but in certain exceptional circumstances it is possible to award restitutionary damages, which are assessed with reference to the benefits obtained by the defendant as a result of breaching the con- tract.[85] But such a restitutionary remedy is not founded on the reversal of the defendant's unjust enrichment but instead on the wrong of the breach of contract; hence this remedial option is considered in Part IV.

Alternatively, once the contract has been discharged for breach, the plaintiff may seek to obtain a restitutionary remedy which is not founded on the breach but is based on total failure of consideration, in the sense that the condition for the transfer of benefits to the defendant has not been and will not be satisfied as a result of the breach of contract. Here

---

[82] See pp. 370–3 below.

[83] See p. 754 below and Virgo, 'The Effects of Illegality on Claims for Restitution in English Law' in *The Limits of Restitutionary Claims: A Comparative Analysis* (ed. Swadling, London: UK/UCCL, 1997) pp. 181–2.

[84] For discussion of when a contract may be discharged for breach, see *Chitty's Law of Contract* (27th edn.), Chapter 24.

[85] *Attorney-General* v. *Blake* [1998] 2 WLR 805. See Chapter 17.

restitution is founded on the reversal of the defendant's unjust enrichment. The relevance of the breach of contract is simply that, once the
repudiatory breach has been accepted, the contract ceases to be operative, so opening the way for the restitutionary claim. But the breach itself
does not constitute the underlying cause of action for the claim.

Where the plaintiff's restitutionary claim is founded on total failure of
consideration, it should make no difference that the plaintiff breached
the contract. This is because the fact that the plaintiff committed a wrong
by breaching the contract should have no effect upon a claim founded on
the reversal of the defendant's unjust enrichment. Unfortunately, the
courts have not always recognised this, so it is necessary to analyse separately the cases where the defendant breached the contract and where
the plaintiff breached the contract.

(i) Breach of contract by the defendant

(1) Restitution of money paid

Where the contract is breached by the defendant the innocent plaintiff
who has accepted the breach will be able to obtain restitution of money
paid on the ground of total failure of consideration. This is illustrated by
Giles v. *Edwards*[86] where the defendant contracted to sell all of his cord-
wood to the plaintiff and agreed that the wood would be cut and corded
before the plaintiff collected it. The plaintiff paid for the wood in advance
but, when he went to collect it, the defendant had corded only part of the
wood. Since the defendant had not done what he had promised to do, it
was held that the plaintiff could repudiate the contract completely
because of the defendant's breach and so recover the advance payment.
Although no ground of restitution was specifically recognised, the result
of the case is consistent with the ground being that of total failure of consideration. This was because the contract was an entire contract, so the
plaintiff's contractual obligation to pay for the wood did not arise until
the defendant had performed his side of the bargain. Consequently, the
defendant's part performance of the contract did not mean that the consideration had only failed partially.[87]

Similarly, where the plaintiff has paid a deposit to the defendant who
then breaches the contract, the plaintiff will be able to recover the
deposit, as well as any other advance payments, on the ground of total
failure of consideration.[88]

---

[86] (1797) 7 Term Rep. 181; 101 ER 920.
[87] Cp. *Stocznia Gdanska SA* v. *Latvian Shipping Co.* [1998] 1 WLR 574.
[88] *Barber* v. *NWS Bank plc.* [1996] 1 WLR 641.

(2) Restitution of non-money benefits

Where the plaintiff has transferred a non-money benefit to the defendant he or she should be able to recover the value of the benefit on the ground of total failure of consideration if the defendant has breached the contract and the plaintiff has accepted that the breach has discharged the contract.[89] This remains, however, a controversial matter because of the assumption that total failure of consideration is appropriate as a ground of restitution only where the defendant has been enriched by the receipt of money. Although no cases have explicitly recognised that the ground of total failure of consideration is applicable where the defendant has received a non-money benefit, because invariably restitutionary analysis is hidden behind the labels of *quantum meruit* or *quantum valebat*, some cases are at least consistent with the proposition that total failure of consideration is available even as regards claims for such benefits.

This is illustrated by *De Bernardy* v. *Harding*[90] where the defendant was in charge of letting seats to see the funeral of the Duke of Wellington. The defendant entered into an agreement with the plaintiff whereby the plaintiff would sell tickets for the funeral abroad. After the plaintiff had incurred expense in making the necessary arrangements the defendant informed him that he would sell all of the tickets himself. The plaintiff then forwarded the names of applicants for tickets to the defendant and sought payment from the defendant in respect of the expenditure he had incurred and the services he had provided. The defendant reimbursed the plaintiff for his expenditure but refused to pay him for his services. It was held that the plaintiff had a choice whether to sue for breach of contract or to accept the discharge of the contract and sue for the work he had done. If the plaintiff had brought a restitutionary claim for the work done, the claim would presumably have succeeded. The plaintiff's services were incontrovertibly beneficial to the defendant, since he had been saved expense which he would inevitably have incurred had the plaintiff not advertised the sale of tickets abroad. It could also be shown that there had been a total failure of consideration, since the plaintiff had not been paid for his services. Although the defendant did reimburse the plaintiff for the expenditure incurred, the receipt of this consideration could be apportioned, since it related only to expenditure rather than to the services which were beneficial to the defendant.

(3) Losing contracts

Where the defendant has breached a contract the plaintiff will be able to obtain restitution on the ground of total failure of consideration even

---

[89] *Lodder* v. *Slowey* [1904] AC 442, PC.
[90] (1853) 8 Exch. 821; 155 ER 1586. See also *Chandler Bros. Ltd.* v. *Harding* [1936] 3 All ER 179.

where the contract was, from the plaintiff's perspective, a bad bargain. Of course, in such a case it will be rare for the defendant to breach such a contract which is advantageous to him or her, but, where such a contract is breached, the plaintiff's restitutionary claim will not be defeated by the fact that, had he or she sued the defendant for breach, no compensatory damages would have been awarded because the plaintiff would not have suffered any loss. This is irrelevant to the plaintiff's restitutionary claim since restitutionary remedies are assessed by reference to the defendant's gain rather than the plaintiff's loss. This is illustrated by *Wilkinson* v. *Lloyd*[91] where the plaintiff agreed to buy shares from the defendant, the transfer being conditional on the defendant obtaining the consent of the directors of the relevant company to the transfer. The plaintiff paid the defendant for the shares without realising that the defendant had not been able to obtain the directors' consent. After he had discovered this, the plaintiff accepted that the contract had been discharged since the defendant had not done all that was necessary to ensure that the shares were transferred into the plaintiff's name. The plaintiff then sued the defendant for repayment of the purchase price on the ground of total failure of consideration, since the plaintiff had not received any of the shares. The plaintiff's action succeeded even though the value of the shares had fallen below the purchase price in the meantime. Similarly, where the enrichment is a non-money benefit, the fact that the benefit was transferred pursuant to a losing contract is an irrelevant consideration when determining whether the plaintiff can bring a restitutionary claim.[92]

It has sometimes been suggested that awarding restitution to a plaintiff who has entered into a losing contract may subvert the allocation of risks under it where the risk of the contract being a bad bargain has been allocated to the plaintiff. So, for example, if the plaintiff agrees to buy goods from the defendant and pays in advance, it may be assumed that the plaintiff is expected to take the risk that the goods may fall in value. This is a difficult question. The better view is that, where it is clear that the contract has allocated the risk of loss to the plaintiff, then the law of restitution should not be used to subvert this, even though the contract has been discharged by the plaintiff for breach.[93] In such a case the plaintiff's claim to restitution would be defeated by the contract. But such a conclusion should only be drawn where the risk has clearly been allocated to the plaintiff by the contract. The simple fact that the plaintiff has

[91] (1845) 7 QB 25; 115 ER 398. See also the American case of *Bush* v. *Canfield* (1818) 2 Conn. 485.

[92] *Lodder* v. *Slowey* [1904] AC 442. See also the American case of *Boomer* v. *Muir* (1933) 24 P 2d. 570.

[93] This is consistent with the approach of the House of Lords in *Pan Ocean Shipping Co. Ltd.* v. *Creditcorp Ltd.* [1994] 1 WLR 161.

paid the defendant in advance should not be sufficient to presume that the risk of loss has been allocated to the plaintiff. If the parties really do intend to allocate the risk of loss in this way then they should do so explicitly by including a particular term to this effect in the contract itself.

(ii) Breach of contract by the plaintiff

Restitution should also be awarded on the ground of total failure of consideration where the contract has been discharged for a breach committed by the plaintiff. The fact that the plaintiff's claim was effectively self-induced, in the sense that had the plaintiff not breached the contract it would not have been discharged and so restitution would not have been available, should not be sufficient to deny the restitutionary claim. The fact that the breach was self-induced could only be relevant if English law regarded breach of contract as so wrong that it should be discouraged by denying restitution to the plaintiff on the ground of public policy. But English law does not generally characterise breach of contract in this way,[94] for, if it did, the usual remedy for breach of contract would be specific performance rather than compensatory damages. So long as the contract-breaker compensates the victim for any loss suffered as a result of the breach, there is no reason of principle or policy why he or she should not claim restitution.

That English law does not prevent the contract-breaker from obtaining restitution is illustrated by the fact that, where the innocent party brings a restitutionary claim founded on total failure of consideration as a result of the breach, the contract-breaker is allowed to bring a counterclaim for restitution on the same ground. If the contract-breaker is allowed to bring a counterclaim, it should follow that he or she can bring a direct claim for restitution once the contract has been discharged for breach. This has in fact been recognised, although there has been some uncertainty whether the ground of restitution is total failure of consideration and the law is more complicated where the enrichment takes the form of a non-money benefit.

(1) Restitution of money paid

Where the plaintiff has paid money to the defendant and then breaches the contract, the preferable view is that the plaintiff is able to recover this money on the ground of total failure of consideration. This is illustrated by *Dies* v. *British and International Mining and Finance Co. Ltd.*[95] The plaintiff entered into a contract with the defendant for the purchase of rifles and ammunition and paid part of the purchase price in advance. The plaintiff did not take delivery of the rifles and ammunition and so the

---

[94] See Chapter 17.   [95] [1939] 1 KB 724.

defendant discharged the contract for breach. The plaintiff then successfully recovered the advance payment from the defendant, subject to
the defendant's claim for damages in respect of loss suffered as a result
of the breach. Unfortunately, the judge specifically rejected total failure
of consideration as the ground of restitution and concluded that the
plaintiff's right to recover the money derived from the terms of the contract itself.[96] This reasoning is unsatisfactory today, but it was under-
standable at the time the case was decided, since restitutionary remedies
were awarded by reference to the implied contract theory. Two years
later that theory was rejected by the House of Lords in *United Australia
Ltd.* v. *Barclays Bank.*[97] The importance of the *Dies* case lies in the fact
that the plaintiff was able to obtain restitution even though he had
breached the contract. Despite the rejection of total failure of consideration as the reason for the restitutionary claim succeeding, total failure of
consideration should be treated as the best explanation of the result now
that the implied contract theory has itself been rejected. For the plaintiff
had paid the money to the defendant without receiving anything which
he had originally expected in return. This is an archetypal case of total
failure of consideration.

That the contract-breaker is able to recover money from the defendant
on the ground of total failure of consideration is further supported by the
decision of the Court of Appeal in *Rover International Ltd.* v. *Cannon
Film Sales Ltd. (No. 3)*,[98] where the defendant had granted the plaintiff a
licence to exhibit nine films on Italian television. The fee for the licence
was to be paid in three instalments. The plaintiff paid the first two instalments and then the defendant purported to terminate the contract for
breach of the contract by the plaintiff and counterclaimed for payment
of the final instalment. It was held that, if the plaintiff had paid this instalment, it would have been able to recover it on the ground of total failure
of consideration, the consideration having failed because the plaintiff
had not received any films from the defendant. Consequently, the defendant could not sue for payment of the instalment from the plaintiff.
Logically, therefore, the contract-breaker would have been able to
recover the first two instalments which it had paid if it had brought a
claim for repayment.

The contract-breaker's restitutionary claim founded on total failure of
consideration is subject to an important qualification, namely that restitution will be denied to the extent that it is excluded by terms in the contract. In such circumstances the law of restitution cannot be used to
subvert the law of contract. This is particularly important in respect of

---

[96] *Ibid*, p. 744.   [97] [1941] AC 1.
[98] [1989] 1 WLR 912. This aspect of the case did not involve Rover International Ltd.
which had entered into a pre-incorporation contract. See p. 392 below.

the recovery of advance payments by the contract-breaker, because there may be a number of different reasons why the contract-breaker made these payments. In particular, a crucial distinction needs to be made between an advance payment, on the one hand, and a non-refundable deposit or payment of a sum which is forfeit if the plaintiff breaches the contract, on the other hand. Where the payment constitutes an advance payment of the purchase price it can be recovered on the ground of total failure of consideration if the plaintiff did not receive any benefit pursuant to the contract.[99] However, if the payment is characterised as a deposit then it cannot be recovered on the ground of total failure of consideration simply because the purpose of such a payment is to operate as security for the plaintiff performing the contract.[100] In other words, the deposit operates by allocating to the plaintiff the risk of the contract not being performed and, if the contract is not performed because of the plaintiff's breach, then, at least as a general rule, he or she cannot resort to the law of restitution to subvert this contractual allocation of risk.[101]

This distinction between advance payments and deposits was recognised in *Howe* v. *Smith*[102] where the plaintiff had paid a sum of money to the defendant and, the plaintiff having breached the contract, it was held that he was not able to recover the payment because it was a deposit. Fry LJ defined a deposit as an 'earnest to bind the bargain so entered into [which] creates by the fear of its forfeiture a motive in the payer to perform the rest of the contract'.[103] Whether a particular payment is a deposit or simply a part payment depends on the construction of the contract.[104]

The only[105] exception to the general rule that deposits are not recoverable by the contract-breaker arises where the deposit is of such an excessive amount that it is deemed to be a penalty. Equity will intervene to relieve the defendant against the consequences of forfeiture of a penalty, at least where it can be shown that the defendant has acted unconscionably.[106] Although Birks has argued that the equitable rules relating

---

[99] *Palmer* v. *Temple* (1839) 9 Ad. and E 508; 112 ER 1304. See also *Mayson* v. *Clouet* [1924] AC 980; *McDonald* v. *Dennys Lascelles* (1933) 48 CLR 457; and *Dies* v. *British and International Mining and Finance Co. Ltd.* [1939] 1 KB 724.

[100] *Howe* v. *Smith* (1884) 27 Ch.D 89; *Monnickendam* v. *Leanse* (1923) 39 TLR 445.

[101] The deposit is recoverable if the contract is not performed because of the defendant's breach. See p. 349 above.

[102] (1884) 27 Ch.D 89.   [103] *Ibid*, p. 101.

[104] *Palmer* v. *Temple* (1839) 9 Ad. and E 508; 112 ER 1304.

[105] Although the plaintiff in *Chillingworth* v. *Esche* [1924] 1 Ch. 97 recovered a deposit from the defendant, this was because the payment was made 'subject to contract' and, since no contract was ever signed, the plaintiff who sought repayment was not in breach of any contract. Consequently, the advance payment was not a true deposit since it was 'an anticipatory payment intended only to fulfil the ordinary purpose of a deposit if and when the contemplated agreement should be arrived at' (Sargant LJ at p. 115).

[106] *Stockloser* v. *Johnson* [1954] 1 QB 476; *Galbraith* v. *Mildenhall Estates* [1965] 2 QB 478.

to relief against forfeiture fall within the law of restitution,[107] the better view is that it is a contractual doctrine which simply operates to strike out particular clauses in the contract and so it does not constitute a ground of restitution in its own right.[108] The effect of this is that, even where a forfeiture clause has been struck out as penal, if the plaintiff wishes to recover the payment he or she must still base the restitutionary claim on one of the recognised grounds of restitution, such as total failure of consideration.

(2) Restitution of non-money benefits

Where the contract-breaker wishes to bring a restitutionary claim in respect of non-money benefits which have been received by the defendant, total failure of consideration should again be available as a ground of restitution. The courts have, however, been reluctant to allow restitution in such circumstances. Such reluctance is unnecessary since, for reasons of symmetry, the recognised grounds of restitution should be applicable regardless of the type of benefit which had been received by the defendant.[109]

That the contract-breaker may have a restitutionary claim against the innocent party in respect of benefits in kind was recognised *obiter* by some members of the House of Lords in *Miles* v. *Wakefield Metropolitan District Council*.[110] In this case the plaintiff registrar refused to conduct marriage ceremonies on Saturday mornings in breach of contract, pursuant to an industrial dispute. The House of Lords decided that the plaintiff's employer was entitled to deduct salary in respect of the period when the plaintiff refused to work. Lords Brightman and Templeman went on to consider what the position would have been if the industrial action had taken the form of a 'go slow'. Because the plaintiff would then have been working in a manner which was designed to harm the employer it would not have been obliged to pay the plaintiff under the contract. But the judges suggested that the plaintiff would have been entitled to a *quantum meruit* in respect of the work which had been accepted by the employer.[111] Whilst the recognition of a *quantum meruit* claim in favour of the contract-breaker is to be welcomed, it is in fact misguided in the circumstances of an industrial dispute which takes the form of a 'go-slow', simply because the contract will not have been terminated and fundamental principles of the law of restitution deny restitutionary remedies founded on total failure of consideration where the contract

---

[107] Birks, *An Introduction to the Law of Restitution*, at p. 214, argues that the ground of restitution might be inequality.

[108] See Burrows, *The Law of Restitution*, p. 273.   [109] See p. 126 above.

[110] [1987] AC 539.   [111] *Ibid*, p. 553 (Lord Brightman), p. 661 (Lord Templeman).

still operates.[112] Despite this, the case remains important because two members of the House of Lords were prepared to accept that a contract-breaker could bring a restitutionary claim in respect of non-money benefits. Although the judges did not identify the relevant ground of restitution, it is clear that total failure of consideration would have been available if the plaintiff had not been paid anything for the work which he or she had done.

The plaintiff's restitutionary claim to non-money benefits may be modified or excluded by contract. This is illustrated by *Sumpter* v. *Hedges*[113] where the plaintiff had contracted to construct a number of buildings on the defendant's land for the payment of a lump sum. The plaintiff completed over half of the work which he had agreed to do,[114] but he was unable to finish because he ran out of money. The defendant accepted the plaintiff's repudiatory breach and the contract was discharged. The defendant completed the building himself, using the materials which the plaintiff had left behind. The plaintiff then sought to recover the value of the work which he had done and the value of materials which had been left behind. The plaintiff's claim succeeded in respect of the materials which had been used by the defendant, but he failed to recover the value of his services. There were two reasons for this decision, one contractual and one restitutionary. The contractual reason was that, because the parties had agreed that the payment would be a lump sum, the contract was an entire contract, so the defendant was not liable to pay the plaintiff for his work under the contract until the work had been completed. The other reason was that the law of restitution could not assist the plaintiff because it was held that for the plaintiff to bring a *quantum meruit* claim it was necessary to identify a fresh contract to pay and the defendant had not done anything from which a fresh contract could be implied.[115]

This decision might therefore be treated as explicable because of the court's reliance on the now discredited implied contract theory. Now that theory has been rejected it may be thought that there is no bar to allowing a restitutionary claim to succeed in such circumstances. *Sumpter* v. *Hedges* was, however, followed in *Bolton* v. *Mahadeva*[116]

---

[112] See Lord Bridge at *ibid*, p. 552.

[113] [1898] 1 QB 673. See also *Munro* v. *Butt* (1858) 8 E and B 738; 120 ER 275 and *Boston Deep Sea Fishing and Ice Co.* v. *Ansell* (1888) 39 Ch.D 339.

[114] The contract price was £565 and the plaintiff had done work which was valued at £333.

[115] In *Boston Deep Sea Fishing and Ice Co.* v. *Ansell* (1888) 39 Ch.D 339, 365 Bowen LJ, held that the contract-breaker was not able to claim a *quantum meruit* because it could not rely on its own wrongful act in breaching the contract. But a contract-breaker can recover money which was paid under the contract, so why should the fact of breach prevent a contract-breaker from claiming a *quantum meruit*?

[116] [1972] 1 WLR 1009.

which was decided after the rejection of the implied contract theory. In *Bolton* v. *Mahadeva* the plaintiff agreed to install a central heating system into the defendant's home but, in breach of contract, he installed a system which did not heat adequately and gave out fumes. It was held that the plaintiff was not entitled to recover any part of the contract price in respect of the goods supplied and the work done, even though the cost of remedying the defect was much less than the original contract price, being £174 whereas the contract price was £560. But again the plaintiff had entered into an entire contract.

It appears that in both of these cases the defendant was unjustly enriched at the plaintiff's expense, since each defendant received part of the benefit which had been requested, namely the building and installation of the central heating system respectively, and there had been a total failure of consideration since neither plaintiff had been paid for the work which he had done.[117] Despite this the result in each case is consistent with general principles of the law of restitution, since restitutionary remedies will not be awarded if they will subvert the law of contract. The contracts in both *Sumpter* v. *Hedges* and *Bolton* v. *Mahadeva* were entire contracts, whereby the defendant is not liable to pay the plaintiff until the work has been completed. The effect of this is that the risk of the plaintiff failing to complete the contract is placed squarely on him or her. Where the risk of failure has been allocated to the plaintiff by the contract it is not for the law of restitution to subvert this allocation. Consequently, whenever a contract is an entire contract it should be presumed that the plaintiff bears the risk of non-completion. This presumption will however be rebutted in three situations where it is not equitable for the defendant to rely on the entire contracts rule to prevent the plaintiff from being paid for the work which he or she has done.

(1) Where the contract has been substantially performed then it would be inequitable for the defendant to argue that the contract has not been completely performed so that he or she is not obliged to pay for the work which was done. In such circumstances the contract-breaker can sue on the contract and the innocent party will be able to bring a counterclaim for damages to the extent that the contract-breaker's actual performance fails to comply with the performance which he or she contracted to provide. This is illustrated by *Hoenig* v. *Isaacs*[118] where the plaintiff agreed to decorate and furnish the defendant's flat for the payment of a lump sum of £750. However, when the defendant inspected the plaintiff's work he

---

[117] Though it seems that the plaintiff in *Sumpter* v. *Hedges* had received some money from the defendant. If so, it would not be possible to conclude that the consideration had totally failed, unless the payment could be apportioned because, for example, it related to the supply of certain materials rather than the provision of the plaintiff's services.

[118] [1952] 2 All ER 176. See also *H. Dakin and Co. Ltd.* v. *Lea* [1916] 1 KB 566.

discovered a number of defects which would have cost just over £55 to remedy. It was held that the plaintiff had substantially performed the contract[119] and so the defendant was liable to pay the plaintiff the contract price subject to a deduction in respect of the cost of making good the defects.

Usually, where the contract-breaker has substantially, but not completely, performed the contract, the breach will not be sufficiently serious to constitute a repudiatory breach, so the plaintiff will be able to sue on the contract rather than bring a claim in restitution. However, in certain circumstances, such as where the contract-breaker is a shipowner who breached a contract by deviating from the agreed route, the very fact of deviation will be treated as a sufficiently serious breach to enable the innocent party to accept the repudiation. In such a case the contract-breaker should be able to bring a restitutionary claim in respect of carrying the cargo for the defendant if the contract was substantially performed. That such a plaintiff would have a restitutionary claim in such circumstances was tentatively accepted by some members of the House of Lords in *Hain SS Co. Ltd.* v. *Tate and Lyle Ltd.*[120]

(2) The defendant may be considered to have been benefited by the plaintiff's part-performance, despite the fact that the work had been provided under an entire contract, if the defendant had freely accepted what the plaintiff had done once the contract had been discharged.[121] The effect of such free acceptance is either that the defendant waives the requirement that the contract must be substantially performed before he or she is obliged to pay the plaintiff or that the defendant is estopped from arguing that the contract was an entire contract.[122] That the defendant is liable to the plaintiff where he or she freely accepted the part performance is illustrated by *Hoenig* v. *Isaacs*[123] where it was held that, since the defendant could have rejected the defective furniture which had been supplied rather than use it, he was prevented from arguing that he was not liable to pay for it on the ground that it was defective.[124] Similarly, by virtue of section 30(1) of the Sale of Goods Act 1979, where the seller of goods has not delivered all the goods which he or she had agreed to supply, the purchaser has an option to reject what has been

---

[119] Although Somervell LJ did say, at p. 179, that the case was close to the borderline of what constitutes substantial performance.

[120] [1936] 3 All ER 597, p. 603 (Lord Atkin), p. 612 (Lord Wright MR), p. 616 (Lord Maugham). The shipowner's restitutionary claim did not arise on the facts of the case because it was held that the cargo owner had waived the breach arising from the deviation from the agreed route.

[121] See, for example, *Steele* v. *Tardiani* (1946) 72 CLR 386, 405 (Dixon J).

[122] See *Miles* v. *Wakefield Metropolitan District Council* [1987] AC 539, 553 (Lord Brightman).

[123] [1952] 2 All ER 176.   [124] See Somervell LJ, *ibid* at pp. 179–80.

delivered, but if the purchaser accepts the goods then he or she must pay for them at the contract rate.

But if free acceptance of the plaintiff's part performance prevents the defendant from relying on the fact that the contract was entire, why did this not enable the plaintiff to obtain restitution in *Sumpter* v. *Hedges* and *Bolton* v. *Mahadeva*? This was because the defendant will be considered to have freely accepted a benefit only if he or she had a free choice whether or not to accept what the plaintiff had provided. In *Hoenig* v. *Isaacs* the defendant did not have to accept the furniture which was supplied by the plaintiff, but in *Sumpter* v. *Hedges*, where the plaintiff had commenced work on the defendant's land, the defendant had no choice but to complete the building, since if the building was left in an uncompleted state it would be a nuisance to the land.[125] Similarly, in *Bolton* v. *Mahadeva* the plaintiff had installed the central heating system in the defendant's house. Again, the defendant had no choice but to accept the system which constituted a fixture and could not have been removed easily.

(3) The defendant will also be prevented from relying on the fact that the contract was an entire contract where he or she was in breach and prevented the plaintiff from performing it.[126]

Even though the entire contracts rule is subject to a number of exceptions, it is still capable of producing unjust results. The denial of restitution in cases such as *Bolton* v. *Mahadeva* means that the defendant obtains the benefit of the plaintiff's part-performance without being obliged to pay anything for it. Although this may simply be the effect of the parties' agreeing that the contract be an entire contract, in many cases the presumption that the plaintiff should bear the risk of loss may be unrealistic, particularly because the parties may be unaware of the consequences of the contract being made entire. Where the parties did not intend to allocate the risk in this way there is no reason why the plaintiff should be prevented from obtaining restitution in respect of goods or services which have been received by the defendant under the contract, even though the contract has not been fully performed. It is for this reason that a recommendation of the Law Commission[127] should be adopted, namely that the contract-breaker who partly performed a contract should be entitled to recover the value of the work provided, even if the contract was entire. The Law Commission proposed that the

---

[125] [1898] 1 QB 673, 676 (Collins LJ). See also *Munro* v. *Butt* (1858) 8 E and B 738; 120 ER 275.

[126] *Munro* v. *Butt* (1858) 8 E and B 738; 120 ER 275; *Hoenig* v. *Isaacs* [1952] 2 All ER 176, 181 (Denning LJ). See also *Appleby* v. *Myers* (1867) LR 2 CP 651.

[127] 'Pecuniary Restitution on Breach of Contract' (Law Com. No. 121, 1983). See Burrows, 'Law Commission Report on Pecuniary Restitution on Breach of Contract' (1984) 47 *MLR* 76.

valuation of the work should be subject both to a *pro rata* contract price ceiling and to the innocent party's right to a set off or to counterclaim for damages in respect of the plaintiff failing to complete the contract. Also, consistent with the general principles relating to the restitutionary action founded on total failure of consideration, the contract-breaker would not be able to obtain restitution unless the contract had been discharged. Finally, the Law Commission recommended that the parties should be able to exclude the right to restitution in the contract itself. The effect of this reform would be that a contract-breaker could obtain a restitutionary remedy regardless of the fact that the contract was an entire contract and had not been fully performed. This would not involve the law of restitution subverting the law of contract since it would be possible to exclude the restitutionary claim in the contract itself. What this really means is that the imposition of risk of failure could only be placed on the plaintiff expressly and not by presumption. This would be a highly desirable reform.

(g) Anticipated and incomplete contracts[128]

Where the plaintiff and the defendant are negotiating a contract and, in the expectation that the contract will be forthcoming, the plaintiff incurs expenditure then, if no contract is made either expressly or impliedly, clearly the plaintiff has no contractual remedy against the defendant, but he or she may be able to bring a restitutionary claim. Similarly, where the plaintiff transfers a benefit to the defendant pursuant to a contract which turns out to be incomplete and so invalid, a restitutionary claim may be available.

This has proved to be a particularly controversial area of the law of restitution, primarily because of the care which must be taken in determining the boundaries between contractual and restitutionary claims. It is vital to ensure that the law of restitution does not subvert the law of contract. Consequently, if it is possible to imply a contract between the parties then the plaintiff should sue on the contract and not in restitution.[129] The danger, however, is that a contract is implied too readily in these anticipated and incomplete contract cases. This makes a mockery

---

[128] For an extensive survey of the law and the issues arising see McKendrick, 'Work Done in Anticipation of a Contract Which does not Materialise' in R*estitution: Past, Present and Future* (ed. Cornish, Nolan, O'Sullivan and Virgo), Chapter 11.

[129] *Turriff Construction Ltd.* v. *Regalia Knitting Mills Ltd.* [1972] EGD 257. This may be the preferable explanation of *Way* v. *Latilla* [1937] 3 All ER 759. See Hedley, 'Work Done in Anticipation of a Contract Which does not Materialise: A Response' in *Restitution: Past, Present and Future* (ed. Cornish, Nolan, O'Sullivan and Virgo), Chapter 12, who considers that liability in these cases should simply turn on whether or not there was an agreement to pay for the work done.

of the law through the introduction of fictional contracts. Consequently, if the facts of the case are such that it is not possible to imply a contract then it is appropriate to consider whether the plaintiff can bring a restitutionary claim instead. But it is also vital to ensure that, if the plaintiff can be considered to have taken the risk that no contract would be made, then the plaintiff's claim should fail. This is an area of the law where the principle that restitution is not available to a volunteer is of crucial importance.[130]

(i) Establishing unjust enrichment

One of the biggest difficulties in establishing a restitutionary claim where the plaintiff has acted in respect of a contract which is anticipated or incomplete relates to proving that the defendant had obtained an enrichment, as has previously been examined.[131] Typically, it will be possible to show that the defendant was enriched either where he or she had received an objective benefit and was prevented from relying on the subjective devaluation principle because of free acceptance,[132] or, in those cases where an objective benefit has not been received, where the defendant was estopped from denying this.[133] In some cases the plaintiff's restitutionary claim will fail simply because it cannot be shown that he or she had been enriched.[134]

Once the question of the defendant's enrichment has been established, the plaintiff's restitutionary claim depends on the identification of a ground of restitution. This has never been specifically examined in the cases, but in virtually every case where restitution has been awarded in the context of anticipated and incomplete contracts the ground of restitution could have been total failure of consideration, since the plaintiff acted in the expectation that he or she would receive a benefit and no benefit was received.

(ii) Establishing total failure of consideration[135]

Where the plaintiff's claim arises from an anticipated contract failing to materialise or a contract being incomplete, the condition on which the transfer of the benefit to the defendant will be contingent is obviously not the performance of a contractual promise, but the defendant may

---

[130] See pp. 39–40 above. [131] See pp. 89–91 above.

[132] See, for example, *William Lacey (Hounslow) Ltd.* v. *Davis* [1957] 1 WLR 932 and *British Steel Corporation* v. *Cleveland Bridge and Engineering Co.* [1984] 1 All ER 504.

[133] See, for example, *Brewer Street Investments Ltd.* v. *Barclays Woollen Co. Ltd.* [1954] 1 QB 428.

[134] See, for example, *Jennings and Chapman Ltd.* v. *Woodman Matthews and Co.* [1952] 2 TLR 409. See also *Regalian Properties plc.* v. *London Docklands Development Corporation* [1995] 1 WLR 212, discussed at p. 363 below.

[135] See Burrows, 'Free Acceptance and the Law of Restitution' (1988) 104 *LQR* 576, 596.

still have promised to transfer a benefit to the plaintiff or the condition may be a non-promissory contingency. Where the defendant has promised a benefit to the plaintiff in return for the receipt of the enrichment, the consideration will only be considered to have failed totally where the defendant is no longer able and willing to perform the promise, typically because of the defendant's refusal to reimburse the plaintiff for the expenditure which has been incurred.[136] This is illustrated by *William Lacey (Hounslow) Ltd.* v. *Davis*[137] where the defendant wished to have his premises rebuilt. The plaintiff submitted an estimate for the work and, although the parties did not enter into a binding contract, the defendant led the plaintiff to believe that a contract would be made. The defendant asked the plaintiff to incur expenditure for a purpose which did not relate to the performance of the anticipated contract, and the plaintiff agreed to do this work in the belief that it would be recompensed out of the profit which it would make under the contract once it was made. When no contract was made the plaintiff successfully brought a *quantum meruit* claim to recover the reasonable value of the services which had clearly benefited the defendant.[138] Although the ground of restitution was not clearly identified in the case, the trial judge appeared to suggest that the ground was mistake. But this is an unsatisfactory explanation. The plaintiff had not made any mistake as to any existing facts; rather it had made a misprediction as to what would happen in the future, and this is not a ground of restitution.[139] Surely the preferable explanation for the success of the restitutionary claim was that the consideration had failed totally, since the condition on which the plaintiff's expenditure was conditional was that it would be reimbursed under the contract and, when no contract was made, the consideration for the plaintiff's expenditure failed totally.

Similarly, in *British Steel Corporation* v. *Cleveland Bridge and Engineering Co. Ltd.*[140] the defendant wanted the plaintiff to supply steel nodes and, after obtaining an estimated price from the plaintiff, it sent the plaintiff a letter of intent to the effect that it intended to enter into a contract with the plaintiff on the defendant's standard terms and requested that the plaintiff commence work on the nodes pending the issue of the contract. No such contract was ever made because the parties failed to agree terms. The plaintiff delivered to the defendant all but one of the steel nodes which the defendant wanted. The defendant

[136] See pp. 331–2 above.

[137] [1957] 1 All ER 932. See also *Sabemo Pty. Ltd.* v. *North Sydney Municipal Council* [1977] 2 NSWLR 880; *Marston Construction Co. Ltd.* v. *Kigass Ltd.* (1989) 15 Con. LR 116; and *David Michael Lusty* v. *Finsbury Securities Ltd.* (1991) 58 BLR 66.

[138] As was recognised by Rattee J in *Regalian Properties plc.* v. *London Docklands Development Corporation* [1995] 1 WLR 212, 225.

[139] See pp. 140–1.   [140] [1984] 1 All ER 504.

refused to pay for them on the ground that they had been delivered late and out of sequence. The plaintiff then sued for the reasonable value of the nodes by a *quantum meruit* and succeeded. It was clear that the defendant had received a valuable benefit.[141] Even though the trial judge, Robert Goff J, did not identify a specific ground of restitution in this case, surely it was total failure of consideration since the plaintiff had not received anything for the work it had done and the nodes it had supplied.

(iii) Agreements which are subject to contract

The consideration may also take the form of a non-promissory contingency, but only if it had been communicated to the defendant, for otherwise the plaintiff will be considered to be acting as a volunteer and will have taken the risk that the contract might not be made. The best example of a case involving a non-promissory contingency is where the plaintiff transfers a benefit to the defendant pursuant to an agreement which is 'subject to contract'. In such a case the transfer of the benefit is conditional on the contract being made and, if no contract materialises, restitution will lie even if the reason for the contract failing to materialise is the refusal of the plaintiff to sign the agreement.[142]

However, in *Regalian Properties plc.* v. *London Docklands Development Corporation*[143] restitution was denied to a plaintiff who had incurred expenditure after entering into an agreement which was subject to contract. In *Regalian* the plaintiff had entered into an agreement with the defendant for the development of land. This agreement was expressly made subject to contract. The defendant requested the plaintiff to obtain designs from architects and encouraged it to incur other preliminary expenditure amounting to almost £3 million so that the plaintiff was in a position to obtain the building lease from the defendant and so that it could perform the contract once it was obtained. Eventually, because of the fall in property prices, no contract was ever made, but the plaintiff sought reimbursement from the defendant. The trial judge held that the plaintiff's claim failed because, as the agreement was subject to contract, the parties were free to withdraw at any time and so the expenditure which was incurred in anticipation of the contract had been incurred at the plaintiff's risk. Whilst the judge was correct to reject the plaintiff's restitutionary claim, the reasons given for his conclusion are not satisfactory, particularly because of the inconsistency with *Chillingworth* v. *Esche*, which was not cited, where the plaintiff did

---

[141] The fact that the nodes had been delivered out of sequence relates to the question of valuation rather than whether or not the delivery of the nodes constituted a valuable benefit. See p. 104 above.

[142] See *Chillingworth* v. *Esche* [1924] 1 Ch. 97.   [143] [1995] 1 WLR 212.

obtain restitution even though the agreement was 'subject to contract'. In fact, *Regalian* is easily distinguishable from *Chillingworth* v. *Esche*, for in that case the plaintiff had paid money to the defendant, so there was an obvious enrichment. In *Regalian*, although the plaintiff had incurred expenditure in preparation for the performance of the contract, this did not benefit the defendant in any way, as was recognised by the trial judge,[144] because the expenditure was incurred to place the plaintiff in a position to obtain and perform the expected contract. If the question of enrichment is put to one side, it was possible to conclude that there had been a total failure of consideration, since the condition on which the plaintiff's expenditure was contingent was the making of a contract, and, since the agreement was expressly made subject to contract, this was a condition of which the defendant was aware. But without any enrichment, the fact that the consideration had failed totally was irrelevant.

Presumably, therefore, if the defendant in *Regalian* had received an enrichment the plaintiff's restitutionary claim would have succeeded, because the case would then appear to be indistinguishable from *Chillingworth* v. *Esche*. But the trial judge in *Regalian* emphasised that the plaintiff's restitutionary claim failed specifically because the agreement was subject to contract and so the plaintiff had incurred the expenditure at its own risk. If this is correct, why was the fact that the agreement was 'subject to contract' in *Chillingworth* considered to be irrelevant, when it was treated as barring the plaintiff's claim in *Regalian*? The only possible explanation for this is that in *Regalian* the fact that the agreement was 'subject to contract' excluded a restitutionary claim. In other words, the phrase 'subject to contract' allocated the risk that no contract would ever be made to the plaintiff. This was indeed recognised by the trial judge:

Each party to such negotiations must be taken to know (as in my judgment Regalian did in the present case) that pending the conclusion of a binding contract any cost incurred by him in preparation for the intended contract will be incurred at his own risk, in the sense that he will have no recompense for those costs if no contract results.[145]

The fact that the negotiations were made 'subject to contract' should only be considered to be relevant, however, if it really can be said that the clause is intended to allocate the risk of no contract being made. If this was indeed the proper interpretation of the facts in *Regalian*, whereas *Chillingworth* v. *Esche* can legitimately be regarded as a case in which there was no intention to allocate the risk of the contract not being made, then the two cases are clearly distinguishable. The different contexts of the two cases suggest that such a distinction can be drawn. *Chillingworth*

---

[144] [1995] 1 WLR 212, 225.   [145] [1995] 1 WLR 212, 231.

v. *Esche* involved the sale of land where agreements are automatically made subject to contract, so it is not possible to assume that the parties have deliberately allocated the risk of no contract being made. In *Regalian*, however, there was no practice of making such agreements subject to contract, so the fact that this is what occurred suggests that there was a deliberate decision to allocate the risk of no contract being made. If this explanation is correct it will mean that the particular context of the agreement will always need to be carefully considered when determining the consequences of the agreement being made subject to contract.

(iv) Introducing a fault requirement

Some of the cases involving benefits transferred pursuant to anticipated contracts which fail to materialise suggest that an alternative approach can be adopted, namely that the award of a restitutionary remedy depends on the relative fault of the parties. This was recognised in *Brewer Street Investments Ltd.* v. *Barclays Woollen Co. Ltd.*[146] where the plaintiff and the defendant had entered into negotiations for the lease of the plaintiff's premises by the defendant. After an agreement was made subject to contract the defendant requested the plaintiff to make certain alterations to the premises. No final agreement was made and the plaintiff sought to recover the costs of the work from the defendant. It was held that, since no final agreement had been made due to the fault of the defendant, the plaintiff's restitutionary claim succeeded.[147]

This principle of fault was also relied on by Sheppard J in the Australian case of *Sabemo Pty. Ltd.* v. *North Sydney Municipal Council*[148] where he held that the defendant was liable to make restitution to the plaintiff in respect of work done on a contract which was anticipated but did not materialise, because the defendant had deliberately decided not to enter into the agreement.[149] Presumably if the defendant had failed to enter into the agreement in circumstances in which he or she was acting in good faith, such as where the defendant reasonably disagreed with the terms of the proposed agreement, then he or she would not be at fault. Sheppard J contemplated that, if neither party was at fault, then each party would have borne the risk that no agreement might be made so that the expenditure could not be recovered.

---

[146] [1954] 1 QB 428. See also *Jennings and Chapman Ltd.* v. *Woodman Matthews and Co.* [1952] 2 TLR 409.

[147] *Ibid*, p. 438 (Romer LJ). Somervell LJ suggested at p. 434 that if the failure to make a final agreement was not due to the fault of either party then the plaintiff's claim would still have succeeded, but he also acknowledged that if the plaintiff had been at fault then the claim would have failed. Denning LJ did not consider either party to have been at fault.

[148] [1977] 2 NSWLR 880.   [149] *Ibid*, p. 900.

English law does not, in fact, recognise a doctrine of good faith and fair dealing in pre-contractual negotiations,[150] despite the decision of the Court of Appeal in *Brewer Street Investments*, for the orthodox position of English law is that the parties are free to make contracts or not. Nevertheless, the introduction of a principle of good faith bargaining into English law would provide an alternative solution to the problem of plaintiffs who incur expenditure in anticipation of a contract which never materialises.

(v) Alternative claims

In some cases in which the plaintiff has incurred expenditure pursuant to an anticipated or incomplete contract the remedy will not lie within the law of restitution at all, because it is not possible to show that the defendant has been enriched. In such circumstances it may be possible for the plaintiff to identify a collateral contract whereby the defendant agrees that he or she will reimburse the plaintiff for the expenditure which has been incurred.[151] It might even be possible for the plaintiff to sue the defendant in tort. So, for example, if the defendant had said that he or she would make a contract but never intended to do so, he or she could be liable to the plaintiff for misrepresentation.

Alternatively, there is growing evidence that the plaintiff may be able to base his or her claim on promissory estoppel, even though the orthodox approach to estoppel in English law is that it operates as a shield rather than a sword, so that it cannot be used to found a cause of action.[152] Whilst the Privy Council in *Attorney-General of Hong Kong* v. *Humphreys Estate*[153] held that on the facts of that case, where the plaintiff had incurred expenditure in respect of an agreement which was 'subject to contract', the plaintiff could not found an action for reimbursement on estoppel, it was accepted that in certain circumstances the defendant's conduct would mean that he or she would be estopped from denying that the parties had entered into a contract, even where the agreement was 'subject to contract'.[154]

(h) Unenforceable contracts

Where the plaintiff transfers a benefit to the defendant under a contract which is unenforceable he or she cannot recover the value of the benefit under the contract, since this would involve the enforcement of what is

---

[150] *Walford* v. *Miles* [1992] AC 128.
[151] *Turriff Construction Ltd.* v. *Regalia Knitting Mills Ltd.* [1972] EGD 257.
[152] *Combe* v. *Combe* [1951] 2 KB 215.   [153] [1987] AC 114.
[154] See *Salvation Army Trustee Co. Ltd.* v. *West Yorkshire Metropolitan County Council* (1980) 41 P and CR 179 and the decision of the High Court of Australia in *Walton Stores (Interstate) Ltd.* v. *Maher* (1988) 164 CLR 387.

unenforceable. It may, however, be possible to bring a restitutionary claim since, being an independent legal obligation, the award of a restitutionary remedy does not involve enforcement of the contract.[155] A contract may be unenforceable for a number of reasons, but often unenforceability arises as a result of failure to comply with statutory formalities relating to the contract. There used to be a number of statutory formalities in English law, particularly by virtue of the Statute of Frauds 1677. Today, most of these formalities have been removed, but they remain particularly important for contracts involving sale of land.[156] Section 2 of the Law of Property (Miscellaneous Provisions) Act 1989 requires contracts for the sale and other dispositions of land to be in writing and to be accompanied by the signature of, or on behalf of, each party to the contract. Failure to comply with these formalities means that the contract is unenforceable, but not invalid.

Where the plaintiff wishes to obtain restitution of a benefit which has been transferred pursuant to an unenforceable contract, the ground of restitution will typically be total failure of consideration. Although such a restitutionary claim will succeed even though the contract has not been set aside,[157] it must be shown that the defendant is no longer ready, able or willing to perform his or her part of the bargain.[158] This is well illustrated by *Monnickendam* v. *Leanse*[159] where the plaintiff had contracted to buy the defendant's house. The plaintiff paid the defendant a deposit but, because the contract was unenforceable for lack of writing, the plaintiff repudiated the contract and sought to recover the deposit. It was held that, because the defendant remained ready and willing to perform the contract, the plaintiff was unable to recover the deposit. But it was accepted that if the contract had been repudiated by the defendant then the plaintiff would have been able to recover the deposit, since this would have meant that the defendant was no longer willing to perform.[160]

Restitution of benefits which have been transferred pursuant to an unenforceable contract may be ordered regardless of whether the enrichment is money[161] or a non-money benefit,[162] though, as always,

---

[155] As was recognised by the House of Lords in *Westdeutsche Landesbank Girozentrale* v. *Islington LBC* [1996] AC 669.

[156] Note also contracts made with minors which are unenforceable against the minor under the Minors' Contracts Act 1987. Where a minor has transferred a benefit to the defendant under such a contract restitutionary relief may be available, but this is properly characterised as being grounded on the minor's incapacity rather than total failure of consideration. See pp. 416–19 below.

[157] As recognised by Deane J in *Pavey and Matthews Pty. Ltd.* v. *Paul* (1987) 162 CLR 221, 256.

[158] See the discussion of *Thomas* v. *Brown* (1876) 1 QBD 714 at p. 331 above.

[159] (1923) 39 TLR 445.   [160] *Ibid*, p. 447 (Horridge J).   [161] See *ibid*.

[162] See *Scarisbrick* v. *Parkinson* (1869) 20 LT 175 and the decision of the Supreme Court of Canada in *Deglman* v. *Guaranty Trust Co. of Canada and Constantineau* [1954] 3 DLR

where the benefit takes the form of services, there are complex questions to consider relating to the identification and valuation of the enrichment. This is particularly well illustrated by *Pulbrook* v. *Lawes*[163] where the plaintiff had entered into an oral agreement with the defendant for the lease of a house, on condition that certain alterations were made to it. The plaintiff paid to have the drawing room painted in a particular way and to have gas pipes installed. After the alterations had been done, the defendant defaulted and no lease was executed. The plaintiff sought to recover the amount he had spent in altering the house, but he was unable to sue the defendant on the contract because it was unenforceable due to lack of writing. However, the plaintiff successfully brought a claim to recover the reasonable value of the work done. The ground of restitution was specifically held to be akin to that of total failure of consideration, which was established because the plaintiff had incurred the expenditure in the expectation that he would take a lease of the house and no lease had been executed. But the difficulty in analysing this case as involving the reversal of the defendant's unjust enrichment relates to the identification of the benefit, particularly because Blackburn J described the work as 'fanciful painting of no benefit to the house'. Although the courts found that some of the work had been requested by the defendant, and it appears to have been assumed that some of the work was beneficial to the house, it is difficult to consider the defendant to have been benefited by all of the work which had been done.

The most complex issue relating to whether restitution can be awarded where a benefit has been transferred pursuant to an unenforceable contract concerns whether the policy which made the contract unenforceable should prevent the restitutionary claim from succeeding as well. In principle, because the obligation to make restitution is an independent obligation imposed by law and does not arise from any agreement between the parties, the restitutionary obligation should not be affected by the policy of the statute which makes the contract unenforceable. This was recognised by the High Court of Australia in *Pavey and Matthews Pty. Ltd.* v. *Paul*[164] where the plaintiff renovated the defendant's cottage, having made an oral contract to do so. The defendant regarded the price for the work as excessive and, having paid part of the price, refused to pay the balance.[165] The plaintiff was not able to sue the

---

785. *Scott* v. *Pattison* [1923] 2 KB 723 has sometimes been treated as a further example, but in that case the plaintiff recovered remuneration in respect of work he would have done had he not been sick. Since he had not actually done this work it is not possible to treat this aspect of the case as restitutionary, since there was no evidence that the defendant had been enriched.

[163] (1876) 1 QBD 284.   [164] (1987) 162 CLR 221.

[165] This means that it is difficult to identify the ground of restitution which was relied on in this case. Since the plaintiff had been partly paid, the ground of restitution could not be

defendant on the contract to recover the balance because, being an oral contract, it was unenforceable as a result of a statutory provision which required such an agreement to be in writing. The plaintiff therefore brought a restitutionary claim for the reasonable value of its services and succeeded. The High Court specifically recognised that by allowing the plaintiff's claim to succeed it was not contravening the policy of the statute. The statute sought to ensure that the terms of building contracts were in writing and clear so that builders could not make spurious claims against customers. But this policy did not affect the plaintiff's restitutionary claim, because the court was not enforcing the defendant's contractual promise to pay the plaintiff but was enforcing an independent obligation to make restitution, an obligation which was triggered by the fact that the defendant had been unjustly enriched at the plaintiff's expense, and this obligation did not depend in any way on proving the terms of the contract. Although in cases such as *Pavey and Matthews Pty. Ltd.* v. *Paul* the statutory policy which made the contract unenforceable does not affect the plaintiff's right to restitution, great care must always be taken to ensure that the policy of the statute is not undermined by awarding restitution. It is therefore vital to identify the policy of the statute carefully in an attempt to determine why the contract was made unenforceable.

Even though it was decided in *Pavey and Matthews* that the obligation to make restitution was independent of and unaffected by the unenforceable contract, this will not always be the case, since there may be circumstances in which the terms of the contract will be highly relevant to the restitutionary claim. For example, the fact that a contract was made shows that the benefits which were provided by the plaintiff were not intended as a gift and the contract may also assist the court in valuing the benefit which was received by the defendant.[166] Similarly, the contract may need to be referred to where the ground of restitution is total failure of consideration, since the contract will assist in identifying what consideration was expected for the transfer of the benefit by the plaintiff.[167] It should be possible to refer to the contract in any of these circumstances as evidence of the parties' intention, save where the

total failure of consideration, unless the money received could be apportioned. The success of the plaintiff's claim was probably because of partial failure of consideration, although this was not acknowledged, and there are some dicta which suggest that the defendant was required to make restitution because she had freely accepted the benefit: (1986) 162 CLR 221, 228 (Mason and Wilson JJ). Whether free acceptance constitutes a ground of restitution is considered in at pp. 121–4 above.

[166] *Pavey and Matthews Pty. Ltd.* v. *Paul* (1987) 162 CLR 221, 257 (Deane J). See also *Scarisbrick* v. *Parkinson* (1869) 20 LT 175.

[167] *Pavey and Matthews Pty. Ltd.* v. *Paul* (1987) 162 CLR 221, 227 (Mason and Wilson JJ), p. 257 (Deane J).

contract is considered to be particularly unreliable. This is most likely to be the case where the contract was made unenforceable because of a policy to prevent abuse of a weak party by a stronger party. Where the contract is unreliable for this reason then it should not be taken into account for the purposes of establishing the restitutionary claim.

(i) Withdrawal from an illegal transaction[168]

Although the general rule is that a plaintiff who has transferred a benefit to the defendant in respect of an illegal transaction cannot bring a restitutionary claim on the ground of total failure of consideration, because he or she continues to be tainted by the illegality,[169] restitution will be available where the plaintiff can establish that he or she is no longer tainted by the illegality. The easiest way to establish this is by showing that the plaintiff has withdrawn from the illegal transaction. This withdrawal principle, otherwise known as the *locus poenitentiae*, has long been recognised as a ground of restitution in its own right,[170] but careful analysis of the principle suggests that it is, at the very least, closely related to the ground of total failure of consideration and should be considered to be founded on the principle of failure of consideration.

The policy behind the withdrawal principle is to deter the plaintiff from performing the illegal transaction by allowing restitution to be awarded before the plaintiff has become tainted by the illegality. Originally the principle would only be applicable if two conditions were satisfied. First, the plaintiff must have withdrawn from the illegal transaction before it had been wholly or substantially executed.[171] Secondly, the plaintiff must have repented of the illegality.[172] However, the withdrawal principle has recently been radically reinterpreted by the Court of Appeal in *Tribe* v. *Tribe*.[173]

In *Tribe* the plaintiff feared that he would be forced to sell his shares in the family business to meet potential liabilities to creditors. Consequently, he transferred them to his son. The son never paid for the shares and was never intended to pay for them. This transfer was an illegal transaction because the plaintiff's purpose was to defraud his creditors. No creditors were deceived, however, because alternative arrangements were made which prevented the liabilities from arising. Once the risk that the assets would be taken had passed, the plaintiff

---

[168] See Virgo in *The Limits of Restitutionary Claims: A Comparative Analysis* (ed. Swadling) pp. 163–7.

[169] See pp. 346–8 above.

[170] See Merkin, 'Restitution By Withdrawal from Executory Illegal Contracts' (1981) 97 *LQR* 420.

[171] *Taylor* v. *Bowers* (1876) 1 QBD 291; *Kearley* v. *Thompson* (1890) 24 QBD 742.

[172] *Bigos* v. *Bousted* [1951] 1 All ER 92. See also *Alexander* v. *Rayson* [1946] 1 KB 169, 190.

[173] [1996] Ch. 107.

requested his son to return the shares to him, but he refused to do so. Since the equitable presumption of advancement applies in respect of transfers of property from a father to his son,[174] it was presumed that the plaintiff had given the shares to his son. To rebut this presumption the plaintiff needed to show that his purpose was not to give the shares to his son absolutely, rather that the son would hold the shares until the threat from his creditors had passed. But this was an illegal purpose and, for reasons of public policy, such purposes cannot rebut the presumption of advancement. However, the Court of Appeal held that the father had in fact withdrawn from the illegal transaction. Consequently, he ceased to be tainted by the illegality and so was able to plead his true intention in transferring the shares to his son to show that he had never intended to give the shares to him absolutely.[175]

In accepting that the plaintiff could rely on the withdrawal principle, the Court of Appeal held that there were two conditions which needed to be satisfied.

(*a*) *No part of the illegal purpose must have been carried into effect.* This did not bar restitution on the facts of the case because it was assumed that the plaintiff's purpose was to deceive creditors and, since no creditors had been deceived, no part of the father's purpose had been carried into effect. Whether this is correct depends on the identification of what the plaintiff's purpose actually was in transferring the shares to his son. It could just as easily, and perhaps more accurately, have been concluded that the plaintiff's purpose was simply to make it appear that he did not own shares and this purpose had been achieved. But clearly the identification of the plaintiff's purpose can be manipulated to secure what is perceived to be a just result, in the same way that the notion of total failure of consideration is manipulated to secure restitution.[176]

(*b*) *The plaintiff must have withdrawn from the illegal transaction.* It is no longer necessary to show that the plaintiff has repented of the illegality and so it was irrelevant that the father had sought restitution only once it was clear that the purpose of the transaction would never be fulfilled and even though there was no evidence of contrition on his part. The conclusion that the father had withdrawn on the facts of this case means that the test of withdrawal is easily satisfied. Withdrawal does not require a voluntary decision on the part of the plaintiff that he or she will have nothing more to do with the illegal transaction, for if this is the test of withdrawal it is clear that the plaintiff had not satisfied it. Rather, all

---

[174] See pp. 637–8 below.

[175] The withdrawal principle was consequently relied on to enable the father to bring a proprietary restitutionary claim. This aspect of the case is discussed at p. 638 below. Despite this, the case remains good authority on the ambit of the withdrawal principle generally.   [176] See pp. 336–41 above.

the plaintiff had done was to make a claim for restitution of the shares once he had realised that the danger of creditors seizing his assets had passed. Consequently, the so-called requirement of withdrawal is meaningless. It will simply be sufficient that the plaintiff has commenced proceedings for restitution before any part of the illegal purpose has been satisfied.

The reinterpretation of the withdrawal principle in *Tribe* v. *Tribe*, in requiring no part of the illegal purpose to have been fulfilled and liberating it from the requirement of repentance, means that today when the plaintiff's restitutionary claim is founded on this principle it is in fact being founded on the ground of total failure of consideration, where the condition on which the benefit is transferred is the performance of a non-promissory contingency. In the same way that consideration will not have failed totally if any part of the contingency is satisfied, so too restitution will not be available by reference to the withdrawal principle if any part of the illegal purpose is fulfilled.

Will the withdrawal principle only operate where the consideration is, as was the case in *Tribe* v. *Tribe*, a non-promissory contingency or will it also be applicable where the consideration involves the performance of a promise by the defendant? For example, if the plaintiff contracted to buy a car from the defendant and paid the defendant in advance and, for some reason, this transaction was illegal and unenforceable, would the plaintiff be able to recover the money paid if the defendant had refused to deliver the car to him or her? It might be argued that, in such circumstances, the withdrawal principle is inapplicable because there has been no failure of the plaintiff's purpose, since he or she presumably still wants the contract to be performed. But since the withdrawal principle appears to be indistinguishable from the ground of total failure of consideration, and since the consideration has failed totally in this situation, the better view is that the amount of money which the plaintiff paid should be restored. It should be irrelevant that the money was paid pursuant to an illegal transaction, save where the transaction involved the commission of a serious criminal offence.

There is only one qualification to the assertion that the withdrawal principle and the ground of total failure of consideration are identical, and this arises where the consideration involves the performance of a non-contractual promise by the defendant. It has already been seen that generally restitution will only be awarded on the ground of total failure of consideration in such circumstances if it can be shown that the defendant is no longer able, ready and willing to perform the promise. This requirement should not be applied where the performance of the defendant's promise will involve him or her in an illegal act. In such circumstances restitution should lie by virtue of the withdrawal principle even if the defendant remains ready, able and willing to do what he or she had promised, simply because awarding restitution in such circumstances would encourage parties not to perform illegal acts.

The next stage in the development of the law in this area is that the courts should recognise that restitutionary claims will succeed in all cases of total failure of consideration, despite the fact that the plaintiff has participated in an illegal transaction. The only qualification should be that restitution will be denied in those cases where the illegality involves the commission of a serious criminal offence, such that no court would wish to assist the plaintiff on the grounds of public policy.[177] If partial failure of consideration is ever recognised as a general ground of restitution in its own right, it too should be available even where the plaintiff has participated in an illegal transaction.

3. PARTIAL FAILURE OF CONSIDERATION

Although the most common ground of restitution which is founded on the principle of failure of consideration is that of total failure of consideration, and even though that ground of restitution has been interpreted in such a way that effectively restitution is being awarded on the ground of partial failure of consideration, in one particular situation the applicable ground of restitution is specifically partial failure of consideration, namely where the contract has been frustrated.

Where benefits have been transferred in respect of a contract which is later frustrated, the restitutionary regime is, for the most part, governed by the Law Reform (Frustrated Contracts) Act 1943. This statute was enacted in the light of the unsatisfactory nature of the common law regime concerning the consequences of a contract being frustrated. Unfortunately the common law regime still applies to particular types of contracts, including certain contracts for the carriage of goods by sea, contracts of insurance and contracts for the sale of goods where the goods have perished.[178] Where the common law applies the ground of restitution continues to be that of total failure of consideration, whereas under the Law Reform (Frustrated Contracts) Act 1943 the ground of restitution is effectively partial failure of consideration, although this phrase is not used in the statute itself.

---

[177] For further discussion of this limitation see p. 754 below.
[178] Law Reform (Frustrated Contracts) Act 1943, s. 2(5).

(a) The definition of frustration

Whenever a contract is frustrated it is discharged automatically.[179] The law relating to when a contract is frustrated is complex,[180] but the essence of frustration was identified by Lord Radcliffe in *Davis Contractors Ltd.* v. *Fareham Urban District Council*:[181]

frustration occurs whenever the law recognises that without default of either party a contractual obligation has become incapable of being performed because the circumstances in which the performance is called for would render it a thing radically different from that which was undertaken by the contract.

A contract will therefore only be frustrated where its performance would be radically different as a result of some extraneous event or change of circumstances which took place without the fault of either party.[182] Consequently, frustration cannot be self-induced.

(b) Restitution of benefits transferred before a contract is frustrated

Before the different restitutionary regimes are examined, there is one matter of great practical importance which must be emphasised, namely that the question of restitutionary relief following the frustration of a contract rarely reaches the courts. This is illustrated by the fact that, since the enactment of the Law Reform (Frustrated Contracts) Act 1943, only two cases have been reported concerning the interpretation of this Act. This may be because the interpretation of the Act is clear, so there is no need to resort to the courts, but, as will be seen, the interpretation of the Act is certainly not free from difficulty. The better explanation for the scarcity of cases is that parties tend to provide for the consequences of frustration in their contracts by a *force majeure* clause or because disputes arising from frustration tend to be settled by arbitration.[183]

(i) The common law

At one stage the attitude of the common law to restitutionary claims following the frustration of a contract was to reject such claims and to let the loss lie where it fell.[184] However, in *Fibrosa Spolka Akcyjna* v.

---

[179] *J. Lauritzen AS* v. *Wijsmuller BV (The Super Servant Two)* [1990] 1 Lloyd's Rep. 1.

[180] For detailed examination of this question see Treitel, *Frustration and Force Majeure* (London: 1994).

[181] [1956] AC 696, 729.

[182] *J. Lauritzen AS* v. *Wijsmuller BV (The Super Servant Two)* [1990] 1 Lloyd's Rep. 1, 10 (Bingham LJ).

[183] See Stewart and Carter, 'Frustrated Contracts and Statutory Adjustment: The Case for a Reappraisal' (1992) 51 *CLJ* 66, 108.

[184] *Chandler* v. *Webster* [1904] 1 KB 493.

Fairbairn Lawson Combe Barbour Ltd.[185] the House of Lords recognised that money which had been paid pursuant to a contract which was subsequently frustrated could be recovered, but only if the consideration for the payment had totally failed. In the *Fibrosa* case the plaintif had entered into a contract with the defendant for the purchase of machinery. The plaintiff paid one third of the purchase price in advance but the contract was frustrated by the outbreak of the Second World War before any of the machinery had been delivered. It was held that the plaintiff could recover the advance payment because the consideration for that payment had failed totally, and also that the defendant was not able to set off the expenditure which it had incurred in preparing the machines for delivery under the contract.

That restitution will not lie where the consideration had partially failed is illustrated by *Whincup* v *Hughes*,[186] where a father paid a sum of money to have his son apprenticed to a watchmaker for six years. The father paid the watchmaker in advance, but the watchmaker died after one year, frustrating the contract. It was held that the father could not recover the advance payment in respect of the remaining five years because the consideration for the payment had partially failed.

Where the enrichment takes the form of a benefit in kind a restitutionary claim will still succeed at common law only where the consideration for transfer of the benefit has failed totally. This is supported by *Société Franco-Tunisienne d'Armement* v. *Sidermar SpA*[187] where the plaintiff had entered into a contract to carry freight via the Suez Canal. However, the Suez Canal was closed, so the plaintiff carried the freight via the Cape of Good Hope instead. Since this was a fundamentally different route it was held that the closure of the Suez Canal had frustrated the contract. The plaintiff was able to recover the reasonable value of the services provided on a *quantum meruit*. Although the ground of restitution was not identified it was presumably total failure of consideration, since the plaintiff had not been paid for carriage of the freight.

Where the benefit in kind is transferred pursuant to an entire contract, where the defendant is not obliged to pay the plaintiff until the plaintiff has completed his or her side of the bargain, then, if the contract is frustrated before the plaintiff has fully performed, any restitutionary claim will fail. This is illustrated by *Appleby* v. *Myers*[188] where the plaintiff had contracted to erect machinery on the defendant's premises, with the price being paid once the work had been completed. After the plaintiff had completed some of the work, the premises and the machinery which had been installed were destroyed by fire, so frustrating the contract. The

---

[185] [1943] AC 32.   [186] (1871) LR 6 CP 78.   [187] [1961] 2 QB 278.
[188] (1867) LR 2 CP 651. See also *Cutter* v. *Powell* (1795) 6 Term. Rep. 320; 101 ER 573.

plaintiff sued to recover the reasonable value of the work which had been done before the fire, but the claim failed, because the contract was an entire contract. As Blackburn B said:[189]

the plaintiffs having contracted to do an entire work for a specific sum, can recover nothing unless the work be done, or it can be shown that it was the defendant's fault that the work was incomplete, or that there is something to justify the conclusion that the parties have entered into a fresh contract.

(ii) The Law Reform (Frustrated Contracts) Act 1943

The main purpose of the Law Reform (Frustrated Contracts) Act 1943 was to remove the perceived injustice of the common law, particularly the denial of restitution where the consideration had only partially failed. A further injustice of the common law was that, although it was possible for the plaintiff to bring a restitutionary claim following frustration, it was not possible to take into account the expenditure which had been incurred by the defendant.[190] Although the 1943 Act provides a solution to both of these difficulties, it is complicated and uncertain in scope. One reason for this complexity results from the difficulty in identifying the Act's rationale. Whilst it seems tolerably clear that the Act creates a statutory regime which is founded on the reversal of the defendant's unjust enrichment,[191] although no reference to restitution or unjust enrichment is included in the Act,[192] it is equally clear that the Act does not simply operate to ensure that the value of any benefit obtained by the defendant under a contract which is subsequently frustrated is restored to the plaintiff. In addition, the Act seeks to apportion losses arising from the frustrating event between the two parties. The real difficulty in analysing the statutory regime relates to the reconciliation of these two different policies of reversing unjust enrichment and loss apportionment.

There are two key provisions in the Act. The first, section 1(2), applies where the defendant has been enriched by the receipt of money and the second, section 1(3), applies where the enrichment takes some other form. Before either provision can be applied it must be shown that the contract has been discharged for frustration and that the contract was governed by English law.[193]

---

[189] (1867) LR 2 CP 651 p. 659.

[190] As was recognised by Viscount Simon LC in the *Fibrosa* case [1943] AC 32, 49.

[191] *BP Exploration Co. (Libya) Ltd.* v. *Hunt (No. 2)* [1979] 1 WLR 783, 799 (Robert Goff J). Cp. Haycroft and Waksman, 'Restitution and Frustration' [1984] JBL 207, 225 who argue that the function of the Act is to apportion losses rather than to reverse unjust enrichment.

[192] Lawton LJ in *BP Exploration Co. (Libya) Ltd.* v. *Hunt (No. 2)* [1981] 1 WLR 232, 243 consequently stated that the court was not assisted in its interpretation of the Act by words which did not appear in the statute.

[193] Law Reform (Frustrated Contracts) Act 1943, s. 1(1).

(1) Restitution of money

Where the plaintiff has paid money to another party to the contract before the contract was frustrated he or she is able to recover such sums 'as money received by [the other party] for the use of' the plaintiff.[194] The effect of this provision is that the plaintiff is given a statutory right to obtain restitution from the defendant. Although the plaintiff does not need to identify specifically the elements of an unjust enrichment action, the statutory right of recovery is consistent with a restitutionary claim to reverse the defendant's unjust enrichment. It is crucial to the statutory claim that the defendant has received money, an incontrovertible benefit, from the plaintiff, so the defendant must have been enriched at the plaintiff's expense. The ground of restitution can be said to be partial failure of consideration, since the right of recovery exists even though the plaintiff has received some benefit under the contract. This means that if a case such as *Whincup* v. *Hughes*[195] was decided today, the father would be able to recover the advance payment even though his son had only been apprenticed for a year.

The plaintiff is able to recover the payment from the defendant under section 1(2) even though this means that the plaintiff will be escaping from a bad bargain, in that, had the contract not been frustrated, the plaintiff would have suffered a loss.[196] The fact that the contract was a bad bargain ceases to be relevant, because the effect of frustration is to discharge the contract so it no longer affects the restitutionary claim.[197]

Although section 1(2) appears to create a wide right of recovery it is subject to a number of limitations:

(1) The plaintiff will only be able to recover money which was paid before the contract was discharged for frustration. However, if the plaintiff had paid the defendant after discharge he or she would be able to obtain restitution on the ground of mistake.[198]
(2) The plaintiff will only be able to rely on section 1(2) where he or she has paid money to somebody who is party to the contract which was frustrated.
(3) It is possible for the parties to contract out of the statutory regime,[199] although the courts will carefully construe the contract to ensure that

---

[194] *Ibid*, s. 1(2). The provision also states that the plaintiff will cease to be liable to pay money to the defendant under the discharged contract.
[195] (1871) LR 6 CP 78.
[196] *BP Exploration Co. (Libya) Ltd.* v. *Hunt (No. 2)* [1979] 1 WLR 783, 800 (Robert Goff J).
[197] A similar rule applies where a contract is discharged for breach. See pp. 350–2 above.
[198] See *Oom* v. *Bruce* (1810) 12 East 225; 104 ER 87.
[199] Law Reform (Frustrated Contracts) Act 1943, s. 2(3).

the parties really did intend to exclude the statutory scheme following the frustration of the contract.[200]

The plaintiff's right to restitution is qualified by the proviso to section
1(2). The effect of this is that, if the defendant incurred expenses in or for
the purpose of the performance of the contract[201] before the contract
was discharged, then the court has a discretion to allow the defendant to
retain all or part of what he or she received from the plaintiff, if it considers it to be just to do so having considered all the circumstances of the
case. Similarly, if the plaintiff was liable to pay the defendant before the
contract was frustrated, the defendant may recover all or some of this
amount in respect of the expenditure which he or she incurred. The burden of proving that the proviso is applicable is on the defendant.[202] The
amount which the defendant is allowed to retain or to recover from the
plaintiff is limited in two ways. First, it must not exceed the expenses
which the defendant has actually incurred. Secondly, it is limited to the
amount which the defendant has received from the plaintiff or which the
plaintiff was liable to pay to the defendant. So, for example, if the plaintiff paid £10,000 to the defendant and was liable to pay a further £5,000 to
the defendant before the contract was frustrated, and the defendant
incurred expenditure of £18,000 in performan e of the contract, then the
defendant will, subject to the exercise of the court's discretion, be able to
retain the £10,000 and recover the £5,000, but will be out of pocket in
respect of the remaining £3,000.

The proviso is a very important limitation on the plaintiff's right to
obtain restitution, but it is a limitation which does not appear to be consistent with the analysis of section 1(2) as a provision which creates a
statutory right of restitution to reverse the defendant's unjust enrichment. In *BP* v. *Hunt*[203] Robert Goff J tried to rationalise the proviso in
restitutionary terms by concluding that it embodied a statutory form of
the defence of change of position. But this conclusion is very difficult to
accept, particularly in the light of the restrictive interpretation of that
defence at common law, where the defendant will be considered to have
changed his or her position only where the defendant incurred expenditure after he or she had received a benefit from the plaintiff, and where
the expenditure was incurred in reliance on the validity of the receipt of
that benefit. The expenditure must also be extraordinary.[204] The proviso
to section 1(2), on the other hand, applies even where the expenditure
was incurred before the defendant received any payment from the plain-

---

[200] *BP Exploration Co. (Libya) Ltd.* v. *Hunt (No. 2)* [1979] 1 WLR 783, 829 (Robert Goff J).
[201] This expenditure is also deemed to include reasonable sums in respect of overhead
expenses or work or services personally performed by the defendant: s. 1(4).
[202] *Gamerco SA* v. *ICM/Fair Warning (Agency) Ltd.* [1995] 1 WLR 1226, 1235 (Garland J).
[203] [1979] 1 WLR 783, 800.				[204] See Chapter 24.

tiff, and it is not necessary to show that the expenditure was extraordinary. It is therefore not possible to say that the proviso imports a defence of change of position into section 1(2).

The proviso is, however, subject to a qualification which provides an important clue as to its purpose. According to the proviso expenditure incurred by the defendant will be relevant only if it was incurred in or for the purpose of the performance of the contract. It follows that the purpose of the proviso is simply to enable the defendant to retain or recover those expenses which were incurred in the expectation that the contract would be performed. This is perfectly justifiable. If the plaintiff is able to recover the payment which he or she made to the defendant under the contract, it is surely only fair that the defendant can reclaim his or her expenditure which was incurred with reference to the contract. So the real function of the proviso is to enable the courts to allocate losses which have arisen as a result of the contract being frustrated.

That the proviso should be interpreted in this way was acknowledged by Garland J in the only case to have considered the application of section 1(2). In *Gamerco SA* v. *ICM/Fair Warning (Agency) Ltd.*[205] the plaintiff had agreed to promote a concert in Madrid involving the band 'Guns N'Roses'. Four days before the concert was due to be held the local authority banned the use of the stadium which had been booked because of fears that the venue was not safe. The plaintiff was unable to find an alternative venue and so the concert was cancelled. This constituted frustration of the contract. The plaintiff had paid the defendant $412,500 pursuant to the contract and wished to recover this sum under section 1(2). However, the defendant had incurred expenditure in relation to the performance of the contract of about $50,000 and wanted to retain this amount. Garland J accepted that the court was obliged 'to do justice in a situation which the parties had neither contemplated nor provided for, and to mitigate the possible harshness of allowing all loss to lie where it has fallen'.[206] This did not, however, mean that the court was obliged to apportion the losses equally between the parties or that the defendant could recoup all of his or her expenditure. The court was, rather, to apportion the losses having regard to all of the circumstances of the case. One of the circumstances which the judge considered to be relevant was that the plaintiff had incurred expenditure of $450,000.[207] Consequently, its loss was much greater than that of the defendant, and

---

[205] [1995] 1 WLR 1226. See Clark, 'Frustration, Restitution and the Law Reform (Frustrated Contracts) Act 1943' [1996] *LMCLQ* 170.

[206] [1995] 1 WLR 1226, 1237.

[207] Presumably the plaintiff could not recover this expenditure from the defendant under s. 1(3) because there was no evidence that the defendant had received a valuable benefit by virtue of the expenditure.

so the judge decided not to allow the defendant to retain any amount in respect of the expenditure which it had incurred.

Although the effect of section 1(2) and the proviso is to enable losses to be apportioned between the parties, it is only partially effective in this regard. For example, the defendant will only be able to recover expenditure to the extent that the plaintiff has paid money, or is liable to pay money, to the defendant before the contract was frustrated. Also, if the plaintiff incurred expenditure in or for the performance of the contract, and this did not involve the payment of money to the defendant or the defendant receiving a valuable benefit, then the plaintiff is unable to recoup this benefit specifically from the defendant. Whether section 1(2) should be replaced by a provision which enables the court to apportion all the losses between the parties, as occurs in other countries,[208] will be examined after the operation of section 1(3) is considered.

(2) Restitution of non-money benefits

The restitution of non-money benefits which have been obtained by the defendant before the contract was frustrated is governed by section 1(3) of the 1943 Act. This is a complex provision but essentially it applies whenever the defendant, who was a party to the contract with the plaintiff, has received a valuable benefit other than money by reason of anything which was done by the plaintiff in, or for the purpose of, the performance of the contract. A defendant who has received such a benefit before the contract was frustrated is liable to pay the plaintiff such sum as the court considers to be just having regard to all the circumstances of the case. This sum must not exceed the value of the benefit to the defendant who obtained it. Section 1(3) requires consideration of three separate matters: first, the identification of the valuable benefit; secondly, the valuation of this benefit; thirdly, the assessment of the sum which it would be just for the defendant to pay to the plaintiff. These three matters will be considered in turn and then their application will be examined with reference to the difficult case of *BP Exploration Co. (Libya) Ltd.* v. *Hunt (No. 2)*.[209] But it is first necessary to consider the rationale of section 1(3).

In *BP Exploration Co. (Libya) Ltd.* v. *Hunt (No. 2)*[210] Robert Goff J assumed that the rationale of section 1(3) was to ensure that the defendant was not unjustly enriched as a result of the contract being frustrated. Others have argued that section 1(3) should be interpreted simply as a mechanism to allocate losses between the parties.[211] The better view

---

[208] Such as the British Columbian Frustrated Contracts Act 1974, the New South Wales Frustrated Contracts Act 1978 and the South Australian Frustrated Contracts Act 1988.

[209] [1979] 1 WLR 783.   [210] *Ibid*, p. 799.

[211] See, for example, McKendrick, 'Frustration, Restitution and Loss Apportionment' in *Essays on the Law of Restitution* (ed. Burrows) p. 147.

is that subsection 1(3), like subsection 1(2), exists both to reverse the defendant's unjust enrichment and to allocate losses suffered as a result of the frustration. This is because section 1(3) involves two distinct elements. The first concerns the identification of the valuable benefit, and this constitutes the ceiling on the plaintiff's award. This element is concerned with the reversal of the defendant's unjust enrichment, since it must be shown that the defendant received a valuable benefit at the plaintiff's expense. As with section 1(2) the ground of restitution can be considered to be partial failure of consideration. Once this valuable enrichment has been identified it is then necessary to identify the just sum which should be awarded. This cannot be greater than the value of the benefit received by the defendant but it could be less. This second aspect of section 1(3) is concerned with the allocation of losses arising from the frustration of the contract. Failure to identify this composite approach to section 1(3) has made its interpretation unnecessarily complex.

To establish a claim under section 1(3) the plaintiff must first show that the defendant has received a valuable non-money benefit under the contract. The statute does not define benefit for these purposes, so the common law definition is presumably applicable. This means that we are only concerned with those benefits which have been received by the defendant and that an objective test of benefit should be adopted.[212] However, as section 1(3) specifically recognises, whether this benefit can be considered to be valuable should be determined with reference to whether the recipient valued it. This constitutes a recognition of the principle of subjective devaluation. So, if the defendant received an objective benefit but did not value it at all, he or she should not be considered to have received a valuable benefit. But if this principle of subjective devaluation is applicable under the Act, then it should be possible to defeat the defendant's reliance on that principle by showing that the benefit was incontrovertibly beneficial or that the defendant had freely accepted it.[213] Equally, if he or she has received something to which he or she attaches a value, but which the reasonable person would not regard as valuable, then the defendant should still be regarded as having received a benefit, by virtue of the principle of subjective valuation.[214]

Where the defendant has received goods, the identification of the valuable benefit will not usually cause any difficulty. However, as always, where the alleged benefit takes the form of the provision of services, the identification of the benefit is more complex. In *BP* v. *Hunt* Robert Goff J accepted that pure services, namely services which do not produce an

---

[212] See pp. 68–9 above.   [213] See pp. 72–86 above.
[214] As recognised by Robert Goff J in *BP Exploration Co. (Libya) Ltd.* v. *Hunt (No. 2)* [1979] 1 WLR 783, 802.

end-product, could constitute a valuable benefit,[215] though obviously such services should only be treated as beneficial where they have been received by the defendant.[216] He also held that where the service results in a valuable end-product then the relevant benefit for the purposes of the Act is the end-product and not the provision of the service. Consequently, it will be the end-product which must be valued and which will provide the ceiling on the award of the just sum, even though the value of the service may be greater than the value of the end-product. This interpretation of the Act has been criticised, and Robert Goff J himself objected to it, but felt bound by the terms of the statute to interpret the phrase 'valuable benefit' in this way.[217] But this interpretation of the Act can be justified on two grounds:

> First, it is clearly consistent with the words of section 1(3) which refers to a valuable benefit being obtained by the defendant and makes no reference to the plaintiff's expenditure in providing the service.
>
> Secondly, since the first two stages of the analysis under section 1(3) are concerned with whether the defendant has been unjustly enriched, the general principles of the law of restitution relating to the identification of a benefit should be applicable. By those principles the defendant should only be considered to be enriched where he or she received a benefit.[218] Where the benefit takes the form of pure services then, by definition, there cannot be an end-product, so the only possible benefit can be the service. But where the service results in the defendant receiving an end-product, it is surely only the end-product which is beneficial to the defendant, since it is the end-product which has derived from the service. It would be unrealistic to say that the defendant's benefit is the service when it is apparent that he or she had actually been benefited by the end-product. This is what the defendant would consider to be the benefit.

Although the plaintiff's expenditure in providing the service may exceed the value of the benefit this is an irrelevant consideration at this stage of the analysis, since we are simply concerned to identify the defendant's enrichment. The plaintiff's expenditure will be a relevant consideration when determining the award of the just sum. However, and this is the real drawback of section 1(3), the award of the just sum is limited by the value of the defendant's valuable benefit, so if the plaintiff's

---

[215] [1979] 1 WLR 783, 802.

[216] This notion that the benefit must have been received by the defendant before it can constitute a valuable benefit was recognised in *Parsons Bros. Ltd.* v. *Shea* (1968) 53 DLR (2d) 86 concerning the interpretation of the Newfoundland Frustrated Contracts Act 1956, which is similar to the 1943 Act.

[217] [1979] 1 WLR 783, 802.

[218] See pp. 68–9 above.

expenditure exceeds the value of this benefit the plaintiff cannot recover all of his or her expenditure. This may be considered to be unjust, but it follows logically from the application of the principle of unjust enrichment. If we are concerned, as well we may be, that the plaintiff's expenditure in providing the service is not being taken into account when identifying the valuable benefit, that is an argument to the effect that the restitutionary response which underlies section 1(3) is inappropriate where a contract has been frustrated. Instead, we should adopt a scheme which is more concerned with the allocation of losses.

Once the benefit has been identified it must then be valued and this value will constitute the ceiling on the award of the just sum. Presumably, the objective value of the benefit will be used but, since the principle of subjective devaluation is incorporated into section 1(3), it follows that if the defendant would not have valued it so highly, then this lower valuation would be adopted unless the benefit were incontrovertibly beneficial or the defendant had freely accepted it.[219] The *pro rata* contract price will presumably be an important evidential factor in determining the value the defendant placed on the benefit.

In *BP* v. *Hunt* [220] Robert Goff J complicated the question of valuing the benefit received by the defendant by considering section 1(3)(a) and (b) at this stage, when those subsections appear to be more relevant to determining the award of the just sum.

By section 1(3)(a) the court is to have regard to the expenditure incurred by the defendant in connection with the performance of the contract before it was frustrated. The consequence of Robert Goff J's assumption that section 1(3)(a) is relevant to the valuation of the defendant's benefit is that any such expenditure which was incurred by the defendant can be deducted from the valuable benefit. But this is inconsistent with the clear words of the section 1(3) which treats the defendant's expenditure relating to the contract as relevant to the assessment of the just sum and not the valuable benefit. Also to treat the defendant's expenditure as relating to the determination of the valuable benefit is inconsistent with Robert Goff J's conclusion that section 1(3)(a) embodies a defence of change of position. If this is correct then section 1(3)(a) should only apply once the benefit has been identified, for the defence of change of position at common law applies only after the plaintiff has established that the defendant had received an enrichment. Consequently, the defendant's expenditure which was incurred in connection with the performance of the contract should only be taken into account when the court is determining the award of the just sum.

---

[219] See Stewart and Carter, 'Frustrated Contracts and Statutory Adjustments: The Case for a Reappraisal' (1992) 51 *CLJ* 66, 92.   [220] [1979] 1 WLR 783, 802–5.

By section 1(3)(b) the court is to have regard to the effect of the frustrating event on the benefit which was received by the defendant. The consequence of Robert Goff J's assumption that section 1(3)(b) is relevant to the valuation of the defendant's benefit is that, if the benefit which was received by the defendant was destroyed by the frustrating event, the inevitable conclusion must be that the defendant had not received a valuable benefit for the purposes of the 1943 Act. If this is correct, it would mean that *Appleby* v. *Myers*[221] would still be decided in the same way today. In that case the plaintiff had installed machinery which was destroyed in a fire and it was held that the plaintiff's restitutionary claim for the value of the machinery supplied and the work done failed completely. According to Robert Goff J the effect of section 1(3)(b) in this type of case is that, since any benefit which the defendant had received was destroyed, the defendant cannot be considered to have received a valuable benefit. Consequently, if the ceiling to the just sum is nothing, then the just sum can be nothing. But this is a highly dubious interpretation of section 1(3)(b) for two reasons. First, because the structure of section 1(3) makes it clear that section 1(3)(b) is only relevant to the determination of the just sum and not the identification of the valuable benefit. Secondly, in the law of restitution the principle of the time factor means that the defendant should only be considered to have been enriched once a benefit has been received. Subsequent events are only relevant when considering whether the defendant has a defence to the plaintiff's claim, such as the defence of change of position. That this principle of the time factor is incorporated within section 1(3) is made clear by the requirement that the valuable benefit must have been received before the contract was frustrated. Since we are considering whether the defendant had received a benefit before the contract was frustrated and what its value was, it is not appropriate to consider the events which happened after the benefit was received; subsequent events, such as the effect of the frustrating event on the benefit, should only be considered when the award of the just sum is determined.

Once the court has determined that the defendant has received a valuable benefit it must then determine the just sum which should be awarded to the plaintiff, a sum which does not exceed the value of the defendant's benefit. The better interpretation of this aspect of section 1(3) is that it is not concerned with the reversal of the defendant's unjust enrichment, but is simply concerned with the allocation of losses between the parties. This is because section 1(3) specifies that the court must have regard to all the circumstances of the case to determine what is a just sum. It is at this stage of the claim under section 1(3) that the particular circumstances in sub-

---

[221] (1867) LR 2 CP 651.

sections (a) and (b) should be taken into account. Consequently, under section 1(3)(a), the court should consider the expenditure which was incurred by the defendant in connection with the contract. Although Robert Goff J assumed in *BP* v. *Hunt*[222] that section 1(3)(a), like the proviso to section 1(2), incorporated a defence of change of position, there is again no warrant for such a conclusion. The defence of change of position requires a change in the defendant's circumstances which occurred in reliance on the validity of the receipt of the benefit from the plaintiff and only after that benefit was received,[223] but neither requirement is incorporated into section 1(3)(a). The real function of section 1(3)(a) is simply to enable the court to take into account any relevant loss which was suffered by the defendant as a result of the contract being frustrated.

The effect of the frustrating event on the valuable benefit should also be taken into account when determining the just sum, as a result of the proper interpretation of section 1(3)(b), whether the effect was to destroy the benefit or simply to reduce its value. Again, the true function of section 1(3)(b) is simply to enable the court to apportion the losses between the parties. So, for example, if the valuable benefit was worth £50,000 when it was received but it was destroyed by the frustrating event so that the defendant was left with nothing, the justice of the case may require the court to reduce the amount which is awarded to the plaintiff to take into account the loss suffered by the defendant. Whether the effect of this destruction is that the defendant would not be required to pay the plaintiff anything or, perhaps more fairly, that the defendant must pay the plaintiff half the value of the benefit, is something which lies completely within the discretion of the court.

This analysis of the just sum is simple, although perhaps it leaves too much to the discretion of the court.[224] But it is at least clear that the purpose of the just sum is to allocate losses between the parties, albeit that this is constrained by the value of the benefit which was received by the defendant. It is most unfortunate therefore that Robert Goff J adopted a very different interpretation of the just sum in *BP* v. *Hunt*, where he assumed that the just sum was determined by the principle of unjust enrichment. In other words, the just sum would be assessed by reference to the value of the benefit which was transferred under the contract.[225]

---

[222] [1979] 1 WLR 783, 806.   [223] See Chapter 24.

[224] The Court of Appeal in *BP Exploration Co. (Libya) Ltd.* v. *Hunt (No. 2)* [1981] 1 WLR 232, 238 held that the determination of the just sum lies in the discretion of the trial judge and an appellate court would only intervene with the trial judge's decision if it was plainly wrong or unjust.

[225] The Court of Appeal was not prepared to interfere with this method for assessing the just sum, although the Court emphasised that it gained no help in interpreting the statute from the use of words which were not included in it, presumably words such as 'unjust enrichment': [1981] 1 WLR 232, 243.

But, since it is clear that Parliament intended the just sum to be, at least potentially, different from the valuable benefit which constitutes the ceiling to an award, Robert Goff J adopted a different meaning of benefit for the purposes of assessing the just sum, namely the value of the benefit which had been *provided* by the plaintiff, rather than the value of the benefit *received* by the defendant. This is highly artificial and confusing and stems from a desire to squeeze the square peg of section 1(3) into the round hole of the law of restitution founded on the reversal of the defendant's unjust enrichment. It would have been so much easier if Robert Goff J had recognised that the function of the just sum is simply to apportion losses between the parties.

When assessing the just sum there are two factors not mentioned in the statute which may be of particular relevance. The first, which was recognised by Robert Goff J, is the terms of the contract. Because of his assumption that the just sum is assessed with reference to the reasonable value of the plaintiff's services, it is obvious that Robert Goff J would treat the contract as 'by far the most useful evidence of a fair remuneration to be awarded in respect of the services rendered'.[226] But even if the assessment of the just sum is not restricted to the value of the plaintiff's services, the terms of the contract remain a key factor in the equation, but not as important as was envisaged by the judge. For he thought that in most cases the just sum would be limited to a rateable proportion of the contract price so that the plaintiff would not be able to escape the consequences of a bad bargain.[227] Whilst the fact that the plaintiff had entered into a bad bargain should be a relevant consideration, it should not be the prime determinant of the just sum since the court must have regard to all the circumstances of the case. The second factor which should be considered, a factor which was specifically rejected by Robert Goff J, is the conduct of both parties, particularly whether they had breached the contract before it was frustrated. In *BP* v. *Hunt* itself the defendant alleged that the plaintiff had committed certain breaches of the contract so that a deduction should be made from the just sum to reflect this. But the trial judge held that, even if it could be shown that the plaintiff had acted unreasonably, this was of no relevance to the assessment of the just sum.[228] But surely, if the plaintiff had the opportunity to minimise his or her loss before the frustrating event occurred and failed to do so, this is a factor which is relevant to the assessment of the just sum.[229] The conduct of the defendant

---

[226] [1979] 1 WLR 783, 822.   [227] *Ibid*, p. 806.

[228] Though if the impossibility of performance of the contract was self-induced then the plaintiff will not be able to argue that it has been frustrated.

[229] See Dickson, 'An Action for Unjust Enrichment' (1983) 34 *NILQ* 106, 122 and Haycroft and Waksman (1984) *JBL* 207, 222.

should similarly be taken into account when determining the sum which it is just to award.

The application of section 1(3) may be excluded by the contract, but the court will only consider the statutory scheme to have been excluded where the parties, being aware of the risks of frustration, clearly intended such exclusion, as was recognised by the House of Lords in *BP* v. *Hunt*.[230] Also, as with section 1(2), there is no scope under section 1(3) for including an interest element in respect of the period during which the defendant had received the benefit of the plaintiff's services. The question of the award of interest can only be considered once the just sum has been assessed.[231]

The application of the principles which underlie section 1(3) can be illustrated by analysing the decision of Robert Goff J in *BP* v. *Hunt* itself. The facts of the case were very complicated, but essentially the dispute related to an oil concession which had been granted to Hunt by the Libyan government. Hunt was unable to develop the concession himself and so he entered into a joint venture with BP whereby he agreed to grant BP half of the concession and to allow it to explore for oil and to develop the concession if oil was found. BP was to pay for the cost of exploration and development but, once the oil came on stream, it was to receive half of the oil and additional 'reimbursement oil' to reimburse it for its contributions to the exploration and development of the concession. BP spent millions of pounds exploring for oil, and it eventually found a large oilfield and began to extract oil. The contract was frustrated when the Libyan government expropriated BP's share of the concession, and two years later Hunt's share was also expropriated. When the contract was frustrated BP had only been reimbursed one third of the oil which was due to it. Consequently, BP sued Hunt under section 1(3) in respect of the valuable benefit which Hunt had received. This was the first case to consider the 1943 Act and, whilst the case went on to be heard by the Court of Appeal[232] and the House of Lords,[233] these appeals related to specific matters and did not concern the general principles underlying the Act. Hence Robert Goff J's judgment continues to be the most important analysis of the operation of section 1(3).

Robert Goff J approached the case in the following way. First, he identified the valuable benefit obtained by Hunt before the contract was frustrated as the end-product of BP's services, namely the enhancement in the value of Hunt's oil concession rather than the value of BP's work in finding and extracting the oil. This is surely correct, since the actual benefit which Hunt himself received was the enhancement in the value of his concession. Secondly, in determining the value of this benefit the judge

---

[230] [1983] 2 AC 352.   [231] *BP* v. *Hunt* [1981] 1 WLR 232, 244 (CA).
[232] [1981] 1 WLR 232.   [233] [1983] 2 AC 352.

considered the effect of the frustrating event, by virtue of section 1(3)(b). Since the expropriation of BP's interest had dramatically reduced the value of Hunt's interest, the judge considered that this had reduced the value of the benefit which Hunt had received to half the oil he had obtained from the oilfield plus the compensation he had obtained from the Libyan government. But this confuses the question of the time factor. All the judge should have been concerned with at this stage was the identification and valuation of the benefit which had been received, subsequent events should only have been relevant to the assessment of the just sum. The judge valued the benefit at $85 million, so this constituted the ceiling on the award. Finally, the judge assessed the just sum by reference to restitutionary principles. Since he assumed that the benefit for these purposes was the services provided by the plaintiff rather than the end-product received by the defendant, he valued the just sum at $35m and, since this was less than the value of the valuable benefit, this was the amount which he ordered Hunt to pay to BP. This just sum was effectively made up of the expenses incurred by BP on behalf of Hunt, as evidenced by the terms of the contract, plus the amount of money and oil which had been paid by BP to Hunt with a deduction for the amount which Hunt had reimbursed BP before the contract was frustrated. Perhaps the award of $35m was entirely appropriate, but it is clear that the basis for assessing this sum was not. The judge should have considered all the circumstances of the case, not just the value of the services provided.

(c) The need for principled reform

Subsection 1(2) and (3) of the 1943 Act are somewhat schizophrenic provisions, embodying as they do both principles of restitution founded on the reversal of the defendant's unjust enrichment and the allocation of losses between the parties. But this attempt to allocate losses is half-hearted. There are a number of situations in which a party will have incurred expenditure but he or she will not be able to reclaim it even if the court considers this to be just. For example, the defendant's expenditure incurred in connection with performance of the contract before it was frustrated can only be recouped if the plaintiff paid or was liable to pay money to the defendant or the defendant received a valuable benefit from the plaintiff. Would it not be better to replace the 1943 Act with a new scheme whereby all the losses of the parties which arise from the contract being frustrated may be apportioned between them?

(i) Arguments against loss apportionment

Burrows is not convinced that there is a need for a statutory regime which involves the apportionment of losses.[234] This is for a number of reasons. For example, the traditional approach of the law of contract is that each party should take the risk of loss arising from frustration rather than having that loss apportioned between them. Also loss apportionment can result in uncertainty, and if we really desire to apportion losses it will be necessary to take into account the relative fault of the parties, adding to the complexity of the analysis. His conclusion is that the case for loss apportionment is unproven and that the award of restitutionary relief achieves sufficient justice following frustration. Stewart and Carter also reject a scheme of loss apportionment on the ground that there is no reason why one party to a contract should act as an insurer for the loss suffered by the other party, by having to bear some or all of the other's loss.[235] They consider that a common law scheme which is simply founded on the principle of reversing unjust enrichment is perfectly adequate. But the refusal of the English courts so far to recognise partial failure of consideration as a ground of restitution surely makes reliance on the common law of restitution inadequate in this context.

(ii) Arguments in favour of loss apportionment

McKendrick, on the other hand, has argued convincingly that we should adopt a scheme of full apportionment of losses.[236] He accepts that, whilst the need to restore benefits to the plaintiff must remain an important part of the relief which is available when a contract is frustrated, this restitution interest is not the only interest which needs to be protected, since it is also necessary to consider the reliance interest. This interest is in particular need of protection in the context of frustrated contracts simply because both parties are equally innocent of the frustration, so it is unfair simply to let the loss lie where it fell. This is not necessarily the case in the other situations in which a contract has been discharged, such as where it was discharged for breach or failure to comply with statutory formalities or when the contract was null and void. However, it does not follow that, in the context of frustrated contracts, losses should be apportioned equally between the parties, simply because one party may have suffered greater losses than the other. Consequently,

---

[234] Burrows, *The Law of Restitution*, p. 287.

[235] 'Frustrated Contracts and Statutory Adjustment: The Case for a Reappraisal' (1992) 51 *CLJ* 66, 109.

[236] 'Frustration, Restitution and Loss Apportionment' in *Essays on the Law of Restitution* (Burrows ed.) p. 169. See also Haycraft and Waksman, 'Restitution and Frustration' (1984) JBL 207 who consider the 1943 Act to be sufficiently flexible to allow for the adjustment of losses without the need for reform.

McKendrick concludes there is a need to take into account the particular circumstances of the case when allocating losses between the parties. In particular, loss apportionment should be excluded if the risk of frustration has been allocated by the parties in the contract itself.

(iii) A middle way

What is needed is a statutory mechanism which adequately protects both the restitutionary and the reliance interests, but without recourse to an unrestrained judicial discretion. The preferable solution is to adopt the model of the British Columbian Frustrated Contracts Act 1974. The general scheme of that Act is that each party must make restitution in respect of anything done by way of contractual performance by the other.[237] For the purposes of this Act a broad definition of benefit is adopted in that a benefit is 'something done in the fulfilment of contractual obligations whether or not the person for whose benefit it was done received the benefit'.[238] Consequently, the defendant should be deemed to have been benefited either where he or she had obtained a benefit from the plaintiff or where the plaintiff had incurred expenditure in relation to the performance of the contract. Whilst such a broad notion of 'benefit' may be somewhat misleading, this simple technique of expanding what is meant by benefit will ensure that the defendant is not allowed to retain any unjust enrichment, and also that the expenditure which the plaintiff incurred may be recovered. If the defendant had also incurred expenditure he or she would either be able to set this off against the plaintiff's claim or bring a claim him- or herself for restitution from the plaintiff. Whilst this statutory regime cannot be considered to be completely restitutionary, since the defendant's liability is not confined to the benefit which he or she received, it would at least operate within the framework of the law of restitution. In addition, the British Columbian Act provides that, where the effect of the frustrating event is to diminish the value of the contractual performance, then the losses should be shared equally between the parties.[239] This is less convincing, since it is more just for losses to be apportioned according to the particular circumstances of the case.

4. VOID CONTRACTS

(a) The uncertainty as to the ground of restitution

Where the plaintiff has transferred a benefit to the defendant pursuant to a contract which is void *ab initio* it should be relatively easy for the

---

[237] British Columbian Frustrated Contracts Act 1974, s. 5(1).
[238] *Ibid*, s. 5(4).   [239] *Ibid*, s. 5(3).

plaintiff to establish that the defendant has been unjustly enriched at the plaintiff's expense. The most appropriate ground of restitution appears to be total failure of consideration. This should be easier to establish where a contract is void *ab initio* than where, for example, the contract has been discharged for breach, since the fact that a contract is null and void means that, as a matter of law, there was no contract, so nothing needs to be set aside before the restitutionary claim can be brought. The plaintiff then only needs to show that the consideration for the benefit which was transferred to the defendant has failed totally.

But what of the case in which the contract is void but the consideration has not failed totally? Is it possible to establish a ground of restitution in this case? There is some evidence that there is indeed a separate ground of restitution which may be available in such circumstances, a ground of restitution which is dependent on the fact that the contract is void *ab initio*, and this is the ground of absence of consideration. Where the plaintiff seeks to show that there has been a total failure of consideration, the essence of his or her claim is that the consideration which he or she expected has failed as a matter of fact. In other words, if the plaintiff transferred a benefit to the defendant, usually on condition that a benefit would be received in return and no benefit was forthcoming, the plaintiff's intention that the defendant should receive the benefit can be treated as vitiated. Where, however, the plaintiff has transferred a benefit to the defendant pursuant to a contract which is null and void, he or she can never receive the expected consideration from the defendant as a matter of law. This is because, if the contract is null and void, the law assumes that there never was a contract. As a result, the plaintiff's intention that the defendant should receive the benefit can be treated as vitiated. If this argument is correct, it means that the defendant can never provide consideration as a matter of law in respect of a void contract, even if the plaintiff did actually receive a benefit from the defendant. This ground of absence of consideration would therefore provide a useful way for avoiding the total failure of consideration requirement.

Determining the appropriate ground of restitution as regards those benefits which are transferred in respect of void contracts is a highly controversial matter. It is clear that total failure of consideration may be a relevant ground of restitution in such a case, and this will be examined first. The potential application of absence of consideration will then be examined, and finally an alternative ground of restitution will be considered.

(b) Total failure of consideration

In many cases in which the plaintiff has transferred a benefit to the defendant under a contract which is void the ground of restitution has either been expressly recognised as total failure of consideration or the fact that the consideration failed totally adequately explains why the plaintiff's restitutionary claim succeeded. Although a contract may be void for a number of different reasons, the question of restitution of benefits transferred in respect of such contracts has arisen in three different contexts in particular.

(i) Pre-incorporation contracts

Where one of the parties to a contract is a company which was not incorporated when the contract was made then, as between these parties,[240] the contract is null and void. That a restitutionary claim may be brought in respect of any benefits which were transferred in respect of such a contact, was recognised by the Court of Appeal in *Rover International Ltd.* v. *Cannon Film Sales Ltd. (No. 3)*.[241] Whilst all of the judges accepted that the plaintiff company, which had paid money to the defendant under a pre-incorporation contract, could recover that money on the ground of mistake,[242] it was only Kerr LJ who specifically recognised that the claim could also be founded on total failure of consideration,[243] though Nicholls LJ did agree with his reasoning, so it presumably represents part of the ratio of the case. The defendant had also benefited from services provided by the plaintiff under the contract and conceded that the plaintiff was entitled to a *quantum meruit*. Although no ground of restitution was identified in respect of this claim, again the ground of restitution should be considered to be either mistake or total failure of consideration.

(ii) Infancy

Before the enactment of the Minors' Contracts Act 1987, contracts which were made with infants were void unless they involved the supply of necessaries.[244] Money which had been paid under a contract which was void for infancy could be recovered if the consideration had totally failed.[245] Similarly, other benefits which had been transferred under a contract made with an infant were recoverable on the ground of total failure of consideration as well. This is illustrated by *Pearce* v. *Brain*[246] where the

---

[240] By the Companies Act 1985, s. 36C a pre-incorporation contract has effect as though it was made with the person who purported to act for the company or as agent for it.

[241] [1989] 1 WLR 912. See also *Cotronic (UK) Ltd.* v. *Dezonie* [1991] BCLC 721 where the plaintiff's restitutionary claim succeeded in respect of building services which had been provided under a pre-incorporation contract. Although the ground of restitution was not identified, it could have been total failure of consideration.

[242] Although the mistake appears to be more of a mistake of law which was not a ground of restitution at the time.

[243] [1989] 1 WLR 912, 924.   [244] See p. 415 below.

[245] As was effectively recognised in *Valentini* v. *Canali* (1889) 24 QBD 166, although on the facts the consideration had not failed totally.

[246] [1929] 2 KB 310.

plaintiff who was an infant contracted with the defendant to exchange his motorcycle for the defendant's car. Since the contract had been made with an infant it was void, but it was accepted that the plaintiff could recover the motorcycle if the consideration for the transaction had failed totally. But since the plaintiff had used the car the consideration had not totally failed.

(iii) Want of authority

A contract may also be void where one of the parties lacks authority to make it.[247] A number of cases recognise that a restitutionary claim may succeed in respect of benefits which have been transferred under such a contract, although the ground of restitution has never been specifically identified. In principle, a plaintiff who transfers benefits to the defendant under a contract which is void for want of authority should be able to obtain restitution on the ground of total failure of consideration. However, the two leading cases in which restitutionary relief was awarded in respect of a contract which was void for want of authority cannot be explained on this ground.

In *Craven-Ellis* v. *Canons Ltd.*[248] the plaintiff purported to enter into a contract with the defendant company whereby it was agreed that the plaintiff would act as managing director for the defendant which would pay the plaintiff for his services. After the plaintiff had done some work for the defendant he claimed his remuneration, but the defendant refused to pay him. The plaintiff was unable to sue the defendant on the contract because it was void for want of authority, since neither the plaintiff nor the other directors who made the agreement on behalf of the defendant possessed the requisite qualification shares which authorised them to make the agreement, as was required by the company's articles of association. The plaintiff consequently sought to recover reasonable remuneration for the work he had done and his claim succeeded. Although the ground of restitution was never identified, it appears that for Greer LJ it was mistake of fact,[249] namely a mistaken belief that a valid contract had been made. This is dubious, however, because the mistake was surely one of law which was not a recognised ground of restitution at the time. It might be considered that the ground of restitution could alternatively have been total failure of consideration, but this could not have been established because, since the directors were not authorised to act for the defendant, the defendant was not aware of the consideration which the plaintiff expected to receive for the

---

[247] *Guinness plc.* v. *Saunders* [1990] 2 AC 663.   [248] [1936] 2 KB 403.

[249] *Ibid*, p. 413, where Greer LJ accepted that the contract was void because of the plaintiff's mistake and so presumably accepted that this constituted the ground of restitution.

provision of his services, and this is a necessary condition before total failure of consideration can be established.[250]

The second case in which restitution was awarded in the context of a contract which was void for want of authority is the decision of the House of Lords in *Guinness plc.* v. *Saunders*,[251] but again it is very difficult to identify the ground of restitution which was applicable. In *Guinness* the plaintiff company had paid the defendant £5.2m for his assistance in a successful take-over bid. This contract was void for want of authority under the company's articles of association, and the plaintiff success-fully recovered the money it had paid to the defendant. Again the ground of restitution was not specifically identified by the court, but it is clear that it was not total failure of consideration because the plaintiff had received some consideration in respect of the payment, although this would not have been an obstacle if absence of consideration was recog-nised as a ground of restitution. Similarly it could not have been mistake as to the existence of a valid contract, because the mistake was surely one of law rather than fact, and mistake of law was not a recognised ground of restitution at the time.[252] The preferable explanation of the case is that restitution was awarded by virtue of the defendant having breached his fiduciary duty as a director of the company. Consequently, restitution was not awarded to reverse the defendant's unjust enrichment, but was simply a remedy arising from the commission of a wrong by the defen-dant.[253]

(c) Absence of consideration

Although in some of the cases in which restitution has been awarded in respect of benefits transferred under a void contract the ground of resti-tution is clearly total failure of consideration, the majority of cases in which restitution has been awarded are simply consistent with this as the ground of restitution. In some other cases, particularly those concerning contracts being void for want of authority, the award of a restitutionary remedy cannot be justified on the ground of total failure of considera-tion. There is consequently scope for arguing that the ground of restitu-tion in some of these cases should in fact have been absence of consideration; since if the contract is void, the plaintiff could never receive the expected consideration under the contract as a matter of law. Whether absence of consideration is a recognised ground of restitution remains unclear, although there are three strands of cases which suggest that such a ground of restitution is recognised in English law.

---

[250] See p. 325 above.				[251] [1990] 2 AC 663.
[252] Birks, 'Restitution Without Counter-Restitution' [1990] *LMCLQ* 330, 332.
[253] See p. 535 below.

(i) Cases which support the recognition of absence of consideration

(1) The annuity cases

In a number of cases in the late eighteenth and early nineteenth centuries restitutionary claims were brought in respect of annuities. The grant of an annuity was a common method of borrowing money whereby the borrower, in return for a sum of money from the lender, agreed to pay an annuity to the lender during the lender's lifetime in lieu of interest and the return of the loan. The Annuity Acts of 1777 and 1813 were passed to regulate the granting of annuities and required compliance with certain formalities, such as registration of the annuity. Failure to comply with these formalities resulted in the contract being treated as null and void. The importance of this in the present context is that it was recognised in a number of cases that restitution of the money paid under the void annuity contracts was possible even though payments had been made by both parties.[254]

Some commentators have explained these cases on the ground of total failure of consideration or mistake.[255] But this is not acceptable. If there was a failure of consideration it was partial, since payments had been received as well as made, and if there was a mistake it was one of law, and English law was clear that, subject to exceptions which were not applicable in these annuity cases, neither partial failure of consideration nor mistake of law was a ground of restitution at the time. So some other ground of restitution needs to be identified. The most appropriate explanation is that of absence of consideration. Since the annuities were null and void the plaintiff could never, as a matter of law, obtain the consideration for his or her payment and so restitution should be awarded.[256]

(2) Payments to discharge a liability which does not exist

In *Woolwich Equitable Building Society* v. *IRC*[257] a majority of the House of Lords recognised that the payment of tax to the Revenue, after a tax demand which the Revenue was not authorised to make, was recoverable. Although the actual ground of restitution was the fact that the tax had been paid to a public authority which was not entitled to receive the money,[258] both Lord Goff and Lord Browne-Wilkinson referred to the

---

[254] See, for example, *Hicks* v. *Hicks* (1802) 3 East 16; 102 ER 502.

[255] Birks, 'No Consideration: Restitution After Void Contracts' (1993) 23 *Univ. WALR* 195, 214; Burrows, ' Swaps and the Friction Between Common Law and Equity' (1995) 3 *RLR* 15, 18.

[256] See *Westdeutsche Landesbank Girozentrale* v. *Islington LBC* [1994] 4 All ER 890, 930 (Hobhouse J).

[257] [1993] AC 70.

[258] See pp. 433–4 below.

fact that the plaintiff would not have received any consideration for the payment.[259] This was because the plaintiff had paid the money to the Revenue in the expectation that this would discharge its tax liability. But since there was no liability to discharge, the plaintiff would never receive any consideration for the payment.

(3) The swaps litigation

The most important example of the ground of absence of consideration in operation arises from the cases in the so-called 'swaps litigation'. In these cases the plaintiffs had entered into interest rate swap transactions with the defendants in circumstances in which such transactions were null and void. Essentially an interest rate swap transaction is a speculative transaction whereby two parties gamble on how interest rates will change. The simplest form of transaction involves an agreement between two parties whereby each party agrees to pay a sum of money to the other over a stated number of years, which is divided into accounting periods. This money is calculated by reference to the interest which would have accrued during each accounting period on a notional capital sum. The rate of interest of one party will be fixed, whereas that of the other party will be floating, meaning that it will be assessed by reference to a variable market rate of interest. Although each party is liable to pay the other at the end of each accounting period, one party will invariably be liable to pay more than the other, so that party will pay what is due to the other party having deducted what that other party owes to him or her. Whether it is the fixed or the floating rate payer who will benefit under such a transaction depends on the movements of the interest rates. Often in the course of a swaps transaction the floating rate of interest will vary above and below the fixed rate of interest, meaning that at some stage in the course of the transaction both parties will be liable to pay the other party. Essentially, such swaps transactions involve the parties gambling on the fluctuation of interest rates.

From the early 1980s local authorities began to enter into such interest rate swap transactions with a number of different financial institutions. However, in 1990 the House of Lords held that such transactions were beyond the statutory powers of the local authorities and so were null and void.[260] This was because participation of local authorities in such transactions could not be considered to be incidental to the power of such authorities to lend and borrow money, simply because these transactions did not involve the lending or borrowing of money. Consequently, the party which had paid the most under such transactions, either the local authority or the financial institution depending on the particular

---

[259] [1993] AC 70, 166 (Lord Goff), 197–8 (Lord Browne-Wilkinson).
[260] *Hazell* v. *Hammersmith and Fulham LBC* [1992] 2 AC 1.

circumstances of the case, brought restitutionary claims to recover the balance of the money paid. A large number of such actions were instigated and certain characteristic actions were identified and were pursued as test cases. The most important of these was *Westdeutsche Landesbank Girozentrale* v. *Islington London Borough Council*,[261] which was heard with *Kleinwort Benson Ltd.* v. *Sandwell Borough Council* before Hobhouse J, although his decision in respect of the latter case was not the subject of an appeal. In both of these cases it was the banks which sought restitution of the balance of the money from the local authorities. The plaintiffs also sued to recover interest due on this sum. The plaintiffs relied on restitutionary claims in equity and at common law. It is the common law claim for money had and received which is relevant to this chapter.

There were two obstacles in the way of the plaintiff's common law claim:

(1) *Sinclair* v. *Brougham.* In *Sinclair* v. *Brougham*[262] the House of Lords held that an action for money had and received could not succeed if the award of restitution would involve the indirect enforcement of an invalid transaction. Consequently, restitutionary relief would be unavailable at common law, as it was in that case, where the plaintiff sought restitution of an *ultra vires* loan, because the value of the restitutionary remedy would be the same as the amount of the loan, so the effect of restitution would be to repay and so enforce the loan. However, in *Westdeutsche Landesbank* both Hobhouse J and the Court of Appeal held that this principle was inapplicable to the facts of the case simply because the interest rate swaps transaction was not a borrowing transaction, but was a futures contract which does not, by its very nature, involve the lending of any money. Consequently, if the defendant local authority was required to make restitution to the bank this would not involve the indirect enforcement of the transaction, since the effect of restitution would simply be to restore the parties to the position they occupied before the transaction was entered into. Even where the transaction involves a loan it now appears that restitution of the money lent can be awarded, simply because it is now recognised that the obligation to make restitution is imposed by law and is independent of the contractual obligation to repay the loan.[263]

---

[261] [1994] 4 All ER 890 (Hobhouse J; [1994] 1 WLR 938 (CA); [1996] AC 669 (HL). The decisions of Hobhouse J and the CA are the most important in respect of the identification and definition of absence of consideration as a ground of restitution. The HL was more concerned with proprietary restitutionary claims: see Chapter 20.

[262] [1914] AC 398.

[263] See Lord Goff in *Westdeutsche Landesbank Girozentrale* v. *Islington LBC* [1996] AC 669, 688.

(2) *Identifying the ground of restitution.* The second obstacle to the plaintiffs' claim concerned the identification of a relevant ground of restitution. The plaintiffs could not rely on mistake since the only mistake made was one of law, concerning the legal validity of the payment, and there was nothing to suggest that any of the exceptions to the mistake of law bar was applicable. Equally, the plaintiffs could not rely on total failure of consideration since, save for two transactions, the plaintiffs had been paid some money in the course of the transaction. However, Hobhouse J recognised that the plaintiffs' restitutionary claim could succeed by virtue of the ground of absence of consideration for the plaintiffs' payment to the defendant. This analysis was endorsed by the Court of Appeal.[264]

(ii) Determining the ambit of absence of consideration

This recognition of absence of consideration as a ground of restitution is not free from difficulty. Despite the explicit recognition of the ground in *Westdeutsche Landesbank* whether the ground really does exist remains uncertain and, even if it does exist, its ambit is unclear. Six particular problems can be identified.

(1) The effect of subsequent decisions

Although absence of consideration was clearly recognised by Hobhouse J and the Court of Appeal in *Westdeutsche Landesbank*, its status must be reconsidered in the light of the House of Lords decision in that case. Unfortunately, the decision of that court is of little assistance, since it was much more concerned with the nature of the plaintiff's equitable claim than with the claim for money had and received. Nevertheless, the judgments of Lords Goff and Browne-Wilkinson do provide some clues as to whether absence of consideration is a valid ground of restitution. Although Lord Goff declined to express any concluded view, he did say that there was considerable force in the criticisms which have been expressed concerning the validity of absence of consideration as a ground of restitution, and he would have preferred that the ground of restitution was failure of consideration.[265] Although this does not constitute a clear rejection of absence of consideration, it seems that, in the light of Lord Goff's earlier description of the requirement that the consideration must have failed totally as unprincipled and producing unfortunate effects, he was assuming that restitution should have been awarded on the ground of partial failure of consideration. However, he did not at any stage explicitly state this, and anyway his comments were

---

[264] [1994] 1 WLR 938. See also *Kleinwort Benson Ltd.* v. *Birmingham City Council* [1996] QB 380, 393 (Evans LJ) and 394 (Saville LJ).
[265] [1996] AC 669, 683.

obiter dicta since the question of the ground of restitution for the purposes of a common law restitutionary action was not the subject of an appeal.

Lord Browne-Wilkinson, on the other hand, did appear to recognise the validity of absence of consideration as a ground of restitution, although he too used the language of failure of consideration. In his analysis of *Sinclair* v. *Brougham*[266] he suggested that the plaintiffs in that case should have succeeded in their common law claim for recovery of money which had been lent to a building society pursuant to a transaction which was *ultra vires* the building society. He specifically recognised that the ground of restitution in that case should have been total failure of consideration.[267] Crucially, he concluded that the consideration in that case had failed totally, even though the building society had done what it had promised to do, because the plaintiffs had paid money to the building society:

in consideration of a promise to repay. That promise was ultra vires and void; therefore the consideration for the payment of the money wholly failed.[268]

In the light of this reasoning he went on to endorse the decision of the Court of Appeal in *Westdeutsche Landesbank* that the money had been paid for a consideration which had wholly failed. But even though Lord Browne-Wilkinson used the language of total failure of consideration, his emphasis on the fact that the transaction was *ultra vires* and void means that his analysis is indistinguishable from that of Hobhouse J. At the very least, Lord Browne-Wilkinson could not be referring to the notion of total failure of consideration as it is normally used, because the plaintiffs had received a factual benefit in that the plaintiffs' money was deposited with the defendant. The only way that this consideration could fail totally is if it failed as a matter of law, since the defendant lacked the capacity to receive the plaintiffs' money. It is this notion of legal failure of consideration, arising from the fact that the contract was null and void, which is identical to the approach of Hobhouse J. His approach is, if anything, clearer and more honest because he is prepared to call it absence of consideration rather than total failure of consideration.

The clear division of opinion between Lords Goff and Browne-Wilkinson, and the failure of the other judges to address this issue, means that it is not possible to conclude that absence of consideration has no role as a ground of restitution in English law. Consequently, the judgments of Hobhouse J and the Court of Appeal continue to be of vital importance to the recognition of absence of consideration as a ground of restitution.

---

[266] [1914] AC 398.   [267] [1996] AC 669, 710.   [268] *Ibid.*

Since the decision of the House of Lords in *Westdeustche Landesbank* the Court of Appeal has had an opportunity to reconsider the nature of the plaintiff's restitutionary claim arising from payments made under an interest rate swap transaction in *Guinness Mahon and Co. Ltd.* v. *Kensington and Cheslea Royal London Borough Council*.[269] In this case the plaintiff bank's restitutionary claim against a local authority succeeded, although the actual ground of restitution is difficult to identify with certainty. Morritt LJ considered that the ground of restitution was total failure of consideration and that this was the ground of restitution which was relied on in *Westdeutsche Landesbank* itself, even though he accepted that consideration had been given by the defendant since it had performed its part of the transaction.[270] But the judge also recognised that the reason there was a total failure of consideration was simply because the contract was *ultra vires*.[271] This is a virtually identical approach to that adopted by Lord Browne-Wilkinson in *Westdeutsche Landesbank*. Waller LJ was less convinced that the approach of the House of Lords in *Westdeutsche Landesbank* supported that of the trial judge and the Court of Appeal. Although he defended the result of the case, he doubted whether absence of consideration was an appropriate ground of restitution.[272] For Robert Walker LJ the choice between total failure of consideration and absence of consideration was simply a matter of terminology.[273] Although the approaches of the judges in this case suggest a tendency to prefer total failure of consideration to absence of consideration, it is clear that all three of them treated the notion of failure of consideration differently in the context of void contracts, essentially because the consideration had failed as a matter of law rather than fact. On any view therefore, it is clear that the cases subsequent to the decisions of the trial judge and the Court of Appeal in *Westdeutsche Landesbank* support the recognition of a ground of restitution which is different from that which is traditionally called total failure of consideration. Indeed, absence of consideration was specifically relied on as a ground of restitution by Sullivan J in *Dorchester upon Medway CC* v. *Kent CC*[274] in respect of a restitutionary claim to recover an *ultra vires* payment.

(2) The relationship between absence and total failure of consideration

Even though absence of consideration was specifically relied on to enable restitution of money to be awarded, it is odd that Hobhouse J in *Westdeutsche Landesbank* awarded restitution on the ground both of

---

[269] [1998] 3 WLR 829. This decision was commended by Lord Hope in *Kleinwort Benson Ltd.* v. *Lincoln CC* [1998] 3 WLR 1095, 1153.

[270] [1998] 3 WLR 829, 835.   [271] *Ibid*, p. 838.   [272] *Ibid*, p. 842.

[273] *Ibid*, p. 850.   [274] *The Times*, 5 March 1998.

total failure of consideration, in respect of those transactions where only the plaintiff had paid money to the defendant without receiving anything in return, and absence of consideration, in respect of those transactions where both the plaintiff and the defendant had paid money to the other party and the plaintiff was simply seeking to recover the net payment from the defendant. If absence of consideration is a valid ground of restitution it should be applicable in all cases where money has been paid under a transaction which is null and void, and the question whether or not the plaintiff received any benefit under the transaction should be irrelevant. The only exception to this is that, if the plaintiff has received a benefit under the transaction, he or she should be required to make counter-restitution of it to the defendant.

(3) Fully executed transactions

One of the interest rate swap transactions in *Kleinwort Benson Ltd.* v. *Sandwell Borough Council*[275] was fully executed, in that the agreed period of the transaction had expired before the House of Lords declared that it was *ultra vires*. But despite this, the plaintiff's restitutionary claim still succeeded on the ground of absence of consideration, because of the assumption that any benefit which the plaintiff had received under the transaction was not validly received since the transaction was considered to be null and void from the start. But should restitutionary relief be available to re-open a transaction once it is complete?

Birks has argued that a distinction should be drawn between those transactions which are closed, meaning that they are fully executed, and those which remain open.[276] He asserts that where a transaction is fully executed it is not possible to conclude that the plaintiff's intention that the defendant should retain the money paid has been vitiated in any way, so there is no reason why restitution should be awarded in such circumstances. In other words, the plaintiff has received exactly that for which he or she had bargained. However, Birks's rejection of the argument that restitution should be awarded even where the transaction has been executed is weakened by his recognition that, where there is a relevant mistake, the plaintiff can obtain restitution on the ground of that mistake even where the transaction has been fully executed.[277] He is forced to accept that restitution will be awarded in such circumstances because, for mistake to operate as a ground of restitution, it is sufficient that the mistake was operative at the time the benefit was received by the defendant. Subsequent events are irrelevant to establish the mistake, although they may enable the defendant to plead a defence of change of position.

---

[275] [1994] 4 All ER 890.
[276] 'No Consideration: Restitution after Void Contracts' (1993) 23 *Univ. WALR* 195, 206.
[277] *Ibid*, p. 229.

In fact, there is no problem in allowing restitution in respect of a fully executed swaps transaction even where the ground of restitution is absence of consideration. This has now been recognised by the court of Appeal in *Guinness Mahon and Co. Ltd.* v. *Kensington and Chelsea Royal London BC.*[278] In this case the plaintiff bank had entered into an interest rate swap transaction with the defendant local authority which the parties agreed would last for five years until 1987. By the end of the agreement the defendant had received over £380,000 more than it had paid. Subsequently, when the House of Lords declared this type of agreement void, the bank sought restitution of the net amount which the defendant had received even though the agreement was fully executed. The court of Appeal held that the plaintiff's claim should succeed because there was no basis for distinguishing between open and closed transactions. This must be right if the basis for restitution is absence of consideration arising from the fact that the transaction was null and void. If there never was any transaction then the fact that the apparent transaction had been completely performed or not is totally irrelevant. In particular the court stressed that if the transaction has been completely performed the defendant has no better right to the money than if the transaction has only been partly performed. This conclusion also avoids the unjust situation which would arise if the plaintiff were able to recover every payment made to the defendant until the penultimate payment, but would not be able to recover a penny once the final payment had been made.

(4) Restitution of gifts

If absence of consideration were applied literally as a ground of restitution it would mean that all gifts could be recovered once they had been made because, generally, no consideration will be provided for such gifts. However, restitution of gifts on this ground was specifically excluded by Hobhouse J and the Court of Appeal, and they were right to do so. Restitutionary claims in respect of gifts made should be defeated by virtue of the fundamental principle which denies restitution where a benefit has been transferred voluntarily.[279]

(5) Nullity of purpose

Whilst it is clear that absence of consideration should be an appropriate ground of restitution where a benefit has been transferred under a contract which is a nullity, is it possible for the plaintiff to rely on absence of consideration where no contract has been made, but the benefit was transferred for a particular purpose which was a nullity? For example, if

---

[278] [1998] 3 WLR 829. This decision was commended by Lord Hope in *Kleinwort Benson Ltd.* v. *Lincoln CC* [1998] 3 WLR 1095, 1153.

[279] See pp. 39–40 above.

the plaintiff has entered into an agreement with the defendant which is subject to contract, it has already been seen that if the plaintiff pays money to the defendant in the expectation that a contract will be made and no contract is forthcoming, the plaintiff may be able to recover the money on the ground of total failure of consideration, even though the defendant never promised that a contract would be made.[280] If, however, the plaintiff received some benefit from the defendant in return for the payment then it is not possible for the plaintiff to rely on the ground of total failure of consideration. But if the contract could never be made as a matter of law, would the plaintiff be able to recover the money on the ground of absence of consideration? This question was identified but was not answered in *Friends' Provident Life Office* v. *Hillier Parker May and Rowland (a firm)*.[281] The better view is that if, as a matter of law, no contract could validly be made then the expected consideration could never be provided and so the plaintiff should be able to obtain restitution on the ground of absence of consideration in exactly the same way as occurred in *Westdeutsche Landesbank* itself.

(6) Restitutionary claims brought by local authorities

The majority of the cases in which restitutionary claims have been made in respect of interest rate swap transactions have involved claims brought by a financial institution against the local authority. But there are some cases where the local authority has successfully sued the financial institution,[282] and the right of the local authority to obtain restitution has been recognised in other cases.[283] There is no reason why absence of consideration should not be available in this context as well. Indeed, if absence of consideration is recognised as a ground of restitution it should be available in all cases in which benefits have been transferred pursuant to a transaction which is null and void, regardless of who the plaintiff is.

(d) Should absence of consideration be recognised as a ground of restitution?

The identification of the most appropriate ground of restitution where the plaintiff has transferred a benefit to the defendant pursuant to a void transaction remains highly controversial. Analysis of the case law

---

[280] See, for example, *Chillingworth* v. *Esche* [1924] 1 Ch. 97, discussed at p. 326 above.
[281] [1995] 4 All ER 260, 269 (Auld LJ).
[282] See in particular *South Tyneside Metropolitan Borough Council* v. *Svenska International plc.* [1995] 1 All ER 545.
[283] *Guinness Mahon Co. Ltd.* v. *Chelsea and Kensington Royal LBC* [1998] 3 WLR 829, 837 (Morritt LJ).

suggests that three grounds of restitution are potentially applicable, namely total failure, absence of consideration and mistake. With the recognition by the House of Lords in *Kleinwort Benson* v. *Lincoln CC*[284] that a mistake of law can ground a restitutionary claim, it will be much easier to establish that the defendant has been unjustly enriched in respect of interest rate swaps transactions which have been held to be void. Consequently, there will be much less need for a ground of absence of consideration. But such a ground may sometimes still be of some significance where a causative mistake cannot be established, for example because the transaction was declared void by statute[285] or the plaintiff suspected that there was no liability to pay the money,[286] and so it is worth examining whether the recognition of a ground of absence of consideration can be justified.

(i) Criticisms of absence of consideration

The chief criticism of the ground of absence of consideration is that it confuses the contractual notion of consideration with the restitutionary notion of consideration.[287] Whereas consideration in the law of restitution is concerned with the condition which the plaintiff imposes for the transfer of a benefit to the defendant, the contractual notion of consideration is the defendant's promise which is required for a contract to be valid. Consequently, if the contract is void as a matter of law then the defendant's promise is invalid as well, and so contractual consideration is absent. But it does not follow from the fact that the contract is void that restitutionary relief should follow automatically, since some reason must be identified to require the defendant to make restitution to the plaintiff, typically that the plaintiff's intention to transfer a benefit to the defendant can be considered to be vitiated: and just because the defendant's promise is void it does not follow that the plaintiff's intention is vitiated. In the swaps cases, the plaintiff paid money to the defendant on condition that, if the defendant became liable to pay the plaintiff under the agreement, this money would be paid to the plaintiff. Typically, this condition was satisfied to some extent so that the plaintiff's intention to benefit the defendant could not be treated as vitiated. This is a strong argument and, whilst it can be countered by saying that the transfer of a benefit to the defendant is conditional on the transaction being valid so that if the contract is invalid the plaintiff's intention can be considered to be vitiated, this notion of vitiation of intention is highly artificial.

---

[284] [1998] 3 WLR 1095.

[285] The House of Lords in *ibid* held that such a mistake of law would not ground a restitutionary claim. For criticism of this conclusion see pp. 163–4 above.

[286] Though restitution of payments made in such circumstances may be defeated by the bar of voluntary submission to an honest claim. See pp. 686–9 below.

[287] See, for example, Swadling 'Restitution for No Consideration' (1994) 2 *RLR* 73, 85.

(ii) An alternative approach

Although the recognition of absence of consideration as a ground of restitution in its own right can be criticised, it does not follow that the award of restitution in those cases in which this ground was relied on, particularly the swaps cases, is necessarily wrong. In fact the result of these cases can be defended but by reference to a different ground of restitution, albeit one that is closely related to the notion of absence of consideration.

Most commentators have assumed that absence of consideration will be applicable where the plaintiff has transferred a benefit under a void contract. But the fact that a contract is void is not the reason why restitution should be made; it is a symptom rather than a cause. The restitutionary response should not be considered to be triggered simply by the fact that the contract is void, but rather restitution should be grounded on the reason the contract was void in the first place. If this is correct it means that absence of consideration should be rejected as a ground of restitution and three alternative grounds of restitution can be identified which can be used to explain the cases.

(1) Incapacity

In many of the cases in which a contract is found to be null and void the reason is that one of the parties lacks capacity to enter into the contract. Where, for example, the plaintiff lacks such capacity, the reason the contract is null and void is to protect the plaintiff, such as a minor, or the public.[288] This policy of protection should be carried through into the law of restitution, so if the party who lacks capacity to enter into the contract has transferred a benefit to the other party restitution should be grounded on the plaintiff's incapacity. This is illustrated by those cases arising from the swaps litigation in which the local authority sought restitution from a bank. Since the local authority lacked capacity to enter into such a transaction because of a policy that it should not take unnecessary risks with local taxpayers' money, it is right that the bank should make restitution of the money it has received, even if the swaps transaction has been fully executed. The policy behind the decision to avoid the transaction must be followed through into the restitutionary claim, where the policy can be vindicated most effectively.[289] This was explicitly recognised by Morritt LJ in *Guinness Mahon and Co. Ltd.* v. *Kensington and Chelsea Royal LBC*:[290]

---

[288] *Guinness Mahon Co. Ltd.* v. *Chelsea and Kensington LBC* [1998] 3 WLR 829, 840 (Morritt LJ).

[289] *Auckland Harbour Board* v. *R.* [1924] AC 318.

[290] [1998] 3 WLR 829, 840. See also *Kleinwort Benson Ltd.* v. *Lincoln CC* [1998] 3 WLR 1095, 1153 (Lord Hope).

the ultra vires doctrine exists for the protection of the public ... the court should [not] apply the law of restitution so as to minimise the effect of the doctrine. If ... there is no claim for a completed swap then practical effect will be given to a transaction which the doctrine of ultra vires proclaims had no legal existence.

As this dictum makes clear, this emphasis on the reason the transaction was void explains why restitution is available in respect of fully executed transactions: the recipient of the benefit has no better right to receive or retain the benefit after the transaction was executed than he or she did before.

Although questions of incapacity are less important today in respect of private law claims, as exemplified by the fact that the *ultra vires* doctrine has been almost completely abrogated in its application to companies, questions of incapacity may still be applicable. This is illustrated by *Rover International Ltd.* v. *Cannon Film Sales Ltd. (No. 3)*[291] where the plaintiff lacked capacity to make a contract since it had not been incorporated at the time. It is therefore possible to argue that the ground of incapacity could have been relied on in that case as well. Consequently, many of the restitutionary claims which have been analysed as involving the absence of consideration should properly be treated as involving the ground of incapacity.[292]

(2) Unauthorised receipt by a public authority

Another ground of restitution which is available where the plaintiff has transferred a benefit to the defendant pursuant to a transaction which is void arises where the defendant is a public authority. In such a case, the receipt of the benefit by the defendant is unauthorised and so it is required to make restitution to the plaintiff, as was recognised by the House of Lords in *Woolwich Equitable Building Society* v. *IRC*.[293] In fact, it is this ground of restitution which was most appropriate in many of the swaps cases in which a bank sought restitution from a local authority, since the consequence of the transactions being held to be *ultra vires* the local authorities was that the receipt of the money by those authorities was unauthorised, and so restitution should have followed by virtue of this factor alone, for otherwise the local authorities would have obtained a windfall.[294]

---

[291] [1989] 1 WLR 912.   [292] Incapacity is examined in Chapter 13.
[293] [1993] AC 70. See Chapter 14.
[294] See *Westdeutsche Landesbank Girozentrale* v. *Islington LBC* [1994] 1 WLR 938, 951 (Leggatt LJ) and *Guinness Mahon Co. Ltd.* v. *Chelsea and Kensington Royal LBC* [1998] 3 WLR 829, 844 (Waller LJ).

(3) Miscellaneous cases: public policy

There are other cases in which a contract is void for reasons other than incapacity but where the policy behind the invalidity needs to be protected by the award of restitutionary relief. This has been explicitly recognised by Birks who has said that:

wherever the law pursues a policy sufficient to avoid a contract that same policy must carry through to restitution of value which has been transferred. In that way 'void contract' would in itself become a policy ground for restitution.[295]

Although Birks went on to add that 'the cases present an obstacle to that approach' this appears not to be the case where the contract is void for incapacity. The problem with recognising a miscellaneous ground of restitution founded on public policy is that it can result in the reasoning which appears in Birks's statement, namely that restitution should follow whenever a contract is null and void. This would be unacceptable,[296] since restitution should lie only when it is an appropriate way of fulfilling the policy which made the contract void in the first place. It may be particularly difficult to determine when such a restitutionary response is appropriate, but perhaps the annuity cases illustrate when such a response can be justified. The annuity transactions in those cases were void because of the failure to comply with statutory formalities rather than the incapacity of either party.[297] But the policy behind the need for such formalities, and consequent invalidity of the transaction if the formalities were not satisfied, was presumably to protect the parties against exploitation. It follows that if the annuity contracts were void it was entirely appropriate to require the parties to make restitution to ensure that they were placed in the position which they originally occupied. In other words, the award of restitution helped to protect parties to annuity contracts from exploitation by stronger parties.

(iii) The advantages of rejecting absence of consideration as a ground of restitution

Even if the ground of absence of consideration is rejected it does not necessarily mean that any of the cases which have been discussed in this context would have been decided any differently. What it would mean is that the potential confusion between the notions of total failure of consideration and absence of consideration would disappear. 'Consideration' would be returned to its purely restitutionary meaning.

---

[295] Birks, *An Introduction to the Law of Restitution*, p. 220.

[296] See *Guinness Mahon Co. Ltd.* v. *Chelsea and Kensington Royal LBC* [1998] 3 WLR 829, 842 (Waller LJ).

[297] *Westdeutsche Landesbank Girozentrale* v. *Islington LBC* [1996] AC 669, 683 (Lord Goff).

The law would be simplified further since, where a contract was null and void because one of the parties lacked capacity to enter into it, the ground of restitution would simply be the incapacity. The focus of the law would shift to looking at the reason the contract was void rather than determining the consequences of the contract being void. This shift would also mean that restitution in the context of executed contracts would be much easier to defend. Finally, in those cases in which the plaintiff had transferred benefits to the defendant in respect of a contract which was null and void, it would still be possible for the plaintiff to obtain restitution on the ground of total failure of consideration if the plaintiff had not received any of the expected consideration for the benefits.

13

Incapacity

1. GENERAL PRINCIPLES

(a) Incapacity of the plaintiff

Where the plaintiff lacks capacity to enter into a transaction this in itself should constitute a ground of restitution to enable him or her to recover any benefits which he or she has transferred to the defendant pursuant to the transaction. Two reasons can be identified to justify the recognition of incapacity as a ground of restitution in its own right.

(i) Absence or vitiation of intent

The effect of the plaintiff's incapacity will be that he or she cannot be considered to have intended that the defendant should receive a benefit. This will either occur because the plaintiff is incapable of forming the necessary intent as a matter of law, as is the case where the plaintiff is a company or a public authority which has been acting *ultra vires*, or because the effect of the incapacity is such that the plaintiff cannot be considered to have exercised a free will in transferring the benefit to the defendant, as is the case where the plaintiff is a minor or mentally incapacitated.[1] As Fullagar J said in *Blomley* v. *Ryan*,[2] 'the primary question [is] as to the reality of the assent' of the incapacitated person.

(ii) Policy demands restitution

The recognition of incapacity as a ground of restitution can also be justified on policy grounds. This is because the rules which state that the plaintiff lacked capacity to transact with the defendant can be interpreted as incorporating a requirement that the incapacitated person should be restored to the position which he or she occupied before the benefit was transferred to the defendant. This interpretation of the incapacity rules is justified because these rules are founded on a policy of protecting people from the consequences of the incapacitated person's actions. This policy of protection clearly operates where the plaintiff is mentally incapacitated or is an infant, where the incapacitated person him- or herself is in need of protection.[3] Where the plaintiff is a company

---

[1] *Johnson* v. *Clark* [1908] 1 Ch. 303, 316 (Parker J).   [2] (1956) 99 CLR 362, 401.

[3] See, for example, Lord Denning MR in *Chaplin* v. *Leslie Frewin (Publishers) Ltd.* [1966] Ch. 71, 90: 'For the protection of the young and foolish . . .'.

or a public authority the policy of protection is still relevant, but here it is the shareholders or the taxpayers respectively who are in particular need of protection from the consequences of the company's or public authority's actions.

(b) Incapacity of the defendant

Where it is the defendant who is incapacitated this incapacity may be relevant to restitutionary claims in two different ways.

(i) Defendant's incapacity as a defence

The incapacity of the defendant has sometimes been considered to operate as a defence to the plaintiff's claim for restitution. Whether incapacity does indeed operate as a general defence to restitutionary claims is considered in Chapter 27.

(ii) Defendant's incapacity as a ground of restitution

The defendant's incapacity may exceptionally constitute a ground of restitution to enable the plaintiff to obtain restitution from the defendant, but it seems that this will only occur where policy demands that the incapacitated defendant should not retain the benefit. This will be the case where, for example, the defendant is a public authority which has received money from the plaintiff in circumstances in which the defendant did not have capacity to receive the money.[4] In other cases, such as where the defendant was suffering from a mental disorder or was a minor, the defendant's incapacity should not constitute a ground of restitution.[5] This is because the plaintiff's intention to benefit the defendant cannot be considered to have been vitiated simply because the defendant was mentally disordered or a minor and the policy of protecting such people does not require them to make restitution to the plaintiff. Similarly, where the plaintiff sought restitution from a company in respect of goods delivered or services rendered pursuant to a contract which was *ultra vires* the company, the fact that the defendant lacked capacity could not constitute a ground of restitution for the plaintiff's claim.[6]

---

[4] As was recognised by the House of Lords in *Woolwich Equitable Building Society* v. *IRC* [1993] AC 70, discussed in Chapter 14.

[5] Though where the plaintiff transfers property to a minor the court has a discretion to enable the plaintiff to recover that property or its substitute where it considers it to be just to do so. See the Minors' Contract Act 1987, s. 3(1), examined at pp. 762–3 below.

[6] *Re Jon Beauforte (London) Ltd.* [1953] Ch. 131. Today the plaintiff would be able to sue the defendant company on the contract even though it was *ultra vires*: Companies Act 1985, s. 35 (as amended by the Companies Act 1989, s. 108(1)).

There is no reason why the plaintiff cannot obtain restitution from the defendant in circumstances in which the defendant lacked capacity to receive the benefit, but the plaintiff's claim will only succeed if he or she can rely on one of the recognised grounds of restitution. For example, the plaintiff may have transferred a benefit to the defendant who was a minor and who has refused to pay for the benefit. Since the contract is unenforceable the plaintiff cannot sue the defendant on the contract but the plaintiff could obtain restitution on the ground of total failure of consideration.[7]

2. THE CATEGORIES OF INCAPACITY

If the plaintiff's incapacity can constitute a ground of restitution it is vital to determine what constitutes incapacity for these purposes. A number of different types of incapacity can be identified, which need to be analysed with some care since there is a great deal of uncertainty both as to the requirements for establishing each form of incapacity and the effect of each type of incapacity on the plaintiff's restitutionary claim.

(a) Mental disorder

Mental disorder covers a wide variety of conditions including people whose mental development has been slow, whose brains have been damaged or who suffer from some type of recognised physical illness, such as the effects of a brain tumour,[8] or psychological condition, such as schizophrenia or senile dementia.[9] Whatever the reason for the plaintiff's mental disorder, whether he or she can be considered to be incapacitated is a question of degree. The fact that a plaintiff is mentally disordered may be relevant to restitutionary claims in four different circumstances.

(i) Protection of the court

Sometimes, where the mental disorder is such that a person is incapable of managing his or her own property and affairs, he or she will be placed under the protection of the court, which will be able to control his or her property and affairs.[10] This has the consequence that any gift made by the mentally disordered person whilst under the protection of the court will be absolutely void,[11] whereas any contract which disposes of the person's property and which was made without the authority of the court

[7] See Chapter 12.
[8] *Simpson* v. *Simpson* [1989] Fam. Law 20.
[9] *Re Beaney* [1978] 1 WLR 770.
[10] Mental Health Act 1983, s. 94.
[11] *Re Walker* [1905] 1 Ch. 160.

does not bind the mentally disordered person, though it may be ratified by the court.[12] Where the transaction has not been ratified, any property which was transferred under it may be recovered by the court on behalf of the mentally incapacitated person.

(ii) Non est factum

In an extreme case where the plaintiff purports to sign a contract and the mental incapacity is such that he or she does not realise the nature of the document which he or she is signing, then the contract will be void on the ground of *non est factum*.[13] Consequently, the plaintiff will be able to obtain restitution of benefits transferred to the defendant either on the ground of mistake or on the ground of total failure of consideration.

(iii) Other transactions

In all other cases the transaction which the plaintiff entered into will be treated as valid unless two conditions are satisfied.

(1) Failure to understand the nature and effect of the transaction

It must first be established that the plaintiff did not understand the nature and effect of the transaction at the time he or she entered into it. The extent to which the plaintiff must fail to understand the transaction depends on the type of transaction which is involved and its potential effect on the plaintiff's circumstances. A particularly important consideration concerns the type and value of any property which the plaintiff transferred to the defendant. So, for example, in *Re Beaney*[14] the deceased, who was suffering from advanced senile dementia, transferred her house, which was her only valuable asset, to her eldest daughter. The transfer was set aside because the deceased had not understood that the consequence of the transaction was to make an absolute gift of the house to her daughter and the effect of this transfer on the claims of her other children had not been explained to her. As Martin Nourse QC said:[15]

[I]f the subject matter and value of a gift are trivial in relation to the donor's other assets a low degree of understanding will suffice. But, at the other extreme, if its effect is to dispose of the donor's only asset of value and thus for practical purposes to pre-empt the devolution of his estate under his will or on his intestacy, then the degree of understanding required is as high as that required for a will and the donor must understand the claims of all potential donees and the extent of the property to be disposed of.

---

[12] *Baldwyn* v. *Smith* [1900] 1 Ch. 588.   [13] See p. 178 above.

[14] [1978] 1 WLR 770. See also *Simpson* v. *Simpson* [1989] Fam. Law 20 and the decision of the High Court of Australia in *Gibbons* v. *Wright* (1954) 91 CLR 423.

[15] *Ibid*, p. 774.

(2) Defendant's knowledge of the incapacity

The second condition is that the defendant must have known that the plaintiff lacked the capacity to understand what he or she was doing.[16] But why should this be relevant, particularly because such a requirement does not apply where the plaintiff is a minor? The only possible explanation for this requirement is that, where the plaintiff is suffering from a mental disorder, the defendant may have no idea of the incapacity, and such a matter is difficult to check, whereas whether the plaintiff is a minor may be checked easily by asking the minor what his or her age is.

(3) Consequences of the conditions being satisfied

Where the mentally incapacitated plaintiff has transferred a benefit to the defendant in circumstances where both these conditions have been satisfied, he or she will be able to recover the benefit. Where, however, the plaintiff has entered into a contract with the defendant in circumstances where both conditions have been satisfied it is first necessary to show that the contract has ceased to operate before restitutionary relief can be awarded. It is unclear whether the plaintiff's incapacity makes the contract either void[17] or voidable.[18] The preferable view is that the contract is voidable,[19] since this is consistent with the effect of the plaintiff's minority on the validity of the contract.[20] Consequently, any contract made by a plaintiff who was mentally incapacitated to the knowledge of the defendant can be rescinded, although this will be subject to the usual bars on rescission, including that the plaintiff must be in a position to make counter-restitution to the defendant.[21] Once the contract has been rescinded the plaintiff will be able to recover all the benefits which he or she had transferred to the defendant.

(iv) Exploitation

Where a mentally incapacitated plaintiff has transferred a benefit to the defendant the plaintiff may be able to obtain restitution of the benefit without relying on his or her incapacity, but instead by establishing that one of the grounds of restitution which are founded on the principle of exploitation can be established.[22] For example, the plaintiff may be able

---

[16] *Imperial Loan Co.* v. *Stone* [1892] 1 QB 599, 601 (Lord Esher MR). This was affirmed by the Privy Council in *Hart* v. *O'Connor* [1985] AC 1000.

[17] See, for example, *Daily Telegraph Newspaper Co. Ltd.* v. *McLaughlin* [1904] AC 776 and *Simpson* v. *Simpson* [1989] Fam. Law 20.

[18] *Imperial Loan Co. Ltd.* v. *Stone* [1892] 1 QB 599, 602 (Lopes LJ) and *Gibbons* v. *Wright* (1954) 91 C.LR 423.

[19] *Anson's Law of Contract* (by J. Beatson), p. 230.   [20] See p. 416 below.

[21] *Molton* v. *Camroux* (1849) 4 Ex. 17; 154 ER 117. For analysis of the bars to rescission see pp. 32–5 below.

[22] See Chapter 10.

to show that the defendant has unduly influenced the plaintiff or that the defendant has acted unconscionably.

(b) Intoxication

Intoxication is treated as a ground of restitution in the same way as mental disorder. So where, for example, the plaintiff was so intoxicated at the time of signing a contract that he or she did not realise that the nature of the contract was different from that which he or she intended to sign, then the doctrine of *non est factum* will be applicable and the contract will be void. In every other case in which the plaintiff was intoxicated at the time of entering into a transaction with the defendant, this will make the transaction voidable so long as the plaintiff was so intoxicated that he or she did not understand the nature and effect of the transaction and the defendant knew that the plaintiff was intoxicated at the time.[23] This means that the plaintiff must have been really drunk, rather than merely tipsy, before he or she can be regarded as incapacitated. Where, however, the intoxicated person is supplied with necessaries he or she must pay a reasonable price for them.[24]

(c) Somnambulism

It has sometimes been suggested that if the plaintiff entered into a transaction with the defendant whilst sleepwalking, then the transaction can be set aside.[25] Sleepwalking is to be treated as a form of temporary mental incapacity. Whilst it is highly unlikely that such a case would ever arise, transactions entered into whilst sleepwalking should be treated in the same way as acts performed whilst intoxicated. Consequently, any transaction entered into whilst sleepwalking should only be rescinded if the plaintiff lacked understanding of what he or she was doing and the other party knew that the plaintiff was sleepwalking. If the plaintiff signed a contract whilst sleepwalking this could be set aside on the ground of *non est factum*, since the plaintiff would not have been aware of the nature of the document which he or she was signing.[26]

---

[23] *Gore* v. *Gibson* (1845) 13 M and W 623; 153 ER 260. See also *Molton* v. *Camroux* (1849) 4 Ex. 17; 154 ER 1107 and *Matthews* v. *Baxter* (1873) LR 8 Exch. 132.

[24] Sale of Goods Act 1979, s. 3(2).

[25] *Gore* v. *Gibson* (1845) 13 M and W 623, p. 627; 153 ER 260, 262 (Alderson B).

[26] *Gibbons* v. *Wright* (1954) 91 CLR 423.

(d) Minority

(i) The problems raised by minority

The role of minority as a ground of restitution raises issues of some complexity. This is largely due to changes in the law concerning the effect of minority on the validity of transactions. The common law on the effect of minority was replaced by a statutory regime in 1874[27] the main effect of which was to treat contracts made with minors as void, subject to certain exceptions. This statutory regime was abolished by the Minors' Contracts Act 1987[28] with the effect that the common law rules on the validity of contracts made with minors have been resurrected. This means that contracts made with minors are no longer void. It also means that those cases which were decided between 1874 and 1987 need to be analysed with some care. To make matters even more confusing, the definition of what constitutes a minor has also changed. Today a minor is defined as a child under 18,[29] whereas the previous age of majority was 21. It follows that there is now less opportunity for contracts to be made with minors, though the issue continues to be of some practical importance.

(ii) The effect of minority on the validity of contracts

Where a minor has transferred benefits to the defendant pursuant to a contract between them and the minor wishes to recover these benefits, the first question which needs to be considered is whether the contract continues to be operative. This is because of the fundamental principle that restitutionary relief is only available where the contract has ceased to operate.[30] Between 1874 and 1987 contracts made with minors were void, so there was nothing to bar the minor's restitutionary claim. Today, the effect of the contract on the minor depends on the nature of the contract. The contract may fall into one of two categories:[31]

(1) Contracts in which the minor acquired an interest of a permanent or continuous nature, such as contracts for the acquisition of interests in land or shares in a company.[32] These contracts are valid and binding until the minor disclaims the contract whilst still a minor or within a reasonable time of having attained the age of majority.[33]

(2) Other contracts which are not continuous do not bind the minor unless they are ratified within a reasonable time after he or she had attained the age of majority.

---

[27] The Infants' Relief Act 1874. [28] S. 4 (2).
[29] Family Law Reform Act 1969, s. 1. [30] See pp. 40–2 above.
[31] See *Anson's Law of Contract* (by J. Beatson) pp. 209–10.
[32] See *Steinberg* v. *Scala (Leeds) Ltd.* [1923] 2 Ch. 452.
[33] *Lovell and Christmas* v. *Beauchamp* [1894] AC 607.

The distinction between these types of contracts makes legal analysis of the effect of the plaintiff's minority on the contract somewhat difficult. Where the contract can be characterised as continuous in its operation it is acceptable to conclude that the contract operates until it is rescinded. Where the contract is not continuous it is not strictly true to say that it needs to be rescinded since it does not bind the minor during his or her minority and will only bind once the age of majority has been attained and the contract is ratified. Since these contracts cannot affect the minor whilst he or she is a minor there is no need to rescind them. These types of contracts cannot therefore constitute an obstacle to the minor's restitutionary claim if he or she transferred benefits to the defendant under the contract.

(iii) The effect of minority on other transactions

Where a minor makes a gift to a person of full capacity the disposition should be regarded as valid until the minor wishes to set it aside.[34]

(iv) The role of minority in restitutionary claims

(1) There must be a total failure of consideration

Where a minor is not bound by a transaction by reason of his or incapacity, it should follow that the minor will be able to obtain restitution of benefits transferred under the transaction as long as one of the recognised grounds of restitution is applicable. Whether the fact that the plaintiff was a minor can operate as a ground of restitution in its own right is a matter of some controversy. The general approach of the cases is that restitution will not lie simply on the ground of minority, since it must also be shown that the consideration for the transfer of the benefit has totally failed.[35] This is illustrated by *Steinberg* v. *Scala (Leeds) Ltd.*[36] where the plaintiff had repudiated a contract for the purchase of shares whilst she was still a minor and then sought to recover the purchase price from the company. Her restitutionary action failed on the ground that there had not been a total failure of consideration, because she had obtained the very thing for which she had bargained, namely a shareholding in the company. This was a valuable benefit, which entitled her to receive a dividend or to attend general meetings of the shareholders. Similarly, in *Pearce* v. *Brain*[37] the plaintiff, who was a minor, exchanged his motorcycle for the defendant's car. After the plaintiff had driven the car for 70 miles it broke down. The plaintiff then sought to recover the

---

[34] *Zouch* v. *Parsons* (1765) 3 Burr. 1794, 1806; 97 ER 1103, 1110.
[35] See Chapter 12 for analysis of total failure of consideration as a ground of restitution.
[36] [1923] 2 Ch. 452. See also *Corpe* v. *Overton* (1833) 10 Bing. 252; 131 ER 901.
[37] [1929] 2 KB 310.

bicycle or its value, but his action failed on the ground that there had not been a total failure of consideration since he had obtained some benefit from the transaction, namely the use of the car for a few days.

(2) The relevance of minority

Where the conditions for establishing total failure of consideration have been satisfied this will constitute the ground of restitution on which the plaintiff bases his or her restitutionary claim. It would seem, therefore, that the fact that the plaintiff was a minor would be irrelevant. This is not, however, the case, since pleading minority in conjunction with total failure of consideration does have one important advantage to the plaintiff. This is because, where the plaintiff is an adult who entered into a contract of a continuous nature and who wishes to obtain restitution on the ground of total failure of consideration, it is first necessary for the plaintiff to repudiate the contract, for example by showing that the defendant had breached it. This might be difficult to establish. Where, however, the plaintiff is a minor who entered into a contract of a continuous nature the plaintiff can rescind or ignore the contract simply by virtue of the fact that he or she was a minor. It is then only necessary to show that there has been a total failure of consideration before the plaintiff can obtain restitution.

(3) Should it be necessary to establish that the consideration has totally failed?

Is it really appropriate to ground restitution on total failure of consideration in those cases in which the plaintiff was a minor at the time of contracting with the defendant? Careful analysis of the cases which recognise the requirement that there must have been a total failure of consideration suggests that they are concerned with the distinct, but apparently similar, principle that restitution should be denied to the plaintiff if he or she is unable to make full counter-restitution to the defendant. If this is correct, it follows that the appropriate ground of restitution in these cases should be that the plaintiff lacked capacity to enter into the contract with the defendant, but restitution should be denied to the plaintiff if he or she is unable to restore all the benefits which had been received from the defendant.[38] This is a much more satisfactory approach to the problem.

That the plaintiff's minority should operate as a ground of restitution in its own right is perfectly acceptable. The reason contracts made with minors are usually unenforceable against them presumably derives from a desire to protect minors from the consequences of entering into

[38] Goff and Jones, *The Law of Restitution*, p. 641. See also Burrows, *The Law of Restitution*, p. 325 and Treitel, 'The Infants Relief Act 1874' (1957) 73 *LQR* 194.

foolish transactions. If this is the policy of the law such protection will only be partial if restitution is denied.[39] There is no reason why the policy which makes the contract unenforceable against the minor should not be followed through to its logical conclusion to ensure that the benefits which were provided under the contract should be restored to the minor, subject to the minor restoring any benefits which he or she had obtained under the contract. But despite this, the law considers that the position of the defendant should not be ignored and, if the plaintiff is unable to restore benefits which were received from the defendant, then it is only just that restitution should be denied. Support for this approach can be found in the decision of the Divisional Court in *Valentini* v. *Canali*[40] where the plaintiff, who was a minor, leased a house from the defendant. The plaintiff agreed to pay £102 for the use of the defendant's furniture and paid £68 on account. After using the house and the furniture for a few months the plaintiff sought to recover the £68. His action failed because, as Lord Coleridge CJ said:[41]

When an infant has paid for something and has consumed or used it, it is contrary to natural justice that he should recover back the money which he has paid. Here the infant plaintiff who claimed to recover back the money which he had paid to the defendant had the use of a quantity of furniture for some months. He could not give back his benefit or replace the defendant in the position in which he was before the contract.

Lord Coleridge did not suggest that restitution should be denied because there had been no total failure of consideration. Rather, restitution was denied because, as he thought, the plaintiff could not make counter-restitution to the defendant.

It is much more consistent with the fundamental principles of the law of restitution that the plaintiff's restitutionary claim should be defeated because he or she cannot make counter-restitution to the defendant, than it is to say that the plaintiff's claim should fail because he or she cannot rely on the ground of total failure of consideration. Similarly, where the plaintiff needs to rescind a contract it has long been accepted that rescission will be barred if the plaintiff cannot make counter-restitution to the defendant. The importance of this analysis is that the more liberal interpretation of the bar that counter-restitution is impossible should be applicable to restitutionary claims founded on the plaintiff's minority.[42] It follows that the plaintiff's restitutionary claim should not be barred simply because he or she cannot make exact counter-restitution to the defendant. It should be sufficient that the plaintiff can restore the value

---

[39] As Lord Denning MR said in *Chaplin* v. *Leslie Frewin (Publishers) Ltd.* [1966] Ch. 71: '[i]f the infant is to be protected, the law must be able to intervene as well after as before the disposition is made'.

[40] (1889) 24 QBD 166.   [41] *Ibid*, p. 167.   [42] See pp. 690–3 below.

of any benefit which he or she has received to the defendant without necessarily having to restore the actual benefit received. This means that in a case such as *Valentini* v. *Canali* the plaintiff would have been able to rescind the contract and recover the money paid to the defendant, if he had made counter-restitution by paying the defendant the reasonable price for hiring the furniture.

(4) Exploitation

Where a minor has transferred a benefit to the defendant he or she may be able to obtain restitution of the benefit without relying on his or her incapacity, but instead by establishing that one of the grounds of restitution which are founded on the principle of exploitation can be established.[43] For example, the minor may be able to show that the defendant had unduly influenced the minor or that the defendant had acted unconscionably in entering into the transaction with him or her.

(e) Corporate incapacity

(i) Restitution at common law

The law on corporate capacity used to be much more important than it is now. Under the common law where a company provided a benefit to the defendant in circumstances which were beyond the company's capacity, the transaction was characterised as *ultra vires* and was null and void,[44] with the consequence that the company could recover the benefit from the defendant.[45] This right of restitution was qualified by the House of Lords in *Sinclair* v. *Brougham*,[46] where it was held that a personal restitutionary claim would fail where the plaintiff sought to recover money which had been lent to the defendant, because awarding restitution in such circumstances would enable the plaintiff effectively to enforce a loan which was null and void. This qualification has since been rejected by the House of Lords in *Westdeutsche Landesbank Girozentrale* v. *Islington LBC*.[47] In those cases in which the plaintiff company which had been acting *ultra vires* obtained restitution from the defendant, it seems that the ground of restitution was the very incapacity of the company itself, the award of restitutionary relief being justified by the need to protect the company's shareholders against abuse of corporate funds.[48]

---

[43] See Chapter 10.

[44] *Ashbury Railway Carriage and Iron Co. Ltd.* v. *Riche* (1875) LR 7 HL 653.

[45] *Brougham* v. *Dwyer* (1913) 108 LT 504. See also *International Sales and Agencies Ltd.* v. *Marcus* [1982] 3 All ER 551, 560 (Lawson J).

[46] [1914] AC 398.   [47] [1996] AC 669.

[48] See Burrows, *The Law of Restitution*, p. 330.

(ii) The implications of statutory reform of the ultra vires *doctrine*

The common law *ultra vires* doctrine has been abrogated by statute.[49] Section 35(1) of the Companies Act 1985 states that:

The validity of an act done by a company shall not be called into question on the ground of lack of capacity by reason of anything in the company's memorandum.

It follows from this provision that, if a company transfers a benefit to another party in circumstances in which the company did not have capacity to do so because the transaction lay outside the company's objects which are contained in its memorandum, the validity of the transfer cannot be called into question. Consequently, the company will not be able to recover the benefit from the other party on the ground of the company's incapacity. There is, however, nothing to stop the company from recovering the benefit by reference to any other ground of restitution.

(f) Incapacity of public authorities

Where a public authority transfers a benefit to the defendant in circumstances in which the authority lacked the capacity to transfer the benefit, the incapacity may operate as a ground of restitution to enable the benefit to be recovered.[50] This is illustrated by *Auckland Harbour Board* v. *R.*[51] where the Privy Council held that money which had been paid out of the consolidated fund[52] by the Minister of Railways was recoverable since he was authorised to make the payment only if the recipient of the money had granted a lease, and the money had been paid even though no lease had been granted. Consequently the payment was unauthorised by Parliament and so it was *ultra vires*. Restitution is justified on the ground of the public authority's incapacity because it protects the public from the consequences of public authorities misusing public funds.[53]

Whilst the ground of restitution is clear and the award of restitution is justifiable the judgment of Viscount Haldane in the *Auckland Harbour Board* case has caused some confusion. He said that payment 'from the consolidated fund made without Parliamentary authority is simply illegal and ultra vires, and may be recovered by the Government if it can, as

---

[49] Companies Act 1985, s. 35, as inserted by the Companies Act 1989, s. 108.

[50] The question whether restitutionary relief is available against a public authority which received a benefit which it lacked the capacity to receive is considered in Chapter 14.

[51] [1924] AC 318. See also *Commonwealth of Australia* v. *Burns* [1971] VR 825 and *Sandvik Australia Pty. Ltd.* v. *Commonwealth of Australia* (1989) 89 ALR 213.

[52] This is the central fund into which taxes are paid: [1924] AC 318, 326.

[53] See *Commonwealth of Australia* v. *Burns* [1971] VR 825, 827 (Newton J).

here, be traced'[54] Does this reference to tracing mean that the State's restitutionary claim is founded on the vindication of the public authority's proprietary rights, with the consequence that restitution will only be obtained if, and to the extent that, the public authority can identify property in the hands of the defendant in which the plaintiff has retained a proprietary interest? This would be unnecessarily restrictive, and the better view is that Viscount Haldane was not using 'traced' in any technical sense. Rather, what he appears to have meant is simply that it is possible to show that money from the consolidated fund had been received by the defendant. In other words, 'traced' is simply being used in the sense of the money being received 'at the expense of' the State.[55]

That a public authority's incapacity may constitute a ground of restitution in its own right has been something which has received little judicial attention. In a number of cases the public authority has based its claim on other grounds of restitution, such as mistake, when incapacity would have served just as well and might even have been easier to establish.[56] This is particularly true of some of the interest rate swap cases, where a local authority sought to obtain restitution of money paid to financial institutions under transactions which the authority did not have capacity to enter into.[57] In these cases the local authority appears to have relied on the ground of absence of consideration, as was first recognised by Hobhouse J in *Westdeutsche Landesbank Girozentrale* v. *Islington LBC*,[58] when it could have simply relied on the ground that the plaintiff lacked capacity to enter into the transaction. At the very least, by basing the restitutionary claim on the plaintiff's incapacity, it is easier to justify the award of restitutionary relief simply because of the policy of ensuring that the interests of those who provided the funds in the first place should be protected against the misuse of the funds.

---

[54] [1924] AC 318, 327.

[55] This was the interpretation which Newton J preferred in *Commonwealth of Australia* v. *Burns* [1971] VR 825, 828.

[56] The recent recognition that the public authority could obtain restitution on the ground of mistake of law provides another route for public authorities to obtain restitution, but the ambit of this ground of restitution remains a matter of some uncertainty. See pp. 162–5 above. Consequently, the ground of incapacity will still be preferable in many cases because it will typically be easier to establish.

[57] See in particular *South Tyneside Metropolitan Borough Council* v. *Svenska International plc.* [1995] 1 All ER 545.

[58] [1994] 4 All ER 890. See pp. 394–403 above

14

Restitution from Public Authorities

1. GENERAL ISSUES

(a) Why should public authorities be treated differently from other defendants?

Whereas every chapter in this Part has been concerned with identifying particular grounds of restitution and the principles which underlie them, this chapter is concerned with the application of these grounds of restitution and principles in one particular context, namely where a restitutionary claim is brought against public authorities.[1] Such separate treatment is justified because there is a growing body of case law which suggests that, where the defendant is a public authority, there are additional questions of policy which need to be taken into account when determining whether the restitutionary claim should succeed. There is a public law dimension to the claim which always requires careful consideration. There are essentially two contradictory questions of public policy which need to be taken into account.

(i) Constitutional considerations

There is a constitutional dimension to restitutionary claims brought against public authorities which derives from the principle that, where a public authority is not entitled to the money which it has received, then the money should be repaid to the citizen from whom it was unlawfully taken. The justification for this principle is that, since the power of the public authority to demand payment from the citizen can only exist under the law, it follows that if the demand was made unlawfully then the public authority has no right to retain what it received and should make restitution to the payer. That public authorities can only demand payment where they are lawfully authorised to do so is a fundamental principle of English law which is enshrined in Article 4 of the Bill of Rights 1689. This states that:

levying money for or to the use of the Crown, by pretence of prerogative, without grant of Parliament, for longer time, or in other manner than the same is or shall be granted is illegal.

[1] For restitutionary claims brought by public authorities there is less complexity, although note the particular issues concerning institutional incapacity, examined at pp. 420–1 above.

This principle continues to be of profound importance today. The effect of it is that public authorities can only demand payment where they have statutory authority to do so. This was recognised in *Attorney-General* v. *Wilts. United Dairies Ltd.*[2] where it was held to be illegal for the Food Controller to require payment of a sum of money as a condition for the grant of a licence to purchase milk. This was because there was no express authority from Parliament to demand the money and so the demand was contrary to the Bill of Rights. As Atkin LJ said:[3]

If an officer of the Executive seeks to justify a charge upon the subject made for the use of the Crown (which includes all the purposes of the public revenue), he must show, in clear terms, that Parliament has authorised the particular charge.

The logical consequence of this constitutional principle is that, where the public authority receives payment as a result of an unlawful demand, it should make restitution to the payer.[4] That the payer should be entitled to restitution as of right seems even more obvious in the light of the fact that, where the Crown pays money out of the consolidated fund without statutory authority, it is able to recover the payment by virtue of its incapacity to make the payment in the first place.[5]

(ii) Implications for the general community

But even though the payer of an unauthorised demand to a public authority appears to have a clear case for restitution by virtue of constitutional considerations, subject to the identification of a ground of restitution, this is complicated by a second consideration of public policy. This derives from the fact that restitutionary claims which concern public authorities are likely to involve large sums of money, whether because one or two claimants seek to recover large sums or because there are numerous claims for relatively minor sums. Where a public authority has received such sums in circumstances in which it can be shown to be unjustly enriched, awarding restitutionary remedies may seriously jeopardise public funds with consequent deleterious effects on the community.[6] It follows that restitutionary claims against public authorities should be deterred, for reasons of public policy.

(iii) Balancing principle and pragmatism

Consequently, the question whether a restitutionary claim can successfully be brought against a public authority involves a clash of principle and pragmatism. For constitutional principle demands that a public

---

[2] (1921) 37 TLR 884 (CA); (1922) 127 LT 822 (HL).   [3] (1921) 37 TLR 884, 886.
[4] *Woolwich Equitable Building Society* v. *IRC* [1993] AC 70, 172 (Lord Goff).
[5] *Auckland Harbour Board* v. *R.* [1924] AC 318. See p. 420 above.
[6] *Glasgow Corporation* v. *Lord Advocate*, 1959 SC 203, 230 (Lord Clyde).

authority which has unlawfully received money should return it, but pragmatism suggests caution, to preserve the security of the public authority's receipts for the greater good, namely the benefit of the general community. These arguments are essentially incompatible but, as will be seen, some form of compromise can be reached by accepting the right of the payer to bring a restitutionary claim but ensuring that the public authority has a number of special defences to protect the security of its receipt.[7] It follows that, when the position of public authorities within the law of restitution is considered, there are two key questions which need to be examined. First, whether the existing grounds of restitution are adequate to enable plaintiffs to obtain restitution from public authorities, or whether special grounds of restitution are needed to ensure that the constitutional principle is adequately protected. Secondly, whether the peculiar position of these authorities requires special defences to be created, to ensure that there is no unnecessary disruption of public finances which could have profoundly detrimental effects on the effectiveness of the public authority.[8]

(b) Defining public authorities

'Public authorities' can be defined widely to include the emanations of the State in whatever form. Consequently, a 'public authority' can include local authorities, the Inland Revenue, quangos and even nationalised industries. Some of the issues raised in this chapter will also be applicable to the recently privatised public utilities. Although, these utilities are in form no different from any other company which is motivated by the need to make profit, so that notions of jeopardising their finances should only be of a secondary concern, these recently privatised companies do maintain a powerful, sometimes monopolistic position, so that they straddle the public and private law divide. This raises important questions of whether any different considerations should apply in respect of restitutionary claims brought against such companies.

(c) Establishing unjust enrichment

Usually a restitutionary claim will be brought against a public authority where the authority received money which it was not authorised to receive. These are called *ultra vires* payments. Where the public authority has received money from the plaintiff, there is no doubt that the author-

---

[7] See pp. 440–1 below.

[8] No special defences are recognised in respect of claims for restitution from public authorities. Whether such special defences should be recognised is considered at pp. 440–1 below.

ity has been enriched at the plaintiff's expense. The crucial question therefore relates to the identification of a ground of restitution. There is no reason, however, why a restitutionary claim against a public authority cannot be concerned with recovering the value of non-money benefits, so long as the test of enrichment has been satisfied.[9] But since virtually every case which involves restitutionary claims being brought against a public authority relates to restitution of *ultra vires* payments, it is this type of claim which will be examined in this chapter. The receipt of a payment may be regarded as *ultra vires* the public authority for three reasons.

(i) Invalid statutory provisions

Where money is paid to a public authority pursuant to an invalid statutory provision, it follows that the money is not lawfully due to the public authority and so it will be characterised as *ultra vires*.[10]

(ii) Unauthorised transactions

Payment to a public authority will also be characterised as *ultra vires* if it is made pursuant to a transaction in which the public authority is not authorised to participate. The best illustration of this type of *ultra vires* payment arises from the interest rate swaps litigation, where financial institutions paid money to local authorities pursuant to interest rate swaps transactions which the House of Lords held that the local authorities did not have capacity to enter.[11]

(iii) Mistake

The final reason why the receipt of a payment might be considered to be *ultra vires* the public authority is a mistake which meant that, even though the public authority was authorised to demand payment of money in principle, the particular payer was not liable to pay the money, either at all or at least not the full amount which was demanded. The public authority's mistake in demanding the payment from the payer may have been a factual mistake as to the assessment of the sum which was due or was a mistake of law arising from the misinterpretation of a particular regulation which was valid but was never intended to apply to such a payer.

In all of these situations, even though the initial payment to the public authority may have been *ultra vires*, it is possible for Parliament to pass retrospective legislation to validate the payment. Such legislation does not contravene the European Convention on Human Rights.[12]

---

[9] See Chapter 4.   [10] *Woolwich Equitable Building Society* v. *IRC* [1993] AC 70.
[11] *Hazell* v. *Hammersmith and Fulham LBC* [1992] 2 AC 1.
[12] *National Provincial Building Society* v. *UK* [1997] STC 1466. See Tiley, 'Human Rights and Taxpayers' (1998) 57 *CLJ* 269.

The question which needs to be considered in this chapter is whether the person who made an *ultra vires* payment to the public authority can sue the authority for restitution and, if so, what the relevant ground of restitution is. Whilst this analysis will concentrate on restitutionary claims at common law, it will also be necessary to examine certain specific statutory provisions which recognise to varying extents a right to obtain restitution of *ultra vires* payments from public authorities.

2. THE GROUNDS OF RESTITUTION

(a) Mistake

With the abolition of the mistake of law bar by the House of Lords in *Kleinwort Benson Ltd.* v. *Lincoln City Council*[13] there is much greater scope for the plaintiff who has made an *ultra vires* payment to a public authority to obtain restitution by reference to an established ground of restitution, namely mistake. This is because many cases involving *ultra vires* payments, but certainly not all,[14] arise because the plaintiff was mistaken as to the law since typically he or she believed that he or she was liable to pay the money to the public authority.

(b) Duress

Where a defendant obtains a benefit as a result of an unlawful demand, then this will constitute a ground of restitution, namely duress.[15] Since the plaintiff's restitutionary claim in respect of *ultra vires* payments to a public authority is by definition unlawful, the plaintiff will be able to obtain restitution on the ground of duress of the person if the payment was caused by the public authority threatening to restrain, or actually restraining, the plaintiff or duress of goods if the public authority threatened to seize, or actually seized, the plaintiff's property. Alternatively, restitution could be grounded on economic duress if the defendant threatened to breach a contract, commit a tort or do some other unlawful act. So, for example, the plaintiff might be able to recover money from the defendant on the ground of economic duress if the plaintiff paid the money as the result of an unlawful threat by the defendant to withdraw a licence if the money was not paid.[16] But the most likely form of duress to

---

[13] [1998] 3 WLR 1095. See Chapter 8.

[14] See *Woolwich Equitable Building Society* v. *IRC* [1993] AC 70 where the plaintiff had not been affected by a mistake, either of fact or of law.

[15] See Chapter 9.

[16] This would also be covered by the ground of restitution known as extortion by colour of office. See pp. 427–9 below.

be applicable in respect of restitutionary claims against public authorities is duress of goods, since often the authority will have the sanction to seize the plaintiff's goods if the money demanded is not paid.[17] Such a threat is unlawful because the authority is not authorised to seize goods in respect of a debt which is not lawfully due. Where, however, the authority threatens to institute legal proceedings to recover the money if it is not paid, this does not constitute duress[18] because the plaintiff is given an opportunity to dispute the legality of the demand in legal proceedings. Consequently, payment in response to such a threat is characterised as a voluntary payment and is not recoverable on the ground of duress.

(c) Extortion by colour of office (*colore officii*)

(i) Defining extortion by colour of office

Extortion by colour of office, also known as *colore officii*,[19] is a ground of restitution which is founded on the general principle of compulsion, like duress.[20] Extortion by colour of office is confined in its operation to restitution from public authorities or public officials. Essentially this ground of restitution arises where 'a public officer demands and is paid money he is not entitled to, or more than he is entitled to, for the performance of his public duty'.[21]

It is unclear to what extent this ground of restitution is different from that of duress. The preferable view is that duress will only be established where the plaintiff can show that the public authority had obtained payment as the result of an unlawful threat. For the purposes of extortion by colour of office it is not necessary for the plaintiff to prove that the public authority had actually threatened the plaintiff in any way. The necessary compulsion can be presumed where a public authority or official has demanded payment from the plaintiff, because of the peculiar powers of enforcement, and even punishment, which are available to such bodies and people if the payment is not made. For example, if the authority demands excessive payment for a licence, the plaintiff may have no choice but to pay the money since the licence is vital to the plaintiff's business. The public authority does not need to threaten that it will not issue the licence if the money is not paid, because it is implicit in the demand that if the money is not forthcoming the plaintiff will not get the

---

[17] See *Maskell* v. *Horner* [1915] 3 KB 106.

[18] *William Whiteley Ltd.* v. *R.* (1910) 101 LT 741.

[19] '*Colore officii*' was described by Glidewell LJ in *Woolwich* v. *IRC* [1993] AC 70, 80 as an 'archaic phrase [which] is at best vague and at worst almost meaningless at the present day'.

[20] See Chapter 9.   [21] *Mason* v. *New South Wales* (1959) 102 CLR 108, 140.

licence. The refusal of the authority to issue the licence would in fact be unlawful because the money demanded was not lawfully due to the public authority.

It follows that the rationale of the extortion by colour of office ground of restitution does not lie in the fact that the defendant has threatened the plaintiff. Rather, it is founded on the fact that public officials and authorities occupy a peculiarly powerful position, such that demands for payment made by such people and organisations have more authority than similar demands made by private individuals. This was recognised by Lord Denning in *Lloyds Bank Ltd.* v. *Bundy*[22] who said that these cases arise where the public official is 'in a strong bargaining position by virtue of his official position or public profession'. It follows that this ground of restitution can be considered to be founded on both the principles of compulsion and exploitation. But the best explanation of extortion by colour of office is that it is founded on the principle of compulsion. This was recognised by Isaacs J in *Sargood Bros.* v. *The Commonwealth*:[23]

> The right to recovery after a demand c*olore officii* rests upon the assumption that the position occupied by the defendant creates virtual compulsion, where it conveys to the person paying the knowledge or belief that he has no means of escape from payments strictly so called if he wishes to avert injury to or deprivation of some right to which he is entitled without such payment.

(ii) Identifying extortion by colour of office

One of the best illustrations of the application of this ground of restitution is *Morgan* v. *Palmer*[24] where publicans in a town who needed licences to sell liquor were required to pay four shillings to the mayor. This continued for over 65 years. It was held that such payments were *ultra vires* and the plaintiff was allowed to recover what he had paid because the parties were not on equal terms. This suggests that the court presumed compulsion simply because the mayor was in a stronger bargaining position.

But this ground of restitution and the principle of implicit compulsion has not always been recognised. For example, in *Twyford* v. *Manchester Corporation*[25] a monumental mason was charged fees in respect of the work he had done in a cemetery owned by the Manchester Corporation when the Corporation had no right to make such charges. The plaintiff's restitutionary claim failed because the defendant had never threatened that the plaintiff would be excluded if he did not pay the sums demanded. This means that the plaintiff could not have established

---

[22] [1975] QB 326, 337.   [23] (1910) 11 CLR 258, 277.
[24] (1824) 2 B and C 729; 107 ER 584. See also *Dew* v. *Parsons* (1819) 2 B and Ald. 562; 106 ER 471 and *Brocklebank Ltd.* v. *R.* [1925] 1 KB 52.
[25] [1946] Ch. 236. See also *Slater* v. *Burnley Corporation* (1888) 59 LT 636.

duress, but there was surely scope for identifying an implied threat to exclude the plaintiff arising from the fact that the defendant was in a much stronger position, possessing as it did powers to exclude the plaintiff if the money was not paid.

(iii) Is extortion by colour of office still a relevant ground of restitution?

Although the ground of extortion by colour of office has proved to be of some significance in respect of restitutionary claims brought against public authorities, it is probably a ground of restitution which will no longer be of any relevance. This is because the House of Lords in *Woolwich Equitable Building Society* v. *IRC*[26] has recognised a new ground of restitution of relevance to restitutionary claims against public authorities, which does all of the work of extortion by colour of office and more. The better view, therefore, is that whilst extortion by colour of office is of historical interest and laid the foundation for the recognition of the new ground of restitution in *Woolwich*, it is a ground which is no longer of any significance to the law of restitution.

(d) Total failure of consideration

Usually failure of consideration will only be applicable as a ground of restitution where the basis for the plaintiff's payment has totally failed.[27] This ground will consequently generally be of no relevance in the context of recovery of *ultra vires* payments, since often the basis on which the plaintiff made the payment will not have failed totally. This is illustrated by *Westdeutsche Landesbank Girozentrale* v. *Islington LBC*[28] where the plaintiff bank had paid the defendant local authority pursuant to a number of *ultra vires* interest rate swaps transactions. As regards most of these transactions the plaintiff could not show that the consideration for its payments had totally failed because it had received money from the defendant as well. However, in respect of two of the transactions restitutionary relief was awarded on the ground of total failure of consideration since the plaintiff had not received any money from the defendant in respect of these transactions.

(e) Absence of consideration

Absence of consideration has been the ground of restitution of particular importance in the context of restitution from public authorities, most notably the interest rate swap cases. Indeed, it was this ground which was relied on by both the trial judge and the Court of Appeal to justify the

---

[26] [1993] AC 70. See p. 432 below.   [27] See Chapter 12.
[28] [1994] 4 All ER 890 (Hobhouse J); [1994] 1 WLR 938 CA.

award of restitution at common law in *Westdeutsche Landesbank Girozentrale* v. *Islington LBC.*[29] It was considered that there was no consideration for the plaintiff's payments to the defendant because the swap transactions were null and void. Since *ultra vires* payments to public authorities are void payments, it follows that absence of consideration is a potentially important ground of restitution in respect of the recovery of such payments from public authorities. There are, however, certain difficulties in applying this ground of restitution to such restitutionary claims.[30] In particular, it may be considered that this ground of restitution is only applicable where the plaintiff has paid money to a public authority pursuant to a contract, where the plaintiff expects to receive a benefit in return for the payment, and not where the plaintiff pays tax or duty to the public authority. In fact, absence of consideration may even be applicable to the recovery of this type of *ultra vires* payment. This is because the plaintiff will have paid the authority in the belief that the payment will have discharged his or her liability to the authority. This is the consideration which the plaintiff expects to receive for the payment. But if the money was not due, it follows that there is no liability which can be discharged, and so there can be no consideration for the plaintiff's payment as a matter of law. Such an argument was recognised by Lord Mansfield in *Campbell* v. *Hall*[31] where the plaintiff recovered duties which he had paid on sugar exported from Grenada on the ground that the duty had been unlawfully demanded because it had never been authorised by Parliament. The duty was recoverable specifically because it had been paid without consideration.[32]

(f) *Ultra vires* receipt

(i) Implicit recognition of the ground of *ultra vires* receipt

Restitutionary claims against public authorities have succeeded in other cases, where none of the established grounds of restitution appear to have been applicable. The success of the plaintiff's claim in these cases can only be justified on the ground of an independent ground of restitution which is peculiar to restitutionary claims against public authorities. This is illustrated by *Steele* v. *Williams.*[33] In this case the plaintiff had taken extracts from a parish register. After he had done so, the parish

---

[29] [1994] 4 All ER 890 (Hobhouse J); [1994] 1 WLR 938 CA. See pp. 396–8 above.

[30] Other difficulties with the ground of absence of consideration are considered at pp. 398–403 above.

[31] (1774) 1 Cowp. 204; 98 ER 1245.

[32] See also *Dew* v. *Parsons* (1819) B and Ald. 562; 106 ER 471 and *Queens of the River Steamship Co. Ltd.* v. *The Conservators of the River Thames* (1899) 15 TLR 474.

[33] (1853) 8 Exch. 625; 155 ER 1502. See also *South of Scotland Electricity Board* v. *British Oxygen Co. Ltd.* [1959] 1 WLR 587.

clerk demanded a sum of money which the plaintiff paid. This money was not lawfully due to the clerk and the plaintiff was held able to recover it. This case has sometimes been treated as one in which the ground of restitution was compulsion involving extortion by colour of office, but there is nothing to suggest that the plaintiff was compelled to make the payment since the demand for payment arose only once the plaintiff had taken the extracts from the register. Consequently the case is better regarded as one in which the ground of restitution was simply the fact that the clerk's demand was unauthorised, making his receipt of the money *ultra vires*.[34]

(ii) Explicit rejection of the ground of *ultra vires receipt*

Other cases have rejected a general right of restitution founded on the receipt of an *ultra vires* payment, primarily because of the fear that allowing restitution for this reason would unsettle public finances.[35] Most importantly, such a general ground of restitution was rejected by the Supreme Court of Canada in *Air Canada* v. *British Columbia*,[36] where a majority of the court rejected the plaintiff taxpayers' claim to recover *ultra vires* payments for three main reasons:

(1) If the plaintiff's claim were allowed to succeed then the State would need to recover the money from a new generation of taxpayers which had not benefited from the provision of State services funded by the tax.
(2) Arranging for the repayment of the original taxpayers and issuing new tax demands would be economically inefficient.
(3) A further consequence of repaying tax to the original taxpayers would be to disrupt public finances.

Whilst all of these factors are possible dangers arising from restitutionary claims being brought against public authorities, they should not prevent the acceptance of a general right of recovery and should be dealt with by developing specific defences for the protection of public authorities where the greater public good requires such protection. This was the approach which was advocated by Wilson J in a powerful dissenting judgment, where she argued that there should be a general right of recovery where money is paid to public authorities which is not lawfully due.[37]

---

[34] Alternatively, the result could be justified by reference to the ground of absence of consideration.

[35] See, for example, *National Pari-Mutuel Association Ltd.* v. *R.* (1930) 47 TLR 110.

[36] (1989) 58 DLR 161.

[37] See also Cornish, 'Colour of Office: Restitutionary Redress against Public Authority' [1987] *JMCL* 41 and Birks, 'Restitution from the Executive: A Tercentenary Footnote to the Bill of Rights' in *Essays on Restitution* (ed. Finn), Chapter 6.

(iii) Explicit recognition of the ground of ultra vires receipt

A new ground of restitution, confined in its application to restitutionary claims brought against public authorities for the recovery of payments made pursuant to an *ultra vires* demand, has been recognised by the House of Lords in the important case of *Woolwich Equitable Building Society* v. *Inland Revenue Commissioners.*[38]

(1) The facts of *Woolwich*

The Inland Revenue had assessed the tax liability of the Woolwich Building Society by reference to regulations made under the Finance Act 1985, regulations which were subsequently held by the House of Lords to be *ultra vires* and so rendering the tax demand invalid.[39] The effect of this was that the plaintiff had paid nearly £57 million more tax to the Revenue than was actually due. The Revenue repaid this money to the plaintiff with interest, but it refused to pay interest in respect of the period in which it first received the payment until the decision of the trial judge that the regulations were void. Consequently, the plaintiff sued to recover this interest, amounting to £6.73 million. The success of the plaintiff's claim depended on whether the Revenue was liable to repay the plaintiff from the moment it received the payment or from the moment when the regulations were held to be void. If the Revenue's liability arose by virtue of its unjust enrichment, then this liability would have existed from the moment at which it received the payment from the plaintiff. Clearly the Revenue had been enriched at the plaintiff's expense. The key question, therefore, was whether the plaintiff's claim fell within one of the recognised grounds of restitution.

In determining which grounds of restitution were applicable a number of features concerning the payment by the plaintiff to the Revenue need to be emphasised. The plaintiff paid the sums demanded by the Revenue, even though it disputed the legality of the demand, because it felt that it had no choice but to pay. This was because on its face the demand was lawful. If the plaintiff had refused to pay the money it would have been the only building society to do so. Consequently, any proceedings brought by the Revenue to recover the tax would have been gravely embarrassing and would have resulted in adverse publicity. If the plaintiff had failed to pay but the Revenue's demand was eventually vindicated, the building society feared it would incur heavy penalties and

---

[38] [1993] AC 70. For commentary see McKendrick, 'Restitution of Unlawfully Demanded Taxes' [1993] *LMCLQ* 88; Beatson, 'Restitution of Taxes, Levies and Other Imposts: Defining the Extent of the *Woolwich* Principle' (1993) 109 *LQR* 401; Virgo, 'The Law of Taxation is Not an Island—Overpaid Taxes and the Law of Restitution' [1993] *BTR* 442.

[39] *R.* v. *Inland Revenue Commissioners, ex p. Woolwich Equitable Building Society* [1990] 1 WLR 1400.

the interest owing to the Revenue would have far outweighed any return that could have been obtained by investment of the disputed sum. Finally, at the time when the payments were made it was not possible to identify the amount which was in dispute. Therefore, the plaintiff decided to pay but lodged a protest with the Revenue when it did so.

(2) Identifying the relevant ground of restitution

The key question for the House of Lords to determine was whether the plaintiff's claim fell within any of the recognised grounds of restitution.

(a) Mistake

Clearly the plaintiff had not paid the tax as the result of a mistake because the plaintiff had disputed its liability to pay the tax from the start, and if there had been a mistake it would have been a mistake of law, which was not a ground of restitution at the time.

(b) Duress

Although the Revenue possessed statutory powers to distrain against the taxpayer's goods if it did not pay the tax without needing to obtain a court order to do so, the Revenue had not actually threatened the plaintiff with distraint. Nevertheless, Lords Browne-Wilkinson and Slynn, whilst accepting that the traditional definition of duress was not satisfied on the facts, felt that the plaintiff was under such pressure to pay the tax that it was compelled to do so, with the result that the payment was not voluntary and so was recoverable.[40] Lord Goff accepted the existence of such pressure but, because the possibility of distraint by the Revenue was very remote, concluded that compulsion could not be established on the facts of the case.[41]

(c) Absence of consideration

Lord Browne-Wilkinson also referred to the fact that the plaintiffs had paid the money for no consideration[42] as a further reason why the plaintiff's restitutionary claim should succeed.

(d) Receipt of an ultra vires payment

The references to duress and absence of consideration were merely supplementary arguments in favour of the plaintiff's right to obtain restitution. The true ground of restitution was that 'money paid by a citizen to a public authority in the form of taxes or other levies paid pursuant to an *ultra vires* demand by the authority is *prima facie* recoverable by the citizen as of right'.[43] The essential feature of this ground of restitution, which was identified by Lord Goff and endorsed by Lords Slynn and

---

[40] [1993] AC 70, p. 198 (Lord Browne-Wilkinson) and p. 204 (Lord Slynn).
[41] *Ibid*, pp. 172–3.   [42] *Ibid*, p. 198.   [43] *Ibid*, p. 177 (Lord Goff).

Browne-Wilkinson,[44] is that restitution should be awarded simply because the tax was unlawfully demanded under an *ultra vires* statute. This exists as a ground of restitution not because the plaintiff's intention that the defendant receive the payment can be regarded as vitiated, though this is possible, but because of fundamental constitutional principles, arising from the Bill of Rights, that no public authority can retain money which it had no authority to receive.[45] This is therefore a policy-oriented ground of restitution.[46] Such a right of recovery is recognised by the law of the European Community in respect of charges levied by Member States contrary to Community law.[47] As Lord Goff recognised, 'at a time when Community law is becoming increasingly important, it would be strange if the right of the citizen to recover overpaid charges were to be more restricted under domestic law than it is under European law'.

(iv) Determining the ambit of the ground of ultra vires receipt

There are a number of outstanding questions about the ambit and effect of this ground of restitution.

(1) Does this ground apply to all types of *ultra vires* payment?

It is unclear whether this ground of *ultra vires* receipt is confined to cases where money was demanded under an invalid statute, as was the case in *Woolwich* itself. Although the point was expressly left open in *Woolwich*, there is no reason why recovery should be confined to such demands.[48] The crucial feature of this ground of restitution is that money was paid to a public authority which was not authorised to receive the payment. This lack of authority may arise, as in *Woolwich*, because a statutory regulation was invalid or it may arise where a valid statute has been misconstrued. The Law Commission have suggested that the notion of an *ultra vires* payment should cover all payments collected by a person or body who was acting outside its statutory authority, whether because it was acting in excess of its statutory power or because of procedural abuses, abuses of power or errors of law.[49]

(2) Is the ground of restitution confined to the recovery of overpaid taxes?

Although *Woolwich* was concerned with the recovery of overpaid tax, this ground of restitution should be applicable to the recovery of any overpaid levy from a public authority, as was recognised by Lord

---

[44] [1993] AC 70, p. 196 (Lord Browne-Wilkinson) and p. 201 (Lord Slynn).
[45] *Ibid*, p. 172 (Lord Goff).   [46] See pp. 124–5 above.
[47] Case 199/82 *Amministrazione delle Finanze dello Stato* v. *SpA San Giorgio* [1983] ECR 3595.
[48] [1993] AC 70, p. 177 (Lord Goff), p. 205 (Lord Slynn).
[49] 'Restitution: Mistakes of Law and Ultra Vires Public Authority Receipts and Payments' (Law Com. No. 227, 1994) p. 66.

Goff.[50] Consequently, this ground of restitution should be applicable to all unlawful demands for payment made for the supply of services by a public authority.

(3) Must the plaintiff have protested about the lawfulness of the demand?

Although in *Woolwich* the plaintiff had protested to the Revenue when it made its payment that the money was not lawfully due, the success of the plaintiff's claim should not be conditional on him or her protesting against the validity of the demand, for in many cases the plaintiff will be unaware that the demand was unlawful. Also a requirement of a protest accompanying the payment would largely confine recovery to those plaintiffs who have the resources to examine the validity of the demand. But the fact that the plaintiff did protest about the validity of the payment is of vital evidential importance, suggesting as it does that the payment was not made voluntarily.

(4) Is the restitutionary claim a matter of public or private law?

A crucial restriction on the ambit of this ground of restitution is that it is confined in its operation to restitutionary claims brought against public authorities, for the rationale of the ground is that any *ultra vires* payment which is received by a public authority must be returned to the payer by virtue of fundamental constitutional principles. Such constitutional principles are inapplicable where the recipient of the payment is not a public authority. The restriction to restitution from public authorities is significant as regards the procedure which must be adopted to obtain restitutionary relief. Until recently it appeared that if plaintiffs wished to challenge a demand from a public authority as an *ultra vires* demand, then, because this constituted a public law claim, they had to do so by virtue of judicial review under RSC, Order 53.[51] It is not, however, possible to obtain restitutionary relief under Order 53.[52] This meant that if the plaintiff wished to obtain restitution from a public authority he or she would have to adopt a dual procedure. The plaintiff would first need to apply by judicial review for a declaration that the demand was unlawful and then seek restitution of the money in separate proceedings. This was the procedure which the Woolwich Building Society had to adopt to obtain restitution from the Revenue. The need for judicial review has important implications in that the limitation period for such an application is three months from the date on which the ground for challenge arises, though this is subject to the discretion of the court.[53]

[50] [1993] AC 70, 177.   [51] *O'Reily* v. *Mackman* [1983] 2 AC 237.
[52] *Wandsworth London Borough Council* v. *Winder* [1985] AC 461.
[53] RSC Order 53, r. 4.

But it has now been accepted by the Court of Appeal that, where the plaintiff wishes to obtain restitution on the ground of *ultra vires* receipt, it is not necessary for the plaintiff first to bring judicial review proceedings.[54] The plaintiff can bring a restitutionary claim at common law to show that the money was not due and, once this has been established, then recover the overpaid tax from the public authority. This is a perfectly acceptable approach, since the dominant issue for the plaintiff relates to the existence of a private law right,[55] namely the right to restitution because the defendant was unjustly enriched at the plaintiff's expense, even though the existence of this right is dependent on the consideration of a public law issue, concerning whether the public authority is authorised to receive the particular payment. This decision of is vital importance, both because it avoids the cumbersome procedure involving both judicial review and a separate claim for restitution, but also because it avoids the very short limitation period which is inherent in an application for judicial review. It consequently makes the ground of *ultra vires* receipt a particularly attractive ground of restitution for the plaintiff to plead.

(5) Relationship between *ultra vires* receipt and absence of consideration

Since the decision of the House of Lords in *Woolwich*, the courts have recognised absence of consideration as a ground of restitution.[56] Does the recognition of this ground of restitution have any effect on the ground recognised in *Woolwich*? The two grounds of restitution do have different spheres of operation, since absence of consideration is applicable as a ground of restitution regardless of who the defendant is, whereas the ground of *ultra vires* receipt can only be relied on where the plaintiff seeks restitution from a public authority. But where the plaintiff does seek restitution of an *ultra vires* payment from a public authority there is a clear overlap between the two grounds of absence of consideration and *ultra vires* receipt. This is illustrated by the fact that the plaintiff's claim in *Woolwich* could have been founded on the ground of absence of consideration, as was acknowledged by Lord Browne-Wilkinson. Also the plaintiff's claim for restitution in *Westdeutsche Landesbank* was founded on absence of consideration, even though the plaintiff was seeking restitution of an *ultra vires* payment from the defendant local authority.

[54] *British Steel* v. *Customs and Excise* [1997] 2 All ER 366.

[55] See *Roy* v. *Kensington and Chelsea and Westminster Family Practitioner Committee* [1992] 1 AC 624 where the House of Lords recognised the importance of the private law right being dominant when determining whether the plaintiff's claim should be characterised as a public law or private law claim.

[56] See pp. 394–403 above.

But it does not follow that the two grounds of restitution should be treated as interchangeable in their application to restitutionary claims against public authorities. It was seen in Chapter 12 that the recognition of a ground of absence of consideration is difficult to defend, it being preferable to treat this as a ground of restitution which is founded on the plaintiff's incapacity to transfer a benefit to the defendant. It follows that, where the plaintiff seeks to obtain restitution of a payment made to a public authority which lacked the capacity to receive the payment, the ground of restitution should be that of *ultra vires* receipt rather than absence of consideration. Effectively this means that the plaintiff can rely on the defendant's incapacity to receive payment when the defendant is a public authority. The reason for this is that, as a matter of public policy, public authorities which lack capacity to receive a payment should not be allowed to retain the payment.

(6) Restricting the right to restitution

Where the plaintiff seeks to obtain restitution from the defendant on the ground of *ultra vires* receipt the right to restitution at common law may be restricted in two ways. First, it may be removed by statute so that the plaintiff will have to rely on the statutory mechanism for restitution.[57] It follows that the common law defences to restitution will not apply and the defendant will be confined to the defences under the statute. Secondly, the parties may have made express provision for restitution of overpayments by contract or such an agreement can be implied.[58] Again, the consequence of this will be that the common law restitutionary mechanism, including the general defences to restitutionary claims, will be excluded because of the fundamental principle that the law of restitution cannot subvert contractual mechanisms for recovery.[59] The effect of the parties making provision for restitution by contract is that the law of contract will govern recovery of the overpayment rather than the law of restitution.

(g) Particular statutory provisions

In addition to restitution of *ultra vires* payments at common law, there are certain statutory provisions concerning the recovery of overpaid taxes and duties.[60] Unfortunately, these provisions are not consistent

---

[57] *British Steel* v. *Customs and Excise* [1997] 2 All ER 366.

[58] *Sebel Products Ltd.* v. *Commissioners of Customs and Excise* [1949] 1 Ch. 409.

[59] See pp. 40–2 above.

[60] These provisions include s. 33 of the Taxes Management Act 1970 (which provides for the recovery of overpaid income tax, corporation tax, capital gains tax and petroleum revenue tax), s. 241 of the Inheritance Tax Act 1984 (which provides for the repayment of overpaid Inheritance Tax) and s. 29 of the Finance Act 1989 (which provides for the repayment of overpaid excise duty and car tax).

about when the plaintiff will be able to recover such overpayments. These differences involve such matters as the conditions which must be satisfied before the money can be recovered, whether there is a right to relief, or whether it is subject to an administrative discretion, the types of defences which are available and whether or not interest should be awarded. The nature of these differences is illustrated by comparing two different statutory provisions.

(i) Taxes Management Act 1970, section 33

Section 33 of the Taxes Management Act 1970 provides for the recovery of overpaid income tax, corporation tax, capital gains tax and petroleum revenue tax only where there has been an excessive assessment by reason of some error or mistake in the tax return. Consequently, this provision was not applicable in the *Woolwich* case, because such an error or mistake had not been made. Where the provision applies the payer has no right to recover the overpaid tax, since the Board of the Inland Revenue is empowered to award such relief as it believes is reasonable and just.[61] No relief is to be granted where the tax return was made in accordance with the practice which was generally prevailing when the return was made.[62] This effectively constitutes a bar to prevent unnecessary disruption of public finances by confining recovery to cases of individual error rather than where the error arose from the general practice adopted by the Revenue.

(ii) Value Added Tax Act 1994, section 80

Section 80 of the Value Added Tax Act 1994 makes provision for the recovery of overpaid VAT.[63] The effect of this statute is that where VAT has been paid in circumstances in which the money was not due to the Customs and Excise Commissioners, they are liable to repay that amount to the payer. Consequently, there is a general right to repayment, regardless of the circumstances of payment, so that recovery is not confined to cases of mistaken payment. Overpaid VAT can only be recovered under this section, so the common law restitutionary regime is excluded. By section 80(3) recovery of the overpaid tax is denied if repayment would unjustly enrich the payer. This constitutes a defence of passing on which would be applicable, for example, where the payer had passed on the burden of the tax to his or her customers.[64]

---

[61] Taxes Management Act 1970, s. 33(2).   [62] *Ibid.*
[63] As amended by the Finance Act 1997, ss. 46–7.
[64] Virgo, 'Restitution of Overpaid V.A.T.' [1998] *BTR* 582. For an illustration of the operation of this unjust enrichment defence see *Marks and Spencer plc.* v. *Customs and Excise Commissioners* [1999] STC 205.

3. REFORM OF THE LAW[65]

The state of the law concerning the recovery of *ultra vires* payments from public authorities is much more satisfactory following the recognition in *Woolwich* of the ground of *ultra vires* receipt. Nevertheless, there is still scope for improvement, particularly arising from the inconsistencies between the various statutory provisions and the common law regime for recovering money from public authorities. The Law Commission has examined the question of restitution of *ultra vires* payments from public authorities, and concluded that the law needs to be reformed.[66]

(a) Recommendations of the Law Commission as to the right to restitution

The Law Commission has recommended that the specific statutory provisions which govern the recovery of most forms of tax, levy or charge paid to public authorities should be amended to ensure that they are founded upon the same principles and subject to the same defences, so that they are as consistent with each other and the common law as possible. The effect is that the ground of *ultra vires* receipt will be left to be developed by the common law, whilst the essence of that ground of restitution will be incorporated into statutory provisions relating to specific taxes and levies.

The Law Commission recommended that the statutory right of recovery should *prima facie* lie where money is paid to the relevant public body in circumstances in which the money was not due. It would follow that the payer would be able to recover the payment either where it was paid by mistake or where the receipt of the money was *ultra vires* the authority for other reasons, such as the invalidity of subordinate legislation. The Law Commission also recommended that overpaid taxes should be recovered as far as possible through the existing statutory tribunals rather than through the courts. Such tribunals possess the experience to deal with the issues relating to specialised types of taxation and would be cheaper and quicker in providing a remedy than pursuing restitutionary claims through the courts.

---

[65] See Virgo, 'Striking the Balance in the Law of Restitution' [1995] *LMCLQ* 362; Beatson, 'Mistakes of Law and Ultra Vires Public Authority Receipts: The Law Commission Report' (1995) 3 *RLR* 280; and Flynn, ' "No Taxation Without Restitution"—The Law Commission's Proposals on the Recovery of Overpaid Taxes' [1995] *BTR* 15.

[66] 'Restitution: Mistakes of Law and *Ultra Vires* Public Authority Receipts and Payments' (Law Com. No. 227, 1994).

(b) Recommendations of the Law Commission as to the special defences

The Law Commission also acknowledged the need for specific defences to limit this *prima facie* right of recovery because of the peculiar circumstances arising from money being repaid by public bodies which may have deleterious effects upon the general public. The need to protect public finances was recognised as a legitimate policy aim,[67] which is justified because in certain cases the amount of tax or charge which must be repaid could amount to millions of pounds, with disastrous consequences for the public authority and the relevant projects which it finances. Although the Law Commission rejected a general defence of serious disruption to public finances, since such a defence would be too uncertain in operation, it did recommend the creation of four specific defences to protect public authorities against serious fiscal disruption.

(i) Failure to exhaust statutory remedies

The Law Commission recommended that restitution should be denied in statutory actions to recover overpaid taxes and charges either where the claimant has already raised the issue on an appeal against an assessment to the relevant tax or charge or where the plaintiff failed to make a claim for repayment in appeal proceedings, when he or she knew or should have known of the ground of claim. The policy behind this defence is to encourage the submission of disputed assessments to appeal before the appropriate statutory tribunal.

(ii) Change in a settled view of the law

Where the claim to restitution is founded on a mistake of law the Commission recommended that restitution should be denied where the payment was made in accordance with a settled view of the law that the money was due and that view was subsequently changed by a decision of a court or tribunal.[68] This defence is not recommended to be applicable where the claim for restitution is founded on the invalidity of subordinate legislation since, in such circumstances, the rationale for restitution is not dependent upon mistake, but rather is founded on the impropriety of the public authority retaining funds without statutory authority. The very fact of the change in a settled view of the law will confirm such impropriety.

But can any defence of change in a settled view of the law ever be justified where restitution is sought from a public authority? If the plaintiff

---

[67] Law Com. No. 227, paras. 10.5–10.8.
[68] Support for such a defence can be found in the judgment of Lord Goff in *Kleinwort Benson Ltd.* v. *Lincoln CC* [1998] 3 WLR 1095, 1122.

seeks restitution of money from the public authority because payment was not due to it, the particular reason the money was not due should be irrelevant. Even if the money was paid on the basis of a settled view of the law which is later proved to be mistaken, restitution should follow simply because it is subsequently acknowledged that the money was not due. The argument of constitutional impropriety in the public authority retaining money which was not due to it should prevail over that founded on the disruption to public funds arising from a mistake as to a settled view of the law.

(iii) Compromise

The Law Commission also recommended that restitution should be denied where the plaintiff's claim had either been contractually compromised or where the payment was made in response to litigation which had been commenced by the public authority, but not where the litigation was merely threatened. Such a defence of compromise is consistent with the general bars to restitutionary claims at common law founded on the plaintiff's voluntary submission to an honest claim.[69]

(iv) Unjust enrichment

Finally, the Law Commission recommended that the public authority should have a defence to the plaintiff's claim where the consequence of the public authority repaying the plaintiff would be that the plaintiff was unjustly enriched. This effectively constitutes a defence of passing on. Although this defence has been rejected as a general defence to restitutionary claims at common law,[70] since the fact that the plaintiff has passed on his or her loss to a third party does not affect the fact that the defendant has obtained a benefit to which he or she was not entitled, the defence can be justified in respect of statutory claims to recover *ultra vires* payments. This is because, since the burden of the payment is actually borne by the third party rather than the plaintiff, the argument in favour of the constitutional impropriety of the public authority retaining the plaintiff's money is weakened, and it follows that it is legitimate to be more concerned about the security of public finances. In practice, however, it will be very difficult to prove that the plaintiff has actually passed on the burden of the payment to third parties.[71]

---

[69] See pp. 686–9 below.
[70] *Kleinwort Benson Ltd.* v. *Birmingham CC* [1997] QB 380. See p. 735 below.
[71] See p. 737 below.

PART IV
RESTITUTION FOR WRONGS

15

General Principles

1. THE ESSENCE OF RESTITUTION FOR WRONGS

In Part III those restitutionary claims which are founded on the reversal of the defendant's unjust enrichment were examined. In this Part, the emphasis shifts to those restitutionary claims which are founded on the commission of a wrong by the defendant. There are four types of wrong-doing which may trigger the award of restitutionary remedies, namely tort, breach of contract, equitable wrongdoing and the commission of a criminal offence. For the purposes of this book the detailed rules which determine whether or not a wrong has been committed will not be examined, since this is adequately dealt with in the specialised works on each of these subjects. What this Part is concerned with is whether, once the plaintiff has shown that the defendant has committed a wrong, the plaintiff can obtain a restitutionary remedy from the defendant. This is a difficult matter to resolve, since there is great uncertainty about which wrongs can and should trigger the award of restitutionary remedies. A further difficulty is that, unlike restitution founded on the reversal of the defendant's unjust enrichment, where the only remedy available is restitutionary, in those cases in which restitution is founded on the commission of a wrong, the plaintiff may be able to obtain other remedies in the alternative, such as remedies to compensate the plaintiff for loss suffered rather than to deprive the defendant of benefits obtained by the commission of the wrong.

(a) The relationship between restitution for wrongs and the reversal of the defendant's unjust enrichment

For those commentators[1] and judges[2] who argue that the law of restitution is only concerned with the reversal of the defendant's unjust enrichment, it is necessary to show how a defendant who has obtained benefits through the commission of a wrong can be considered to be unjustly

---

[1] Burrows, *The Law of Restitution*, at p. 376, treats restitution for wrongs as founded on the reversal of the defendant's unjust enrichment. This was originally the view of Birks: see *An Introduction to the Law of Restitution* at p. 313, but he has since changed his mind. See 'Misnomer' in *Restitution: Past, Present and Future* (ed. Cornish, Nolan, O'Sullivan and Virgo), Chapter 1.

[2] See, in particular, Peter Gibson LJ, in *Halifax Building Society* v. *Thomas* [1996] Ch. 217, 224.

enriched at the plaintiff's expense. Clearly such a defendant can be considered to have been enriched and, because this arose from the commission of a wrong, it is possible to conclude that the enrichment was unjustly obtained. But the difficulty arises from establishing that this enrichment was obtained at the plaintiff's expense because, typically, the defendant's enrichment will not have been subtracted from the plaintiff. For this reason, if restitution for wrongs is to be explained by reference to the reversal of unjust enrichment principle, it is necessary to re-define the notion of 'at the plaintiff's expense' where the plaintiff's claim is founded on the commission of a wrong, so that, rather than showing that the defendant's benefit was taken from the plaintiff, it is sufficient that the benefit derived from the commission of a wrong which involved the breach of a duty owed to the plaintiff.[3] It follows that restitutionary remedies are available to the plaintiff so long as the defendant's benefit can be shown to have resulted from the wrong even though the benefit was not subtracted from the plaintiff.

It is, however, highly artificial to regard restitution for wrongdoing as founded on the principle of reversing unjust enrichment,[4] particularly because the notion of the enrichment being obtained at the plaintiff's expense has to be artificially extended to cater for those wrongs which do not involve any benefit being subtracted from the plaintiff. It is easier and more accurate simply to analyse restitution for wrongdoing in the following way.

(i) The plaintiff is a victim of a wrong

The plaintiff must be the victim of a wrong which was committed by the defendant. It is not necessary to show that the defendant was enriched at the plaintiff's expense or that the plaintiff can found his or her claim on a recognised ground of restitution. It is simply sufficient that the plaintiff can sue the defendant for wrongdoing.

(ii) The wrong triggers restitutionary remedies

The wrong must have been of a type which has been recognised as triggering restitutionary remedies. Questions of policy need to be carefully examined to determine whether the award of a remedy which is measured by reference to the defendant's gain really is appropriate as a response to the commission of that type of wrong.

---

[3] See Burrows, *The Law of Restitution*, at p. 376 and Birks, *An Introduction to the Law of Restitution* at p. 42.

[4] See p. 10 above and *Morris* v. *Tarrant* [1971] 2 QB 143, 162 (Lane J). That restitution for wrongs is not founded on the unjust enrichment principle was recognised by Millett J in *Macmillan Inc.* v. *Bishopsgate Investment Trust plc. (No. 3)* [1995] 1 WLR 978, 988.

(iii) The defendant obtained a benefit

The defendant must have obtained a benefit as a result of the commission of the wrong, for without proof of such a benefit it will not be possible to award the plaintiff any gain-based remedy.[5] To determine whether the defendant has been benefited for the purposes of a restitutionary claim founded on wrongdoing, the definition of enrichment which is applicable to an action founded on the reversal of unjust enrichment should apply.[6] This means that the defendant must generally have received an objective benefit which it is not possible subjectively to devalue, for example because the enrichment is incontrovertibly beneficial or he or she has freely accepted it. That the principle of subjective devaluation is applicable where a restitutionary claim is founded on the commission of a wrong was recognised by the Court of Appeal in *Ministry of Defence* v. *Ashman*.[7] Usually, however, where the defendant has committed a wrong the defendant will have obtained money, which is incontrovertibly beneficial.

It follows from this analysis that the underlying cause of action for a claim of restitution for wrongs should be considered to be founded on the wrong itself and not on the unjust enrichment of the defendant. In other words, the defendant's liability to make restitution to the plaintiff is parasitic on the wrong.[8]

(b) The advantages of treating restitution for wrongs as not being founded on the unjust enrichment principle

There are a number of advantages which follow from the treatment of restitution for wrongs as not being founded on the principle of unjust enrichment. First, it reflects the approach which is generally adopted in practice, whereby restitutionary remedies are awarded for wrongdoing without any attempt to analyse the case in terms of unjust enrichment. There is particularly no need to show that the plaintiff's claim falls within any of the established grounds of restitution, it being sufficient that the claim is founded on a recognised form of wrongdoing.

Secondly, the rejection of an unjust enrichment analysis emphasises that the key questions of principle and policy which are of concern to the law of restitution in this context relate to the determination of the appropriate remedy for the wrong rather than the definition of the wrong.

Thirdly, the recognition that the relevant cause of action is the wrong rather than the defendant's unjust enrichment has consequences for

---

[5] *Hambly* v. *Trott* (1776) 1 Cowp. 371, 376; 98 ER 1136, 1139 (Lord Mansfield).
[6] See Chapter 4 above.   [7] [1993] 2 EGLR 102.
[8] Friedmann, 'Restitution for Wrongs: The Basis of Liability' in *Restitution: Past, Present and Future* (eds. Cornish, Nolan, O'Sullivan and Virgo) p. 133.

pleading and proof, for the application of defences and for the application of the rules of private international law to restitutionary claims.[9] As
regards pleading and proof, the plaintiff must establish the elements of
the wrong rather than unjust enrichment.[10] As regards defences, the fact
that the plaintiff's claim is founded on the commission of a wrong rather
than unjust enrichment should affect the operation of defences, such as
limitation periods, which are dependent on the nature of the cause of
action.[11] As regards private international law, the fact that the plaintiff's
claim is characterised as being founded on wrongdoing will determine
the rules of jurisdiction and choice of law which are applicable.

(c) Alternative analysis

Since the underlying causes of action for restitution for wrongdoing and
restitution for unjust enrichment are different, it may be possible for the
plaintiff to establish both types of claim on the same set of facts. This has
been called 'alternative analysis'.[12] So, for example, if the plaintiff is
induced to pay £100 to the defendant as a result of a fraudulent misrepresentation, the plaintiff may base his or her restitutionary claim on the
fact that the defendant has been unjustly enriched at the plaintiff's
expense, with the ground of restitution being the induced mistake.[13]
Alternatively, the plaintiff may wish to base the claim on the tort of
deceit. Usually the result of the claim will be the same regardless of the
cause of action which is chosen, but sometimes it will be a matter of
importance to the plaintiff whether the claim is founded on the commission of a wrong or the reversal of the defendant's unjust enrichment. One
of the most significant factors affecting how the action is framed relates
to what the plaintiff needs to prove to establish the cause of action. It
may, for example, be easier to prove that the defendant has been unjustly
enriched than that the defendant has committed a wrong, primarily
because liability for unjust enrichment is strict, whereas liability for a
number of wrongs requires proof of fault.

The fact that alternative analysis is possible means that some of the old
cases in particular need to be treated with care because, although they
may appear to have decided that a restitutionary remedy could be
awarded for the type of wrong which was committed, the cause of action
might today be interpreted as having been founded on unjust enrichment.

---

[9] See Virgo 'What is the Law of Restitution About?' in *ibid*, pp. 318–28.
[10] See Adkins Court Forms (1992) pp. 625 ff.   [11] See Chapter 28.
[12] Birks, *An Introduction to the Law of Restitution*, p. 44.   [13] See p. 166 above.

(d) Does restitution for wrongs really form part of the law of restitution?

Regardless of whether restitution for wrongs is considered to be based on the principle of unjust enrichment or the fact that the defendant has committed a wrong, it is clear that the plaintiff can obtain remedies which are assessed by reference to the benefit obtained by the defendant as a result of the commission of the wrong. But should these remedies really be characterised as restitutionary? In many of the cases where a gain-based remedy is awarded to the plaintiff, the benefit which was obtained by the defendant did not derive from the plaintiff, so how can the benefit be *restored* to the plaintiff? It is more accurate to say that, rather than the defendant being liable to restore a benefit to the plaintiff, he or she must disgorge the value of the benefit to the plaintiff.[14] But this is simply a matter of fine-tuning. It is perfectly legitimate to treat disgorgement for wrongdoing as falling within the law of restitution, since it is clear that the remedies which are awarded are restitutionary in the broadest sense, in that they are assessed by reference to the value of the benefit which was obtained by the defendant from the commission of the wrong, rather than by reference to the loss suffered by the plaintiff.[15]

(e) The relationship between restitution for wrongs and proprietary restitutionary claims

Where the defendant has wrongly taken the plaintiff's property the plaintiff may have two alternative restitutionary actions, one founded on wrongdoing and the other on the vindication of property rights.[16] For example, if the defendant takes the plaintiff's car without permission and then sells it, the tort of conversion will have been committed. The plaintiff may seek a restitutionary remedy founded on the conversion, or

---

[14] See Farnsworth, 'Your Loss or My Gain? The Dilemma of the Disgorgement Principle in Breach of Contract' (1985) 94 *Yale LJ* 1339, 1342 and Smith, 'The Province of the Law of Restitution' (1992) 71 *CBR* 672, 696.

[15] Cp. *Target Holdings Ltd.* v. *Redferns (a firm)* [1996] AC 421 where Lord Browne-Wilkinson, at p. 434, described the remedy of ordering the reconstitution of a trust as 'restitution'. Whilst this may be accurate in a descriptive sense, since reconstituting a trust involves restoring it to its state before trust property was misappropriated, the use of 'restitution' is unfortunate in this context since reconstitution of a trust is a compensatory remedy, because it is assessed by reference to what the trust lost rather than what the defendant gained. See Rickett, 'Equitable Compensation: The Giant Stirs' (1996) 112 *LQR* 27, 28. See also *Swindle* v. *Harrison* [1997] 4 All ER 705 where the Court of Appeal described the remedy of equitable compensation for breach of fiduciary duty as 'restitutionary'. Such a description is incorrect because equitable compensation is assessed by reference to the plaintiff's loss rather than the defendant's gain. See Elliott, 'Restitutionary Compensatory Damages' (1998) 6 *RLR* 135.

[16] See, for example, *Lipkin Gorman (a firm)* v. *Karpnale Ltd.* [1991] 2 AC 548.

alternatively may bring a proprietary restitutionary claim to recover the proceeds of the sale of the car, such a claim being founded on the plaintiff's continuing title in the car and its traceable product.[17]

This distinction between proprietary claims and claims founded on wrongs is not, however, as neat a distinction as first appears, because a number of forms of wrongdoing require proof that the defendant has interfered with the plaintiff's proprietary rights, which in turn requires proof that the plaintiff has a continuing interest in the particular property. This is illustrated by the tort of conversion. But where the plaintiff sues for the tort of conversion, even though he or she must be shown to have an interest in the property converted, the cause of action is still founded on the tort and not on the vindication of property rights. It follows that the award of restitutionary remedies following the commission of the tort of conversion are properly considered in this Part, rather than in Part V where restitutionary proprietary claims are examined. It should be emphasised, however, that this is merely a matter of convenience for the exposition of the subject and because of the legacy of history as to how causes of action are characterised. It does not mean that the commission of the tort of conversion has nothing to do with proprietary restitutionary claims.[18]

The overlap between restitution for wrongs and proprietary restitutionary claims may arise in another context. Sometimes, where the defendant commits an equitable wrong, the court may recognise that the defendant holds the benefit obtained from the wrong on constructive trust for the plaintiff.[19] The consequence of this is that the plaintiff will have an equitable proprietary interest in the property held by the defendant, so the plaintiff will be able to bring a restitutionary proprietary claim to vindicate this property right.[20]

2. THE PRINCIPLES UNDERLYING THE AWARD OF RESTITUTIONARY REMEDIES FOR WRONGS

(a) The fundamental principles

There are two conflicting principles which relate to the award of a restitutionary remedy for the defendant's wrongdoing.[21] The first is that the

---

[17] See Chapter 20.

[18] See also the analysis of the equitable action for knowing receipt of trust property which, because of the need to prove fault on the part of the defendant, could be analysed as a claim founded on the commission of an equitable wrong, whereas it is treated in this book simply as a claim to vindicate property rights. See p. 668 below.

[19] See pp. 539–44 below.   [20] See Chapter 21.

[21] See *Halifax Building Society* v. *Thomas* [1996] Ch. 217, 229 (Glidewell LJ).

defendant should not profit from his or her wrongdoing.[22] If this principle is accepted and is taken to its logical conclusion it follows that, whenever the defendant obtains a benefit as a result of the commission of a wrong, he or she should be required to disgorge that benefit regardless of the type of wrong committed. The second principle contradicts the first since it denies restitutionary relief to the plaintiff where the effect of requiring the defendant to disgorge the benefit would be that the plaintiff profits from the commission of the wrong by the defendant. If this principle prevailed it would mean that restitutionary relief was unavailable in any case in which the plaintiff has suffered no loss as a result of the defendant's wrongdoing. This would result in a dramatic restriction in the scope for the award of restitutionary relief for wrongdoing, since in a number cases the defendant will have obtained a benefit from the commission of a wrong in circumstances where the plaintiff will have suffered little or no loss.

One method of reconciling these two principles is by concluding that any benefit obtained by the defendant should be paid to the State rather than to the plaintiff. This can already occur where the defendant has committed a criminal offence and he or she is deprived of any benefit obtained through the imposition of a fine or the confiscation of the proceeds of the crime.[23] But this is because it is the function of the State to enforce the criminal law. Also the criminal sanction is preserved for particularly culpable conduct which deserves punishment. This is not the case with most forms of wrongdoing which involve the infringement of private rights. There is some evidence, however, that the courts would prefer to leave the matter to the State, so that, if no statutory provision has been made for disgorgement, it is felt that the law of restitution should not be used to provide a remedy.[24] But, as Birks has recognised:

[if] the courts continue to subscribe to that view they will acquiesce in a trend towards the disempowerment of the individual and the alienation of the citizen from the legal system. Faith in the law and in individual action within the law will give way to helpless grumbling against the bureaucracy.[25]

In fact the law of restitution itself has been able to reach a compromise between the two conflicting principles, by recognising that a restitutionary response is appropriate only in respect of certain types of wrongdoing. Where the defendant has committed one of these types of wrongs the law of restitution considers that it is preferable that the plaintiff

---

[22] *Attorney-General* v. *Guardian Newspapers Ltd. (No. 2)* [1990] 1 AC 109, 286 (Lord Goff).
[23] See pp. 568–70.
[24] See, in particular, *Halifax Building Society* v. *Thomas* [1996] Ch. 217, 229 (Peter Gibson LJ) and 230 (Glidewell LJ). See also *Chief Constable of Leicestershire* v. *M* [1989] 1 WLR 20, 23 (Hoffmann J).
[25] 'The Proceeds of Mortgage Fraud' (1996) 10 *TLI* 2, 5.

should obtain the benefit of the wrongdoing rather than allowing the defendant to profit from the commission of the wrong, even though the result may be that the plaintiff profits from the commission of the wrong by the defendant. Consequently, it is necessary to determine which types of wrongdoing will trigger a restitutionary response. A number of factors can be identified which will assist in the determination of this.[26]

(b) Determining which wrongs will trigger a restitutionary response

(i) Interference with property

Where the wrongdoing involves the defendant obtaining a benefit by using or interfering with the plaintiff's property restitutionary relief is likely to be available. The award of restitution in such circumstances is consistent with the two principles which underlie restitution for wrongs. First, the defendant will have obtained a benefit as a result of the commission of a wrong which involves interference with somebody else's property rights. Secondly, since the profits derived from the use of the plaintiff's property, it is appropriate that the defendant disgorges the benefit to the plaintiff. So, for example, where the defendant takes the plaintiff's car and hires it out without the plaintiff's permission, it is appropriate that the money received by the defendant should be paid to the plaintiff since it constitutes the fruits of the plaintiff's property.

The award of restitutionary remedies where the defendant obtains a benefit as the result of wrongful interference with the plaintiff's property is justified by the fact that English law considers property rights to be deserving of particular protection from interference; the so-called right to exclusive enjoyment of property. This was recognised by Lord Shaw in *Watson, Laidlaw and Co. Ltd.* v. *Pott, Cassels and Williamson*[27] who said that 'wherever an abstraction or invasion of property has occurred, then, unless such abstraction or invasion were to be sanctioned by law, the law ought to yield a recompense under the category or principle . . . either of price or of hire'. In a very important analysis of the principles which underlie restitution for wrongs, Jackman[28] has also identified the principle of interference with property as being of prime importance in explaining many of the cases in which a restitutionary remedy has been awarded for wrongdoing. He justifies the award of restitutionary remedies for such wrongdoing as a means of protecting what he calls facilitative institutions. He considers property to be an institution which needs to be protected by the law and the award of restitutionary remedies

---

[26] See Jackman, 'Restitution for Wrongs' (1989) 48 *CLJ* 302.
[27] (1914) 31 RPC 104, 119. See also *Surrey County Council* v. *Bredero Homes Ltd.* [1993] 1 WLR 1361, 1369 (Steyn LJ).
[28] 'Restitution for Wrongs' (1989) 48 *CLJ* 302, 305–11.

ensures proper respect for the institution since it is a mechanism for deterring harm to it, by ensuring that all benefits which the defendant derives from the property should be disgorged to the plaintiff.

The problem with this property principle relates to the determination of what constitutes property rights. This is the weakness of Friedmann's analysis of the award of restitutionary remedies for wrongdoing.[29] He concludes that restitutionary remedies are particularly appropriate where the effect of the wrong is interference with the plaintiff's property rights. But, to explain many of the cases in which restitutionary relief has been awarded, he adopts a very wide interpretation of property to include 'quasi-property', a phrase which covers 'interests in ideas, information, trade secrets and opportunity'.[30] But if the notion of property is extended in this artificial way it is unclear when this extension should end. Whilst interference with property rights is a useful principle for determining when restitutionary relief is available it is not the only principle and the notion of property rights must not be extended artificially.[31]

(ii) Deterrence and ethical standards[32]

(1) Abuse of a relationship of trust and confidence

Where the defendant abuses a relationship of trust and confidence between him or her and the plaintiff, the award of restitutionary relief will be available.[33] It is not every relationship between the parties which deserves such protection, but where there is a relationship of trust and confidence this is, to use Jackman's terminology, a facilitative institution which deserves particular protection from the law.[34] This is because the key characteristic of such relationships is that the plaintiff is dependent on the defendant for advice and management, so the defendant is placed in a particularly powerful position where there is a constant temptation

---

[29] 'Restitution of Benefits Obtained Through the Appropriation of Property or the Commission of a Wrong' (1980) 80 *Columbia Law Review* 504.

[30] *Ibid*, p. 512.

[31] More recently Friedmann has developed his theory to conclude that the defendant will be required to disgorge benefits to the plaintiff where the defendant has interfered with the plaintiff's property interests even though this does not involve the commission of a wrong: 'Restitution for Wrongs: The Basis of Liability' in *Restitution: Past, Present and Future* (eds. Cornish, Nolan, O'Sullivan and Virgo). He therefore concludes that the award of restitutionary relief in such cases involves an independent restitutionary claim. But such cases are better treated as either involving claims founded on the reversal of the defendant's unjust enrichment or the vindication of proprietary rights. If the plaintiff cannot establish that the defendant has been unjustly enriched, committed a wrong or received the plaintiff's property, then the plaintiff's claim for restitution should fail.

[32] Friedmann, 'Restitution of Benefits Obtained Through the Appropriation of Property or the Commission of a Wrong' (1980) *Columbia Law Review* 504, 551–6.

[33] See Chapter 18.　　　　　[34] 'Restitution for Wrongs' (1989) 48 *CLJ* 302, 311–17.

for him or her to exploit the plaintiff. It is to deter the defendant from succumbing to this temptation that restitution of any benefits obtained by breach of trust or confidence will be awarded to the plaintiff.[35] This is why a restitutionary remedy may be awarded even though there is no evidence that the defendant did actually abuse the relationship of trust and confidence.

(2) Illegal and immoral conduct

Where the wrong committed by the defendant involves the commission of an illegal or immoral act it is entirely appropriate for the defendant to disgorge benefits acquired from the commission of the wrong to the plaintiff. The award of restitutionary relief in such circumstances is justified by the need to deter defendants from committing such wrongs. It is for this reason that restitutionary relief is appropriate where the defendant has obtained a benefit by committing a criminal act.[36]

(3) The defendant's culpability

Although it has sometimes been suggested that restitutionary remedies should be available where the defendant's conduct in committing the wrong is particularly blameworthy, the nature of the defendant's culpability cannot operate as a principle to identify those wrongs for which restitutionary relief is available, simply because the defendant's culpability will vary from case to case. The Court of Appeal recognised in *Attorney-General* v. *Blake*[37] that the fact that the defendant has deliberately committed a wrong is not a reason in its own right to award restitution. But once it has been determined by reference to other principles that restitutionary relief is appropriate for a particular type of wrongdoing, the defendant's culpability may be taken into account to determine the type of relief which is appropriate on the facts of that particular case. So, for example, the fact that the defendant deliberately committed a wrong may be a reason why the defendant should be required to disgorge all benefits received as a result of the wrongdoing.

   In the United States the defendant's culpability is a factor which has influenced the type of restitutionary relief which is awarded. So, for example, where the defendant deliberately trespassed onto the plaintiff's land, he was liable to account to the plaintiff for all the profits which arose from the trespass,[38] whereas it has been suggested that if the defendant is an unintentional wrongdoer he or she will only be liable to pay the plaintiff the reasonable value of the benefit obtained from the

   [35] See Birks, *An Introduction to the Law of Restitution*, p. 332.
   [36] See Chapter 19.   [37] [1998] 2 WLR 805, 818.
   [38] *Edwards* v. *Lee's Administrators* (1936) 265 Ky. 418. See also *Olwell* v. *Nye and Nissen Co.* (1946) 26 Wash. 2d. 282.

commission of the wrong.[39] There is some evidence in this country too that the defendant's culpability will be taken into account when determining the type of restitutionary remedy which should be awarded.[40]

(iii) Inadequacy of compensatory remedies

In those cases in which the typical remedy awarded for the commission of a wrong is damages to compensate the plaintiff for loss suffered as a result of the wrong, restitutionary remedies are appropriate where such compensatory remedies are inadequate. This is the main reason why restitutionary remedies may exceptionally be available where the defendant has obtained a benefit as a result of breaching a contract.[41]

3. THE TYPES OF RESTITUTIONARY REMEDIES FOR WRONGDOING

Once it has been accepted that the wrong committed by the defendant was of a type for which restitutionary relief is available, it is then necessary to determine what type of restitutionary remedy should be awarded. There are a number of different restitutionary remedies which are available.

(a) Money had and received

Where the defendant has obtained money as a result of the wrong he or she may be required to pay this to the plaintiff by means of an action for money had and received. This is a common law[42] restitutionary remedy, even though it is still described as an 'action'. It is a prerequisite for this remedy to be awarded that the money which the defendant obtained as a result of the commission of the wrong was subtracted from the plaintiff. So, for example, if the defendant wrongly obtained the plaintiff's money by deceit, the defendant may be required to repay the money to the plaintiff by means of the action for money had and received.[43]

---

[39] *Ibid.*

[40] *Jegon* v. *Vivian* (1871) LR 6 Ch.App. 742, 761 (Lord Hatherley LC). The defendant's culpability has also proved to be an important factor in deciding what remedies should be awarded for breach of confidence. See pp. 546–9 below.

[41] See Chapter 16.

[42] It is, therefore, not available where the defendant commits an equitable wrong.

[43] Alternatively, the plaintiff may bring a restitutionary claim founded on unjust enrichment, the ground of restitution being an induced mistake. See pp. 166–7 above.

(b) Account of profits

Where the defendant has obtained a profit as a result of the commission of a wrong he or she may be ordered to render an account and pay this profit to the plaintiff. This remedy is clearly restitutionary, since it requires the defendant's gain to be ascertained and transferred to the victim of the wrong.[44] An account of profits is a discretionary equitable remedy[45] and consequently it may be defeated by equitable defences such as laches.[46] It may also be unavailable to the plaintiff if his or her conduct can be regarded as unconscionable, as will be the case where the plaintiff stood by whilst the defendant made the profit and the plaintiff then claimed that he or she was entitled to those profits.[47] Although the remedy of an account of profits is equitable it is not confined in its operation to equitable wrongs, since it is clearly available in respect of some torts.[48] It is often difficult to ascertain exactly what profits the defendant made as a result of the wrongdoing, since usually the profits will have been increased by the contribution of the defendant's own ideas, property and money. Consequently, the courts do not require absolute accuracy in the determination of the profits which derived from the commission of the wrong.[49]

(c) Restitutionary damages

(i) The ambit of restitutionary damages

The term 'restitutionary damages' is apt to mislead since 'damages' suggests the award of a compensatory remedy which is assessed by reference to the plaintiff's loss, but the addition of the word 'restitutionary' immediately contradicts this. If, however, 'damages' is interpreted simply to mean a financial remedy, the addition of the word 'restitutionary' clarifies that this is a remedy which is assessed by reference to what the defendant obtained as a result of committing a wrong,[50] whereas compensatory damages are assessed by reference to the loss suffered by the plaintiff.

[44] See *My Kinda Town Ltd.* v. *Soll and Grunts Investments* [1982] FSR 147, 156 where Slade J said that the purpose of ordering an account of profits is 'to prevent an unjust enrichment of the defendant'. This can be correct only if 'unjust enrichment' is used in a purely descriptive sense rather than as a substantive principle. See pp. 8–9 above.

[45] *Seager* v. *Copydex Ltd.* [1967] 1 WLR 923, 932 (Lord Denning MR).

[46] See pp. 775–7 below.   [47] *Re Jarvis (deceased)* [1958] 1 WLR 815, 820 (Upjohn J).

[48] See, in particular, the torts which involve interference with intellectual property rights, discussed at pp. 491–2 below.

[49] *Watson, Laidlaw and Co. Ltd.* v. *Pott, Cassels and Williamson* (1914) 31 RPC 104, 114 (Lord Atkinson). See also *My Kinda Town Ltd.* v. *Soll* [1982] FSR 147, 159 (Slade J).

[50] Birks, 'Restitutionary Damages for Breach of Contract: *Snepp* and the Fusion of Law and Equity' [1987] *LMCLQ* 421.

Although the distinction between compensatory and restitutionary damages has been ignored in some cases,[51] the Court of Appeal in *Attorney-General* v. *Blake*[52] had no hesitation in calling the restitutionary remedy which is awarded for breach of contract 'restitutionary damages'. This accords with the recommendation of the Law Commission that the judiciary should use this term to describe the remedy.[53] Rapid implementation of Law Commission proposals is unusual, but in this case the judiciary adopted the recommendation the day after it was made.

Even though the notion of restitutionary damages is starting to be recognised by the judiciary it is clear that it is not a term of art. Typically, those judges and commentators who recognise the notion of restitutionary damages consider it to be wide enough to encompass all financial restitutionary remedies which are awarded in respect of wrongdoing.[54] This is particularly the view of the Law Commission.[55] If this is correct it means that the notion of restitutionary damages encompasses money had and received and the remedy of an account of profits. But since these remedies have a distinct meaning it is preferable to confine the notion of restitutionary damages to a particular form of financial remedy which is different from those other two remedies, namely where the defendant has not obtained a positive benefit from the commission of the wrong but has simply saved money.[56] Where the defendant has saved money as a result of committing a wrong he or she may be ordered to pay the equivalent of the amount saved to the plaintiff, and this should properly be characterised as restitutionary damages. This would mean that the remedies of money had and received and account of profits will be applicable where the defendant has obtained a positive benefit through the commission of the wrong, whereas the remedy of restitutionary damages will be applicable where the defendant has obtained a negative benefit by saving money.

(ii) Are 'restitutionary damages' really restitutionary?

Whether the award of damages in circumstances in which the defendant has saved money is necessarily a restitutionary remedy is a particularly controversial matter, since in many cases it is possible to characterise the

[51] *Ministry of Defence* v. *Ashman* [1993] 2 EGLR 102, 105 (Hoffmann LJ).

[52] [1998] 2 WLR 805, 819.

[53] Law Commission, 'Aggravated, Exemplary and Restitutionary Damages' (Law Com. No. 247, 1997) pp. 51–2.

[54] See in particular Birks, 'Civil Wrongs: A New World' in *Butterworths Lectures 1990–1991* (London: Butterworths, 1992) p. 71.

[55] Law Com. No. 247, 1997, p. 51.

[56] See Mason and Carter, *Restitution Law in Australia* (Sydney: Butterworths, 1995) p. 607.

remedy as both compensatory and restitutionary. This is primarily because the method which is adopted to determine the amount which the defendant saved through the commission of the wrong is what he or she would have had to pay to the plaintiff to obtain that which was actually obtained by committing the wrong. So, for example, if the defendant had taken the plaintiff's property without the plaintiff's permission and so saved the cost of hiring the property, the measure of damages will be the amount the defendant would have had to pay to the plaintiff to hire the property. It has been argued by Sharpe and Waddams[57] that the damages which the plaintiff receives in such circumstances are compensatory rather than restitutionary. This is because such damages seek to compensate the plaintiff for the loss of the opportunity to bargain with the defendant for an appropriate fee for the use of the plaintiff's property. The authors argue that the damages should be assessed as equal to the full profits made by the defendant, because the defendant in breaching the contract 'has prevented anyone from knowing how much in fact would have been paid for the right taken'.[58] Such a compensatory analysis may be appropriate in a number of cases, at least where the plaintiff would have been willing to hire the property to the defendant or somebody else, but a principle of lost opportunity to bargain cannot be used to explain the function of the remedy which has been awarded in every case in which the defendant has saved money by interfering with the plaintiff's property. This is because damages have been awarded in a number of cases in which the defendant has interfered with the plaintiff's property even though there was no evidence that the plaintiff would have bargained with the defendant, and sometimes it is clear that the plaintiff would definitely not have bargained with the defendant.[59] If the damages which were awarded in these cases are to be treated as compensatory rather than restitutionary it is necessary to introduce a fiction that the plaintiff would have been prepared to bargain with the defendant, even though this might be contradicted by the evidence. Such artificiality can be avoided simply by concluding that the plaintiff may be awarded damages which are assessed by reference to the amount saved by the defendant as a result of the wrongdoing.

---

[57] 'Damages for Lost Opportunity to Bargain' (1982) 2 *OJLS* 290. See *Inverugie Investments Ltd.* v. *Hackett* [1995] 1 WLR 713.

[58] 'Damages for Lost Opportunity to Bargain' (1982) 2 *OJLS* 290, 296.

[59] See in particular *Strand Electric and Engineering Co. Ltd.* v. *Brisford Entertainments Ltd.* [1952] 2 QB 246 and *Penarth Dock Engineering Co. Ltd.* v. *Pounds* [1963] 1 Lloyd's Rep. 359.

(d) Constructive trust

In certain circumstances in which the defendant has obtained profits through the commission of an equitable wrong the defendant will be required to hold the profits on constructive trust for the plaintiff.[60] Although the recognition that the defendant holds property on constructive trust for the plaintiff is not a remedy as such,[61] the recognition of the constructive trust does have remedial consequences because the plaintiff will be able to vindicate his or her equitable proprietary right by recovering the property which is held on trust. Where the defendant holds property on constructive trust this can have a number of advantages for the plaintiff. For example, because the plaintiff will have an equitable proprietary interest in the profits it follows that he or she will have priority over the defendant's unsecured creditors if the defendant becomes insolvent before the profits are paid to the defendant. It will also mean that the plaintiff will be able to claim the fruits of the profits from the defendant. So, for example, if the profits which are held on constructive trust are invested in shares, the plaintiff will be able to claim the shares and any dividends which have been paid in respect of them.

When the defendant will be considered to hold the profits on constructive trust is a matter of particular controversy. One view is that all profits which the defendant is liable to disgorge to the plaintiff should be held on constructive trust for the plaintiff, by virtue of the maxim that equity treats as done what ought to have been done. In other words, once the defendant has obtained profits as a result of the commission of a wrong these profits are deemed by equity to belong to the plaintiff from that moment and so are held on constructive trust for the plaintiff.[62] An alternative view is that the defendant should only be considered to hold profits on constructive trust for the plaintiff where those profits derive from the commission of an equitable wrong relating to the plaintiff's property. This more restrictive approach is preferable since it minimises the proprietary consequences arising from the conclusion that the defendant holds property on trust for the plaintiff.[63]

---

[60] See pp. 539–44 and 628–35 below.
[61] See pp. 635–7 below for examination of the notion of the remedial constructive trust.
[62] See *Attorney-General for Hong Kong* v. *Reid* [1994] 1 AC 324.
[63] This is discussed further in at pp. 539–44 below.

(e) Exemplary damages[64]

Where the defendant has committed one of a limited number of torts,[65] such as defamation, assault and false imprisonment, the court may award the plaintiff exemplary damages in addition to any damages which are awarded to compensate the plaintiff for any loss suffered. Exemplary damages will only be awarded in very special circumstances, but for present purposes the most important of these is where the defendant committed the tort calculating that he or she would make a profit which might well exceed any compensation which was payable to the plaintiff.[66] Whilst exemplary damages cannot be regarded as a completely restitutionary remedy, since the measure of exemplary damages is not necessarily confined to the profit which the defendant made from the commission of the tort, such damages can be characterised as 'a blunt instrument to prevent unjust enrichment by unlawful acts'.[67] Despite this, the unsatisfactory nature of exemplary damages as a weapon in the restitutionary armoury is reflected in the rationale behind the award of such damages, which is not simply to deprive the defendant of any benefit made from the wrongdoing, but is primarily to punish the defendant for such cynical wrongdoing and to deter the defendant from engaging in such unacceptable conduct in future.[68] Consequently, such damages are an inaccurate way of ensuring that the defendant does not profit from the wrongdoing.

(f) Restoration of property

Another restitutionary remedy which arises where the defendant has committed a wrong is for the court to order that any property which the defendant obtained through the commission of the wrong should be restored to the plaintiff. This is illustrated by section 3(3)(a) of the Torts (Interference with Goods) Act 1977 which applies where the defendant tortiously obtained and retained goods belonging to the plaintiff. This provision enables the court to order the defendant to restore the goods to the plaintiff, although this remedy is available only to the extent that damages are an inadequate remedy.

---

[64] For analysis of the law relating to the award of exemplary damages and recommendations as to reform see 'Aggravated, Exemplary and Restitutionary Damages' (Law Com. No. 247, 1997) pp. 53–184.

[65] The category of torts for which exemplary damages can be awarded is closed: *AB* v. *South West Water Services Ltd.* [1993] QB 507.

[66] See *Rookes* v. *Barnard* [1964] AC 1129, 1226 (Lord Devlin).

[67] *Broome* v. *Cassell and Co. Ltd.* [1972] AC 1027, 1130 (Lord Diplock).

[68] *Rookes* v. *Barnard* [1964] AC 1129, 1221 (Lord Devlin).

(g) Injunctions

Whilst the grant of an injunction cannot be considered as a restitutionary remedy as such, because the function of an injunction is to require the defendant to act or to refrain from acting in a particular way, it is a remedy which may be of relevance in the context of restitutionary claims for wrongs. This is illustrated by *Attorney-General* v. *Blake*[69] where an injunction was granted to prevent the defendant from receiving the proceeds of a crime, namely the proceeds of a book which had been written in breach of the Official Secrets Acts. Whilst this injunction was not strictly a restitutionary remedy, since the defendant was not required to disgorge the royalties to anybody, the effect of the injunction was to prevent the defendant from receiving the proceeds of the crime in the first place. In other words, the function of the injunction was to prevent the defendant from profiting from the crime.

4. THE RELATIONSHIP BETWEEN RESTITUTIONARY AND COMPENSATORY REMEDIES FOR WRONGDOING[70]

(a) Election between inconsistent remedies

Sometimes the plaintiff will be able to claim a compensatory remedy as well as a restitutionary remedy for the same wrong. In such cases it is a fundamental principle of the law of remedies that the plaintiff is not able to recover both types of remedy to the extent that they are inconsistent.[71] Where the remedies are inconsistent with each other the plaintiff must elect between them. Once the plaintiff has made this election any claim to the other remedy which was not chosen is lost forever.[72]

(b) When must the election be made?

Although the normal time for election is by the time the judgment is given in the plaintiff's favour and is being entered against the

---

[69] [1998] 2 WLR 805.

[70] See 'Aggravated, Exemplary and Restitutionary Damages' (Law Com. No. 247, 1997) pp. 47–9 for analysis and criticism of the law.

[71] *Sutherland* v. *Caxton* [1936] Ch. 323, 336 (Farwell J); *Mahesan s/o Thambiah* v. *Malaysia Government Officers' Co-operative Housing Society Ltd.* [1979] AC 374; *Island Records Ltd.* v. *Tring International plc.* [1996] 1 WLR 1256, 1258 (Lightman J); *Tang Man Sit* v. *Capacious Investments Ltd.* [1996] AC 514, 521.

[72] *United Australia Ltd.* v. *Barclays Bank Ltd.* [1941] AC 1. See also *Island Records Ltd.* v. *Tring International plc.* [1996] 1 WLR 1256, 1258 (Lightman J).

defendant,[73] this rule only applies where the plaintiff was in possession of all the necessary information to be able to make the election. As Lightman J recognised in *Island Records Ltd. v. Tring International plc.*:[74]

a party should in general not be required to elect or be found to have elected between remedies unless and until he is able to make an informed choice. A right of election, if it is to be meaningful and not a mere gamble, must embrace the right to readily available information as to his likely entitlement in case of both the two alternative remedies.

Such a delay in making the election is more likely to be countenanced where the judgment is a default or summary judgment,[75] where the plaintiff may not have had sufficient information on the profits made by the defendant when the judgment was given. But a delay will also be countenanced where, as occurred in *Island Records*, a split trial procedure is adopted, whereby the issues of liability and assessment of remedies are separated, with the second hearing only being held if the decision on liability is favourable to the plaintiff. Delay in exercising the right of election will not be countenanced, however, if the delay is unreasonable, since it prejudices the defendant.[76] But where the delay is reasonable, the court will be prepared to defer entry of judgment for a reasonable time to allow the plaintiff to obtain the necessary information to make an informed election. The court will even be prepared to make discovery and other orders to provide the plaintiff with the necessary information.[77]

(c) *Tang Man Sit* v. *Capacious Investments Ltd.*

The unusual facts of *Tang Man Sit* v. *Capacious Investments Ltd.*[78] provided the Privy Council with the opportunity to consider when the plaintiff can be considered to have elected between inconsistent remedies. In *Tang Man Sit* a landowner had agreed to assign some houses to the plaintiff, but the deed of assignment was never executed. The landowner then let the houses without the plaintiff's approval. After the death of the landowner the plaintiff sued the landowner's personal representative for breach of trust. The plaintiff claimed an account of the profits which the landowner had made from letting the houses in breach of trust. But the plaintiff also claimed compensation for the lost market rental on the houses, for the fall in the value of the properties resulting from the

---

[73] See *United Australia Ltd.* v. *Barclays Bank Ltd.* [1941] AC 1, 19 (Viscount Simon LC).
[74] [1996] 1 WLR 1256, 1258. See also *Warman International Ltd.* v. *Dwyer* (1995) 182 CLR 544, 570.
[75] *Tang Man Sit* v. *Capacious Investments Ltd.* [1996] AC 514.
[76] *Island Records Ltd.* v. *Tring International plc.*, [1996] 1 WLR 1256, 1259 (Lightman J).
[77] *Ibid.*   [78] [1996] AC 514.

houses being encumbered by tenancies and for damage arising from their occupation. The trial judge found for the plaintiff and ordered the defendant both to account for the profits made and to compensate the plaintiff for the loss suffered, this loss to be assessed subsequently. The plaintiff recovered part of the profits and also proceeded with the assessment of the loss suffered. It discovered that the compensation for loss would be much greater than the profits which the defendant had made and so the plaintiff sought to recover the damages from the defendant, giving credit for the profits which it had already received. The issue for the Privy Council was whether the plaintiff had elected to receive the profits with the consequence that it was unable to recover damages for loss.

The Privy Council first recognised that the remedies of compensation and account of profits were inconsistent. This was because the account of profits represented the money which the defendant had received from the use of the properties in breach of trust, whereas compensation represented the financial return the plaintiff would have received for the same period had it been able to use the properties; the wrong which enabled the defendant to gain the profit also caused loss to the plaintiff. Because of the inconsistency between the remedies the plaintiff was required to elect between them. The question then was at what point the plaintiff is required to make an election.

Even though the trial judge had already entered judgment for the plaintiff, the Privy Council held that the plaintiff had not exercised the right of election until it claimed compensation rather than restitution. The delay in making the election was not considered to be unreasonable because the form of the trial judge's order was for both an account of profits and compensation. This meant that the plaintiff's acceptance of the profits from the defendant did not constitute an election, particularly because the plaintiff was proceeding with the necessary steps for the assessment of damages and the defendant had not paid the profits to the plaintiff under the misapprehension that the plaintiff had accepted profits rather than compensatory damages.

(d) Determining when compensatory and restitutionary remedies are inconsistent

It does not follow from the decision of the Privy Council in *Tang Man Sit* that restitutionary and compensatory remedies are always inconsistent,[79] although great care must be taken to ensure that the two remedies are compatible. For example, in *Tang Man Sit* itself if the plaintiff had

---

[79] That an account of profits and compensation is not necessarily inconsistent was accepted by the Privy Council at [1996] AC 514, 522. Cp. Lightman J in *Island Records Ltd.* v. *Tring International plc.* [1995] 1 WLR 1256, 1258.

elected to take the profits it is clear that it could not also have claimed compensation for the income it had lost from being unable to lease the properties, since the defendant's profits arose from the same event which caused the plaintiff's loss, namely that the defendant had leased the properties rather than the plaintiff. But there would have been nothing to stop the plaintiff claiming, in addition to the restitutionary remedy of an account of profits, compensation in respect of the capital loss to the properties arising from the breach of trust, namely that the tenancies had resulted in wear and tear to the properties and that the value of the properties had decreased by reason of their being leased.

The crucial question in determining the compatibility of the remedies is whether the award of a restitutionary remedy reduces the plaintiff's loss. If it does, it follows that compensatory and restitutionary remedies are inconsistent and the plaintiff must elect between them. This is illustrated by *Maheson s/o Thambiah* v. *Malaysia Government Officers' Co-operative Housing Society Ltd.*[80] where the defendant, in return for a bribe, had caused the plaintiff to buy land at an overvalue. The plaintiff sued the defendant both for the amount of the bribe and for damages for fraud for the loss caused by the purchase. It was held by the Privy Council that the two remedies were incompatible because, if the plaintiff recovered the amount of the bribe, this would have reduced its loss in buying the land at an overvalue. Consequently the plaintiff had to elect between the two remedies.

5. CAUSATION

Before the plaintiff is able to obtain restitution for wrongs he or she must show that any benefit which was obtained by the defendant arose from the wrongdoing. This question of causation is of crucial importance to our understanding of when restitutionary remedies may be awarded for wrongs, which remedy can be awarded and how it should be assessed.

(a) The general principle of causation

As a general rule the 'but for' test of causation applies in respect of restitutionary claims founded on wrongdoing. Consequently, the defendant will only be liable to disgorge a benefit to the plaintiff where the plaintiff can show that the defendant would not have obtained the particular benefit but for the commission of the wrong.[81] So, for example, in *My*

---

[80] [1979] AC 374.

[81] Goff and Jones, *The Law of Restitution*, p. 783. See Farnsworth, 'Your Loss or My Gain? The Dilemma of the Disgorgement Principle in Breach of Contract' (1985) 94 *Yale LJ* 1339, 1343.

Kinda Town Ltd. v. *Soll*[82] where the defendant had committed the tort of passing off by using as a name for a restaurant one which was similar to that used by the plaintiff, it was held that the defendant was liable to account for the profits it had made from customers who had confused the defendant's restaurant with those of the plaintiff. This was simply because, but for the commission of the tort, these profits would not have been obtained. Clearly in cases such as this it may be a particularly difficult matter to determine which benefits obtained by the defendant are attributable to the commission of the wrong.

(b) Assessing the defendant's contribution

In those cases in which the benefits obtained by the defendant resulted in part from the commission of the wrong and also from his or her own additional input, this input should be reflected in the remedy which the plaintiff is awarded. This may be achieved by apportioning the profits which arose from the wrong, to reflect the fact that some part of the profits were made by virtue of the defendant's input.[83] Alternatively, where the defendant is liable to account for all of the profits made as a result of the commission of the wrong, he or she may be awarded a personal allowance to reflect the reasonable value of his or her contribution, at least where the defendant's conduct is not reprehensible.[84] A further option is to conclude that the plaintiff is only entitled to receive the profits made by the defendant for a certain period, thereafter the profits are deemed not to have derived from the commission of the wrong.[85]

(c) The principle of remoteness of benefit

In the same way that remedies which seek to compensate the plaintiff for loss suffered are subject to a principle of remoteness, the award of restitutionary remedies is limited by a principle of remoteness of benefit. Without such a limiting principle all benefits which accrue to the defendant as a result of the wrongdoing would be liable to be transferred to the plaintiff. This could constitute over-protection of the plaintiff from the effects of the defendant's wrongdoing by emphasising the principle that no wrongdoer should profit from the commission of the wrong, without sufficient consideration of whether all of this profit should properly be

---

[82] [1982] FSR 147, reversed as to liability in the Court of Appeal: [1983] RPC 407.

[83] See *Attorney-General* v. *Guardian Newspapers (No. 2)* [1990] 1 AC 109, 266 (Lord Brightman).

[84] *Boardman* v. *Phipps* [1967] 2 AC 46. See also *Warman International Ltd.* v. *Dwyer* (1995) 128 ALR 201, 211. Cp. *Guinness* v. *Saunders* [1990] 2 AC 663.

[85] See *Warman International Ltd.* v. *Dwyer* (1995) 128 ALR 201.

transferred to the plaintiff. It is for this reason that a principle of remoteness of benefit is needed, the effect of which is that the defendant will only be liable to disgorge benefits to the plaintiff if they were obtained in circumstances which were not too remote from the commission of the wrong. The nature of the problem is illustrated by the following example. If the defendant takes £10,000 from the plaintiff without consent it is obvious that the benefit which was obtained by the defendant as a result of the wrong was £10,000. But what if the defendant used part of the money to buy shares and the value of the shares increased? Can the plaintiff successfully argue that this increase in value arose from the wrongdoing, or should this profit be regarded as too remote from the commission of the wrong? This depends on how the notion of remoteness is defined.

There was no need to consider specifically the question of remoteness of benefit in those claims which are founded on the reversal of the defendant's unjust enrichment, because the principle of remoteness is implicit in the requirement that the defendant's enrichment was obtained at the plaintiff's expense. The effect of this requirement is that the defendant will only be required to make restitution to the plaintiff of those benefits which are equivalent to what was subtracted from the plaintiff.[86] Equally, where the plaintiff seeks to obtain a proprietary restitutionary remedy there is no need to consider the application of the principle of remoteness, simply because all traceable gains accruing to the defendant which are derived from the plaintiff's property must be transferred to the plaintiff.[87] It is only where the plaintiff's restitutionary claim is founded on the defendant's wrongdoing that the issue of remoteness of benefit arises, and even here the question of remoteness will not be relevant in respect of all the restitutionary remedies which are available for wrongdoing. For example, if the plaintiff claims to recover money had and received by the defendant, the very nature of the remedy means that it is only available in respect of that money which the defendant had obtained directly from the plaintiff. Similarly, where the plaintiff claims restitutionary damages in respect of money saved by the defendant as a result of committing the wrong, the only question is what the defendant would have spent had the wrong not been committed. It is in respect of the remedy of account of profits that the question of remoteness of gain needs to be considered explicitly.

Although the matter is not free from doubt, the preferable test of remoteness is that a benefit is not too remote from the commission of the wrong where it arises directly from it.[88] Benefits which arise indirectly

---

[86] See Chapter 5.   [87] See Chapter 20.

[88] This test of remoteness appears to have been endorsed by the Court of Appeal in *Attorney-General* v. *Blake* [1998] 2 WLR 805, 819.

from the commission of the wrong should be considered to be too remote and so do not need to be disgorged.[89] The application of this principle of remoteness may be illustrated by an example where the defendant wrongfully takes the plaintiff's car. All the benefits which the defendant gains from the use of the car should be considered to arise directly from the wrongdoing. So, if the defendant hires the car to third parties, any money obtained from such hiring should be disgorged to the plaintiff. Similarly, if the defendant used the car and so saved necessary expenditure, the value of this negative benefit should be paid to the plaintiff in the form of restitutionary damages. If, however, the defendant obtained £500 from the use of the car and bought shares with this money then any dividends paid to the defendant need not be disgorged to the plaintiff, since they did not arise directly from the wrongful use of the plaintiff's car. The only qualification to this will arise if the plaintiff could establish a proprietary claim to the profits obtained by the defendant, as would occur if the profits were found to be held on constructive trust, and then the plaintiff would be able to claim all the profits made from the use of the car, regardless of whether they arose directly or indirectly.[90]

Support for this principle that indirect benefits are too remote can be found in the decision of the Court of Appeal in *Halifax Building Society* v. *Thomas*.[91] One of the issues in that case concerned whether a restitutionary claim could be made in respect of the proceeds of sale of a flat which had been purchased by the defendant with a loan from the plaintiff building society. This loan had been made as a result of the defendant's fraudulent misrepresentation as to his identity. When the flat was sold by the plaintiff there was a surplus after the loan had been discharged. It was held that the defendant could claim this surplus because it had not been made at the expense of the plaintiff.[92] Whilst this reasoning cannot be defended since, had the defendant received the proceeds of sale, the plaintiff's restitutionary claim would have been founded on tort rather than unjust enrichment so there was no need to show that the benefit was received at the plaintiff's expense, the intuitive response of the court was correct. This is because the surplus proceeds of sale were not obtained directly from the commission of the wrong, but were indirectly obtained once the defendant had used the loan to

---

[89] Birks call this the principle of the first non-subtractive receipt: Birks, *An Introduction to the Law of Restitution*, p. 352. The distinction between direct and indirect benefits is a more elegant way of describing the same idea.

[90] See, for example, *Attorney-General of Hong Kong* v. *Reid* [1994] 1 AC 324.

[91] [1996] Ch. 217. See also *Boyter* v. *Dodsworth* (1796) 6 TR 681; 101 ER 770; *Ex p. Vaughan* (1884) 14 QBD 25; and *Chief Constable of Leicestershire* v. *M* [1989] 1 WLR 20.

[92] [1996] Ch. 217, 227 (Peter Gibson LJ).

purchase the flat, by virtue of the fact that the value of the flat had increased.[93]

(d) More than one victim[94]

There is one particular problem of causation which arises where there are a number of potential plaintiffs.[95] In such circumstances it will some-times be very difficult, if not impossible, to show that the benefit obtained by the defendant derived from the commission of a wrong against a particular plaintiff. For example, if the defendant owns a factory which discharges pollutants into the air, causing a nuisance to nearby residents, but no loss to them, and the defendant saved £10,000 as a result of failing to install the necessary devices which would have drasti-cally reduced pollution, what should be the measure of the plaintiffs' remedy? This will depend on who sues the defendant. If only one resi-dent sues, but ten have been affected, should the one person who sues recover the full amount which the defendant saved or only a proportion? If the plaintiff is awarded only a proportion, how should this be ascer-tained?

Where it is possible to apportion the defendant's benefit amongst all potential plaintiffs, then this is the proper course to take. So, for example, in *Jaggard* v. *Sawyer*[96] the defendant had breached a covenant which had been made with nine other people. Only one of these sued the defendant and the remedy which was awarded was ascertained by identifying the full amount which the defendant would have been liable to pay if all the victims had sued and then one ninth of this amount was allocated to the plaintiff. But this was an easy case, since the number of potential plain-tiffs was readily ascertained. In other cases it might be very difficult to predict how many people had been affected by the defendant's wrong. Consequently it will not be possible to ascertain how the benefit obtained by the defendant as a result of the commission of the wrong should be allocated to any particular plaintiff who sued the defendant. In

---

[93] See Watts, 'The Limits of Profit-Stripping for Wrongs' (1996) 112 *LQR* 219, 220. If, how-ever, the court had recognised that, had the defendant received the proceeds of sale, they were received in circumstances in which the defendant had been acting unconscionably, it would follow that the proceeds would have been held on constructive trust and so the defendant would have been liable to disgorge all the proceeds to the plaintiff regardless of whether they arose directly or indirectly from the commission of the wrong. See pp. 630–4 below.

[94] 'Aggravated, Exemplary and Restitutionary Damages' (Law Com. No. 247, 1997) pp. 50–1.

[95] There is no problem where there is more than one defendant, since each defendant will simply be liable to disgorge the benefit which he or she had obtained as a result of the commission of the wrong. See *ibid*, 49.

[96] [1995] 1 WLR 269.

such circumstances there are only two possible solutions. The first is that the plaintiff should be denied restitutionary remedies completely. This is the view of Goff and Jones[97] and, in respect of exemplary damages, the Court of Appeal has held that such damages will not be awarded where there are a large number of plaintiffs.[98] Alternatively, the defendant should be required to disgorge all benefits to the plaintiff who successfully sues first. Such an approach has been recommended by the Law Commission as being appropriate where the defendant is liable to pay exemplary damages.[99] Since the fundamental principle of the law of restitution for wrongs is that the defendant should not profit from the commission of the wrong, this approach would also be appropriate in the context of restitutionary remedies where it is not possible to apportion the defendant's gain between different plaintiffs.

6. THE AVAILABLE DEFENCES FOR RESTITUTION FOR WRONGS

Where the plaintiff claims restitution from the defendant in circumstances in which the defendant has committed a wrong, the question of which defences are available to the defendant is a matter of some complexity, depending on the nature of the plaintiff's restitutionary claim. There are three fundamental principles which need to be borne in mind when determining what defences are available to the defendant.

(a) Restitutionary claim founded on the defendant's wrongdoing

Where the plaintiff's restitutionary claim is founded on the commission of a wrong by the defendant, any defence which applies to the wrong should also apply to the restitutionary claim. So, for example, if the effect of the defence is to extinguish the cause of action then there can be no wrong on which the plaintiff's claim can be based. For example, as regards limitation periods, the relevant limitation period should be that which relates to the particular wrong rather than unjust enrichment.[100] Similarly, when tortious causes of action were defeated by the *actio personalis* bar, by virtue of which the personal representatives of a deceased wrongdoer could not be liable for a wrong committed by the deceased,

---

[97] Goff and Jones, *The Law of Restitution*, p. 786.

[98] *AB* v. *South West Water Services Ltd.* [1993] QB 507.

[99] 'Aggravated, Exemplary and Restitutionary Damages' (Law Com. No. 247, 1997) p. 189.

[100] *Beaman* v. *ARTS Ltd.* [1948] 2 All ER 89 (Denning J). *Chesworth* v. *Farrar* [1967] 1 QB 407, where the plaintiff was allowed to bring a restitutionary claim despite the fact that the tortious limitation period had passed, is better regarded as a case where the cause of action was the vindication of a proprietary right, rather than wrongdoing.

this bar would defeat the plaintiff's claim even where he or she sought restitutionary relief.[101]

(b) Application of the general defences to restitutionary claims

In addition, where the plaintiff's restitutionary claim is founded on the defendant's wrong then, because the plaintiff seeks restitutionary relief, the general defences to restitutionary claims should also be applicable.[102] The most important of these is the defence of change of position.[103] The effect of this defence is that, if the defendant has changed his or her position in reliance on the receipt of a benefit, then restitution should be barred to the extent that the defendant's position has changed. But this is subject to a very important qualification, namely that the defence will only operate to the extent that the defendant has changed his or her position in good faith.[104] Presumably the fact that the defendant has committed a wrong will not automatically mean that change of position will be defeated, because it does not follow automatically from the fact that the defendant is a wrongdoer that he or she was acting in bad faith. But the fault of the defendant in committing the wrong will clearly be a relevant consideration in determining the applicability of the defence. So, for example, if the defendant intentionally committed a tort, the defence of change of position should be denied to him or her.

(c) Restitutionary claim founded on the reversal of the defendant's unjust enrichment

Where the plaintiff's restitutionary claim is founded on the reversal of the defendant's unjust enrichment even though the defendant has also committed a wrong, then by virtue of the principle of alternative analysis, any defence which applies to an action founded on the wrong would appear not to be applicable to the claim founded on unjust enrichment. This is because the plaintiff does not need to establish the wrong in order to show that the defendant has been unjustly enriched. It follows that the plaintiff could avoid the application of defences which relate to the wrong by founding the claim on unjust enrichment instead. But, before the court allows this to happen, it should carefully consider whether the policy which underlies the defence should be extended to a claim founded on unjust enrichment. This is exactly what the House of Lords

---

[101] *Hambly* v. *Trott* (1776) 1 Cowp. 371, 375; 98 ER 1136, 1139 (Lord Mansfield).
[102] See Part VI.   [103] See Chapter 24.
[104] *Lipkin Gorman (a firm)* v. *Karpnale Ltd.* [1991] 2 AC 548, 580 (Lord Goff). See p. 727 below.

did in *The Universe Sentinel*.[105] In this case the plaintiff sought to recover money which had been paid to the defendant trade union as a result of its threats that, unless the money was paid, it would prevent the plaintiff's ship from sailing. The plaintiff's claim was founded on the reversal of the defendant's unjust enrichment, the ground of restitution being economic duress. The plaintiff could also have sued the defendant for the tort of interfering with contract, but it had not done so because there was a statutory immunity in favour of the defendant in respect of torts which were committed in the furtherance of a trade dispute. The question for the House of Lords was whether the policy underlying this statutory provision should be extended to the action founded on unjust enrichment. It was held that the immunity should be extended to the plaintiff's claim.[106] This was an appropriate decision because the statutory immunity was not dependent on the nature of the cause of action on which the plaintiff's claim was based, but was concerned with whether the defendant should be held liable for any remedy in respect of conduct which related to a trade dispute.

7. RECOMMENDATIONS FOR REFORM

The Law Commission has recently examined the law of restitution for wrongs.[107] It considered that it is preferable to leave the development of the law of restitution for wrongs to the common law and it is surely right to reach this conclusion, since the law concerning the award of restitutionary remedies for wrongs is still at an early stage of development, so that it would be inappropriate to curtail development by the judges. But the Law Commission did conclude that, since it recommends that the award of exemplary damages should be placed on a statutory footing, it should follow that restitutionary damages should be available whenever exemplary damages could be awarded. Consequently, the Law Commission recommended that legislation should provide that restitutionary damages may be awarded where the defendant has committed a tort, an equitable wrong or a statutory wrong and the defendant's conduct showed a deliberate and outrageous disregard of the plaintiff's rights.[108] The Law Commission also recommended that the award of such damages should be a matter for the judge and that this statutory

---

[105] *Universe Tankships Inc. of Monrovia* v. *International Transport Workers Federation* [1983] AC 366. See also *Dimskal Shipping Co. SA* v. *International Transport Workers Federation, The Evia Luck* [1992] 2 AC 152, 167 (Lord Diplock).

[106] In fact the money was recoverable simply because it was paid in respect of matters which did not relate to a trade dispute.

[107] 'Aggravated, Exemplary and Restitutionary Damages' (Law Com. No. 247, 1997).

[108] *Ibid*, p. 43.

power should not infringe any other power to award restitutionary damages.

If the development of the law of restitution for wrongs is left to the common law, how should that law be developed? The answer is that it should continue to be developed in a piece-meal fashion with continuous regard to the principles which underlie the award of restitutionary remedies for wrongdoing. Although it may be felt that restitutionary remedies should be available regardless of the type of wrong which is committed, this is a dangerous approach, simply because each type of wrongdoing raises very different issues of policy as to the remedy which is appropriate. For example, the award of restitutionary damages for breach of contract and the commission of a criminal offence raise very different questions which need to be examined in respect of the particular wrong itself. Nevertheless, the analysis of the Law Commission and the identification of the fundamental principles in this chapter should mean that judges can be more confident in awarding restitutionary remedies for wrongs in the future.

16

Restitution for Torts

1. GENERAL PRINCIPLES

Where the plaintiff is the victim of a tort the most common remedy is damages to compensate him or her for loss suffered. But this is not the only remedy which is available. For certain torts exemplary damages may be awarded to punish the defendant for cynically committing them[1] and other remedies are available which are purely restitutionary in effect, notably restitutionary damages and money had and received. The most important question relating to the award of restitutionary remedies for torts is whether they are available regardless of the tort which is committed or whether they are available only in respect of certain torts. If the latter is the case, it is then necessary to identify the criterion which is used to identify those torts for which restitutionary relief is available. The focus for this discussion is the so-called doctrine of 'waiver of tort' which has been particularly influential in the development of the law in this area.

(a) The doctrine of waiver of tort

The doctrine of waiver of tort has had a malign influence on the rational development of the law of restitution for wrongs by virtue of its ambiguity and tendency to mislead. In *United Australia Ltd.* v. *Barclays Bank Ltd.*[2] Lord Romer described the phrase 'waiver of tort' as picturesque but inaccurate. The doctrine can be interpreted in three different ways.

(i) Waiver of a compensatory remedy

The usual interpretation of the doctrine is that the plaintiff can elect not to claim compensation for the tort and can choose instead to recover a restitutionary remedy, such as the recovery of money had and received or restitutionary damages.[3] It is, however, totally misleading to say that a plaintiff who elects a restitutionary remedy is waiving the tort. In fact, it is vital that the plaintiff does not waive the tort because the tort constitutes the cause of action on which the plaintiff's restitutionary claim is

---

[1] See *Rookes* v. *Barnard* [1964] AC 1129.   [2] [1941] AC 1, 34.

[3] This is the interpretation adopted by Goff and Jones, *The Law of Restitution*, see p. 773. Cp. Hedley, 'The Myth of "Waiver of Tort" ' (1984) 100 *LQR* 653.

founded.[4] All the plaintiff is doing is waiving the right to obtain remedies assessed by reference to the loss suffered, and instead he or she elects remedies which are assessed by reference to the benefit gained by the defendant as a result of committing the tort.

That this is the proper analysis of this interpretation of the waiver of tort doctrine is supported by its history. The need to waive the tort originated as a device to enable the plaintiff to obtain a restitutionary remedy from the defendant where the cause of action was the defendant's wrongdoing. Such a waiver was required because, if the plaintiff wished to obtain restitution from the defendant, it used to be necessary to identify a promise by the defendant to repay the plaintiff. But if the defendant had committed a tort against the plaintiff such a promise to repay would be incongruous, save where the plaintiff had ratified the wrong first. Such ratification was therefore required if the plaintiff wished to bring a restitutionary claim. Eventually the ratification of the wrong became a fiction, but at least it provided a route to implying a contract and so obtaining restitutionary remedies.

With the rejection of the implied contract theory by the House of Lords in *United Australia Ltd.* v. *Barclays Bank Ltd.*[5] the demise of the doctrine of waiver of tort should have followed automatically. If it was no longer necessary to imply a promise to make restitution it should have followed that it was no longer necessary to show that the plaintiff had ratified the wrong before he or she could obtain restitutionary relief for the defendant's tort. But unfortunately the House of Lords in that case did not appreciate the logical consequence of the rejection of the implied contract theory, since the court affirmed the continued existence of the waiver of tort doctrine.

In the *United Australia* case the plaintiff had received a cheque which had been fraudulently endorsed by its secretary, who did not have authority to do so, in favour of M Ltd., a company with which the secretary was associated. M Ltd. paid the cheque into its account with the defendant bank. The defendant collected the proceeds of the cheque and placed them to the credit of M Ltd.'s account. The plaintiff then sought to recover the value of the cheque from M Ltd. by suing both for money had and received and money lent. Before the plaintiff had obtained final judgment, the action against M Ltd. was automatically stayed after M Ltd. entered into compulsory liquidation. The plaintiff then sued the defendant for damages for negligence and for the conversion of the cheque. The defendant pleaded that it could not be sued by the plaintiff because, by initially commencing proceedings against M Ltd., the plaintiff had elected to waive the tort. This argument was rejected by the

---

[4] *Chesworth* v. *Farrar* [1967] 1 QB 407, 417 (Edmund Davies J).   [5] [1941] AC 1.

House of Lords, so the plaintiff was able to sue the defendant and obtain compensatory damages for the tort of conversion. On the facts of the case it was particularly easy to conclude that the commencement of proceedings against M Ltd. had not involved waiver of the tort by the plaintiff, since the tort of conversion committed by M Ltd. was separate from that committed by the defendant. In other words, the remedies which the plaintiff sought were cumulative rather than alternative, being founded on different acts of conversion.[6] The plaintiff would only have been prevented from seeking compensation for its loss against the defendant if the plaintiff had fully recouped all of its loss in the earlier proceedings against M Ltd.[7] But the court specifically recognised that its decision would have been the same if the plaintiff had initially sued the defendant for money had and received and then, before final judgment was given, had commenced proceedings against the same defendant for compensation. This is because the commencement of proceedings does not involve an election between restitutionary and compensatory remedies.[8] Compensation would only have been denied to the plaintiff if it had elected to take the restitutionary remedy, for it would then have been bound by that election. The implication of this decision, therefore, is that the plaintiff would have irrevocably waived the tort only once it had elected to take a restitutionary remedy. It follows from this that the court implicitly recognised that the waiver of tort doctrine is concerned with waiving the usual compensatory remedy for the tort, rather than waiving the underlying cause of action.

That the doctrine of waiver of tort relates to choosing between alternative remedies has been accepted in subsequent cases, most notably by Edmund Davies J who said in *Chesworth* v. *Farrar*[9] that:

A person upon whom a tort has been committed has at times a choice of alternative remedies, even though it is a *sine qua non* regarding each that he must establish a tort has been committed. He may sue to recover damages for the tort, or he may waive the tort and sue in quasi-contract to recover the benefit received by the wrongdoer.

Even if the doctrine is interpreted in this way it is misleading to speak of 'waiver of tort'. It is clear that the plaintiff does not need to waive anything, since he or she simply needs to elect between restitutionary and compensatory remedies. Crucially, the plaintiff must ensure that he or she does not waive the tort itself for that is the underlying cause of action regardless of the remedy which the plaintiff seeks. As Birks has said,

---

[6] See Lord Wright in *United Australia Ltd.* v. *Barclays Bank Ltd.* (1941) 57 *LQR* 184, 190.

[7] [1941] AC 1, 20 (Viscount Simon LC). See also *Tang Man Sit* v. *Capacious Investments Ltd.* [1996] AC 514, 523.

[8] See *ibid*, discussed in at p. 462 above.   [9] [1967] 1 QB 407.

'[waiver of tort] has become a loose and anachronistic description of the decision by the victim of such a tort to seek restitution'.[10]

(ii) Waiver of the cause of action

The doctrine of waiver of tort can be interpreted in another way, as recognised by Peter Gibson LJ in *Halifax Building Society* v. *Thomas*,[11] who defined the doctrine 'as meaning that the plaintiff chooses not to sue in tort for damages but sues instead in restitution for the recovery of the benefit taken by the wrongdoer'. Although the phrase 'sues instead in restitution' is ambiguous, what the judge appears to have meant is that the plaintiff could waive a cause of action in tort in favour of a cause of action 'in restitution'. In other words, where the plaintiff is the victim of a tort then, rather than found the restitutionary claim on the defendant's wrongdoing, he or she may be able to bring an action which is founded on the reversal of unjust enrichment. This sense of waiver of tort therefore involves alternative analysis. So, for example, if the defendant induced the plaintiff to pay money to him or her by virtue of a fraudulent misrepresentation, the plaintiff may sue the defendant for the tort of deceit or may instead base a restitutionary claim on the defendant's unjust enrichment, with the ground of restitution being induced mistake. Similarly, if the defendant has falsely imprisoned the plaintiff and made it a condition of release that the plaintiff should pay a sum of money to the defendant, the plaintiff can base a restitutionary claim either on the tort of false imprisonment or, within the action founded on reversing unjust enrichment, on the ground of duress of the person.[12]

Although the plaintiff's election to base the claim on unjust enrichment rather than tort makes it appear that he or she has waived the tort, this is true only in a purely descriptive sense. It is not true in any technical sense, because simply basing the claim on unjust enrichment does not extinguish the tort. As was recognised by the House of Lords in *United Australia Ltd.* v. *Barclays Bank Ltd.*,[13] the plaintiff's claim in tort will only be extinguished once final judgment has been obtained against the defendant. Until that point the plaintiff is able to discontinue the proceedings based upon unjust enrichment and commence proceedings founded on the tort. Where the plaintiff founds his or her claim in restitution on the defendant's unjust enrichment the plaintiff is not waiving the tort but is simply ignoring it.[14]

---

[10] Birks, *An Introduction to the Law of Restitution*, p. 317.   [11] [1996] Ch. 217, 227.
[12] *Duke de Cadaval* v. *Collins* (1836) 4 A and E 858; 111 ER 1006.   [13] [1941] AC 1.
[14] Birks, 'Restitution and Wrongs' (1982) 35 *CLP* 53, 55.

(iii) Ratification of the defendant's wrongdoing

The only true case of waiver of tort occurs where the plaintiff has actually ratified the defendant's wrongdoing.[15] This notion of waiver of tort will be applicable only where the defendant purported to act as the plaintiff's agent but lacked the authority to do so. For example, if the defendant sold the plaintiff's car purporting to act as the plaintiff's agent but without authority to do so, there are two options which are available to the plaintiff. He or she could sue the defendant for the tort of conversion and obtain compensatory or restitutionary remedies. Alternatively, the plaintiff could ratify the sale with the result that the plaintiff retrospectively authorised the defendant's actions. Consequently, the defendant would be subject to the usual obligations of an agent, including the obligation to account to the plaintiff for the purchase price which had been received from the purchaser. Since the effect of the ratification by the plaintiff is to extinguish the tort,[16] it follows that once the plaintiff has ratified the wrong he or she is unable to sue the defendant on the tort. It is for this reason that such ratification is properly called waiver of tort and the doctrine should properly be confined to this specific context.

(b) Is there a role for the doctrine of waiver of tort in the modern law of restitution?

Apart from the exceptional case where the plaintiff has truly ratified the defendant's wrongdoing, the doctrine of waiver of tort should be rejected. Where the plaintiff chooses to base the restitutionary claim on unjust enrichment rather than the tort, references to the doctrine of waiver can only cause confusion. The alternative analysis principle is a perfectly acceptable way of describing what the plaintiff is actually doing. Where the plaintiff chooses to claim a restitutionary remedy rather than compensation for the tort, any reference to waiver of tort is totally misleading, since it suggests that the plaintiff's cause of action is not founded on the tort where he or she seeks a restitutionary remedy. This is patently untrue. The doctrine should be confined to the agency context and it should otherwise be removed from the law of restitution.

---

[15] This has been called 'extinctive ratification' by Birks, *An Introduction to the Law of Restitution*, p. 315.

[16] *Verschures Creameries Ltd.* v. *Hull and Netherlands Steamship Co. Ltd.* [1921] 2 KB 608. See *United Australia Ltd.* v. *Barclays Bank Ltd.* [1941] AC 1, 28 (Lord Atkin).

(c) Restitutionary remedies for torts

(i) General principles

Once it is accepted that restitutionary remedies are potentially available for the victim of a tort, it is still necessary to determine in what circumstances the commission of a tort may trigger the award of such remedies. When considering this question a number of key principles can be identified.

(1) The compensation principle

The general principle underlying the award of remedies for the commission of a tort is that the plaintiff who establishes that a tort has been committed will recover damages which are equivalent to the loss which he or she has suffered.[17] This is the compensation principle.

(2) Nominal damages

Usually where the plaintiff has suffered no loss as a result of the tort he or she will only be awarded nominal damages.[18]

(3) Compensation for proprietary loss

Where the plaintiff has suffered a pecuniary loss in the value of his or her property or a right to property as a result of the tort, the damages will usually be assessed by reference to the diminution in value of the property or the right.[19] So again the assumption is that damages will compensate the plaintiff for loss suffered.

(4) The user principle

Sometimes damages will be awarded for tortious interference by the defendant with the plaintiff's property or proprietary right even though the plaintiff has not suffered any pecuniary loss as a result of the interference. In these circumstances the damages which are awarded to the plaintiff are assessed by reference to what the defendant would have paid for the use of the property if he or she had negotiated with the plaintiff for the use of the property or the proprietary right. This is the so-called 'user principle'.[20] It is a matter of some controversy whether the damages which are awarded by reference to this principle should be characterised as compensatory or restitutionary. In a number of cases in which the user principle has been applied the remedy could be charac-

---

[17]   *Stoke-on-Trent City Council* v. *W. and J. Wass Ltd.* [1988] 1 WLR 1406, 1410 (Nourse LJ). See also *Ministry of Defence* v. *Ashman* [1993] 2 EGLR 102, 105 (Hoffman LJ).

[18]   *Stoke-on-Trent City Council* v. *W. and J. Wass Ltd.* [1988] 1 WLR 1406, 1410 (Nourse LJ).

[19]   *Ibid.*

[20]   *Ibid*, p. 1416 (Nicholls LJ).

terised either as compensating the plaintiff for the loss arising from the defendant's use of the property without paying for it or as depriving the defendant of a benefit, namely what the defendant saved by not paying the plaintiff for the use of the property. Indeed, in *Inverugie Investments Ltd.* v. *Hackett*[21] the Privy Council said that the user principle 'need not be characterised as exclusively compensatory, or exclusively restitutionary: it combines elements of both'. Despite this there is a tendency in the cases to characterise the damages which are awarded by reference to the user principle as essentially compensatory.

This is well illustrated by the decision of the Court of Appeal in *Strand Electric and Engineering Co. Ltd.* v. *Brisford Entertainments Ltd.*[22] where the defendant had hired switchboards from the plaintiff for use in the defendant's theatre. After the contract of hire had come to an end the defendant retained the equipment and the plaintiff sued for the tort of detinue.[23] It was accepted that the defendant was liable and the court held that the measure of damages should be assessed by reference to what the defendant would have had to pay to hire the equipment for the period during which the tort was being committed. For Somervell and Romer LJJ these damages were intended to compensate the plaintiff for the loss it had suffered by virtue of the fact that the defendant's detention of the equipment had meant that the plaintiff was unable to make a profit from hiring the equipment to somebody else. But this identification of loss was highly artificial since it appeared that the plaintiff would not have been willing to hire out the equipment for the period during which the defendant had possession of it.[24] Consequently, Denning LJ's justification for the award of damages is preferable. He said that the damages were restitutionary and were assessed by reference to the benefit which the defendant had received by retaining the property without having to pay for its hire.

(5) Identification of loss to establish the tort

Sometimes whether the plaintiff has suffered loss as a result of the defendant's actions will be of crucial importance in determining whether the plaintiff can sue the defendant for a tort, since the identification of loss suffered by the plaintiff is a crucial element for establishing the cause of action. In such situations the question of loss suffered is an issue of substance rather than remedy. This type of tort was recognised by the Court of Appeal in *Stoke-on-Trent City Council* v. *W. and J. Wass Ltd.*[25] which

---

[21] [1995] 1 WLR 713, 718.   [22] [1952] 2 QB 246.

[23] Today, this would be the tort of conversion.

[24] It is for this reason that Sharpe and Waddam's analysis of such cases as involving the award of compensatory damages for the lost opportunity to bargain cannot be defended: 'Damages for Lost Opportunity to Bargain' (1982) 2 *OJLS* 290. See p. 458 above.

[25] [1988] 1 WLR 1406.

concerned the tort of nuisance which the plaintiff local authority alleged the defendant had committed by holding a market in close proximity to a market held by the plaintiff. Whereas the plaintiff had statutory authority to hold a market, the defendant lacked any authority to do so. Since the markets were held on the same day the defendant was held to be liable, even though it could not be shown that the plaintiff had suffered any loss; such loss was presumed. But it was accepted that if the markets had not been held on the same day the defendant would only be liable to the plaintiff if it could be shown that the plaintiff had suffered loss. If no loss had been suffered then 'there is no cause of action'[26] and without a cause of action there could be no question of remedies being awarded, whether compensatory or restitutionary, since no tort could be established.

(6) Wrongdoers should not profit from the commission of a tort

Where the plaintiff has not suffered any loss at all, and cannot be presumed to have suffered any loss, the compensation principle, if taken literally, will mean that the only available remedy is nominal damages. But, where the defendant has obtained a benefit as a result of the tort, it is appropriate to require him or her to disgorge that benefit to the plaintiff because of the principle that wrongdoers should not profit from their wrong. Whilst the award of restitutionary remedies for torts has been implicitly recognised in some cases, where the plaintiff has been awarded a remedy even though he or she has not suffered any loss,[27] there is little explicit support in English law for the award of restitutionary remedies in such circumstances. Indeed, in *Stoke-on-Trent City Council* v. *W. and J. Wass Ltd.*[28] the Court of Appeal doubted the existence of restitutionary relief for torts, save where the defendant had committed the tort of trespass. As Nourse LJ said:[29]

> where no loss has been suffered no substantial damages of any kind can be recovered . . . It is possible that the English law of torts, more especially of the so-called 'proprietary torts', will in due course make a more deliberate move towards recovery based not on loss suffered by the plaintiff but on the unjust enrichment of the defendant . . . But I do not think that that process can begin in this case and I doubt whether it can begin at all at this level of decision.

But analysis of the old cases on waiver of tort and other cases involving remedies for torts suggest that the award of restitutionary remedies for torts is more widespread than Nourse LJ contemplated.[30] Nevertheless,

---

[26] [1988] 1 WLR 1406, p. 1419 (Nicholls LJ).
[27] As in *Strand Electric and Engineering Co. Ltd.* v. *Brisford Entertainments Ltd.* [1952] QB 246.
[28] [1988] 1 WLR 1406.   [29] *Ibid*, at p. 1415.
[30] See in particular Hoffman LJ in *Ministry of Defence* v. *Ashman* [1993] 2 EGLR 102, 105.

as Nourse LJ recognised, it seems that restitutionary remedies are not available for all torts, but will only be available in respect of the 'proprietary torts' which involve the defendant interfering with the plaintiff's property or proprietary rights. This stems from the fundamental principle that property is a facilitative institution which requires particular protection from unacceptable interference.[31] This protection can take the form of requiring a wrongdoer to disgorge any benefit obtained from interfering with the plaintiff's property.

(ii) The obstacle of Phillips v. Homfray[32]

Care must be taken when analysing old cases which are consistent with restitutionary remedies being awarded for torts, both because a number of these cases are ambiguous as to whether the remedy awarded was intended to be compensatory or restitutionary, and also because it is sometimes unclear whether the underlying cause of action is tort or the reversal of the defendant's unjust enrichment. In addition, there are some cases which appear to suggest that restitutionary remedies cannot be available where the defendant has committed a tort. The most influential of these are the cases which arose from the litigation in *Phillips* v. *Homfray*. The complex litigation in *Phillips* v. *Homfray*, which lasted for over 20 years in the late nineteenth century, has been one of the major obstacles to the recognition of restitutionary remedies for torts. In fact, careful analysis of the various decisions which make up this litigation shows that they do not prevent restitutionary remedies being awarded for torts.

(1) The course of the litigation

In *Phillips* v. *Homfray* the deceased had committed the tort of trespass by drawing coal from the plaintiff's land and using passages under that land to transport this coal and coal which had been mined from his own land. The Court of Appeal[33] held that the plaintiff was entitled to recover the value of the coal which the deceased had mined from the plaintiff's land and was also entitled to a remedy in respect of the use of the passages under the land for the transfer of the coal. The court ordered that an inquiry should be held to ascertain the amount and value of coal which had been mined from the plaintiff's land and what the cost for the use of the passages should be. The deceased died before this inquiry was held. As the law stood at the time, the deceased's personal representatives

---

[31] Jackman, 'Restitution for Wrongs' (1989) 48 *CLJ* 302, 305–11. See p. 452 above.

[32] See Gummow, 'Unjust Enrichment, Restitution and Proprietary Remedies' in *Essays on Restitution* (ed. Finn) pp. 60–7. See also Birks, *Civil Wrongs: A New World*, pp. 65–7.

[33] (1871) LR 6 Ch. App. 770.

could not be liable for any tort committed by the deceased,[34] so the case returned to the Court of Appeal to determine whether the deceased's personal representatives were entitled to have the inquiry discharged.[35] The Court of Appeal was required to consider only whether the deceased's estate remained liable to the plaintiff in respect of the deceased's use of the passages under the plaintiff's land. This effectively turned on a question of alternative analysis, namely whether the plaintiff's claim was dependent on the tort of trespass, which would not have survived the deceased's death, or whether the plaintiff's action could be founded on the defendant's unjust enrichment, an action which would have survived the death of the deceased. The court held that the plaintiff's action was founded on the tort of trespass, and so it did not survive the death of the deceased. The court relied on two additional reasons for its decision that the plaintiff did not have a restitutionary claim which survived the deceased's death.[36]

(1) The court first concluded that the deceased had not received a benefit by using the passages under the plaintiff's land. The court assumed that the deceased would have benefited from the trespass only if he had acquired property or the proceeds of property from the plaintiff as a result of the trespass. It did not consider that the negative benefit, which arose from the fact that the deceased had saved money by not paying the plaintiff for the use of the passages, was a real benefit for these purposes.[37] It followed that a restitutionary claim was unavailable because there was nothing for the deceased's estate to disgorge to the plaintiff.

(2) The court also held that the plaintiff could not waive the trespass, primarily because it was not possible to imply a contract that the deceased would pay for the use of the passages where the deceased had never intended to pay for such use.

(2) Analysis of the case

If this decision is taken at face value it appears to constitute a major restriction on the ability to award restitutionary remedies for torts, both because of the restrictive interpretation of what constitutes an enrichment and because of the suggestion that restitutionary relief is only available where it is possible to imply a contract to pay the plaintiff for the use of his or her property. The conclusion that such a contract cannot be implied if the defendant never intended to pay for the use of the plaintiff's property constitutes a fundamental obstacle to the success of restitutionary claims arising from the commission of a tort, simply

---

[34] This bar is called *actio personalis moritur cum persona*. It was abolished by the Law Reform (Miscellaneous Provisions) Act 1934.

[35] (1883) 24 Ch.D 439.   [36] *Ibid*, p. 466 (Bowen and Cotton LJJ).

[37] Cp. Baggallay LJ at p. 471–2.

because in most cases the defendant does not intend to pay for the unauthorised use of the plaintiff's property, hence the defendant's conduct is characterised as wrongful. Careful analysis of the Court of Appeal's decision, however, shows that it was wrongly decided for two reasons and that it should not be interpreted as barring restitutionary claims founded on torts.

(1) It is clear that if the plaintiff's claim was founded on tort then it should have been barred by the *actio personalis* bar, since this bar related to the underlying cause of action. It is for this reason impossible to defend the assertion of the Court of Appeal that, if the deceased had obtained property or proceeds from the plaintiff as a result of the trespass, a restitutionary claim would lie against the estate. This assertion is indefensible because, even where the deceased has obtained a positive benefit from the tort, the underlying cause of action is still the tort and any claim on the tort must be barred by the *actio personalis* bar. Whether the benefit which the defendant obtained was positive or negative is totally irrelevant. The question is simply whether a tort can be established and, on the facts of the case, it was not possible to do so. But it does not follow from this that all restitutionary claims founded on tort are barred, at least where the defendant has obtained a negative benefit. *Phillips* v. *Homfray* turned on the application of a defence which was peculiar to certain tort claims and, anyway, that defence has since been abolished.

(2) Even though the plaintiff could not rely on the commission of a tort to establish a restitutionary claim, it does not follow that the plaintiff could not bring any restitutionary claim, because he or she may have brought a claim founded on the defendant's unjust enrichment. Although the Court of Appeal held that such a claim could not be established because it was not possible to imply a contract, such reasoning has since been rejected.[38] Could the plaintiff have established that the deceased had been unjustly enriched at his expense? As regards the identification of an enrichment, the suggestion of the Court of Appeal that the saving of expenditure cannot constitute an enrichment is inconsistent with the modern approach to the definition of enrichment.[39] If the court's suggestion was correct it would mean that restitution would never lie for pure services or where the plaintiff has discharged the defendant's debt by paying a third party. Surely the deceased had been incontrovertibly benefited by saving a necessary expense, since the only way of getting the coal out of the mine was by paying the plaintiff for the use of the passages under his land.[40] Clearly this benefit had been obtained at the plaintiff's expense and the relevant ground of restitution could have

---

[38] *United Australia Ltd.* v. *Barclays Bank Ltd.* [1941] AC 1.   [39] See Chapter 4.
[40] This was recognised by Baggallay LJ at (1883) 24 Ch.D 439, 471.

been that of ignorance, because the plaintiff was unaware that the defendant was trespassing under his land.[41] It therefore seems that the defendant had been unjustly enriched at the plaintiff's expense.

But it is also necessary to consider whether the policy of the *actio personalis* bar should be applicable to such a restitutionary action. It seems that this bar only applied to claims which were founded on tort and had no application to a claim founded on reversing the defendant's unjust enrichment. This is supported by the final case in the *Phillips* v. *Homfray* saga, which concerned the question whether the plaintiff could recover the value of the coal which the deceased had extracted from the plaintiff's land.[42] The Court of Appeal accepted that if this claim had been founded on the tort of trespass it would have been barred by the *actio personalis* bar, but, since the action was characterised by the judges as an equitable action to recover the benefits which the defendant had received by wrongfully taking the plaintiff's coal, the underlying cause of action was not tort. In fact this aspect of the plaintiff's claim could be analysed as founded on the plaintiff's continuing proprietary interest in the coal which had been taken without his knowledge,[43] so the restitutionary claim was founded on the vindication of property rights rather than tort and so was not affected by the *actio personalis* bar.

(3) Conclusions: *Phillips* v. *Homfray* is a red herring

The implications of this analysis is that the controversial decision in the *Phillips* v. *Homfray* saga, namely the case which was decided in 1882, is wrongly decided, both because it was wrong to suggest that the plaintiff had not been enriched and because the plaintiff's claim was not necessarily founded on the commission of a tort by the deceased. Careful analysis of the series of cases which formed the *Phillips* v. *Homfray* litigation suggests that there is nothing in any of the decisions which prevents the award of restitutionary remedies for tort.

2. TORTS FOR WHICH RESTITUTIONARY REMEDIES ARE AVAILABLE

Once it is accepted that restitutionary remedies are indeed available where the defendant commits a tort, it is then necessary to determine which torts will trigger a restitutionary response. Those torts which are committed when the defendant interferes with the plaintiff's property rights are most likely to trigger such a response, but there is some evidence that other torts which are not proprietary may trigger a similar response.

---

[41] See Chapter 7.　　　[42] [1892] 1 Ch. 465.　　　[43] See p. 605 below.

(a) Trespass to land[44]

(i) Are restitutionary remedies available for trespass to land?

It is clear that where the plaintiff has suffered loss as a result of the defendant's trespass on his or her land, the defendant will be required to compensate the plaintiff for this loss. So, for example, where the defendant has travelled across the plaintiff's land without permission to do so, he or she will be required to pay damages which are assessed by reference to the fee which he or she would have had to pay to obtain the plaintiff's permission to use the land.[45] Such a remedy may be characterised as compensatory. But there has been great uncertainty about whether the plaintiff can ever be awarded a remedy which is assessed solely by reference to the defendant's gain arising from the trespass. This doubt has largely arisen from the decision of the Court of Appeal in *Phillips* v. *Homfray*,[46] which has been wrongly interpreted as deciding that restitutionary remedies are not available for the tort of trespass to land. But some cases, even though they do not explicitly recognise that a restitutionary remedy is available, can only be explained on the basis that the damages which were awarded were restitutionary.[47]

It is now clear that restitutionary damages are available where the defendant has trespassed on the plaintiff's land, as was recognised by a majority of the Court of Appeal in *Ministry of Defence* v. *Ashman*.[48] The conclusion was unanimously affirmed by the Court of Appeal in *Ministry of Defence* v. *Thompson*.[49] In the *Ashman* case the defendant and her husband, who was a member of the Royal Air Force, had occupied premises which were owned by the plaintiff. The defendant's husband moved out of the property but the defendant continued to occupy the premises with her two children. The plaintiff asked the defendant to vacate the property, but she refused to do so because she had nowhere

[44] See Cooke, 'Trespass, Mesne Profits and Restitution' (1994) 110 *LQR* 420.

[45] *Jegon* v. *Vivian* (1871) LR 6 Ch. App. 742 and *Phillips* v. *Homfray* (1871) LR 6 Ch. App. 770.

[46] (1883) 24 Ch.D 439. See pp. 481–4 above. See also *Attorney-General* v. *De Keyser's Royal Hotel* [1920] AC 508 and *Morris* v. *Tarrant* [1971] 2 QB 143.

[47] See *Whitwham* v. *Westminster Brymbo Coal and Coke Co.* [1896] 1 Ch. 894; *Penarth Dock Engineering Co. Ltd.* v. *Pounds* [1963] 1 Lloyd's Rep. 359, 362 (Lord Denning); *Bracewell* v. *Appleby* [1975] Ch. 408; and *Swordheath Properties Ltd.* v. *Tabet* [1979] 1 WLR 285. Note also ss. 27 and 28 of the Housing Act 1988 whereby a restitutionary remedy is available where a landlord unlawfully evicts a tenant, this remedy being assessed by reference to the increase in the value of the landlord's property as a result of the eviction: *Jones* v. *Miah* (1992) 24 HLR 578, 587.

[48] [1993] 2 EGLR 102. Lloyd LJ, at p. 106, doubted whether restitutionary damages were available for the trespass to land because of the decision in *Phillips* v. *Homfray* (1883) 24 Ch.D 439.

[49] [1993] 2 EGLR 107. See also *Re Polly Peck International plc.* [1997] 2 BCLC 630. Noted by Jaffey, 'Restitution and Trespass to Land' (1997) 5 *RLR* 79.

else to go. The plaintiff then claimed possession of the premises and damages for trespass. The issue for the Court of Appeal was whether these damages should be assessed by reference to the market rent for such premises, by the subsidised rent which a serviceman would actually pay for the premises or by some other measure. Hoffmann LJ recognised that, although the usual measure of damages for tort is to compensate the plaintiff for loss suffered, it is possible for the plaintiff to elect to recover restitutionary damages measured by reference to the value of the benefit obtained by the defendant as a result of committing the tort.[50]

(ii) Valuing the defendant's benefit

Where the plaintiff has elected to claim restitutionary damages for the plaintiff's trespass to his or her land, as the plaintiff had done in *Ministry of Defence* v. *Ashman*,[51] it is then only necessary to value the benefit which the defendant received; there is no need to consider the plaintiff's loss or what it would have done had the defendant vacated the property when requested. Hoffmann LJ recognised that, when the defendant's benefit is valued, it is usually the objective value of the benefit which is relevant.[52] This would be the rent payable on the open market, which is the amount the defendant saved by continuing to occupy the plaintiff's premises. But this objective value can be subjectively devalued by the defendant if the particular benefit might not be worth so much to the defendant as to anyone else.[53] It was considered that the defendant could subjectively devalue the value of the benefit because she had no choice but to stay in the premises until the local authority was willing to re-house her, so she could not be considered to have freely accepted the benefit.

Although the Court of Appeal did not specifically consider whether the benefit to the defendant in occupying the premises was incontrovertibly beneficial to her, the court did in effect find that she had in fact been incontrovertibly benefited by remaining on the premises, since she was getting accommodation for herself and her children which she would necessarily have had to pay for. It follows that the court should have concluded that the defendant could not have subjectively devalued the benefit which she had received. But it is not enough simply to identify an incontrovertible benefit; such a benefit must also be valued. It could not be valued at the market rate since, even if the defendant had been able to

[50] [1993] 2 EGLR 102, 105. Kennedy LJ at p. 104, described this approach as 'somewhat analogous to quasi-contractual restitution'. But there is no analogy; this is restitution.

[51] [1993] 2 EGLR 102.

[52] This is consistent with the general approach to the determination of enrichment for the purposes of the action founded on the reversal of the defendant's unjust enrichment. See p. 62 above.

[53] [1993] 2 EGLR 102, 105 (Hoffmann LJ).

find somewhere else to live, she would not necessarily have spent that much money. Since she was willing to pay for local authority housing, this was considered to be the reasonable value of the benefit she had received and constituted the measure of the restitutionary damages which were awarded. Consequently, the defendant was held to have received a benefit which was valued by reference to the amount which she would have been prepared to pay for other accommodation; this was her incontrovertible benefit. If the defendant had been seeking private rented accommodation then the market rate would have been the appropriate value of the benefit.[54] Logically, if the defendant had been looking for free accommodation with a friend she could not be considered to have received any valuable benefit at all, so the plaintiff would be confined to compensatory damages.

The question of valuation of the benefit was considered further in the *Thompson* case, the facts of which were virtually identical to those of *Ashman*, where it was held that the actual value to the defendant of the benefit of continuing to occupy the plaintiff's premises was the higher of the rent which the defendant had previously paid for the premises and what she would have had to pay for local authority accommodation which was suitable to her needs.[55] These two measures were relevant because it was clear that the defendant was willing to pay both these sums. The previous rent was what the defendant had 'voluntarily been willing to pay for that house and, therefore, must have been the minimum value of the benefit of occupation'[56] and the cost of local authority accommodation was what the defendant intended to pay once such accommodation had been found, and so this cost constituted what the defendant had saved by committing the trespass on the plaintiff's land.

Usually, the value to the defendant of the use of the plaintiff's premises will be equivalent to its ordinary letting value.[57] The facts of the *Ashman* and *Thompson* cases were unusual, primarily because the actual rent of the premises was well below its market value. But, despite the unusual facts, the decisions are of crucial importance because, as Hoffmann LJ recognised, it is now time to 'call a spade a spade' and recognise the existence of restitutionary remedies for torts.[58] Such recognition of restitutionary remedies will not cause any injustice to the plaintiff, because, if his or her loss is greater than the defendant's actual benefit, the plaintiff

[54] Cooke, 'Trespass, Mesne Profits and Restitution' (1994) 110 *LQR* 420, 428.
[55] *Ministry of Defence* v. *Thompson* [1993] 2 EGLR 107 (Hoffmann LJ). In the *Ashman* case the damages were assessed by reference to the rent for local authority housing because this would have been slightly higher than what the defendant had been paying for the occupation of the plaintiff's premises.
[56] [1993] 2 EGLR 107, 108 (Hoffmann LJ).
[57] As occurred in *Swordheath Properties Ltd.* v. *Tabet* [1979] 1 WLR 285.
[58] [1993] 2 EGLR 102, 105.

can simply elect to claim compensatory rather than restitutionary damages.

(iii) Inverugie Investments Ltd. *v.* Hackett

The acceptance by the Court of Appeal in *Ashman* and *Thompson* that restitutionary damages are available where the defendant has trespassed on the plaintiff's land appears to have been qualified, or perhaps even rejected, by a subsequent decision of the Privy Council. In *Inverugie Investments Ltd.* v. *Hackett*[59] the plaintiff, who leased apartments within a Bahamian hotel complex, was ejected from the complex by the defendant who owned it. The defendant then used the apartments which had been leased by the plaintiff over the next 15 years for hotel guests. The average occupancy of the apartments over this period was only about 40 per cent. The plaintiff sued the defendant for trespass to land and sought damages which were to be assessed by reference to a reasonable rent for the apartments. The defendant conceded that the plaintiff was entitled to a reasonable rent, so the only question for the Privy Council was how this rent should be assessed. The Privy Council affirmed that, when assessing damages for trespass, it is irrelevant that the plaintiff could not have let the property to anybody else or could not have used it for him- or herself.[60] It was sufficient that the defendant's tort had deprived the plaintiff of the use of the property. Consequently, the defendant was required to pay for its use of the plaintiff's apartments, and this was to be assessed by reference to the reasonable rental value of all of the apartments which the plaintiff had leased throughout the whole period the defendant was committing the trespass, after deduction of what the plaintiff had saved in not having to pay rent as a result of the defendant's trespass. It was irrelevant that the premises had not been fully occupied. Crucially, the court said of the 'user principle', which provided the basis for the award of the damages in this case, that it 'need not be characterised as exclusively compensatory, or exclusively restitutionary; it combines elements of both'.[61]

The decision of the Privy Council in *Inverugie Investments* raises two difficulties.

First, Lord Lloyd, speaking for the Board, distinguished the Court of Appeal's decision in *Ashman* on the basis that the cause of action in that case was not tort, but was restitution as an independent cause of action.[62] This is simply wrong and is inconsistent with the underlying theory of restitution for wrongs, whereby the cause of action is the wrong but the plaintiff is entitled to elect to have either a restitutionary or a compensatory remedy.

---

[59] [1995] 1 WLR 713.   [60] *Ibid*, p. 717.   [61] *Ibid*, p. 718.
[62] [1995] 1 WLR 713, 715.

Secondly, we are left with an important question concerning the characterisation of the remedy which was awarded. Is it accurate for the court to say that the damages are both compensatory and restitutionary? It might be considered that the damages which were awarded sought to compensate the plaintiff for loss suffered from the tort. But the plaintiff's actual loss was confined to the amount of income which it did not receive from the apartments and, since the occupancy throughout the 15-year period was only about 40 per cent, awarding the plaintiff the full rental value of the apartments would have over-compensated him. It might be argued that the plaintiff had lost the opportunity to bargain with the defendant, but if he had bargained with the defendant for the use of the apartments, the fact that the apartments would not have been used throughout the year would have been taken into account in reaching the bargain. Should the damages be characterised as restitutionary instead? The difficulty with a restitutionary analysis is that the Privy Council found that the defendant had not derived a benefit from all of the apartments all of the time, but it was still expected to pay a reasonable rent for the use of the apartments throughout the period during which the tort had been committed. Despite this, the damages which were awarded can be justified by reference to restitutionary principles. This is because, by having the use of the plaintiff's apartments throughout the year, the defendant should be regarded as having received an objective benefit, namely the opportunity to obtain income from the use of the apartments. Since the defendant had not received a financial benefit in respect of all the apartments throughout the period of the trespass, it could seek subjectively to devalue this objective benefit by 60 per cent, representing the period for which it did not receive any income from the apartments. But subjective devaluation may be defeated by the principles of incontrovertible benefit and free acceptance. Clearly the defendant had not been incontrovertibly benefited but, by virtue of its actions in ejecting the plaintiff, it could be considered to have freely accepted the benefit, because, in ejecting the plaintiff, the defendant should be considered to have taken the risk that the apartments would not be occupied throughout the year. Such an argument could not have been relied on in *Ministry of Defence* v. *Ashman*,[63] since in that case the defendant had no choice but to commit the tort of trespass. But where the defendant does have a choice whether or not to commit the tort, as will usually be the case, the nature of the defendant's conduct should prevent him or her from subjectively devaluing the benefit which had been obtained. Although such reasoning was not relied on in *Inverugie Investments*, it is consistent with fundamental principles of the law of restitution and does

[63] [1993] 2 EGLR 102.

enable a result to be reached which is intuitively correct. Most importantly, this reasoning enables the damages which were awarded to be
characterised as restitutionary and avoids the absurd conclusion that
they were both restitutionary and compensatory.

(b) Trespass to goods

Where the defendant has committed the tort of trespass to goods the
remedy which is awarded will be assessed in a similar way to that which
is awarded for trespass to land. Consequently, the better view is that
restitutionary remedies are available which are assessed by reference
either to the amount the defendant gained from the tort or the amount
saved by not paying the plaintiff for the use of the property. This is illustrated by *Oughton* v. *Seppings*[64] where a sheriff's officer committed the
tort of trespass to goods by seizing the plaintiff's horse and selling it. The
plaintiff recovered the proceeds of sale in an action for money had and
received without any investigation being undertaken as to the actual loss
he had suffered. The remedy, therefore, appears to have been assessed
simply by reference to the benefit gained by the defendant.

(c) Conversion

Where the defendant has converted the plaintiff's goods, for example by
selling them, the remedy for the commission of such a tort is restitutionary because the defendant must pay the value of the proceeds of sale to
the plaintiff without any inquiry being undertaken as to what the market
value of the goods was at the time of sale, which would be the measure of
the plaintiff's loss.[65] In other words, the remedy for conversion can be
assessed by reference to the defendant's gain rather than the plaintiff's
loss. This is illustrated by *Lamine* v. *Dorrell*[66] where the defendant had
committed the tort of conversion by selling the plaintiff's debentures
without permission. It was held that the plaintiff could recover the sale
price in an action for money had and received, without any attempt to
ascertain what the market value of the debentures was. Similarly, in
Chesworth v. *Farrar*[67] the plaintiff's landlord converted the plaintiff's

---

[64] (1830) 1 B and Ad. 241; 109 ER 776. See also *Strand Electric and Engineering Co. Ltd.* v.
Brisford Entertainments Ltd. [1952] 2 QB 246, 254–5 (Denning LJ).

[65] Cooke, 'Trespass, Mesne Profits and Restitution' (1994) 110 *LQR* 420, 421. Usually, the
market value and the proceeds of sale will be the same, but this is not necessarily the case.
The plaintiff will elect restitutionary relief where the proceeds of sale were greater than the
market value of the goods.

[66] (1701) 2 Ld. Raym. 1216; 92 ER 303. See also *United Australia Ltd.* v. *Barclays Bank Ltd.*
[1941] AC 1.

[67] [1967] 1 QB 407.

property and the plaintiff recovered the sale price of the goods without any attempt to ascertain what the market value of the goods was at the time of the sale. This remedy was acknowledged to be restitutionary because it was held that the limitation period for tort did not apply to the plaintiff's claim.[68] Where the defendant has converted the plaintiff's property by simply using it without selling it, the plaintiff's remedy can be restitutionary damages, assessed by reference to what the defendant saved by not having to pay the plaintiff for the use of the property.[69]

(d) Interference with intellectual property rights

Where the defendant interferes with the plaintiff's intellectual property rights the defendant's liability will be tortious. Originally, however, the liability was equitable and this equitable legacy continues to have an influence upon the remedies which are available. Today, the defendant's liability for interference with intellectual property rights may arise either by statute or the common law. Statutory relief exists for breaches of copyright[70] and patents,[71] whereas the remedies for infringement of trade marks[72] and passing-off[73] continue to be governed by the common law.

It is generally accepted that, where the defendant interferes with any type of intellectual property right, a restitutionary remedy is available, whether it is measured by reference to the profits which the defendant made from infringing the right or to what the defendant would have had to pay to obtain the plaintiff's consent to interfere with the right. The awarding of restitutionary remedies in this context is consistent with the principles relating to the award of restitutionary remedies for wrongdoing, on the basis that restitution is justified by the policy of protecting property rights. There is, however, no consistency between the different regimes governing intellectual property rights as to which type of restitutionary remedy is available and what the conditions are for awarding such remedies. Because of this inconsistency, each type of intellectual property right will be considered in turn.

---

[68] This aspect of the decision is criticised at p. 772 below.

[69] See the decision of Denning LJ in *Strand Electric and Engineering Co. Ltd.* v. *Brisford Entertainments Ltd.* [1952] QB 246. See also *Hillesden Securities Ltd.* v. *Ryjak Ltd.* [1983] 2 All ER 184.

[70] Copyright, Designs and Patents Act 1988, s. 96(2). See also s. 229(2) of the Act which allows an account of profits to be awarded where the defendant has infringed a design right.

[71] Patents Act 1977, s. 61(1)(d).

[72] *Edelsten* v. *Edelsten* (1863) 1 De GJ and Sm. 185; 46 ER 72.

[73] *Lever* v. *Goodwin* (1887) 36 Ch.D 1.

(i) Breach of copyright

Where the defendant has profited from the breach of copyright he or she will be liable to account to the plaintiff for the profits obtained, regardless of the fault of the defendant in breaching the copyright.[74] Damages are also available as a remedy for breach of copyright, but not if the defendant's infringement was innocent, in the sense that the defendant did not know and had no reason to know of the existence of the copyright.[75] It is unclear whether this means that restitutionary damages are unavailable for such innocent breaches of copyright. In addition, where the infringement is innocent but the defendant profited from it then, although the defendant is liable to account, the court will be prepared to make an allowance for the defendant's skill and effort in making the profit.[76]

(ii) Infringement of patents

Where the defendant has knowingly or negligently infringed a patent then an account of profits or an award of damages is available.[77] But where the patent was innocently infringed the plaintiff is unable to obtain either.[78]

(iii) Passing off

An account of profits will only be awarded if the defendant deliberately passed off the plaintiff's goods.[79]

(iv) Infringement of trade marks

An account of profits will only be awarded if the defendant deliberately interfered with the plaintiff's trade mark.[80] Where the defendant innocently infringed the plaintiffs' trade mark the plaintiff will still be able to obtain a compensatory remedy.[81]

Whilst there is an unacceptable inconsistency in the award of restitutionary relief for those torts which are concerned with interference with intellectual property rights, it is clear that the culpability of the defendant is generally a relevant consideration when determining the type of restitutionary remedy which should be awarded.

---

[74] Copyright, Designs and Patents Act 1988, s. 96(2). A similar provision applies to an infringement of a design right: *ibid*, s. 229(2).

[75] *Ibid*, s. 97(1). Similar provision is made for innocent infringement of a design rights: *ibid*, s. 233(1).

[76] *Redwood Music Ltd.* v. *Chappell and Co. Ltd.* [1982] RPC 109.

[77] Patents Act 1977, s. 61(1).   [78] *Ibid*, s. 62(1).

[79] *My Kinda Town Ltd.* v. *Soll* [1982] FSR 147.

[80] *Edelsten* v. *Edelsten* (1863) 1 De GJ and S 185; 46 ER 72.

[81] *Gillette UK Ltd.* v. *Edenwest Ltd.* [1994] RPC 279.

(e) Nuisance

Whether restitutionary remedies are available where the defendant commits the tort of nuisance is a particularly controversial matter. In *Carr-Saunders* v. *Dick McNeil Associates Ltd.*[82] the defendant committed a nuisance by erecting extra storeys to its property which reduced the amount of natural light to the plaintiff's property. The plaintiff was awarded damages in lieu of an injunction, and these damages appeared to be assessed by reference to the amount necessary to compensate the plaintiff for loss of use and amenity. However, Millett J did say that, if there had been evidence of the profit which the defendant gained by committing the tort, this would have been taken into account in assessing the award of damages. This suggests that a remedy assessed by reference to the defendant's benefit arising from the tort may be available where a nuisance is committed.

The decision of the Court of Appeal in *Stoke-on-Trent City Council* v. *W. and J. Wass Ltd.*[83] suggests, however, that restitutionary remedies are not available where the defendant has committed a nuisance. In this case the defendant had deliberately committed a nuisance by operating a market in close proximity to the plaintiff's market and so infringing the plaintiff's right to hold a market in a particular area. The plaintiff was granted an injunction to restrain further infringement of this proprietary right. Although the plaintiff had not been shown to have suffered any loss of custom by virtue of the tort, the trial judge awarded the plaintiff damages which were assessed by reference to a licence fee which the plaintiff would have charged the defendant to operate its market. This remedy could be characterised as either compensatory, by virtue of the licence fee which the plaintiff had not been able to charge, or restitutionary, by reference to the amount saved by the defendant in not having to pay a licence fee. But the Court of Appeal overruled the trial judge's decision and awarded nominal damages, on the basis that generally damages for tort could only compensate the plaintiff for actual loss suffered.

In the light of the general principles which have been identified in this chapter, *Wass* should be considered to have been wrongly decided, simply because the defendant obtained a benefit by wrongly interfering with the plaintiff's proprietary right. Nuisance should be considered to be a proprietary tort for which restitutionary relief is available. It should have followed, therefore, that the defendant was liable to account to the plaintiff for the profits which it had obtained by virtue of committing the tort, or, as the trial judge recognised, should have been liable to pay for a licence fee to operate the market.

---

[82] [1986] 2 All ER 888.   [83] [1988] 1 WLR 1466.

(f) Deceit

Some cases are consistent with the assertion that a plaintiff will be able to obtain a restitutionary remedy where the defendant has committed the tort of deceit. For example, in *Hill* v. *Perrott*[84] the defendant had fraudulently induced the plaintiff to sell goods to a third party who was insolvent and so was unable to pay for them. The defendant then obtained the goods from the third party. It was held that a contract would be implied to prevent the defendant from profiting from the fraud, and so the defendant was required to pay the plaintiff for the goods.[85] This restitutionary remedy is clearly consistent with the general principle relating to restitutionary remedies being awarded where the tort committed by the defendant has interfered with the plaintiff's proprietary rights, since, but for the defendant lying to the plaintiff, he would not have been induced to sell the goods to the third party.[86]

A recent decision of the Court of Appeal, however, appears at first sight to cast doubt on the proposition that restitutionary remedies are available where the defendant has deceived the plaintiff.[87] In *Halifax Building Society* v. *Thomas*[88] the defendant had obtained a mortgage advance from the plaintiff by means of a fraudulent misrepresentation that he was somebody else with a better credit rating. This was a criminal offence. The defendant used the mortgage advance to purchase a flat. After the defendant had defaulted on his interest payments and the plaintiff had discovered the misrepresentation, the plaintiff sold the flat. The plaintiff used the proceeds of sale to discharge the loan and was left with a surplus. The plaintiff claimed that it was entitled to retain the surplus on the ground that, if the defendant had received the proceeds of sale, it would have been liable to account to the plaintiff for all of the proceeds because they had been obtained by wrongdoing.[89] The Court of

---

[84]   (1810) 3 Taunt. 274; 128 ER 109.

[85]   Restitution might be justified in this case by reference to the unjust enrichment principle, with the ground of restitution being induced mistake, although it would be difficult to establish that the defendant's benefit had been obtained at the plaintiff's expense, since it was actually obtained from the third party. It is far easier to explain the case as one involving restitution for the tort of deceit.

[86]   See also *Abbotts* v. *Barry* (1820) 2 Brad. and B 369; 129 ER 1009 where, on similar facts, the defendant was held liable to account to the plaintiff for the proceeds of sale of the goods which he had received from the third party and then sold. Here the justification for restitution was the fact that a sale which had been induced by fraud did not involve transfer of title, so the restitutionary remedy was awarded to vindicate the plaintiff's continuing proprietary interest in the goods.

[87]   Note also the dictum of Lord Steyn in *Smith New Court Securities Ltd.* v. *Citibank NA* [1997] AC 254, 283 that the only method of assessing damages for the tort of deceit is by reference to the plaintiff's financial loss.

[88]   [1996] Ch. 217.

[89]   In fact, the defendant had been convicted of a criminal offence and a confiscation order was made for the proceeds of the crime. One reason for the failure of the plaintiff's

Appeal rejected this argument on the ground that the plaintiff had relied on its contractual rights in selling the flat and so had affirmed the mortgage. Probably what the court meant by this was that, by electing to affirm the mortgage when it knew that the defendant had obtained the mortgage by fraud, the plaintiff had literally waived the tort of deceit with the consequence that the tort was extinguished and so there was no wrong on which the plaintiff's restitutionary claim could be based. But whether this is correct depends on what is required for waiver of the tort. Could it really be said that the plaintiff's failure to rescind the transaction meant that it had ratified the wrongdoing? This cannot be the case since, if the flat had been sold at a loss so the proceeds of sale would not have discharged the loan completely, the plaintiff would still have been able to sue the defendant in tort. In other words, the failure to rescind the transaction did not constitute a waiver of the tort and so the court's decision must be considered to be incorrect.[90]

The Court of Appeal in *Halifax Building Society* v. *Thomas* said nothing to suggest that restitutionary remedies are unavailable in principle where the defendant has committed the tort of deceit. It follows, therefore, that if the defendant had sold the flat and was left with a surplus after the mortgage advance had been repaid, the plaintiff should have been able to recover this profit from the defendant. Allowing restitutionary relief in such a case is consistent with the notion that such relief is confined to the proprietary torts, because the effect of the defendant's deceit was that the plaintiff was induced to lend its money to the defendant. There is, however, one particular difficulty in allowing the plaintiff to recover the surplus proceeds of sale in such circumstances, and this relates to the question of remoteness. Could it really be said that the surplus arose directly from the commission of the wrong? Peter Gibson LJ suggested that the profit could not be said to arise directly from the wrong because the profit was not obtained at the plaintiff's expense.[91] Whilst a notion of 'at the plaintiff's expense' is inappropriate in such a case, because the cause of action is the wrong and not unjust enrichment, the judge's conclusion was correct; the making of the profit would have been too remote from the commission of the wrong. The loan was received from the building society as a direct result of the wrongdoing, but the surplus proceeds of sale could only be considered to be an

---

claim to retain the surplus proceeds of sale was because the defendant could not have profited from his wrongdoing by reason of the confiscation order. See Chapter 19 for discussion of this aspect of the case.

[90] See Mitchell, 'No Account of Profits for a Victim of Deceit' [1996] *LMCLQ* 314, 316. See also Birks, 'The Proceeds of Mortgage Fraud' (1996) 10 *TLI* 2, 3.

[91] [1996] Ch. 217, 227.

indirect result of the wrong once the house had been sold.[92] Consequently, the Court of Appeal's decision that the plaintiff was not entitled to retain the surplus proceeds of sale was the right result but for the wrong reason. Where, however, the defendant obtains a benefit as a direct result of the deceit, he or she should be required to disgorge this benefit to the plaintiff, although usually where the defendant has obtained a benefit from the plaintiff by deceit, the plaintiff will be able to bring a restitutionary claim founded on the reversal of the defendant's unjust enrichment, where the ground of restitution is the induced mistake.[93]

3. IS THERE A GENERAL PRINCIPLE IN FAVOUR OF THE AWARD OF RESTITUTIONARY REMEDIES FOR TORTS?

Analysis of the cases show that the possibility of a restitutionary remedy being awarded for a tort will only arise where the defendant's wrongdoing involves interference with the plaintiff's property in some way. If this is the general principle then restitutionary remedies will not be available where, for example, the defendant commits the torts of assault, battery, false imprisonment, malicious prosecution or defamation; the plaintiff will be confined to compensatory, or perhaps exemplary, damages rather than a purely restitutionary remedy.[94] Usually where these torts have been committed the defendant will not have obtained a benefit, so the question of the availability of restitutionary remedies could not arise.[95] But for some other non-proprietary torts the defendant may have obtained a benefit from the commission of the tort and so it might be appropriate to require the defendant to disgorge this benefit to the plaintiff. This may sometimes be the case with the tort of negligence[96] where, for example, the defendant negligently causes injury to the plaintiff as a result of economising on safety precautions. It is also possible that the defendant might benefit from the commission of the tort of defamation where, for example, it can be shown that a newspaper's circulation rose dramatically as a result of the publication of defamatory remarks about the plaintiff. Similarly, where the defendant commits the tort of inducing

---

[92] Whether it should make any difference that the surplus was the proceeds of crime is discussed at pp. 562–3 below. The Court of Appeal also rejected an argument that the defendant should be considered to have held the proceeds of sale on a constructive trust. This aspect of the case is also discussed in at pp. 563 below.

[93] Jackman, 'Restitution for Wrongs' (1989) 48 *CLJ* 302, 310.

[94] In *United Australia Ltd.* v. *Barclays Bank Ltd.* [1941] AC 1, 12 Viscount Simon LC suggested that the torts of defamation and assault could not be 'waived'.

[95] *Hambly* v. *Trott* (1776) 1 Cowp. 371, 376; 98 ER 1136, 1139 (Lord Mansfield).

[96] Cp. Jackman, 'Restitution for Wrongs' (1989) 48 *CLJ* 302, 311.

a breach of contract, he or she may have obtained a benefit as a result of the wrongdoing.[97]

It is consequently necessary to consider whether it is possible to justify confining restitutionary relief to the proprietary torts. Is there a case for extending the law so that a restitutionary remedy is potentially available for all torts? Goff and Jones argue that it should be sufficient that the commission of any type of tort has caused the defendant to gain a benefit which would not have been gained but for the commission of the tort.[98] Although it is clear that this view does not yet represent English law,[99] it is a view which should be recognised by the courts. Wherever the defendant has obtained a benefit as a result of the commission of a tort the plaintiff should be able to elect a restitutionary remedy whereby the defendant is required to disgorge to the plaintiff the benefit obtained. Restitution is justified simply because no wrongdoer should be allowed to benefit from the commission of a wrong and the plaintiff is an appropriate recipient of the benefit because he or she is the victim of the wrong. This principle should be of general application regardless of the type of tort which the defendant has committed, since there is no policy reason why restitutionary remedies should not be available in such circumstances.

The potential importance of recognising that restitutionary relief should be available regardless of the tort committed by the defendant is illustrated by the remedies which are available for the tort of defamation. As the law stands, because defamation is concerned with injury to reputation rather than injury to property, restitutionary remedies are not available. Although exemplary damages can be awarded, they are a very blunt tool to deprive the defendant of benefits obtained from the tort, since their rationale is punishment rather than ensuring that the defendant does not profit from the commission of the tort.[100] It would be much more appropriate to recognise that a restitutionary remedy is available simply to ensure that the defendant is not allowed to profit from the commission of the tort. Exemplary damages may sometimes be appropriate but, as the Law Commission has recognised, such damages should be awarded only in exceptional circumstances.[101]

---

[97] That restitutionary remedies are available where the defendant has induced a breach of contract was recognised in the American case of *Federal Sugar Refining Co.* v. *US Sugar Equalisation Board Inc.* (1920) 268 F 575.

[98] Goff and Jones, *The Law of Restitution*, p. 781.

[99] *Stoke-on-Trent City Council* v. *W. and J. Wass Ltd.* [1988] 1 WLR 1406, 1415 (Nourse LJ).

[100] *Rookes* v. *Barnard* [1964] AC 1129, 1221 (Lord Devlin).

[101] 'Aggravated, Exemplary and Restitutionary Damages' (Law Com. No. 247, 1997), p. 197.

17

Restitution for Breach of Contract

1. GENERAL PRINCIPLES

Where the defendant has breached a contract the orthodox remedial response is that the plaintiff can obtain damages which are assessed by reference to the loss suffered by the plaintiff.[1] Usually the purpose of such damages is to place the plaintiff in the position he or she would have been in had the contract not been breached.[2] This involves the protection of what has been called the 'expectation interest'.[3] Sometimes, where it is not possible to ascertain what position the plaintiff would have occupied had the contract not been breached, the purpose of the award of damages is to place the plaintiff in the position which he or she would have occupied had the contract not been entered into. In such cases the plaintiff will be reimbursed for the expenditure which he or she had incurred before the contract was breached.[4] This involves the protection of the so-called 'reliance interest'.[5] What we need to consider in this chapter is whether there is a third interest which can be protected by the award of damages where the defendant has breached a contract, namely the restitution interest.[6] In other words, in those cases in which the plaintiff did not suffer any loss as a result of the breach of contract but the defendant obtained a benefit, or where the value of the defendant's benefit arising from the breach exceeds any loss suffered by the plaintiff, is it possible for the remedy which is awarded for the breach of contract to be ascertained by reference to the value of the benefit which had been obtained by the defendant?

---

[1] *Surrey County Council* v. *Bredero Homes Ltd.* [1993] 1 WLR 1361, 1364 (Dillon LJ). See also *Johnson* v. *Agnew* [1980] AC 367, 400 (Lord Wilberforce).

[2] *Robinson* v. *Harman* (1848) 1 Ex. 850, 855; 154 ER 363 (Parke B).

[3] It is more accurately described as the 'performance interest': Friedmann 'The Performance Interest in Contract Damages' (1995) 111 *LQR* 628.

[4] *Anglia Television Ltd.* v. *Reed* [1972] 1 QB 60.

[5] See Fuller and Perdue, 'The Reliance Interest in Contract Damages' (1936–37) 46 *Yale LJ* 52.

[6] This was recognised by Steyn LJ in *Surrey County Council* v. *Bredero Homes Ltd.* [1993] 1 WLR 1361, 1369. See also Fuller and Perdue (1936–37) 46 *Yale LJ* 52, 54.

(a) The general principle denying restitution for breach of contract

A number of cases have recognised that restitutionary remedies are not available where the defendant has breached a contract.[7] This was recognised most clearly by Megarry V-C in *Tito* v. *Waddell (No. 2).*[8] In this case the defendant mining company had contracted with the plaintiffs, the inhabitants of Ocean Island, to replant the island once it had completed its mining operations there. The defendant failed to replant the island and the plaintiffs sued for breach of contract. They were awarded only nominal damages since they had not suffered any loss as a result of the breach. This was because the plaintiffs were no longer living on the island, so they would not have incurred expenditure themselves in replanting the island. Also, the difference between the value of the island with and without replanting was trivial. The plaintiffs had claimed that the measure of damages should be the amount of money which the defendant had saved in failing to replant the island as it had promised, but Megarry V-C rejected this restitutionary measure. He said:[9]

If the defendant has saved himself money, as by not doing what he has contracted to do, that does not of itself entitle the plaintiff to recover the saving as damages: for it by no means necessarily follows that what the defendant has saved the plaintiff has lost.

The judge assumed that damages for breach of contract could only be measured by reference to the plaintiff's loss and he considered this to be an absolute rule without exceptions.

(b) *Attorney-General* v. *Blake*: the new approach

Despite the general principle against the award of restitutionary remedies for breach of contract, the Court of Appeal in *Attorney-General* v. *Blake*[10] has recently recognised that restitutionary remedies can indeed be available where the defendant has breached a contract, but only in the most exceptional circumstances. Whilst this decision is of vital importance, it must be emphasised that this aspect of the Court of Appeal's judgment was *obiter dicta*.[11] Despite this, the court recognised in the clearest terms that in certain exceptional circumstances it is entirely appropriate for the courts to award damages which are assessed by

---

[7] See, for example, *Teacher* v. *Calder* [1899] AC 451, 467 (Lord Davey); *The Siboen and the Sibotre* [1976] 1 Lloyd's Rep. 293, 337 (Kerr J) and *Surrey County Council* v. *Bredero Homes Ltd.* [1993] 1 WLR 1361, 1364 (Dillon LJ).

[8] [1977] Ch. 106. [9] *Ibid*, p. 332. [10] [1998] 2 WLR 805.

[11] The issue was actually raised by the Court itself and, even though the plaintiff did not wish to advance a claim for restitutionary remedies, the Court still considered what would have happened had the claim for the award of such remedies been made.

reference to the benefit obtained by the defendant as a direct result of the breach of contract. This is because, if the court is unable to award restitutionary remedies for breach of contract, the plaintiff might be deprived of an effective remedy for the breach because 'of a failure to attach a value to the plaintiff's legitimate interest in having the contract duly performed'.[12] In other words, the value to the plaintiff of having the contract performed may outweigh the loss which he or she would actually suffer if the contract were not performed. In such circumstances the only effective remedy is one which is assessed by reference to the benefit obtained by the defendant as a result of breaching the contract rather than the loss suffered by the plaintiff.

(i) Fundamental principles

The court identified two principles which should be relied on to identify the exceptional circumstances where restitutionary remedies are an appropriate remedy for breach of contract.

(1) Inadequacy of compensatory damages

Where the award of compensatory damages is inadequate in the light of what the plaintiff wanted the contract to achieve, the plaintiff has a particular interest in the performance of the contract and, if the contract is not performed, it is appropriate that the plaintiff's remedy is assessed by reference to what the defendant has gained by failing to perform it. Although the determination of whether compensatory damages are adequate is a matter of some uncertainty,[13] the recognition of this principle is important since it will ensure that the award of restitutionary remedies does not undermine the fundamental principle that the usual remedy for breach of contract should be damages which seek to compensate the plaintiff for loss suffered. Compensatory damages will be considered to be inadequate when, for example, the contract relates to unique goods which may be impossible to value.

(2) Benefit obtained directly from the breach of contract

The defendant should only be required to disgorge those benefits which were acquired directly from the breach of the contract. Benefits which are too remote from the breach need not be disgorged since they are not considered to be tainted by the defendant's wrongdoing in breaching the contract.

---

[12] [1998] 2 WLR 805, 817. See Friedmann, 'The Performance Interest in Contract Damages' (1995) 111 *LQR* 628 and Coote, 'Contract Damages, *Ruxley* and the Performance Interest' (1997) 56 *CLJ* 537.

[13] See Chen-Wishart, 'Restitutionary Damages for Breach of Contract' (1998) 114 *LQR* 363.

(ii) *Circumstances where restitutionary remedies may be available*

The recognition of these two principles meant that the court was able to recognise two specific circumstances where justice required the award of restitutionary remedies where a contract has been breached.

(1) Failure to provide what the defendant contracted to provide

Where the defendant agreed to provide a particular service for the plaintiff but, after the plaintiff had paid the full price for it, the defendant actually provided a less extensive service, it is entirely appropriate that the defendant should be required to disgorge to the plaintiff the amount saved by breaching the contract. This is because in this type of case compensatory damages could be considered to be an inadequate remedy, because the plaintiff has shown by requesting the particular performance that he or she has an interest in it being performed, and the benefit obtained by the defendant, namely the amount saved, arises directly from the breach of the contract.

This situation is illustrated by the facts of the American case of *City of New Orleans* v. *Fireman's Charitable Association*,[14] where the defendant entered into a contract with the plaintiff to provide a fire-fighting service and the plaintiff paid the full contract price for this service. The defendant did not in fact provide as full a service as it had promised, since it did not provide the stipulated number of firemen and horses or the agreed length of hose-pipe. The defendant saved a great deal of money as a result of this skimped performance, but there was nothing to suggest that this had caused any loss to the plaintiff, since it had not prevented the defendant from putting out any fires. Consequently, it was held that the plaintiff could recover only nominal damages. The Court of Appeal in *Blake* considered that this was a case where justice demanded the award of substantial damages which would be assessed by reference to the amount saved by the defendant in breaching the contract.

If restitutionary remedies are available for this type of breach of contract, they will be particularly relevant where the plaintiff enters into a contract to provide for a pleasurable amenity and what the plaintiff receives under the contract is not what he or she has expected to receive. In such circumstances it may be particularly difficult to assess the plaintiff's loss, with the consequence that the award of compensatory damages may be an inadequate remedy. Restitutionary damages may therefore be a more appropriate remedy. This is illustrated by the facts of *Ruxley Electonics and Construction Ltd.* v. *Forsyth*,[15] a decision of the House of Lords. The defendant had agreed to build a swimming pool for the plaintiff for nearly £18,000. It was agreed that the pool was to be seven

---

[14] (1891) 9 So. 486.   [15] [1996] AC 344.

feet six inches deep at the diving end, but when it was built it was only six feet nine inches deep at the deepest end. This did not affect the value of the pool or prevent it from being safe to dive into since there was no diving board. The cost of deepening the pool was £21,560, since the pool would need to be demolished and reconstructed. The House of Lords held that, where the cost of rebuilding is out of all proportion to the benefit to be obtained, it is unreasonable to assess damages by reference to the cost of rebuilding. Instead, the proper measure of damages is the diminution in the value of the work arising from the breach of contract. Since there was no diminution in value in this case the plaintiff would receive only nominal damages. The plaintiff was, however, awarded a sum of £2,500 for loss of amenity, since the plaintiff had not obtained what he had bargained for under the contract.

In fact, in cases such as *Ruxley*, as an alternative to the award of compensatory damages for diminution in value and lost amenity, the plaintiff may instead be awarded a restitutionary remedy which is assessed by reference to the amount which the defendant has saved in not building a swimming pool as deep as had been promised. Whilst such an award would not have been applicable on the facts of *Ruxley*, since there was nothing to suggest that the defendant had obtained a benefit by breaching the contract, where such a benefit has been obtained in this type of case it is surely appropriate to award a restitutionary remedy. This was already recognised by the House of Lords in *East Ham Corporation* v. *Bernard Sunley and Sons Ltd.*[16] where Lord Cohen referred, without criticism, to the notion of damages assessed by reference to the difference in cost to the builder of the actual work done and the work specified. If such a difference could have been identified on the facts of *Ruxley* surely this would have been an appropriate measure of damages. It would be a remedy which is proportionate to the extent of the breach, and one which encourages the potential contract-breaker not to cut corners in performing the contract. The award of restitutionary damages would also have been consistent with *Blake* since compensatory damages might be considered to be an inadequate remedy and any benefit obtained by the defendant would have arisen directly from the breach of contract.

In some cases where the defendant has failed to do what he or she agreed to do, it is possible for the court to avoid the need to consider whether restitutionary remedies are appropriate by artificially constructing a loss but, as the Court of Appeal recognised in *Blake*, it is simpler and more open to award restitutionary remedies.[17] The potential for artificially constructing a loss is illustrated by a decision of the Court of Appeal in *White Arrow Express Ltd.* v. *Lamey's Distribution Ltd.*[18] where

---

[16] [1966] AC 406.   [17] [1998] 2 WLR 805, 818.
[18] *The Times*, 21 July 1995. See Beale, 'Damages for Poor Service' (1996) 112 *LQR* 205.

the plaintiff had contracted for and paid extra for a deluxe delivery service but had received only a basic service. It was held that, if the plaintiff were to claim more than nominal damages, it must quantify the difference between the market value of what it had contracted for and the market value of what was provided. This meant that if the market value of the basic service was less than the market value of the deluxe service then the plaintiff would have suffered a loss to the extent of the difference in value. Since the market value of the basic and deluxe delivery services was the same the plaintiff could obtain only nominal damages. Sir Thomas Bingham MR illustrated the basic principle with reference to the following example. '[If] B orders and pays in advance for a five-course meal costing £50 and is served a three-course meal costing £30, he has suffered loss'. But this is an easy case. What of the case in which the plaintiff has not suffered any quantifiable loss but the defendant has made a gain? It is in this context that restitutionary remedies are appropriate to deprive the defendant of the benefit obtained by not providing what he or she had contracted to provide. So, for example, if the plaintiff has paid £50 for a luxury three-course meal made with the freshest of ingredients, but gets only a meal made from tinned ingredients, has the plaintiff really suffered a loss? He still got a three-course meal, so it would be artificial to conclude that he had suffered a loss. It is much easier to assess the plaintiff's remedy by reference to what the defendant had saved by breaching the contract. So, if in *White Arrow Express* itself it could have been shown that the defendant had saved money by not providing the deluxe service, the difference in value between the two services should have been the measure of what the defendant was required to disgorge to the plaintiff.[19]

(2) Doing what the defendant contracted not to do

Where the defendant agreed not to do something and then obtained a benefit as a result of doing precisely what he or she had agreed not to do the Court of Appeal in *Blake* recognised that it would be appropriate for the plaintiff to disgorge any benefits obtained from breaching the contract to the plaintiff. This actually occurred in *Blake* itself, since the defendant had disclosed information in his autobiography which he had previously agreed that he would not disclose and obtained benefits, in the form of royalties, as a direct result of this breach of contract. The award of restitutionary remedies in this case could have been justified because the benefit derived directly from the breach of contract and

---

[19] The plaintiff may have been able to bring a claim founded on the defendant's unjust enrichment, with the ground of restitution being total failure of consideration, if it was possible to apportion the consideration between the basic and deluxe services. See pp. 338–41 above.

because the plaintiff had suffered no loss and so compensatory damages would not adequately protect the plaintiff's interest in the performance of the contract.

(c) Additional methods for obtaining restitutionary remedies following breach of contract

If the view of the Court of Appeal in *Attorney-General* v. *Blake* prevails, it follows that restitutionary remedies are potentially available where the defendant has breached a contract. But the Court of Appeal recognised that such remedies would be available only in two limited circumstances. In fact, there are a number of other techniques whereby restitutionary remedies can be awarded where the defendant has breached a contract. The extent to which all of these mechanisms remain relevant after *Blake* is a matter of uncertainty.

(i) Alternative analysis

A fundamental distinction needs to be drawn between restitution *following* breach of contract and restitution *for* breach of contract. Where the claim is for restitution following termination of the contract for breach, the plaintiff's cause of action is not the breach of contract but the reversal of the defendant's unjust enrichment. Consequently, the plaintiff must establish that the defendant has obtained a benefit at the plaintiff's expense and in circumstances which fall within one of the established grounds of restitution, which will typically be total failure of consideration.[20] So, for example, if the plaintiff contracted to buy a car from the defendant for £3,000, which the plaintiff paid in advance, but the defendant fails to deliver the car, the plaintiff can repudiate the contract for breach and recover the £3,000 on the ground of total failure of consideration. Where the plaintiff's claim is founded on unjust enrichment the only relevance of the breach of contract is that it enables the plaintiff to set the contract aside. The plaintiff's cause of action is not founded on the breach of contract itself but is founded instead on the defendant's unjust enrichment.

(ii) Contractual term specifying a restitutionary remedy

The parties may insert a clause into the contract which stipulates that damages for breach of contract shall be assessed by reference to the benefit gained by the defendant as a result of the breach rather than the plaintiff's loss. That such a clause is effective to justify the award of restitutionary remedies for breach of contract was recognised by the Privy

---

[20] See Chapter 12.

Council in *Reid-Newfoundland Co.* v. *Anglo-American Telegraph Co.*[21] In this case the defendant had entered into a contract with the plaintiff to use a telegraph wire for the transmission of messages which related to the defendant's railway business. To ensure that the wire was not used to transmit messages which related to other aspects of the defendant's business, a term was included in the contract to the effect that the defendant could not use the wire to transmit commercial messages 'except for the benefit and account' of the plaintiff. The defendant used the wire for the transmission of messages which were unrelated to its railway business and was held liable to account to the plaintiff for the profits which accrued to it from the use of the wire. Such a remedy was appropriate because of the clause which had been inserted into the contract, the effect of which was that any profit which was made by the defendant in breach of the agreement was deemed to have been received for the benefit of the plaintiff. The right to restitutionary remedies in such cases derives from the contract itself, rather than unjust enrichment or the commission of a wrong and so does not properly form part of the law of restitution.[22]

(iii) Identification of a fiduciary relationship

In certain cases it is possible to identify a fiduciary relationship between two contracting parties.[23] Where such a relationship can be found, the underlying cause of action will be breach of fiduciary duty rather than breach of contract. Since the usual remedy for breach of fiduciary duty is a restitutionary remedy and because the identification of a fiduciary relationship is open to manipulation, this is a potentially important mechanism for obtaining restitutionary relief arising from a breach of contract, although the courts are loathe to identify a fiduciary relationship in a purely commercial context.[24] The relevance of identifying a fiduciary relationship between two contracting parties is illustrated by *Reading* v. *Attorney-General*[25] where the plaintiff, a sergeant in the British army stationed in Egypt, sought to recover money which had been seized from him by his employer, the Crown. The Crown had seized the money because it constituted bribes which the plaintiff had received for assisting in the smuggling of liquor. The House of Lords held that the Crown could retain this money because it constituted profits which the plaintiff had obtained in breach of his contract of employment, and to support

[21] [1912] AC 555. See also *Surrey County Council* v. *Bredero Homes Ltd.* [1993] 1 WLR 1361, 1364 (Dillon LJ).

[22] See p. 41 above.

[23] For examination of the notion of a fiduciary relationship see pp. 521–34 below.

[24] See *Hospital Products Ltd.* v. *US Surgical Corporation* (1984) 156 CLR 41 (High Court of Australia). See p. 43 above.

[25] [1951] AC 507.

this conclusion the Court concluded that the plaintiff owed fiduciary duties to his employer. It follows from this that, had the sergeant retained the bribes, the Crown could have sued him for breach of fiduciary duty and recovered the bribes which he had obtained.[26]

(iv) Tortious wrongdoing

Sometimes, where the defendant has breached a contract with the plaintiff, the defendant will also have committed a proprietary tort[27] so that the plaintiff will be able to obtain a restitutionary remedy founded on the tort rather than the breach of contract. For example, in *Penarth Dock Engineering Co. Ltd.* v. *Pounds*[28] the plaintiff sued the defendant for breach of contract and the tort of trespass to property by virtue of the defendant's failure to remove a pontoon from the plaintiff's dock. The plaintiff was awarded damages which were measured by reference to the amount which the defendant had saved in not having to pay rent for the dock. Although it seems that the plaintiff's primary claim was for breach of contract it is clear that Lord Denning MR felt able to award a restitutionary remedy because the defendant had also committed the tort of trespass, for which restitutionary relief was clearly available.

(v) Interference with the plaintiff's proprietary rights

Where the consequence of the breach of contract is that the defendant interferes with the plaintiff's proprietary rights, restitutionary remedies may be available because of the general policy of the law which seeks to protect such rights from wrongdoing by requiring the defendant to disgorge those benefits which were obtained by interfering with the plaintiff's property.[29] There are four key cases where the question of the award of restitutionary remedies for breaches of contract which involved interference with proprietary rights has been considered.

In *Wrotham Park Estate Co. Ltd.* v. *Parkside Homes Ltd.*[30] the defendant had built houses on a piece of land without obtaining the prior consent of the plaintiff, a neighbouring landowner, as was required by a restrictive covenant which had been registered as a land charge. As a result of this breach of covenant the plaintiff sought an injunction requiring the houses which had been built to be demolished. This was refused on the ground that it would constitute an unacceptable waste of much needed houses, but damages were awarded in lieu of the injunction. These damages were assessed by reference to the amount of money

---

[26] The bribes would, in fact, be held on constructive trust for the plaintiff. See *Attorney-General of Hong Kong* v. *Reid* [1994] 1 AC 324.

[27] See Chapter 16.

[28] [1963] 1 Lloyd's Rep. 359. See also *Bracewell* v. *Appleby* [1975] Ch. 408.

[29] See p. 452 above.   [30] [1974] 1 WLR 798.

which the plaintiff could reasonably have demanded from the defendant to relax the covenant. This was calculated to be 5 per cent of the profits which it was reasonably anticipated that the defendant would make from building the houses.

This decision has proved to be controversial and in assessing it three key questions need to be considered.

(1) Can the damages which were awarded to the plaintiff be regarded as restitutionary rather than compensatory? Although the plaintiff had not suffered actual financial loss from the breach of the covenant, because the value of its land was unaffected by the development, the damages could still be characterised as compensating the plaintiff for the loss of the opportunity to bargain with the defendant to relax the covenant.[31] But this would be highly artificial because it was clear that the plaintiff would never have agreed to relax the covenant.[32] The damages are better regarded, therefore, as restitutionary, since they represent the value of the benefit to the defendant from the breach, namely the amount saved by the defendant in not paying for the relaxation of the covenant. This conclusion is strengthened by the fact that the trial judge specifically relied on a number of tort cases where the remedy awarded can only be characterised as being restitutionary.

(2) If it is correct that the damages which were awarded were restitutionary, the second question which needs to be considered is why the defendant was not liable to account for all of the profits it made by building the houses in breach of the restrictive covenant? This was presumably because of the principle of causation, the effect of which is that the defendant should only be liable to account for those profits which would not have been made but for the breach of the contract. In *Wrotham Park* the defendant's breach of covenant only related to the failure to obtain the plaintiff's consent to relax the covenant. It could never be proved that all of the defendant's profits arose from this breach, since most of the profits arose from the defendant's input in building the houses. Consequently, the defendant was liable to disgorge only those profits which derived from the breach. But in a case such as this it is virtually impossible to determine which profits derived from the breach. The formula which was adopted, namely 5 per cent of the profits, is artificial but it is at least realistic since it represents a reasonable sum which would have been demanded by somebody in the position of the plaintiff before agreeing to relax the covenant.

---

[31] This was how Megarry V-C explained the case in *Tito* v. *Waddell (No. 2)* [1977] Ch. 106, 335, as did Millett LJ in *Jaggard* v. *Sawyer* [1995] 1 WLR 269, 291. See also Sharpe and Waddams, 'Damages for Lost Opportunity to Bargain' (1982) 2 *OJLS* 290 and Stoljar, 'Restitutionary Relief for Breach of Contract' (1989) 2 *JCL* 1.

[32] This was recognised by Brightman J at [1974] 1 WLR 798, 815.

(3) The final and most important question about the *Wrotham Park* case is, if the damages which were awarded were restitutionary, why were they awarded in this particular case? The preferable explanation is simply that the defendant's breach of covenant constituted interference with the plaintiff's proprietary rights. The relevant proprietary right was the restrictive covenant itself, as reflected by the fact that the covenant was registered as a land charge and created a right for the benefit of the plaintiff as the owner of the neighbouring land. By awarding a restitutionary remedy the trial judge was protecting this particular proprietary right and this is consistent with the fundamental principles which underlie the award of restitutionary remedies for wrongdoing where the protection of property rights is a fundamental objective.

In *Surrey County Council* v. *Bredero Homes Ltd.*[33] the plaintiffs, two local authorities, sold land to the defendant subject to a covenant that the defendant would develop the land only in accordance with the planning permission which it had already obtained and which provided for the building of 72 houses. The plaintiffs were prepared to waive this covenant on the receipt of a sum of money from the defendant. But in breach of the covenant, and without negotiating a variation of it with the plaintiffs, the defendant applied for new planning permission to enable it to build 78 houses, and it received this permission from one of the plaintiffs. The plaintiffs did not apply for an injunction to stop the extra houses from being built but, once they had been built, they claimed damages for breach of the covenant. The trial judge awarded the plaintiffs nominal damages because they had suffered no loss from the breach. The plaintiffs then appealed to the Court of Appeal on the ground that, by virtue of the decision in *Wrotham Park*, they should be awarded restitutionary damages which they argued should be assessed either by reference to the profit obtained by the defendant from building the additional six houses or a sum of money which the defendant would reasonably have paid to obtain the plaintiffs' consent to relax the covenant. The Court of Appeal rejected this argument and held that, since the plaintiffs had suffered no loss, they were not able to recover substantial damages for the defendant's breach. So the effect of the case is to affirm the general principle that the function of the award of damages for breach of contract is to compensate the plaintiff for loss suffered.

But the Court of Appeal still needed to distinguish the decision in *Wrotham Park* and each judge adopted a different way of doing so. Dillon LJ distinguished that case on the basis that the damages were awarded in equity in lieu of an injunction, whereas in the *Surrey County Council* case the plaintiffs had never sought an injunction and were sim-

---

[33] [1993] 1 WLR 1361.

ply seeking damages for breach of contract at common law.[34] But he did not explain why this should make any difference. Steyn LJ, on the other hand, acknowledged that restitutionary damages could be awarded where the defendant had breached a contract and accepted that the damages in *Wrotham Park* were restitutionary.[35] Even more importantly, he stated that the award of restitutionary damages in that case was justified because the defendant had invaded the plaintiff's property rights,[36] but he asserted that in the *Surrey County Council* case the defendant's conduct did not 'involve any invasion of the plaintiff's interests even in the broadest sense of that word'.[37] Despite the clear difference of approach between Dillon and Steyn LJJ, Rose LJ said that he agreed with both judgments and purported to distinguish *Wrotham Park* on the patently irrelevant ground that in that case the plaintiff objected to the defendant's building work from the start.

In the light of the general principles which underlie the award of restitutionary remedies for wrongdoing, the approach of Steyn LJ is much to be preferred. In *Surrey County Council* it is clear that the defendant had not interfered with any of the plaintiffs' proprietary rights,[38] since the covenant in that case was simply a contractual promise, whereas the right in *Wrotham Park* was a restrictive covenant, which is a proprietary right which attaches to land. So the effect of both cases appears to be that, whilst damages for breach of contract are normally assessed by reference to the plaintiff's loss, they may be assessed by reference to the benefit obtained by the defendant as a result of the breach where the effect of the breach is to interfere with the plaintiff's proprietary rights. Unfortunately, a later decision of the Court of Appeal on this issue, *Jaggard* v. *Sawyer*,[39] appears to prevent such a simple reconciliation of *Wrotham Park* and *Surrey County Council* from being made.

In *Jaggard* v. *Sawyer* the plaintiff and the defendant each owned a house in a private road. They were both parties, with all of the other householders in the road, to a covenant that they would use their land only as a private garden and would keep the road in good repair. The defendant bought land next to his house, intending to build a house on it. Since this land did not have direct access to the road, he obtained planning permission to build a drive in his garden to connect this house to the private road. The plaintiff objected but did not obtain an injunction to stop the house or drive from being built. Once the new house had been built, the plaintiff then sought an injunction to prevent the defendant from using the plaintiff's part of the road to gain access to the new house. The plaintiff based her claim on the defendant's breach of the

---

[34] *Ibid*, p. 1367.   [35] *Ibid*, p. 1369.   [36] *Ibid*.   [37] *Ibid*.
[38] As both Dillon and Steyn LJJ expressly recognised at pp. 1365 and 1371 respectively.
[39] [1995] 1 WLR 269.

covenant and trespass to her part of the private road. The Court of Appeal declined to order an injunction but awarded damages in lieu of an injunction. These damages were assessed by reference to what the defendant would have had to pay all of the parties to the covenant to secure their consent to relax it. Since there were nine other parties to the covenant, the plaintiff received one ninth of this amount.

Although the result is consistent with that in *Wrotham Park*, Millett LJ was adamant that the damages were compensatory and not restitutionary.[40] But despite this, the remedy can be explained by reference to the general principles which have been identified relating to the award of restitutionary remedies for wrongs for two reasons.[41] First, the covenant related to the enjoyment of the plaintiff's property and so breach of the covenant could be considered to involve an interference in the plaintiff's proprietary right. Secondly, since the plaintiff's claim was also founded on the tort of trespass to the plaintiff's land, for which it is clear that restitutionary remedies can be awarded,[42] this could just as easily have been the basis for awarding a restitutionary remedy on the facts of the case.

Although the question of the appropriate remedy for interference with property rights did not arise in *Blake*, the Court of Appeal did suggest in that case that the award of restitutionary damages in *Wrotham Park* could not be justified on the ground that the defendant had interfered with the plaintiff's proprietary right arising from the restrictive covenant because 'the measure of damages cannot depend on whether the proceedings are between the original parties to the contract or their successors in title'.[43] But this assumes that the restrictive covenant in *Wrotham Park* bound only the original parties, whereas in fact the covenant bound successors in title because it was registered as a land charge.[44] But although this analysis of the *Wrotham Park* case is unconvincing, the effect of *Blake* on the award of remedies for breach of contract means that it is no longer necessary to show that the effect of the breach of contract is interference with the plaintiff's property rights. For it is now simply sufficient to show that compensatory remedies are an inadequate remedy and that the benefit obtained by the defendant derived directly from the breach of contract. This is exactly what happened in *Wrotham Park*. In that case the defendant's benefit was obtained as a direct result of the breach of covenant, since, in building houses without the plaintiff's permission, the defendant did what it had promised not to do, and compensatory damages would have been inadequate because the plain-

---

[40] [1995] 1 WLR 269, 291. See also Sir Thomas Bingham MR at p. 281.

[41] See Goodhart, 'Restitutionary Damages for Breach of Contract: The Remedy That Dare Not Speak Its Name' (1995) 3 *RLR* 3.

[42] See p. 485 above.   [43] [1998] 2 WLR 805, 817.

[44] See *Tulk* v. *Moxhay* (1848) 2 Ph. 774; 41 ER 1143.

tiff had not suffered any loss. The remedy which was awarded in *Jaggard* v. *Sawyer* can similarly be characterised as restitutionary since, when the defendant used his land to build a driveway, he was doing that which he had promised not to do and the benefit he obtained, namely what he had saved in not having to pay the plaintiff to obtain her permission for the change of use, was obtained as a direct result of the breach of covenant.

More controversially, a further implication of the observations of the court in *Blake* is that the failure to award restitutionary damages in *Surrey County Council* v. *Bredero Homes Ltd.*[45] was incorrect. For in that case the defendant had built houses in breach of a covenant to develop the land only in accordance with the planning consent. Since the defendant had done what it had promised not to do it should have been liable to disgorge to the plaintiffs what it had saved by breaching the covenant.

Whilst a convincing case can be made that restitutionary remedies should be available where the defendant's breach of contract has involved interference with the plaintiff's property rights, simply because of the policy to protect such rights from interference, such a principle is uncertain, particularly because the notion of a proprietary right can be interpreted widely.[46] So, for example, it could be argued that purely contractual rights are choses in action and so can be characterised as proprietary rights.[47] Consequently, it is far more appropriate to justify the award of restitutionary remedies in such cases by reference to a different principle and the decision of the Court of Appeal in *Blake* provides a mechanism by which this can be done.

2. SHOULD RESTITUTIONARY REMEDIES GENERALLY BE AVAILABLE FOR BREACH OF CONTRACT?

If the *obiter* dicta of the Court of Appeal in *Blake* are considered to represent the state of English law on the award of restitutionary remedies for breach of contract, it follows that such remedies will be available whenever compensatory damages are inadequate and the defendant has obtained a benefit as a direct result of the breach of contract. But it is still necessary to consider whether this limited approach to the award of restitutionary remedies is satisfactory or whether such remedies should be available more generally. A number of commentators have argued

[45] [1993] 1 WLR 1361.

[46] As was recognised by Steyn LJ in *Surrey County Council* v. *Bredero Homes* [1993] 1 WLR 1361, 1370.

[47] See Barak J in *Adras Building Material Ltd.* v. *Harlow and Jones GmbH* (1995) 3 *RLR* 235, 270 (a decision of the Israeli Supreme Court) who suggested that a contractual right was a property right and so restitutionary damages could be awarded for infringing this right.

that restitutionary remedies should be generally available for breach of contract. Most importantly, Goff and Jones argue that restitution should lie in all cases in which the defendant has made a gain which he or she would not have made but for the breach of contract, although they do suggest that the court should have a discretion to deny restitution in certain cases.[48]

(a) How wrongful is a breach of contract?

To determine whether restitutionary remedies should generally be available for breaches of contract in English law, it is necessary to reconsider some of the basic principles which relate to the award of restitutionary remedies for wrongdoing. The key principle which justifies the award of restitutionary remedies for wrongs is that the wrongdoer should not be allowed to profit from the wrong.[49] What needs to be considered is whether the nature of breach of contract is such that any defendant who profits from the breach should not be allowed to retain that profit. Although breach of contract cannot be considered to be of the same magnitude of wrongfulness as committing a tort or crime or even a breach of fiduciary duty, it is wrongful, as has been recognised for the purposes of economic duress.[50] In many cases, however, a breach of contract is only technically wrongful and sometimes a breach of contract may even be economically efficient and so can be considered to be justified, so long as the plaintiff is adequately compensated for any loss suffered.[51] A breach of contract will be efficient where, for example, a vendor has contracted to sell goods to the plaintiff but sold them instead to a third party who valued them more than the plaintiff and so was prepared to pay more for them. There is no obvious reason why a breach of contract should be deterred by awarding restitutionary remedies to deprive the defendant of any benefit obtained from the breach, where the breach can serve a useful economic function. The problem with this argument concerns the identification of those cases in which a breach of contract can be considered to be economically efficient, since in the vast majority of cases the costs which arise from the breach will exceed any benefits derived from it.[52] This includes costs arising from contracts

---

[48] Goff and Jones, *The Law of Restitution*, p. 522.   [49] See p. 451 above.

[50] See p. 208 above. See also *Ahmed Angullia bin Hadjee Mohamed Sallah Angullia* v. *Estate and Trust Agencies (1927) Ltd.* [1938] AC 624, 640 (Lord Romer).

[51] See Posner, *Economic Analysis of Law* (4th edn., Boston, Mass.: Little Brown & Co., 1992) pp. 117–26. For criticism of the theory of efficient breach see Friedmann, 'The Efficient Breach Fallacy' (1989) 18 *JLS* 1; Smith, 'Disgorgement of the Profits of Breach of Contract: Property, Contract and "Efficient Breach" ' (1992) 24 *Canadian Business Law Journal* 121; and O'Dair, 'Restitutionary Damages for Breach of Contract and the Theory of Efficient Breach: Some Reflections' (1993) 46 *CLP* 113.

[52] See Friedmann, n. 51 above, p. 7.

which the plaintiff may have made with other parties and which the plaintiff is forced to repudiate or renegotiate as a result of the defendant's breach.[53]

(b) Identifying situations where the breach of contract is sufficiently wrongful

There are, in fact, three different situations in which the nature of the defendant's breach of contract may be considered to be sufficiently wrongful to justify the award of restitutionary remedies.

(i) Cynical breach of contract

Sometimes the defendant's conduct in breaching the contract may be considered to be so cynical that he or she should not be allowed to profit from the breach.[54] Whilst this argument is superficially attractive, it is virtually impossible to apply in practice, because of the uncertainty in determining what constitutes a cynical breach of contract. Is this merely a deliberate breach of contract or one where the defendant calculates that, after compensating the plaintiff for any loss suffered, he or she would still make a profit from the breach? But in either case what is really wrong with breaching the contract in such circumstances? A cynical breach can still be an efficient breach, and reference to the motive of the defendant in breaching the contract is 'contrary to the general approach of [the English] law of contract'.[55] It would also result in greater uncertainty in the assessment of damages, something which should be avoided if at all possible in the context of commercial contracts. Consequently, no exception to the general rule against the award of restitutionary remedies for breach of contract should be founded on the fact that the defendant's breach was cynical. This conclusion was accepted by the Court of Appeal in *Attorney-General* v. *Blake*,[56] essentially because it does not follow from the fact that the defendant's breach was deliberate that any benefits obtained by him or her necessarily derived from the breach of contract or that compensatory damages are an inadequate remedy for the breach.

(ii) Defendant entered into a more profitable contract

It has sometimes been suggested that restitutionary remedies are appropriate where the defendant has breached the contract with the plaintiff

---

[53] *Ibid*, p. 13.

[54] This principle was recognised in Ireland in *Hickey* v. *Roche* (1993) 1 *RLR* 196. It has been advocated by Birks, 'Restitutionary Damages for Breach of Contract: *Snepp* and the Fusion of Law and Equity' [1987] *LMCLQ* 421.

[55] *Surrey County Council* v. *Bredero Homes Ltd.* [1993] 1 WLR 1361, 1370 (Steyn LJ).

[56] [1998] 2 WLR 805, 818.

in order to enter into a more profitable contract with someone else. Those who support this view tend to regard the decision of the Israeli Supreme Court in *Adras Building Material Ltd.* v. *Harlow and Jones GmbH*[57] as representing the ideal solution to the problem. In *Adras* the plaintiff agreed to buy 7,000 tons of steel from the defendant. The defendant supplied some of this steel to the plaintiff, but it then received an offer from a third party to buy the remaining steel for a higher price. Consequently the defendant agreed to supply the remaining steel to the third party. The plaintiff sued the defendant for breach of contract and claimed that it should obtain restitution of the difference between the original contract price and the price obtained by the defendant from the resale to the third party. A majority of the Supreme Court found for the plaintiff and recognised a general right to the award of restitutionary damages whenever the defendant obtained a benefit as a result of a breach of contract. But great care must be taken before the restitutionary principles recognised in *Adras* are transplanted into English law, primarily because the approach of Israeli law to breach of contract is fundamentally different from that of English law. For Israeli law expects contractual promises to be performed and it is for this reason that, as was recognised in *Adras* itself, the general remedy for breach of contract is specific performance. On the other hand, the attitude of English law to the binding nature of promises is much more ambivalent. In England when the defendant breaches a contract the usual remedial response is to award damages and only certain types of contract are specifically enforceable.[58] This fundamentally different attitude means that, although the unrestricted award of restitutionary damages might be entirely appropriate in Israel, this is not necessarily the case in this country.

In fact, the Court of Appeal in *Attorney-General* v. *Blake*[59] specifically rejected the case where the defendant has breached a contract with the plaintiff to enter into a more profitable contract with a third party as one where restitutionary remedies were appropriate. The Court was right to do so. There is no particular reason why restitutionary remedies are appropriate in such a case, because it does not necessarily follow that compensatory damages are an inadequate remedy. Neither does it follow from the fact that the defendant has benefited from entering into a contract with a third party that this benefit was obtained directly from the breach of contract. Rather, the breach of contract placed the defendant in a position in which he or she was able to obtain the benefit from

[57] (1988) 42 (1) PD. See (1995) 3 *RLR* 235.
[58] *Co-operative Insurance Society Ltd.* v. *Argyll Stores (Holdings) Ltd.* [1998] AC 1, 11 (Lord Hoffmann).
[59] [1998] 2 WLR 805.

the third party. Consequently, the benefit was obtained indirectly and so the defendant should not be required to disgorge it to the plaintiff.

(iii) Specifically enforceable contracts

A third circumstance in which restitutionary relief may be an appropriate remedy for a breach of contract is where the contract which is breached is specifically enforceable. That restitutionary relief may be available in such circumstances is consistent with the principles recognised by the Court of Appeal in *Blake*. This is because contracts are only specifically enforceable where compensatory damages are an inadequate remedy. The only remaining question, therefore, is whether the benefit obtained by the defendant can be considered to arise directly from the breach of contract.

That restitutionary remedies should be available where the defendant has breached a specifically enforceable contract has been advocated by a number of commentators.[60] This is because, where a contract is considered to be specifically enforceable, the policy of the law is in favour of the performance of the contract. If the defendant fails to perform the contract in circumstances in which the contract can no longer be specifically enforced, it is entirely appropriate that the defendant should make restitution to the plaintiff, both because breach of specifically enforceable contracts should be deterred and because, if the defendant does breach such a contract, he or she should not be allowed to profit from the clear wrong of doing so. In fact, where restitutionary remedies are awarded for breach of contract this is simply a monetised form of specific performance, assuming that if the contract had been performed the plaintiff would have obtained the benefit which the defendant had obtained.

Unfortunately the principle that restitutionary remedies for breach of contract should be available where the defendant has breached a specifically enforceable contract was rejected by Steyn LJ in *Surrey County Council* v. *Bredero Homes Ltd.*,[61] where he said that restricting the award of restitutionary relief to where the remedies of specific performance and injunctions:

---

[60] See Beatson, *The Use and Abuse of Unjust Enrichment*, p. 17. This is also recognised by Birks, 'Restitutionary Damages for Breach of Contract: *Snepp* and the Fusion of Law and Equity' [1987] *LMCLQ* 421, 442. See also Waddams, 'Restitution as Part of Contract Law' in *Essays on the Law of Restitution* (ed. Burrows) pp. 208–12; O'Dair 'Restitutionary Damages for Breach of Contract and the Theory of Efficient Breach: Some Reflections' (1993) 46 *CLP* 1134. See also Nolan, 'Remedies for Breach of Contract: Specific Enforcement and Restitution' in *Failure of Contracts: Contractual, Restitutionary and Proprietary Consequences* (ed. Rose, Oxford: Hart Publishing, 1997) p. 35.

[61] [1993] 1 WLR 1361, 1371.

would have been available . . . seems to me a bromide formula without any rationale in logic or common sense. Given a breach of contract, why should the availability of a restitutionary remedy, as a matter of legal entitlement, be dependent on the availability of the wholly different and discretionary remedies of injunction and specific performance.

But this misses the point. Whilst it is true that the award of specific performance and injunctions lie in the discretion of the court, such remedies can only be awarded in certain well defined circumstances, essentially where compensatory damages would be an inadequate remedy and primarily where the contract relates to the creation or protection of proprietary interests. The fact that a contract is specifically enforceable should be considered to be sufficient indication that the defendant should be deprived of any benefit which he or she obtained in breaching the contract.

If this is correct, it is clearly necessary to determine in what circumstances a contract will be specifically enforceable. There are five particular characteristics of such contracts.[62] First, compensatory damages must be an inadequate way of protecting the plaintiff's interests. Secondly, the plaintiff must have a legitimate interest in the performance of the contract. Thirdly, the plaintiff's interest must not be capable of protection by reasonable mitigating action by the plaintiff. Fourthly, the specific performance must not require constant supervision by the courts, as will be the case where the defendant is required to perform a contract over a period of time rather than where he or she is simply required to achieve a particular result.[63] Finally, specific performance will not be ordered where the plaintiff's conduct is such that equitable relief is not merited or where the making of such an order would conflict with fundamental social and economic policies which are opposed to the compulsion of performance, such as the policy against compelling a defendant to employ the plaintiff.

The importance of the distinction between contracts which are and which are not specifically enforceable was recognised by Purchas LJ in *Williams* v. *Roffey Bros. and Nicholls (Contractors) Ltd.*[64] who stated that, save for contracts which are specifically enforceable, it is perfectly acceptable for a party to a contract deliberately to breach that contract if he or she is able to cut losses as a result. The decision of the Israeli Supreme Court in *Adras* also reflects the significance of the distinction,

---

[62] See Beatson, *The Use and Abuse of Unjust Enrichment*, p. 17.

[63] *Co-operative Insurance Society Ltd.* v. *Argyll Stores (Holdings) Ltd.* [1998] AC 1, 12 (Lord Hoffmann). Lord Hoffmann also recognised that a contractual obligation would not be specifically enforced if the terms of the order could not be precisely drawn: *ibid*, pp. 13–14.

[64] [1991] 1 QB 1.

since in that case restitutionary damages were awarded only because of the assumption of Israeli law that all contractual promises should be performed, hence the fact that in Israel specific performance is the primary contractual remedy. The special treatment of specifically enforceable contracts is also supported by many of the English cases which have examined the question of the award of restitutionary remedies. The emphasis of some of these cases on the question whether an injunction is an available remedy is an entirely appropriate consideration, since where an injunction is available in principle then the contract is specifically enforceable. So, for example, in *Wrotham Park* and *Jaggard* v. *Sawyer* the award of what appears to have been restitutionary damages was correct, because the performance of the covenants in those cases was specifically enforceable in the discretion of the court.

(c) Conclusions

It follows from this analysis that, for the moment at least, restitutionary remedies are available for breach of contract in three particular circumstances: first, where the defendant has failed to provide what he or she agreed to provide under the contract; secondly, where the defendant has promised to do something which he or she had specifically promised not to do; thirdly, where the defendant has breached a contract which is capable of specific performance. Other situations may be recognised in the future where restitutionary relief is available, but this can only be the case where compensatory damages are an inadequate remedy and where the defendant has obtained a benefit as a direct result of the breach of contract.

18

Restitution for Equitable Wrongdoing

1. GENERAL PRINCIPLES

(a) The rationale behind the award of restitutionary remedies for equitable wrongdoing

Where the defendant has committed a tort or breached a contract restitutionary remedies tend to be available only in exceptional circumstances. Where, however, the defendant has breached an equitable duty which he or she owed to the plaintiff, restitutionary relief is much more common. There are two reasons for this. First, the equitable jurisdiction relating to the award of remedies tends to be much more flexible and adaptable than the equivalent common law jurisdiction. Secondly, the policies which justify the award of restitutionary remedies for wrongdoing are much more likely to come into play where the defendant commits an equitable wrong.[1] This is because the typical equitable duty which the defendant owes to the plaintiff arises from a relationship of trust and confidence. As Jackman has recognised,[2] the nature of such relationships gives the defendant an opportunity to abuse and exploit the plaintiff, so that the relationship is in particular need of protection. Consequently, it is necessary to deter the defendant from exploiting the relationship, and this is done by ensuring that, at the very least, the value of any benefit which the defendant obtained from the breach of duty should be paid to the plaintiff to whom the duty was owed. It is irrelevant that the plaintiff did not suffer any loss by reason of the breach of duty, since the function of the award of restitutionary remedies is to ensure that the defendant does not benefit from the commission of the equitable wrong. But such remedies also exist to deter the defendant from committing the wrong in the first place, and so expose the plaintiff to the risk of loss, by requiring the defendant to disgorge all benefits obtained from the commission of the wrong to the plaintiff.

There is one other principle which underlies the award of restitutionary remedies for wrongs which is also particularly important in the context of equitable wrongdoing, and this relates to the moral nature of the defendant's breach of duty. For analysis of the cases suggests that where the defendant is particularly culpable in breaching his or her equitable

---

[1] See pp. 453–4 above.   [2] 'Restitution for Wrongs' (1989) 48 *CLJ* 302, 311.

duty then a more extensive form of restitutionary remedy may be available. Also where the defendant is not considered to be culpable in breaching his or her duty it seems that an equitable allowance will be awarded to him or her to reflect the value of the defendant's contribution to the benefit which he or she obtained.[3]

(b) Types of remedy which are available for equitable wrongdoing

Where the defendant has committed an equitable wrong it follows that the remedies which are available are equitable.

(i) Account of profits

Usually where the defendant obtains a profit as a result of committing an equitable wrong the remedy which is awarded will be an account of profits. This is a personal remedy so the defendant is simply liable to pay to the plaintiff the value of the benefit which he or she obtained from the wrong.

(ii) Proprietary remedies

The courts are increasingly accepting that a proprietary remedy will be available following the commission of an equitable wrong by recognising that the nature of the wrong is such that any benefit gained is held on constructive trust for the plaintiff.[4] Where property is held on constructive trust it follows that the plaintiff has a proprietary interest in the property which he or she can vindicate by means of a restitutionary proprietary claim.[5] One of the most controversial matters relating to the award of restitutionary remedies for equitable wrongdoing relates to the determination of when proprietary relief should be available.

(iii) Interest

Where the plaintiff is awarded a restitutionary remedy for equitable wrongdoing then the equitable jurisdiction to award compound interest will be triggered.[6] This has an important role in ensuring that the defendant wrongdoer is deprived of all the benefits which he or she obtained as a result of the wrongdoing.

(iv) Equitable compensation

Although the normal remedy for equitable wrongdoing is restitutionary, it does not follow that other forms of remedy are excluded. Most

---

[3] Compare *Boardman* v. *Phipps* [1967] 2 AC 46 and *O'Sullivan* v. *Management Agency and Music Ltd.* [1985] QB 428 with *Guinness* v. *Saunders* [1990] 2 AC 663.
[4] The nature of the constructive trust is examined at p. 459 above
[5] See Chapter 21.
[6] *Westdeutsche Landesbank Girozentrale* v. *Islington LBC* [1996] AC 669. See pp. 25–8 above.

importantly, the notion of equitable compensation is increasingly being recognised by English law.[7] Although this remedy has sometimes been called restitutionary,[8] since the effect of the remedy is to restore the plaintiff to the position which he or she would have occupied had the wrong not been committed, the remedy has nothing to do with the law of restitution as such, simply because it is not assessed by reference to the gain made by the defendant but is instead assessed by reference to the loss suffered by the plaintiff. It is nonetheless important to be aware of the existence of equitable compensatory remedies, because the existence of such remedies in equity's armoury will no doubt circumscribe the importance of restitutionary remedies. It is still unclear, however, to what extent the prevalence of restitutionary remedies for equitable wrongdoing will be affected by the growing recognition of equitable compensation.

2. THE CATEGORIES OF EQUITABLE WRONGDOING

Although a wide variety of equitable wrongdoing can be identified, there are essentially four different categories of such wrongdoing.[9] They are breach of fiduciary duty, abuse of relationships of confidence, unconscionability and dishonestly assisting in a breach of trust. Rather than concentrating on the nature of the equitable wrongs themselves, the analysis which follows will seek to determine when restitutionary remedies will be awarded for such wrongdoing and the type of restitutionary remedies which are awarded.

(a) Breach of fiduciary duty

Where the defendant is in a fiduciary relationship with the plaintiff the defendant is in a position to exploit the plaintiff and so, by virtue of the policy of protecting such relationships against abuse, restitutionary remedies are available where the defendant has breached his or her fiduciary duty. Before examining the types of duty which fiduciaries owe to

[7] See, in particular, *Nocton* v. *Lord Ashburton* [1914] AC 932, 956–7 (Viscount Haldane LC); *Bishopsgate Investment Management Ltd.* v. *Maxwell (No. 2)* [1994] 1 All ER 261, *Target Holdings Ltd.* v. *Redferns (a firm)* [1996] AC 421, *Mahoney* v. *Purnell* [1996] 3 All ER 61, *Bristol and West Building Society* v. *Mothew* [1998] Ch. 1, 17 (Millett LJ) and *Swindle* v. *Harrison* [1997] 4 All ER 705. See also the decision of the High Court of Australia in *Warman International Ltd.* v. *Dwyer* (1995) 128 ALR 201.

[8] See *Swindle* v. *Harrison* [1997] 4 All ER 705, 714 where Evans LJ described the equitable remedy for restoring the plaintiff to the position he or she occupied before the defendant committed a fraudulent wrong as 'restitution'.

[9] See Davies, 'Restitution and Equitable Wrongs: An Australian Analogue' in *Consensus ad Idem* (ed. Rose) p. 163.

their principals, it is first necessary to examine when a fiduciary relationship can be identified. [10]

(i) The identification of fiduciary relationships

There is no legal definition of when the defendant can be considered to be a fiduciary.[11] There are, however, certain types of relationships which are always treated as fiduciary. So, for example, trustees, personal representatives, directors, agents, partners and joint tenants will always be treated as owing some kind of fiduciary duty to their principal. But the classes of fiduciary relationships are not closed, and so if the relationship between the parties does not fall within any of the recognised classes, the particular nature of the relationship needs to be carefully examined to determine whether it is sufficiently similar to the recognised classes to enable it to be treated as a fiduciary relationship. In *Bristol and West Building Society* v. *Mothew*[12] Millett LJ identified the essential characteristics of fiduciary relationships:

A fiduciary is someone who has undertaken to act for or on behalf of another in a particular matter in circumstances which give rise to a relationship of trust and confidence. The distinguishing obligation of a fiduciary is the obligation of loyalty.

This is the touchstone against which the defendant's relationship with his or her principal should be assessed to determine whether the defendant owes fiduciary obligations so that the relationship can be characterised as fiduciary.

Whilst it is clear that an express trustee is a fiduciary, there is a great deal of uncertainty whether resulting and constructive trustees should be similarly characterised. As regards resulting trustees[13] it seems that whether such a trustee is a fiduciary depends on the reason a resulting trust was recognised. So, for example, if the resulting trust arose from the failure of an express trust it is appropriate to treat the resulting trustee as a fiduciary.[14] Whether the constructive trustee should be regarded as a fiduciary is a controversial matter, but the preferable view is that the essence of the constructive trust is simply that there is a separation of legal and equitable title and that it does not automatically follow from this that the constructive trustee is subject to fiduciary duties because he or she has not knowingly subjected him or herself to

[10] Hayton, 'Fiduciaries in Context: An Overview' in *Privacy and Loyalty* (ed. Birks) p. 292.
[11] But see Glover, 'The Identification of Fiduciaries' in *Privacy and Loyalty* (ed. Birks), Chapter 10, who attempts to identify the hallmarks of a fiduciary relationship.
[12] [1998] Ch. 1, 18. See also Birks, 'Equity in the Modern Law: An Exercise in Taxonomy' (1996) 26 *Univ. WALR* 1, 18.
[13] See pp. 617–28 below.
[14] See Chambers, *Resulting Trusts* (Oxford: Clarendon Press, 1997), pp. 196–200.

fiduciary obligations.[15] But it is possible for a constructive trustee to be subject to such fiduciary obligations where he or she knew the facts by virtue of which the constructive trust was imposed.

One of the most important questions relating to the identification of a fiduciary relationship is the extent to which parties to commercial trans-actions can be considered to owe fiduciary duties to other parties to the transaction. This was examined by the Privy Council in *Re Goldcorp Exchange plc.*,[16] where a restrictive interpretation of fiduciary duties was adopted.[17] In that case the plaintiffs had bought bullion from the defen-dant company. The bullion had not been allocated to the plaintiffs, who consequently argued that the defendant had breached its fiduciary duty to them. This argument was easily rejected because the court was unable to identify duties which could be characterised as fiduciary rather than merely contractual. The identification of fiduciary duties, especially in a commercial context, can have profound consequences on the risks inherent in such relationships and it is to be hoped that the recognition in this case that fiduciary duties are fundamentally different from merely contractual obligations will prevent the concept from being abused purely from a desire to secure a just result. As Lord Mustill memorably said, 'high expectations do not necessarily lead to equitable remedies'.[18] Millett LJ, as he then was, has emphasised extra-judicially that:

It is the first importance not to impose fiduciary obligations on parties to a purely commercial relationship who deal with each other at arm's length and can be expected to look after their own interests.[19]

But the restrictive approach to the recognition of fiduciary relation-ships in the *Goldcorp* case has not always been adopted. Sometimes it seems that the inherent uncertainty about what constitutes a fiduciary relationship has been manipulated to ensure that the defendant is liable to make restitution to the plaintiff. This is illustrated by *English* v. *Dedham Vale Properties Ltd.*[20] In this case the defendant was a property development company which wanted to purchase the plaintiff's land. The purchase price which was agreed reflected the fact that planning permission for development of the site was unlikely, but before the con-tracts were exchanged the defendant applied for planning permission

---

[15] See Millett, 'Restitution and Constructive Trusts' (1998) 114 *LQR* 399, 405.
[16] [1995] 1 AC 74.
[17] See also *Hospital Products International* v. *United States Surgical Corporation* (1984) 156 CLR 41 (High Court of Australia).
[18] [1995] 1 AC 74, 98.
[19] 'Equity's Place in the Law of Commerce' (1998) 114 *LQR* 214, 217–18. Cp. Sir Anthony Mason, 'The Place of Equity and Equitable Remedies in the Contemporary Common Law World' (1994) 110 *LQR* 238, 245–6.
[20] [1978] 1 WLR 93.

and obtained it, but it failed to inform the plaintiff of this. Once the plaintiff had discovered that the defendant had obtained planning permission, it successfully claimed the profit which the defendant had made as a result of the development, on the ground that the defendant owed the plaintiff fiduciary duties. It was held that the defendant was a fiduciary because it was deemed to have been acting as an agent on behalf of the plaintiff when it obtained planning permission. But this is a highly artificial finding of such a relationship since there was nothing on the facts to suggest that either party had ever contemplated that the defendant was acting as the plaintiff's agent. As Birks has suggested, the finding of a fiduciary relationship simply seems to be a convenient method of ensuring that the defendant was liable to make restitution to the plaintiff.[21]

(ii) The nature and ambit of fiduciary obligations[22]

A number of different principles can be identified relating to the nature and ambit of fiduciary obligations.

(1) In an important dictum from an American case Frankfurter J said:

To say that a man is a fiduciary only begins the analysis: it gives direction to further inquiry. To whom is he a fiduciary? What obligation does he owe as a fiduciary? In what respects has he failed to discharge these obligations? And what are the consequences of his deviation from duty?[23]

In other words, it is not enough to decide that the defendant is a fiduciary: this is simply the initial question. This has now been recognised explicitly in English law. In *Attorney-General* v. *Blake*[24] the Court of Appeal recognised that there is more than one category of fiduciary relationship and that different categories of relationship possess different characteristics and attract different kinds of fiduciary obligation.[25] Crucially, it is dangerous to assume that all fiduciaries are subject to the same duties in all circumstances.[26]

(2) It was also recognised in *Attorney-General* v. *Blake*[27] that a particular relationship may fall within more than one category of fiduciary relationship. Also the different categories of relationship may last for varying periods and the duties owed by the fiduciary will differ depending on the category of relationship which is being considered.

---

[21] Birks, *An Introduction to the Law of Restitution*, p. 331.

[22] For detailed examination of the nature and ambit of fiduciary duties see Finn, *Fiduciary Obligations*.

[23] *Securities and Exchange Commission* v. *Chenery Corporation* (1943) 318 US 80, 85–6.

[24] [1998] 2 WLR 805.

[25] *Ibid*, p. 814. See also *Bristol and West Building Society* v. *Mothew* [1998] Ch. 1. For more general analysis of the nature of fiduciary obligations see Millett, 'Equity's Place in the Law of Commerce' (1998) 114 *LQR* 214, 218–23.

[26] *Henderson* v. *Merrett Syndicates Ltd.* [1995] 2 AC 145, 206 (Lord Browne-Wilkinson).

[27] [1998] 2 WLR 805, 814.

(3) In *Bristol and West Building Society* v. *Mothew*[28] Millett LJ recognised that not every breach of duty by a fiduciary is a breach of fiduciary duty. Rather, fiduciary duties are 'those duties which are peculiar to fiduciaries and the breach of which attracts legal consequences differing from those consequent upon the breach of other duties'.[29] So, for example, although all fiduciaries are under an obligation to use proper skill and care in the discharge of their duties, the breach of this obligation is not a breach of a fiduciary duty simply because the obligation arises from the fact that the defendant has assumed responsibility to another person and not from the fact that the defendant is a fiduciary.

(4) All fiduciary duties are proscriptive in effect.[30] This means that the duties do not identify what fiduciaries must do, but rather identify what they should not do.

(5) For a fiduciary to be liable for breach of fiduciary duty he or she must have breached the duty by an intentional act; unconscious omission is not sufficient.[31] But, crucially, a fiduciary will be held liable without needing to prove that he or she acted dishonestly.[32]

(iii) The categories of fiduciary relationship

There are three distinct categories of fiduciary relationship. Each of these relationships possess different characteristics and attract different kinds of fiduciary obligation.[33]

(1) The relationship of trust and confidence

The Court of Appeal in *Attorney-General* v. *Blake*[34] emphasised that the most important category of fiduciary relationship is the relationship of trust and confidence. The essence of this relationship is that the fiduciary undertakes to act in the interests of the principal or occupies a position in which he or she is obliged to act in the interests of the principal.[35] In other words, the fiduciary must be loyal to the principal.

The identification of this relationship of trust and confidence is illustrated by *Attorney-General* v. *Blake*.[36] George Blake had been a member of the British Secret Intelligence Service but he was also an agent of the Soviet Union. He was convicted of unlawfully communicating information to the Soviets but he escaped to Moscow where he wrote his autobiography. In this book he disclosed information about the secret service.

---

[28] [1998] Ch. 1, 16.   [29] *Ibid.*

[30] *Attorney-General* v. *Blake* [1998] 2 WLR 805, 816.

[31] *Bristol and West Building Society* v. *Mothew* [1998] Ch. 1, 19 (Millett LJ).

[32] *Warman International Ltd.* v. *Dwyer* (1995) 128 ALR 201, 208. Cp. the liability for dishonestly assisting a breach of fiduciary duty where fault must be proved. See pp. 553–5 below.

[33] Millett, 'Equity's Place in the Law of Commerce' (1998) 114 *LQR* 214, 219.

[34] [1998] 2 WLR 805, 814.   [35] *Ibid.*   [36] [1998] 2 WLR 805.

This breached an agreement not to disclose information gained as a result of his employment by the Crown and it also constituted a breach of the Official Secrets Acts. The book was published in the United Kingdom without the permission of the Crown. The Attorney-General sued, on behalf of the Crown, to recover all the sums which had been received or were receivable by the publisher. One argument made by the Attorney-General was that, if Blake had received these profits, he would have been liable to account for them to the Crown because they were made in breach of fiduciary duty. The Court of Appeal accepted that there was a fiduciary relationship of trust and confidence between Blake and the Crown because Blake was employed to act in the best interests of the Crown. But it also recognised that this duty lasts only as long as the relationship of trust and confidence continues and that such a relationship ends once the employee ceases to be employed by the employer. Consequently, once Blake ceased to be employed by the Crown he no longer owed a duty of loyalty to it as a fiduciary. The only way that a duty of loyalty would subsist despite the termination of employment was where the employee had entered into a contractual undertaking not to damage the employer's interests once the employee had left his or her employment. But if this agreement were breached liability would be founded on breach of contract rather than breach of fiduciary duty.

Where there is a relationship of trust and confidence the conduct of the fiduciary is constrained by two fundamental principles.

(1) *The no-conflict principle.* The no-conflict principle has two elements: first, that where a fiduciary finds him- or herself in a position in which his or her personal interest conflicts with his or her duty to the principal then the fiduciary must prefer the duty to the principal to his or her personal interest;[37] secondly, fiduciaries should avoid placing themselves in a position where their duty to one principal conflicts with their duty to another principal save where both principals have given their fully informed consent to such a conflict.[38]

(2) *The no-profit principle.* The no-profit principle prohibits fiduciaries from obtaining an advantage by virtue of their position as fiduciary either for themselves or for a third party, save where the principal has given his or her fully informed consent to the fiduciary obtaining the advantage. So, for example, the fiduciary is prohibited from making a profit by using an opportunity or knowledge which he or she acquired by virtue of his or her position as a fiduciary.

Whether these two principles are mutually exclusive is a controversial matter. One view is that whenever the fiduciary makes a profit in breach of his or her fiduciary duty this will inevitably involve a contravention of

---

[37] *Swain* v. *The Law Society* [1982] 1 WLR 17, 36 (Oliver LJ).
[38] *Clark Boyce* v. *Mouat* [1994] 1 AC 428, 435.

the no-conflict principle. The preferable view, however, is that the two principles should always be considered separately. Certainly, the no-conflict principle can be contravened without the fiduciary making any profit. Equally, where the fiduciary is alleged to have made a profit in breach of the fiduciary duty it should not be necessary to establish that this also involved a conflict of interest.[39] The fact that the fiduciary made an unauthorised profit should be sufficient to impose liability.

Nolan has argued that a number of the specific duties which are founded on the no-conflict principle are better characterised as disabilities, in the sense that the fiduciary is disabled from acting against the interests of his or her principal.[40] He further argues that where the plaintiff seeks a restitutionary remedy from the fiduciary in respect of a benefit which was obtained in contravention of the no-conflict principle, this restitutionary claim should be treated as being founded on the unjust enrichment principle rather than restitution for wrongs. So, for example, if the fiduciary purchases property from the principal at an undervalue, the defendant's liability to make restitution will be founded on his or her unjust enrichment, since the defendant will have obtained a benefit at the plaintiff's expense, as the benefit was subtracted from the plaintiff. Nolan fails to identify a recognised ground of restitution which will be applicable in such circumstances, but he suggests that a ground of restitution should be recognised because the plaintiff's consent to benefit the defendant can be considered to be impaired.[41] Whilst this is a persuasive argument, particularly because it is consistent with a number of cases, its success depends on how the liability of a fiduciary is analysed. Should a fiduciary who infringes the no-conflict principle be characterised as a wrongdoer? Since the liability of the defendant depends on the fact that he or she was a fiduciary and failed to reach the high standards which are expected of a fiduciary, it is preferable to treat infringement of the no-conflict principle as a form of wrongdoing, for which restitutionary relief is available. This is not, however, inconsistent with Nolan's thesis since the principal could still base a claim on the unjust enrichment principle by means of alternative analysis.

A number of specific duties can be identified which are derived from the no-conflict and the no-profit principles.[42]

(1) *The self-dealing rule.* By virtue of this rule a fiduciary is barred from dealing for himself and for the principal in the same transaction.[43] If this

---

[39] Harpum, 'Fiduciary Obligations and Fiduciary Powers—Where Are We Going?' in *Privacy and Loyalty* (ed. Birks) p. 148.

[40] 'Conflicts of Interest, Unjust Enrichment and Wrongdoing' in *Restitution: Past, Present and Future* (ed. Cornish, Nolan, O'Sullivan and Virgo), p. 99. See *Tito* v. *Waddell (No. 2)* [1977] Ch. 106, 248 (Megarry V-C).

[41] *Ibid*, p. 93.   [42] See Goff and Jones, *The Law of Restitution*, chapter 33.

[43] *Tito* v. *Waddell (No. 2)* [1977] Ch. 106, 241 (Megarry J).

duty is breached the transaction can be rescinded and the fiduciary is liable to account to the principal for any profits which were made.

(2) The fair dealing rule. By virtue of this rule the fiduciary is barred from transacting with the principal unless the fiduciary can show that the transaction is fair and that he or she has made full disclosure of all facts material to the transaction.[44] If this duty is breached any transaction into which the fiduciary has entered is liable to be rescinded by the principal and the fiduciary is liable to account for any profits which he or she has made.[45]

(3) Acting for more than one principal. Where the fiduciary is acting for more than one principal there is scope for a number of breaches of fiduciary duties.

Where a fiduciary has acted for two principals whose interests potentially conflict and who have not given their informed consent to the fiduciary acting for the other principal, then, since the fiduciary's duty to one principal may conflict with his or her duty to the other, this constitutes a breach of fiduciary duty.[46] There will not be a breach of fiduciary duty, however, if the principal who complains of the potential conflict knew that the fiduciary was acting for another principal, as will be the case where the fiduciary was a solicitor who was acting for both lender and borrower and both of the clients knew that the solicitor was acting for the other party.[47]

Fiduciaries will also have breached their fiduciary duty if, when acting for more than one principal, they consciously further the interests of one to the prejudice of the other.[48] So, for example, if a solicitor is acting for both lender and borrower and makes a misrepresentation of fact to the lender which the fiduciary knows will influence its decision to make a loan, then this constitutes a breach of the fiduciary duty which is owed to the lender. This is because the solicitor is abusing his or her fiduciary relationship with the lender by obtaining an advantage for the other principal.[49]

There will also be a breach of fiduciary duty if there is an actual conflict of duty so that the fiduciary cannot fulfil his or her obligations to one principal without failing in his or her obligations to the other principal,

[44] *Ibid.* See the discussion of fiduciary relationships of influence at p. 532 below.

[45] In *Re Cape Breton Co. Ltd.* (1889) 29 Ch.D 795 it was held that where the fiduciary sells property to the plaintiff who has affirmed the transaction the fiduciary is not liable to account for his or her profits, since the act of affirming the transaction means that the liability of the fiduciary is extinguished.

[46] *Clarke Boyce* v. *Mouat* [1994] 1 AC 428.

[47] *Bristol and West Building Society* v. *Mothew* [1998] Ch. 1, 19 (Millett LJ).

[48] *Ibid.*

[49] *Bristol and West Building Society* v. *May May and Merrimans* [1996] 2 All ER 801, 817–18 (Chadwick J).

as will be the case where the fiduciary advises one of the principals to a proposed transaction on the merits of the transaction.[50]

If any of these fiduciary duties is breached the plaintiff will have a restitutionary claim against the fiduciary. Any transaction which is entered into between the two principals as a result of a breach of fiduciary duty may be set aside by the principal who is prejudiced, as long as the other principal was party to the breach of duty.[51]

(4) *Interference with the plaintiff's property.* Probably the clearest case in which restitutionary remedies are available for breach of a fiduciary duty is where the fiduciary obtains a benefit from the use of the plaintiff's property. This is illustrated by *Brown* v. *IRC*[52] where the defendant solicitor received clients' money which he deposited in a bank account. The defendant then used the interest for his own purposes. This constituted a breach of fiduciary duty because the defendant had used income which belonged to the clients for himself and without the authority of the clients. This was a clear breach of the no-profit principle.

(5) *Exploitation of opportunities.* Where the fiduciary has obtained a benefit not by the use of the plaintiff's property specifically but by exploiting an opportunity which came to the fiduciary in that capacity, this also constitutes the breach of a fiduciary duty because he or she profited from his or her position as fiduciary. The fiduciary will be liable to disgorge to the principal any profits obtained by such a breach of duty, regardless of the fact that the fiduciary acted reasonably and in good faith. It is irrelevant that the principal would not have been able to exploit the opportunity him or herself.[53]

Liability in such circumstances is particularly well illustrated by the decision of the House of Lords in *Boardman* v. *Phipps*.[54] In this case one of the defendants, a solicitor to a trust, realised that a company in which the trust held a minority of the shares was badly managed. Since the trust did not have sufficient capital to take over the company and so reconstruct it, the solicitor used his own money to buy shares himself. One of the beneficiaries of the trust also contributed his own money to buy shares. Through the exercise of his own skill, but also by means of information which he had obtained in his capacity as fiduciary, the solicitor turned the company into a highly profitable business. It was held that both the solicitor and the beneficiary had breached their fiduciary duty to the trust. They were both treated as fiduciaries because they were deemed to be acting as agents for the trust. The breach of fiduciary duty

---

[50] *Bristol and West Building Society* v. *Mothew* [1998] Ch. 1, 19 (Millett LJ).
[51] *Moody* v. *Cox and Hatt* [1917] 2 Ch. 71.   [52] [1965] AC 244.
[53] *Boardman* v. *Phipps* [1967] 2 AC 46.
[54] Ibid. See also *Cook* v. *Deeks* [1916] 1 AC 554 and *Regal (Hastings) Ltd.* v. *Gulliver* [1967] 2 AC 134n.

arose from the fact that they had made a personal profit by virtue of their position as fiduciaries, without gaining the fully informed consent of the trustees for their plans. Consequently they were held liable to account to the trust for the profits they had made, although the solicitor was awarded an allowance which was assessed by reference to the value of his services to the trust.

Boardman v. *Phipps* is a difficult case to justify. It was accepted by the majority that the defendants had not interfered with the plaintiff's property, since the information which they had obtained in their capacity as fiduciaries could not be treated as trust property. Neither were the defendants acting in bad faith, as was reflected by the fact that the solicitor was awarded an allowance for the work which he had done. Consequently, the imposition of a liability to make restitution can only be justified by the policy of deterring fiduciaries from making a profit from their position as fiduciaries. But was there really anything wrong with what the defendants did? There was nothing to suggest that they had abused their relationship of trust and confidence. The trust would not have received any more money from its shares in the company if the defendants had not intervened, and the defendants took the risk with their own money that they would be able to improve the company's fortunes. But the defendants were still held liable to account for their profits to the trust. This hardly seems fair. Whether the decision of the House of Lords should be considered to be correct depends on the message we think we should be giving to fiduciaries. If we wish to make it clear that fiduciaries should be expected to give their full attention to the person to whom they owe their duties, and that they should never place themselves in a position in which they could possibly abuse their position, the decision in *Boardman* v. *Phipps* must be correct. Alternatively, where there is no hint of fraud in the conduct of the defendant, surely it is much more realistic and just to commend the defendant for what he or she had done rather than to hold him or her liable to make restitution to the plaintiff. This was the view of the minority in the case, who held that the defendants should not be liable to account to the plaintiff for the profits they had made because they had been acting in good faith and because the beneficiaries had made it clear that they were not interested in a scheme to obtain the majority of the company's shares.[55]

(6) *Receipt of a bribe.* Where a fiduciary has received a bribe to induce him or her to act against the interests of the principal this is one of the

[55] See also the corporate opportunity cases which have held that directors should not be liable for taking opportunities which were offered to their company where the company declined the opportunity and the director made full and frank disclosure of his or her desire to take the opportunity. See, for example, *Peso-Silver Mines Ltd.* v. *Cropper* (1966) 58 DLR (2d.) 1 (Supreme Court of Canada) and *Queensland Mines Ltd.* v. *Hudson* [1978] 52 ALJR 379 (PC).

clearest cases in which the fiduciary should be considered to have broken his or her fiduciary duty, by contravening both the no-conflict and the no-profit principles. Restitutionary relief in such cases is justified simply on the ground that fiduciaries should be deterred from accepting bribes, and so being influenced to act against the best interests of the people to whom they owe fiduciary duties. One of the best ways of deterring such conduct is by depriving the defendant of the bribe which he or she received. This is illustrated by *Reading* v. *Attorney-General*[56] where the defendant was a sergeant in the British Army serving in Egypt. He was bribed to sit on lorries whilst wearing military uniform so that alcohol could be illegally transported without being stopped by the police. The defendant was convicted of a crime. Most of the bribes which he had received were seized by the Crown and he sought to recover them. His action failed because he had been acting in breach of his fiduciary duty and so he would have been liable to account for the bribes to the Crown.[57]

(2) The relationship of confidentiality

The fiduciary relationship of confidentiality will arise where information is imparted by the principal to a fiduciary in confidence.[58] Although such a relationship of confidentiality may arise when one person is employed by another, the relationship does not depend on employment. Consequently, this fiduciary relationship will continue even where the employee is no longer employed by the employer. This was recognised by the Court of Appeal in *Attorney-General* v. *Blake*[59] where the court, relying on an earlier decision of the House of Lords,[60] recognised that members of the Secret Intelligence Service such as Blake owe a life-long duty of confidence to the Crown. This means that if the fiduciary breaks the confidence he or she will be considered to have breached a fiduciary duty.

The essential obligation arising from the relationship of confidentiality is that the fiduciary must maintain the confidentiality of the information which he or she possesses. But this obligation lasts only as long as the information itself remains confidential. This was recognised by the Court of Appeal in *Blake*. Since the information which Blake had published in his autobiography was no longer confidential, it followed that he had not breached his fiduciary duty of confidence by disclosing this information.

---

[56] [1951] AC 507. See also *Attorney-General* v. *Goddard* (1929) 98 LJKB 743.
[57] The controversial question of the nature of the remedy which should be awarded where the fiduciary has received a bribe is examined at pp. 540–4 below.
[58] *Attorney-General* v. *Blake* [1998] 2 WLR 805, 815.   [59] *Ibid.*
[60] *Attorney-General* v. *Guardian Newspapers Ltd. (No. 3)* [1990] 1 AC 109.

Liability for abusing a fiduciary relationship of confidentiality is different from liability for the action for breach of confidence,[61] as was recognised by the Court of Appeal in *Blake*.[62] The crucial distinction between these two forms of liability is that the former depends on there being a relationship between the parties which can be characterised as fiduciary in nature, whereas the action for breach of confidence simply depends on the defendant having confidential information in circumstances in which there was a duty to protect the confidentiality. Also, whereas liability for abusing a fiduciary relationship of confidence is strict,[63] liability in the action for breach of confidence depends on the defendant being at fault in some way.[64]

(3) The relationship of influence

Another type of fiduciary relationship is that of influence.[65] This will arise where the nature of the relationship between the parties is such that one party is utterly dependent on the other, so that the other party is in a position to exploit the former who is peculiarly vulnerable to the exploitation. Any relationship can potentially be characterised as one of influence.[66] Relationships which might particularly be characterised in this way include the relationship of solicitor and client,[67] trustee and beneficiary and agent and principal.

This type of fiduciary relationship is illustrated by *Tate* v. *Williamson*[68] where the deceased, who was in financial difficulties having 'contracted habits of extravagance at University',[69] sought the advice and assistance of his great-uncle, who deputed his nephew, the defendant, to help the deceased. The deceased offered to sell his reversionary interest to the defendant, who agreed to buy it for £7,000. Before the agreement for purchase was signed the defendant received notification that the interest was valued at £20,000, but he did not disclose this information to the deceased. It was held that the relationship between the parties was such that the defendant was under a duty to communicate to the deceased all the information he had which related to the value of the property. The defendant's failure to inform the deceased of the valuation meant that the transaction was set aside. The relationship between the parties was characterised as fiduciary, because the defendant had placed himself in

---

[61] See p. 545 below.   [62] [1998] 2 WLR 805, 814.

[63] See, for example, *Warman International Ltd.* v. *Dwyer* (1995) 128 ALR 201.

[64] See p. 546 below.

[65] This has sometimes been described as a relationship of confidence, but such a description fails to distinguish this relationship from the other two types of fiduciary relationship.

[66] *BCCI* v. *Aboody* [1990] QB 923, 964.   [67] See *Wright* v. *Carter* [1903] 1 Ch. 27.

[68] (1866) LR 2 Ch. App. 55.

[69] The deceased died, at the age of 24, from his addiction to drink.

such a position of influence by undertaking to arrange the deceased's debts that he was under fiduciary duties which prevented him from purchasing the deceased's property without making full disclosure. In a very important dictum Lord Chelmsford LC identified the essential features of this fiduciary relationship:

Wherever two persons stand in such a [fiduciary] relation that, while it continues, confidence is necessarily reposed by one, and the influence which necessarily grows out of that confidence is possessed by the other, and this confidence is abused, or the influence is exerted to obtain an advantage at the expense of the confiding party, the person so availing himself of his position will not be permitted to retain the advantage, although the transaction could not have been impeached if no such confidential relation had existed.[70]

Fiduciary relationships of influence should be defined restrictively and should be confined to those exceptional cases in which the relationship between the parties is such that the plaintiff can be regarded as being totally dependent on the defendant for advice. *Tate* v. *Williamson* was an example of such a case.

Where the principal enters into a transaction either with the fiduciary or a third party in circumstances in which the fiduciary might have influenced the principal to enter into the transaction, it is presumed that the fiduciary exploited the principal, and so the burden is on the party who wishes to enforce the transaction to show that it was fair.[71] This is illustrated by *Demerara Bauxite Co. Ltd.* v. *Hubbard*[72] where a solicitor purchased property from his former client, in circumstances in which the antecedent relationship of influence between the parties continued. Lord Parmoor identified the crucial feature of this type of fiduciary relationship:

in the absence of competent independent advice a transaction . . . between persons in the relationship of solicitor and client, or in a confidential relationship of a similar character, cannot be upheld, unless the person claiming to enforce the contract can prove, affirmatively, that the person standing in such a confidential position has disclosed, without reservation, all the information in his possession, and can further show that the transaction was, in itself, a fair one, having regard to all the circumstances.[73]

The transaction will be treated as valid, therefore, only where there has been full disclosure of everything which is or may be material to the principal's decision to enter into the transaction and where the other party can show that the transaction itself was fair, particularly that the transaction was not at an undervalue.[74] Since the determination of whether the transaction was fair requires consideration of all the circumstances

---

[70] (1866) LR 2 Ch. App. 55, 61.   [71] *Moody* v. *Cox and Hatt* [1917] 2 Ch. 71.
[72] [1923] AC 673.   [73] *Ibid*, p. 681.   [74] *Wright* v. *Carter* [1903] 1 Ch. 27.

of the case, it follows that the question of fairness depends on whether the transaction was substantively fair, namely that the terms were fair; and procedurally fair, namely that the means which were used to induce the principal to enter into the transaction were fair. Consequently, whether the principal was advised to obtain independent and competent advice will be a particularly important consideration in determining whether the transaction was fair.

There is an obvious similarity between liability for undue influence and liability for abusing a fiduciary relationship of influence, since in both cases the defendant's liability is founded on the actual or potential exploitation of the plaintiff. But the boundary between the two forms of liability is uncertain,[75] particularly because where there is a relationship of influence there will also be the potential for undue influence. It has, however, been recognised that whilst the two forms of liability overlap, they do not coincide.[76] The crucial distinction between the two forms of liability is that a fiduciary relationship of influence will only be recognised where the principal is utterly dependent on the fiduciary.

It follows from the fact that, although liability for breach of a fiduciary relationship of influence is more restrictive than liability for undue influence, where the relevant fiduciary relationship can be identified, the plaintiff who seeks restitution has two options open to him or her. First, the plaintiff could bring a restitutionary claim founded on the reversal of the defendant's unjust enrichment, with the ground of restitution being the actual or presumed undue influence.[77] Alternatively, the plaintiff could bring a restitutionary claim against the fiduciary founded on the breach of fiduciary duty. Although the plaintiff has a choice which restitutionary route to adopt, a claim founded on abuse of a relationship of influence does have certain advantages over the doctrine of undue influence.

First, unlike the doctrine of actual undue influence, it is not necessary to show that the principal was actually influenced by the fiduciary to enter into the relevant transaction. It is sufficient that the relationship between the parties was such that the fiduciary could have influenced the principal.

Secondly, unlike the doctrine of presumed undue influence, it is not necessary for the principal to show that the transaction was manifestly disadvantageous to the plaintiff. Once the relationship of influence has been identified, manifest disadvantage is assumed and the burden is on the defendant to show that the transaction was not unfair to the

---

[75] *CICB Mortgages plc.* v. *Pitt* [1994] 1 AC 200, 209 (Lord Browne-Wilkinson).

[76] See *Moody* v. *Cox and Hatt* [1917] 2 Ch. 71, 79 (Lord Cozens-Hardy MR) and *BCCI* v. *Aboody* [1990] QB 923, 962.

[77] See pp. 253–65 above.

plaintiff. The heavy burden of proving that the transaction is fair is shifted where there is a relationship of influence simply because of the potential for abuse of such relationships by the fiduciary.[78]

(iv) The nature of the restitutionary remedies which are available for breach of fiduciary duty[79]

(1) Account of profits

The orthodox approach to the award of restitutionary remedies for breach of fiduciary duty is to require the defendant to account to the plaintiff for the profits which he or she obtained as a result of the breach.[80] Normally an account of profits will simply be a personal remedy, with the defendant being required to disgorge the value of the profits obtained from the breach of duty.

The problem with ordering that an account of profits be taken relates to the determination of which profits derive from the breach of fiduciary duty itself. Three mechanisms have been identified which can assist in the assessment of the profits for which the defendant should account to the plaintiff.

(a) Shifting the burden of proof

In the important decision of *Warman International Ltd.* v. *Dwyer*[81] the High Court of Australia recognised that where the defendant had profited from his or her breach of fiduciary duty the defendant must account for all the profits arising from the breach, the burden being placed on the defendant to show that it is inequitable to account for the whole of the profits. Essentially this means that the defendant must show that the profits were too remote from the commission of the breach of fiduciary duty. This shift in the burden of proof is presumably justified by the stringent policy that fiduciaries should not profit in any way from their breach of duty. Consequently, it is presumed that all profits were derived from the breach, and it is for the defendant to show that this was not the case.

(b) Limiting the period for which the account must be taken

Where the nature of the breach of fiduciary duty is that the defendant earns a profit over a period of time, and is still earning the profit at the time of the trial, a difficult question arises whether the defendant is

---

[78] *BCCI* v. *Aboody* [1990] QB 923, 963, and *CICB Mortgages plc.* v. *Pitt* [1994] 1 AC 200, 209 (Lord Browne-Wilkinson). See p. 284 above.
[79] It is now possible to award equitable compensation for breach of fiduciary duty: *Swindle* v. *Harrison* [1997] 4 All ER 705.
[80] *Nocton* v. *Lord Ashburton* [1914] AC 932, 956–7 (Viscount Haldane LC).
[81] (1995) 128 ALR 201, 212.

required to account for all of the profits which have been made and also those which may be made in the future. This was a matter which was examined in *Warman* v. *Dwyer* where the High Court of Australia recognised that, where it is equitable to do so, the defendant may be required to account only for the profits generated over a specified period of time. This was the type of account which was ordered in *Warman* v. *Dwyer* itself, where the defendant was required to account only for those profits which the plaintiff would have made over a limited period of time had the defendant not breached the fiduciary duty.[82]

(c) The equitable allowance

Alternatively, the defendant fiduciary may be awarded an equitable allowance in respect of those profits which were earned by virtue of the defendant's own efforts, and this sum will be deducted from the amount for which the defendant has to account to the plaintiff.[83] This allowance will be awarded only where it is equitable to do so. Although the award of the equitable allowance to a fiduciary who has breached his or her fiduciary duty was recognised by the House of Lords in *Boardman* v. *Phipps*,[84] a subsequent decision of the same court, *Guinness plc.* v. *Saunders*[85] casts doubt on the legitimacy of the award of an allowance to the fiduciary in such circumstances. In *Guinness plc.* v. *Saunders* the sum of £5.2 million had been paid to a director of Guinness for the advice and services he had given in respect of the take-over of another company by Guinness. It was accepted that this money had been received by the director in breach of his fiduciary duty, and consequently he was liable to repay it to Guinness. But the director argued that he was entitled to an equitable allowance for the services which he had supplied to the company. The House of Lords rejected this claim on two grounds: first, because equity had no power to grant an allowance to a director who had breached his or her fiduciary duty if the articles made no provision for such a payment.[86] The reason for this is that the court is reluctant to interfere with the affairs of the company. Consequently, the decision to award an allowance should be a matter for the company and not for the court. Secondly, because of the fundamental principle that trustees are not entitled to be remunerated for their services except where such remuneration is provided for in the trust deed, it was considered to follow that a fiduciary should not be awarded an equitable allowance save

---

[82] The High Court also suggested that the profits may be split between the plaintiff and the defendant but that this would normally be appropriate only where there was an antecedent profit sharing arrangement: *ibid.* In the context of breach of fiduciary duty it is highly unlikely that such an arrangement would have been made.

[83] See *Boardman* v. *Phipps* [1967] 2 AC 46 and *Warman International Ltd.* v. *Dwyer* (1995) 128 ALR 201, 212.

[84] *Ibid.*   [85] [1990] 2 AC 663.   [86] *Ibid*, p. 692 (Lord Templeman).

in the most exceptional circumstances, where the award of such an allowance would not encourage the fiduciary to put him- or herself in a position in which his or her personal interest conflicted with the duty which was owed to the principal.[87] Since the nature of the director's breach of duty was to place him in a position in which his personal interest conflicted with his duty to the company it followed that the equitable allowance was denied to him. But neither of these reasons is convincing. First, why should the allowance be unavailable where the fiduciary is a director? If the defendant has incurred expense and provided services, particularly where the expense and services have benefited the plaintiff company, why should this not be taken into account when determining the extent of the defendant's liability to the plaintiff? Secondly, the award of the equitable allowance should not be considered as encouraging the fiduciary to place him- or herself in a position in which personal interest and duty to the principal conflict. This is because the equitable allowance does not enable the fiduciary to profit from his or her breach of duty; rather it should simply ensure that the fiduciary is remunerated for expense incurred and services provided. There can surely be no objection to a fiduciary being remunerated, since this would not encourage the fiduciary to breach his or her fiduciary duty. It has in fact been recognised that there is nothing wrong with the court granting an allowance to remunerate a fiduciary for services provided to the principal.[88] The real objection arises where the fiduciary is allowed to profit from the breach of duty.[89]

The major difficulty with the award of an equitable allowance to a fiduciary arises from the uncertainty about the reason for awarding the allowance. In fact, two justifications can be identified.

First, it might be possible to conclude that the award of an equitable allowance constitutes a mechanism for ensuring that the principal is not unjustly enriched at the fiduciary's expense. This unjust enrichment may arise because, if the effect of the fiduciary's time and money is that the principal obtains a benefit, the principal will have been enriched at the fiduciary's expense. But it will also be necessary to identify a ground of restitution. The best explanation is that restitution would be founded on the principle of failure of consideration. In the typical case the fiduciary would expect to be remunerated for the services which he or she provides by the profit which he or she obtains from the breach of duty. But if the fiduciary is required to disgorge all of these profits to the principal

---

[87] [1990] 2 AC 663, 701 (Lord Goff).

[88] *Dale* v. *IRC* [1954] AC 11, 27 (Lord Normand). See Harpum in *Privacy and Loyalty* (ed. Birks) p. 159.

[89] But note *O'Sullivan* v. *Management Agency and Music Ltd.* [1985] QB 428 where the Court of Appeal contemplated that the allowance might include a profit element.

there will be a total failure of consideration and so restitutionary relief should be awarded. Although this analysis of the equitable allowance can be used to explain why the allowance was awarded in certain cases in which the principal was benefited by what the fiduciary had done,[90] this explanation has never been recognised and, crucially, the nature of the allowance which is awarded does not appear to be assessed by reference to the value of the benefit obtained by the principal. Rather, the allowance seeks only to remunerate the fiduciary for his or her work and skill.[91] Also this explanation of the equitable allowance is inapplicable in any case in which the principal has not obtained a benefit from the fiduciary simply because the principal will not have been enriched at the fiduciary's expense.

The alternative, and preferable, explanation of the equitable allowance is that, where the fiduciary has made a profit as a result of the exercise of his or her time and skill, it is not possible to say that all of the fiduciary's profits derived from the commission of the wrong. Since the fiduciary is required to disgorge only those profits which did arise from the wrongdoing, it follows that the equitable allowance seeks to apportion profits so that the principal recovers only those profits which derive from the breach of fiduciary duty and the fiduciary is allowed to retain those profits which can be considered to derive from his or her work and skill. It will, of course, be very difficult to apportion the profits exactly, but at least the existence of the allowance gives the court the opportunity to determine in general terms how much of the profits derived from the fiduciary's input, so that the fiduciary is not required to disgorge these profits to the principal because they did not derive from the commission of the wrong. This explanation of the award of the allowance was expressly recognised by the High Court of Australia in *Warman International Ltd.* v. *Dwyer*[92] where the court emphasised that:

[W]hen it appears that a significant proportion of an increase in profits has been generated by the skill, efforts, property and resources of the fiduciary, the capital which he has introduced and the risks he has taken, so long as they are not risks to which the principal's property has been exposed. Then it may be said that the relevant proportion of the increased profits is not the product or consequence of the plaintiff's property but the product of the fiduciary's skill, efforts, property and resources.

---

[90] Most notably *Boardman* v. *Phipps* [1967] 2 AC 46. But if the equitable allowance does seek to ensure that the principal is not unjustly enriched it should also have been awarded in *Guinness plc.* v. *Saunders* [1990] 2 AC 663 where the principal had also been benefited by the defendant's services.

[91] See *Boardman* v. *Phipps* [1967] 2 AC 46, 102 (Lord Cohen) and 112 (Lord Hodson).

[92] (1995) 128 ALR 201, 212.

If the equitable allowance seeks to apportion the profits between those which derive from the breach and those deriving from the fiduciary's own input, it should follow that the fiduciary in *Guinness plc.* v. *Saunders* should have been awarded an allowance, because he had provided some valuable services for the remuneration which he had received. But the denial of the allowance in this case can be justified on another ground, although it was a ground which was not specifically recognised. Although the House of Lords assumed throughout that the director had been acting in good faith, there was clearly a suspicion of *mala fides*, since criminal charges had been brought as a result of the acquisition of the company by Guinness and an application had been made to extradite the director to the United States. If the House of Lords had been satisfied on the balance of probabilities that the director had been acting in bad faith then it would have been appropriate, in the exercise of the equitable jurisdiction, to decline to award an equitable allowance.

(d) Redefining remoteness

It has sometimes been argued[93] that it should follow from the policy that a wrongdoer should not be allowed to profit from his or her wrongdoing that a fiduciary who has committed certain breaches of fiduciary duty, most notably where he or she has received a bribe, should be liable to account to the principal for both the value of the bribe and any income obtained from it. In other words, the usual rule of remoteness, namely that wrongdoers should be liable to account only for benefits which arose directly from the wrongdoing, should be relaxed in the context of fiduciaries who have been bribed. Whether the remoteness rules should be redefined in such circumstances is essentially a question of policy as to how severely we should treat fiduciaries who accept bribes. Since such fiduciaries are clearly particularly culpable[94] there is some merit in the view that they should be liable to account for all the benefits which they obtained from their breach of duty, regardless of whether the benefits arose directly or indirectly. So, for example, in a case such as *Attorney-General for Hong Kong* v. *Reid*,[95] where the defendant fiduciary had obtained a bribe which he used to buy land, it might be concluded that the defendant should be liable to account for the value of the land to the principal since the land represents value which the defendant received indirectly as a result of committing the wrong. Such a solution has the advantage that the defendant is deprived of all benefits which arose from the commission of the wrong, but the principal is not given any propri-

---

[93] By Burrows, for example: see *The Law of Restitution*, p. 412.
[94] See *Attorney-General for Hong Kong* v. *Reid* [1994] 1 AC 324, 330 (Lord Templeman).
[95] *Ibid.*

etary interest in the profits so that he does not gain priority over the defendant's unsecured creditors if the defendant became insolvent.[96]

(2) Proprietary remedies following the recognition of a constructive trust

Whilst the personal restitutionary remedy of an account of profits is the usual remedy for a breach of fiduciary duty, in certain circumstances the courts will recognise that the profits were held by the fiduciary on constructive trust for the principal. It follows that the principal will have an equitable proprietary interest in the profits which he or she can vindicate by virtue of proprietary restitutionary remedies.[97] This has the advantage to the principal that he or she has priority over the fiduciary's unsecured creditors if the fiduciary becomes insolvent. Also the principal is entitled not just to the value of the profits obtained by the fiduciary but also the fruits of those profits. Whether the profits are held on constructive trust for the principal is therefore a vitally important, but also a highly controversial, matter. Two distinct approaches can be identified to determine when the profits of a breach of fiduciary duty are held on constructive trust.

(a) The narrow interpretation

According to the narrow, orthodox, view the profits of a breach of fiduciary duty are be held on constructive trust for the principal only where the defendant has made the profit by interfering with the plaintiff's proprietary rights. The recognition of a constructive trust in such circumstances is defensible because the profits made by the defendant can be considered to represent the fruits of the plaintiff's property. Consequently, it is entirely appropriate that the plaintiff should have an equitable proprietary interest in the profits.

In addition, it is justifiable that the defendant should hold property on constructive trust where the consequence of the defendant's breach of fiduciary duty is that the defendant obtains property which the principal would have obtained had the defendant not breached his or her duty. Goode has described the property which the defendant obtains in such circumstances as a 'deemed agency gain',[98] which should be held on constructive trust for the principal simply because the demands of the fiduciary relationship are such that it should be assumed that the defendant obtained the property for his or her principal rather than for him- or

---

[96] Cp. the decision of the Privy Council in *Reid* where it was recognised that the defendant held the land on constructive trust for the principal. See p. 541 below.

[97] See Chapter 21.

[98] See Goode, 'Property and Unjust Enrichment' in *Essays on the Law of Restitution* (ed. Burrows) p. 230.

herself. This is illustrated by *Keech* v. *Sandford*[99] where the defendant
trustee held a lease on trust for the beneficiary. When the time came to
renew the lease the landlord refused to renew it in favour of the trust but
was prepared to renew it in favour of the trustee personally. This was
held to constitute a breach of fiduciary duty, with the result that the
trustee held the lease on constructive trust for the beneficiary. This conclusion can be justified because the trustee had obtained property
which, because of practice at the time, the beneficiary expected would be
renewed as a matter of right.[100] Similarly, in *Cook* v. *Deeks*[101] the directors of the plaintiff company were negotiating a contract with a third
party on behalf of the company. Rather than signing the contract on
behalf of the company some of the directors signed it on behalf of themselves. It was held that the directors were liable for a breach of fiduciary
duty and held the profits they had made on constructive trust for the
company. Again this result can be justified because, had the defendants
not breached their duty, the company would have obtained the contract,
so the defendants' gain could be presumed to have been made on behalf
of the company.

(b) The wide interpretation

Recent cases have, however, suggested that whenever the defendant has
made a profit as a result of breaching his or her fiduciary duty those profits should be held on constructive trust for the plaintiff, even though the
fiduciary has not interfered with any of the plaintiff's proprietary rights.
It follows from this that the victim in all cases of breach of fiduciary duty
could bring a proprietary restitutionary claim against the fiduciary and a
third party who has received assets in which the principal has an equitable proprietary interest.

The battleground for the determination of whether a constructive trust
should be recognised in all cases of breach of fiduciary duty has been
those cases in which a fiduciary has received a bribe. In *Lister and Co.* v.
Stubbs[102] it was held that the defendant, a foreman who bought supplies
for the plaintiff and who had accepted bribes from one of the suppliers in
return for his placing orders with that supplier, was liable to account to
the plaintiff for the value of the bribe. The defendant had invested some
of the bribes in land, but it was held that the plaintiff did not have an
equitable proprietary interest in the land. It followed that the relation-

---

[99] (1726) Sel. Cas. Temp King 61; 25 ER 223.
[100] Oakley, 'The Liberalising Nature of Remedies for Breach of Trust' in *Trends in
Contemporary Trust Law* (ed. Oakley, Oxford: Clarendon Press, 1996) p. 235.
[101] [1916] 1 AC 554.
[102] (1890) 45 Ch.D 1. See also *Metropolitan Bank* v. *Heiron* (1880) LR 5 Ex. D 319;
Attorney-General's Reference (No. 1 of 1985) [1986] QB 491; and *Islamic Republic of Iran* v.
Denby [1987] 1 Lloyd's Rep. 367.

ship between the parties was not one of trustee and beneficiary but simply one of debtor and creditor.

However, in *Attorney-General for Hong Kong* v. *Reid*[103] the Privy Council recognised that where the defendant fiduciary received a bribe he or she held that bribe on constructive trust for the principal. The defendant fiduciary in this case held a number of public offices in Hong Kong, including that of Director of Public Prosecutions. He had accepted a number of bribes to induce him to frustrate the prosecution of a number of criminals. He purchased land with this money and the plaintiff claimed that it had an equitable proprietary interest in this land. The Privy Council agreed and ordered that the land was held by the defendant on constructive trust for the plaintiff. In reaching this conclusion the Privy Council specifically rejected *Lister* v. *Stubbs* for the following reason. Where a defendant receives a bribe in beach of his or her fiduciary duty it is clear that he or she is liable to account to the principal for the value of the bribe immediately it is received, simply because it is the receipt of the bribe which constitutes the breach of duty. There is consequently a personal liability to account to the principal. However, by virtue of the equitable maxim that equity looks on as done that which ought to be done, equity presumes that the fiduciary has accounted for the value of the bribe when it is received. It follows, therefore, that equity considers the principal to have an equitable proprietary interest in the bribe immediately it is received, with the result that the defendant holds the bribe on constructive trust for the principal. The plaintiff in *Reid* was able to vindicate its equitable proprietary interest in the bribe against the land which the defendant had bought because the plaintiff could trace its proprietary interest into the land.

The decision of the Privy Council in *Attorney-General of Hong Kong* v. *Reid* raises a number of questions.

(1) Does *Reid* represent English law? Being a decision of the Privy Council *Reid* is not binding on the English courts.[104] The decision was, however, approved by Sir Richard Scott V-C in *Attorney-General* v. *Blake*,[105] but he did not feel able to follow it because it was a decision of the Privy Council. The case was also recognised by Peter Gibson LJ in *Halifax Building Society* v. *Thomas*.[106] There are some earlier cases

---

[103] [1994] 1 AC 324.

[104] A principle which has recently been emphasised in the criminal law context concerning the definition of provocation where the decision of the Privy Council in *Luc Thiet Thuan* [1997] AC 131 has expressly not been followed by the Court of Appeal: *R.* v. *Campbell* [1997] 1 Cr.App.R 199, 207 (Lord Bingham CJ); *R.* v. *Parker* [1997] Crim. LR 759; and *R.* v. *Smith* [1998] 4 All ER 387.

[105] [1996] 3 All ER 903, 912. The Court of Appeal in *Blake* did not consider *Reid*: [1998] 2 WLR 805.

[106] [1996] Ch. 217, 229.

which appear to be consistent with the approach adopted in *Reid*. Most importantly, in *Boardman* v. *Phipps*[107] the trial judge appears to have held[108] that the shares which the defendants had purchased in breach of fiduciary duty should be held on constructive trust, and nothing was said by the Court of Appeal or the House of Lords to suggest that this was wrong.[109] This conclusion is not consistent with the narrow view of when a constructive trust should be recognised, since the defendants had not profited by interfering with the plaintiff's property and had not made a deemed agency gain. Consequently, the House of Lords appears to have adopted the wider view.[110] But there are other cases in which the defendant's profit was obtained in breach of fiduciary duty without interfering with the principal's property or making a deemed agency gain where the defendant was simply required to account for the value of the profit made.[111]

Despite the virtually unanimous assumption of those who have commented on the decision of the Privy Council in *Reid* that it does represent English law, it clearly remains a matter of great uncertainty whether an English judge would necessarily follow *Reid*. As will be seen, the consequences of recognising that the principal has an equitable proprietary interest in the profits suggest that *Reid* should not be followed in English law.

(2) Is the application of *Reid* confined to restitutionary claims to bribes? If *Reid* is followed in English law, there is no reason to think that its application will be confined to where the fiduciary receives a bribe. Peter Gibson LJ in *Halifax Building Society* v. *Thomas*[112] recognised that the decision was applicable generally where the defendant breached a fiduciary duty. This must be correct. The essential justification for the conclusion that a bribe should be held on constructive trust for the principal is that this follows from the maxim that equity looks on as done

---

[107] [1967] 2 AC 46.

[108] See Crilley, 'A Case of Proprietary Overkill' (1994) 2 *RLR* 57, 61–2.

[109] Lord Guest specifically held that the defendants held the shares as constructive trustees and were liable to account to the plaintiffs: [1967] 2 AC 46, 117. But he also recognised that information was property, which would justify the recognition of a constructive trust. This was rejected by the majority.

[110] See Hayton, 'Developing the Law of Trusts for the 21st Century' (1990) 106 *LQR* 87, 101, who concludes that the reference to a 'constructive trust' simply meant that the defendants were personally liable to account for their profit. This interpretation is consistent with the narrow view of when a 'proprietary constructive trust' will be recognised, but it also emphasises the unacceptable ambiguity in the use of the phrase 'liable as a constructive trustee'. See Millett, 'Restitution and Constructive Trusts' (1998) 114 *LQR* 399, 400.

[111] See *Regal (Hastings) Ltd.* v. *Gulliver* [1967] 2 AC 134 n. and *Industrial Developments Consultants Ltd.* v. *Cooley* [1972] 1 WLR 443.

[112] [1996] Ch. 217, 229. See also *Attorney-General* v. *Blake* [1996] 3 All ER 903, 912 (Sir Richard Scott V-C).

that which ought to be done. But this maxim appears to be applicable regardless of the fiduciary duty which was breached. For whenever the fiduciary obtains a profit in breach of fiduciary duty he or she is person-ally liable to account to the principal for that profit. It follows that, by virtue of the equitable maxim, equity will consider the principal to have an equitable proprietary interest in those profits.

(3) Should the profits of a breach of fiduciary duty be held on con-structive trust? The conclusion of the Privy Council that the defendant held the bribe on constructive trust for the principal is highly dubious. The conclusion of the court is clearly inconsistent with the narrow view of the constructive trust, since the defendant had not interfered with property which already belonged to the principal. The only way that the court could justify its conclusion was by applying the equitable maxim that equity treats as done that which ought to be done and it was only by deeming the bribe to have been paid to the principal that the court fash-ioned an equitable proprietary interest. But why should the equitable maxim be applied in this way? As Crilley has recognised:

In *Reid*, the maxim that equity regards as done that which ought to be done was applied. This 'technique' transformed Reid from a debtor into a constructive trustee. Yet, unless there was already in existence a specifically enforceable oblig-ation to transfer the actual money he received, there is nothing on which the maxim can bite.[113]

So the crucial question is whether there is a specifically enforceable obligation to transfer the bribe to the defendant. The defendant never had an interest in the bribe since it was received from a third party, so it is difficult to see how such an obligation can be identified. It follows that the finding of a constructive trust depends on a fiction, namely that equity regards as done that which ought to be done. It is no longer suffi-cient to rely on the ritual recantation of a maxim to justify a result; we must look behind the maxim and find reasons why the recognition of a constructive trust is appropriate. There is no obvious reason of policy or principle why an equitable proprietary interest should be recognised.[114]

A further objection to the result in *Reid* is that, by recognising that the principal has a proprietary interest in the bribe, it follows that he or she gains priority over the fiduciary's unsecured creditors if the fiduciary becomes insolvent. Is this justifiable? Lord Templeman sought to justify this result by arguing that the unsecured creditors of the fiduciary should not be placed in any better position than the fiduciary.[115] But this is a

---

[113] 'A Case of Proprietary Overkill' (1994) 2 *RLR* 57, 65–6.
[114] See Goode in *Essays on the Law of Restitution* (ed. Burrows), chapter 9, and Cowan, Edmunds and Lowry, 'Lister and Co. v. Stubbs: Who Profits?' [1996] *JBL* 22.
[115] [1994] 1 AC 324, 331.

highly dubious statement,[116] particularly because it means that unsecured creditors who have given value, and so will suffer loss if they are not paid, are in a weaker position than the principal, who has not given value for the bribe and so will not have suffered any loss.[117]

Consequently, there is no reason that the defendant should be given such proprietary protection. It is sufficient that the fiduciary is liable to account to the principal for the value of the bribe received. If the fiduciary becomes bankrupt the principal should be treated simply as an unsecured creditor. It follows that, regardless of the nature of the breach of fiduciary duty, there is no reason why the principal should obtain priority over the fiduciary's unsecured creditors, save where it is clear that the profit made by the fiduciary was made from the use of the principal's property.

The real advantage of the decision of the Privy Council in *Reid* is that it ensures that the fiduciary who has profited from the breach of fiduciary duty is not allowed to retain any part of that profit. The result is therefore consistent with the fundamental principle underlying the law of restitution for wrongs, namely that wrongdoers should not be allowed to profit from the commission of the wrong.[118] But this result can be achieved in another way without recognising that the principal has a proprietary interest in the profits. All that needs to be done is to reinterpret the remoteness of gains principle so that all fiduciaries who have breached their duty are liable to account for all profits which arose from the breach of duty, regardless of whether the profit arose directly or indirectly.[119] Such a result would be consistent with the clear policy of deterring fiduciaries from being tempted to breach their duty. The threat that the fiduciary would not be allowed to retain any profit obtained from the breach, save where an equitable allowance could be awarded, would have an important deterrent effect. It would not follow that the profits deriving from the breach of duty should never be held on constructive trust, since the narrow interpretation of that trust would be retained, namely that the principal should be recognised as having an equitable proprietary interest in the fiduciary's profits if the profits derived from interference with the principal's property or can be considered to be a deemed agency gain.

---

[116] See Crilley, 'A Case of Proprietary Overkill' (1994) 2 *RLR* 57, 69.

[117] Rotherham, 'The Recovery of the Profits of Wrongdoing and Insolvency: When is Proprietary Relief Justified?' [1997] 1 *CFILR* 43, 47. See also Goode in *Essays on the Law of Restitution* (ed. Burrows) p. 224.

[118] Crilley, 'A Case of Proprietary Overkill' (1994) 2 *RLR* 57.

[119] See p. 538 above.

(b) Breach of confidence

Breach of confidence is treated as an equitable wrong rather than a tort.[120] This type of equitable wrongdoing will arise whenever the defendant is in a confidential relationship with the plaintiff and breaches that confidence by disclosing confidential information. Where the plaintiff alleges that the defendant has broken this confidence the plaintiff will bring an action for breach of confidence, the remedy for which may be restitutionary. Holding the defendant liable for breaking a confidence is justified as a means of maintaining the integrity of relationships of confidence.[121] This was recognised by Lord Keith in *Attorney-General* v. *Guardian Newspapers Ltd. (No. 2)*:[122]

[As] a general rule, it is in the public interest that confidence should be respected, and the encouragement of such respect may in itself constitute a sufficient ground for recognising and enforcing the obligation of confidence even where the confider can point to no specific detriment to himself.

A careful distinction needs to be drawn between liability for abusing a fiduciary relationship of confidence[123] and the action for breach of confidence. If a fiduciary breaches the confidence his or her liability will be strict.[124] Where, however, the defendant owes a duty of confidence but is not a fiduciary, liability will be founded on the action for breach of confidence and the defendant must be shown to be at fault in some way.[125]

(i) The identification of the duty of confidence[126]

A duty of confidence may be imposed expressly or impliedly by contract.[127] So, for example, where the defendant is an employee or agent of the plaintiff he or she may be under a contractual duty not to use confidential information obtained from the plaintiff without the plaintiff's consent. In such cases liability for breach of confidence will be founded on an action for breach of contract. Alternatively, and of primary interest in this chapter, a duty of confidence may arise in equity. In *Coco* v. *A.N.*

---

[120] *Attorney-General* v. *Guardian Newspapers (No. 2)* [1990] 1 AC 109, 281 (Lord Goff). Despite this there is a clear analogy between liability for breach of confidence and tortious liability, particularly the tort of interference with intellectual property rights. But this is only an analogy, since breach of confidence does not involve any interference with property rights, as confidential information is not property. Note that the Law Commission has recommended the enactment of a statutory tort of breach of confidence: 'Breach of Confidence' (Law Com. No. 110, 1981).

[121] See Jackman, 'Restitution for Wrongs' (1989) 48 *CLJ* 302, 315.

[122] [1990] 1 AC 109, 256.   [123] See p. 530 above.

[124] See, for example, *Warman International Ltd.* v. *Dwyer* (1995) 128 ALR 201.

[125] See p. 546 below.

[126] See Gurry, *Breach of Confidence* (Oxford: Clarendon Press, 1984) Part IV, and Jones, 'Restitution of Benefits Obtained in Breach of Another's Confidence' (1970) 86 *LQR* 463.

[127] See *Faccenda Chicken* v. *Fowler* [1987] Ch. 117.

Clark (Engineers) Ltd.[128] Megarry J identified the three prerequisites for the action for breach of confidence:

(1) The defendant must have received information which possessed the necessary quality of confidence.

(2) This information must have been imparted in circumstances which imported an obligation of confidence. There is no comprehensive definition of when the defendant will owe a duty of confidence to the plaintiff, but it is clear that such a duty may arise in a wide variety of circumstances. So, for example, a duty of confidence may relate to trade secrets,[129] national security[130] and even personal confidences.[131] Essentially, a duty of confidence will arise where there was a relationship of trust between the plaintiff and the defendant, such as the relationship between doctor and patient, or where the defendant obtained information directly or indirectly from the confider which the defendant then or subsequently knew or believed to be confidential.[132]

(3) The defendant must have made unauthorised use of this information to the detriment of the plaintiff. Unauthorised use may take the form of the defendant disclosing the information or using it to obtain a benefit. The defendant either must have deliberately breached his or her duty of confidence or should have realised that he or she was breaching the duty of confidence.[133] Obviously the duty cannot be breached once the information has ceased to be secret and confidential.[134] Even if the defendant has disclosed confidential information he or she may be able to rely on a defence, such as disclosure being in the public interest.[135]

(ii) Restitutionary remedies for breach of confidence

Restitutionary remedies for breach of confidence take two forms, namely an account of profits and restitutionary damages. But, whilst restitutionary remedies are common for this type of action, they are not the only remedies available. Sometimes compensatory damages may be awarded for breach of the equitable duty of confidence,[136] as may an injunction to

---

[128] [1969] RPC 41, 47. These conditions were affirmed by the Court of Appeal in *Murray* v. *Yorkshire Fund Managers Ltd.* [1998] 1 WLR 951.

[129] *Saltman Engineering Co. Ltd.* v. *Campbell Engineering Co. Ltd.* (1948) 65 RPC 203.

[130] *Attorney-General* v. *Guardian Newspapers Ltd. (No. 2)* [1990] AC 109.

[131] *Argyll* v. *Argyll* [1967] 1 Ch. 302.

[132] See Capper, 'Damages for Breach of the Equitable Duty of Confidence' (1994) 14 *LS* 313.

[133] *Coco* v. *A.N. Clark (Engineers) Ltd.* [1969] RPC 41, 47.

[134] See *Attorney-General* v. *Blake* [1998] 2 WLR 805.

[135] *Hellewell* v. *Chief Constable of Derbyshire* [1995] 4 All ER 473.

[136] *Dowson and Mason Ltd.* v. *Potter* [1986] 2 All ER 418. See Capper 'Damages for Breach of the Equitable Duty of Confidence' (1994) 14 *LS* 313, 330. See also the decision of the New

stop a confidential relationship from being abused and also damages in lieu of an injunction.[137]

(1) Account of profits

Where the defendant has made a profit from the breach of confidence he or she may be liable to account for this profit to the plaintiff. Such a remedy is more likely to be available where the defendant has knowingly breached the confidence. This is illustrated by *Peter Pan Manufacturing Corporation* v. *Corsets Silhouette Ltd.*[138] where the defendant had manufactured and sold bras knowingly using confidential information which it had obtained from the plaintiff. The defendant was held liable to account to the plaintiff for the profits which it had made as a result of breaking the confidence.

(2) Restitutionary damages

Where the defendant has innocently used confidential information it seems that, rather than being liable to account to the plaintiff for the profit obtained as a result of the breach of confidence, the restitutionary remedy will take the form of damages assessed by reference to what the defendant saved in not paying the plaintiff for the use of the information. This is illustrated by *Seager* v. *Copydex Ltd. (No. 2)*[139] where the defendant inadvertently used confidential information in manufacturing a carpet-grip. The basis for assessing the damages was held to depend on the nature of the information which was confidential. If the information which the defendant had used was of a type which could be provided by any competent consultant, it was held that damages should be assessed by reference to the fee which the defendant saved by not employing such a consultant. Such damages can easily be characterised as restitutionary, since they are assessed by reference to the gain made by the defendant, namely what he or she had saved in not paying a consultant. Alternatively, if the information can be characterised as special, in that it could not have been obtained by employing a consultant, the damages should be assessed by reference to the market price for the information. To determine the market price it is necessary to consider what a willing purchaser would have paid a willing seller for the information. This method of assessing the damages can be characterised either as compensatory, by reference to what the plaintiff lost in being unable to sell

Zealand Court of Appeal in *Aquaculture Corporation* v. *New Zealand Green Mussel Co. Ltd.* [1990] 3 NZLR 299.

[137] *Attorney-General* v. *Guardian Newspapers Ltd. (No. 2)* [1990] AC 109, 286 (Lord Goff). See *Saltman Engineering Co. Ltd.* v. *Campbell Engineering Co. Ltd.* (1948) 65 RPC 203.

[138] [1963] 3 All ER 402. See also *Attorney-General* v. *Guardian Newspapers Ltd. (No. 2)* [1990] 1 AC 109.

[139] [1969] 1 WLR 809.

the information to the defendant,[140] or restitutionary, by reference to what the defendant saved in not having to pay the plaintiff for the information. Since it does not need to be shown that the plaintiff would have been prepared to sell the information to the defendant the better view is that such damages are restitutionary.[141]

(3) Proprietary remedies following the recognition of a constructive trust

It seems obvious that where the defendant makes a profit by use of confidential information the profit should not be held on constructive trust for the plaintiff because there is no reason why the plaintiff should be considered to have an equitable proprietary interest in the profits. This is essentially because confidential information cannot be considered to be property,[142] so the defendant has not made a profit by interfering with the plaintiff's property.[143] Even if the approach of the Privy Council in *Attorney-General of Hong Kong* v. *Reid*[144] is correct, whereby a fiduciary holds the profits of a breach of fiduciary duty on constructive trust for the principal, it does not follow that the defendant in an action for breach of confidence necessarily holds the profits arising from the breach on constructive trust for the plaintiff. This is because the principle in *Reid* applies only where the defendant is liable to account to the plaintiff for profits and only when the liability to account arises at the point when the defendant receives the profits. This is not the case where the defendant obtains profits in breach of confidence, simply because the defendant will not automatically be liable to account for the profits. Rather, whether the defendant is liable to account depends on the exercise of the court's discretion, having examined all the circumstances of the case, particularly the culpability of the defendant. There is, therefore, no scope for the operation of the equitable maxim that equity treats as done that which ought to be done.[145]

---

[140] This is how this method of assessment was characterised in *Dowson and Mason Ltd.* v. *Potter* [1986] 2 All ER 418. In the first decision of the Court of Appeal in *Seager* v. *Copydex* [1967] 2 All ER 415, it was held that the appropriate remedy was compensatory damages. The question in the second case related to how these damages should be assessed.

[141] See p. 458 above.

[142] *Boardman* v. *Phipps* [1967] 2 AC 46. Cp. *Prince Albert* v. *Strange* (1849) 2 De G and Sm. 652; 64 ER 293 (Knight Bruce V-C).

[143] But it follows that if the defendant obtains an asset in breach of the duty of confidence that asset may be held on constructive trust for the plaintiff. See Lord Goff in *Attorney-General* v. *Guardian Newspapers Ltd. (No. 2)* [1990] 1 AC 109 who suggested that the copyright over the confidential information obtained by the defendant should be held on constructive trust for the plaintiff.

[144] [1994] 1 AC 324. See p. 541 above.

[145] In *Halifax Building Society* v. *Thomas* [1996] Ch. 217, 229, Peter Gibson LJ recognised that the decision of the Privy Council in *Reid* applied only where the defendant had breached a fiduciary duty.

However, in *LAC Minerals Ltd.* v. *International Corona Resources Ltd.*[146] the Supreme Court of Canada held that a constructive trust would be imposed as a remedy for a breach of confidence, so that the plaintiff had a proprietary interest in the defendant's profits. But the imposition of a constructive trust in such circumstances is explicable simply by the fact that this was a decision of a Canadian court, where the notion of a remedial constructive trust has been recognised. In this country, the constructive trust is properly considered to be a substantive institution rather than a remedy, so that it will only be invoked where the plaintiff has an equitable proprietary interest in property held by the defendant by operation of law, and there is no reason of law why such a proprietary interest should be recognised in the profits made as a result of breach of confidence.

(c) Unconscionability

Another type of equitable wrongdoing arises where the defendant's conduct can be characterised as unconscionable. Where the defendant has acted unconscionably the courts may be prepared to award restitutionary remedies to the plaintiff. Such a jurisdiction is particularly well developed in the Antipodes and Canada, but there is some evidence for its recognition in this country as well. The problem with this type of wrongdoing arises from its inherent uncertainty. Nevertheless, certain specific types of equitable liability can be identified which are founded on the fact that the defendant has acted unconscionably. The most important example of such liability is equitable estoppel.

(i) Equitable estoppel

Although the orthodox attitude of English law is that estoppel can operate only as a shield and not as a sword, meaning that the plaintiff can rely on the estoppel only to prevent the defendant from pleading a defence and not to found a cause of action,[147] there is an exceptional type which can be relied on to found a cause of action.[148] This form of estoppel has variously been called proprietary estoppel, estoppel by acquiescence and estoppel by encouragement, though it appears that these terms are simply describing the same principle.[149] Although the expression

---

[146] (1989) 61 DLR (4th) 14.

[147] Cp the doctrine of promissory estoppel: *Central London Property Trust* v. *High Trees House* [1947] KB 130.

[148] See *Attorney-General of Hong Kong* v. *Humphreys Estate (Queen's Garden) Ltd.* [1987] AC 114, 127 (Lord Templeman) and *Salvation Army Trustee Co. Ltd.* v. *West Yorkshire Metropolitan County Council* (1980) 41 P and CR 179. That estoppel may operate as a cause of action has also been recognised by the High Court of Australia in *Walton Stores (Interstate) Ltd.* v. *Maher* (1988) 164 CLR 387.

[149] *Crabb* v. *Arun District Council* [1976] Ch. 179, 194 (Scarman LJ).

'proprietary estoppel' is most often used to describe this form of estoppel, this is in fact misleading, since the estoppel is not confined to claims to property. Consequently, the expression 'equitable estoppel' is a preferable term.

Liability for this form of estoppel will arise where the defendant has made a representation on which the plaintiff relies to his or her detriment. In such circumstances the defendant will be bound by his or her representation because, where the plaintiff has acted to his or her detriment in reliance on it, 'it would be unconscionable and unjust to allow the defendants to set up their undoubted rights against the claim being made by the plaintiff'.[150] The function of equitable estoppel is illustrated by the following example of Lord Kingsdown in *Ramsden* v. *Dyson*:[151]

> If a man under a verbal agreement with a landlord for a certain interest in land, or, what amounts to the same thing, under an expectation, created or encouraged by the landlord, that he shall have a certain interest, takes possession of such land, with the consent of the landlord, and upon the faith of such promise or expectation, with the knowledge of the landlord and without obligation by him, lays out money upon the land, a court of equity will compel the landlord to give effect to such promise or expectation.[152]

Since this form of liability is founded on the unconscionable nature of the defendant's conduct,[153] it follows that equitable estoppel is properly characterised as constituting a form of equitable wrongdoing. The remedy which is available may take a variety of forms, including damages to compensate the plaintiff for loss suffered, but exceptionally restitutionary remedies may be available.

(1) Establishing the estoppel

To establish liability for equitable estoppel a number of conditions need to be satisfied. The defendant must have created or encouraged a belief or expectation on the part of the plaintiff that he or she would receive some benefit, and the plaintiff must have relied on this to his or her detriment and to the knowledge of the defendant.[154] Sometimes it has been recognised that, rather than the defendant encouraging the plaintiff's mistaken expectation, it is sufficient that the defendant has acquiesced

---

[150] *Crabb* v. *Arun District Council* [1976] Ch. 179, 194 (Scarman LJ). See also *Ward* v. *Kirkland* [1967] Ch. 194, 235 (Ungoed-Thomas J); *Holiday Inns Inc.* v. *Broadhead* [1974] 232 EG 951, 1087 (Robert Goff J); *Taylor Fashions Ltd.* v. *Liverpool Victoria Trustees Co. Ltd.* [1982] QB 133, 151 (Oliver J); and *Gillett* v. *Holt* [1998] 3 All ER 917, 928 (Carnwath J).

[151] (1866) LR 1 HL 129, 170.

[152] See also *Inwards* v. *Baker* [1965] 2 QB 29, 36–7 (Lord Denning MR), 38 (Danckwerts LJ).

[153] Halliwell, 'Estoppel: Unconscionability as a Cause of Action' (1994) 14 *LS* 15.

[154] *Gillett* v. *Holt* [1998] 3 All ER 917, 929 (Carnwath J).

in this mistake.[155] Finally, the defendant must have done something or refrained from doing something which prevented the plaintiff's expectation from being fulfilled.[156]

(2) Identifying the appropriate relief

Once liability for equitable estoppel has been established the court will determine what is the minimum equity to do justice to the plaintiff. The range of remedial relief for equitable estoppel was identified by Brennan J in *Waltons Stores (Interstate) Ltd.* v. *Maher*:[157]

Sometimes it is necessary to decree that a party's expectations be specifically fulfilled by the party bound by the equity; sometimes it is necessary to grant an injunction to restrain the exercise of legal rights either absolutely or on condition; sometimes it is necessary to give an equitable lien on property for the expenditure which a party has made on it.

In identifying the minimum equity the court will consider all the circumstances of the case, but particularly the nature of the defendant's conduct[158] and the competing interests of the parties.[159] The relief must not be disproportionate to the plaintiff's detriment.[160]

Normally the relief which is awarded to satisfy the plaintiff's equity cannot be characterised as restitutionary, but the response is tailored simply to satisfy the plaintiff's expectations which were induced by the defendant.[161] For example, in *Dillwyn* v. *Llewelyn*[162] the defendant purported to give land to the plaintiff and approved of the plaintiff's construction of a building on the land. The gift was invalid and so the defendant remained owner of the land. But since the plaintiff had spent money constructing the building in reliance on his expectation of title, and the defendant knew this, it was considered to be unconscionable for the defendant not to satisfy the plaintiff's belief that he owned the land. Consequently, the defendant was required to transfer the land to the plaintiff. This was not a restitutionary remedy, since the remedy was not assessed by reference to the defendant's gain as a

---

[155] *Ramsden* v. *Dyson* (1866) LR 1. HL 129, 140–1 (Lord Cranworth).
[156] *Attorney-General of Hong Kong* v. *Humphreys Estate (Queen's Garden) Ltd.* [1987] 1 AC 114.
[157] (1988) 164 CLR 387, 419.
[158] *Pascoe* v. *Turner* [1979] 1 WLR 431, 436 (Cumming-Bruce LJ).
[159] See, for example, *Sledmore* v. *Dalby* (1996) 72 P and CR 196 where, having balanced the interest of the parties and considered the lapse of time since the original act which gave rise to the equity, it was held that there was no longer any estoppel operating against the defendant.
[160] (1996) 72 P & CR 196, 204 (Roch LJ).
[161] Cooke, 'Estoppel and the Protection of Expectations' (1997) 17 *LS* 258.
[162] (1862) 4 De GF and J 517; 45 ER 1285.

result of his wrongdoing, but it was a remedy which existed simply to fulfil the plaintiff's expectations.[163]

But exceptionally the relief which is awarded can be characterised as restitutionary. For example, in *Chalmers* v. *Pardoe*[164] the defendant, who had leased land from the Native Land Trust Board of Fiji, agreed that the plaintiff could build a house on part of the land. The defendant also agreed that he would ensure that the plaintiff became tenant of the land on which the house was built. The plaintiff consequently built the house, but the defendant declined to take the necessary steps to enable the plaintiff to become the tenant. The Privy Council would have been prepared to grant an equitable charge on the land for the benefit of the plaintiff but, because the prior consent of the Native Land Trust Board had not been obtained, the transaction was illegal. However, the Privy Council did say that, because it was against conscience that the defendant should retain the benefit of the building, he would be required to repay to the plaintiff the sums expended upon the construction of the house. Clearly, therefore, this remedy can be characterised as restitutionary since, rather than fulfilling the plaintiff's expectations, the remedy simply sought to restore the benefit which had been received by the defendant.

Birks properly treats cases such as this as falling within the law of restitution, but he also assumes that the nature of the claim is founded on the reversal of the defendant's unjust enrichment, with the ground of restitution being mistake.[165] But this is very difficult to justify, particularly because the remedy which is awarded in these cases need not be restitutionary. The preferable view is that in all of these cases the plaintiff's restitutionary claim is founded on the defendant's unconscionable conduct which is identified by the estoppel, and the relief which is awarded lies in the discretion of the court. As with all examples of restitution founded on wrongdoing, the restitutionary remedy is only one type of remedy which is open to the court.

(ii) Other forms of unconscionability

It was noted in Chapter 10 in the context of the principle of exploitation that the unconscionable nature of the defendant's conduct may constitute a ground of restitution within the action to reverse the defendant's

---

[163] See also *Inwards* v. *Baker* [1965] 2 QB 29; *Crabb* v. *Arun RDC* [1976] Ch. 179; *Salvation Army Trustee Company* v. *West Yorkshire Metropolitan County Council* (1981) 41 P & CR 179.

[164] [1963] 1 WLR 677. See also *The Unity Joint Stock Mutual Banking Association* v. *King* (1858) 25 Beav. 72; 53 ER 563 and *Lee-Parker* v. *Izzett (No. 2)* [1972] 1 WLR 775. *Hussey* v. *Palmer* [1972] 1 WLR 1286 is another case in which the relief can be characterised as restitutionary, since the plaintiff was content to recover her expenditure rather than to receive an interest in the property to which she had contributed.

[165] Birks, *An Introduction to the Law of Restitution*, pp. 290–3.

unjust enrichment.[166] If unconscionability is recognised in this country as a form of equitable wrongdoing of general application, as is increasingly being recognised in Australia in the form of the unconscionable bargain doctrine,[167] it follows that the plaintiff may have two types of restitutionary claim available to him or her. The first is founded on the reversal of the defendant's unjust enrichment, and the second on the principle of restitution for wrongs. There have been some recent indications that this more general form of equitable wrongdoing founded on the defendant's unconscionable conduct may indeed be recognised in this country.[168] This is a cause of concern, because of the inherent uncertainty of the notion of unconscionable conduct, unless some clear principles can be identified to assist in the determination of when the defendant's conduct can be treated as unconscionable.

(d) Dishonestly inducing or assisting in a breach of trust or fiduciary duty

Where the defendant has dishonestly assisted a trustee or fiduciary to breach his or her duty, or has induced such a breach of duty, the defendant will be liable to the plaintiff to whom the duty was owed.[169] The defendant's liability for dishonest assistance is a form of accessorial liability, since the defendant is a secondary party to the wrong committed by the trustee or fiduciary who breaches his or her duty. It follows that the accessory is tainted by this wrongdoing and so his or her liability is also a form of equitable wrongdoing.

(i) Establishing liability for dishonest assistance

To establish liability for dishonest assistance the following conditions must be met:

(1) There must have been a breach of trust or of fiduciary obligation, but this need not have been a dishonest and fraudulent breach on the part of the trustee or fiduciary.

(2) The defendant must either have procured the breach of trust or fiduciary obligation or assisted in the breach.

(3) The defendant must have been acting dishonestly. This was recognised by the Privy Council in *Royal Brunei Airlines* v. *Tan*.[170] Dishonesty is interpreted as an objective test, so the defendant is

---

[166] See pp. 286–97 above.

[167] See *Commercial Bank of Australia Ltd.* v. *Amadio* (1983) 151 CLR 447. See also *Garcia* v. *National Australia Bank Ltd.* (1998) 72 AJLR 1242. See pp. 277–8 above.

[168] See *Mahoney* v. *Purnell* [1996] 3 All ER 61, discussed at p. 282 above. See Rickett, 'Equitable Compensation: The Giant Stirs' (1996) 112 *LQR* 27, 30.

[169] *Royal Brunei Airlines Sdn. Bhd.* v. *Tan* [1995] 2 AC 378.   [170] *Ibid.*

considered to have acted dishonestly if he or she failed to act as an honest person would have acted in the circumstances.[171] Unfortunately, it is not yet certain that this case will be followed in England. In fact, in a case decided after *Tan*, the trial judge accepted that the defendant must have acted dishonestly before he or she could be liable as an accessory, but he added that the defendant must also know of the existence of the trust or the fiduciary duty.[172] There is consequently still some doubt about the degree of culpability which must be established before the defendant can be held liable as an accessory.

(ii) Determining the remedy which is awarded

Once the defendant has been found liable for dishonestly assisting or inducing a breach of trust or fiduciary duty it is then necessary to determine the appropriate remedy which should be awarded.

(1) The constructive trust

Once it is shown that the accessory is liable for dishonest assistance he or she is said to be a constructive trustee. But this recognition of a constructive trust is not consistent with the normal notion of a constructive trust which applies only where the defendant is in receipt of identifiable property in which the plaintiff has an equitable proprietary interest.[173] Where the defendant has simply been an accessory to the breach of trust or breach of fiduciary duty he or she will not necessarily have received any property which can be the subject of a constructive trust.[174] It is for this reason that reference to constructive trusts in the context of liability for dishonest assistance is misleading. It has sometimes been recognised that reference to a constructive trust in this context is simply a formula for equitable relief to be granted.[175] But the reference to constructive trust is still misleading and potentially confusing. It would be better if the language of constructive trusteeship were removed completely from this area of the law, and it was specifically recognised that the real remedy which is awarded for this type of equitable wrong is a financial remedy. The difficult question is how this remedy is to be assessed.

(2) Is the remedy restitutionary or compensatory?

Normally the remedy will compensate the plaintiff for loss suffered as a result of the breach of trust or fiduciary duty, but is it ever possible to

---

[171] *Royal Brunei Airlines Sdn. Bhd* v. *Tan* [1995] 2 AC 378, 389.

[172] *Brinks* v. *Abu-Saleh (No. 3), The Times*, 23 October 1995.

[173] *Westdeutsche Landesbank Girozentrale* v. *Islington LBC* [1996] AC 669, 705 (Lord Browne-Wilkinson).

[174] If the defendant has received property he or she may be liable for knowing receipt. See p. 668 below.   [175] *English* v. *Dedham Vale Properties Ltd.* [1978] 1 WLR 93.

award a restitutionary remedy which is assessed by reference to the gain made by the defendant as a result of inducing or assisting in the breach of duty? In the decision of the Privy Council in *Royal Brunei Airlines* v. *Tan*[176] it was held that liability for dishonest assistance is not restitutionary, unlike liability for knowing receipt.[177] Whether this assertion is correct depends on what is meant by restitution in this context. To the extent that the defendant who is liable for dishonest assistance will not have obtained a benefit which was taken from the plaintiff, it is correct to say that the defendant's liability is not restitutionary, since there is nothing for the defendant to restore to the plaintiff. But it does not follow that restitutionary remedies are necessarily excluded in this context. It is perfectly possible to conceive of cases where the defendant who was liable for assisting or inducing a breach of trust or fiduciary duty obtained a benefit as a result. Consequently, by virtue of the fundamental principle that no wrongdoer should be allowed to profit from his or her wrong, it should follow that the defendant can be required to disgorge this benefit to the plaintiff. This has actually been recognised by the High Court of Australia in *Warman International Ltd.* v. *Dwyer*[178] where two companies were liable for dishonestly assisting a breach of fiduciary duty and were held liable to account for the profits which they had made.

(iii) Knowing receipt

In addition to liability for dishonest assistance in a breach of trust, equity recognises an action for knowing receipt of trust property in breach of trust. This form of liability is properly analysed as founded on the vindication of the plaintiff's equitable property right, so it is examined in Chapter 21. However, since liability for knowing receipt depends on the defendant having been at fault, a strong case can be made for treating this as a form of wrongdoing which should be treated in exactly the same way as the action for dishonest assistance.[179] It would follow that equity recognises a common liability for all accessories who participate in a breach of trust, either by assisting in the breach or receiving trust property in breach of trust. This form of wrongdoing would be the equitable equivalent of the tort of interfering with contractual relations. The real advantage of this equitable action for knowing receipt would be that the defendant could be personally liable both to account for profits and also to compensate the plaintiff for loss suffered. Consequently, the remedy would not necessarily be restitutionary.

---

[176] [1995] 2 AC 378, 386. [177] See p. 668 below. [178] (1995) 128 ALR 201.
[179] Lord Nicholls, 'Knowing Receipt: The Need For A New Landmark' in *Restitution: Past, Present and Future* (ed. Cornish, Nolan, O'Sullivan and Virgo) pp. 243–4.

19

Criminal Offences

1. GENERAL PRINCIPLES AND POLICIES

When an offender has committed a criminal offence the law of restitution may be relevant in two ways.[1] First, the offender may have received a benefit as a result of the commission of the crime, so the question for the law of restitution is whether there is a cause of action which will enable the victim or the State to recover the proceeds of the crime. Secondly, a consequence of the offender committing the crime may be that he or she is entitled to obtain a benefit, under a life assurance policy for example. Here the question for the law of restitution is whether the offender can be prevented from obtaining this benefit. Whether the victim or the State can claim the proceeds of the crime or the offender can obtain a benefit arising from the commission of the crime will depend upon the application of the same fundamental principle, namely that no wrongdoer should be allowed to profit from the commission of a wrong.[2] Since there is no clearer wrong than the commission of a criminal offence, the application of the 'no profit principle' means that, as a general rule, the victim of the crime or the State should recover the proceeds of the crime from the offender and the offender should not be entitled to obtain a benefit which he or she would otherwise be able to claim as a result of the commission of the crime.

2. RESTITUTIONARY CLAIMS BROUGHT BY THE VICTIM

(a) The general principle

It is a fundamental principle of the law of restitution that no criminal can retain a benefit which accrues to him or her as a result of the commission of a crime.[3] Similarly, anybody who obtains the proceeds of crime from

---

[1] See generally Virgo, 'The Law of Restitution and the Proceeds of Crime—A Survey of English Law' (1998) 6 *RLR* 34.

[2] This principle was recognised by Lord Hardwicke LC in *Bridgeman* v. *Green* (1755) 2 Ves. Sen. 627, 628; 28 ER 399, 400. See p. 451 above.

[3] *St. John Shipping Corp.* v. *Joseph Rank Ltd.* [1957] 1 QB 267, 292 (Devlin J). See also *Attorney-General* v. *Guardian Newspapers Ltd. (No. 2)* [1990] 1 AC 109, 286 (Lord Goff).

the criminal will be liable to make restitution, as was recognised by Lord Commissioner Wilmot in *Bridgeman* v. *Green*:[4]

Let the hand receiving it be ever so chaste, yet if it comes through a corrupt polluted channel, the obligation of restitution will follow it . . . [5]

But despite the clear recognition of this fundamental principle it does not follow automatically that the victim of the crime is necessarily entitled to recover the benefit which the defendant had obtained, since the victim must base his or her restitutionary claim on one of the principles which underlie the law of restitution.

(b) Claims founded on unjust enrichment

The victim may be able to bring a restitutionary claim on the basis that the criminal was unjustly enriched at the victim's expense. This is because the commission of a criminal offence may enable the victim to establish one of the recognised grounds of restitution. So, for example, if the defendant falsely imprisoned the plaintiff and demanded the payment of money from him or her as a condition of release, the defendant has committed the crimes of false imprisonment[6] and blackmail,[7] but the plaintiff can recover the money paid on the ground of duress of the person.[8]

(c) Claims founded on the vindication of property rights

Alternatively, the victim may be able to establish a restitutionary claim against the criminal on the basis that the victim seeks to vindicate his or her continuing proprietary rights. This will often be the case where the defendant steals the plaintiff's property or handles stolen property, as occurred in *Lipkin Gorman (a firm)* v. *Karpnale Ltd.*,[9] where money was stolen from a firm of solicitors by a partner, who gambled with the money at the defendant's casino. The plaintiff recovered much of the

---

[4] (1757) Wilm. 58, 65; 97 ER 22, 25.

[5] Though the application of this principle will be subject to the defence of *bona fide* purchase: see Chapter 22. Consequently, if the recipient of the benefit provided value and was unaware that the benefit constituted the proceeds of crime, the victim's restitutionary claim would be barred. This defence is applicable because the victim's claim against anybody other than the criminal will necessarily be a claim to vindicate proprietary rights. See Chapter 20.

[6] This is a common law offence. See Smith and Hogan, *Criminal Law* (8th edn., London: Butterworths, 1996) pp. 431–42.

[7] Theft Act 1968, s. 21.

[8] See, for example, *Duke de Cadaval* v. *Collins* (1836) 4 Ad. and El. 858; 111 ER 1006. See p. 198 above.

[9] [1991] 2 AC 548. See p. 606 below.

money which had been stolen on the basis that the defendant had received money which belonged to the plaintiff. It was irrelevant that the defendant in this case was not the criminal, it being sufficient that the defendant had received the proceeds of crime from the criminal.[10]

(d) Claims founded on wrongdoing

(i) Torts and breaches of fiduciary duty

Finally, the victim of the crime may found his or her restitutionary claim on the commission of a wrong. Where the crime also constitutes the commission of a restitution-yielding tort then it is clear that the plaintiff may sue the criminal in tort and seek a restitutionary remedy. So, for example, where the defendant commits a crime involving deception, such as obtaining property by deception, this also constitutes the tort of deceit and so the plaintiff can obtain a restitutionary remedy from the criminal in respect of that tort.[11] Alternatively, the crime committed by the criminal may involve breach of fiduciary duty, so the victim will be able to bring a restitutionary claim against the defendant based upon that breach.[12]

(ii) Founding a claim on the crime itself

(1) Objections to restitutionary claims founded on the commission of crimes

Where the victim of the crime is unable to sue the criminal for the commission of a tort or breach of fiduciary duty is it possible to found a restitutionary claim on the crime itself? In principle the answer should be 'yes' because the commission of a crime is an even more heinous form of wrongdoing. There are no cases, however, where a victim has brought a restitutionary claim founded on the commission of a crime. The main reason for this is that in many cases the victim of the crime will have a claim for compensation from the defendant. Where the victim's loss is equivalent to the defendant's gain and it is clear that the victim can

---

[10] Where the plaintiff wishes to recover stolen property from a thief the court may require the defendant to return the property, its substitute or its value to the victim: Theft Act 1968, s. 28.

[11] See *Halifax Building Society* v. *Thomas* [1996] Ch. 217 where the defendant was convicted of conspiring to obtain a mortgage advance by deception. On the facts the plaintiff's restitutionary claim to recover the proceeds of the crime failed because it had elected to affirm the mortgage despite the defendant's fraud. But if the mortgage had not been affirmed and it could have been shown that the defendant had obtained a benefit as a result of the crime the claim should have succeeded.

[12] See, for example, *Reading* v. *Attorney-General* [1951] AC 507 and *Attorney-General for Hong Kong* v. *Reid* [1994] 1 AC 324.

recover compensation for loss suffered as a result of the crime, whether at common law or by virtue of particular statutory provisions,[13] there is no need to bring a somewhat speculative claim for restitution.

Sometimes, however, the defendant's gain might exceed the plaintiff's loss and so a restitutionary claim would be attractive. But that such a restitutionary claim might be brought was doubted by Glidewell LJ in *Halifax Building Society* v. *Thomas*:[14]

The proposition that a wrongdoer should not be allowed to profit from his wrongs has an obvious attraction. The further proposition, that the victim or intended victim of the wrongdoing, who has in the event suffered no loss, is entitled to retain or recover the amount of the profit is less obviously persuasive.

Two reasons can be suggested for this reluctance to allow the victim to recover the proceeds of the crime.

First, the award of restitutionary remedies is much easier to justify where the defendant has committed a tort or broken a fiduciary duty than where a crime has been committed. This is because in those cases where the defendant committed a tort or broke a fiduciary duty it is clear that the defendant has broken a duty which was owed to the victim. Where, however, the defendant has committed a crime the law treats this as involving the breach of a duty which is owed to the State, hence the power of the State to punish the criminal. But, despite this, in those cases where the victim has been harmed by the commission of a crime it is surely appropriate to conclude that this involves a breach of duty which was owed to the victim. In fact, a number of offences depend upon the identification of breach of such a duty before the criminal can be convicted.[15] The fact that the defendant has harmed the victim, either physically or by interfering with his or her property, and has obtained a benefit as a result should be sufficient to enable the victim to claim the defendant's benefit.

Another reason for the judicial reluctance to recognise that the victim of a crime can recover the proceeds of the crime from the criminal is that the policy of preventing the criminal from profiting from the crime is a matter for Parliament, using the mechanisms of fines and confiscation. It is often asserted that it is not for the courts to interfere with this policy by extending the law to deprive the criminal of the proceeds. This

---

[13] Such as the power of a criminal court to order the offender to pay compensation to the victim in respect of personal injury, loss or damage resulting from the offence: Powers of Criminal Courts Act 1973, s. 35 (as amended by the Criminal Justice Act 1982, s. 67 and the Criminal Justice Act 1988, s. 104(1)). Compensation may also be obtained from the Criminal Injuries Compensation Board: Criminal Justice Act 1988, ss. 108–17.

[14] [1996] Ch. 217, 229.

[15] See, for example, the definition of gross negligent manslaughter after the decision of the House of Lords in *R.* v. *Adomako* [1995] 1 AC 171.

was recognised by Peter Gibson LJ in *Halifax Building Society* v. *Thomas*:[16]

In considering whether to extend the law of constructive trusts in order to prevent a fraudster benefiting from his wrong, it is also appropriate to bear in mind that Parliament has acted in recent years . . . on the footing that without statutory intervention the criminal might keep the benefit of his crime. Moreover, Parliament has given the courts the power in specific circumstances to confiscate the benefit rather than reward the person against whom the crime has been committed.[17]

But whilst it is clear that the State has the prime interest in ensuring that criminals do not profit from their crimes, it does not follow that the judges lack a subsidiary power to deprive criminals of the proceeds of their crimes where the statutory powers of fines and confiscation are inadequate to deprive the criminal of all the proceeds. The inadequacy of the statutory powers is exemplified by the fact that fines cannot be used to deprive criminals of benefits which they obtain after they have been convicted and sentenced, or benefits of which the court might not have been aware were obtained by the criminal. Also the statutory powers of confiscation are limited to where the crime committed by the defendant was serious and they cannot be invoked unless the defendant has been convicted.[18] There is surely a role for the law of restitution as developed by the judiciary to serve an interstitial function to ensure that the criminal does not retain the proceeds of crime.[19]

(2) The case for recognising restitutionary claims founded on the commission of crimes

There is consequently no obvious objection to the common law and equity recognising that the victim of a crime should have a right to obtain the proceeds of the crime from the criminal, although this right should be subsidiary to the power of the State to obtain such proceeds. This restitutionary right of the victim is justified for two main reasons.

First, it is a fundamental policy of English law that no defendant should profit from his or her crime. Where the State has not deprived the criminal of these profits it is entirely appropriate that the victim should

---

[16] [1996] Ch. 217, 229. See also Glidewell LJ at p. 230.

[17] See also Hoffmann J in *Chief Constable of Leicestershire* v. *M.* [1989] 1 WLR 20, 23.

[18] As illustrated by *Attorney-General* v. *Blake* [1998] 2 WLR 805.

[19] See Glidewell LJ in *Halifax Building Society* v. *Thomas* [1996] Ch. 217, 230: '[t]he enactment of this legislation does not, of course, lead inevitably to the conclusion that neither common law nor equity provides a means by which [the criminal] could be prevented from enjoying the profit of the crime'. Though he did add that 'the readiness of Parliament to address the problem by legislation weakens the case for providing a solution by judicial creativity'.

be allowed to instigate such an action as 'the instrument of a social purpose'.[20]

The second justification is just as important. In many cases where the plaintiff is the victim of a crime he or she will have suffered harm for which compensation is not available in the normal way. Enabling the plaintiff to obtain the proceeds of the crime will therefore act as some sort of recompense for the harm which has been suffered.

So, for example, if a third party paid the defendant £1,000 to assault the plaintiff, it is surely entirely appropriate that the plaintiff recovers £1,000 from the defendant, both because the defendant should not be allowed to profit from the crime and because this operates as some form of compensation for the injury and trauma suffered by the victim. As Birks has said, in such circumstances the recovery of the proceeds of crime which exceeds the plaintiff's loss 'is not an undeserved windfall but . . . a remedy for an individual wrong'.[21]

(3) The nature of the restitutionary relief

If the defendant is held liable to make restitution to the victim as a result of the commission of a crime the remedy which will be awarded will typically be an account of the profits obtained as a result of the commission of the crime. It is, however, possible that the court will conclude that the defendant holds the proceeds of crime on constructive trust for the victim, so it follows that the victim can bring a restitutionary claim to recover the property which is held on constructive trust. The potential importance of the constructive trust in the context of restitutionary claims founded on the commission of a crime arises from the judgment of Lord Browne-Wilkinson in *Westdeutsche Landesbank Girozentrale* v. *Islington LBC*.[22] The judge recognised that 'when property is obtained by fraud equity imposes a constructive trust on the fraudulent recipient: the property is recoverable and traceable in equity'.[23] Whether this reflects the state of English law as to when a constructive trust will be recognised is a controversial matter,[24] but, if it is correct, it follows that the constructive trust will be particularly important where the defendant has committed any crime, such as theft or deception, which can be considered to involve fraudulent conduct on the part of the defendant. Indeed, Lord Browne-Wilkinson specifically recognised that a thief who stole a bag of coins would hold those coins on constructive trust for the victim.[25] In fact, the commission of any crime can be considered to involve unconscionable conduct with the consequence that the proceeds of the crime will be held on constructive trust for the victim. But it is still too

---

[20] Birks, 'The Proceeds of Mortgage Fraud' (1996) 10 *TLI* 1, 5.   [21] *Ibid.*
[22] [1996] AC 669.   [23] *Ibid*, p. 716.   [24] See pp. 630–5 below.
[25] [1996] AC 669, 716.

early to be sure exactly when the courts will recognise that property is held on constructive trust.

(iii) Obstacles to restitutionary claims founded on crimes

If the victim does bring a restitutionary claim to obtain the proceeds of the crime there are four main obstacles which must be surmounted before such a claim can succeed, and these obstacles will dramatically limit the scope of such a claim.

(1) Causation and remoteness

The general rule of causation in respect of wrongs is the 'but for' test.[26] The application of this test to a claim for restitution of the proceeds of crime means that the victim must show that, but for the commission of the crime, the benefit would not have been obtained by the defendant. For reasons of consistency with other claims for restitution for wrongs this test of causation should apply to claims to the proceeds of crime. Similarly, the general principle of remoteness should apply to claims for restitution of the proceeds of crime, namely that the benefit must have arisen directly from the commission of the wrong. This was recognised in *Halifax Building Society* v. *Thomas*,[27] where the defendant had obtained a mortgage advance by deception and had used this to purchase a flat which had subsequently increased in value. Peter Gibson LJ said:[28]

> Further I am not satisfied that in the circumstances of the present case it would be right to treat the unjust enrichment of [the criminal] as having been gained 'at the expense of' [the plaintiff], even allowing for the possibility of an extended meaning for those words to apply to cases of non-subtractive restitution for a wrong . . . I do not overlook the fact that the policy of law is to view with disfavour a wrongdoer benefiting from his wrong, the more so when the wrong amounts to fraud, but it cannot be suggested that there is a universally applicable principle that in every case there will be restitution of benefit from a wrong . . . On the facts of the present case . . . the fraud is not in itself a sufficient factor to allow [the plaintiff] to require [the criminal] to account for it.

This was therefore a case in which the plaintiff could not simply rely on the fact that it was the victim of a fraud to obtain the proceeds of the crime. The explanation for this can be found in the earlier case of *Chief Constable of Leicestershire* v. *M*.[29] the facts of which were almost identical to those of *Halifax Building Society* v. *Thomas*, in that the offender had made profits from the sale of properties he had purchased with the assistance of a mortgage advance which he had obtained by deception. Hoffmann J did not accept that these profits constituted the proceeds of

---

[26] See p. 464 below.   [27] [1996] Ch. 217.   [28] *Ibid*, p. 227.
[29] [1989] 1 WLR 20.

crime because the profit was not itself obtained by deception but rather was made from the money which was obtained by deception. In other words, the money was too remote from the crime.

The effect of these two decisions appears to be that if the victim is to recover the proceeds of crime from the criminal it must be shown that the proceeds were obtained directly from the crime, rather than indirectly, as will occur where the criminal has profited from investing the proceeds of the crime. This strict approach to the question of remoteness of benefit is at least consistent with the approach which is adopted where the plaintiff's restitutionary action is founded on tort or breach of fiduciary duty.[30] If the victim of a crime can recover only those benefits which the defendant obtained directly from the commission of the offence, it follows that the victim should recover all those benefits which the criminal obtained directly from the victim, and presumably also those benefits which the criminal was promised as an inducement to commit the crime, such as a bribe to commit an assault, simply because the bribe was only paid to the criminal because he or she had committed the crime.

If, however, the court concludes that, by virtue of the defendant's fraudulent conduct, he or she holds the proceeds of crime on constructive trust for the plaintiff, the question of remoteness of benefit will be much less important. This is because all profits obtained as a result of the crime will be subject to the constructive trust, regardless of whether they arose directly or indirectly. This is illustrated by the decision of the Privy Council in *Attorney-General for Hong Kong* v. *Reid*,[31] in which the court concluded that the defendant held the bribe he had received on constructive trust for the plaintiff. This meant that the plaintiff had an equitable proprietary interest in the bribe, and subsequently the property which had been purchased with the bribe. In fact, the recognition of a constructive trust would have avoided the problem of remoteness in *Halifax Building Society* v. *Thomas*[32] because it could be concluded that the property which the defendant purchased using the mortgage advance was held on constructive trust for the plaintiff building society, since the defendant had obtained the mortgage advance through the commission of a crime and so had acted fraudulently. If the property were held on constructive trust it would follow that the proceeds of the sale of the house would also be subject to the constructive trust, regardless of the fact that the property had increased in value.

---

[30] It also accords with the test of remoteness which is adopted for the purposes of the forfeiture rule, examined at p. 579 below.

[31] [1994] 1 AC 324.   [32] [1996] Ch. 217.

(2) The operation of the *in pari delicto* defence

It is an accepted principle of the law of restitution that no court will allow a restitutionary claim to be brought where it is founded on an illegal act.[33] This is known as the *in pari delicto* defence.[34] In principle this means that the victim of the crime will not be able to rely on the commission of a crime to obtain restitution from the criminal. This will not, however, usually be the case, because there is an accepted exception to this defence where the parties are not equally responsible for the illegal act. Usually the victim will not have participated in the commission of the crime and so he or she will not have been tainted by the illegality.[35]

(3) The relationship with the public law powers of the Attorney-General

It was recognised by the Court of Appeal in *Attorney-General* v. *Blake*[36] that the Attorney-General can bring a public law claim to ensure that criminals are prevented from receiving the proceeds of the crime.[37] Although the Court of Appeal did not specifically consider whether the Attorney-General could bring a claim to deprive the criminal of the proceeds of the crime once they had been received, the Court did appear to suggest that such a claim was not available. But in the light of the fundamental principle that no criminal should be allowed to profit from his or her crime, this is a very odd conclusion to reach. In fact, because of that principle, if the Attorney-General can prevent the criminal from receiving the proceeds of the crime, it should follow that, where the criminal has received the proceeds of the crime, the Attorney-General should be able to bring a restitutionary claim to deprive the criminal of these proceeds. But if this were correct, would the victim's private law claim not conflict with the Attorney-General's public law claim? Indeed, in *Blake* the Court of Appeal recognised that the Attorney-General was an appropriate person to institute a claim against the criminal, because it was one of his or her functions to enforce the criminal law. It was recognised by the Court that, since the Attorney-General would only intervene where it was right to do so, there were adequate safeguards against the abuse of the jurisdiction to prevent the criminal from receiving the proceeds of the crime.

But whilst it is proper that the Attorney-General is the only person who should be able to intervene to prevent the defendant from obtaining a benefit, since the Attorney-General is the guardian of the criminal law, it does not follow that the victim of the crime should be prevented from bringing a claim to require the defendant to disgorge those benefits

---

[33] *Holman* v. *Johnson* (1775) 1 Cowp. 341, 343; 98 ER 1120, 1121 (Lord Mansfield).
[34] See Chapter 26.   [35] See *Kiriri Cotton Co. Ltd.* v. *Dewani* [1960] AC 192.
[36] [1998] 2 WLR 805.   [37] See p. 571 below.

which have been received as a result of committing the crime. Because of the principle that no criminal should profit from the crime and because the victim was harmed by the defendant, it is entirely appropriate that the victim should have a right to sue the criminal for restitutionary relief. This right should only be circumscribed by statute or where the Attorney-General considers that it is not in the public interest for the victim to sue the defendant or where the Attorney-General has commenced proceedings to recover the proceeds of crime from the defendant.

(4) The Human Rights Act 1998

Since the statutory mechanisms for the recovery of the proceeds of crime apply only where the defendant has been convicted of a crime, it follows that the common law claim brought by the victim for restitution of the proceeds of crime will be most significant where the defendant has not been convicted. But does the civil liability of the defendant to make restitution of the proceeds of crime to the victim infringe the European Convention on Human Rights, which has been incorporated into English law by the Human Rights Act 1998? It might be concluded that such civil liability does infringe the European Convention because the defendant is being treated as a criminal, even though he or she has not been convicted of a crime.[38] This imposition of civil liability lacks the safeguards of criminal procedure, most notably by virtue of the different standards of proof, the civil standard of proof being proof on the balance of probabilities whereas the criminal standard is proof beyond reasonable doubt. Whether such civil restitutionary liability will be considered to infringe the criminal's human rights is a matter of some uncertainty. This was an issue which was ignored by the Court of Appeal in *Attorney-General* v. *Blake*,[39] although when that case was decided the European Convention had not been incorporated into English law. It is to be hoped that, because restitutionary liability is a civil liability which does not involve the defendant being charged with an offence, and because the restitutionary remedy does not seek to punish the defendant, the imposition of such liability is not considered to infringe the rights of the criminal which are protected by the European Convention.

(iv) The potential implications of recognising restitutionary claims founded on crimes

The potential implications of a claim to recover the proceeds of crime where the cause of action is simply the crime itself can be illustrated by

[38] See, in particular, Article 6(2) of the European Convention on Human Rights: '[e]veryone charged with a criminal offence shall be presumed innocent until proved guilty according to law'.
[39] [1998] 2 WLR 805.

reference to two situations where a benefit has been obtained as a result of the commission of a crime.

(1) *Rosenfeldt* v. *Olson*

The first example is the decision of the British Columbia Court of Appeal in *Rosenfeldt* v. *Olson*.[40] In this case the accused was suspected of murdering 11 children. In order to secure his agreement to plead guilty to murder and to disclose the location of the bodies, the police agreed to pay $100,000 to be held on trust for the benefit of the accused's wife and their child. The parents of seven of the accused's victims claimed that this money was impressed with a constructive trust for their benefit. Their claim failed on the ground that the accused's wife and child had not been unjustly enriched at the expense of the parents. This was because the money which had been paid had not been subtracted from the victims. But this decision shows the dangers of assuming that the only cause of action within the law of restitution is that founded on unjust enrichment. It is obvious that the recipients of the money had not been unjustly enriched at the expense of the parents, but it could still have been argued that the parents' restitutionary claim should be founded on the accused's crime. But, even if a claim which was founded on the crime was recognised, it was clear that the benefit had not been obtained as a direct result of the accused committing the crime, and so, in accordance with general principles of remoteness, it was correct that the restitutionary claim failed.[41]

(2) Recovering the literary proceeds of crime

If a restitutionary claim founded on the commission of a crime is recognised, such a claim is particularly important where a criminal, usually a killer, obtains money by selling his or her story to a newspaper or television company or publishes a book about the crime.[42] Should the victim, or where relevant his or her personal representatives, be allowed to recover this money? A number of States in the United States and in Australia have enacted laws to prevent convicted criminals from retaining profits by marketing their stories, with the profits usually being made

---

[40] (1986) 25 DLR (4th) 472.

[41] Even though the accused had committed particularly heinous crimes, and so perhaps a more liberal test of remoteness of benefit might be adopted, as discussed below, there is no reason why a different test of remoteness should be adopted where the plaintiff seeks to recover the proceeds of crime from a third party, such as the accused's spouse and child.

[42] Goff and Jones, *The Law of Restitution*, p. 811. See also Freiberg, 'Confiscating the Literary Proceeds of Crime' [1992] *Crim. LR* 96. Freiberg gives the example of Pottle and Randle who obtained £30,000 in respect of the publication of their book, *The Blake Escape: How We Freed George Blake and Why*.

available for the benefit of the victims of the crime and their families.[43] No specific statutory provision has been made for this problem in this country,[44] but will the common law prevent the criminal from retaining profits by marketing stories in this way? Clearly, but for the commission of the crime the defendant would not have had a story to sell, and so would not have obtained the money, so the 'but for' test of causation is satisfied. But there are two potential objections to the defendant having to make restitution to the victim.

First, the defendant might argue that the money which he or she received for selling the story was obtained only indirectly from the crime, since the money derived from the story rather than from the commission of the crime itself. The benefit would therefore be too remote. One response to this argument is to assert that, as a matter of public policy, a criminal who has obtained any benefit as a result of the commission of heinous crimes, such as murder, should not be allowed to argue that the benefit was too remote from the crime.[45] Alternatively it could be argued that, since the commission of the crime was a vital element of the criminal having a story to sell in the first place,[46] the profits flowed directly from the crime.

The defendant may also argue that he or she assisted in the writing of the story and so may claim that, even if part of the benefit which he or she obtained were to be disgorged to the plaintiff, there should be an apportionment to reflect his or her personal contribution. Whilst such an argument would succeed where the plaintiff's claim was founded on the defendant's breach of fiduciary duty,[47] it should be defeated where the plaintiff's claim is founded on a crime committed by the defendant, again for reasons of public policy that a defendant who has committed a serious crime should not be allowed to benefit in any way from its commission.

(v) Restitution from third parties

Whilst the victim might be able to establish a restitutionary claim to recover the proceeds of the crime from the criminal, it will be even more

---

[43] See Okuda, *Criminal Antiprofit Laws: Some Thoughts in Favor of their Constitutionality* (1988) 76 *Cal. LR* 1353 and Freiberg, n. 42 above, at p. 97.

[44] Although such profits may be the subject of a confiscation order being made under the Criminal Justice Act 1988, as discussed at p. 569 below.

[45] Note the similar principle that the court will never allow a plaintiff to obtain restitution on the ground of unjust enrichment where he or she has committed a serious crime, simply for reasons of public policy. See *Tappenden* v. *Randall* (1801) 2 Bos. and Pul. 467, 471; 126 ER 1388, 1390 (Heath J); *Kearley* v. *Thomson* (1890) 24 QBD 742, 747 (Fry LJ).

[46] Okuda, 'Criminal Antiprofit Laws: Some Thoughts in Favor of their Constitutionality' (1988) 76 *Cal. LR* 1353, 1360.

[47] See, for example, *Boardman* v. *Phipps* [1967] 2 AC 46 and *O'Sullivan* v. *Management Agency and Music Ltd.* [1985] QB 428.

difficult to establish such a claim against anybody else who assisted the criminal in obtaining the proceeds without being party to the offence.[48] For example, a ghost writer or publisher who assists in the writing and publication of the defendant's story should not be liable to disgorge the benefits they obtained from the publication of the story.[49] This is because any benefit which the ghost writer or the publisher obtained was surely too remote from the commission of the crime in the first place. The reach of restitution would be too wide if it embraces claims against both the criminal and anybody who assisted the criminal in obtaining a benefit from the crime without themselves being guilty of a crime in their own right.

Where, however, the third party receives property from the criminal which is held on constructive trust for the plaintiff, the plaintiff will be able to bring a restitutionary claim to vindicate his or her proprietary rights.[50] Where the third party receives property from the criminal in which the plaintiff does not have a continuing proprietary interest, but the third party is aware that the property represents the proceeds of crime, the third party may be considered to have acted unconscionably so that he or she will hold the property on constructive trust for the victim.

3. RESTITUTIONARY CLAIMS BROUGHT BY THE STATE

There are a number of statutory mechanisms whereby benefits obtained by an offender as a result of committing a crime may be liable to be disgorged to the State. Disgorgement of the proceeds of crime to the State should be considered to fall within the law of restitution, since, by committing a crime, the offender has committed a wrong against the State by breaching his or her duty to abide by the criminal law of the land. Since detailed analysis of these provisions concerning disgorgement to the State is adequately dealt with in specialised works on the subject,[51] it will

[48] The victim will have a restitutionary claim against an accessory who obtained a benefit as a result of the commission of a crime because the accessory is guilty of a crime in his or her own right.

[49] Invariably those States in the United States which have statutes prohibiting the criminal from profiting from the commission of the crime do not prohibit the publisher, ghost writer or producer from retaining profits derived from the criminal's story: Okuda, 'Criminal Antiprofit Laws: Some Thoughts in Favor of their Constitutionality' (1988) 76 *Cal. LR* 1353.

[50] See Chapter 21. This will be subject to the defence of *bona fide* purchase: see Chapter 22. The third party could also be liable for knowingly receiving the proceeds of crime which are subject to a constructive trust (see pp. 668–71 below) or dishonestly assisting the criminal in breaching the trust (see pp. 553–5 above). See Oakley, *Constructive Trusts* (3rd edn., London: Sweet and Maxwell, 1997) p. 222 ff.

[51] See in particular *Mitchell, Taylor and Talbot on Confiscation and the Proceeds of Crime* (2nd edn., London: Sweet and Maxwell, 1997).

be sufficient here simply to identify the key provisions relating to confiscation of the proceeds of crime.

(a) Confiscation orders

The most important of the statutory mechanisms to recover the proceeds of crime concerns the duty of the court to order that benefits obtained by an offender as a result of the commission of certain crimes should be confiscated by the State.[52] Essentially, where an offender has been convicted of an indictable offence[53] which is not a drug-trafficking offence, and the prosecutor has given written notice to the court that he or she considers a confiscation order to be appropriate or the court considers such an order to be appropriate, the court must make an order that the offender pay such sum to the Crown as the court thinks fit.[54] The sum which is ordered to be confiscated is limited to the lesser of the benefit which the defendant obtained or the amount which appears to the court to be that which may be realised at the time the order is made.[55] Although confiscation orders cannot be made in respect of profits obtained from drug-trafficking offences, this is only because a more draconian power to confiscate profits exists in respect of such offences.[56]

Where the victim of the crime has instituted or intends to institute civil proceedings against the defendant in respect of loss, injury or damage sustained in connection with the defendant's criminal conduct, the court has a power rather than a duty to make a confiscation order.[57] Where the defendant has been convicted of one offence and the court considers that the defendant has obtained benefits from a course of criminal conduct, the court may order that all of these benefits should be confiscated even though some of them arise from crimes in respect of which the defendant has not been convicted and which have never been formally taken into consideration in criminal proceedings.

This statutory obligation to make confiscation orders applies regardless of the value of the benefit which the defendant obtained. 'Benefit' for these purposes includes pecuniary advantages as well as property obtained as a result of the commission of the crime.[58] In other words, if

---

[52] Part VI, Criminal Justice Act 1988, as amended by the Proceeds of Crime Act 1995.

[53] A Magistrates' Court may also make a confiscation order in respect of a limited number of summary offences.

[54] Criminal Justice Act 1988, s. 71, as amended by the Proceeds of Crime Act 1995, s. 1.

[55] Criminal Justice Act 1988, s. 71(6).

[56] Drug Trafficking Act 1994, s. 2(3). This is a more draconian power because of the statutory assumption that all of the drug trafficker's assets are the proceeds of crime and so are liable to confiscation.

[57] Criminal Justice Act 1988, s. 71(1C) as inserted by the Proceeds of Crime Act 1995, s.1.

[58] Criminal Justice Act 1988, s. 71(4), (5).

the offender has saved money as a result of the crime this negative enrichment constitutes a benefit for the purposes of the Act. The benefit must be obtained 'as a result of or in connection with' the commission of the crime.[59]

The power to make a confiscation order is particularly important where the offender has committed so-called 'victimless' crimes, such as insider dealing,[60] where there is no victim who can claim compensation or restitution from the offender. The power to make a confiscation order will also be available to confiscate profits made by a criminal in respect of the publication of a book about the crime or the sale of the story to a newspaper or a television company.

(b) Ancillary powers

Even before the offender is convicted the High Court has power to make a restraint order,[61] to prevent the offender from dissipating his or her property, or a charging order,[62] to secure a future confiscation order.[63]

4. DENIAL OF BENEFITS ARISING FROM THE COMMISSION OF CRIMES

(a) Does the denial of benefits to a criminal form part of the law of restitution?

Where one consequence of an offender committing a crime is that he or she is entitled to receive a benefit, the general principle that no offender should profit from wrongdoing means that the benefit should be denied to him or her. But does the analysis of this application of the no-profit principle properly fall within a work on the law of restitution? Burrows suggests that it does not, simply because the law of restitution is concerned with the transfer of benefits to the plaintiff, whereas the question which is being considered here is whether the conduct of the offender is such as to prevent the benefit from being received by the criminal in the first place.[64] Goff and Jones disagree[65] and they are right to do so.

---

[59] Criminal Justice Act 1988, s. 71(4).
[60] Contrary to the Criminal Justice Act 1993, Part V.
[61] Criminal Justice Act 1988, s. 77.   [62] *Ibid*, s. 78.
[63] A charging order was made over the houses of Potter and Randle on the ground that the benefit which they obtained from the publication of a book about their part in George Blake's escape from prison was one which arose from the commission of the crime. No confiscation order was made because proceedings against Potter and Randle were discontinued. See Freiberg, 'Confiscating the Literary Proceeds of Crime' [1992] *Crim. LR* 96.
[64] Burrows, *The Law of Restitution*, p. 380.
[65] Goff and Jones, *The Law of Restitution*, p. 802.

Although the denial of benefits to a criminal is not restitutionary, in the sense that it does not involve the application of restitutionary remedies, it is appropriate to examine the rules relating to the denial of benefits to a criminal in a book on restitution. This is because both preventing the defendant from receiving the proceeds of the crime and transferring the proceeds of crime to the victim or to the State are motivated by the same policy consideration, namely that no criminal should be allowed to profit from the crime. The same question of public policy arises regardless of whether it is considered before or after the defendant has obtained the proceeds of the crime.

(b) The Attorney-General's public law claim

In the important case of *Attorney-General* v. *Blake*[66] the Court of Appeal recognised that the Attorney-General could bring a public law claim to ensure that no criminal received the proceeds of crime.[67]

George Blake had been a member of the Secret Intelligence Service, but he was also an agent of the Soviet Union. He was consequently convicted of unlawfully communicating information to the Soviets, but he escaped to Moscow where he wrote his autobiography. In this book he disclosed information about the secret service. This constituted a breach of section 1 of the Official Secrets Act, because Blake had disclosed official information without lawful authority. The book was published in the United Kingdom by Jonathan Cape Ltd. without the permission of the Crown. The Attorney-General sued, on behalf of the Crown, to recover all the sums which had been received or were receivable by the publisher.

Since the royalties which had been paid to Blake and which remained payable by the publishers had arisen from the publication of the autobiography, they were the proceeds of crime. But since Blake had not been convicted of a crime in respect of the submission of his manuscript to the publisher, the statutory regime for confiscation of the proceeds was inapplicable. The Attorney-General argued that an equivalent power existed at common law. This raised three separate issues.

(i) The nature of the Attorney-General's claim

The Attorney-General is the guardian of the public interest and has a particular duty to vindicate the criminal law. Consequently, it has been recognised that the Attorney-General can apply to the civil courts to obtain an injunction to uphold the criminal law.[68] This jurisdiction to grant an injunction was extended by the Court of Appeal in *Blake* to the

---

[66] [1998] 2 WLR 805.
[67] See Virgo, 'Clarifying Restitution for Wrongs' [1998] *RLR* 118.
[68] See *Gouriet* v. *Union of Post Office Workers* [1978] AC 435.

case where a crime had already been committed, to ensure that the defendant did not benefit from the consequences of that crime. The exercise of such a power was justified on the ground that the criminal courts in this case were powerless to prevent the defendant from benefiting from the crime, because he had not been convicted of an offence relating to the disclosure of information in his autobiography. If the civil courts were also unable to intervene it would follow that Blake could flout the criminal law with impunity and bring it into disrepute by being able to obtain and retain the proceeds of his crime.

(ii) Can the Attorney-General bring a private law claim for restitution of the proceeds of crime?

The Court of Appeal recognised that the Attorney-General could bring such a public law claim in his own capacity as guardian of the public interest and not as a representative of the Crown. But could the Attorney-General bring a private law claim on behalf of the Crown, to enable the Crown to recover the proceeds of the crime from the defendant?[69] The Court of Appeal considered that the Attorney-General could not have obtained restitutionary damages in this case, since it concluded that it had jurisdiction only to grant a remedy which had prospective effect by preventing the defendant from obtaining the proceeds of the crime.[70] But why cannot the court have jurisdiction to award restitutionary remedies which have retrospective effect, and so prevent the criminal from retaining the proceeds of the crime? Whilst it is perfectly acceptable to conclude that, where the statutory regime for confiscating the proceeds of crime applies, it is inappropriate for there to be a parallel development of the common law regime,[71] it does not follow that the common law has no role to play where the statutory regime is inapplicable.[72] Otherwise the effect of *Blake* is that the common law can prevent a criminal from receiving the proceeds of crime, but it cannot require the criminal to disgorge the proceeds once they have been received. This is illogical and contradicts the clear policy, specifically recognised by the Court of Appeal,[73] that criminals should not be allowed to profit from their crimes.

(iii) Determination of the remedy

The Court of Appeal recognised that it had jurisdiction to grant an injunction which should be fashioned to ensure that Blake did not

---

[69] Whether the Attorney-General's public law claim excludes the victim's private law claim for restitution of the proceeds of crime is considered at pp. 564–5 above.

[70] [1998] 2 WLR 805, 822.

[71] *Chief Constable of Leicestershire* v. *M.* [1989] 1 WLR 1015, 1018 (Hoffmann J) and *Halifax Building Society* v. *Thomas* [1996] Ch. 217, 229 (Peter Gibson LJ).

[72] See pp. 560–1 above.   [73] [1998] 2 WLR 805, 822.

receive any benefit which arose directly from the commission of the crime. The injunction which was granted stated that the defendant was restrained from receiving or authorising anybody to receive on his behalf any benefit which resulted from or in connection with the publication of his book. Two observations can be made about this remedy.

First, the Court of Appeal refused to determine what was to happen to the proceeds of the crime. It suggested that if the unpaid royalties, which the publisher had received but was unable to pay to Blake, could be used for a purpose which was not contrary to the public interest, the court could authorise that use on the application of the Attorney-General. In other words, since Blake's book could still be sold, the publisher could continue to receive Blake's royalties, but it had to retain this money until the Attorney-General decided what should happen to it.

Secondly, the court recognised that the injunction would relate only to those benefits which derived directly from the commission of the crime. Although this is consistent with the rules of remoteness which apply to other types of restitutionary claim founded on the commission of a wrong[74] and with the statutory regime on the confiscation of the proceeds of crime,[75] is it really appropriate to exclude benefits indirectly obtained from the crime from the operation of the injunction? What if, for example, the publisher had invested the royalties for Blake in shares and had received dividend payments? Could Blake claim these dividends? According to the Court of Appeal he could, because the dividends were not directly obtained from the commission of the crime. But where the defendant has committed a crime there is a very strong case that the normal rules of remoteness should not apply, so that the defendant is required to disgorge all benefits which derive either directly or indirectly from the commission of the crime.[76]

(c) The forfeiture principle

(i) The ambit of the forfeiture principle

It is a fundamental principle of English law that a criminal is not able to enforce rights or to recover benefits which accrue to him or her as a result of the commission of certain types of criminal offence.[77] This is a rule of public policy. As Fry LJ said in *Cleaver* v. *Mutual Reserve Fund Life Association*:[78]

---

[74] See p. 466 above.

[75] S. 71(4) of the Criminal Justice Act 1988 requires confiscation of the value of property which was obtained as a result of or in connection with the commission of the crime.

[76] See p. 567 above.

[77] *Cleaver* v. *Mutual Reserve Fund Life Association* [1892] 1 QB 147, 156 (Fry LJ); *Beresford* v. *Royal Insurance Co.* [1938] AC 586, 598 (Lord Atkin).

[78] [1892] 1 QB 147, 156.

The principle of public policy invoked is in my opinion rightly asserted. It appears to me that no system of jurisprudence can with reason include amongst the rights which it enforces rights directly resulting to the person asserting them from the crime of that person.

Where the defendant is entitled to benefits as a result of an unlawful killing, the rule which precludes him or her from obtaining those benefits is called the forfeiture rule.[79] But the principle which underlies the forfeiture rule is not confined to where the crime which has been committed is an unlawful killing. Fry LJ recognised in *Cleaver* that the general principle may also be invoked where the criminal has committed a crime involving fraud.[80] The forfeiture principle is in fact potentially applicable in respect of all crimes, but the courts have accepted that it is only the commission of certain types of criminal conduct which will trigger its operation.[81] The test which the courts have adopted is whether the offender intentionally committed the crime. This was recognised by Lord Denning MR in *Hardy* v. *Motor Insurers' Bureau*,[82] where he said that 'no person can claim reparation or indemnity for the consequences of a criminal offence where his own wicked and deliberate intent is an essential ingredient in it'.

Whilst the application of the forfeiture principle prevents the criminal from obtaining all benefits which accrue as a result of the commission of the crime, the vast majority of the cases are concerned with whether the criminal can obtain an indemnity under an insurance policy. Consistent with the forfeiture principle, such an indemnity will be denied where the criminal intentionally committed the crime,[83] but not where it was committed negligently or innocently.[84] So, for example, it has long been recognised that a criminal who deliberately sets fire to his or her own property to obtain insurance money for damage to the property will not be able to recover the money from the insurance company.[85] The forfeiture principle also prevents those who claim through the criminal from recovering benefits which arise from the commission of a crime.[86]

---

[79] *Re K. (deceased)* [1986] Ch. 180, 185 (Vinelott LJ).   [80] [1892] 1 QB 147, 156.
[81] See Lord Wright in *Beresford* v. *Royal Insurance Co. Ltd.* [1937] 2 KB 197, 220.
[82] [1964] 2 QB 745, 760.
[83] *Haseldine* v. *Hoskin* [1933] 1 KB 822. See also *Geismar* v. *Sun Alliance and London Insurance Ltd.* [1978] QB 383, 395 (Talbot J).
[84] *Tinline* v. *White Cross Insurance Association Ltd.* [1921] 3 KB 327; *James* v. *British General Insurance Co. Ltd.* [1927] 2 KB 311. See also *Euro-Diam Ltd.* v. *Bathurst* [1990] QB 1, 40 (Kerr LJ).
[85] *Beresford* v. *Royal Insurance Co. Ltd.* [1938] AC 586, 595 (Lord Atkin).
[86] *The Amicable Society for a Perpetual Life Assurance Office* v. *Bolland* (1830) 4 Bligh (NS) 194; 5 ER 70.

(ii) The relationship between the forfeiture principle and the in pari
delicto *defence*

The principle that criminals, or those claiming through criminals, are not
able to obtain benefits arising from a crime is closely related to the principle that a court will not enable a party to obtain restitution of benefits
transferred pursuant to an illegal transaction; the *in pari delicto*
defence.[87] Indeed, both of these principles are founded on the same general principle of *ex turpi causa non oritur actio*, namely that the courts
will not assist criminals and similar wrongdoers.[88] Also both principles
are principles of public policy rather than of justice.[89] Consequently,
they may sometimes lead to unfair results.

Nevertheless, the forfeiture principle and the *in pari delicto* defence
remain distinct, there being a number of important differences between
them. For example, a transaction may be illegal without necessarily
involving the commission of a crime. Also the *in pari delicto* defence is
applicable only once a benefit has been transferred, whereas the forfeiture principle applies before any benefit has been received. Most
importantly, it is much easier to defend the forfeiture principle because
the criminal is clearly a wrongdoer, whereas the plaintiff who seeks to
recover a benefit which has been obtained by the defendant under an
illegal transaction may have been an innocent party. The effect of these
differences is that, whilst it is necessary to acknowledge the common
policy behind the forfeiture principle and the principle denying restitution on the ground of illegality, the two principles should be kept separate because they apply in different circumstances.

(iii) The rationale of the forfeiture principle

A number of explanations have been given for the existence of the forfeiture principle.[90] One explanation is that it exists to deter potential criminals from committing crimes in order to obtain benefits as a result.[91]
This may explain why the application of the forfeiture principle is
confined to where the criminal has intentionally committed the crime,
since it is only in this situation that the threat of forfeiture of benefits is
likely to have any deterrent effect at all. But it is most unlikely that this
principle of the civil law would constitute any greater deterrent than
that already provided by the criminal law. Another explanation of the

[87] *Holman* v. *Johnson* (1775) 1 Cowp. 341, 343; 98 ER 1120, 1121 (Lord Mansfield).
[88] See *Euro-Diam Ltd.* v. *Bathurst* [1990] QB 1, 35 (Kerr LJ).
[89] *Dunbar* v. *Plant* [1998] Ch. 412, 422 (Mummery LJ).
[90] See Shand, ' Unblinkering the Unruly Horse: Public Policy in the Law of Contract'
(1972) 30 *CLJ* 144.
[91] *Beresford* v. *Royal Insurance Co. Ltd.* [1938] AC 586, 598 (Lord Atkin); *Gray* v. *Barr*
[1971] 2 QB 554, 581 (Salmon LJ); *Re H. (deceased)* [1990] 1 FLR 441, 446 (Peter Gibson J).

principle is that it stems from a desire to punish the criminal for committing the crime, but it is surely inappropriate for the civil law to punish the criminal, this being a function for which only the criminal courts are suited. If the civil courts seek to punish the criminal in addition to the punishment which is imposed by the criminal courts, there is an obvious danger of excessive punishment.[92] A final explanation of the forfeiture principle is that it is justified on the ground that no criminal should be able to resort to the law to recover benefits to which he or she has become entitled as a result of his or her crimes.[93] This is probably the main reason for the existence of the rule, namely a general distaste that the law should be used to assist criminals in any way.[94]

(d) The forfeiture rule[95]

It is in connection with the commission of unlawful killings where the forfeiture principle has proved to be most important. Here the principle is called the forfeiture rule, as has been recognised by the Forfeiture Act 1982. Section 1 of the Act states that:

the 'forfeiture rule' means the rule of public policy which in certain circumstances precludes a person who has unlawfully killed another from acquiring a benefit in consequence of the killing.

Originally any benefits which accrued to an offender as a result of the commission of murder and other felonies were forfeited to the Crown, but this rule was abolished by the Forfeiture Act 1870. Consequently, the effect of the forfeiture rule today is that the benefits which accrue to the criminal as a result of an unlawful killing are forfeited to the person who is entitled to them once the claims of the criminal, or those claiming through the criminal, are discounted. The uncompromising rigidity of this forfeiture rule has often been criticised,[96] and its application has now been qualified by the Forfeiture Act 1982.[97]

---

[92] As recognised by Devlin J in *St John Shipping Corp.* v. *Joseph Rank Ltd.* [1957] 1 QB 267, 292.

[93] *Gray* v. *Barr* [1970] 2 QB 626, 640 (Geoffrey Lane J). See also *Euro-Diam Ltd.* v. *Bathurst* [1990] QB 1, 35 (Kerr LJ).

[94] As Wilmot CJ said in *Collins* v. *Blantern* (1767) 2 Wils. 347, 350; 95 ER 859, 852: 'no polluted hand shall touch the pure fountains of justice'.

[95] For general discussion of this rule see Earnshaw and Pace, 'Let the Hand Receiving It Be Ever So Chaste' (1972) 37 *MLR* 481.

[96] See, for example, Chadwick, 'A Testator's Bounty to His Slayer' (1914) 30 *LQR* 211.

[97] But the rule continues to be applied strictly in other jurisdictions which have no equivalent statutory provision. See, for example, *Troja* v. *Troja* (1994) 33 NSWLR 269 (NSW CA).

(i) The types of unlawful killing which trigger the forfeiture rule

It is clear that the forfeiture rule applies in respect of benefits which accrue as the result of the defendant committing the crime of murder,[98] in other words where the defendant has caused the death of a person intending either to kill or to cause serious injury to the victim.[99] It is irrelevant that the murderer was not motivated by a desire to profit from the killing, the very fact of committing murder being sufficient to preclude the killer from obtaining any benefits as a result.[100]

Whether the forfeiture rule is applicable to all forms of manslaughter has been a controversial matter. In *Dunbar* v. *Plant*[101] the Court of Appeal accepted by a majority that the forfeiture rule should apply to all cases of manslaughter, since there was no logical basis for distinguishing between different types of unlawful killing. If this is correct, it follows that the forfeiture rule is potentially applicable where the defendant commits voluntary manslaughter, whether by provocation, diminished responsibility or pursuant to a suicide pact,[102] and also where the killer commits involuntary manslaughter, whether constructive manslaughter or gross negligent manslaughter. The rule would even apply, as was accepted in *Dunbar* v. *Plant* itself, where the defendant was guilty of aiding and abetting a suicide.

It is not, however, correct to say that there is no logical basis for distinguishing between different types of unlawful killing, for it has been recognised on a number of occasions that a distinction can be drawn on the basis of the killer's culpability.[103] Consequently, it has been recognised that the forfeiture rule should be applicable only where the killer committed a crime intentionally or deliberately and it is irrelevant that the actual killing was unintentional or that the crime did not involve violence or threats of violence.[104] This test covers all cases of murder and voluntary manslaughter, which is simply murder committed in certain extenuating circumstances. So, for example, if the defendant is convicted

[98] See, for example, *Cleaver* v. *Mutual Reserve Fund Life Association* [1892] 1 QB 147.

[99] The forfeiture rule will not be applicable to a person who committed murder or any other unlawful killing but was found to be insane, simply because such a person is acquitted of the crime by virtue of insanity: Criminal Procedure (Insanity) Act 1964, s. 1. See *Re Houghton* [1915] 2 Ch. 173; *Re Pitts* [1931] 1 Ch. 546.

[100] *Cleaver* v. *Mutual Reserve Fund Life Association* [1892] 1 QB 147.

[101] [1998] Ch. 412. That the forfeiture rule should apply to all cases of manslaughter had been recognised previously. See, for example, *In the Estate of Hall* [1914] P 1, 7 (Hamilton LJ) and *Re Giles (deceased)* [1972] Ch. 544.

[102] See the Homicide Act 1957, ss. 2–4.

[103] *Gray* v. *Barr* [1970] 2 QB 626, 640 (Geoffrey Lane J). See also *Gray* v. *Barr* [1971] 2 QB 554, 569 (Lord Denning MR); *R.* v. *Chief National Insurance Commissioner, ex p. Connor* [1981] 1 QB 758, 766 (Lord Lane CJ); *Re K. (deceased)* [1985] Ch. 85, 98 (Vinelott J); *Re H. (deceased)* [1990] 1 FLR 441 (Peter Gibson J).

[104] See *Dunbar* v. *Plant* [1998] Ch. 412, 425 (Mummery LJ).

of manslaughter by reason of diminished responsibility, the forfeiture rule will prevent him or her from obtaining any property under the victim's will.[105] Constructive manslaughter would also be caught by the rule, since that crime requires the defendant to have committed an unlawful act intentionally.[106] It would also cover the case where the defendant was guilty of aiding and abetting the victim to commit suicide, since the defendant would have been committing the crime intentionally.[107] The test will not, however, cover the crime of gross negligence manslaughter, since that crime does not require proof of any intentional conduct.

Even though a distinction can be drawn between different types of unlawful killing on the basis of culpability, the better view is that of the majority in *Dunbar* v. *Plant*, so the forfeiture rule should apply to all types of unlawful killing. This is appropriate because the enactment of the Forfeiture Act in 1982 has meant that the forfeiture rule can be modified where justice demands.[108] If such an Act did not exist it would be appropriate to interpret the forfeiture rule restrictively to minimise unjust results. Since, however, the judges have a power to modify the application of the rule where appropriate, it is not necessary to interpret the rule itself restrictively.

If the forfeiture rule is to apply to all forms of manslaughter it should also apply to other forms of unlawful killing, such as causing death by dangerous driving,[109] even though this does not require proof of intent to commit the crime. The forfeiture rule should also apply to other forms of liability relating to unlawful killing, such as where the defendant is an accessory to an unlawful killing or where the defendant has attempted to kill or is involved in a conspiracy to kill or has incited an unlawful killing.

(ii) Proving the killer's guilt

For the forfeiture rule to apply it must be shown that the killer was guilty of an unlawful killing. As a general rule, if the killer has been convicted of an unlawful killing in criminal proceedings, this conviction is admissible evidence in civil proceedings and will be sufficient proof of guilt for the purposes of those proceedings, though it is still possible for the killer to show in the civil proceedings that he or she was not guilty of the unlawful killing.[110] But if the defendant is acquitted in criminal proceedings, all this means is that the defendant's guilt was not proved beyond all reasonable doubt. It is still possible for the defendant to be deprived of

---

[105] *Re Giles* [1972] Ch. 544; *Re Royse* [1985] Ch. 22.   [106] *R.* v. *Church* [1966] 1 QB 59.
[107] *Dunbar* v. *Plant* [1998] Ch. 412, 425 (Mummery LJ).   [108] See p. 585 below.
[109] Contrary to the Road Traffic Act 1988, s. 1 (as substituted by the Road Traffic Act 1991, s. 1).
[110] Civil Evidence Act 1968, s. 11.

benefits arising from the crime in civil proceedings where the standard of proof is the more easily satisfied test of the balance of probabilities.[111] So, in *Gray* v. *Barr*,[112] although the killer had been acquitted of homicide, he was still denied an indemnity from his insurers by virtue of the forfeiture rule. This rule will even be applicable if the killer had never been tried for the particular offence.[113]

(iii) Application of the forfeiture rule

(1) Entitlement to the benefit must be caused by the killing

For the forfeiture rule to be applicable to prevent the criminal from obtaining benefits it must be shown that the unlawful killing directly caused the criminal to become entitled to the benefits.[114] The usual 'but for' test of causation is applicable for these purposes. So it must be shown that the consequence of the killing is that the killer became entitled to benefits to which he or she would not otherwise have been entitled or that the killer had become entitled to benefits sooner than he or she would otherwise have done.[115] The forfeiture rule should be applicable where the killer has simply accelerated the acquisition of the benefit because, by killing the victim, the killer has deprived the victim of the opportunity to change his or her mind about the destination of the benefit and has removed the possibility that he or she might have predeceased the victim.[116] In certain circumstances it will be difficult to show that the killer became entitled to benefits because of the unlawful killing. For example, if the killer unlawfully wounded the victim who, before he or she died, made a will in favour of the killer, it is not possible to say that the killer became entitled to the benefits as a result of the killing, since the benefits accrued as a result of the victim's acts after the fatal injury had been caused. Similarly, if before he or she died the victim had the opportunity to alter the devolution of his or her estate but failed to do so, it might be argued that the killer became entitled to benefits as a result of the victim's omission rather than the killing.[117] But it would be possible to conclude that the victim's omission had broken the chain of causation

---

[111] *Dunbar* v. *Plant* [1998] Ch. 412. The Court of Appeal has recently affirmed that the standard for proving in civil proceedings that the killer was guilty of murder is the civil standard on the balance of probabilities: *Francisco* v. *Diedrick, The Times*, 3 April 1998.

[112] [1971] QB 554. [113] *Dunbar* v. *Plant* [1998] Ch. 412.

[114] *Cleaver* v. *Mutual Reserve Fund Life Association* [1892] 1 QB 147, 156 (Fry LJ); *St John Shipping Corp.* v. *Joseph Rank Ltd.* [1957] 1 QB 267, 292 (Devlin J). Cp. *Re H. (deceased)* [1990] 1 FLR 441, 442, where Peter Gibson J said that the forfeiture rule prevented the killer from benefiting directly *or indirectly* from the crime.

[115] Youdan, 'Acquisition of Property by Killing' (1973) 89 *LQR* 235.

[116] Maddaugh and McCamus, *The Law of Restitution* (Aurora: Canada Law Bank Inc., 1990) p. 486.

[117] Youdan, 'Acquisition of Property by Killing' (1973) 89 *LQR* 235, 236.

only where the victim knew that he or she had the opportunity to alter the devolution of property and consciously failed to do so. In the absence of clear evidence to this effect, this will be a very difficult matter to prove.

There will be a point at which the killing is too remote a cause of the benefits accruing to the killer, and in such circumstances the forfeiture rule will not operate to deprive the killer of such benefits. This is illustrated by a South African case[118] where a father killed his parents who had bequeathed property to his child and the child died shortly after the parents had been killed. It was held that the father could inherit the property which the child had been bequeathed by its grandparents. Although it could be argued that, but for the father killing his parents, the child would not have received the property and so the father would not have been able to inherit, the killing had ceased to be an operative cause, since the father did not receive the property from his parents directly. Consequently, the forfeiture rule was held to be inapplicable.

(2) The types of benefits to which the forfeiture rule may apply

Where the forfeiture rule is applicable it may prevent the killer from obtaining a number of different benefits. For example, a killer is not entitled to benefit under the will[119] or intestacy[120] of the deceased. Similarly, a killer is not entitled to benefit from a life insurance policy on the victim's life.[121] The forfeiture rule has even been applied to deprive a killer of social welfare payments, such as a widow's pension, to which he or she would otherwise have been entitled.[122]

(3) Application of the forfeiture rule to cases in which the victim is prevented from changing a will

In certain circumstances it may be possible to show that the victim was intending to change his or her will and so deprive the killer of property which had been bequeathed to the killer under the will. In such a situation the forfeiture rule does not strictly apply. This is because the killer was already entitled to the benefits and so did not become entitled to them as a result of the killing. Consequently, the forfeiture rule will not prevent title to the benefits from passing to the killer. But, because the killer's actions prevented the victim from changing his or her will, a constructive trust should be imposed so that the killer holds the property on trust for the 'person who, in the view of equity, has the best right to it'.[123]

---

[118] *Ex p. Steenkamp* (1952) (1) SA 744 (T).   [119] *Re Giles (deceased)* [1972] Ch. 544.
[120] *Re Sigsworth* [1935] 1 Ch. 89.
[121] *Cleaver* v. *Mutual Reserve Fund Life Association* [1892] 1 QB 147. In *Gray* v. *Barr* [1971] 2 QB 554 the forfeiture rule prevented the killer from claiming an indemnity from his insurers in respect of his liability for the unlawful death of the victim.
[122] *R.* v. *Chief National Insurance Commissioner, ex p. Connor* [1981] 1 QB 758.
[123] Youdan, 'Acquisition of Property by Killing' (1973) 89 *LQR* 235, 257.

(4) Application of the forfeiture rule to cases where there is a joint tenancy

A particular problem arises in respect of the application of the forfeiture rule where there is a joint tenancy. For example, where a husband and wife are joint owners of the matrimonial home and the wife kills her husband, what happens to their respective interests in the property? The effect of a joint tenancy is that each joint tenant is assumed to own the whole of the legal interest over the relevant property, subject to the co-existing and co-extensive rights of the other joint tenants. This means that, if there are two joint tenants and one of them dies, the other is automatically entitled to the property absolutely. But if one of the joint tenants dies as a result of being unlawfully killed by the other joint tenant, should the forfeiture rule come into operation and so prevent the killer from obtaining the property? This problem does not arise where there is a tenancy in common, since in such a case the property is owned equally by the tenants in common, so that if one tenant kills the other, the killer will not be deprived of the interest which he or she already possesses, but the forfeiture rule will prevent him or her from obtaining the interest of the deceased to which he or she might otherwise have been entitled.[124] But the application of the forfeiture rule is more complicated where there is a joint tenancy, essentially because the effect of killing the other joint tenant is that the killer's rights are enlarged rather than created as a result of the commission of the crime. There are two possible solutions to this problem.

The first solution is that the killer should be allowed to retain his or her beneficial interest in half of the property for life, but on his or her death the interest should revert to the beneficiaries of the victim's estate. This has the advantage that the killer's estate is eventually deprived of the beneficial interest in his or her half of the property and this is justified because, by killing the victim, the killer has deprived the victim of the chance of surviving him or her, and so of becoming entitled to the whole of the property.[125] Consequently, it should be assumed that the victim would have survived the killer and so would have taken the property absolutely by virtue of survivorship. But this smacks of double punishment since, in addition to the punishment of the killer for the unlawful killing, the killer's estate will also be deprived of property to which the killer was already entitled before the crime was committed. There is no warrant for extending the operation of the forfeiture rule in this way. To make matters worse, the effect of this punishment of depriving the killer's estate of the property is that the killer's beneficiaries are effectively being

---

[124] *Davitt* v. *Titcumb* [1990] Ch. 110.
[125] Jones, *Restitution in Public and Private Law*, p. 69.

punished for the crime, whereas the killer was allowed to enjoy the benefit of half of the property for the rest of his or her life.

The second, and preferable, solution to the problem is that the killer should be entitled to retain half of the beneficial interest in the property, but the other half of the beneficial interest should pass to the deceased's next of kin.[126] The best way of achieving this solution is as follows. By the usual rule of survivorship the entire legal interest in the property will be vested in the killer. The killing should, however, be treated as a severance of the joint tenancy so that the beneficial interest vests in the victim and the killer as tenants in common.[127] Where there are three joint tenants, one of whom kills the other, again the killer should not be deprived of his or her existing proprietary interest, but the principle of survivorship should still operate in favour of the other joint tenant, who would consequently obtain the victim's interest in the property.[128]

The advantage of this solution to the problem of joint tenants who kill is that the forfeiture rule prevents the killer from benefiting from the commission of the crime without depriving the killer, or those claiming through him or her, of an existing proprietary right. Consequently, in the case of a wife who has killed her husband, the forfeiture rule should not be used to deprive her of her own interest in the matrimonial home, since this right did not arise as a result of the killing. Rather, she should be prevented from acquiring her deceased husband's share of the matrimonial home. The effect of this solution is still that the killer is deprived of an existing right, namely the right of a joint tenant to gain the entire estate should the other joint tenant predecease him or her, but this is entirely appropriate since, by virtue of the killing, any chance that the other joint tenant might have naturally predeceased the killer has been removed.

(5) Application of the forfeiture rule where the victim is a life tenant

A similar problem to that of killings by joint tenants arises where property has been settled on one person for life with remainder to another person, and that person unlawfully kills the former. The effect of the death is that the killer is entitled to the estate immediately, but this would mean that the killer would be profiting from the crime, and this is contrary to public policy.[129] But if the forfeiture rule is invoked to prevent the killer from obtaining the property he or she will be deprived of a proprietary interest which already existed before the killing. To reconcile these conflicting policies it is necessary to identify the true benefit which the

---

[126] *Re K. (deceased)* [1985] Ch. 85, 100 (Vinelott J).
[127] This solution was approved in *Dunbar* v. *Plant* [1998] Ch. 412, 418 (Mummery LJ).
[128] See Street J in *Rasmanis* v. *Jurewitsch* [1968] 2 NSWLR 166, 168.
[129] *Cleaver* v. *Mutual Reserve Fund Life Association* [1892] 1 QB 147, 157 (Fry LJ).

killer obtains by unlawfully killing the life tenant. This benefit is that the killer accelerates the enjoyment of the life interest. The best method for preventing the killer from enjoying this benefit is by determining what the life tenant's life expectancy was and preventing the killer from enjoying the property until it is likely that the victim would have died naturally.[130] Consequently, the killer should hold the property on a constructive trust in favour of the victim's estate until the victim was expected to have died naturally.

The position is more complicated where the killer's interest is contingent on his or her surviving the life tenant. It could be argued that, in such circumstances, the act of killing the victim means that it should be presumed that the killer would not have outlived the life tenant, so the killer should be deprived of his or her whole interest in the property. But this constitutes a forfeiture of an existing proprietary interest, since even a contingent remainder is alienable and valuable.[131] A preferable solution is to have regard to the victim's life expectancy.[132] Until the end of the period of the victim's life expectancy the property should be treated as though the victim had not died and so should be held on constructive trust for the benefit of the victim's estate. If at the end of this period the killer is still alive, the contingency should be treated as fulfilled and the killer should take the property. If the killer dies before the end of this period the victim's beneficiaries should take the property absolutely.

(6) Claims of third parties

Whether third parties are able to claim benefits which accrue as a result of the commission of an unlawful killing turns on whether the third parties' claim relates to a benefit which accrued to the killer as a result of the crime. If the claim is so related it will be defeated by the forfeiture rule, because the effect of the rule is that the killer cannot obtain the benefit, and if he or she does not have the benefit the third party cannot claim it either.[133] Such benefits are tainted by the crime and so are caught by the forfeiture rule. If, however, the third party has an independent claim to the benefit he or she will not be affected by the forfeiture rule because the claim is untainted by the crime.

The typical example of a case in which the third party's claim is tainted by the crime is where personal representatives of the killer wish to claim benefits to which the killer would have been entitled had the forfeiture rule not been applicable. If the killer could not obtain the benefits by virtue of the forfeiture rule, then neither can the personal representatives. This is

---

[130] Youdan, 'Acquisition of Property by Killing' (1973) 89 *LQR* 235, 250.
[131] *Ibid.* [132] *Ibid*, p. 251.
[133] *Cleaver* v. *Mutual Reserve Fund Life Association* [1892] 1 QB 147, 155 (Lord Esher MR); *In the Estate of Cunigunda (otherwise Cora) Crippen (deceased)* [1911] P 108, 112.

illustrated by *Beresford* v. *Royal Insurance Co.*[134] where the personal representatives of a person who had committed suicide were unable to recover policy moneys from an insurance company, with which the suicide had obtained a life insurance policy. This is because at the time suicide was a crime and it was contrary to public policy that the personal representatives should recover the fruits of the crime, namely the money which was due as a result of the death of the suicide victim.

An example of a case in which a third party was able to claim benefits because the claim was untainted by the commission of the crime is the decision of the Court of Appeal in *Cleaver* v. *Mutual Reserve Fund Life Association*,[135] where a wife killed her husband who had a policy of life insurance with the defendants. The executors of the deceased claimed the sum insured from the defendants. Whilst it was admitted that the wife could not benefit from this money, because of the forfeiture rule, this rule could not be relied on to prevent the defendants from paying the money to the deceased's executors whose claim did not depend on whether the wife was entitled to money under the insurance policy. It was only once the executors had received this money that they would have been prohibited from paying it to the wife by virtue of the forfeiture rule.

(7) Allocation of benefits which are caught by the forfeiture rule

If the killer and those claiming through the killer are unable to obtain benefits by virtue of the forfeiture rule, such benefits should be considered to be retained by the victim's estate and so should be transferred to those people who are beneficiaries of that estate, except for the killer. Normally benefits, such as property, will pass to the victim's residuary legatee[136] or to those who are entitled to the property if the victim died intestate.[137] If the killer was the sole residuary legatee the property should be distributed as though the victim had died intestate.[138] If the property was left to a class of beneficiaries, one of whom was the killer, his or her share should be divided equally between the other members of the class.[139]

It has sometimes been suggested that, rather than the victim's estate passing to the next person in succession after the criminal, it should pass as *bona vacantia* to the Crown.[140] But there is no reason why the forfeiture rule should be used to deprive the successor of his or her rights to the estate, since these rights were not created by the commission of the crime, but rather arise from the law of intestacy or by virtue of the terms

---

[134] [1938] AC 586.   [135] [1892] 1 QB 147.
[136] As occurred in *Re Peacock* [1957] Ch. 310.   [137] *Re Sigsworth* [1935] Ch. 89.
[138] *Re Pollock* [1941] 1 Ch. 219; *Re Callaway* [1956] Ch. 559.
[139] *Re Peacock* [1957] Ch. 310.   [140] See *Re Callaway* [1956] Ch. 559.

of the victim's will. In other words, the successor's rights are not tainted by the commission of the crime.

(8) Proprietary implications of the forfeiture rule[141]

A consequence of the principle that no criminal should profit from his or her crime is that title to property which would otherwise accrue to the criminal, or to those claiming through him or her, cannot pass. But this response is not free from difficulty. This is because in many cases, whether by virtue of statute or the common law, legal title should indeed pass to the criminal, and there is no provision in the statute or common law to the effect that an exception should be made where the passing of property is triggered by the criminal's own act. For the forfeiture rule to work it must be assumed that, for reasons of public policy, every legal rule contains an implied term to the effect that no criminal who, by the commission of the crime, has triggered the passing of property should be allowed to benefit from the crime.[142] It would be a much more honest response to apply the relevant statutory and judicial laws literally, without artificial interpretation. This would mean that legal title to property would pass to the criminal. But, because of the principle that no criminal should profit from his or her crime, equity should ensure that an equitable interest in the property is created in favour of the victim, by virtue of the killer's unconscionable conduct, with the result that the criminal should hold the property on a constructive trust for the victim's estate.[143] This would have the advantage that the operation of the forfeiture rule would not conflict with the clear words of statute and judicial precedent but would continue to fulfil the policy that no criminal should profit from his or her crime.

A consequence of this would be that, if the property which had been acquired by or through the criminal had been received by a third party, beneficiaries of the victim of the crime, would be able to recover the property. But this is subject to the qualification that the property could not be recovered from a third party who was a *bona fide* purchaser for value.[144]

(iv) The Forfeiture Act 1982

The inflexible common law forfeiture rule has now been modified by the 1982 Forfeiture Act. Although this Act does not apply where the

---

[141] See Chapter 20.

[142] See for example *Re Royse* [1985] Ch. 22 in which it was assumed that the application of the Inheritance (Provision of Family and Dependants) Act 1975 was subject to the forfeiture rule, even though the Act makes no provision for this rule.

[143] Youdan, 'Acquisition of Property by Killing' (1973) 89 *LQR* 235, 253. This would be consistent with Lord Browne-Wilkinson's interpretation of the constructive trust in *Westdeutsche Landesbank Girozentrale* v. *Islington LBC* [1996] AC 669, 716. See p. 630 below.

[144] See Chapter 22.

defendant has committed murder,[145] in every other case in which the forfeiture rule has precluded a person who has unlawfully killed another person from acquiring any interest in property, the application of that rule may be modified by order of the court.[146] Obviously this power to modify the forfeiture rule will be relevant only where the forfeiture rule is applicable in the first place, so it remains necessary to consider the application of the forfeiture rule at common law. But the Forfeiture Act is not automatically applicable simply because the forfeiture rule applies. The Act will apply only where the killer has committed an unlawful killing either as principal or accessory,[147] but it does not apply to inchoate offences which relate to unlawful killing, such as attempts to kill the victim. The Act applies only where somebody is prevented by the forfeiture rule from acquiring an interest in property. The notion of 'interest in property' includes any beneficial interest in property which the offender would have acquired under the will of the deceased or on his or her intestacy,[148] and property which was held on trust for any person and which the offender would have acquired as a result of the death of the deceased.[149] This would cover the case where one joint tenant kills the other and, subject to the operation of the forfeiture rule, would have obtained the property absolutely by virtue of the principle of survivorship. The definition of 'interest in property' means that the Act does not apply to benefits which would have been obtained under an insurance policy had not the forfeiture rule been applicable, save where the proceeds of the policy are held on trust for the killer.[150]

The court will modify the forfeiture rule only if it is satisfied that, having regard to the conduct of the killer and of the deceased and to any other circumstances of the case which appear to be material, the justice of the case requires the rule to be modified.[151] The forfeiture rule may be disapplied completely[152] or it may be modified in part.[153] In exercising his or her discretion whether or not the forfeiture rule should be modified the trial judge must not seek to do justice between the parties to the dispute, but should rather consider whether the culpability of the defendant justified the strict application of the forfeiture rule.[154] In *Dunbar* v. *Plant*[155] Mummery LJ said that:

---

[145] Forfeiture Act 1982, s. 5.

[146] *Ibid*, s. 2(1). The Act applies regardless of when the unlawful killing occurred: s. 7(4). It applies even though the killer has not been convicted of an offence: *Dunbar* v. *Plant* [1998] Ch. 412.

[147] *Ibid*, s. 1(2).   [148] *Ibid*, s. 2(4)(a).   [149] *Ibid*, s. 2(4)(b).

[150] *Dunbar* v. *Plant* [1998] Ch. 412.   [151] Forfeiture Act 1982 s. 2(2).

[152] *Ibid*, s. 2(1). See, for example, *Dunbar* v. *Plant* [1998] Ch. 412.

[153] Forfeiture Act 1982, s. 2(5).

[154] *Dunbar* v. *Plant* [1998] Ch. 412.   [155] *Ibid*, pp. 427–8.

The court is entitled to take into account a whole range of circumstances relevant to the discretion, quite apart from the conduct of the offender and the deceased: the relationship between them; the degree of moral culpability for what has happened; the nature and gravity of the offence; the intentions of the deceased; the size of the estate and the value of the property in dispute; the financial position of the offender; and the moral claims and wishes of those who would be entitled to take the property on the application of the forfeiture rule.

The application of the Forfeiture Act is well illustrated by the decision of the Court of Appeal in *Re K. (deceased)*,[156] in which a wife, having killed her husband, was convicted of manslaughter for which she received a sentence of two years' probation. This lenient sentence was justified by the particular circumstances of the killing. The wife had been battered by her husband for a number of years. On the day of the killing her husband had beaten her again and, intending to frighten him away, she picked up a loaded shotgun, released the safety catch and aimed it at him. The gun accidentally went off and killed him. The wife claimed that she was entitled to an interest under her husband's will and was also entitled to the matrimonial home. The Court, having accepted that the forfeiture rule was applicable, held that the wife should be granted complete relief from the forfeiture of all the benefits which had accrued to her on the death of her husband. A number of factors were considered to be relevant to the exercise of the court's discretion.

(1) The most important factor was the degree of moral culpability of the wife in committing the crime; her offence was considered to be at the least serious end of the spectrum of manslaughter offences. This was because she had been provoked to kill her husband and this had been reflected in the sentence of probation which she had received.
(2) The moral culpability of the wife and of her husband were compared. Whilst the wife had been loyal to her husband, it was considered to be relevant that he had abused her for a number of years.
(3) The relative financial position of the wife as compared with that of the other people who were entitled under the husband's will was taken into account. The court stressed that the husband had made appropriate provision for his wife and was under no moral duty to make provision for anybody else.
(4) The conduct of the other beneficiaries under the husband's will was also considered, particularly since a number of them had confirmed, after the death of the husband, that the terms of the husband's will should be respected, despite the potential application of the forfeiture rule.[157]

---

[156] [1986] Ch. 180.   [157] See also *Re H. (deceased)* [1990] 1 FLR 441.

Further, in *Dunbar* v. *Plant*[158] the Court of Appeal exercised its discretion to disapply the forfeiture rule completely in a case in which the defendant had aided and abetted the suicide of her fiancee, where he had killed himself pursuant to a suicide pact. It was held that the forfeiture rule should not be applied to prevent the defendant from obtaining benefits from the deceased's estate for a number of reasons. The most important reason was that the nature of the defendant's crime was such that she had not received any penal sanction for it, consequently her culpability did not justify the application of the forfeiture rule. Also the deceased had intended that the relevant benefits, namely the proceeds of an insurance policy and his interest in their house, should be received by the defendant on his death.[159]

By virtue of the enactment of the Forfeiture Act 1982 the injustice which arose from the strict adherence to the principle that no criminal could benefit from the commission of a criminal offence has been alleviated to some extent. But that Act is not totally satisfactory. It should, for example, be extended to cases of murder, since there are some cases of murder in which the killer's true culpability does not warrant the strict application of the forfeiture rule. For example, in certain cases of mercy killing, where one spouse kills the other to alleviate his or her suffering, there is no reason why the killer should be prevented from obtaining benefits which would otherwise have accrued to him or her on the death of the victim. Different murders can involve different degrees of culpability and this should be reflected in the way the forfeiture rule is applied in such cases. It is also most unfortunate that the Act does not apply to relieve the forfeiture of benefits which would have been received under an insurance policy had not the forfeiture rule been applicable. Most importantly, the Forfeiture Act places the judiciary in a particularly difficult position, since the Act gives no assistance on how the judges' discretion should be exercised. Consequently, in all reported cases concerning the application of the Act the judges have disapplied the forfeiture rule completely rather than modify the application of the rule.[160]

---

[158] [1998] Ch. 412.

[159] Mummery LJ dissented on the ground that weight should be given to the moral claims and wishes of the deceased's family.

[160] The only case in which the forfeiture rule was modified rather than disapplied was the decision of the trial judge in *Dunbar* v. *Plant*, but the Court of Appeal overruled this decision. Other cases in which the rule was disapplied completely include *Re K.* [1986] Ch. 180 and *Re S.* [1996] 1 WLR 235.

PART V

PROPRIETARY RESTITUTIONARY CLAIMS

20

Establishing Proprietary Restitutionary Claims

1. THE NATURE

The examination of the law of restitution so far has concentrated on two different principles on which restitutionary claims can be founded, namely unjust enrichment and wrongdoing. This Part will examine the third and final principle on which such claims may be based, namely the vindication of the plaintiff's property rights.

(a) Questions of terminology

(i) Distinguishing between proprietary claims and remedies

The analysis of proprietary restitutionary claims which is adopted in this book draws a fundamental distinction between proprietary claims and proprietary remedies.[1] All restitutionary claims which are founded on the vindication of the plaintiff's proprietary rights[2] are properly classified as proprietary claims, since they are dependent solely upon the identification and protection of proprietary rights. But the restitutionary remedies by virtue of which these property rights are vindicated are not necessarily proprietary, since, depending upon the particular circumstances of the case, the appropriate remedy may be either proprietary or personal.[3] So, for example, if a proprietary remedy is awarded the plaintiff may recover particular property,[4] whereas if a personal restitutionary remedy is awarded the plaintiff will recover only the value of particular property.[5] It is consequently vital to bear in mind the distinction between the claim and the remedy; just because the plaintiff brings a proprietary restitutionary claim it does not necessarily follow that he or she will obtain a proprietary restitutionary remedy.

[1] This distinction was recognised by Millett LJ in *Trustee of the Property of F.C. Jones and Sons (a firm)* v. *Jones* [1997] Ch. 159, 168.

[2] Such a description of the underlying principle does have some judicial support. See, for example, *Tinsley* v. *Milligan* [1994] 1 AC 340, 368 (Lord Lowry).

[3] The most important example of a case in which the plaintiff obtained a personal restitutionary remedy for a proprietary restitutionary claim is the decision of the House of Lords in *Lipkin Gorman (a firm)* v. *Karpnale Ltd.* [1991] 2 AC 548. See p. 665 below.

[4] For discussion of this and other proprietary restitutionary remedies see pp 657–64 below.

[5] See pp. 664–73 below.

(ii) Classifying proprietary restitutionary remedies

One further question of terminology needs to be considered. Birks[6] has called proprietary restitutionary remedies the 'second measure' of restitution, or value surviving, to distinguish them from personal remedies, which he considers to be the 'first measure' of restitution, or value received, and this terminology has been adopted by a number of commentators. This classification of the 'first' and 'second' measures of restitution is not, however, particularly useful, since use of the words 'first' and 'second' does not accurately reflect the essential difference between personal and proprietary remedies. Consequently, no reference is made in this book to the first and second measures of restitutionary remedies. Instead, the traditional distinction between personal and proprietary remedies will be adopted, since these terms identify the crucial distinction between the two types of remedy. For personal remedies operate against one person, the defendant, who received the plaintiff's property, whereas proprietary remedies operate against the property which the defendant has and in which the plaintiff has a proprietary interest. The key distinction between the two types of claim, as recognised by Goode, is that personal remedies are founded on the *obligation* to pay, whereas proprietary remedies are founded on the continuing *ownership* of the relevant asset.[7]

(b) The nature of the cause of action

When the plaintiff wishes to vindicate his or her proprietary rights, he or she simply needs to establish that, when the defendant received the property in question, the plaintiff had an interest in it, either legal or equitable. The plaintiff may have such a proprietary interest either because the nature of the transfer to the defendant means that title to the property did not pass to the defendant or because the circumstances existing at the time of the transfer are such that a proprietary interest is recognised by operation of law.

(i) Distinguishing between vindication of property rights and reversal of unjust enrichment

The most important feature of the action to vindicate property rights is that it forms part of the law of property and has nothing to do with the principle of reversing the defendant's unjust enrichment.[8] Consequently, it is not necessary to show that the defendant has been

---

[6] Birks, *An Introduction to the Law of Restitution*, p. 75.
[7] Goode, 'Ownership and Obligation in Commercial Transactions' (1987) 103 *LQR* 433.
[8] See p. 12 above.

unjustly enriched at the plaintiff's expense. Once the plaintiff has shown that the defendant has property, whether it be chattels, land, intellectual property or, most importantly, money, in which the plaintiff had a proprietary interest at the time of receipt, nothing else needs to be proved to establish the plaintiff's cause of action. If the defendant has the plaintiff's property he or she should return it, or its value, to the plaintiff.

Many commentators who have written about the law of restitution would disagree with this analysis since they treat proprietary restitutionary claims as founded on the principle of reversing unjust enrichment.[9] They argue that since property is a benefit which generally cannot be subjectively devalued it is possible to establish that the defendant who received the property has been enriched. Also, if the plaintiff had a proprietary interest in the property at the time of its receipt by the defendant, this shows that the property was received at the plaintiff's expense. The stumbling block in this unjust enrichment analysis relates to the identification of the ground of restitution. Some commentators suggest that the applicable grounds of restitution are the same as those which were discussed in Part III.[10] Other commentators create new grounds of restitution to enable them to explain the reported cases. For example, Burrows is forced both to rely on the ground of ignorance and to create a ground of restitution which he calls 'retention of property belonging to the plaintiff without his consent'.[11] But such artifice is completely unnecessary. The reported cases do not use such reasoning and they have no need to do so, simply because it is sufficient to establish that the defendant has received property in which the plaintiff has a proprietary interest.

The perfect example of this analysis being adopted is the decision of the House of Lords in *Lipkin Gorman (a firm)* v. *Karpnale*[12] where one of the partners of the plaintiff firm of solicitors stole money from the plaintiff and gambled with it at the defendant's casino. The plaintiff brought a restitutionary claim for money had and received against the defendant. The House of Lords held that the plaintiff's claim should succeed simply because it had a continuing proprietary interest in the money at the time it was received by the defendant.[13] There was no need to establish a claim founded on the reversal of the defendant's unjust enrichment, since the claim was founded on the vindication of property rights and had nothing

---

[9] See in particular Burrows, *The Law of Restitution*, Chapter 13. A number of judges would agree. See, for example, Millett LJ in *Boscawen* v. *Bajwa* [1996] 1 WLR 328, 334.

[10] This is the approach of both Birks, *An Introduction to the Law of Restitution*, and Goff and Jones, *The Law of Restitution*.

[11] Burrows, *The Law of Restitution*, Chapter 13.   [12] [1991] 2 AC 548.

[13] In fact, by virtue of the tracing rules, the plaintiff did not have a continuing proprietary interest, but counsel for the defendant surprisingly conceded the point. See p. 646 below.

to do with unjust enrichment.[14] It is for this reason that no ground of restitution was identified by the House of Lords, even though a number of commentators have sought to identify one from the facts of the case.[15] In the light of this conclusion that *Lipkin Gorman* has nothing to do with unjust enrichment and everything to do with vindication of proprietary rights it is ironic that the case has become the leading authority on the recognition of unjust enrichment as a cause of action in English law.

Birks has specifically rejected this analysis of proprietary restitutionary claims. He has asserted that it is incorrect to compare unjust enrichment with property rights because the former is an event and the latter is a response to an event.[16] Consequently, he concludes that unjust enrichment can trigger property rights. The problem is that Birks does not give any convincing examples of cases in which property rights were indeed triggered by the fact that the defendant was unjustly enriched at the plaintiff's expense. It is, anyway, unnecessarily complicating to assert that property rights are triggered by unjust enrichment in any substantive sense. [17] It is much simpler to say that property rights arise from a variety of events and, once it has been shown that the plaintiff does indeed have a property right which has been interfered with by the defendant, this itself constitutes the event by virtue of which restitutionary remedies can be awarded.[18]

(ii) The relationship between the law of restitution and the law of property

One of the most difficult questions involving the ambit of the law of restitution concerns the relationship between it and the law of property. There are three possible views of the nature of this relationship.

(1) The law of restitution and the law of property are distinct

The law of restitution is completely separate from the law of property. This means that where it is alleged that the plaintiff has retained an interest in the defendant's property, the determination of this and the remedy which is applicable to vindicate this interest is purely a matter for the law of property and has nothing to do with the law of restitution. This means

[14] See also *Macmillan Inc.* v. *Bishopsgate Investment Trust plc. (No. 3)* [1996] 1 WLR 387. See Virgo, 'Reconstructing the Law of Restitution' (1996) 10 *TLI* 36.

[15] See Birks, 'The English Recognition of Unjust Enrichment' [1991] *LMCLQ* 473, 483 and McKendrick, 'Restitution, Misdirected Funds and Change of Position' (1992) 55 *MLR* 377.

[16] Birks, 'Property and Unjust Enrichment: Categorical Truths' [1997] *NZ Law Rev.* 623. See also Birks, 'Misnomer' and Swadling, 'What is the Law of Restitution About? Four Categorical Errors' both in *Restitution: Past, Present and Future* (ed. Cornish, Nolan, O'Sullivan and Virgo).

[17] See p. 12 above.

[18] See Grantham and Rickett, 'Trust Money as an Unjust Enrichment: A Misconception' [1998] *LMCLQ* 514, 519.

that the potential reach of the law of restitution is very limited. This extreme and restrictive interpretation of the ambit of the law of restitution is not reflected in the case law.

(2) Restitutionary proprietary rights are created by operation of law

The law of restitution is relevant only where the proprietary interest is created by operation of law rather than by the consent of the parties. This is the view in particular of Birks who has said that '[t]here is no such thing as a restitutionary right generated by consent'.[19] This means, for example, that where an express trust is constituted this 'can never create a restitutionary beneficial interest'.[20] If this view is correct, it is necessary to draw a distinction between pure proprietary rights which are pre-existing and consensual, and restitutionary proprietary rights which are created by operation of law, the law of restitution being relevant only to the latter. These restitutionary proprietary rights will arise where, for example, the plaintiff's property has been substituted by another asset. Birks assumes that the plaintiff's right to claim the substitute asset is a restitutionary proprietary right, because the plaintiff has a right to this asset only by operation of law. If, however, the defendant had retained the original asset, the plaintiff's right to claim this asset would have been a pure proprietary right.[21] But no convincing reason is given why we should divide up proprietary rights into pure and restitutionary rights. Such a division is highly artificial because, regardless of the reason for the existence of the right, all these rights are proprietary and may trigger restitutionary remedies.[22] Whether or not the plaintiff has a proprietary right is a matter for the law of property, and it is only once such rights have been recognised that the question of restitutionary relief becomes relevant. If we create artificial distinctions between pure proprietary rights and restitutionary proprietary rights the danger is that we ignore the fundamental policy of the law which is to protect property rights, regardless of how the right arose.

---

[19] Birks, *An Introduction to the Law of Restitution*, p. 54. See also Nolan, 'Change of Position', p. 177; Barker, 'After Change of Position: Good Faith Exchange in the Modern Law of Restitution', p. 211, both in *Laundering and Tracing* (ed. Birks) and Swadling, 'Restitution and *Bona Fide* Purchase' in *The Limits of Restitutionary Claims: A Comparative Analysis* (ed. Swadling), p. 79.

[20] Birks, *An Introduction to the Law of Restitution*, p. 54.

[21] See Birks, 'On Taking Seriously the Difference Between Tracing and Claiming' (1997) 11 *TLI* 2, 8.

[22] See Grantham, 'Doctrinal Bases for the Recognition of Proprietary Rights' (1996) 16 *OJLS* 561, 574.

(3) The vindication of proprietary rights forms part of the law of restitution

All questions concerning the vindication of proprietary rights are restitutionary and so should fall within the ambit of the law of restitution. This is the preferable view. The reason for this derives from the fundamental nature of the law of restitution. That body of law which we call restitution is simply concerned with the determination of when restitutionary remedies can be awarded.[23] In the context of proprietary claims, before the question of the availability of restitutionary relief can arise, we need to ascertain that the plaintiff has proprietary rights in the property received by the defendant. It should make no difference whether the right arose consensually or by operation of law. So long as the plaintiff has a proprietary interest there is at least the potential of a restitutionary remedy being awarded.[24] Consequently, it is not possible to conclude that the law of restitution and the law of property are distinct bodies of law, since the law of restitution is available to vindicate proprietary rights where the defendant has interfered with those rights. Rather, it is the law of unjust enrichment and the law of property which are totally distinct. This is because the recognition and creation of property rights is a matter for the law of property and has nothing to do with the unjust enrichment principle.

Since proprietary restitutionary claims depend on the identification of a proprietary interest in the plaintiff, whether arising consensually or by operation of law, the law relating to the identification of such interests needs to be examined before it is possible to consider whether restitutionary relief is available. This requires analysis of the law of real property, personal property and the law of trusts. In a textbook on the law of restitution there simply is not enough space to examine such matters, which are dealt with perfectly well by the specialised books on these areas.[25] But a book on the law of restitution does need to identify the general principles relating to the recognition and creation of proprietary rights before going on to examine how these rights can be vindicated by restitutionary remedies.[26]

---

[23] See p. 3 above.

[24] Burrows, *The Law of Restitution*, at p. 370, is also prepared to consider all proprietary claims as falling within the law of restitution. But now see, 'Restitution: Where Do We Go From Here?' (1997) 50 *CLP* 95, 112.

[25] See, especially, Worthington, 'Proprietary Interests in Commercial Transactions' and Goode, *Commercial Law*, chapter 8.

[26] See pp. 601–41 below.

(iii) The relationship between proprietary restitutionary claims and restitution for wrongs

There are certain wrongs which are dependent on proof that the defendant has interfered with the plaintiff's proprietary rights, primarily the tort of conversion. Should restitutionary claims relating to such a tort be treated as founded on the wrong or as involving the vindication of proprietary rights? This is a difficult question, but the preferable view is that such claims are best treated as founded on the wrong.[27] This is for two reasons: first, because the wrong itself must be specifically pleaded, and secondly because the remedy which is available is not necessarily restitutionary, but may involve the award of compensatory damages. This is a characteristic of a claim founded on wrongdoing rather than vindication of proprietary rights.

Where the plaintiff seeks a restitutionary remedy in respect of a wrong committed by the defendant the remedy is usually personal. There are, however, cases in which the defendant has been awarded a proprietary restitutionary remedy and the event which triggered this was a wrong.[28] In such cases there is clearly an overlap between restitution for wrongs and the vindication of property rights. It is preferable, however, to treat such claims as ultimately founded on the wrong, since it is the wrong which triggers the recognition of the plaintiff's proprietary right.[29]

(c) The nature of the restitutionary remedy

The remedies which are available to the plaintiff to enable him or her to vindicate proprietary rights may be either personal or proprietary, though in each case the remedy is restitutionary since it enables the plaintiff either to recover the value of the property or to assert a proprietary interest in the actual property or its product or substitute.[30]

(i) Personal restitutionary remedies[31]

The personal restitutionary remedies which are available where the plaintiff seeks to vindicate a proprietary right include recovery of the value of money received by the defendant under the common law action of money had and received[32] and the equitable remedy of account of profits. Where the plaintiff seeks a personal remedy he or she only needs

---

[27] See p. 450 above.

[28] See, for example, *Attorney-General for Hong Kong* v. *Reid* [1994] 1 AC 324 where the Privy Council recognised that the plaintiff had a proprietary restitutionary remedy by virtue of the defendant's breach of fiduciary duty.

[29] See *ibid.*   [30] See *Boscawen* v. *Bajwa* [1996] 1 WLR 328, 334 (Millett LJ).

[31] See pp. 664–73 below.

[32] As occurred in *Lipkin Gorman (a firm)* v. *Karpnale Ltd.* [1991] 2 AC 548.

to show that, when the defendant received the relevant property, the plaintiff had a proprietary interest in that property. The fact that the defendant has dissipated the property after its receipt does not necessarily defeat the plaintiff's claim, though dissipation of the property may enable the defendant to plead the defence of change of position.[33]

(ii) Proprietary restitutionary remedies[34]

The proprietary restitutionary remedies, sometimes known as remedies *in rem*, enable the plaintiff to assert his or her property rights over an asset which is held by the defendant. There are two types of proprietary restitutionary remedy: first, remedies by virtue of which the plaintiff can recover the property which is held by the defendant; secondly, remedies which recognise that the plaintiff has a security interest in property which is held by the defendant. Both types of remedy can be awarded only if the plaintiff continues to have a proprietary interest in an asset which is held by the defendant at the time the plaintiff commences the restitutionary claim. Proprietary remedies are not concerned with returning the value of what the defendant has received to the plaintiff, but they are concerned simply with the assertion of proprietary rights against particular property. It follows that, if the defendant dissipated the property which he or she had received before the plaintiff brought his or her claim, the plaintiff is forced to rely on personal remedies. Proprietary restitutionary remedies may, however, still be awarded even though the specific property has been dissipated, so long as the defendant retains a product of the property or a substitute for it.[35]

(1) The advantages of proprietary restitutionary remedies

Proprietary restitutionary remedies have three main advantages over personal restitutionary remedies.

(1) Where the defendant has become bankrupt or insolvent a personal remedy may be useless. This is because the effect of a personal remedy is to create a debt owed by the defendant to the plaintiff. Until the debt has been paid the plaintiff is a creditor of the defendant, but he or she will not have any security interest in the defendant's property. Consequently, the plaintiff's claim for payment will not be distinguished from those of the other general creditors of the defendant as regards the distribution of the defendant's assets. If the defendant has sufficient assets to pay off all the creditors this will not be a hardship. But, if the defendant has insufficient assets to pay off all the creditors, the plaintiff may not receive the

---

[33] See Chapter 24.   [34] See pp. 657–66.

[35] Whether the plaintiff can assert a proprietary right against a product of or substitute for the plaintiff's original property depends upon the application of the tracing rules. See pp. 642–55 below.

full amount which is due, and he or she may not receive anything at all. This is because when assets are distributed upon the debtor's insolvency or bankruptcy they are distributed according to a list of priorities. Unsecured creditors will not receive anything until the claims of creditors with proprietary rights and preferential creditors have been satisfied and the expenses of the insolvency proceedings paid. Consequently, if the plaintiff can show that he or she has a proprietary interest in some of the assets in the defendant's possession, the plaintiff will rank above the general unsecured creditors in the distribution of the defendant's assets and, subject to the nature of the proprietary interest, their claim is more likely to be satisfied.[36] In particular, in those cases in which it is clear that the defendant never received title to the relevant property, that property should not form part of the general pool of assets which are available for distribution amongst the defendant's general creditors.[37] For where the defendant has never enjoyed the legal or beneficial ownership of the property in question there is no reason why his or her creditors should benefit from the fact that he or she received the property in which the plaintiff had retained a proprietary interest.

(2) A proprietary remedy is also advantageous where it is not possible to assess accurately the true value of the property which is in the defendant's possession. For example, where the defendant receives an original work of art which has been stolen from the plaintiff, it may simply be impossible to value the picture accurately and, even if it were possible, receiving the monetary value of the picture may be an inadequate remedy for the plaintiff, who may wish to recover the work of art itself because of its æsthetic or sentimental value. This advantage of a proprietary remedy will not be relevant where the plaintiff is seeking restitution of money, since money has no intrinsic value, save where it no longer constitutes currency.

(3) A final advantage of some proprietary remedies arises where the property which has been obtained by the defendant has increased in value. In such circumstances, the plaintiff would clearly prefer to assert his or her rights against the property itself and so gain the benefit of the increased value. Where, however, the property has fallen in value, the plaintiff will wish to claim a personal restitutionary remedy which would be assessed by reference to the value of the property at the time it was received by the defendant.

---

[36] The extent of the priority which the plaintiff will gain over other creditors will depend upon the type of proprietary remedy which is awarded. See pp. 657–64 below.

[37] Goode, 'Ownership and Obligation in Commercial Transactions' (1987) 103 *LQR* 433, 439.

(2) Policy issues

Since an important consequence of awarding proprietary restitutionary remedies is that the plaintiff will gain priority over the defendant's unsecured creditors if the defendant becomes bankrupt or insolvent, the award of such a remedy will be to the prejudice of these other creditors. Therefore, the court must always be vigilant against affording the plaintiff excessive protection at the expense of the defendant's other creditors. This has been recognised in a number of cases. For example, in *Re Stapylton Fletcher Ltd*.[38] Judge Paul Baker QC said:

> The court must be very cautious in devising . . . interests and remedies which erode the statutory scheme for distribution on insolvency. It cannot do so because of some perceived injustice arising as a consequence only of the insolvency.[39]

Ultimately, the court must simply strive to balance the interests of two innocent parties, namely the plaintiff and the defendant's creditors.

In striving to balance these interests one of the most important considerations relates to whether or not the plaintiff can be considered to have taken the risk of the defendant's insolvency or bankruptcy. For if the plaintiff did take the risk, or can be deemed to have taken it, there is no reason why the plaintiff's claim should be preferred to that of the defendant's other creditors, and so he or she should rank equally with those creditors.[40] The principal situation in which it is acceptable to prefer the plaintiff's claim over those of the defendant's other creditors is where the plaintiff was completely unaware that property had been taken from him or her, for example where a thief has stolen some of the plaintiff's property. In such a case it is perfectly acceptable that the plaintiff be afforded proprietary protection since he or she was not given the opportunity to arrange for the restitutionary claim to be secured. Equally, if the plaintiff made arrangements for security but for some reason this security is invalid, it should be acceptable that the plaintiff be afforded a degree of proprietary protection to fulfil his or her legitimate expectations that any claim against the defendant would be secured.

(d) The framework for analysing a typical proprietary restitutionary claim

When the plaintiff seeks a restitutionary remedy to vindicate a proprietary right there are a number of different questions which need to be

[38] [1994] 1 WLR 1181, 1203.

[39] See also *Re Polly Peck International plc. (No. 2)* [1998] 3 All ER 892, 827 (Mummery LJ).

[40] This will be the case, for example, where the plaintiff entered into a transaction with the defendant which was void *ab initio*. See Lord Goff in *Westdeutsche Landesbank Girozentrale* v. *Islington LBC* [1996] AC 669, 684.

considered in a specific order. The preferable mode of analysis is as follows:

(1) Does the plaintiff have a proprietary interest in an asset, whether an existing one or one which can be created by operation of law?
(2) Can the plaintiff follow or trace this proprietary interest from his or her own hands to those of the defendant, even though other property has been substituted for the plaintiff's property or it has become mixed with property belonging to somebody else?
(3) What is the nature of the plaintiff's claim to this property and what is the appropriate remedy to vindicate the plaintiff's proprietary rights?[41] If the plaintiff seeks a proprietary restitutionary remedy it is necessary to show that the defendant has retained property in which the plaintiff can identify his or her proprietary interest.
(4) Does the defendant have a defence to defeat or restrict the plaintiff's action?

Although this process of analysis is not necessarily reflected in the cases, where the different stages are often indistinguishable, it is essential that a clear and logical method of reasoning is adopted. For without it, the result will be confusion and inconsistency, as is reflected in the decided cases themselves.

2. IDENTIFICATION OF THE PROPRIETARY INTEREST

The first question which must be considered to establish a proprietary restitutionary claim is whether the plaintiff has a proprietary interest in the property which was received by the defendant. This notion of a subsisting proprietary interest has usefully been described by Birks as the proprietary base,[42] which indicates that it is the necessary foundation upon which the proprietary claim will be built. The proprietary base may be established in two different ways. First, the plaintiff will have a continuing proprietary interest where the nature of the transfer was such that title to the property did not pass to the defendant. In this type of case the plaintiff's proprietary interest will have been retained.[43] Secondly, even though the legal title may have passed to the defendant, the plaintiff will have a proprietary interest in the property received by the

---

[41] This will be affected by whether the plaintiff's claim is brought in equity or at common law.

[42] Birks, *An Introduction to the Law of Restitution*, pp. 378–85. A phrase which was adopted by Millett J in *Macmillan Inc.* v. *Bishopsgate Investment Trust plc. (No. 3)* [1995] 1 WLR 978, 989.

[43] Sometimes legal title will pass to the defendant but it will be revested in the plaintiff, for example by rescission. See pp. 611–12 below.

defendant where the circumstances surrounding the transfer were such that it is possible to recognise that the plaintiff has an equitable interest in the particular property. In this type of case the plaintiff's proprietary interest will have been created.[44]

(a) Retention of a proprietary interest[45]

In determining whether the plaintiff has retained title in the property which was received by the defendant it is necessary to examine the rules of property law concerning the transfer of title.[46]

(i) The general rules for the passing of title

The fundamental principle relating to the passing of title, regardless of whether the transaction is one of sale or gift, is that title will pass only where the parties intend it to pass.[47] Usually the parties will intend title to pass where the property is delivered to the purchaser or donee, either actually or constructively. Constructive delivery includes where title deeds are delivered or goods are set aside for storage.[48] Where there is no evidence of the parties' actual intent they will be presumed to intend that title will pass on delivery.

Title can only pass, however, where the property was in existence at the time of the transfer and was ascertainable, even though it had not been ascertained.[49] It is for this reason that the claim of the main group of plaintiffs in *Re Goldcorp Exchange Ltd.*[50] failed. In *Goldcorp* some of the plaintiffs had entered into a contract to purchase bullion from a company which had gone into insolvent liquidation. It was essential to these plaintiffs' claims to the bullion that they had a proprietary interest in it. This was because a bank had lent money to the company and it had obtained a security interest in the bullion by means of a floating charge. Since the company had insufficient assets to satisfy the claims of both the plaintiffs and the bank, the plaintiffs needed to show that they had a proprietary interest which ranked above that of the bank. The difficulty which faced the plaintiffs was that, although they had paid the purchase price for the bullion and had agreed with the company that it would store

[44] See Grantham, 'Doctrinal Bases for the Recognition of Proprietary Rights' (1996) 16 *OJLS* 561 who characterises these two approaches in terms of the 'property approach' and the 'duty approach'.

[45] See Worthington, *Proprietary Interests in Commercial Transactions*, chapter 6.

[46] For analysis of the rules relating to the passing of title in money see Fox, 'The Transfer of Legal Title to Money' (1996) 4 *RLR* 60.

[47] *Middleton* (1873) LR 2 CCR 38, 43. See the Sale of Goods Act 1979, s. 17.

[48] *Re Stapylton Fletcher Ltd.* [1994] 1 WLR 1181.

[49] See the Sale of Goods Act 1979, s. 16. Ascertainment may occur by exhaustion: Sale of Goods (Amendment) Act 1995, s.1(2) amending the Sale of Goods Act 1979.

[50] [1995] 1 AC 74. See also *Re London Wine Co. (Shippers) Ltd.* [1986] PCC 121.

the bullion on their behalf, the bullion had not been specifically allocated to them. It was for this reason that the Privy Council held that the property in the bullion had not passed to the plaintiffs. Since the plaintiffs' bullion could not be ascertained it was not possible to conclude that the plaintiffs had a proprietary interest in any particular property.[51]

Alternatively, the plaintiffs in *Re Goldcorp Exchange Ltd.* argued that they had a proprietary interest in the bullion by virtue of estoppel. Their argument was that, since the company had promised to allocate the bullion to each plaintiff, it was estopped from denying that it had done so and consequently it could be assumed that the plaintiffs did have a proprietary interest in the bullion. This argument was summarily dismissed by the Privy Council, because estoppel could give the plaintiffs only the pretence of a title where no title exists and such a fictional title could not give the claimants priority over the bank's real proprietary interest in the bullion. Estoppel is essentially a rule of evidence and cannot be used to conjure a title. This is surely right. It is one thing to estop the defendant by virtue of the representations which it has made and which have been relied upon by the plaintiff to its detriment. It is a completely different thing to bind a third party by virtue of the defendant's representations. In other words, estoppel can be used as a defence but cannot be used to establish a cause of action.[52]

A second group of claimants in *Re Goldcorp Exchange Ltd.* were in a somewhat different position, because they had bought bullion from a different company which had since been taken over by Goldcorp. Before this take-over occurred their bullion had been ascertained and appropriated and it was conceded, rightly, that this was sufficient to pass title to the claimants. Consequently, they had a proprietary base on which their proprietary claim could be founded.[53]

The law relating to the passing of title where a purchaser has bought part of an identified bulk has been amended by the Sale of Goods (Amendment) Act 1995. By virtue of this Act it will be presumed that the parties intended that title should pass where the purchaser has bought part of an identified bulk and has paid part of the price in advance.[54] This

---

[51] Cp. *Re Stapylton Fletcher Ltd.* [1994] 1 WLR 1181 where the property in identical bottles of wine was held to have passed to the purchasers of wine, even though the bottles had not been appropriated to each customer, it being sufficient that the purchasers' bottles were kept separate from the vendor's trading stock. The effect of this was that the purchasers held the wine as tenants in common.

[52] *Re Stapylton Fletcher Ltd.* [1994] 1 WLR 1181, 1203 (Judge Paul Baker QC).

[53] In fact, the proprietary claim of this group of claimants failed because they were unable to identify the bullion in which they had a proprietary interest.

[54] Sale of Goods (Amendment) Act 1995, s. 1(3). For discussion of this and other aspects of the Act see Ulph, 'The Sale of Goods (Amendment) Act: Co-ownership and the Rogue Seller' [1996] *LMCLQ* 93.

presumption of intention can be rebutted by evidence that title was to pass at a later date.

Even where the plaintiff has initially retained legal title, that title will automatically pass as soon as the plaintiff's property, or its product or substitute, ceases to be identifiable.[55] This will be determined by reference to the tracing rules.[56]

(ii) Circumstances in which title will not pass

In addition to the general rules on when title in property will pass, there are certain recognised situations in which title will not pass to the defendant. Sometimes the plaintiff will make it clear that he or she has no intention that title in the particular property should pass to the defendant. This is illustrated by those transactions in which the plaintiff agrees to sell property to the purchaser but includes a reservation of title clause to ensure that legal title to the property does not pass to the purchaser until he or she has paid for it.[57] If the purchaser sells the plaintiff's property without the plaintiff's consent he or she will not obtain title to the proceeds of sale. Similarly the plaintiff will not intend title to pass to the defendant where the transaction is a bailment.

Also, title will not pass to the defendant either where the plaintiff lacks an intention that title should pass or where the plaintiff's intention can be treated as vitiated. Such vitiation of intention will arise only in certain exceptional cases. Analysis of the categories of cases in which the plaintiff's intention is vitiated suggests that they mirror the recognised grounds of restitution within the action founded on the reversal of unjust enrichment. But it must be emphasised that these categories have a different function in the context of proprietary restitutionary claims and are consequently defined in a different way from the recognised grounds of restitution. For in this context we are not concerned with whether the plaintiff actually intended to benefit the defendant. Rather, we are concerned to determine whether the plaintiff actually intended that title in the property should pass to the defendant.

(1) Ignorance[58]

Where the plaintiff is unaware that his or her property has been taken by the defendant, or that it was taken by a third party and has subsequently been received by the defendant, the plaintiff clearly does not intend that

---

[55] *Westdeutsche Landesbank Girozentrale* v. *Islington LBC* [1996] AC 669, 703 (Lord Browne-Wilkinson).

[56] See pp. 642–55 below.

[57] This is called a *Romalpa* clause after the case which first recognised the validity of such clauses: *Aluminium Industrie Vaassen BV* v. *Romalpa Aluminium Ltd.* [1976] 1 WLR 676. See Worthington, *Proprietary Interests in Commercial Transactions*, chapter 2.

[58] See Chapter 7.

title to the property should pass to the defendant and so he or she retains a proprietary interest. So, for example, where the plaintiff's property is stolen, title will not pass to the thief.[59] In a number of cases the plaintiff, who was ignorant that his or her property had been taken, was able to bring a restitutionary claim against the defendant who was either the direct or the indirect recipient of the property. In each of these cases the courts emphasised that the effect of the plaintiff's ignorance was that it prevented title from passing to the defendant.

(a) Direct recipients

In *Neate* v. *Harding*[60] the defendants went into the house of the plaintiff's mother and took the plaintiff's money. It was held that the plaintiff could recover the amount of money which had been taken in an action for money had and received. Pollock CB emphasised that the money belonged to the plaintiff and continued to belong to him even though it had been taken by the defendants. As he said: '[t]he owner of property wrongfully taken has a right to follow it . . . treat it as his own, and adopt any act done to it'.[61] In *Merry* v. *Green*[62] the court specifically relied on the plaintiff's ignorance to explain why the plaintiff's property had not passed to the defendant. In this case the plaintiff had sold a bureau in a public auction to the defendant, who later discovered that a purse containing money was hidden in a secret drawer inside it. It was held that the plaintiff could recover the value of the money since he had never intended it to be delivered to the defendant.

(b) Indirect recipients

In a number of cases the plaintiff has been able to bring a restitutionary claim against a defendant who has received property belonging to the plaintiff via a third party in circumstances in which the plaintiff was unaware that the third party had taken the property. In each case the success of the claim depended on proof that when the defendant received the property the plaintiff continued to have a proprietary interest in it. Consequently, the award of restitutionary relief could be justified because the defendant had interfered with the plaintiff's continuing ownership of the property. This is illustrated by *Clarke* v. *Shee and Johnson*[63] in which the plaintiff's clerk had received payments from the plaintiff's customers which he used to buy lottery tickets from the defen-

---

[59] *R.* v. *Ilich* (1987) 69 ALR 231, 244 (Wilson and Deane JJ). This is also implicit in the decision of the House of Lords in *Lipkin Gorman (a firm)* v. *Karpnale Ltd.* [1991] 2 AC 548.

[60] (1851) 6 Exch. 349; 155 ER 577. See also *Holiday* v. *Sigil* (1826) 2 Car. and P 177; 172 ER 81 and *Moffat* v. *Kazana* [1968] 3 All ER 271.

[61] (1851) 6 Exch. 349, 350; 155 ER 577, 578.

[62] (1841) 7 M and W 623; 151 ER 916.

[63] (1774) 1 Cowp. 197; 98 ER 1041. This case was specifically affirmed by the House of Lords in *Lipkin Gorman (a firm)* v. *Karpnale Ltd.* [1991] 2 AC 548.

dants, without the knowledge of the plaintiff. The plaintiff successfully recovered this money from the defendants in an action for money had and received. Lord Mansfield specifically recognised that the plaintiff's action succeeded because he was able to identify his money in the hands of the defendants.[64]

Another important decision in this context is that of Denning J in *Nelson* v. *Larholt*.[65] In this case the plaintiff beneficiaries of the deceased brought an action to recover money which had been paid to the defendants without their knowledge by the deceased's executors. Denning J held that the plaintiffs' action succeeded both in equity and in an action for money had and received. In an important dictum he identified the essential principle relating to the recovery of money which has been taken from the plaintiff without his or her knowledge:[66]

If [money] is taken from the rightful owner, or indeed, from the beneficial owner, without his authority, he can recover the amount from any person into whose hands it can be traced, unless and until it reaches one who receives it in good faith and for value and without notice of the want of authority . . . This principle has been evolved by the courts of law and equity side by side . . . It is no longer appropriate, however, to draw a distinction between law and equity . . . The right here is not peculiar to equity or contract or tort, but falls naturally within the important category of cases where the court orders restitution, if the justice of the case so requires.

This suggestion that the approaches of law and equity have fused is unduly optimistic, but this remains an important dictum since it recognises that the plaintiff has a proprietary restitutionary claim where his or her money has been taken without authority.

The best example of this principle in operation is the decision of the House of Lords in *Lipkin Gorman* v. *Karpnale*[67] where it was accepted that the plaintiff retained a proprietary interest in the money which had been stolen from it by one of its partners and which had been received by the defendant. Consequently, the plaintiff was able to recover the value of the money in an action for money had and received by virtue of its proprietary rights. Clearly the plaintiff did not intend title in the money to pass because it was unaware that the money had been taken. A similar analysis was adopted by the Court of Appeal in *Macmillan Inc.* v. *Bishopsgate Investment Trust plc. (No. 3)*,[68] concerning a restitutionary claim for the recovery of shares which had been taken from the plaintiff without its knowledge.

---

[64] See also *Marsh* v. *Keating* (1834) 1 Bing. NC 198; 131 ER 1094; *Calland* v. *Loyd* (1840) 6 M and W 26; 151 ER 307.

[65] [1948] 1 KB 339.   [66] *Ibid* at pp. 342–3.   [67] [1991] 2 AC 548.

[68] [1996] 1 WLR 387. See p. 13 above.

(2) Mistake

Where the plaintiff has made a mistake[69] this prevents title in property from passing to the defendant only where the mistake is fundamental, since it is only such mistakes which can be regarded as sufficiently serious to vitiate the plaintiff's intention that title should pass to the defendant.[70] The notion of a fundamental mistake is notoriously uncertain, but it is possible to define the principle to some extent. The question whether title passes to the defendant when the plaintiff is affected by a mistake is one which has been rigorously examined in the context of the crime of theft, where it is necessary to determine whether the property mistakenly transferred by the victim can be considered to belong to the victim or to the defendant.[71] A number of criminal cases have recognised that a mistake will be fundamental in three situations,[72] with the consequence that the plaintiff's intention to transfer the property to the defendant will have been vitiated, so that title to the property will not pass. These cases should be regarded as applicable to the law of restitution as well, because the question for both the criminal law and the law of restitution is the same: when does a mistake prevent title from passing?

(a) Mistake as to the identity of the recipient

That a mistake as to the identity of the recipient of the property will constitute a fundamental mistake is illustrated by *Middleton*,[73] a criminal case in which the defendant, who wished to withdraw money from his post office savings account, was handed a sum of money by the post office clerk. This sum was more than was standing to the defendant's credit at the time. The clerk paid this amount of money because he had referred to a letter which authorised the payment, but the letter referred to another depositor. It was held that in these circumstances the mistake of the clerk was such that it prevented the title in the money from passing to the defendant. The clerk's mistake was fundamental since he was

---

[69] Presumably, after the decision of the House of Lords in *Kleinwort Benson Ltd.* v. *Lincoln CC* [1998] 3 WLR 1095, regardless of whether the mistake is a mistake of law or fact.

[70] *Barclays Bank* v. *Simms* [1980] QB 677, 689 (Robert Goff J). See also *Chambers* v. *Miller* (1862) 13 CBNS 125; 143 ER 50.

[71] The offence is now defined by the Theft Act 1968, s. 1. The question whether the victim has retained title for the purposes of theft is less important today because, by virtue of s. 5(4) of the Theft Act 1968, if the defendant is under an obligation to restore property received by mistake, that property is deemed to belong to the person who is entitled to restitution.

[72] See the decision of the High Court of Australia in *Ilich* v. *R.* (1987) 69 ALR 231, 243 (Wilson and Dawson JJ). See also Williams, 'Mistake in the Law of Theft' (1977) 36 *CLJ* 62, 64.

[73] (1873) LR 2 CCR 38. See also *Cundy* v. *Lindsay* (1878) 3 App. Cas. 459 and *R.E. Jones Ltd.* v. *Waring and Gillow Ltd.* [1926] AC 670, 696 (Lord Sumner).

mistaken about the identity of the defendant, and this mistake vitiated his intent to pay the defendant.[74] The plaintiff's mistake as to identity will, however, only vitiate the plaintiff's intention where the identity of the recipient is a matter of fundamental importance.[75]

(b) Mistake as to the identity of the property

That a mistake as to the identity of the property will constitute a fundamental mistake was recognised in *Ashwell*,[76] where the defendant was convicted of stealing a sovereign. The defendant had asked the victim to lend him a shilling but the victim handed over a sovereign thinking that it was a shilling. Cave J held that 'as there was a mistake as to the identity of the coin no property passed'.[77]

(c) Mistake as to the quantity of the property

Whether a mistake as to the quantity of the property which is transferred should be regarded as a fundamental mistake is a matter of some controversy, but where the plaintiff transfers more property to the defendant than he or she intended this must be a fundamental mistake because the plaintiff did not intend to transfer the excess property to the defendant. Birks has described such a mistake as one 'which all men would agree that it decisively vitiated the intention to give'.[78] This view has also been endorsed in a number of judicial pronouncements.[79] There are, however, other cases which suggest that a mistake as to quantity does not prevent title from passing.[80]

That a mistake as to the quantity of the property transferred can constitute a fundamental mistake was recognised by the High Court of Australia in *Ilich* v. *R.*,[81] in which the defendant was charged with stealing money from the victim. The defendant assumed that money which had been left on a table by the victim constituted payment by the victim for the work the defendant had done as a locum in a veterinary practice and so the defendant took it. He later realised that he had been overpaid. The High Court accepted that the victim had made a fundamental mis-

---

[74] (1873) LR 2 CCR 38.

[75] *Citibank NA* v. *Brown Shipley and Co. Ltd.* [1991] 2 All ER 690, 699 (Waller J).

[76] (1885) 16 QBD 190. See also *Middleton* (1873) LR 2 CCR 38, 45.

[77] (1885) 16 QBD 190, 201. This was doubted in *Potisk* (1973) 6 SASR 389 on the basis that the mistake did not relate to the identity of the metal disc which was handed over but its value, and so the mistake should not have been treated as fundamental. But surely the identity of a coin depends on the value which is ascribed to it, so that a mistake as to the type of coin handed over is a fundamental mistake.

[78] Birks, p. 158. See also Williams, 'Mistake in the Law of Theft' (1977) 36 *CLJ* 62, 64.

[79] See *Eldan Services Ltd.* v. *Chandag Motors Ltd.* [1990] 4 All ER 459, 462 (Millett J) and *Friends' Provident Life Office* v. *Hillier Parker May and Rowden* [1995] 4 All ER 260, 275 (Auld J). See also *Russell* v. *Smith* [1958] 1 QB 27.

[80] See, for example, *Moynes* v. *Coopper* [1956] 1 QB 439.

[81] (1987) 69 ALR 231.

take in overpaying the defendant and so in principle title to the money did not pass.[82]

Whether a similar result would be reached in this country must be considered in the light of the difficult case of *Chase Manhattan Bank NA* v. *Israel-British Bank (London) Ltd.*[83] In this case the plaintiff bank mistakenly paid $2 million to the defendant bank, thinking that it was liable to pay the money to the defendant, but forgetting that the money had already been paid. The plaintiff sought to recover the money. Since the defendant had gone into liquidation and did not have sufficient assets to pay off all of its unsecured creditors, it was crucial for the plaintiff to establish that it had a proprietary interest in the money so that it could claim a proprietary restitutionary remedy, and so achieve priority over the general creditors. The trial judge held that the plaintiff had an equitable proprietary interest in the money which had been paid to the defendant, with the result that the money was held on constructive trust for the plaintiff.[84] It is implicit in this decision that legal title to the money had passed to the defendant. But why did title pass when the plaintiff's mistake related to the amount of money paid and so could be considered to have been fundamental? In fact, a finding of fundamental mistake should have been easier to reach in *Chase Manhattan* than it was in *Ilich* because, when determining whether there is a fundamental mistake as to quantity, the nature of the transaction between the parties is significant. A distinction should be drawn between those cases in which the plaintiff intends the defendant to have some money but simply overpays him, and those cases where the plaintiff pays the defendant twice in two separate transactions. The best example of a simple case of overpayment is *Ilich* itself, where arguably the mistake was not sufficiently fundamental after all. This was because the victim intended to give the defendant only part of the money, but it was not possible to identify which money was intended to pass and which was paid by mistake.[85] Consequently, the victim's intention that title to the money should pass should not have been treated as vitiated. But the facts of *Chase Manhattan* were very different, because in that case it was possible to identify which money the plaintiff did not intend the defendant to have, namely the whole of the second payment. As regards the payment of this money the plaintiff's mistake should have been treated as fundamental so that the plaintiff retained legal title to the money.[86] Despite this identification of a

[82] On the facts of the case title did pass because the defendant was considered to be a *bona fide* purchaser for value. See Chapter 22.

[83] [1981] Ch. 105. [84] On this aspect of the decision see p. 630 below.

[85] This was recognised by Brennan J in *Ilich* (1987) 69 ALR 231, 254.

[86] This analysis is supported by a number of theft cases in which it was held that title passed to the defendant where money had simply been overpaid. See, for example, *Moynes* v. *Coopper* [1956] 1 QB 439 and *Attorney-General's Reference (No. 1 of 1983)* [1985] QB

fundamental mistake, the reason legal title was considered to have passed to the defendant in this case was presumably not because of the nature of the mistake but simply because the plaintiff's money had been paid into the defendant's bank account and so it was not possible to identify it at law.[87]

The preferable view therefore is that whenever the plaintiff makes a fundamental mistake as to the identity of the recipient or the identity or the quantity of the property which has been transferred, title to that property will not pass because the plaintiff's intention to transfer title will have been vitiated by a fundamental mistake. All other mistakes are mistakes as to motive only and will not prevent property from passing. So, for example, a mistake as to a liability to pay money to the defendant will not prevent title from passing, because it is not sufficiently fundamental to vitiate the plaintiff's intention that title to the money should pass to the defendant. The mistake will, instead, have a lesser consequence, namely to vitiate the plaintiff's intention to benefit the defendant so that the plaintiff will be able to recover the amount of money paid by mistake by reference to the unjust enrichment principle.[88]

(3) Misrepresentation

Where the defendant has induced a mistake to be made by the plaintiff so that he or she transfers property to the defendant, generally title will pass to the defendant,[89] save where the mistake which has been induced can be characterised as fundamental.[90] This is defined in the same way as for spontaneous mistakes. Where the induced mistake was not fundamental but was induced by a fraudulent misrepresentation it will be possible to rescind at law any transaction entered into as a result of the misrepresentation and revest title in the plaintiff.[91]

(4) Powerlessness

Although powerlessness has never been specifically recognised as a reason why the plaintiff did not intend title to be transferred to the defendant, it is obvious that, in the same way that the plaintiff lacks such an intention where he or she is ignorant of the transfer, similarly the plaintiff will lack such an intention where he or she is powerless to resist the transfer. So, for example, if the defendant enters the plaintiff's house, ties

---

182. Cp. *R.* v. *Shadrokh-Cigari* [1988] Crim. LR 465, a case of overpayment where it was held that property did not pass because of the supposed application of *Chase Manhattan*. But *Chase Manhattan* was distinguishable because it involved a double payment rather than a simple overpayment.

[87] See p. 646 below.   [88] See Chapter 8.

[89] *Clough* v. *North Western Rly. Co.* (1871) LR 7 Exch. 26 and *Moynes* v. *Coopper* [1956] 1 QB 439, 445 (Lord Goddard CJ).

[90] *Cundy* v. *Lindsay* (1878) 3 App. Cas. 459.   [91] See p. 612 below.

him up and then takes his property, title in that property will not pass to the defendant because clearly the plaintiff did not intend title to pass.

(5) Compulsion

Compulsion will not operate to vitiate the plaintiff's intention that title should pass save in the most exceptional case in which the pressure is so extreme that the plaintiff had no choice but to do as the defendant demanded.[92] For example, if the defendant threatened to kill the plaintiff if he or she failed to pay a sum of money to the defendant, then, since the pressure is so extreme, the plaintiff had no choice but to do as the defendant demanded, and so any apparent intention of the plaintiff that the defendant should obtain title to the money should be treated as vitiated.

An example of such a case is *Duke de Cadaval* v. *Collins*,[93] where the plaintiff was arrested by the defendant, on the false ground that he owed the defendant £10,000. To secure his release the plaintiff paid the defendant £500. It was held that the plaintiff could recover this money in an action for money had and received. Lord Denman CJ held that 'the property in the money . . . never passed from the plaintiff, who parted with it only to relieve himself from the hardship and inconvenience of a fraudulent arrest'.[94] The restitutionary claim was therefore brought to vindicate the plaintiff's continuing proprietary interest. Since a threat to continue to deprive the plaintiff of his liberty is a particularly serious threat, Lord Denman's analysis is perfectly acceptable, since the plaintiff could be treated as having no choice at all but to pay the defendant. Where the threat is less extreme, such as a threat to meddle with the plaintiff's property or reputation, title to money paid as a result of the threat will presumably pass to the defendant, and so the plaintiff's restitutionary claim can only be founded upon the reversal of unjust enrichment.[95] Consequently, it is highly unlikely that duress of goods or economic duress could ever be considered to be so serious as to vitiate the plaintiff's intention that title in the property should pass to the defendant.

(iii) Particular circumstances in which title will be revested in the plaintiff

Sometimes where title has passed to the defendant it may subsequently be revested in the plaintiff. The most important example of this is where

---

[92] Fox, 'The Transfer of Legal Title to Money' (1996) 4 *RLR* 60, 68. Usually, where compulsion operates, the plaintiff does have a choice whether or not to submit, albeit not a free choice. See Chapter 9.

[93] (1836) 4 Ad. and E 858; 111 ER 1006.   [94] *Ibid*, p. 864; p. 1009.

[95] See Chapter 9.

the plaintiff has transferred property to the defendant pursuant to a contract which he or she is subsequently able to rescind at law.[96] Rescission at common law is a self-help mechanism which automatically revests title in the plaintiff.[97] It follows that the plaintiff will be able to claim the property which was transferred to the defendant. Whilst the ambit of rescission at law is a matter of some controversy, the preferable view is that it is available only where the defendant induced the plaintiff to enter into the transaction as a result of a fraudulent misrepresentation.

If, of course, the property has been dissipated, rescission of the transaction cannot have any proprietary consequences, since there will not be any title which can be revested in the plaintiff.[98]

Where property has been transferred under a contract which has been breached or frustrated then, once the contract has been repudiated by the other party, it is terminated only from the moment of repudiation and does not operate to revest title in the plaintiff. The difference between rescission and repudiation is that rescission operates to undo the transaction, whereas repudiation terminates the transaction for the future.

(iv) Particular circumstances in which title will pass

Although in most cases in which the plaintiff transfers property to the defendant title will pass to the defendant, it is worth emphasising three situations in which title will pass because it may be thought that the nature of the transfer will prevent this.

(1) Failure of consideration

(a) Total failure of consideration
Where the plaintiff has transferred property to the defendant in the expectation that a benefit will be received in return and this benefit is not forthcoming, this failure of consideration will not revest title in the plaintiff.[99] This was recognised by the Privy Council in *Re Goldcorp Exchange Ltd.*[100] where the plaintiffs had paid money for bullion which was never allocated to them. Even though the consideration for their payment had failed totally it was held that title to the money had passed to the defendant company and could not be revested. Consequently, the plaintiffs were confined to a restitutionary claim founded on the reversal of the

---

[96] See p. 30 above.

[97] See, in particular, *Car and Universal Finance Co. Ltd.* v. *Caldwell* [1965] 1 QB 524.

[98] Although the defendant will be liable to make restitution of the value of any benefit received under the transaction. See p. 31 above.

[99] Though failure of purpose may operate to create an equitable proprietary interest in the plaintiff. See p. 622 below.

[100] [1995] 1 AC 74.

defendant's unjust enrichment, with the ground of restitution being total failure of consideration.[101] This is surely right. The plaintiffs initially intended title to pass in the expectation that a benefit would be received. The failure to receive a benefit subsequently was not a sufficient reason to revest title in the plaintiffs.

(b) Absence of consideration[102]

Sometimes there may appear to be greater scope for a proprietary restitutionary claim to be made where the consideration for a transaction is absent, such as where the plaintiff transfers property to the defendant pursuant to a transaction which turns out to be null and void. In such circumstances the plaintiff cannot receive any consideration for the transfer by operation of law. Whether it is possible in such a case to treat the plaintiff's intention that title should be transferred to the defendant as vitiated was an issue which arose in the interest rate swaps litigation, where money was paid by banks and local authorities pursuant to interest rate swap transactions which were held to be null and void because they were *ultra vires* the local authorities. Even though the transaction was void *ab initio* the House of Lords in *Westdeutsche Landesbank Girozentrale* v. *Islington LBC*[103] recognised that title to the money did pass under the transactions so that the plaintiff was unable to bring a proprietary claim to recover it.[104]

Whether *Westdeutsche Landesbank* is correct depends on whether the plaintiff's intention to transfer title should be considered to have been vitiated when, as a matter of law, the transaction was null and void from the start. In *Westdeutsche Landesbank* Lord Goff considered the proper analogy to be with a case of breach of contract where there has been a total failure of consideration.[105] This is not convincing, because where a contract has been set aside for breach, it is obvious that title to property will already have passed. Where, however, the contract is void *ab initio*, the situation is different because there never was an underlying transaction. Despite this difference, the decision of the House of Lords is surely correct. The question with which we are concerned is whether the plaintiff's intention to transfer title can be regarded as vitiated. At the time *Westdeutsche Landesbank* was decided a plaintiff could not rely on mistake of law to establish a restitutionary claim. Consequently, the plaintiff relied on failure of consideration, specifically absence of consideration. But, simply because the plaintiff cannot receive consideration under the

---

[101] See Chapter 12. This claim was worthless because the defendant was insolvent.
[102] See p. 394 above.   [103] [1996] AC 669.
[104] That title passes under an *ultra vires* transaction was accepted in *Ayers* v. *South Australian Banking Corp.* (1871) LR 3 PC 548.
[105] [1996] AC 669, 689 (Lord Goff).

transaction as a matter of law is not a reason for vitiating his or her inten-tion that title should pass.[106] The House of Lords has, however, subse-quently recognised that a mistake of law may ground a restitutionary claim.[107] It follows that where a plaintiff transfers a benefit to the defen-dant in the belief that the underlying transaction was valid, when it was in fact void, the plaintiff was mistaken at the time the benefit was trans-ferred. If this can be considered to be a fundamental mistake this is suf-ficient to vitiate the plaintiff's intention that title to property should pass to the defendant. It is, however, unlikely that such a mistake is funda-mental since it is not a mistake as to the identity of the defendant or the property or even as to the quantity of the property transferred. It is sim-ply a mistake as to the liability to pay the defendant and this is not a fun-damental mistake, since it is a mistake only as to motive.[108]

(2) Illegality

If the plaintiff has paid money to the defendant pursuant to an illegal transaction, the fact of illegality will not prevent the title in the property from passing to the defendant. This was recognised in *Singh* v. *Ali*.[109] This is presumably because, even though the transaction itself is void for reasons of public policy, the plaintiff intended that property should pass and the law recognises this intention. But such a conclusion contradicts the basic policy of the law relating to illegal transactions which is simply that such transactions should have no effect.[110]

(3) Incapacity

(a) Minority

Where the plaintiff transfers property to the defendant the fact that the plaintiff is a minor will not prevent title to the property from being trans-ferred.[111] Similarly, where the plaintiff transfers property to the defen-dant, the fact that the defendant is a minor will not prevent title from being transferred. However, as regards this latter situation, the effect of section 3(1) of the Minors' Contracts Act 1987 is that a minor may be

---

[106] Save, perhaps, where the court considers that, since public policy demands that the transaction should be void, public policy should also demand that title to the property should be revested in the plaintiff. But this is a difficult argument because of the inherent uncertainty in determining what public policy demands.

[107] *Kleinwort Benson Ltd.* v. *Lincoln CC* [1998] 3 WLR 1095.

[108] See p. 610 above.

[109] [1960] AC 167. See also *Belvoir Finance* v. *Stapleton* [1971] QB 210. Cp. Higgins, 'The Transfer of Property Under Illegal Transactions' (1962) 25 *MLR* 149 who argues that prop-erty should not pass under illegal transactions. Restitution of property which has been transferred pursuant to an illegal transaction is examined at pp. 637–41 below.

[110] See p. 641 below.

[111] *Chaplin* v. *Leslie (Frewin) Publishers Ltd.* [1966] Ch. 71.

required to transfer to the other party to the contract any property which was acquired by the minor under the contract or any property which represents the original property, as long as the court considers it to be just and equitable that such a transfer is made. No case has yet considered the meaning of this statutory provision, so it remains unclear when it will be just and equitable to make such a transfer of property. However, if the provision is interpreted literally it seems that it is confined to proprietary restitutionary claims. Consequently, if the minor has disposed of the property which has been obtained, and there is no other property which represents it, restitution under the statute will be denied. The statute will also only be applicable where property has been transferred pursuant to a contract and will not extend to the recovery of gifts.

(b) Institutional incapacity

Where the plaintiff transfers property to the defendant and one of the parties to the transaction is an institution which lacks capacity to participate in it, this should not prevent title from passing. It has, however, been suggested that where a public authority makes a payment which it lacks capacity to make it will have a proprietary claim to recover what it has paid.[112] This appears to be inconsistent with *Westdeutsche Landesbank* which suggest that title will pass even though it is transferred pursuant to an *ultra vires* transaction. The only possible justification for concluding that title should not pass where a public authority lacks capacity to transfer the property is by reference to public policy. Consequently, it may be concluded that the policy which makes the transaction *ultra vires* in the first place, namely the protection of taxpayers, should be followed through to its logical conclusion to ensure that the public authority cannot lose its proprietary rights.

(4) Exploitation

Since the grounds of restitution which are founded on exploitation are equitable it follows that the defendant's exploitation of the plaintiff will not prevent legal title from passing to the defendant.[113]

(v) Retention of equitable title

Where a trust has been constituted, whether expressly or as a matter of law, the trustee will hold property on trust for the beneficiary. This means that the trustee has the legal title to the property and the beneficiary has an equitable interest in the property. If the trustee transfers the property to a third party without the beneficiary's consent, the

---

[112] See Lord Goff in *Woolwich Equitable Building Society* v. *IRC* [1993] AC 70, 177, commenting on *Auckland Harbour Board* v. *The King* [1924] AC 318.
[113] *Allcard* v. *Skinner* (1887) 36 Ch.D 145, 190 (Bowen LJ).

beneficiary will retain an equitable interest in the property which he or she can vindicate against the third party. This is illustrated by *Re Diplock*[114] in which the executors of the deceased's estate mistakenly paid part of the money from the estate to third parties. The beneficiaries of the estate who were actually entitled to receive the property were able to bring a proprietary claim to recover it since they had retained an equitable proprietary interest in it.

(b) Creation of a proprietary interest[115]

Even where title to the property has passed to the defendant it may still be possible for the courts to recognise that the plaintiff has a proprietary interest in the property because the circumstances of the transfer may be such that an equitable proprietary interest will be recognised. The essential nature of equitable proprietary rights was identified by Lord Browne-Wilkinson in *Westdeutsche Landesbank Girozentrale* v. *Islington London Borough Council*:[116]

A person solely entitled to the full beneficial ownership of money or property, both at law and in equity, does not enjoy an equitable interest in that property. The legal title carries with it all rights. Unless and until there is a separation of the legal and equitable estates, there is no separate equitable interest.

In other words, an equitable proprietary interest will not exist until there has been an event which enables the equitable title to be separated from the legal title. This will occur when the circumstances of the transfer of the property to the defendant enable the court to conclude that the property is held on trust by the defendant for the plaintiff.

The determination of when equitable proprietary interests will be recognised is a highly controversial matter, but a number of principles can be identified.

(i) The express trust

The usual mechanism for the creation of an equitable proprietary interest is the express trust. Where a trust has been constituted the trustee will have the legal title to the property which is the subject of the trust and the beneficiary will have an equitable interest in the property. Whether an express trust has been validly created will depend on whether it has satisfied the three certainties, namely certainty of intent, certainty of subject matter and certainty of object.[117] It follows from this, for exam-

---

[114] [1948] Ch. 465.
[115] See Worthington, *Proprietary Interests in Commercial Transactions*, chapters 7 and 8.
[116] [1996] AC 669, 706.
[117] Parker and Mellows, *The Modern Law of Trusts* by A.J. Oakley (7th edn., London: Sweet and Maxwell, 1998), pp. 82–105.

ple, that an express trust will be recognised only if the property which is alleged to be subject to the trust is ascertainable.[118] It is for this reason that in *Re Goldcorp Exchange Ltd.*,[119] where the plaintiffs had purchased bullion which had not been specifically allocated to them, the Privy Council held that the property was not held on an express trust. For in such circumstances, where the actual identity of the bullion which had been purchased remained uncertain, it was not possible to say which part of the bulk was subject to the trust. This principle was qualified by the Court of Appeal in *Hunter* v. *Moss*.[120] In this case the defendant, who owned 950 of the 1,000 issued shares of a company, made an oral declaration that he would hold 5 per cent of the company's issued shares on trust for the plaintiff. Subsequently, the defendant argued that the trust was incompletely constituted because there was no certainty as to its subject matter. But the Court held that the trust was completely constituted because the shares were indistinguishable, and so it was sufficient that the defendant owned enough shares to constitute the trust without needing to identify which ones were subject to the trust.

(ii) The resulting trust[121]

(1) The nature of the resulting trust

The resulting trust is a potentially important mechanism for recognising equitable proprietary interests. Where a resulting trust exists the defendant holds the relevant property on trust for the plaintiff. This means that the plaintiff has an equitable proprietary interest in the property, an interest which can be vindicated by an equitable proprietary claim. One of the most important and controversial questions concerning proprietary restitutionary claims relates to the determination of when the defendant will hold property on a resulting trust. There are two distinct approaches to this question.

(1) *The positive intent analysis.* According to the first approach a resulting trust will arise only where the transferor of property can be considered to have intended that the property would be held on trust for him or her on the occurrence of certain events.[122] The intention of the transferor

---

[118] *Westdeutsche Landesbank Girozentrale* v. *Islington LBC* [1996] AC 669, 705 (Lord Browne-Wilkinson).

[119] [1995] 1 AC 74.   [120] [1994] 1 WLR 452.

[121] For a general examination of the role of the resulting trust see Chambers, *Resulting Trusts* (Oxford: Clarendon Press, 1997).

[122] *Tinsley* v. *Milligan* [1994] 1 AC 340, 371 (Lord Browne-Wilkinson) and *Westdeutsche Landesbank Girozentrale* v. *Islington LBC* [1996] AC 669, 708 (Lord Browne-Wilkinson). See Swadling, 'A New Role for Resulting Trusts?' (1996) 16 *LS* 110. Cp. constructive trusts which are imposed by law regardless of the plaintiff's intention.

may be express or implied.[123] According to this analysis the resulting trust will only be recognised in two situations:[124] first, where the plaintiff gratuitously transferred property to the defendant or provided consideration for the transfer of property to the defendant;[125] secondly, where an express trust fails to dispose of all of the property which was conveyed to the trustees. In both cases the equitable proprietary interest in the property can be considered to result back to the plaintiff, so that the defendant holds the property on trust for the plaintiff.

(2) *The absence of intent analysis.* An alternative analysis of the resulting trust is that this trust depends on there being an absence of intention to benefit the recipient rather than an actual intention to create the trust. According to this analysis the resulting trust arises by operation of law rather than the plaintiff's positive intent. It is this approach which is propounded by Chambers in particular in his book on resulting trusts.[126] This analysis of the resulting trust is consistent with a number of cases in which a resulting trust was recognised, even though the intention of the transferor to create a trust could not be established, because, for example, it was clear that the transferor did not want a resulting trust[127] or the intention was unenforceable.[128] Despite this, this analysis of the resulting trust is inconsistent with a number of cases, most notably the decision of the House of Lords in *Westdeutsche Landesbank* where Lord Browne-Wilkinson expressly adopted the orthodox approach to the recognition of the resulting trust.[129]

The chief consequence of recognising the intention to create a trust analysis of the resulting trust is that the resulting trust is interpreted restrictively. As a result of this the third mechanism for recognising equitable proprietary interests, the constructive trust, is interpreted much more broadly.[130] As far as the plaintiff is concerned, whether the defendant is characterised as a resulting or constructive trustee is not decisive, since the crucial question is whether the plaintiff can be considered to

---

[123] In *Westdeutsche Landesbank Girozentrale* v. *Islington LBC* [1996] AC 669, 708 Lord Browne-Wilkinson stated that resulting trusts give 'effect to the common intention of the parties'. This is incorrect. Whatever analysis of the resulting trust is adopted, it is clear that we are concerned only with the transferor's intent. Lord Browne-Wilkinson's reference to the common intent of the parties arose from a confusion between the so-called 'common intent constructive trust' and the resulting trust. See p. 635 below.

[124] *Ibid*, p. 689 (Lord Goff) and p. 708 (Lord Browne-Wilkinson).

[125] Chambers, *Resulting Trusts*, p. 11. See pp. 621–2 below.

[126] It has also been accepted by Millett LJ (as he then was) extra-judicially. See "Restitution and Constructive Trusts' (1998) 114 *LQR* 399, 400.

[127] *Vandervell* v. *IRC* [1967] 2 AC 291 where the consequence of recognising that property which had been transferred was subject to a resulting trust was to defeat a tax avoidance scheme.

[128] *Hodgson* v. *Marks* [1971] Ch. 892.

[129] [1996] AC 669, 689. See also Lord Goff at p. 708.

[130] *Ibid*, pp. 715–16. See pp. 628–37 below.

have an equitable proprietary interest in property held by the defendant, and it will not matter to the plaintiff how this proprietary interest arises. Nevertheless, the debate about the ambit of the resulting and constructive trusts and their relationship is of practical and theoretical importance. It is consequently necessary to consider which of the two analyses should be adopted and why. The following factors are particularly important.

(1) By virtue of the significant implications of recognising that the defendant holds property on trust for the plaintiff it is important to be clear how the different trusts are defined and when they will be recognised. The restrictive interpretation of the resulting trust according to the intent to create a trust analysis means that the ambit of the trust is fairly easy to determine. But a consequence of this restrictive definition is that the constructive trust is interpreted widely. This wider interpretation, however, causes a great deal of uncertainty, especially because the defendant will typically be considered to be a constructive trustee where he or she acted unconscionably.[131] This is a notoriously vague concept. If, however, the absence of intent analysis of the resulting trust is adopted, it follows that the constructive trust can be interpreted more restrictively. Consequently, the resulting trust will become the chief mechanism for the recognition of equitable proprietary interests. This will lead to greater certainty in the law since it is easier to establish whether the plaintiff's intent to benefit the defendant was absent or vitiated than it is to determine whether the defendant had acted unconscionably.

(2) A further consequence of expanding the role of the resulting trust and restricting the role of the constructive trust is that the rules on the creation of equitable proprietary interest will become more consistent with the rules on the passing of legal title. Essentially title will not pass to the defendant when the plaintiff's intention to pass title can be considered to be absent or vitiated. A similar scheme arises from the wider interpretation of the resulting trust, where the trust will be recognised where the plaintiff's intention to benefit the defendant can be considered to be absent or vitiated.

(3) Another advantage of Chambers' analysis of the resulting trust is that it avoids the artificiality of the intention to create a trust analysis. This is because that analysis depends on the identification of the plaintiff's intention that property in the possession of the defendant should be held on trust for the plaintiff. But it is highly unlikely that such an intention can be identified from the facts, so it is necessary to imply or presume the intention. This is typically highly artificial and contravenes one

---

[131] See p. 630 below.

of the fundamental principles of the law of restitution, namely the principle against fictions.[132] The emphasis in Chambers' analysis on the absence of the plaintiff's intention avoids this artificiality, since this analysis simply depends on identifying circumstances in which the plaintiff's intention to benefit the defendant can be considered to be vitiated or absent and this is ultimately a question of fact rather than fiction.

(4) The absence of intent analysis of the resulting trust is also consistent with the reported cases. As Chambers emphasises it explains a number of cases where property was held on a resulting trust even though it was not possible to establish that the plaintiff had intended the property to be held on resulting trust.[133] But Chambers' thesis also explains those cases where it appears that the plaintiff did intend the property to be held on resulting trust. This is because where the plaintiff has such an intent he or she will also lack the intention that the defendant should receive absolutely the property which was transferred.

(5) The biggest drawback with Chambers' thesis, however, concerns whether the recognition of a wider doctrine of resulting trust will give plaintiff's excessive proprietary protection.[134] If the defendant is to be considered to hold property on resulting trust whenever the plaintiff's intention to benefit the defendant is vitiated, it follows that the defendant will hold property on resulting trust in virtually every case in which the defendant can be considered to be unjustly enriched. This is because the rationale of most of the recognised grounds of restitution is that the defendant's enrichment will be unjust where the plaintiff's intention to benefit the defendant has been vitiated in some way. But if the plaintiff has an equitable proprietary interest in virtually every case in which the defendant has been unjustly enriched this will give the plaintiff the opportunity to obtain proprietary restitutionary remedies in virtually all cases of unjust enrichment. This is excessive proprietary protection and it is unacceptable because it would unsettle the security of transactions and would prejudice the position of the defendant's creditors.

This is a serious concern and it follows that, if Chambers' thesis is to be recognised, it is vital to define restrictively the notion of the vitiation of the plaintiff's intent. This can be done by clearly distinguishing between restitutionary claims founded on the vindication of property rights and claims founded on unjust enrichment. It follows that, just because the plaintiff's intention to benefit the defendant has been vitiated for the purposes of identifying a ground of restitution, it does not necessarily mean that the plaintiff's intention to benefit the defendant has been vitiated for the purposes of identifying a resulting trust. A more restrictive

---

[132] See p. 43 above.　　　　　　　　　　　　　　　　　[133] See p. 618 above.
[134] *Westdeutsche Landesbank Girozentrale* v. *Islington LBC* [1996] AC 669, 716 (Lord Browne-Wilkinson).

interpretation of when the plaintiff's intention will be vitiated needs to be adopted before a resulting trust can be recognised.

Although the arguments are finely balanced, the absence of intent analysis of the resulting trust is preferable, although more work needs to be done to determine when the plaintiff's intention to benefit the defendant should be treated as vitiated for these purposes. It is clear, however, that this analysis of the resulting trust cannot yet be considered to be recognised in English law, by virtue of the decision of the House of Lords in *Westdeutsche Landesbank*. The effect of the House of Lords' decision is that resulting trusts have no greater role beyond that of the traditional categories.[135] It is consequently necessary to consider when the resulting trust will be recognised according to the traditional interpretation of the trust. Nevertheless, there is clear dissatisfaction with Lord Browne-Wilkinson's analysis of the relationship between resulting and constructive trusts amongst commentators, including senior members of the judiciary.[136] It follows that the House of Lords may at the earliest opportunity wish to restrict the ambit of the constructive trust and expand the ambit of the resulting trust. But this does not yet represent the state of English law in this field.

(2) The traditional categories of resulting trust

The orthodox method for characterising resulting trusts is to divide the trust into two categories.[137] First there is the presumed resulting trust which depends on the presumed intention of the transferor, and secondly there is the automatic resulting trust which arises without reference to the intention of the transferor.

(a) Presumption of resulting trust[138]

Where the plaintiff transfers property to the defendant or purchases property which is vested in the defendant's name alone or in their joint names, and the plaintiff does not receive any consideration for this transaction, it will be presumed that the plaintiff intended the property to be held on resulting trust for the plaintiff.[139] It is, however, possible for

---

[135] The Court specifically rejected Birks's notion of the restitutionary resulting trust which he suggested would arise whenever the plaintiff had transferred property to the defendant in the absence of consideration and without intending a gift. See Birks, 'Restitution and Resulting Trusts' in *Equity: Contemporary Legal Developments* (ed. Goldstein, Jerusalem: Faculty of Law, Hebrew University of Jerusalem, 1992) p. 335. This suggestion had also been criticised by Swadling, 'A New Role for Resulting Trusts?' (1996) 16 *LS* 110. Chambers' thesis is, however, founded on Birks's article.

[136] Lord Millett in particular. See Millett LJ, 'Review of Chambers' *Resulting Trusts*' (1998) 6 *RLR* 283.

[137] See *Re Vandervell (No. 2)* [1974] Ch. 269, 289 (Megarry J).

[138] See Chambers, *Resulting Trusts*, chapter 1.

[139] See *Tinsley* v. *Milligan* [1994] 1 AC 340, 371 (Lord Browne-Wilkinson).

the defendant to rebut the presumption that the defendant was intended to be trustee, for example by showing that a gift was intended.[140] This presumption of a resulting trust will not arise, however, where the nature of the relationship between the parties is such that the plaintiff can be presumed to have intended the transfer of property to be a gift. This is the so-called 'presumption of advancement'. The burden is then on the plaintiff to rebut the presumption of gift. The presumption of advancement will arise, for example, where the plaintiff transfers property to his wife[141] or child.[142]

Chambers fits the presumed resulting trust into his theory of the resulting trust by careful analysis of what is being presumed in these circumstances. He concludes that the presumption is that the plaintiff did not intend the transfer of a property to be an absolute gift to the defendant, rather than a presumption that the plaintiff intended the property to be held on resulting trust.[143]

(b) Automatic resulting trusts[144]

Where the plaintiff transfers property to the defendant on an express trust, and that trust either fails or its purpose is satisfied, the property will be held on resulting trust for the plaintiff. This is illustrated by *Re Ames' Settlement*[145] where, pursuant to a pre-nuptial marriage settlement, property was transferred after the marriage had been performed. However, this marriage was retrospectively annulled, the trust failed and so the property was held on resulting trust for the covenantor. Similarly, where a trust has been constituted and the purpose of the trust has been fulfilled any trust property remaining will be held on resulting trust for the person who constituted the trust in the first place.[146]

Where it is impossible or impractical to effect restitution to the plaintiff the property which has been received by the defendant will pass to the State by way of *bona vacantia*. So, for example, where money is raised by anonymous street collections for a particular purpose and that purpose fails, it is impossible to identify the donors of the money so the money will pass to the State.[147]

Chambers fits the automatic resulting trust into his theory of the resulting trust on the basis that where an express trust fails or the purpose of the trust is satisfied the plaintiff does not intend the defendant to

---

[140] Swadling, 'A New Role for Resulting Trusts?' (1996) 16 *LS* 110, 111. This was affirmed by the House of Lords in *Westdeutsche Landesbank Girozentrale* v. *Islington LBC* [1996] AC 669. See in particular Lord Browne-Wilkinson at p. 708.

[141] *Tinker* v. *Tinker* [1970] P 136.   [142] *Tribe* v. *Tribe* [1996] Ch. 107.

[143] Chambers, *Resulting Trusts*, p. 21.   [144] *Ibid*, chapter 2.

[145] [1946] 1 Ch. 217.   [146] See, for example, *Re Abbott* [1900] 2 Ch. 326.

[147] *Re West Sussex Constabulary's Widows, Children and Benevolent (1930) Fund Trusts* [1971] Ch. 1.

retain the property absolutely.[148] He considers that there is, in fact, no distinction between presumed and automatic resulting trusts because those cases which have been analysed as involving an automatic resulting trust are properly analysed as cases in which the plaintiff should be presumed not to have intended the defendant to enjoy the property beneficially.[149] It follows that this presumption can be rebutted by evidence that the plaintiff did intend the defendant to enjoy the benefit of the property.

(c) Three difficult problems

(i) The *Quistclose* trust[150]

In *Barclays Bank Ltd.* v. *Quistclose Investments Ltd.*[151] the House of Lords recognised that where the plaintiff lends money to the defendant for a particular purpose and that purpose fails the money would be held on trust for the plaintiff. It follows that the plaintiff has an equitable proprietary interest in the money. The application of the *Quistclose* principle is illustrated by the facts of the case itself. Quistclose had lent money to Rolls Razor Ltd. specifically to enable Rolls Razor to pay a dividend. The money was paid into a bank account which was specially opened for the purpose. Rolls Razor became insolvent, so the dividends could not be paid. The bank wished to use the money in the account to discharge debts owed by Rolls Razor to it. Quistclose said that the bank could not do this because Quistclose had an equitable interest in the money. The House of Lords accepted this argument. It held that when money is lent for a particular purpose, the lender has an equitable right to see that the money is applied for that purpose. If the purpose fails and the parties have agreed expressly or impliedly that in such circumstances the money should be repaid to the lender, the money will be held on trust for the lender.[152]

The nature of this trust and the ambit of this *Quistclose* principle are matters of particular controversy.[153] One of the most controversial questions concerns the proper characterisation of the trust. Chambers has suggested that it is a resulting trust because it arises where the consideration for the payment to the defendant has failed.[154] The alternative view is that the money will be held on trust for the plaintiff only if this is what

---

[148] Chambers, *Resulting Trusts*, p. 66.   [149] *Ibid.*

[150] See Worthington, *Proprietary Interests in Commercial Transactions*, chapter 3.

[151] [1970] AC 567. See also *Carreras Rothman Ltd.* v. *Freeman Matthews* [1985] 1 All ER 155. See Chambers, *Resulting Trusts*, chapter 3.

[152] [1970] AC 567, 581–2 (Lord Wilberforce).

[153] See Chambers, *Resulting Trusts*, chapter 3, for detailed analysis of these difficulties. See also Millett, 'The Quistclose Trust: Who Can Enforce It?' (1985) 101 *LQR* 269.

[154] *Resulting Trusts*, chapter 3.

the parties intended, whether expressly or impliedly. In other words, the money is held on an express trust rather than a resulting trust. This is more consistent with the analysis of the House of Lords in *Quistclose* itself. That a *Quistclose* trust is an express trust was recognised by Ferris J in *Box* v. *Barclays Bank plc*.[155] In that case the plaintiffs had paid money to a company on the understanding that it would be invested on their behalf with the defendant bank on the money market. The money was not invested in this way and so the plaintiffs argued that it was subject to a *Quistclose* trust. This claim failed, however, because there was no evidence of an intention that the company would hold the money on trust for the plaintiffs. In his analysis of the *Quistclose* principle the judge made a number of important observations:

(1) He accepted without comment that this type of trust is not confined to where a lender has lent money to enable the borrower to pay other creditors.[156] The present case was very different from the typical *Quistclose* scenario, since the plaintiffs had paid money to the company for their own benefit, but this did not prevent the trust from being recognised.

(2) Ferris J explicitly recognised that the *Quistclose* trust is an express trust. In a case such as *Box* the proper characterisation of the trust is a matter of great importance. Since the judge considered the trust was express he concluded that it could not be recognised because there was no intent to hold the money on trust. But if the trust is characterised as a resulting trust then the actual intention of the parties is irrelevant once it has been shown that the plaintiff intended the money to be paid only for a particular purpose which had failed. Consequently, a resulting trust analysis might have enabled the judge to find that the money was indeed held on trust for the plaintiffs once the money had been deposited in a different way from that which they had intended.

(3) Finally, and most controversially, the judge assumed that the *Quistclose* trust could be recognised simply where the purpose for which the money had been paid had not been satisfied, rather than that it had become impossible to fulfil. If this is correct it follows that the ambit of the *Quistclose* trust has been expanded dramatically. It effectively means that property which has been transferred for a particular purpose may be held on trust whenever the purpose has not been carried out, even though the purpose may still be carried out. This raises particularly difficult questions of fact in determining at what the point the trust can be considered to have arisen. The prefer-

---

[155] *The Times*, 30 April 1998.
[156] This is also advocated by Chambers, *Resulting Trusts*, p. 85.

able view therefore is that the *Quistclose* trust should be confined to its traditional role, namely where it has become impossible to fulfil the purpose for which the money was paid.

(ii) Qualified intention

Even according to Chambers's thesis the resulting trust arises only where the defendant was not free to use the property for his or her own benefit.[157] So in most cases in which consideration has failed a resulting trust will not be recognised because the defendant did indeed receive the property absolutely. If Chambers's thesis is correct, however, it follows that if the defendant never received the property beneficially the failure of consideration may be sufficient to trigger a resulting trust.[158] Chambers considers the *Quistclose* trust to be such an example.

This raises a very difficult and important question about benefits which are transferred pursuant to a contract which is void *ab initio*. Since such transactions are never valid it may be concluded that the defendant never received the property beneficially and so such benefits should be held on resulting trust for the plaintiff. The decision of the House of Lords in *Sinclair* v. *Brougham*[159] is consistent with this argument since the Court recognised that property which was transferred pursuant to a void transaction would be held on resulting trust. In this case the plaintiffs had deposited money with a building society which did not have capacity to borrow the money. It was held that, because this transaction was *ultra vires* and so null and void, the building society held the money on trust for the depositors, who consequently had an equitable proprietary interest which gave them priority over the claims of the building society's shareholders. This case was, however, overruled by the House of Lords in *Westdeutsche Landesbank Girozentrale* v. *Islington London Borough Council*[160] which held that no resulting trust arises when property is transferred to the defendant under a void contract.

In *Westdeutsche Landesbank* the plaintiff bank had paid the defendant local authority a sum of money in respect of an interest rate swap transaction which was held to be null and void because the defendant lacked capacity to enter into it. The defendant conceded that it was liable to repay this money to the plaintiff, so the only question before the House of Lords was whether the plaintiff could claim compound interest from the defendant in respect of the amount which was due to it. Compound interest is available only in respect of equitable claims,[161] so the plaintiff

---

[157] *Ibid*, p. 145.   [158] *Ibid*, chapter 6.   [159] [1914] AC 398.
[160] [1996] AC 669, 713 (Lord Browne-Wilkinson) with whom Lords Slynn (at p. 718) and Lloyd (at p. 738) concurred. Lord Goff was simply prepared to distinguish the case: *ibid*, p. 688.
[161] As was affirmed by the House of Lords in *Westdeutsche Landesbank*. See p. 26 above.

needed to establish that it had an equitable proprietary interest in the money which the defendant had received. The plaintiff sought to show this by arguing that, since the transaction was void, its purpose had failed and so the money was held on resulting trust for the plaintiff. This was rejected by the House of Lords for a number of reasons: first, because if a resulting trust was recognised it would give unacceptable priority to the plaintiff if the defendant became insolvent, priority which would not be available if the transaction was merely voidable; secondly, because of a reluctance to import equitable principles into commercial dealings;[162] thirdly, because the plaintiff, having entered into a commercial transaction, took the risk of the defendant's insolvency.[163]

This is surely correct.[164] Where the plaintiff intends to transfer a benefit to the defendant for a particular purpose and that purpose can never be satisfied, there is no obvious reason why the property should be held on resulting trust for the plaintiff. Legal title will have passed to the defendant in such circumstances,[165] and similarly the failure of the transaction should never trigger the creation of an equitable proprietary interest. It should make no difference whether the consideration failed subsequently or there was an absence of consideration. Where the transaction has failed the plaintiff should not obtain an equitable proprietary interest save where he or she intended that property should be held on trust for him or her in such circumstances.[166]

(iii) Vitiated intent

Chambers has argued that the logical consequence of his thesis, that property will be held on resulting trust whenever the defendant has received identifiable property and the plaintiff did not intend the defendant to receive the benefit of the property, is that property will be held on resulting trust whenever the plaintiff's intention to transfer a benefit to the defendant can be considered to be absent or vitiated.[167] He considers that the plaintiff's intention will be treated as vitiated for the purposes of recognising a resulting trust whenever it can be treated as vitiated for the purposes of establishing a recognised ground of restitution.[168] This is because Chambers assumes that the resulting trust is an equitable response to the defendant's unjust enrichment. This argument is flawed for the following reasons:

---

[162] [1996] AC 669, 704 (Lord Browne-Wilkinson).   [163] *Ibid*, p. 684 (Lord Goff).

[164] Chambers supports the decision of the House of Lords but only because he considers this to be a case where the consideration failed after the defendant had received the money absolutely: *Resulting Trusts*, p. 162. This assumes that there had been a failure rather than an absence of consideration.

[165] See p. 613 above.

[166] See *Barclays Bank Ltd.* v. *Quistclose Investments Ltd.* [1970] AC 567.

[167] *Resulting Trusts*, chapter 5.   [168] *Ibid*, p. 127.

(1) The resulting trust has nothing to do with the reversal of unjust enrichment, save where that principle is used in a descriptive sense.[169] Rather, since the consequence of recognising that property is held on resulting trust is that the plaintiff has an equitable proprietary interest, the resulting trust arises in the context of restitutionary claims to vindicate proprietary rights.[170] Consequently, the analogy should be drawn with the rules on the passing of legal title rather than with the interpretation of grounds of restitution. That the resulting trust has nothing to do with the unjust enrichment principle is reflected in the fact that Chambers has real difficulty in fitting the traditional categories of resulting trust into the unjust enrichment model. This is because there is no clear ground of restitution which justifies the recognition of the resulting trust in these cases.

(2) If the resulting trust is recognised whenever the defendant receives the plaintiff's property in circumstances in which the plaintiff's intention to benefit the defendant can be considered to be absent or vitiated for whatever reason, this will result in excessive proprietary protection.[171] This is unacceptable because it will prejudice the defendant's creditors and undermine the security of transactions.[172]

It should not follow, however, that the resulting trust will never arise where the plaintiff's intention can be considered to be vitiated. In the same way that legal title to property will not pass to the defendant where the nature of the transfer is such that the plaintiff's intention to transfer the property can be regarded as absent, so too the plaintiff's intention that the defendant should receive the property absolutely should be considered to be absent, so that the property is held on resulting trust for the plaintiff. The resulting trust will, however, be relevant only where legal title has passed to the defendant despite the absence of the plaintiff's intention that property should pass. This will be the case, for example, where the plaintiff's property cannot be traced at law, because it has been deposited in a bank account for example,[173] or where the plaintiff's money has passed to the defendant as currency.[174] So, for example, if the plaintiff paid money to the defendant as a result of a fundamental mistake, legal title to the money does not pass to the defendant.[175] If, however, the plaintiff is unable to identify his or her money at law in the defendant's hands he or she may still be able to identify it in equity. But the defendant should be considered to hold property on resulting trust for the plaintiff only if the mistake was so fundamental that the plaintiff's intention to transfer the property to the defendant can be considered to

---

[169] See p. 12 above. [170] Cp. Chambers, *Resulting Trusts*, p. 131.
[171] See p. 620 above. [172] *Ibid.* [173] See p. 646 below.
[174] See pp. 675–6 below. [175] See p. 607 above.

have been vitiated.[176] Similarly, if the plaintiff was ignorant of the transfer of his or her property to the defendant this should be sufficient to treat the property as held on resulting trust if it is no longer possible to identify the property at law. This is simply because, in cases of ignorance, the plaintiff has no intention at all that the defendant should receive the benefit of the property.

That the absence of the plaintiff's intention to transfer property to the defendant may be sufficient for the courts to recognise that the defendant holds the property in trust for the plaintiff was recognised by the Court of Appeal in *Allcard* v. *Skinner*,[177] where the plaintiff, a nun, was presumed to have been unduly influenced by her mother superior to transfer property to the convent. It was recognised that the plaintiff was able to recover so much of the property which the mother superior continued to hold 'on the ground that it was property the beneficial interest in which she had never effectually parted with'.[178] Whilst it would have been more accurate to say that the effect of the defendant's exploitation was that the equitable proprietary interest was created rather than retained, since such an interest cannot exist until legal title has passed from the plaintiff,[179] this dictum does suggest that property may be held on trust where it is transferred as a result of the defendant's exploitation of the plaintiff. But it does not follow, as Chambers assumes, that all property transferred as a result of exploitation, duress, mistake, incapacity or ignorance should be held on resulting trust for the plaintiff. Rather, property should be held on resulting trust only where the circumstances of the transfer were such that the plaintiff's intention to transfer the property to the defendant can be considered to be absent or vitiated.

(iii) The constructive trust[180]

(1) The nature of the constructive trust

A further mechanism by which the plaintiff can obtain an equitable interest in property held by the defendant is the constructive trust. This is a notoriously ambiguous concept. There are two separate notions of this trust.[181]

First, there is the institutional constructive trust which is a true trust which arises by operation of law on the occurrence of a particular event by virtue of which the plaintiff acquires an equitable proprietary right in

---

[176] This would therefore explain how the mistaken payment in *Chase Manhattan Bank* v. *Israel-British Bank (London) Ltd.* [1981] Ch. 105 could be considered to be held on trust for the plaintiff. See pp. 609–10 above.

[177] (1887) 36 Ch.D 145.   [178] *Ibid*, p. 172 (Cotton LJ).   [179] See p. 616 above.

[180] See, generally, Oakley, *Constructive Trusts* (3rd edn., London: Sweet and Maxwell, 1997).

[181] See Lord Browne-Wilkinson in *Westdeutsche Landesbank Girozentrale* v. *Islington LBC* [1996] AC 669, 714.

property held by the defendant. These events have the common characteristic that the defendant's conscience can be considered to have been affected by the circumstances surrounding the transfer of property.[182] According to this notion of the constructive trust the court simply recognises that the trust has already arisen, without having any discretion as to whether or not to do so.

The alternative notion of the constructive trust is that it is simply 'a judicial remedy giving rise to an enforceable equitable obligation: the extent to which it operates retrospectively to the prejudice of third parties lies in the discretion of the court'.[183] In other words, it is simply a remedy which can be awarded when it is considered to be appropriate to do so.

The orthodox view in English law is that the constructive trust is a substantive institution which will be recognised in certain circumstances.[184] These circumstances will be examined first, and then the question whether a remedial constructive trust should be recognised in English law will be considered.

(2) Circumstances when an institutional constructive trust will be recognised

(a) Breach of fiduciary duties[185]
Where the defendant owes fiduciary duties to the plaintiff and receives property in breach of duty, the defendant may be required to hold that property on constructive trust for the plaintiff. The best, and most important example, of a constructive trust being imposed in such circumstances is *Attorney-General for Hong Kong* v. *Reid*,[186] where the defendant, who was an officer of the Crown and so owed it fiduciary duties, received bribes which the Privy Council decided should be held on constructive trust for the Crown. This was because the defendant was liable to account to the plaintiff for the profits made from the breach of his fiduciary duty and, by virtue of the equitable maxim that equity treats as done that which ought to be done, the defendant was deemed to have accounted to the plaintiff for the value of the bribe immediately it had been received. It followed that the Crown was deemed to have an equitable proprietary interest in the bribes from the moment they had been

---

[182] See Millett, 'Restitution and Constructive Trusts' (1998) 114 *LQR* 399, 400.

[183] *Westdeutsche Landesbank Girozentrale* v. *Islington LBC* [1996] AC 669, 715 (Lord Browne-Wilkinson). See also *Re Polly Peck International plc. (No. 2)* [1998] 3 All ER 812, 823 (Mummery LJ) and 830 (Nourse LJ).

[184] See, for example, *Metall und Rohstoff AG* v. *Donaldson, Lufkin and Jenrette Inc.* [1990] 1 QB 391, 478–80 and *Halifax Building Society* v. *Thomas* [1996] Ch. 217, 229 (Peter Gibson LJ).

[185] See pp. 520–34 above.   [186] [1994] 1 AC 324.

received by the defendant, and so they were held on constructive trust for the Crown. The implication of this decision is that, whenever the defendant receives property in breach of fiduciary duty, the defendant will hold that property on constructive trust. This gives excessive proprietary protection to the person to whom the fiduciary duty is owed.[187] Consequently, the preferable view is that a fiduciary who has profited from breaching his or her fiduciary duty should be considered to hold those profits on constructive trust for the principal only where the profits derive from the fiduciary's interference with the principal's property or where the profits can be deemed to have been gained on behalf of the principal.[188]

(b) Unconscionability on the part of the defendant

Constructive trusts will also be recognised more generally in circumstances in which the defendant's conduct can be considered to be unconscionable, even though the defendant did not owe fiduciary duties to the plaintiff. This appears to be the effect of an important dictum of Lord Browne-Wilkinson in *Westdeutsche Landesbank Girozentrale* v. *Islington LBC*[189] relating to the case of *Chase Manhattan Bank NA* v. *Israel-British Bank (London) Ltd.*[190] In *Chase Manhattan Bank* it was held that where the plaintiff had mistakenly paid the defendant the same amount of money twice, although legal title in the money which had been mistakenly paid had passed to the defendant, it was still possible for the court to recognise that the plaintiff had an equitable proprietary interest in the money. As Goulding J said:[191]

a person who pays money to another under a factual mistake retains an equitable property in it and the conscience of the other is subjected to a fiduciary duty to respect his proprietary rights.

Even though the plaintiff's mistake could be characterised as fundamental,[192] presumably legal title to the money had passed to the defendant because it was no longer possible to identify the plaintiff's money at law as it had been mixed in the defendant's bank account. It is unclear, however, how Goulding J could conclude that the plaintiff had an equitable proprietary interest in the money which had been received by the defendant. One explanation is that the plaintiff's intention to benefit the defendant had been vitiated by the fundamental mistake so that the

---

[187] This is discussed in more detail in pp. 541–4 above. See also Grantham, 'Doctrinal Bases for the Recognition of Proprietary Rights' (1996) 16 *OJLS* 561, 580–2.

[188] See, for example, *Cook* v. *Deeks* [1916] AC 554.

[189] [1996] AC 669, 714–15. See also Lord Browne-Wilkinson at p. 705 and *Hussey* v. *Palmer* [1972] 1 WLR 1286, 1290 (Lord Denning MR).

[190] [1981] Ch. 105.   [191] *Ibid*, p. 119.   [192] See pp. 609–10 above.

[193] See p. 627 above.

money was held on resulting trust for the plaintiff.[193] Lord Browne-Wilkinson in *Westdeutsche Landesbank Girozentrale* v. *Islington London Borough Council*[194] stated, however, that Goulding J was wrong to conclude that the plaintiff had an equitable proprietary interest in the money from the moment that it had been received by the defendant. He did, however, suggest an alternative explanation of how an equitable proprietary interest in the money could have been acquired. He suggested that the plaintiff subsequently obtained an equitable proprietary interest in the money by virtue of a constructive trust. This derived from the fact that the defendant knew that the plaintiff had paid the money to it by mistake within two days of the defendant having received the money. As Lord Browne-Wilkinson said:

Although the mere receipt of the moneys, in ignorance of the mistake, gives rise to no trust, the retention of the moneys after the recipient bank learned of the mistake may well have given rise to a constructive trust.[195]

In other words, the justification for the recognition of an equitable proprietary interest was that the defendant's conscience had been affected by its knowledge of the mistake whilst it was in possession of the money which had been paid by the plaintiff. The defendant's subsequent failure to return the money once it was aware of the mistake constituted unconscionable conduct and it was this conduct which should be considered to have triggered the judge's recognition that the defendant held the property on constructive trust for the plaintiff.

This notion of the constructive trust being founded on the defendant's unconscionable conduct will arise in other circumstances. So, for example, a constructive trust will be recognised where the defendant has obtained property by fraud[196] or where property has been transferred to the defendant on the understanding that the defendant will give effect to another party's rights and it is unconscionable for the defendant subsequently to deny that other party's rights.[197] Similarly, if the defendant steals the plaintiff's money the plaintiff will have an equitable proprietary interest in it by virtue of a constructive trust because the defendant's conscience will have been affected at the time of receipt. This was specifically recognised by Lord Browne-Wilkinson in *Westdeutsche Landesbank*.[198] The problem with the recognition of a constructive trust in a case such as this relates to what has happened to the legal title in the money. It has already been seen that where the plaintiff's money is stolen

---

[194] [1996] AC 669, 715.
[195] *Ibid.* See also *Neste Oy Ltd.* v. *Lloyds Bank plc.* [1983] 2 Lloyd's Rep. 658.
[196] *Stocks* v. *Wilson* [1913] 2 KB 235, 244 (Lush J).
[197] *Ashburn Anstalt* v. *Arnold* [1989] Ch. 1.
[198] [1996] AC 669, 716. See also *Bankers Trust Co.* v. *Shapira* [1980] 1 WLR 1274.

his or her legal title in the money will not pass to the defendant until it ceases to be traceable.[199] But if the legal title has not passed, how can the equitable title be considered to have been separated from it? This was not considered by Lord Browne-Wilkinson. One possible solution is that the plaintiff should be allowed to elect to treat the title as having passed, so that an equitable proprietary interest would be created, to enable the plaintiff to gain the advantages of having an equitable proprietary interest, including the advantages of more liberal tracing rules and more extensive remedies. But such a notion of election is highly artificial. It would be far easier simply to say that an equitable proprietary interest cannot exist as a matter of law unless the plaintiff intended legal title to pass, or where the property in which the plaintiff has retained legal title ceases to be traceable.

If a constructive trust can be recognised once the defendant becomes aware that the plaintiff has made a mistake, can a constructive trust be recognised in other circumstances in which the transfer of property to the defendant can be treated as vitiated in some way? For example, if the defendant realises that the plaintiff has paid him or her under a void contract, there is no reason why the defendant cannot be considered to have acted unconscionably in not repaying the money to the plaintiff if the defendant would be considered to have acted unconscionably if he or she knew that the money had been paid by mistake. Consequently, on the facts of *Westdeutsche Landesbank* the defendant would presumably have held the money on constructive trust for the plaintiff had the money not ceased to be traceable before the defendant knew that the transaction was void.

If a constructive trust can be recognised where the defendant knew that the transaction was void, what of the case where the defendant knows that the consideration for the transaction would fail totally? There seems no obvious reason why a constructive trust could not exist in such circumstances. Consequently, if *Re Goldcorp Exchange*[200] were decided today it might be possible to conclude that the defendant held a quantity of bullion on constructive trust for the purchasers because it had been 'behaving in a systematically unconscientious way. It had not the least intention of honouring its contracts in the manner which it made them.'[201] Whether this constitutes sufficient evidence of unconscionable conduct will be discussed next, but the crucial point is that, in principle, a constructive trust could be recognised even where there was a total fail-

---

[199] This is the effect of *Lipkin Gorman (a firm)* v. *Karpnale Ltd.* [1991] 2 AC 548.
[200] [1995] 1 AC 72. See p. 617 above.
[201] Birks, 'Trusts Raised to Reverse Unjust Enrichment: The *Westdeutsche* Case' (1996) 4 *RLR* 3, 21.

ure of consideration.

Since this test for the recognition of a constructive trust depends on the conscience of the defendant being affected in some way it is vital to be clear what constitutes unconscionable conduct for these purposes. This raises two distinct questions.

(*1*) *The degree of fault.* What degree of fault is required on the part of the defendant before his or her conduct can be considered to be unconscionable? If the plaintiff paid money by mistake or because the transaction was invalid it is clear that the defendant's knowledge of the mistake or the invalidity of the transaction will be sufficient to treat him or her as acting unconscionably. Presumably, it will also be sufficient that the defendant believes or suspects that the plaintiff was mistaken or that the transaction was invalid. But should it be sufficient that the defendant ought to have known of the mistake or the invalidity? If it is sufficient, this would dramatically widen the ambit of proprietary restitutionary claims. But due to the policy of the law to restrict proprietary claims, particularly because of the adverse effect they have on the defendant's creditors,[202] the better view is surely that the rules for the imposition of constructive trusts should be interpreted very restrictively. Consequently, the defendant's conscience should be considered to be affected only where he or she was subjectively aware of the plaintiff's mistake or the invalidity of the transaction.[203]

(*2*) *The question of timing.* At what point must the defendant's conscience be affected? Clearly if the defendant knew of the mistake or the invalidity of the transaction at the time of receipt it is appropriate to recognise that the property is held on constructive trust for the plaintiff. Lord Browne-Wilkinson's interpretation of *Chase Manhattan* suggests that acquiring knowledge of the mistake two days after receipt of the money would have been sufficient to characterise the defendant's conduct as unconscionable. But what if the defendant discovers the mistake months or even years later? The natural limit to the period during which we should consider whether the defendant's conscience has been affected is once the defendant has lost the property which he or she received from the plaintiff or the proceeds of or substitute for that property.[204] In other words, the question of recognising a constructive trust is bound up with the question of following and tracing; if the plaintiff's property ceases to be identifiable according to the following and tracing rules a constructive trust cannot be imposed, simply because there will

---

[202] See p. 600 above.

[203] In *Westdeutsche Landesbank* [1996] AC 669, 705 Lord Browne-Wilkinson appeared to accept that the defendant's conscience will be affected only where he or she knew 'of the factors which are alleged to affect' his or her conscience.

[204] *Ibid*, p. 707 (Lord Browne-Wilkinson); *Re Goldcorp Exchange Ltd.* [1995] 1 AC 74.

be no identifiable fund to which the trust can attach. This is the reason a constructive trust was not recognised on the facts of *Westdeutsche Landesbank*, because when the defendant learnt that the swaps transaction was void the plaintiff's money had ceased to be identifiable.[205]

But if this analysis is right it may mean that the recognition of an equitable proprietary interest in *Sinclair* v. *Brougham*[206] may have been correct after all.[207] For in that case, when the defendant discovered that it lacked capacity to receive deposits, the money it had received from the depositors was still traceable. This method of resurrecting *Sinclair* v. *Brougham* clearly was not intended by the House of Lords in *Westdeutsche Landesbank*. The only way that this result can be avoided, with the added benefit of dramatically restricting the recognition of equitable proprietary interests through constructive trusts, is by saying that the question whether or not the defendant's conscience has been affected should be judged only at the time the relevant property was received by the defendant. This would mean that both *Sinclair* v. *Brougham* and *Chase Manhattan* should be rejected. This is inevitable; either they are both right or they are both wrong. This restrictive approach to the recognition of equitable proprietary interests also avoids the artifice of saying that the defendant owns a piece of property absolutely and only subsequently will an equitable proprietary interest be carved from it for the benefit of the plaintiff. Whether such an interest can be recognised should be judged only at the time of receipt.

(c) Rescission

A further situation in which the courts may recognise that property is held on constructive trust for the plaintiff is where he or she is able to rescind in equity a transaction with the defendant.[208] In *Lonrho plc.* v. *Fayed (No. 2)*[209] Millett J recognised that when a contract obtained by fraudulent misrepresentation is rescinded the property which was transferred pursuant to the contract will be held on constructive trust for the transferor. In *El Ajou* v. *Dollar Land Holdings plc.*,[210] however, although Millett J affirmed that when a transaction is rescinded an equitable title can vest in the plaintiff retrospectively, he characterised the trust which arises as a result of the rescission as a resulting trust rather than a constructive trust. Characterisation of the trust as a resulting trust explains why the effect of the rescission is to vest equitable title in the plaintiff

---

[205] [1996] AC 669, 689 (Lord Goff), 707 (Lord Browne-Wilkinson).

[206] [1914] AC 348. See p. 625 above.

[207] See Birks, 'Trusts Raised to Reverse Unjust Enrichment: The *Westdeutsche* Case' (1996) 4 *RLR* 3, 22.

[208] See p. 31 above. For rescission at law see p. 30 above.

[209] [1992] 1 WLR 1, 12. See also *Daly* v. *Sydney Stock Exchange* (1986) 65 ALR 193, 204 (Brennan J).   [210] [1993] 3 All ER 717, 734.

retrospectively. It is also consistent with Chambers's thesis that a result-ing trust will arise when the plaintiff did not intend the defendant to receive the property absolutely.[211] Where the plaintiff rescinds a trans-action because his or her intention to benefit the defendant was vitiated in some way, it follows that the plaintiff cannot have intended that the defendant should have received the property.

Regardless of whether the defendant is characterised as a resulting or constructive trustee it is clear that, until the transaction is rescinded, the plaintiff has a mere equity to rescind the transaction.[212] It is for this rea-son that the plaintiff will be barred from rescinding the transaction if a third party acquires an equitable interest in the property for value and without notice of the plaintiff's right to rescind.[213]

(d) Miscellaneous cases where constructive trusts will be recognised
The defendant will hold property on constructive trust in a number of other circumstances. For example, where the plaintiff enters into a con-tract for the sale of land, once the contract is made the defendant will hold the land on constructive trust for the plaintiff.[214] Where the parties have an express or implied common intention that the plaintiff will have an interest of some kind in property, the property will be held on con-structive trust for that party.[215] Where property is held subject to a secret trust the preferable analysis is that the property is held on constructive trust.[216] Where a criminal obtains property as the result of the commis-sion of a criminal offence, this property may be held on constructive trust for the victim of the crime.[217]

(3) The remedial constructive trust

Whereas an institutional constructive trust arises by operation of law from the date of the event which gives rise to it, the remedial constructive trust arises through the exercise of the judge's discretion whenever it is considered to be just to recognise that the plaintiff has an equitable pro-prietary interest.[218] If the remedial constructive trust were recognised in English law, it would be applicable in any case in which the defendant had received property from the plaintiff in circumstances in which the

---

[211] See p. 618 above.

[212] *Phillips* v. *Phillips* (1862) 4 De GF and J 208; 45 ER 1164. Cp. Chambers, *Resulting Trusts* who suggests at p. 171 that the plaintiff who has a right to rescind has an equitable proprietary interest which is held on resulting trust.

[213] *Westminster Bank Ltd.* v. *Lee* [1956] Ch. 7.

[214] Oakley, *Constructive Trusts*, chapter 6.

[215] *Gissing* v. *Gissing* [1971] AC 886. This would be better treated as a form of resulting trust. See *Tinsley* v. *Milligan* [1994] 1 AC 340, 371 (Lord Browne-Wilkinson).

[216] Oakley, *Constructive Trusts*, chapter 5.   [217] See p. 561 above.

[218] *Westdeutsche Landesbank Girozentrale* v. *Islington LBC* [1996] AC 669, 714 (Lord Browne-Wilkinson).

defendant had committed an equitable wrong, or perhaps any form of wrongdoing, or where the defendant was unjustly enriched. Such a remedy could have a profound effect on the law of restitution, since it would enable judges to create equitable proprietary interests where it was felt that the justice of the case demanded. This would enable the court to transfer to the plaintiff an asset which belongs to the defendant, and in which the plaintiff did not have a pre-existing legal or equitable interest.[219] The key difference between the institutional and the remedial constructive trust is that to recognise a remedial constructive trust it is not necessary to establish that the plaintiff has a pre-existing proprietary right; the purpose of the remedial constructive trust is to create such a proprietary right.[220]

A possible disadvantage of the remedial constructive trust is that creating equitable proprietary rights where it is considered to be just to do so may prejudice the rights of the defendant's creditors. But, being a discretionary remedy, it could be fashioned in such a way that no proprietary interest was created, but the plaintiff was simply able to recover all the profits made by the defendant. In particular, the remedy need not be awarded if any innocent third party would suffer. If, however, the court did decide to create an equitable proprietary interest in the defendant's property, this would be another mechanism whereby the plaintiff could establish a proprietary base for the purposes of establishing a restitutionary claim to vindicate property rights.

Although the orthodox interpretation of the constructive trust is that it is a substantive institution, there is growing support for the recognition of the remedial constructive trust. For example, in *Westdeutsche Landesbank* Lord Browne-Wilkinson suggested that perhaps the notion of the remedial constructive trust should be introduced into English law because it would enable proprietary relief to be tailored to the particular circumstances of the case,[221] although he refused to decide the point since it was not directly in issue. In *Re Goldcorp Exchange Ltd.*[222] Lord Mustill in the Privy Council recognised the power of the court to create equitable proprietary interests by virtue of the remedial constructive trust.

The existence of such a remedy within the law of restitution does, at first sight, appear to be particularly attractive, since it enables just results to be achieved. But surely such a remedy is at odds with some of the fun-

---

[219] Birks, 'Trusts Raised to Reverse Unjust Enrichment: The *Westdeutsche* Case' (1996) 4 *RLR* 3, 14.

[220] *Re Polly Peck International plc. (No. 2)* [1998] 3 All ER 812, 830 (Nourse LJ).

[221] [1996] AC 669, 716. Cp. 'Constructive Trusts and Unjust Enrichment', an address delivered to the Holdsworth Club in 1991 (see (1996) 10 *TLI* 98, 99) where Lord Browne-Wilkinson considered that the remedial constructive trust was contrary to principle.

[222] [1995] 1 AC 74, 104.

damental principles which underlie the law of restitution. One of the most important of those principles is that the award and ambit of remedies should be certain and predictable. The recognition of the remedial constructive trust would force the law of restitution down the track towards palm-tree justice. This is especially unacceptable in the context of commercial transactions. We need to have clear rules whether or not equitable proprietary rights have been created and the remedial constructive trust is antithetical to such clarity and predictability.[223] Birks has accurately described the remedial constructive trust as a remedy which is 'ugly, repugnant alike to legal certainty, the sanctity of property and the rule of law'.[224] The remedial constructive trust should have no place in the remedial armoury of English law. Recently the Court of Appeal has refused to recognise that the remedial constructive trust forms part of English law, primarily because it was considered that the variation of property rights should be a matter for Parliament rather than for the discretion of the judge, especially where the creation of an equitable proprietary right by a judge would exclude assets from distribution to the unsecured creditors of the defendant.[225]

(c) The vindication of proprietary rights despite illegality

(i) The principle of no reliance on the illegality

In certain cases in which the plaintiff may have retained legal title in property which was transferred to the defendant or in which an equitable proprietary interest may be recognised, the plaintiff will not be able to vindicate his or her proprietary rights because the transaction was tainted by illegality. This is because it is a fundamental principle of the law of restitution that a plaintiff is not able to obtain restitution if he or she needs to rely on the fact that the transaction was illegal to establish the restitutionary claim.[226] So, for example, where the plaintiff transfers property to his wife motivated by an illegal purpose, such as a desire to prevent the property from being taken by his creditors, the equitable presumption of advancement applies, whereby it is presumed that the transfer of property was intended as a gift.[227] The plaintiff will be unable to rebut this presumption of gift, however, because to do so would

---

[223] See Millett, 'Equity—The Road Ahead' (1995) 9 *TLI* 35, 42.

[224] 'Property and Unjust Enrichment: Categorical Truths' [1997] *NZ Law Rev.* 623, 641. See also Millett, ' Restitution and Constructive Trusts' (1998) 114 *LQR* 399.

[225] *Re Polly Peck International plc. (No. 2)* [1998] 3 All ER 812. See especially Mummery LJ at p. 827.

[226] *Holman* v. *Johnson* (1775) 1 Cowp. 341, 343; 31 ER 934, 942 (Lord Mansfield). For analysis of when a transaction will be considered to be tainted by illegality see Chapter 26.

[227] *Tinker* v. *Tinker* [1970] P 136. The presumption also applies in respect of transfers by a parent to a child. See, for example, *Tribe* v. *Tribe* [1996] Ch. 107. See p. 370 above.

require disclosure of his or her illegal purpose in making the transfer, and so the property will remain with the defendant.[228] But in certain exceptional circumstances the plaintiff will be able to vindicate his or her proprietary right where he or she can identify a proprietary base without needing to plead the fact that the underlying transaction was illegal. There are three principle examples of this.

(1) Rebutting the presumption of advancement

Where the presumption of advancement applies the plaintiff will be able to rebut it by showing that he or she did not intend the transfer of a benefit to the defendant to be a gift, even though the plaintiff had participated in an illegal transaction, if the plaintiff can establish that he or she had not been tainted by the illegality. This will be the case where, for example, the plaintiff can show that he or she withdrew from the illegal transaction before any part of the illegal purpose was fulfilled.[229]

(2) Presumption of resulting trusts

In other cases in which the plaintiff has transferred property to the defendant for an illegal purpose the nature of the relationship between the parties may be such that it can be presumed that the defendant holds property on resulting trust for the plaintiff. [230] The plaintiff will be able to vindicate his or her equitable proprietary right because he or she does not need to rely on the illegality to establish the presumption. The defendant may wish to rebut the presumption by showing that the plaintiff had intended the property to be transferred to fulfil an illegal purpose, but he or she will not be able to do so because such an argument requires the defendant to plead the plaintiff's illegal purpose and this is not permissible.

The leading case to recognise that the plaintiff can bring a proprietary restitutionary claim where he or she does not need to rely on the illegality is the decision of the House of Lords in *Tinsley* v. *Milligan*.[231] In this case Miss Tinsley and Miss Milligan had been lovers. They bought a house together but it was put in the sole name of Tinsley on the understanding that they would have joint beneficial ownership. This arrange-

---

[228] See, for example, *Gascoigne* v. *Gascoigne* [1918] 1 KB 223; *Re Emery's Investment Trusts* [1959] Ch. 410; *Palaniappa Chettiar* v. *Amnasalam Chettiar* [1962] AC 294; *Tinker* v. *Tinker* [1970] P 136.

[229] As was recognised by the Court of Appeal in *Tribe* v. *Tribe* [1996] Ch. 107. See p. 370 above.

[230] See pp. 621–2 above.

[231] [1994] 1 AC 340. See also *Petherpermal Chetty* v. *Mundy Servai* (1908) 24 TLR 462, *Rowan* v. *Dann* [1992] 64 P and CR 202 and *Lowson* v. *Coombes* [1999] 2 WLR 720. The principle was also recognised by the Ontario Court of Appeal in *Gorog* v. *Kiss* (1977) 78 DLR (3d.) 690.

ment was to enable Milligan to perpetrate a fraud on the Department of Social Security by making false benefit claims. Tinsley made similar fraudulent claims. Subsequently the relationship ended and Tinsley brought an action for possession of the house, asserting that she had sole ownership of it. Milligan counterclaimed that she had joint beneficial ownership of the property because the nature of the relationship between them was such that a resulting trust could be presumed. The issue was simply whether the defendant was able to assert her equitable proprietary interest under this resulting trust when the purpose of the arrangement had been to enable her to perpetrate a fraud. By a majority it was held that Milligan's counterclaim should succeed on the specific ground that she did not need to rely on the illegality to assert her title.[232] She simply needed to show that she had contributed to the purchase price and that there had been a common understanding of joint owner-ship. This meant that a resulting trust could be presumed in her favour without needing to refer to the illegality. The only way Tinsley could rebut this was by reference to the fact that the transaction was illegal, and this was not possible as a matter of public policy.[233]

(3) Limited proprietary interests

A further situation in which the plaintiff will be able to recover property without relying on the illegality is where the illegal transaction created a limited proprietary interest. So, for example, in *Bowmakers Ltd.* v. *Barnet Instruments Ltd.*[234] the plaintiff had hired out machine tools to the defendant under three separate hiring agreements, each with an option to purchase. The defendant sold two of the tools and refused to return the other one to the plaintiff after the plaintiff had demanded its return because the defendant had failed to keep up with the hire payments. The plaintiff sued the defendant for conversion of the tools and the defen-dant pleaded illegality as a defence, on the ground that the supply of the tools contravened certain statutory regulations. Despite this, the plain-tiff's claim succeeded on the ground that the claim was founded on its continuing title and it was not necessary for it to found its claim on the illegal transaction. Such a conclusion is easy to justify as regards the two machines which the defendant had sold in breach of the hiring agree-ment, because the sale terminated the agreement so that the plaintiff

---

[232] Lord Goff dissented on the ground that to obtain relief in equity the applicant must come with clean hands. In fact, the clean hands maxim is a principle of justice which is designed to prevent those guilty of serious misconduct from securing a discretionary equi-table remedy, such as an injunction or specific performance: *Dunbar* v. *Plant* [1998] Ch. 412, 422 (Mummery LJ). It follows that the maxim should not be relevant where a party seeks to vindicate an equitable proprietary right.

[233] Cp. the decision of the High Court of Australia in *Nelson* v. *Nelson* (1995) 70 ALJR 47.

[234] [1945] 1 KB 65.

was able to assert its own title without needing to have recourse to the illegality to set the agreement aside. The result is much more difficult to justify as regards the third machine which the defendant had retained, simply because the failure to keep up with the payments did not terminate the defendant's limited interest as bailee. The only way the plaintiff could defeat this interest was by relying on the illegality, but this is not allowed as a matter of public policy. The result can be justified only by assuming that the contract of hire-purchase contained a covenant which terminated the hire agreement if the defendant failed to keep up with its payments.

This principle is also applicable where an illegal lease has been created. Such a lease will vest a limited interest in the lessee.[235] If the lessee defaults on the payment of rent the landlord will not be able to rely on the lease to sue for payment, since this would involve the enforcement of the illegal lease, which would clearly be contrary to public policy.[236] However, once the lease ends, by effluxion of time or because of a breach of a covenant in the lease entitling the landlord to terminate it, the lessee's limited interest will end and the landlord will be able to rely on his or her legal title to seek recovery.[237]

(ii) A critique of the no reliance on illegality principle

Although the ratio of *Tinsley* v. *Milligan* appears to be that Milligan was able to vindicate her equitable proprietary right because she did not need to rely on the underlying illegal transaction by reference to which the property had been transferred into the name of Tinsley alone,[238] this explanation is difficult to justify. This is because Milligan had to rely on the underlying illegal transaction to both establish that legal title had been transferred to Tinsley and that the nature of the transaction was such that the presumption of resulting trust could be invoked. That such reliance on the illegal transaction to establish a proprietary claim is legitimate was recognised by Lord Browne-Wilkinson himself when he said that:[239]

a plaintiff can at law enforce property rights so acquired provided that he does not need to rely on the illegal contract for any purpose other than providing the basis of his claim to a property right . . . it is irrelevant that the illegality of the underlying agreement was either pleaded or emerged in evidence: if the plaintiff has acquired legal title under the illegal contract that is enough.

Although Lord Browne-Wilkinson was referring to claims to vindicate legal proprietary rights, he also recognised that no distinction should be

---

[235] *Feret* v. *Hill* (1854) 15 CB 207; 139 ER 400.
[236] *Alexander* v. *Rayson* [1936] 1 KB 169, 186.
[237] See also *Gordon* v. *Chief Commissioner of Metropolitan Police* [1910] 2 KB 1080.
[238] [1994] 1 AC 340, 372 (Lord Browne-Wilkinson).   [239] *Ibid*, 370.

drawn between the rules at law and in equity. It follows that Milligan could indeed rely on the illegal transaction to establish that legal title had been transferred to Tinsley alone. It might be argued that the effect of Lord Browne-Wilkinson's dictum is that a party can rely on an illegal transaction but cannot rely on an illegal purpose when he or she wishes to vindicate property rights. But, once it has been accepted that the plaintiff can rely on an illegal transaction, why should he or she be prevented from relying on his or her actual, albeit illegal, intention as well to identify what the parties really intended should happen to the property? Indeed, in *Silverwood* v. *Siverwood*[240] the Court of Appeal accepted that the plaintiff *could* rely on the illegal purpose of the parties to rebut the defendant's defence that the transferor of the property had intended it to be a gift to the defendant.

In fact, the principle that the plaintiff can enforce proprietary rights only if he or she has no need to rely on the illegality is a myth.[241] The better view is that the law does permit reliance on illegality for the purposes of establishing title, whether at law or in equity. This can be illustrated by a number of examples. One of these arises where the transferor transfers property pursuant to an illegal transaction. It has long been recognised that such a transaction is effective to pass title to the transferee.[242] It should follow that, if title has passed to the transferee but the property itself remains with the transferor, the transferee is able to rely on the illegal transaction itself to enforce his or her proprietary rights.[243] Similarly, if the bailor of property or the lessor of land wishes to recover the property which has been transferred under an illegal contract, he or she will often need to find some reason under the contract why possession should be recovered, such as breach of a covenant or the effluxion of time. In other words, the transferor will need to rely on the illegal contract to show that the transferee's right to possession has ceased.

It follows that the principle that the plaintiff can vindicate property rights as long as he or she does not need to rely on the illegality should be rejected as artificial. The plaintiff should be able to vindicate proprietary rights even though he or she has been tainted by illegality save where the illegality is of a particular serious kind.[244]

---

[240] (1997) 74 P and CR 453, 457 (Peter Gibson LJ).
[241] Enonchong, 'Title Claims and Illegal Transactions' (1995) 111 *LQR* 135, 155.
[242] *Singh* v. *Ali* [1960] AC 167.
[243] Enonchong, 'Title Claims and Illegal Transactions' (1995) 111 *LQR* 135, 140. See *Singh* v. *Ali* [1960] AC 167, 176–7 and *Tinsley* v. *Milligan* [1994] 1 AC 340, 366 (Lord Jauncey).
[244] See Chapter 26.

3. THE FOLLOWING AND TRACING RULES

(a) The function of following and tracing

Once the plaintiff can establish that he or she has retained a legal interest in property or that an equitable interest can be recognised, it is then
necessary for the plaintiff to show that he or she had a proprietary interest in the property which had been received by the defendant. To establish this, the plaintiff will need to rely on the following and tracing rules.

(i) The essence of following

The essence of following is that the plaintiff is able to show that the actual
property in which the plaintiff has a proprietary interest has been
received by the defendant.[245] If the identity of the plaintiff's property has
been lost or the property has been destroyed he or she will no longer be
able to follow it. Where the plaintiff transfers the property directly to the
defendant there is no difficulty in following it. Where, however, the property is received indirectly by the defendant the question of following may
be more difficult. It is for this reason that particular rules have been formulated which assist the plaintiff in following his or her property into the
defendant's hands. [246]

(ii) The essence of tracing

The essential function of the tracing rules is to enable the plaintiff to
show that the value of the property in which he or she originally had a
proprietary interest has been received by the defendant, even though the
defendant did not receive the original property. In other words, the tracing rules enable the plaintiff to identify property in the defendant's
hands which the plaintiff has not previously owned but which can be
considered to represent the plaintiff's original property. Only once the
plaintiff has done this can he or she claim the property in the hands of the
defendant or the value of that property.[247] So, for example, if the plaintiff
paid £10,000 to a friend because of a fundamental mistake and the friend
then used that money to buy a car, which he then sold for £15,000 and
used the proceeds of sale to buy shares which he gave to his daughter, the
plaintiff may wish to claim the shares from the daughter. To establish
such a claim, the plaintiff will need to show both that he retained a proprietary interest in the original £10,000 which he paid by mistake and
that this proprietary interest can be traced into the car, the proceeds of
the car and ultimately into the shares, so that the value in the original

---

[245] Smith, *The Law of Tracing* (Oxford: Clarendon Press, 1997) p. 4.
[246] See pp. 643–4 below.   [247] Smith, *The Law of Tracing*, p. 3.

£10,000 now subsists in the shares. Whether the plaintiff can establish this depends on the tracing rules.[248]

Although tracing has sometimes been regarded as a remedy in its own right,[249] such a characterisation is mistaken. For the tracing rules are simply a process[250] which enables the plaintiff to identify property in the hands of the defendant in which the plaintiff has or had a proprietary interest. Only once the plaintiff has established this does the question of the appropriate remedy to vindicate this proprietary right arise. The essence of the tracing process was identified by Millett LJ in *Boscawen* v. *Bajwa*:[251]

It is the process by which the plaintiff traces what has happened to his property, identifies the persons who have handled or received it, and justifies his claim that the money which they handled or received (and, if necessary, which they still retain) can properly be regarded as representing his property.

Consequently, a fundamental distinction needs to be made between tracing property and then making a claim to that property.[252]

The tracing rules are particularly complex, essentially because of the fundamental differences between tracing at law and in equity. As will be seen, this distinction is indefensible. It is another example of the historical divisions of the past being perpetuated without reason. Although some commentators have argued that there is no longer any distinction between tracing at law and in equity,[253] it is not yet possible to reach such a conclusion. Despite the fusion of the administration of law and equity last century, the distinction between tracing at law and in equity remains.

(b) Following

The rules on following simply exist to enable the plaintiff to establish that the defendant has received the plaintiff's property. The rules themselves cause no great difficulty and are usefully described and analysed by Smith in his book, *The Law of Tracing*.[254] The rules are particularly important when the plaintiff's property has been mixed with the defendant's, where it is necessary to determine whether the plaintiff's property has lost its identity and so cannot be followed.[255] It will not be possible to follow the plaintiff's property where it has been subsumed into another asset, has become a fixture or has been merged with

---

[248] See pp. 644–55 below.   [249] See *Sinclair* v. *Brougham* [1914] AC 398.
[250] *Boscawen* v. *Bajwa* [1996] 1 WLR 328, 334 (Millett LJ).
[251] *Ibid.*   [252] See Smith, *The Law of Tracing*, pp. 11–14.
[253] See especially *ibid*, p. 5 and Khurshid and Matthews, 'Tracing Confusion' (1979) 95 LQR 78.
[254] Part II.   [255] *Ibid*, pp. 70 ff.

another asset to form a new one.[256] Where it is no longer possible to follow the plaintiff's property it may be possible to trace the value of the property into a substitute asset.

(c) Tracing at common law

(i) The basic rules

The common law tracing rules are logical but restrictive. The fundamental principle underlying these rules is that the common law will enable the plaintiff to identify the value of his or her property in the substitutes for that property, so long as the substitutes have not become mixed with other property so that they lose their identity.[257] So, to take the simplest case, if the defendant stole the plaintiff's car and sold it, the plaintiff would be able to trace his or her continuing proprietary interest into the proceeds of sale, assuming that they still exist and have not been polluted by irretrievable mixing with any other money. If the defendant used the proceeds of sale to buy another car, without contributing any part of the purchase price him- or herself, then the plaintiff could trace into that car and then bring a proprietary restitutionary claim to it. The ability of the plaintiff to claim the substitute for the original property is called the exchange-product theory.

The logic behind these tracing rules is clear. To the extent that the substitute directly represents the original property there can be no objection to allowing tracing into its substitute. If the plaintiff's original property ceases to exist, the plaintiff has no choice but to trace the value of the original property into its substitute. For example, if the defendant took the plaintiff's car and sold it to a third party who drove the car and crashed it so that it was destroyed, the plaintiff cannot recover the car, but he can instead trace into the substitute, the proceeds of sale, in the hands of the defendant. Where, however, the original property and the proceeds of sale continue to exist, the plaintiff has a choice whether he or she claims the original property or the proceeds of sale.[258] This is simply a matter for the plaintiff to decide whether or not to claim the original property or the substitute. It has nothing to do with adoption or ratification.[259] In *Boscawen* v. *Bajwa*,[260] albeit in the context of an equitable proprietary claim but the same issue arises there as with common law tracing, Millett LJ preferred to analyse the ability of the plaintiff to decide

---

[256] Smith, *The Law of Tracing*, p. 104.
[257] *Taylor* v. *Plumer* (1815) 3 M and S 562; 105 ER 721. See p. 647 below.
[258] *Marsh* v. *Keating* (1834) 1 Bing (NC) 198; 131 ER 1094.
[259] *Lipkin Gorman (a firm)* v. *Karpnale Ltd.* [1991] 2 AC 548, 573 (Lord Goff).
[260] [1996] 1 WLR 328, 342. See also *Lipkin Gorman (a firm)* v. *Karpnale Ltd.* [1991] 2 AC 548.

whether to claim the original property or its substitute as involving an election between remedies. In other words, the plaintiff is allowed to elect whether the remedy should be to recover the original property or its substitute. This is surely correct and is consistent with the doctrine of election between remedies in the context of restitution for wrongs.[261]

This election analysis has a number of advantages. In particular it explains why the plaintiff cannot bring proprietary claims against both the original property and the substituted property. By assuming that the plaintiff has a power to shift the proprietary interest from the original property to its substitute and that this can occur only once the power of election has been exercised, it follows that the plaintiff is able to bring only one proprietary claim at a time. But this election analysis does cause problems of its own.[262] For example, if the effect of this analysis is that the plaintiff has no interest in the substitute until the power of election has been exercised, it should follow that if the defendant who is in possession of the substitute becomes insolvent before the plaintiff has made the election the plaintiff's right to the substitute ought to be extinguished.[263] Further, if the defendant has exercised skill and labour in effecting a profitable exchange, it is not possible to reflect this in a claim at law because there is no scope for the award of an allowance. The defendant might, however, be able to bring a claim founded on unjust enrichment, with the ground of restitution being mistake as to the ownership of the property.

(ii) Tracing into profits

Usually where the plaintiff has traced property at common law he or she simply traces into the substitute for the property. It has now been recognised by the Court of Appeal in *Trustee of the Property of F.C. Jones* v. *Jones*[264] that the plaintiff can trace at law into the profits made from his or her property. In this case the partners in a firm of potato growers committed an act of bankruptcy. One of the partners drew cheques from a partnership bank account and paid them to his wife, who in turn paid the cheques into her account with a firm of commodity brokers. This money was applied on the potato futures market and the wife made a large profit which she deposited in a special account at her bank. This money was never mixed with her own money. The trustee in bankruptcy of the partnership claimed this whole amount. It was clear that the trustee was

---

[261] See p. 461 above.

[262] See Khurshid and Matthews, 'Tracing Confusion' (1979) 95 *LQR* 78 and Andrews and Beatson ' Common Law Tracing: Springboard or Swan-song?' (1997) 113 *LQR* 21, 24.

[263] Grantham, 'Doctrinal Bases for the Recognition of Proprietary Rights' (1996) 16 *OJLS* 561, 570.

[264] [1997] Ch. 159.

legally entitled to the money in the partnership bank account from the date of the bankruptcy.[265] The question was whether he could trace at law into the wife's bank account.[266] It was held that he could because there was a chain of straight substitutions from the money in the partnership account to the chose in action representing the funds deposited at the wife's bank account. It did not matter that the original money paid from the partnership bank account had nearly quintupled in value; the trustee in bankruptcy was entitled to claim this profit simply because it derived from the original money without being mixed with any other money of the wife.

(iii) Tracing into mixed products

The major limitation on the efficacy of tracing at common law is that it is not possible to trace into a mixed product,[267] save where it is possible to separate the components of the product. There are two reasons why tracing into a mixed fund at common law is not possible: first, because of the inadequacies of the common law proprietary remedies, especially that it is not possible to charge a mixed fund;[268] secondly, because the common law adopts a rigidly logical approach to tracing. Where there has been an irretrievable mixing it is simply not possible to say in what property the plaintiff has a proprietary interest. Consequently, where such mixing has occurred the plaintiff's legal title to the property will be extinguished.

The main application of this restriction on tracing at common law arises where the plaintiff's money becomes mixed in the defendant's bank account, so that it is not possible to say which money belongs to the plaintiff and which to the defendant. It has sometimes been suggested that the effect of the restriction on common law tracing into mixed products is that if the plaintiff's money is paid into a bank account tracing will automatically fail. But this is not the case. The common law is willing to trace into a bank account, even though the property in which the plaintiff has a proprietary interest has changed its identity from a sum of money to a debt owed by the bank to the account holder. But since this debt represents completely the sum of money which originally existed,

---

[265] This is no longer the law: Insolvency Act 1986, ss. 278 and 306.

[266] An equitable proprietary claim could not be established because statute had passed the entire interest in the partnership money to the trustee in bankruptcy, so it could not have been held on trust by the wife.

[267] *Taylor* v. *Plumer* (1815) 3 M and S 562; 105 ER 721; *Agip (Africa) Ltd.* v. *Jackson* [1991] Ch. 547; *El Ajou* v. *Dollar Land Holdings* [1993] 3 All ER 717. Smith in 'Tracing in *Taylor* v. *Plumer*: Equity in the Court of King's Bench' [1995] *LMCLQ* 240 has argued that *Taylor* v. *Plumer* actually turned on tracing in equity. This was recognised by Millett LJ in *Trustee of the Property of F.C. Jones* v. *Jones* [1997] Ch. 159, 169 but he still affirmed the rule that tracing at law is barred if the property has been mixed with other property.

[268] *Agip (Africa) Ltd.* v. *Jackson* [1991] Ch. 547, 563 (Fox LJ).

assuming that no other money had been credited to this account either before or after the plaintiff's money had been credited to it, the debt can simply be regarded as the substitute for the plaintiff's money. A good example of tracing in such circumstances is *Banque Belge pour l'Etranger v. Hambrouck*[269] where the first defendant forged a number of cheques so that £6,000 was debited from the account of his employer at the plaintiff bank, and this sum was then credited to his own bank account. The first defendant then drew sums from this account which he paid to his mistress, and she paid these sums into her own bank account. The plaintiff bank sought to recover this money from the mistress. At the time of the bank's action the mistress's account was credited with the sum of £315. The Court of Appeal held that the plaintiff was able to trace into this credit because only the proceeds of the fraud had been paid into the account of the first defendant and his mistress, so that there had not been any mixing of money. It did not matter that the tracing process did not relate to sums of money throughout, since at various stages credits were substituted for actual money. This was irrelevant because the credits simply represented the money and neither the credits nor the money were ever tainted by any other money or credits which did not derive from the fraud.

Modern banking practice is such that it is increasingly difficult to trace into and through a bank account. This is particularly because of telegraphic transfers, which mean that the plaintiff is unable to show that the money received by the defendant necessarily represents the plaintiff's money. This limitation on the efficacy of tracing at common law was recognised in *Trustee of the Property of F.C. Jones v. Jones*[270] where Millett LJ affirmed that it was not possible to trace through inter-bank clearing, and that tracing at law would be defeated where value is passed by an electronic funds transfer. This is unacceptable. There is no reason why common law tracing should be defeated by mixing and, at the very least, the approach in equity should be adopted at law, so that it should be possible to trace into a mixed product.[271]

(d) Tracing in equity

The main advantage of tracing in equity is that it will not be defeated by the irretrievable mixing of property.[272] This difference in approach between law and equity has sometimes been expressed in terms that the

---

[269] [1921] 1 KB 321.　　　　　　　　　　　　　　　[270] [1997] Ch. 159, 168.

[271] See *Banque Belge pour l'Etranger* v. *Hambrouck* [1921] 1 KB 321, 335 (Atkin LJ). For more radical proposals for reform of the tracing rules see p. 655 below.

[272] *Re Hallett's Estate* (1880) 13 Ch.D 696; *Sinclair* v. *Brougham* [1914] AC 398; *Agip (Africa) Ltd.* v. *Jackson* [1991] Ch. 417.

common law views property as physical assets whereas equity is able to view property metaphysically. Consequently, where money in which the plaintiff has a proprietary interest is mixed in a bag with the defendant's money so that it is not possible to say which coins or notes belong to which party, tracing at law will fail because the common law cannot identify the actual coins or notes in which the plaintiff has a proprietary interest. But equity is able to assume that the plaintiff's property continues to exist in the mixture, albeit that it is not possible to say which coins or notes belong to which party. The reason equity can do this is that, when the plaintiff has traced his or her property into a mixed fund, an equitable charge will be placed on the whole fund as security for the plaintiff's claim.[273] Consequently, equity does not specifically regard part of the money as actually belonging to the plaintiff; rather equity is prepared to assume that the plaintiff simply has an equitable interest in the mixture by means of a charge on the fund.

Since equity is prepared to trace into and through a mixed fund, complex rules have been developed to determine how such tracing can occur. This will be examined after a further distinction between tracing at law and equity has been considered, namely that to trace in equity it is necessary to identify a fiduciary relationship.

(i) The fiduciary requirement

The disadvantage of tracing in equity is that to trigger the equitable rules it is necessary to show that the property in which the plaintiff had an equitable proprietary interest passed to the defendant through the hands of a fiduciary in breach of duty.[274] It is not, however, necessary to show that the defendant owed fiduciary duties to the plaintiff, since it suffices that the fiduciary was an intermediary between the plaintiff and the defendant.[275] Initially the equitable tracing rules arose in the context of breach of trust by a trustee where the fiduciary requirement was easily established. The simplest case is where a trustee takes property from the trust and uses it for his own purposes. Since the common law could not be used to provide a remedy, because the law did not recognise the trust, equity intervened to enable the beneficiaries to identify the prop-

---

[273] *Re Hallett's Estate* (1880) 13 Ch.D 696, 708–10 (Jessel MR); *Sinclair* v. *Brougham* [1914] AC 398, 420–2 (Viscount Haldane LC), 441–2 (Lord Parker of Waddington), 459–60 (Lord Sumner).

[274] *Ibid*; *Re Diplock* [1948] 1 Ch. 465; *Agip (Africa) Ltd.* v. *Jackson* [1991] Ch. 547, 566 (Fox LJ), *El Ajou* v. *Dollar Land Holdings plc.* [1993] 3 All ER 717, 733 (Millett J). This requirement has recently been affirmed by the Court of Appeal in *Boscawen* v. *Bajwa* [1996] 1 WLR 328, 335 (Millett LJ). *Re Diplock* was specifically affirmed by Lord Browne-Wilkinson in *Westdeutsche Landesbank Girozentrale* v. *Islington LBC* [1996] AC 669, 714.

[275] *Re Diplock* [1948] 1 Ch. 465. See also *Boscawen* v. *Bajwa* [1996] 1 WLR 328.

erty to which they were entitled. The rules were then extended from trustees to include all fiduciaries.[276]

Whilst the requirement that the property must have passed through the hands of a fiduciary in breach of his or her duty has been recognised in many cases, what is actually meant by this is much more extensive than the traditional concept of a fiduciary relationship. *Sinclair* v. *Brougham*[277] is a perfect example of the artifice of the fiduciary requirement. For in that case it was assumed that the directors of the defendant building society, which had engaged in an *ultra vires* banking business, owed fiduciary duties to the depositors who had deposited money with it. Such an interpretation of the fiduciary relationship is contrary to the orthodox view that directors only owe fiduciary duties to their company, save where a specific fiduciary relationship can be identified, but there was no evidence of such an explicit relationship on the facts. The recognition by Lord Browne-Wilkinson in *Westdeutsche Landesbank Girozentrale* v. *Islington LBC*[278] that even a thief can be characterised as a fiduciary, since the thief's conscience will have been affected so that the property which was stolen is held on constructive trust for the victim, means that the fiduciary requirement will be even easier to satisfy. Essentially, anybody can be treated as a fiduciary so long as he or she can be considered to have been acting unconscionably. It follows that the requirement of a fiduciary relationship as a precondition for equitable tracing has become even more artificial. This is particularly the case because it seems that it is no longer necessary specifically to show that the fiduciary breached his or her duty. This can be assumed simply from the fact that the defendant received the plaintiff's property in circumstances in which he or she ought to have returned it to the plaintiff.

In fact, careful analysis of the judgment of Lord Browne-Wilkinson in *Westdeutsche Landesbank* suggests that he rejected the requirement that the equitable tracing rules will only be applicable where there is a fiduciary relationship. This is because, although he appears to have suggested that a thief can be treated as a fiduciary, he stated this in the context of an argument which he ultimately rejected.[279] Certainly the judge's dictum is ambiguous, but if he had sought to remove this long-standing requirement he would probably have done so explicitly. His comments were *obiter* anyway. Consequently, Lord Browne-Wilkinson's judgment should be treated as a strong indication of the need to remove the fiduciary relationship requirement for tracing in equity, but it is not

---

[276] *Re Hallett's Estate* (1880) 13 Ch.D 696.   [277] [1914] AC 398.
[278] [1996] AC 669, 716.
[279] *Ibid*; Birks, 'On Taking Seriously the Difference Between Tracing and Claiming' (1997) 11 *TLI* 2, 3.

yet possible to say categorically that the requirement has been removed from English law.

Since the fiduciary relationship is so artificial it follows that the time has come to conclude that it should be rejected as no longer serving any useful purpose. The requirement has been expressly rejected in New Zealand.[280] Tracing in equity has moved a long way from its origins where a trustee breached his or her trust. Today, tracing is particularly important in connection with money laundering and widespread commercial fraud. Equitable tracing needs to adapt to be of use in such circumstances, and rejection of the fiduciary relationship requirement would be the best way of achieving this. It does not follow that there would no longer be any need to consider whether or not the plaintiff's property had been received by a fiduciary, since this may be a significant consideration when determining whether the plaintiff has an equitable proprietary interest which he or she could vindicate. This should be the only condition for the equitable tracing rules to apply, namely that the plaintiff can establish an equitable proprietary base.[281]

(ii) Mixing of money

Since equity allows tracing of money into and through a mixed fund, complex rules have developed to balance the interests of the different contributors to the fund. Different rules exist depending on whether the plaintiff's money has been mixed with the money of a fiduciary or of an innocent third party.

(1) Mixing with the fiduciary's money

Where the fiduciary has mixed the plaintiff's money with his or her own money, the plaintiff's claim to the mixed fund will prevail over that of the fiduciary.[282] Where money has been taken from the mixed fund so that there is insufficient to satisfy the plaintiff's claim, and it is not possible for the plaintiff to prove whether the money spent from the fund was that of the plaintiff or of the fiduciary, the plaintiff may rely on one of two alternative presumptions, whichever is more favourable to the plaintiff. The first presumption is that the fiduciary spent his or her own money first, so where the fiduciary has spent money from the mixed fund the plaintiff will be able to trace into the sum remaining in the fund.[283] The

---

[280] *Elders Pastoral Ltd.* v. *Bank of New Zealand* [1989] 2 NZLR 180.

[281] See *Westdeutsche Landesbank Girozentrale* v. *Islington LBC* [1994] 1 WLR 938, 947 (Dillon LJ) and 953 (Leggatt LJ). Although this decision was overruled by the House of Lords nothing was said about this point. See also Grantham, 'Doctrinal Bases for the Recognition of Proprietary Rights' (1996) 14 *OJLS* 61, 65 and Smith, *The Law of Tracing*, pp. 123–30.

[282] *Re Diplock* [1948] 1 Ch. 465, 539. If the fiduciary claims that a particular asset represents his or her own property the onus is on the fiduciary to prove this: *Lupton* v. *White* (1805) 15 Ves. Jun. 432; 33 ER 817.   [283] *Re Hallett's Estate* (1880) 13 Ch.D 696.

alternative presumption is that the fiduciary spent the plaintiff's money first, so where the fiduciary has used money from the fund to purchase an asset and dissipated the remaining amount, the plaintiff can trace into the purchased asset.[284] The reason for these presumptions is that, where a wrongdoer mixes his money with that of the plaintiff, he or she has created an evidential difficulty as to what has happened to the plaintiff's money. In such a case the difficulty will be resolved against the interests of the wrongdoer, save where the wrongdoer can rebut the presumption.[285]

(2) Mixing with the money of a third party

Where the plaintiff's money is mixed with that of an innocent volunteer[286] the general rule is that the money will be assumed to belong to both parties.[287] Also, if the value of the mixed fund has fallen, the loss will be borne by the parties in proportion to their contribution to the fund. An exception to this general rule that the fund belongs to the parties arises where the money has been paid into a current bank account so that the rule in *Clayton's Case*[288] applies,[289] namely that the money which was first paid into the bank account is deemed to be that which is first paid out of it. So, for example, if the plaintiff's £1,000 is paid into a current account which is already credited with the innocent volunteer's £1,000 and the sum of £1,000 is subsequently withdrawn, then it will be presumed that it was the innocent volunteer's money which was withdrawn. However, the rule in *Clayton's Case* is only a presumption and will not be relied on if it is impractical or unjust to do so.[290]

(iii) Restrictions on equitable tracing

The general rules of equity require tracing into a specific asset or fund where it is possible to say that the asset or fund represents the plaintiff's money. Consequently, equitable tracing will fail or will be restricted in the following circumstances.

---

[284] *Re Oatway* [1903] 2 Ch. 356. The plaintiff can also claim a proportionate share of the resulting profits: *Re Tilley's Will Trusts* [1967] 1 Ch. 1179.

[285] Birks, 'On Taking Seriously the Difference Between Tracing and Claiming' (1997) 11 *TLI* 2, 5.

[286] Meaning someone who had not given consideration for the property received and who had no reason to suspect that somebody else had a proprietary interest in it. If the defendant did know or had reason to suspect that somebody else had a proprietary interest in the property the defendant will be treated as a fiduciary: *Boscawen* v. *Bajwa* [1996] 1 WLR 328, 337 (Millett LJ).

[287] *Sinclair* v. *Brougham* [1914] AC 398. See also *Re Diplock* [1948] 1 Ch. 465, 524.

[288] (1817) 1 Mer. 572; 35 ER 781.   [289] *Re Diplock* [1948] 1 Ch. 465.

[290] *Barlow Clowes International Ltd.* v. *Vaughan* [1992] 4 All ER 22, where the rule in *Clayton's Case* was not applied because the large number of claims made the operation of the rule impractical. A rateable basis of distribution was adopted instead.

(1) Dissipation of the asset or fund

Where the fund has been dissipated and no specific asset can be identified which derives from it, tracing will fail. So, for example, where the plaintiff's money is paid into an overdrawn bank account there will be no asset which can be considered to represent the plaintiff's property.[291]

(2) Lowest intermediate balance

If the plaintiff's money is mixed with other money, for example in a bank account, and at some stage the balance of that account is less than the amount of the plaintiff's money which had been paid into it, the amount which the plaintiff can recover is limited to the maximum amount which can be regarded as representing the plaintiff's money.[292] So if the defendant paid £1,000 of the plaintiff's money into his own bank account, which already had £1,000 in it, and the defendant then dissipated £1,500, the maximum value which the plaintiff can trace is £500. This is because the first £1,000 which was spent is deemed to have been the money of the defendant. But since another £500 was spent, this must have been the plaintiff's money, leaving only £500 left to satisfy the plaintiff's claim. The only exception to this rule is where the defendant subsequently paid money into the bank account with the clear intent to make good the dissipation of the plaintiff's money.

(3) Backward tracing

The orthodox view is that a plaintiff is not able to assert a proprietary interest against property in the defendant's possession where the defendant was already in possession of that property before receiving the plaintiff's money, because in such circumstances the defendant's property cannot be regarded as representing the plaintiff's money, even if the plaintiff's money was used to pay for the property.[293] In other words, it appears that so-called 'backward tracing' is not available to the plaintiff. So, for example, if the plaintiff's money is used by the defendant to discharge a debt which the defendant owed, the plaintiff will not be able to trace into the property which the defendant had acquired in exchange for the debt.

However, in *Foskett* v. *McKeown*[294] Sir Richard Scott V-C tentatively recognised the principle of backward tracing, although he declined to

---

[291] *Re Goldcorp Exchange Ltd.* [1995] 1 AC 74; *Bishopsgate Investment Management Ltd.* v. *Homan* [1995] Ch. 211.

[292] *James Roscoe (Bolton) Ltd.* v. *Winder* [1915] 1 Ch. 62; *Re Goldcorp Exchange Ltd.* [1995] 1 AC 74; *Bishopsgate Investment Management Ltd.* v. *Homan* [1995] Ch. 211.

[293] *Ibid*, p. 221 (Leggatt LJ).

[294] [1998] 2 WLR 298, 315. See also *Bishopsgate Investment Management Ltd.* v. *Homan*, p. 217 (Dillon LJ) and *Boscawen* v. *Bajwa* [1996] 1 WLR 328, 341 (Millett LJ).

decide the point. Hobhouse LJ[295] and Morritt LJ[296] explicitly rejected the proposition that the doctrine of tracing could be used to follow value into a previously acquired asset. The issue arose in the following circumstances. A trustee misappropriated trust money and used it to pay some of the premiums on a life assurance policy. The issue for the court was whether the plaintiff, one of the beneficiaries of the trust, could claim a proportionate share of the £1 million which was paid on the death of the trustee. For the plaintiff's claim to succeed he needed to show that trust money had been used to pay the premiums, by means of the tracing rules. The difficulty was that the trustee had paid an annual premium of £10,220 out of an account which was in credit only to the extent of £596.74. Shortly after the premium was paid there was a transfer into the overdrawn account of a sum of money which was sufficient to put the account in credit. Sir Richard Scott V-C was prepared to accept that, if the plaintiff could show that this was his money, then the fact that this money was paid into the bank account shortly after the payment of the premium would not prevent the plaintiff from tracing his money into the premium which was paid. As the judge said:

The availability of equitable remedies ought . . . to depend upon the substance of the transaction in question and not upon the strict order in which associated events happen.[297]

If this view is accepted it will mean that 'backward tracing' may be possible.[298] If an asset is acquired by the defendant with money obtained from an overdraft or a loan it should be possible to trace into this asset. There is, in fact, a decision of the Court of Appeal which supports this approach. In *Re Diplock*[299] money had been paid by mistake to the Heritage Craft Schools, and this money was used to pay a debt which had been incurred to enable the recipient to improve a building. It was held that, even though the money had actually been used to discharge the debt, it had effectively been used to pay for the improvements and so it was possible to trace the value of the money into the improvements. This is consistent with the courts examining the substance of the transaction rather than being confined to a consideration of events in the exact order in which they occurred.

---

[295] [1998] 2 WLR 298, 321.

[296] *Ibid*, p. 327. See also *Bishopsgate Investment Management Ltd.* v. *Homan* [1995] Ch. 211, 217 (Dillon LJ).

[297] *Ibid*, p. 315. This had previously been advocated by Smith, 'Tracing into the Payment of a Debt' (1995) 54 *CLJ* 290.

[298] *Bishopsgate Investment Management Ltd.* v. *Homan* [1995] Ch. 211, 217, *per* Dillon LJ. Leggatt LJ, at p. 221, rejected any notion of 'backward tracing'. Henry LJ agreed with both judgments.

[299] [1948] Ch. 465, 548–9.

(iv) A move to a more pragmatic approach?

Despite the orthodox approach of equitable tracing which requires clear representation of the value of the plaintiff's property in the asset or fund which is in the defendant's possession or under his or her control, dicta in some recent cases suggest that it is possible to trace into the defendant's general assets even though no specific asset can be identified as representing the plaintiff's money.[300] This has been described as the 'swollen assets theory', since the defendant's assets have been swollen by the receipt of property to which the plaintiff had a proprietary claim. Tracing into the defendant's general assets is justified on the basis that, if the defendant has dissipated those assets in which the plaintiff had a proprietary interest, and because the defendant could have dissipated other assets which he or she owned, it is right that the plaintiff should be able to make a claim against those other assets. Such a flexible approach to tracing is not consistent with the orthodox tracing rules and has recently been confined to the specific situation in which a bank trustee wrongly deposits trust money with itself in a mixed rather than a non-existent fund.[301] The courts have been right to reject the general incorporation of the swollen assets theory into the tracing rules, since such a theory confuses the fundamental distinction between proprietary claims where the plaintiff seeks a personal remedy and those where he or she seeks a proprietary remedy. For where the plaintiff seeks a personal remedy, it is sufficient for the plaintiff to establish that the defendant received property in which the plaintiff had a proprietary interest; it is irrelevant that this property was dissipated subsequently. Where, however, the plaintiff seeks a proprietary remedy, it is imperative that he or she establishes that the defendant has particular assets which can be considered to represent the plaintiff's property. It is only where particular assets can be identified which represent the plaintiff's original property that it is appropriate that the plaintiff should gain priority over the defendant's general creditors.

Nevertheless, recent cases do suggest a trend towards the development of a more pragmatic approach to the equitable tracing rules. For example, where the plaintiff's money is paid into different bank accounts an equitable charge will be placed on each account even though the plaintiff was unable to identify which sums went into which account.[302] Similarly, recent suggestions that backward tracing should be recognised

---

[300] See in particular *Space Investments Ltd.* v. *Canadian Imperial Bank of Commerce Trust Co. (Bahamas) Ltd.* [1986] 1 WLR 1072, 1074 (Lord Templeman).

[301] *Re Goldcorp Exchange Ltd.* [1995] 1 AC 74, 105 (Lord Mustill); *Bishopsgate Investment Management Ltd.* v. *Homan* [1995] Ch. 211. See Gullifer, 'Recovery of Misappropriated Assets: Orthodoxy Re-established?' [1995] *LMCLQ* 446, 447.

[302] *El Ajou* v. *Dollar Land Holdings plc.* [1993] 3 All ER 717.

indicate a greater willingness to use tracing rules to secure what is perceived to be a just result.[303]

(e) The future of the tracing rules

Whilst many of the rules relating to tracing can be justified as a logical response to the problems of identification of property, there remains much about these rules which is unsatisfactory. Primarily, the artificial distinction between the rules at common law and equity should be rejected. What we require in a modern law of restitution is a unified approach to tracing which incorporates the acceptable features of both regimes.[304] It should follow that it is always possible to trace into a mixed fund, but without needing to prove that the property has passed through a fiduciary relationship.

It is only by adopting such a unified regime that the tracing rules will be able to cope with the complex problems thrown up by the modern commercial environment. For the problem of identifying property essentially arises today in the context of money laundering and commercial fraud. The tracing rules need to adapt to be able to cope with a commercial world with rapidly developing technological and financial conditions. Banking has developed dramatically since the nineteenth century, for there are now 'efficient clearing systems which can process in seconds huge numbers of high-unit transactions and facilitate global transfers of accounts from one financial centre to another as the former closes for the day while the other is opening'.[305] The inadequacy of the tracing rules for the modern world is illustrated by the fact that common law tracing is unable to follow money where it has passed through a clearing system, as will invariably occur where money is laundered through bank accounts, because the money will have become mixed with other money. Also, the requirement for tracing in equity that the money has passed through a fiduciary relationship has resulted in highly artificial responses in commercial transactions, where the relationship between parties is usually one of debtor and creditor without the addition of any fiduciary obligations. If a unified system for tracing were adopted it would mean that the law of restitution would be much more effective in the context of commercial fraud.

---

[303] See p. 653 above.
[304] See *Nelson* v. *Larholt* [1948] 1 KB 339, 342–3 (Denning J) and *Bristol and West Building Society* v. *Mothew* [1996] 4 All ER 698, 716 (Millett LJ). See also Andrews and Beatson, 'Common Law Tracing: Springboard or Swansong?' (1997) 113 *LQR* 21, 25; Birks, 'On Taking Seriously the Difference between Tracing and Claiming' (1997) 11 *TLI* 2; and Millett, 'Restitution and Constructive Trusts' (1998) 114 *LQR* 399, 409.
[305] Goode, 'Ownership and Obligation in Commercial Transactions' (1987) 103 *LQR* 433, 436.

21

Restitutionary Claims and Remedies to Vindicate Property Rights

1. GENERAL PRINCIPLES

(a) Proprietary and personal remedies

Once a plaintiff has established that he or she has a legal or equitable proprietary interest which can be followed or traced into property which is or was in the defendant's possession or under the defendant's control, the plaintiff can establish a restitutionary claim to vindicate his or her proprietary rights.[1] The questions which need to be examined in this chapter are what is the nature of the plaintiff's claim to this property and what is the appropriate remedy to vindicate this proprietary right? These remedies can take two forms. The first are proprietary remedies where the plaintiff is able to recover the property itself, or at the very least acquire a security interest in the property in the defendant's hands. The second are personal remedies where the defendant is able to recover only the value of the property received by the defendant. Typically proprietary remedies are preferable, since they all give the plaintiff priority over the defendant's unsecured creditors if the defendant becomes insolvent and some of these remedies enable the plaintiff to recover the fruits of the property. But all proprietary remedies are worthless once the property in which the plaintiff has a proprietary interest has been dissipated. It is in this situation that personal remedies become particularly attractive.

(b) Distinguishing between claims and remedies

A distinction needs to be drawn between the plaintiff's claim and the remedy which is available to vindicate that claim. It is assumed for the purposes of this chapter that the plaintiff is able to identify a proprietary base and so has a proprietary right, and is able to follow or trace this proprietary right into property which is held by the defendant. The only remaining questions, therefore, relate to the nature of the claim which the plaintiff can bring to vindicate his or her proprietary rights and then the most appropriate remedy which is available to achieve this objective.

---

[1] See Chapter 20.

To determine which claim and which remedy are appropriate it is necessary to consider the nature of the right and the personality of the recipient of the property in which the plaintiff has the right.

2. PROPRIETARY CLAIMS AND REMEDIES

(a) Common law proprietary claims and remedies

As a general rule, the common law has no proprietary remedies. Consequently, if the plaintiff has retained legal title in property which has been received by the defendant, the plaintiff can claim only the value of this property rather than the property itself.[2] One true exception to this is that the plaintiff is able to recover land from the defendant.[3] There is also the remedy of delivery up of goods under section 3(3) of the Torts (Interference with Goods) Act 1977, which is a proprietary remedy available where the defendant has committed a tort involving interference with the plaintiff's property rights. But this remedy is available only where damages are inadequate.[4]

There are certain other exceptional circumstances in which one party may be able to recover specific property from other party in legal proceedings. For example, in *Greenwood* v. *Bennett*[5] it was recognised that the court could order that a car should be transferred to the original owner in interpleader proceedings, where the holder of the car was requesting the court to determine who had the better claim to it.

(b) Equitable proprietary claims and remedies

Equity has developed much more extensive proprietary remedies. Some of these remedies have little, if anything, to do with the law of restitution, such as an order for specific performance or an injunction. Other remedies clearly operate within the law of restitution to enable the plaintiff to vindicate his or her equitable property rights, most notably the equitable lien and the constructive trust. When considering whether equitable proprietary remedies should be awarded there is one matter of vital importance which must not be forgotten, namely that these remedies are available only where the plaintiff can establish an *equitable* proprietary base in the property retained by the defendant.

---

[2] *Trustee of the Property of F.C. Jones and Sons (a firm)* v. *Jones* [1997] Ch. 159, 168 (Millett LJ).

[3] In an action for ejectment. See Goff and Jones, *The Law of Restitution*, p. 94.

[4] See also the Minors' Contracts Act 1987, s. 3. See pp. 614–15 above.

[5] [1973] QB 195. See p. 76 above.

(i) Constructive trust

The recognition that the defendant holds property on constructive trust for the plaintiff may have two different implications.

(1) Transfer of property

Where the plaintiff can show that he or she has an equitable proprietary interest in property which is in the hands of the defendant, the court may declare that the property is held on constructive trust for the plaintiff, and it will order the defendant to transfer this property to the plaintiff.[6]

(2) Proportionate share

A constructive trust may also be imposed where the plaintiff is considered to have a proportionate share in the property which is in the defendant's possession. This remedy is more attractive to the plaintiff than an equitable charge[7] where the property has increased in value. Where the plaintiff's money has been used by the defendant, who has also used his or her own money, to purchase an asset the plaintiff can claim a share of this asset which is proportionate to the amount of money which was contributed by the plaintiff.[8] Similarly, the remedy is available where the defendant mixes money from two innocent parties and uses this money to buy an asset.[9] In such circumstances the claims of both plaintiffs are equal, so it is not appropriate for one to have priority over the other. Rather, they should share the asset proportionately, bearing *pro rata* any increase or decrease in its value.[10]

(3) Remedial constructive trust

If the remedial constructive trust were ever recognised in English law it would mean that the courts would be given a discretion to determine what form the proprietary remedy should take. For example, the proprietary consequences of recognising the constructive trust might be mitigated so that the plaintiff would not be given priority over any of the

---

[6] *Boscawen* v. *Bajwa* [1996] 1 WLR 328, 334 (Millett LJ). In *Foskett* v. *McKeown* [1998] 2 WLR 298, 310, Sir Richard Scott V-C said that the property would be held on resulting trust. But in the light of the restrictive interpretation of the resulting trust by the House of Lords in *Westdeutsche Landesbank Girozentrale* v. *Islington LBC* [1996] AC 669 this will be the appropriate conclusion only where the plaintiff's property has been used by the defendant to enable him or her to purchase property. In such circumstances there will be a presumption that the property was held on resulting trust for the plaintiff. See p. 621 above.

[7] See p. 659 below.

[8] *Re Tilley's Will Trusts* [1967] Ch. 1179. Since this involves the use of the plaintiff's money to purchase an asset it may be more accurate to describe the property as being held on a resulting rather than a constructive trust.

[9] *Edinburgh Corporation* v. *Lord Advocate* (1879) 4 App. Cas. 823, 841 (Lord Hatherley).

[10] *Re Diplock's Estate* [1948] Ch. 465, 532 (Lord Greene MR). See also *Foskett* v. *McKeown* [1998] 1 WLR 298, 310 (Sir Richard Scott V-C).

other creditors of the defendant. But the most recent pronouncements on this issue suggest that the remedial constructive trust should not be recognised in English law.[11]

(ii) Equitable charge or lien

An alternative remedy to the recovery of particular property or the award of a proportionate share is to impose a charge on the property to secure repayment of the amount which the defendant owed to the plaintiff. This enables the plaintiff to recover the value received and retained by the defendant plus interest, but does not enable the plaintiff to recover any more. In *Foskett* v. *McKeown*[12] Sir Richard Scott V-C recognised that the imposition of an equitable charge over an asset was a restitutionary remedy.

Where the plaintiff's money has been used by the defendant to improve or maintain the defendant's property it is not appropriate for the court to require the defendant to hold the property on constructive trust for the plaintiff since the plaintiff cannot be considered to have a beneficial interest in it, as would be the case where the plaintiff's property was used to acquire an asset. Instead the court may treat the property as charged with a sum which represents the amount by which the value of the defendant's property has been increased by the use of the plaintiff's money.[13] Similarly, where the defendant has used the plaintiff's money to improve or maintain the property of a third party a charge over the property may be available, but only if it would not be unfair to the innocent third party.[14] Where the plaintiff's money has been used by the defendant to purchase an asset the plaintiff can claim a proportionate share in the property, but there is nothing to stop the plaintiff from claiming a charge over it if he or she wants.[15] A charge is an appropriate remedy in such a case if the value of the asset has not increased.

The use of a charge as a restitutionary remedy is illustrated by *Foskett* v. *McKeown*[16] where a trustee used just over £20,000 of trust money in breach of trust to pay two of the premiums on a life assurance policy. On the death of the trustee the proceeds of this policy, over £1 million, were paid by the life assurance company to the defendants. The plaintiff, one of the beneficiaries of the trust, was able to trace the money in which he had an equitable proprietary interest into the premiums and the proceeds of the policy. The key question for the Court of Appeal was

[11] *Re Polly Peck International plc. (No. 2)* [1998] 3 All ER 812.
[12] [1998] 2 WLR 298, 310.   [13] *Boscawen* v. *Bajwa* [1996] 1 WLR 328, 335 (Millett LJ).
[14] *Re Diplock's Estate* [1948] Ch. 465, 547 (Lord Greene MR); *Foskett* v. *McKeown* [1998] 2 WLR 298, 310 (Sir Richard Scott V-C).
[15] *Re Hallett's Estate* (1880) 13 Ch.D 696, 711 (Jessel MR).
[16] [1998] 2 WLR 298. This decision has been appealed to the House of Lords.

whether the appropriate remedy to be awarded to vindicate this equitable proprietary right should be a charge over the proceeds of the policy to enable the plaintiff to recover his money plus interest, or whether he was entitled to a proportion of the proceeds calculated by reference to the amount of his money which was used to pay the premiums. It was held that the plaintiff was entitled to a charge and not a proportionate share. The main reason for this was that the plaintiff's money was considered to have been used to improve rather than to purchase the life insurance policy.[17] But the charge was also an appropriate remedy because, although it was considered to be just that the plaintiff should recover his money which was used to keep the policy on foot, it was not considered to be just to divest the defendants of a proportionate part of their beneficial interest in the policy, when they were innocent of any participation in the breach of trust. This is consistent with fundamental principles concerning the imposition of equitable proprietary remedies where the dispute is essentially between two innocent parties.

The equitable charge has also been used as a restitutionary remedy in other cases in which its use is much more difficult to defend. For example, in *Cooper* v. *Phibbs*[18] the plaintiff contracted with the defendants to take a lease of a fishery. Both parties were mistaken in entering into this contract since neither party realised that the fishery already belonged to the plaintiff. Consequently, the contract could be rescinded for mistake. But it was held that rescission would be subject to a declaration that the defendants should be given a charge over the fishery to secure the value of improvements which had been made by their father who mistakenly believed that the land belonged to them. The purpose of this charge was to enable the defendants to recover the value of services which had mistakenly been provided for the eventual benefit of the plaintiff. It is difficult to justify the award of a proprietary restitutionary remedy in such a case when there was clearly no evidence that the defendants had any proprietary interest in the land which needed to be vindicated. The defendants should simply have been awarded the reasonable value of the improvements to the land.

---

[17] Cp. Morritt LJ, *ibid* at p. 332, who considered that where the plaintiff's money had been used to pay a premium it should be considered to have contributed to the purchase of an asset rather than to the maintenance of an existing asset. The conclusion of the majority, however, was correct because the nature of this particular life assurance policy was that the proceeds of the policy would have been paid to the defendant even if the premiums had not been paid. It followed that the plaintiff's money simply maintained the policy and did not contribute to its purchase.

[18] (1867) LR 2 HL 149.

(iii) Subrogation[19]

(1) The function of subrogation

Subrogation is a remedy which is designed to ensure 'a transfer of rights from one person to another . . . by operation of law'.[20] Essentially the function of the remedy is to enable the plaintiff to rely on the rights of a third party against a defendant, or the rights of a defendant against a third party. This is often described as the plaintiff being allowed to stand in the shoes of the third party. The typical case in which subrogation will be an appropriate remedy in the context of a proprietary restitutionary claim is where the plaintiff's money is used by the defendant to discharge a debt which the defendant owed to a secured creditor. In such circumstances the plaintiff can be subrogated to the secured creditor's charge and gain the benefit of that security as against other creditors of the borrower. This remedy of subrogation is available to the plaintiff even though the creditor's security has been discharged because one consequence of the remedy is that the creditor's security is metaphorically resurrected for the benefit of the lender. In effect the benefit of the charge is treated as though it had been assigned to the plaintiff[21] so that the plaintiff will obtain the benefit of that charge.

In the leading case of *Banque Financière de la Cité* v. *Parc (Battersea) Ltd.*[22] the House of Lords recognised that there were essentially two forms of subrogation which were recognised in English law. The first is that which arises by virtue of the express or implied intentions of the parties. Since this right to subrogation arises by virtue of contract, it has nothing to do with the law of restitution.[23] Secondly, the equitable remedy of subrogation may be awarded by operation of law as a restitutionary remedy specifically to reverse the defendant's unjust enrichment.[24] Although the matter was not discussed by the House of Lords, subrogation will also be available where the plaintiff's restitutionary claim is founded on the vindication of proprietary rights, and is in fact most likely to arise in such circumstances.

In the *Banque Financière* case the House of Lords recognised that, on the unusual facts of that case, the remedy of subrogation was available to reverse the defendant's unjust enrichment and it operated as a personal

[19] For examination of the remedy of subrogation see pp. 23–5 above. For detailed analysis see Mitchell, *The Law of Subrogation*.

[20] *Orakpo* v. *Manson Investments Ltd.* [1978] AC 95, 104 (Lord Diplock).

[21] *Banque Financière de la Cité* v. *Parc (Battersea) Ltd.* [1998] 2 WLR 475, 488 (Lord Hoffmann). See also *Boscawen* v. *Bajwa* [1996] 1 WLR 328, 333 (Millett LJ).

[22] [1998] 2 WLR 475.

[23] *Hobbs* v. *Marlowe* [1978] AC 16, 39 (Lord Diplock). See p. 41 above.

[24] [1998] 2 WLR 475, 483 (Lord Hoffmann). See also *Boscawen* v. *Bajwa* [1996] 1 WLR 328, 335 (Millett LJ).

remedy, so that the plaintiff obtained priority only over the defendant and not as regards any of the other creditors of the debtor company.[25] Usually, however, the remedy operates as a proprietary remedy since the plaintiff obtains the benefit of the third party's security completely. Consequently, to the extent that the third party had priority over other creditors of the defendant, the plaintiff will gain equal priority.

(2) The principles underlying the remedy of subrogation

(1) The restitutionary remedy of subrogation arises by operation of law and does not depend on the parties' intention that the remedy should be available.[26] Since the remedy arises by operation of law it does not follow that the proprietary consequences do not operate until the court has made the necessary order. Rather, the court order simply satisfies the pre-existing equity.[27] This is a very important matter in the context of priorities.

(2) If subrogation is to operate as a proprietary remedy by subrogating the plaintiff to a security interest it is necessary to consider whether the justice of the case requires such a result.[28] One of the key considerations in determining what is a just result is whether the plaintiff intended to obtain the benefit of a security when he or she paid money, even though the plaintiff did not intend to make any payment to the person who ultimately benefited from it.[29] So, for example, if the plaintiff had paid money but did not intend to obtain any security interest it would not be just to subrogate the plaintiff to a security.[30] If the plaintiff did intend to obtain a security it would be appropriate to subrogate the plaintiff to a security.[31] The burden of proving that the plaintiff intended the loan to be secured should be on the plaintiff, since this is consistent with basic principles concerning the establishment of causes of action for the purposes of the law of restitution.[32]

The application of this principle is illustrated by *Boscawen* v. *Bajwa*[33] where a building society lent money to the purchasers of a house, with the loan being secured by a first legal charge. This money was paid to the purchaser's solicitors, was then transferred to the vendor's solicitors and was used to discharge a mortgage on the property. The sale of the house fell through. The vendor's creditors obtained a charging order against

---

[25] [1998] 2 WLR 475, 480 (Lord Steyn) and 489 (Lord Clyde). See p. 24 above.

[26] *Ibid*, p. 483 (Lord Hoffmann).

[27] *Boscawen* v. *Bajwa* [1996] 1 WLR 328, 342 (Millett LJ).   [28] *Ibid*, p. 339.

[29] *Ibid*.   [30] See *Paul* v. *Speirway Ltd.* [1976] Ch. 220.

[31] See *Butler* v. *Rice* [1910] 2 Ch. 277 and *Ghana Commercial Bank* v. *Chandiram* [1960] AC 732.

[32] *Banque Financière de la Cité* v. *Parc (Battersea) Ltd.* [1998] 2 WLR 475, 486 (Lord Hoffmann).

[33] [1996] 1 WLR 328.

the property and claimed an order for possession and sale of it. The building society, on the other hand, claimed that it was entitled by subrogation to the rights of the vendor as mortgagee and so it was entitled to a charge on the proceeds of sale which ranked above the vendor's creditors. The Court of Appeal found for the building society for the following reasons. The building society could trace its money in equity into the payment which was used to discharge the mortgage by the vendor. The requirement that the money must have passed through the hands of a fiduciary was satisfied because, when the money was paid to the purchaser's solicitors to be transmitted to the vendor's solicitors, the money was held in trust for the building society. The remedy which was ordered to enable the building society to vindicate its property rights was the remedy of subrogation because it was held that the vendor's solicitor must have intended to keep the mortgage alive for the benefit of the building society. The Court of Appeal emphasised that it was concerned with the solicitor's intention to keep the security alive, because the building society's money had not been paid directly to discharge the vendor's mortgage. This seems unnecessarily complicated. The crucial question should simply have been what the building society's intention was in paying the money, and it had clearly intended to obtain the benefit of a security. It followed that a proprietary subrogation remedy was entirely appropriate.

(3) The plaintiff may still obtain the benefit of a creditor's security against the defendant by means of the subrogation remedy even though the security has been discharged.[34] This was recognised by Millett LJ in *Boscawen* v. *Bajwa*[35] who accepted that a discharged charge can be resurrected.[36] So, for example, if the plaintiff's money has been used by the defendant to discharge a debt owed by the defendant to a third party, it will be possible for the plaintiff to obtain the benefit of any security of the creditor, even though that security has been discharged. An aspect of the decision of the Court of Appeal in *Re Diplock*[37] appears, however, to suggest a contrary conclusion. In that case money had mistakenly been paid to the Leaf Homeopathic Hospital, and was used to discharge a mortgage over the hospital's property. It was held that the plaintiffs could not trace into a discharged debt[38] and so be subrogated to the mortgage. But this result is best explained as turning on a question of evidence rather than law, namely that it could not be shown that the plaintiff's money had

---

[34] That the plaintiff can obtain the benefit of a creditor's *undischarged* security was recognised by the House of Lords in *Banque Financière de la Cité* v. *Parc (Battersea) Ltd.* [1998] 2 WLR 475.

[35] [1996] 1 WLR 328, 341.

[36] This is illustrated by *Nottingham Permanent Building Society* v. *Thurston* [1903] AC 6.

[37] *Re Diplock* [1948] 1 Ch. 465, 549–50.

[38] The question of backward tracing is discussed at pp. 652–3 above.

been used to discharge the mortgage. If the money could not be traced into the mortgage there was no basis for a proprietary restitutionary remedy to be awarded.[39] Alternatively, the denial of the remedy could be explained on the basis that the hospital had innocently changed its position.[40]

(4) The plaintiff may not be awarded the remedy of subrogation for reasons of public policy. This is illustrated by *Orakpo* v. *Manson Investments Ltd.*[41] where the plaintiff was not subrogated to the rights of a third party because this would have been contrary to the policy of the Moneylenders Acts.

(5) It is possible to exclude the remedy of subrogation expressly by contract. Similarly, the contract between the plaintiff and the defendant may impliedly exclude the remedy of subrogation. This is illustrated by *Capital Finance Co. Ltd.* v. *Stokes*[42] where the plaintiff and the defendant had agreed that the plaintiff should obtain a security by way of a legal charge. This charge was unenforceable because it had not been registered, but it was held that, because a legal charge was a better interest than an equitable lien, the agreement between the parties prevented the plaintiff from being subrogated to a third party's equitable lien against the defendant. In other words, the intention that the plaintiff should have the benefit of a legal charge prevented the plaintiff from being subrogated to a lesser equitable charge.

3. PERSONAL CLAIMS AND REMEDIES

This section is concerned with those cases in which the plaintiff seeks to secure a personal restitutionary remedy in circumstances in which it is an essential element of the claim that he or she has a legal or equitable proprietary interest in the property which the defendant had received, and sometimes continues to retain.

(a) Personal claims and remedies at common law

(i) Tort

For certain types of torts for which the plaintiff will be awarded a personal remedy it is necessary for the plaintiff to establish that the defendant interfered with property in which the plaintiff has a legal proprietary interest. So, for example, if the plaintiff wishes to recover damages for the tort of conversion it may be necessary to show that he or

---

[39] See Smith, 'Tracing Into The Payment of a Debt' (1995) 54 *CLJ* 290, 295.
[40] *Boscawen* v. *Bajwa* [1996] 1 WLR 328, 341 (Millett LJ).		[41] [1978] AC 95.
[42] [1969] 1 Ch. 261.

she has a legal proprietary interest in property[43] and that property, or its substitute, was converted by the defendant acting in some way which is inconsistent with the plaintiff's proprietary rights. Although the remedy which is awarded will typically be compensatory damages, the plaintiff may wish to waive the tort and bring a restitutionary claim to recover the value of the property which the defendant converted.[44]

(ii) Action for money had and received

In some cases where the plaintiff is bringing an action for money had and received at common law it is an essential element of the claim that the plaintiff had a proprietary interest in the property which the defendant received. This will be the case where the plaintiff brings a restitutionary claim against the defendant who received the plaintiff's property via a third party. In such a case the plaintiff is unable to bring a claim founded on unjust enrichment because it will not be possible to show that the defendant has been enriched at the plaintiff's expense.[45] The plaintiff will instead seek to show that the defendant has received property in which the plaintiff has retained a proprietary interest. It is sufficient that the plaintiff has received the property in which the plaintiff has a legal proprietary interest; it is not necessary to show that the defendant has retained this property.[46]

The key case which illustrates this type of proprietary restitutionary claim for which the plaintiff seeks a personal restitutionary remedy is *Lipkin Gorman (a firm)* v. *Karpnale Ltd.*[47] In that case money had been stolen from the plaintiff firm of solicitors by one of its partners who had gambled with it at the defendant's casino. The House of Lords held that the defendant was liable to make restitution to the plaintiff. The nature of this claim has been a matter of particular controversy. Some have argued that it was founded on the reversal of the defendant's unjust enrichment, with the ground of restitution being that the plaintiff was ignorant that its money had been stolen.[48] An alternative view is that this claim was simply concerned with the vindication of the plaintiff's property rights in the money, those rights having been retained because the

[43] A possessory interest is sufficient: *MCC Proceeds Inc.* v. *Lehman Bros. International (Europe)* [1998] 4 All ER 675.

[44] See pp. 490–1 above. Alternatively, the court may order that the property is returned to the plaintiff. See the Torts (Interference with Goods) Act 1977, s. 3(2), discussed at p. 657 above.

[45] See Chapter 5.

[46] See *Agip (Africa) Ltd.* v. *Jackson* [1990] Ch. 265, 285 (Millett J).

[47] [1991] 2 AC 548. See also *Clarke* v. *Shee and Johnson* (1774) 1 Cowp. 197; 98 ER 1041 and *Trustee of the Property of F.C. Jones and Sons (a firm)* v. *Jones* [1997] Ch. 159.

[48] Birks, 'The English Recognition of Unjust Enrichment' [1991] *LMCLQ* 473 and McKendrick, 'Restitution, Misdirected Funds and Change of Position' (1992) 55 *MLR* 377.

money had been stolen.[49] This latter analysis was adopted by Ferris J in *Box* v. *Barclays Bank plc.*[50] where he recognised that the plaintiff's claim in *Lipkin Gorman* was founded on the fact that the money in which it had legal title could be traced into the defendant's hands.[51]

This analysis of *Lipkin Gorman* as a case which involved a proprietary restitutionary claim rather than a claim founded on the reversal of unjust enrichment is consistent with the leading judgments in the case itself. For none of the judges identified a ground of restitution on which the plaintiff's claim could be founded. Rather, Lord Goff in particular referred to the fact that the plaintiff had a subsisting interest in the money.[52] Consequently, *Lipkin Gorman* should be treated as a case where the reason the plaintiff's claim for money had and received succeeded was simply that the defendant had received money in which the plaintiff had a legal proprietary interest, rather than that the defendant was unjustly enriched in any substantive sense.

(iii) Action for debt

It was recognised by the Court of Appeal in *Trustee of the Property of F.C. Jones and Sons (a firm)* v. *Jones*[53] that, where the plaintiff could establish that the defendant had received property in which the plaintiff had legal title, the plaintiff could bring an action for debt against the defendant and obtain an order for payment of the money. This is a personal claim, which has the same practical consequences as the action for money had and received, namely that the plaintiff is able to recover the value of the money which was received by the defendant.

(b) Personal claims and remedies in equity

Where the defendant has received property in which the plaintiff has an equitable proprietary interest there are a number of personal claims and remedies which enable the plaintiff to recover the value of his or her property.

---

[49] See Virgo, 'What is the Law of Restitution About?' in *Restitution: Past, Present and Future* (ed. Cornish, Nolan, O'Sullivan and Virgo) pp. 314–16.

[50] *The Times*, 30 April 1998.

[51] In fact the plaintiff's money had probably become mixed with other property so that it could no longer be traced at law, but the defendant conceded that it was possible to trace the money.

[52] See also *Clarke* v. *Shee and Johnson* (1774) 1 Cowp. 197, 200; 98 ER 1041, 1043 (Lord Mansfield).

[53] [1997] Ch. 159. See Davern, 'Common Law Tracing, Profits and the Doctrine of Tracing Back' (1997) 5 *RLR* 92, 94.

(i) Administration of estates

The House of Lords in *Ministry of Health* v. *Simpson*[54] recognised an apparently limited personal restitutionary action in equity, whereby beneficiaries of a deceased's estate were able to recover money which had been paid to the defendants by the personal representatives who were administering the estate and who mistakenly believed that the money was properly paid to the defendants. This equitable action has two unusual features. First, unlike many equitable claims which depend on the defendant's conscience having been affected in some way before equitable liability is imposed, the defendant's liability is strict. Secondly, the plaintiff beneficiaries are able to bring an action against the recipients of the estate only once they have exhausted their remedies against the personal representatives. This limitation is difficult to defend, but it may simply be because the personal representatives can be considered to have been at fault in making the mistake in the first place and, being an equitable claim, this form of liability should prevail over strict liability.

The proper analysis of this equitable action is a matter of some controversy, but the preferable view is that it simply involves a restitutionary claim which is founded on the vindication of the plaintiff's proprietary rights.[55] This is because dicta in subsequent cases suggest that any person who received the property which had mistakenly been transferred from the estate will be liable to make restitution unless he or she was a *bona fide* purchaser for value,[56] and this defence of *bona fide* purchase is applicable only to proprietary restitutionary claims.[57] It follows from this that the imposition of strict liability can be defended because, where the defendant has interfered with the plaintiff's property rights he or she should make restitution to the plaintiff regardless of fault. It is not, however, possible to justify the requirement that the plaintiff must have exhausted his or her remedies against the personal representatives, since in vindicating this proprietary interest the plaintiff's claim should be brought against the defendant first. Since there is no requirement at common law that the plaintiff should exhaust his or her remedies against the person who transferred the benefit to the defendant, it is difficult to defend the introduction of such a requirement in this equitable action.

---

[54] [1951] AC 251.

[55] Although in *Commissioner for Stamp Duties (Queensland)* v. *Kingston* [1965] AC 694, 712, the Privy Council recognised that the plaintiff beneficiaries had no proprietary interest until the assets had been distributed properly.

[56] See, for example, *Nelson* v. *Larholt* [1948] 1 KB 339, 342 (Denning J) and *Baker (G.L.) Ltd.* v. *Medway Building and Supplies Ltd.* [1958] 1 WLR 1216, 1220 (Danckwerts J).

[57] See Chapter 22.

Although this specific equitable action has generally arisen in the context of property transferred in the course of administering estates, the recognition of strict liability in equity may prove to be a useful model from which a more general strict liability action could be developed; an action which could be relied on by a plaintiff whenever the defendant has interfered with his or her equitable proprietary rights. There is, in fact, authority which suggests that such a development is possible. In *G.L. Baker Ltd.* v. *Medway Building and Supplies Ltd.*[58] this equitable strict liability claim was applied even though assets were distributed from an *inter vivos* trust rather than in the course of the administration of an estate.

(ii) Action for knowing receipt[59]

The equitable action for knowing receipt can be considered to be the equitable equivalent of the common law claim for money had and received. Both claims are dependent on proof that the defendant has received property in which the plaintiff had a proprietary interest: either a legal interest for the action for money had and received or an equitable interest for the action for knowing receipt. A further similarity between the two actions is that both claims will succeed so long as it can be shown that the defendant received property in which the plaintiff had a proprietary interest, it not being necessary to show that the defendant has retained this property. Further, the remedy which is awarded for both types of claim is a personal restitutionary remedy since it is assessed by reference to the value of the property which the defendant received at the time of its receipt. Despite these similarities between the two claims there is one fundamental difference between them relating to the need to prove fault before liability can be imposed. Whereas liability in the action for money had and received is strict, liability for the action for knowing receipt depends on proof that the defendant was at fault in some way. The degree of fault which must be proved is a matter of particular controversy. But the reason why fault must be established is also a controversial matter which requires consideration.

(1) The conditions of liability

In order to establish liability for knowing receipt the following conditions need to be met:

(a) The defendant must have received property in breach of trust or received trust property and then misapplied it.

---

[58] [1958] 1 WLR 1216.

[59] See Lord Nicholls of Birkenhead, 'Knowing Receipt: The Need for A New Landmark' in *Restitution: Past, Present and Future* (ed. Cornish, Nolan, O'Sullivan and Virgo), chapter 15.

(b) The property must be received by the defendant for his or her own use and benefit.[60] This means that if the property is received by the defendant merely as agent, as will be the case where a bank receives money on behalf of a customer, the defendant could be liable for dishonest assistance in breach of trust[61] but not for knowing receipt, unless the defendant subsequently misappropriates the property for his or her own use.

(c) The defendant must have been at fault in receiving the property in breach of trust.

There are two lines of authority as to the degree of fault which needs to be established.

(a) *Subjective test.* The defendant may be liable only if he or she was dishonest, which means that the defendant knew or suspected that the property had been received in breach of trust.[62] This is a subjective test of fault.

(b) *Objective test.* The defendant will be liable if he or she received the property in circumstances in which he or she failed to make the inquiries which a reasonable person would have made whether the property had been transferred in breach of trust.[63] This is an objective test of fault.

The authorities generally point to the need to show subjective fault on the part of the defendant before he or she can be held liable for knowing receipt. This is apparently because it is considered that the defendant should be liable only where he or she acted unconscionably in receiving the property.[64] This is inconsistent with liability for dishonest assistance where, although it is necessary to show that the defendant was dishonest in assisting a breach of trust, this dishonesty is interpreted objectively since it is necessary to consider whether the defendant had acted as an honest person would have

---

[60] *Agip (Africa) Ltd.* v. *Jackson* [1990] 1 Ch. 265, affirmed [1991] Ch. 547, CA.

[61] See pp. 553–5 above.

[62] *Carl-Zeiss Stiftung* v. *Herbert Smith and Co. (a firm) (No. 2)* [1969] 2 Ch. 276; *Competitive Insurance Co. Ltd.* v. *Davies Investments Ltd.* [1975] 1 WLR 1240; *Re Montagu's Settlement Trusts* [1987] Ch. 264; *Barclays Bank plc.* v. *Quincecare Ltd.* [1992] 4 All ER 363, 374 (Steyn J); *Eagle Trust plc.* v. *SBC Securities* [1992] 4 All ER 488; *Cowan de Groot Properties Ltd.* v. *Eagle Trust plc.* [1992] 4 All ER 700. In *Hillsdown plc.* v. *Pensions Ombudsman* [1997] 1 All ER 862, Knox J, at p. 903, affirmed the subjective test of fault but said that the defendant could be liable for knowing receipt even though he or she did not appreciate that a breach of trust was involved. This would undermine the essentially subjective test of fault.

[63] *Belmont Finance Corp. Ltd.* v. *Williams Furniture Ltd. (No. 2)* [1980] 1 All ER 393; *International Sales and Agencies Ltd.* v. *Marcus* [1982] 3 All ER 551; *Agip (Africa) Ltd.* v. *Jackson* [1990] Ch. 265, 291 (Millett J); *El Ajou* v. *Dollar Land Holdings plc.* [1993] 3 All ER 717, 739 (Millett J). See also *The Citadel General Assurance Co.* v. *Lloyds Bank of Canada* [1997] 3 SCR 805 (Supreme Court of Canada).

[64] *Re Montagu's Settlement Trusts* [1987] Ch. 264, 285 (Megarry V-C).

done.[65] This inconsistency between these two forms of liability is particularly difficult to justify in the light of the different nature of liability for dishonest assistance and knowing receipt. This was recognised by La Forest J in *The Citadel General Assurance Co.* v. *Lloyds Bank of Canada*,[66] a decision of the Supreme Court of Canada, where he stated that 'whereas the accessory's liability is "fault-based", the recipient's liability is "receipt-based" '.[67] Since the recipient's liability is predicated on the fact that the defendant has received property for his or her own benefit in which the plaintiff had an equitable proprietary interest,[68] it should follow that either no fault is required before the defendant is held liable to make restitution to the plaintiff[69] or, at the very least, an objective test of fault is sufficient.[70]

(2) The remedy for knowing receipt

Once these conditions have been satisfied the defendant will be held liable to the plaintiff as a constructive trustee. This notion of constructive trust is, however, highly misleading. This constructive trust is not being used in this context as a mechanism for transferring property to the plaintiff. Rather, it is simply a mechanism which is relied on for holding the defendant personally liable to account for the value of the property received.[71] It would be far easier to remove all references to the constructive trust in the context of liability for knowing receipt and to refer instead simply to a personal liability to account.

(3) The advantages of the action for knowing receipt

Bearing in mind that liability in the action for money had and received is strict, whereas liability for knowing receipt depends on proof of fault, it might be wondered why a plaintiff would wish to bring an action for knowing receipt in equity rather than the common law action for money had and received. There are, however, two advantages of the equitable action. First, the plaintiff's proprietary interest may be recognised only in

---

[65] *Royal Brunei Airlines Sdn. Bhd.* v. *Tan* [1995] 2 AC 378. See pp. 553–4 above.

[66] [1997] 3 SCR 805.

[67] *Ibid*, p. 836. See also *Royal Brunei Airlines Sdn. Bhd.* v. *Tan* [1995] 2 AC 378, 386.

[68] *Agip (Africa) Ltd.* v. *Jackson* [1990] Ch. 265, 292 (Millett J). See also Millett, 'Tracing the Proceeds of Fraud' (1991) 107 *LQR* 71, 83 and Gardner, 'Knowing Assistance and Knowing Receipt: Taking Stock' (1996) 112 *LQR* 56, 85.

[69] See p. 671 below.

[70] The Supreme Court of Canada in *The Citadel General Assurance Co.* case adopted an objective test of carelessness to determine whether the defendant was liable for receiving trust property in breach of trust.

[71] *Westdeutsche Landesbank Girozentrale* v. *Islington LBC* [1996] AC 669, 707 (Lord Browne-Wilkinson). See also *Paragon Finance plc.* v. *Thakrar* [1999] 1 All ER 400, 409 (Millett LJ).

equity, so it will not be possible for the plaintiff to show that he or she had retained a legal proprietary interest in the property which had been received by the defendant. Secondly, even if the plaintiff had initially retained a legal proprietary interest, this interest may have been lost subsequently, as will occur where the plaintiff's money has been paid into a mixed account. In such circumstances it may still be possible for the plaintiff to identify an equitable proprietary interest in the property which was received by the defendant, so that the plaintiff could bring an equitable claim for knowing receipt.

(4) The future of the action for knowing receipt

The real problem with the action for knowing receipt is that liability involves both restitution for wrongdoing, because of the need to establish that the defendant was at fault in some way, and restitution founded on the vindication of proprietary rights, which depends on the defendant having received property in which the plaintiff has an equitable proprietary interest. The time has come to rationalise the action for knowing receipt by dividing it up into two separate actions, one founded on wrongdoing and the other on the vindication of property rights. This has been advocated by Lord Nicholls of Birkenhead in a seminal article on the action for knowing receipt.[72]

(a) Vindication of equitable property rights

An equitable action should be recognised which would be the exact counterpart of the action for money had and received. In other words, a strict liability version of the action of knowing receipt should be recognised. If the essence of such an action is that the defendant has interfered with the plaintiff's equitable proprietary rights by the receipt of property it is surely appropriate that the defendant's liability is strict.[73] This would help to reduce the chasm between legal and equitable claims and would bring us closer to the utopia of an assimilated legal system. The model for such a claim should be the claim recognised in *Ministry of Health* v. *Simpson* concerning the administration of estates.[74] It would not follow that questions of the defendant's fault are completely irrelevant, since such questions would be considered when determining whether the defendant can rely on defences such as change of position[75] and *bona fide* purchase.[76] But these defences are also available to claims for money

---

[72] 'Knowing Receipt: The Need for A New Landmark' in *Restitution: Past, Present and Future* (ed. Cornish, Nolan, O'Sullivan and Virgo), chapter 15.

[73] *Ibid*, p. 238. See also Birks, 'Misdirected Funds: Restitution from the Recipient' [1989] *LMCLQ* 296 and Harpum, 'Knowing Receipt and Knowing Assistance: The Basis of Equitable Liability' in *The Frontiers of Liability* (ed. Birks, 1, Oxford: Clarendon Press, 1994) p. 9.

[74] See p. 667 above.   [75] See Chapter 24.   [76] See Chapter 22.

had and received which are founded on the vindication of the plaintiff's legal proprietary rights.[77]

(b) Restitution for wrongs

Even if a strict liability version of the 'knowing' receipt action were recognised, a case could still be made for the recognition of a claim founded on the defendant's knowing receipt of property in breach of trust. Liability for such an action should depend on the defendant acting dishonestly, in the sense that the defendant's conduct would be characterised by an honest person as dishonest conduct. Fault would therefore be the same as the action for dishonest assistance in a breach of trust.[78] The real advantage of recognising the equitable wrong of knowing receipt would be that the defendant could be personally liable both to account for all benefits received and also to compensate the plaintiff for loss suffered.[79] Consequently, the remedy would not necessarily be restitutionary.

(iii) Subrogation

The House of Lords in *Banque Financière de la Cité* v. *Parc (Battersea) Ltd.*[80] recognised that subrogation may operate as a personal remedy.[81] Consequently, on the facts of that case, the plaintiff was able to rely on a third party's security rights against the defendant, but only as against the defendant and not as against any of the defendant's other creditors. More simply the personal remedy of subrogation may operate to assign a third party's personal rights against the defendant to the plaintiff.[82] This will be a particularly useful remedy where the plaintiff's direct restitutionary claim against the defendant is barred and the plaintiff's money has been used by the defendant to discharge a debt owed to a third party creditor. This is illustrated by *Re Wrexham, Mold and Connah's Quay Railway Co.*[83] where the plaintiff could not sue the defendant directly because the borrowing transaction was *ultra vires*, but it was held that the plaintiff could rely on the rights of a third party to sue the defendant. The role of subrogation as a personal restitutionary remedy is much less important today, however. When the law of restitution was founded on the notion of an implied contract, the remedy of subrogation provided a useful mechanism for enabling the plaintiff to secure restitution, even

---

[77] See *Lipkin Gorman (a firm)* v. *Karpnale Ltd.* [1991] 2 AC 548.
[78] See pp. 553–5 above.
[79] Lord Nicholls of Birkenhead in *Restitution: Past, Present and Future*, p. 244.
[80] [1998] 2 WLR 475.
[81] Although the remedy was awarded in that case to reverse the defendant's unjust enrichment, rather than to vindicate the plaintiff's proprietary rights. See p. 24 above.
[82] *Boscawen* v. *Bajwa* [1996] 1 WLR 328, 333 (Millett LJ).
[83] [1899] 1 Ch. 440.

though a contract could not be implied between the plaintiff and the defendant because, for example, the defendant lacked the capacity to enter into the transaction. But, with the rejection of the implied contract theory and the recognition that the obligation to make restitution is imposed by operation of law, the role of subrogation as a personal remedy is much less important. For today the plaintiff will be able to obtain restitution directly from the defendant by means of an action founded on unjust enrichment regardless of the fact that either party to the transaction lacked the capacity to enter into the transaction.[84]

(c) The future of personal claims and remedies

The inconsistency between the common law and equity as regards the nature and ambit of personal claims and remedies to vindicate proprietary rights is unacceptable. Ideally the three actions of money had and received, knowing receipt and administration of estates should be assimilated into one action, which would be available whenever the defendant has interfered with the plaintiff's proprietary rights and regardless of whether those rights were legal or equitable. The key characteristic of this action would be that liability is strict. The fault of the defendant would be considered but only at the stage of determining whether the defendant can successfully rely on one of the defences to proprietary restitutionary claims.

---

[84] As was recognised by the House of Lords in *Westdeutsche Landesbank Girozentrale* v. *Islington LBC* [1996] AC 669.

22

The Defence of Bona Fide *Purchase*

It might be thought that the proper place for analysis of the defence of
bona fide purchase is Part VI where the general defences to restitutionary
claims are considered. It is, however, more appropriate to examine the
defence in this Part, because it is not one which is generally available to
all restitutionary claims. Rather, the defence of *bona fide* purchase is
available only to defeat those claims which are based on the plaintiff's
legal or equitable property rights, in other words proprietary restitutionary claims.[1] The defence is not available where the plaintiff's claim is
founded on the reversal of the defendant's unjust enrichment, neither is
it available where the defendant's claim is founded on the commission of
a wrong, save where the wrong involves the plaintiff proving that the
defendant had interfered with property in which the plaintiff has a proprietary interest.

1. THE FUNCTION OF THE DEFENCE

The function of the *bona fide* purchase defence is to make good defects
in the defendant's title to property.[2] The defence constitutes an exception to the *nemo potest dare quod non habet* principle by virtue of which
the transferee cannot obtain rights to property which are better than
those of the transferor. Consequently, where the transferor of property
does not have good title to that property the defendant can be considered to have obtained good title if the conditions for the *bona fide* purchase defence have been satisfied. It is for this reason that the operation
of the defence is confined to those restitutionary claims which involve
the vindication of the plaintiff's property rights.[3] Where the defence

[1] Swadling, 'Restitution and *Bona Fide* Purchase' in *The Limits of Restitutionary Claims: A Comparative Analysis* (ed. Swadling) p. 79. See also Key, '*Bona Fide* Purchase as a Defence in the Law of Restitution' [1994] *LMCLQ* 421.

[2] See *Boscawen* v. *Bajwa* [1996] 1 WLR 328, 334 (Millett LJ). See also Swadling, n. 1 above, p. 103. Cp. O'Dell, 'Restitution, Coercion by a Third Party and the Proper Role of Notice' (1997) 56 *CLJ* 71.

[3] Swadling, n. 1 above, assumes that the law of restitution is founded only on the princi-ple of unjust enrichment and so he is forced to conclude that, since the *bona fide* purchase defence has only a proprietary function, it cannot apply to the law of restitution. But once it is accepted that the law of restitution also involves the vindication of proprietary rights it is clear that the defence of *bona fide* purchase can have a role within the law of restitution.

applies, the defendant cannot be considered to have interfered with the plaintiff's proprietary rights simply because, at the time when the defendant received the property, he or she is considered to have obtained good title to it so that the plaintiff's property rights are extinguished. It follows that there are no longer any property rights of the plaintiff which can be vindicated.

The operation of the *bona fide* purchase defence can be justified by the need to protect the security of commercial transactions. Where the defendant has obtained property in good faith and for value then, as between the owner of the property and the recipient, the latter should have the better claim to the property, since he or she should be secure in the validity of the receipt of the property if there is nothing to put him or her on notice that the transferor did not have a good title to transfer.[4]

2. AMBIT OF THE DEFENCE

The ambit of the *bona fide* purchase defence depends on whether the plaintiff's proprietary restitutionary claim is brought at common law or in equity.

(a) Common law

(i) The defence is generally inapplicable

The *bona fide* purchase defence has a very limited ambit at common law. In respect of most proprietary restitutionary claims the defence is inapplicable because of the operation of the *nemo dat* principle. So, for example, where a car is transferred to the defendant by a third party in circumstances in which that third party does not have legal title to the car, the defendant is not able to obtain any better title to the car, even if he or she could be characterised as a *bona fide* purchaser for value because the defendant had paid for the car and was not aware of the third party's lack of title.[5]

(ii) Proprietary restitutionary claims to money[6]

Where, however, the defendant receives money which has passed into circulation as currency the plaintiff's title is destroyed and the defendant obtains title to the money if he or she receives it in good faith and for

---

[4] *Bishopsgate Motor Finance Corp.* v. *Transport Brakes Ltd.* [1949] 1 KB 322, 336–7 (Denning J).

[5] See *Greenwood* v. *Bennett* [1973] QB 195.

[6] Fox, '*Bona Fide* Purchase and the Currency of Money' (1996) 55 *CLJ* 547.

value.[7] In other words, the *bona fide* purchase defence is applicable to
extinguish the plaintiff's title to the money so that any proprietary restitutionary claim brought by the plaintiff in respect of the money will be
defeated. The reason the defence is recognised where the defendant has
received money as a *bona fide* purchaser has been identified by Fox, who
states that:

[it] helps money to circulate readily in the economy in that it reduces the need for
recipients to make detailed inquiries into the title of people who tender money in
payment of debts or to buy goods.[8]

(b) Equity

The *bona fide* purchase defence is generally applicable in respect of restitutionary proprietary claims which are brought in equity, regardless of
the nature of the property which the defendant received. Consequently,
where the defendant has purchased a legal estate for value without
notice of the plaintiff's equitable proprietary rights the plaintiff's proprietary right is extinguished, regardless of the nature of the property which
the defendant has purchased.[9] Where, however, the defendant has
obtained an equitable proprietary interest for value the defence will not
be available, because of the rule that the first equitable interest in time
takes priority.[10]

(c) Rescission

It has been recognised that where a plaintiff wishes to rescind a contract
he or she will not be able to do so if the property which the plaintiff transferred under the contract has been obtained by a *bona fide* purchaser for
value.[11] This bar to rescission applies regardless of whether the plaintiff
wishes to rescind the contract at common law or in equity and regardless
of the property which the plaintiff seeks to recover. The rationale behind
the bar is that, if the subject matter of the contract has been obtained by
a *bona fide* purchaser for value, it will not be possible to return the parties to the position which they occupied before the contract was made.
The result of this will be that the plaintiff's claim for restitution of the
property will be barred, since it is not possible to obtain restitution if the
contract continues to operate between the parties.

---

[7] *Miller* v. *Race* (1758) 1 Burr. 452, 457–8; 97 ER 398, 401. See also *Clarke* v. *Shee and Johnson* (1774) 1 Cowp. 197; 98 ER 1041, *Banque Belge pour l'Etranger* v. *Hambrouck* [1921] 1 KB 321, 329 (Scrutton LJ) and *Ilich* v. *R.* (1987) 69 ALR 231.

[8] 'Bona Fide Purchase and the Currency of Money' (1996) 55 *CLJ* 547, 565.

[9] *Cave* v. *Cave* (1880) 15 Ch.D 639.

[10] *Macmillan Inc.* v. *Bishopsgate Investment Trust plc.* [1995] 1 WLR 978, 1000 (Millett J).

[11] *Phillips* v. *Brooks Ltd.* [1919] 2 KB 243. See p. 34 above.

3. CONDITIONS FOR ESTABLISHING THE DEFENCE

The burden of establishing the *bona fide* purchase defence is placed on the defendant[12] who must show that two conditions have been satisfied. Once these conditions have been satisfied the defence operates absolutely, barring the plaintiff's proprietary restitutionary claim completely, although the plaintiff may still be able to found a restitutionary claim on the defendant's unjust enrichment or the commission of a wrong by the defendant.

(a) Good faith

The defendant must show that he or she acted in good faith in receiving the property from the transferor. What is meant by good faith depends on whether the plaintiff's restitutionary claim is brought at common law or in equity.

(i) Common law

At common law the notion of good faith is equated with honesty.[13] It is therefore a subjective test which will not be satisfied if the defendant knew or suspected that the transferor had a defective title to the property which was transferred.

(ii) Equity

In equity the notion of good faith is defined more widely than at common law to include an objective test of constructive notice. The defendant will be deemed to have notice of the plaintiff's equitable proprietary interest if the defendant failed to make inquiries which would have been made by a reasonable person in his or her position.[14] Notice will also be imputed to the defendant if his or her agent had actual or constructive notice of the defect in title, as long as the agent acquired notice in the course of the transaction involving the transfer of property which the plaintiff wishes to recover. The defendant will not, however, be prevented from relying on the defence simply because he or she had notice of a doubtful claim of the plaintiff to recover the property.[15]

---

[12] *Re Nisbet and Pott's Contract* [1906] 1 Ch. 386. Cp. *Polly Peck International plc.* v. *Nadir (No. 2)* [1992] 4 All ER 769.

[13] *Nelson* v. *Larholt* [1948] 1 KB 339.

[14] *Ibid*. See also *Macmillan Inc.* v. *Bishopsgate Investment Trust plc.* [1995] 1 WLR 978, 1000 (Millett J).

[15] *Carl-Zeiss Stiftung* v. *Herbert Smith (No. 2)* [1969] 2 Ch. 276.

(b) Purchase for value

The defendant will be able to rely on the defence only if he or she provided value for the transfer of title to the property in which the plaintiff
claims a proprietary interest. Value includes the giving of money or
money's worth or marriage consideration.[16] It is not necessary for the
courts to consider whether the value which was given for the property
was adequate; it is sufficient that some value was given. This value
requirement means that the defence cannot be relied on by the recipient
of a gift, simply because such a recipient will not have provided any consideration for the transfer. The value which is provided by the defendant
may be provided before or after the property was transferred to him or
her, so long as when the property was transferred to the defendant or the
value was provided by the defendant, whichever was the later, he or she
was not fixed with notice of the plaintiff's proprietary interest.[17] The
defendant cannot be considered to have provided value for the property
if it was transferred pursuant to an illegal transaction.[18]

4. OPERATION OF THE DEFENCE

The defence has a number of peculiar characteristics.

(a) A complete defence

Where the conditions for establishing the defence have been satisfied the
plaintiff's restitutionary claim is barred completely, rather than being
barred merely to the extent that the defendant has provided consideration for the property.[19] It is consequently a different types of defence
from that of change of position which operates only to the extent that the
defendant's position has changed.[20]

(b) The defence may be applicable even though the defendant was not a *bona fide* purchaser

Usually the *bona fide* purchase defence will be pleaded by the defendant
who seeks to establish that he or she satisfied its conditions. But this

---

[16] *Pullan* v. *Koe* [1913] 1 Ch. 9.   [17] *Ratcliffe* v. *Barnard* (1871) LR 6 Ch. App. 652.
[18] *Lipkin Gorman (a firm)* v. *Karpnale Ltd* [1991] 2 AC 548. See also *Clarke* v. *Shee and Johnson* (1774) 1 Cowp. 197; 98 ER 1041.
[19] *Ilich* v. *R.* (1987) 69 ALR 231, 245 (Wilson and Dawson JJ). See also *Lipkin Gorman* v. *Karpnale* [1991] 2 AC 548.
[20] See Chapter 24.

need not be the case. It is possible that the plaintiff's property was transferred to a third party in circumstances in which the plaintiff's intention to transfer title can be considered to be vitiated but the third party recipient can be considered to be a *bona fide* purchaser of the property. Consequently, the third party will have obtained a good title to the property which he or she will be able to transfer to the defendant. The plaintiff's claim against the defendant to vindicate property rights cannot succeed in such circumstances simply because the plaintiff's title to the property has been defeated by reason of the third party being a *bona fide* purchaser for value. Once that interest has been defeated it cannot subsequently be resurrected against the defendant.

(c) The defence applies regardless of whether the plaintiff seeks a personal or proprietary restitutionary remedy

The defence will be operative regardless of whether the remedy which the plaintiff seeks is personal or proprietary. This is because the time at which the question of *bona fide* purchase is considered is when the defendant received the property or its proceeds. If at this point the defendant was in good faith and had provided value for the property, the plaintiff's title will be defeated and he or she will be unable to show that the defendant retained property in which the plaintiff had a proprietary interest or even that the defendant had received such property.

That the defence is available where the plaintiff seeks personal restitutionary remedies was recognised by the House of Lords in *Lipkin Gorman (a firm)* v. *Karpnale Ltd.*[21] where the plaintiff's action for money had and received was founded on its continuing proprietary interest. The House of Lords accepted that this action might have been defeated if the defendant had been a *bona fide* purchaser, although the defence could not be established on the facts since the money had been transferred pursuant to an unlawful gambling transaction, so the defendant could not be considered to have provided value. Similarly, it has been recognised that the equitable action for restitution arising from the mistaken payment of assets in the administration of an estate can be defeated if the recipient of property from the estate was a *bona fide* purchaser for value.[22]

---

[21] [1991] 2 AC 548. See also *Clarke* v. *Shee and Johnson* (1774) 1 Cowp. 197; 98 ER 1041 and *Nelson* v. *Larholt* [1948] 1 KB 339.

[22] *Ministry of Health* v. *Simpson* [1951] AC 251 and *Re J. Leslie Engineers Co. Ltd.* [1976] 1 WLR 292, 299 (Oliver J).

PART VI

THE GENERAL DEFENCES AND BARS TO RESTITUTIONARY CLAIMS

23

Fundamental Principles and General Bars

1. THE FUNCTION AND AMBIT OF GENERAL DEFENCES AND BARS

During the examination of the three different types of restitutionary claims in Parts II, III, IV and V certain specific defences were considered.[1] These defences are, however, of only limited application. There are a number of other defences and bars which are of general application to all, or almost all, restitutionary claims. These are called the general defences and bars and they will be examined in this Part.

(a) The distinction between defences and bars

The distinction between defences and bars is a matter of particular theoretical and practical importance. The crucial difference between the two is that, whereas a bar relates to the establishment of the plaintiff's cause of action, a defence arises only once the plaintiff has established the cause of action. It follows from this that the plaintiff bears the burden of proving that one of the bars to restitutionary claims is not applicable and, if the plaintiff is unable to show this, then his or her claim will fail.[2] If, however, the plaintiff can establish the claim the burden then shifts to the defendant to plead and prove that one of the general defences is applicable.

(b) The principles underlying the general defences and bars

Two fundamental principles can be identified to justify the recognition of the general defences and bars.

(i) Justice favours the defendant retaining the benefit

The principle which justifies the recognition of the general defences in particular is that, because of the particular circumstances of the case, the justice of the defendant retaining a benefit outweighs the justice of the plaintiff recovering it.[3] This was recognised by Lord Mansfield in *Moses*

---

[1] Such as the defence of *bona fide* purchase in Chapter 22 and the defence of good consideration in Chapter 8 (see p. 169 above).

[2] Though usually this will be a live issue only once the defendant has asserted that one of the bars applies.

[3] See *Baylis* v. *Bishop of London* [1913] 1 Ch. 127, 140 (Hamilton LJ).

v. *Macferlan*[4] when he said that '[the defendant] may defend himself by every thing which shews that the plaintiff, *ex aequo et bono*, is not entitled to the whole of the demand, or to any part of it'. It is as a result of this principle, for example, that the plaintiff's restitutionary claim will be defeated to the extent that the defendant's position has changed in reliance on the validity of the receipt of the benefit.[5] Similarly the plaintiff's claim may be defeated if he or she has participated in an illegal transaction,[6] simply because such participation weakens the plaintiff's claim that the defendant ought to make restitution of any benefit.

(ii) Security of receipt

A second principle can also be identified which can be used to justify the recognition of both the general defences and general bars. This is the principle that the defendant's receipt of a benefit should be secure.[7] What this means is that, when a defendant receives a benefit, he or she should not be subjected to any unnecessary insecurity when deciding what to do with the benefit because he or she may have to make restitution to the plaintiff. One of the prime functions of the general defences and bars is to identify those circumstances in which it is reasonable for the defendant to treat the benefit as his or her own to do with as he or she wishes. So, for example, where the plaintiff has voluntarily transferred a benefit to the defendant it is entirely appropriate that the defendant should be entitled to believe that the benefit is secure so that he or she will not be obliged to make restitution to the plaintiff.[8]

(c) Classification of defences as 'enrichment-related' and 'unjust-related'

Birks in particular has classified the general defences as either 'enrichment-related' or 'unjust-related'.[9] The purpose of this classification is to show that the general defences have different functions. The so-called 'enrichment-related' defences operate where the defendant is not considered to be enriched as result of events occurring after the receipt of a benefit, whereas the 'unjust-related' defences operate where it is not considered to be just that the defendant should make restitution to the plaintiff. But nothing is to be gained from such artificial classification. This is primarily because the unjust enrichment principle is not the only

---

[4] (1760) 2 Burr. 1005, 1010; 97 ER 676, 679.   [5] See Chapter 24.

[6] See Chapter 26.

[7] Birks, 'The Fourth Part of the Principle' in *Restitution—The Future*, p. 123.

[8] See pp. 686–9 below.

[9] Birks, 'The Fourth Part of the Principle' in *Restitution—The Future*, p. 126. See also Nolan, 'Change of Position' in *Laundering and Tracing* (ed. Birks) p. 136.

type of restitutionary claim, since such claims can also be founded on the commission of a wrong or the vindication of proprietary rights. In respect of those claims it is inappropriate to analyse defences in terms of whether they are oriented towards enrichment or 'unjust factors'. A further objection is that such classification operates artificially to restrict the analysis of these defences, principally because a number of them can be analysed as showing both that the defendant is no longer enriched and that it is not just for the defendant to make restitution to the plaintiff.[10] Ultimately, as Lord Mansfield recognised in *Moses* v. *Macferlan*, all defences are related to the justice of the defendant making restitution and this should be the key issue with which we should be concerned.

2. GENERAL BARS TO RESTITUTIONARY CLAIMS

(a) Exclusion of the right to restitution by contract

It follows from the principle that the obligation to make restitution is always subordinate to the law of contract[11] that the right to obtain restitution can be excluded by an agreement between the parties. This may occur expressly, as where the parties have entered into a valid compromise,[12] or it may occur impliedly. An example of an implied exclusion of the right to restitution is where the plaintiff pays a deposit to the defendant for the purchase of a house. Since a deposit is paid as a guarantee that the plaintiff will perform the contract it follows that if the contract fails because of the plaintiff's withdrawal from it, save where the deposit is characterised as a penalty, the plaintiff will not be able to recover the deposit, even though there has been a total failure of consideration.[13] This is simply because the implicit effect of the deposit is to deprive the plaintiff of his or her right to recover it.

Such exclusions of the right to obtain restitution at first sight appear to be covered by the Unfair Contract Terms Act 1977, but the Act is inapplicable to exclusions of the right to restitution. This is because the application of the Act is confined to those cases in which a party has excluded his or her liability arising in contract,[14] whereas the obligation to make restitution does not arise from contract but is an independent obligation imposed by law.[15]

[10] See in particular the defence of change of position examined in Chapter 24.
[11] See pp. 40–2 above.   [12] See p. 688 below.   [13] See pp. 353–5 above.
[14] Unfair Contract Terms Act 1977, s. 3. The Act is, however, applicable where a party has purported to exclude his or her liability in tort. Consequently, it would be relevant where the plaintiff's restitutionary claim is founded on the commission of a tort, the liability for which the defendant has sought to exclude.
[15] See Tettenborn, *Law of Restitution in England and Wales*, p. 245.

(b) Voluntary transfers[16]

Where the plaintiff voluntarily transfers a benefit to the defendant he or she will be considered to have waived the right of recovery and so any restitutionary claim will be barred.[17] Restitution is barred in these circumstances essentially because of the policy of finality, to ensure that disputes, once settled, are not re-opened. This bar of voluntary submission to the defendant's claim may arise in a number of different circumstances.

(i) True voluntary transfers

Although the plaintiff may have a restitutionary claim against the defendant in principle, the plaintiff's claim will fail where he or she can be considered to have acted voluntarily in transferring a benefit to the defendant.[18] This was recognised by Lord Reading in *Maskell* v. *Horner*:[19]

If a person with knowledge of the facts pays money, which he is not in law bound to pay, and in circumstances implying that he is paying it voluntarily to close the transaction, he cannot recover it. Such a payment is in law like a gift, and the transaction cannot thereafter be re-opened.

Where the plaintiff's claim is founded on the defendant's unjust enrichment the question whether the plaintiff acted voluntarily in transferring a benefit to the defendant is generally indistinguishable from the question of causation, and so there is no need for it to be considered separately. For example, if the plaintiff was compelled to pay the defendant the plaintiff will be considered to have acted voluntarily only if the compulsion had not actually caused the plaintiff to make the payment. But if the compulsion did not cause the plaintiff to make the payment it cannot constitute a ground of restitution anyway. The burden is consequently on the plaintiff to prove that he or she acted involuntarily, in other words that the compulsion caused the payment to be made.[20] Sometimes it may appear that the plaintiff acted voluntarily, for example because the payment was accompanied by a declaration that the payment was vol-

---

[16] This bar has sometimes been called 'submission to an honest claim'. This is misleading because the bar is applicable even though the defendant has not made a claim. Arrowsmith prefers to call the bar 'waiver': 'Mistake and the Role of the "Submission to an Honest Claim"' *Essays on the Law of Restitution* (ed. Burrows) p. 38. But since the essence of the bar is that the transfer was made voluntarily it seems unnecessarily confusing to call it anything other than 'voluntary transfer'. This is the preferred expression of the High Court of Australia in *David Securities Pty. Ltd.* v. *Commonwealth Bank of Australia* (1992) 175 CLR 353, 374.

[17] *Woolwich Equitable Building Society* v. *IRC* [1993] AC 70, 165 (Lord Goff).

[18] Note also the principle of officiousness, examined at pp. 39–40 above.

[19] [1915] 3 KB 106, 118.

[20] *Mason* v. *New South Wales* (1959) 102 CLR 108, 144 (Windeyer J).

untary, but it is always necessary to consider whether the appearance of voluntariness had been compelled by the defendant as well.[21] If it had been compelled it should be discounted.

Similarly, if the plaintiff paid the defendant as a result of a mistake the plaintiff will be able to obtain restitution only if the mistake was a sufficient cause of the payment and, if it was not, the plaintiff can be considered to have acted voluntarily. This was recognised by Robert Goff J in *Barclays Bank Ltd.* v. *W.J. Simms (Southern) Ltd.*[22] when he said that restitution for mistake would be denied where 'the payor intends that the payee shall have the money at all events whether the fact be true or false, or is deemed in law so to intend'. Ultimately, whether the plaintiff is considered to have acted voluntarily depends on the plaintiff's belief when he or she paid the defendant.

Where the plaintiff has made a payment to the defendant which is accompanied by a protest that the payment was not due, it does not automatically follow that the payment was made involuntarily,[23] though a protest will provide some evidence of involuntariness. The absence of a protest does not necessarily mean that the plaintiff can be regarded as having made a voluntary payment.[24]

(ii) Deemed voluntary transfers

In certain circumstances a transfer will be deemed to have been made voluntarily as a matter of law. This is exemplified by *Morgan* v. *Ashcroft*[25] where the plaintiff's mistaken payment to the defendant was held to be irrecoverable because it was made pursuant to a gambling transaction. Such a transaction is unenforceable because it is illegal and so, as a matter of law, the payment to the defendant was deemed to have been made voluntarily.

(iii) Compulsion of legal process

If the plaintiff pays money to the defendant under compulsion of legal process, the plaintiff will be deemed to have paid the money voluntarily.[26] Compulsion of legal process means that the defendant had threatened either expressly or impliedly to commence legal proceedings to recover the money if the plaintiff does not pay[27] or where the plaintiff paid the money once the defendant has actually commenced legal

---

[21] *The Universe Sentinel* [1983] AC 366, 387 (Lord Diplock).
[22] [1980] QB 677, 695. See also Parke B in *Kelly* v. *Solari* (1841) 9 M and W 54, 59; 152 ER 24, 26 and Lord Abinger CB *ibid*, 58; 26.
[23] *Twyford* v. *Manchester Corporation* [1946] Ch. 236.
[24] *Maskell* v. *Horner* [1915] 3 KB 106.   [25] [1938] 1 KB 49.
[26] *Moore* v. *Vestry of Fulham* [1895] 1 QB 399.
[27] *Cook* v. *Wright* (1861) 1 B and S 559; 121 ER 822.

proceedings by securing the service of a writ upon the plaintiff.[28] Payment made in response to such compulsion is deemed as a matter of law to have been voluntary simply because the plaintiff was given the opportunity to contest his or her liability in proceedings but gave way and paid the defendant.[29] It makes no difference whether the plaintiff thought that the money was not lawfully due to the defendant or mistakenly believed that it was due. The policy which underlies this bar is that in favour of the security of receipts and a desire to ensure that there is an end to litigation.[30]

The general bar to restitutionary claims where payment was made as a result of compulsion of legal process is qualified where the defendant was not acting in good faith in demanding the payment, for example where the defendant knew that he or she did not have a right to receive the payment.[31]

(iv) Settlements and compromises[32]

Where the plaintiff settles or compromises[33] the defendant's claim for payment the plaintiff will be barred from obtaining restitution from the defendant because the policy of the law is to uphold the settlement of claims.[34] A settlement constitutes a bargain between the parties and should be invalidated only in extreme circumstances, namely where the contractual test for mistake can be regarded as satisfied, in other words where there is a shared fundamental mistake,[35] or where the defendant induced the settlement by fraud, duress, undue influence or lack of good faith.[36]

In determining whether the plaintiff has settled or compromised the defendant's claim, Andrews identifies four key principles:[37]

(1) A settlement may consist either of an agreement to pay the defendant or actual payment in response to a claim by the defendant. Payment may itself constitute a contractual settlement of the claim, since the consideration for the settlement will be the defendant's promise that he or she will abandon the claim, at least where the

---

[28] *Hamlet* v. *Richardson* (1833) 9 Bing. 644; 131 ER 756.

[29] *Moore* v. *Vestry of Fulham* [1895] 1 QB 399, 402 (Lord Halsbury).

[30] *Marriott* v. *Hampton* (1797) 7 TR 269; 101 ER 969 (Lord Kenyon).

[31] *Ward and Co.* v. *Wallis* [1900] 1 QB 675.

[32] Andrews, 'Mistaken Settlements of Disputable Claims' [1989] *LMCLQ* 431. See also Arrowsmith in *Essays on the Law of Restitution* (ed. Burrows) pp. 29–32.

[33] The terms 'settlements' and 'compromise' are not terms of art and can be used interchangeably.

[34] For analysis of the arguments in favour of the policy in favour of upholding settlements see Andrews, 'Mistaken Settlements of Disputable Claims' [1989] *LMCLQ* 431, 432–5.

[35] *Holmes* v. *Payne* [1930] 2 KB 301.

[36] See *The Universe Sentinel* [1983] AC 366, 387 (Lord Diplock).

[37] 'Mistaken Settlements of Disputable Claims' [1989] *LMCLQ* 435–8 and 449.

defendant believes that he or she has a claim against the plaintiff.[38] Where the defendant does not believe that he or she has a valid claim new consideration will need to be provided for the settlement to be valid.[39] To avoid the suggestion that the plaintiff has settled the claim he or she should protest at the time of paying the defendant.

(2) A settlement may exist even though the parties have not commenced litigation.[40]

(3) There may be a settlement even though the defendant could not have sustained a proper legal claim against the plaintiff.

(4) The parties can settle a dispute which has not yet been fully spelt out. In determining whether there has been a settlement of such a dispute it is necessary to see whether a promise to pay or an actual payment was made by the plaintiff when there was some doubt whether the money was due, so that it was reasonable for the defendant to suppose that the payment closed the matter.

(c) *Res judicata* or issue estoppel

(i) *The function of* res judicata

Once there is a final judgment of a court relating to any restitutionary action the general bar of *res judicata* will be applicable.[41] The effect of this is that the parties are estopped from litigating the matter which was determined by the court, even if one of the parties considers the judgment to be wrong. The policy behind this bar to restitutionary claims is again that of finality of litigation, in that once a matter has been determined by a court it should not be re-opened in separate proceedings.

This bar was recently considered by the Irish Supreme Court in *Dublin Corporation* v. *Building and Allied Trade Union.*[42] In this case the plaintiff sought to recover a sum of money it had paid to the defendant for a piece of land on the condition that the defendant reinstated its own property adjacent to the land. This payment had been made following an award made by an arbitrator. The defendant failed to reinstate its land and the plaintiff sought to recover part of the money it had paid. The plaintiff's claim failed completely by reason of *res judicata*. Keane J stated that the consequence of the arbitrator's award was that the parties were estopped between themselves from litigating these issues again.[43]

---

[38] Beatson, 'Duress as a Vitiating Factor in Contract' (1974) 33 *CLJ* 97, 103.

[39] Macdonald, 'Duress by Threatened Breach of Contract' [1989] *JBL* 460, 466.

[40] *Brisbane* v. *Dacres* (1813) 5 Taunt. 143, 160; 128 ER 641, 648 (Heath J).

[41] *Moses* v. *Macferlan* (1760) 2 Burr. 1005, 1009; 97 ER 676, 678 (Lord Mansfield).

[42] [1996] 2 ILRM 547. See O'Dell, 'Restitution and *Res Judicata* in the Irish Supreme Court' (1997) 113 *LQR* 245.

[43] *Ibid*, p. 555–6.

The application of *res judicata* to the facts is difficult to defend, since the plaintiff's claim for restitution in the second proceedings could not have been raised before the arbitrator, since at that point the plaintiff had not paid any money to the defendant.[44] In other words, the particular issue which formed the basis of the plaintiff's claim, namely that the land had not been reinstated, had not been determined in earlier proceedings. There was, therefore, no ground for holding that the plaintiff was estopped from asserting that the consideration for its payment had failed.

(ii) Limitations on the res judicata bar

There are certain exceptional circumstances in which a claim can be brought even though the matter has already been determined by a court. The most obvious example of this is where new evidence has become available since the first hearing.[45] Although in *Moses* v. *Macferlan*[46] Lord Mansfield recognised the existence of the *res judicata* bar, it was not applied on the facts of the case, so the plaintiff was able to recover money which he had been compelled to pay to the defendant by a court in earlier proceedings. It seems that this was because the judgment which had been obtained by the defendant in the earlier proceedings had been procured by fraud.[47] Consequently, the defendant's fraudulent conduct may mean that the plaintiff cannot be estopped by an earlier judgment.

(d) Counter-restitution is not possible[48]

It is a condition of all restitutionary claims that, before the plaintiff can recover any benefit from the defendant, he or she must return to the defendant any benefit which he or she had received from the defendant. To the extent that such counter-restitution is not possible the plaintiff's restitutionary claim will be barred. Although this bar is potentially applicable to all restitutionary claims where the plaintiff has received a benefit from the defendant, it is in the context of claims founded on the reversal of the defendant's unjust enrichment where the requirement to make counter-restitution has been particularly important.

(i) Determining what constitutes counter-restitution

The orthodox approach to the requirement that the plaintiff must make counter-restitution is that only precise counter-restitution can suffice.

---

[44] See O'Dell, 'Restitution and *Res Judicata* in the Irish Supreme Court' (1997) 113 *LQR* 245, 249.

[45] *Arnold* v. *National Westminster Bank* [1989] 1 Ch. 63, 67 (Browne-Wilkinson V-C).

[46] (1760) 2 Burr. 1005, 1009; 97 ER 676, 678.   [47] *Ibid*, p. 1012; 680.

[48] McKendrick, 'Total Failure of Consideration and Counter-Restitution: Two Issue or One?' in *Laundering and Tracing* (ed. Birks), chapter 8.

Consequently, the courts had no difficulty in recognising that where the plaintiff has received money from the defendant, exact counter-restitution is possible by repaying the value of this money. Where the plaintiff has received goods from the defendant counter-restitution can be made by returning the goods to the defendant. Returning the property constitutes sufficient counter-restitution even if the value of the property has declined, so long as this was not due to the plaintiff's fault, and the plaintiff will not be required to compensate the defendant for the depreciation in value.[49] But where the plaintiff has received goods which have been consumed or has received services then, because such benefits cannot be returned to the defendant, the orthodox interpretation of the counter-restitution requirement is that the plaintiff's claim must fail because he or she cannot make precise counter-restitution to the defendant. Since the courts are not prepared to value these benefits, it follows that if the actual benefit received cannot be returned to the defendant then the plaintiff's claim must inevitably fail.

There is growing evidence that the courts now accept that the plaintiff need not make precise counter-restitution to the defendant, it being sufficient that the plaintiff pays the defendant the value of the benefits which he or she has received. This is illustrated by *Erlanger* v. *New Sombrero Phosphate Co.*[50] where it was accepted that, because of equity's power to do what is practically just between the parties, it is sufficient that the plaintiff makes substantial rather than precise counter-restitution. The effect of this is that where, for example, the plaintiff has received the benefit of services from the defendant he or she may be required to pay a sum of money to the defendant representing the reasonable value of the services.[51]

This wide interpretation of how counter-restitution can be made is clearly adopted in equity. This interpretation should be adopted at common law as well, by virtue of the principle that the common law follows equity.[52] It follows from this wider interpretation of counter-restitution that the bar of counter-restitution, being impossible, will be applicable only in the most exceptional circumstances where the benefit received by the plaintiff cannot be valued. In fact, if this wide interpretation of counter-restitution is univerally recognised it is difficult to conceive of any case in which the plaintiff's restitutionary claim will be barred because he or she is unable to make counter-restitution to the defendant.[53]

[49] *Newbigging* v. *Adam* (1888) 13 App. Cas. 308.
[50] (1878) 3 App. Cas. 1218.
[51] See also *Boardman* v. *Phipps* [1967] 2 AC 46 and *O'Sullivan* v. *Management Agency and Music Ltd.* [1985] QB 428.
[52] See Halson, 'Rescission for Misrepresentation' (1997) 5 *RLR* 89, 91.
[53] Birks 'Overview' in *Laundering and Tracing* (ed. Birks) p. 338.

(ii) Circumstances in which the requirement to make counter-restitution is inapplicable

In certain situations in which the plaintiff has received a benefit from the defendant he or she will not be required to make counter-restitution to the defendant.

(1) Benefit voluntarily transferred

The receipt of a benefit from the defendant will not bar the plaintiff's restitutionary claim where the benefit was one which the defendant voluntarily conferred without any obligation to do so, or where the defendant was obliged to confer the benefit but it should have been conferred without charge.

(2) Public policy

The plaintiff will not be required to make counter-restitution for reasons of public policy where the transfer of the benefit by the defendant was pursuant to an illegal transaction.[54]

(iii) Circumstances in which restitution is denied even though the plaintiff can make counter-restitution

In the context of the action founded on the reversal of the defendant's unjust enrichment the plaintiff's restitutionary claim may sometimes be barred where he or she has received a benefit from the defendant even though the plaintiff can make counter-restitution of the value of the benefit to the defendant. Whether the restitutionary claim is barred in such circumstances will depend on the ground of restitution on which the plaintiff's claim is founded.

(1) Total failure of consideration

Where the plaintiff's claim is founded upon the ground of total failure of consideration it is clear that if the plaintiff has received a benefit from the defendant this will mean that the consideration has not totally failed and so the restitutionary claim must fail. There is no question whether or not counter-restitution is impossible; the receipt of any benefit will defeat the claim.[55] If it was accepted that counter-restitution was available in respect of such a claim it would follow that the ground of restitution was being converted from one of total failure of consideration to one of partial failure, because the plaintiff's claim would not be defeated even though he or she had received a benefit as long as the plaintiff could restore the value of this benefit to the defendant.[56]

---

[54] See *Smith* v. *Cuff* (1817) 6 M and S 160; 105 ER 1203.   [55] See Chapter 12.

[56] As is recognised in respect of restitutionary claims arising from a frustrated contract. See the Law Reform (Frustrated Contracts) Act 1943, discussed at pp. 376–88 above.

(2) Mistake

The ability to make counter-restitution appears to be denied to the plaintiff where his or her claim is founded on mistake and good consideration has been received from the defendant. The fact that the plaintiff has received consideration from the defendant apparently bars the plaintiff's claim completely.[57] But surely, if the plaintiff has received a benefit from the defendant which can be valued, the plaintiff's restitutionary claim should be allowed to succeed so long as the value of the benefit is transferred to the defendant.[58]

---

[57] *Barclays Bank Ltd.* v. *W.J. Simms Son and Cooke (Southern) Ltd.* [1980] QB 677, 695 (Robert Goff J). See p. 171 above.

[58] See *Laird Securities* v. *Commonwealth Bank of Australia* (1992) 175 CLR 353, 392 (Brennan J).

24

Defences Arising from Changes in the Defendant's Circumstances

Sometimes the defendant's circumstances will change to such an extent after he or she has obtained a benefit that it is no longer just for the defendant to make full restitution of the benefit received. In such cases the defendant may be able to rely on one of three defences to defeat or circumscribe the plaintiff's restitutionary claim, namely estoppel, payment by an agent to his or her principal and change of position. The availability of each defence will depend on the reason why the defendant's circumstances have changed.

1. ESTOPPEL

Estoppel is a defence which is not confined in its application to restitutionary claims, but it has had an important role in this context. In the light of the recent recognition of the defence of change of position, however, it seems that the role of estoppel as a general defence to restitutionary claims will be much less important, although it cannot yet be considered to be irrelevant. Essentially the estoppel defence will be applicable where the defendant detrimentally changes his or her position in reliance on a representation made by the plaintiff that a benefit was validly received. Where estoppel is established the plaintiff's restitutionary claim will be barred completely, because it is a procedural defence which prevents the plaintiff from arguing that the elements of the restitutionary claim have been established.

Although the defence of estoppel is potentially applicable to all three types of restitutionary claim, it is particularly relevant to claims founded on the reversal of the defendant's unjust enrichment, and especially where the ground of restitution is mistake, simply because it is in this context that there is greater opportunity for the plaintiff to make a representation to the defendant that the enrichment was validly received. In fact, all the reported cases concerning the application of estoppel to restitutionary claims relate to the recovery of mistaken payments. But there is no reason why the defence cannot apply where the plaintiff's claim is founded on other grounds of restitution and concerns other types of enrichment.

(a) The conditions for establishing the defence of estoppel

The leading case on the estoppel defence is *United Overseas Bank* v. *Jiwani*,[1] where McKenna J identified three conditions which need to be satisfied before the defence is applicable.[2] He also emphasised that the burden of proving these elements is, as with all defences, placed on the defendant.

(i) *The defendant is led to believe that he or she is entitled to the benefit*

The plaintiff must either have made an unequivocal representation of fact that the defendant was entitled to receive the particular benefit or have owed a duty of accuracy to the defendant which the plaintiff breached. McKenna J assumed that these were alternative conditions, so it is sufficient that either is established. It has, however, sometimes been assumed that these are not alternatives, and so both a representation and a duty of accuracy must be identified in every case.[3] This would be unnecessarily limiting, particularly because the courts will only be able to find that a plaintiff owed a duty of accuracy to the defendant in the most exceptional of cases. Consequently, the view of McKenna J is to be preferred.

(1) Representation of fact

Where the plaintiff is alleged to have represented that the defendant was entitled to receive the benefit, the representation must be collateral to the transfer, in the sense that it cannot be implied from the mere fact that the plaintiff voluntarily transferred the benefit to the defendant.[4] So, for example, where a bank honours a cheque which is a forgery it does not represent that the cheque was genuine,[5] although an estoppel might be established if the plaintiff was put on notice as to the validity of the cheque.

The representation may either have been made expressly or may be implied from the circumstances surrounding the transfer, but in either case it must be clear and unequivocal and the plaintiff must have intended that the defendant act on it.[6]

The best example of an express representation is the situation where, having transferred the benefit to the defendant, the plaintiff confirms

---

[1] [1976] 1 WLR 964.   [2] *Ibid*, p. 968.
[3] See *R.E. Jones Ltd.* v. *Waring and Gillow Ltd.* [1926] AC 670, 693 (Lord Sumner); *Weld-Blundell* v. *Synott* [1940] 2 KB 107, 114 (Asquith J); *Lloyd's Bank Ltd.* v. *Brooks* (1950) 6 Legal Decisions Affecting Bankers 161, 168.
[4] *R.E. Jones Ltd.* v. *Waring and Gillow Ltd.* [1926] AC 670.
[5] *National Westminster Bank Ltd.* v. *Barclays Bank International Ltd.* [1975] QB 654.
[6] *Sidney Balson Investment Trust Ltd.* v. *E. Karmios and Co. (London) Ltd.* [1956] 1 QB 529, 540 (Denning LJ).

that it was properly transferred. This is illustrated by *Deutsche Bank (London Agency)* v. *Beriro and Co.*[7] where the plaintiff mistakenly informed the defendant that a bill of exchange had been collected and consequently the plaintiff paid a sum of money to the defendant. When the plaintiff discovered its mistake it sought to recover the money from the defendant, but it was estopped from asserting that the money had been paid by mistake because of the express representation which it had made that the bill had been collected.

The decision of the Court of Appeal in *Holt* v. *Markham*[8] illustrates how a representation may be implied from the circumstances surrounding the payment. In this case the plaintiff paid the defendant air officer more money than he was entitled to receive. Two years later the plaintiff claimed recovery of the money on the ground that the defendant was retired and so he was not entitled to receive all of the money. Whilst it was correct that the defendant was not entitled to receive the money, it was not because he was retired. The defendant informed the plaintiff of this, but he did not hear anything further for another two months. By the time the plaintiff eventually contacted the defendant to inform him that he was not entitled to receive the money for another reason, he had lost the money which he had received by investing it in a failed business venture. Although the Court of Appeal held that the plaintiff's mistake was one of law and not fact, so restitution was not available,[9] it also held that, even if the mistake had been one of fact, the plaintiff would have been estopped from relying on the mistake. Two different types of representation were identified by the judges. First, Scrutton LJ concluded that there was an inherent representation that the plaintiff would inform the defendant of any mistake it had made in paying the money to the defendant within a reasonable time of the money being paid.[10] This is highly artificial since it amounts to the implication of a representation from the mere fact that the plaintiff had paid the money to the defendant. Such an implied representation is acceptable only where the plaintiff owes a duty of accuracy to the defendant and there was nothing to suggest that such a duty existed in this case. More convincing was the reasoning of Bankes and Warrington LJJ who identified an implied representation that the money had been properly paid to the defendant from the fact that the plaintiff had failed to respond to the defendant's letter.[11]

The representation on which the defendant relies must have been made by the plaintiff and not a third party. This is the effect of the deci-

---

[7] (1895) 73 LT 669. See also *Avon County Council* v. *Howlett* [1989] 1 WLR 605.
[8] [1923] 1 KB 504.
[9] Mistake of law does now ground a restitutionary claim. See p. 139 above.
[10] [1923] 1 KB 504, 514.   [11] *Ibid*, p. 511 (Bankes LJ) and p. 512 (Warrington LJ).

sion of the House of Lords in *R.E. Jones Ltd.* v. *Waring and Gillow Ltd.*[12] where the plaintiff had been induced to pay money to the defendant as a result of a fraudulent misrepresentation made by a third party. It was held that the defence of estoppel was inapplicable, presumably because any representation as to the validity of the payment to the defendant came from the fraudster and not the plaintiff and the plaintiff was not responsible for the fraudster's representations.[13]

(2) Duty of accuracy

In exceptional circumstances it will be possible to establish an estoppel even though the plaintiff did not make an actual representation of fact to the defendant, if the plaintiff owed a duty of accuracy to the defendant which he or she breached. Although it is preferable to distinguish such a duty of accuracy from representations of fact, the effect of the plaintiff owing a duty of accuracy to the defendant is that, when the plaintiff transfers a benefit to the defendant, there is an inherent representation that the benefit was properly transferred.

Whether such a duty of accuracy exists will depend on the nature of the relationship between the plaintiff and the defendant. Such a duty is likely to arise where the plaintiff occupies a position of superiority over the defendant because he or she possesses all the information and expertise to assess the validity of the transfer of the benefit. The identification of such a duty of accuracy is illustrated by *Skyring* v. *Greenwood*[14] where the defendant was an army paymaster who had credited a Major Skyring with certain allowances. Although the defendant was informed in 1816 that Skyring was not eligible to receive these allowances, the defendant continued to credit Skyring with them until he died in 1821. When Skyring's executors sought to recover the sums which had been credited to him, the defendant refused to pay on the ground that the deceased had not been eligible to receive them. The executors' action succeeded because the defendant had been under a duty to inform the deceased that he was not entitled to the allowance immediately the defendant had been informed that this was the case. Although the court specifically stated that it did not consider the defendant to have been estopped from denying that the money credited was actually due to the deceased, this was surely the effect of the decision. The defendant's breach of duty in failing to communicate with the deceased meant that he was estopped from arguing that the deceased was not eligible to receive the allowance. The existence of this duty of accuracy was also recognised in *Avon County Council* v. *Howlett*[15]

---

[12] [1926] AC 670.   [13] *Ibid*, p. 692 (Lord Sumner).
[14] (1825) 4 B and C 281; 107 ER 1064.
[15] [1983] 1 WLR 605, 612 (Eveleigh LJ), 621 (Slade LJ). This was *obiter* because the plaintiff had conceded that it had made a representation to the defendant.

where it was suggested that a local government officer owed a duty of accuracy to an employee in respect of the payment of the employee's salary.

It is only in exceptional cases that the court will recognise that the plaintiff owes a duty of accuracy to the defendant. So, for example, in *National Westminster Bank Ltd.* v. *Barclays Bank International Ltd.*[16] it was accepted that a bank does not owe a duty of accuracy when it honours a cheque, at least where there is nothing to suggest that the cheque was not genuine. Where, however, the plaintiff is aware of certain facts relating to the validity of the transfer of the payment to the defendant he or she may be under a duty to disclose these facts to the defendant. So, for example, in *Greenwood* v. *Martins Bank Ltd.*,[17] where the plaintiff's wife had withdrawn the plaintiff's money by forging his signature, it was held that he was estopped from relying on the forgery to recover his money from the defendant because, once he was aware of what his wife had done, he owed the defendant a duty to disclose the forgeries.

(ii) Reliance by the defendant

The defendant must have relied on the plaintiff's representation, whether this be a collateral representation or a representation derived from a breach of the plaintiff's duty of accuracy. The effect of this condition is that the defendant will not be able to rely on the estoppel defence if he or she knew that he or she was not entitled to receive the benefit or was suspicious as to the validity of the transfer of the benefit but did not inform the plaintiff of these suspicions,[18] or where the defendant simply did not believe the plaintiff's representation. In each of these circumstances it is not possible to conclude that the defendant relied on the plaintiff's representation. So, for example, if the plaintiff mistakenly paid the defendant twice and the defendant knew that the second payment was not due, the plaintiff cannot be estopped from claiming restitution of the mistaken payment even if the plaintiff had represented to the defendant that the second payment was due. This is illustrated by *United Overeseas Bank* v. *Jiwani*[19] itself, where the court found that the defendant had not honestly believed that the money which had been credited to his account was actually due to him, so the estoppel defence failed.

The requirement that the defendant must have relied on the plaintiff's representation means that, for example, if the plaintiff mistakenly paid money to the defendant and this money was subsequently stolen from the defendant, there is no role for the defence of estoppel, simply because the defendant did not act in reliance on the validity of the

---

[16] [1975] QB 654, 662 (Kerr J).   [17] [1933] AC 51.
[18] *Larner* v. *LCC* [1949] 2 KB 683.   [19] [1976] 1 WLR 964.

receipt. But this is a situation where the defence of change of position would be available.[20]

(iii) Change of circumstances

The defendant's circumstances must have changed in such a way as to make it inequitable to require him or her to make restitution to the plaintiff. This notion of change of circumstances involves two separate considerations.

(1) Causation

The defendant must establish that, but for the receipt of the benefit from the plaintiff, his or her circumstances would not have changed in the way which they did. This is illustrated by the facts of *United Overseas Bank* v. *Jiwani*,[21] where the defendant, having been paid by the plaintiff by mistake, used this money to purchase a hotel. One reason the defence of estoppel failed was that the defendant could not show that his circumstances had changed as a result of his belief that the money was properly paid. This was because, even if the defendant had not received the money from the plaintiff, he would still have purchased the hotel, borrowing the money if necessary.

Similarly, if the defendant spends money on ordinary living expenses which he or she would have incurred anyway, the defence cannot be established. But the fact that the defendant spent the money on ordinary living expenses will not automatically prevent the defence from being established if it can be shown that the defendant would not have incurred this expenditure but for the receipt of the money. This was recognised by the Court of Appeal in *Avon County Council* v. *Howlett*[22] where the plaintiff substantially overpaid sickness benefits to the defendant teacher as a result of a mistake. The defendant and his wife adjusted their expenditure in the light of this overpayment, for example by purchasing a second-hand car and a new suit, and they put some of the money away in savings. Thus, the overpayment was not spent on any extraordinary items, but was absorbed by small improvements in the defendant's daily quality of life. This was held to be a sufficient detrimental reliance to establish estoppel, in that the defendant had spent more money than he would otherwise have done had the overpayment not been received.

(2) Detriment

It must also be shown that the change of circumstances was to the defendant's detriment. So, if the defendant received £1,000 from the plaintiff

---

[20] See pp. 712–15 below.   [21] [1976] 1 WLR 964.   [22] [1983] 1 WLR 605.

by mistake and, in reliance on the plaintiff's representation that the money was due, used the money to buy shares which he or she would not have purchased but for the receipt of the money, and these shares increased in value, the defence of estoppel will not be open to the defendant simply because he or she has not suffered detriment as a result of the purchase. If, however, the defendant's investment was a bad one, this constitutes a detrimental change of circumstances. Consequently, in *Holt* v. *Markham*[23] the defendant had detrimentally changed his position by investing money which he had received from the plaintiff in a company which went into liquidation. In *Deutsche Bank (London Agency) Ltd.* v. *Beriro and Co.*[24] the defendant's position changed because he paid the money which had been received from the plaintiff to a third party. This constituted a detrimental change of circumstances because the defendant was unable to recover the money from the third party.

Whilst the defendant's detrimental change of circumstances usually arises as a result of an act on the part of the defendant, the change may also arise by virtue of an omission. This is illustrated by *Avon County Council* v. *Howlett*[25] where, as a result of being overpaid sickness benefit, the defendant failed to claim social security benefit to which he would otherwise have been entitled. It was recognised that this constituted a detrimental change of circumstances.[26] Similarly, in *Greenwood* v. *Martins Bank Ltd.*[27] it was accepted that the defendant had detrimentally relied on the plaintiff's representation that his wife had not committed a forgery, by virtue of the defendant's failure to sue the wife in respect of the forgery when it had the opportunity to do so.

(iv) The justice of the case

Even where the defendant has detrimentally changed his or her position in reliance on the plaintiff's representation, the defence of estoppel may still fail if, as was acknowledged by McKenna J in *United Overseas Bank* v. *Jiwani*,[28] it is not just to require the defendant to make restitution to the plaintiff. This will be the case where, for example, the defendant was under a duty to inform the plaintiff of his or her mistake and failed to do so. This occurred in *Larner* v. *LCC*,[29] where the defendant failed to inform his employer of changes in his service pay which meant that the employer mistakenly paid him more money than he was entitled to receive. Similarly, the defence will fail if the defendant was a wrongdoer or he or she had made a misrepresentation to the plaintiff which con-

---

[23] [1923] 1 KB 504.   [24] (1895) 73 LT 669.   [25] [1983] 1 WLR 605.
[26] *Ibid*, p. 621 (Slade LJ).   [27] [1933] AC 51.   [28] [1976] 1 WLR 964, 968.
[29] [1949] 2 KB 683. This qualification was also recognised by Slade LJ in *Avon County Council* v. *Howlett* [1983] 1 WLR 605, 621.

tributed to the plaintiff mistakenly transferring the benefit to the defendant.[30]

(b) The consequence of the plaintiff being estopped

The effect of successfully pleading estoppel is that the plaintiff's restitutionary claim is barred completely, even though the defendant may not have spent all of the money which was received. In other words the defence does not operate *pro tanto*[31] unlike the defence of change of position.[32] The effect of this is illustrated by *Avon County Council* v. *Howlett*[33] where the plaintiff's claim to recover £1,007 which had mistakenly been paid to the defendant was defeated, even though the defendant had pleaded that he had only changed his position to the extent of £546. Estoppel is considered to operate as a complete defence to the plaintiff's restitutionary claim simply because it is an evidentiary rule which prevents the plaintiff from adducing facts which contradict the representation on which the defendant has relied to his detriment.[34] Whilst this obviously makes the defence more attractive to defendants, it is liable to produce unjust results, for if the defendant has been unjustly enriched by the receipt of £1,000 and, in reliance on the plaintiff's representation, parts with £200, he or she remains unjustly enriched to the extent of £800. Surely it is not just that the defendant should retain this sum, simply because he or she has relied on the plaintiff's representation to some extent. The potential injustice arising from the operation of the defence was recognised by the judges in *Avon County Council* v. *Howlett*,[35] particularly where the defendant's change of position is small in comparison with the value of the enrichment which he or she received. There are a number of ways of avoiding this extreme result.

(1) *De minimis*

If the defendant's position changed in only a very small way, this should not be sufficient to estop the plaintiff from denying the truth of the representation. Consequently, the defence should be subject to a *de minimis* qualification.

---

[30] *George Whitechurch Ltd.* v. *Cavanagh* [1902] AC 117, 145 (Lord Brampton); *National Westminster Bank Ltd.* v. *Barclays Bank International Ltd.* [1975] QB 654, 676 (Kerr J).
[31] This was affirmed by Lord Goff in *Lipkin Gorman (a firm)* v. *Karpnale Ltd.* [1991] 2 AC 548, 579. See also *Avon County Council* v. *Howlett* [1983] 1 WLR 605, 622 (Slade LJ) and *Greenwood* v. *Martins Bank Ltd.* [1932] 1 KB 371 (CA), affirmed [1933] AC 51 (HL).
[32] See p. 709 below.   [33] [1983] 1 WLR 605.   [34] *Ibid*, p. 622 (Slade LJ).
[35] *Ibid*, p. 608 (Cumming-Bruce LJ) and p. 624 (Slade LJ).

(2) Apportionment of payments

Burrows has suggested that a single representation of fact made by the plaintiff might be divided into a number of different representations which operate only to the extent that the defendant's position changed.[36] This suggestion is surely unworkable where the plaintiff has made only one payment to the defendant, as occurred in *Avon County Council* v. *Howlett*, because it would be a fiction to assert that the plaintiff made more than one representation as to the validity of the single payment. But where a number of payments have been made it should be possible to consider each payment separately to determine to what extent the defendant's circumstances have changed in respect of each payment.[37]

(3) Imposition of conditions

The court might be prepared to make the application of the defence conditional on the defendant accepting that he or she would return that part of the benefit to the plaintiff in respect of which his or her circumstances have not changed,[38] although Slade LJ left open whether the court had jurisdiction to obtain such an undertaking from the defendant.

(4) Shifting the burden of proof

Cumming-Bruce LJ in *Avon County Council* v. *Howlett*[39] suggested that the burden of proof might be shifted, so that once the defendant has shown that he or she suffered some detriment in reliance on the plaintiff's representation, the plaintiff must then prove that the defendant's circumstances changed only in respect of part of the benefit which he or she received. But such a recommendation is unlikely to work in practice, since the plaintiff is unlikely to know, let alone be able to prove, to what extent the defendant's circumstances have actually changed.

(5) Unconscionability

In *Avon County Council* v. *Howlett*[40] Eveleigh LJ suggested that in certain circumstances it might be unconscionable for the defendant to retain that part of the benefit in respect of which his or her position had not changed, but he did not identify what these circumstances might be. Cumming-Bruce LJ also recognised that restitution might still lie on the

---

[36] Burrows, *The Law of Restitution*, p. 437.

[37] Note the similar approach in respect of the ground of restitution of total failure of consideration where it is possible to apportion the consideration. See pp. 338–41 above.

[38] Such a solution was advocated by Viscount Cave LC and Lord Atkinson in *Jones Ltd.* v. *Waring and Gillow Ltd.* [1926] AC 670, 688, but in that case such an undertaking was voluntarily proferred by the defendant.

[39] [1983] 1 WLR 605, 609. [40] *Ibid*, p. 612.

ground that it would be inequitable for the defendant to retain part of the benefit which he or she had received, but he declined to rule on when such an equity would be recognised.[41] Slade LJ was much less certain about the relevance of broad concepts of justice and equity, which he considered to be misleading and uncertain in application.[42] Despite these concerns about the uncertainty of a rule that the defendant should be required to make restitution only to the extent that it is equitable to do so, it must not be forgotten that this is the principle which underlies the analogous doctrine of proprietary estoppel, whereby the court will allow an estoppel to operate only to the extent that it is necessary to do justice.[43] Consequently, reference to a principle of unconscionability is probably the most appropriate method to avoid the potential injustice which would arise from the defence of estoppel operating automatically as a complete bar to the plaintiff's restitutionary claim.

(c) Is there a continuing role for the estoppel defence?

In the light of the recognition of the defence of change of position, a defence which operates only to the extent that the defendant's circumstances have in fact changed, there is a very strong argument for saying that there is no longer any role for estoppel as a defence to restitutionary claims.[44] Indeed, in *RBC Dominion Securities Inc.* v. *Dawson*[45] the Newfoundland Court of Appeal held that the recognition of the defence of change of position meant that the defence of estoppel was no longer available in respect of restitutionary claims.

It is not possible, however, to conclude in this country that the recognition of the change of position defence means that there is no longer a role for the defence of estoppel to restitutionary claims. Indeed, in recognising the defence of change of position in *Lipkin Gorman* v. *Karpnale*[46] Lord Goff assumed that there was a continuing role for the defence of estoppel. The two defences do operate in a different way, in that estoppel requires proof of a representation and change of position requires a more extraordinary change of circumstances than is the case for estoppel. But the crucial difference between the two defences is that estoppel

---

[41] *Ibid*, p. 608.   [42] *Ibid*, p. 621.
[43] See p. 551 above. In *Walton's Stores (Interstate) Ltd.* v. *Maher* (1988) 164 CLR 387 the High Court of Australia recognised the doctrine of equitable estoppel, which was an amalgam of proprietary and promissory estoppel, whereby relief would be awarded only to the extent of the defendant's detriment. See Key, 'Excising Estoppel by Representation as a Defence to Restitution' (1995) 54 *CLJ* 525, 533.
[44] See *ibid*, p. 526.   [45] (1994) 111 DLR (4th) 230.
[46] [1991] 2 AC 548, 578 (Lord Goff). In *South Tyneside Metropolitan BC* v. *Svenska International plc.* [1995] 1 All ER 545 Clarke J assumed that the defence of estoppel continued to be applicable despite the recognition of the defence of change of position.

defeats the plaintiff's claim completely whereas change of position defeats the plaintiff's claim only to the extent that the defendant's position has changed. It follows that estoppel will continue to be the defence which the defendant will prefer to plead as long as he or she can establish the necessary representation.[47] If, however, the courts eventually decide that the estoppel defence should not bar the plaintiff's restitutionary claim completely, it is likely that the defence will cease to have any function in the law of restitution.

2. TRANSFER OF A BENEFIT BY AN AGENT TO HIS OR HER PRINCIPAL

Where an agent has received a benefit from the plaintiff on behalf of his or her principal, the plaintiff can sue the agent for restitution of the benefit even where the principal is disclosed.[48] The restitutionary action against the agent may be defeated, however, if he or she has transferred the benefit to his or her principal. In such circumstances the plaintiff will be forced to bring a restitutionary claim against the principal.

(a) Features of the agent's defence

(i) The defendant must have received the benefit as agent

The agent's defence will not be available if the defendant received the benefit as principal, simply because in such circumstances he or she has received the benefit for his or her own use.[49] The defendant will not be considered to have received the benefit as agent in two particular circumstances.

(1) Where the defendant did not have authority to receive the benefit on behalf of the supposed principal he or she will not be considered to have received the benefit as agent.[50]

---

[47] The Law Commission has favoured the retention of the estoppel defence despite the recognition of the defence of change of position: 'Restitution: Mistakes of Law and Ultra Vires Public Authority Receipts and Payments' (Law Com. No. 227, 1994) pp. 48–9 and 141.

[48] See, for example, *Buller* v. *Harrison* (1777) 2 Cowp. 565; 98 ER 1243 and *Kleinwort Sons and Co.* v. *Dunlop Rubber Co.* (1907) 97 LT 263. It has sometimes been suggested that the plaintiff can only sue the principal and not the agent to recover the benefit, because when the agent receives the benefit it is deemed to have been received by the principal. See, for example, *The Duke of Norfolk* v. *Worthy* (1808) 1 Camp. 337; 170 ER 977 and *Ellis* v. *Goulton* [1893] 1 QB 350. But if this were correct there would be no need to have a specific defence where an agent transfers a benefit to the principal.

[49] *Newall* v. *Tomlinson* (1871) LR 6 CP 405; *Baylis* v. *Bishop of London* [1913] 1 Ch. 127; *Kleinwort Sons and Co.* v. *Dunlop Rubber Co.* (1907) 97 LT 263.

[50] See *Sorrell* v. *Finch* [1977] AC 728.

(2) The defence is not available, even where the agent had authority to receive the benefit, if the agent was acting on behalf of an undisclosed principal, so that the plaintiff was unaware that he or she was dealing with an agent.[51] Where, however, the agent is acting on behalf of an undisclosed principal it may still be possible to defeat the plaintiff's restitutionary claim by reliance on the separate defence of change of position which is not affected by such a limitation.

(ii) The benefit must be transferred to the principal

The defence will only be available to the agent if he or she had transferred the benefit which he or she received from the plaintiff to the principal. Usually it will be obvious that the benefit has been transferred. For example, where the agent received money from the plaintiff it is sufficient to show that the agent paid this money to the principal. But the agent can be considered to transfer a benefit to the principal in other ways. This was recognised by Lord Atkinson in *Kleinwort Sons and Co.* v. *Dunlop Rubber Co.*[52] when he said that it is sufficient that the agent:

had paid over the money which he received to the principal, or settled such an account with the principal as amounts to payment, or did something which so prejudiced his position that it would be inequitable to require him to refund.

Essentially, the defence will be available only to the extent that the agent's circumstances have changed because the principal has effectively received the benefit from the agent.[53] So, for example, the agent can be deemed to have transferred money to the principal if the agent expended the money on behalf of the principal and with the principal's authority, for example by paying it to a third party.[54] The defence will not, however, be available if the agent simply credited the principal with the payment,[55] because a credit entry can easily be reversed without the principal even knowing of its existence.

(iii) The agent must not know of the grounds for a restitutionary claim

The agent's defence will fail if the agent transferred the benefit received from the plaintiff to the principal once the agent had become aware of the grounds of the plaintiff's restitutionary claim.[56]

---

[51] See *Sadler* v. *Evans* (1766) 4 Burr. 1984, 1986; 98 ER 34, 35; *Baylis* v. *Bishop of London* [1913] 1 Ch. 127, 133 (Cozens-Hardy MR) and *Agip (Africa) Ltd.* v. *Jackson* [1990] Ch. 265, 288 (Millett J). Cp. *Transvaal and Delagoa Bay Investment Co. Ltd.* v. *Atkinson* [1944] 1 All ER 579 where the defence succeeded even though the agent was acting on behalf of an undisclosed principal, but the point was not argued.

[52] (1907) 97 LT 263, 265.   [53] *Ibid.*

[54] *Holland* v. *Russell* (1863) 4 B and S 14; 122 ER 365. See also *Transvaal and Delagoa Bay Investment Co. Ltd.* v. *Atkinson* [1944] All ER 579.

[55] *Buller* v. *Harrison* (1777) 2 Cowp. 565; 98 ER 1243; *Cox* v. *Prentice* (1815) 3 M and S 344; 105 ER 641.   [56] *Buller* v. *Harrison* (1777) 2 Cowp. 565; 98 ER 1243.

(iv) The agent must not be implicated in wrongdoing

The agent will not be able to rely on the defence if he or she received the benefit as a result of the commission of a wrong to which he or she was a party or where he or she was aware of the commission of the wrong.[57] So, for example, where the agent received money pursuant to an illegal transaction he or she will not be able to rely on the defence if he or she paid this money to the principal.[58] Similarly the defence will not be available where the agent extracted money from the plaintiff by duress.[59] The defence is denied to the agent in such circumstances simply because it is inequitable for a wrongdoer, or somebody who has been tainted by the wrong, to rely on such a defence to defeat the plaintiff's restitutionary claim.[60]

(v) No need to show detriment

It has been a matter of some controversy whether the agent's defence will only be established if the agent suffered detriment as a result of transferring the benefit to the principal. In *Kleinwort Sons and Co.* v. *Dunlop Rubber Co.*[61] Lord Loreburn LC emphasised that the defence would be applicable only if the agent's position could be considered to have been altered to his or her disadvantage. But, although usually the transfer of a benefit will indeed be disadvantageous to the agent, this will not always be the case and, where there is no detriment, the defence should still be available.[62] So, for example, where the agent uses the money which has mistakenly been paid to him by the plaintiff to discharge a debt which the principal owed to the agent, this should be considered to involve a transfer of the benefit to the principal even though the agent has not suffered any loss as a result of it.[63]

(vi) The defence operates pro tanto

The defence will be applicable only to the extent that the benefit has been transferred to the principal. So, for example, if the agent receives £1,000 from the plaintiff by mistake and pays £750 of this to the principal, the agent remains liable to repay the outstanding £250 to the plaintiff.

---

[57] *Snowdon* v. *Davis* (1808) 1 Taunt. 359; 127 ER 872.
[58] *Townson* v. *Wilson* (1808) 1 Camp. 396; 170 ER 997.
[59] *Snowdon* v. *Davis* (1808) 1 Taunt. 359; 127 ER 872.
[60] See Goff and Jones, *The Law of Restitution*, pp. 837–8.   [61] (1907) 97 LT 263, 264.
[62] *Australia and New Zealand Banking Group Ltd.* v. *Westpac Banking Corporation* (1988) 164 CLR 662.
[63] *Continental Caoutchouc and Gutta Percha Co.* v. *Kleinwort Sons and Co.* (1904) 90 LT 474.

(vii) The defence is available to all restitutionary claims

The agent's defence is applicable regardless of the type of restitutionary claim brought by the plaintiff. So, for example, the defence has succeeded where the plaintiff's claim has been founded on the reversal of unjust enrichment, where the ground of restitution was spontaneous mistake,[64] induced mistake[65] and duress of goods,[66] though in the latter two cases the defence succeeded only because the agent was unaware of the wrongdoing. Millett J recognised in *Agip (Africa) Ltd.* v. *Jackson*[67] that the defence would also succeed where the plaintiff brought an action for money had and received founded on the vindication of proprietary rights. But in the same case Millett J held that there was no scope for the defence to operate where the plaintiff's claim was founded on the equitable action for knowing receipt.[68] This distinction between common law and equitable claims, which are founded on the same underlying principle, namely the vindication of property rights, presumably arises from the fact that the agent in the action for knowing receipt is implicated in wrongdoing.

(b) The rationale of the agent's defence

The rationale of the agent's defence is a matter of some uncertainty. A number of explanations of the defence can be identified.

(i) The defendant is no longer enriched

In *Continental Caoutchouc and Gutta Percha Co.* v. *Kleinwort Sons and Co.*[69] Collins MR said that the reason for the defence is that the agent 'is a mere conduit-pipe [who] had not had the benefit of the windfall'. In other words, the defence operates because, as a result of events subsequent to the receipt of the enrichment by the agent, he or she is no longer enriched. Whilst this is certainly true of most cases in which the agent's defence has succeeded, it is not the explanation for all these cases because there is no requirement that the agent suffered any detriment in transferring the benefit to the principal. Also, if the operation of the defence simply depended on whether or not the defendant had retained an enrichment, it would not be possible to justify the limitation on the operation of the defence that it applies only if the principal was disclosed. In addition, because of the recognition of the defence of change of position, if the rationale of the agent's defence was simply that the

---

[64] *Holland* v. *Russell* (1863) 4 B and S 14; 122 ER 365.
[65] *Transvaal and Delagoa Bay Investment Co. Ltd.* v. *Atkinson* [1944] 1 All ER 579.
[66] *Owen and Co.* v. *Cronk* [1895] 1 QB 265. [67] [1990] Ch. 265, 288.
[68] *Ibid*, 289. [69] (1904) 20 TLR 403, 405.

agent was no longer enriched, it would be very difficult to distinguish between the two defences, with the probable result that the agent's defence would be assimilated into the change of position defence.[70] There is no reason to think that this is the case.

(ii) The justice of the case

An alternative explanation of the defence, as suggested by Lord Atkinson in *Kleinwort Sons and Co.* v. *Dunlop Rubber Co.*,[71] is that it is founded on equitable principles whereby it is unjust to require the agent to make restitution where he or she has transferred the benefit to the principal. But such a notion of justice is too vague a principle on which to found the defence, although it is clearly an influential factor in determining its ambit.

(iii) Determining the proper party to sue

Another explanation of the defence is that it simply exists as a means of determining which is the better party to sue, the agent or the principal.[72] This was recognised by the High Court of Australia in *Australia and New Zealand Banking Group Ltd.* v. *Westpac Banking Corporation*[73] where it was held that the defence was applicable where the principal had 'effectively received the benefit of the payment with the consequence that prima facie liability to make restitution has become his'. In other words, where the benefit which was received by the agent has effectively been transferred to the principal, it is the principal who is the proper person against whom the plaintiff's restitutionary claim should be brought. But this justification of the defence does not explain all its requirements, most notably the fact that the defence is limited to where the principal is disclosed.

(iv) Estoppel

The preferable explanation of the defence is that it is founded on estoppel. According to this explanation the agent will continue to be liable to the plaintiff unless the plaintiff can be estopped from bringing a restitutionary claim against the agent. Such an estoppel would be established if the plaintiff knew that he or she was dealing with an agent and so authorised the transfer of the benefit to the principal.[74] This does at least explain why the defence operates only where the principal has been dis-

---

[70] See p. 731 below.   [71] (1907) 97 LT 263, 265.

[72] Millett, 'Tracing the Proceeds of Fraud' (1991) 107 *LQR* 71, 76.

[73] (1988) 164 CLR 662, 674. See also *Portman Building Society* v. *Hamlyn Taylor and Neck (a firm)* [1998] 4 All ER 202.

[74] Swadling, 'The Nature of Ministerial Receipt' in *Laundering and Tracing* (ed. Birks) pp. 257–9.

closed, but it does not explain why the defence operates even where there has been no detrimental reliance. Consequently, this must be a form of estoppel in which it is sufficient that the agent has relied on the plaintiff's representation so that the agent transferred a benefit to the principal, it not being necessary to show that the agent suffered any detriment as a result.

3. CHANGE OF POSITION[75]

(a) Recognition of the defence

Although the notion of a defence of change of position has existed in some limited embryonic form for some time,[76] its existence had been in doubt, since a number of cases had specifically rejected such a defence in English law.[77] The defence has now been expressly recognised by the House of Lords in *Lipkin Gorman (a firm)* v. *Karpnale Ltd.*[78] It was widely defined by Lord Goff as being:

---

[75] For general examination of this defence see Jones, 'Change of Circumstances in Quasi-Contract' (1957) 73 *LQR* 48; Nolan, 'Change of Position' in *Laundering and Tracing* (ed. Birks); Birks, 'Change of Position: The Nature of the Defence and its Relationship to Other Restitutionary Defences' in *Restitution: Developments in Unjust Enrichment* (ed. McInnes, Sydney: LBC Information Services, 1996).

[76] See, in particular, *Larner* v. *LCC* [1949] 2 KB 683, 688 (Denning LJ); *Spiers and Pond Ltd.* v. *Finsbury MPC* (1956) 1 Ryde's Rating Cases 219; and *Barclays Bank* v. *W.J. Simms, Son and Cooke (Southern) Ltd.* [1980] QB 677, 695 (Robert Goff J). For other positive references to the defence of change of position see *R.* v. *Tower Hamlets London Borough Council, ex p. Chetnik Developments Ltd.* [1988] AC 858, 882 (Lord Goff); *Rover International Ltd.* v. *Cannon Film Sales Ltd. (No. 3)* [1989] 1 WLR 912, 925 (Kerr LJ); and *Citibank NA* v. *Brown Shipley and Co. Ltd.* [1991] 2 All ER 690, 701 (Waller J). Note also the limited application of the defence of change of position in respect of equitable proprietary claims: *Re Diplock* [1948] Ch. 465. See also the application of the defence in respect of forged bills of exchange (examined in Goff and Jones, *The Law of Restitution*, at pp. 838–41) and the paymaster cases in the context of estoppel, where the readiness to imply a representation meant that the court was effectively basing a defence on the defendant's detrimental reliance. In *BP Exploration Co. (Libya) Ltd.* v. *Hunt (No. 2)* [1979] 1 WLR 783, at pp. 800 and 804, Robert Goff J explained the operation of the proviso to s. 1(2) and (3) of the Law Reform (Frustrated Contracts) Act 1943 as founded on the principle of change of position. See pp. 376–88 above.

[77] See, in particular, *Baylis* v. *Bishop of London* [1913] 1 Ch. 127, where it was held that, save for the agent's defence, which was inapplicable on the facts because the principal was undisclosed, there was no general defence in English law where the defendant had transferred the benefit which had been received from the plaintiff. See also *Standish* v. *Ross* (1849) 3 Exch. 527, 534; 154 ER 954, 957 (Parke B); *Durrant* v. *The Ecclesiastical Commissioners for England and Wales* (1880) 6 QBD 234; *Ministry of Health* v. *Simpson* [1951] AC 251, 276 (Lord Simonds); and *Rover International Ltd.* v. *Cannon Film Sales Ltd. (No. 3)* [1989] 1 WLR 912, 935 (Dillon LJ).

[78] [1991] 2 AC 548, 558 (Lord Bridge), 568 (Lord Ackner), 578 (Lord Goff).

available to a person whose position has so changed that it would be inequitable in all the circumstances to require him to make restitution, or alternatively to make restitution in full.[79]

This harks back to the principle expounded by Lord Mansfield in *Moses* v. *Macferlan*[80] to justify the recognition of defences to a restitutionary claim, namely that the defendant 'may defend himself by everything which shows that the plaintiff *ex aequo et bono* is not entitled to the whole of the demand, or to any part of it'. Where the defendant's position changed after he or she received a benefit it is only fair that this should be taken into account in determining whether and to what extent the defendant should make restitution to the plaintiff.

Despite this clear recognition of the defence its ambit remains uncertain, particularly because the House of Lords declined to elaborate on its details, preferring that this should be determined on a case-by-case basis.[81] A few cases have been decided since *Lipkin Gorman* which have elaborated to some limited extent on the ambit of the defence. The laws of certain Commonwealth countries where the defence has been recognised can also be considered to determine how the defence should be defined.[82] But there are still a number of fundamental questions which remain unresolved. One of the most important is whether the defence applies to all restitutionary claims. Although Goff and Jones assume that the defence is generally applicable,[83] this was not expressly recognised in *Lipkin Gorman* by Lord Goff who said that it was not appropriate in that case 'to identify all those actions in restitution to which change of position may be a defence'.[84] A further vital question concerns the identification of the rationale of the defence, for until that is clearly recognised it will be impossible to determine the ambit of the defence.[85] It will also be necessary to examine how the change of position defence relates to the other restitutionary defences which are triggered by changes in the defendant's circumstances.[86]

Despite the uncertainty about the ambit and role of the defence, its recognition is of vital importance to the development of the law of restitution. For, by recognising that the change of the defendant's position after he or she has received a benefit is relevant to the success of the

[79] [1991] 2 AC 548, 580.
[80] (1760) 2 Burr. 1005, 1010; 97 ER 676, 679.
[81] [1991] 2 AC 548, 558 (Lord Bridge) and 579 (Lord Goff).
[82] See, in particular, the decision of the Supreme Court of Canada in *Rural Municipality of Storthoaks* v. *Mobil Oil Canada Ltd.* (1975) 55 DLR (3d.) 1, 13 and the decision of the High Court of Australia in *David Securities Pty. Ltd.* v. *Commonwealth Bank of Australia* (1992) 175 CLR 353, 385. The defence has also been recognised in New Zealand by the New Zealand (Judicature) Act 1908, s. 94B, as inserted by s. 2 of the Judicature (Amendment) Act 1958.
[83] Goff and Jones, *The Law of Restitution*, p. 819.
[84] [1991] 2 AC 548, 580. This is examined at pp. 725–30 below.
[85] See p. 725 below.   [86] See pp. 730–2 below.

plaintiff's restitutionary claim, it is possible to adopt a wider interpretation of the underlying cause of action, particularly the grounds of restitution for purposes of the action founded on the reversal of the defendant's unjust enrichment.[87] The recognition of the defence will make it easier for the plaintiff to establish a restitutionary claim, because the interests of the defendant can be better protected by considering whether it is just for the defendant to make restitution in the light of any change in his or her position.

(b) The conditions for establishing the change of position defence

The essential feature of the change of position defence, as identified by Lord Goff in *Lipkin Gorman*,[88] is that the defendant's position has so changed that it is inequitable to require him or her to make restitution to the plaintiff. If this dictum is taken literally it follows that the defence is potentially available wherever the defendant's position has changed for the worse after he or she had received the benefit, subject to the determination of whether it is equitable to require the defendant to make restitution. But placing the emphasis on what is equitable makes the defence far too wide and uncertain. Indeed, the fear that the defence would be too vague and unpredictable was one of the main reasons it had previously been rejected. As Hamilton LJ said in *Baylis* v. *Bishop of London*,[89] 'we are not now free in the twentieth century to administer that vague jurisprudence which is sometimes attractively styled "justice as between man and man"'.

In fact, it is possible to interpret the defence of change of position in a much more principled way. The operation of the defence appears to be founded on two key principles.

(1) There must be a causative link between the receipt of the benefit by the defendant and his or her change of position, so that, but for the receipt of the benefit, the defendant's position would not have changed.

(2) The defendant's position must have changed in circumstances which make it inequitable for him or her to make restitution to the plaintiff. Specific principles can be identified to assist in the determination of what is equitable for these purposes.

Both these principles underlie the defence because it is only where the defendant's position has changed by virtue of the receipt of the

---

[87] See *Lipkin Gorman (a firm)* v. *Karpnale Ltd.* [1991] 2 AC 548, 581 (Lord Goff).

[88] *Ibid*, p. 580.

[89] [1913] 1 Ch. 127, 140. See also Cohen, 'Change of Position in Quasi-Contracts' (1931–2) 45 HLR 1333, 1361.

enrichment and where it is just for the defendant to rely on the defence that it is possible to conclude that the defendant's interest in the security of his or her receipt should prevail over the interest of the plaintiff in obtaining restitution.

It should be emphasised that these two principles underlie one defence of change of position and do not, as some commentators have argued, form two separate defences of change of position, one enrichment-related and one unjust-related.[90] The identification of two types of change of position defence is needlessly complicated, and Birks has since described the existence of the unjust-related form as 'doubtful'.[91]

(i) Causation

The first requirement for the establishment of the defence is that there must have been a causal link between the receipt of the benefit by the defendant and his or her change of position. This causal link can be established in two ways: first, where it can be established that the defendant no longer retains the specific benefit which was received from the plaintiff; and secondly where the defendant's position has changed in other ways as a result of his or her reliance on the validity of the receipt of the benefit from the plaintiff. The reason for distinguishing between the two tests of causation is simply because the second test depends on proof that the defendant detrimentally relied on the validity of the receipt to change his or her position, whereas the first test does not require any proof of reliance on the validity of the receipt.[92]

(1) Loss of benefit test of causation[93]

According to the lost benefit test, the defence of change of position is open to the defendant if he or she no longer retains the actual benefit which had been received from the plaintiff.[94] So, for example, if the plaintiff paid £1,000 to the defendant by mistake and, whilst the defendant was walking home, he or she was robbed of the money, then the defence should in principle be available. Whether the defence will actually succeed depends on whether the circumstances are such that it

---

[90] See, for example, Birks in *Restitution—The Future*, pp. 123 ff. and Nolan in *Laundering and Tracing* (ed. Birks) pp. 135 ff.

[91] In *Restitution: Developments in Unjust Enrichment* (ed. McInnes) p. 63.

[92] This first test of causation is not recognised in Australia, where change of position can only be established where the defendant has acted 'on the faith of the receipt'. See *David Securities Pty. Ltd.* v. *Commonwealth Bank of Australia* (1992) 175 CLR 353, 385. See also *State Bank of New South Wales* v. *Swiss Bank* (1995) 39 NSWLR 350, noted by Chambers, 'Change of Position on the Faith of the Receipt' (1996) 4 *RLR* 103.

[93] See Nolan in *Laundering and Tracing* (ed. Birks) p. 148.

[94] This interpretation of the defence is also recognised in German law. See Zweigert and Kötz, *An Introduction to Comparative Law* (3rd edn., Oxford: Clarendon Press, 1998) p. 582.

would be inequitable to require the defendant to make restitution to the plaintiff, but the fact that the money was stolen will probably be suffi-cient for the defence to operate.[95] Similarly, if the enrichment is destroyed, for example by fire, the defence should in principle be avail-able.[96] Although this test of causation was not specifically recognised by the House of Lords in *Lipkin Gorman*, nothing was said in that case to suggest that it is not relevant.[97]

(a) Establishing the benefit was lost

The essential feature of this test of causation is that the defendant no longer has the benefit which he or she received from the plaintiff. Usually causation is established once the defendant can show that he or she no longer has the benefit because, but for the receipt of the benefit, the defendant could not have lost it. Although this test of causation is for-mulated in terms of whether the defendant has retained the benefit which was received from the plaintiff, it does not follow that this form of the defence is available only where the plaintiff has brought a proprietary restitutionary claim. Even where the plaintiff's claim is founded on the reversal of the defendant's unjust enrichment the claim may be defeated by the fact that the defendant no longer retains the enrichment which was received, simply because the fact that the defendant no longer has the enrichment may make it inequitable to require the defendant to make restitution.

(b) Retention of the product of the benefit

If the defendant has retained a product of the benefit, for example where he or she uses money received from the plaintiff to buy a car, it should not be possible to conclude that the defendant has lost the benefit, sim-ply because he or she has retained the value of the original benefit, albeit in a different form.[98] However, in *RBC Dominion Securities Inc.* v. *Dawson*[99] the Newfoundland Court of Appeal held that the defence of change of position could apply even where the defendant had substi-tuted property for the original benefit received from the plaintiff. But this is surely inconsistent with the essential feature of the defence of change of position, namely that it is only inequitable for the defendant to make restitution to the plaintiff to the extent that the defendant's position has

---

[95] See pp. 720–5 below.

[96] Although in such a case if the benefit was transferred under a contract the doctrine of frustration applied and the restitutionary claim would be governed by the Law Reform (Frustrated Contracts) Act 1943. See pp. 376–88 above.

[97] This test of causation was recognised by Clarke J. in *South Tyneside BC* v. *Svenska International* [1995] 1 All ER 545, 563.

[98] The second test of causation, namely detrimental reliance on the validity of the receipt of the benefit, may be applicable instead. See p. 716 below.

[99] (1994) 111 DLR (4th) 230.

changed. Where the defendant has merely substituted one benefit for that received from the plaintiff it is not clear why the defence of change of position should succeed, since the defendant has retained the value of the benefit so that he or she has not necessarily suffered any detriment. It is surely detriment suffered by the defendant which makes it inequitable for the defendant to make full or any restitution.[100]

(c) Fall in value of the benefit

If the defendant receives an asset from the plaintiff or receives money which the defendant uses to purchase an asset, and the value of that asset falls, the defence should be applicable to the extent that the value has fallen.[101] That the defence of change of position may operate in this way may be illustrated by the decision of the Court of Appeal in *Cheese* v. *Thomas*,[102] where the plaintiff and the defendant had jointly contributed to the purchase of a house. This transaction was set aside on the ground of presumed undue influence, and the question before the court related to how the relief should be determined in the light of the fact that the value of the house had fallen. It was held that this loss in value should be borne by both parties in proportion to their respective contributions to the purchase of the house. Although the court justified this loss apportionment by reference to an inherent equitable discretion to do practical justice, Chen-Wishart[103] has argued that the result is consistent with the application of the change of position defence, because, although the defendant was unjustly enriched by the receipt of money from the plaintiff, this was 'reduced by the subsequent loss to the value of the house in the recession'.[104] Consequently, the result of *Cheese* v. *Thomas* suggests that the change of position defence may be applicable even where the value of the enrichment received from the defendant has fallen in value, but, as always, this will only be the case if it is equitable for the defendant to rely on the defence.

(d) The change of position must be extraordinary

Although it appears that the causation test is easily established where the defendant no longer has the benefit which he or she received from the plaintiff, this is not the case. There is an additional requirement which also needs to be considered before causation is established, namely that the loss of the benefit did not occur in the ordinary course of events. The loss must be extraordinary. The reason for this requirement is illustrated by the following example. If the defendant received a sum of money by

---

[100] See p. 724 below.
[101] See *Lipkin Gorman (a firm)* v. *Karpnale Ltd.* [1991] 2 AC 548, 560 (Lord Templeman).
[102] [1994] 1 WLR 129. See pp. 279–81 above.
[103] 'Loss Sharing, Undue Influence and Manifest Disadvantage' (1994) 110 *LQR* 173.
[104] *Ibid*, p. 178.

mistake from the plaintiff and the defendant used this money to pay for his or her usual living expenses, it is not possible to conclude that but for the receipt of the money the defendant would not have spent money on living expenses, because if the money had not been received the defendant would have paid the expenses from his or her existing resources. Consequently, in such circumstances the test of causation can be satisfied only where the expenditure is extraordinary. This requirement was specifically recognised by Lord Goff in *Lipkin Gorman*.[105] As Lord Goff recognised in that case, the effect of this requirement will be that the defence is available only in exceptional cases.[106]

The defendant's change of position will clearly be considered to be extraordinary where he or she no longer has the benefit for reasons outside his or her control. So, if the benefit has been stolen or destroyed, the change of position should always be considered to be extraordinary. The test of extraordinary change of position will be most relevant where the benefit is money and the defendant has spent that money. In this situation the defendant's expenditure will be extraordinary, where, for example, he or she engaged in a special project or undertook a special financial commitment as a result of the receipt of the benefit from the plaintiff.[107]

The test of extraordinary change of position is assessed subjectively, by reference to changes in the defendant's particular circumstances. It follows that if the defendant uses money received from the plaintiff on normal living expenditure this can still be considered to be extraordinary expenditure if the defendant would not have incurred the expense but for the receipt of the money from the plaintiff. A similar test is adopted in respect of the defence of estoppel, as is illustrated by *Avon County Council* v. *Howlett*,[108] in which the defence was established even though the defendant had spent money which had mistakenly been paid to him on everyday items, because he would not have purchased these items if he had not received the money. That a similar approach is adopted in respect of the defence of change of position is illustrated by the decision of the Newfoundland Court of Appeal in *RBC Dominion Securities Inc.* v. *Dawson*,[109] in which the defence applied to the extent that the defendant had used the money received from the plaintiff in respect of clothes and furnishings which she had bought or refurbished only because she would not have bought or refurbished these items if the money had not been received.

---

[105] [1991] 2 AC 548, 580. See also *David Securities* v. *Commonwealth Bank of Australia* (1992) 175 CLR 353, 386.

[106] *Ibid.*

[107] *Rural Municipality of Storthoaks* v. *Mobil Oil Canada Ltd.* (1975) 55 DLR (3d.) 1, 13 (Martland J).

[108] [1983] 1 WLR 605. See p. 699 above.   [109] (1994) 111 DLR (4th) 230.

(2) The detrimental reliance test of causation

(a) The basic test

The alternative test of causation is satisfied where, even though the defendant has retained the particular benefit which he or she received from the plaintiff, he or she relied on the validity of the receipt of the benefit and suffered detriment in other ways. For example, if the defendant received £1,000 from the plaintiff and the defendant placed this sum in a separate bank account, then, if he or she spent £500 of his or her own money which would not have been spent but for the receipt of the £1,000 from the plaintiff, the defendant's position is considered to have changed to the extent of £500. Since the defendant would not have incurred the expenditure but for the receipt of the £1,000 it follows that the receipt of that money caused the defendant to change his or her position. In other words, the defendant has suffered detriment by relying on the validity of the receipt of the benefit from the plaintiff.

This test of causation has been recognised in some countries,[110] and it was adopted in *Lipkin Gorman* where a thief had stolen money from the plaintiff and had gambled with this money at the defendant's casino. The defendant was considered to have changed its position by paying winnings to the thief. The detrimental reliance test of causation had been satisfied because, but for the defendant's belief that the thief was entitled to gamble with the money, it would not have paid the winnings to the thief.

Usually the defendant's change of position will take the form of the defendant incurring expenditure as a result of the receipt of a benefit from the plaintiff. But the defendant's position may change in other ways. For example, he or she may have received money from the plaintiff in the mistaken belief that the plaintiff owed him or her the money, whereas it was actually owed to the defendant by a third party. If the defendant relied on the validity of the receipt from the plaintiff and did not discover that the money was owed by the third party until the statutory limitation period had passed, the defendant's position has changed, since he or she cannot recover the money from the third party. Consequently, if the plaintiff seeks restitution of the money, he or she should be able to rely on the defence of change of position.[111]

---

[110] See, for example, the New Zealand Judicature Act 1908, s. 94B as amended. Proof of reliance on the validity of the receipt is also required in Canada (*Rural Municipality of Storthoaks* v. *Mobil Oil Canada Ltd.* (1975) 55 DLR (3d.) 1, 13, *per* Martland J), and Australia (*David Security Pty. Ltd.* v. *Commonwealth Bank of Australia* (1992) 175 CLR 353, 385).

[111] Cp. *Durrant* v. *The Ecclesiastical Commissioners for England and Wales* (1880) 6 QBD 234 where the defence of change of position was rejected in such circumstances. If these facts arose today the defence should be available to the defendant.

(b) General hardship is not sufficient

It is not sufficient to satisfy this test of causation that the defendant suffered general hardship after receiving the benefit from the plaintiff, where the hardship did not relate to the receipt of that benefit. For example, if the defendant received £1,000 from the plaintiff by mistake, and a month later the defendant was made redundant or was the victim of a burglary,[112] it is not possible to establish change of position because the change in the defendant's circumstances is unrelated to the receipt of the enrichment from the plaintiff. There is no causal connection between the receipt of the benefit and the detriment suffered by the defendant.

(c) The relevance of an extraordinary change of position

Although Lord Goff suggested in *Lipkin Gorman*[113] that the defence could be established only where the defendant's change of position was extraordinary, this should be considered to be a requirement only where the defendant relies on the first test of causation. Where the defendant relies on the detrimental reliance test of causation it should not be necessary to show that the defendant's position was extraordinary, simply because the defendant may be able to prove that he or she detrimentally relied on the validity of the receipt of the benefit even though the change of position was not extraordinary. Nevertheless, the fact that the change of position was extraordinary will make it much easier for the defendant to prove that, but for the receipt of the benefit, his or her position would not have changed. It follows that the extraordinary nature of the defendant's change of position is a factor which suggests detrimental reliance, but it should not be treated as a requirement in its own right.[114]

(d) Anticipatory change of position

One matter relating to the operation of the detrimental reliance test has proved to be particularly controversial, namely whether the defence is available where the defendant's position changed before he or she received the benefit from the plaintiff, but in anticipation that the benefit would be received. This question arose in *South Tyneside MBC* v. *Svenska International plc.*,[115] where the plaintiff local authority had entered into an interest rate swap transaction with the defendant bank

---

[112] Where the £1,000 itself is stolen in the burglary the defendant satisfies the first test of causation since he or she no longer has the benefit. See p. 712 above.

[113] [1991] 2 AC 548, 580. See also *David Securities* v. *Commonwealth Bank of Australia* (1992) 175 CLR 353, 386.

[114] Nolan in *Laundering and Tracing* (ed. Birks) p. 162.

[115] [1995] 1 All ER 545. See Nolan, 'Change of Position in Anticipation of Enrichment' [1995] *LMCLQ* 313. See also *Westdeutsche Landesbank Girozentrale* v. *Islington LBC* [1994] 4 All ER 890, 948 (Hobhouse J).

and, after such transactions had been held by the House of Lords to be *ultra vires* and void,[116] sought restitution of the net sums which it had paid. The defendant argued that it was not liable to make restitution because, in reliance on the validity of the original swap contract, it had incurred expenditure by buying or selling securities to match and cancel out its liabilities under the swaps transaction, and it argued that this constituted a detrimental change of position. What made the defendant's argument original was that it had incurred the relevant expenditure before any enrichment had been received from the plaintiff. The trial judge, Clarke J, rejected any defence of anticipatory change of position in a case in which the underlying transaction was null and void, although he did recognise that there might be some unidentified cases in which such a defence might operate where the transaction was not a nullity.[117] The fact that the transaction was a nullity enabled the judge to draw a distinction between cases where the defendant incurred expenditure before and after the enrichment had been received. Where the change of position occurred after the receipt of the enrichment it was possible to conclude that the defendant had relied on the validity of the receipt of the enrichment, whereas where the defendant's position had changed before the enrichment was received he or she could only be considered to have relied on the validity of the transaction and, since the transaction was a nullity, the defendant's reliance was invalid. The effect of the decision is that the defendant who incurs expenditure before the enrichment has been received must be regarded as taking the risk as to whether or not the transaction is valid.

This emphasis on the fact that the transaction was a nullity to determine whether change of position could be established is surely irrelevant. Clarke J accepted that the defence would be available where the defendant changed his or her position after the enrichment was received, even though the enrichment was transferred under a transaction which was a nullity.[118] The defence succeeds because the defendant thought that the benefit had been validly received, and it is irrelevant that this is not in fact the case. The same reasoning should apply where the defendant's change of position occurred before the benefit was received, so long as the defendant thought that the transaction was valid. It should again be irrelevant that the transaction is invalid so that the benefit could as a matter of law never be validly received.

It does not follow from the rejection of a distinction founded on whether the transaction is null and void that the defence of anticipatory change of position should necessarily be recognised, since all that we have concluded so far is that Clarke J's reasons are inadequate. Clarke J

---

[116] *Hazell* v. *Hammersmith and Fulham LBC* [1992] 2 AC 1. See p. 396 above.
[117] [1995] 1 All ER 545, 565.   [118] *Ibid*, p. 567.

did not examine the question of principle whether anticipatory change of position should be sufficient to ground the defence. Burrows has argued that the defence of anticipatory change of position should not be recognised in English law.[119] This is because, since the function of the defence is to uphold the security of receipts so that a defendant having received a benefit is entitled to regard it as his or hers to keep, the defence should operate only where the defendant's position has changed after the benefit has been received. Where the defendant's position changes in anticipation that a benefit will be received, the application of the defence would protect the defendant's reliance on the expectation of receipt, and Burrows does not consider that this expectation of receipt deserves to be protected. As he has said:[120]

... if the law is not willing to give the plaintiff a remedy for expectation or reliance losses incurred in expectation of a payment when the payment is never made, it is not clear why it should be willing to do so through a defence to restitution of the payment.

But this misses the point. The issue of change of position is not concerned with the question whether a cause of action can be established; it is simply a matter of defence and, as recognised by Lord Goff in *Lipkin Gorman*, the fundamental principle which underlies the defence is whether or not it is equitable to make restitution. If the defendant has incurred expenditure by virtue of an expectation that a benefit will be received it is surely appropriate to consider whether it is equitable for him or her to make restitution once the benefit has been received.

The better view is that, so long as the defendant's change of position was made in reliance on the expectation that a benefit will be received, the defence of change of position should succeed, subject to the question whether this is just and equitable,[121] even though the defendant's position changed before the benefit was received. This is simply because the necessary causation can be established even where the defendant's position changed before the benefit was received, because of his or her reliance on the expectation that a benefit would be received from the plaintiff.

That the notion of anticipated change of position should be recognised in English law is supported by the operation of that defence in *Lipkin Gorman* itself, where the defence succeeded even though the defendant had started to change its position before it had received all of the plaintiff's money.[122] The defendant's defence of change of position in that case was founded on the fact that it had paid winnings to the thief

---

[119] See Burrows, *The Law of Restitution*, p. 424. [120] *Ibid.* [121] See p. 719 below.
[122] Although Lord Goff described this result as just rather than logical: [1991] 2 AC 540, 583.

who was using the plaintiff's money to make bets. The House of Lords did not adopt a strict approach to the determination of the extent of the defendant's change of position for, if it had, the payment of winnings on a bet would have constituted a change of position only in respect of that bet and the defendant would not have changed its position in respect of any losing bets. Instead, the House of Lords was prepared to adopt a global view to avoid the factual difficulties of determining the actual extent by which the defendant's position had changed in respect of each individual bet. This meant that the defendant was considered to have changed its position even if it had paid out more to the thief on the earlier bets than the later ones, so that its change of position anticipated later receipts from the thief. Although the defendant only anticipated rather than expected future receipts from the thief, the approach of the House of Lords is defensible as a practical solution to a difficult evidential problem.

(ii) Whether it is inequitable to make restitution

Once it has been shown that, but for the receipt of the benefit from the plaintiff, the defendant's position would not have changed, it must then be shown that the particular circumstances of the change of position are such that it would be inequitable to require the defendant to make full, or even any, restitution of the benefits received to the plaintiff. Whilst equitable considerations of fairness and justice may appear to make the defence unnecessarily uncertain and unprincipled, and is inconsistent with Lord Goff's dictum that where restitution is denied 'it is denied on the basis of legal principles',[123] a number of factors can be identified to assist in the determination of whether the defendant's change of position is such as to make restitution inequitable. It must be emphasised that the notion of what is equitable needs to be clearly ascertained. It is not acceptable for the defendant to argue that he or she should not make restitution simply because he or she is suffering from some particular hardship, such as illness or redundancy. This is catered for by the requirement that the defence can arise only if the causation test is first satisfied. Notions of injustice then operate to restrict the application of the defence.

(1) Bad faith

Lord Goff expressly recognised in *Lipkin Gorman* that a defendant will not be able to rely on the defence if he or she acted in bad faith.[124] The scope of the concept of bad faith is a matter of some uncertainty, but it

---

[123] [1991] 2 AC 540, 583, 578.   [124] *Ibid*, p. 580.

would clearly prevent reliance on the defence where the defendant committed fraud or duress or had been participating in an illegal transaction.

(2) Wrongdoing

Lord Goff also acknowledged that the defence would be unavailable if the defendant was a wrongdoer.[125] This limitation on the operation of the defence is more difficult to justify, since the nature of wrongdoing is so variable. It should not necessarily follow from the fact that the defendant has committed a wrong that the defence should necessarily be denied to him or her.[126] Rather, the court should have regard to the nature of the wrongdoing. So, for example, if the defendant intentionally committed a tort the case for concluding that the defence is unavailable should be stronger than if the defendant negligently committed a tort.

(3) Knowledge and notice of the plaintiff's restitutionary claim

The defendant should be unable to rely on the defence if he or she changed his or her position knowing that he or she was liable to make restitution to the plaintiff. So the defence should not be available if the defendant was aware that the plaintiff had made a mistake in paying money to him or her.[127] Similarly, the defence should be unavailable if the defendant knew that there was a risk, albeit small, that he or she was not entitled to the money.[128]

It is unclear whether the defence should be denied to the defendant if he or she ought to have known that he or she was liable to make restitution. Birks has suggested that the defence should not be available in such circumstances because the defendant's claim for security of receipt is weakened by his or her constructive notice of the plaintiff's restitutionary claim.[129] Whether this is correct depends ultimately on whether the fact that a reasonable person would have been aware of the plaintiff's claim makes it inequitable for the defendant to rely on the defence of change of position when the defendant had not considered that the plaintiff would have such a claim. Perhaps this should simply be treated as a factor which should be placed in the balance when determining whether it is equitable for the defence to succeed.

(4) Fault of the defendant in changing his or her position

The conduct of the defendant in changing his or her position should also be taken into account when determining whether the defence should be

---

[125] *Ibid.* [126] Birks in *Laundering and Tracing* (ed. Birks) p. 324.

[127] *RBC Dominion Securities Inc.* v. *Dawson* (1994) 111 DLR (4th) 230, 238 (Cameron JA).

[128] *South Tyneside MBC* v. *Svenska International plc.* [1995] 1 All ER 545, 569 (Clark J).

[129] Birks in *Restitution: Developments in Unjust Enrichment* (ed. McInnes) p. 58. Now see Birks, 'Notice and Onus in *O'Brien*' (1998) 12 *TLI* 2, 10.

available. If the defendant was not responsible for the change of circumstances as will be the case where, for example, the benefit was stolen or destroyed without any fault on the part of the defendant, this strongly suggests that the defence should succeed. But if the defendant was negligent in changing his or her position it is more controversial whether the defendant should be able to rely on the defence. The Law Commission has recommended that the defence should be available even though the recipient was careless in changing his or her position, so long as he or she was honest.[130] This is the preferable view. It is surely equitable for the defendant to rely on the defence even though he or she was careless in changing his or her position, especially because the carelessness of the plaintiff in mistakenly transferring the benefit to the defendant does not prevent him or her from establishing a restitutionary claim in the first place.[131]

(5) Relative fault of the parties

Although the fault of the defendant in changing his or her position should not operate to prevent him or her from relying on the change of position defence at all, it does not follow that the defendant's fault is irrelevant when determining the extent to which the defendant can be considered to have changed his or her position. Support for this can be found in the decision of Hobhouse J in *Westdeutsche Landesbank Girozentrale* v. *Islington LBC*.[132] This approach is also adopted in New Zealand where the relative fault of the parties is assessed in the same way as contributory negligence in tort claims to determine to what extent the defendant's liability should be reduced by virtue of the defence. So, for example, where the plaintiff pays money to the defendant by mistake and the defendant pleads the defence of change of position, the success of this defence will depend on who was more responsible for making the mistake.[133]

If it is accepted that the relative fault of the parties should be taken into account when assessing the extent to which the defendant can be considered to have changed his or her position, it will be necessary to apportion blame between the parties. So, for example, if the plaintiff paid the defendant £1,000 by mistake in circumstances in which the court was able to conclude that both parties were equally responsible for the mistake, and the defendant had spent that money on a holiday which he or

---

[130] 'Restitution: Mistakes of Law and Ultra Vires Public Authority Receipts and Payments' (Law Com. No. 227, 1994), para. 2.23 (p. 19). See also Chambers, 'Change of Position on the Faith of the Receipt' (1996) 4 *RLR* 103.

[131] See, for example, *Kelly* v. *Solari* (1841) 9 M and W 54; 152 ER 24. See p. 145 above.

[132] [1994] 4 All ER 890, 950.

[133] *Thomas* v. *Houston Corbett and Co.* [1969] NZLR 151.

she would not have taken had he or she not received the money, and assuming that there were no other circumstances which affected the determination of whether it was equitable to allow the defence, the defendant would be liable to pay the plaintiff £500. This is because, since the parties were equally at fault, the defence should operate in respect of only half of the money spent. It will, of course, be difficult for the courts to ascertain the degree of fault of the parties and, as Burrows has suggested, any notion of apportionment of blame in determining the extent of the defendant's change of position would restrict the possibility of out-of-court settlements.[134] Nevertheless, consideration of the relative fault of the parties should be an important factor in determining the appropriate operation of the defence. It may be considered to be more convenient to adopt a blanket rule that the defendant should be prevented from relying on the defence whenever his or her conduct can be considered to be more blameworthy than that of the plaintiff. But even this will require careful consideration of the facts of the case in determining the relevant fault of the parties.

(6) Risk allocation

The question of risk allocation may also be pertinent to the determination of the operation of the defence. If it can be concluded that the plaintiff should take the risk of any detrimental change in the defendant's position this suggests that the defence should succeed. Alternatively, if the defendant can be considered to have taken the risk this suggests that the defence should fail.[135]

The importance of risk allocation is illustrated by *Goss* v. *Chilcott*[136] where the defendants were held liable to repay the amount of a loan to the plaintiff on the ground of total failure of consideration. When the defendants had received the loan in the first place they lent it to a third party in a separate transaction and were unable subsequently to obtain repayment from the third party. The defendants therefore pleaded the defence of change of position to defeat the plaintiff's restitutionary claim. The Privy Council rejected this defence primarily because the defendants knew throughout that they were liable to repay the loan, and in lending the money to the third party they deliberately took a risk that he would be unable to repay them. Essentially what the defendants were doing was seeking to shift their loss to the plaintiff and, if they had been allowed to do this, it would have been unjust to the plaintiff, because the defendants had voluntarily taken the risk that they would lose their money.

---

[134] Burrows, *The Law of Restitution*, p. 430.
[135] *South Tyneside Metropolitan BC* v. *Svenksa International plc.* [1995] 1 All ER 545, 569 (Clarke J).
[136] [1996] AC 788.

(7) Detrimental change of position

The defence is available to the defendant only if his or her position changed to his or her detriment.[137] So, for example, if the defendant received £1,000 from the plaintiff which he or she used to buy shares, which would not have been purchased but for the receipt of the money, it seems obvious that, if the shares have increased in value, the defendant cannot rely on the defence of change of position because it would not be equitable to do so. If the shares have decreased in value the defendant's position has detrimentally changed to the extent of that loss of value.[138] Similarly, where the defendant uses money received from the plaintiff to pay off a debt, even if the defendant discharged the debt earlier than he or she would otherwise have done because of the money received from the plaintiff, this does not constitute a sufficient change of position because the defendant would not have suffered any detriment.[139] This is simply because, by using the money to discharge a debt which has already been incurred, the defendant has benefited from the receipt of the money.

The question whether the defendant has suffered detriment is particularly difficult to determine in two situations.

(a) Retention of benefit

The defence is easier to establish in those cases in which the defendant received money and spent it without receiving anything in return, such as where the defendant donated the money to a charity, because the defendant has clearly suffered detriment. But where the money has been spent on property which the defendant retains and which is readily realisable without loss, it is surely not inequitable for the defendant to make restitution to the plaintiff. Since the defendant retains the value of the benefit he or she cannot be considered to have suffered any detriment.[140]

(b) Acquisition of a cause of action against a third party

Where the consequence of the defendant's change of position is that he or she acquires a cause of action against a third party can he or she really be considered to have suffered detriment?[141] For example, if the plaintiff

---

[137] *Rover International Ltd.* v. *Cannon Film Sales Ltd. (No. 3)* [1989] 1 WLR 912, 925 (Kerr LJ). See also the decision of Lord Loreburn in *Kleinwort Sons and Co.* v. *Dunlop Rubber Co.* (1907) 97 LT 263, 264.

[138] See *Lipkin Gorman (a firm)* v. *Karpnale Ltd.* [1991] 2 AC 548, 560 (Lord Templeman).

[139] See *RBC Dominion Securities Inc.* v. *Dawson* (1994) 111 DLR (4th) 230, 241 (Cameron JA).

[140] Though this view was not accepted in *ibid*, where the defendant had used the money to buy a table, chairs, a lamp and a video recorder. This was held to be sufficient to constitute a detrimental change of position.

[141] Nolan in *Laundering and Tracing* (ed. Birks) pp. 170–2.

pays £1,000 to the defendant by mistake and this money is stolen by a thief, it might be concluded that the defendant's position has not changed because he or she has a restitutionary claim against the thief to recover the money. If the defendant has actually recovered the money from the thief it is obvious that the defendant's position has not detrimentally changed. Although it did change, it has no longer changed, so it would be inequitable to allow the defendant to rely on the defence. But this is the easy case. What if the plaintiff sued the defendant for restitution before the defendant sued the third party? Should the fact that the defendant has a potential claim against the third party mean that his or her position has not changed? Since the success of the defendant's claim is speculative, the preferable view is that he or she should still be considered to have suffered a detrimental change of position, so that he or she will not be required to make restitution to the plaintiff. The plaintiff may, however, seek the remedy of subrogation whereby the defendant's cause of action against the third party can be vested in the plaintiff.[142] If this remedy were not awarded the defendant could be unjustly enriched at the plaintiff's expense if the defendant did eventually recover the money from the third party. The consequence of this analysis is that the plaintiff ultimately bears the risk of the defendant losing the enrichment and being unable to recover it from the third party.

(c) The application of the defence

Now that the defence of change of position has been recognised one of the most important questions which remains is whether it applies to all types of restitutionary claim. If it does not, it is then necessary to determine to which claims it applies and why.

(i) Claims founded on the reversal of the defendant's unjust enrichment

Although it is clear that the change of position defence is applicable to all claims founded on the reversal of the defendant's unjust enrichment,[143] it is not clear what the function of the defence is in respect of such a claim. Does the defence focus on the question whether the defendant can be considered to have been enriched or on whether the retention of the enrichment is sufficiently unjust? This is a particularly important question, because it will affect the way the defence is interpreted when it is applied to claims founded on the reversal of the defendant's unjust enrichment.

---

[142] *Ibid*, p. 172.
[143] This was assumed in *South Tyneside MBC* v. *Svenska International plc.* [1995] 1 All ER 545, even though the defence was not established on the facts of the case.

Birks[144] has argued that the defence is enrichment-oriented since this is consistent with the principle of subjective devaluation. This argument is illustrated by the following example. If the defendant uses money received from the plaintiff to purchase benefits which he or she would not have bought but for the receipt of the money, then, if the defendant is liable to repay the plaintiff, he or she is effectively forced to pay for benefits which he or she did not value. This follows from the fact that the defendant would not have spent his or her own money on such benefits, but was prepared to spend only the supposed windfall received from the plaintiff. But this emphasis on change of position as negating the defendant's enrichment is not useful for two reasons:

(1) The question of enrichment within the action founded on the reversal of the defendant's unjust enrichment is concerned only with the determination of whether or not the defendant was enriched at the time a benefit was received. Once the defendant has been shown to have received a benefit it is obvious that he or she has been enriched, and subsequent events cannot affect this.

(2) Lord Goff in *Lipkin Gorman* emphasised that the defence would be available where it was inequitable to require the defendant to make full restitution of any benefits received. This suggests that questions of justice are of paramount importance in determining whether or not the defence will apply. If this were not the case, there would be no need to emphasise good faith and the fault of the parties in considering the application of the defence.

Consequently, the real function of the defence of change of position is to identify those cases in which the justice of the defendant not making restitution outweighs the justice of the plaintiff obtaining restitution. In fact, it is not useful to relate the application of the defence to the elements of the unjust enrichment principle at all. It is much more accurate to analyse the defence with reference to the remedial question whether it is appropriate to require the defendant to make full restitution to the plaintiff in the light of subsequent events.

Although the defence is applicable in principle to all claims founded on the reversal of the defendant's unjust enrichment, the actual application of the defence may be affected by the nature of the ground of restitution on which the plaintiff relies. In particular, where the ground of restitution involves some form of reprehensible conduct on the part of the defendant, such as duress of the person or goods or where the defendant's conduct is unconscionable, he or she may be characterised as

---

[144] Birks, *An Introduction to the Law of Restitution*, p. 441. See also Burrows, *The Law of Restitution*, p. 421 and Nolan in *Laundering and Tracing* (ed. Birks) p. 136 who says that the defence is 'principally an enrichment related defence'.

having acted in bad faith or as a wrongdoer and so may be prevented from relying on the defence.

(ii) Restitution for wrongs

Where the defendant has obtained a benefit as a result of the commission of some form of wrongdoing, it appears that the defendant is not able to rely on the defence of change of position, because Lord Goff in *Lipkin Gorman* specifically recognised that the defence was not open to a wrongdoer.[145] But the defence should not automatically be denied to the defendant just because he or she committed a wrong, because the unlawfulness of wrongs varies a great deal. The defence should be denied only where the defendant's wrongdoing can be treated as equivalent to acting in bad faith. Clearly, therefore, if the defendant is a thief or has accepted a bribe it is likely that the defence will be denied to him or her, particularly because such a wrongdoer was acting in bad faith. But on the other hand a confidant who unwittingly betrayed a confidence should not be treated as having acted in bad faith. Consequently there is no reason why such a defendant should be prevented from relying on the defence, even though he or she had committed a wrong.

(iii) Restitutionary claims founded on the vindication of proprietary rights

When the application of the defence of change of position to proprietary claims is considered it is necessary to examine claims for personal and proprietary restitutionary remedies separately.

(1) Personal restitutionary remedies

It is clear that where the plaintiff's claim is founded on the fact that the defendant has received property in which the plaintiff had retained a proprietary interest then, if the defendant is no longer in possession of that property or its traceable proceeds, the plaintiff will be confined to a personal restitutionary remedy, and in such circumstances the defendant will be able to rely on the defence of change of position. The authority for this is *Lipkin Gorman (a firm)* v. *Karpnale Ltd.*[146] itself. Although the defendant in that case was held to be liable in a claim for money had and received to make restitution to the plaintiff, where the plaintiff's claim was founded on the vindication of its proprietary rights in the money which the defendant received from the thief, the defendant's liability was reduced by the defence of change of position.

---

[145] [1991] 2 AC 546, 580. In that case the defence was not available to the defendant in respect of a claim founded on the tort of conversion.
[146] *Ibid.*

Whether the defence applies to all claims founded on the vindication of the plaintiff's proprietary rights where the plaintiff seeks a personal remedy is a matter of some uncertainty. For example, in *Ministry of Health* v. *Simpson*[147] it was held that the defence was not available in respect of a personal claim brought by an executor or administrator to recover estate moneys which had been wrongfully disbursed. Although this decision was mentioned in *Lipkin Gorman,* it was not overruled. The better view is that, since *Ministry of Health* v. *Simpson* was decided before the change of position defence had been recognised, it should no longer be considered to be good law. There is no reason of policy or principle why the defence should apply to certain proprietary claims for personal restitutionary remedies and not to others.

(2) Proprietary restitutionary remedies

It is where the plaintiff seeks a proprietary restitutionary remedy that the application of the defence of change of position is much more uncertain. Whilst it is clear that, if the defendant no longer retains the plaintiff's property or its traceable proceeds, the plaintiff will not obtain a proprietary remedy, this is not because of the application of the defence. Rather, it is simply because the plaintiff is not able to establish the essential elements of his or her claim, namely that the defendant retains property in which the plaintiff has a proprietary interest. The more difficult question arises where the defendant does retain the plaintiff's property or its traceable proceeds, but the defendant argues that his or her position detrimentally changed as a result of reliance on the validity of the receipt. Should the plaintiff's claim be affected by the defence of change of position in such circumstances? For example, if the defendant received £500 from the plaintiff in circumstances in which the plaintiff retained a proprietary interest in the money and the money remained traceable, and then the defendant in reliance on the legitimate receipt of this payment paid £200 of his or her own money to a charity, can the defendant rely on the defence of change of position to reduce the liability to the plaintiff to repayment of £300? Quite often there will be no need to consider whether the defence is available in such circumstances, since the plaintiff's claim will typically be defeated completely by the defence of *bona fide* purchase.[148] But that defence will not cover all cases, particularly where the property was simply given to the defendant who did not provide any consideration for it.

Ultimately, whether the defence of change of position should be applicable in such circumstances simply turns on whether we prefer to emphasise the proprietary element of the plaintiff's claim, which

---

[147] [1951] AC 251. See p. 667 above.   [148] See Chapter 22.

demands that the plaintiff's property be returned, or the restitutionary aspect of the claim, which demands consideration of whether it is equitable that the defendant should make restitution where the defendant's position has changed in reliance on the validity of the receipt. A number of authors have contended that the defence should be applicable even where the plaintiff seeks a proprietary remedy,[149] and this is the preferable view.[150] Although the plaintiff's restitutionary claim is founded on his or her continuing proprietary rights, the success of this claim should still be subject to equitable considerations. This would avoid drawing distinctions according to whether the plaintiff seeks a personal or proprietary remedy. This is illustrated by the decision of the Court of Appeal in *Re Diplock's Estate*,[151] which concerned an equitable proprietary claim. In that case, it was not sufficient for the plaintiffs to show that their money had been used by the defendant for building improvements. Whether an equitable proprietary remedy could be awarded depended on whether it was equitable in the circumstances of the case to grant a restitutionary remedy, and this required consideration of such matters as whether the improvements had added to the market value of the building. Essentially, the decision whether a proprietary restitutionary remedy would be awarded was dependent on whether, in the light of subsequent events, it was just that the defendant should be required to make restitution to the plaintiff. Thus, the court was essentially considering whether the plaintiff's claim was defeated by change of position.[152]

There is one final problem which needs to be addressed if the defence of change of position is to be applied to cases in which the plaintiff seeks a proprietary restitutionary remedy, namely whether the particular remedy involved can be adjusted to cater for the defendant's change of position. This is illustrated with reference to two types of proprietary restitutionary remedy.

(*1*) *Charge.* The creation of a charge over the relevant property can easily be adjusted to accommodate the change of position defence, since the sum secured by the charge can be diminished to reflect the extent to which the defendant's position will have changed.[153]

(*2*) *Claiming the entire beneficial interest.* Where the plaintiff seeks the remedy of a declaration that the entire beneficial interest of an asset is held on trust for him or her it is much more difficult to adjust this remedy to accommodate the defence of change of position. The only way this

---

[149] Goff and Jones, *The Law of Restitution*, p. 203, Burrows, *The Law of Restitution*, p. 431 and Nolan in *Laundering and Tracing* (ed. Birks) p. 178.

[150] This was also accepted by Lord Browne-Wilkinson in *Westdeutsche Landesbank Girozentrale* v. *Islington LBC* [1996] AC 669, 716.

[151] [1948] 1 Ch. 465, 546.

[152] See Millett LJ in *Boscawen* v. *Bajwa* [1996] 1 WLR 328, 341.

[153] Birks in *Restitution: Developments in Unjust Enrichment* (ed. McInnes) p. 56.

can be done effectively is by compelling the plaintiff to make good the defendant's change of position as a condition of the remedy being awarded.[154]

The consequence of this analysis is that the change of position defence should be applicable to all restitutionary claims, regardless of the principle on which the claim is founded. This is because the defence is properly analysed as a defence which relates to the extent of the restitutionary remedy which is awarded rather than to the negation of the plaintiff's cause of action. Once the plaintiff has established the cause of action the onus then shifts to the defendant in all restitutionary claims to establish that it is not equitable for the defendant to make restitution because of the change in his or her position.

(d) The relationship between change of position and other defences

There is growing evidence that change of position is playing an important role in the modern law of restitution. But one of the most difficult questions following the recognition of the defence is what effect its recognition will have on a number of the other defences which have been applied to restitutionary claims, particularly estoppel, the agent's defence and *bona fide* purchase.

(i) The relationship between change of position and estoppel

In principle there is no reason why the defences of change of position and estoppel should be incompatible, since they operate differently.[155] The defence of estoppel is applicable only where the defendant has detrimentally relied on the plaintiff's representation that the benefit was properly received.[156] Also this defence, being a rule of evidence, operates to bar the plaintiff's claim completely. The defence of change of position, on the other hand, does not depend upon the identification of a representation and operates only to the extent that the defendant's position has changed in reliance on the receipt of the benefit. A further difference between the two defences may be that, because a representation needs to be proven to establish estoppel, a lesser quantum of detrimental reliance is required for that defence than is required to establish change of position. This is because proof of the plaintiff's representation changes the balance of the equities between the parties, so that there should be no need to show that the defendant's change of circumstances was extraordinary. These differences mean that it is possible to justify the

---

[154] Birks in *Restitution: Developments in Unjust Enrichment* (ed. McInnes) p. 56.
[155] Cp. *RBC Dominion Securities Inc.* v. *Dawson* (1994) 111 DLR (4th) 230, 237 (Cameron JA).
[156] See pp. 695–703 above.

continued existence of a defence of estoppel despite the recognition of change of position.

(ii) The relationship between change of position and the agent's defence

The recognition of the defence of change of position might mean that there is no longer any role for the agent's defence where he or she has received a benefit which is effectively transferred to the principal.[157] But again the differences between the two defences are such that the agent's defence continues to be relevant. These differences include that, for the agent's defence, it is not necessary to show that the agent's circumstances have changed detrimentally, neither is it necessary to prove any extraordinary change of circumstances on the part of the agent, it being sufficient that he or she transferred the benefit to the principal because he or she was under a duty to do so.

Since the defences are compatible it follows that an agent could rely on both as defences to one restitutionary claim. So, for example, if the plaintiff paid the agent £1,000 by mistake, intending this sum to be paid to the principal, and the agent paid only £800 to the principal, the agent's defence will apply in respect of this amount. If the principal informed the agent that he or she could retain the remaining £200 as commission, and the agent donated this sum to charity, he or she could invoke the defence of change of position in respect of that amount.

(iii) The relationship between change of position and bona fide purchase[158]

One consequence of the recognition of the defence of change of position is that the continuing existence of the defence of *bona fide* purchase has been called into question. It has been suggested that *bona fide* purchase is the paradigm example of change of position[159] and that the two defences are founded on the same principle, namely that the defendant has changed his or her position in circumstances which make it inequitable to require the defendant to make restitution to the plaintiff.[160] But although Lord Goff recognised in *Lipkin Gorman* that change of position was akin to the defence of *bona fide* purchase, he did not

---

[157] Birks treats the defence as a particular manifestation of change of position: Birks, 'Overview' in *Laundering and Tracing*, p. 345.

[158] For analysis of the *bona fide* purchase defence see Chapter 22. On the relationship between *bona fide* purchase and change of position see Barker, 'After Change of Position: Good Faith Exchange in the Modern Law of Restitution' in *Laundering and Tracing* (ed. Birks) chapter 7.

[159] Millett, 'Tracing the Proceeds of Fraud' (1991) 107 *LQR* 71, 82.

[160] Birks, 'The English Recognition of Unjust Enrichment' [1991] *LMCLQ* 473. Birks has since recanted, in *Restitution: Developments in Unjust Enrichment* (ed. McInnes) p. 65.

regard the defences as identical.[161] This is the better view.[162] There are enough differences between the two to justify their continued treatment as separate defences:

(1) The *bona fide* purchase defence is a complete defence to the plaintiff's restitutionary claim in the same way as estoppel, whereas change of position will operate only to the extent that the defendant's position has actually changed.

(2) The change of position defence will apply only where the defendant has detrimentally changed his or her position, whereas there is no need to show any detriment to establish the defence of *bona fide* purchase.

(3) Most importantly, whereas the change of position defence is a general defence which is applicable to all restitutionary claims, the *bona fide* purchase defence is a specific defence which applies only where the plaintiff's restitutionary claim is founded on the vindication of property rights. This is because the rationale of the *bona fide* purchase defence is to give the defendant indefeasible title to property in which the plaintiff had a proprietary interest.

Since the requirements for establishing the two defences and the policies underlying them are so different, the recognition of change of position should not affect the continued existence of the *bona fide* purchase defence.

---

[161] [1991] 2 AC 548, 580–1.
[162] See Key, '*Bona Fide* Purchase as a Defence in the Law of Restitution' [1994] *LMCLQ* 421 and Nolan in *Laundering and Tracing* (ed. Birks) p. 186.

25

Passing On and Mitigation of Loss

Whereas the defences of estoppel, transfer by an agent to his or her principal and change of position are assessed by reference to changes in the circumstances of the defendant, usually after he or she has received a benefit, the question which needs to be considered in this chapter is whether there are, and if not whether there should be, any defences in English law which operate by reference to changes in the circumstances of the plaintiff after the defendant received the benefit. There are two possible defences which, if they are recognised, operate in this way, namely passing on and mitigation of loss.

1. PASSING ON[1]

(a) The general principle

If the defence of passing on is recognised in English law it applies where the plaintiff has suffered loss by virtue of transferring a benefit to the defendant and the plaintiff has passed this loss on to a third party. It is in respect of restitutionary claims founded on the reversal of the defendant's unjust enrichment that the case for a defence of passing on is clearest. To establish such a claim the plaintiff must show that the defendant has been enriched at the plaintiff's expense. But if the plaintiff has recouped his or her loss following the transfer of a benefit to the defendant by passing that loss on to a third party, it appears that the defendant's enrichment has been at the expense of the third party and not the plaintiff. If the defendant made restitution in full to the plaintiff in such circumstances this would mean that the plaintiff becomes unjustly enriched at the expense of the third party by the receipt of a windfall gain. This can be illustrated by the following example. The defendant public authority demands the payment of a statutory duty from the plaintiff. The plaintiff pays this money to the defendant and then recoups it from its customers by increasing the price of its goods. The plaintiff later discovers that the defendant had no authority to demand the duty and so the plaintiff seeks restitution from the defendant. Since

---

[1] See Rose, 'Passing On' in *Laundering and Tracing* (ed. Birks) chapter 10 and McInnes ' "Passing On" in the Law of Restitution: A Reconsideration' (1997) 19 *Sydney LR* 179.

the plaintiff has not suffered any loss, because the initial loss was passed on to the customers, the defendant's enrichment does not appear to have been at the plaintiff's expense, but is instead at the expense of the customers, since they have ultimately borne the burden of the defendant's unauthorised demand. It would seem to follow therefore, as a matter of principle, that the plaintiff's restitutionary claim should be defeated to the extent that the loss suffered by the plaintiff has been passed on to a third party. But, as will be seen, this principled argument has generally not been recognised by the judges.

(b) Judicial examination of the defence

(i) Recognition of the defence

The defence of passing on has been recognised in some jurisdictions. For example, it was recognised by the Supreme Court of Canada in *Air Canada* v. *British Columbia*[2] and also by the European Court of Justice. In *Amministrazione delle Finanze dello Stato* v. *SpA San Giorgio*[3] it was held that Community law does not prevent Member States from 'disallowing repayment of charges which have been unduly levied where to do so would entail unjust enrichment of the recipients', as would occur where, for example, unduly levied charges have been incorporated into the price of goods and passed on to purchasers. However, the effect of Community law is that it simply 'does not prevent' Member States from adopting a passing on defence. The *San Giorgio* case is not authority for the proposition that Member States must adopt such a defence.[4]

The defence exists in English law in certain statutory provisions which relate to the recovery of overpaid VAT, excise duty and car tax. For example, recovery of overpaid VAT is denied if repayment would unjustly enrich the person who paid the VAT. [5] This presumably encompasses a defence of passing on, which would be applicable where, for example, the taxpayer had passed on the burden of the VAT to its customers.[6]

---

[2] (1989) 59 DLR (4th) 161, 193–4 (La Forest J). The defence was rejected by Wilson J at p. 170 on the ground that the only question before the court related to the establishment of the unjust enrichment of the defendant. But it does not necessarily follow that the passing on defence is irrelevant, since it must still be considered whether the defendant was unjustly enriched *at the plaintiff's expense.*

[3] Case 199/82 [1983] ECR 3595.   [4] *Ibid*, Mancini AG at 3636.

[5] Value Added Tax Act 1994, s. 80(1), as amended by the Finance Act 1997, s. 46. See Virgo, 'Restitution of Overpaid VAT' [1998] *BTR* 582. See *Marks and Spencer plc.* v. *Customs and Excise Commissioners* [1999] STC 205. See also Finance Act 1989, s. 29(3), which contains a similar defence in respect of the recovery of overpaid excise duty and car tax.

[6] This was recognised by Evans LJ in *Kleinwort Benson Ltd.* v. *Birmingham CC* [1997] QB 380, 389.

(ii) Rejection of the defence

The defence has been expressly rejected in Australia.[7] Whether it is recognised at common law in England has been a controversial matter. Although the point was left open by Lord Goff in *Woolwich Equitable Building Society* v. *IRC*,[8] the defence was expressly rejected by the Court of Appeal in *Kleinwort Benson Ltd.* v. *Birmingham CC*.[9] This was one of the interest rate swap cases, in which the defendant local authority argued that the plaintiff, a bank which was seeking restitution of money paid under a void interest rate swaps transaction to the defendant, had passed on the financial loss arising from the swap transaction by entering into hedging transactions to protect the plaintiff against the risks which are inherent in a swaps transaction. The Court of Appeal rejected this argument for two reasons:

(1) If restitutionary remedies were concerned with what the plaintiff has lost then the passing on defence would be highly relevant, because the fact that the plaintiff has passed on his or her loss would mean that he or she would require less compensation from the defendant. But because the law of restitution is concerned with recovery of what the defendant has gained, it follows that the fact that the plaintiff has passed on his or her loss is an irrelevant defence to a restitutionary claim.[10] This was well expressed by Saville LJ who said that:

> [The defendant] does not cease to be unjustly enriched because the payer for one reason or another is not out of pocket. His obligation to return the money is not based on any loss the payer may have sustained, but on the simple ground that it is unjust that he should keep something to which he has no right.[11]

(2) Where the plaintiff's restitutionary claim is founded on the reversal of the defendant's unjust enrichment it has to be shown that the defendant was unjustly enriched at the plaintiff's expense. But this requirement of 'at the plaintiff's expense' means only that the benefit received by the defendant derived from the plaintiff. It does not mean that the defendant's gain was ultimately received at the expense of the plaintiff. This is effectively a question of timing. The

---

[7] By the High Court of Australia in *Mason* v. *New South Wales* (1959) 102 CLR 108 and *Commissioner of State Revenue* v. *Royal Insurance Australia Ltd.* (1994) 126 ALR 1.

[8] [1993] AC 70, 178.

[9] [1997] QB 380. See also *Kleinwort Benson* v. *South Tyneside MBC* [1994] 4 All ER 972 (Hobhouse J).

[10] See Rose in *Laundering and Tracing* (ed. Birks) p. 274.

[11] [1997] QB 380, 394. Evans LJ recognised at p. 393 that, even if the restitutionary claim was concerned with compensating the plaintiff for the loss it had suffered, the hedging transaction which the plaintiff had entered into was too remote and so need not be considered.

defendant's obligation to make restitution to the plaintiff arises once the defendant has received an enrichment in circumstances of injustice. What the plaintiff does after the defendant has received the enrichment is irrelevant to the plaintiff's claim.

Although the defence of passing on was rejected on the facts of the case, its availability was left open generally and particularly as regards claims for the recovery of tax and other duties.[12] Evans LJ did not consider these cases to be relevant to the swaps cases because they involve public law claims, but this is a surprising statement since most of the swaps cases also involve a public law element, involving restitutionary claims brought against public authorities. Indeed, *Kleinwort Benson* itself involved a claim brought against a public authority. A preferable basis for distinguishing the swaps cases from the tax cases is that, in the tax cases where the plaintiff taxpayer has passed on the burden of the tax to his or her customers, the plaintiff can be considered to have collected the tax from his or her customers on behalf of the tax authority.[13] Consequently, it is permissible to treat the tax authority as having been enriched at the expense of the customers, because the plaintiff is simply acting as the agent for the authority,[14] so the customers should be able to sue the authority directly. This analysis will, however, depend on the nature of the tax liability.[15]

(c) Should the defence of passing on be recognised?

The state of English law is such that, save where specific provision has been made by statute, the defence of passing on does not exist as a defence to restitutionary claims. But should such a defence be recognised? A number of factors can be identified which suggest that the defence should not be recognised.

(i) Restitution is concerned with depriving the defendant of any gain

Whatever principle is used to ground the plaintiff's restitutionary claim, the remedy which is awarded is assessed simply by reference to the gain obtained by the defendant. It follows that the law of restitution is not concerned that the plaintiff's loss following the enrichment of the defendant has been passed on to third parties.[16] This is the crux of the decision of the Court of Appeal in the *Kleinwort Benson* case and is the most important reason for rejecting the passing on defence.

---

[12]   [1997] QB 380, 389 (Evans LJ).   [13]   *Ibid.*
[14]   See p. 108 above. See also *Commissioner of State Revenue* v. *Royal Insurance Australia Ltd.* (1994) 126 ALR 1, 14 (Mason CJ).
[15]   Virgo, 'Restitution of Overpaid VAT' [1998] *BTR* 582, 587–8.
[16]   See p. 105 above.

(ii) The difficulty of proving that the loss has been passed on

Even if the defence of passing on were recognised it would be virtually impossible, save in the clearest of cases, for the defendant to establish that the plaintiff has indeed passed on the loss to a third party.[17] For example, if the plaintiff has paid money to the defendant and seeks to recoup this loss from his or her customers by increasing prices, it does not follow that the plaintiff will necessarily be able to recoup the loss. This was recognised by Advocate General Mancini in the *San Giorgio* case:

[The] passing on of charges is not generally relevant because of the innumerable variables which affect price formation in a free market and because of the consequent impossibility of definitively relating any part of the price exclusively to a certain cost.[18]

Consequently, even though the plaintiff may have increased the price of goods to recoup the enrichment which was transferred to the defendant, this may in turn have had an impact on sales volume resulting in an overall loss. It follows that the plaintiff would not have passed on the loss to his or her customers.

Burrows has suggested that one solution to this evidential problem is to create a presumption that the plaintiff has passed on the loss and place the burden on the plaintiff to rebut this presumption.[19] But, as Burrows acknowledges, this is unacceptable because the burden of proving restitutionary defences should be borne by the defendant.

(iii) It is not equitable to recognise a defence of passing on

The most important principle underlying the recognition of defences to restitutionary claims is that in certain recognised circumstances it is not equitable to require the defendant to make restitution to the plaintiff. In *Kleinwort Benson Ltd.* v. *Birmingham CC*[20] Morritt LJ relied on the question of what was just and equitable as a reason for rejecting the passing on defence. He acknowledged that a consequence of rejecting the defence is that the plaintiff may be left with a windfall where he or she was able to pass on the loss to a third party but, crucially, Morritt LJ asserted that:

the plaintiff has a better title than the defendant to any 'windfall' available, not least so as to be in a position to satisfy any claim made against him by those from whom 'the windfall' was ultimately derived.[21]

---

[17] See McInnes, ' "Passing On" in the Law of Restitution: A Reconsideration' (1997) 19 *Sydney LR* 179, 199 and Virgo, 'Restitution of Overpaid VAT' [1998] *BTR* 582, 588–9.

[18] Case 199/82 [1983] ECR 3595, 3629.

[19] Burrows, *The Law of Restitution*, p. 476.   [20] [1997] QB 380, 401.

[21] *Ibid.* Cp. *Air Canada* v. *British Columbia* (1989) 59 DLR (4d.) 161,193, where La Forest J said that 'the law of restitution is not intended to provide windfalls to plaintiffs who have suffered no loss'.

Consequently, as between the plaintiff and the defendant it is the plaintiff who should benefit from the fact that a loss has been passed on to a third party.

2. MITIGATION OF LOSS[22]

Even though the defence of passing on has been rejected in English law, it is still necessary to consider whether a similar but sufficiently distinct defence should be recognised, namely the defence of mitigation of loss. If this defence were recognised it would mean that the plaintiff who has transferred a benefit to the defendant would be required to minimise his or her loss and, to the extent that this loss has been minimised, the defendant's obligation to make restitution should be reduced.

This defence was considered by the Court of Appeal in *Kleinwort Benson Ltd.* v. *Birmingham CC*[23] where it was specifically rejected. In fact, the plaintiff's conduct in the *Kleinwort Benson* case involved mitigation of loss rather than passing on the actual loss which the plaintiff had suffered since the plaintiff had entered into a hedging transaction with a third party simply to minimise the risk of loss it might suffer. The conclusion of the court that there was no duty on the plaintiff to mitigate his or her loss[24] and that there was no defence of mitigation of loss[25] is clearly correct, and for reasons which are similar to those which suggest that the defence of passing on should not be recognised. Crucially, the law of restitution is simply concerned with the award of those remedies which exist to deprive the defendant of benefits obtained. It is concerned only with the gain made by the defendant and not the loss suffered by the plaintiff.[26]

If a defence of mitigation of loss were recognised it would limit the extent of the plaintiff's restitutionary remedy; consequently there is no incentive for the plaintiff to mitigate his or her loss, even though this would often be economically efficient and so should be encouraged. Consequently, the failure to recognise mitigation of loss as a defence may be that the plaintiff is more likely to mitigate his or her loss.

The only possible qualification of this rejection of the defence of mitigation of loss may arise where the plaintiff's restitutionary claim is founded on the commission of a wrong by the defendant, such as a tort. Where the plaintiff seeks a compensatory remedy from the defendant who has committed a tort the plaintiff must mitigate his or her loss, and so it could be argued that the plaintiff is required to mitigate his or her

---

[22] See Burrows, *The Law of Restitution*, pp. 475–6.   [23] [1997] QB 380.
[24] *Ibid*, p. 393 (Evans LJ).   [25] *Ibid*, p. 394 (Saville LJ) and p. 399 (Morritt LJ).
[26] Rose in *Laundering and Tracing* (ed. Birks) p. 276.

loss even where the plaintiff seeks a restitutionary remedy.[27] But this is a flawed argument. The plaintiff is required to mitigate his or her loss only where a compensatory remedy is sought since such a remedy is assessed only by reference to the plaintiff's loss. Where the plaintiff seeks a restitutionary remedy, albeit that the claim is founded on the commission of a tort, the remedy is only assessed by reference to the defendant's gain obtained from committing the tort. The fact that the plaintiff has or might have mitigated his or her loss is irrelevant. In fact, in many cases in which the defendant obtained a benefit as a result of the commission of a wrong the plaintiff will have suffered little if any loss.

3. REJECTION OF DEFENCES TRIGGERED BY CHANGES IN THE PLAINTIFF'S CIRCUMSTANCES

The conclusion of this chapter is that no defences should be recognised in the law of restitution which are triggered by changes in the plaintiff's circumstances. Since there are clearly a number of defences which are triggered by changes in the defendant's circumstances, is the rejection of the defences of passing on and mitigation of loss defensible? The answer is 'yes', and the reason for this stems from the fundamental nature of the law of restitution. That body of law which we call the law of restitution is simply concerned with the award of remedies to deprive the defendant of benefits. These remedies are defendant-focused and so changes in the defendant's circumstances after the receipt of the benefit should be taken into account to determine whether it is equitable for the defendant to make full restitution. Changes in the plaintiff's circumstances are of no consequence to the question whether the defendant should be deprived of a particular benefit. Exactly the same principle applies as regards compensatory remedies, but in reverse. The function of compensatory remedies is to compensate the plaintiff for loss suffered; they are therefore plaintiff-focused. Consequently, changes in the plaintiff's circumstances after loss has been suffered will be taken into account when assessing the remedy which is to be awarded, in the form of the doctrine of mitigation of loss. But changes in the defendant's circumstances are of no consequence. It follows that the nature of the defence which is recognised is affected by the function of the remedy which is awarded.

---

[27] A duty to mitigate loss in such circumstances was contemplated by Evans LJ in *Kleinwort Benson Ltd.* v. *Birmingham CC* [1997] QB 380, 393.

26

Illegality

1. GENERAL PRINCIPLES

All restitutionary claims regardless of the underlying cause of action are subject to a defence of illegality. This stems from the fundamental principle of law, known as *ex turpi causa non oritur actio*,[1] that the courts will generally not assist the plaintiff to obtain a remedy where his or her action is founded on an illegal transaction. This principle was recognised by Lord Mansfield in *Holman* v. *Johnson*[2] where he said that:

No Court will lend its aid to a man who founds his cause of action upon an immoral or illegal act. If from the plaintiff's own stating or otherwise, the cause of action appears to arise *ex turpi causa*, or the transgression of a positive law of this country, there the Court says he has no right to be assisted. It is upon this ground the Court goes; not for the sake of the defendant, but because they will not lend their aid to such a plaintiff.

There is, however, another principle which is particularly relevant to restitutionary claims, and this is known as the *in pari delicto est conditio defendentis* defence. If the plaintiff seeks restitution in connection with a transaction which was tainted by illegality the claim may be defeated by the *in pari delicto* defence. By virtue of this defence, where the parties are equally at fault as regards their participation in the illegal transaction the defendant should be allowed to retain the enrichment. This defence was specifically identified by Lord Mansfield in *Holman* v. *Johnson*.[3] He justified such a rule by reference to 'general principles of policy', even though this was 'contrary to the real justice' as between the two parties in that it enabled the defendant to retain any enrichment regardless of the circumstances of the case. Consequently, the *in pari delicto* defence operates as a general defence to restitutionary claims, although it is subject to a number of qualifications.

(a) Definition of illegality

There is no accepted definition of what constitutes illegality. The word has often been used, not as a term of art, but simply to describe a state of

---

[1] 'No action can arise from a base cause'.
[2] (1775) 1 Cowp. 341, 343; 98 ER 1120, 1121. See also *Muckleston* v. *Brown* (1801) 6 Ves. Jun. 52, 69; 31 ER 934, 942 (Lord Eldon LC).
[3] *Ibid.*

affairs which is contrary to law; but mere unlawfulness does not equate with illegality. A cognate principle is sometimes referred to, known as public policy, by virtue of which restitutionary claims may be defeated. But typically the court will conclude that the plaintiff's claim should be defeated by virtue of public policy without further elaboration. Reference to public policy creates uncertainty, both because the requirements of public policy are uncertain and because any notion of public policy is liable to change over the years.

A number of principles can be identified to determine whether a particular transaction is illegal.

(i) Illegality at common law

At common law a transaction will be illegal for three reasons:

(1) Where the transaction involves the commission of a legal wrong, whether criminal or civil.

(2) Where the transaction involves conduct which may be considered to be immoral or contrary to public policy. This includes, for example, champertous agreements[4] and agreements concerning the sale of offices and honours.[5] A matter of recent concern is whether interest rate swaps transactions are contrary to public policy. If such transactions involve gambling they would be contrary to public policy and so would be void. However, it has been held that, since the primary purpose of such transactions is to raise money rather than to wager, they are not void as being contrary to public policy.[6]

(3) The transaction itself may be legal but it may be tainted by an illegal purpose as will be the case where, for example, the plaintiff transfers property to the defendant to make it appear that the plaintiff has no interest in the property.[7]

(ii) Illegality by statute

A statute may make a transaction illegal either by expressly or impliedly prohibiting a particular transaction, so the transaction is unenforceable, or by prohibiting a particular method of performance of the transaction, so that the transaction is unenforceable only if that method of performance is adopted.

(iii) The significance of the parties' knowledge of the illegality

Where the formation or performance of a transaction is prohibited by statute or the common law the transaction is unenforceable by either

---

[4] See *Giles* v. *Thompson* [1994] 1 AC 142.
[5] *Parkinson* v. *College of Ambulance* [1923] 2 KB 1.
[6] See *Morgan Grenfell and Co. Ltd.* v. *Welwyn Hatfield DC* [1995] 1 All ER 1.
[7] See, for example, *Tribe* v. *Tribe* [1996] Ch. 107.

party regardless of whether or not he or she knew of the illegality.[8] In other cases whether the transaction is enforceable depends on the parties' intention or knowledge. So, for example, if both parties intend to commit an illegal act in the course of performing an otherwise legal transaction, or one party so intends and the other is aware of this illegal purpose, the transaction is unenforceable by both of them.[9] If just one of the parties had such an intention then he or she would not be able to enforce the transaction, but this would have no effect on the other party's right of enforcement, so long as he or she was ignorant of the illegal purpose.[10] If one party has an illegal purpose and the other subsequently discovers it, the latter can refuse to take any further part in the transaction and he or she will have a restitutionary claim in respect of the work he or she had already lawfully done.[11]

(b) The consequences of a transaction being tainted by illegality

(i) *The* in pari delicto *defence*

If a transaction is tainted by illegality then, as a general rule, a plaintiff who has transferred a benefit to the defendant pursuant to the transaction will not be able to obtain restitution of that benefit from the defendant, because the defendant will be able to plead the *in pari delicto* defence.[12] The application of this defence is illustrated by *Parkinson* v. *College of Ambulance*[13] where the plaintiff had given a donation to a charity on the understanding that he would receive a knighthood as a result. When no knighthood was forthcoming he sought restitution of the money on the ground of total failure of consideration, but the claim failed because the contract was illegal as being contrary to public policy.

But the *in pari delicto* defence should not be interpreted in such a way as to bar the plaintiff's restitutionary claim automatically if he or she had been tainted by illegality. The defence was always intended to be applied flexibly, as is illustrated by its application in *Holman* v. *Johnson*[14] itself. This case concerned an action to recover the price of goods supplied by the plaintiff, who knew that the goods were to be smuggled into England. The plaintiff's claim succeeded because mere knowledge of the smuggling was held not to be sufficient to bar his claim and because he was not

---

[8] *Re Mahmoud and Ispahani* [1921] 2 KB 716.
[9] *Pearce* v. *Brooks* (1866) LR 1 Ex. 213.
[10] *Archbolds (Freightage) Ltd.* v. *Spanglett Ltd.* [1961] QB 374.
[11] *Clay* v. *Yates* (1856) 1 H and N 73; 156 ER 1123.
[12] See *Muckleston* v. *Brown* (1801) 6 Ves. Jun. 52, 69; 31 ER 934, 942 (Lord Eldon LC) and *Gordon* v. *Chief Constable of Metropolitan Police* [1910] 2 KB 1080, 1090 (Vaughan Williams LJ).
[13] [1923] 2 KB 1. See also *Mohamed* v. *Alaga and Co. (a firm)* [1998] 2 All ER 720.
[14] (1775) 1 Cowp. 341, 343; 98 ER 1120, 1121.

guilty of any offence. Lord Mansfield recognised that the *in pari delicto* defence should be applied flexibly, and this is inherent in the test which he formulated. For a test stating that the assistance of the court will be denied where the parties are *par delictum* is a test judged by reference to the relative blameworthiness of the parties. Consequently, if one party is less blameworthy than the other the court should assist that party. Despite this, in the nineteenth and twentieth centuries the defence came to be applied more rigorously, so much so that it was used to bar the plaintiff's claim whenever he or she had been tainted by illegality. For example, in *Wild* v. *Simpson*[15] Atkin LJ gave the example of a taxi-driver who was engaged to drive to a particular destination and who was informed by the passenger halfway through the journey that he was going to perpetrate a burglary at the destination. Atkin LJ suggested that if the driver proceeded with the journey he would not be able to recover his fare, or even half of it, since the driver's claim for restitution would have been tainted by illegality. But surely he was much less blameworthy than the passenger, so there is no reason why his claim for restitution should be defeated.

(ii) Denial of restitution in equity

A principle restricting recovery in cases of illegality also exists in equity in the form of the maxim that the plaintiff who comes to equity must come with clean hands.[16] This means that if the plaintiff's conduct is regarded as improper relief in equity will be refused. In the leading case on this maxim, *Dering* v. *Earl of Winchelsea*,[17] it was held that such improper conduct does not arise if there is merely moral impropriety; the impropriety must arise in a legal sense. Such impropriety does not, however, necessarily equate with illegality. Where there is illegality the transaction will be unenforceable both at law and in equity,[18] but where there is no illegality equity may still deny relief by virtue of the unclean hands maxim.

The question of the operation of this equitable maxim was considered by Lord Goff in his dissenting judgment in *Tinsley* v. *Milligan*,[19] where he concluded that it was not possible to vindicate proprietary rights in equity where those rights had arisen under an illegal transaction, simply because the claimant must come with clean hands. In fact, Lord Goff's interpretation of the clean hands maxim was mistaken because that

---

[15] [1919] 2 KB 544, 566.

[16] See *Groves* v. *Groves* (1829) 3 Y and J 163, 174; 148 ER 1136, 1141 (Lord Alexander CB); *Tinker* v. *Tinker* [1970] P 136, 143 (Salmon LJ); *Tinsley* v. *Milligan* [1994] 1 AC 340, 357 (Lord Goff); and *Nelson* v. *Nelson* (1995) 70 ALJR 47, 68 (Dawson J).

[17] (1787) 1 Cox 318; 29 ER 1184.   [18] *Ayerst* v. *Jenkins* (1873) LR 16 Eq. 275.

[19] [1994] 1 AC 340.

maxim has a particular function which is very different from that of the *in pari delicto* defence. This was recognised by Mummery LJ in *Dunbar* v. *Plant*.[20] He recognised that, whereas the *in pari delicto* principle is a principle of public policy[21] which must be strictly applied by the court, the clean hands maxim is a principle of justice which is designed to prevent those guilty of serious misconduct from securing an equitable remedy, such as specific performance[22] or an injunction.[23] The consequence of making this distinction between principles of public policy and principles of justice is that the clean hands maxim applies only where the plaintiff seeks a discretionary equitable remedy and it does not apply where the plaintiff seeks equitable remedies as a matter of right, such as where the plaintiff seeks to vindicate an equitable proprietary right.[24]

(c) The policy behind the *in pari delicto* defence

A number of reasons have been recognised for denying the plaintiff restitutionary remedies where he or she has been tainted by illegality.[25]

(i) Deterrence

Illegal conduct is regarded as being contrary to public policy and so should be deterred.[26] But it is difficult to see how this policy of deterrence justifies the denial of restitutionary relief to a plaintiff who has participated in an illegal transaction.[27] This is because whether the denial of restitution will actually deter a party from entering into an illegal transaction will depend on a variety of factors, including knowledge of the illegality and the value of the transaction. In fact, if the person who expects to receive a benefit is aware of the illegality and of the policy denying restitution he or she is much more likely to participate in the transaction, knowing that any benefit which is received may be retained.[28] But this is a highly artificial argument, since it is unlikely that either party will be aware of the *in pari delicto* defence and its implications.[29] Even if the parties were so aware, it would be very difficult for them to predict

---

[20] [1998] Ch. 412, 422.

[21] As had been recognised by Lord Mansfield in *Holman* v. *Johnson* (1775) 1 Cowp 341, 343; 98 ER 1120, 1121.

[22] See, for example, *Coatsworth* v. *Johnson* (1886) 54 LT 520.

[23] See *Argyll (Duchess)* v. *Argyll (Duke)* [1967] Ch. 302, although the maxim did not apply on the facts because the plaintiff's unacceptable conduct was considered to be too remote.

[24] This is consistent with the approach of the majority in *Tinsley* v. *Milligan* [1994] 1 AC 340, examined at pp. 638–9 above.

[25] See Grodecki, '*In Pari Delicto Potior Est Conditio Defendentis*' (1955) 71 LQR 254, 265–73.

[26] *Euro-Diam Ltd.* v. *Bathurst* [1990] QB 1, 35.

[27] *Tinsley* v. *Milligan* [1994] 1 AC 340, 368 (Lord Lowry).

[28] *Nelson* v. *Nelson* (1995) 70 ALJR 47, 88 (McHugh J).

[29] See *Tribe* v. *Tribe* [1996] Ch. 107, 134 (Millett LJ).

whether or not restitution would be denied because of the uncertain operation of the exceptions to the defence. Also, in those cases where there is serious illegality of a criminal nature, it is unlikely that the denial of restitution will be a greater deterrent than that of the criminal law.

(ii) Morality

The denial of restitution has sometimes been justified on the ground that participation in an illegal transaction is immoral and should effectively be punished by denying relief.[30] Such an argument is unconvincing because participation in illegal transactions does not necessarily mean that the plaintiff is acting immorally, for he or she may have contravened only a relatively minor regulatory provision.

(iii) The dignity of the court

Sometimes, for prudish reasons, the court may feel unwilling to award the plaintiff restitutionary relief where he or she has been tainted by illegality, for fear of the court itself being tainted by such illegality.[31] This is an unsatisfactory justification for the defence because it suggests that the court is more concerned with its own dignity than the need to secure justice between the parties.

Analysis of these different justifications of the *in pari delicto* defence suggests that there is no convincing policy reason in favour of denying restitution to a plaintiff who is tainted by illegality. In fact, this appears increasingly to be the conclusion of the courts which often seek to grant restitution to such plaintiffs whilst maintaining that they are honouring the *in pari delicto* defence. They have done this by developing a number of exceptions to the defence.

2. METHODS FOR AVOIDING THE OPERATION OF THE *IN PARI DELICTO* DEFENCE

It has been seen throughout this book that in a number of instances restitutionary remedies may be awarded despite the fact that the plaintiff has participated in an illegal transaction. In these cases illegality is not a ground of restitution itself.[32] Rather, other grounds of restitution exist which can be justified on the basis that the policy behind the *in pari delicto* defence is inapplicable.

---

[30] *Tinsley* v. *Milligan* [1992] Ch. 310, 334 (Ralph Gibson LJ).
[31] *Collins* v. *Blantern* (1767) 2 Wils. 347, 350; 95 ER 850, 852 (Wilmot CJ).
[32] Cp. Burrows, *The Law of Restitution*, p. 334.

(a) The vindication of proprietary rights despite illegality[33]

In *Tinsley* v. *Milligan*[34] the House of Lords recognised that the plaintiff can vindicate proprietary rights even though he or she has participated in an illegal transaction, so long as he or she can vindicate the right without needing to rely on the illegality itself. This is, however, a highly dubious principle because a number of situations have been recognised in which the plaintiff can rely on an illegal transaction to vindicate property rights.[35] It follows that the so-called exception to the *in pari delicto* defence, that the plaintiff can vindicate proprietary rights so long as he or she does not need to rely on the illegality to establish the claim, should be rejected as artificial. The plaintiff should be able to vindicate proprietary rights even though he or she has been tainted by illegality save where the illegality is of a particularly serious kind.[36]

(b) The parties are not *in pari delicto*

The plaintiff's restitutionary claim will also succeed even though the claim arises from participation in an illegal transaction, where the parties are not *in pari delicto*, which will usually be the case where the defendant is more responsible for participating in the illegal transaction than the plaintiff.

(i) Mistake[37]

Where the plaintiff's mistake related to the fact that the transfer of a benefit was illegal he or she can found a restitutionary claim on the ground of mistake.[38] If the plaintiff was mistaken as to the illegality it is possible to conclude that he or she is not tainted by it and so there is no reason why the restitutionary claim should fail. This will be the case even where both parties are unaware of the illegality.[39]

(ii) Compulsion[40]

The plaintiff will be able to bring a restitutionary claim by virtue of compulsion despite the fact that he or she has been tainted by illegality.[41]

(iii) Actual or potential exploitation[42]

In certain circumstances the defendant will be deemed to be more responsible for participation in the illegal transaction than the plaintiff if

---

[33] See pp. 637–41 above.   [34] [1994] 1 AC 340.   [35] See p, 641 above.
[36] See pp. 754–6 below.   [37] See p. 166 above.
[38] *Oom* v. *Bruce* (1810) 12 East 225; 104 ER 87.   [39] *Ibid.*
[40] See p. 191 above.   [41] *Astley* v. *Reynolds* (1731) 2 Stra. 915; 93 ER 939.
[42] See pp. 297–9 above.

the defendant occupied a position where he or she could actually or potentially exploit the plaintiff's weaker position. This arises in two situations: first, where the defendant has acted oppressively;[43] secondly, where statute imposes an obligation on one party to ensure that the transaction complied with the law. [44]

(iv) Restitution for wrongs

The principle that restitutionary relief will be available if the parties are not *in pari delicto* will also be relevant where the plaintiff's restitutionary claim is founded on wrongdoing. For where the plaintiff is innocent of the wrong and it was the defendant who had acted illegally the defendant cannot rely on illegality to retain an enrichment.[45]

(c) Withdrawal from an illegal transaction[46]

Where the plaintiff has withdrawn from an illegal transaction before any part of it has been performed the plaintiff can bring a restitutionary claim, with the ground of restitution effectively being that of total failure of consideration.[47] Restitution is justified in such circumstances on the ground that the plaintiff is no longer tainted by the illegality and from a policy of deterring the performance of illegal contracts. But if this exception is founded on the principle of failure of consideration, an anomaly of some importance is created in the law of restitution, since it has been accepted in a number of cases that where the plaintiff brings a restitutionary claim grounded on total failure of consideration the fact that the plaintiff is tainted by illegality will defeat the plaintiff's claim.[48] Other cases have, however, expressly recognised that the plaintiff's claim will succeed in such circumstances.[49] At the very least, the recognition of a principle that the plaintiff can obtain restitution where he or she has simply withdrawn from the illegal transaction makes the bar on restitutionary claims grounded on failure of consideration where the plaintiff is tainted by illegality very difficult to defend.

---

[43] See, for example, *Smith* v. *Cuff* (1817) 6 M and S 160; 105 ER 1203.
[44] See, for example, *Kiriri Cotton Co. Ltd.* v. *Dewani* [1960] AC 192.
[45] See, for example, Chapter 19.   [46] See pp. 370–3 above.
[47] See *Tribe* v. *Tribe* [1996] Ch. 107.
[48] See, for example, *Evanson* v. *Crooks* (1911) 106 LT (NS) 264; *Parkinson* v. *College of Ambulance* [1925] 2 KB 1; *Berg* v. *Sadler and Moore* [1937] 2 KB 158; and *Bigos* v. *Bousted* [1951] 1 All ER 92. See also *Taylor* v. *Bhail* [1996] CLC 377.
[49] *Bloxsome* v. *Williams* (1824) 3 B and C 232; 107 ER 720; *Shaw* v. *Shaw* [1965] 1 WLR 537 (Lord Denning MR).

(d) A limitation upon the methods for avoiding the *in pari delicto* defence

In each of these situations in which the plaintiff is able to bring a restitutionary claim despite his or her participation in an illegal transaction the claim will still be defeated if the nature of the illegality is particularly serious.[50] This is because in such cases of serious illegality it will be against public policy for the court to assist the plaintiff to obtain restitution. So, for example, a court would never order restitution of money paid to the defendant to kill a third party simply because the agreement would be too grossly immoral for the court to consider assisting the plaintiff.[51]

The decision of the Court of Appeal in *Taylor* v. *Bhail*[52] can be justified on similar grounds. In that case the plaintiff builder agreed with the defendant that he would put in an estimate for building work which was £1,000 above the actual cost of the estimated work, to enable the defendant to defraud his insurance company. The plaintiff's claim that he should be paid for the work which he had actually done failed. This can be justified on the basis that the plaintiff and the defendant had committed the serious crime of conspiracy to defraud.[53] As Millett LJ recognised such insurance fraud is a serious problem which needs to be deterred,[54] and so restitutionary relief was denied simply on the ground of public policy.

3. REFORM OF THE LAW

It has been widely acknowledged that the law relating to the defence of illegality as it applies to restitutionary claims is unsatisfactory. Indeed, in *Tinsley* v. *Milligan*[55] Lord Goff said, 'I would be more than happy if a new system could be evolved which was both satisfactory in its effect and capable of avoiding the kind of result which flows from the established rules of law'. The defence is undoubtedly unsatisfactory since it produces results which are often harsh, capricious and uncertain, and consequently it is in desperate need of reform. There are a number of options available.

---

[50] See *Bowmakers Ltd.* v. *Barnet Instruments Ltd.* [1945] 1 KB 65, 72 (du Parcq LJ).
[51] *Tappenden* v. *Randall* (1801) 2 Bos. and Pul. 467, 471; 126 ER 1388, 1390 (Heath J); *Kearley* v. *Thomson* (1890) 24 QBD 742, 747 (Fry LJ).
[52] [1996] CLC 377.   [53] *Ibid*, p. 381 (Russell LJ).
[54] *Ibid*, p. 384.   [55] [1994] 1 AC 340, 363.

(a) A general discretion to award restitutionary relief despite illegality

One possible reform is to replace the existing law with a discretionary power to enable the courts to award restitution if the justice of the case so demands.[56] This discretion may arise either at common law or by statute.

(i) Common law

(1) The public conscience test

The courts have experimented with a new exception to the *in pari delicto* defence by analysing all of the circumstances of the case to determine whether or not restitutionary or other relief should be awarded. The test the courts have concentrated on is one of public policy, specifically whether the public conscience would be affronted if relief were granted. This test originated in *Thackwell* v. *Barclays Bank plc*.[57] In that case an action for negligence and conversion of a cheque failed by reason of the *ex turpi causa* principle, but only after the court had considered all the circumstances of the case, including the quality of the illegality, in deter- mining whether by granting a remedy to the plaintiff it would be seen to be assisting or encouraging the plaintiff in his criminal act. A remedy was eventually denied to the plaintiff because he had been a knowing party to a fraudulent transaction. Clearly the courts perceived the existing law relating to the granting of relief where the plaintiff was tainted by illegal- ity as often producing unjust results, hence the desire to adopt a flexible test enabling judges to exercise their discretion to secure the right result.

The public conscience test was also applicable to restitutionary claims, as was recognised by the Court of Appeal in *Tinsley* v. *Milligan*,[58] but the House of Lords unanimously rejected this approach on the ground that it was inconsistent with the authorities and too uncertain.[59] The court was surely right to do so. The public conscience test is vague and would result in inconsistent and incoherent law.[60] The law of restitution in par- ticular must be developed in a principled way, to avoid allegations of palm-tree justice. Justice is dependent on a high degree of certainty and

[56] See Dickson, 'Restitution and Illegal Transactions' in *Essays on the Law of Restitution* (ed. Burrows) p. 195.

[57] [1986] 1 All ER 676. See also *Saunders* v. *Edwards* [1987] 1 WLR 1116; *Euro-Diam Ltd.* v. *Bathurst* [1990] QB 1; and *Howard* v. *Shirlstar Container Transport Ltd.* [1990] 1 WLR 1292.

[58] [1992] Ch. 310.   [59] See also *Nelson* v. *Nelson* (1995) 70 ALJR 47, 89 (McHugh J).

[60] See *Tinsley* v. *Milligan* [1994] 1 AC 340, 363 (Lord Goff). But the Court of Appeal in sub- sequent cases has still referred to the public conscience test. See *Silverwood* v. *Silverwood* (1997) 74 P and CR 453, 458 (Nourse LJ) and *Reeves* v. *Commissioner of Police* [1998] 2 WLR 401, 415 (Buxton LJ) 426, (Lord Bingham of Cornhill CJ).

predictability, and this is lacking if the public conscience test is adopted. But the attitude of the judges and their perception of the law as producing injustice should not be ignored. There remains a need for a shift of emphasis to avoid the unfair results of the existing law.

(2) The policy of the statute

An alternative test has been recognised by the High Court of Australia in *Nelson* v. *Nelson*,[61] on the ground that it is more principled than the public conscience test. According to *Nelson* v. *Nelson* the decision to grant relief to a plaintiff who has participated in an illegal transaction should be determined by reference to the policy of the statute by virtue of which the relevant transaction was found to have been illegal or tainted by illegality. This approach is well summarised by McHugh J who said that:[62]

courts should not refuse to enforce legal or equitable rights simply because they arose out of or were associated with an unlawful purpose unless:
    (a) the statute discloses an intention that those rights should be unenforceable in all circumstances; or
    (b) (i) the sanction of refusing to enforce those rights is not disproportionate to the seriousness of the unlawful conduct;
    (ii) the imposition of the sanction is necessary, having regard to the terms of the statute, to protect its objects or policies; and
    (iii) the statute does not disclose an intention that the sanctions and remedies contained in the statute are to be the only legal consequences of a breach of the statute or the frustration of its policies.

On the facts of the case, the plaintiff had provided money to buy a house which was put in the name of her son and daughter. This was done to enable the plaintiff to preserve an entitlement to a subsidy to finance the purchase of another house. She received this subsidy without disclosing that she had an interest in the first property. She therefore had an illegal purpose. The house was sold and the plaintiff claimed the proceeds of sale. It was held by the High Court that the presumption of advancement applied in a mother and child relationship,[63] so the plaintiff was presumed to have given the house to her children. Consequently, if she wished to recover the proceeds of sale she had to rebut this presumption. English law would not have allowed her to rebut the presumption since this would have required her to rely on her illegal purpose to explain why she did not intend her initial payment to be a gift.[64] But the High Court was prepared to allow her to rely on her real

---

    [61] (1995) 70 ALJR 47. See Enonchong 'Illegality and the Presumption of Advancement' (1996) 4 *RLR* 78.
    [62] (1995) 70 ALJR 47, p. 89.
    [63] Cp. the English authorities of *Bennett* v. *Bennett* (1879) 10 Ch.D 474 and *Re Ashton* [1897] 2 Ch. 574.
    [64] See *Tinsley* v. *Milligan* [1994] 1 AC 340.

purpose to rebut the presumption, since it considered allowing the mother to recover the proceeds of sale would not frustrate the policy of the statute. This was because the State had a power to recover any subsidy which it had paid to somebody who was not entitled to receive it, and also because the relevant statute did not contain any criminal sanction for making an application for a subsidy to which the applicant was not entitled. To ensure that the policy of the Act was not frustrated it was ordered that the plaintiff could recover the proceeds of sale only once she had repaid the subsidy to the State.

Although the approach of the High Court of Australia to the question of granting relief to a participant in an illegal transaction is more principled than an approach which is founded on the public conscience test, it is nonetheless essentially a discretionary approach. References in particular to the express or implied policy of the statute mean that the Australian judges are giving themselves a great deal of discretion to reach what they perceive to be a just result because of the great difficulty in determining what the implied policy of a particular statutory provision actually is. The application of this approach is even more difficult where the illegality is recognised at common law through the operation of public policy. An approach whereby restitutionary relief depends on identifying the policy behind the invocation of public policy is a nonsense. Consequently, the approach of the High Court of Australia must also be rejected on the ground of uncertainty.

(ii) Statutory reform

In both New Zealand[65] and Israel[66] the courts have been given a statutory power to award restitutionary remedies to a party to an illegal transaction. The New Zealand provision allows the courts to grant restitutionary and other relief to a party to an illegal contract 'as the Court in its discretion considers just'. Relevant factors in the exercise of this discretion include the conduct of the parties, the object of the enactment, the gravity of the penalty and the plaintiff's knowledge of the facts and law. Creating such a general discretion by statute is superficially attractive, since it allows the courts to assess all the circumstances of the case to see whether the plaintiff deserves to receive restitutionary relief. Despite this, such a reform is unacceptable since it will create too much uncertainty in an area of the law in which certainty and consistency are vital. The introduction of a general statutory discretion is unlikely to be of any long-term assistance since it is likely that a body of case law will develop which would suffer from the same inconsistencies as the common law, as has been the case in New Zealand.[67]

[65] The Illegal Contracts Act 1970, s. 7.   [66] Contract Law (General Part) 1973, s. 31.
[67] See Coote, 'Validation under the Illegal Contracts Act' (1992) 15 *NZULR* 80.

(b) Disgorgement to a third party

An alternative reform is to give the court a power to remove any benefit received by the defendant and, where both the plaintiff and the defendant are *in pari delicto*, divert that benefit or part of it to a third party, such as the State or a charity. This is a form of relief which was adopted in *Nelson* v. *Nelson*[68] where, as a condition of restitutionary relief being granted, the plaintiff was required to restore to the State the subsidy which she had received. This is a perfectly acceptable exercise of the court's equitable jurisdiction to grant relief on terms by virtue of which the victim of the illegal transaction is able to recover what it has lost even though it was not a party to the proceedings. Such a result can be justified by the policy that wrongdoers, especially criminals, should not be allowed to profit from their wrongdoing.[69]

But the notion of forfeiting a benefit to a third party can be interpreted more widely, so that benefits are forfeited to third parties even though they were not victims of the illegality. This interpretation of forfeiture raises difficult problems at a theoretical level, since it appears to confuse the functions of restitution as a civil law action, concerned with the relative claims of the parties, and the criminal law, concerned with the intervention of the State.[70] For this reason, the defendant should be required to disgorge benefits to a third party only where that party is a victim of the illegal transaction, regardless of whether the victim is party to the proceedings.

(c) Rejection of the *in pari delicto* defence

(i) Arguments in favour of abolishing the defence

The preferable reform is in fact the simplest, namely that the *in pari delicto* defence should be rejected. This would have a profound effect on this body of law. At the moment there is an effective presumption against restitution where transactions are tainted by illegality. As a result of a wide definition of illegality and an ever-increasing number of statutory regulations making many transactions illegal, restitutionary relief has been denied in many cases in which justice demanded that the plaintiff's claim should have succeeded.[71] The abolition of the *in pari delicto* defence would go a long way to avoiding injustice. A number of arguments can be identified in favour of removing the *in pari delicto* defence.

(1) Abolition of the defence would mean that restitution in circumstances of illegality will accord with the general restitutionary model,

---

[68] (1995) 47 ALJR 47.   [69] See Chapter 19.
[70] Grodecki, '*In Pari Delicto Potior Est Conditio Defendentis*' (1955) 71 *LQR* 264, 267.
[71] See Wigmore (1891) 25 *Am. L Rev.* 712.

without needing to resort to technical and artificial arguments, such as whether the plaintiff's right is untainted by the illegality, and without reference to complex and uncertain grounds of restitution such as that of withdrawal.

(2) The abolition of the defence would mean that restitutionary relief will typically be awarded by reference to recognised principles rather than by the exercise of unpredictable judicial discretion.

(3) The policy of deterrence is just as likely to be fulfilled by allowing restitution to a plaintiff who has been tainted by illegality as by denying relief to such a person.[72]

(4) In those cases in which restitutionary relief was awarded under the existing law such relief would still be awarded if the *in pari delicto* defence were removed, but the result would have been obtained more easily, since there would no longer be any need to justify restitution where the plaintiff is implicated in the illegality. More importantly, in many of those cases in which restitution has been denied the result would have been different if the defence had been removed, and rightly so, since the award of restitutionary relief is usually required as a matter of justice. A good example of the harshness of the existing law arises from the facts of *Wild* v. *Simpson*,[73] where a solicitor entered into an illegal agreement with a client, whereby the client agreed to pay a percentage of whatever he recovered to the solicitor. The solicitor sought to recover his costs but his action failed simply because the contract of service was illegal. This hardly seems fair. The solicitor had done work for the client but was unable to recover anything for this because of the illegal nature of the original agreement. It is right that the illegal agreement itself is not enforced, so the solicitor would not be allowed to sue for a percentage of what the client recovered, but this should not affect the restitutionary claim.

(ii) The consequences of abolishing the in pari delicto *defence*

Abolition of the *in pari delicto* defence would have the following consequences.

(1) Transactions would still be unenforceable

Abolition of the defence would have no effect upon the *ex turpi causa* principle, so that the courts would still refuse to enforce illegal transactions.

(2) Restitutionary claims would be established as normal

If the defence were abolished it would still be necessary to rely on the recognised grounds of restitution to establish a restitutionary claim. So,

[72] *Smith* v. *Bromley* (1760) 2 Doug. 696n., 698; 99 ER 441, 444 (Lord Mansfield).
[73] [1919] 2 KB 544.

where the plaintiff's claim was founded on the reversal of the defendant's unjust enrichment, the plaintiff would still need to establish a ground of restitution such as mistake, but mistake would be available even if the plaintiff had not made a mistake as to the existence of the illegality. The ground of restitution involving exploitation will still be relevant where it can be shown that the defendant acted oppressively or took advantage of the plaintiff who was the beneficiary of statutory protection. The real advantage of the abolition of the *in pari delicto* defence would be to allow restitution specifically on the ground of total failure of consideration. There would consequently no longer be any need for a ground of restitution founded on the plaintiff's withdrawal from the illegal transaction. Equally, where the plaintiff wishes to vindicate a proprietary right which was tainted by illegality he or she would be able to do so without reference to the artificial principle that he or she did not need to rely on the illegality to establish the claim.

(3) Retention of a discretion to deny restitution in cases of extreme turpitude

The courts would need to retain the discretion, which has long been recognised,[74] that restitutionary relief should be denied to the plaintiff where the illegal transaction involves extreme turpitude. This is for reasons of public policy, namely deterrence, morality and the preservation of the dignity of the court. Although the retention of such a discretion may be criticised as too uncertain, it is important to retain an element of flexibility to deal with the infinite variety of cases of illegality. A number of principles can be formulated to assist in the determination of what constitutes serious illegality.

(1) The plaintiff should be considered to have participated in a transaction involving extreme turpitude only where the plaintiff has committed a crime. This is consistent with the decision of Lord Mansfield in *Holman* v. *Johnson*[75] where the plaintiff's claim succeeded precisely because he had not committed a criminal offence. If particular conduct has not been made criminal it should not be treated as though it were criminal by denying restitutionary relief to the plaintiff. But the mere fact that the plaintiff is a criminal should not bar him or her from obtaining restitution as a matter of course. This principle has been recognised in other areas of the law. So, for example, in *Revill* v. *Newbery*[76] it was recognised that a burglar, who was shot by the owner of a shed whilst the burglar was about to break into it, could be compensated for his injuries even though he had been injured whilst committing a crime. If such a criminal can get compensation for personal injury, the case for the court

[74] See p. 748 above.   [75] (1775) 1 Cowp. 341; 98 ER 1120.
[76] [1996] QB 567.

awarding restitutionary relief to a criminal should be even stronger. Consequently, the fact that the plaintiff has committed a crime should be a condition of restitution being denied to the plaintiff, but it is not enough in its own right to deny restitution. Other principles need to be considered as well.

(2) The plaintiff should not be awarded restitutionary relief if the consequence of this is that he or she will profit from the commission of a crime.[77] So, for example, if the plaintiff obtained money from a drug deal which he paid to his grandmother to hide it from the authorities, he should not be able to recover these proceeds since they constitute the proceeds of a crime.

(3) If the plaintiff has obtained a benefit or avoided a loss as a result of the commission of a crime it ought to be made a condition of him or her obtaining restitution that he or she restore that benefit or compensate the victim for the loss suffered. This ought to be the case even if the benefit has been obtained at the expense of somebody who is not party to the proceedings. So, for example, in a case such as *Tribe* v. *Tribe*,[78] in which the plaintiff had transferred shares to his son to induce the plaintiff's creditors to believe that he had no valuable assets, if the creditors had been induced to believe that the plaintiff did not own any shares and they suffered loss as a result, it ought to be a condition of the plaintiff recovering the shares from the defendant that he reimburse the creditors for their loss. Such restitution on terms has been recognised in a number of cases.[79] Where it is not possible to evaluate the benefit which the plaintiff has received as a result of the commission of the wrong, or the loss suffered by the victim, it might then be appropriate to deny restitution to the plaintiff.[80]

(4) There comes a point where the nature of the crime committed by the plaintiff is so extreme that public policy demands that he or she should not receive the assistance of the court in obtaining restitutionary relief. In such circumstances restitution is denied not on the grounds of principle but simply through the exercise of the court's discretion. The need for a residual discretion in the court to deny restitution is inevitable, but the consequent uncertainty can be minimised if the discretion is exercised only in the most exceptional circumstances, having

---

[77] *Beresford* v. *Royal Insurance Co. Ltd.* [1937] 2 KB 197.

[78] [1996] Ch. 107.

[79] See, for example, *Lodge* v. *National Union Investment Co.* [1907] 1 Ch. 800 and *Nelson* v. *Nelson* (1995) 70 ALJR 47. Cp. *Kasumu* v. *Baba-Egbe* [1956] AC 539 where restitution on terms was denied because it was inconsistent with the policy of the statute by virtue of which the transaction was illegal. For general discussion of the award of restitutionary relief on terms see Enonchong, 'Illegality and the Presumption of Advancement' (1996) 4 *RLR* 78, 86–7.

[80] *Nelson* v. *Nelson* (1995) 70 AJLR 47, 92 (McHugh J).

regard to the nature of the harm involved, the plaintiff's culpability and the maximum sentence available. So, for example, the court should not allow a plaintiff to vindicate his or her proprietary rights in respect of property which is held on resulting trust where the plaintiff had contributed to the purchase of a house which was vested in the sole name of the defendant, in circumstances in which the house was intended to be used as a base for terrorist activities.[81]

(d) The next step

The Law Commission has recently published a consultation paper on the effect of illegality on contracts and trusts.[82] In this paper the Law Commission provisionally recommended that the existing complex law on the effect of illegality on transactions should be replaced by a discretion whether transactions should be enforced, property rights should be recognised and benefits should be restored.[83] But the Law Commission emphasises that this discretionary approach should be structured. In particular it states that:

We therefore provisionally propose that, in exercising its discretion, a court should consider: (i) the seriousness of the illegality involved; (ii) the knowledge and intention of the party . . . seeking to recover benefits conferred under [the transaction]; (iii) whether refusing to allow standard rights and remedies would deter illegality; (iv) whether refusing to allow standard rights and remedies would further the purpose of the rule which renders the transaction illegal; and (v) whether refusing to allow standard rights and remedies would be proportionate to the illegality involved.[84]

If such a reform were adopted illegality would probably continue to operate as a general defence to restitutionary claims, but the courts would be given greater opportunity to avoid unjust results by allowing the plaintiff's restitutionary claim to succeed despite the taint of illegality. The real concern with the proposals of the Law Commission is whether even a 'structured discretion' will result in too much uncertainty in an area where clarity is vital.

---

[81] See *Tinsley* v. *Milligan* [1994] 1 AC 340, 362 (Lord Goff). See also *Taylor* v. *Bhail* [1996] CLC 377.

[82] 'Illegal Transactions: The Effect of Illegality on Contracts and Trusts' (Law Com. No. 154, 1999).

[83] *Ibid*, pp. 9–10.   [84] *Ibid*, p. 9.

27

Incapacity

1. QUESTIONS OF POLICY

It was seen in Chapter 12 that incapacity can operate as a ground of restitution in its own right, in that it enables the plaintiff who is incapacitated to secure restitution where the incapacity arises from mental disorder, minority or institutional incapacity. In each of these cases there is a strong policy of protection to ensure that the person who is incapacitated does not suffer from entering into foolish transactions. The question which needs to be considered in this chapter is whether the fact that the defendant was incapacitated in some way can operate as a defence to defeat the plaintiff's restitutionary claim, regardless of the nature of that claim. This raises two contradictory policy questions.

(a) Does an incapacitated defendant deserve to be protected from restitutionary claims?

The effect of recognising a defence of incapacity is that the defendant is able to retain benefits which he or she would otherwise be required to restore to the plaintiff. Does the fact that the defendant is incapacitated in itself require the defendant to be protected from restitutionary claims? Giving the incapacitated defendant a defence to a restitutionary claim is more difficult to justify than recognising incapacity as a ground of restitution for a plaintiff who is incapacitated. This is because where the defendant is incapacitated and is not prejudiced by being required to make restitution to the plaintiff, there is no obvious reason why the defendant's incapacity should bar the plaintiff's claim. Where the defendant would be prejudiced in making restitution this is usually because the defendant's circumstances have changed and so he or she can rely on the defence of change of position.[1]

(b) Would the award of a restitutionary remedy to the plaintiff subvert the law of contract?

Usually the question of the defendant's incapacity arises where the plaintiff and defendant have entered into a contract which has been

---

[1] See Chapter 24.

vitiated by the defendant's incapacity. The plaintiff may have transferred a benefit to the defendant pursuant to the transaction which the plaintiff will then wish to recover. The consequent question of policy is whether the granting of a restitutionary remedy to the plaintiff against the incapacitated defendant can be considered to subvert the law of contract by virtue of which the contract was treated as vitiated in the first place. This is an important issue since it is a fundamental principle of the law of restitution that the award of restitutionary remedies must not subvert the law of contract.[2] If the contract was vitiated because of a policy of protecting the defendant from the consequences of his or her incapacity, perhaps this policy must be carried through to the law of restitution as well, so that the plaintiff's restitutionary claim fails.

Both of these policy questions must be borne in mind when considering whether different types of incapacity should operate as defences to restitutionary claims.

2. MINORITY

(a) Restitutionary claims founded on the reversal of unjust enrichment

(i) The supply of necessaries

Where the plaintiff has supplied a minor, who is defined as anybody under the age of 18,[3] with necessary goods or services pursuant to a contract, the plaintiff is able to recover the reasonable value of these necessaries[4] even though the contract itself is unenforceable.[5] It is clear therefore that the plaintiff's restitutionary claim will succeed and the minor has no defence of incapacity.

(ii) The supply of non-necessary benefits

Where the plaintiff has transferred benefits to a minor which cannot be characterised as necessaries the plaintiff is unable to enforce the contract against the minor.[6] The traditional view is that the plaintiff will not be able to bring a restitutionary claim against the minor for the value of the benefit transferred because the defendant has a defence of incapacity. Although this defence of minority has been recognised in a number of cases, careful analysis of these cases suggests that their conclusions

---

[2] See pp. 40–2 above.   [3] Family Law Reform Act 1969, s. 1.
[4] See the Sale of Goods Act 1979, s. 3(2), which applies to the sale and delivery of goods which can be characterised as necessaries.
[5] See pp. 313–14 above.   [6] See p. 415 above

are highly dubious in the light of recent developments in the law of restitution.

(1) Decisions which recognise a defence of minority

The leading case which suggests that the defendant's minority is a defence to restitutionary claims is *Cowern* v. *Nield*,[7] where the plaintiff paid the defendant, who was a minor, a sum of money for goods which the defendant subsequently failed to deliver. The plaintiff sued to recover the money on the ground of total failure of consideration, but the claim failed because the court concluded that it was not possible to imply a contract between the minor and the plaintiff since this would result in the indirect enforcement of a contract which was void. Similarly in *R. Leslie Ltd.* v. *Shiell*[8] the plaintiff had lent money to the defendant minor, who had made a fraudulent misrepresentation as to his age. The plaintiff sought to recover this money but was unable to do so, again on the ground that the court would not indirectly enforce a contract which was void by reason of the defendant's incapacity.[9]

The problem with the reasoning in these cases is that it is founded on the fact that the court would not imply a contract to make restitution where the defendant lacked the capacity to make a contract. But the implied contract theory of restitutionary claims was rejected by the House of Lords in *United Australia Ltd.* v. *Barclays Bank Ltd.*[10] It is now clear that the obligation to make restitution is imposed as a matter of law[11] and has nothing to do with the enforcement of any actual or implied contract between the parties. It follows that if the plaintiff had been awarded restitutionary relief in these cases where the defendant was a minor this would not have infringed the policy of the law which stated that any contract made between the parties was unenforceable.

(2) Should a defence of minority be recognised?

Although the reasoning of the cases which have recognised a defence of minority can be rejected, it is still necessary to consider whether, as a matter of policy, the defendant's minority should operate as a defence to the plaintiff's restitutionary claim. Whilst it is true that minors require some protection against the consequences of entering into foolish transactions which they are not able to detect because of their immaturity, the minor should not be over-protected, since this may cause injustice to the party with full capacity. It follows that the plaintiff's restitutionary claim against a minor should be defeated only where there is a danger of the

---

[7] [1912] 2 KB 419. See also *Bristow* v. *Eastman* (1794) 1 Esp. 172; 170 ER 317.
[8] [1914] 3 KB 607.   [9] *Ibid*, p. 612 (Lord Sumner).   [10] [1941] AC 1.
[11] See *Westdeutsche Landesbank Girozentrale* v. *Islington LBC* [1996] AC 669, 688 (Lord Goff).

minor being unduly prejudiced by virtue of the obligation to make restitution. Such prejudice will not arise where the minor still has the benefit or its product which the plaintiff had transferred to him or her, since the minor can justifiably be expected to return that which he or she has no right to retain. Where, however, the minor has dissipated the benefit he or she could be prejudiced if he or she were required to make restitution to the plaintiff, since the minor will need to find the value of the benefit from his or her own resources. But in circumstances such as this there is no need for the plaintiff's restitutionary claim to be defeated by a defence of incapacity, because the defence of change of position would presumably be applicable. Perhaps that defence should be interpreted more flexibly where the defendant is a minor, to give him or her greater protection against restitutionary claims than is available where the defendant is an adult. So where, for example, the minor has received a sum of money from the plaintiff to purchase necessaries and the minor wastes the money on extravagant parties, this may enable the minor to rely on the defence of change of position even though the defence would not have been available had the defendant been an adult because it would not have been equitable to allow the defence to succeed.[12] Consequently, the fact that the defendant was a minor should be taken into account when determining whether or not it is equitable for the change of position defence to succeed.

There was no obvious policy reason why the plaintiff's restitutionary claim should have failed in both *Cowern* v. *Neild*[13] and *R. Leslie Ltd.* v. *Shiell*[14] because there was nothing to suggest that the award of a restitutionary remedy would have prejudiced the minor. In *Cowern* v. *Nield* the minor had received money for goods which he had failed to deliver and, assuming that he had not changed his position, he should have been required to repay this money to the plaintiff. Equally, in *R. Leslie Ltd.* v. *Shiell* if the minor had been obliged to repay the plaintiff the sum of money he had borrowed at a reasonable rate of interest the plaintiff could not be considered to have taken advantage of the defendant's minority in any way.

It follows that there is no role for a defence of minority where the plaintiff's claim is founded on the defendant's unjust enrichment, since the defence of change of position, interpreted more liberally than normally, would give the defendant adequate protection against the plaintiff's restitutionary claim.

---

[12] See pp. 720–5 above.   [13] [1912] 2 KB 419.   [14] [1914] 3 KB 607.

(b) Restitutionary claims founded on wrongdoing

(i) Tort

Where the defendant has obtained a benefit as a result of the commission of a wrong there is no reason why the fact that the defendant was a minor should defeat the plaintiff's restitutionary claim. A minor does not deserve particular protection against restitutionary claims where he or she has obtained a benefit as a result of wrongdoing. This has been recognised in a number of cases. For example, in *Bristow* v. *Eastman*[15] the defendant was held liable for embezzling money from his employer. Here the underlying wrong was either the tort of conversion or deceit. It was specifically held that minority was not a defence to this action, since the action was founded on the commission of a tort.

Where, however, the tort on which the plaintiff's claim is founded is connected with a contract made with a minor, it has been held that, because the contract is unenforceable, the action grounded on the tort will also be barred, since if such a claim were allowed to succeed it would result in the indirect enforcement of the contract. This is illustrated by *Stocks* v. *Wilson*,[16] where the defendant, who was a minor, fraudulently misrepresented his age and consequently induced the plaintiff to sell and deliver to him furniture, paintings and artefacts for £300. The defendant sold some of these items and used the rest as security for a loan. The defendant failed to pay the plaintiff the agreed contract price. The plaintiff sued the defendant for breach of contract, and failed because the contract was unenforceable as a result of the defendant's minority. The plaintiff also sued the defendant for damages for deceit, and this action also failed because the deceit related to the contract. Similarly, in *Leslie* v. *Sheill*[17] where the plaintiff had been induced to contract with the minor by his fraudulent misrepresentation as to his age, it was held that the plaintiff could not obtain a remedy for the tort of deceit because such a remedy would indirectly enforce the contract which had been made.

The reasoning of the judges in both of these cases is unconvincing because the remedy which the plaintiff sought was founded on tort and not contract. The fact that the tort related to the formation of the contract is irrelevant, particularly where the plaintiff seeks a restitutionary remedy, since the effect of this remedy is not to enforce any contract which was made as a result of the commission of the tort, but simply to deprive the defendant of any benefits obtained from the commission of the wrong.

---

[15] (1794) 1 Esp. 171; 170 ER 317.   [16] [1913] 2 KB 235.   [17] [1914] 3 KB 607.

(ii) Equitable wrongdoing

Where the plaintiff's claim is founded on an equitable wrong the fact that the defendant is a minor is not a defence to the claim.[18]

(iii) Crime

Where the defendant has profited from the commission of the crime he or she should be required to disgorge any benefits derived from the crime by virtue of the principle that no criminal should be allowed to profit from a crime. This principle is so fundamental to the law of restitution that the defendant should be required to disgorge the profit even though he or she was a minor.

(iv) Breach of contract

Where the plaintiff's restitutionary claim is founded on the defendant's breach of contract, the fact that the defendant is a minor is a relevant consideration, because the policy of the law of contract should prevail even though the plaintiff seeks a restitutionary remedy. Since a contract is unenforceable against a minor it should follow that where the minor breaches the contract he or she cannot be considered to have committed a wrong. Consequently, if no wrong has been committed, there is no scope for the plaintiff to bring a restitutionary claim founded on restitution for wrongs. Here the defendant's minority does not operate as a defence to the plaintiff's claim; it simply prevents the plaintiff from establishing that claim in the first place.

(v) Conclusions

It follows that the defendant's minority should not operate as a defence to the plaintiff's restitutionary claim where that claim is founded on the commission of a wrong. But it is important to ensure that the award of a restitutionary remedy does not unduly prejudice the defendant. The mechanism for this is through the flexible application of the defence of change of position.

(c) Restitutionary claims founded on the vindication of property rights

Although in principle if the plaintiff wishes to recover property from the defendant it should be irrelevant that the defendant was a minor when he or she received the property, the defendant's minority must be taken into account when the property has been transferred under a contract. This is because, by virtue of section 3(1) of the Minors' Contracts Act

---

[18] *Stocks* v. *Wilson* [1913] 2 KB 235.

1987, the court has a discretion to order that the plaintiff can recover his or her property from such a defendant where it considers it to be just and equitable to do so. It follows that the law does contemplate that the plaintiff will be able to vindicate his or her proprietary rights against a minor, although the plaintiff does not have a right to a restitutionary remedy since the award of the remedy lies in the discretion of the court.

3. MENTAL INCAPACITY

Mental incapacity may take a variety of forms.[19] It may be permanent, as where the defendant is insane, or temporary, as where the defendant was drunk at the time of entering a transaction with the plaintiff. Whether mental incapacity can operate as a defence to restitutionary claims is something which has received little judicial attention. The leading case on the point is *Re Rhodes*[20] which, at first sight, appears to suggest that such a defence is recognised because the plaintiffs' restitutionary claim failed. The plaintiffs, who were relatives of the defendant, had paid some of the charges arising from the defendant living in a mental asylum. The plaintiffs sought to recover these charges from the defendant on the ground that they were necessaries, but this claim failed. This was not, however, because the defendant was incapacitated, but simply because the plaintiffs were not able to show that they intended to be repaid by the defendant. In other words, the plaintiffs had acted officiously. There was nothing in the case to indicate that the claim would otherwise have failed simply because the defendant was incapacitated.

Since the defendant's minority does not operate as a defence to restitutionary claims, there is no reason why a defence of mental incapacity should be recognised, particularly because both forms of incapacity have a similar function, namely to protect the incapacitated person from the adverse consequences of entering into foolish transactions. Where a mentally incapacitated defendant has received a benefit from the plaintiff there is no reason why the defendant should retain that benefit simply because of the incapacity. The only significance of the defendant's incapacity is, where his or her circumstances have changed since the benefit was received, the defence of change of position should be applied in a more flexible way than it would be if the defendant had full capacity.

---

[19] See p. 411 above.   [20] (1890) 44 Ch.D 94.

4. INSTITUTIONAL INCAPACITY

The question of incapacity has been particularly important in the context of companies which have entered into transactions which they do not have capacity to make. Such *ulta vires* transactions are null and void.[21] In a number of cases the courts have had to consider whether the fact that the defendant company was incapacitated constituted a bar to the plaintiff's restitutionary claim. Although this is no longer a relevant question, because by virtue of section 35 of the Companies Act 1985 the plaintiff can enforce a transaction which is beyond the capacity of the company, the old cases remain relevant since they assist in determining what the position of the common law is as to the defence of incapacity generally. Also the question of incapacity remains highly relevant in respect of other institutions which remain subject to the *ultra vires* doctrine, most notably public authorities.[22]

(a) Rejection of a defence of institutional incapacity

The general attitude of the common law has been that the fact that the defendant institution lacks capacity to enter into a transaction does not operate as a bar to the plaintiff's restitutionary claim. This is justifiable on policy grounds. The prime purpose of the *ultra vires* doctrine is to ensure that shareholders and creditors are protected from the consequences of the institution entering into speculative transactions. But this policy of protection is not furthered in any way by the defendant institution being able to retain benefits which had been obtained in respect of an *ultra vires* transaction. This approach is reflected in *Re Phoenix Life Assurance Co.*[23] where a company issued marine insurance policies to the plaintiff, which the company lacked capacity to do. When the company was wound up the plaintiff sought to enforce claims on these policies. Although the claims on the policies themselves were barred, because they were void as a result of the company's lack of capacity to issue them, the plaintiff was still able to recover the premiums in an action for money had and received, the ground of restitution being total failure of consideration. The plaintiff's claim was not affected in any way by the defendant's incapacity.

That institutional capacity should not be a defence to restitutionary claims at all is reflected in the litigation arising from public authorities

---

[21] *Ashbury Railway Carriage and Iron Co. Ltd.* v. *Riche* (1875) LR 7 HL 653.
[22] See in particular *Woolwich Equitable Building Society* v. *IRC* [1993] AC 70 and the litigation arising from interest rate swaps transactions.
[23] (1862) 2 J and H 441; 70 ER 1131. See also *Flood* v. *Irish Provident Assurance Co.* (1912) 46 ILT 214.

entering into interest rate swap transactions. These transactions were null and void because the local authorities lacked capacity to enter into them.[24] Consequently, where a financial institution sought restitution from the local authorities a defence of institutional incapacity, had it existed, would have defeated the plaintiff's claim. But restitution was not denied in any of the swaps cases on the ground of incapacity. Indeed restitutionary relief was awarded in many of the cases despite the defendant's incapacity.[25]

(b) Implicit recognition of a defence of institutional incapacity

There are, however, certain cases in which the defendant's incapacity has effectively operated as a defence to the plaintiff's restitutionary claim. The most important of these is the decision of the House of Lords in *Sinclair* v. *Brougham*[26] where the plaintiffs sought to recover money which they had lent to a building society which was carrying on a banking business even though it lacked capacity to do so. The House of Lords held that the plaintiffs' personal claim for restitution failed, because the award of restitutionary relief would have indirectly contradicted the *ultra vires* bar, by enabling the plaintiffs to recover their loan when the transaction was null and void. This did not, however, prevent the plaintiffs' proprietary claim in equity from succeeding, presumably because the award of a proprietary restitutionary remedy did not involve effective enforcement of the loan, since the plaintiffs could only recover what the defendant had retained rather than what the defendant had received.

Although *Sinclair* v. *Brougham* seems to deny personal restitutionary relief to the plaintiff, at least where he or she seeks restitution of money lent to the defendant, as a result of the defendant's incapacity making the transaction null and void, such a conclusion is no longer defensible. This was the conclusion of a majority of the House of Lords in *Westdeutsche Landesbank Girozentrale* v. *Islington London Borough Council*,[27] in which it was recognised that, since the obligation to make restitution is imposed by law, the award of a restitutionary remedy does not effectively enforce the loan transaction. It follows that, where the plaintiff has lent money to the defendant in a transaction which is void because of the defendant's incapacity, that incapacity cannot bar the plaintiff's claim.

[24] *Hazell* v. *Hammersmith and Fulham LBC* [1992] 2 AC 1.
[25] See, in particular, *Westdeutsche Landesbank Girozentrale* v. *Islington LBC* [1994] 1 WLR 938 (CA).
[26] [1914] AC 398.
[27] [1996] AC 669, 710 (Lord Browne-Wilkinson), p. 718 (Lord Slynn) and p. 738 (Lord Lloyd). Cp. Lord Goff at p. 688.

5. SHOULD A DEFENCE OF INCAPACITY BE RECOGNISED?

This analysis has shown that there is no justification for the law of restitution to recognise a defence of incapacity. The failure even to consider such a defence in the swaps cases illustrates its unimportance. It is to be hoped that the modern developments in the law of restitution will mean that in future the question of incapacity as a defence can be stated simply: there is no such defence.

28

Limitation Periods and Laches

For reasons of public policy most civil actions are subject to a time bar the effect of which is that, once a particular period of time has passed, the defendant can no longer be sued on that action. One of the main reasons for having time bars is so that the threat of an action does not continually hang over the defendant, so that, once the limitation period has passed, he or she can be certain that the benefit has been validly received and will not need to be returned to the plaintiff. The existence of time bars also act as an incentive for plaintiffs to bring claims as soon as possible. This is particularly advantageous since, as time passes, evidence may become less reliable and more difficult to obtain.

There are two distinct legal regimes relating to the barring of restitutionary actions by the passage of time. The first and most important is contained in the Limitation Act 1980, which specifies particular limitation periods for different types of actions. Unfortunately the Act does not, with certain minor exceptions, contain any specific provision relating to restitutionary claims, so the question of what is the appropriate period of limitation is a matter which is not free from difficulty.[1] The second regime is the equitable defence of laches, which determines whether an equitable action is time barred by reference to the justice of the case, all the surrounding circumstances considered. The Limitation Act applies to all common law claims and closely related equitable claims, whereas the defence of laches applies to what might be called purely equitable claims. Where the Limitation Act applies there is no scope for the application of the laches defence.[2]

1. LIMITATION PERIODS

The Limitation Act 1980 contains a variety of arbitrary limitation periods which apply to particular causes of action. Unlike the laches defence, these limitation periods must be applied strictly without the court having any discretion to determine whether the conduct of the parties is

---

[1] A similar problem has arisen in respect of the allocation of jurisdiction under the Brussels Convention 1968 where no specific provision is made for restitutionary claims. See *Kleinwort Benson Ltd.* v. *Glasgow CC* [1997] 3 WLR 923.

[2] *Re Baker* (1881) 20 Ch.D 230.

such that the periods should or should not be enforced. Where the plaintiff can sue under a number of different causes of action, such as unjust enrichment and equitable wrongdoing, the fact that one action is time barred does not prevent the plaintiff from relying on the other one.[3] The question of the appropriate limitation period for restitutionary claims needs to be examined in respect of each type of claim.

(a) Reversal of the defendant's unjust enrichment

(i) The usual limitation period

No specific provision is made in the Limitation Act 1980 for restitutionary claims which are founded on the reversal of the defendant's unjust enrichment. Consequently, it might be argued that no limitation period should be applicable to such claims.[4] But surely as a matter of policy the plaintiff's claim should fail when sufficient time has lapsed to remove the injustice of the defendant retaining the benefit which was received from the plaintiff.[5] Therefore, some limitation period is necessary, bearing in mind that the equitable doctrine of laches is generally inapplicable to such claims since it applies only where the plaintiff seeks equitable relief. A limitation period must be identified therefore by analogy with one of the causes of action for which the Limitation Act does make specific provision.

By section 5 of the Limitation Act 1980 actions which are founded on simple contract are barred after six years. The predecessor of this provision[6] was interpreted by Lord Greene MR in *Re Diplock*[7] as covering actions for money had and received, although 'the words used cannot be regarded as felicitous'. This conclusion was affirmed by Hobhouse J in *Westdeutsche Landesbank Girozentrale* v. *Islington LBC*[8] on the ground that such actions should be treated as akin to contract, and so a limitation period of six years is applicable. This is artificial and harks back to the implied contract theory, but since no specific provision is made for this type of restitutionary claim in the Limitation Act, it seems to be the best solution available. It is certainly better than concluding that such restitutionary actions are subject to no limitation period at all. In fact this conclusion is consistent with the Limitation Act 1623, section 3 of which provided a limitation period of six years for all assumpsit claims, and this provision continued to apply until 1939.

Specific provision is made in the Limitation Act 1980 for the recovery of money by virtue of any statute, where the limitation period is six years

---

[3] *Nelson* v. *Rye* [1996] 1 WLR 1378, 1389 (Laddie J).   [4] *Ibid*, p. 1390.
[5] McLean 'Limitation of Actions in Restitution' (1989) 48 *CLJ* 472, 475.
[6] Limitation Act 1939, s. 2(1)(a).   [7] [1948] Ch. 465, 514.
[8] [1994] 4 All ER 890, 943.

as well.[9] Consequently, restitutionary claims for money under the Law Reform (Frustrated Contracts) Act 1943 are subject to a limitation period of six years. Consistency demands that a similar limitation period should apply to all claims founded on the reversal of unjust enrichment, regardless of the ground of restitution on which the plaintiff relies.

(ii) Qualification of the general limitation period for particular restitutionary claims

Even though the limitation period for restitutionary claims founded on the reversal of the defendant's unjust enrichment should usually be six years, it is clear that for particular types of claim different considerations may apply.

(1) Claims in equity

Where the restitutionary relief which the plaintiff seeks is equitable the Limitation Act 1980 is inapplicable,[10] and so the equitable doctrine of laches applies.[11] Consequently, where the plaintiff seeks a restitutionary remedy on the ground of undue influence or the defendant's unconscionable conduct then, because such claims are equitable even though they are founded on the reversal of the defendant's unjust enrichment, it is the doctrine of laches rather than the Limitation Act which applies.[12]

(2) Contribution

Where the plaintiff brings a contribution claim under the Civil Liability (Contribution) Act 1978[13] the claim is subject to a limitation period of two years from the date on which the statutory right of action accrues.[14]

(3) Salvage

The limitation period for salvage claims is two years from the date on which the salvage services were rendered.[15]

(iii) The determination of when time starts to run

The limitation period begins to run from the date the cause of action accrues. For the purposes of a claim founded on the reversal of the defendant's unjust enrichment this is usually the point at which the defendant receives the enrichment.[16] Sometimes, however, the cause of action can

---

[9] Limitation Act 1980, s. 9.

[10] *Ibid*, s. 36(1).

[11] See p. 775 below.

[12] *Allcard* v. *Skinner* (1887) 36 Ch.D 145.

[13] See pp. 242–5 above.

[14] Limitation Act 1980, s. 10(1). To determine when the cause of action accrues see s. 10(2)–(4).

[15] Maritime Conventions Act 1980, s. 8. For a discussion of salvage claims see pp. 320–1 above.

[16] *Kleinwort Benson* v. *South Tyneside MBC* [1994] 4 All ER 972, 978 (Hobhouse J).

be established only after the defendant has received the enrichment, as will be the case where the ground of restitution is total failure of consideration. In such cases, time will begin to run only once the relevant ground of restitution can be established.[17] So, for example, it has been held that a restitutionary claim founded on frustration will accrue only once the consideration for the transaction failed.[18] Despite certain dicta that a restitutionary cause of action will accrue only once the plaintiff has demanded return of the enrichment,[19] the better view is that there is no such requirement, for otherwise the plaintiff would be able to postpone the date from which the limitation period begins to run until it suits him or her to inform the defendant of the restitutionary claim.[20]

There are a number of specific rules relating to the time from which the limitation period begins to run in certain cases.

(1) Plaintiff subject to incapacity

Where the plaintiff is under some form of disability, which means that he or she is a minor or is suffering from mental incapacity,[21] the limitation period will not begin to run until he or she has ceased to be under a disability or has died, and it will then run for a period of six years.[22]

(2) Claim founded on spontaneous or induced mistake

Where the claim is founded upon the defendant's fraud,[23] or the defendant has deliberately concealed from the plaintiff any fact relating to the plaintiff's action,[24] or where the claim relates to mistake[25] the limitation period will not begin to run until the plaintiff has discovered the fraud, concealment or mistake or could have discovered it with reasonable diligence. In *Peco Arts Inc.* v. *Hazlitt Gallery Ltd.*[26] it was held that, to determine whether the plaintiff could have discovered the fraud, concealment or mistake with reasonable diligence, it was necessary to consider whether the ordinary prudent person would have done so in the particular circumstances of the case.

The effect of this provision is that it is always necessary to identify with

---

[17] *Guardian Ocean Cargoes Ltd.* v. *Banco de Brasil (No. 2)* [1994] 2 Lloyd's Rep. 152, 160 (Saville LJ).

[18] *BP Exploration Co. (Libya) Ltd.* v. *Hunt* [1983] 2 AC 352, 373 (Lord Brandon).

[19] See *Freeman* v. *Jeffries* (1869) LR 4 Exch. 189 at p. 198 (Martin B) and p. 200 (Bramwell B).

[20] See *Baker* v. *Courage and Co.* [1910] 1 KB 56, 65 (Hamilton J).

[21] Limitation Act 1980, s. 38(2).

[22] *Ibid*, s. 28.   [23] *Ibid*, s. 32(1)(a).   [24] *Ibid*, s. 32(1)(b).

[25] *Ibid*, s. 32(1)(c). A claim will relate to mistake only where the mistake forms an essential part of the claim: *Phillip-Higgins* v. *Harper* [1954] 1 QB 411, 419 (Pearson J). This will be the case where the plaintiff's restitutionary claim is founded on mistake. In *Kleinwort Benson Ltd.* v. *Lincoln CC* [1998] 3 WLR 1095 the House of Lords recognised that this provision also applies to mistakes of law.

[26] [1983] 1 WLR 1315.

care what the ground of restitution is on which the plaintiff's claim is based. For if, for example, it is founded on mistake, time will not start to run from when the defendant has received an enrichment, but will begin only once the plaintiff has or should have discovered the mistake. Provision is made only for fraud, mistake and deliberate concealment. This is unfortunate. Where, for example, the plaintiff has been subjected to duress surely time should not begin to run until the duress has ceased, for the plaintiff who has succumbed to the defendant's threats cannot be expected to commence restitutionary proceedings until the threats have ceased to operate.[27]

(3) Recovery of debts or other liquidated pecuniary claims

Where the plaintiff seeks to recover a debt or any other liquidated pecuniary claim and the defendant has acknowledged the plaintiff's claim or has made any payment in respect of it, time will begin to run only from the date of acknowledgement or payment.[28] The acknowledgement or payment by the defendant will be relevant only if it relates to the particular debt or other liquidated pecuniary claim which the plaintiff seeks to be paid.[29]

This provision should be applicable to all claims for money had and received and claims for money paid to the use of the defendant because these are liquidated pecuniary claims which are assessed by reference to the amount of money received by the defendant. In principle the provision could not be extended to cover claims for the reasonable value of services or goods because such remedies depend on the assessment of the court as to the value of the benefit received by the defendant and so do not constitute a liquidated claim. But in *Amontilla Ltd.* v. *Telefusion plc.*[30] it was held that a *quantum meruit* claim for the reasonable value of building services constituted a liquidated pecuniary claim within section 29(5). This is a highly dubious decision simply because a *quantum meruit* claim cannot be characterised as a liquidated claim.

(iv) Should a different general limitation period be recognised?

Is six years an appropriate limitation period for most restitutionary claims founded on unjust enrichment? All limitation periods are arbitrary but, as Burrows has tentatively suggested, it may be argued that in the light of the recognition of the defence of change of position, the limitation period for restitutionary claims could be longer than for contract

---

[27] See McLean, 'Limitation of Actions in Restitution' (1989) CLJ 472, 481. Cp. the equitable doctrine of laches which will not apply in cases of undue influence until the plaintiff has ceased to be unduly influenced by the defendant. See p. 776 below.

[28] Limitation Act 1980, s. 29(5).

[29] *Kleinwort Benson* v. *South Tyneside MBC* [1994] 4 All ER 972, 981 (Hobhouse J).

[30] (1987) 9 Constr. LR 139.

and tort claims, simply because the defence of change of position exists to give the defendant some security in the validity of his or her receipt.[31] But it is too early to say whether the defence will have that effect, particularly because it seems that change of position will be interpreted restrictively. Consequently, it is entirely appropriate that the limitation period for restitutionary claims is consistent with that for other causes of action involving civil obligations.

(b) Restitution for wrongs

(i) Restitutionary claims founded on the commission of tort or breach of contract

Where the plaintiff's restitutionary claim is founded on tort or breach of contract the limitation period should be six years. This is because the underlying cause of action for the plaintiff's claim is the tort or the breach of contract, and so the limitation period for those causes of action should apply even where the plaintiff seeks a restitutionary remedy. By sections 2 and 5 of the 1980 Limitation Act actions which are founded on tort and contract respectively are subject to a six-year limitation period. If the wrong is statute-barred then there is no longer a cause of action on which the plaintiff's claim can be based.[32]

Unfortunately, this simple analysis has not been reflected in the cases. The most important decision is *Chesworth* v. *Farrar*,[33] where the plaintiff brought an action for money had and received to recover the proceeds of sale of converted goods. The question for the court was whether this was a cause of action in tort, for if it was a limitation period of six months was applicable, this being the limitation period in respect of tortious actions against the estate of a deceased tortfeasor.[34] The court adopted a purposive construction of the legislation to determine whether the tort limitation period applied to a restitutionary claim and concluded that it did not. Rather, because the plaintiff's action was analogous to a contractual action, a limitation period of six years applied, although the judge did recognise that it was crucial for the plaintiff's restitutionary claim that he established that the tort of conversion had been committed. But if the plaintiff's claim depended on proof of the commission of a tort, surely the limitation period for that tort was applicable. This is because the purpose of a limitation period is to bar the cause of action rather than the particular remedy. If the cause of action cannot be sued on it follows that the plaintiff cannot obtain any remedy, regardless of the type of remedy which he or she seeks. The decision in *Chesworth* v. *Farrar* must be

---

[31] Burrows, *The Law of Restitution*, p. 439.
[32] *Beaman* v. *ARTS Ltd.* [1948] 2 All ER 89, 92–3 (Denning J).
[33] [1967] 1 QB 407.   [34] Such a limitation period no longer exists.

wrong.

That this is the proper conclusion is supported by section 23 of the Limitation Act which states that, where the plaintiff seeks the remedy of account, the relevant limitation period is that of the underlying cause of action. In other words, this provision acknowledges that the limitation period is determined by the underlying cause of action and not the remedy sought. Consequently, if the plaintiff seeks an account of profits following the infringement of a copyright the limitation period for the account is the same as that for the infringement of copyright.[35]

Where the plaintiff's claim is founded on tort or breach of contract the cause of action accrues from the date the wrong was committed. Burrows has suggested that time should start from the date the enrichment is received or the tort or breach of contract occurs, whichever is the later.[36] This would be consistent with the similar rule which applies where the plaintiff's claim is founded on the reversal of the defendant's unjust enrichment. But this assumes that where the plaintiff seeks a restitutionary remedy founded on a wrong he or she is suing in respect of a different cause of action. This is plainly wrong, and so there is no need for any different rule relating to the accrual of the cause of action where the plaintiff seeks to obtain a restitutionary remedy in respect of tort or breach of contract.

The date for the commencement of the limitation period will, however, be delayed if any of the particular statutory provisions under the Limitation Act is applicable. For example, where the plaintiff is the victim of fraud, as is the case where the defendant has committed the tort of deceit, the limitation period is postponed until the plaintiff has discovered the fraud or could have discovered it with reasonable diligence.[37] Similarly, where the plaintiff's claim is dependent on proof of a mistake, as is the case where the plaintiff sues in respect of a misrepresentation, the limitation period begins to run only once the plaintiff has or should reasonably have discovered the mistake.[38]

(ii) Restitutionary claims founded on equitable wrongs

Where the plaintiff's claim is founded on the commission of one of the equitable wrongs generally the Limitation Act 1980 is inapplicable[39] and the equitable doctrine of laches applies. So, for example, the Limitation Act 1980 does not generally apply to claims for breach of fiduciary duty.[40]

---

[35] *Nelson* v. *Rye* [1996] 1 WLR 1378, 1389 (Laddie J).
[36] Burrows, *The Law of Restitution*, p. 449.   [37] Limitation Act 1980, s. 32(1)(a).
[38] *Ibid*, s. 32(1)(c).   [39] *Ibid*, s. 36(1).
[40] *Nelson* v. *Rye* [1996] 1 WLR 1378, 1390 (Laddie J). This conclusion was considered, however, by Millett LJ to be incorrect in *Paragon Finance plc.* v. *D.B. Thakerar & Co. (a firm)* [1999] 1 All ER 400, 415–16, at least where the fiduciary is not a trustee.

There are, however, particular statutory provisions in respect of certain claims founded on equitable wrongdoing. So, for example, where the plaintiff sues the defendant for non-fraudulent breach of trust, there is a six-year statutory limitation period,[41] although this will not apply where the claim is brought against a fraudulent trustee.[42]

(c) Vindication of proprietary rights

Determining the appropriate limitation period for restitutionary claims which are founded on the vindication of proprietary rights is a matter of some complexity, depending on the nature of the property in which the plaintiff has a proprietary interest and the nature of the plaintiff's restitutionary claim. The following principles are particularly relevant to the determination of the appropriate limitation period for such claims.

(i) Land

Where the plaintiff brings an action to recover land such a claim is subject to a limitation period of 12 years.[43] Once the limitation period has passed the title of the owner of the land is automatically extinguished,[44] so the plaintiff ceases to have a proprietary base on which he or she can found a proprietary restitutionary claim.

(ii) Restitutionary claims in respect of converted goods

Where the plaintiff's property has been converted, the plaintiff's claim is subject to a six-year limitation period because conversion is a tort. Where, however, the property is converted again before the plaintiff is able to recover it, there is no new limitation period for the second conversion.[45] So, for example, if D1 converts the plaintiff's property on 1 January 1994 and D2 converts the same property on 1 January 1999, the plaintiff has only one year to sue D2. Once the limitation period has passed in respect of any action relating to conversion the plaintiff's title to the property is extinguished.[46]

(iii) Recovery of stolen property

Where the plaintiff brings a restitutionary claim in respect of stolen property such a claim is not subject to a six-year limitation period.[47]

(iv) Equitable proprietary claims

Most equitable proprietary claims are not subject to a limitation period

---

[41]   Limitation Act 1980, s. 21(3).

[42]   *Ibid*, s. 21(a). 'Trustee' includes resulting and constructive trustees: Trustee Act 1925, s. 68(17), incorporated by Limitation Act 1980, s. 38(1).

[43]   Limitation Act 1980, s. 15.   [44]   *Ibid*, s. 17.   [45]   *Ibid*, s. 3(1).

[46]   *Ibid*, s. 3(2).   [47]   *Ibid*, s. 4(1).

under the 1980 Act and will only be barred by virtue of the doctrine of laches. The 1980 Act does, however, make specific provision for claims to recover trust property from anybody other than the trustee, such claims being subject to a limitation period of six years.[48] But there is no limitation period in respect of claims to recover trust property or the proceeds of trust property from a trustee.[49] Claims to the personal estate of a deceased person are barred after 12 years from the date on which the right to receive the share or interest accrued,[50] though no limitation period applies where the trustee was fraudulent.[51]

2. LACHES

(a) The function of the laches defence

Laches is an equitable doctrine which defeats the plaintiff's equitable claim where he or she is dilatory in suing the defendant.[52] The defence applies in all cases where the plaintiff seeks an equitable remedy, such as an account of profits, rescission[53] and equitable proprietary remedies. The rationale for the defence is that the plaintiff's claim should be defeated where there is such delay in commencing proceedings that it would be unjust to the particular defendant to allow a plaintiff to enforce his or her rights.

The function of the defence was identified by the Privy Council in *Lindsay Petroleum Co.* v. *Hurd*[54] in the following terms:

the doctrine of laches in courts of equity is not an arbitrary or technical doctrine. Where it would be practically unjust to give a remedy, either because the party has, by his conduct, done that which might fairly be regarded as equivalent to a waiver of it, or where by his conduct and neglect he has . . . put the other party in a situation in which it would not be reasonable to place him if the remedy were afterwards to be asserted . . . lapse of time and delay are most material. But in every case, if an argument against relief, which otherwise would be just, is founded upon mere delay . . . the validity of that defence must be tried upon principles substantially equitable. Two circumstances, always important in

---

[48] Limitation Act 1980, s. 21(3).

[49] *Ibid*, s. 21(1)(b). 'Trustee' includes resulting and constructive trustees, and personal representatives. See Trustee Act 1925, s. 68(17). The reference to constructive trustee here means that no limitation period applies in respect of actions for knowing receipt because the defendant who is held liable is a constructive trustee. But see Millett LJ in *Paragon Finance plc.* v. *D.B. Thakerar & Co. (a firm)* [1999] 1 All ER 400, 409.

[50] Limitation Act 1980, s. 22(a). See *Re Diplock* [1948] Ch. 465.

[51] *Ibid*, s. 21(1)(a). This provision will be applicable even where the trustee is not the defendant: *Baker Ltd.* v. *Medway Building and Supplies Ltd.* [1958] 1 WLR 1216.

[52] The doctrine of laches is preserved by the Limitation Act 1980, s. 36(2).

[53] *Allcard* v. *Skinner* (1887) 36 Ch.D 145.   [54] (1874) LR 5 PC 221, 239–40.

such cases, are, the length of the delay and the nature of the acts done during the interval, which might affect either party and cause a balance of justice or injustice in taking the one course or the other, so far as relates to the remedy.

(b) Establishing laches

(i) Relevant factors

When deciding whether the laches defence should bar the plaintiff's restitutionary claim the judge must exercise his or her discretion to decide where the balance of justice lies. A number of factors have been identified to assist in the exercise of this discretion. Particularly important factors are the extent of the delay, the degree of prejudice suffered by the defendant as a result of the delay, the extent to which this was caused by the plaintiff and whether the plaintiff knew that the defendant would suffer prejudice from the delay.[55] Lengthy delay will usually not be sufficient in itself to bar relief. Neither is it necessary to show that the prejudice suffered by the defendant was caused by the delay. Although laches is a separate defence from that involving limitation periods, the statutory limitation period is a useful indicator of what constitutes a reasonable time in which the action should be commenced.[56]

Where the plaintiff has been subject to undue influence time will start to run only once the plaintiff is free to exercise an independent choice, in other words once the undue influence has ceased to operate.[57] But once the influence has been removed, the plaintiff only has a reasonable time in which to bring proceedings.

(ii) Relevance of the plaintiff's knowledge of his or her claim

Laches will be established only where the plaintiff knew of his or her claim, or was aware of the possibility that he or she might have such a claim.[58] So, for example, in *Lindsay Petroleum Co.* v. *Hurd*[59] the plaintiff successfully rescinded a conveyance of land on the ground of fraudulent misrepresentation, even though he sought to rescind the conveyance 15 months after it had been made. This was because the plaintiff had acted promptly once he had discovered the fraudulent misrepresentation. However, in *Leaf* v. *International Galleries*[60] rescission on the ground of innocent misrepresentation was barred since five years had passed since the plaintiff had entered into the transaction. But the plaintiff had discovered that the defendant had made an innocent misrepresentation only shortly before he sought to rescind the contract and he could not

---

[55] *Nelson* v. *Rye* [1996] 1 WLR 1378, 1398 (Laddie J).
[56] *Allcard* v. *Skinner* (1887) 36 Ch.D 145.   [57] *Ibid*, p. 187 (Lindley LJ).
[58] *Ibid*, p. 192 (Bowen LJ).   [59] (1873) LR 5 PC 221.
[60] [1950] 2 KB 86.

reasonably have discovered this any earlier. Perhaps the stricter approach to the application of the doctrine which was adopted in this case can be justified on the ground that the misrepresentation was innocent rather than fraudulent, so that the balance of justice was not so much in the plaintiff's favour.

(iii) Nelson *v.* Rye

An important decision which illustrates how the judge determines whether the plaintiff's restitutionary claim should be defeated by the defence of laches is *Nelson* v. *Rye*.[61] In this case the plaintiff was a professional musician who had appointed the defendant to manage his affairs. It was agreed that the defendant would pay the plaintiff annually the net profits which the plaintiff had earned. After 10 years the defendant terminated the relationship without having paid the plaintiff any of the profits which were due to him. 14 months later the plaintiff commenced proceedings to recover these profits on the ground of breach of fiduciary duty. The plaintiff's claim was only partially successful since it was held that, in respect of the profits due from the first five years of the business relationship, his delay in bringing proceedings had caused the defendant substantial prejudice so that it would be unreasonable and unjust to allow the plaintiff to assert his right to an account for this period. This was because the judge found that the plaintiff had wilfully refused to involve himself in his financial affairs. The judge concluded that the defendant had suffered prejudice as a result of the delay because he was unable to give evidence about what was actually due to the plaintiff after the deduction of expenses he had been prejudiced by the delay, since he had destroyed many invoices and receipts which were more than six years old, and his memory would become less reliable over the passage of time.

3. REFORM OF THE LAW ON LIMITATION PERIODS

The Law Commission has published a consultation paper on the reform of the law on limitation periods.[62] In that paper the Law Commission provisionally recommends that a core regime should regulate limitation periods for claims, including restitutionary claims. According to this regime there would be an initial limitation period of three years from the date on which the plaintiff knew or ought reasonably to have known of the existence of the cause of action. In addition, however, the plaintiff would not be able to bring a claim more than 10 years after the date of the

---

[61] [1996] 1 WLR 1378.   [62] 'Limitation of Actions' (Law Com. No. 151, 1998).

act or omission which gave rise to his or her claim. The courts would not have a discretion to disapply this limitation period. If the law on limitation periods were reformed in this way it would bring much needed certainty to an area of the law which is of great practical importance but is unnecessarily complicated.

Bibliography

ANDREWS, N., 'Mistaken Settlements of Disputable Claims' [1989] *LMCLQ* 431
—— and BEATSON, J., 'Common Law Tracing: Springboard or Swan-song?' (1997) 113 *LQR* 21
ARISTOTLE, *Nichomachean Ethics* (ed. Ross, D., Oxford: Oxford University Press, 1984)
ARROWSMITH, S., 'Mistake and The Role of the "Submission to an Honest Claim" ' in *Essays on the Law of Restitution* (ed. Burrows, A.S., Oxford: Clarendon Press, 1991) p. 17
ASHWORTH, A., *Principles of Criminal Law* (2nd edn., Oxford: Clarendon Press, 1995)
ATIYAH, P.S., *The Rise and Fall of Freedom of Contract* (Oxford: Clarendon Press, 1979)
—— 'Economic Duress and the "Overborne Will" ' (1982) 98 *LQR* 197
BAKER, J., 'The History of Quasi-Contract in English Law' in *Restitution: Past, Present and Future* (ed. Cornish, W., Nolan, R., O'Sullivan, J., Virgo, G., Oxford: Hart Publishing, 1998) p. 37
BAMFORTH, N., 'Unconscionability as a Vitiating Factor' [1995] *LMCLQ* 538
BARKER, K., 'Restitution of Passenger Fare' [1993] *LMCLQ* 291
—— 'Unjust Enrichment: Containing the Beast' [1995] *OJLS* 457
—— 'After Change of Position: Good Faith Exchange in the Modern Law of Restitution' in *Laundering and Tracing* (ed. Birks, P.B.H., Oxford: Clarendon Press, 1995) p. 191
—— 'Rescuing Remedialism in Unjust Enrichment Law: Why Remedies are Right' (1998) 57 *CLJ* 301
—— 'Equitable Title and Common Law Conversion: The Limits of the Fusionist Ideal' (1998) 6 *RLR* 150
—— '*O'Brien*, Notice and the Onus of Proof' in *Restitution and Banking Law* (ed. Rose, F., Oxford: Mansfield Press, 1998) p. 78
BEALE, H., 'Points on Misrepresentation' (1995) 111 *LQR* 385
—— 'Damages for Poor Service' (1996) 112 *LQR* 205
BEATSON, J., 'Duress as a Vitiating Factor in Contract' (1974) 33 *CLJ* 99
—— *The Use and Abuse of Unjust Enrichment* (Oxford: Clarendon Press, 1991)
—— 'Restitution of Taxes, Levies and Other Imposts: Defining the Extent of the *Woolwich* Principle' (1993) 109 *LQR* 401
—— 'Mistakes of Law and *Ultra Vires* Public Authority Receipts: The Law Commission Report' (1995) 3 *RLR* 280
—— *Anson's Law of Contract* (27th edn., Oxford: Oxford University Press, 1998)
BIGWOOD, R., 'Undue Influence: "Implied Consent" or "Wicked Exploitation"?' (1996) 16 *OJLS* 503
BIRKS, P.B.H., '*Negotiorum Gestio* and the Common Law' (1971) 24 *CLP* 110
—— 'The Recovery of Carelessly Mistaken Payments' (1972) 25 *CLP* 179
—— 'Restitution and Wrongs' (1982) 35 *CLP* 53

BIRKS, P.B.H., 'Restitution and the Freedom of Contract' (1985) 38 *CLP* 141

—— 'Restitutionary Damages for Breach of Contract: *Snepp* and the Fusion of Law and Equity' [1987] *LMCLQ* 421

—— 'Misdirected Funds: Restitution from the Recipient' [1989] *LMCLQ* 296

—— *An Introduction to the Law of Restitution* (revised edn., Oxford: Clarendon Press, 1989)

—— 'The Travails of Duress' [1990] *LMCLQ* 342

—— 'Restitution without Counter-Restitution' [1990] *LMCLQ* 330

—— 'Restitution from the Executive: A Tercentenary Footnote to the Bill of Rights' in *Essays on Restitution* (ed. Finn, P., Sydney: The Law Book Co., 1990) p. 161

—— 'The English Recognition of Unjust Enrichment' [1991] *LMCLQ* 473

—— 'In Defence of Free Acceptance' in *Essays on the Law of Restitution* (ed. Burrows, A.S., Oxford: Clarendon Press, 1991) p. 109

—— *Restitution—The Future* (Sydney: The Federation Press, 1992)

—— 'Civil Wrongs: A New World' in *Butterworth Lectures 1990–1* (London: Butterworths, 1992)

—— 'Restitution and Resulting Trusts' in *Equity: Contemporary Legal Developments* (ed. Goldstein, S.R., Jerusalem: Faculty of Law, Hebrew University of Jerusalem, 1992), p. 335

—— 'No Consideration: Restitution after Void Contracts' (1993) 23 *Univ. WALR* 195

—— 'The Proceeds of Mortgage Fraud' (1996) 10 *TLI* 2

—— 'Equity in the Modern Law: An Exercise in Taxonomy' (1996) 26 *Univ. WALR* 1

—— 'Failure of Consideration' in *Consensus ad Idem* (ed. Rose, F. London: Sweet and Maxwell, 1996) p. 179

—— 'Change of Position: The Nature of the Defence and its Relationship to Other Restitutionary Defences' in *Restitution: Developments in Unjust Enrichment* (ed. McInnes, M.P., Sydney: LBC Information Services, 1996) p. 49

—— 'Property and Unjust Enrichment: Categorical Truths' [1997] *NZ Law Rev.* 623

—— 'On Taking Seriously the Difference Between Tracing and Claiming' (1997) 11 *TLI* 2

—— 'Misnomer' in *Restitution: Past, Present and Future* (ed. Cornish, W., Nolan, R., O'Sullivan, J., Virgo, G., Oxford: Hart Publishing, 1998) p. 1

—— 'Notice and Onus in *O'Brien*' (1998) 12 *TLI* 2

—— 'The Law of Restitution at the End of an Epoch' (1999) 28 *Univ. WALR* 13

—— and BEATSON, J., 'Unrequested Payment of Another's Debt' (1976) 92 *LQR* 188

—— and CHIN, N.Y., 'On the Nature of Undue Influence' in *Good Faith and Fault in Contract Law* (ed. Beatson, J., and Friedmann, D., Oxford: Clarendon Press, 1995) p. 57

BROWNE-WILKINSON, N., 'Constructive Trusts and Unjust Enrichment' (1996) 10 *TLI* 98

BURROWS, A.S., 'Contract. Tort and Restitution—A Satisfactory Division or Not?' (1983) *LQR* 217

—— 'Law Commission Report on Pecuniary Restitution on Breach of Contract' (1984) 47 *MLR* 76

—— 'Free Acceptance and the Law of Restitution' (1988) 104 *LQR* 576

—— *The Law of Restitution* (London: Butterworths, 1993)

—— 'Restitution from Assignees' (1994) 2 *RLR* 52

—— 'Swaps and the Friction Between Common Law and Equity' (1995) 3 *RLR* 15

—— 'Restitution: Where Do We Go From Here?' (1997) 50 *CLP* 95

—— and McKENDRICK, E., *Case and Materials on the Law of Restitution* (Oxford: Oxford University Press, 1997)

BUTLER, P.A., 'Mistaken Payments, Change of Position and Restitution' in *Essays on Restitution* (ed. Finn, P., Sydney: The Law Book Co., 1990) p. 87

CAPPER, D., 'Damages for Breach of the Equitable Duty of Confidence' (1994) 14 *LS* 313

—— 'Unconscionable Bargains' in *One Hundred and Fifty Years of Irish Law* (ed. Dawson, Greer, and Ingrams, London: SLS/Round Hall Sweet and Maxwell, 1996), p. 45

—— 'Undue Influence and Unconscionability: A Rationalisation' (1998) 114 *LQR* 479

CARTER, J.W., 'Ineffective Transactions' in *Essays on Restitution* (ed. Finn, P., Sydney: The Law Book Co., 1990) p. 206

CARTWRIGHT, J., 'An Unconscionable Bargain' (1993) 109 *LQR* 530

CHADWICK, J., 'A Testator's Bounty to his Slayer' (1914) 30 *LQR* 211

CHAMBERS, R., 'Change of Position on the Faith of the Receipt' (1996) 4 *RLR* 103

—— *Resulting Trusts* (Oxford: Clarendon Press, 1997)

CHEN-WISHART, M., 'Loss Sharing, Undue Influence and Manifest Disadvantage' (1994) 110 *LQR* 173

—— 'The *O'Brien* Principle and Substantive Unfairness' (1997) 56 *CLJ* 60

—— 'Restitutionary Damages for Breach of Contract' (1998) 114 *LQR* 363

Chitty's Law of Contract (27th edn., London: Sweet and Maxwell, 1994)

COHEN, 'Change of Position in Quasi-Contracts' (1931–2) 45 *Harv. LR* 1333

COOKE, E., 'Trespass, Mesne Profits and Restitution' (1994) 110 *LQR* 420

—— 'Estoppel and the Protection of Expectations' (1997) 17 *LS* 258

COOTE, B., 'Validation Under the Illegal Contracts Act' (1992) 15 *NZULR* 80

—— 'Contract Damages, *Ruxley* and the Performance Interest' (1997) 56 *CLJ* 537

CORNISH, W.R., 'Colour of Office: Restitutionary Redress Against Public Authority' [1987] *JMCL* 41

COWAN, D.S., EDMUNDS, R., and LOWRY, J., '*Lister and Co.* v. *Stubbs*: Who Profits?' [1996] *JBL* 22

CRETNEY, S., 'Mere Puppets, Folly and Imprudence: Undue Influence for the Twenty-First Century' (1994) 2 *RLR* 3

CRILLEY, D., 'A Case of Proprietary Overkill' (1994) 2 *RLR* 57

DAVERN, R., 'Common Law Tracing, Profits and the Doctrine of Tracing Back' (1997) 4 *RLR* 92

DAVIES, D., 'Restitution and Equitable Wrongs: An Australian Analogue' in *Consensus ad Idem* (ed. Rose, F., London: Sweet and Maxwell, 1996) p. 158

DAWSON, J.P., 'Economic Duress—An Essay in Perspective' (1947) 45 *Mich. LR* 253

—— '*Negotiorum Gestio*: The Altruistic Intermeddler' (1961) 74 *Harv. LR* 817

DICKSON, B., 'An Action for Unjust Enrichment' (1983) 34 *NILQ* 106

—— 'Restitution and Illegal Transactions' in *Essays on the Law of Restitution* (ed. Burrows, A., Oxford: Clarendon Press, 1991) p. 171

EARNSHAW, T.K., and PACE, P.J., 'Let the Hand Receiving It Be Ever So Chaste' (1974) 37 *MLR* 481

ELLIOTT, S.B., 'Restitutionary Compensatory Damages' (1998) 6 *RLR* 135

ENONCHONG, N., 'Title Claims and Illegal Transactions' (1995) 111 *LQR* 135

—— 'Illegality and the Presumption of Advancement' (1996) 4 *RLR* 78

—— *Illegal Transactions* (London: LLP Ltd., 1998)

EVANS, SIR W., 'An Essay on the Action for Money Had and Received' (1998) 6 *RLR* 1

FARNSWORTH, E.A., 'Your Loss or My Gain? The Dilemma of the Disgorgement Principle in Breach of Contract' (1985) 94 *Yale LJ* 1339

FINN, P.D. (ed.), *Fiduciary Obligations* (Sydney: Law Book Co., 1977)

—— 'Equitable Doctrine and Discretion in Remedies' in *Restitution: Past, Present and Future* (ed. Cornish, W., Nolan, R., O'Sullivan, J., Virgo, G., Oxford: Hart Publishing, 1998) p. 251

FLYNN, L., 'No Taxation Without Redistribution—The Law Commission's Proposals on the Recovery of Overpaid Taxes' [1995] *BTR* 15

FOX, D., 'The Transfer of Legal Title to Money' (1996) 4 *RLR* 60

—— '*Bona Fide* Purchase and the Currency of Money' (1996) 55 *CLJ* 547

FREIBERG, A., 'Confiscating the Literary Proceeds of Crime' [1992] *Crim. LR* 96

FRIEDMANN, D., 'Payment of Another's Debt' (1983) 99 *LQR* 534

—— 'Restitution of Benefits Obtained Through the Appropriation of Property or the Commission of a Wrong' (1980) 80 *Columbia Law Review* 504

—— 'The Efficient Breach Fallacy' (1989) 18 *JLS* 1

—— 'The Performance Interest in Contract Damages' (1995) 111 *LQR* 628

—— 'Restitution for Wrongs: The Basis of Liability' in *Restitution: Past, Present and Future* (ed. Cornish, W., Nolan, R., O'Sullivan, J., Virgo, G., Oxford: Hart Publishing, 1998) p. 133

FULLER, L.L., and PERDUE, W.R., 'The Reliance Interest in Contract Damages' (1936–7) 46 *Yale LJ* 52

GARDNER, S., 'Knowing Assistance and Knowing Receipt: Taking Stock' (1996) 112 *LQR* 56

—— 'Wives' Guarantees of their Husbands' Debts' (1999) 115 *LQR* 1

GARNER, M., 'The Role of Subjective Benefit in the Law of Unjust Enrichment' (1990) 10 *OJLS* 42

GLOVER, J., 'The Identification of Fiduciaries' in *Privacy and Loyalty* (ed. Birks, P.B.H., Oxford: Clarendon Press, 1997) p. 269

GOFF, R., and JONES, G.H., *The Law of Restitution* (5th edn., London: Sweet and Maxwell, 1998)

GOODE, R.M., 'The Bank's Right to Recover Money Paid on a Stopped Cheque' (1981) 97 *LQR* 254

—— 'Ownership and Obligation in Commercial Transactions' (1987) 103 *LQR* 433

—— 'Property and Unjust Enrichment' in *Essays on the Law of Restitution* (ed. Burrows, A.S., Oxford: Clarendon Press, 1991) p. 215

—— *Commercial Law* (2nd edn., Harmondsworth: Penguin Books, 1995)

GOODHART, W., 'Restitutionary Damages for Breach of Contract: The Remedy that Dare Not Speak Its Name' (1995) 3 *RLR* 3

GRANTHAM, R.B., 'Doctrinal Bases for the Recognition of Proprietary Rights' (1996) *OJLS* 561

—— and RICKETT, C.E.F., 'Property and Unjust Enrichment: Categorical Truths or Unnecessary Complexity?' [1997] 2 *NZ Law Rev.* 668

—— 'Restitution, Property and Mistaken Payments' (1997) 5 *RLR* 83

—— 'Trust Money as an Unjust Enrichment: A Misconception' [1998] *LMCLQ* 514

GRODECKI, J.K., '*In Pari Delicto Potior Est Conditio Defendentis*' (1995) 71 *LQR* 254

GULLIFER, L., 'Recovery of Misappropriated Assets: Orthodoxy Re-established?' [1995] *LMCLQ* 446

GUMMOW, W.M.C., 'Unjust Enrichment, Restitution and Proprietary Remedies' in *Essays on Restitution* (ed. Finn, P., Sydney: The Law Book Co., 1990) p. 47

GURRY, F., *Breach of Confidence* (Oxford: Clarendon Press, 1984)

HALLIWELL, M., 'Estoppel: Unconscionability as a Cause of Action' (1994) 14 *LS* 15

HALSON, R., 'Opportunism, Economic Duress and Contractual Modifications' (1991) 107 *LQR* 649

—— 'Rescission for Misrepresentation' (1997) 5 *RLR* 89

HARPUM, C., 'Knowing Receipt and Knowing Assistance: The Basis of Equitable Liability' in *The Frontiers of Liability* (ed. Birks, P.B.H., Oxford: Clarendon Press, 1994) Vol. 1, p. 9

—— 'Fiduciary Obligations and Fiduciary Powers—Where Are We Going?' in *Privacy and Loyalty* (ed. Birks, P.B.H., Oxford: Clarendon Press, 1997) p. 283

HAYCROFT, A.M., and WAKSMAN, D.M., 'Frustration and Restitution' [1984] *JBL* 207

HAYTON, D., 'Developing the Law of Trusts for the Twenty-First Century' (1990) 106 *LQR* 87

—— 'Fiduciaries in Context: An Overview' in *Privacy and Loyalty* (ed. Birks, P.B.H., Oxford: Clarendon Press, 1997) p. 283

HEDLEY, S., 'The Myth of "Waiver of Tort"' (1984) 100 *LQR* 653

—— 'Unjust Enrichment as the Basis of Restitution—An Overworked Concept' (1985) 5 *LS* 56

—— 'Unjust Enrichment' (1995) 54 *CLJ* 578

—— 'Ten Questions for "Unjust Enrichment" Theorists' [1997] 3 *Web JCL* 1

—— 'Work Done In Anticipation of a Contract Which Does Not Materialise: A Response' in *Restitution: Past, Present and Future* (ed. Cornish, W., Nolan, R., O'Sullivan, J., Virgo, G., Oxford: Hart Publishing, 1998) p. 195

HIGGINS, M.J., 'The Transfer of Property under Illegal Transactions' (1962) 25 *MLR* 149

HOOLEY, R., 'Taking Security after *O'Brien*' [1995] *LMCLQ* 346

—— and O'SULLIVAN, J., 'Undue Influence and Unconscionable Bargains' [1997] *LMCLQ* 17

HOPE, E.W., 'Officiousness' (1929) 15 *Cornell LQ* 25

JACKMAN, I.M., 'Restitution for Wrongs' (1989) 48 *CLJ* 302

JACKSON, R.M., *The History of Quasi-Contract in English Law* (Cambridge: Cambridge University Press, 1936)

JAFFEY, P., 'Restitution and Trespass to Land' (1995) 5 *RLR* 79

JONES, G., 'Change of Circumstances in Quasi-Contract' (1957) 73 *LQR* 48

JONES, G., 'Restitution of Benefits Obtained in Breach of Another's Confidence' (1970) 86 *LQR* 463

—— *Restitution in Public and Private Law* (London: Sweet and Maxwell, 1991)

Kennedy's Law of Salvage (Steel and Rose, 5th edn., London: Stevens, 1985)

KEY, P., '*Bona Fide* Purchase as a Defence in the Law of Restitution' [1994] *LMCLQ* 421

—— 'Excising Estoppel by Representation as a Defence to Restitution' (1995) *CLJ* 525

KHURSHID, S., and MATTHEWS, P., 'Tracing Confusion' (1979) 95 *LQR* 78

KLIPPERT, G.B., 'The Juridical Nature of Unjust Enrichment' (1980) 30 *University of Toronto LJ* 356

LANGBEIN, J.H., 'The Later History of Restitution' in *Restitution: Past, Present and Future* (ed. Cornish, W., Nolan, R., O'Sullivan, J., Virgo, G., Oxford: Hart Publishing, 1998) p. 57

LAW COMMISSION, *Pecuniary Restitution on Breach of Contract* (Law Com. No. 110, 1981)

—— *Restitution: Mistakes of Law and Ultra Vires Public Authority Receipts and Payments* (Law Com. No. 227, 1994)

—— *Aggravated, Exemplary and Restitutionary Damages* (Law Com. No. 247, 1997)

—— *Limitation of Actions* (Law Com. C.P. No. 151, 1998)

—— *Illegal Transactions: The Effect of Illegality on Contracts and Trusts* (Law Com. No. 154, 1999)

MACDONALD, E., 'Duress by Threatened Breach of Contract' [1989] *JBL* 460

MADDAUGH, P.D., and McCAMUS, J.D., *The Law of Restitution* (Aurora: Canada Law Book Inc., 1990)

MASON, A.M., 'The Place of Equity and Equitable Remedies in the Contemporary Common Law World' (1994) 110 *LQR* 328

MASON, K., and CARTER, J.W., *Restitution Law in Australia* (Sydney: Butterworths, 1995)

MATTHEWS, P., 'Money Paid Under a Mistake of Fact' (1980) 130 *NLJ* 587

—— 'Stopped Cheques and Restitution' [1982] *JBL* 281

McINNES, M.P., '"Passing On" in the Law of Restitution: A Reconsideration' (1997) 19 *Sydney LR* 179

—— 'At the Plaintiff's Expense—Quantifying Restitutionary Relief' (1998) 57 *CLJ* 472

McKENDRICK, E., 'Incontrovertible Benefit—A Postscript' [1989] *LMCLQ* 401

—— 'Frustration, Restitution and Loss Apportionment' in *Essays on the Law of Restitution* (ed. Burrows, A.S., Oxford: Clarendon Press, 1991) p. 147

—— 'Restitution. Misdirected Funds and Change of Position' (1992) 55 *MLR* 377

—— 'Restitution of Unlawfully Demanded Taxes' [1993] *LMCLQ* 88

—— 'Total Failure of Consideration and Counter-Restitution: Two Issues or One?' in *Laundering and Tracing* (ed. Birks, P.B.H., Oxford: Clarendon Press, 1995) p. 217

—— 'Mistakes of Law—Time for Change' in *The Limits of Restitutionary Claims: A Comparative Analysis* (ed. Swadling, W.J., London: UKNCCL, 1997) p. 212

—— 'Work Done In Anticipation of a Contract Which Does Not Materialise' in *Restitution: Past, Present and Future* (ed. Cornish, W., Nolan, R., O'Sullivan, J., Virgo, G., Oxford: Hart Publishing, 1998) p. 163

McLEAN, H.M., 'Limitation of Actions in Restitution' (1989) 48 *CLJ* 472

MEAD, G., 'Free Acceptance: Some Further Considerations' (1989) 105 *LQR* 460

—— 'Restitution Within Contract' (1991) 11 *LS* 172

MEE, J., 'Undue Influence, Misrepresentation and the Doctrine of Notice' (1995) 54 *CLJ* 536

MERKIN, R., 'Restitution by Withdrawal from Executory Illegal Contracts' (1981) 97 *LQR* 420

MILLETT, P., 'The *Quistclose* Trust: Who Can Enforce It?' (1985) 101 *LQR* 269

—— 'Tracing the Proceeds of Fraud' (1991) 107 *LQR* 71

—— 'Equity—The Road Ahead' (1995) 9 *TLI* 35

—— 'Equity's Place in the Law of Commerce' (1998) 114 *LQR* 214

—— 'Restitution and Constructive Trusts' (1998) 114 *LQR* 399

—— Review of Chambers' *Resulting Trusts* (1998) 6 *RLR* 283

MITCHELL, A.R., TAYLOR, S.M.E., and TALBOT, K.V., *On Confiscation and the Proceeds of Crime* (2nd edn., London: Sweet and Maxwell, 1997)

MITCHELL, C., *The Law of Subrogation* (Oxford: Clarendon Press, 1995)

—— 'No Account of Profits for the Victim of Deceit' [1996] *LMCLQ* 314

—— 'The Civil Liability (Contribution) Act 1978' (1997) 5 *RLR* 527

NAHAN, N.Y., 'Rescission: A Case for Rejecting the Classical Model?' (1997) 27 *Univ. WALR* 66

NEEDHAM, C.A., 'Mistaken Payments: A New Look at an Old Theme' (1978) 12 *Univ. of Brit. Col. LR* 159

NICHOLLS, D., 'Knowing Receipt: The Need for a New Landmark' in *Restitution: Past, Present and Future* (ed. Cornish, W., Nolan, R., O'Sullivan, J., Virgo, G., Oxford: Hart Publishing, 1998) p. 231

NOLAN, R.C., 'Change of Position' in *Laundering and Tracing* (Oxford: Clarendon Press, 1995) p. 135

—— 'Change of Position in Anticipation of Enrichment' [1995] *LMCLQ* 313

—— 'Remedies for Breach of Contract: Specific Enforcement and Restitution' in *Failure of Contracts: Contractual, Restitutionary and Proprietary Consequences* (ed. Rose, F., Oxford: Hart Publishing, 1997) p. 35

—— 'Conflicts of Interest, Unjust Enrichment and Wrongdoing' in *Restitution: Past, Present and Future* (ed. Cornish, W., Nolan, R., O'Sullivan, J., Virgo, G., Oxford: Hart Publishing, 1998) p. 163

O'DAIR, R., 'Restitutionary Damages for Breach of Contract and the Theory of Efficient Breach: Some Reflections' (1993) 46 *CLP* 113

O'DELL, E., 'Restitution, Coercion by a Third Party and the Proper Role of Notice' (1997) 56 *CLJ* 71

—— 'Restitution and *Res Judicata* in the Irish Supreme Court' (1997) 113 *LQR* 245

O'SULLIVAN, J., 'Undue Influence and Misrepresentation after *O'Brien*: Making Security Secure' in *Restitution and Banking Law* (ed. Rose, F., Oxford: Mansfield Press, 1998) p. 42

OAKLEY, A.J., 'The Liberalising Nature of Remedies for Breach of Trust' in *Trends in Contemporary Trust Law* (ed. Oakley, A.J., Oxford: Clarendon Press, 1996) p. 217

—— *Constructive Trusts* (3rd edn., London: Sweet and Maxwell, 1997)

—— *Parker and Mellows: The Modern Law of Trusts* (7th edn., London: Sweet and Maxwell, 1998)

OKUDA, S., 'Criminal Antiprofit Laws: Some Thoughts in Favour of their Constitutionality' (1985) 76 *Cal. LR* 1353

PHANG, A., 'Economic Duress: Recent Difficulties and Possible Alternatives' (1997) 5 *RLR* 53

POSNER, R., *Economic Analysis of Law* (4th edn., Boston, Mass.: Little, Brown and Co., 1992)

PROKSCH, L., 'Rescission on Terms' (1996) 4 *RLR* 71

REID, 'The Judge as Law-Maker' (1972–3) 12 *JSPTL* (NS) 22

RICKETT, C.E.F., 'Equitable Compensation: The Giant Stirs' (1996) 112 *LQR* 27

—— 'The Financier's Duty of Care to a Surety' (1998) 114 *LQR* 17

ROSE, R., 'Restitution for the Rescuer' (1989) 9 *OJLS* 167

—— 'Passing On' in *Laundering and Tracing* (Oxford: Clarendon Press, 1995) p. 261

—— 'General Average as Restitution' (1997) 113 *LQR* 569

ROTHERHAM, C., 'The Recovery of the Profits of Wrongdoing and Insolvency: When is Proprietary Relief Justified?' [1997] 1 *CFILR* 43

SHAND, J., 'Unblinkering the Unruly Horse: Public Policy in the Law of Contract' (1972) 30 *CLJ* 144

SHARPE, R.S., and WADDAMS, S.M., 'Damages for Lost Opportunity to Bargain' (1982) 2 *OJLS* 290

SIMESTER, A., 'Unjust Free Acceptance' [1997] *LMCLQ* 103

SMITH, J.C., and HOGAN, B., *Criminal Law* (8th edn., London: Butterworths, 1996)

SMITH, L.D., 'Three-Party Restitution: A Critique of Birks's Theory of Interceptive Subtraction' (1991) 11 *OJLS* 481

—— 'The Province of the Law of Restitution' (1992) 71 *CBR* 672

—— 'Disgorgement of the Profits of Breach of Contract: Property, Contract and "Efficient Breach"' (1992) 24 *Canadian Business Law Journal* 121

—— 'Tracing in *Taylor* v. *Plumer*: Equity in the Court of King's Bench' [1995] *LMCLQ* 240

—— 'Tracing into the Payment of a Debt' (1995) 54 *CLJ* 290

—— *The Law of Tracing* (Oxford: Clarendon Press, 1997)

SMITH, S., 'Contracting Under Pressure: A Theory of Duress' (1976) 76 *CLJ* 343

STEWART, A., and CARTER, J.W., 'Frustrated Contracts and Statutory Adjustment: The Case for a Reappraisal' (1992) 51 *CLJ* 66

STOLJAR, S.J., 'Unjust Enrichment and Unjust Sacrifice' (1987) 50 *MLR* 603

—— *The Law of Quasi-Contract* (2nd edn., Sydney: The Law Book Co., 1989)

—— 'Restitutionary Relief for Breach of Contract' (1989) 2 *JCL* 1

SUTTON, R.J., 'Payments of Debts Charged Upon Property' in *Essays on the Law of Restitution* (ed. Burrows, A.S., Oxford: Clarendon Press, 1991) p. 71

Swadling, W.J., 'Restitution for No Consideration' (1994) 2 *RLR* 73

—— 'The Nature of Ministerial Receipt' in *Laundering and Tracing* (Oxford: Clarendon Press, 1995) p. 243

—— 'A Claim in Restitution?' [1996] *LMCLQ* 63

—— 'A New Role for Resulting Trusts?' (1996) 16 *LS* 110

—— 'Restitution and *Bona Fide* Purchase' in *The Limits of Restitutionary Claims: A Comparative Analysis* (ed. Swadling, W.J., London: UKNCCL, 1997) p. 29

—— 'What is the Law of Restitution About?: Four Categorical Errors in Restitution' in *Restitution: Past, Present and Future* (ed. Cornish, W., Nolan, R., O'Sullivan, J., Virgo, G., Oxford: Hart Publishing, 1998) p. 331

Tettenborn, A.M., *Law of Restitution in England and Ireland* (2nd edn., London: Cavendish Publishing, 1996)

—— 'Lawful Receipt—A Justifying Factor?' (1997) 5 *RLR* 1

Tiley, J., 'Human Rights and Taxpayers' (1998) 57 *CLJ* 269

Treitel, G.H., 'The Infants' Relief Act 1874' (1957) 73 *LQR* 194

—— *Frustration and Force Majeure* (London: Sweet and Maxwell, 1994)

Ulph, J., 'The Sale of Goods (Amendment) Act: Co-ownership and the Rogue Seller' [1996] *LMCLQ* 93

Verse, D.A., 'Improvements and Enrichments: the Law of Restitution' (1998) 6 *RLR* 85

Virgo, G.J., 'The Law of Taxation is Not an Island—Overpaid Taxes and the Law of Restitution' [1993] *BTR* 442

—— 'Striking the Balance in the Law of Restitution' [1995] *LMCLQ* 362

—— 'Reconstructing the Law of Restitution' (1996) 10 *TLI* 20

—— 'The Effects of Illegality on Claims for Restitution in English Law' in *The Limits of Restitutionary Claims: A Comparative Analysis* (ed. Swadling, W.J., London: UKNCCL, 1997) p. 141

—— 'Undue Influence and Misrepresentation after *O'Brien*: Making Security Secure: A Commentary' in *Restitution and Banking Law* (ed. Rose, F., Oxford: Mansfield Press, 1998) p. 70

—— 'What is the Law of Restitution About?' in *Restitution: Past, Present and Future* (ed. Cornish, W., Nolan, R., O'Sullivan, J., Virgo, G., Oxford: Hart Publishing, 1998) p. 305

—— 'The Law of Restitution and the Proceeds of Crime—A Survey of English Law' (1998) 6 *RLR* 34

—— 'Clarifying Restitution for Wrongs' (1998) 6 *RLR* 118

—— 'Restitution of Overpaid VAT' [1998] *BTR* 582

Waddams, S.M., 'Restitution as Part of Contract Law' in *Essays on the Law of Restitution* (ed. Burrows, A.S., Oxford: Clarendon Press, 1991) p. 197

Wade, J.W., 'Restitution of Benefits Conferred Without Request' (1966) 19 *Vanderbilt LR* 1183

Watts, P., 'Does a Subcontractor Have Restitutionary Rights Against the Employer?' [1995] *LMCLQ* 398

—— 'The Limits of Profit-Stripping for Wrongs' (1996) 112 *LQR* 219

Wigmore (1891) 25 *Am. L Rev.* 712

Williams, G., 'Mistake in the Law of Theft' (1977) 36 *CLJ* 62

WINFIELD, P.H., 'Mistake of Law' (1943) 59 *LQR* 327

WORTHINGTON, S., 'Proprietary Interests in Commercial Transactions' (Oxford: Clarendon Press, 1996)

WRIGHT, LORD, *Legal Essays and Addresses* (Cambridge: Cambridge University Press, 1939)

——'*United Australia Ltd.* v. *Barclays Bank Ltd.* (1941) 57 *LQR* 184

YOUDAN, T.G., 'Acquisition of Property by Killing' (1973) 89 *LQR* 235

ZWEIGERT, K., and KOTZ, H., *An Introduction to Comparative Law* (trans, Weir, T., 3rd edn., Oxford: Clarendon Press, 1998)

Index